THE OXFORD HANDBOOK OF

SPACE SECURITY

THE OXFORD HANDBOOK OF

SPACE SECURITY

Edited by

SAADIA M. PEKKANEN *and* P.J. BLOUNT

OXFORD
UNIVERSITY PRESS

OXFORD
UNIVERSITY PRESS

Oxford University Press is a department of the University of Oxford. It furthers
the University's objective of excellence in research, scholarship, and education
by publishing worldwide. Oxford is a registered trade mark of Oxford University
Press in the UK and certain other countries.

Published in the United States of America by Oxford University Press
198 Madison Avenue, New York, NY 10016, United States of America.

Library of Congress Cataloging-in-Publication Data
Names: Pekkanen, Saadia M., editor. | Blount, P. J., editor.
Title: The Oxford handbook of space security / [edited by] Saadia M.
Pekkanen and P.J. Blount.
Description: New York, NY : Oxford University Press, [2024] |
Includes bibliographical references. |
Identifiers: LCCN 2023017649 (print) | LCCN 2023017650 (ebook) |
ISBN 9780197582671 (hardback) | ISBN 9780197582688 (epub) |
ISBN 9780197582701
Subjects: LCSH: Space security.
Classification: LCC JZ5695 .O94 2024 (print) | LCC JZ5695 (ebook) |
DDC 327—dc23/eng/20230607
LC record available at https://lccn.loc.gov/2023017649
LC ebook record available at https://lccn.loc.gov/2023017650

DOI: 10.1093/oxfordhb/9780197582671.001.0001

Printed by Sheridan Books, Inc., United States of America

Contents

PART III: STATECRAFT AND STRATEGY

PART IV: STRATEGIC IMPLICATIONS OF CAPABILITIES

PART V: PROSPECTS

About the Contributors

Mohamed Amara is the General Counsel of the UAE Federal Geographic Information Center, a member of the International Institute of Space Law (IISL), and a former General Counsel for the UAE Space Agency.

Setsuko Aoki is a Professor of Law at Keio University Law School, Vice Director of the Center for Space Law at Keio University, and former Vice-President of the International Institute of Space Law.

Natália Archinard is Deputy Head of the Science, Transport and Space Section at the Federal Department of Foreign Affairs of Switzerland.

Mathieu Bataille is a Research Fellow and Lead on Security and Defence at the European Space Policy Institute in Vienna, Austria, addressing primarily the topics of security and defence from and in space.

Aaron Bateman is an Assistant Professor of history and international affairs at George Washington University and is a core faculty member of the Space Policy Institute.

Jairo Becerra is the Director of the Socio-Legal Research Center at the Catholic University of Colombia, member of the International Institute of Space Law (IISL), and Latino American Regional Organizer of the Manfred Lachs Space Law Moot Court Competition.

Olavo de O. Bittencourt Neto is a Professor of International Law at the Catholic University of Santos (Brazil), arbitrator for Space Related Disputes at the Permanent Court of Arbitration (CPA-PCA), and a member of the Board of the International Institute of Space Law (IISL).

P.J. Blount is a Lecturer in Law in the School of Law and Politics at Cardiff University. He serves as the Executive Secretary of the International Institute of Space Law.

Nickolas J. Boensch is a Program Manager at BryceTech.

Mariel Borowitz is an Associate Professor in the Sam Nunn School of International Affairs at the Georgia Institute of Technology and head of the Nunn School Program on International Affairs, Science, and Technology.

Stephen Buono is Collegiate Assistant Professor in the Social Sciences at the University of Chicago, where he is a Harper & Schimdt Fellow in the Society of Fellows. He was previously an Ernest May Fellow in History and Policy at Harvard University.

Tai Ming Cheung is a Professor in the School of Global Policy and Strategy at the University of California San Diego and director of the University of California Institute on Global Conflict and Cooperation.

Malcolm Davis is a Senior Analyst in Defence Strategy and Capability at the Australian Strategic Policy Institute (ASPI) in Canberra, Australia.

Raymond Duvall is the Morse-Alumni Professor of Political Science, Emeritus, at the University of Minnesota.

Davis Ellison is a Strategic Analyst at The Hague Centre for Strategic Studies and a PhD Candidate in the Department of War Studies at King's College London.

Martin Elvis is an Astrophysicist at the Center for Astrophysics | Harvard & Smithsonian, a Fellow of the American Association for the Advancement of Science, a Member of the Aspen Center for Physics, and is past-Chair of the Hubble Space Telescope Users' Committee and of the High Energy Division of the American Astronomical Society.

Yasuhito Fukushima is a Senior Research Fellow at the National Institute for Defense Studies, Japan, and a previous visiting scholar at the University of California Institute on Global Conflict and Cooperation.

Desislava Gancheva is a Policy Advisor at the Australian Space Agency and a graduate of the University of Adelaide Law School.

Šumit Ganguly is Distinguished Professor of Political Science and holds the Tagore Chair in Indian Cultures and Civilizations at Indiana University, Bloomington. In 2022–2023, he was a Visiting Fellow at the Hoover Institution at Stanford University.

Carl Graefe is a PhD Candidate at the University of Minnesota.

Laura Grego is a Senior Scientist and the Research Director in the Global Security Program at the Union of Concerned Scientists and a Visiting Scholar at the Massachusetts Institute of Technology Laboratory for Nuclear Security and Policy.

Peter L. Hays is a Defense Contractor supporting the Space Staff in the Pentagon, an Adjunct Professor at the Space Policy Institute at George Washington University, and Space Chair at Marine Corps University.

Mark Hilborne is a Lecturer at King's College London in the Defence Studies Department at the Joint Services Command and Staff College.

Tomas Hrozensky is a Senior Research Fellow and Lead on European Engagement at the European Space Policy Institute in Vienna, Austria, focusing extensively on policy issues in space safety and sustainability.

Hanbeom Jeong is a Professor at Korea National Defense University, serves as the president of the Korean Space Association for National Defense, and is a member of the Security Space Working Committee at the Korea National Space Council.

John J. Klein is a Senior Fellow and Strategist at Falcon Research, Inc., and Adjunct Professor at George Washington University's Space Policy Institute, Georgetown University's Strategic Studies Program, and the Institute of World Politics.

Alanna Krolikowski is an Assistant Professor of Political Science at the Missouri University of Science and Technology (Missouri S&T).

Paul B. Larsen is a former Professor of Space Law (visiting and adjunct) Georgetown University Law Center and Southern Methodist University, and a Senior Legal Counsel for the US Government Interagency Committee on GPS.

Su-Mi Lee is an Associate Professor and the Chair of the Department of Political Science at the University of Hawai'i at Hilo and serves as a member of the Peaceful Unification Advisory Council of the Republic of Korea.

Pavel Luzin is a Visiting Scholar at the Fletcher School of Law and Diplomacy, Tufts University, and a Senior Fellow at the Jamestown Foundation.

Larry F. Martinez is a Professor Emeritus in the Department of Political Science at California State University, Long Beach, and serves as the International Institute of Space Law (IISL) observer to the United Nations Committee on the Peaceful Uses of Outer Space (COPUOUS).

James Clay Moltz is a Professor in the Department of National Security Affairs at the Naval Postgraduate School and former Dean of the Graduate School of International and Defense Studies.

Forrest E. Morgan is a Senior Lecturer at Carnegie Mellon University, a former Space Operator for the US Air Force, and a former Senior Political Scientist at RAND Corporation.

Samuel Oyewole is a Lecturer at the Department of Political Science, Federal University Oye-Ekiti, Nigeria.

Scott Pace is a Professor of the Practice of International Affairs and Director of the Space Policy Institute at the Elliott School of International Affairs, George Washington University.

Deganit Paikowsky is a Lecturer at the International Relations Department at the Hebrew University of Jerusalem and a Non-resident Scholar at the Space Policy Institute of George Washington University.

Prashanth Parameswaran is a Fellow at the Woodrow Wilson International Center for Scholars, and Founder of the weekly ASEAN Wonk newsletter focused on foreign and security developments across Southeast Asian and the Indo-Pacific region.

Xavier Pasco is the Director of the Fondation pour la Recherche Stratégique (FRS) and the European Editor of the international academic review *Space Policy*.

Saadia M. Pekkanen is the Job and Gertrud Tamaki Endowed Professor and the Founding Director of the Space Law, Data and Policy Program (SPACE LDP) at the University of Washington.

Kevin Pollpeter is a Senior Research Scientist at the Center for Naval Analyses.

Rajeswari Pillai Rajagopalan is the Director of the Centre for Security, Strategy and Technology (CSST) at the Observer Research Foundation, New Delhi. She is also a senior defense writer for *The Diplomat* and a former Technical Advisor to the United Nations Group of Governmental Experts (GGE) on the Prevention of an Arms Race in Outer Space (PAROS).

Michael Raska is an Assistant Professor and Coordinator of the Military Transformations Programme at the S. Rajaratnam School of International Studies (RSIS), Nanyang Technological University in Singapore.

Nikola Schmidt is the Head of the Centre for Governance of Emerging Technologies and Senior Researcher at the Institute of International Relations in Prague, Czech Republic.

Sagee Geetha Sethu is an Assistant Professor of Law and the Program Head of Amity Law School at Amity University, Dubai.

Matthew Stubbs is a Professor at the University of Adelaide Law School and a core expert of the international research project to develop the *Woomera Manual on the International Law of Military Space Activities and Operations*.

Tim Sweijs is a Senior Research Fellow at the Netherlands' War Studies Research Centre and the Director of Research at The Hague Centre for Strategic Studies.

Koji Tachibana is an Associate Professor of Philosophy at Chiba University, Japan, and an International Associate Scholar at Georgetown University Medical Center.

Brad Townsend is a Senior Engineer with the Aerospace Corporation supporting the United States Space Force's new Space Warfighting Analysis Center and a former Army Space Officer and Advisor on Space Policy and Strategy to the Chairman of the Joint Chiefs.

Florian Vidal is a Research Fellow at the UiT The Arctic University of Norway in Tromsø. He is also an Associate Fellow at the LIED (Laboratoire Interdisciplinaire des Energies de Demain), Paris Cité University, and at the French Institute of International Relations (IFRI), France.

Wang Guoyu is an Associate Professor at the Law School of Beijing Institute of Technology (BIT), Dean of the Academy of Air, Space Policy and Law of BIT, Deputy

Director of China National Space Administration Space Law Center, and a Board Director of the Institute of International Space Law (IISL).

Jessica West is a Senior Researcher at the Canadian peace research institute Project Ploughshares, a Research Fellow at the Kindred Credit Union Centre for Peace Advancement, and a Senior Fellow at the Centre for International Governance Innovation (CIGI). In her positions, she interacts regularly with key United Nations bodies tasked with space security and space safety issues.

Wendy N. Whitman Cobb is a Professor of Strategy and Security Studies at the US Air Force's School of Advanced Air and Space Studies (SAASS).

James J. Wirtz is a Professor of National Security Affairs at the Naval Postgraduate School, Monterey, California.

Xiaodan Wu is an Associate Professor of the Law Faculty, China Central University of Finance and Economics, and a researcher at the Institute of Defense Economics and Management, China Central University of Finance and Economics.

Zhou Bo is a Senior Fellow of the Center for International Security and Strategy, Tsinghua University, and China Forum expert. A Senior Colonel, ret., he was Director of the Center for Security Cooperation of Office for International Military Cooperation of the Ministry of National Defense of the People's Republic of China.

PART I

OVERVIEW

CHAPTER 1

....

INTERNATIONAL RELATIONS THEORY AND THE EVOLUTION OF "PEACEFUL PURPOSES" IN OUTER SPACE

....

SAADIA M. PEKKANEN AND P.J. BLOUNT

INTRODUCTION

....

THE driving questions in international relations (IR) theory are about why states go to war and what makes them stay at peace. We believe these questions are especially pertinent in the contemporary transformations of the space domain, which is marked by a rising number of players, unprecedented commercial innovations, and creeping weaponization in the context of great power competition (Pekkanen 2019). They also deserve attention at a time when geopolitical shifts and technological changes have led states to more offensive stances in the space environment, eroding the legal contents of peaceful purposes as set out in the foundational 1967 Outer Space Treaty (OST) (Blount 2019). The specific goal of *The Oxford Handbook of Space Security* is to fill a perceived gap in the IR literature engaging with space security.

To our minds, the topic of space security falls by definition under the broader field of inquiry of international security, which itself falls under the broader umbrella of IR. Whether explicit or not the topic of space security has received sustained global attention in the fields of law (von der Dunk, 2015; Lyall and Larsen, 2018; Masson-Zwaan and Hofmann, 2019) and policy as shown in comprehensive edited volumes (Schrogl et al., eds., 2015; Steer and Hersch, eds. 2021). The tendrils of space security are also illuminated in works focused on the historical, political, and economic dynamics of the space race between the United States and the former Soviet Union (McDougall 1985; Burrows 1998; Siddiqi 2000, 2010; MacDonald 2017). Other scholars have examined the workings, as well as the purpose and imagination, of space politics, security, and strategy; and they have done so in conversation with distinct IR analytics and discourses, often with sobering implications for them (Gray 1996; Dolman 2002; Klein 2006, 2019; Johnson-Freese 2007, 2019; Sheehan 2007; Moltz 2008; Bormann and Sheehan, eds. 2009; Coletta and Pilch, eds. 2009; Hays 2011; Mutschler 2013; Dawson 2018; Bowen 2020, 2022; Deudney 2020; Townsend 2020).

Alongside these works, and to the best of our knowledge, this edited handbook is the first to comprehensively shine the light of IR analytics specifically on the topic of space security writ large. This framing is used to push forward both theoretical and applied knowledge on space security, and opens up new trajectories of research in this complex area. Just as early analyses tended to focus upon space and the Cold War, we focus on space security in the contemporary era's return to great power competition; as then, so now, by this we do not mean to suggest that there are no other equally worthy agendas to focus on in the space realm, such as civil exploration or commercial innovations (Goldsen 1963, 5).

But we maintain that the dual-use nature of the underlying space technologies, much of which of which can be transposed from civilian to military purposes, complicate the prospects for the peaceful uses of outer space in virtually every activity (Johnson-Freese 2007, 27–50). This foundational technical reality affects also the projection and imagination of IR in space because, whether soldiers or explorers, "without the right technology—which is more or less the same technology for both parties—nobody can get to it, operate in it, scrutinize it, dominate it, or use it to their advantage and some else's disadvantage. Absent that technology, neither side can achieve its end . . . the technology all sides seek is both cutting-edge and potentially dual-use" (Tyson and Lang 2018, 20–21).

We therefore approach space security as a complex assemblage of societal risks and benefits that result from space-based technologies and capabilities. For the purposes of this book, we explicitly distinguish space security to mean the interaction between space technology and international and national security processes and issues framed by IR analytics. Our emphasis also includes concepts such as freedom of action in and through space, safety and security of space operations, and security and threats that manifest as a result of space capabilities (Sheehan 2015, 8–10).

We are particularly interested in whether the space domain can remain peaceful, a theme which allows us to connect to the past and project to the future. Since before the launch of *Sputnik I*, "peaceful purposes" (and the interchangeable "peaceful uses") has been used as a frame within which state action in outer space is legitimated. The States Parties to the OST both recognize and desire the common interest of all in the "exploration and use of outer space for peaceful purposes" right in the preamble. As a normative concept, peaceful purposes has long served as a threshold between legitimate and illegitimate space activities, and its usage is ubiquitous in international forums and discussions concerning space activities (Blount 2018). Article IV of the OST is the firmest articulation of the norm through its application to the moon and other celestial bodies. While this is a limited application in the treaty text, the entire provision underpins the broader notion of peaceful purposes as applicable to the whole of space. Article IV states:

> States Parties to the Treaty undertake not to place in orbit around the Earth any objects carrying nuclear weapons or any other kinds of weapons of mass destruction, install such weapons on celestial bodies, or station such weapons in outer space in any other manner.
>
> The Moon and other celestial bodies shall be used by all States Parties to the Treaty exclusively for peaceful purposes. The establishment of military bases, installations and fortifications, the testing of any type of weapons and the conduct of military manoeuvres on celestial bodies shall be forbidden. The use of military personnel for scientific research or for any other peaceful purposes shall not be prohibited. The use of any equipment or facility necessary for peaceful exploration of the Moon and other celestial bodies shall also not be prohibited.

Despite its role as a foundational normative principle, the term peaceful purposes lacks a static definition, and instead is wrapped in the narratives and practices advanced by states that seek to legitimate their own activities, though it is ubiquitous in state practice concerning space activities and used by states of all types to frame their activities. Two examples show this diversity of usage stretched over time. First, in the early speeches concerning US plans for space activities, the United States characterized space as a place for "peaceful purposes" (Eisenhower 1960). Second, in 2009, under threat of UN security sanctions for developing a ballistic missile program, North Korea announced that it would be launching a satellite into space and stated that this launch was in accordance with the principle of the "peaceful uses of outer space" (KCNA 2009). Beyond usage by states, the phrase is observable in nearly all UN documents adopted addressing space activities.

The ubiquitous yet diverse usage of this phrase as a legitimating narrative means that peaceful purposes have a fluid and evolving meaning that is highly subject to the zeitgeist on space in the theory and practice of IR today. The dynamic nature of this framing norm results in a number of conceptual issues as both states and commentators attempt to perceive and respond to the nature of IR in space. Shifts in geopolitics and technological developments can reorient states in their relationship to the peaceful uses of outer space, and at present both of these phenomena are shaping the international space order. The renewal of great power military rivalry and the arrival of deep-pocketed private-sector entrepreneurs are two prominent reasons why we should pay serious attention to where activities are in the space domain and where they might boldly go (Deudney 2020, 22–25).

These are the driving forces with which this volume on space security grapples. And we do not do so alone. Who thinks what about space security, where it is headed, and why that might matter at this historical stage is what we set out to illuminate with our contributors. Our contributors are based in both established and emerging spacefaring countries spread around the world. They give us ground-up knowledge on how states, technology, and prospects for peaceful purposes come together in their areas of expertise under IR rubrics.

With this as backdrop, we do three things in this overview chapter. First, we discuss our approach to IR analytics, and specifically the ways in which we have structured the handbook. Second, we lay out a summary of principal findings from each of our contributors. And finally, we set out some takeaways for both theorists and practitioners at a time when a space war is not unimaginable and its aftermath for the world order unclear.

WHAT IR THEORY IS RELEVANT TO SPACE SECURITY?

We structured this handbook using the lens of states and IR theory. As in much of the study of IR, whether it is being acclaimed or criticized, the state is central to the study of space security and is long likely to remain so as it navigates the related uncertainties of domestic and transnational realities (Lake 2008). As we noted at the outset, the international security environment is currently in a period of significant transformation as innovative processes and structural shifts are rapidly changing underlying assumptions about space-related capabilities and their uses. This means that states, whether established or emerging in the space domain, are currently readjusting how they understand and use space as a security mechanism both in space and terrestrially.

Broadly, our goal in this volume is to theorize the development, trajectory, and governance of space security at the nexus of the state. We seek to analyze the contemporary role of states and specific pressure points currently driving their decisions, trajectories, and alignments in the international space order. As well, we seek to frame those analyses with IR theories, frameworks, concepts, and constructs. Our purpose is to build an understanding of why states do the things they do and what the significance of their actions might be in practice for peaceful purposes in the space domain.

In search of that understanding, we favor an analytically eclectic and problem-focused approach (Katzenstein and Sil 2008; Sil and Katzenstein 2010a, 2010b; Pace 2023). Given our longstanding and interdisciplinary engagement with the topic, this approach is very much in line with our own intellectual orientation. Our sense of space security is that there is no one paradigm—such as the familiar IR triad of realism, liberalism, and constructivism—that can explain all its deeply intertwined strands. Nor is the triad the only way to approach space security. Along with the works by our contributors outside of this handbook, we also noted the oeuvres by other scholars and experts that falls under the broad rubric of IR theory and outer space. Taken together, over time, the important point is that they suggest any number of other analytical devices could also prove fruitful in engaging with space security (Roberts 1988; Pfaltzgraff 2011; Mutschler 2015; Stroikos 2022).

Nor do we think that trumpeting the importance of one paradigmatic approach over another at the outset is useful to contributors, such as those in this volume who bring their own degrees of IR training, thinking, and perspectives to the subject matter from around the world. We therefore consciously eschew the overly structured paradigmatic route and let our contributors dip into paradigms, constructs, frameworks (or not) as they see fit in their own areas of expertise. Our sensibility is infused with the pragmatist ethos, alert to the wide scope of messy problems, and mindful of the limits of substantive causal complexity in studying them (Sil and Katzenstein 2010a, 412). In this handbook, we are aiming for analyses that are historically contingent, grounded, and policy relevant.

To draw together and extract some meaningful conclusions from a work of this size we clarified the core concepts as well as the scope of the enterprise. The expanse of what we think of as the field of IR is virtually limitless and it is not one thing alone. The field evolves over time, is shaped by systemic and historical circumstances, and involves the actions, reactions, and interactions of major, middle, and emerging powers with their wide varieties of domestic politics. A good indication of the range of topics the IR field can involve is the signature Oxford Handbook series itself.

On point is *The Oxford Handbook of International Relations*. It showcases general debates that stretch across new and diverse theoretical perspectives and their particular ethical considerations. It highlights a wide range of approaches to methods: sociological, psychological, quantitative, case studies, and historical. It also includes subfields and other disciplines, such as international political economy, strategic studies, foreign-policy decision-making, ethics, and international law. It encompasses reflections on the theory-practice divide and calls for a more relevant discipline, which we believe is also applicable to the next big frontier (Reus-Smit and Snidal 2008).

There are prominent IR subfields such as those exemplified by *The Oxford Handbook of International Security* which, in addition to grounding these debates, illuminates disagreements about what security is and how it should be studied (Gheciu and Wohlforth, eds. 2018). The scope of what is already studied under the heading of international security includes national security, leadership, norms, economics, nuclear proliferation, arms control, energy, crime, terrorism, intelligence, cybersecurity, development, alliances, regional and international organizations, and so on.

There are also country or region-focused IR subfields, as represented in *The Oxford Handbook of the International Relations of Asia* (Pekkanen, Ravenhill, and Foot 2014). Here the field of IR is split into its two major wings, international political economy and international security, each of which then thematically covers the foreign policies of the principal countries as well as sets of regional interactions. All of these handbooks grapple with the central IR issues of war and peace, conflict and cooperation, and because they are products of their historical times, also flag new challenges, opportunities, and trajectories.

None of them delve into space, much less space security—which brings us to the one at hand. In it, echoing many of the substantive themes in the previous handbooks noted above, we too seek engagement with material and ideational factors in IR theory that shape how and why states do the things they do in the space domain. While, as noted, our contributors were encouraged to use the constructs and approaches in IR theory they deemed appropriate to their domain of inquiry we requested that they also engage, to the extent possible, with the following core concepts.

- **The role of the state as a central actor in space security.** Although a state-centric theoretical approach may not have primacy for each chapter, the goal of any approach used should help to elucidate how states manage their interactions in the space domain. We requested that the chapter clarify the role and motives of states and/or other dominant actors that help define and shape space security.

- **The role of "peaceful purposes" or "peaceful uses" in framing the space security environment.** These are critical concepts in the existing law and policy space-related scholarship as noted above. We requested that the chapter should seek to analyze whether and how this concept has influenced space security activities by states and others.

- **The role of changing technology in shaping state approaches to security in, through, and from space.** Technological change is a critical element in understanding the threat landscape in both the national security and international peace and security levels. We asked our contributors to reflect on how evolving technology has affected the evolving nature of threats and conditioned responses by states.

WHAT DO WE LEARN FROM OUR CONTRIBUTORS?

We also used the substantive themes from previous handbooks to delineate the scope of this volume. The problem of interest to us in this book is: what do our specialist contributors see as the principal threats to peaceful purposes in the space domain, and what are the forces and actors they see in shaping its prospects in the foreseeable future? Below we provide a brief summary across the five parts, extracting some of the key points directly from our contributors' abstracts as we look across the scoped topics and countries.

Overview

In the first section, the **overview**, the handbook orients readers to space security with some historical and legal background that is interwoven with the role of international organizations.

Stephen Buono and Aaron Bateman set the stage with a brief overview of international space security as it developed primarily out of the US-Soviet rivalry during the Cold War. With a focus on anti-satellite (ASAT) weapons, they chart both the development of US and Soviet military space policy and the concurrent achievements of multilateral space diplomacy at the United Nations (UN). The first epoch in space security (1957–1991), they argue, can be divided into two general periods: one marked by the quest for stability and legal norms, the other by the search for safety and growing threats. Setsuko Aoki discusses legally binding and non-legally binding international frameworks for enhancing space security and concludes that non-legally binding norms could possibly enhance space security. For more than half a century, international law has only prohibited states' freedoms in stationing weapons of mass destruction in outer space and the threat or use of force from, to, and in outer space. While there is no clear picture of laws of armed conflict applicable to space, she suggests that the recent UN General Assembly Resolution on Responsible Behaviors is a promising way to generate new norms for space security.

Theoretical Approaches and Perspectives

In the second section, the handbook turns to a set of **theoretical perspectives and approaches.**

P.J. Blount begins with securitization theory, which holds that security threats are constructed through narratives that move issues into the realm of security. He argues this is germane to how narratives surrounding the space domain have led to the increasing conceptualization of space activities as securitized. Through an analysis of narratives deployed out of the US military and diplomatic establishment, he shows that the understanding of space as a security issue is being transformed. Carl Graefe and Raymond Duvall suggest one crucial possibility in space security is that states might attempt to control portions of space for exclusive use in security competition with other states. Using a critical theoretical perspective, they challenge arguments that the unique properties of space prevent exclusionary politics because of high costs and risks and that, as such, they facilitate the domain's prospective democratization. Instead, they highlight that the differential dynamics of cost reductions in attempted mastery over space operations may lead to the means for and establishment of a colonial regime of selective exclusion in outer space.

Wendy N. Whitman Cobb points out capabilities that are intrinsic to the global economy, such as communications, financial transactions, and environmental and weather monitoring, depend on space-based systems. She argues that economic interdependence between states is heavily supported by these space systems, and that raises the cost of potential conflict in the domain. This commercial space peace theory not only has implications for how conflict in space may be discouraged by increasing the commercialization of space but also for the ways in which IR writ large may deal with the power of private companies. Pavel Luzin surveys the topic of soft power, contrasting elements of space cooperation, competition, and space security. In his view, even the US–Soviet space race demonstrated that soft power employed by both actors contributed to space security. Further, he suggests that competitive approaches toward soft power tend toward a positive-sum game, as exemplified in the space partnerships established by the United States. He finds a similar story is underway in the new space realities involving competition between actors' soft powers and their agendas for space exploration and international space cooperation.

Tai Ming Cheung and **Yasuhito Fukushima** argue that techno-security innovation is a crucial but overlooked phenomenon in studies of the development of the space sector. Its key characteristics include the catalytic role played by external threat perceptions in affecting top-level leadership intervention, the presence of self-reliant techno-nationalistic impulses in decision-making, and the emphasis on civil-military integration. These factors are apparent in the US and Chinese techno-security space innovation systems, and their impact can be expected to become more prominent as US-China great power techno-security competition intensifies. Although their approaches differ, both countries believe civil-military integration is pivotal in gaining a decisive edge. **Xiaodan Wu** analyzes domestic policy as a powerful shaping force for space security. She argues not only that a range of military, science and technology (S&T), political, and economic national interests are intertwined in outer space, but that they can also be influenced by seemingly trivial and irrelevant factors. Matters are further complicated because national policy formulation is supported by an array of governmental and non-governmental actors, all interacting within a state's space governance mechanism, and all influenced both by the political climate and the state's space development model. Space security is sustained by the interplay of these domestic elements and achieved at the nexus of international competition and cooperation.

Tim Sweijs and **Davis Ellison** assert that the evolution of space as a warfighting domain is keeping brisk pace alongside its increasing economic and societal importance. They reason that a clear understanding of the strategic dynamics in space is a necessary prerequisite to enhancing the stability and peaceful uses of space. They draw on previous thinking from other military domains to propose three foundational concepts for developing a strategic theory for space: power, access, and command. They consider the theory's relation to orbital uses for space as well as in the emerging commercial and military uses of cislunar and deep space. **Saadia M. Pekkanen** argues that great power competition between the United States and China is also indicated by a bipolarity of space alliances. The United States is responding to a swirl of material and perceptual threats and forging alliances that are actively balanced by those of its peer competitor, China. With a focus on space stations, including in cislunar space, she maps how two sets of alliances are extending into space, how they are organized and led, and what they portend for stability. She cautions that congruence from follower states cannot be taken for granted by either side. **Forrest E. Morgan** asserts that the military forces of Western states, which typically conduct expeditionary operations, have become increasingly dependent on support from orbital assets. To reduce their effectiveness in war, potential adversaries are developing counterspace capabilities. As satellites are difficult to defend, the question is whether adversaries can be deterred from attacking them. Applying the fundamentals of punishment- and denial-based deterrence, he finds that strategies to deter attack on national security space systems face several difficult challenges. But emerging trends in technology and commercialization may lead to mixed strategies that make deterrence in space more robust, promoting responsible behavior.

Jessica West observes that the prevention of an arms race in outer space (PAROS) has been on the international agenda for decades with little progress. Arms control poses an intractable challenge for space governance, which cannot just be attributed to technical challenges or lack of political will. She contends the failure to restrict weapons use in space is also a consequence of an abiding myth of the peacefulness of outer space. This myth makes deployment of weapons in space taboo for most, but also permits military competition for some, cloaked by a fog of peace. **Koji Tachibana** finds that the peaceful use of space is central to space security. He argues that the underlying governance regime is structured on non-binding soft law instruments, meaning that states tend not to comply if they deem it not to be in their national interests. He argues that to realize the idea of peaceful uses, a certain shared understanding of ethics is required to encourage compliance by states. He scrutinizes the ethics most appropriate to ensuring space security and comes to the conclusion that virtue ethics–based cosmopolitanism satisfies the needed conditions.

Statecraft and Strategy

The goal of this section is to advance theoretically informed knowledge about **statecraft and strategy** related to space security, and to get a better grip on how it is both understood and unfolding in countries and regions around the world.

Scott Pace takes up an analytically eclectic lens to examine the broad sweep of US international activities in space. He asserts that both its dependence on space-derived information and an increase in potential adversary threats to its space assets has driven the United States to protect its national security interests in space by creating a distinct military service for space, the United States Space Force. Notably, its national space policy addresses not just deterrence in the space domain but also measures to shape the international space environment in a manner conducive to US interests. **Kevin Pollpeter**'s focused argument is that China's search for space security is rooted in a technonationalist strategic culture that conditions it to think and act in realist terms that emphasize competition, conflict, and the balance of power. He asserts that China's space program is inherently tied to the People's Republic of China's (PRC) leadership's view of the international security situation and that China's build-up of military space capabilities cannot be divorced from the PRC leadership's view of the need to protect China from international security threats, particularly those perceived as coming from the United States.

Florian Vidal asserts that, while long in disarray, Russia has renewed its space geopolitical ambitions, moving toward a narrative of autarky. To pursue this aim, the space field is part of the national security architecture in the face of Russia's rivalry with Western powers and the rise of China. The Ministry of Defense manages critical infrastructure, as the space domain is a way for Moscow to maintain its deterrence. Russia engages in counter-space capabilities to disrupt the space activities of its main competitors and to meet strategic and security objectives by strengthening Russian activities in low Earth orbit (LEO). For **Saadia M. Pekkanen**, the space domain present threats, challenges, opportunities, and uncertainties for all states. Using the lens of grand strategy, she illuminates how Japan is producing prosperity and security in its national interest under these conditions. Given its deeply developmental and historically realist orientation, the Japanese state is doing so by proactive positioning on all fronts in the space domain— economic, military, diplomatic. Through whatever means, processes, and forums available, the Japanese state's all-fronts vision keeps it attentive to locking in specific national advantages, big or small, concrete or nebulous. **Rajeswari Pillai Rajagopalan** and **Šumit Ganguly** mark India as an established space power with its own launch capabilities and space exploration programs. Among the most significant changes they note is the evolution of India's position from a moral and principled stance of non-militarization of outer space to one that is conditioned by pragmatism and national security considerations. This includes accepting some forms of militarization, though not outright weaponization. Compelled by changing regional security dynamics, the larger global space developments, and China's counterspace capabilities, India is expanding its space activities to address the growing military and security requirements necessary for its defense.

Xavier Pasco notes that France has long recognized the strategic value of a national space effort, propelled by perceptions of its prime importance for defence and security for key national players. The earlier development and consolidation of the national deterrence force also reinforced military space efforts based on the principle of strategic autonomy. While France balances national autonomy and regional cooperation, this explains the priority it gives to an independent access to space as well as the high level of investment it devotes to military Earth observation satellites as compared to its European neighbors. **Mark Hilborne** finds that British space policy seeks to simultaneously address concerns over the security of its own space assets and space-dependent critical national infrastructure, its role within its principal alliances, and the need to serve the growing economic and societal benefits that depend on space. At the same time, the UK is seeking a greater voice in the international governance of space as a means to enhance its diplomatic leverage. To reconcile these divergent aims, the UK government has sought a cross-sector approach to space policy. **Mathieu Bataille** and **Tomas Hrozensky** assert that while socio-economic benefits used to be the predominant driver of EU (European Union) activities in space, recent developments show the rising prominence of a security dimension. All components of the EU Space Programme have a security aspect, and space is increasingly integrated in EU security and defence frameworks. Space is also prominently identified as a key contributor to European strategic autonomy, and there is an emphasis on ensuring the strategic autonomy of the space sector itself. They attribute this evolution to the EU's hedging behavior in response to changes occurring in the international landscape.

Deganit Paikowsky sheds light on the driving forces for advancing space strategies and securitizing space in West Asia through the theoretical lens of membership in the space club. Membership in the space club was always considered a measure of power and high standing. But global politics and technological advancement have introduced significant changes in global space activities. As well, membership in the space club has expanded. She provides an overview of overall space activity in West Asia, and compares the perspectives on club membership of Israel, an established spacefaring nation, with that of the UAE, an emerging spacefaring nation. **Samuel Oyewole** examines the development of space strategies for military-security purposes in countries in Africa. He also discusses their rationales in the framework of African realism, and the implications for national and international security. Drawing on the experiences of Egypt, South Africa, and Nigeria, he contends that the military dimension of African space strategies are driven by a mixture of national and regional interests that are premised on security realities and ideational values. This development has encouraged cooperation amid competition, as Africanist values of progress, peace, brotherhood, and regionalism are crisscrossing realism's ideas of power, security, and status in military space strategies in the region. **Olavo de O. Bittencourt Neto** and **Jairo Becerra** find that the Latin American perspective on space security reflects local particularities and blends military, economic, environmental, and societal dimensions. They examine Brazil, Argentina, and Colombia, assessing their space policies and national concerns. Space programs are conducted by some but not all Latin American nations, with different organizational structures and budgets. Regional space cooperation mechanisms have appeared over the past few decades but have not yet provided sufficient regional coordination.

Prashanth Parameswaran examines the state of play in Southeast Asia space security and strategy over the past few years and finds regional actors have been looking to increase their investments in space technologies and accompanying capabilities. He argues that the increasing pursuit of space capabilities by a wider range of Southeast Asian states over the past few years can be understood in three phases of multi-decade long thinking in this domain, and that it is driven by four key factors: technological diffusion, rising commercial opportunities, intra-regional competition, and a more sobering regional and global geopolitical environment. **Su-Mi Lee and Hanbeom Jeong** review the thirty-year history of South Korea's space programs, using a realist approach to analyze the principal milestones, policies, and development. While there are economic considerations, they argue South Korea's desire to develop space programs can be attributed largely to its security concerns about threats from North Korea. They uncover how distrust in the anarchical international system leads South Korea to pursue self-reliance while signing up for space cooperation with the United States to reinforce and expand the scope of the ROK-US security alliance. **Matthew Stubbs** and **Desislava Gancheva** draw attention to how Australia and New Zealand are making a transition from passive consumers of space services to active space powers. They examine developments such as New Zealand's commercial domestic launch capability through Rocket Lab and Australia's increasing investments in sovereign satellite capabilities. They also consider Australian and New Zealand multilateral engagement on space security. They see the influence of an eclectic mixture of factors in this evolution—economic development, internal and external balancing, cosmopolitanism, neorealism, and neoliberalism—driving the transition of Australia and New Zealand as active space powers.

Strategic Implications of Capabilities

In this section, our contributors take up the challenge of assessing the **strategic implications of capabilities** for interstate stability or instability.

Laura Grego assesses anti-satellite (ASAT) and other space-based weapons. The ability to negate satellite capabilities can help a state be sure a potential adversary cannot use space assets to enhance terrestrial military power in a conflict or to retain exclusive use of orbits or celestial bodies without being challenged. ASAT weapons may have potential deterrence effects, but cannot assure dominance of the space environment. The pursuit of dominance is likely to lead to arms racing and potentially serious crisis instability problems. **Larry F. Martinez** examines the merging of cyber capabilities with space technologies and the resulting military implications. Cybersecurity is connected to the manipulation of software code to disrupt digitally dependent societal or security infrastructures on Earth and in space. As a consequence, cybersecurity is becoming a prime factor in militarizing outer space and its governance. This strategic shift to cyber-intensive forms of coercive force challenges fundamental paradigms about the role of states in space security, the distinctions between defensive and offensive cyber operations, and approaches by states to cyber and space security as critical elements of their overall strategic doctrine. **Michael Raska** and **Malcolm Davis** point to how the diffusion of AI-enabled systems and technologies affects space capabilities that shape warfighting. Specifically, they address the "AI wave" in space operations, reflected in AI-enabled mega-constellations of small satellites combined with machine-enhanced battlespace management and command and control. The diffusion of these emerging and disruptive capabilities poses new challenges for human involvement, decision-making, and professional military training.

Brad Townsend looks at the challenges associated with tracking and removing debris, as well as how the extension of national security competition into space could affect the space environment. He finds that there are clear signs that a security dilemma-driven competition exists in space. One catastrophic consequence of this could be uncontrolled debris generation brought about by conflict. He believes it is both possible and necessary to avoid such an outcome. He concludes with recommendations to ensure the future sustainability of Earth orbits. For normal space operations, elevating debris mitigation guidelines to the level of international law combined with developing enforcement mechanisms for malign actors will reduce debris generation. Further, extending the laws of armed conflict to ban usage of debris-generating weapons in orbit will mitigate the threat of armed conflict extending into space. **Wang Guoyu** argues for the concept of space security global governance (SSGG) as a timely and effective means to preserve space sustainability. He suggests that the escalation of the misperceptions and misunderstandings among powers is more urgent than other factors that have an impact on space sustainability. He argues that states should pursue sincerity and wisdom in seeking common understandings of key terms, like space safety, security, stability, and sustainability. They should also pursue a common recognition of the applicability of the applicable *lex lata* to build up practical coordinative mechanisms and pursue a new international regime for SSGG. **P.J. Blount** takes up the concept of space traffic management (STM) through the lens of the norm life cycle. He suggests that the present system of space traffic coordination is structured through the norm of information sharing. For true STM to emerge, it will be critical for states, commercial actors, and epistemic communities to continue the discursive practices that advance norms. He suggests that this is a multivariate process that happens in different levels of international governance by a variety of actors in a number of different forums.

Alanna Krolikowski and Martin Elvis consider the state of existing governance structures for space resources, identifying a need for institutional development. They analyze states' different interests in governance to explain the international community's bifurcation into two emerging camps, each advocating a distinct approach to regime building. The first camp, led by the United States, is creating permissive and voluntary institutions to facilitate near-term commercial exploitation. The second, loosely coalescing around Russia, China, and numerous lesser spacefaring states, aims to gradually develop a more restrictive and binding regime. This cleavage portends a contested and fragmented international order governing space resource exploitation. **Mariel Borowitz** finds that space activity has been, and largely remains, the province of state actors. But she asserts that data from Earth observation satellites can contribute to human security—focusing on security at the level of the individual and addressing issues such as environmental security, food security, and health security. The trend toward open data policies, the growth of the commercial remote sensing sector, and the increasing availability of data analysis tools and training have created more opportunities for non-state actors to utilize satellite data and to affect prospects for human security in meaningful ways. **Peter L. Hays** and **James J. Wirtz** discuss how space systems provide support for intelligence, surveillance, and reconnaissance activities that are vital to national security. These systems must be integrated into existing force structures, military doctrines, operations, and even logistical procedures before they can reach their full potential. Military space assets are increasingly interwoven with commercial systems, creating strategic and governance challenges for legal regimes that currently demand revision. Despite the fragility of space systems, the apparent dominance of the offense in space, and the inadequacies of the OST regime in the face of many new space security challenges, states appear to have little collective appetite for addressing challenges in the divisive international politics.

Mohamed Amara and Sagee Geetha Sethu argue that national development depends on social, economic, and political components, and that security, writ large, is also an essential contributory element. A top national priority for most countries is to use space technology for the advancement of security, mainly human security. Many states focus on adopting space programs toward this particular end. They provide a comparative analysis of the space programs of emerging spacefaring countries, namely the UAE, Indonesia, Mexico, and South Africa to understand which elements of human security are priorities for these states and the underlying reasons for their focus. **Paul B. Larsen** examines the implications of Global Navigation Satellite Systems (GNSS) that are in geopolitical crisis. The United States, Russia, EU, and China have established international satellite positioning, navigation, and timing systems. With the exception of the European Galileo, they are all linked to confrontational national military operations, yet all provide free services that have become pillars of economic and social society. GNSS services are threatened by intentional harmful interference that undermines their reliability and places stress on the regulatory structure. He surveys the governance mechanisms intended to reduce interference and its impacts.

John J. Klein and Nickolas J. Boensch argue that NewSpace is playing a key role in the changing global security landscape. Many security professionals anticipate that entrepreneurial interest and investment in space companies will lead to significant changes in civil, military, and commercial use of and access to space. NewSpace, then, is essential for achieving a competitive advantage among rival states. While NewSpace companies are a source of innovation and benefit, there are security risks associated with these new capabilities and services. Ultimately, the multitude of benefits coming from NewSpace outweigh any associated risks to security. **Nikola Schmidt** examines planetary defense, the activity of defending the planet Earth from asteroids and comets, through a cosmopolitan framework. Though planetary defense is a transnational or global problem, the current state of planetary defense governance favors undesirable unilateral actions with international security consequences. He argues that planetary defense can be understood and used by every state as a unique opportunity to practice a responsible foreign policy based on cosmopolitan ideas built on scientific efforts. The lens of security cosmopolitanism shows how the international community can effectively govern global security issues and how such policies can contribute to human flourishing.

Prospects

The final section assesses **prospects** for the future of space security, giving us solution-driven perspectives from Europe, the United States, and China.

Natália Archinard suggests ways forward in the global governance of space activities. She presents the majors international initiatives in this area in the last two decades, describing the corresponding positions of different states or groups of states. She explains why finding consensus on international agreements in the areas of space security, safety, and sustainability proves to be challenging for these states. However, with an overview of recent trends in the space sector, she identifies areas in which small steps could advance the global governance of space activities. **James Clay Moltz** assesses future prospects for peaceful outcomes in space by surveying the history of international cooperation, current political dynamics, and emerging technological challenges.

He examines a set of political, technical, and geostrategic factors that are creating new concerns about space conflict. He highlights a series of markers to track peaceful prospects in the years ahead based on international success or failure in dealing with orbital debris, space weapons, and the rise of new actors and companies. He recommends ways forward for preventing conflict and promoting more institutionalized forms of space security. **Zhou Bo** and **Wang Guoyu** find that the landscape of outer space governance is divided into two approaches. China and Russia seek a binding treaty of non-weaponization and no arms race in space, but the US-led western states assert the unavoidability of space weaponization and the appropriateness of non-legally binding rules for responsible behavior. These views are not necessarily incompatible, and they favor a dual-track approach in which all parties agree to the goal of negotiating a binding treaty of non-weaponization and no arms race while encouraging discussions on responsible behaviors that could serve the goal of preventing an arms race in outer space.

WHAT ARE THE TAKEAWAYS?

One of the key goals of this handbook is to use IR analytics to frame our understanding of space security. Our contributors examine how discrete states, regions, and other actors approach space security, giving us also global viewpoints that bring material, ideational, and perceptual elements from IR theory into play. They give readers a holistic view of space security and the contextual and analytical tools needed to understand and situate the potential future developments in the area. This understanding is, in our mind, essential because it presents a variety of different paths and outcomes that states may shape, take, and pursue. We end with some takeaways for space security and IR that are ripe for further consideration by scholars, practitioners, and decision-makers.

- **All actors matter, but states matter more.**
  It is true that states interact with a variety of other actors including commercial actors and international institutions. But at the end of the day, space security is state-centric. It has a terrestrial scope that has a significant impact on what goals actors pursue and how they pursue them in the economic, political, and military realms. Further, while states may be legally banned from claiming territory in space, space is still uniquely aligned to territory. As the security stance within these terrestrial geographies change, this affect how states conceptualize their security goals in and through the space domain.

- **Technology frontiers are many, but entanglement with commerce creates new threats.**
  New and accelerating changes in technology are a critical driver in shaping how states perceive, construct, and move to respond to threats. The dual-use nature of space technologies means that many new space ventures may come to the fore as

commercial concepts but must be assessed as part of national security architectures when evaluating the level of threat from an adversary. Commercial-military fusion means such technologies can be wielded as state power and can become legitimate objects of targeting in war. This technology entanglement affects the calculus of war.

- **"Peaceful purposes" has evolved in international relations, but in misguided ways.**
  Norms, such as peaceful purposes. are malleable and are shaped by how states use and interpret them across time and across different political and power configurations. A core activity in the international politics of space is the contestation of norms using narratives deployed through law and policy instruments, through diplomacy, and through acceptance or rejection of normative interpretation by other states. Through such processes, norms can be strengthened or weakened. The latter situation is where we are, as the normative content of the "peaceful uses of outer space" is being transformed and stretched. Norm-degradation is real and has consequences. A cascade of exits from the OST is a possible one.

- **Bipolarity is emerging in the international space order, and hard power matters.**
  The United States and China are the two dominant poles in space activities, far above the rest. They are seeking to balance each other through internal systems of techno-security industrial innovation, affecting their material power. There are limits to their external attractiveness and persuasion, however. Technological development happens within the context of the state system, and autonomy is prized by many other competent and innovative space powers with their own developmental and defense interests. Further, space governance is still centered in the multilateral arena, and numerous states participate in constituting the overall nature of space security. In line with their own national interests and visions, they also actively contribute to state practice and norm building in the space domain.

- **Conflict in space is not inevitable, but it is increasingly unavoidable.**
  Contemporary geopolitics is pushing the international community further down a path toward a conflict in, through, and at the nexus of space. If such a conflict were to manifest, there is little certainty as to its nature and outcome, which could range from an environmentally destructive kinetic war to one in which satellites are attacked through non-kinetic means, such as electronic and cyber. Any such conflict will likely be tied to a corresponding terrestrial conflict and be driven by that connection both tactically and strategically.

- **Building mutually assured transparency is necessary.**
  A theme repeatedly returned to in this handbook is the need for norms that establish what constitutes legitimate activity within the space domain. Such norms,

found in the OST, have been critical to sustaining space security into the current era. As technology changes and the international arena continues to transform, there is increasing pressure to come to some sort of normative agreement on legitimate behavior that brings in the major space powers along with broad multilateral support. Greater transparency in space activities, and reinforcement of already supported normative frames, would serve as an initial building block to consider in such discussions. However, this would require space actors to come to the diplomatic table in good faith. The strategic and tactical implications of the changing technological context of space suggests that there is an increasing need to understand the dynamics of space diplomacy.

REFERENCES

Blount, P.J. 2019. "The Shifting Sands of Space Security: The Politics and Law of the Peaceful Uses of Outer Space." *Indonesian Journal of International Law* 17, no. 1: 1–18.

Blount, P.J. 2018 "Space Security Law." In *Oxford Encyclopedia of Interplanetary Science*. Oxford University Press. https://oxfordre.com/planetaryscience/display/10.1093/acrefore/978019 0647926.001.0001/acrefore-9780190647926-e-73;jsessionid=486534B1186073302265DB222 5708F56#acrefore-9780190647926-e-73-bibItem-0071.

Bowen, Bleddyn E. 2020. *War in Space: Strategy, Spacepower, Geopolitics*. Edinburgh: Edinburgh University Press.

Bowen, Bleddyn E. 2022. *Original Sin: Power, Technology, and War in Outer Space*. New York, NY: Oxford University Press.

Bormann, Natalie, and Michael Sheehan, eds. 2009. *Securing Outer Space*. New York: Routledge.

Burrows, William E. 1998. *This New Ocean: The Story of the First Space Age*. New York: Modern Library.

Coletta, Damon, and Frances T. Pilch, eds. 2009. *Space and Defense Policy*. New York: Routledge.

Dawson, Linda. 2018. *War in Space: The Science and Technology Behind Our Next Theater of Conflict*. Cham, Switzerland: Springer.

Deudney, Daniel. 2020. *Dark Skies: Space Expansionism, Planetary Geopolitics and the Ends of Humanity*. New York: Oxford University Press.

Dolman, Everett C. 2002. *Astropolitik: Classical Geopolitics in the Space Age*. New York: Frank Cass.

Eisenhower, Dwight D. 1960. Address Before the 15th General Assembly of the United Nations. https://www.presidency.ucsb.edu/documents/address-before-the-15th-general-assembly-the-united-nations-new-york-city.

Gheciu, Alexandra, and William C. Wohlforth, eds. 2018. *The Oxford Handbook of International Security*. New York: Oxford University Press.

Goldsen, Joseph M. 1963. "Outer Space in World Politics." In *Outer Space in World Politics*, edited by Joseph M. Goldsen, 3–24. (New York: Frederick A. Praeger).

Gray, Colin S. 1996. "The Influence of Space Power Upon History." *Comparative Strategy*, 15, no. 4: 293–308.

Hays, Peter L. 2011. *Space and Security*. Santa Barbara: ABC-CLIO.

Jakhu, Ram S., and Joseph N. Pelton, eds. 2017. *Global Space Governance: An International Study*. Cham, Switzerland: Springer.

Johnson-Freese, Joan. 2007. *Space as a Strategic Asset*. New York: Columbia University Press.

Johnson-Freese, Joan. 2017. *Space Warfare in the 21st Century: Arming the Heavens*. New York: Routledge.

Katzenstein, Peter J., and Rudra Sil. 2008. "Eclectic Theorizing in the Study and Practice of International Relations." In *The Oxford Handbook of International Relations*, edited by Christian Reus-Smit and Duncan Sindal, 109–30. New York: Oxford University Press, 2008.

KCNA. 2009. "KCNA Report on DPRK's Accession to International Space Treaty and Convention." March 2. https://web.archive.org/web/20090402023049/http://www.kcna.co.jp/item/2009/200903/news12/20090312-11ee.html.

Klein, John J. 2006. *Space Warfare: Strategy, Principles and Policy*. New York: Routledge.

Klein, John J. 2019. *Understanding Space Strategy: The Art of War in Space*. New York: Routledge.

Lake, David A. 2008. "The State and International Relations." In *The Oxford Handbook of International Relations*, edited by Christian Reus-Smit and Duncan Snidal, 41–61. New York: Oxford University Press.

Lyall, Francis, and Paul B. Larsen. 2018. *Space Law: A Treatise (Second Edition)*. New York: Routledge.

MacDonald, Alexander. 2017. *The Long Space Age: The Economic Origins of Space Exploration*. New Haven: Yale University Press.

Masson-Zwaan, Tanja, and Mahulena Hofmann. 2019. *Introduction to Space Law (Fourth Edition)*. The Netherlands: Wolters Kluwer.

McDougal, Myres S., Harold D. Lasswell, and Ivan A Vlasic. 1963. *Law and Public Order in Space*. New Haven and London: Yale University Press.

McDougall, Walter A. 1985. *The Heavens and the Earth: A Political History of the Space Age*. New York: Basic Books.

Moltz, James Clay. 2008. *The Politics of Space Security: Strategic Restraint and the Pursuit of National Interests*. Stanford: Stanford University Press.

Mutschler, Max M. 2013. *Arms Control in Space: Exploring Conditions for Preventive Arms Control*. New York: Palgrave MacMillan.

Mutschler, Max M. 2015. "Security Cooperation in Space and International Relations Theory." In *Handbook of Space Security: Policies, Applications and Programs*, edited by Kai-Uwe Schrogl, Peter L. Hays, Jana Robinson, Denis Moura, and Christina Giannopapa, 41–56. Vol. 1. New York: Springer Reference.

Pace, Scott. 2023. "U.S. Space Policy and Theories of International Relations: The Case for Analytical Eclecticism." *Space Policy*. https://doi.org/10.1016/j.spacepol.2022.101538.

Pekkanen, Saadia M. 2019. "Governing the New Space Race." *American Journal of International Law Unbound* 113: 92–97. https://www.cambridge.org/core/journals/american-journal-of-international-law/article/governing-the-new-space-race/14BD9B37A7A15A8E225A5355BB29E51B.

Pekkanen, Saadia M., John Ravenhill, and Rosemary Foot, eds. 2014. *The Oxford Handbook of the International Relations of Asia*. New York: Oxford University Press.

Pfaltzgraff, Robert L., Jr. 2011. "International Relations Theory and Spacepower." In *Toward a Theory of Spacepower: Selected Essays*, edited by Charles D. Lutes and Peter L. Hays with Vincent A. Manzo, Lisa M. Yambrick, and M. Elaine Bunn, 37–56. Washington, DC: National Defense University Press.

Reus-Smit, Christian, and Duncan Snidal, eds. 2008. *The Oxford Handbook of International Relations*. New York: Oxford University Press.

Roberts, Darryl. 1988. "Space and International Relations." *The Journal of Politics* 50, no. 4: 1075–90.

Schrogl, Kai-Uwe, Peter L. Hays, Jana Robinson, Denis Moura, and Christina Giannopapa, eds. 2015. *Handbook of Space Security: Policies, Applications and Programs*, Vol. 1 and Vol. 2. New York: Springer Reference.

Sheehan, Michael. 2007. *The International Politics of Space*. New York: Routledge.

Sheehan, Michael. 2015. "Defining Space Security." In *Handbook of Space Security: Policies, Applications and Programs*, edited by Kai-Uwe Schrogl, Peter L. Hays, Jana Robinson, Denis Moura, and Christina Giannopapa, 7–21. Vol. 1. New York: Springer Reference.

Siddiqi, Asif A. 2000. *Challenge to Apollo: The Soviet Union and the Space Race, 1945–1974*. Washington, DC: National Aeronautics and Space Administration.

Siddiqi, Asif A. 2010. *The Red Rockets' Glare: Spaceflight and the Soviet Imagination, 1857–1957*. New York, NY: Cambridge University Press.

Sil, Rudra, and Peter J. Katzenstein. 2010a. "Analytic Eclecticism in the Study of World Politics: Reconfiguring Problems and Mechanisms across Research Traditions." *Perspectives on Politics* 8, no. 2: 411–31.

Sil, Rudra, and Peter J. Katzenstein. 2010b. *Beyond Paradigms: Analytic Eclecticism in the Study of World Politics*. New York: Palgrave Macmillan.

Stares, Paul B. 1985. *The Militarization of Space: U.S. Policy, 1945–1984*. Ithaca: Cornell University Press.

Steer, Cassandra, and Matthew Hersch, eds. 2021. *War and Peace in Outer Space: Law, Policy, and Ethics*. New York: Oxford University Press.

Stroikos, Dimitrios. 2022. "International Relations and Outer Space." *Oxford Research Encyclopedia of International Studies*. https://doi.org/10.1093/acrefore/9780190846 626.013.699.

Townsend, Brad. 2020. *Security and Stability in the New Space Age: The Orbital Security Dilemma*. New York: Routledge.

Tyson, Neil deGrasse, and Avis Lang. 2018. *Accessory to War: The Unspoken Alliance between Astrophysics and the Military*. New York: W. W. Norton & Company.

von der Dunk, Frans, with Fabio Tronchetti, eds. 2015. *Handbook of Space Law*. Cheltenham and Northampton: Edward Elgar.

CHAPTER 2

···

A SHORT HISTORY OF SPACE SECURITY

···

STEPHEN BUONO AND AARON BATEMAN

SPACE has always been about security. The first man-made object to breach earth's atmosphere was a weapon of war, the Nazis' A-4 missile. When the first successful test of these *vergeltungswaffen* reached an altitude of 56 miles on October 3, 1942, Peenemünde director Walter Dornberger exclaimed, "Today, the spaceship is born!" (Gangale 2018).[*] Within three years, hundreds of "spaceships" had rained down on the United Kingdom (UK), France, and Belgium in a storm of terror. Once the USSR officially kickstarted the space age in 1957, the implications for national safety were multivariate but no less obvious. Satellite reconnaissance offered to penetrate secretive military-industrial complexes and verify arms control agreements. Global television broadcasting meant propaganda in every hut. Space weapons menaced the imagination. In the later years of the twentieth century, as near-earth orbits became increasingly populated with satellites, space was linked to security far beyond military dimensions. We now rely on space-based infrastructure to communicate, navigate our ships, planes, and cars, conduct e-commerce and banking transactions, monitor our crops, and predict the onset of natural disasters. Space security is about physical security, economic security, and even food security.

What follows is a condensed account of this history, particularly its origins and development in the Cold War. Surveying the first half-century of space security, one notices both a general trend and a sharp dividing line. The trend is that from 1957 to the present, the definition of space security—that is to say, the variety of issues huddling under its umbrella—gradually expanded. In the mid-1950s, when cosmic flight first became a reality, space security implied mainly security from intercontinental ballistic missiles

·············

[*] There is disagreement about where "air" ends and "space" begins. NASA and the US Air Force have suggested the two blend together at 50 miles, whereas the Fédération Aéronautique Internationale, the National Oceanic and Atmospheric Administration, and a host of other agencies argue that the Kármán line (roughly 62 miles) is the boundary.

(ICBMs), which plied space during their heinous trajectories. Americans troubled by *Sputnik* were less concerned with the satellite than with the massive rocket that had propelled it into orbit. But it did not take long for the list to grow. Satellites quickly required legal and technological protections, for Washington and Moscow detonated nuclear weapons at orbital altitudes and developed robust anti-satellite (ASAT) programs, the latter a key focus of this chapter given their continued relevance in the post–Cold War period. International space law blossomed as an academic and professional discipline. By the mid-1960s a host of other problems emerged, including the vulnerability of the space environment itself. Today, "space security" captures everything from orbital debris to extraterrestrial resources to safety from asteroids. The dawn of private spaceflight promises to complicate matters even further (Sheehan 2015).

The topographer of space security will also notice a sharp cleavage separating this history. Despite massive military space budgets and pervasive discourse about a competitive, antagonistic "space race," the first period—running from 1957 to 1975—was one of relative military restraint and significant diplomatic achievement. Lavish space-weapon projects languished under the tarp. International space law grew and matured. For all the bluster with which Nikita Khrushchev hailed space technology as a revolution in Soviet military power, in practical terms he fell in step with three consecutive US presidents and a host of international organizations building a political consensus about keeping war out of space. By 1966, the USSR, the United States, and dozens of other countries around the world agreed in a landmark treaty that space should be exempted from political competition and violence. The Apollo-Soyuz Test Project in 1975—in which a US spacecraft docked with a Soviet capsule—seemed to mark the transition of détente to the cosmos. Astronaut and cosmonaut embraced.

But signs, tokens, and myths were these. Space politics proved no more immune to the whims of history than earthly politics. The second period of space security (1975–1991) mapped neatly onto the deterioration of US-Soviet relations from the mid-to-late 1970s. Out of fear that NASA's shuttle program reflected a dangerous military capacity, the USSR reinitiated its co-orbital anti-satellite program in 1976; Gerald Ford's administration, in turn, concluded that treating space as a "sanctuary" was "neither enforceable nor verifiable," and conducted its own battery of ASAT tests (Memorandum from David Elliot to Brent Scowcroft 1976). Jimmy Carter and Leonid Brezhnev attempted to salvage the impasse in a series of talks in 1978 and 1979, but to no avail. Instead, space technology came to be viewed not as a surrogate for the Cold War but a means to wage and win it: a race to the high ground. Research into kinetic-kill vehicles, directed-energy weapons, and other space weapons proliferated. The fever peaked in 1983 when Ronald Reagan announced the Strategic Defense Initiative (SDI), a spaceborne system for ballistic missile defense equipped with sensors, guidance systems, and high-energy lasers.

The collapse of the USSR in 1991 did bring a measure of stability to international space security, but the future was no less ambiguous. Though Washington and the new regime in Moscow hoped to steer space technology away from military applications, the decisive role that satellites played in the First Gulf War kept those considerations at the front of official policy. And while US leaders no longer had to fear the boogeyman of Soviet space weapons, they did little to address either the proliferation of potentially hostile space powers, such as China, or the sheer increase in the quantity of space activities unfolding across the globe, both public and private.

In the realm of space security, then, the end of the Cold War amounted to the most dangerous threat—direct conflict between great powers—making room for a host of other phenomena, less understood at first but no less challenging. The bipolar structure of space security gave way to a multilateral one in which budding space powers like China, India, and Japan as well as post-colonial nations desiring a stake in the future helped shape the international space security regime. And although states continued to play the central role in space, private communications and spaceflight firms grew in importance, drove change, and thus filled out a diverse table of stakeholders. Whether this diffusion of influence in space security will continue or succumb to a great-power (dare one say Cold War) retrenchment in space is one of the central questions of this volume. We will be living with the consequences for decades.

THE SEARCH FOR STABILITY, 1957–1975

In the beginning, there were rockets. When in the 1920s pioneering theorists and engineers in Russia, Europe, and the United States began working out the potential for liquid-fuel rockets to ferry human beings into space, none then used the term "space security," yet from the start the implications of these instruments for war and peace were near at hand. Most of the progenitors of human spaceflight—including Konstantin Tsiolkovsky in Russia, Robert Goddard in the United States, and Herman Oberth in Germany—were well attuned to the ways in which the dream of space travel might be adapted to the cause of violence, and several actively sought patronage for their research from the military. Historians have well documented the origins of the US and Soviet space programs in the interwar work of plucky rocket societies and tinkerers, and it requires no recapitulation here (Mc Dougall 1985; Siddiqi 2003; Bainbridge 1976; Gainor 2008; Geppert 2008; Buckeley 1991). Suffice it to say: space security was born decades before the first satellites reached orbit. As the technical foundations of modern rocketry developed, so too did theoretical speculations about its significance to international security. Writers across the West at once recognized the revolutionary military potential of rockets as long-distance ordnance and hoped they would serve the interests of peace, either by making war prohibitively terrible or else by uniting humanity in the interests of scientific discovery and adventure (Buono 2023). Engineer Arthur Cleaver, president of the British Interplanetary Society, envisioned space exploration as an "outlet" for the innate aggression of *homo sapiens*, a moral equivalent to war (Cleaver 1948). Science-fiction authors and philosophers such as David Lasser, Arthur C. Clarke, and Olaf Stapledon provided an imaginative tableau in which earthly animosities would simply melt away once human beings had reached space in unison (Kilgore 2003). Particularly after the shock of atomic weaponry in 1945—and, of course, the inevitable conclusion that states would adapt rockets to carry the bomb—these and other writers urged that disarmament in space would lead to disarmament back on earth.

Though the centrality of the rocket still held when the space age began in earnest on October 4, 1957, space security quickly became a complicated affair. For when the USSR launched *Sputnik I*, space policy did not constitute, as it does today, a distinct realm of international relations warranting its own strategic debates, academic specialists, and budgets; rather, it was indistinguishable from Soviet and US national security, particularly military policy and nuclear deterrence. *Sputnik* solidified a security paradigm in which every conceivable realm of human organization and ingenuity became a battleground of competence. US space strategy in the Eisenhower years is a case in point. The United States had to wage a total cold war against the USSR *and* maintain the integrity of its institutions and budget; build its space program using military personnel and technology *and* prevent the Pentagon from taking control over civilian missions; meet Moscow's technological challenge *and* keep space weapon free. Thus did a dual-track space policy develop: pursuit, on the one hand, of the technical means in space to preserve the US nuclear deterrent (especially the ability to spy on the Soviet arsenal with satellites) and, on the other, a legal regime that would maintain the United States' image as a promoter of peace and cooperation in space (McDougall 1985).

Soviet space strategy was equally complex, as it depended on the unique parameters demanded by Marxist-Leninist ideology (which revered technology and pitched it as the engine of socialism) and what Walter McDougall calls "The Khrushchevian Synthesis" (which linked the space-technological revolution with the story of the USSR itself). Within this milieu, Soviet space security sought to: (1) propound the military superiority of the USSR and the technological-organizational superiority of communism; (2) keep pace with the United States in the military applications of space to head off US "space control"; (3) resist, either through technology or politics, the use of spy satellites; and (4) leverage ICBM production to cut conventional military costs and—for Khrushchev specifically—limit the power of the armed forces. As with the United States, these goals dictated that there be two space races: the civilian one defined by space spectaculars, firsts, and manned missions, and the military one defined by the contribution of space systems to the balance of power (McDougall 1985).

And so began what scholars have since the 1980s referred to as "the militarization of space," which, though it threatened to dominate international space security from the outset, proceeded in surprisingly benign fashion (Geppert, Brandau, and Siebeneichner 2020; Stares 1985a; Kalic 2012; Mowthorpe 2004; Gupta 1985). Believing that outer space would soon constitute a new dimension of armed conflict, engineers, officers, and, in the US case, aerospace firms, promoted every military space system under the sun, from bombardment satellites and space planes to lunar bases and orbiting battle stations. But fiscal, technical, and political constraints made the most fantastical projects an impossibility, lending some measure of stability to US-Soviet relations in space. The USSR, for example, developed a prototype "fractional orbital bombardment system" (FOBS), but it remained unarmed and in any case inferior to land- and submarine-launched ballistic missiles. The US Air Force (USAF) poured billions of dollars into the Dyna-Soar space glider—which would air-launch into space, "bounce" of the atmosphere, and deploy missiles against targets on Earth and in space—only to cancel the program in 1963. Indeed, far from developing space weapons projects that would revolutionize war, the two sides instead developed ancillary systems that bolstered the existing military apparatus: satellites for early warning, reconnaissance, arms control verification, communications, navigation, weather forecasting, and geodetic data gathering (Stares 1985b).

To hedge their bets against enemy domination of space, both superpowers did explore methods to torpedo enemy satellites. In the United States, interservice rivalry gave rise to a range of viable ASAT systems. Martin Aircraft teamed up with the USAF to birth Bold Orion, which deployed an air-launched missile from a Boeing B-47. In October 1959, Bold Orion became the vessel for the world's first ASAT test when a prototype came within four miles of *Explorer IV* as it reached its apogee over Cape Canaveral. Over the next five years the USAF pushed numerous other plans: Project SAINT (a co-orbital "inspection" system doubling as an ASAT weapon); Program 437 (a modified Thor missile tipped with a nuclear warhead); and, most evocatively, Dyna-Soar. The US Navy, not to be outdone, forwarded its own air-launched system, Project Hi-Ho, as well as proposals, grouped under the name Early Spring, involving the use of direct-ascent submarine-launched ballistic missiles. Even the US Army joined in. From November 1957 it argued that the three-stage, solid-fueled Nike-Zeus missile could be easily prepared for the ASAT role. Code-named MUDFLAP (later Project 505), the program received the go-ahead in May 1962 (Chun 2006).

In the USSR, early ASAT studies split between two designs, each promoted by a titan of the Soviet space program. Sergei Korolev pushed for his R-7 rocket to carry an interceptor that would collide directly with the target. Vladimir Chelomei, chief designer at OKB-52, forwarded a self-guided, co-orbital vehicle that would explode once in proximity to the target. In contrast to the mishmash of programs unfolding in the United States, in 1960 the Kremlin, prompted by the U-2 affair and public revelations about Project SAINT, committed to Chelomei's design and designated it the IS (Istrebitel Sputnikov, or "destroyer of satellites") program. The first test flight occurred in November 1963, and the Soviets successfully intercepted their own satellite five years later. Clandestine tests would continue for the rest of the decade (Siddiqi 1997; Zak 2013; Mowthorpe 2007).

Anti-satellite tests in the late 1950s and early 1960s raised an important new issue in space security: how might space wars or, at the very least, conflicts begun *in* space, affect the orbital environment? Scientists, journalists, and laypeople alike reacted with a mix of curiosity and alarm when in March 1959 the *New York Times* revealed that the Atomic Energy Commission and the Pentagon had conducted nuclear weapons tests in outer space the previous fall. The Department of Defense (DoD) had designed the test series, codenamed Project Argus, to ascertain the fitness of high-altitude detonations for the ASAT role and ballistic missile defense: if the emitted electrons from such denotations became trapped in the earth's naturally occurring bands of geomagnetic radiation, perhaps they might destroy enemy satellites, disrupt the sensitive electronic components of ICBMs, or disrupt radio communications. But what of the planet? "The Earth is so minute on the cosmic scale and its environment is controlled by the delicate balance of such great natural forces," thought British astronomer Bernard Lovell, "that one must view with dismay a potential interference with these processes before they are investigated by the delicate tools of the true scientist" (Fleming 2020).

By the time of the *Times*'s exposé, the United States, the USSR, and the UK had agreed to a nuclear test moratorium out of both political convenience and genuine concerns about fallout. It lasted only three years. In September 1961 the USSR restarted its testing regimen, including blasts far above the Kármán line (roughly 62 miles) separating the Earth's atmosphere from the infinite reaches beyond. The Kennedy administration was not far behind. Particularly concerning was the United States' Starfish Prime test, which set off 1.5 megatons 250 miles above the Central Pacific on July 9, 1962. The blast dispersed a cloud of radioactive particles that chaffed and burnt out the solar batteries of six satellites, including the world's first communication satellite, *Telstar I*, which had begun beaming television to Europe that same week (Wolverton 2018). The USSR conducted its own cosmic test series—"Project K"—in 1961 and 1962. The electro-magnetic pulse (EMP) emitted by one test induced a powerful current that fused 350 miles of telephone lines and ignited a fire that burned down a nearby power plant (Moltz 2019).

Did this not constitute the "militarization of outer space?" Only briefly. In the mid-1960s it was not militarization but rather arms control that characterized the space security regime. Concerns over the impact that exospheric nuclear tests would have on the civilian space program, including the risk such tests posed to astronauts, helped drive support for the 1963 Limited Test Ban Treaty (LTBT), which banned nuclear tests in outer space, underwater, and in the atmosphere (Higuchi 2020). Only months later the superpowers attached their signatures to a landmark United Nations General Assembly (UNGA) resolution calling upon states to refrain from stationing nuclear weapons in orbit, on celestial bodies, or in outer space generally. Banning both space nuclear weapons tests and the stationing of nuclear weapons in space effectively nullified a half-decade of US research on satellite bombardment.

The rising tide of space diplomacy crested in 1966 when the United States and the USSR submitted to the UN Committee on the Peaceful Uses of Outer Space (COPOUS) competing drafts of a treaty governing activities on the moon and other celestial bodies. The Soviet document was much broader (it encompassed all of space) and more closely tied to the earlier UNGA resolutions, thus the COPUOS Legal Subcommittee used it as the basis for negotiations. The talks took merely six months to complete, a speed that contradicted the difficult issues involved. The resulting Outer Space Treaty (OST)—known formally as the Treaty on Principles Governing the Activities of States in the Exploration and Use of Outer Space, including the Moon and Other Celestial Bodies—was a diplomatic triumph. It circumscribed political conflict over space to an extent and in language that would have made the architects of the defunct League of Nations Charter green with jealousy. Its very first article decreed that signatories would explore and use space "for the benefit and in the interests of all countries," regardless of their individual contributions to spaceflight. Space would henceforth be "the province of all mankind" (Graham and LaVera 2003; Buono 2020).

From a security perspective, the most important clauses derive from Articles II and IV. The former, assuaging widespread concerns about a neocolonial race to the moon, stated unequivocally that outer space, including heavenly bodies, is ineligible to sovereign claims by use or occupation. The latter article enshrined earlier resolutions into binding international law, banning the placement of weapons of mass destruction in space or on celestial bodies and declaring that such bodies would be used "exclusively for peaceful purposes." The treaty forbids the construction of military bases or installations, the testing of all weapons, and the conduct of military maneuvers on celestial bodies.

It is no exaggeration to say that the entry of the OST into force is, to date, the most significant milestone in the history of global space security (Aoki, this volume). The agreement, which more than 100 countries have signed, has assumed a "quasi-constitutional" role in the governance of space (Vedda 2017) In the seventeen years following 1967, the OST acted as bedrock for four additional international space treaties: the 1968 Rescue Agreement, which provides for the assistance of distressed astronauts; the 1972 Liability Convention, which provided assurance to those who suffer damages caused by space objects; the 1975 Registration Convention, which compels states to keep a record of objects launched into space and to inform the UN Secretary-General of that record; and the 1984 Moon Agreement that established the moon and its natural resources "the common heritage of mankind."

Alongside the OST, the culmination of the US moon program in the late 1960s and early 1970s appeared to confirm the arrival of a more cooperative, irenic space politics divested from the Cold War. Though *Apollo 11* astronauts Neil Armstrong and Edwin Aldrin planted the US flag in the lunar surface, they also brought with them miniature flags from every UN member nation so they might be gifted to world leaders upon return to earth. Before departing the moon, they also left a small silicone disc inscribed with well wishes from more than seventy countries; a gold olive branch; and, in defiance of the space race, two medals commemorating Soviet cosmonauts Yuri Gagarin and Vladimir Komarov, who had recently died in tragic crashes. Memorably, they also left a plaque recording that when "men from planet Earth" had first set foot upon the moon, they had come "in peace for all mankind." The transplantation to outer space of US-Soviet détente was punctuated most evocatively six years later, in July 1975, when an Apollo spacecraft docked with a Soyuz capsule, an event crowned by "handshakes in space."

THE SEARCH FOR SAFETY, 1975–2001

The cosmic honeymoon was short lived. Within five months of the Apollo-Soyuz victory, anxieties about the Soviet ASAT program resurfaced after the USSR renewed testing of its co-orbital ASAT. The US intelligence community reported that the Soviet ASAT had become fully operational in 1971 and was likely "capable of intercepts at up to 2,500 nm altitude," meaning that imagery and electronic intelligence satellites were within reach. Due to its altitude limitations, the USSR's ASAT could not attack early warning, communications, and intelligence satellites in geosynchronous orbit, but analysts warned that that "the Soviets have also demonstrated a capability to perform some of the orbital operations required to intercept a satellite in geostationary orbit" (Interagency Intelligence Memorandum on Soviet Dependence on Space Systems 1975).

The growing body of intelligence on Soviet ASAT developments pushed the Ford administration in early 1976 to form a special panel to investigate the reduction of satellite vulnerability, the military uses of space over the next fifteen years, and the United States' own possible development of ASAT weapons. Physicist Solomon Buchsbaum, once a presidential science advisor, oversaw the study. He and his team concluded that the US government should take additional measures to enhance the survivability of its military and intelligence satellites, prompting Ford to sign National Security Decision Memorandum (NSDM) 333 to make critical space systems more resilient (NSDM 333). Given the importance of satellites for US national security, NSDM 333 was long overdue.

But the panel went much further with its recommendations. In the 1970s, both the United States and the USSR had begun to use military and intelligence satellites to more directly support tactical operations. The USSR had launched a constellation of ocean surveillance satellites that could provide targeting information on US and allied naval vessels in near-real-time (Siddiqi 1999). Additionally, in late 1976 the Ford administration would oversee the launch of KH-11, the first US electro-optical satellite that could rapidly downlink imagery and send it to the president's desk in minutes rather than having to wait weeks for film-return canisters from older satellite reconnaissance systems. Consequently, Buchsbaum and his colleagues had concluded that "this trend toward effective integration of space assets into military combat operations will continue and that real-time space capabilities will become increasingly important—even essential to the effective use of military forces" (Memorandum from David Elliot to Brent Scowcroft 1976).

Due to this shift toward tactical usage, enemy satellites would become important targets in wartime, which required having ASATs to destroy them. According to the final report, non-interference provisions in the SALT and ABM Treaties did not apply to wartime situations and the targeting of satellites that were not primarily used for arms control verification. Due to these factors, Buchsbaum and his colleagues argued that "treating space as a sanctuary, [was] neither enforceable nor verifiable" and that "the Soviets should not be allowed an exclusive sanctuary in space" (Memorandum from David Elliot to Brent Scowcroft 1976).

In his last few days in office Ford signed NSDM 345, which directed the development of a non-nuclear ASAT to "selectively nullify certain militarily important Soviet space systems, should that become necessary." The president, moreover, approved the creation of a non-kinetic ASAT mechanism to electronically attack satellite command and control links with the stated goal of being "able to use such an anti-satellite capability in a reversible, less provocative way at lower crisis thresholds" (NSDM 345). The Soviet ASAT capability, coupled with the shift toward the tactical usage of satellites, prompted Ford and his senior advisors to view space security in more competitive terms (NSDM 345).

When Jimmy Carter defeated Ford in the 1976 presidential election, he, in contrast, was not convinced of the military utility of ASATs. Rather than focusing on being able to destroy Soviet satellites, he wanted to negotiate limits leading to the elimination of US and Soviet ASATs. The president believed that an ASAT competition would be costly and threaten satellites that were needed to verify arms control treaties. Carter wrote in a March 1977 letter to Soviet General Secretary Leonid Brezhnev that he sought an "agreement not to arm satellites nor to develop the ability to destroy or damage satellites" (Letter from President Carter to Soviet General Secretary Brezhnev 1976). Due to his arms control objectives, the president placed NSDM 345 in abeyance pending a policy review (PRM-23 1977).

Despite the administration's emphasis on arms control, the joint chiefs argued for continued development of an ASAT in response to the Soviet ASAT and maintained that such a capability would indeed have deterrent value. Most importantly, they wanted the means to negate the Soviet ocean-surveillance satellites that could threaten NATO's ability to maintain its sea lines of communication. The service chiefs warned that the USSR could "gain superiority in space" if the United States did not act (Memorandum from the Chairman of the Joint Chiefs of Staff to Secretary of Defense Brown 1977). Intelligence analysts, however, continued to doubt that a US ASAT would actually deter the USSR in wartime (Interagency Intelligence Memorandum on Soviet Dependence on Space Systems 1975). Intelligence reporting in 1978 suggested, nevertheless, that the USSR could develop ASATs designed to attack higher altitude satellites, which would threaten critical early warning and nuclear command and control infrastructure. This situation would be a source of even greater instability (National Intelligence Estimate 1978). To highlight the ASAT problem, the head of the Central Intelligence Agency (CIA), Admiral Stansfield Turner, said hyperbolically that "the Russians can kill us in space" (New York Daily News 1978).

National Security Advisor Zbigniew Brzezinski warned Carter of the psychological power of space weapons, saying that a Soviet demonstration of a laser ASAT could have an even more negative impact on the US people than Sputnik (Memorandum for Brzezinski 1977). This advice came at a time of growing anxiety in the public sphere about war in space. In the late 1970s, people feared outer space being transformed into a battlefield due to reports about Soviet "killer satellites" (Siebeneichner 2018). The BBC series "The Real War in Space" (1978) featured interviews with high-ranking US officials and scientists who talked of the growing danger associated with laser weapons and ASATs. Media reports also claimed that the USSR had "achieved a technical breakthrough" with a laser "capable of neutralizing the entire United States ballistic missile force" (New York Times 1977).

As a result of increased public attention on space weapons, a US inter-agency working group acknowledged that "exaggerated statements in the US press about lasers" had "raised public concerns about a possible arms competition in space" (PRM/NSC-23 1977). It appeared that there was a fleeting opportunity to prevent the militarization of space from entering into a full-fledged arms race. Not everyone was convinced, however, that space weapons were inherently dangerous or destabilizing. There were space enthusiasts who embraced futuristic ideas about lasers in space for missile defense. Maxwell Hunter, a Lockheed engineer who would develop close ties to Senator Malcom Wallop (D-WY), argued that "lasers in space could produce a revolution in warfare by ending the long-standing dominance of offensive weapons" and that it was therefore "a genocidal hoax" to treat space as a sanctuary (PRM/NSC-23 1977).

US allies had begun to pay closer attention to space security issues in this time period as well. A classified UK study observed that "in view of NATO's increasing reliance on military satellites for intelligence gathering, navigation and C3 [command, control, and communications], the deployment of an effective Soviet system could pose a general threat to Western security" (FCO 66/1343. n.d.). In light of this situation, UK ambassador to NATO John Killick expressed the concern that if either the United States or the USSR used its ASATs, "the side whose satellites have been put of action [might] have to contemplate first use of nuclear weapons for fear of themselves becoming the victim of a first pre-emptive strike" (FCO 66/1137 1978). In a word, there was fear that ASATs would increase the likelihood of nuclear war.

In 1978 and 1979 US and Soviet representatives met multiple times to discuss potential limits on ASATs. As Moscow and Washington began, the UN Committee on Disarmament advocated the prevention of an arms race in outer space (Alves 1991). To place greater pressure on Moscow to agree to ASAT constraints, Carter authorized the development of kinetic and non-kinetic ASAT capabilities and removed the restriction on testing against objects in space. Progress in the negotiations was slow, and there were many disagreements over what even constituted an ASAT. For instance, the USSR was concerned about the US space shuttle being used as a weapon (Telegram from US Embassy in Finland 1978). While US officials remained hopeful that an agreement was indeed possible, the Soviet invasion of Afghanistan in 1979 brought the talks to a standstill. Consequently, moving into the 1980s, the space security situation appeared even more tenuous.

Upon coming into office, Ronald Reagan began the largest peacetime military buildup in US history. His administration approached space as yet another domain that required greater military resources to dissuade the USSR from acting against US interests. To this end, Reagan's first space policy signed in July 1981 directed the DoD to develop an ASAT to "deter threats" to US space systems and "to deny the adversary the use of space-based systems" in wartime (Reagan 1982). Ideas about using ASATs for space control were being solidified during this period (Newberry 1997). The perceived need to "operationalize" space would lead to the establishment of Air Force Space Command in 1982 and then US Space Command in 1985 (Report of Commission to Assess United States National Security Space Management and Organization 2001).

One of Reagan's most controversial acts was his March 1983 speech calling for scientists to develop a capability to render nuclear weapons "impotent and obsolete" (Reagan 1983). Although he did not explicitly mention space capabilities, this was clearly what he had in mind. Shortly thereafter, the president established the Strategic Defense Initiative (SDI), a research program to develop technologies that could be used to destroy ballistic missiles in all phases of flight. Developing space-based defenses would, however, violate the 1972 ABM Treaty. The United Kingdom expressed concern that SDI would lead to a "free for all in space" (PREM 19/11881984). British, French, and West German officials were especially worried about the implications of space-based missile defense for strategic stability (Allied Attitudes towards the Strategic Defense Initiative 1985). Because of SDI, missile defense largely defined space security in the 1980s.

In late 1983, the USSR proposed a moratorium on ASAT testing leading to their full elimination. US administration officials recognized, however, that limits on ASATs would hamper the development of SDI because they both depended on the same technologies (Minutes of a National Security Planning Group Meeting 1984). Kenneth Adelman, the head of the Arms Control and Disarmament Agency, advocated "rules of the road" for space to alleviate US-Soviet tensions in this general area, but there was little support for this from other administration officials (Minutes of a National Security Council Meeting 1985). The White House sought to deploy its air-launched Miniature Homing Vehicle (MHV) ASAT as soon as possible and conducted a debris-producing test in 1985. After this, Congress placed restrictions on testing against objects in space; faced with ASAT testing constraints, the Pentagon cancelled MHV in 1988 (Weeden 2014).

Largely due to the intense controversy over space-based missile defense, space security became more global in the 1980s. The Pontifical Academy of Sciences in Vatican City hosted an international conference in 1984 that examined humanity's future in space, including its security dimensions (Pontifical Academy of Sciences 1984). The establishment of SDI led to reinvigorated support in the United Nations for creating a Prevention of an Arms Race in Outer Space (PAROS) ad-hoc committee. As the United States and the USSR commenced bi-lateral talks on space issues, multilateral discussions were taking place at the United Nations Committee on Disarmament (Alves 1991).

In the US-Soviet arms control talks, disagreements about space weapons (both missile defense and ASATs) had become one of the most contentious issues. The superpower summit held in Reykjavik in 1986 fell apart because Mikhail Gorbachev and Ronald Reagan could not agree on terms for restricting space-based missile defense development and testing (Thatcher-Reagan 1986). In an effort to make progress on strategic arms issues, Gorbachev de-linked SDI from talks on intermediate-range nuclear forces (Charles 2010). This change led to Moscow and Washington signing the Intermediate Nuclear Forces (INF) Treaty in 1987. US-Soviet divergence on space weapons remained an obstacle to the strategic nuclear weapons dialogue (START) that would not be resolved until 1990.

AN ERA OF UNCERTAINTY: POST–COLD WAR SPACE SECURITY

Early in his presidency, George H.W. Bush embraced a space-based missile defense concept called Brilliant Pebbles that involved "smart" interceptors capable of tracking and targeting ballistic missiles (Baucom 2004). This was a lighter and cheaper model for space-based missile defense. There was, however, still widespread opposition in Congress, and among the European allies, to interceptors in space because of the implications for the ABM Treaty (PREM 19/3650 1992). As relations with the USSR improved, lawmakers questioned the need for an expansive strategic defense effort.

The First Gulf War, in which a US-led coalition drove Saddam Hussein's army out of Kuwait, placed a spotlight on both space and missile defense. Space systems (e.g., GPS, intelligence satellites, and early warning) were so successfully integrated into tactical operations that Air Force Chief of Staff Merrill McPeak said that this was the first "space war" (Kelly 1993). The perception that Patriot missile defense batteries successfully intercepted significant numbers of Iraqi Scud missiles launched at Saudi Arabia and Israel led to an upsurge in congressional support for missile defense, though space-based missile defense remained contentious. Early in 1991, Bush adopted a more limited strategic defense system called Global Protection Against Limited Strikes that would involve fewer numbers of Brilliant Pebbles in orbit, coupled with land-based defenses, to protect against ballistic missile attacks from so-called rogue regimes.

Due to the role of satellites in the successes of the First Gulf War, some US officials maintained that the United States needed to be able to execute space control operations, despite improving relations with Moscow (Rohlman 1993). To this end, the March 1992 National Military Strategy identified space as "the 'High Ground' that we must occupy" (Department of Defense 1993). Congress, nevertheless, continued to cut funding for strategic defense, especially space-based interceptors, and ASATs. Between 1990 and 1993, Brilliant Pebbles suffered significant failures during three flight tests, which did not help the case of space-based missile defense advocates. During Bill Clinton's presidency, missile defense was further reoriented toward ground- and sea-based theater defense and ASATs received minimal financial support.

The collapse of the USSR and the ending of the Cold War inaugurated a new era in the history of space security. From the perspective of US officials, the only serious threat to US space interests was gone. At this same time, the number of spacefaring nations was rising and a commercial space economy was expanding. Even though Washington and Moscow had cooperated in addressing many security issues associated with nuclear weapons, the denouement of the Cold War did not lead to a better framework for regulating state and non-state activities in space. At best, there was the tacitly accepted norm (between Washington and Moscow) of no longer conducting debris-producing ASAT tests. Fundamentally, little work was done in the 1990s to prepare for the anticipated growth in international space activities.

Even with the USSR gone and no clear threat within sight, a special commission to assess US national security space management and organization warned in January 2001 of a "space pearl harbor" (Report of Commission to Assess United States National Security Space Management and Organization 2001). The report's authors advocated reducing the vulnerability of national security space systems. Exactly nine months later, terrorists carried out the September 11 attacks that ultimately led to the US Global War on Terror. Due to these events, space security took a back seat to other national security priorities.

Unlike during the Cold War, bipolarity does not define the present state of space security because space is increasingly accessible to a broad range of actors. The burgeoning commercial space economy highlights the reality that space activities are no longer confined to states with immense budgets. Despite these discontinuities, the Cold War still offers relevant lessons for analyzing space security. First and foremost, there is an unrelenting tension between space weapons advocates and proponents of arms control placing limits on them. Perhaps most importantly, the Cold War teaches us that space security cannot be dealt with in isolation from other national security problems. Although there are many unknowns about the future of space security, we can be certain that it will be increasingly shaped by competition and the potential for conflict. Developing more effective mechanisms for space governance and collective security will, moreover, be challenged by the inclination to use space (and counter-space) systems to seek military advantages.

References

"Allied Attitudes towards the Strategic Defense Initiative." 1985. CREST, CIA-RDP85T01058R000202390001-0. February 8, 1985.

Alves, Pericles Gasparini. 1991. *Prevention of an Arms Race in Outer Space: A Guide to the Discussions in the Conference on Disarmament*. New York: United Nations.

Bainbridge, William Sims. 1976. *The Spaceflight Revolution: A Sociological Study*. Seattle, WA: Krieger Publishing Company.

Baucom, Donald. 2004. "The Rise and Fall of Brilliant Pebbles." *The Journal of Social, Political, and Economic Studies* 29, no. 2: 143–90.

Buckeley, Rip. 1991. *The Sputniks Crisis and Early United States Space Policy: A Critique of the Historiography of Space*. Bloomington: Indiana University Press.

Buono, Stephen. 2020. "Merely a 'Scrap of Paper'? The Outer Space Treaty in Historical Perspective." *Diplomacy & Statecraft* 31, no. 2: 360–72.

Buono, Stephen. 2023. "The Interplanetary School of IR." *International History Review*. DOI: 10.1080/07075332.2023.2251487

Charles, Elizabeth. 2010. "The Game Changer: Reassessing the Impact of SDI on Gorbachev's Foreign Policy, Arms Control, and US-Soviet Relations." PhD diss., George Washington University.

Chun, Clayton K. S. 2006. *Shooting Down a "Star": Program 437, the US Nuclear ASAT System, and Present-Day Copycat Killers*. Cadre Paper No. 6. Montgomery, AL: Air University Press.

Cleaver, Arthur. 1948. "The Interplanetary Project." *Journal of the British Interplanetary Society* 7: 21–39.

Department of Defense. 1993. "National Military Strategy of the United States." March 17, 1993.

FCO 66/1137. 1978. Minute from Killick to Mallaby, "Anti-Satellite Weapons: US/Soviet Exchanges." May 11. UK National Archives.

FCO 66/1343. n.d. FCO briefing, "Anti Satellite Weapons—The Current Situation." UK National Archives.

Fleming, James R. 2020. "Iowa Enters the Space Age," *Annals of Iowa* 79, no. 4 (Fall): 301–24.

Ford, Gerald. 1976. "NSDM-333, Enhanced Survivability of Critical U.S. Military and Intelligence Space Systems." July 7. *Foreign Relations of the United States, 1969–1976.* Volume E-3. *Documents on Global Issues, 1973–1976.*

Ford, Gerald. 1977. "NSDM-345, U.S. Anti-Satellite Capabilities." January 18. *Foreign Relations of the United States, 1969–1975.* Volume XXXV, *National Security Policy, 1973–1976.*

Gainor, Chris. 2008. *To a Distant Day: The Rocket Pioneers.* Lincoln: University of Nebraska Press.

Gangale, Thomas. 2018. *How High the Sky? The Definition and Delimitation of Outer Space and Territorial Airspace in International Law.* Leiden, Netherlands: Brill.

Geppert, Alexander C. T. 2008. "Space Personae: Cosmopolitan Networks of Peripheral Knowledge, 1927–1957." Journal of Modern European History 6, no. 2: 262–86.

Geppert, Alexander C. T., Daniel Brandau, and Tilman Siebeneichner, eds. 2020. *Militarizing Outer Space: Astroculture, Dystopia and the Cold War.* New York: Palgrave Macmillan.

Graham, Thomas, Jr., and Damien J. LaVera. 2003. "Treaty on Principles Governing the Activities of States in the Exploration and Use of Outer Space, Including the Moon and Other Celestial Bodies, Signed at Washington, London, and Moscow, January 27, 1967." In *Cornerstones of Security: Arms Control Treaties in the Nuclear Era*, edited by Thomas Graham, Jr. and Damien J. LaVera, 35. Seattle, WA: University of Washington Press.

Gupta, Rakesh. 1985. *Militarization of Outer Space—A Case of US Policy.* New Delhi: Patriot Publisher.

Higuchi, Toshihiro. 2020. *Political Fallout: Nuclear Weapons Testing and the Making of a Global Environmental Crisis.* Stanford, CA: Stanford University Press.

Interagency Intelligence Memorandum on Soviet Dependence on Space Systems. 1975. CREST, CIA-CREST, DOC_0000380221. October 6, 1975.

Issues Paper Prepared by the PRM-23 Interagency Group. 1977. August 9. *Foreign Relations of the United States, 1977–1980.* Volume XXVI, *Arms Control and Nonproliferation.*

Kalic, Sean N. 2012. *U.S. Presidents and the Militarization of Outer Space, 1946–1967.* College Station, TX: Texas A&M University Press.

Kelly, Ricky B. 1993. "Centralized Control of Space: The Use of Space Forces by a Joint Force Commander." Master's thesis, School of Advanced Air Power Studies.

Kilgore, De Witt Douglas. 2003. *Astrofuturism: Science, Race, and Visions of Utopia in Space.* Philadelphia: University of Pennsylvania Press.

Letter from President Carter to Soviet General Secretary Brezhnev. 1977. March 4. *Foreign Relations of the United States, 1977–1980.* Volume VI, *Soviet Union.*

McDougall, Walter. 1985. . . . *the Heavens and the Earth: A Political History of the Space Age.* New York: Basic Books.

Memorandum for Brzezinski. 1977. "Soviet and US High-Energy Laser Weapons Programs." November 28. *Foreign Relations of the United States, 1977–1980.* Volume XXVI. *Arms Control and Nonproliferation.*

Memorandum from David Elliot to Brent Scowcroft. 1976. Final Report of the Ad Hoc NSC Space Panel—Part II: US Anti-Satellite Capabilities. November 3. Gerald R. Ford Library.

Memorandum from the Chairman of the Joint Chiefs of Staff to Secretary of Defense Brown. 1977. "Anti-Satellites." July 29. *Foreign Relations of the United States, 1977–1980.,* Volume XXVI. *Arms Control and Nonproliferation.*

Minutes of a National Security Planning Group Meeting. 1984. "Next Steps in the Vienna Process." September 18. *Foreign Relations of the United States, 1981–1988*. Volume IV. *Soviet Union, 1983–1985*.

Minutes of a National Security Council Meeting. 1985. "Nuclear Arms Control Discussions." March 27. *Foreign Relations of the United States, 1981–1988*. Volume XI. *START I*.

Moltz, James Clay. 2019. *The Politics of Space Security: Strategic Restraint and the Pursuit of National Interests*. 3rd ed. Stanford, CA: Stanford University Press.

Mowthorpe, Matthew. 2004. *The Militarization and Weaponization of Space*. New York: Lexington Books.

Mowthorpe, Matthew. 2007. "The Soviet/Russian Antisatellite (ASAT) Programme During the Cold War and Beyond," *Journal of Slavic Military Studies* 15, no. 1: 17–28.

National Intelligence Estimate 11-3/8-77. 1978. "Soviet Capabilities for Strategic Nuclear Conflict Through the Late 1980s." CREST, CIA-DOC_0000268138. April.

Newberry, Robert. 1997. "Space Doctrine for the 21st Century." Montgomery, AL: Air Command and Staff College.

New York Times. 1977. "Soviet Breakthrough Is Reported in Work on an Anti-Missile Beam." May 3, 1977.

PREM 19/1188. 1984. Heseltine and Howe Minute to MT. "Anti-Satellite Systems and Arms Control." June 19. UK National Archives.

PREM 19/3650. 1992. Minute from Prentice to Wall. "GPALS." July 22. UK National Archives.

PRM/NSC-23. 1977. "Summary of Significant Discussion and Conclusions of a Policy Review Committee Meeting. Coherent Space Policy." *Foreign Relations of the United States*, August 9. Volume XXVI. *Arms Control and Nonproliferation*.

Pontifical Academy of Sciences. 1984. "The Impact of Space Exploration on Mankind." October 1–5. Rome, Italy.

Reagan, Ronald. 1983. "Address to the Nation on Defense and National Security." March 23. Ronald Reagan Presidential Library.

Reagan, Ronald. 1982. NSDD-42, "National Space Policy." July 4. CREST, CIA-RDP84B00148R000100320009-2.

Report of the NSC Ad Hoc Panel on Technological Evolution and Vulnerability of Space. 1976. October. US National Security Council Institutional Files 1974–1977. Gerald R. Ford Presidential Library.

Report of Commission to Assess United States National Security Space Management and Organization. 2001. January 11, https://aerospace.csis.org/wp-content/uploads/2018/09/RumsfeldCommission.pdf.

Rohlman, William H. 1993. "A Political Strategy for Antisatellite Weaponry." Master's thesis, The Industrial College of the Armed Forces.

Sheehan, Michael. 2015. "Defining Space Security." In *Handbook of Space Security*, edited by Kai-Uwe Schrogl, Peter Hays, Jana Robinson, and Denis Moura, 20–40. New York: Springer.

Siddiqi, Asif. 2003. *Sputnik and the Soviet Space Challenge*. Gainesville, FL: University Press of Florida.

Siddiqi, Asif. 1999. "Staring at the Sea: The Soviet RORSAT and EORSAT Programmes." *Journal of the British Interplanetary Society* 52, no. 11: 397–416.

Siddiqi, Asif. 1997. "The Soviet Co-Orbital Anti-Satellite System: a Synopsis." *Journal of the British Interplanetary Society* 50, no. 6: 225–40.

Siebeneichner, Tilmann. 2018. "Spacelab: Peace, Progress and European Politics in Outer Space, 1973–85." In *Limiting Outer Space*, edited by Alexander Geppert, 259–83. New York: Palgrave Macmillan.

Stares, Paul B. 1985a. *The Militarization of Space: U.S. Policy, 1945–1984*. Ithaca, NY: Cornell University Press.

Stares, Paul. 1985b. "US and Soviet Military Space Programs: A Comparative Assessment," *Daedalus* 114, no. 2: 127–45.

Telegram from US Embassy in Finland. 1978. "ASAT First Round." June 20. *Foreign Relations of the United States*, 1977–1980., Volume XXVI. *Arms Control and Nonproliferation*.

Thatcher-Reagan (record of conversation). 1986. Executive Secretariat, NSC: System File, 8607413–Oct 86. Ronald Reagan Presidential Library.

"The Real War in Space." 1978. BBC.

Vedda, James. 2017. "The Outer Space Treaty: Assessing Its Relevance at the 50-Year Mark." May. Center for Space Policy and Strategy.

Weeden, Brian. 2014. "Through a Glass, Darkly: Chinese, American, and Russian Anti-Satellite Testing in Space." *The Space Review*, March 17, 2014.

Wieghart, James. 1978. "Russians Can Kill Us in Space, CIA Chief Says." *New York Daily News*, February 1, 1978.

Wolverton, Mark. 2018. *Burning the Sky: Operation Argus and the Untold Story of the Cold War Nuclear Tests in Outer Space*. New York: Overlook Press.

Zak, Anatoly. 2013. "The Hidden History of the Soviet Satellite-Killer," *Popular Mechanics*, November 1, 2013. https://www.popularmechanics.com/space/satellites/a9620/the-hidden-history-of-the-soviet-satellite-killer-16108970/.

CHAPTER 3

∙∙

LEGAL FRAMEWORKS FOR SPACE SECURITY

∙∙

SETSUKO AOKI

INTRODUCTION

∙∙

THIS chapter describes the development and present status of legal frameworks for space security as well as near term prospects.

Basic legal frameworks for enhancing space security were formulated within several years of the first successful launch of an artificial satellite in October 1957. Little has changed since then concerning the rules of legally binding instruments adopted in the United Nations (UN). This lack of change may be mainly because of a series of successful bilateral arms control agreements between the then superpowers, the United States and the Union of the Soviet Socialist Republics (USSR), and no occurrence of an international armed conflict in outer space to date. It may also be due to the consensus-based decision-making system taken in the UN Committee on the Peaceful Uses of Outer Space (UNCOPUOS) (UN Doc. A/AC.105/PV.2 1962) and the Conference on Disarmament (CD) (Froehlich and Seffinga 2020, 24).

The seeming stability and peace in outer space ended with the sudden anti-satellite (ASAT) test by China in January 2007. Until that time, international society seemed to think that intentional and physical destruction of space objects would not take place again, for neither the United States nor the USSR/Russia had conducted an ASAT test of this kind for more than two decades. That optimism was shattered by China. Worse, as the Chinese ASAT test was carried out in an incredibly high orbit of about 865 kilometers altitude, it generated large numbers of space debris to stay in orbits for decades to a century to come, which also brought about space safety concerns (Kelso 2014).

Today, more serious concerns have been noted both in space security and space safety. For the former, various malicious military activities have been reported, including stalking an adversary's valuable military satellites for several months to monitor its capabilities, and various new types of ASAT tests using non-kinetic weapons and ever more refined cyber means (Chow 2017, 82–116). ASAT tests with physical destruction of its own satellites continue as well. India became the fourth nation of this category in March 2019 and Russia resumed a destructive ASAT test in November 2021, for the first time since 1982. For the latter, large-constellation programs being pursued in the low Earth orbit (LEO) have contributed significantly to congested space, in addition to the long-noted increasing number of space actors inevitably causing space safety challenges.

This chapter evaluates the present legal frameworks for space security. First, it examines the contents and characteristics of legally binding international rules. Second, it analyzes non-legally binding international rules and norms relating to space activities. National space strategies and policies which have influenced or may influence the establishment of future legally and non-legally binding frameworks for space security are also briefly highlighted in various parts. Finally, the chapter concludes that there is hope for enhancing space security through non-legally binding norms complimented by concrete measures in the form of technically based guidelines.

There are various definitions for discussing "space security" (Pekkanen and Blount, this volume). Some definitions focus on the issue of military space security, others encompass both military and civilian aspects including environmental security (Sheehan 2015, 7–21). For the purposes of this chapter, the term space security is used to describe the situation in which trust is shared in the international society that any actors may be able to engage in their space activities without the fear of intentional and/or malicious interference by other actors. "Space activities," both crewed and robotic, mean an aggregation of activities including leaving Earth to go to outer space, operations in outer space, and returning to Earth from outer space. While the term "norm" is used more often for non-legally binding rules than legally binding rules, the word "norm" denotes both legally binding rules and non-legally binding rules depending on the context.

LEGALLY BINDING INTERNATIONAL RULES FOR SPACE SECURITY

The Establishment of Basic Space Norms in 1963

Basic norms for space security were formulated in 1963 when the Treaty Banning Nuclear Weapon Tests in the Atmosphere, in Outer Space and Under Water (PTBT), entered into force and the two critically important UN General Assembly (UNGA) Resolutions were adopted.

PTBT obligates States Parties not to carry out any nuclear weapon test explosion, or any other nuclear explosion, in the atmosphere, under water, or in outer space (Art. I1. (a)). Interestingly, the adoption of the PTBT overlapped the time when both the United States and the USSR had fully come to realize the value of reconnaissance satellites to monitor nuclear explosions in outer space (Moltz 2008, 137; Temple 2005, 383). This shows that from the beginning of the space age, outer space had been extensively used for enhancing national security and verification of arms control agreements, although it was not until 1978 when US President Carter disclosed that surveillance satellites had been widely used (Stares 1985, 186).

As for the two UNGA Resolutions, the first was the UNGA Resolution 1884 adopted on October 17, 1963, which called upon all states to "refrain from placing in orbit around the earth any objects carrying nuclear weapons or any other kinds of weapons of mass destruction, installing such weapons on celestial bodies, or stationing such weapons in outer space in any other manner" (para.2 (a)). This expression became, in its entirety, Article IV (1) of the Treaty on Principles Governing the Activities of States in the Exploration and Use of Outer Space, including the Moon and Other Celestial Bodies (Outer Space Treaty or OST) of 1967, which remains the most important arms control provision relating to space to date. The second was the UNGA Resolution 1962 on December 13, 1963, the nine principles of which were taken almost intact in the Outer Space Treaty as the basic principles for space activities including military space activities.

In this period, there had been heated discussions on the meaning of the "peaceful" uses of outer space, sometimes only between the United States and the USSR, and other times in international forums, including especially the UN. The kernel of the argument was whether "peaceful" should equate with "non-military" or "non-aggressive." Except in the very early period through 1958, the United States interpreted "peaceful" as "non-aggressive," and the Soviet position was "peaceful" being "non-military." According to the "peaceful" = "non-aggressive" interpretation, military activities are permitted except in so far as they are expressly forbidden by international law. Consequently, any space activity not falling within the "threat or use of force" prohibited in Article 2(4) of the UN Charter would be "peaceful" use of space (Vlasic 1991, 38–40). The interpretation of "peaceful" is important as it is only the "non-aggressive" interpretation that legalizes the use of military satellites and the intercontinental ballistic missiles (ICBMs) that navigate through outer space before hitting the target on the Earth. As the United States had always been ahead of the USSR on the operation of military satellites, with its first photo reconnaissance satellite launched in 1959 (Temple 2005, 142–75), the USSR tabled a proposal to ban satellites for the collection of intelligence information in the Legal Subcommittee (LSC) of the UNCOPUOS in 1962 (UN Doc. A/AC.105/L.2 1962). However, when its stable operation of reconnaissance satellites became possible, the Soviet objections subsided. By the mid-1960s, both states took the position that "peaceful" meant "non-aggressive," which greatly influenced the drafting of the OST in 1966 (Cheng 1997, 220–26).

The Most Important Framework for Space Security: Outer Space Treaty

Dichotomy in Outer Void Space and on Celestial Bodies

As Article IV of the Outer Space Treaty has been the most important arms control provision in space security, the meaning of this Article IV (1) (2) is to be studied in some detail along with recent state practice.

Article IV of the Space Treaty reads:

> States Parties to the Treaty undertake not to place in orbit around the Earth any objects carrying nuclear weapons or any other kinds of weapons of mass destruction, install such weapons on celestial bodies, or station such weapons in outer space in any other manner.
> The Moon and other celestial bodies shall be used by all States Parties to the Treaty exclusively for peaceful purposes. The establishment of military bases, installations and fortifications, the testing of any type of weapons and the conduct of military manoeuvres on celestial bodies shall be forbidden. The use of military personnel for scientific research or for any other peaceful purposes shall not be prohibited. The use of any equipment or facility necessary for peaceful exploration of the Moon and other celestial bodies shall also not be prohibited.

It is apparent that the strictness of arms control between "outer void space" (a term invented by Professor Bin Cheng) (Cheng 1997, 529) and on the moon and other celestial bodies considerably differs. Freedom of military uses seems reserved to a large degree in outer void space whereas the scope of military activities on the moon and other celestial bodies seems either completely prohibited or considerably restricted to the extent that it could be said to be substantially prohibited at least in view of the present space technology and activities on celestial bodies. The details of provisions of Article IV with today's interpretation and its implications in practice considering the dual-use nature of space technology are described below.

Prohibited and Permissible Military Actions in Outer Void Space

In outer void space, only the stationing or orbiting around the Earth of a weapon of mass destruction (WMD) is prohibited. WMD was defined by the UN Commission for Conventional Armaments in 1948 (UN Doc. S/C.3/32/Rev.1 1948) as "atomic explosive weapons, radio-active material weapons, lethal chemical and biological weapons, and any weapons developed in the future," which have comparable destructive effect to such existent weapons. This was the understanding of the scope of WMDs from the time of making the OST to date with little or no changes. Today, although possible new types of WMDs have been discussed in the UN Disarmament Commission and the CD, little has been changed, at least on the scope of nuclear weapons (Lyall and Larsen 2018, 460–61).

Article IV (1) shows that the use of an ICBM is not banned by the OST as it neither orbits around the Earth nor would otherwise be stationed in outer space (US Senate 1967, 26). Likewise, the predominant interpretation around the time of making the OST was that Fractional Orbital Bombardment System (FOBS) being developed by the USSR was not also banned because such systems would deorbit before making an entire rotation of the Earth (Ikeda 1971, 135–39). However, because of their apparently destabilizing effect, FOBS was prohibited by some bilateral treaties including the Treaty Between the United States and the USSR on Further Reduction and Limitation of Strategic Offensive Arms (START I) in 1991 (Arts. V 18. (c)), which expired in December 2009. The interpretation that FOBS is not prohibited by the OST seems to remain, as when it was reported in October 2021 that China had conducted weapon tests involving a FOBS that deployed a hypersonic glide vehicle (HGV) (Sevastopulo and Hille 2021), there was no accusations that China had violated Article IV of the OST, although mounting concerns were expressed about the further decrease in space security (Hitchens 2021).

The stationing of conventional weapons in outer void space is also not prohibited under the OST. Nor is it prohibited to test conventional weapons in orbit, which explains the difficulty in stopping destructive ASAT tests.

Test and Use of WMD in Outer Space

In this regard, a more sensitive question would be the legality of a nuclear weapon test in outer space if it is conducted through suborbital or FOBS-type trajectories. In any areas of outer space, PTBT bans nuclear explosion test. However, since some states such as China, France, and the Democratic People's Republic of Korea (DPRK) are not parties to the PTBT, and the Comprehensive Nuclear-Test-Ban Treaty (CTBT) has not entered into force, unless there is a customary rule of international law that prohibits nuclear explosion tests in outer space, it may be difficult to categorically conclude that nuclear tests are altogether forbidden in any location in outer space. However, France seems to have unilaterally accepted the obligation not to take nuclear explosion tests in outer space as France made public its intention in 1974 that it would convert to underground nuclear testing after a series of final tests in the atmosphere (ICJ 1974, 266–67) and is understood to be under the same obligation as States Parties to the PTBT. It is likely to be concluded that a nuclear weapon test in outer space is prohibited if such a weapon has already been orbiting around the Earth or otherwise stationed in outer space, because if a nuclear weapon must not be placed in orbit around the Earth, a nuclear weapon test explosion cannot be possible in orbit. However, it may be difficult to forbid non-parties to the PTBT to conduct a nuclear explosion test in a suborbital or FOBS-type trajectories under the OST.

Likewise, although the possibility or effectiveness of such tests is highly doubtful, at least at the state of development level of today's science, some latitude of interpretation may exist for a test of a biological weapon or chemical weapon in suborbital and FOBS-type trajectories, because neither the Biological Weapons Convention (1972) nor Chemical Weapons Convention (1993) explicitly bans a weapon test in outer space.

As to the use of nuclear weapons in outer space, its legality or illegality would be judged on whether it meets the right of self-defense criteria in Article 51 of the UN Charter (ICJ 1996, 263). Along with the use of other WMDs, this question would not be addressed under OST but under the law of self-defense—*jus ad bellum*.

In sum, arms control in outer void space has been restricted to the prohibition of stationing WMDs (substantially nuclear weapons) and the "threat or use of force," which is an established rule of customary international law reflected under Article 2(4) of the UN Charter (ICJ 1986, 187–90; ICJ 2004, 87) with the exception of the right to self-defense. This led to the argument in various forums including, especially in the CD, that norms in outer space have been insufficient and that all weapons in outer space and the use of force toward space objects shall be prohibited to stabilize outer space (West, this volume). Noting the dual-use nature of space technology that disables any efforts to define "weapons" in space (Pekkanen 2021), it would not be an effective measure to pursue. A radically different approach seems needed, which will be addressed later in this chapter.

Arms Control on Celestial Bodies

In contrast, the permissible scope of activities could be more ambiguous on the moon and other celestial bodies due to the less clear wording of the prohibited activities and the dual-use nature of space activities. The drafting history shows that the original US proposal intended to demilitarize celestial bodies. It was modeled on Article I of the 1959 Antarctic Treaty, which accomplished demilitarization of Antarctica (Vlasic 1991, 40–41). However, because the US proposal did not include the phrase "inter alia" stated in Article I of the Antarctic Treaty, it could be interpreted that the list of prohibited actions was exhaustive, while this was not the intention of the US proposal. In addition, the present wording of the second sentence of Article IV (2) taken from the Soviet proposal may further contribute to the interpretation that the prohibited activities list is exhaustive, irrespective of the true intention of the USSR, which remained unclear during and after the negotiation of the OST (Cheng 1997, 247). If the prohibited activities are definitive, then residual military activities may be permissible so long as they do not constitute "threat or use of force" under Article 2 (4) of the UN Charter. Conversely, if they are construed as exemplified, there would be no leeway for any military activities, thus demilitarization was accomplished.

As the agreed interpretation of the United States and the USSR was "peaceful" equals "non-aggressive," it is possible that the list of prohibited activities was a definitive one in accordance with the normal reading, and some military activities are permissible. However, the expression in the first sentence of Article IV (2) is not just for "peaceful purposes" but for "exclusively for peaceful purposes." Thus, some commentators opine that irrespective of the interpretation of "for peaceful purposes," the addition of the adverb "exclusively" leaves no room to interpret this as "non-aggressive" (Hobe, Schmidt-Tedd, and Schrogl 2009, 82). If this interpretation is taken, then the second sentence of Article IV (2) means that explicitly prohibited actions cannot but represent an exemplified list. If construing the adverb "exclusively" adds nothing from the legal point of view, because "peaceful" meaning "non-aggressive" had been the predominant interpretation supported also by state practice, the second sentence is to be read that prohibited activities are definitive, and residual military activities could be permissible (Aoki 2017, 202).

In sum, there is no clear answer whether non-military use has been obligated on celestial bodies. Some commentators pointed out in the 1960s that it would be difficult to identify an activity that did not fall under the clearly prohibited activities, and therefore the moon and other celestial bodies were "substantially" demilitarized (Meyer 1968, 29). The issue is if the status of the substantially demilitarized area, irrespective of the interpretation of the "exclusively for peaceful purposes," could remain intact in the future when competition to establish the cislunar space would be intense (Miller 2021). The reading of the third and fourth sentences of Article IV (2) indicates that States Parties may obtain the outcome of scientific research and any other activities for "peaceful purposes" conducted by their nationals including military personnel, using any equipment or facility for "peaceful purposes." Space technology is conspicuously dual use in nature. Since the fourth sentence can be read as the confirmation of the lawfulness of the peaceful conversion of state-of-the-art military equipment or facility, together with the legality of military personnel engaging in any activities for peaceful purposes, obtaining knowledge and using application technologies that could contribute to militarization on celestial bodies could be permissible for States Parties. The original intention of arms control on celestial bodies may not be completely useless, though it seems insufficient in an age in which not only exploration but also use of the moon and other celestial bodies has begun. There would be no state-of-the-art space technology that could not have military implications, especially when it is obtained by military personnel. For the use of celestial bodies, it seems that more concrete international rules and norms should be formulated to provide clearer standards of actions to states to maintain and promote space security.

Arms Control under the Moon Agreement: What Is "On the Moon"?

Given that only eighteen states have ratified or acceded to the Agreement Governing the Activities of States on the Moon and Other Celestial Bodies (MA) as of 2021, arms control provisions in the MA tends to be assessed as not so important, because regulations in its Article 3 are similar in contents to Article IV of OST, at least at first glance. However, if note is taken of the provisions that the MA "shall also apply to other celestial bodies within the solar system, other than the Earth" (Art. 1(1)) and that the reference to the "Moon" in the MA shall include "orbits around or other trajectories to or around it" (Art. 1(2)), the prohibition on the "establishment of military bases, installations and fortifications, the testing of any type of weapons and the conduct of military manoeuvres on the Moon" (Art. 3 (4)) could extend to some areas of outer void space. In this regard, the clarification process of UNCOPUOS/LSC, just before the adoption of the MA, reached the agreement that the outer void space to which the MA was applicable would be the orbits and trajectories, except those in Earth orbits only and trajectories of space objects between the Earth and such orbits (UN Doc. A/34/20 1979, 11).

Therefore, it is possible that ASAT tests would also be banned in outer void space pursuant to the MA, which would be a big leap from arms control provisions under the OST. Views are divided, however, as to whether such an interpretation is applicable to space arms control, and the objection by China and Russia in this regard may have to be taken into consideration (Aoki 2017, 205).

Important Norms for Behaviors for Space Activities

Other than Article IV of the OST and Article 3 of the MA, which most directly relate to space security, some provisions in the OST are more relevant than other provisions in promoting space security. The implications in such provisions are briefly touched upon in this section.

Non-appropriation of outer space by any means (Art. II) is undoubtedly of critical importance to maintaining security in outer space by negating the possibility of colonialization. Moreover, the OST emphasizes the principles of cooperation, mutual assistance, and the duty to give due regard to the corresponding interests of all other states (Art. IX) to reconcile possibly contradicting principles to explore and use outer space "for the benefit and in the interests of all countries," on the one hand, and which is free for all states, on the other hand (Art. I). Further, principles for avoiding harmful contamination and potentially harmful interference with other states' space activities are set forth, and avoidance of potentially harmful interference shall be attained through prior international consultations (Art. IX). To promote the principle of international cooperation, a State Party shall provide information of its space activities to the UN Secretary-General (UNSG) and international society in general to the greatest extent feasible and practicable (Art. XI).

Since these principles are too abstract to apply to a specific case that could influence space security, subsequent UNGA Resolutions such as the 1996 Space Benefit Declaration (UN Doc. A/RES/51/122 1996) and UNCOPUOS technically based guidelines have been adopted for the effective implementation of OST. This will be discussed later in this chapter.

Space Security Enhanced by the Bilateral Agreements

ABM Treaty and After

The United States and USSR significantly influenced space security for the first fifty years of military space activities through a series of strategic nuclear arms control agreements and other measures. Among them, the 1972 Treaty Between the United States and the USSR on the Limitation of Anti-Ballistic Missile Systems (ABM Treaty) was of special importance for space security, as both states promised not to develop, test, or deploy anti-ballistic missile (ABM) systems or components that are sea-based, air-based, space-based, or mobile land-based (Art. V 1.). For thirty years from May 1972 to June 2002, when it was effectively terminated, the ABM Treaty had been the most stringent arms control provision in outer space as the development, testing, and deployment of conventional weapons in outer space had been clearly prohibited.

The idea of prohibiting any weapons in outer space has been pursued by Russia jointly with China since especially 2002 in the CD. The first such was the announcement of the future draft Treaty on the Prevention of the Deployment of Weapons in Outer Space, the Threat or Use of Force Against Outer Space Objects (CD/1679 2002), which was followed by the 2008 Draft Treaty on Prevention of the Placement of Weapons in Outer Space and of the Threat or Use of Force against Outer Space Object (PPWT) (CD/1839 2008) and revised PPWT submitted in 2014 (CD/1985 2014). To be more precise, however, it must be said that it is not only since 2002 but since the establishment of the CD that the USSR and later Russia pursued the banning of any weapons in outer space (CD/274 1982; CD/476 1984; West, this volume).

Russia's military space policy, or at least parts of it, is reflected in the Russian Military Doctrine approved in December 2014 (Russian Federation 2014). In this document, Russia regards "the intention to place weapons in outer space" (para. 12 d) as one of the external military risks and aims "to promote the conclusion of an international treaty on prevention of placement of any types of weapons in outer space" (para. 21 m) and "to adopt in the UN framework provisions" (para. 21 n) for securing the security and safety of outer space operations, along with deploying various space objects to support its armed forces (para. 32 d, g). Russian stances in the CD and various forums in the UN, as well as its other national practice, seem to have straightforwardly followed the views reflected here. Thus, it is likely that Russia would continue to pursue PPWT as the most favorable option, and this would not persuade relevant spacefaring states, as the latter states hold the views that "weapons in outer space" cannot be precisely defined due to the inherent dual nature of space technology. Conspicuously different views among relevant states cannot inspire optimism for future space security in general, to say the least.

Rule of No Interference with Military Satellites

A series of bilateral treaties for nuclear strategic arms control, including the ABM Treaty, contain the verification clauses for monitoring observance with each treaty in the name of "national technical means of verification" (NTM), except the Treaty Between the United States and the Russian Federation on Strategic Offensive Reductions (SORT) in 2002. NTM is not defined in any of the treaties concerned. Nor is stated that NTM includes surveillance satellites in any treaty or related official documents. However, the fact that satellite surveillance/monitoring had been an important—in some cases, the most important—element of the NTM was widely known among the intelligence community (US National Reconnaissance Office 1971) and was even given a reassurance in a US governmental website (US Secretary of State 2000; US Department of State 2009).

The standard type of provisions are as follows: (1) each Party shall use NTM at its disposal in a manner consistent with generally recognized principles of international law; (2) each Party undertakes not to interfere with the NTM of the other Party; and (3) each Party undertakes not to use concealment measures which impede verification by NTM (for instance, ABM Treaty, Art. XII; START I, Art. IX). As the Treaty between the United States and the Russian Federation on Measures for the Further Reduction and Limitation of Strategic Offensive Arms (New START Treaty) was extended in February 2021 for another five years, the NTM provisions are effective at present (New START Treaty, Art. X).

It is not only bilateral nuclear arms control agreements, a multilateral Treaty on Conventional Armed Forces in Europe (CEF Treaty) also contains the mechanism of "national or multinational technical means of verification" (Art. XV 1.) with a similar commitment found in the above-mentioned US-USSR/Russian NTM mechanisms.

From the point of view of space security, the implications of these NTM or even multinational technical means provisions may be evaluated that satellite surveillance/

monitoring for the verification of arms control agreements is a useful tool for that purpose when both the goals of States Parties and targets to monitor are sufficiently clear and other settlement of differences/disputes mechanisms are established, as is the case in the US-USSR/Russia nuclear arms control agreements. However, it has to be noted that this is strictly the treaty-based mechanism, and there is no such general rule to prohibit ASAT between the two states or more than two states. In parallel, various multinational satellite monitoring systems have been proposed in international forums including an International Satellite Monitoring Agency (ISMA) by France (UN Doc. A/S-10/AC.1/7 1978) and PAXSAT systems by Canada (e.g. CD/786 1987; CD/1785 2006) during the past four decades. It remains uncertain if multilateral satellite monitoring systems of arms control agreements would be possible or even useful for enhancing space security (Aoki 1992, 208–52, 263–66).

International Law Applicable to International Armed Conflicts in Outer Space

Reaction to the Reality that Space Has Become a New Operational Domain

Beyond the peacetime utilization of military satellites for monitoring the military activities of potential adversaries, since the Gulf War in 1990, space systems have been extensively used to wage a terrestrial armed conflict effectively (Freeland 2015, 99). Facing up to the reality that space has become a new operational domain, military powers have established and restructured space command, space force, and equivalent thereto to strengthen military capabilities in space. China established the Strategic Support Force (SSF) in 2015 within the People's Liberation Army (PLA). SSF is responsible for most of the space warfare mission as well as for cyber, electronic, and psychological warfare (US-China Economic and Security Review Commission 2019, 291). Also in 2015, Russia reestablished Space Forces. The United States restructured and newly established the US Space Command (USSPACECOM) and Space Force in August and December 2019 respectively. Likewise, France's restructuring of its Air and Space Force had been completed by September 2020, and the United Kingdom established a separate Space Command in 2021. Several other nations followed the trends: Japan established the Space Operation Squadron in the Air Self-Defense Force in 2020 (Pekkanen 2022), and Germany created a space command in the German Space Situational Awareness (SSA) Centre in 2021.

The North Atlantic Treaty Organization (NATO) extended the scope of the applicability of Article 5 (self-defense) of the North Atlantic Treaty from "on land, sea, air or cyberspace" to an attack "to, from, or within space" in June 2021. The North Atlantic Council will decide when such an attack leads to the invocation of Article 5 of the treaty on a case-by-case basis (NATO 2021, para. 33). In any domain, occurrence of an armed attack is the prerequisite for a state or states to resort to the right of self-defense (UN

Charter, Art. 51), but there are not formal legal criteria to decide what concrete effects makes up an "armed attack" to, from, or within outer space. This will have to be studied along with the criteria of "use of force" in space, as "scale and effects" are to determine whether a particular action amounts to an "armed attack" or "use of force" (ICJ 1986, 93). Another important question should also be addressed. When a satellite is physically destroyed in outer space by kinetic or non-kinetic means, it certainly amounts to at least use of force. However, when satellite is only functionally destroyed or degraded by non-kinetic means, whether this is determined to be a use of force depends on various elements including the effects brought about on the ground. This is a common question to be addressed, both for space armed conflicts and cyber armed conflicts.

The Ambiguity of the Law of Armed Conflict in Outer Space

Made decades after the advent of the space age, none of the general treaties that regulates behavior during armed conflict—*jus in bello*—explicitly refer to outer space as the scope of application in addition to "on land, at sea or in the air" (e.g., Protocol Additional to the Geneva Conventions of 12 August 1949, and Relating to the Protection of Victims of International Armed Conflicts (AP I) 1977, Art. 49 (4)). However, it is widely confirmed that *jus in bello* will also apply to an international armed conflict to, from, or in outer space once it occurs, as established rules of international law covering a certain situation—for example armed conflicts—will also be applicable to a new domain in which human activity has extended, as exemplified by the application of the UN Charter to space activities (Schmitt 2006, 115–46; Mačák 2018, 12).

The contour of *jus in bello* regarding to, from, or in outer space is highly ambiguous for several reasons. This subsection briefly touches upon the question of applicable scope of *jus in bello* using the term the law of armed conflict (LOAC), because it undoubtedly contains the law of neutrality different from international humanitarian law (IHL).

Due in part to no occurrence of armed conflict in outer space to date, it is not clear how peacetime international space law would continue to apply in time of armed conflict other than that it would in general continue to apply, and that the application of some kinds of rules would be suspended or restricted according to the nature of the armed conflict. The maxim that *lex specialis derogat legi generali* (a special law prevails over general law) is not useful enough to reconcile space law and LOAC as this maxim is only effective when applied to treaties in the same field, which space law and LOAC do not satisfy. Ultimately, a policy decision would be required to determine which body of law would apply in a certain situation of an armed conflict (Stephens 2018, 80–84, 90–92).

The law of neutrality would be of especial significance in contemplating an armed conflict in outer space because of the extensive use of dual-use commercial satellites by armed forces for the past three decades. Rights and obligations of a neutral state, which is also the state of registry of a dual-use commercial satellite, would be questioned in the case of an armed conflict in outer space. It follows that the clarification would be required as to whether a commercial satellite serving as part of military operations would be regarded as a "military objective" by virtue of "use," since military objectives would be determined by "their nature, location, purpose or use" making an effective contribution to military action (AP I, Art. 52 (2)). Granting that the answer is in the affirmative, all feasible precautions in the choice of means and methods of attack shall be taken to avoid causing excessive incidental loss of civilian life or damage to civilian objects in relation to the military advantage anticipated (AP I, Art. 57 (2)). If a satellite is used both for telemedicine and military communications, this should be duly taken into consideration: one effort to clarify this situation is the ongoing development of the Woomera Manual on the International Law of Military Space Operations (Stephens 2018, 99).

ENMOD Convention as the Bridge between Arms Control and LOAC

The Convention on the Prohibition of Military or Any Other Hostile Use of Environmental Modification Techniques (ENMOD Convention) has two aspects: it is primarily categorized as a LOAC treaty as it regulates the behavior of states in a military or hostile environment, but it also has elements of an arms control agreement intended to prevent a certain action in peacetime. The ENMOD Convention was drafted in the Conference on the Committee on Disarmament (CCD), external to the UN, to address the issue of artificial modification of the environment for military or other hostile purposes. Prior coordination by the United States and USSR was so successful that both tabled identical draft articles to the CCD in 1975. Consequently, the ENMOD Convention was adopted in the CCD the next year, which was followed by the approval of this convention in UNGA in 1976 (UN Doc. A/RES/31/72 1976). Other than the OST, this is probably the only arms control agreement relating to outer space to which China, Russia, and the United States are States Parties.

States Parties undertake "not to engage in military or any other hostile use of environmental modification techniques having widespread, long-lasting or severe effects as the means of destruction, damage or injury to any other State Party" (Art. I 1.). The threshold of "widespread, long-lasting or severe effects" is clarified in the Understandings Regarding the Convention adopted at the same time as the ENMOD Convention. It reads: "(a) 'widespread': encompassing an area on the scale of several hundred kilometers; (b) 'long-lasting': lasting for a period of months, or approximately a season; (c) 'severe': involving serious or significant disruption on harm to human life, natural and economic resources or other assets" (UN Doc. A/31/27 vol 1 1976, 91). "Environmental modification techniques" is defined as any technique for changing the dynamics, composition, or structure of the Earth or of outer space through the deliberate manipulation of natural processes (Art. II).

The question remains whether there could be a convincing scenario satisfying the conditions mentioned above in outer space, especially in view of the definition of "environmental modification techniques." If massive space debris is deliberately generated by destroying a state's satellite to damage an adversary's military satellite constellations and it changes an orbital environment exceeding several hundred cubic kilometers for several decades—at least two of the three thresholds are met-, could this be assessed as being brought about by the use of an environmental modification technique? The answer seems to largely depend on the interpretation of the "dynamics, composition or structure" and "natural processes" of outer space. Today, it may yet be difficult to devise a convincing scenario to which the ENMOD Convention could apply, but tomorrow's space technology may enable the effective use of environmental modification techniques in outer space.

Currently, the greatest merit of the ENMOD Convention seems to lie in its preventive function: it prevents states from developing an environmental modification technique to employ it in a military or hostile action in outer space in the future. Further, another merit cannot be underestimated: the threshold of the violation of the ENMOD Convention is much lower than that of Article 35 (3) of AP I, which bans "methods or means of warfare which are intended, or may be expected, to cause widespread, long-term and severe damage to the natural environment." An action does not become unlawful under AP I unless it satisfies all three conditions: "widespread, long-term and severe damage," different from the case of the ENMOD Convention, where one of the three conditions is sufficient and "long-term" under API is understood as "decades and not . . . months" (ICRC 1987, 417–18). This happens because the goals of the two treaties are different in that the goal of the ENMOD Convention is to prevent the use of an environmental modification technique as a weapon, while AP I aims at protecting the natural environment so as to prohibit the unnecessary injury of the civilian population as an IHL (ICRC 1987, 414).

In conclusion, the ENMOD Convention seems useful for maintaining space security both in peacetime and in a time of armed conflict.

Non-Legally Binding International Rules for Space Security

As of January 2022, one hundred states are members of UNCOUPOS where all decisions have to be consensus based. Recalling that only forty-seven states were members when the last of the UN space treaties, MA was adopted in 1979 (UN Doc. A/RES/32/196B 1977; UN Doc. A/RES/35/16 1980), there seems substantially no possibility of adopting a new UN treaty today and in the foreseeable future. Therefore, only non-legally binding norms may be formulated in response to current security threats to, from, and in outer space. This section describes and evaluates the effectiveness of major non-legally binding rules and norms made within and outside the UN. First, non-legally binding but politically important norms are analyzed. Then, technically based guidelines made in the UN are referred to. Although these guidelines are not norms, but only practical specifications for the safe use of space, there is always the possibility that a new political norm may be born therefrom. Finally, on-going efforts in UNGA that are most likely to succeed are introduced.

HCOC

The Hague Code of Conduct against Ballistic Missile Proliferation (Hague Code of Conduct or HCOC) is evaluated here as one of the most important non-legally binding norms for space security in view of the number of subscribing states and its contents. This is a transparency and confidence building measures (TCBM) on the development and launch of ballistic missiles and space launch vehicles (SLVs). The idea of this mechanism had started in an export control regime, Missile Technology Control Regime (MTCR), and the final product, the Hague Code of Conduct adopted in 2002, is open for all states to be a subscribing state. Regular meetings are held in Vienna, Austria; 93 states signed in 2002; as of December 2021, 143 states have become subscribing states. Among major spacefaring states, China is the only one that has not signed it, while India joined the HCOC in 2016. UNGA continues to support the HCOC, adopting resolutions to that effect multiple times (UN Doc. A/RES/59/91 2004; UN Doc. A/RES/67/42 2013; UN Doc. A/RES/69/44 2014; UN Doc. A/Res/71/33 2016; UN Doc. A/Res/73/49 2018).

Subscribing states voluntarily commit themselves to provide pre-launch notifications of launches of SLVs and test flights of their ballistic missiles (4 a. iii.), annual declarations of SLV policies, and information on preceding year SLV launches and test flights, as well as to invite international observers to their launch sites (4 a. ii.).

UN GGE Recommendations

Reports of the results of discussions by the group of governmental experts (GGE) on confidence building measures (CBM)—renamed TCBM in 2005—commissioned by UNSG have been published twice: in 1993 (UN Doc. A/48/305 1993) and 2013 (UN Doc. A/68/189 2013). The 2013 Report recommends that UN Member States pursue certain measures, specified below, and hold regular discussions on the review and implementation of such recommended measures in the UNCOPUOS, UN Disarmament Commission, and CD. The main recommended measures are: (1) information exchange on national space security matters including policies and military space expenditures; (2) information exchange on operations of space objects and planned launches to avoid mishaps, misperceptions, and mistrust; (3) notification of high-risk activities, emergency situations, and intentional orbital breakups of space objects: and (4)) voluntary familiarization visit to launching sites.

COPUOS States Members have been reporting on their implementations on voluntary basis, especially under the agenda item "ways and means of maintaining outer space for peaceful purposes" (UN Doc. A/76/20 2021, paras. 34–39) as recommended by UNGA Resolutions on TCBM in outer space (UN Doc. A/RES/76/55 2021, para. 3). It is widely understood that such voluntary reporting has nurtured a friendly environment that enabled joint ad hoc meetings on possible challenges to space security and sustainability by the first committee (dealing with disarmament and international security) and fourth committee (whose mandate is special political and decolonization matters, to which the COPUOS annually reports its work) of the UNGA in 2017 and 2019 (UN Doc. A/RES/76/55 2021, para.7). These meetings are historic, given the long understanding that the mandate of COPUOS and therefore the fourth committee was restricted to peaceful uses of outer space only, and that discussing space security was reserved for the first committee only. Under the increasingly blurred demarcation between space security and safety, it is a promising sign that COPUOS has the opportunity to strengthen "a unique and fundamental role in global governance and international cooperation on outer space" (UN Doc. A/76/20 2021, para. 4). Due to the inherent dual-use nature of space technology (Pekkanen 2021), this change in the function of COPUOS seems nothing but an inevitable and desirable course for reaching a practical solution.

Technically Based Guidelines That May Develop into New Norms

The Scientific and Technical Subcommittee (STSC) of COPUOS adopted Space Debris Mitigation Guidelines by consensus in February 2007 after six years of discussions (UN Doc. A/62/20 2007). Among its seven guidelines, Guideline 4 may be of especial importance for space security, although it was not intended to express a norm but only to set out a technically based guideline for the safe use of outer space. Guideline 4 recommends that "intentional destruction of any on-orbit spacecraft and launch vehicle orbital stages or other harmful activities that generate long-lived debris should be avoided" and that "[w]hen intentional break-ups are necessary, they should be conducted at sufficiently low altitudes to limit the orbital lifetime of resulting fragments" (UN Doc. A/62/20 2007, Annex).

The latest of a series of technically based guidelines is UNCOPUOS Guidelines for the Long-Term Sustainability of Outer Space Activities (LTS Guidelines), also devised in COPUOS/STSC. While this twenty-one sets of LTS Guidelines and the COPUOS Space Debris Mitigation Guidelines do not contain norms due to its technical nature, it is possible that both guidelines might be developed into new non-legally binding norms in the future based on state practice. Five guidelines in Section A (policy and regulatory framework for space activities) and ten guidelines in Section B (safety of space operations) of the LTS Guidelines are especially promising in this regard, as more concrete and detailed rules could be developed than guidelines in Sections C (international cooperation, capacity-building and awareness) and Section D (scientific and technical research and development) through the STSC discussions currently conducted.

The US National Space Traffic Management (STM) Policy (Space Policy Directive-3) (White House 2018) and the STM guidelines to be completed by the European Union in the near future (European Union 2020) will greatly influence the specifications of the Section B LTM Guidelines. With the help of such national and regional rule-setting and subsequent national implementation, the otherwise technical guidelines may generate new norms for orbital space activities. It may also be noteworthy that the agreed statements at the G-7 Leaders' Summit held in the United Kingdom (UK) in June 2021 included undertakings by seven states and the European Union to focus on the development of "common standards and best practices and guidelines related to sustainable space operations alongside the need for a collaborative approach for space traffic management and coordination" (Carbis Bay G7 2021, para. 35). This might also help in formulating some new STM norms from the LTS Guidelines.

UNGA Resolution on Responsible Behaviors

This is the latest and likely to be the most important initiative to be developed into a new norm regarding space activities in the mid-twenty-first century. The UK-led UNGA Resolution Reducing Space Threats through Norms, Rules and Principles of Responsible Behaviours (Resolution on Responsible Behaviors) (UN Doc. A/RES/75/36 2020) was adopted on a vote of 164 in favor, 12 against (including China and Russia), with 6 abstentions (including India). While the draft PPWT proposed by Russia and China in the CD focuses on the prohibition of placing weapons in outer space and the threat or use of force against an "outer space object" (CD/1985 2014, Art. I (a)), this UNGA resolution does not focus on any specific weapons, irrespective of the place deployed or to be tested. Rather, the approach of this resolution is to nurture common understanding on the threats and security risks to space systems and what actions and activities "could be considered responsible, irresponsible or threatening and their potential impact on international security," and then share ideas for developing norms, rules and principles in this regard (UN Doc. A/RES/75/36 2020, para. 5). This approach is chosen based on the fact that "space systems" comprise not only spacecraft operating in outer space but also ground facilities and communication links, and attacks from Earth to space, space to space, space to Earth, and through the cyber domain to space would have to be addressed comprehensively to reduce space threats. Further, not only weapons specifically designed and manufactured for attacking space systems but also dual-use satellites could be used to destroy or degrade space systems (Pekkanen 2021; Rajagopalan 2021; ESPI 2021).

Twenty-five states (including China, India, Russia, and the United States) and the European Union submitted their views on these issues, following which a second UNGA Resolution with the same title was adopted in December 2021. This authorized an open-ended working group to meet in 2022 and 2023 to deepen the discussion and submit a report to the UNSG (UN Doc. A/RES/76/231 2021, paras. 5–6). This new initiative has just begun, but already seems most promising as it is supported by an overwhelming number of states and others have sent their national reports anyway and are not opposed to it.

The US Secretary of Defense published a memorandum on the "Tenets of Responsible Behavior in Space" in July 2021. This specified five tenets of responsible behavior according to which Department of Defense (DoD) Components will conduct space operations and are also ordered "to develop and coordinate guidance regarding these tenets

and associated specific behaviors for DoD operations in the space area of responsibility"
(US Secretary of Defense 2021, 1). It is rare for a military department to take such a bold
step a that may translate into new norms in space operations.

The UK, which led the initiative, announced the promotion of responsible behaviors
(Goal 2: Promote the values of Global Britain) as one of the five goals of its National
Space Strategy released in September 2021 (United Kingdom 2021, 19).

CONCLUSION

For more than half a century, there has been little change in established legally binding
rules of international law for space security. As in 1967, Article IV of OST is at the
center of international rules in space security today. Nor has there been any clearer understanding of LOAC rules governing an armed conflict to, from, and in outer space,
should one occur. History shows that it is next to impossible to make a new legally
binding treaty relating to space activities in the foreseeable future. Thus, any possible
new norms to enhance space security are expected to come through non-legally binding
instruments. At present, the UNGA Resolution on Responsible Behaviors seems most
promising in generating norms for enhancing space security, because of its focus on responsible and irresponsible behaviors in outer space, not forbidding weapons placed in
outer space. Since the dual-use nature is especially conspicuous in space activities, this is
an appropriate direction. The final result of a set of norms on responsible and irresponsible behaviors remains uncertain, but one thing is clear: New norms, to be listed, would
have to be complemented by concrete measures for effective national implementation,
a major part of which would be the specifications of the LTS and other technically based
guidelines as well as HCOC and other relevant TCBM instruments.

Established international norms are indispensable, but ultimately, they have to be
translated into national implementation to enhance space security. Thus, we can expect
virtuous cycles between national, regional, and international policy discussions. In this
regard, national and regional guidelines and policies on STM are hopefully also being
developed in major spacefaring nations.

REFERENCES

Agreement Governing the Activities of States on the Moon and Other Celestial Bodies. 1979.
    December 18. 1363 UNTS 3 (MA).
Antarctic Treaty. 1959. 402 UNTS 71.
Aoki, Setsuko. 2017. "Law and Military Uses of Outer Space." In *Routledge Handbook of Space
    Law*, edited by Ram S. Jakhu and Paul Stephan Dempsey, 197–224. London, New York:
    Routledge.

Aoki (Ushioda), Setsuko. 1992. "Satellite-Based Multilateral Arms Control Verification Schemes and International Law." PhD diss., Montreal Institute of Air and Space Law, McGill University. https://escholarship.mcgill.ca/concern/theses/qr46r261d.

Carbis Bay G7 Summit Communiqué. 2021. June 13. https://www.consilium.europa.eu/media/50361/carbis-bay-g7-summit-communique.pdf.

CD/274. 1982. April 7. Conference on Disarmament.

CD/476. 1984. March 20. Conference on Disarmament.

CD/786. 1987. August 24. Conference on Disarmament.

CD/1679. 2002. June 28. Conference on Disarmament.

CD/1785. 2006. June 21. Conference on Disarmament.

CD/1839. 2008. February 29. Conference on Disarmament.

CD/1985. 2014. June 12. Conference on Disarmament.

Cheng, Bin. 1997. *Studies in International Space Law*. Oxford; New York: Clarendon Press.

Chow, Brian G. 2017. "Stalkers in Space: Defending the Threat." *Strategic Studies Quarterly* (Summer): 82–116. https://www.airuniversity.af.edu/Portals/10/SSQ/documents/Volume-11_Issue-2/Chow.pdf.

Comprehensive Nuclear-Test-Ban Treaty (CTBT). 1996. September 10.

Convention on the Prohibition of the Development, Production and Stockpiling of Bacteriological (Biological) and Toxin Weapons and on their Destruction 1972. April 10, 1015 UNTS 163 (BWC).

Convention on the Prohibition of the Development, Production, Stockpiling and Use of Chemical Weapons and on their Destruction 1993. January 13, 1974 UNTS 317 (CWC).

Convention on the Prohibition of Military or Any Other Hostile Use of Environmental Modification Techniques 1977. May 18. 1108 UNTS 151 (ENMOD Convention).

European Union. 2020. Space Traffic Management for XXI Century Space Operations. https://cordis.europa.eu/project/id/101004319.

ESPI. (European Space Policy Institute). 2021 "UN Resolution on Norm of Responsible Behaviours in Space—a Step Forward to Preserve Stability in Space." *ESPI Briefs* 54, November. https://espi.or.at/publications/espi-executive-briefs/category/5-espi-executive-briefs.

Freeland, Steven. 2015. "The Laws of War in Outer Space." In *Handbook of Space Security*, edited by Kai-Uwe Schrogl et al., 81–112. Vol. 1. New York: Springer.

Froehlich, Annette, and Vincent Seffinga, eds. 2020. *The United Nations and Space Security: Conflicting Mandates Between UNCOPUOS and the CD*. Switzerland: Springer.

Hague Code of Conduct against Ballistic Missile Proliferation (the Hague Code of Conduct: HCOC). 2002. https://www.hcoc.at/.

Hitchens, Theresa. 2021. "It's a FOBS, Space Force's Saltzman Confirms amid Chinese Weapons Test Confusion." November 29, 2021. https://breakingdefense.com/2021/11/its-a-fobs-space-forces-saltzman-confirms-amid-chinese-weapons-test-confusion/.

Hobe, Stephan, Bernhardt Schmidt-Tedd, and Kai-Uwe Schrogl, eds. 2009. *Cologne Commentary on Space Law*. Vol. 1. Cologne: Carl Heymanns Verlag.

ICJ. 1974. Nuclear Test Case (Australia v. France). Rep. 253.

ICJ. 1986. Military and Paramilitary Activities in and against Nicaragua (Nicaragua v. USA) (Merits). Rep 226.

ICJ. 1996. Legality of a Threat or Use of Nuclear Weapons (Advisory Opinion). Rep 14.

ICJ. 2004. Legal Consequences of the Construction of a Wall in the Occupied Palestinian Territory (Advisory Opinion). Rep 136.

ICRC (International Committee of the Red Cross). 1987. *Commentary on the Additional Protocols of 8 June 1977 to the Geneva Conventions of 12 August 1949*. USA; Canada: Kluwer Academic Publishers.

Ikeda, Fumio. 1971. *Treatise on Space Law*. Tokyo: Seibundo.

Kelso, T. S. 2014. "Analysis of the 2007 Chinese ASAT Test and the Impact of Its Debris on the Space Environment." *Technical Papers 2007 AMOS Conference*, 321–30, Maui, Hawaii, July 10.

Lyall, Francis, and Paul, B. Larsen. 2018. *Space Law: A Treatise*. 2nd ed. London; New York: Routledge.

Mačák, Kubo. 2018. "Silent War: Applicability of the Jus in Bello to Military Space Operations" *International Law Studies* 94: 1–38.

Meyer, Alex. 1969. "Interpretation of the Term 'Peaceful' in the Light of the Space Treaty." *Proceedings of the 11th (1968) Colloquium on the Law of Outer Space*, 24–29. Washington, DC: AIAA.

Miller, Amanda. 2021 "Cislunar Space." *Air Force Magazine*. October 7, 2021. https://www.airforcemag.com/article/cislunar-space/.

Moltz, James Clay. 2008. *The Politics of Space Security: Strategic Restraint and the Pursuit of National Interests*. Stanford, CA: Stanford University Press.

NATO (North Atlantic Treaty Organization). 2021. Brussels Summit Communiqué. June 14. https://www.nato.int/cps/en/natohq/news_185000.htm.

Pekkanen, Saadia M. 2021. "Challenges to Building Responsible Behaviour in Space." *Space Tracker*, October 18, 2021. https://www.orfonline.org/expert-speak/challenges-to-building-responsible-behaviour-in-space/.

Pekkanen, Saadia M. 2022. "Neoclassical Realism in Japan's Space Security." In *The Oxford Handbook of Japanese Politics*, edited by Robert J. Pekkanen and Saadia M. Pekkanen, 763–90. New York: Oxford University Press.

Protocol Additional to the Geneva Convention of 12 August 1949, and relating to the Protection of Victims of International Armed Conflicts. 1977. December 12. 1125 UNTS 3 (Additional Protocol I).

Rajagopalan, Rajeswari Pillai. 2021. "Space Security Governance: Could a New Working Group Narrow the Divide?" November 5. https://www.orfonline.org/research/space-security-governance/.

Russian Federation. 2014. The Military Doctrine of the Russian Federation. Press Release, December 25. English Translation, June 29, 2015. https://rusemb.org.uk/press/2029.

Schmitt, Michael N. 2006. "International Law and Military Operations in Space." *Max Planck UNYB* 10: 89–125.

Stephens, Dale. 2018. "The International Legal Implications of Military Space Operations: Examining the Interplay between International Humanitarian Law and the Outer Space Legal Regime." *International Law Studies* 94: 76–101.

Sheehan, Michael. 2015. "Defining Space Security." In *Handbook of Space Security: Policies, Applications and Programs*, edited by Kai-Uwe Schrogl et al., 7–21 New York: Springer.

Stares, Paul. 1985. *The Militarization of Space: US Policy 1945–1984*. Ithaca, NY: Cornell University Press.

Sevastopulo, Demetri, and Kathrin Hille. 2021. "China Tests New Space Capability with Hypersonic Missile" *Financial Times*. https://www.ft.com/content/ba0a3cde-719b-4040-93cb-a486e1f843fb.

Temple, L. Parker. 2005. *Shades of Gray: National Security and the Evolution of Space Reconnaissance*. Reston, VA: AIAA.

Treaty Banning Nuclear Weapon Tests in the Atmosphere, in Outer Space and Under Water. 1963. August 14. 489 UNTS 43 (PTBT).

Treaty between the United States of America and the Union of Soviet Socialist Republics on the Limitation of Anti-Ballistic Missile Systems. 1972. May 26. 944 UNTS 13 (ABM Treaty) (terminated June 13, 2002).

Treaty between the United States of America and the Union of Soviet Socialist Republics on Further Reduction and Limitation of Strategic Offensive Arms. 1991. July 31. (START I).

Treaty between the United States and the Russian Federation on Strategic Offensive Reductions. 2002. May 24. (SORT) (expired February 5, 2011).

Treaty between the United States of America and the Russian Federation on Measures for the Further Reduction and Limitation of Strategic Offensive Arms. 2010. April 8. (New START Treaty).

Treaty on Conventional Armed Forces in Europe. 1990. November 19. 30 ILM 1 (1991) (CFE Treaty).

Treaty on Principles Governing the Activities of States in the Exploration and Use of Outer Space, including the Moon and Other Celestial Bodies. 1967. January 27. 610 UNTS 205 (Outer Space Treaty or OST)

UN Doc. A/RES/1884 (XVIII). 1963. October 17.

UN Doc. A/RES/1962(XVIII). 1963. December 13.

UN Doc. A/34/20. (1979).

UN Doc. A/RES/31/72. 1976. December 10.

UN Doc. A/RES/32/196B. 1977. December 20.

UN Doc. A/RES/35/16. 1980. November 3.

UN Doc. A/RES/51/122. 1996. December 13.

UN Doc. A/RES/59/91. 2004. December 3.

UN Doc. A/RES/67/42. 2013. January 4.

UN Doc. A/RES/69/44. 2014. December 11.

UN Doc. A/Res/71/33. 2016. December 9.

UN Doc. A/Res/73/49. 2018. December 12.

UN Doc. A/RES/75/37. 2020. December 16.

UN Doc. A/RES/76/55. 2021. December 13.

UN Doc. A/RES/76/231. 2021. December 30.

UN Doc. A/31/27 vol 1. 1976.

UN Doc. A/AC.105/PV.2. 1962. March 19.

UN Doc. A/48/305. 1993. October 15.

UN Doc. A/62/20. 2007.

UN Doc. A/68/189. 2007. 29 July 2013.

UN Doc. A/76/20. 2021.

UN Doc. A/76/77. 2021. July 13.

UN Doc. A/S-10/AC.1/7. 1978.

United Kingdom. 2021. National Space Strategy. September.

US-China Economic and Security Review Commission. 2019. November. 2019 Report to Congress of the US-China Economic and Security Review Commission. https://www.uscc.gov/annual-report/2019-annual-report-congress; https://www.uscc.gov/sites/default/files/2019-11/2019%20Annual%20Report%20to%20Congress.pdf.

US Department of State. 2009. January 20. On Narrative of SALT II Verification. https://www.state.gov/t/isn/5195.htm.

US National Reconnaissance Office. 1971. November 5. Memorandum for Mr. John P. Shaw. https://www.nro.gov/Portals/65/documents/foia/declass/NROStaffRecords/692.PDF.

US Secretary of Defense. 2021. July 7. Memorandum on Tenets of Responsible Behavior. https://media.defense.gov/2021/Jul/23/2002809598/-1/-1/0/TENETS-OF-RESPONSIBLE-BEHAVIOR-IN-SPACE.PDF.

US Senate Committee on Aeronautical and Space Sciences. 1967. "Outer Space Treaty Analysis and Background Data Staff Report." 90th Congress, 1st session. Committee print. Washington, DC: U.S. Government Printing Office.

Vlasic, Ivan A. 1991. "The Legal Aspects of Peaceful and Non-Peaceful Uses of Outer Space." In *Peaceful and Non-Peaceful Uses of Space*, edited by Bhupendra Jasani, 37–55. New York: Taylor & Francis.

White House. 2018. Space Policy Directive-3, National Space Traffic Management Policy June 18. https://aerospace.org/sites/default/files/policy_archives/Space Policy Directive 3 - STM 18Jun18.

PART II

THEORETICAL APPROACHES AND PERSPECTIVES

CHAPTER 4

....

THE DISCOURSE OF SPACE SECURITIZATION

....

P.J. BLOUNT

INTRODUCTION

....

A core technological challenge in human spaceflight is the docking of spacecraft on-orbit. Designing docking mechanisms that can be employed by multiple states and operators is essential to facilitating cooperation in space and increasing the safety of astronauts. The challenges presented by this technology first came to the fore during the execution of the 1975 *Apollo-Soyuz* mission, which saw a US *Apollo* spacecraft dock with a Soviet *Soyuz* spacecraft in a symbolic moment of cooperation connected to the so-called détente during the Cold War. The docking system designed for this mission had to enable more than just the technical docking of the two spacecraft; it also had to fit within the political narratives of the two states. Docking systems at that point had generally been designed asymmetrically with one side of the system being characterized as female and the other side being characterized as male. In the *Apollo-Soyuz* mission the decision as to which state would receive which side of such a docking system was politically fraught as neither would have easily agreed to being the "penetrated" side of the equation (Jenks 2021). This necessitated and led to the development of an androgynous, symmetric docking system. Setting aside the significant misogyny in the political rhetoric surrounding this situation, what this illustrates is the power of narrative (as well as the narrative of power) in international relations (IR). The political narrative surrounding the technology became a driving force in the design decisions made as it affected the nature of the political relations between the two states involved.

This example is proffered to illustrate that narrative is an important factor in the construction of the normative world we inhabit (Cover 1983), and such narratives indeed hold sway in the field of IR among states. This significance of narrative constructions has been recognized by securitization theorists who suggest that narratives shape the way in which we understand the normative frames that govern security issues. This chapter takes up securitization theory and applies it in the context of the space domain. It argues that narratives of security have played a significant, if not dominant, role in IR in the space context, and that these narratives are active in the construction of the normative structures in the space domain. Specifically, it will suggest that securitization in space has resulted in a move from narratives of co-operation to narratives of competitiveness and that this is reflected in the normative struggles within space security.

This chapter will first, briefly, explain securitization theory as a tool of analysis for security issues in IR. Next it will give an account of the changing narratives of space security, addressing specifically the significant shift from rhetoric surrounding the "peaceful uses of outer space" to rhetoric concerning the "congested, contested, and competitive" nature of outer space. Finally, the chapter will discuss and analyze this shift within the context of securitization and examine the future prospects for the maintenance of stability in the space domain.

SECURITIZATION

Securitization theory emerged in the early mid-1990s and early 2000s from a conceptual underpinning in speech act theory (Waever 2015, 122). At a very basic level, securitization theorists argue that security issues in IR are constructed rather than inherent, and it is the rhetoric that is used to frame issues as being related to security that results in them being understood as security issues. Under this theory, security and threats to security are the result of "discursive politics" rather than the inherent qualities of a particular issue area (Balzacq 2010, 15). The analysis of discourse reveals how "a particular issue comes to be spoken and thought of as a security issue" (Peoples 2011, 77). It likely goes too far to extend securitization theory to an extreme and reject other factors beyond narratives in the construction of security issues. Regardless, there is significant value in understanding how narratives influence understandings of security issues and their framing within governance processes.

Securitization theory focuses on the "rhetorical structure of decision-makers when framing an issue and attempting to convince an audience to lift the issue above politics" (Eroukhmanoff 2017, 105). This framing constitutes a speech act that constructs the understanding of the issue through the "*symbolic power* of words, that is the power of constituting the given through utterances, of making people see and believe, of confirming and transforming the vision of the world and, thereby, action on the world and the world itself" (Balzacq 2010, 3, citing Bourdieu). In other words, "words do not merely describe reality, but constitute reality, which in turn triggers certain responses" (Eroukhmanoff 2017, 106). The language that we use to describe the world also helps to construct our understanding of the world, and threats become "constructed" by language (106). This is an "intersubjective process" and rooted in competing discourses that can frame an issue (Buzan, Wæver, and Wilde 1998, 30). In the securitization process "the concept of security permits the activation of a new context, or converts the existing one into something different" (Balzacq 2010, 11).

Securitization is a process that occurs through a securitizing actor, which has the ability to shape the discourse surrounding an issue through an "articulated assemblage of practices whereby heuristic artefacts . . . are contextually mobilized" (Balzacq 2010, 3). This discourse targets an audience with a message concerning security risk to the "referent object," which in the military realm is "usually the state" (Buzan, Wæver, and Wilde 1998, 22). The audience is central to securitization theory as it represents the social group that is targeted by the securitizing discourse. Audience in this context is understood narrowly as an "empowering audience," which is an audience with "direct causal connection" to an issue and has the ability to enable action by the securitizing actor (Balzacq 2010, 8–9). This audience needs to "subscribe . . . to a threat image for it to produce political effects" (8), and together with the securitizing actor they "reach a common structured perception of an ominous development" (12).

Securitization occurs when "an audience collectively agrees on the nature of the threat" (Eroukhmanoff 2017, 106). This leads to a heightening of the threat in terms of the urgency with which it must be addressed, and results in issues being "treated with the same degree of urgency as military threats have been historically" (Peoples 2011, 80). The language used to construct the threat changes the response by actors addressing the threat. Securitization literature has traditionally focused on issues that are "presented as existential threat[s]" and how the securitization of an issue leads to the acceptance of states of exception and the connected reduction of democratic processes in response to the threat (Buzan, Wæver, and Wilde 1998, 21, 24; Eroukhmanoff 2017, 106). However, narrative construction of threats need not always reach into the realm of a state of exception, and securitization might be better understood as a process rather than an outcome. The narrative construction of threats works within a nuanced spectrum that runs from the non-politicized to the politicized to the fully securitized (Buzan, Wæver, and Wilde 1998, 23–24). Though at the securitized end of the spectrum emergency measures that threaten established governance structures may become accepted, shifts along the spectrum show how responses to security issues are impacted by the words chosen to describe and frame these issues and how such issues are situated within normative frameworks. Further, it is not suggested herein that securitization is the only way in which security issues arise or should be understood. Other approaches maintain significant explanatory power, but it is suggested that narratives of securitization are important in understanding how responses to security issues are shaped, especially within normative frameworks. Finally, it should also be noted that narratives of securitization must be resonant within the context of external factors, such as technological development (Balzacq 2010, 13). For instance, the development of nuclear weapons does not become a security issue merely through discursive processes, but our understanding of that security issue is shaped by framing narratives that are significant drivers in stabilization and escalation processes.

Indeed, the analysis that follows is not intended to show that space security issues have moved into the undemocratic space of a state of exception (though that possibility certainly exists), but rather that the shift from describing space as a cooperative environment to describing it as a competitive environment has impacted how states have positioned themselves in their responses to these threats.

THE SANCTUARY THAT NEVER WAS

In a fascinating study of US documents relating to space security, Dickey argues that the shift in US policy from space as a sanctuary to space as a contested domain occurred significantly earlier than previously thought, moving the change from the 1980s to the 1970s (Dickey 2020, 2–3). Dickey's study highlights the significant role of narrative in the construction of space as a security issue, and she suggests that the shift from "sanctuary" thinking to contestation driven narratives was a major driver of US approaches to space. But within Dickey's text there is a fascinating footnote that brings this into focus. Dickey notes that the first use of "sanctuary" to describe space that she identified was in a US military document rejecting the notion (9). This is an interesting rhetorical turn because it indicates that the dominant narrative of space as contested co-opted the idea of sanctuary as a way to reject previous US policy. "Sanctuary" as a shorthand for the earlier US policy is important as it served to frame and delegitimize this policy with the easily rejectable idea of sanctuary. The pre-contestation policy never understood space as a sanctuary, that is as a refuge from danger, but rather it pursued space security as nuanced and saw cooperative efforts with adversaries as a tool within this policy. Dickey notes that there is significant ambiguity in the idea of space as a sanctuary and that there is a lack of consensus underlying its meaning (2), which further indicates its lack of salience as a formal US policy. As a function of a securitization narrative, to characterize the existing policy—which did emphasize "political, diplomatic, and strategic methods of preventing or avoiding conflict" (2)—as "sanctuary" eased the rejection of this policy by shaping the perception of it. It was and is quite clear that space has never been a sanctuary and has historically been linked to national security (Peoples 2011, 83), which was evident from the early 1960s when states conducted nuclear tests in the space domain (Moltz 2008, 46–47), but the perception of a norm based policy was easily weakened by aligning it with a narrative constructed around the idea of sanctuary. This weakening opened the door for rhetoric that endorsed the need for US "dominance" in space (Peoples 2011, 85).

This section seeks to evaluate how narrative shifts from peace and cooperation to contestation and competition represent a process of "constructing shared understanding" of what constitutes threats and security in the space domain. Specifically, it will examine the United States as a securitizing actor using rhetoric to shape the discourse for the audience of the, admittedly ambiguous, international space community. The two examples addressed in this section are both examples of narratives of security that began within the US national context but were successfully pushed into the supranational context. Securitization is rooted in the "study of discourse and political constellations" (Buzan,

Wæver, and Wilde 1998, 25), and an examination of how the United States through its military space policy has been able to push national narratives into acceptance within international discourse will reveal the securitization tendencies in the issue area of space security. This section will first investigate the pedigree of the narrative of cooperation surrounding the peaceful uses of outer space and its emergence at the beginning of the space age. It will then turn its attention to the contemporary narrative of space as a contested and competitive domain. The similarities in the spread of these narratives serve as a useful example of the ongoing securitization of the space domain.

Peaceful Purposes

Space as a domain for peaceful purposes and peaceful uses has a deep heritage in the normative discourse surrounding the space environment. As a normative frame, the emergence of peaceful purposes can be traced to the very beginnings of the space age, and it was embraced by the international community shortly after the launch of *Sputnik I*. Though it was quickly embraced as an international norm, the norm itself has never had clear and settled content and has been a central locus for normative contestation (Blount 2019). Even at the beginning of the Space Age the content of the norm was unsettled as the two Cold War superpowers began to understand how space affected their strategic positions. This section gives a brief account of the initial use of peaceful purposes as a normative frame and its emergence from the policy of the United States and acceptance at the international level.

After the reworking of the structure of international governance post–World War II, one of the core goals of the new system was the "maintenance of international peace and security" (Charter of the United Nations, Art. 1). This system faced immediate challenges to this goal from the intertwined development of nuclear weapons and the evolving Cold War between the United States and the USSR. Seeking a resolution to the impending arms race surrounding nuclear weapons, US President Eisenhower gave a speech titled "Atoms for Peace" to the United Nations General Assembly (UNGA) in 1953. This speech sought to gain support for an International Atomic Energy Agency that would ensure that atomic and nuclear capabilities were used for "peaceful pursuits of mankind" and for "peaceful uses" (Eisenhower 1953). This idea would be rephrased as "peaceful purposes" and would become a clear theme in the Eisenhower administration's approach to atomic weapons, and be repeated in speeches and letters (see for example Eisenhower 1960).

The USSR rejected the US proposal on atomic weapons, but in January 1958, shortly after the launch of *Sputnik I*, President Eisenhower sent a letter to Nikolai Bulganin, Chairman of the Soviet Council of Ministers, in which he proposed that space should "be used only for peaceful purposes" (Eisenhower 1958). In this letter, Eisenhower links this idea to his failed proposal to couple nuclear capabilities with "peaceful purposes" and states that "[t]here are about to be perfected and produced powerful new weapons which, availing of outer space, will greatly increase the capacity of the human race to destroy itself" (Eisenhower 1958). This push by the US administration would be significantly more successful than its Atoms for Peace initiative. In the National Aeronautics and Space Act of July 1958, the US Congress codified "that it is the policy of the United States that activities in space should be devoted to peaceful purposes for the benefit of all mankind" (NAS Act, 1958, Sec. 102). The US position would find acceptance in the international community, including the USSR, in the first UNGA Resolution 1348 (XIII), Question of the Peaceful Uses of Outer Space (United Nations 1958). This resolution uses the phrases "peaceful uses" or "peaceful purposes" a total of ten times and establishes the ad hoc Committee on the Peaceful Uses of Outer Space. Resolution 1348 (XIII) was the first UNGA resolution on space, and every subsequent resolution addressing space matters has included the phrase peaceful purposes or peaceful uses. The idea still holds significant sway as a normative threshold for space activities and states invoke peaceful purposes when attempting to legitimize their activities in space. As an example, North Korea frames its space activities as being for peaceful purposes despite widespread criticism that the space program is a cover for ballistic missile development (KCNA 2009).

"Peaceful" as a framing narrative for space may be somewhat misleading. Only sporadically have states suggested that the notion of peaceful is equivalent to non-military, and contemporary state practice completely negates such an interpretation. The idea of peace in the general normative discourse of international governance allows for the development and maintenance of defensive military capabilities, which are understood to be consistent with "peaceful" as long as they are not used in an aggressive manner in contravention of the ban on the use or threat of force found in UN Charter Art. 2 (4). In the space domain, there has never been a direct definition of "peaceful purposes" and though treated as a threshold for legality of space activities, the term is not found as a treaty obligation. Instead, peaceful purposes exists as a framing norm found within customary international law; however, herein the concern is not with its legal power, but with its power as a framing narrative for space activities. This framing narrative is directly connected to the legal system from which this norm springs; but recognizing it as a narrative acknowledges the contestation of meaning and content that exists within the norm itself.

Though there is no strict legal or political definition of peaceful purposes, the term is most often linked to ideas of communication and cooperation. This can be seen in its usage in the UNGA Resolutions that use peaceful purposes as a frame for the substance of the resolutions, which often emphasize communication and cooperation as methods for maintaining the peaceful uses of outer space. More significantly, this can be seen in the preamble to the Outer Space Treaty, which invokes the idea of peaceful purposes as a raison d'être for the treaty. The treaty itself places significant emphasis on ideas of international cooperation as well as communication among space actors (Blount 2018). Though these obligations are soft in nature, they are framed as significant tools in maintaining stability in space for the maintenance of international peace and security.

Within the context of securitization theory, the narrative of peaceful purposes that was pursued as a normative frame for space activities shows a clear attempt to shift space away from being securitized. The implementation of the cooperative approach to peace that emerged in the early space age could be viewed as a countervailing process of de-securitization. That is not to suggest that space lacked security dimensions that could only emerge through a process of securitization; space clearly had significant implications for national and international security. Rather, this process was intended to anchor space into a normative framework that addressed security dimensions in a de-escalatory way. By framing space as a place for cooperative peace, the goal was not to create a sanctuary but to avoid states of exception that result from normative breakdowns. The trend that Dickey notes emerging in the 1970s is the effective introduction of a new narrative that considers space to be contested. Importantly, the narrative line that she traces is domestic and existed within US military policy rather than in the narratives of foreign policy that carried the message of peaceful purposes. The narrative of contestation, though, would eventually bleed over into the international arena and take hold there, creating an escalatory shift along the securitization spectrum.

Congested, Contested, and Competitive

While the normative framing around a narrative of cooperation and peace still maintains importance today within the space domain, there have been clear pushes toward narratives that securitize space. This has already been noted with regards to the shift from space as a sanctuary to space as a domain of contestation. This section will take up this account through the narrative of space as "congested, contested, and competitive." Like peaceful purposes, this phrase also finds its roots in US policy discourse surrounding the space domain and also shows a similar trend of being pushed into the international narratives surrounding the space environment.

Though it most certainly has a policy pedigree that pre-exists (see for example, Peoples 83–87), the first significant use of the phrase "congested, contested, and competitive" appears in the United States Department of Defense (DoD) National Security Space Strategy of January 2011. This document argues that the "current and future strategic environment is driven by three trends—space is becoming increasingly congested, contested, and competitive" (Department of Defense 2011, 1). The rhetorical nature of this phrase can be seen in the DoD's explanation of these trends. With regards to the congested nature of space, DoD places emphasis on China's 2007 anti-satellite (ASAT) weapon and the debris that it caused, and only places the increasing number of space actors as a secondary cause of congestion (1–2). Contestation in space is explicitly adversarial, with the US strategy noting that space systems "face a range of man-made threats that may deny, degrade, deceive, disrupt, or destroy assets" from both state and non-state actors alike (3). The competitive nature of space is linked to an erosion of US leadership and market share in space that leads to a potential challenge to "assured access to critical technologies" (3).

Two things should be noted about the way in which this phrase is deployed in the National Space Security Strategy. First, this rhetoric, emerging from within the military context, is explicitly non-cooperative. It frames commercial advances from foreign competitors as a challenge to national security, rather than an advance for the use of space for all humankind. Second, this narrative is explicitly US centric. While the idea of congestion may be translated as a challenge to other actors in space, both the contested and competitive elements are understood in relation to US national security interests rather than the interests of the international space-faring community. Interestingly, within US national civil space policy this idea is not replicated in either the 2010 Space Policy of the Obama administration or the 2020 Space Policy of the Trump administration (White House 2010; 2020). It is explicitly part of the US military approach to space. Despite this explicitly military framing at the US domestic level, this phrase has had impact in driving the narratives surrounding space at the international level and has been deployed within scholarly and UN discussions on space security.

Within the scholarly community, since 2009 when there were no usages of this phrase, there has been sustained use of the phrase in academic articles based on Google Scholar data (Figure 4.1). Though this analysis is only quantitative, it shows at a minimum that the phrase has become part of the common discourse surrounding space security issues. Interestingly, this data reveals three returns (but only two unique publications) for the phrase in 2010 before its publication in the 2011 US Security Space Strategy indicating that it had some usage in the community before 2011. While scholarly discourse is not of itself evidence of securitization, it does illustrate that the narrative has taken root in the concerned community, and can link to notions of norm growth out of epistemic communities (Haas 1992). Evidence that this has borne fruit can be found in the United Kingdom's Defence Space Strategy, which states that "[w]e are seeing the space domain become more competitive, congested and contested" (Ministry of Defense 2022, 9).

More telling has been the adoption of the phrase by delegations to the UN. Searching the UN Documents website shows that since 2011, the phrase has appeared in sixteen UN documents, and has been used by delegations including the Canada (United Nations 2021c), European Union (United Nations 2021a; 2021b; 2021c; 2022b; 2022c),

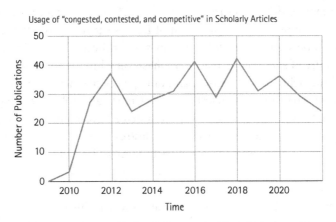

Usage of "congested, contested, and competitive" in Scholarly Articles

FIGURE 4.1 Use of "congested, contested, and competitive" in scholarly articles.

Source: Google data.

Ireland (United Nations 2021c), Japan (United Nations 2020; 2021a), Luxembourg (United Nations 2021c), the Netherlands (United Nations 2020; 2021c; 2022c), Poland (United Nations 2020), Slovenia (United Nations 2021c), South Korea (United Nations 2020; Conference on Disarmament 2021b; United Nations 2021c; 2022a; 2022c; 2022d), the United Arab Emirates (United Nations 2017), United Kingdom (Conference on Disarmament 2021a), and the United States (Conference on Disarmament 2011; United Nations 2019a; Conference on Disarmament 2021a; United Nations 2021c) as well as by non-governmental observers (UNIDIR in, United Nations 2021d; Mcgill University in, United Nations 2022e). It is notable that the bulk of these usages are found in 2021 and 2022.

The list of nations deploying this phrase does display a bias of usage by allies of the United States, but at least one use of the phrase stands out as a multilateral adoption. In 2013, the UN Group of Governmental Experts on Transparency and Confidence-Building Measures in Outer Space Activities (GGE TCBMs) included it in the overview section of its final report, stating:

> The result of the increase in space actors and space users is that the space environment, especially key Earth orbits, has become increasingly utilized over the past few decades. As a consequence, the outer space environment is becoming increasingly congested, contested and competitive. In the context of international peace and security, there is growing concern that threats to vital space capabilities may increase during the next decade as a result of both natural and man-made hazards and the possible development of disruptive and destructive counterspace capabilities. (United Nations 2013, para. 6)

While the three Cs rhetoric has not yet become a dominant theme in the discourse of space, it is clear that US efforts at deploying the rhetoric have been successful, as it has entered the parlance of the UN debates on space security in different forums, including the First Committee, the GGE TCBMs, and the Open Ended Working Group on Reducing Space Threats. This is an interesting development, as the phrase has evolved out of its original context in the US Security Space Strategy. Specifically, the ideas of contested and competitive would seem to require a significant shift in meaning for an international deployment, since they originally were used in a quite specific manner in relation to US interests.

Significant to the discussion of securitization is the way in which this narrative actually changes our understanding of space security, because it goes further than a simple narrative of contestation. The contested element clearly originates within the military sphere and can be related to the idea of conflict. To state that space is contested indicates a move away from peaceful purposes as a normative frame and suggests, specifically, a security threat from an adversarial power within the domain. This shift heightens the understanding of threat within the traditional domain of security. Congested and competitive, on the other hand, suggest security threats in areas that sit outside the traditional realm of security through the military lens.

First, congested refers directly to environmental factors in the space domain and safety factors for space operations. This concept, as brought forward by DoD, concerns the impact on operations caused by both uncontrolled debris as well as the proliferation of space actors. It effectively securitizes the operational environment. The issue of a crowded space domain is not a new one, but it originated in the civil discourse of space as space agencies, and specifically the National Aeronautics and Space Agency (NASA), began to articulate the problem in the late 1970s and early 1980s (Morin and Richard 2021, 568). The increase in orbital debris caused by the 2007 Chinese ASAT provided a significant link between the space environment and security. Space is not unique in this area and follows a trend of securitizing environmental issues. For example, climate change has increasingly been articulated as a security issue (see for example, United Nations 2009; White House 2015).

Second, the notion of competitive is linked, by DoD, directly to economic and commercial aspects of the space environment. It is not used as a synonym for the adversarial conflict implied by the contested notion. Instead, it implicates the increasing number of commercial actors that are engaging with space activities and shifts purely economic activity into the sphere of security. These competitors are not adversarial but pose threats to military operations in a variety of ways. They increase congestion, a trend that is currently playing out with very large constellations. They also, through the development of new technology, create threats as a result of their dual-use nature. For instance, commercial active debris removal technologies can easily be employed to engage in harmful interference with other operators, and as has been seen in the conflict in Ukraine, commercial actors can provide critical military support to terrestrial operations. Commercial actors engaging in conflicts is not a new phenomenon by any means (see Singer 2011), but the dynamic contained in the notion of a competitive space domain is different. Rather than these actors being private military contractors employed by militaries, competitive implies that these actors are a security threat in that they compete with military actors.

Taken together the narrative power in these three terms shifts toward the securitization of the space domain in that it both escalates traditional security threats and brings non-traditional threats within the security paradigm. The shift of this narrative from the US context to the international context creates the potential for the emergence of a new securitized supranational framing for normative behavior in space, but one that is burdened with its US centric military roots. This requires questioning of the supranational norm as to who is contesting space and who is competing for space. The adversarial and oppositional implications of this phrase create significant issues for its application as a normative frame. In the international usages of the phrase discussed above, these questions aren't answered. Instead, they seem to flow from the idea of congestion: that is, because space is congested it is also contested and competitive. Congestion is a much more accepted value concerning space and can be found used within the context of the Long Term Sustainability of Space (United Nations 2019b, Annex II) as well as in statements by non-US allies. The three Cs, though, shift the argument away from one in which space is simply crowded to one in which nameless bad actors are challenging the user of the phrase in its space ambitions. The result of such usage is the rhetorical securitization of space by "an audience that collectively agrees on the nature of the threat" (Eroukhmanoff 2017, 106). This process does not create new security issues, but it changes the discourse on how those issues can be addressed, pushing them further on the securitization spectrum.

SPACES OF EXCEPTION

This chapter has addressed securitization as a process rather than an end result. In this process narrative contestation is used to shape how an issue can be addressed through changes in the normative discourse. Traditional securitization scholarship is often concerned with the end result when an issue is considered to become "securitized." This occurs through "means of an argument about the priority and urgency of an existential threat," in which "the securitizing actor has managed to break free of procedures or rules he or she would otherwise be bound by, we are witnessing a case of securitization" (Buzan, Wæver, and Wilde 1998, 25). In other words, when an issue has become fully securitized it moves out of bounding normative frameworks and into the realm of a state of exception giving the security actor ability to act freely. While it would be improper to suggest that space has become fully securitized in this sense, it is notable that much of the current contestation in this area is about the nature of the normative framework itself. Normative here is not intended to be a synonym for legal. The legal regime governing space is a permissive one that puts few direct limitations on states (Blount 2018, 47), but the normative framework that surrounds space activities has served to instill restraint in the actors within this domain. Norms in this sense shape the bounds of what is acceptable behavior in space as opposed to what is legal behavior in space.

There has, of course, always been contestations in the space domain, but the evolving nature of the complex interactions among operators in space in the post–Cold War era is illustrative of the potential escalation toward securitization. Touch points include the US rejection of new legal rules in space from the early 2000s until quite recently (White House 2006), the ongoing embrace of counterspace capabilities by a number of states (Weeden and Samson 2022), the establishment of military branches directly connected to space operations (Blount 2019), and the increasing rhetoric surrounding the development and use of offensive weapons in space (Blount 2019). Two salient examples can help to bring this into focus. First, the US declaration that space is a "warfighting" domain (Smith 2017; United States Space Force 2020, 10). This statement has domestic implications "for force structure [and] budget decisions," but it also has significant impact on "public and international perceptions" (Dolman 2022, 82). A second recent example can be found in Russia's assertions over targeting US commercial satellites being used by Ukraine in the ongoing conflict resulting from Russia's 2022 invasion of Ukraine (Bingen and Johnson 2022). While the targeting of these satellites would likely be legal under the law of armed conflict, such activities would run counter to the cooperative and peaceful normative framework deployed early in the space age. Both of these examples serve to place space activities on a rhetorical footing of war, which is representative of the ultimate normative breakdown and results in a state of exception. The United States does this rhetorically and Russia takes up that thread and suggests actual action.

The pugilistic rhetoric that states are deploying helps to shift the narrative surrounding space away from a peaceful domain marked by communication, coordination, and cooperation and into a being a domain marked by congestion, contestation, and competitiveness. Of course, rhetoric is not the only driver in this situation, and activities such as the spate of ASAT tests beginning in 2007 also serve to increase the heightened awareness of space as a security issue. At the same time, narrative and rhetoric are important tools used by security actors to normalize their activities by altering the frameworks of acceptable behavior in which they function.

The shift toward the securitization of space is not a complete one, though, and there are signs that states may still de-securitize their narratives. Specifically, the rhetoric by the United States as one of the key provocateurs in this area has begun to soften. Specific examples include US support of the UK-led UNGA Resolution on Reducing Space Threats through Norms, Rules and Principles of Responsible Behaviours and the US revival of the voluntary moratorium on destructive ASAT testing (White House 2022). Both of these acts run counter to previous US policy and could make a move away from securitizing processes in space. Whether or not these actions by the United States will be sufficient to draw down the securitization process is yet to be seen and cannot be isolated from other international processes such as potential Russian escalation in an ongoing armed conflict. As conflict and potential conflict over territorial contestations remains a driver in IR and a significant challenge to the rules based international order, the potential for advancing securitization processes in space and terrestrially remains a threat. To this end, it is important to understand not simply the traditional security drivers for states, but also the normative discourse that surrounds these drivers and the framing of acceptable behavior.

CONCLUSION

Narratives about norms are important tools in our construction of space security, and understanding how those narratives operate is important in understanding how states perceive their relation to the space environment and to other operators. While it is important to recognize that narratives are not the only drivers in the security dimension of space, or any issue area, they serve as significant tools for bounding the acceptable actions of actors within that domain. As Reisman observed in his analysis of international incidents as a function of international law, "shared notions of what is right influence perception, reaction, and capacity for mobilization" (Reisman 1984, 2).

Space has not yet ossified into a securitized realm, a situation that can hopefully be avoided. However, there is a need for states to engage in maintaining the peaceful and cooperative environment of space, and in order to hold back raw assertions of power there is a need to construct normative narratives that, in fact, restrain states. In the early days of the space age these narratives were constructed around peace and cooperation founded on a common understanding of the space environment (Moltz 2008, 46). Today may not be so dissimilar. The work occurring around the idea of sustainability has been critical in addressing these issues from a civil or peaceful perspective (see Wang, this volume), but that common understanding of the fragility of the space environment and the risk of escalation in space can also serve as a common foundation to deploy normative frameworks surrounding space security. In order to avoid the state of exception in space, states—as security actors—need to be cognizant of the narratives they push and how those narratives affect the normative framework surrounding restraint and stability in space. As technology changes and actors proliferate, the shaping of core values in space will become increasingly important in maintaining the space domain for the benefit of all humankind.

REFERENCES

Balzacq, Thierry. 2010. "A Theory of Securitization: Origins, Core Assumptions, and Variants." In *Securitization Theory*, edited by Thierry Balzacq, 1–30. London: Routledge.

Bingen, Kair A., and Kaitlyn Johnson. 2022. "Russia Threatens to Target Commercial Satellites." CSIS. November 10, 2022. https://www.csis.org/analysis/russia-threatens-target-commerc ial-satellites.

Blount, P.J. 2018. "Innovating the Law: Fifty Years of the Outer Space Treaty." In *Innovation in Outer Space: International and African Legal Perspective*, edited by Mahulena Hofmann and P. J. Blount, 31–52. Baden-Baden: Nomos Verlagsgesellschaft mbH & Co. KG.

Blount, P.J. 2019. "The Shifting Sands of Space Security: The Politics and Law of the Peaceful Uses of Outer Space." *Indonesian Journal of International Law* 17, no. 1: 1–18.

Buzan, Barry, Ole Wæver, and Jaap de Wilde. 1998. *Security: A New Framework for Analysis.* Boulder, CO: Lynne Rienner.

Charter of the United Nations. 1945.

Conference on Disarmament. 2011. February 8. Final Record of the 1203rd Plenary Meeting, Held at the Palais des Nations, Geneva, on Tuesday. U.N. Doc. CD/PV.1203.

Conference on Disarmament. 2021a. Final Record of the One Thousand Five Hundred and Seventy-Sixth Plenary Meeting, U.N. Doc. CD/PV.1576.

Conference on Disarmament. 2021b. Final Record Of The One Thousand Five Hundred and Seventy-Seventh Plenary Meeting. U.N. Doc. CD/PV.1577.

Cover, Robert M. 1983. "Foreword: Nomos and Narrative." *Harvard Law Review* 97: 4–68.

Department of Defense. 2011. *National Security Space Strategy*.

Dickey, Robin. 2020. September. "The Rise and Fall of Space Sanctuary in U.S. Policy." Aerospace Corporation.

Dolman, Everett, 2022. "Space Is a Warfighting Domain." *Aether: A Journal of Strategic Airpower & Spacepower* 1, no. 1: 82–90.

Eisenhower, Dwight D. 1953. "Atoms for Peace." https://www.iaea.org/about/history/atoms-for-peace-speech.

Eisenhower, Dwight D. 1958. Letter to Nikolai Bulganin, Chairman, Council of Ministers, U.S.S.R. https://www.presidency.ucsb.edu/documents/letter-nikolai-bulganin-chairman-council-ministers-ussr.

Eisenhower, Dwight D. 1960. Address before the 15th General Assembly of the United Nations. https://www.presidency.ucsb.edu/documents/address-before-the-15th-general-assembly-the-united-nations-new-york-city.

Eroukhmanoff, Clara. 2017. "Securitization Theory." In *International Relations Theory*, edited by Stephen McGlinchey, Rosie Walters, and Christian Scheinpflug, 104–9. Bristol: e-International Relations.

Haas, Peter M. 1992. "Introduction: Epistemic Communities and International Policy Coordination." *International Organization* 46, no. 1: 1–35.

Jenks, Andrew. 2021. "Sex and Cold-War Technological Fixes, Part I." *NYU Jordan Center* (blog). March 9, 2021. https://jordanrussiacenter.org/news/technological-fixes-and-sex-in-the-cold-war-part-i/.

KCNA. 2009. March 2. "KCNA Report on DPRK's Accession to International Space Treaty and Convention." https://web.archive.org/web/20090402023049/http://www.kcna.co.jp/item/2009/200903/news12/20090312-11ee.html.

Ministry of Defense. 2022. "Defence Space Strategy: Operationalising the Space Domain."

Moltz, James Clay. 2008. *The Politics of Space Security: Strategic Restraint and the Pursuit of National Interests*. Stanford, CA: Stanford Security Studies.

Morin, Jean-Frédéric, and Benjamin Richard. 2021. "Astro-Environmentalism: Towards a Polycentric Governance of Space Debris." *Global Policy* 12, no. 4: 568–73.

Peoples, Columba. 2011. "The Securitization of Outer Space: Challenges for Arms Control." *Contemporary Security Policy* 32, no. 1: 76–98.

Reisman, W. Michael. 1984. "International Incidents: Introduction to a New Genre in the Study of International Law." *Yale Journal of International Law* 10: 1.

Singer, Peter Warren. 2011. *Corporate Warriors: The Rise of the Privatized Military Industry*. Ithaca, NY: Cornell University Press.

Smith, Marcia. 2017. "Top Air Force Officials: Space is Now a Warfighting Domain." SpacePolicyOnline.com. https://spacepolicyonline.com/news/top-air-force-officials-space-now-is-a-warfighting-domain/.

United Nations. 1958. General Assembly Resolution 1348 (XIII), Question of the Peaceful Uses of Outer Space.

United Nations. 2009. Climate Change and Its Possible Security Implications: Report of the Secretary-General. U.N. Doc. A/64/350.

United Nations. 2013. Group of Governmental Experts on Transparency and Confidence-Building Measures in Outer Space Activities. U.N. Doc. A/68/189.

United Nations. 2017. Views of States Members of the Committee on the Peaceful Uses of Outer Space on Transparency and Confidence-Building Measures in Outer Space Activities. U.N. Doc. A/AC.105/1145.

United Nations. 2019a. Official records of the 18th Plenary Meeting of the First Committee. U.N. Doc. A/C.1/74/PV.18.

United Nations. 2019b. June 12–21. Report of the Committee on the Peaceful Uses of Outer Space Sixty-Second Session. U.N. Doc. A/74/20.

United Nations. 2020. First Committee Compendium of Submissions. U.N. Doc. A/C.1/75/INF/5.

United Nations. 2021a. Compendium of Submissions: General Assembly, 76th Session, 1st Committee: Note / by the Chair. U.N. Doc. A/C.1/76/INF/5.

United Nations. 2021b. General Assembly Official Records, 76th Session: 1st Committee, 7th Meeting, Tuesday, October 12, 2021, New York. U.N. Doc. A/C.1/76/PV.7.

United Nations. 2021c. Reducing Space Threats through Norms, Rules and Principles of Responsible Behaviours. U.N. Doc. A/76/77.

United Nations. 2021d. Review of the i Implementation of the Recommendations and Decisions Adopted by the General Assembly at Its Tenth Special Session. U.N. Doc. A/76/175.

United Nations. 2022a. Disarmament Commission 379th Meeting Tuesday, April 5, 2022. U.N. Doc. A/CN.10/PV.379.

United Nations. 2022b. European Union (EU) Joint Contributions to the Works of the Open-Ended Working Group on Reducing Space Threats through Norms, Rules and Principles of Responsible Behaviours. U.N. Doc. A/AC.294/2022/WP.2.

United Nations. 2022c. Further Practical Measures for the Prevention of an Arms Race in Outer Space. U.N. Doc. A/77/80.

United Nations. 2022d. Regarding the Works of the Open-Ended Working Groupon Reducing Space Threats through Norms, Rules, and Principles of Responsible Behaviours. U.N. Doc. A/AC.294/2022/WP.15.

United Nations. 2022e. Written Contribution to the Open-Ended Working Group (OEWG) on Reducing Space Threats through Norms, Rules and Principles of Responsible Behaviours. U.N. Doc. A/AC.294/2022/NGO/5.

United States Space Force. 2020. Spacepower: Doctrine for Space Forces.

Wæver, Ole. 2015. "The Theory Act: Responsibility and Exactitude as Seen From Securitization." International Relations 29, no. 1: 121–27.

Weeden, Brian, and Victoria Samson. 2022. Global Counterspace Capabilities: An Open Source Assessment. Washington, D.C.: Secure World Foundation.

White House. 1960, Executive Order 10870—Designating the Facilities of the National Aeronautics and Space Administration at Huntsville, Alabama, as the George C. Marshall Space Flight Center. https://www.presidency.ucsb.edu/documents/executive-order-10870-designating-the-facilities-the-national-aeronautics-and-space.

White House. 2006. US National Space Policy.

White House. 2010. National Space Policy of the United States of America.

White House. 2015. Findings from Select Federal Reports: The National Security Implications of a Changing Climate.

White House. 2020. National Space Policy of the United States of America.

White House. 2022. Fact Sheet: Vice President Harris Advances National Security Norms in Space. https://www.whitehouse.gov/briefing-room/statements-releases/2022/04/18/fact-sheet-vice-president-harris-advances-national-security-norms-in-space/.

CHAPTER 5

CRITICAL SPACE SECURITY
Space Is Not Special

CARL GRAEFE AND RAYMOND DUVALL

INTRODUCTION

THE history of the modern state is intimately bound with processes of securing exclusive control over designated territory, frequently through colonization. These processes of territorial securitization are not limited to history, nor do they stop at the edge of the atmosphere in our space age. Though there are unique physical properties associated with outer space, these do not necessarily translate into unique political outcomes for extraterrestrial spaces. To the contrary, the relative absence to date of overtly conflictual dynamics of "territorial" conquest and colonization in space is dependent on the continued underdevelopment of states' capacity in this domain, and not on the absence of a colonial aspiration for conquest and exclusive control. Anyone interested in the politics of space security needs to take seriously the future eventuality of a state or group of states developing the means to carve out extraterrestrial spaces for their exclusive use: the means to colonize space. In this chapter we highlight that possibility. Specifically, we critically evaluate several dynamics in the securitization of outer space to reveal prospective futures of exclusion and extraterrestrial imperialism.

The labeling of theoretical perspectives in the study of international relations (IR) is a fraught exercise. When invited to contribute a chapter on "critical" space security, we approached our assignment in terms of the general commitments of broadly critical perspectives, rather than seeking to privilege one or another variant of Critical (with a capital C) Theory. In our view, broadly critical perspectives share some fundamental constitutive principles. In an incisive recent contribution, Beate Jahn points to two "core principles." In her words, the first of those is that "[t]he emancipatory goal of transforming society as a whole must . . . become a regulative ideal [of scholarship]." Second, "critical theory aims to change thinking . . . it reflects on the way in which knowledge production itself is complicit in the constitution of social and political issues" (Jahn 2021, 1284). In an earlier formulation, pointing to those core principles, albeit in somewhat different terms, Duvall and Varadarajan say "[c]ritical theories . . . share a commitment to challenging the naturalness of the existing world order and the acceptability of its dominant relations and practices of power. Critical theory focuses analysis on the effects of power on the differential ability of actors to control their own circumstances. It also goes beyond that theoretical contribution to provide impetus for practical political action in challenging, confronting, and disrupting existing relations of power. Thus, in the contemporary era, critical IR theory is relevant, among other ways, as a stimulus to resist empire in its many guises" (Duvall and Varadarajan 2003, 75). It is in that spirit that we think of the current chapter as offering a decolonial critique.

Our argument will unfold in three parts. First, we assess the validity and sustainability of arguments that use the unique properties of outer space to arrive at a conclusion that the domain will remain removed from the overtly conflictual dynamics of colonization and exclusive territorial control. We show that general acceptance of ever-broadening (and less peaceful) definitions of "peaceful purposes" reflects the extension of a colonial mindset whereby "peace" includes the normalized violence of the dominant state(s). Second, we outline how securitization of space assets can be translated into a regime of selective exclusion in outer space. The creeping securitization of space assets gradually establishes a territoriality in outer space that mirrors the exclusive politics of the international territorial system on Earth, a process of territorial assimilation integral to processes of colonization. Finally, we deploy a decolonial critical perspective to begin considering how a regime of selective exclusion in outer space could impact international politics. Exclusivity operates in two fashions in the territoriality of the international system. First, individual territorial units (states) claim and exercise sovereign control over specific spaces to the exclusion of all others. Second, because territorial sovereignty is a necessity for recognition in the system, all other ways of being are excluded or take a backseat once proprietary territoriality is introduced. The upshot of these three processes is that a future space politics pivoting on exclusionary zones looms as a real possibility.

CONTINUED PEACEFUL PURPOSES

Space politics has often been viewed as exemplary, at least with respect to the absence, to date, of overt physical hostilities—open warfare—in efforts to control spatial domains. This relative peace is due to multiple factors, but one should be wary of projecting these dynamics onto futures in outer space. Many arguments used to explain this relatively peaceful state of space politics rely on factors that may or may not represent continuing challenges to future states as state capacity increases. Indeed, many of the factors claimed to be acting toward the preservation of peace in space in fact incentivize specific logics of securitization.

Securitization refers to processes through which a subject is identified and labeled as a matter of "national security" and hence calls for strong or forceful response. To call something a security issue is to securitize it and to legitimate a powerful response to it. Our argument is that the various arguments that circulate to claim the inherent "peacefulness" of outer space serve to the contrary to identify space as a securitized domain (on the logics of securitization, see, among other sources, Buzan, Weaver, and de Wilde 1998). When these securitizing efforts are paired with the rhetoric of peaceful purposes, a changing interpretation of peace is produced that imports exclusionary state practices into the space domain. Thus, while some argue that increasing state capacity (and the falling costs of operating in space that accompany it) is a democratizing force in outer space, we contend that increasing mastery of the space environment opens the door for exclusive "territorial" politics.

In this section we briefly critique three of the most influential lines of argument that associate the space environment with peaceful political outcomes. The first is that orbital mechanics make fighting war in the space domain difficult and raise the risks and costs to such a degree that no space power would be willing to act aggressively for fear of damaging their own assets, an assumption that is already being brought clearly into doubt by the accelerating pace at which kinetic anti-satellite tests are conducted. The second is the commercial peace argument, where private operators require a stable environment to attract investment and this is assumed to lead to the establishment and preservation of a rules-based space regime, an assumption emblematic of the until-now prevailing liberal international order, an order that is increasingly precarious. The third is that the space domain is so intricately tied to nuclear stability that no state is willing to significantly destabilize the status quo in space for fear of disrupting nuclear stability.

Orbital Mechanics

Cascading orbital collisions is an often-cited reason to avoid kinetic conflict in orbital spaces. Debris created by the kinetic destruction of a satellite puts other space assets, including allied or neutral assets, at risk. It is already the case that such an eventuality has not prevented several states from moving forward with anti-satellite technologies. Far from being a hard disincentive to conflict initiation in space, however, the mechanics of the space environment may incentivize developing greater capacity for spatial control. Controlling the space around one's own assets has the dual benefit of guarding against weapons deployed by an adversary or debris resulting from tests, accidents, and conflicts between other parties. Indeed such a desire for spatial control is a potential breeding ground for new and innovative ways to selectively destroy or impair unfriendly space systems.

Gopalaswamy and Kampani (2014), in their early and ultimately unsuccessful efforts to dissuade Indian policymakers from pursuing a kinetic ASAT option, offer several alternatives such as blinding/dazzling, jamming, and spoofing. In the intervening years between their writing and today, states have innovated other options for engaging violently in space. Blount points to three contemporary advancing fields that might offer states the capacity to engage combatively in space: (1) proximity and rendez-vous operations; (2) cyberspace; and (3) very large constellations. Recent war gaming has demonstrated the central role some of these strategies—especially proximity and rendezvous operations—play in planning and preparing for modern great power confrontation (Sokolski 2022). Blount explains how these technologies offer challenges to the previously technologically bound conception of "peaceful purposes" and push the understanding of the phrase toward a "non-aggressive" rather than the more limiting "non-military" understanding (Blount 2019). We would remind readers that this ongoing redefinition of the meaning of peace, noted by Blount, is an extension of the long tradition of moving the "necessary" violence of the state out of the "non-peaceful" and into the "peaceful" category, thereby entrenching the legitimacy of violence produced by a state.

The "peace" in "peaceful purposes" references "peace" within a specific ordering of the world and that ordering involves the production of violent capacities to protect and secure the territorial interests of powerful states (see the discussion of Maldonado-Torres 2020 in Trevino 2020 for a detailed discussion concerning the coloniality of the term "peaceful purposes"). Thus, although the physical properties of outer space have thus far seemingly helped to prevent overt belligerence in that domain, those properties do not create enduring conditions that necessarily constrain states to the maintenance of a collaborative future. Instead they produce incentives to innovate new ways of violent engagement and spatial control that are already blurring the lines of what peace in space even means. Because many of the various innovative ways for engaging with space assets of another state may not involve kinetic explosions and splashy shows of violence, they can obfuscate the political processes of territorialization that we are already seeing unfold.

Commercial Peace

Another argument that forecasts a peaceful future for outer space is that capitalism in orbit will serve as a pacifying force. There are two major branches to this argument. The first emphasizes interconnectedness. Space assets are highly integrated into the function of a globalized economy on which all space powers depend. Conflict initiation in space holds unique potential to disrupt economic activity and is therefore thought to be too costly to risk. The other branch of this argument focuses on the entrance of private capital into space-based markets, such as the much-celebrated space tourism ventures that have recently enjoyed success. The argument goes that stability must be demonstrated before significant continued private investment can occur. In this view, space exploration or space tourism firms throughout the world, as well as those involved in well-established private satellite operations, will pressure their governments to establish a rules-based order that protects investments and the profits they generate (Whitman Cobb 2020).

National-capitalist competition seems more likely, however, especially as the lines between commercial and state actors are typically blurred in space operations. To date, for
example, no private actor has gotten to orbit without governmental support, and this is
unlikely to change even with the emerging development of "private" space exploration
and tourism ventures. The Outer Space Treaty (OST) puts liability for objects cleared
for launch by national administrations on the states themselves. This hands-off-but-
government-sponsored-and-contracted-and-overseen kind of arrangement is reminiscent of the company-states of imperial Europe. Company-states often operated with a
type of sovereign authority that is usually only afforded to states in the international
system. Most notably, company-states frequently controlled large tracts of territory
(Phillips and Sharman 2020). In many ways the space age company-state is marked by
a mirrored arrangement. The dual-use nature of space assets and their standing as critical defense infrastructure means that satellites are simultaneously assets of a corporation and assets of a nation-state. Entities such as launch providers, telecommunications
companies, and commercial satellite imaging firms are highly political organizations
that participate in diplomacy, shape norms, and inform law both domestically and internationally. Due to provisions in the OST, it is not possible for a state to formally stake
claim to extraterrestrial territory. However, once a nation's (or company's) space assets
are in place, there are functionally no legal methods for removing them, making the
prohibition against appropriation less relevant in the actual conduct of international
politics in space. Private actors can then hold space (or even extract resources, provided
they are registered in one of the small but growing group of states that has enacted legislation to encourage prospecting in space) on behalf of the state that "granted them their
(launch) charter."

In a recently published article Victoria Samson shows how recent trends in space development have favored the company side of the company-state in ways that have potential to destabilize international politics, by giving firms (and their accompanying states)
avenues to subvert rules and understandings from earlier eras of space governance that
might be contrary to their interests (Samson 2022). Motivating this company-state arrangement in the space age is the fundamental logic of expanded capital accumulation
described by Rosa Luxemburg, following Karl Marx, in an earlier era of capitalist competition (Luxemburg 2003). And just as in that era the logic led to heightened aggressiveness in nationalist competition, such a belligerent pairing of state and company can
be expected in the "private" capitalization of space.

Connection to Nuclear Stability

Another factor some offer as a putatively stabilizing force in outer space is the important
functions the domain plays in issues of nuclear security. Moltz, for example, argues that
the role space assets play in the nuclear security infrastructure of powerful states (early
warning systems, extra-atmospheric interception, the primary pathway for payload delivery, stockpile and production monitoring, etc.) produces an inherent stability for the

space domain (Moltz 2014). The argument is that hostile engagement in space would produce serious risk to these valuable, strategic, nuclear stabilizing functions. The destructive capability of nuclear weapons makes this risk an existential threat, which states are strongly inclined to avoid. Such a line of argumentation, while seemingly plausible, misses a key point. Specifically it takes the role of the space domain in nuclear strategy as given, when instead it should be remembered that space's connection to nuclear strategy is not inherent, but rather the product of path dependent choices that were (and continue to be) made by humans. Günter Anders offers a robust critical assessment of nuclear weapons and technology that is highly germane to this point.

Anders helps illuminate the artificial nature of the existence of nuclear weapons and their relationship to space by identifying some of the ways we naturalize current nuclear strategy. Anders points out that we have a tendency to anthropomorphize technology that creates an illusory association to organic life. For example, we speak of "generations" of bombs and delivery systems as if advancement through these generations is a "self-directed" process (Anders 1956, 1986; see also Van Munster and Sylvest 2019). When we use rhetoric like this, we externalize human participation in the processes that have created the current nuclear paradigm, naturalizing and normalizing its form and giving justification for its continuation. The same is true when we position nuclear stability as an environmental factor of the space domain. Nuclear weapons in general, and also the specific (space related) form we have given them, are far from natural. To the contrary, nuclear weapons are human instruments whose function can be interrogated to analyze the proposed relationship between nuclear stability and the stability of the space domain.

In contrast to popular theory in IR, which focuses on nuclear weapons as systems that are not used, Anders sees nuclear weapons as constantly in use. The existence of nuclear weapons produces a constant globalized threat of extreme violence. In response to this constancy of nuclear conflict, Anders famously reformulates Clausewitz claiming; "What today is wrongly called 'peace' is but the continuation or preparation of war by other means" (Anders 1958; English translation in Van Munster and Sylvest 2019). This statement by Anders points us directly back to processes of securitization. Thinking of nuclear weapons and their attendant infrastructures as constantly in use illuminates how nuclear stability can be constantly used as an instrument for securitization. Everpresent threat drives ever-expanding necessity to make safe and ever-growing acceptance of novel means by which safety can be pursued. The reminder from Anders that the association between space and nuclear weapons is not a natural phenomenon should stand as evidence of how processes of securitization can jump to new domains. "We need to use space to make the world safe from nuclear weapons" has become "we need to make space safe because of nuclear weapons." By choosing to connect nuclear weapons and outer space, opportunities for further securitization are produced. And while the pursuit of safety might be a noble goal in a vacuum, *how* space might be made safe and for *whom* it is being made safe are critical questions that remain. The remainder of this chapter will address these questions by focusing on territorialization, the demarcation of space for exclusive use, as the product of ongoing securitization in outer space.

From Securitization to Territorial Exclusion

If, as we argued in the previous section, the alleged principal pillars of stable peace in space cannot be counted on for the long-term future, then the question arises: how is one to assess prospects for that future? A process that can lead from the multilateralism enshrined in early space law to an increasingly militarized and exclusionary protection of hybrid state-corporate assets is a politically contingent process of securitization: the identification and labeling of developments in space domains as actual or potential threats to national security. Bound tightly to terrestrial processes of interstate competition, securitization drives toward the development of the means for selective exclusion by a powerful spacefaring state or group of spacefaring states. Exclusion is the primary method for deriving security in international politics, a legacy of the formation of the specifically bounded territorial entity that is the modern state. In this section we argue that securitization in the space sector can translate directly into an exclusive politics that effectively territorializes outer space. The ultimate quest for a state that has committed to the securitization and territorialization of outer space is logically the development of the means of selective exclusion. Once the means to selective exclusion have been obtained, the colonization of space begins in earnest.

Securitization

Williams conceptualizes the generic process of securitization as "The socially and politically successful speech act that labels an issue a security issue, removing it from the realm of normal day-to-day politics, casting it as an existential threat calling for and justifying extreme measures" (Williams 1998, 435). With respect to the domain of outer space, Klimburg-Witjes documents this process of securitization unfolding in Europe with respect to tension between the European Space Agency (ESA) and the European Union concerning how much military and security work the ESA can carry out given its original mandate as a civilian organization. The Galileo constellation is offered as the beginning point for a process of securitization of European space activity. Klimburg-Witjes shows how the motivation for Galileo stems from a security crisis when European forces were denied access to critical satellite data from the United States during the Balkan conflicts in the 1990s (Klimburg-Witjes 2021). The necessity of a space presence for the operation of a modern military allows the European Union to push civilian organizations into military functions and encourages the hybridity that is a defining factor of space operations for all states. In this example, the uses of ESA and Galileo to achieve military objectives are the "extreme measures" justified by the labeling of gaps in military intelligence as an existential threat. In turn, objects in space are now being positioned as threatened; one possible "extreme measure" that could be deployed to meet this so-called threat is territorialization.

In the United States, securitization results in the adaptation of military strategy to encompass the space domain in ways that are consequential for the spatiality of outer space. The term "unfettered access" is a favored one in US military doctrine that securitizes areas of the global commons. The doctrine of maintaining unfettered access requires the application of control (see for example, Joint Publication 3-14 *Space Operations*, 2018). In the maritime domain this is Sea Control; in the space domain this is Space Control. The trajectory of US sea control casts instructive light for imagining US space control (see for example, Sumida 2011). US sea control is achieved by floating overwhelming force and pinning adversarial fleets into defensive coastal positions while conducting freedom of navigation acts through waters deemed to be of importance. However, the United States has at times taken control at sea further than this through the unilateral establishment of new kinds of property rights in international law.

In 1945 President Truman issued the Truman Proclamation that extended the maritime boundaries of the United States 200 miles into the open ocean. This was patterned on the Pan-American Security Zone that the United States set up during the Panama Conference of 1939 to protect trade with the Allies and to open the entire Western Atlantic to the control of the US Navy. Both the Pan-American Security Zone and the Truman Proclamation were made in response to the securitization of offshore activities during times of intense interstate competition. Functionally, the Truman Proclamation extended the borders of the United States 200 miles into the open ocean, legitimating the (forceful if necessary) exclusion of agents of other states and offering the security of exclusion to things like offshore oil platforms as well as merchant trade networks. The innovation of new forms of property rights in international law is US tradition and expresses a willingness to innovate systems of spatial control in contravention to international norms, customs, or laws. In pointing to this US experience, we do not argue that the logic of the dynamic is uniquely American. To the contrary, we offer it as an example of a more general process that is likely to affect securitization in space by any powerful state. Securitization translates directly into stratagems of spatial control, whose ultimate expression is legitimated exclusion through territorialization. We need to recognize, however, that this form of spatial control is enabled by a legacy of colonialism and imperialism baked into the spatial ordering of the international system. In the next section we will explore how territorial exclusion connects with coloniality through an exploration of Trevino's concept of the American Cosmic Order (Trevino 2020).

Territorial Exclusion and Coloniality

Territorialization of outer space is made possible by its securitization and the operating logics of control in international politics. Natalie Trevino helps cast light on how the spatial elements of the contemporary international order are associated with colonial legacies. In "The Cosmos is not Finished," she shows how frontierism is projected forward into the space age through the use of the metaphor of space as the "Final Frontier." The application of the frontier metaphor assimilates outer space into traditional conceptions of geographic space and orients it in a colonial fashion as a place for extraction, exploitation, and settlement. Trevino outlines the US understanding of outer space, and indeed its place in the cosmos, as being defined through the "Killian Formula." Delineated in James Killian's memo on the organization of the United States' space interests, that formula states that exploitation is the sum of exploration and control (Exploitation = Exploration + Control) (Trevino 2020). It is the control side of this formula that points to territorialization understood in the context of contemporary international politics. An area that is territorialized undergoes a process whereby general space is cordoned off into demarcated zones in which exclusive violence is legalized and legitimated. Already assets in space have zones which when violated trigger evasive maneuvers to avoid collisions (the "pizza box" zone for the international space station is a popular example). It is not difficult to imagine a future where "evasive maneuvers" are replaced with "protective measures" or some other rhetorical formation that refocuses the provision of security to space assets on keeping others out of one's zone (see Bateman 2022 for a specific recent application of "protective measures").

Trevino begins the explanation of what she calls the American Cosmic Order by deploying Quijano's concept of coloniality in combination with Krupp's theory of cosmic orders. Coloniality is the matrix of power relationships left over from the history of colonialism. These power relationships operate on nearly all aspects of human lives (Quijano 2007). One of the key legacies of colonialism in international politics is the spatial ordering of the world. Karin Mickelson outlines the development of the colonial origins of the spatial ordering of the world by exploring how international law creates a mental "map" in the imaginations of policy makers. The map is defined by a typology composed of four categories of space ordered according to how it is governed and made available for use: *terra nullius*, *res communis*, "Common Heritage of Mankind" (CHM), and sovereign territory. Mickelson demonstrates that these categories and the expressed need for such categorization stems from a colonial gaze on the natural world, according to which the sole distinguishing feature between *res communis* and common heritage categories is the extent of environmental management and protection through collective management. Whereas in territory defined by a *res communis* understanding exploitation of natural resources is not externally managed, common heritage territories have in place some regime for collective management of the space and the resources it holds, usually resulting in the regulation of extraction rights. Thus for Mickelson Antarctica, though not formally governed by the legal CHM regime, should be thought of as a CHM space in the map of international law (see Keyuan 1991 for clarification of the CHM principle and its application to areas beyond national jurisdiction such as Antarctica). The gathering momentum toward resource extraction in outer space without the establishment of a regime for collective management reinforces a perspective that space is not immune from the colonial legacies deeply embedded in IR, but is instead another domain to be assimilated into the set of practices that normalizes boundary drawing and incorporates violent exclusion into its understandings of peace, stability, security, and prosperity.

Trevino argues that the colonial understanding most relevant to outer space is US frontierism. The spatiality of frontierism is a spatial logic unique to the US experience. Whereas the spatiality of European colonialism was defined by an inside-outside division fueled by the myth of Europe, the spatial logic of US colonialism focused on *the frontier*, the place of conversion where "wilderness" was assimilated into civilization (Trevino 2020 citing Webb 1952). Trevino accounts for this major difference through an analysis of the impact of Puritan understandings on the American Cosmological Order. The Puritan understanding of settling America as the mission of turning a "wild" continent into a "civilized" one was translated into the secular and civil project of settling the frontier. Thus a fundamentally cosmological understanding of the order of the universe was spatially affixed onto the point of transition from "wild" to "American," the frontier. This understanding of what America is and its place in the world and the cosmos is translated into the space age. A telling example of this translation is the deployment of the frontier metaphor.

To talk of the "Final Frontier" is to depict outer space as an antagonistic "outside" that one can pit oneself against, master, and then justifiably exploit. "The American Cosmic Order produces and perpetuates state-sanctioned violence and the violence of capitalism, because it requires an 'outside' to exploit and abuse as part of the colonial project of the Frontier" (Trevino 2020, 61). The same logic that positions a continent populated by millions as "wilderness" to be conquered and brought to order positions outer space as a domain subject to mastery and possession. The attendant ethno and anthropocentric logics of value are carried along (Mickelson 2014; Trevino 2020). Furthermore, the notion of the civilizing project is translated with the frontier metaphor. Ultimately the wilds are to be assimilated into civilized space. Borders must replace the frontier and the fundamental jurisdictional question, the primary allocation of "mine and thine," must be answered before "outside" space is truly assimilated into the international system (see Schmitt and Ulmen 2006 for a detailed discussion on the spatial foundations of international order and law). The spatial project that is implicit in the frontier metaphor, when coupled with the processes of securitization outlined above, points to a territorialization of outer space based on the violent exclusion of those who are not wanted, trusted, or deemed responsible enough to be there. A focus on the American Cosmic Order is necessary because the process implied by the frontier metaphor is generalizable to other major space powers and precludes all other ways of being and relating to outer space. As long as there is one or more space powers with intent to territorialize and exploit, all other visions for the future must contend with those powerful states.

Ultimately the American Cosmic Order displaces the responsibility of exploitation from humans onto the cosmos. This act of displacement takes us full circle. By claiming that movement toward spatial control is a natural reaction to the natural environmental conditions presented by outer space, strategists enjoy absolution from the consequences of violence, as violent exclusion is normalized and legitimized as necessary for the achievement of "peace" in such a potentially harsh "world."

In the remainder of this chapter, we sketch a scenario of possible, even perhaps likely, futures that emerge from the space security politics that we have described in the foregoing discussion. Our intent is *not* to suggest that the *specific* details of this speculative exercise in scenario building are the essence of our theoretical argument. Instead, our interest is in the underlying logic, not the substantive specifics, and our intent is to highlight the often hidden inequalities and colonial relations built into the logic and workings of the space security politics described in the preceding sections.

EXCLUSIVE SPACE POLITICS AND THE IMPLICATIONS OF THE SPACE CLUB

Since the first successful space launches, there has been a "Space Club" of states that possess the means to access space, initially a club of two, which has now grown to include several additional members, although far from all states. Despite the informality of this club, its members have appreciable power to shape the international space regime by virtue of their established access to the domain and the attendant ability to set or challenge precedent, norms, laws, and customs. If or as the means to selective exclusion in space are developed, membership in the Space Club would no longer be determined solely by achievement of a capacity to launch successfully into space. Selective exclusion is the capability for a state or group of states to constrain the access all others have to meaningfully use outer space. It is the means to control space, in space. An entity that maintains possession of the means to selective exclusion holds the power to control admission into (and expulsion out of) the Space Club. Submission to the power that holds the means to selective exclusion would become the primary pathway to membership. Thus, the transition from an unintentionally exclusive space regime to one of intentional selective exclusion means a reordering of international politics to a more explicitly imperial arrangement.

The consideration of what a monopoly of weaponized low-Earth orbit might look like is offered in Havercroft and Duvall's response to Dolman's theory of astropolitik (Duvall and Havercroft 2008; Havercroft and Duvall 2009). Whereas they articulate a theory of a state possessing a monopoly of Earth-directed space power (weaponization of orbit with the strategic capability of projecting force down the gravity well) reconstituting global politics through the redefinition of state sovereignty through the effectuation of a diffuse global "empire," we seek here to imagine how the monopoly of a space-directed space power (the ability to selectively exclude other states from securing orbital positions or accessing deep space) might impact international order. The primary change is the stripping away of factors that obscure power relationships in the world system. Before the means to selective exclusion from space are developed, the compromised sovereignty of less powerful states can be passed off as a lack of achievement, a "natural" phenomenon. With the development of the means to selective exclusion, the dichotomy between the powerful and the less powerful becomes one that would be much more explicitly enforced. Through the attendant loss of meaningful self-determination and the explicit enforcement of markedly distinct economic roles in the space regime, the realities of an imperial solar system would emerge as more starkly visible.

In this exercise we are attempting to highlight that the potentialities of future space security politics are illuminated by current power relationships in IR. This in turn means that the interrogation of Earthly power offered by critical scholars can be comfortably extended to extraterrestrial domains. Our argument is meant to serve as an invitation for greater engagement with theorizing the space age from critical scholars as well as a warning to crafters of space policy: bringing politics as usual along for the space ride only advances the imperial world order as it now exists into space.

Meaningful Self Determination

The establishment of a space regime in which a few states hold the means to selective exclusion would establish a sharp dichotomy of states in international politics. Whereas those who find themselves in the Space Club would be able to participate fully in shaping the future of spacefaring, another group of states would be consigned to be Earthbound. Earthbound states cannot use outer space to solve their problems unless granted permission by the Space Club. In an era where human connectivity is facilitated by orbital pathways and opportunity is found in the yawning vacuum, a lack of access to space means a lack of meaningful self-determination for the Earthbound. In this scenario of intentional and enforced exclusion, the myth of an international competition between states that can be "won" through significant achievement could no longer obfuscate the power operating to exclude some for the benefit of others. Indeed, the dichotomy of states would be as stark as "intentionally confined to Earth" versus "cleared to venture out among the planets."

The changes to the meanings of state sovereignty that we are sketching here as likely resulting from the development of the means for selective exclusion are subtly different from those put forth by Havercroft and Duvall concerning a monopoly of space-based power projection capabilities. Whereas they see a transformation of state sovereignty because of a loss of the monopoly of force within the boundaries of the state, we see a degradation of state sovereignty because of the loss of its relationship to territories and spaces *outside* of the state's formal territorial footprint. If space is a territory that is considered *res communis* and a state is excluded from being able to act meaningfully in space, the excluded state is, in effect, no longer considered to be of the community of states. Members of the Space Club become first among (only nominal) "equals" in international society.

The possibilities for meaningful self-determination of Earthbound states should also be considered within the context of global climate change. As some scholars note, an exodus imperative looms as a real possibility for spacefaring states who can move practices of extraction and maybe even production off-world, leaving the Earthbound with a world stripped of the possibility for enrichment by traditional means because ecological precarity will force the prioritization of the maintenance of the ecological ability to sustain life. Bruno Latour's *Down to Earth* outlines examples of such detachment of the imaginations of the wealthy and powerful from Earthly futures (Latour 2018). This perspective has potential to shed light on security concerns and the prioritization of space security. In order to complete a decoupling from Earthbound politics, the means to selective exclusion would become a necessity for the powerful (see Mann and Wainwright 2018 for more on the connection between global climate change and space security).

The compromise of sovereignty via the degradation of meaningful self-determination occurs then on two fronts. The first is the loss of the ability to meaningfully interact with outside sites of opportunity. The second is the loss of bargaining power in the ecological balancing act that is maintaining spaceship Earth.

Confinement, Earth, Deep Space, and Selective Exclusion

With an enforced dichotomy between Earthbound and spacefaring, a division of labor is established between the two that pushes costs and responsibilities onto the Earthbound while consolidating benefits and resources to the spacefaring. The Earth, with its comparative advantage at producing and sustaining life, hereby becomes the responsibility of the Earthbound, while the material profits from deep space activities would be consolidated in spacefaring states. Because spacefaring states could access Earth, but Earthbound states could not meaningfully interact with extraterrestrial spaces, the terms of trade would not favor the Earthbound. This is not an unfamiliar structure to the world system. Indeed, the fundamental conceptual framework of Core-Periphery or, more recently, Global North-Global South, that has been so important to the development of critical strands of IR theory would be effectuated unambiguously and in spades. Geographer Julie Klinger ties critical environmental geography with processes of space colonization and terrestrial economic inequity. Her work illuminates the extension of the spatial ordering of the international economic system into outer space through the terrestrial and extraterrestrial impacts of the space economy (Dunnet et al. 2019; Klinger 2021).

The composition of the membership of the Space Club has a significant impact on determining how space is used. Although we have been particularly attentive to the American Cosmic Order while imagining a world system defined by selective exclusion from outer space, it is our responsibility as critical scholars to recognize that other political imaginaries exist for international politics and space politics specifically. The clearest alternative to a colonized space politics would be a bolstering of the common heritage principle that includes meaningful collective spatial management and attention to concerns of equity among states. This alternative political imaginary that takes seriously the implications of an outer space domain managed for the common heritage of all mankind could be said to have found clear expression at the meeting of Non-Aligned States in Bandung Indonesia in 1955.

Heloise Weber articulates a perspective that sees Bandung as being the introduction of a specific and concrete international development regime that was posed as an alternative explicitly to combat colonialism and the coloniality of the international system even after formal decolonization was well underway. In Weber's words; "I conclude that the "spirit of Bandung" resonates today not only as a memory of political struggle but also in concrete struggles for development otherwise" (Weber 2016, 155). Weber traces how the principles of solidarist internationalism that were made into a concrete movement at Bandung find voice later in the New International Economic Order (NIEO) proposals adopted by the UN General Assembly in the 1970s.

Stephen Mau completes the connection by drawing explicit lines from the equity principles underlying NIEO to the common heritage of mankind (Mau 1984). Mau shows that the equity principles voiced at Bandung and in the NIEO declaration speak directly to the pooled management of a resource-rich domain and the opportunities it presents to the world that defines the CHM principle. In fact, one might argue that the birth of the common heritage principle was during the negotiations of the Antarctic Treaty System (ATS) in 1956–57 where India under Prime Minister Nehru (also critical in organizing Bandung) made an influential intervention. Sanjant Chaturvedi argues that the only reason the ATS falls short of the vision of international management of territory with explicit goals of international equity is because the treaty doesn't fully address the territorial claims on the continent. This reading reinforces that the spatial aspects of the common heritage principle are paramount and that a system that seeks to secure outer space absent these commitments to collective spatial management also necessarily falls short of the CHM principle (Chaturvedi 2013). In Mau's view, in terms of international law the inheritor of this tradition is the Agreement Governing the Activities of States on the Moon and Other Celestial Bodies (the Moon Treaty). The Moon Treaty explicitly addresses the issues of equity that embody the true spirit of the common heritage of mankind principle. Mau argues, and it is relatively widely accepted, that it is precisely this explicit support of issues of economic equity and an advancement for international management to achieve equity goals that is the reason the powerful spacefaring states have not supported the Moon Treaty (Mau 1984).

Thus, it is not for a lack of political imagination that one can see a path that points toward selective exclusion, boundary drawing, and colonization of extraterrestrial space. Indeed, the principles that point in a countervailing direction have been articulated on the international stage, in some of its greatest deliberative forums, for half a century or longer, but to little lasting or deep impact. Rather, as Weber illustrates in the second part of the exploration of Bandung as the advancement of a specific vision for an international development regime focused on economic justice, the liberal international order and its neoliberal innovations present specific "politics of epistemic erasure" that deliberately circumvents alternative political imaginaries and seeks to naturalize the international system as it is (Weber 2016). The securitization of outer space is a prime example of this process. By seeking to separate the security of aspects of the international system from questions of economic equity, securitizing narratives place control in the hands of those with the extraordinary power to make things safe for (their colonial) "peace" in space.

CONCLUSION: SPACE IS NOT SPECIAL

To reflect critically on the politics of space security we have argued, points the analyst toward attending to familiar patterns of the exercise of power in colonial histories and how the legacy of those histories affects contemporary terrestrial security politics. Critical approaches push us to historicize the presentation of the outer space environment as a dangerous one in need of pacification within the larger patterns of the history of colonialism in international politics. Because the pattern of securitization, territorialization, and exclusion is a familiar one, we can imagine similar trend lines of securitization with respect to outer space and connect them to analogous processes in contemporary world politics.

The diffusion of responsibility and the naturalization of exclusive violence are logical and familiar conclusions to the current developments we are seeing in space security politics. The consequences of these developments would be further bifurcation of the international system, with externalized costs placed on less powerful states and the consolidation of benefits to the more powerful states. One potentially significant change that might result from the maturation of exclusive politics in outer space, however, is a revelation of the emptiness of the myth that the gap between states is a natural one accounted for by varying levels of achievement and not an explicitly designed and enforced system of oppression and exclusion. Such a revelation would be testimony to the kind of critical insight expressed by President Sukarno in his welcoming address to the Bandung meeting:

> I beg of you not to think of colonialism only in the classic form which we in Indonesia, and our brothers in different parts of Africa and Asia, knew. Colonialism also has its modern dress, in the form of economic control, intellectual control, actual physical control by a small alien community within a nation. It is a skillful and determined enemy, and it appears in many guises. It does not give up its loot easily. (Phạm and Shilliam 2016 citing Sukarno 1955)

REFERENCES

Anders, Gunter. 1956. "Reflections on the H Bomb." *Dissent* 3, no. 2: 146–55.
Anders, Günter. 1958. "Der Mann auf der Brücke. Tagebuch aus Hiroshima und Nagasaki." In *Hiroshima ist überall*, edited by Gunter Anders, 1–189. Munich: C.H. Beck.
Anders, Günter. 1986. "Denn Sie wissen nicht, was Sie tun: Philosophische Überlegungen zu Reagan, SDI und Wissenschaft und Business." *Frankfurter Rundschau*. May 15, 1986.
Bateman, Aaron. 2022. "Anti-satellite Weapons Are Creating Space Hazards. Here's a Way to Limit the Damage." *Bulletin of the Atomic Scientists*. January 21, 2022.
Blount, P.J. 2019. "The Shifting Sands of Space Security: The Politics and Law of The Peaceful Uses of Outer Space." *Indonesian Journal of International Law* 17, no. 1. https://doi.org/10.17304/ijil.vol17.1.776.

Buzan, Barry, Jaap de Wilde, and Ole Wæver. 1998. *Security: A New Framework for Analysis*. Boulder, CO: Lynne Rienner Publishers.

Chaturvedi, Sanjay. 2013. "Rise and Decline of Antarctica in Nehru's Geopolitical Vision: Challenges and Opportunities of the 1950s." *The Polar Journal* 3 (December): 301–15. https://doi.org/10.1080/2154896X.2013.868087.

Dunnett, Oliver, Andrew S. Maclaren, Julie Klinger, K. Maria D. Lane, and Daniel Sage. 2019. "Geographies of Outer Space: Progress and New Opportunities." *Progress in Human Geography* 43, no. 2: 314–36. https://doi.org/10.1177/0309132517747727.

Duvall, Raymond, and Jonathan Havercroft. 2008. "Taking Sovereignty out of This World: Space Weapons and Empire of the Future." *Review of International Studies* 34, no. 4: 755–75. https://doi.org/10.1017/S0260210508008267.

Duvall, Raymond, and Latha Varadarajan. 2003. "On the Practical Significance of Critical International Relations Theory." *Asian Journal of Political Science* 11, no. 2: 75–88.

Gopalaswamy, Bharath, and Gaurav Kampani. 2014. "India and Space Weaponization: Why Space Debris Trumps Kinetic Energy Antisatellite Weapons as the Principal Threat to Satellites." *India Review* 13, no. 1: 40–57. https://doi.org/10.1080/14736489.2014.873678.

Havercroft, Jonathan, and Raymond Duvall. 2009. "Critical Astropolitics: The Geopolitics of Space Control and the Transformation of State Sovereignty." In *Securing Outer Space*, edited by Natalie Bormann and Michael Sheehan, 42–58. New York: Routledge.

Jahn, Beate. 2021. "Critical Theory in Crisis? A Reconsideration." *European Journal of International Relations* 27, no. 4: 1274–99. https://doi.org/10.1177/13540661211049491.

Keyuan, Zou. 1991. "The Common Heritage of Mankind and the Antarctic Treaty System." *Netherlands International Law Review* 38, no. 2: 173–98. https://doi.org/10.1017/S0165070X00003740.

Klimburg-Witjes, Nina. 2021. "Shifting Articulations of Space and Security: Boundary Work in European Space Policy Making." *European Security* (March): 1–21. https://doi.org/10.1080/09662839.2021.1890039.

Klinger, Julie Michelle. 2021. "Environmental Geopolitics and Outer Space." *Geopolitics* 26, no. 3: 666–703. https://doi.org/10.1080/14650045.2019.1590340.

Latour, Bruno. 2018. *Down to Earth: Politics in the New Climatic Regime*. Hoboken, NJ: Wiley.

Luxemburg, Rosa. 2003. *The Accumulation of Capital*. Routledge Classics. London; New York: Routledge. 2003.

Maldonado-Torres, Nelson. 2020. "Notes on the Coloniality of Peace." *fondation-frantz fanon* (blog). June 4, 2020. https://fondation-frantzfanon.com/notes-on-the-coloniality-of-peace/.

Mann, Geoff, and Joel Wainwright. 2018. "Planetary Sovereignty." In *Climate Leviathan: A Political Theory of Our Planetary Future*, edited by Geoff Mann and Joel Wainwright, 129–53. Brooklyn, NY: Verso.

Mau, Stephen D. 1984. "Equity, the Third World and the Moon Treaty Lead Article." *Suffolk Transnational Law Journal* 8, no. 2: 221–58.

Mickelson, Karin. 2014. "The Maps of International Law: Perceptions of Nature in the Classification of Territory." *Leiden Journal of International Law* 27, no. 3: 621–39. https://doi.org/10.1017/S0922156514000235.

Moltz, James Clay. 2014. *Crowded Orbits*. New York: Columbia University Press. http://www.degruyter.com/document/doi/10.7312/molt15912/html.

Munster, Rens van, and Casper Sylvest. 2019. "Appetite for Destruction: Günther Anders and the Metabolism of Nuclear Techno-Politics." *Journal of International Political Theory* 15, no. 3: 332–48. https://doi.org/10.1177/1755088218796536.

Phillips, Andrew, and J. C. Sharman. 2020. "Company-States and the Creation of the Global International System." *European Journal of International Relations* 26, no. 4: 1249–72. https://doi.org/10.1177/1354066120928127.

Quijano, Aníbal. 2007. "Coloniality and Modern Rationality." *Cultural Studies* 21, nos. 2–3: 168–78. https://doi.org/10.1080/09502380601164353.

Quynh N., Pham, and Robert Shilliam. 2016. "Reviving Bandung." In *Meanings of Bandung: Postcolonial Orders And Decolonial Visions*, edited by Quynh N. Pham and Robert Shilliam, 3–19. London: Rowman & Littlefield.

Samson, Victoria. 2022. "The Complicating Role of the Private Sector in Space." *Bulletin of the Atomic Scientists* 78, no. 1: 6–10. https://doi.org/10.1080/00963402.2021.2014229.

Schmitt, Carl, and G. L. Ulmen. 2006. *The Nomos of the Earth in the International Law of the Jus Publicum Europaeum*. New York: Telos Press.

Scott, Kevin D., ed. 2018. April 10. "Joint Publication 3-14 Space Operations: Incorporating Change I."

Sokolski, Henry. 2022. "A China-US War in Space: The After-Action Report." *Bulletin of the Atomic Scientists* 78, no. 1: 11–16. https://doi.org/10.1080/00963402.2021.2014230.

Sumida, Jon. 2011. "Old Thoughts, New Problems: Mahan and the Consideration of Space Power." In *Toward a Theory of Space Power*, edited by Charles D. Lutes and Peter L. Hays, 3–13. Washington, DC: Institute for National Strategic Studies.

Trevino, Natalie B. 2020. "The Cosmos Is Not Finished." PhD diss., The University of Western Ontario.

Webb, Walter Prescott. 1952. *The Great Frontier*. Boston: Houghton Mifflin.

Weber, Heloise. 2016. "The Political Significance of Bandung for Development: Challenges, Contradictions and Struggles for Justice." In *Meanings of Bandung: Postcolonial Orders and Decolonial Visions*, edited by Quỳnh N. Phạm and Robbie Shilliam, 153–64. London: Rowman & Littlefield.

Whitman Cobb, Wendy N. 2020. *Privatizing Peace: How Commerce Can Reduce Conflict in Space*. Abingdon, UK; New York: Routledge.

Williams, Michael C. 1998. "Modernity, Identity and Security: A Comment on the 'Copenhagen Controversy.'" *Review of International Studies* 24, no. 3: 435–39. https://doi.org/10.1017/S026021059800435.

CHAPTER 6

COMMERCIAL SPACE PEACE THEORY

Economic Interdependence and Conflict in Space

WENDY N. WHITMAN COBB

OVER the past three decades, globalization has been a major subject of study in the international relations (IR) and larger political science community. As it has increased, the degree to which countries have deepened and strengthened their interdependence has consequently increased. However, one of the more significant assets that has enabled this growth has been relatively unappreciated: space-based assets that are, in many ways, the backbone of the global economy. Global Positioning Satellites (GPS) provide precise timing that underpins financial transactions across the globe, communications satellites provide instantaneous connections between peoples and countries, and weather satellites provide much needed information that is used for everything from local forecasts to emergency preparedness and response. The fact that space assets are underappreciated and underacknowledged as a vital part of globalization highlights two reinforcing ideas: the general lack of awareness among the public and policy practitioners of the importance of space and space-based assets and, consequently, the lack of consideration given to the space domain in the IR literature.

With the establishment in the United States and other countries of independent and specialized space forces and the subsequent open acknowledgement of space as a warfighting domain, IR scholars must grapple with how space activities affect global relations as well as the extent to which space activities are consonant with more terrestrial ones. Indeed, as General John Hyten pointed out in 2017, the question is not necessarily about war in space but war that *extends into* space (Hirsch 2018). This highlights that space warfighting cannot be considered in its own silo, but rather must be considered in tandem with terrestrial military action (Bowen 2020). In this chapter, I draw on my previous work (Whitman Cobb 2020) proposing an extension of economic peace theories to the space domain. My commercial space peace theory argues that because the global economy is significantly dependent on space assets, open, kinetic conflict in the space domain will be prohibitively costly. As such, states have a large incentive to avoid this situation so as to avoid harming their own economic prospects.

By way of preview, the chapter begins with a brief examination of the economic peace literature followed by a discussion of the economic value of space. I then discuss several of the propositions that make up the commercial space peace theory and consider their implications for the growing commercialization of space, the role and growth of non-state actors in space, and how IR can take more seriously the space domain in its work.

LOGICS OF PEACE

Theories of Economic Interdependence

The idea that economic interdependence reduces conflict is a long one in IR. Before beginning, it is useful to define what is meant here by interdependence. For our purposes, I take the definition of interdependence from Robert Keohane and Joseph Nye who define interdependence to be a situation of "mutual dependence" influenced by two dimensions, sensitivity and vulnerability (Keohane and Nye 2012, 7). "Sensitivity is the extent to which one country is affected by the actions of another, whereas vulnerability is the extent to which a country can insulate itself from the costly effects of events that occur elsewhere" (McMillan 1997, 34). Importantly, Keohane and Nye's notion of interdependence is different than the larger concept of globalization. Colloquially understood as a "shrinking of the world" making relationships and transactions between people and countries all the easier, it can be examined through trade, foreign investment, and money flows among other things (for a review of the notion of globalization within the IR literature, see Kacowicz and Mitrani 2016).

With this in mind, consider Keohane and Nye's concept of interdependence with respect to GPS. A previous disruption to the system in 2016 of just thirteen millionths of a second caused a cascade of disruptions from the United States to the United Kingdom and Canada (Glass 2016). For example, because of the integral role it plays in timing across the globe, problems in the GPS system can quickly spread, demonstrating a high degree of sensitivity. As for vulnerability, while alternative positioning, navigation, and timing (PNT) systems exist including the European Union's Galileo, Russia's GLONASS, and China's BeiDou, none are as widely used or available as GPS (Glass 2016). Because of this widespread adoption and use, it would be very difficult indeed for individual state economies to insulate themselves from the effect of GPS issues. This is especially true because of how important timing is in global financial transactions.

In returning to the notion of economic interdependence, the underlying hypothesis is that increasing economic ties between countries discourages conflict that would harm a state's overall economy. While World War I dampened the enthusiasm for ideas such as those described by Norman Angell (1912), in more recent years, scholars have returned to the role that economics plays in mediating conflict through different types of economic mechanisms. Growing out of the democratic peace studies of the 1990s, various writers examined the role of trade (Polachek 1980; Polachek, Robst, and Chang 1999; Oneal and Russett 1999; Dorussen 1999; Morrow 1999; McDonald 2004; Hegre, Oneal, and Russett 2010), state interdependence (McMillan 1997; Mansfield and Pollins 2001; Keohane and Nye 2012), capitalism (Schneider and Gleditsch 2010; Mousseau 2010; Mueller 2010; Russett 2010; Rosecrance 2010; Gartzke and Hewitt 2010), market integration (Gartzke and Li 2003; Gartzke 2007), the expectations of future trade (Copeland 2015), and globalization (Murshed and Mamoon 2010; Choi 2010).

Like any good scholarly debate, however, the thesis that economic interdependence reduces conflict has also gathered its critics. Paul Krugman (1996), for example, objects on the principle that states themselves are not engaging in trade, firms are. While this is true, governments do have various incentives (electoral being just one) to ensure a strong and growing economy and, in doing so, are capable of making policy that either facilitates or disrupts economic relations among business entities (Bearce and Omori 2005; McDonald 2007; Brown and Stein 1982; Weingast, Shepsle, and Johnsen 1981; Mayhew 1974; Kleinberg and Fordham 2013). The failure of economic ties to prevent World War I has also been used to weaken the economic interdependence argument, though various scholars have pushed back on this citing, among other things, the out-break of the war in states that were not as economically interdependent (Schumpeter 1955; Chatagnier and Castelli 2016; Gartzke and Lupu 2012; McDonald 2004). Finally, globalization and the trade asymmetries it can produce have also been highlighted as a potential *cause* of conflict rather than a means of reduction.

Commercial Space Peace

While there may indeed be limits to how much economic interdependence can re-duce conflict on earth, space presents a different situation. As space scholars have long recognized, the space domain is unique as compared to terrestrial ones (Mendenhall 2018). The cost of getting and operating there is high, the physics are significantly dif-ferent, and assets there are incredibly vulnerable to space weather, increasing amounts of debris, and more recently, threat of attack from other countries. While military actions in space must have terrestrial consequences for them to matter tactically and strategically (Bowen 2020), I argue economic interdependence may have greater power to dampen conflict *in* space because of the unique nature of space assets and the degree to which they underpin the global economy (Whitman Cobb 2020).

Given the often dangerous and difficult operating conditions of outer space (see Townsend, this volume), it might be rather surprising that the backbone of the global economy is predicated on such vulnerable machines operating in such a treacherous environment. The space industry is currently valued somewhere around US$350 billion, but some predict this to surge toward US$1 trillion by 2040 (Morgan Stanley 2021). This figure likely underestimates the importance of space to the global economy as it includes only those services with specific ties to space, like television broadcasting, satellite communications, and satellite hardware. Because space has been traditionally viewed as a sanctuary where military conflict has been absent (though utilized for military purposes), there has been little fear that important economic assets might be threatened (Moltz 2019). Given this, over the past fifty years, space-based assets have come to provide critical economic services. While it is out of the scope of this chapter to go into significant detail, three areas may be discussed in brief: communications, remote sensing, and PNT (for a wider discussion, see Whitman Cobb 2020).

Communications is a broad heading for a variety of activities to include person-to-person and point-to-point connections but also broadcasting services like television and radio and the relay of different types of information like weather. Taking television alone, broadcasting satellites make up almost US$100 billion of the overall space economy with satellite radio adding an additional US$5 billion in 2018 (FAA 2018). More recently, the further miniaturization of satellite technology and the advent of cheaper launch methods is enabling the establishing of large satellite constellations like Starlink, which is planned to eventually include over 12,000 satellites operating in low earth orbit. The function of Starlink and other planned constellations like Amazon's Kuiper is to provide internet services across the globe thereby further growing the communications portion of the space economy.

Remote sensing is a similarly large category that encompasses things like weather, environmental monitoring, the identification of natural resources like oil and gas, and even monitoring of economic behavior like traffic or shipping patterns. Remote sensing has proven vital in warning of weather emergencies, responding to natural disasters, and even tracking the fallout from Covid-19 (Hudecheck et al. 2020). The United States Geological Service (USGS) estimated that the economic value of its Landsat system increased from US$2.19 billion in 2011 to US$3.45 billion in 2017 (USGS 2021). They further note that Landsat imagery has been used "in many ways including efforts to contain wildfires, increase worldwide crop production, identify famine risks, conserve water, control forest-killing diseases, and reduce climate change impacts" (USGS 2021).

Finally, PNT systems such as GPS provide valuable functions beyond just getting users from point to point. The super precise atomic clocks provide a timing service that enables financial transactions to be accurately made and synchronize activities like emergency services. One study found that a GPS outage would cost the US economy upward of US$1 billion a day for the first month, with costs only increasing (O'Connor et al. 2019). On the other hand, a 2021 report from RAND argues that this threat is perhaps overblown, noting the difficulty in attacking the entire system and the availability of backup systems (Hitchens 2021a). The report, however, lacks specific cost estimates while acknowledging that smaller scale disruptions are possible and no single technology would be able to fill the capability that GPS currently provides. Even if the entire GPS system does not come crashing down, such interruptions can still be costly to a global economic system that has come to rely on it. Additionally, there are an increasing number of examples where jammed GPS signals have led to off-track pilots who were relying on its signals (Harris 2021). While such incidents may not be economically costly, in the short run, they could be potentially dangerous in industries, like aviation, that rely on them for safety.

Much like the economic peace literature, commercial space peace theory also proposes that economics increases the cost of conflict therefore reducing the chances for it. Where these theories differ however, is in terms of unit of analysis and the mechanism of action. Instead of flows of trade or investment between states, this theory looks at the system as a whole and how interdependent states are on a global economy enabled by space systems. Rather than relationships between countries, it is the fact that the global economy is dependent on space that reduces conflicts (Whitman Cobb 2020). Assuming that states have an interest in improving their economic situation, they in turn have an interest in seeing the global economy succeed. This is not quite unlike the situation in the early space race period when the USSR and the United States realized that space imposes a certain environmental interdependence—that preserving the space domain in a way that enabled continued operations was worth more than the costs of conflict there (Moltz 2019). In a similar manner, this theory also suggests that states should rationally and strategically refrain from active conflict in space because of the economic interdependence that space has come to support.

Before examining some of the major propositions further in depth, there are two assumptions the theory makes. First, I assume that states are the central actors in the space domain. To be sure, the number of non-state actors with space capabilities and assets is increasing. SpaceX, for example, owns and operates the largest number of satellites as of mid-2021 with over sixteen hundred Starlink satellites, and more continue to be added. Independent launch capabilities offered by SpaceX and other companies, including the United Launch Alliance, also give these companies significant power. Even with this growth, the space domain is likely to remain dominated by states for several reasons. For one, the Outer Space Treaty (OST) makes states responsible for all actions in outer space including those undertaken by non-state entities under their control. As such, companies like SpaceX must receive permission from the US government to operate and the United States assumes responsibility for what private US parties do in space. Additionally, while the costs of accessing space and building space assets has come down considerably in recent years, the barrier to entry remains high. While this is not necessarily the case in the cyber domain where scholars have predicted a decline in the role and power of the state (Hirst and Thompson 1995; Thurow 2000; for the application of this argument to space, see Newlove-Eriksson and Eriksson 2013), the cost still makes space operations prohibitive for all but a few wealthy individuals and states. Finally, though commercial companies are growing, states still serve as a major, if not the largest, customer of space-related services (Pekkanen 2019). While non-state actors such as private companies might be empowered to act on behalf of a state, the fact remains that space will continue to be dominated by state actors for some time.

Second, I assume that states are rational actors. While there are critiques and caveats to the assumption of rationality that have been explored elsewhere, for the purposes of establishing a basic model, the assumption is included here. I now turn to examining two of the major arguments of the commercial space peace theory, state interest in economic success and the high economic costs of conflict in space.

REFLECTIONS AND EVIDENCE ON THE PROPOSITIONS FROM COMMERCIAL SPACE PEACE

States are interested in promoting economic success, which is increasingly dependent on space. With the understanding that previous economic peace theories have ignored this premise, this theory begins with the idea that states have a fundamental responsibility for and interest in their own economic success. This is perhaps even clearer in the space domain where leaders have often invoked the economic incentives and spin offs that come with state investments in science and technology. Not only did then-Vice President Lyndon B. Johnson cite the economic benefits of space spending in 1963 (Brinkley 2019), but, more recently, then-Vice President Mike Pence did so as well, stating in 2019 that the United States must remain first in space to "propel our economy," in addition to other international benefits.

Further, democratic governments are interested in economic success for electoral purposes. Elected officials (for the most part) are interested in being elected and reelected and must satisfy their voters, many of whom look to their own economic improvements (Mayhew 1974). Space has become a vital part of economic development and support since technological spin-offs often add to economic benefits. Despite critics who see space spending as wasteful diversions from other potential investments, no money is spent in space, rather, it is spent on Earth. For instance, a 2013 report found that National Aeronautics and Space Agency (NASA) develops sixteen hundred new technologies a year and for "every dollar NASA spends on employees, businesses, universities, and others generates $2.60 of output in the economy, as compared to the federal non-military average of $2.30 and the federal military average of $2.00" (Tauri Group 2013, 10). While one might suspect that this incentive is decreased in autocratic and authoritarian states whose leaders do not have to stand for election, as Bruce Bueno de Mesquita and colleagues show in their selectorate theory, there is still a population that authoritarian leaders must satisfy (Bueno de Mesquita et al. 1999; 2004). Though the selectorate is smaller and thus easier to please, authoritarian leaders still need the acquiescence of this group, which can be kept content with economic resources and benefits. If space investments can be used to stimulate and support economic growth, then states of multiple types will see that as a beneficial investment.

Indeed, this has been the case for authoritarian China in recent years as it moved to encourage a commercial space sector in 2014 (Lu et al. 2019). Though several dozen commercial companies have emerged since, many, if not most, remain significantly tied to the government. The question becomes, then, if erstwhile private, commercial companies are still agents of the state, why does the Chinese government seek to encourage their growth? In an expansive analysis of the Chinese commercial space industry, the authors identify several drivers including the economic potential of commercial state and economic development (Lu et al. 2019). They write, "Chinese aspirations with respect to investments in space are being driven by slowing economic growth, and a sense that China needs to encourage the growth of new high-value-added industrial sectors" (23). In this, we find further evidence that even authoritarian governments have an incentive in pursuing economic development and therefore a motivation for preserving the domain in which they may pursue that.

As China's experience with fostering a commercial space industry shows, not only do authoritarian leaders have an interest in fostering economic development as it goes to their own success, but states are increasingly realizing that overall economic success is dependent on space systems. With recent proposals to classify space-based assets as critical infrastructure, the United States also seems to have come to a similar conclusion (Foust 2021). As the global economy becomes even more dependent on space-based systems, this leads to the next major argument of the commercial space peace theory.

The more dependent on space the economy, the greater the economic costs of conflict in space. In considering this premise, we can think about a hypothetical space attack. Putting aside what effect the attack would have on terrestrial actions, state A initiates a kinetic attack on a key communications satellite for state B. While military forces around the world plan and train for contingencies such as the loss of communication or intelligence information, the debris from the attack remains in orbit where it could easily impact with other satellites. Should the debris strike other, uninvolved satellites such as those for GPS or communications, the global economy would reasonably be affected by it. State A, to the extent that its economy is intertwined with the global economy, would then see economic losses from such actions. In other words, even though the attack in space was limited and limited to military assets only, the potential economic fallout from such an action might reverberate throughout the globe and ultimately cause more harm than good to State A. As Roger Handberg (2017, 420) writes, "Globalization has been fostered through satellite technologies. Their disruption can be devastating for all parties, regardless of who is the winner of loser."

In a situation as this one, the United States would no doubt be the most vulnerable simply because it possesses the highest number of currently operating satellites with more than 2500 (UCS Satellite Database 2023). This will likely continue to be the case as US companies like SpaceX continue to build out their megaconstellations of satellites. However, a singular attack on a satellite can have far greater ramifications beyond the moment of impact. As demonstrated by the 2021 Russian ASAT test, kinetic conflict greatly increases debris that can in turn collide with other satellites or spacecraft. This increases the chance of a collisional cascade as predicted by the Kessler syndrome and makes operations for satellites of all countries far more difficult (Kessler and Cour-Palais 1978). Further, though the United States may have the highest number of satellites, we must also consider the types of services they provide, services which the entire globe has come to depend upon. While we have already considered the case of GPS, even SpaceX's Starlink is now providing space-based internet access to more than ninety thousand users in twelve countries with those numbers projected to grow (Sheetz 2021). Thus, the impact of a singular attack will have consequences that go beyond that moment in time.

The high pace of technological advances in space will likely contribute to the global economy's further dependence on space. For one, as companies begin to deploy large satellite constellations, they will become an increasingly important part of the global economy. Aside from Starlink or Amazon's Kuiper, remote imaging services provided by companies like Leo Labs and Planet are increasingly being used by companies of all types to track and manage earthly activity. Michael Hudecheck and colleagues (2020) highlight how they were able to use data on night-time light emissions to measure the economic and social impact of Covid-19. Among their findings is evidence to "suggest that Chinese citizens started self-isolating before the government quarantines—earlier than commonly believed." As such, they argue that remote sensing data of this type can be used not only to track and monitor economic activity but give early indications, in near real time, of potential threats. As a means of managing, processing, and making sense of such large amounts of incoming data, companies have also had to develop analytical and machine processing systems that can quickly identify changes in satellite images to bring them to the attention of the customer. The result is that remote imaging and sensing satellites are a growing portion of the overall space economy which further enable economic growth on the ground (SIA 2020).

Another area of increasing technological change is in the realm of space tourism. While space tourism is unlikely to make up a large share of the space economy (at least in the near future), it certainly ups the ante in terms of potential costs of conflict. Conflict that threatens astronauts on the International Space Station or the missions of various space flight participants (as non-formally trained space tourists are being called) might not have a significant economic impact, but it would certainly have an impact on a state's international reputation and prestige. For instance, we might envision a scenario where an attack occurs while a SpaceX-launched tourist mission is in orbit. If it potentially threatened the mission and the participants on board, the state that initiated the attack would likely suffer reputational costs. Given that prestige and reputation are a significant driver of state behavior in space (Launius 2012; Moltz 2019; Muir-Harmony 2020), it would impose a certain cost.

One potential objection to this premise is that asymmetric dependence on space might actually encourage open conflict. As states like Russia and China have observed the degree to which the US military is dependent on space, they have increased their own space capabilities with an eye toward taking advantage of it in the event of a conflict. However, states like Russia and China are themselves highly integrated into the global economic system, thus any attacks would have the possibility of backfiring economically if not militarily. While there have been some efforts at decoupling economic ties particularly between China and the United States in the wake of the Covid-19 pandemic, it is not at all clear that it will be possible or would isolate a country like China from global economic downturns (Morrison 2021). What is perhaps of greater concern are rogue states like North Korea and Iran who are, for all intents and purposes, *not* a part of the global economy. Their rudimentary missile and space capabilities are established enough that they could carry out kinetic anti-satellite attacks or even detonate a nuclear weapon in outer space, causing widespread disruption and chaos (Harrison et al. 2021). Given the lack of economic consequences that would flow to them, they are likely to be less inhibited by the potential for economic costs.

One intriguing implication of this premise is that there are a whole population of states that are essentially space powers though they do not have independent launch or extensive space capabilities. Because a state's economy is tied into the global economy, a state without a significant space presence may still be indirectly affected by kinetic conflict. As negotiations on norms of behavior in space continue with no apparent resolution in sight, engaging this larger set of actors with a deep interest in preserving the space environment may add needed momentum. Even if a state has nothing to lose in space or on the ground (for instance a ground station that is monitoring and communicating with space-based systems), a state without a major space presence can still lose economically in the case of conflict.

The benefits of active conflict in space must be greater than the economic consequences of it. The final premise of the commercial space peace thesis represents its main implications: the economic costs of conflict in outer space are likely to be high, with a significant potential to spread throughout the global economy and thus affect the initiator of any attack. States, then, if they are behaving rationally, should be discouraged from engaging in such actions because of the significant cost. This is not to say that states will never find military conflict in space to be worth the cost; some states, seeing an advantage open for the taking may very well conclude that the risk is worthwhile enough to bear whatever costs may come whether that be economically or in the loss of the ability to operate in space at all. In an era that finds a return to great power competition, there might even be further motivations for first strikes in space. However, what is different about this era of great power competition compared to the Cold War is that economic interdependence between the United States and China and between all states and the global economy is far greater. Thus, to the extent that the costs of conflict are increasing, particularly as economic ties to space are strengthened, states should rationally choose not to avail themselves of those options.

The commercial space peace theory does not address the likelihood or desirability of space weaponization, merely that space weapons (in most cases) should not be used due to their cost. In recent years, US officials have claimed that both Russia and China have already weaponized space, however, no unclassified evidence is available to date (Garamone 2020). It is also possible the United States has done so as well, but with no public acknowledgement (Hitchens 2021b). While these types of claims and rhetoric certainly point toward a growing arms race in space, it is still possible that weapons can exist and not be used, much like the nuclear arsenal. It would certainly be in the rational interest of major space powers and near-peer states in particular to protect space assets and thus the global economy and their place in it, but it does not necessarily remove the threat of weapons themselves.

The commercial space peace theory also does not suggest that new treaties or institutions are necessarily needed to govern the commons that is space. While these efforts have been ongoing for some time, little progress has been made over the past several decades in terms of defining space weapons or preventing their placement and/or usage. There has been some movement in this field in recent years with the US-led Artemis Accords, but this agreement focuses on principles for the exploitation and exploration of the Moon and not the larger domain itself. Certainly, formal international agreements would be beneficial in terms of enforcement and clear understanding, but they might not be necessary given the invisible hand of economic interest.

Following from that, a policy implication from this theory is that increasing commercialization of space and further integration of space-based assets into the global economy would be one means of increasing the costs of conflict and thereby reducing its chances. While I discuss the ways in which commercial companies themselves have an interest in preventing space conflict and how they might achieve that elsewhere (Whitman Cobb 2020), one direct means is through contracting for services. This does several things: it creates a market for space services that companies can step in to provide and it can reduce costs for the state as private companies continue to innovate. Additionally, Brad Townsend (2020) suggests that contracting out for space security purposes might also alleviate a growing security dilemma as capabilities that might be seen as hostile if operated by a state would instead be controlled by a private company. One example of this might be debris removal. Technologies that could potentially remediate space debris are inherently dual use—if you can take a piece of debris out of orbit, you can also remove an active satellite. However, if states themselves do not own and operate this technology, it might not be seen as threatening to other space actors. As an aside, this would necessitate some international agreement on debris, as even debris remains the property of the state that launched it and thus removing it from outer space would require their approval.

States can also create the legal regimes necessary to foster private space companies and engage in efforts like the Artemis Accords, which begin to lay the foundation for exploration of the moon.

CONCLUSION

The belief that increased economic ties between actors lead to peace is an old one: Immanuel Kant famously theorized in the late 1700s that republican forms of government would hesitate to engage in war because citizens "would be very cautious in commencing such a poor game" due to its inevitable costs. While I doubt that Kant would have considered outer space activities as a natural extension of his argument, the idea remains the same: the economic costs of war in space, made all the more significant by its relationship to the global economy, are so great that they should rationally discourage any potential hostile action there.

While significant parts of scholarship on space have been rooted in rather realist notions of state power and the expansion of it (for instance, Dolman 2002), the commercial space peace theory shows that much remains to be done in terms of IR and space. While scholars can and should look at how IR theories can be applied in space, they must keep in mind just how physically different the domain is. It is tempting to apply lessons learned and models of behavior from Earth to space—analogies such as Antarctica, law of the seas and air, and even laws of the sea bed have generated comparisons. However, as Elizabeth Mendenhall (2018) points out, space is significantly different from any of these others areas. As such, scholars must appreciate the uniqueness of space and not simply translate findings from one domain to another.

These differences, properly recognized, may also lead to new insights on the relationship between states and, perhaps importantly moving forward, how non-state actors like private companies might be further integrated into global governance systems. For example, as states become further dependent on companies for access to space, these companies will see a significant increase in their own power. By denying certain states launch access or restricting what states can or cannot launch, they are exercising a certain power over the space domain. With the reluctance of states to engage with one another in setting out more detailed rules of the road for space, there may come a time where space companies act cooperatively to do so in their stead. What would it mean to have private companies behaving in this manner? How might states manage such events? Could it possibly be the thing that motivates them to engage more in diplomatic efforts? How might we empower non-state actors in a productive way at the international level? On the other side, how can we prevent companies from behaving badly on an international scale? All of these questions suggest new areas of thought for IR in general in an age of globalization.

Recent events in space and the growing threat of weaponization are threatening the notion called for in the OST—that space be used for peaceful purposes. If, as scholars of the economic and commercial peace propose, economic ties are a means of achieving more peaceful relations, then preserving the ability of the global economy and states to benefit from it contributes to the OST's mission of preserving peaceful purposes. Heated rhetoric from leaders in the United States, China, and Russia, however, threaten both peaceful purposes of space and the global economy. With little movement on the diplomatic front, economic relations among the entire global community may serve as a means through which peaceful purposes can be maintained. It requires little of leaders and policymakers beyond a recognition of the intricate ways in which the economy and the space domain are linked and the immense cost that conflict would inflict.

DISCLAIMER

The views presented here are solely the author's and do not necessarily reflect the official policy or position of the United States government, Department of Defense, or any of its related agencies.

References

Bearce, David H., and Sawa Omori. 2005. "How Do Commercial Institutions Promote Peace?" *Journal of Peace Research* 42, no. 6: 659–78. https://doi.org/10.1177%2F0022343305057886.

Bowen, Bleddyn E. 2020. *War in Space: Strategy, Spacepower, Geopolitics*. Edinburgh: Edinburgh University Press.

Brinkley, Douglas. 2019. *American Moonshot: John F. Kennedy and the Great Space Race*. New York: Harper Collins.

Brown, Thad A., and Arthur A. Stein. 1982. "Review: The Political Economy of National Elections." *Comparative Politics* 14, no. 4: 479–97. https://doi.org/10.2307/421633.

Bueno de Mesquita, Bruce, James D. Morrow, Randolph M. Siverson, and Alastair Smith. 1999. "An Institutional Explanation of the Democratic Peace." *The American Political Science Review* 93, no. 4: 791–807. https://doi.org/10.2307/2586113.

Bueno de Mesquita, Bruce, James D. Morrow, Randolph M. Siverson, and Alastair Smith. 2004. "Testing Novel Implications from the Selectorate Theory of War." *World Politics* 56, no. 3: 363–88. https://doi.org/10.1353/wp.2004.0017.

Chatagnier, J. Tyson, and Emanuele Castelli. 2016. "A Modern Peace? Schumpeter, the Decline of Conflict, and the Investment-War Trade-Off." *Political Research Quarterly* 69, no. 4: 852–64. https://doi.org/10.1177%2F1065912916670270.

Choi, Seung-Whan. 2010. "Beyond Kantian Liberalism: Peace through Globalization." *Conflict Management and Peace Science* 27, no. 3: 272–95. https://doi.org/10.1177%2F073889421 0366513.

Copeland, Dale C. 2015. *Economic Interdependence and War*. Princeton, NJ: Princeton University Press.

Dolman, Everett C. 2002. *Astropolitik: Classical Geopolitics in the Space Age*. New York: Frank Cass.

Dorussen, Han. 1999. "Balance of Power Revisited: A Multi-Country Model of Trade and Conflict." *Journal of Peace Research* 36, no. 4: 443–62. https://doi.org/10.1177%2F00223433 99036004004.

FAA. 2018. January. "The Annual Compendium of Commercial Space Transportation: 2018." https://www.faa.gov/about/office_org/headquarters_offices/ast/media/2018_AST_Com pendium.pdf.

Foust, Jeff. 2021. "House Bill Would Designate Space as Critical Infrastructure." *Space News*. June 4, 2021. https://spacenews.com/house-bill-would-designate-space-as-critical-infrastructure/.

Garamone, Jim. 2020. "Esper: Air Force, Space Force, Leading Charge to New Technologies." *US Department of Defense*. September 16, 2020. https://www.defense.gov/Explore/News/ Article/Article/2349408/esper-air-force-space-force-leading-charge-to-new-technologies/.

Gartzke, Erik. 2007. "The Capitalist Peace." *American Journal of Political Science* 51, no. 1: 166–91. https://doi.org/10.1111/j.1540-5907.2007.00244.x.

Gartzke, Erik, and J. Joseph Hewitt. 2010. "International Crises and the Capitalist Peace." *International Interactions* 36, no. 2: 115–45. https://doi.org/10.1080/03050621003784846.

Gartzke, Erik, and Quan Li. 2003. "Measure for Measure: Concept Operationalization and the Trade Interdependence Conflict Debate." *Journal of Peace Research* 40, no. 5: 553–71. https://doi.org/10.1177%2F00223433030405004.

Gartzke, Erik, and Yonatan Lupu. 2012. "Trading on Preconceptions: Why World War I Was Not a Failure of Economic Interdependence." *International Security* 36, no. 4: 115–50. https://doi.org/10.1162/ISEC_a_00078.

Glass, Dan. 2016. "What Happens If GPS Fails?" *The Atlantic.* June 13, 2016. https://www.thea
tlantic.com/technology/archive/2016/06/what-happens-if-gps-fails/486824/.

Handberg, Roger. 2017. "Is Space War Imminent? Exploring the Possibility." *Comparative Strategy* 36, no. 5: 413–25. https://doi.org/10.1080/01495933.2017.1379832.

Harris, Mark. 2021. "FAA Files Reveal a Surprising Threat to Airline Safety: The US Military's GPS Tests." *IEEE Spectrum.* January 21, 2021. https://spectrum.ieee.org/aerospace/aviation/faa-files-reveal-a-surprising-threat-to-airline-safety-the-us-militarys-gps-tests.

Harrison, Todd, Kaitlyn Johnson, Joe Moye, and Makena Young. 2021. April. "Space Threat Assessment 2021." *CSIS Aerospace Security Project.* https://csis-website-prod.s3.amazonaws.com/s3fs-public/publication/210331_Harrison_SpaceThreatAssessment2021.pdf?gVYhCn79enGCOZtcQnA6MLkeKlcwqqks.

Hegre, Havard, John R. Oneal, and Bruce Russett. 2010. "Trade Does Promote Peace: New Simultaneous Estimates of the Reciprocal Effects of Trade and Conflict." *Journal of Peace Research* 47, no. 6: 763–74. https://www.jstor.org/stable/20798962.

Hirsch, Steve. 2018. "There is no 'War in Space.'" *Air Force Magazine.* May 29, 2018. https://www.airforcemag.com/article/there-is-no-war-in-space/.

Hirst, Paul, and Grahame Thompson. 1995. "Globalization and the Future of the Nation State." *Economy and Society* 24, no. 3: 408–42. https://doi.org/10.1080/03085149500000017.

Hitchens, Theresa. 2021a. "USG Should Beware Exaggerated Threat to GPS: RAND." *Breaking Defense.* June 9, 2021. https://breakingdefense.com/2021/06/usg-should-beware-exaggerated-gps-threats-rand/.

Hitchens, Theresa. 2021b. "What Satellite Attach Weapon Might the US Reveal Soon?" *Breaking Defense.* August 24, 2021. https://breakingdefense.com/2021/08/what-satellite-attack-weapon-might-the-us-reveal-soon/.

Hudecheck, Michael, Charlotta Siren, Dietmar Grichnik, and Joakim Wincent. 2020. "Monitoring the Covid-19 Crisis from Space." *MIT Sloan Management Review.* April 17, 2020. https://sloanreview.mit.edu/article/monitoring-the-covid-19-crisis-from-space/.

Kacowicz, Arie M., and Mor Mitrani. 2016. "Why Don't We Have Coherent Theories of International Relations about Globalization?" *Global Governance* 22, no. 2: 189–208. https://doi.org/10.1163/19426720-02202002.

Keohane, Robert O., and Joseph S. Nye, Jr. 2012. *Power and Interdependence.* 4th ed. Boston: Longman.

Kessler, Donald J., and B.G. Cour-Palais. 1978. "Collisional Frequency of Artificial Satellites: The Creation of a Debris Belt." *Journal of Geophysical Research* 83, no. A6: 2637–46. https://doi.org/10.1029/JA083iA06p02637.

Kleinberg, Katja B., and Benjamin O. Fordham. 2013. "The Domestic Politics of Trade and Conflict." *International Studies Quarterly* 57, no. 3: 605–19. https://doi.org/10.1111/isqu.12016.

Krugman, Paul. 1996. *Pop Internationalism.* Cambridge, MA: MIT Press.

Launius, Roger. 2012. "Imprisoned in a Tesseract: NASA's Human Spaceflight Effort and the Prestige Trap." *Astropolitics* 10, no. 2: 152–75. https://doi.org/10.1080/14777622.2012.696015.

Lu, Irina, Evan Linck, Bhavya Lal, Keith W. Crane, Xueying Han, and Thomas J. Colvin. 2019. "Evaluation of China's Commercial Space Sector." *Institute for Defense Analyses.* September 2019. https://www.ida.org/-/media/feature/publications/e/ev/evaluation-of-chinas-commercial-space-sector/d-10873.ashx.

Mansfield, Edward D., and Brian M. Pollins. 2001. "The Study of Interdependence and Conflict: Recent Advances, Open Questions, and Directions for Future Research." *The Journal of Conflict Resolution* 45, no. 6: 834–59. https://doi.org/10.1177%2F0022002701045006007.

Mayhew, David. 1974. *Congress: The Electoral Connection.* New Haven, CT: Yale University Press.

McDonald, Patrick J. 2004. "Peace through Trade or Free Trade?" *The Journal of Conflict Resolution* 48, no. 4: 547–72. https://doi.org/10.1177%2F0022002704266117.

McDonald, Patrick J. 2007. "The Purse Strings of Peace." *American Journal of Political Science* 51, no. 3: 569–82. https://doi.org/10.1111/j.1540-5907.2007.00268.x.

McMillan, Susan M. 1997. "Interdependence and Conflict." *Mershon International Studies Review* 41, no. 1: 33–58. https://doi.org/10.2307/222802.

Mendenhall, Elizabeth. 2018. "Treating Outer Space Like a Place: A Case for Rejecting Other Domain Analogies." *Astropolitics* 16, no. 2: 97–118. https://doi.org/10.1080/14777 622.2018.1484650.

Moltz, James Clay. 2019. *The Politics of Space Security: Strategic Restraint and the Pursuit of National Interests.* Stanford, CA: Stanford University Press.

Morgan Stanley. 2021. "A New Space Economy on the Edge of Liftoff." *Morgan Stanley.* February 17, 2021. https://www.morganstanley.com/Themes/global-space-economy.

Morrison, Allen J. 2021. "The Strategic Challenges of Decoupling." *Harvard Business Review.* May–June 2021. https://hbr.org/2021/05/the-strategic-challenges-of-decoupling.

Morrow, James D. 1999. "How Could Trade Affect Conflict?" *Journal of Peace Research* 36, no. 4: 481–89. https://doi.org/10.1177%2F0022343399036004006.

Mousseau, Michael. 2010. "Coming to Terms with the Capitalist Peace." *International Interactions* 36: 185–213. https://doi.org/10.1080/03050621003785074.

Muir-Harmony, Teasel. 2020. *Operation Moonglow: A Political History of Project Apollo.* New York: Basic Books.

Mueller, John. 2010. "Capitalism, Peace, and the Historical Movement of Ideas." *International Interactions* 36: 169–84. https://doi.org/10.1080/03050621003785066.

Murshed, Syed Mansoob, and Dawood Mamoon. 2010. "Not Loving Thy Neighbour as Thyself: Democracy and Military Expenditure Explanations Underlying India-Pakistan Rivalry." *Journal of Peace Research* 47, no. 4: 463–76. https://doi.org/10.1177%2F0022343310364577.

Newlove-Eriksson, Lindy, and Johan Eriksson. 2013. "Governance beyond the Global: Who Controls the Extraterrestrial?" *Globalizations* 10, no. 2: 277–92. https://doi.org/10.1080/14747731.2013.786250.

Norman Angell. 1912. *The Great Illusion: A Study of the Relation of Military Power in Nations to Their Economic and Social Advantages.* London: Heineman.

O'Connor, Alan C., Michael P. Gallagher, Lyle Clark-Sutton, Daniel Lapidus, Zack T. Oliver, Troy J. Scott, Dallas W. Wood, Manuel A. Gonzalez, Elizabeth G. Brown, Joshua Fletcher. 2019. "Economic Benefits of the Global Positioning System (GPS)." *RTI International.* June 2019. https://www.rti.org/sites/default/files/gps_finalreport.pdf.

Oneal, John R., and Bruce Russett. 1999. "The Kantian Peace: The Pacific Benefits of Democracy, Interdependence, and International Organizations, 1885–1992." *World Politics* 52, no. 1: 1–37. https://doi.org/10.1017/S0043887100020013.

Pekkanen, Saadia M. 2019. "Governing the New Space Race." *AJIL Unbound* 113: 92–97. https://doi.org/10.1017/aju.2019.16.

Polachek, Solomon William. 1980. "Conflict and Trade." *The Journal of Conflict Resolution* 24, no. 1: 55–78. https://doi.org/10.1177%2F002200278002400103.

Polachek, Solomon W., John Robst, and Yuan-Ching Chang. 1999. "Liberalism and Interdependence: Extending the Trade-Conflict Model." *Journal of Peace Research* 36, no. 4: 405–22. https://doi.org/10.1177%2F0022343399036004002.

Rosecrance, Richard. 2010. "Capitalist Influences and Peace." *International Interactions* 36, no. 2: 192–98. https://doi.org/10.1080/03050621003785108.

Russett, Bruce. 2010. "Capitalism or Democracy? Not So Fast." *International Interactions* 36, no. 2: 198–205. https://doi.org/10.1080/03050621003785165.

Schneider, Gerald, and Nils Petter Gleditsch. 2010. "The Capitalist Peace: The Origins and Prospects of a Liberal Idea." *International Interactions* 36: 107–14. https://doi.org/10.1080/03050621003784689.

Schumpeter, Joseph. 1955 [1919]. *Imperialism and Social Classes: Two Essays by Joseph Schumpeter.* Cleveland, OH: Meridian Books.

Sheetz, Michael. 2021. "SpaceX says Starlink Has About 90,000 Users as the Internet Service Gains Subscribers." *CNBC.* August 3, 2021. https://www.cnbc.com/2021/08/03/spacex-starl ink-satellite-internet-has-about-90000-users.html.

SIA. 2020. "Satellite Industry Grows at Record-Setting Pace." *Satellite Industry Association.* July 2, 2020. https://sia.org/satellite-industry-grows-at-record-setting-pace-and-dominates-glo bal-space-economy/.

Tauri Group. 2013. April. "NASA Socio-Economic Impacts." https://www.nasa.gov/sites/defa ult/files/files/SEINSI.pdf.

Thurow, Lester C. 2000. "Globalization: The Product of a Knowledge-Based Economy." *The Annals of the American Academy of Political and Social Science* 570 (July): 19–31. https://doi. org/10.1177%2F000271620057000102.

Townsend, Brad. 2020. *Security and Stability in the New Space Age: The Orbital Security Dilemma.* New York: Routledge.

"UCS Satellite Database." 2023. Union of Concerned Scientists., https://www.ucsusa.org/ resources/satellite-database.

USGS. 2021. March 4. "Landsat's Economic Value to the Nation Continues to Increase." https:// www.usgs.gov/center-news/landsat-s-economic-value-nation-continues-increase?qt-news_science_products=3#qt-news_science_products.

Weingast, Barry R., Kenneth A. Shepsle, and Christopher Johnsen. 1981. "The Political Economy of Benefits and Costs: A Neoclassical Approach to Distributive Politics." *Journal of Political Economy* 89, no. 4: 642–64. https://doi.org/10.1086/260997.

Whitman Cobb, Wendy N. 2020. *Privatizing Peace: How Commerce Can Reduce Conflict in Space.* New York: Routledge.

CHAPTER 7

SOFT POWER AND COOPERATION FOR SPACE SECURITY

PAVEL LUZIN

SPACE security is comprehended usually in terms of hard power. However, the concept of soft power may give us an understanding of how different international agendas for outer space affairs and the space cooperation ties based on them are related to security issues and also influence them. Three aspects of the soft power concept have remained stable over this evolution, that it: functions through directly or indirectly "transforming the attitudes of target audiences in foreign countries"; "has a longer operational time horizon compared to hard power and is more suited to the attainment of general rather than specific goals"; and does not lie exclusively within the control of a country's government, but is "shared with civil society" (Bakalov 2019, 134).

The different perceptions of soft power represented by the United States, Europe, the People's Republic of China (PRC), Japan, Russia, and India will impact the competition among them regarding space affairs for the next decade or so. This suggests that the space security environment will be unstable and the leadership of the United States will be contested by US adversaries. However, competition between the space powers includes soft power, among other things, and usually means a positive-sum game rather than a zero-sum one. As both a political target and a tool for adversarial actors seeking to advance their interests, soft power will likely limit these actors' will to escalate tensions into outer space.

However, Russia's aggression against Ukraine in 2022 has put the Russian space program into disarray and made its soft power a matter of history. Today, it is not clear if Russia will be able to restore soft power in space affairs in the foreseeable future or what framework of space activity it will be able to realize at all. Consequently, Russia's behavior in outer space may be unpredictable in the coming years, but the current turbulence in the world order gives us a better understanding of connections between space security and soft power in outer space affairs.

This chapter is in four parts. The first part explores the definition of soft power in the context of space affairs. The second part discusses how this concept has evolved related to outer space activities. The third part examines the agenda and perceptions of the soft power contenders, namely the United States, Europe, Japan, India, China, and Russia. The fourth part concludes, setting out some applications for space security.

DEFINING SOFT POWER IN SPACE AFFAIRS

The concept of soft power was developed by Joseph S. Nye Jr. in 1990 (Nye 1990). According to him, soft power differs from hard power, which consists of both military power and economic power. There are two related definitions of soft power: (1) it is the ability to obtain desired outcomes through attraction or persuasion rather than coercion or payment (Nye 2004); (2) it is the ability to affect others through the co-optive means of framing the agenda, persuading, and eliciting positive attraction in order to obtain preferred outcomes (Nye 2011, 20–21). Usually, soft power is based on culture, political values, programs, and a state's image (or an image of some other international political actor).

In the context of space security and whole outer space affairs, soft power may be defined as the *ability to promote the global agenda for space explorations and security, to develop and to maintain international space cooperation ties, and to increase one's own international prestige through demonstration of ambitious and impressive achievements in space activity*. The definition of soft power also includes a state being able to adapt its space activity in the most effective way in relation to the space agenda proposed by another state and *to become an attractive partner within such agenda*. The best examples of such adaptation are presented by Japan and India, which develop their space activities within the agenda generally proposed by the United States. Japan is a key US and European partner in outer space for decades, and India pretends to take this role as well through increasing space cooperation with the West. That means they contribute to the western agenda of space exploration and through this contribution they increase their soft power and consequently their weight in global space affairs. As a result, soft power here does not necessarily mean political leadership in space affairs and the developing of a state's own agenda, but presumes that partners become "stakeholders" of the common agenda and consequently, have a common understanding of space security.

It is also evident that space science and technologies play a key role in maintaining soft power (as they do regarding hard power) because they materialize the idea and value of progress, they are related to culture, and they create global interest for those actors who realize advanced space projects and develop new space technologies.

Even if such actors are private space companies or universities, they contribute to the soft power of the states where they realize business activity. This point derives from an institutional environment that depends on political factors and makes private commercial space activity possible, as from international space law where states take responsibility for all kinds of space activities conducted from their lands.

In this way, successful, impressive, attractive, and inspiring space projects have an influence on public opinion as a whole and on opinion within different professional communities in other countries (scientists, industrial professionals, investors, entrepreneurs, and so on). That means soft power in space affairs develops and maintains relations between the states themselves together with ties of cooperation between the academic and business sectors related with space activity.

Consequently, if any single state creates a friendly environment for private space activity it invests in its soft power among other things, regardless of whether or not there is a well-developed and advanced governmental space program. At the same time soft power is not necessarily a driver for international accord in space activity: agendas compete in space affairs, and that is especially true for space security. However, this competition is a positive-sum game rather than a zero-sum game.

It is also evident that soft power should not be considered a purpose for national space policy itself but as deriving from a successful space program and the efficient organizational (institutional) structure of space activity. Therefore, increasing soft power indicates that space policy is well developed and well realized, and a lack of soft power indicates that space policy faces some limitations or even troubles. Taking into account that an unsustainable or/and ineffective national space policy may pose a threat to the common space security environment, the lack of soft power in space affairs may be an indicator of actual space security challenges. This is especially true if a state with unsustainable space activity demonstrates ambitions in foreign policy.

THE EVOLUTION OF SOFT POWER IN SPACE AFFAIRS

Soft power existed long before Joseph S. Nye Jr. coined the term (Nye and Welch 2014, 51–53). It has become relevant for space affairs and space security since October 4, 1957, when the USSR orbited the first artificial satellite. Though hard power competition dominated space affairs during the Cold War, and especially before prohibition of orbital nuclear tests together with nuclear tests in air and sea in 1963, the space race between the USSR and the United States was also a race to build and deploy soft power mechanisms. From 1957 to 1991, the most evident factor of soft power was international prestige for each superpower when one of them was doing something in outer space for the first time: the first satellite; the first human spaceflight; human expeditions to the Moon; robotic missions to Venus, Mars, and other celestial bodies; orbital human stations; and the Space Shuttle. In turn, the international agenda regarding space activity was defined mostly by hard power because of the nuclear arms race during the period, and international space law that appeared in 1960s was closely related with the issue of nuclear arms.

Both multinational space exploration projects and private initiatives in outer space have been developed and put soft power in space affairs at the forefront on par with hard power after the end of the Cold War. Nevertheless, the ability to develop international space cooperation has become significant since the very beginning of the space era. The appearance of Intelsat in 1964, firstly as the International Telecommunications Satellite Consortium (1964–1973) then as the International Telecommunications Satellite Organization (since 1973), was led by the United States in an effort to create common rules and standards and to share satellite services among the partner nations. The Soviet-led Intersputnik International Organization of Space Communications appeared in 1971 with almost the same purposes as Intelsat and originally involved the USSR and several socialist republics (Agreement on the Establishment of the Intersputnik International System and Organization of Space Communications 1971).

These two organizations combined elements of hard power (especially regarding aspects of economy) and soft power because the member states were motivated to participate in these organizations by their own interests and through their own decisions and for the prestige of such participation, not by the dominance of leading superpower, either the United States or the USSR.

For instance, the preamble of the INTELSAT Agreement of August 20, 1971, says that one aim of the member states' is to develop a satellite communication system "which will provide expanded telecommunications services to all areas of the world and which will contribute to world peace and understanding" (Agreement Relating to the International Telecommunications Satellite Organization "INTELSAT" 1971). In turn, the preamble of the Intersputnik Agreement of November 15, 1971, says that the member states recognize "the need to contribute to the strengthening and development of comprehensive economic, scientific, technical, cultural and other relations by communications as well as by radio and television broadcasting via satellites," and they act "in the interests of the development of international co-operation based on respect for the sovereignty and independence of states, equality and non-interference in the internal affairs as well as mutual assistance and mutual benefit" (Agreement on the Establishment of the Intersputnik International System and Organization of Space Communications 1971).

Besides the INTELSAT and Intersputnik, both the United States and the USSR engaged their allies in human space flights, and in both cases it was about sharing the technical and scientific capabilities with allied nations that allowed them to realize their own space ambitions.

In this way, the two superpowers achieved their political and economic purposes through attraction, persuasion, and co-optive means. Washington and Moscow engaged their allies in the US and Soviet space programs respectively, established long-term space cooperation ties, and supported their allies' will to become emerging space powers with increasing their own prestige in international relations and contributing to peace as well as cultural development.

The significant role of soft power for space affairs was apparent during the Apollo–Soyuz Test Project that was being realized in 1972–1975 and was completed by the orbital docking of the US and the Soviet manned spacecrafts, Apollo and Soyuz respectively, on July 17, 1975. The mission had mostly a symbolic sense in times of *détente* during the Cold War, and the United States and the USSR gained from this project in terms of soft power. Space cooperation for peaceful purposes appeared to be possible even between these enemies, and the project laid some significant foundations (for instance, trust) for the US–Russia space partnership seventeen years later. Also, the two superpowers improved their reputation as responsible actors in outer space in the eyes of each other and in the eyes of other states: a situation in which a competition of soft powers brought each competitor a win.

After 1991 when the USSR collapsed and the Cold War ended, the ability to promote a common space agenda and to develop multilateral cooperation ties in space activity became as important as an economic statement and the amount of space expenditures which are converted into space missions, scientific outcomes and technologies, and consequently into the global reputation and prestige. This explains well why the United States was able to achieve global leadership in space affairs: it engaged other leading space powers including Russia into the US space program because of both hard and soft power and promoted the global agenda for space exploration.

The most prominent project here is the International Space Station that was initiated in 1992, launched in 1998, and will be de-orbited at the end of 2020s. Besides its economic and technological, this project, proposed by the United States, was politically attractive, prestigious, and relevant to the wide spectrum of interests of other participants from the very beginning, and it was also based on the positive international reputation of each participant in the eyes of others (Eisenhower 2004). And one of the political consequences here was that the soft power of the United States helped maintain the soft power of Canada, the European Union (EU), Japan, and Russia in space affairs. Moreover, along with a permanent seat in the UN Security Council and nuclear arms, space partnership with the United States allowed Russia to maintain its great power status after the collapse of the USSR. In this way, soft power even contributed into Russia's hard power. Most significant, however, was that the engagement of Russia into US-led space activity created a bilateral and multilateral mutual understanding of space affairs and contributed to space security. Even contradictions with regard to the US missile defense program and military uses of outer space that were escalating in late 1990s did not disrupt the space security environment during the period.

The global agenda for space exploration was also led by the United States: space astronomy, the moon, Mars, and the deep space missions, the revolution in satellite technologies, and preparing the ground for commercial space activity. All space powers, including China and the growing number of emerging ones, conduct their space programs within the US paradigm, even if they do not have any significant space cooperation ties with the United States.

However, the achievements of the US space program, technological progress, fast growing commercial space sector, and the appearance of tens of emerging space powers led to a paradoxical situation by the end of 2010s. On the one hand, it has become as complicated to compete with as to cooperate with the United States in outer space. Many actors may be consumers of the US space program's results and clients of the US space industry, but they cannot be significant US partners because of the lack of technologies and human capital.

On the other hand, US commercial space companies are able to provide services to foreign governments, but they may establish cooperation ties only with foreign commercial entities, not with the foreign space agencies. Consequently, the global agenda for space activity promoted by the United States is attractive and will remain attractive in coming decades, but the entry price here has become much higher than it was during the 1990s–2000s. For instance, the focus on the moon, including human spaceflights there, and on Mars instead of on low Earth orbit creates a gap between developed and developing space powers that is hard to bridge.

At the same time, a number of factors are changing the political environment of space exploration: the increasing number of actors developing national space programs as the environment for private space activity has changed in recent decades; the role of the PRC as a major challenger for US leadership in different areas including outer space; and the fatal failure of Russia's economic modernization and democratization that has brought it to aggression and seen the collapse of its space partnership with the United States, Europe, Canada, and Japan that was established three decades ago. In this way, the reality of space affairs during the 2020s–2030s is not only multilateral competition between not only the hard power of different nations but also between their soft power. This competition for soft power definitely influences the nature of space security.

COMPETITIVE SOFT POWERS IN OUTER SPACE

The competition for soft power in outer space derives as much from the different agendas in this field as from the different perceptions of soft power and different approaches toward it. This section discusses how this is playing out with respect to the major spacefaring countries.

The US perception of soft power is identical to the definition devised by Joseph S. Nye. In this way, the common agenda for space affairs and strong space cooperation ties play the major role here. The US space agenda in relation to soft power presumes several key points: (1) transferring cooperation with its key partners from the International Space Station to the Gateway station in the Lunar orbit (this concerns mostly Canada, Europe, and Japan, but some room for Russia is presumed and depends on US–Russia relations in coming years); (2) realizing and further promoting the Artemis Accords and its principles for cooperation in civil space exploration and use of the moon, Mars, comets, and asteroids for peaceful purposes (NASA n.d.); (3) increasingly relying on the private commercial space sector and improving the domestic and global environment for it; (4) reconsidering the rules of use of low Earth orbit to make it safer for all actors in the face of the deployment of satellite constellations comprising thousands of spacecrafts each and the growing among of orbital debris.

The aforementioned gap between developed and developing space powers within the agenda is one of the key political issues here. However, there are some ways to bridge it. The first way is integration of current and potential partners into supply/manufacturing chains, as the United States already does regarding the European contribution to the Orion spacecraft. Briefly, the United States may give stakes in US space projects to foreign partners. Such stakes do not mean "payments" for loyalty, but voluntary though systemic contributions of partners to the US space program, as well as interdependence through engagement.

The second major way is relying on space companies to expand in the global market, develop their ambitious projects, and create their own supply chains and cooperation ties with foreign space companies and customers. All this activity develops the global agenda of space exploration and makes joining with the US and, more widely the western, space market attractive to other states. On their side, these states are interested in developing domestic institutional environments for commercial space activity so companies can find a market niche and cooperate with US space companies as partners and contractors. Also, these efforts to develop domestic institutional environments for commercial space activity are aimed at attracting investments from US companies in local commercial space projects and startups.

Therefore, the US commercial space sector unintentionally proposes a political choice/prospect for developing countries: either become stakeholders of the western space market with all necessary institutional improvements, including political, or maintain their current political economy reality where a significant advance in space activity would be hardly possible. Though, the last option almost inevitably means that space programs will mostly be about image for such countries and they will prefer to use the agenda of space cooperation to get political and economic gains from space powers such as the PRC or Russia. As a result, there is a choice between soft power and hard power in space affairs, and the soft power option needs certain political economy preconditions like a market environment, liberalization, and democratization.

Besides the United States with its space leadership and soft power in space affairs, EU member states together with the United Kingdom, as key US partners in space exploration through cooperation between NASA, the European Space Agency (ESA), and the North Atlantic Treaty Organization (NATO), present their own specifics in terms of soft power. The European approach firstly presumes the integration of partners into common projects and then into the common market of space services and goods. This last means that European states develop an institutional environment for private initiatives in space affairs following the United States. The EU member states together with the ESA initiated a policy of developing a private commercial space sector in the 2010s. These efforts produced sustainable results by the 2020s, and they will be continued in the coming decades. The increasing level of space cooperation within Europe together with commercialization of space activity creates scientific, economic, and political benefits for all participants and makes it attractive for non-EU states to establish and maintain ties with Europe.

Therefore, ESA as an efficient international institution is a source of soft power in space affairs for all of its members, including bilateral space projects with third parties. Moreover, the ESA develops a European institutional environment for the private space sector, based on improvements of regulations and a system of ESA and national grants, that is attractive for investors, engineers, and startups from outside of the EU. Together with a well-developed scientific and educational environment, it increases European soft power in space affairs on the international level as well as on non state levels like business and academia. All this allows Europe to keep its political autonomy in space affairs under doubtless US leadership in outer space.

Japan as a developed space power and another key US space partner also has its own and usually underestimated soft power potential in space activity. It has been able to create not only an advanced space program but also the institutional environment for private space activity. In distinction to Europe, government efforts in support of space startups and research teams are combined with investments from major corporations. Moreover, Japan's space agency, JAXA, provides startups with access to its facilities. As a result, Japan has developed an institutional model that may be applied in other countries which have a developed industrial sector. India became the first country that applied this model, and South Korea is also doing so. The main long-term outcomes of such an approach include access to the US and European space markets, a developing cooperation with the western private space sector and with NASA and ESA, and a growing share in the global space market. Moreover, all this builds a bridge for space cooperation between those states that realize the same approach toward the developing of their space sectors. Consequently, Japan as the advanced space power may become a leader of cooperative space activity in the Asia Pacific (Pekkanen 2020), and an international space cooperation network of developing space powers that involves startups and universities from different countries without a dominant state actor is also possible within this model. All this demonstrates that the domestic institutional environment for space activity is also a source of soft power, especially if it is universal enough and can be adopted by foreign actors.

India is also developing its space program, pretending to become one of the key US partners in outer space in coming decades so as to establish its own network of space cooperation that will include governments and the private space sector. Significant achievements and advances in space exploration, especially in moon and Mars exploration, together with adaptation of the Japanese model are making India an attractive space partner for developed space powers. Here, increasing soft power potential in space affairs becomes an organic result of long-term policy with concrete purposes. Consequently, in the case of further advances in space exploration, including the developing of a manned program, India could even replace Russia in the international manned space program in the post-International Space Station era, as soon as in the 2030s, regardless of whether or not Russia will be able to keep its remaining space cooperation ties with the United States and Europe, in the case of any domestic political transformation, ending the aggression against Ukraine, and demilitarization.

At the same time, India's case is another example of how soft power in space affairs works: the adopted global (US) agenda of space exploration together with the Japanese model of a private space sector may be attractive because they promise economic and political benefits in the long term, but the race for these promised benefits is prestigious by itself and increases India's own soft power in space affairs. As a result, India becomes a stakeholder of the global agenda of space exploration. Nevertheless, all this also maintains US leadership in space exploration through enlarging the number of its beneficiaries. Therefore, it develops a predictable political environment in space affairs among the US partners and gives a solid contribution to space security by itself.

The PRC has made a significant advance in its own space activity and now it pretends to propose a competitive space agenda that may become relevant for emerging space powers, that is, for the developing countries. Its space program reproduces the universal paradigm of space exploration that is realized by the United States and Europe and was realized by the USSR and then Russia: orbital station, moon and Mars exploration with a long-term prospect for human missions there, and so on. However, the PRC is hardly attractive as an international leader in outer space. Firstly, it is an authoritarian state with a long-term tradition of buying loyalty instead of creating coalitions of interdependent actors. Secondly, it tries to avoid or at least to minimize dependence on its partners in every field, and the same is true for space affairs including interdependence, which seems to be also unacceptable for the PRC's leadership. Thirdly, the PRC does not have a universal cultural and ideological base in distinction from the United States and even from the USSR.

Moreover, there are some significant differences in the PRC's perception of soft power itself. The common view of Beijing's soft power presumes that the PRC political leadership concentrates its efforts on a systemic information campaign (propaganda) in order to improve the state's global image (Shambaugh 2015, 101–4), to increase foreign respect for it in the long term, and consequently, to make the PRC a preferred partner of other actors (Nye et al. 2009, 19–20). Also, a major aspects of soft power in Beijing's view is an ability to control the terms of discussions (Kalimuddin and Anderson 2018, 120–21).

In this way, the PRC has become much more open in demonstrating its space activity (including achievements on planned projects) since the 2010s. More important, the PRC seized the initiative in promoting foreign participation in its space program, especially in the Tiangong manned multimodal space station. Such participation will mean recognition of the PRC's claims for political leadership in space exploration. Beijing uses public communication channels, bilateral diplomatic channels (Zhao 2021; Clark 2021), and the United Nations Office for Outer Space Affairs in its efforts to achieve this goal (UNOOSA n.d.).

The PRC also has a private commercial space sector policy, which on the one hand is mostly intended to foster development of space technologies, for the growth of the domestic market of space services and goods, and for increasing its export potential. In other words, this policy is aimed toward contributing to the PRC's hard power. However, on the other hand, the private space sector demonstrates the prestige and efficiency of the PRC's political economy system and makes it attractive globally.

At the same time, the PRC diversifies its messages in trying to become an attractive partner in outer space (Blanchard and Lu 2012, 571–75). For developed countries, especially in Europe, it is oriented mostly toward scientific communities like universities and research centers that would become mediators between the PRC and their governments. For the developing countries of Asia, Africa, and Latin America, Beijing's message is oriented mostly toward their political elites that may be attracted by the opportunity to make their states emerging space powers in cooperation with Beijing (Ngugi 2020). This opportunity presumes recognition of the PRC's leadership (and submission to it by default, without any additional coercion) but does not mean any obligations regarding improvements of domestic governance and economic regulations. Also, the PRC's approach does not presume any interdependence between space partners. Consequently, space security will be guaranteed only if other states will recognize and accept Beijing's leadership in space affairs and its role as guarantor of space security.

Consequently, the PRC's potential in soft power is limited and realized mostly in its international image as an alternative developed space power rather than in leadership based on long-term space ties of cooperation. However, this image may be converted into soft influence on the elites and bureaucracies in other authoritarian countries and on the international bureaucracy as well.

In its turn, Russia tries to reconsider its space partnership with the United States and the whole West and searches for a new path in outer space. The degradation of its political economy radicalized the Russian elite and led to the massive aggression against Ukraine and against the whole post–Cold War international order. As a result, Russia completely destroyed its soft power potential in space affairs and can be neither a contributor to the well-institutionalized space partnership with the United States, Europe, Canada, and Japan with own specific advances within the common space activity and own exploration projects which also engage foreign partners, nor an alternative space power that is able to propose and realize its own space agenda or at least single space projects attractive to other space powers. Moreover, the degradation of the domestic institutional environment in Russia makes it impossible for Russia to restore its role in space and its soft power potential in the foreseeable future.

Generally speaking, Russia's soft power in space affairs derives from its participation in the International Space Station and other projects led by the United States and/or Europe and from its contribution into the space programs of other nations. However, the confrontation with the West makes the long-term prospects of Russia-US and Russia-EU space cooperation ties uncertain, and that raises the issue of Russia's ability to remain among the leading space powers at all.

Russia's perception of soft power is focused mostly on reputation, positive impressions, and public opinion, and this looks close enough to that of the PRC. However, by contrast with Beijing and even more so with the United States, Russia considers soft power a political tool rather than a political purpose (Borisov 2020) and hard power issues the main area for using soft power as a tool.

Because of a growing lack in space exploration activity, Russia focuses more and more on securitization of the political agenda toward outer space, and it is trying to use its remaining, but fast eroding, status of developed space power to promote its vision and interests among developing countries and international institutions (international bureaucracy). Consequently, such an instrumental approach toward soft power in space affairs (but not only there) predetermines the focus on information/propaganda campaigns and on efforts to use anti-US and anti-western resentment, especially among the elites of the developing and often authoritarian or semi-authoritarian countries.

Nevertheless, at the tactical level and according to its basic approach toward soft power, Russia is forced to pay more attention to achieving positive results in its space activity and to demonstrating such achievements to the international community. However, there is also a strategic level that requires Russia to keep its space partnership with the West beyond the ISS-era at any cost. That means Russia definitely needs to develop some minor international agenda for space affairs and cooperation, and this agenda must be coherent to the US (western) agenda (Luzin 2013, 27–28). That also means that all Russia's efforts toward securitization of space affairs may appear to be false.

However, all this remains impossible while Russia continues its aggression against Ukraine and its radical behavior toward the global order. Moreover, the objective weaknesses of the Russian space program and even the still ongoing degradation of the Russia's statehood will not allow Russia to propose its own cohesive global agenda for space exploration and for long-term space cooperation in the foreseeable future. Given current circumstances, it doesn't matter at all whether Russia will turn to considering soft power as a target or will continue to consider it as a tool.

APPLICATIONS FOR SPACE SECURITY

At the beginning of the 2020s, there were two space security agendas related to soft power. The first one is the agenda of the United States and NATO allies that has been developing since 2019. It is aimed toward NATO itself and presumes an increasing level of space cooperation and sharing the responsibility for the alliance's space security among its members (NATO 2021). Despite the fact that the United States remains the dominant space power within NATO in terms of quantity and quality of satellite constellations (UCS 2021), the coordination of military space activity and efforts for common space security indicates again the interdependence of these allies. So, relying on allies in space security (the hard power field), the United States increases its soft power.

At the same time, NATO allies engaged in extending cooperation in defense space programs to develop interdependence in space security. That means the United States relies on the space assets of other states and needs to increase the level of trust with the leading space powers within the alliance. Consequently, the status of the United States as a trusted partner in defensive space activity may be defined in terms of soft power, and space security that is based on cooperation and interdependence is de facto based on soft power.

Therefore, the soft power of one actor is not enough, even if this actor plays the leading role, and any partner state in the coalition must be an actor that assures any other ally that it can rely on its space capabilities for maintaining common space security. This assurance may be achieved only if such partners represent their positive long-term intentions, good will, and predictable and positive political economy environment. In this way, being an attractive partner for common space security efforts has a long-term structural and/or institutional nature and almost does not depend on temporary, psychological, and/or propaganda factors.

One more source for US soft power in space security is the well-developed US private space sector that may provide the national armed forces of the whole alliance with advanced services and goods, like Earth observation and imaging, launch vehicles, advanced satellite communications, and space tracking. This means an efficient contribution of the market-oriented businesses with civil technologies to space security and maintains the attractiveness of the outer space agenda proposed by the United States. Moreover, the US private space sector generates a global space agenda by itself and creates an environment where other nations try to develop their own private space sector that would be able to cooperate with US space companies and to integrate into their space projects. But a sustainable environment for the private space sector is possible only within a market economy and democratic states.

The interesting fact here is that access to commercial space infrastructure applicable for defense use is also available only to those states that are democratic and market oriented, and which realize their foreign policies according to the international rules. The case of Ukraine, which got access to the satellite systems of Planet Labs, Maxar Technologies, Starlink, and ICEYE soon after the Russian invasion in February 2022, confirms this point well. That's how Ukraine was able to surpass Russia in military space capabilities and to integrate sufficiently commercial space services provided by the western companies into its combat operations. Again, this demonstrates an institutional nature of soft power regarding space security issues.

The second agenda was proposed by Russia and the PRC almost a decade ago, with its core aspect the draft of the Treaty on the Prevention of the Placement of Weapons in Outer Space, the Threat or Use of Force against Outer Space Objects (PPWT) for the whole international community (MFA of the PRC 2014). Despite that fact that there is no significant prospect of the draft being signed because of its structure and disputable terms, it represents a political proposal, some principles, and starting positions for international negotiations in space security. For instance, Russia has signed declarations with a number of developing countries on no first placement of weapons in outer space since 2014 (MFA of the Russian Federation 2020). Moscow also actively promotes this in the United Nations (United Nations General Assembly 2022). Among other things, this diplomatic activity contributes to Russia's soft power: it maintains its image as a responsible actor at least in some areas of international affairs despite the fact that Russia is an aggressor and a violator of international law. It even may be considered as a tool for persuading primarily the West to discuss and bargain on space security issues.

Nevertheless, the PRC considers the PPWT draft mostly as a starting point for a global discussion on the future of space security. It does not search for immediate or even short-term political results in this field, but its long-term purpose is maintaining itself as a one of the key stakeholders of international space law and regulations and one of the key beneficiaries of space activity. The PRC also wants to maintain and extend its international cooperation ties regarding deep space exploration that includes the moon, Mars, and missions to asteroids and beyond but without establishing real interdependence in this field. Here, Beijing is going to bring its predictability and adherence to the rule-based approach in space security on predictable and guaranteed access of the PRC's space industry to western technology and academic sectors and to the global space market where the United States and Europe dominate.

The common point in the approaches of the PRC and Russia is a focus on political image and on inter-governmental relations. They are trying to convince the international community that their agenda in space security must be considered by the West as reasonable and responsible and that it also correlates with the political interests of developing countries, or with political interest of their elites. In this way, this approach is rather manipulative. However, the main difference is that the PRC's approach to space security is oriented more toward its economic, technology, and political strategy (including the military aspect). It is conservative enough, but much more institution based. Though, the main problem here is that both the PRC and Russia consider space security only in terms of military competition, not cooperation, and they do not implement trust in their foreign political culture. These agendas demonstrate two competitive political paradigms. The western paradigm, being the liberal one, presumes the creation of a predictable space security environment through international cooperation: moving from the national level to the international through the common agenda of space activity. The Russian and Chinese paradigm, being the authoritarian one, presumes the creation of a predictable space security environment through international regulation: moving from the international level to the national through the common agenda of space threats, even if the threats are created by those who propose the regulation. If the first paradigm means increasing the opportunities of those who share the purposes and values of space activity, then the second paradigm means limiting opportunities to those who have advanced space programs, space technologies, international cooperation, and the ability to promote and realize a global agenda for space exploration and security.

However, after February 24, 2022, when Russia invaded Ukraine, it became clear how fragile soft power is, especially with regard to authoritarian states that consider soft power mostly in terms of political manipulation rather than in terms of long-term and expanding cooperation and interdependence. Russia completely destroyed its soft power in almost all fields including space affairs. It is neither an attractive partner nor a space power with a good image among the international community, nor a leading space power at all. Russia's aggression also means a decrease in its ability to influence the global space agenda. This has also damaged the space security environment because the political radicalization of Russia may make it a "space troublemaker."

Therefore, soft power in space affairs should be considered as deriving from a long-term space strategy, sustainable space policy, efficient space activity, responsible foreign policy, and positive political economy environment, which means a market economy and democratic governance. In the absence of all these factors, soft power in space affairs is just impossible. So, soft power cannot be regarded as a purpose in itself, it should be viewed as an indicator of the efficiency of space policy and, broadly speaking, of the political economy system.

As a result, the contribution of soft power to space security may be significant as regards cooperation between states in civil and defense space activities based not only on political interests but also on mutual long-term trust and good will and improvements of countries' institutional environment so as to extend and improve international space cooperation ties with wide engagement of actors from business and academic sectors.

REFERENCES

Agreement on the Establishment of the Intersputnik International System and Organization of Space Communications. 1971. November 15. Intersputnik. https://intersputnik.int/upload/en/Establishment_Agreement.pdf.

Agreement Relating to the International Telecommunications Satellite Organization "INTELSAT." 1971. August 20. United Nations. https://treaties.un.org/doc/Publication/UNTS/Volume%201220/volume-1220-I-19677-English.pdf.

Bakalov, Ivan. 2019. "Whither Soft Power? Divisions, Milestones, and Prospects of a Research Programme in the Making." Journal of Political Power 12, no. 1: 129–51.

Blanchard, Jean-Marc F., and Fujia Lu. 2012. "Thinking Hard about Soft Power: A Review and Critique of the Literature on China and Soft Power." Asian Perspective 36, no. 4: 565–89. http://www.jstor.org/stable/42704806.

Borisov, Alexei Vladimirovich. 2020. "Myagkayasila" Rossii: spetsifikaponimaniya i otsenki"["Soft Power of Russia: Specifics of Understanding and Estimations"]. Mirovayapolitika 1: 1–11. DOI: 10.25136/2409-8671.2020.1.32217. https://nbpublish.com/library_read_article.php?id=32217.

Clark, Stephen. 2021. "China Repeats Call for International Astronauts to Join Space Station Crews." Spaceflight Now. October 15, 2021. https://spaceflightnow.com/2021/10/15/china-repeats-call-for-international-astronauts-to-join-future-space-station-crews/.

Eisenhower, Susan. 2004. Partners in Space: US-Russian Cooperation after the Cold War. Washington, DC: The Eisenhower Institute.

Kalimuddin, Mikail, and David A. Anderson. 2018. "Soft Power in China's Security Strategy." Strategic Studies Quarterly 12, no. 3: 114–41. http://www.jstor.org/stable/26481912.

Luzin, Pavel. 2013. "Outer Space as Russia's Soft-Power Tool". Security Index: A Russian Journal on International Security 19, no. 1: 25–29. DOI: 10.1080/19934270.2013.757117. https://www.tandfonline.com/doi/abs/10.1080/19934270.2013.757117?journalCode=rsec20.

MFA of the PRC (Ministry of Foreign Affairs of the People's Republic of China). 2014. June 16. "Treaty on the Prevention of the Placement of Weapons in Outer Space, the Threat or Use of Force against Outer Space Objects (Draft)." https://www.fmprc.gov.cn/mfa_eng/wjb_663 304/zzjg_663340/jks_665232/kjfywj_665252/t1165762.shtml.

MFA of the Russian Federation (Ministry of the Foreign Affairs of the Russian Federation. 2020. July 7. "Prevention of Placement of Weapons in Outer Space [Предотвращение размещения оружия в космосе])." https://archive.mid.ru/mnogostoronnij-razoruzences kij-mehanizm-oon/-/asset_publisher/8pTEicZSMOut/content/id/1127371.

NASA. n.d. The Artemis Accords: Principles for a Safe, Peaceful, and Prosperous Future. https://www.nasa.gov/specials/artemis-accords/index.html.

NATO. 2021. "NATO's Approach to Space." Last updated June 21, 2021. https://www.nato.int/cps/en/natohq/topics_175419.htm.

Ngugi, Brian. 2020. "Kenya, Chinese Space Station Deal Alarms US." Business Daily. September 25, 2020. https://www.businessdailyafrica.com/bd/economy/kenyachinese-space-station-deal-alarms-us-2371670.

Nye, Joseph S., Jr.1990. Bound to Lead: The Changing Nature of American Power. New York: Basic Books.

Nye, Joseph S., Jr. 2004. Soft Power: The Means to Success in World Politics. New York: Public Affairs.

Nye, Joseph S. 2011. The Future of Power. New York: Public Affairs.

Nye, Joseph S., Wang Jisi, Richard Rosecrance, and Gu Guoliang. 2009. "Hard Decisions on Soft Power: Opportunities and Difficulties for Chinese Soft Power." Harvard International Review 31, no. 2: 18–22. http://www.jstor.org/stable/42763291.

Nye, Joseph S., Jr., and David A. Welch. 2014. Understanding Global Conflicts & Cooperation: Intro to Theory and History. Harlow, UK: Pearson.

Pekkanen, Saadia M. 2021. "China, Japan, and the Governance of Space: Prospects for Competition and Cooperation." International Relations of the Asia-Pacific 21, no. 1: 37–64. https://doi.org/10.1093/irap/lcaa007.

Shambaugh, David. 2015. "China's Soft-Power Push: The Search for Respect." Foreign Affairs 94, no. 4: 99–107. http://www.jstor.org/stable/24483821.

Union of Concerned Scientists. 2021. UCS Satellite Database. Updated May 1, 2021. https://www.ucsusa.org/resources/satellite-database.

United Nations General Assembly. 2022. December 7. Resolution 77/42 No First Placement of Weapons in Outer Space. https://documents-dds-ny.un.org/doc/UNDOC/GEN/N22/739/41/PDF/N2273941.pdf?OpenElement.

UNOOSA (United Nations Office for Outer Space Affairs). n.d. "The United Nations/China Cooperation on the Utilization of the China Space Station (CSS)." https://www.unoosa.org/oosa/en/ourwork/access2space4all/China-Space-Station/CSS_Index.html.

Zhao Lei. 2021. "China's Heavenly Palace Welcomes International Cooperation." China Daily, June 17, 2021. https://global.chinadaily.com.cn/a/202106/17/WS60ca84e9a31024adobac9 8be.html.

CHAPTER 8

....

TECHNO-SECURITY SPACE INNOVATION

....

TAI MING CHEUNG AND YASUHITO FUKUSHIMA

INTRODUCTION

....

TECHNOLOGICAL innovation for national security needs, or what can be termed techno-security innovation, has been transformative in the development of the space sector from its genesis in World War II to the present day. But for the unremitting push and pull of military and broader national security interests and requirements, humankind's engagement with space would almost certainly have been slower, smaller, and simpler than what has actually taken place. The USSR and the United States each used rockets modified from ballistic missiles for their first satellite launches in the late 1950s. Also, one of the primary motivations for the United States to start launching satellites was to revolutionize the means of reconnaissance. As is well known, satellite positioning systems, which have become indispensable for social and economic activities, were originally developed for military purposes.

Despite the far-reaching impact of techno-security innovation on the space sector, there has been little systematic and detailed analysis of the nature and characteristics of techno-security innovation in the space domain. The classified nature of many defense and national security space programs has been a major impediment restricting access to critical information. Occasional officially sanctioned historical case studies offer insightful narratives (Dick and Launius 2006; 2007), but they fall far short of the rigorous scholarship that is needed to fill the gaping holes in this segment of the space security studies field.

This chapter is a modest effort to begin examining the nature and defining characteristics of space-centric techno-security innovation. We will begin by tapping into the general scholarship on defense and techno-security innovation to obtain relevant insights to inform analysis and definition of its space sub-variant. Next, we will identify a number of distinguishing characteristics of space-related techno-security innovation.

This will be followed by case studies of the pursuit and nature of techno-security space innovation in the United States and China, assessing the implications for their great power competition. The chapter concludes with a discussion of the policy implications deriving from the US-China techno-security competition.

THE DEFINITION, NATURE, AND CHARACTERISTICS OF TECHNO-SECURITY SPACE INNOVATION

A paucity of academic study of defense and national security related innovation in the space domain means that it is necessary to draw insights gleaned from related areas to provide a definition of techno-security space innovation and distinguish its nature and key characteristics. Of most relevance is the examination of defense innovation, which has received considerable academic and policy interest and attention. A mainstream definition of defense innovation is "the transformation of ideas and knowledge into new or improved products, processes, and services for military and dual-use applications" (Cheung, Mahnken, and Ross 2014, 17). This definition primarily concerns entities and activities engaged in defense and dual-use research, development, engineering, and acquisition.

Techno-security innovation is a new concept that incorporates defense innovation and extends the scope of coverage into a broader understanding of national security and how it interacts with the science, technology, and innovation domains (Cheung 2022). This would include, for example, intelligence, domestic security, and geo-strategic and geo-economic activities such as great power competition.

For the space sector, while defense-related innovation is a major engine of space-related innovation, there are also numerous national security related activities that are closely related to the military and defense spheres but have broader security and strategic applications. The most significant are intelligence-gathering, reconnaissance, and communications operations and geo-strategic competition (Johnson 2006, 481–548). Consequently, techno-security space innovation is a more accurate and inclusive label to capture this diverse array of security-centric activities taking place in the space domain. Techno-security space innovation can be defined as the transformation of ideas and knowledge into new or improved products, processes, and services in space activities for military, intelligence-gathering, and dual-use applications.

The nature and characteristics of defense innovation and techno-security innovation share many common attributes with techno-security space innovation, of which five of the most prominent will be discussed here. First, traditionally, the approach to innovation is state-led, and top-down, and this is important: it means that state institutions such as government and military agencies, state-affiliated research entities, and state-owned or state-backed enterprises have played a commanding role in the innovation process.

A second related feature is that this state-dominated, top-down development model is heavily shaped by the historical circumstances in which defense innovation and techno-security space innovation initially flourished, which was during the Cold War between the 1950s and early 1990s. In the twenty-first century, and especially since the mid-2010s, there have been intensifying efforts to pursue more decentralized market-driven, bottom-up approaches. The case study of the United States later in this chapter highlights the growing importance of the private commercial sector for techno-security space innovation (Moltz 2019, 78).

A third attribute that was heavily influenced by the Cold War environment is the techno-nationalist nature of techno-security space innovation. The development of defense and security-related space technological capabilities was overwhelmingly confined to national borders throughout the Cold War era with limited international cooperation. The external collaboration that did take place was confined to close allies. This strong techno-nationalist ethos has continued to exert a powerful influence in the post–Cold War era, although one bright spot of techno-globalist cooperation is the commercial space sector.

A fourth feature is that defense and security-driven innovation is resource intensive and requires extensive financial, human, material, and societal inputs that span multiple years. A major consequence of this costly burden is that the barriers to entry to defense, techno-security, and techno-security space innovation, especially in the development of disruptive capabilities, are very high and prohibitive to all but a handful of great powers, namely the United States and China, with Russia lagging well behind. An important caveat, though, is that if countries feel sufficiently threatened and are willing and able to make these investments, they could pursue such innovation in a way that focuses on more specific capabilities and functions. This has been the case with some middle powers, of which Japan is a shining example. Japan has long nurtured a robust space industry that can serve as the foundation for disruptive techno-security space innovation (Pekkanen and Kallender-Umezu 2010). In the face of growing threats from China and North Korea, the Japanese government in 2022 decided to construct an indigenous satellite constellation to detect and track moving targets in order to acquire the intelligence, surveillance, reconnaissance, and targeting capabilities needed to conduct counterstrike missions.

A fifth trait is that innovation in the defense, techno-security, and techno-security space domains has been mostly in the form of "big science" or "big engineering" programs. This means the organization of large-scale, highly complex, and advanced technological undertakings, which often required the establishment of special institutional mechanisms to mobilize and concentrate resources and expertise to carry out mega-scale projects. In the United States, for example, the national laboratory system was created during the Cold War for the development of the country's nuclear weapons capabilities. This has also been the case for techno-security space innovation, such as the development and management of US national security space assets with the creation of the National Reconnaissance Office (NRO).

INNOVATION SYSTEMS FRAMEWORK FOR EXAMINING TECHNO-SECURITY SPACE INNOVATION

Defense and techno-security innovation, whether in general or specifically in the space domain, is an extremely complex undertaking involving multiple sets of factors and dynamics. Efforts have been made in the study of defense innovation to develop a conceptual framework to identify and categorize an extensive array of factors that shapes how innovation takes place within the defense innovation ecosystem. This analytical approach is readily applicable for the techno-security space domain.

This framework is based upon looking at the innovation process through an innovation systems perspective derived from the concept of the national innovation system, which seeks to explain the variation in national styles of innovation (Nelson 1993). National innovation systems are defined as complex, constantly evolving ecosystems that include "all important economic, social, political, organizational, institutional and other factors that influence the development, diffusion and use of innovations" (Edquist 2006).

A defense innovation system is defined as "a network of organizations and institutions that interactively pursue science, technology, and innovation-related activities to further the development of defense interests and capabilities" (Cheung 2021, 4). Organizations are entities that are directly or indirectly involved in the innovation process, such as research institutions, universities, state agencies, military units, and defense enterprises. Institutions are institutional arrangements that determine the nature of interactions between organizations within the system, such as norms, routines, habits, established practices, and other rules of the road.

The techno-security space innovation system can be defined as the network of organizations and institutions that interactively pursue science, technology, and innovation-related activities to further the development of techno-security space interests and capabilities.

A study of the defense innovation conceptual framework by Tai Ming Cheung identifies seven categories of factors that play a prominent role in influencing the innovation process (Cheung 2021, 5–8). The first category covers powerful catalytic factors that produce conditions for enabling far-reaching change and disruption. These factors are normally external to the innovation system. Their intervention occurs at the highest and most influential levels of the ecosystem and can produce the conditions for enabling transformative change and disruption. Without these catalytic factors, the innovation system would find it very difficult, if not impossible, to engage in higher end innovation and would remain tied to routine modes of incremental innovation. In the techno-security space domain, the most obvious example of a catalytic event was the launch of the Soviet Sputnik spacecraft in 1957.

A second category is input factors. Material, financial, technological, and human talent are the most important contributions that flow into the innovation system. Resource allocations, technology transfers, high-quality scientific and engineering personnel, and civil-military integration are important input factors.

Institutional factors are a third key category. Institutions are rules, norms, routines, established practices, laws, and strategies that regulate the relations and interactions between actors (individuals and groups) within and outside of the innovation system. Rules can be formal (laws, regulations, and standards) or informal (routines, established practice, and common habits). Norms are shared prescriptions guiding conduct between participants within the system. Strategies are plans and guidance that are devised by actors within and outside the innovation system.

Organizational factors constitute a fourth set of key factors. This refers to formal structures with an explicit purpose. They include firms, state agencies, universities, research institutes, and a diverse array of organized units. Individuals are also counted within this category.

A fifth category involves networks and subsystems. Social, professional, virtual, and other types of networks allow actors, especially individuals, the means to connect with each other within and beyond innovation systems, both domestically and internationally. Networks provide effective channels of sharing information, often more quickly and comprehensively than traditional institutional linkages and they help to overcome barriers such as rigid compartmentalization.

A sixth category covers contextual factors, which are a diverse set of factors that influence and shape the overall innovation environment. Contextual determinants that exert strong influence include historical legacy, the domestic political environment, development levels, and the size of the country and its markets.

The final category is output factors that are responsible for determining the nature of the products and processes that come out of the innovation system. They include the production process, commercialization, the role of market forces such as marketing and sales considerations, and the influence of end-user demand.

THE PURSUIT OF TECHNO-SECURITY SPACE INNOVATION BY THE UNITED STATES AND CHINA IN THE ERA OF GREAT POWER COMPETITION

Great power competition between the United States and China began in earnest in the early 2010s. This is high-stakes zero-sum strategic rivalry between the United States and China over global leadership. The United States worries that its global dominance is under threat from China, while China aims to catch up and surpass the United States.

Both countries recognize that innovation is the key to winning this competition, and space is one of its major arenas. All space sectors, from civil to commercial to national security, are subject to this competition. In the national security space sector, the United States and China are pursuing innovation to gain superiority over each other. The following case studies provide a brief background for each country, focusing on the pursuit, evolution, and nature of their techno-security space innovation systems, which bears on their great power competition today.

THE US PURSUIT OF TECHNO-SECURITY SPACE INNOVATION

The techno-security space innovation that is being pursued by the United States in its great power competition with China is intended to be of a transformative nature. Its primary goal is to maintain US superiority in the space domain by significantly revamping the space architectures of the Department of Defense (DoD) and NRO with a central focus on ensuring resiliency. These far-reaching efforts by the United States were catalyzed by adverse changes in the global security environment that were perceived to be undermining US national security. Heightened attention by US national leaders to these security challenges helped to pave the way for the adoption of new initiatives.

The 1991 Gulf War prompted the United States to incorporate space capabilities into its conventional arsenal. Since then, space capabilities have played an important role in supporting US global military superiority, which is most visibly demonstrated by the operation of long-endurance unmanned aerial vehicles using satellite communications and precision strikes enabled by the Global Positioning System that have become synonymous with the US high-tech way of warfare.

In the mid-2010s, however, the US government became concerned that any US satellites up to geostationary orbit were beginning to be threatened by the growing counterspace capabilities of China and Russia. These fears were shared across the entire US national security space community and also all the way to the top of the national chain of command—to the president. (Hitchens and Johnson-Freese 2016, 3).

The primary way that the United States decided to address these rising threats was to improve the resilience of space capabilities. This saw provisions included in the 2011 National Security Space Strategy jointly submitted to the US Congress by Defense Secretary Robert Gates and National Intelligence Director James Clapper. However, it was the 2014 Strategic Portfolio Review (SPR) for Space, an initiative of senior DoD leaders Ashton Carter and Robert Work, that prompted the DoD to begin to more seriously prepare for a conflict in space (Hays 2016, 23; Weeden 2016, 83–84). Deputy Assistant Secretary of Defense for Space Policy Douglas Loverro, in congressional testimony in 2016 stated that through the SPR, DoD had developed a concept called Assured Space Operations. Also, NRO Director Betty Sapp, told the Subcommittee on

Strategic Forces of the House Armed Services Committee in 2015 that the organization was working on building a more resilient mission architecture.

THE EVOLVING US TECHNO-SECURITY SPACE INNOVATION SYSTEM

The US techno-security space innovation system has been undergoing far-reaching changes since the mid-2010s in its pursuit of disruptive innovation. The most distinctive feature of this change is that the DoD and NRO have sought to incorporate innovation by the private sector. In other words, they emphasize the input factor of civil-military integration through a bottom-up approach where the government follows the private sector in the pursuit of innovation.

This inclusive attitude has applied to defense innovation across the board since the mid-2010s. In a 2014 speech announcing the Defense Innovation Initiative (DII)—an initiative that was expected to develop into the Third Offset Strategy—Defense Secretary Chuck Hagel stated that it was well known that the DoD no longer had exclusive access to the most advanced technologies and could not promote or control the development of new technologies as it once did and that he would actively seek proposals from the private sector, including companies and research institutions that had little to do with the DoD.

The shift in the heart of the defense innovation process from the public to the private sector also applies to the space domain. This is most evident in the rise of NewSpace, especially as startups create innovative technologies and services (Moltz 2019, 79). SpaceX, which began offering launch services using reusable rockets and satellite internet services with a large constellation, is at the forefront of this trend. In his 2016 congressional testimony, Loverro stated that to ensure the resilience of space capabilities, the commercial/entrepreneurial space sector, which provides a natural and sustained space advantage for the United States, must be fully leveraged.

The NRO has also emphasized the importance of leveraging the commercial sector's capabilities. NRO Director Chris Scolese said in a public discussion in 2022 that "We kind of have a motto of 'buy what we can, build what we must'" and has indicated that he intends to make the best use of private sector technology and services.

Institutional factors are changing that are helping to promote techno-security innovation. Following the issuance of the DII memorandum in 2014, the DoD began formulating policies and strategies with great power competition, with China and Russia at the top of institutional priorities. According to Work, who oversaw DII as Deputy Defense Secretary, the initiative was a comprehensive effort aimed at maintaining and expanding US military superiority by renewing all aspects of national defense, including strategy, operations, organization, technology, and intelligence. The primary concern behind the DII was that China and Russia were strengthening their anti-access/area denial (A2/AD) capabilities, including those in the space domain. One capability that Hagel specifically cited in his DII speech was the development of new counterspace capabilities by Russia and China. The DoD became concerned that these Chinese and Russian efforts could hinder US power projection into East Asia, Europe, and other regions and reduce US military superiority. By positioning space as one of the top priorities of the DII, DoD sought to accelerate its efforts to improve its resilience of space capabilities.

In addition, the DoD has sought to expedite access to innovations by startups and other private sector firms that are outside of the traditional defense acquisition system and which represents a formidable barrier to entry. The Defense Innovation Unit (DIU) and the Space Development Agency (SDA), for example, utilize the Other Transaction Authority, which can be used for research, development, and prototyping (Eftimiades 2022, 21).

Organizational factors have also undergone significant changes since the mid-2010s. In 2015, as part of DII, Defense Secretary Carter established the Defense Innovation Unit Experimental (DIUx) to build relationships with the private sector technology community to more effectively leverage the innovation ecosystem in Silicon Valley and other innovation clusters around the United States. DIU, which dropped its experimental label in 2018 after being made permanent, has positioned space as a central part of its portfolio. In addition, Congress in 2018 created the position of Undersecretary of Defense for Research and Engineering in response to concerns about the decline of US defense technological superiority. That same year, the Office of the Undersecretary of Defense for Research and Engineering designated space as one of ten technology areas that should be prioritized for rapid modernization to a more defensible and resilient space posture.

The most far-reaching organizational innovation in the US military space domain took place in 2019 with the establishment of SDA, the US Space Command (USSPACECOM) that is the Unified Combatant Command with the space domain as its area of responsibility, and the US Space Force (USSF) that organizes, trains, and equips space forces. SDA defines itself as DoD's "constructive disruptor for space acquisition." SDA aims to be a fast follower of private sector innovation and to build the Proliferated Warfighter Space Architecture (PWSA), a proliferated low Earth orbit constellation of satellites that can be expected to be highly resilient to kinetic physical attacks. The USSF was created with the expectation of improving the space acquisition process. As part of this effort, USSF launched SpaceWERX in 2021 and began outreach to startups with innovative ideas and technologies by holding Space Force Pitch Days.

A noteworthy feature of the US techno-security space innovation system is the high mobility of human resources across the national security, civil, and commercial sectors. Extensive human interaction and connections exist across the DoD, the intelligence community, civil space agencies, national laboratories, Federally Funded Research and Development Centers, University Affiliated Research Centers, and industry. The fact that civilians outside the government have security clearances is a significant strength for the United States in promoting techno-security space innovation. For example, the

USSF Space Warfighting Analysis Center holds industry days exclusively for clearance holders to share information on the threats and challenges they face to draw innovative ideas from the private sector.

Finally, the US techno-security space innovation system is characterized by contextual factors such as its identity as the global leader in space development and the strong authority of Congress. But Congress has a mixed track record for supporting techno-security space innovation. On occasion, it has acted as a catalyst by creating new positions and increasing budgets, for example, increasing SDA's FY2022 budget by $550 million, allowing the launch of the Tranche 1 Tracking Layer, which are satellites able to detect and track missiles, to begin a year earlier than originally scheduled for 2026 (Albon 2022). But Congress has also been a major barrier to innovation by regularly delaying the passage of spending bills, which seriously impeded the work of DoD, NRO, and other actors in the techno-security space ecosystem.

CURRENT STATUS AND OUTLOOK FOR THE UNITED STATES

The DoD and NRO-led efforts since the 2010s to fundamentally improve the resilience of space capabilities by transforming their space architectures have not yet been accomplished. USSF Vice Chief of Space Operations David Thompson acknowledged in a 2021 interview that many of the space systems the USSF currently operates and is about to begin operating were not designed to operate under threat by capable peers (Cohen 2021). Also, in 2022, John Hyten, who had recently retired as vice chairman of the Joint Chiefs of Staff, noted that the USSF remained unsuccessful in reforming the space acquisition process (Erwin 2022).

Against this backdrop, USSF Chief of Space Operations John Raymond stated in 2022 that transitioning to a more resilient architecture will be a big focus area for USSF for the next decade (Hitchen 2022a). One test of whether disruptive innovation is close to becoming a reality will be whether the SDA will be able to build the PWSA as envisioned and scheduled. Assistant Secretary of the Air Force for Space Acquisition and Integration Frank Calvelli in 2022 praised the SDA's acquisition model and said the Space Systems Command could emulate this approach, pointing out that the current situation of taking seven years to develop a geostationary satellite was an old approach (Hitchen 2022b).

NRO identifies resilience as one of the five elements in its strategic priorities, and continues to work on building a "comprehensive, proliferated overhead architecture." The acquisition process used by the NRO is generally well regarded by Congress and is currently perhaps more able to promote disruptive innovation than the DoD. In December 2021, NRO Director Scolese revealed that two demonstration satellite programs that NRO was operating had taken less than three years from conceptual examination to launch.

Moreover, output factors are critical in translating this architectural shift into military superiority. In particular, warfighters such as USSPACECOM and US Indo-Pacific Command (INDOPACOM) must be able to utilize space capabilities effectively in their operations. To this end, developing new operational concepts will also play an essential role in the success or failure of techno-security space innovation. SDA intends to involve its future satellites in joint exercises, such as INDOPACOM's Northern Edge, and these efforts will contribute to the development of operational concepts.

China's Pursuit of Techno-Security Space Innovation

China's pursuit of techno-security space innovation is expansive and highly ambitious. It is committed to not only rapidly catching up with the United States in the space domain but also surpassing it and becoming the global technological champion. To achieve this audacious goal, China is emphasizing the importance of original innovation and not just the absorption-based development model that has been its traditional and highly successful approach to national and defense technological advancement.

Two catalytic factors have had a profound impact in shaping the nature and trajectory of China's techno-security space innovation. First is the highly influential role of Xi Jinping, China's powerful paramount leader since 2012, who has vigorously led the country's efforts to ramp up its techno-security development efforts in general and in the space sector specifically. When Xi took the reins of power, he put forward the goal of achieving national rejuvenation under his rule. A distinctive feature of Xi's thinking is his emphasis on the pursuit of security alongside economic development.

The second catalytic factor is China's dire threat assessment of the security environment that it faces, which has made the push to develop advanced techno-security capabilities a pressing national priority. This requirement can be traced to the 1990s starting with the 1991 Gulf War, which forced a far-reaching realization by the People's Liberation Army (PLA) that it was woefully unprepared to fight modern high-tech wars. This was followed by acute tensions across the Taiwan Strait from the mid-1990s as Taiwan sought to chart a more independent path toward statehood. The US bombing of the Chinese embassy in Belgrade in 1999 made clear to the Chinese leadership that the ever-present threat posed by the global reach of US military technology and power could be easily targeted against China without a credible deterrence. This severe techno-security threat led the Chinese authorities to urgently but quietly embark on a major build-up of strategic and advanced military capabilities so as to be able to establish an effective A2/AD posture, of which techno-security space assets such as anti-satellite weapons and reconnaissance satellites were a key priority. This negative threat assessment toward the United States has deepened and become more alarming with the onset of great power competition between the two countries since the early 2010s.

To achieve the rejuvenation of the Chinese nation and respond to a complex security environment, Xi initiated a significant reform of the PLA beginning in the mid-2010s. At the Nineteenth Party Congress in 2017, Xi set a goal of basically completing the PLA's modernization by 2035 and turning it into a world-class military force by mid-century that could compete with the United States.

Xi has emphasized the central role of innovation in his goal of transforming China's defense establishment. At the outset of his rule, Xi said that the world was in the middle of a new global military revolution that was developing "at a speed so fast, in a scope so wide, at a level so deep, and with an impact so great that it has rarely been witnessed since the end of World War II," which meant that China had to "advance with the times and vigorously promote military innovation" (Ding 2014). China's techno-security space innovation is an essential part of this effort.

At the same time, Xi has emphasized space development for both the military and civil sectors. Xi has talked about pursuing the dream of making China a premier space power, which is part of his broader dream of building a strong China. Xi's ideas were incorporated into white papers on China's space activities and programs that were published in 2016 and 2021. Both of these white papers list innovative development as the leading principle of the country's space activities.

China's Evolving Techno-Security Space Innovation System

The Chinese techno-security space innovation ecosystem is a state-led, top-down apparatus that is dominated by two state-owned corporations: China Aerospace Science and Technology Corporation (CASC) and China Aerospace Science and Industry Corporation (CASIC). These two powerfully connected firms have enjoyed an ironclad grip on the techno-security space research, development, and acquisition system since their establishment in the 1990s, and they are intent on maintaining their monopolistic control for the foreseeable future.

The Chinese authorities appear to be willing to allow new non-state actors into the space sector in order to promote innovation and competition, although so far this has been primarily confined to the commercial civilian domain. The number of Chinese commercial companies engaged in space development and utilization jumped from twenty-four in 2015 to over a hundred by 2019 (Curcio, Deville, and Lan 2021, 34), triggered by the Chinese government's decision in 2014 to open the space sector to private capital. As of 2020, the Chinese commercial space ecosystem is the second largest in the world, measured by fund-raising (Curcio, Deville, and Lan 2021, 30). Although the Chinese NewSpace sector is still in its infancy and lags far behind its US counterpart in innovative and technological capacity, it does have the potential to introduce new market-driven sources of competition that would be crucial in the long-term development of the Chinese techno-security space innovation system.

The Xi administration's focus on Military-Civil Fusion (MCF) is an essential input factor in China's techno-security space innovation system. Xi announced the elevation of MCF to a top national strategy in 2015. Xi toured the PLA Strategic Support Force (PLASSF) in 2016 and urged it to emphasize the integrated development of military and civilian capabilities.

In 2017, the State Council identified space as a priority area for MCF development alongside the cyber and maritime domains (Iwamoto and Yatsuzuka 2020, 69). In 2019, the State Administration for Science, Technology, and Industry for National Defense (SASTIND) and the Central Military Commission's Equipment Development Department (EDD) jointly published regulations for the manufacture, test flight, and launch of commercial rockets. The regulations stipulate that companies should be encouraged to make the best use of national resources in technological research, manufacturing equipment and facilities, and launch sites. Those efforts demonstrate that China's closed techno-security space innovation system is slowly being prized open to allow room for more competition.

MCF in the space domain has already begun to produce modest results. Among the ten major MCF achievements highlighted by the official Xinhua News Agency in 2015, one success story was a laser gyro that can be applied to the Long March rocket, the Beidou Navigation Satellite System, and the Gaofen-2 earth observation satellite (Iwamoto and Yatsuzuka 2020, 68). In addition, older generations of space technology are being declassified and allowed to be transferred from the military and state-owned enterprises to private companies. iSpace, founded in 2016, became the first Chinese private company to successfully launch a satellite on one of its rockets in 2019, with assistance from CASC, CASIC, EDD, and SASTIND.

The leading military actor in the techno-security innovation system is the PLASSF that was created as part of a far-reaching organizational reform of the PLA high command in 2015. The main entity within the PLASSF responsible for the space portfolio is the Space Systems Department, which took over and consolidated the space-related missions of the PLA General Armament Department and the PLA General Staff Department, which were abolished. The missions of the Space Systems Department are believed to include launch and support; satellite telemetry, tracking, and command; space information support; and attack and defense in space (Costello and McReynolds 2019, 455). The 2019 Defense White Paper notes that the PLASSF is responsible for testing new technologies, which suggests that the force also has a role in the research and development of space assets. Xi told the PLASSF in 2016 that it should strive to be the best in the world and stressed that "innovation is what we need most in building the strategic support force. Innovation is the fundamental solution." According to the 2019 Defense White Paper, the PLASSF is a "new type of combat force" as well as an "important driver for the growth of new combat capabilities."

Current Status and Outlook for China

China's efforts to become a leading techno-security space innovation power has been making concerted progress since the beginning of the twenty-first century, and the pace and trajectory are continuing to accelerate under the tenure of Xi Jinping. While China still lags behind the United States technologically, it has already surpassed Russia in the number of operational satellites, and there are ambitious plans for the launch of many more satellites in the coming years. In 2020, the National Development and Reform Commission designated satellite internet as the new infrastructure (Jones 2021). In response, the China Satellite Network Group was established in 2021, and a satellite constellation called Guowang, consisting of about thirteen thousand satellites, is planned.

China is also beginning to demonstrate its ability to succeed in the development of original new-to-the-world space technological capabilities for both civilian and military applications. In 2017, for example, China became the first country in the world to perform intercontinental quantum key delivery, with its experimental quantum science satellite Mozi transmitting encrypted data and delivering video. Such capability has profound military potential.

Meanwhile, as China expands its space capabilities, ensuring its resilience has become a significant challenge. China is well aware of this need to protect its space-based assets, as evidenced by the 2020 National Defense Law that clearly states space is a critical security domain. Substantial efforts to improve the resilience of space capabilities will be a crucial development priority for China in the years ahead, especially as great power competition with the United States in the space domain becomes more intense. Moreover, the PLA will need to develop the management of its operational space capabilities to be able to effectively utilize its rapidly growing space assets and achieve military superiority.

The Future of US-China Techno-Security Space Competition

As US-China competition in techno-security space innovation ramps up, who will emerge as the long-term winner is uncertain. While the United States in the early 2020s remains the undisputed leader in space innovation in the national security, civil, and commercial sectors, this continuing dominance is by no means assured. The DoD and NRO have yet to successfully achieve drastic transformations in space architectures. They also have not yet formulated operational concepts that can effectively utilize such architectures and link them to military superiority. As the US techno-security space community steps up its efforts to push ahead with this far-reaching transformative enterprise, concerns are being expressed by some leading US space strategists that China is improving its space capabilities faster than the United States (Olson et al. 2022, 11). China's MCF strategy is viewed as a means to robustly accelerate the growth of China's private space companies and provide a much-needed resource for the PLA.

The US-China competition over techno-security space innovation for military superiority is a long-distance marathon that will require an enormous outlay of resources and credible long-term commitment by political leaderships over decades. The winner will be the country that has the deepest pockets and the political stamina to stay in this contest the longest.

CONCLUSION

Techno-security innovation is a crucial but overlooked phenomenon in the study of the development of the space sector. This chapter represents a modest initial effort to put forward analytical insights and approaches drawn from the broader examination of defense innovation and techno-security innovation and applying them to the space domain. In doing so, a number of key characteristics of techno-security space innovation can be discerned. They include the catalytic role played by external threat perceptions and top-level leadership intervention, the powerful presence of self-reliant techno-nationalistic impulses driving decision-making, and the emphasis on civil-military integration.

These factors are readily apparent in the case studies looking at the US and Chinese techno-security space innovation systems, and their impact can be expected to grow more prominent as US-China great power techno-security competition intensifies. Both countries believe that civil-military integration is pivotal for gaining a competitive edge, although their approaches differ greatly. For the United States, the private sector is taking the lead role in driving innovation, while the government and defense sector appears content to be a fast follower. By contrast in China, top-down state-led development remains the dominant innovation model, although the emphasis on MCF means that there is growing attention and access being given to private actors. As much of space technology and service applications are inherently dual-use in nature, civil-military integration is likely to be an especially important source of innovation and technological advancement.

Several policy implications are worth pointing out. First, the increasingly adversarial nature of the US-China great power contest is likely to significantly accelerate the pace and scope of techno-security space innovation between the two countries, which will be one of the central arenas of competition. Whether other countries can afford the enormous cost and huge scale of effort to be able to keep up with the United States and China is debatable. So, the technological gap between the United States and China and other leading space powers such as Russia, Japan, and Europe could widen over the next several decades.

Second, and related to this first point, is whether the United States and China will each pursue techno-security innovation in general, and in space more specifically, on their own or cooperate closely with allies. Both the United States and China have traditionally been stridently techno-nationalist in the building of their technological capabilities for national security applications, but in an era of globalization, commercialization, and the widespread diffusion of knowledge and talent, it is far more difficult and costly for governments to pursue advanced technological projects within their own borders. As the United States steps up its techno-security competition with China, a core component of its strategy is to forge alliances and partnerships with key allies, in particular with its Five Eyes partners (United Kingdom, Australia, Canada, and New Zealand) along with France, Germany, and Japan. The principal external option for China is establishing closer military and technological cooperation with Russia, as well as with leading developing countries utilizing the framework of the Asia-Pacific Space Cooperation Organization and the Belt and Road Initiative. These countries could include Pakistan, Saudi Arabia, and Brazil.

The final issue is whether this adversarial US-China techno-security competition will eventually lead to a comprehensive bifurcation of the United States and Chinese technology orders and spill over into armed conflict. Deep distrust between the two countries, the widening imposition of export controls and other structural barriers to cooperation, and the pursuit of self-reliant policies suggest that the United States and China are spiraling toward a permanent rupturing of ties between their science, technology, and innovation systems. This has largely already occurred in the space domain. This slide into a Cold War–style techno-security stand-off though does not presage militarized conflict between the two countries. For this to occur, other catalytic factors, such as a major escalation in tensions across the Taiwan Strait, would need to be in place. For now, the techno-security competition between the United States and China remains largely peaceful in nature, although fraught with growing tensions and friction.

REFERENCES

Albon, Courtney. 2022. "How the Space Development Agency 'Could Have Died Any Number of Ways.'" *Defense News*. December 8, 2022. https://www.defensenews.com/battlefield-tech/space/2022/12/05/how-the-space-development-agency-could-have-died-any-number-of-ways/.

Curcio, Blaine, Jean Deville, and Chen Lan. 2021. February. "Commercial Space Ecosystem and Trends in China." *New Space in Asia: Experts Views on Space Policy and Business Trends in Asian Countries*. ESPI Report 77, 30–52. https://www.espi.or.at/wp-content/uploads/2022/06/ESPI-Public-Report-77-New-Space-in-Asia-Full-Report.pdf.

Costello, John, and Joe McReynolds. 2019. "China's Strategic Support Force: A Force for a New Era." In *Chairman Xi Remakes the PLA*, edited by Phillip C. Saunders, Arthur S. Ding, Andrew Scobell, Andrew N.D. Yang, and Joel Wuthnow, 437–515. Washington, DC: National Defense University Press. https://ndupress.ndu.edu/Portals/68/Documents/Books/Chairman-Xi/Chairman-Xi_Chapter-12.pdf?ver=2019-02-08-112005-803.

Cohen, Rachel S. 2021. "The Space Force Met Its 18-month Deadline to Get up and Running. Here's What's Next." *Air Force Times*. August 19, 2021. https://www.airforcetimes.com/news/your-air-force/2021/08/19/the-space-force-met-its-18-month-deadline-to-get-up-and-running-heres-whats-next/.

Cheung, Tai Ming. 2021. "A Conceptual Framework of Defence Innovation." *Journal of Strategic Studies* 44, no. 6: 775–801. https://doi.org/10.1080/01402390.2021.1939689.

Cheung, Tai Ming. 2022. *Innovate to Dominate: The Rise of the Chinese Techno-Security State.* Ithaca, NY: Cornell University Press.

Cheung, Tai Ming, Thomas G. Mahnken, and Andrew L. Ross. 2014. "Frameworks for Analyzing Chinese Defense and Military Innovation." In *Forging China's Military Might: A New Framework for Assessing Innovation*, edited by Tai Ming Cheung, 15–46. Baltimore, MD: Johns Hopkins University Press.

Ding, Feng, 2014. "Xi Jinping Addresses Politburo 17th Collective Study Session, Emphasizes Need to Accurately Grasp New Trends in the World's Military Development, Advance with the Times to Vigorously Promote Military Innovation." *Xinhua News Agency*. August 30, 2014. http://www.xinhuanet.com//politics/2014-08/30/c_1112294869.htm.

Dick, Steven J., and Roger D. Launius, eds. 2006. *Critical Issues in the History of Spaceflight*. Washington, DC: National Aeronautics and Space Administration.

Dick, Steven J., and Roger D. Launius, eds. 2007. *Societal Impact of Spaceflight*. Washington, DC: National Aeronautics and Space Administration.

Edquist, Charles. 2006. "Systems of Innovation: Perspectives and Challenges." In *The Oxford Handbook of Innovation*, edited by Jan Fagerberg, David C. Mowery, and Richard R. Nelson, 181–208. Oxford: Oxford University Press.

Eftimiades, Nicholas. 2022. May. "Small Satellites: The Implications for National Security." Atlantic Council, 1–35. https://www.atlanticcouncil.org/wp-content/uploads/2022/05/Small_satellites-Implications_for_national_security.pdf.

Erwin, Sandra. 2022. "Hyten: Space Force 'Hasn't Cracked the Code' on Faster Acquisitions." *SpaceNews*. July 11, 2022. https://spacenews.com/hyten-space-force-hasnt-cracked-the-code-on-faster-acquisitions/.

Hays, Peter L. 2016. July. "United States Military Uses of Space: Issues and Challenges." *Space Security: Trends and Challenges*: 9–26.

Hitchens, Theresa. 2022a. "Space Force's Top Priority for Next Decade: Resiliency, Says CSO Raymond." *Breaking Defense*. March 3, 2022. https://breakingdefense.com/2022/03/space-forces-top-priority-for-next-decade-resiliency-says-cso-raymond/.

Hitchens, Theresa. 2022b. "SDA a 'Model' that Could Shake up All Space Acquisition: Calvelli." *Breaking Defense*. September 20, 2022. https://breakingdefense.com/2022/09/sda-a-model-that-could-shake-up-all-space-acquisition-calvelli/.

Hitchens, Theresa, and Joan Johnson-Freese. 2016. "Toward a New National Security Space Strategy: Time for a Strategic Rebalancing." Atlantic Council Strategy Paper No. 5, 1–60. https://www.atlanticcouncil.org/wp-content/uploads/2015/08/AC_StrategyPapers_No5_Space_WEB1.pdf.

Iwamoto, Hiroshi, and Masaaki Yatsuzuka. 2020. November. "China's Military-Civil Fusion Strategy." *China's Military Strategy in the New Era*. NIDS China Security Report 2021, 61–81. http://www.nids.mod.go.jp/publication/chinareport/pdf/china_report_EN_web_2021_A01.pdf.

Jones, Andrew. 2021. "China Establishes Company to Build Satellite Broadband Megaconstellation." *SpaceNews*. May 26, 2021. https://spacenews.com/china-establishes-company-to-build-satellite-broadband-megaconstellation/.

Johnson, Stephen B. 2006. "The History and Historiography of National Security Space." In *Critical Issues in the History of Spaceflight*, edited by Steven J. Dick and Roger D. Launius, 481–548. Washington, DC: National Aeronautics and Space Administration.

Moltz, James Clay. 2019. "The Changing Dynamics of Twenty-First Century Space Power." *Journal of Strategic Security* 12, no. 1: 15–43. https://doi.org/10.5038/1944-0472.12.1.1729.

Nelson, Richard R., ed. 1993. *National Innovation Systems: A Comparative Analysis*. New York: Oxford University Press.

Olson, John M., Steven J. Butow, Eric Felt, and Thomas Cooley. 2022. August. "State of the Space Industrial Base BASE 2022: Winning the New Space Race for Sustainability, Prosperity and the Planet." https://assets.ctfassets.net/3nanhbfkropc/6L5409bpVlnVyu2I I5FOFnc/7595c 4909616df92372a1d31be609625/State_of_the_Space_Industrial_Base_2022_Report.pdf.

Pekkanen, Saadia, and Paul Kallender-Umezu. 2010. *In Defense of Japan: From the Market to the Military in Space Policy*. Stanford, CA: Stanford University Press.

Weeden, Brian. 2016. July. "U.S. Policy, Programs, and Diplomatic Initiatives in Response to Space Debris and Counterspace Threats." *Space Security: Trends and Challenges*: 77–89.

CHAPTER 9

....

THE INTERPLAY OF DOMESTIC POLICY AND INTERNATIONAL SPACE SECURITY

....

XIAODAN WU

The Importance of Domestic Policy for Space Security

....

THE dawning of the space era significantly and eternally altered the international security environment by introducing a new domain, ripe with possibility and peril. Outer space is an area with mixed sovereignty and competitive national interests. States' perception of space security in the form of domestic policy and their interplay at the international level are a powerful shaping force for space security.

National space policies need to fit within a nation's domestic and foreign policy, as well as its overall development goals and priorities. A thorough assessment of national interests and how they interact at the international level amid great power competition is necessary to explain the puzzle pieces of space security. This chapter follows a state-centric approach, because states are the primary actors of space activities despite the recent diversity trend, and takes into consideration a range of interests, elements, and actors when formulating domestic policies. The focus is space powers because they are the primary shaping force in governance and cooperation, although the dynamics of space security has expanded to include more states. The chapter begins with a focus on the multifaceted dimension of national interests and irrelevant factors; the role of various actors provides theoretical insights into why and who might fashion states' understanding of space security. It then analyzes states competition and cooperation interplay under the guidance of domestic policies and the prospect of space security affected by domestic politics.

The Expansion of National Interests in Space Security

The Multifaceted Dimensions of National Interests

As space system are integrated and used for various purposes, vital national interests started with a focus on the military, scientific and technological, and political dimensions and are now extending to societal concerns, economic gains, and commercial benefit (Sheehan 2015). The multifaceted nature of national interests is owing to the dual-use nature of outer space and the expanding scope of the term security entailed by its unique security dynamics.

First, space technologies have been viewed as an integral and increasingly strategic component for securing national security and the global strength to influence space security. The major reason for the emergence of space programs is the states' perception of technology's importance to their national security. All spacefaring states recognize and follow the same methodology: technological determinism promoting space nationalism.

Second, the inception and development of space activities are closely connected to military capability and national defense. All countries recognize the immense value of military space assets as the apex of national security, and all the industrially advanced states eagerly pursue their own space infrastructures (Dolman 2002, 61). The dual-use nature of space technology makes it unrealistic to compel the abandonment of space technology that could be used as a weapon or impossible to designate the use of outer space for civilian purposes only. Ideas and actions for space weapons have risen and fallen, suggesting the powerful continuing forces within space powers responding to perceived threats. The increasing dependence on space and its assets for military operations make the states realize their vulnerabilities in space. In reverse, this strengthens the need for space defenses to protect access and the freedom to operate in space (Morgan 2010).

Third, the political dimension could accommodate all the other dimensions in its broadest sense. But its primary connotation is linked to the fact that space accomplishments are a considerable source of national pride and a central measure of national power and international status. Part of states' motivation to enter new frontiers has to do with national prestige, such as technology leadership implications, and its perceived momentum as a power. Countries made significant investments in space activities when there appeared no real business rationale to achieve a world first record or beat competitors. Human spaceflight is the ultimate brass ring for prestige (Harrison 2013, 127). The technology leadership connotations that accrue with spaceflight are enough to override opposition, as happened in the United States and China. There have been economic critiques of manned spaceflights during the construction process of China's space station. Previously, opposition had focused on the appropriateness of this ambitious endeavor owing to the lack of necessary resources. Currently, however, objections are based on the advantages of artificial intelligence whereby risks and cost could be decreased substantially and the available resources could rather be used for the improvement of people's livelihood. The recent "first" satellites of some states are claimed for civilian and commercial use only. This indicates a change in the historical focus of space industry, but the inherent dual-use nature ensures its military and political significance (Selding 2016).

Fourth, space assets and systems, key enablers for a wide variety of applications, have become critical infrastructure for the functioning of modern societies (Georgescu 2020). Nearly all states harness the benefits of space operational application services for communications, transportation, financial networks, environment monitoring, resource management scientific exploration, and more. Space is essentially the main global way of collecting, transmitting, and distributing information, making a decisive contribution to the ability to achieve national security with a holistic approach (Adriaensen 2020).

After the initial phase of accessibility, the next logical advance is economic gain. Space is beginning to offer commercial opportunities. NewSpace, or more broadly, commercial space, is rapidly outpacing traditional government in innovation, operations, markets, and investment. New uses and users of outer space are changing the military dominated nature of space activities. Commercial companies are pressing the limits on space security in traditional areas, such as satellite launching and servicing, and highlighting the need for strengthening space security in new areas, such as asteroid and lunar exploitation (Johnson-Freese 2017, 158).

Unbounded and Endless National Interests

A range of national interests are intertwined in outer space. The dual-use nature of space activities renders it impossible to tell which factor dominates or matters in a specific program. Most countries do not have the financial or industrial luxury of having a civil space program separate from a military one and thus consider dual-use technology development as a good return on government investment (Johnson-Freese 2017, 41). Countries usually adopt a comprehensive and layered strategy toward achieving their goals of space security rather than one focused on the military dimension (Krepon 2003, 3). There is no clear distinction between military and civilian use of outer space but a close link between them, in that the development of one is viewed as requiring the simultaneous expansion of the other to effectively serve national security (Lupton 1998, 5).

National considerations for space security could be influenced and defined by seemingly trivial and irrelevant factors far beyond space industry. The biggest challenge posed to the United States by China's space program was considered to be its demographics: the youngest cadre of space scientists and engineers of any space power (Harvey 2004, 237; Moltz 2019, 290). Another example is that it was the national mentality of long-standing craving for scientific and technical self-sufficiency driving China's growth into a space power (Johnson-Freese 2006; Stroikos 2018). Since its defeat in the First Opium War (1839–1842), successive generations of intellectuals, reformers, and revolutionaries tied the survival of Chinese civilization to the ability to understand science and apply technology. From the outset of the People's Republic of China in 1949, both government and ordinary people have viewed self-reliance as essential to reducing the country's vulnerability to external aggression and pressure. This is the deep-rooted reason for the consistent and wide support for designating the highest priority to the space program. The legal and policy constraints based on the political considerations of Western countries substantially limits China's space cooperation; meaningful events include its exclusion from the International Space Station (ISS), the abortion of the Sino-EU Galileo project, and the adoption of the US cooperation-banning bill toward China since 2011. This echoed China's initial intention not to repeat the brutal, ravaging experience of colonialism and imperialism and acted as a spur in its determination to construct Tiangong Station, complete the Beidou navigation system (BDS), and advance the lunar and Mars exploration program.

ACTORS AFFECTING POLICYMAKING DISCOURSE

Spacefaring nations and some nations aiming at achieving this status have their own national space policy, which provide an original source of information about their national interests in and understanding of space security. A comparison between China and the United States, two space powers vastly different in major aspects of the development model and governance mechanisms, demonstrates who and what affects space policymaking discourse.

Diverse Actors

National policy formulation is supported by an array of actors, including the executive, the legislature, and military organs within the state-government structure and the external lobbyists, such as industrial enterprises and epistemic communities. US government agencies and offices with a role in national security have expanded from inner policymakers to entire bureaucracies, and the sheer numbers of individuals, institutions, organizations, bureaucracies and companies with a vested interest in space security continues to expand into to a huge complex (Johnson-Freese 2017, 105). China's space industry extends from governmental and military organs to research and production units in enterprises, universities, and research institutions. They have formed a complicated structure and relationship in strategy formulation, policy adoption, and decision-making.

Much of policymaking is dependent on the opinions and outlook of experts for projections and solutions to problems. No policymakers can be expected to be functionally knowledgeable on space issues. Actions or inactions of national leaders are the result of decisions in the face of different groups of interests pushing for particular technologies or activities and advocating for a varied focus on and priority of space security. Thus, the epistemic communities, within and without the state-government structure, are important influencers in many ways (Haas 1992). Scientific experts and organizations are relied upon to assist, from program design and policy drafting to the delicate negotiations between states and international cooperation. In China, scientists are the initiators, designers, researchers, and contractors of space programs. They are influential throughout the entire process of the space program, from seizing the initiative to proposing a program to feasibility studies for policy approval, and from its initiation to its completion, while usually paving the way forward for the next one.

Non-governmental Organizations (NGOs) have come to have a large impact on the policymaking discourse (Reibaldi 2015). The participation of think tank organs, government sponsored or not, has been a solid practice in US national policy formulation. The government-sponsored study of space policy by the Rand Corporation can be traced back to 1946. Commercial companies, especially in the United States, are beginning to play central roles in the process of forging a state's perception of space security. In China, two state-owned enterprises—China Aerospace Science and Industry Corporation (CASIC) and China Aerospace Science and Technology Corporation (CASTC)—are the backbone of space capacities and programs. The China National Space Administration (CNSA) was established in 1993 within the China Aerospace Industry Corporation (the former CASTC), before it was assigned as an internal division of the Commission of Science, Technology and Industry for National Defense (COSTIND) in 1998. Their (original) administrative responsibilities and functions afforded them power in policy drafting. Some of their documents are treated as quasi-official policy, such as the long-term development roadmap for a space transportation system issued by CASTC in 2017.

Actors' Interaction in Policymaking Discourse

All the actors interact within a state's space governance mechanism. Their roles are largely influenced by the political climate and, ultimately, are determined by a state's development model of space activities: market-oriented or government dominated.

Beginning with President Eisenhower, every US administration has had its space policy. There is continuity and consistency verifying the core elements of US space security. Each policy has stressed international cooperation and peaceful intention, while every policy has reserved the right of self-defense in space (Dolman 2020). There is divergence reflecting the presidents' personal thinking on space security, including their character and ideational frame. Since 2001, all the administrations emphasize the new space security threats and issues brought forth by technological development and actor expansion and diversification, but their approaches are different. The Obama administration adopted a more international approach, with more active engagement in global discussion, and a refocus on global cooperation; the space policies of the Bush and Trump administrations reflected a nationalist approach and a more unilateral tone.

The US process for formulating national policy is the most open and mature, providing for observable interactions among a full range of participants and conceptualizing different interests and concerns. It basically facilitates the interaction of a top-down centralized governance structure and bottom-up commercial-led development. The actors involved and their roles verify the change in political climate and development priority. During the Cold War, diplomats pushing for cooperative outcomes held little sway and scientists doubting the sagacity of ambitious space weapons efforts faced opposition from non-experts with more political clout (Moltz 2019, 121). It was not surprising that the military had played a prominent role. In the 1950s and 1960s, the US Air Force proposed—and the United States adopted—an ad hoc approach and reactive posture to the creation of space treaties, through coordination with the president, the Department of Defense, the State Department, and the National Space Council (Goldsen 1959; Terrill, 1999). Commercial space created a different mode of actor interactions. Another consistency in space policies since the 1980s is promoting and encouraging the development of commercial space, which has been echoed by the US Congress's efforts to stimulate a start-up sector through easing regulations and opening new fields previously blocked by legislation and national security concerns. Since 2010, the relevant policy documents have unfolded a steady elevation of the importance of commerce, including the progression of policy and law making with respect to space resources. The space policy documents of the Trump administration consistently repeated the linkage of economy and partnership with the commercial sector. The emphasis of the US lunar program is not inspiration or exploration but resource exploitation for economic advantage (Goswami 2020, 122). The clear intent to exploit space resources materialized in the private sector with the formation of Planetary Resources in 2012, Deep Space Industries in 2013, and other companies. In 2015, urged by these companies, free-market supporters in Congress passed the Commercial Space Launch Competitiveness Act, protecting US citizens' property rights in exploration and recovery of space resources. It was "a major victory for the private space community," which thereby gained national legitimacy (Goswami 2020, 140).

The fundamental feature of the planned economy in China's space activities originated in the 1950s, a result of concentrating nationwide effort and resources on this key undertaking (Wu 2018). This pragmatic choice has proved effective in supporting and developing space programs beyond China's capabilities. Within this development model, transparency is not a concern. The involvement of policy drafters and approving entities and their working procedures are not clear. Very limited information can be found on the small groups leading in the space domain, so little is known on how they are selected and organized. According to the scarce official information available, a leading group for the coordination of space planning was formed in 1989 including high-level, key stakeholders from the scientific community, enterprises, and military and governmental organs. A similar joint leading group was established in 2004 for the lunar exploration program, and there is news about a similar arrangement for human spaceflight, Earth observation satellites, and heavy-lift launch vehicles. As in the White Papers series on space activities, Chinese space policy can be characterized as that of a planned economy with intrinsic opacity. These papers are nominal statements of policy, but are primarily focused on accomplishments and goals, and not how the government and military use or plan to use space, nor on the organizations that are charged with policy implementation (Pollpeter et al. 2015).

There is no visible, personal touch of national leaders in these policy documents. But recent legislative work has revealed President Xi Jinping's understanding of space security, which is marked by an emphasis on space security in a more assertive tone. China never officially admits the existence of military space activities and satellites for military purposes, although safeguarding space security interests has been listed as one of the aims of national defense in its White Papers on National Defense. In 2014, President Xi Jinping put forward the holistic concept as the guiding principle of national security strategy. Article 32 of the 2015 National Security law clarified space security as a constituent element in the holistic concept and the role of space capacity was emphasized in ensuring national security. A new provision in the Law on National Defense, as revised in 2020, further stipulates that necessary measures shall be taken to preserve China's interests in outer space. This implies the possibility of taking military measures in outer space.

The commercial-led development approach taken in other nations has been inspirational for China (Long 2012; Zhang 2015; Luo, 2017; Li 2018; Zhao 2019). Since 2014, a number of policy documents lay out a more market-oriented approach (Chinese State Council 2014; Chinese National Development and Reform Commission 2015; Chinese State Council 2017). Nowadays, more than a hundred companies are active in offering space products and services, ranging from satellite manufacturing and orbital launches to satellite data and applications (Nie 2020). Commercial space is at an initial phase of development, and the new companies are barely influential in the policymaking discourse.

How the Domestic Policy Interplay Shapes Space Security

This section sets out the main constructs that affect domestic policymaking.

The Interplay Paradigm: Competition and Cooperation

An intriguing dilemma in outer space is the thematic paradox of cooperation born of competition (Dolman 2002, 168). Sovereign states strive to preserve their autonomy and self-defense ability, but also tend to self-restrain and cooperate. It is difficult to isolate a single case of cooperation without finding a basis in competition and conflict. The interplay of competition and cooperation sets the stage for dialogue and sustains the overall direction of international space security.

The motivation for cooperation is essential to this interplay toward space security. All countries have a vested interest in sustaining the space environment and this is the commonality all countries must build on (Johnson-Freese 2017, x). The primary motivation is the interdependent and mutual vulnerable nature of space environment, which could result in pragmatic policy changes to limit competition (Moltz 2019, 60). Space security is a cooperative endeavor to achieve a shared benefit and a logical approach for states who wish to co-exist (West 2020). Cooperation is critical for states to learn and understand each other, including their decision-making processes, institutional policies and operating procedures, political reasoning and constraints. Engagement on a regular and consistent basis is a prerequisite for opportunities to moderate their competition, promote mutual trust capable of transcending political pressures, and create interests that could inhibit aggressive and reckless behavior (Keohane 1984). Advancing scientific research and providing access to and benefits from space activities and applications provide another impetus to cooperate (Basiuk 1977, 7; Hoffmann 1982, 28).

Space activities have initiated a journey into a global consciousness through inspiring and consolidating humanity unity and ecological interconnectivity (Dolman 2002, 83). Space activities have given visual content to a previously vague abstraction: everyone can see the earth whole in its fragility and loneliness (Kranzberg 1985, 13; Deudney 1983, 5). The term "mankind" is frequently used in space treaties, as in that the exploration and use of outer space shall be the "province of all mankind," astronauts shall be regarded as "envoys of mankind" in the Outer Space Treaty, and the moon and its resources are the "common heritage of mankind" in the Moon Agreement. These expressions might seem ostensible, overridden by, or contrary to state practice. However, this collective consciousness and its uniting force cannot be ignored in maintaining space security. There are stable pattern of selective cooperation focusing on deepening military alliances and strategic partnerships. There are also truly global efforts to make space a benefit for mankind. UN General Assembly Resolutions have repeatedly stressed that assisting in bridging down the inequality of national capability could strengthen space security. GPS, GLONASS, and BDS comprise the worldwide radio navigation system used by the International Maritime Organization. A building block toward the UN 2030 agenda for sustainable development is making satellite applications available to all countries.

Interplay Examples and Uncertain Result

Instantiation examination of US-Soviet relations during the Cold War and Sino-US relation in the twenty-first century provides crucial clues to understanding the interplay among states and its results.

During the Cold War, the US-Soviet relationship shaped the space security environment, evolving from military-led, competitive approaches to negotiated, cooperative approaches (Moltz 2019, 12). Support of cooperative space security and continued restraints on deployed weapons remained engrained in enough critical nodes of power within both the US and Soviet governments, despite the occasional rise of space security concerns in the form of renewed weaponry testing or strategic defense initiatives (176). Following the devastating effect of nuclear testing in space and the sobering impact of the Cuban Missile Crisis, the two governments recognized the need to push past domestic obstacles to more meaningful space cooperation in the 1960s. The conclusion of the 1967 Outer Space Treaty marked a singular departure from unilateralist policies on both sides and a clear effort to build an institutionalized and multilateral framework for space security. A gradual norm of noninterference with each other's reconnaissance and early-warning satellites began to emerge by the late 1960s, institutionalized in the Anti-Ballistic Missile Treaty and the first Strategic Arms Limitation Agreement of 1972. Their bilateral and multilateral negotiations was evidence of their recognition of responsibility toward each other and the international community to not extend the arms race into outer space. They created a legacy of cooperation to limit competition, which established the political prerequisites for new projects in the post–Cold War period, such as the long-term integration of manned programs in the ISS.

The United States has viewed China as a near-peer competitor (Hays 2020), a strategic competitor (the 2017 National Security Strategy and the 2018 National Defense Strategy), and even a rival (Goldstein 2015, 349) since the launch of its first taikonaut in 2003. The spokespersons of China's Ministry of Foreign Affairs denied the existence of a race and any rivalry and refuted the designation of China as a competitor as inaccurate and untenable. Their claim was that the United States exaggerates the threat posed by China to adopt an increasingly aggressive strategy and brings a Cold War mentality to outer space by emphasizing its military aspects. Academic commentary focuses on how to avoid a space race and Thucydides' trap through Sino-US engagement and cooperation (Guo 2018; Huang 2019; Li, 2021). The lack of mutual confidence is due to a mixture of reasons, including their long-existing ideological prejudice and the low-level transparency of China's space activities (Wu 2015). Space cooperation between the two countries has been tortuous and minimal since the 1980s and has reduced to almost zero since 2011. Competition remains within the negotiated frameworks, except for the indirect confrontation in the ASAT tests, but there is a strengthening trend. China's 2007 ASAT test triggered strong objections and criticism worldwide, mainly for two reasons: an increase in space debris in near Earth orbit and lack of information from the Chinese government (Marchisio 2009). This was answered by the United States' shooting down of its re-entering satellite in 2008 without generating debris and providing advance briefing to foreign governments.

The net result of cooperation is the limitation of competition, mostly through self-restraint to redirect efforts into safer and more sustainable access to and uses of outer space. Spacefaring nations have viewed restraint as the best option for maintaining the vital interest of stability in space, and they have exercised certain strategic restraints to reduce impacts on space security (Johnson-Freese 2017, 8). Usually, triggering events can promote changes in the definitions of national security, stimulate the process of learning, and shift intentions and behavior. However, this "learning against one's will" highlights the fragility of space security and its dependence on political relationships and climates (Moltz 2019, 326).

Increasing ASAT capacity demonstrates the uncertainty in the interplay between competition and cooperation. Space nationalism arises when there are overriding security fears and unfamiliarity with existing norms (Moltz 2019, 175). This applies to both the 1985 US test and the 2007 Chinese test. As for self-restraint, the US Air Force canceled the ASAT test program in 1988 (Hays 2002, 111). China altered its behavior as a result of widespread international pressure, and did not repeat the debris-producing test. The spin-off effect of the US 1985 test and China's 2007 test has been a changed mindset about the space environment, which activated and focused attention on the debris problem and helped to increase and rally collective awareness and cooperation to address the debris threat. The former led to a tacit norm of no destructive ASAT testing—not violated from 1985 to 2007—and initiated NASA's process of internationalizing debris mitigation and management principles as a consistent cooperation practice toward improving collective security. The latter mobilized and unified the space community, accelerating the approval of the long-awaited UNCOPUOS Space Debris Mitigation Guidelines in 2007. How to prevent the reoccurrence of kinetic destruction of spacecraft is a basic requirement of space security; nonetheless, there is no legal prohibition. The 2007 and 2008 tests set some precedent: they are permissible under certain circumstances, with mitigation of debris production, and the bar raised for international transparency (Marchisio 2009). But this was neither evenly nor entirely followed during the further tests of India and Russia in 2019, 2020, and 2021.

Increasing Intensity and Complexity of Interplay

Space power competition and the democratization of space (Baiocchi 2015) amid the expansion of national interests and the enlargement of the space industry are increasing the intensity and complexity of interplay. There is renewed need to strengthen the role of cooperation as a binding component of space security to reduce uncertainty and the potential for conflict (Pankova 2021).

In recent years, great power competition in US policy has become an ever-increasing nexus of national security focus, and space has reemerged as a central arena, primarily with China and Russia as competitors. "Competition" means a return to state powers using various tools not to support a cooperative system but to seek control and beset each other (Maclennan 2020). Certain interplay entails a danger that competition may turn into confrontation. First, there is a rising tide of global space nationalism and militarism in response to mutual distrust and perceptions of nefarious intent in space (Johnson-Freese 2017, x). Recent efforts to reorganize and modernize in the military field demonstrate both the utility and integration of space assets into operational use. China, France,

Japan, and India have initiated and the United States and Russia have resumed active consideration of space-based, anti-ballistic missile defenses, anti-satellite weapons tests, and the establishment of space military forces. The Russian Space Force was established in 1992, with responsibility for construction and operation of military space infrastructure, and its amalgamation with the air force in 2015 created the Aerospace Force (VKS). The US Space Force was re-established in 2019, tasked with war-fighting missions and operations in and from space. This was followed by the creation of the French Space Command and the establishment of the Japanese space force. The possibility of outer space being a war-fighting domain is becoming real, such assertions being made by the United States, NATO, Russia, France, the United Kingdom, and India.

In addition, divergence between space powers and other states has stalled and undermined international negotiated security, while new actors and unconventional utilization challenge the boundaries of traditional governance regimes and old legal frameworks. Making progress is increasingly difficult and complicated. The relative utility of bottom-up versus top-down approaches to international negotiation in the prevention of arms race in outer space (PAROS) has distracted from the core issue, the compatibility and complementarity of these approaches. The United States tends to favor the development of transparency and confidence building measures (TCBMs) and has been resolute in its objections to a legally binding treaty. China and Russia advance a treaty proposal, the draft Treaty on the Prevention of the Placement of Weapons in Outer Space, the Threat or Use of Force against Outer Space Objects (PPWT), a highly structured proposal that could serve as a building block for a security regime (Proposals on Treaty 2014; Jaramillo 2009). The United States criticized its shortcomings vigorously in detail (Rocca 2008), while Russia and China have shown a certain sincerity in reaching a compromise. China's openness to a provision banning ground-based, anti-satellite weapons has been ignored, while the United States has repeatedly stressed the need to address the issue of ASAT tests (Buck 2014). Meanwhile, the space powers will be actual competitors in their lunar exploration efforts, the US Artemis program versus the Chinese International Lunar Research Station, with the addition of a Russian partnership. In 2021, international negotiations began in UNCOPUOS to plug loopholes in space treaties regarding resource exploitation and utilization. This will require unusual political attention, based on their focus on lunar exploitation for political or economic gains, and the experience of negotiating for seabed resources during the Third UN Conference on the Law of the Sea (Wu 2019).

In parallel, less space competent nations are more concerned about space security, evidenced by the enlargement of COPUOS member states and their statements and votes within the UN framework. They are increasingly important in agreeing on security-enhancing measures. China's concept of "a community of shared future for mankind" could be helpful in negotiating new norms or providing a revolutionary interpretation of existing treaties (Statement by Ambassador Shi Zhongjun 2018) and has been incorporated into several UN General Assembly resolutions on PAROS since 2017. Together with opening its space station and lunar station to all countries instead of certain partners, this narrative has gained China success in space diplomacy (Pollpeter

2020). Despite criticism of China's motivation by the United States (Vote Explanation 2018), this concept is suitable for space activities; it could be constructive in the debate over international space governance and could strengthen cooperation for the benefit of mankind.

The interplay between competition and cooperation could create necessary and sufficient conditions for the sustainable development of space security. Currently, the key is improving its organizational structure, including the principles, the strategy, the organization form, and the mechanisms of international cooperation to foster dialogue and unite all the major players to move in the same direction under the primary objective of co-existence. Space power cooperation will proceed mainly between blocs: the United States and its allies, and China and Russia cooperation. The United States is trying to build a US-centric system of space relations on the basis of bilateral cooperation. China and Russia are open to cooperation with the BRICS countries, ESA, or the United States itself. Sino-American relations are at a crossroads between cooperation or discord and may be constructive or destructive to international space security. A bilateral or a tripartite dialogue should be launched to overcome the imbalance in competition and cooperation.

REFERENCES

Adriaensen, Maarten. 2020. "Supporting Services for Security and Defense." In *Handbook of Space Security: Policies, Applications and Programs*, edited by Kai-Uwe Schrogl, 701–702. 2nd ed. New York: Springer.

Baiocchi, Dave, and William Welser IV. 2015. "The Democratization of Space." *Foreign Affairs* 94, no. 3: 98–104.

Basiuk, Victor. 1977. *Technology, World Politics, and American Policy*. New York: Columbia University Press.

Buck, Christopher L. 2014. October 27. Statement by the Delegation of the United States of America at the UNGA First Committee, Thematic Discussion on Disarmament Aspects of Outer Space.

Chinese National Development and Reform Commission. 2015. The Medium and Long-term Plan for the Development of Civil Space Infrastructure.

Chinese State Council, 2014. The Guiding Opinions on Innovating the Investment and Financing Mechanism for the Key Fields and Encouraging Social Investment No. 60. 2014.

Chinese State Council, 2017. The Guidelines on Deepening Civil-Military Integration in Science and Technology and Industry for National Defense.

Deudney, Daniel. 1983. *Whole Earth Security: A Geopolitics of Peace*. Washington, DC: World Watch Institute.

Dolman, Everett C. 2002. *Astropolitik: Classical Geopolitics in the Space Age*. London: Frank Cass.

Dolman, Everett C. 2020. "War, Policy and Space Power: US Space Security Priorities." In *Handbook of Space Security: Policies, Applications and Programs*, edited by Kai-Uwe Schrogl, 368–79. 2nd ed. Switzerland: Springer.

Goldsen, Joseph M. 1959. *International Political Implications of Activities in Outer Space: A Report of A Conference*. R-0362-RC. Santa Monica: RAND.

Goldstein, Lyle J. 2015. *Meeting China Halfway: How to Defuse the Emerging US-China Rivalry*. Washington DC: Georgetown University Press.

Georgescu, Alexandru. 2020. "Critical Space Infrastructures." In *Handbook of Space Security: Policies, Applications and Programs*, edited by Kai-Uwe Schrogl, 227–30. 2nd ed. New York: Springer.

Goswami, Namrata, and Peter A. Garrestson. 2020. *Scramble for the Skies: The Great Power Competition to Control the Resources of Outer Space*. London: Lexington Books.

Guo, Xiaobing. 2018. "Does Great Power Competition Insist on Irreconcilable Adversaries? The Beijing Xiangshan Forum Provides a Solution." *People's Daily Overseas Edition*. http://opinion.haiwainet.cn/n/2018/1024/c353596-31421197.html.

Haas, Peter M. 1992. "Introduction: Epistemic Communities and International Policy Coordination." *International Organization* 11, no. 1: 1–35.

Harrison, Roger G. 2013. "Unpacking the Three C's: Congested, Competitive, and Contested Space." *Astropolitics* 11, no. 3: 127.

Harvey, Brian. 2004. *China's Space Program: From Conception to Manned Spaceflight*. Chichester: Praxis.

Hays, Peter L. 2002. "United States Military Space: Into the Twenty-First Century." Occasional Paper No. 42. Colorado Springs: U.S. Air Force Academy, Institute for National Security Studies.

Hays, Peter L. 2020. "Spacepower Theory and Organizational Structures." In *Handbook of Space Security: Policies, Applications and Programs*, edited by Kai-Uwe Schrogl, 50. 2nd ed. Switzerland: Springer.

Hoffmann, Erik P, and Robbin F. Laird. 1982. *The Scientific-Technological Resolution and Soviet Foreign Policy*. New York: Pergamon Press.

Huang, Zhicheng. 2019. "Will There Be a Lunar Race between China and the US?" *Space International*, no. 4: 1–5.

Jaramillo, Cesar. 2009. "In Defense of the PPWT Treaty: Towards a Space Weapons Ban." https://ploughshares.ca/pl_publications/in-defence-of-the-ppwt-treaty-toward-a-space-weapons-ban.

Johnson-Freese, Joan. 2017. *Space Warfare in the 21st Century: Arming the Heavens*. London: Routledge.

Johnson-Freese, Joan, and Adrew. S. Erickson. 2006. "The Emerging China-EU Space Partnership: A Geotechnolgical Balancer." *Space Policy* 22, no. 1: 13.

Keohane, Robert O. 1984. *After Hegemony: Cooperation and Discord in the World Political Economy*. Princeton: Princeton University Press.

Kranzberg, Melvin. 1985. "The Top Line: Space as Man's New Frontier." In *International Space Policy: Legal, Economic, and Strategic Options for the Twentieth Century and Beyond*, edited by Daniel S. Rapp, and John R. McIntyre, 13–30. New York: Quorum Books.

Krepon, Michael, and Christopher Clary. 2003. *Space Assurance or Space Dominance: The Case against Weaponizing Space*. Washington, DC: The Henry L. Stimson Center.

Li, Huping. 2021. "Thucydides' Trap and Sino-US Interaction in Space." *Guoji Zhanwang* no. 6: 35–47.

Li, Qiaoyi. 2018. "China on the Way to Becoming a Major Space Power." *Global Times*. https://www.globaltimes.cn/page/201812/1133887.shtml.

Long Jiang, Lin Xiao, and Guojiang Sun. 2012. "Lessons from SpaceX's Business Model for China's Space Industry." *Aerospace China* no. 11: 13–14.

Luo, Heng, Feng Zhao, and Tang Liang. 2017. "Research on the Development Status of U.S. Commercial Space." *Aerospace China* no. 4: 8.

Lupton, David. E. 1998. *On Space Warfare: A Space Power Doctrine.* Montgomery, AL: Air University Press.

Maclennan, Jack. 2020. "The Problem with Great-Power Competition." https://mwi.usma.edu/problem-great-power-competition.

Marchisio, Sergio. 2009. "Article IX." In *Cologne Commentary on Space Law,* edited by Stephan Hobe, Bernhard Schmidt-Tedd, Lai-Uwe Schrogl, 180. Cologne: Carl Heymanns Verlag.

Moltz, James Clay. 2019. *The Politics of Space Security: Strategic Restraint and the Pursuit of National Interests.* 3rd ed. Stanford, CA: Stanford University Press.

Morgan, Forrest E. 2010. *Deterrence and First-Strike Stability in Space: A Preliminary Assessment.* Santa Monica: RAND.

Nie, Mingyan. 2020. "Space Privatization in China's National Strategy of Military-Civilian Integration: An Appraisal of Critical Legal Challenges." *Space Policy* 52: 1–8.

Pankova, Ludmila V., Olga V. Gusarova, and Dmitry V. Stefanovich. 2021. "International Cooperation in Space Activities amid Great Power Competition." *Russia in Global Affairs* 19, no. 4: 97–117.

Pollpeter, Kevin, Eric Anderson, Jordan Wilson, and Fan Yang. 2015. *China Dream, Space Dream: China's Progress in Space Technologies and Implications for the United States.* A Report Prepared for the U.S.-China Economic and Security Review Commission.

Pollpeter, Kevin, Timothy Ditter, Anthony Miller, and Brian Waidelich. 2020. *China's Space Narrative: Examining the Portrayal of the U.S.-China Space Relationship in Chinese Sources and Its Implications for the United States.* Montgomery, AL: China Aerospace Studies Institute.

Reibaldi, Giuseppe, and Max Grimard. 2015. "Non-Governmental Organizations Importance and Future Role in Space Exploration." *Acta Astronautica* 114: 130–37.

Selding, Peter B. 2016. "First Belarusian Satellite Has A Mission of Profit, Not Prestige." https://spacenews.com/belarus-puts-up-its-first-satellite-for-profit-not-prestige.

Sheehan, Michael. 2015. "Defining Space Security." In *Handbook of Space Security: Policies, Applications and Programs,* edited by Kai-Uwe Schrogl, 9–29. New York: Springer.

Stroikos, Dimitrios. 2018. "Engineering World Society? Scientists, Internationalism, and the Advent of the Space Age." *International Politics* 55, no. 1: 73–90.

Terrill, Delbert R. 1999. *The Air Force Role in Developing International Outer Space Law.* Alabama: Air University Press.

The Proposals on Treaty on the Prevention of the Placement of Weapons in Outer Space, the Threat or Use of Force against Outer Space Objects (PPWT), CD/1839, 29 February 2008, CD/1985. 2014. June 12.

The Statement by Ambassador Shi Zhongjun at the UNISPACE+50 High-Level Segment. 2018. 22 June. www.fmprc.gov.cn/ce/cgvienna/eng/hyyfy/t1570762.htm.

The US Ambassador Christina B. Rocca. 2008. Letter Dated August 19, 2008, from the Permanent Representative of the USA, CD/1847. Conference on Disarmament. August 26, 2008.

The US Commercial Space Launch Competitiveness Act 114th Congress (2015–2016). 2015. November 25. www.congress.gov/bill/114th-congress/house-bill/2262/text.

The U. S National Space Policy Documents. www.history.nasa.gov/spdocs.html.

The US Vote Explanation on Draft Resolution of No First Placement of Weapons in Outer Space. October 30, 2017 and November 6, 2018. The US Vote Explanation on Draft Resolution of Further Practical Measures for the Prevention of an Arms Race in Outer Space, October 20, 2017. https://usun.usmission.gov.

West, Jessica L. 2020. "Space Security Cooperation: Changing Dynamics." In *Handbook of Space Security: Policies, Applications and Programs*, edited by Kai-Uwe Schrogl, 145–48. 2nd ed. Switzerland: Springer.

White Papers on China's Space Activities. 2006, 2011, 2016, 2021. Information Office of State Council. http://www.scio.gov.cn/zfbps/index.htm.

White Papers on China's National Defense. 2008, 2010 and 2019. Information Office of State Council, http://www.scio.gov.cn/zfbps/index.htm.

Wu, Xiaodan. 2015. "China and Space Security: How to Bridge the Gap between Its Stated and Perceived Intentions." *Space Policy* 33: 20–28.

Wu, Xiaodan. 2018. "China's Space Law: Rushing to the Finish Line of Its Marathon." *Space Policy* 46: 39.

WU, Xiaodan. 2019. "International Law on Space Resources: Legality, Prospects and China's Strategy." *Manned Spaceflight* 25, no. 4: 558–59.

Zhang, Zhenhua. 2015. "Development of and Lessons from Foreign Commercial Space," *Aerospace China*, no. 11: 38–39.

Zhao, Lei. 2019. "Space Industry Soars to New Height." *China Daily*. http://www.chinadaily.com.cn/a/201901/10/%20WS5c36836ba3106c65c34e38d5.html.

CHAPTER 10

....

THE NEXT FRONTIER

Strategic Theory for the Space Domain

....

TIM SWEIJS AND DAVIS ELLISON

INTRODUCTION

....

MOST strategists agree that although the nature of war may be enduring, its character is prone to change because it is shaped by political, technological, social, and cultural conditions that vary across time and space. War, as Clausewitz observed, is the violent continuation *of* politics by other means (Clausewitz 1989, 87). It is the ultimate expression of contestation *between* polities which in today's world are states. Although states compete over security, prosperity, and ideology, they only infrequently resort to war and instead manage to maintain peaceful relations. Space, too, has been an arena of interstate competition in which states have been able to stave off outright conflict through consultation and cooperation, keeping in line with the lofty objective articulated in the space treaty concluded during the First Space Age, to use space for peaceful purposes (UN Office for Outer Space Affairs 1966). The important question is whether that will continue to be the case at the dawn of the Second Space Age. With the increasing relevance of space for prosperity and security, states are actively positioning themselves to exploit space to protect and promote what they consider vital interests. The emergence of space as a warfighting domain in its own right is prompting a small but growing community of scholars and strategists to reflect on the relevance of extant strategic theories about war and explore the contents of strategic theory for space, heeding Ben Bahney's call for modifying and updating past theories as "starting points for thinking about space" (Bahney 2020, 18).

If the purpose of strategy is to understand how means and ways relate to ends in practice, the purpose of strategic theory is to understand how means and ways relate to ends in theory. Although theory is typically formal and focused on furnishing general insights, it also needs to be concrete to be relevant and take into account domain specific dynamics. Even if it is early days when it comes to human space exploration, it is clear that space too will be a domain of economic, political, and military contestation and perhaps conflict. As always, strategic theory is evolving alongside strategic practice with developments in one influencing the other. Given the rapid pace of progress in the space domain, the moment has come to examine the implications of the emergence of space for existing strategic theory and reflect on its implications for its peaceful use by states and non-state actors. We agree with previous strategists that "the unique geography of space must find expression in unique technology, operations, and tactics" but, we disagree in that we argue that these unique characteristics in fact carry important clues about an "unique logic of strategy" (Gray and Sheldon 1999, 26).

In making this argument this chapter explains why and how space is qualitatively different as a domain compared to other warfighting domains because of both the particular geospatial and physical characteristics of space and its relationship to other warfighting domains in the conduct of contemporary war. It outlines what a space strategy is, and what it is not, on the basis of which it argues that existing strategic theorems need to be revisited, refined, and complemented. Rather than developing a full-fledged strategic theory—which is beyond its scope—the chapter considers three important tenets of military strategic theory, power, access, and command, and examines how these need to be re-conceptualized and operationalized in the space domain. The chapter concludes with reflections on prospects for the continued exploitation of space for peaceful purposes, with new strategic theory setting an intellectual framework, or "playing field," for these purposes. It finally provides recommendations for future research.

Why and How Is Space Important?

Space assets are essential to support basic positioning, navigation, and timing (PNT) that modern day economies, societies and militaries rely on. Launching costs of space assets into low Earth orbit (LEO) have decreased over 700-fold from around US$1,000,000 in the 1950s to US$1,400 today and are expected to decrease further (van Manen, Sweijs, and Bolder 2021). This is opening up space as an arena to a quickly growing number of public and private actors, with a burgeoning global space industry offering a range of terrestrial services. At the same time, public and private actors are seeking to unlock sources of extra-terrestrial value through the exploitation of space-based resources. Historically, state led/backed ventures to exploit economic resources outside national borders have typically been accompanied by military expansion to enforce and guarantee that control. It is therefore no coincidence that major powers have launched ambitious space programs and set up space commands and space forces. At present, space assets are already indispensable enablers in the conduct of contemporary war on earth at the same time as they are critical in preventing nuclear war through their role in strategic stability. Understanding how space is important necessitates a brief overview of how the different orbital levels of space play such important roles in the modern economy and in military affairs. This also helps explain why there is an inherent dynamic that is leading state and private actors to exploit space for economic purposes at the same time as it is driving the further militarization of space (Dawson 2018). The most used, and crowded, orbits are geosynchronous equatorial orbit (GEO), highly elliptical orbits (HEO), medium Earth orbit (MEO), and LEO (European Space Agency 2020). Each level is leveraged for different economic and military purposes. Satellites in GEO are typically used for communication purposes and monitoring functions. As they cover a large range of the Earth's surface, they are best designed for constant observation of specific and broad terrestrial regions and areas. For the military, this makes GEO ideal for detecting missile trajectories and nuclear tests, as they can persistently observe large, continent-sized areas on the ground, while also being able to specifically target specific areas for collection, such as nuclear power plants in Iran or launch sites in North Korea (Moltz 2014, 22).

Assets in MEO orbit serve equally important functions for both economic prosperity and international security. Satellites in MEO cover a range of navigation purposes, from air traffic control to providing directions to smartphones. The critical US Navstar Global Positioning System (GPS), Russian Glonass, European Galileo, and Chinese BeiDou navigational satellites rely on these orbits to function. MEO is thereby critical for the conduct of contemporary warfare, as military forces continue to rely not only on precision navigation but also on privately provided space services, such as mobile network access, that operate at this level (Ceruzzi 2021).

MEO is also an overarching term under which highly elliptical orbits (HEO), also known as Molniya orbits, fall. The benefit that satellites in this position can provide is that, due to the long, elliptical shape of their path, they have a long dwell time over the hemisphere of interest, while moving very quickly over the other (Ilčev 2018). This makes them ideal for early warning systems such as the US Space-Based Infrared System. When multiple satellites are simultaneously employed, it allows for persistent coverage over a given area (Defense Intelligence Agency 2022). The security and reliability of HEO-based early warning satellites is a core element of strategic stability because the ability to identify and track missile launches and trajectories is part of the infrastructure underlying a nuclear power's second-strike capability (Acton 2018, 56–99). Disruptions of nuclear command, control, communications, computers, information, surveillance, reconnaissance (C4ISR) assets can be interpreted to constitute the early stages of a nuclear attack which can incentivize a nuclear power to launch a strike first (Morgan 2010; Bidwell, Bruce, and Bruce 2018). This thus undermines crisis stability because states no longer trust that their second-strike capability is intact (Colby and Schelling 2013). In case of entanglement of nuclear and conventional C4ISR assets, it can also trigger inadvertent escalation because of uncertainty about whether the potential attack is targeting conventional or nuclear infrastructure (Acton 2018, 64–65; Posen 1991). This is especially dangerous in a context in which the major nuclear powers have vastly diverging views on entanglement (Arbatov 2017, 30).

Satellites in LEO are primarily used for high-resolution images of the Earth's surface, remote sensing tasks, and Earth observation missions. Their proximity to Earth makes them useful for reconnaissance missions. It is possible that assets in LEO will one day be used to facilitate commerce or trade of space resources back to Earth, such as minerals and manufactured consumables. This proximity and high level of traffic in LEO also makes them vulnerable to chokepoints and ground-based interference. Due to this broad civil and military reliance on LEO satellites, there is a real risk of misperception, as it is challenging to limit impact to only one particular military or intelligence target.

Overall, without the ability to operate space assets, military powers are effectively "deaf, blind, and mute" (Sweijs and Osinga 2019, 109). In fact, the leveraging of space-based assets has paid significant dividends for both the effectiveness and efficiency of modernized forces. The importance of space in conventional conflict became clearly manifest in Operation Desert Storm in the First Gulf War of 1991, during which space assets provided precise, reliable, and accurate surveillance to improve situational awareness and effectively synchronize and coordinate military forces (Philips 1996, 16). The importance of space assets to support terrestrial operations was seen again in Afghanistan in 2001, where the United States and United Kingdom (UK) leveraged satellite-supported precision missiles with devastating effect on Taliban forces. This combination of "low" and "high" became an ideal type of capability combination for the Pentagon in the early 2000s and continues to shape thinking today. During the Russian war against Ukraine from February 2022 onward, a public-private partnership of the US Agency for International Development and Elon Musk's SpaceX has provided vital satellite constellations that have been used by the Ukrainian government and its armed forces to maintain communications in the face of jamming attempts by the Russians (Suess 2022). In other words, space has allowed conventional armed forces to be more precise, coordinated, and resilient than in the past. In the years to come, the convergence of small satellites and big data analytics is expected to increase ubiquitous situational awareness. This will facilitate the detection and attribution of transgressive state behavior both in the context of war and outside of it including in the grey zone (Pekkanen, Aoki, and Mittleman 2022).

Space is also growing into an independent domain in itself. Non-kinetic space weapons have come to play increasingly important roles in interstate competition as they have reduced the previously prohibitive costs of space operations. Specifically dedicated space forces have been established by various major and middle powers, such as the United States, France, China, Russia, and Iran. NATO recognized space as an operational domain in 2019. Trends in military thinking have evolved along with technology, identifying adversaries' space-based communications and command and control systems as the center of gravity to be targeted early in a conflict. Space is therefore attracting an increasing amount of attention by various strategic actors, ranging from the multi-domain operations current in Western states, to China's "system confrontation" approach (Diaz de Leon 2021, 93–94; Engstrom 2018). This does not necessarily bode well for the peaceful purposes of space, though the following sections will identify how the differences in this environment affect the strategies used by actors to attain their objectives, thereby shaping the field on which such peaceful purposes are pursued.

WHY AND HOW IS SPACE DIFFERENT?

Space is different as a domain of economic and military competition primarily due to its physical qualities. It is a partial vacuum in which there is little to no oxygen, greatly reduced gravitational pull toward Earth, and in which varying bands of solar radiation pose risks to health and technology alike. For humans to spend longer periods of time in space requires a significant degree of training and acclimation. These difficulties only expand in cislunar and deep space, regions in which terrestrial powers are continuing to expand their ambitions.

The degree of this difference is relevant for the character of competition and conflict and thereby for strategic theory that seeks to apply theoretical tenets derived from terrestrial experience. Space, if approached as an independent warfighting domain, poses challenges to traditional military doctrines. First, and at the most basic level, kinetic action risks causing such significant damage from debris fields that nearly any large-scale action is cost prohibitive for actors that rely on continued use of space themselves. Using analogies from the maritime and air domains, multiple anti-satellite missile attacks would be the equivalent of missiles polluting huge swathes of Earth's oceans and airspace. Merely adopting doctrinal thinking from other domains therefore misunderstands the challenges faced when planning operations in space.

A second element is the important role of space in support of operations in the other warfighting domains, especially since the much-heralded Revolution in Military Affairs from the 1990s onward. A wide variety of military activities are conducted from space, including navigation, precision targeting, surveillance, and command and control. Nearly all modernized land, sea, and air services rely on space-based assets for one or more of these functions. As national modernization programs to digitally integrate services have progressed, some have warned this has grown into an over-reliance. Some observers have noted that this has created a situation of mutually assured vulnerability, which could affect how actors conduct military operations in and from space. The reliance that other domains have on space assets shows how fundamentally "cross-domain" space as an environment is (Lindsay and Gartzke 2022, 763–64). This mutual vulnerability could lead states to act more cautiously, though it also creates the incentive to pursue increased capabilities for non-kinetic interference, in the form of electronic warfare assets.

A third element that makes space different as a domain is the way in which its physical properties make current modes of operational and strategic planning either immensely more difficult or highly cost prohibitive. As space powers are diversifying their space assets and increasing their numbers to make them more redundant, the challenge of sufficiently degrading an opponent's space capabilities while safeguarding one's own has negated a search for a center of gravity in space. Transparency is also a problem given space's vastness. Though assets in space can be observed, the clandestine nature of the activities themselves cannot be continuously tracked and attribution poses a challenge.

The sheer distance between assets and the speed at which they travel makes "guessing what is at the other side of the hill" even more difficult, and necessitates significant investment (Ratcliffe 2017). The physical characteristics of space, the emergence of non-kinetic space weapons, and the concurrent growth of independent space forces signals that space is an inherently different operating environment and national defense organizations are adjusting to this reality.

What Is a Space Strategy and Why Is There Need for One?

The capabilities and capacities of space forces are expanding, orbit is becoming ever more crowded, and cislunar and deep space exploration is becoming more and more tied to resource exploitation and interstate competition. Space strategies formulate objectives, means, and ways, and act as a focusing element for the myriad official entities in space to address these challenges. Strategy making is fundamentally about prioritization of ends, ways, and means. A strategy without choices is little more than aspiration. In addition, the level at which the strategy applies is relevant, with an important distinction between grand strategy and military strategy. Grand strategy in the context of this chapter is understood as something akin to policy, something that establishes how states, or other political units, prioritize and mobilize which military, diplomatic, political, economic, and other sources of power to ensure what they perceive as their interests. Military strategy, the development and employment of armed forces for political purposes, falls within the framework of grand strategy (Hooft 2017). The focus here is on the development of military strategies within a broader framework for national decisions related to space power. This is challenging because the dynamics of air, sea, land, and cyber power cannot be so easily transcribed into space. There are several additional complicating factors to strategy making in the space domain. First, there are a wide array of actors in space, and gaining meaningful agreement as to what the objectives are in space is a challenge. This can risk the coherency of strategy. Freedman observes that "many 'strategy' documents actually avoid the topic, lack focus, cover too many dissimilar or only loosely connected issues and themes, address multiple audiences to the satisfaction of none, and reflect nuanced bureaucratic compromises." (Freedman 2013, 610–11). Second, strategy's "principles may be guidelines . . . they are not rules" (Strachan 2019, 188). Developing a cross-government or cross-service strategy does not in and of itself solve the problems it addresses. The bureaucratic difficulties of implementation and the factor of contingency will intervene. These challenges are reflective of Bowen's admonition against conflating strategic theory with the entire breadth of politics itself, where strategy takes the form of a policy framework for "astropolitics" in general, rather than providing a theory by which military security in space can be created and maintained (Bowen 2020, 42–43). From a military-strategic perspective, this could take the form of the desired effects in space, with an underlying theory of how they could be achieved. Importantly, it should offer a link between otherwise disparate military and civilian activities. Against that background, a space strategy should make causal claims about how certain actions or choices will lead to a successful outcome (Jakobsen 2022, 177–91). For the space domain, this should take the form of claims that argue for how space assets can be leveraged to build power relative to others and should also be explicit about the trade-offs entailed in its pursuit. This is an especially poignant element in the space domain, where the physical challenges can swiftly punish hubristic thinking. Power in space, even for great powers, faces limitations. To make causal claims toward success requires an underpinning logic that identifies what space power is for and how it can be leveraged effectively. The following section will introduce concepts that point in this direction.

DOES SPACE REQUIRE NEW STRATEGIC THEORY?

Strategic theory offers an intellectual framework for how to think about the application of space power, a vital underpinning element to understanding how peaceful purposes might be achieved. This is differentiated from a generalist theory of space power, which falls short of equipping the scholar or practitioner with the bridging question of "how?" Answering the question of whether space requires a new strategic theory requires consideration about what past theories can or cannot provide for this new domain. This certainly includes more classical thought on strategy in general but is particularly engaged with writings that have made claims about the role of space and the ways in which it should be used. In an age when extra-terrestrial human activity is rapidly expanding, we need to move beyond the notion that space is only as important inasmuch as it impacts terrestrial events. Gray recognized this and noted the exception to his prediction, arguing that war in space could extend beyond "terrestrial values," and that notions of space power will continue to expand theoretically based on sea and airpower foundations (Gray 1996, 300).

For space, Clausewitzian notions on the nature of war certainly hold. There is no doubt that passion, reason, chance, and friction play as much a role in space as they do on Earth. Similar observations about strategy in general hold as well, particularly that strategy is an output of civil-military relations (Strachan 2006). These do not necessarily bear on the need for new theorizing in relation to space. That the *character* of competition and specifically war in space is quite different is what challenges past strategic theory. Warfighting domains have specific characteristics both shaping and constraining how means and ways are combined in the service of attaining political objectives. Warfare on land is therefore different from warfare on and from sea and in and through the air, based not just on the fact that physical movement in these domains faces varying constraints (compare moving *on* land, *in* water, and *through* air) and opportunities (compare speed of movement, proximity, staying power) but also on how instruments of military power can be combined in peace and war time against fellow members of the species *Homo sapiens* that lives on land rather than in one of the other warfighting domains. Cyber sets itself apart from the three physical domains because distance and time and physical laws apply in entirely different ways in this domain.

Rather than developing a full strategic theory, we consider three traditional concepts in strategic theory, power, access, and command, and examine how these can be usefully conceived of in the space domain. These three concepts are central tenets for a strategic theory for space at the dawn of the Second Space Age. Space power is rooted in the ability to achieve effects in space to support or to obtain objectives on Earth and beyond it. Space power rests first and foremost on access to this domain, otherwise it is impossible to achieve effects in space, similar to the idea that access to the sea is a *conditio sine qua non* of maritime power projection. In addition to access, command of space is needed, even if only temporarily, either to attain freedom of maneuver or to deny an opponent the freedom of maneuver. A reflection on these key tenets is foundational to the development of a strategic theory for space. In addition, they offer a frame that extends beyond the explicitly military realm and can link political (i.e., civilian) and military efforts.

ON POWER IN SPACE

Any strategic theory has an underpinning logic of what power is and how it should be pursued. Power, in Max Weber's foundational formulation rests in "the ability of an individual or group to achieve their own goals or aims when others are trying to prevent them from realising them" (Weber 1947, 152). But power and the sinews of power differ from one domain to another, and certainly manifest in different ways. Coastal and maritime states have recognized that their power rests in their access to and control of the sea. Land powers' depth of their geography, and the size of their populations, lie at the heart of their power (Sloan 2017, 62–63). These differences have also been recognized by strategists in the past. Thucydides divided Athens and Sparta into sea and land powers respectively (Platias 2002). UK historian David Armitage described Napoleonic France as the "elephant" on land and Georgian Britain as the "whale" on the sea (Armitage 2007). Power narrowly conceived has also been defined in conventional military terms. Michael Handel, writing in 1981, conceived of military power in formulaic terms, describing it as a function of quantity and material and non-material qualities that combine for the goal of a state "meet[ing] its goals and needs" (Handel 1981, 226). Other scholars, such as Stephen Biddle, have shared this capability focused approach to power, understanding military power as "the ability to destroy hostile forces while preserving one's own; the ability to take and hold ground; and the time required to do so" (Biddle 2004, 6). These notions, while perhaps useful to understanding force balances in terrestrial warfare, do not readily translate to space.

What constitutes "space power," then? Scholars of strategic theory have often relied on analogies from other domains. In the maritime domain, sea power was considered to exist in the combination of naval and commercial power. Mahan argued that, among other elements such as geography, the power of a state lay within its ability to protect its economic prosperity from military threats, including through a large navy, colonies, and forward basing (Mahan 1987, 73–74). In the air, Douhet, in a similar vein as Biddle, argued that a state must possess an independent air force in order to "bring against the enemy that quantity and quality of offensives which will suffice to crush the enemy's material and moral resistance" (Douhet 2009, 96). Much in these considerations is necessary for space power, though not sufficient in and of themselves.

Current thinking on space power has embraced a combination of sea and air power approaches. Bowen has argued that "spacepower is the use and denial of thousands of machines in Earth orbit that provide important data gathering and communications services for governments, militaries, and economic infrastructure on Earth itself" (Bowen 2022, 14). States have begun to adopt this in practice, with the 2020 US Defense Space Strategy describing space power as "the sum of a nation's capabilities to leverage space for diplomatic, information, military, and economic activities in peace or war in order to attain national objectives" (Department of Defense 2020). These remain, however, fundamentally state-centric theories of space power. Others warn against such a state-centric orientation. James Clay Moltz argues that the globalized space industry has "shifted notions of space power from the national to the international contexts," thereby diffusing power in space away from the state (Moltz 2019, 68). Peter Hayes and Charles Lutes have argued similarly that space power theory should "consider the role of space activity in relation to the larger strategic and international environment. Spacepower theory is not simply a military theory, it is a strategic theory based upon human activity as applied to the space domain" (Hays and Lutes 2007, 206). Our theoretical proposition recognizes these broader aspects, and stresses that military strategies for space cannot be written in a vacuum but should take this broader outlook into account.

Overall, these reflections identify two common elements that make up space power: capabilities and the impact on Earth. First, power in space must be underpinned by the capability to operate in space. Second, power in space does not exist in and of itself, but rather must have benefit to military and civilian pursuits on Earth. In addition, we posit that a simplified understanding of space power then is having the capability to achieve space-based impact for pursuits on Earth and *beyond it*. This applies to both state-centric and non-state centric views. We also observe that the centricity of Earth will evolve as lunar exploration and even colonization extends strategic considerations beyond Earth itself.

On Access to Space

But how then can space power be wielded? First and foremost here is the ability to access space. While intuitive, it is a fundamental element to strategy in space that cannot be taken for granted. Access is made up of three core functions: the ground segment, data links, and the space assets themselves. The ground segment is made up of ground stations (for radio communications), mission control centers, remote terminals, test facilities, launch facilities, and ground networks. Data links are the actual secure communications themselves, the spectrum of networks themselves that link space assets to the various ground segment elements. Finally, are the space assets themselves, be they satellites, spacecraft, or space stations (Paulauskas 2020).

The concept of maintaining access as a core element of strategic thought is not new. Maintaining secure lines of communication for an army on land was a fact stressed in a full chapter by Clausewitz in *On War* (Clausewitz 1989, 345). At sea, Corbett noted on secure lines that in "embracing the lines of fleet supply, they correspond in strategical values not to military lines of supply, but to those internal lines of communication by which the flow of national life is maintained ashore" (Corbett 2004, 96). In the air, Douhet writes of the importance of maintaining, "a network of air lines . . . made up of large links connecting great arteries . . . it must be of a kind to facilitate the development of civil aviation and the utilization of military aviation" (Douhet 2009, 90). The maintenance of secure lines of communication is as vital in space as in all other domains, though the vital difference of space is that these lines in the form of data links must be maintained *at all times* in order for space systems to function, though this can be mitigated through establishing redundancy between links to mitigate any disruptions.

A central challenge in maintaining access through these secure lines of communication, from both an offensive and defensive perspective, is that accessing an opponents' space systems is, paradoxically as it may sound, a much simpler operation than in other domains. There is no Maginot line that can be built as on land, no air-defense bubble such as the one that has prevented Russia's air dominance over Ukrainian air space in 2022, and no waterways or coastal defenses as those that form a buffer between Taiwan and China's land forces (Clayton 2010; Bronk, Reynolds, and Watling 2022; Wuthnow, Grossman, and Saunders 2022). No, in space access is secured in the form of resilient space systems based on redundant space-based assets, the ability to rapidly acquire and place new satellites in orbit, and the leveraging of networked satellite constellations rather than larger legacy platforms. This requires close collaboration both with private actors and allied states (Moltz 2019, 66–94). The relative power of industry in space is central to space access. The future will tell if this leads to an emergence of state-like Dutch East India–style companies in space, or whether nation-states will start nationalizing and exerting full control over these capabilities (Bowen 2022, 39–42). Access, then, does not end at the moment it is achieved, but must be maintained and will require, if achieved outside of the context of independently owned assets, constant coordination and collaboration with national, international, and private actors. Otherwise a state can hardly be considered a space power of any style, major or minor. If space power resides on the ability to access space, access is critical for achieving command in space.

ON COMMAND OVER SPACE

Corbett, in writing on command of the sea, described that it "means nothing but the control of maritime communications," and "it is not identical in its strategical conditions with the conquest of territory" (Corbett 2004, 88–89) Drawing from this maritime analogy, command of space would be akin to the control of space-based lines of communication. But is this sufficient?

Command consists of control and denial. Understanding command of space as the control of communications, in a broad sense, remains apt, though it does require refinement, particularly if stations and at some point colonies in space become less reliant on Earth-based support. Extending from the analogies of the maritime domain, command in space would rest in the ability to control one's own lines of communication and to deny them to others if necessary. This is consistent with past theory, borrowing from Bowen's argument that "acts of space warfare must contribute to a command of space, which can constitute controlling space infrastructure and/or denying its use" (Bowen 2020, 272). Gray and Sheldon base their argument on a similar conception, that as states seek to control the systems upon which they rely, others will seek to deny them that control (Gray and Sheldon 1999, 31). This conception of command remains useful, and we use it here as a base to consider command in the space domain. We also keep in mind Corbett's consideration that, as at sea, command is in constant dispute, and should not be taken to equate with unrivalled dominance (Corbett 2004, 86).

Control is the ability to use one's space systems without external hindrance. It begins by simply maintaining access, which includes being able to navigate satellites through crowded orbital space, replace and repair damaged assets, and interdict hostile attempts to interfere with one's own capabilities. These three aspects alone pose major challenges and require significant amounts of coordination between the ground segment and the space-based assets themselves. Maintaining the capacities to execute this level of control is arguably the area of greatest attention and investment by civilian and military space agencies. Space domain awareness systems which can track debris fields, other satellites, and potential hostile activity are a vital element. These are made up of ground-based radars and space-based sensors which work in tandem to track overall space traffic and identify anomalies (Weeden 2010). Other means of maintaining control have been established since at least the late 1980s. The now-defunct US Office of Technology Assessment identified miniaturization, decoys, evasive maneuvers, shielding, electronic countermeasures, and in-orbit spare satellites as passive ways to ensure space control (United States Congress Office of Technology Assessment 1985). Both space domain awareness and many of the options identified here function in the face of both hostile activity and orbital debris (Hitchens 2007, 173–86).

Denial, ostensibly the other side of the same coin, has much lower barriers to entry. Denial in space is about the ability to prevent an opponent from executing control over their own space systems and attack yours. Both direct ascent anti-satellite missiles and co-orbital assets have proliferated, while the ability to interfere with or disable orbital assets via non-kinetic means has spread. Space operations, once limited to a handful of major space powers, have now grown as options to include a larger group of middle powers including Iran, Japan, South Korea, Israel, and Australia (Harrison et al. 2022). The ability to target the ground segment of an opponent's space system via a cyber-attack is a particularly powerful, lower-cost alternative to developing anti-satellite missile systems. Given the lower barrier for denying space, strategic theory centered on denial is central for smaller and middle powers, and vital for larger space powers to consider.

Returning to maritime thinking, there is a caveat to there being no terrain to control. The varying orbits in space, the moon, and extra-terrestrial bodies such as asteroids challenge this presumption. Command at LEO, GEO, MEO, HEO, including Lagrange point orbits entails different levels of effort to achieve control and to deny access to others. Certain capabilities, such as early-warning satellites, are stationed in only one particular orbit. If that were to be interfered with, or even denied entirely while one's own access is maintained, that orbital "terrain" has effectively been taken, if only temporarily. In line with Corbett's initial consideration on command, we argue that command in space does not only entail control over orbital activities but will in the future involve taking and holding extra-terrestrial territory. The notion that there is no terrain to be taken or lost in space is entirely inapplicable when extra-terrestrial bodies such as the moon come into consideration. The prospect of competition and even conflict for the lunar surface and resources between the Artemis Accord group (led by the United States) and the Russian-Chinese International Lunar Research Station project will certainly have an impact on thinking for space strategy and command in space. Command will then have to evolve not only to maintain lines of communication in space, but also to seize territory on the surface of the moon—as on Earth, so in space. Traditional concepts of war from imperial history, particularly the denial of an opponent's access to extra-terrestrial resources to weaken them militarily and economically, will continue to apply. Blockading an enemy will move from their ports to jamming their data links and attacking their space assets. That imperial-style competition for the control of extra-terrestrial territory is a challenge for peaceful purposes goes without saying and points toward the need to develop international norms and regulations.

Conclusion

The question was posed at the beginning of this chapter of whether the Second Space Age will fare as well as the First Space Age in promoting peaceful purposes. States are actively positioning themselves to exploit space and protect vital interests. The evolution of space as a warfighting domain is keeping brisk pace alongside its increasing economic and societal importance. That the geopolitics of Earth is evolving into astropolitics and thereby extending competition into outer space and, soon, onto celestial bodies, does not bode well for peaceful purposes.

Because space is different, existing strategic theory and past analogies are not suffi-cient to adequately capture the dynamics of this environment. A clear understanding of the strategic dynamics in space is a necessary prerequisite to enhance stability and peaceful uses of space going forward. To that purpose, we have offered here the founda-tional concepts of what can constitute a strategic theory for space. Central to a strategic theory for space are the concepts of space power, access, and command.

Building from theories of air and sea power, we posit that a simplified understanding of space power is having the capability to achieve space-based impact for pursuits on Earth and beyond it, a definition that applies both to state-centric and non-state-centric views. We also observe that Earth's centrality in a strategic theory for space will diminish as space exploration and colonization will make greater inroads in the years to come. Power in space then will be a reflection of an actor's ability to build capabilities and exer-cise them effectively in the pursuit of political goals.

The second concept underpinning a strategic theory for space is access. Access is made up of three core functions: the ground segment, data links, and the space assets themselves. The concept of maintaining access as a core element of strategic thought is not new. Access, then, does not end at the moment it is achieved, but must be maintained and if achieved outside of the context of independently owned assets, becomes a topic of constant coordination and collaboration with national, international, and private ac-tors. For both minor and major powers, space access is fundamental. This could lead to increased dependency on larger state powers or simply lead to a division between haves and have-nots for space.

Finally, strategic theory for space requires a clear conception of command. Command consists of control and denial. The control of communications, in a broad sense, remains relevant, though we note a need for refinement as stations or even colonies in space be-come less reliant on Earth. Extending from the analogies of the maritime domain, com-mand in space would rest in the ability to control one's own lines of communication and to deny them to others if necessary. It should be recognized that command in space, as at sea, and in the air, is transitory as full dominance is neither theoretically possible nor feasible in practice. The mutual vulnerability of states' assets in space makes command a continuously contested element in orbit, though it remains an area for exploration how this would extend to extra-terrestrial bodies such as the moon.

So, what can strategic theory do to answer the question of peaceful purposes for space? Sound strategic theory, thereby taking into account power, access, and com-mand, is a basis for these peaceful pursuits. It effectively sets both the intellectual and practical "playing field" within which peaceful (i.e., commercial, scientific, explora-tory) use is undertaken. If there is clarity on the ways in which military space activities in particular relate to broader ends, it establishes the framework for prioritization and decisions related to the development and employment of space forces, the nature and scope of arms control negotiations, and the rules and norms to guide responsible beha-vior to facilitate space's use for peaceful purposes.

What then are the next steps for strategy in space in both theory and practice? A first step is to flesh out a more fully articulated, layered, and differentiated strategic theory for space based on the concepts presented here. This is a complex task, which will not only have to develop its own causal logics for thinking about strategy in space but also further contend with the legacies of past thought in other domains. It entails engaging with the roles of private actors in both grand and military strategy, as they have emerged as foreign policy actors in their own right (Slaughter 2017). In addition, there is need for more rigorous comparative case analysis of strategic approaches to space including of small and middle powers. There is a growing literature on such comparative approaches from a grand strategic perspective (Balzacq, Dombrowski, and Reich 2019), which should be extended to military strategy and for space specifically.

Informed by adequate strategy theory, this offers those tasked with the practice of strategy-making an intellectual framework for identifying and prioritizing options for space activities. There is reason for optimism that such choices can have material effect. Recent initiatives initially spearheaded by the UK government to establish rules for responsible behavior in space within a United Nations context (Rajagopalan 2020), through the United Nations, to limit ASAT testing (UN Office of Disarmament Affairs 2021), and the multinational effort to develop the Woomera Manual the International Law of Military Space (Woomera Manual Project 2018) are signs that the pursuit of peaceful purposes has not fallen fully by the wayside. At the same time, modernization and testing of militarized space assets continues and rival programs for moon bases have accelerated. Only time will tell in practice, but new strategic theory can offer the guide to build new codes of conduct, find common ground, and reduce risk to activity in space (van Hooft, Boswinkel, and Sweijs 2022).

Acknowledgments

The authors would like to thank Adam Meszaros and Giovanni Cisco for their research assistance.

References

Acton, James M. 2018. "Escalation through Entanglement: How the Vulnerability of Command-and-Control Systems Raises the Risks of an Inadvertent Nuclear War." *International Security* 43, no. 1: 56–99. https://doi.org/10.1162/isec_a_00320.

Arbatov, Alexey. 2017. "Entanglement: Russian and Chinese Perspectives on Non-Nuclear Weapons and Nuclear Risks." Carnegie Endowment for International Peace.

Armitage, David. 2007. "The Elephant and the Whale: Empires of Land and Sea." *Journal for Maritime Research* 9, no. 1: 23–36.

Bahney, Benjamin, ed. 2020. "Space Strategy at a Crossroads: Opportunities and Challenges for 21st Century Competition." Center for Global Security Research, Lawrence Livermore National Laboratory. https://doi.org/10.2172/1635784.

Balzacq, Thierry, Peter Dombrowski, and Simon Reich. 2019. *Comparative Grand Strategy: A Framework and Cases*. Oxford: Oxford University Press.

Biddle, Stephen. 2004. *Military Power: Explaining Victory and Defeat in Modern Battle*. Princeton: Princeton University Press. https://doi.org/10.2307/j.ctt7s19h.

Bidwell, Christopher A., Bruce Bruce, and MacDonald Bruce. 2018. "Emerging Disruptive Technologies and Their Potential Threat to Strategic Stability and National Security." Federation of American Scientists.

Bowen, Bleddyn E. 2020. *War in Space: Strategy, Spacepower, Geopolitics*. 1st ed. Edinburgh: Edinburgh University Press.

Bowen, Bleddyn E. 2022. *Original Sin: Power, Technology and War in Outer Space*. Oxford: Oxford University Press.

Bronk, Justin, Nick Reynolds, and Jack Watling. 2022. "The Russian Air War and Ukrainian Requirements for Air Defence." Royal United Services Institute.

Ceruzzi, Paul. 2021. "Satellite Navigation and the Military-Civilian Dilemma: The Geopolitics of GPS and Its Rivals." In *Militarizing Outer Space: Astroculture, Dystopia and the Cold War*, edited by Alexander C.T. Geppert, Daniel Brandau, and Tilmann Siebeneichner, 343–67. London: Palgrave Macmillan. https://doi.org/10.1057/978-1-349-95851-1_13.

Clausewitz, Carl von. 1989. *On War*. Translated by Michael Eliot Howard and Peter Paret. Rev. ed. Princeton, NJ: Princeton University Press.

Clayton, Anthony. 2010. "André Maginot." *The RUSI Journal* 155, no. 3: 72–75. https://doi.org/10.1080/03071847.2010.499630.

Colby, Elbridge, and Thomas C. Schelling. 2013. "Defining Strategic Stability: Reconciling Stability and Deterrence." Strategic Stability: Strategic Studies Institute, US Army War College. https://www.jstor.org/stable/resrep12086.5.

Corbett, Julian S. 2004. *Principles of Maritime Strategy*. Dover ed. Mineola, NY: Dover Publications.

Dawson, Linda. 2018. *War in Space: The Science and Technology Behind Our Next Theater of Conflict*. Cham: Springer International Publishing. https://doi.org/10.1007/978-3-319-93052-7.

Defense Intelligence Agency. 2022. "Challenges to Security in Space." Defense Intelligence Agency.

Department of Defense. 2020. "2020 Defense Space Strategy Summary." Department of Defense.

Diaz de Leon, Jose. 2021. "Understanding Multi-Domain Operations in NATO." *NATO Joint Warfare Centre Three Swords Magazine* 37: 91–94.

Douhet, Giulio. 2009. *The Command of the Air*. University of Alabama Press ed. Fire Ant Books. Tuscaloosa, Al: University of Alabama Press.

Engstrom, Jeffrey. 2018. "Systems Confrontation and System Destruction Warfare: How the Chinese People's Liberation Army Seeks to Wage Modern Warfare." RAND Corporation. https://www.rand.org/pubs/research_reports/RR1708.html.

European Space Agency. 2020. March 30. "Types of Orbits." The European Space Agency. https://www.esa.int/Enabling_Support/Space_Transportation/Types_of_orbits#GEO.

Freedman, Lawrence. 2013. *Strategy: A History*. Oxford: Oxford University Press.

Gray, Colin S. 1996. "The Influence of Space Power upon History." *Comparative Strategy* 15, no. 4: 293–308.

Gray, Colin S, and John B Sheldon. 1999. "Space Power and the Revolution in Military Affairs. A Glass Half Full?" *Air University Airpower Journal* 13, no. 3: 23–38.

Handel, Michael. 1981. "Numbers Do Count: The Question of Quality versus Quantity." *Journal of Strategic Studies* 4, no. 3: 225–60. https://doi.org/10.1080/01402398108437082.

Harrison, Todd, Kaitlyn Johnson, Makena Young, Nicholas Wood, and Alyssa Goessler. 2022. "Space Threat Assessment 2022." Center for Strategic & International Studies. http://aerosp ace.csis.org/wp-content/uploads/2022/05/Harrison_SpaceThreatAssessment2022_WEB_ v3-compressed.pdf.

Hays, Peter L., and Charles D. Lutes. 2007. "Towards a Theory of Spacepower." *Space Policy* 23, no. 4: 206–209. https://doi.org/10.1016/j.spacepol.2007.09.003.

Hitchens, Theresa. 2007. "Debris, Traffic Management, and Weaponization: Opportunities for and Challenges to Cooperation in Space." *The Brown Journal of World Affairs* 14, no. 1: 173–86.

Hooft, Paul. 2017. "Grand Strategy." *Oxford Online Bibliographies.* https://www.oxfordbibliog raphies.com/display/document/obo-9780199743292/obo-9780199743292-0218.xml.

Hooft, Paul van, Lotje Boswinkel, and Tim Sweijs. 2022. "Shifting Sands of Strategic Stability: Towards A New Arms Control Agenda." The Hague Centre for Strategic Studies.

Ilčev, Stojče Dimov. 2018. "Introduction." In *Global Satellite Meteorological Observation (GSMO) Theory*, edited by Stojče Dimov Ilčev, 1–70. Vol. 1. Cham: Springer International Publishing. https://doi.org/10.1007/978-3-319-67119-2_1.

Jakobsen, Peter Viggo. 2022. "Causal Theories of Threat and Success—Simple Analytical Tools Making It Easier to Assess, Formulate, and Validate Military Strategy." *Scandinavian Journal of Military Studies* 5, no. 1: 177–91. https://doi.org/10.31374/sjms.164.

Lindsay, Jon R., and Erik Gartzke. 2022. "Politics by Many Other Means: The Comparative Strategic Advantages of Operational Domains." *Journal of Strategic Studies* 45, no. 5: 743–76. https://doi.org/10.1080/01402390.2020.1768372.

Mahan, A. T. 1987. *The Influence of Sea Power Upon History, 1660–1783*. Rev. ed. New York: Dover Publications.

Manen, Hugo van, Tim Sweijs, and Patrick Bolder. 2021. "Strategic Alert: Towards a Space Security Strategy." The Hague Centre for Strategic Studies.

Moltz, James Clay. 2014. *Crowded Orbits: Conflict and Cooperation in Space*. New York: Columbia University Press.

Moltz, James Clay. 2019. "The Changing Dynamics of Twenty-First-Century Space Power." *Strategic Studies Quarterly* 13, no. 1: 66–94.

Morgan, Forrest E. 2010. "Deterrence and First-Strike Stability in Space: A Preliminary Assessment." RAND Corporation. https://www.rand.org/pubs/monographs/MG916.html.

Paulauskas, Kestutis. 2020. "NATO Review—Space: NATO's Latest Frontier." *NATO Review.* March 18, 2020. https://www.nato.int/docu/review/articles/2020/03/18/space-natos-latest-frontier/index.html.

Pekkanen, Saadia M., Setsuko Aoki, and John Mittleman. 2022. "Small Satellites, Big Data: Uncovering the Invisible in Maritime Security." *International Security* 47, no. 2: 177–216. https://doi.org/10.1162/isec_a_00445.

Philips, Theresa M. 1996. "Space Support at the Operational Level: How Have We Learned the Lessons of Desert Storm?" Report. Naval War College.

Platias, Athanassios. 2002. "Grand Strategies Clashing: Athenian and Spartan Strategies in Thucydides' "History of the Peloponnesian War.'" *Comparative Strategy* 21, no. 5: 377–99. https://doi.org/10.1080/01495930290043137.

Posen, Barry R. 1991. *Inadvertent Escalation: Conventional War and Nuclear Risks*. Ithaca, NY: Cornell University Press. https://www.jstor.org/stable/10.7591/j.ctt1xx51d.

Rajagopalan, Rajeswari Pillai. 2020. "Assessing the British Proposal on Space Security." *The Diplomat*. October 12, 2020. https://thediplomat.com/2020/12/assessing-the-british-propo sal-on-space-security/.

Ratcliffe, Susan. 2017. "Duke of Wellington." In *Oxford Essential Quotations*, edited by Susan Ratcliffe, 192. Oxford: Oxford University Press.

Slaughter, Anne-Marie. 2017. *The Chessboard and the Web: Strategies of Connection in a Networked World*. New Haven, CT: Yale University Press.

Sloan, Geoffrey. 2017. "British Foreign Policy and the Heartland: Challenge and Nemesis." In *Geopolitics, Geography and Strategic History*, edited by Geoffrey Sloan, 62–86. London: Routledge.

Strachan, Hew. 2006. "Making Strategy: Civil–Military Relations after Iraq." *Survival* 48, no. 3: 59–82. https://doi.org/10.1080/00396330600905510.

Strachan, Hew. 2019. "Strategy in Theory; Strategy in Practice." *Journal of Strategic Studies* 42, no. 2: 171–90. https://doi.org/10.1080/01402390.2018.1559153.

Suess, Juliana. 2022. "Jamming and Cyber Attacks: How Space Is Being Targeted in Ukraine." *RUSI*. April 5, 2022. https://www.rusi.orghttps://www.rusi.org.

Sweijs, Tim, and Frans Osinga. 2019. "VIII. Maintaining NATO's Technological Edge." *Whitehall Papers* 95, no. 1: 104–18. https://doi.org/10.1080/02681307.2019.1731216.

UN Office for Outers Space Affairs. 1966. December 19. "Treaty on Principles Governing the Activities of States in the Exploration and Use of Outer Space, Including the Moon and Other Celestial Bodies." United Nations Office for Outer Space Affairs. https://www.unoosa. org/oosa/en/ourwork/spacelaw/treaties/outerspacetreaty.html.

UN Office of Disarmament Affairs. 2021. July. "Report of the Secretary-General on Reducing Space Threats through Norms, Rules and Principles of Responsible Behaviors (2021)." UNODA. https://www.un.org/disarmament/topics/outerspace-sg-report-outer-space-2021/.

United States Congress Office of Technology Assessment. 1985. *Anti-Satellite Weapons, Countermeasures, and Arms Control*. Washington, DC: US Government.

Weber, Max. 1947. *The Theory of Social And Economic Organization*. New York: Free Press.

Weeden, Brian, Paul Cefola, Jaganath Sankaran. 2010. "Global Space Situational Awareness Sensors." *Secure World Foundation*. https://swfound.org/media/15274/global%20ssa%20 sensors-amos-2010.pdf.

Woomera Manual Project. 2018. "The Woomera Manual on the International Law of Military Space Operations." https://law.adelaide.edu.au/woomera/system/files/docs/Woomera%20 Manual.pdf.

Wuthnow, Joel, Derek Grossman, and Phillip C. Saunders. 2022. *Crossing the Strait: China's Military Prepares for War with Taiwan*. Washington, D.C.: National Defense University.

CHAPTER 11

···

UNBUNDLING THREATS

Balancing and Alliances in the Space Domain

···

SAADIA M. PEKKANEN

ALLIANCES are emerging as a key feature in the space security landscape. The focus of this essay is on how they are organized and led, where they are headed, and what they suggest for peaceful prospects in outer space affairs. The international relations (IR) of space today are marked by the resurgence of great power competition, and the United States and China have emerged as the two dominant poles in it (Shirk 2008, 2022; Foot and Walter 2011; Friedberg 2011; Christensen 2015; Allison 2017; Medeiros 2019; Westad 2019; Shifrinson 2020; Brands and Gaddis 2021; Brands and Beckley 2021; Cheung 2022). They also head a bipolarity of space alliances, meaning two blocs extending into space that reflect the geopolitics around them (Pekkanen 2021). On one side is the United States, coordinating like-mindedness in space matters, with longstanding allies like NATO, the United Kingdom, and Japan, along with newer configurations like QUAD and AUKUS. On the other side is China, partnering with Russia and Pakistan, members of the Asia Pacific Space Cooperation Organization (APSCO), and participants in the Space Information Corridor anchored in the Belt-and-Road Initiative (Pekkanen 2017; Pollpeter 2020, 16; Pollpeter et al. 2020, 20–23; Schrogl and Giannopapa 2020, 54).

The bipolarity perspective, while controversial, is gaining ground (Mearsheimer 2001, 337–46; 2021; Zhang 2012, 131; Allison 2017; Allison 2021; Tunsjø, 2018a; 2018b; Maher 2018; Shirk 2022, 276–77; Zhao 2022; Lind 2023). Irrespective of how they rank relative to each other, the United States and China are "much more powerful than the rest" (Tunsjø 2018a, 5). This includes their standing in the space domain, where they are widely perceived as the two principal countries contesting over military might and industrial innovation. In this domain, as "In the great-power politics of bipolar worlds, who is a danger to whom is never in doubt;" and in the new space race China is the "obsessing danger" for the United States and vice versa since each can damage the other in ways other states cannot match (Waltz 1979, 170).

Bipolarity in a system, where only internal capabilities matter, is not the same as blocs headed up by the two dominant powers but, in my judgment, they deserve attention together in the space domain (Waltz 1979, 168–69; Ripsman, Taliaferro, and Lobell 2016, 45). In practice, we can readily observe that the great power competition between the United States and China in the space domain—where they are by far the most capable space powers—is indicated by their quest for allies. Their dominant status is creating a bipolarization of alliances in which states cluster into two blocs. I assess that bipolarity and bipolarization appear to be coinciding in the international space order today (Rapkin et. al. 1979).

It is the practice, reality, and significance of the diverging space alliances which I explore in this essay. At this historical stage, then, the policy question is whether the rise of China's space power and the alarm it instills in the United States makes conflict inevitable between them and their respective blocs of allies. Some say it does, but nothing is inevitable in international relations. If historical experience is a guide, then competition—even war—extending in space is of concern (Hyten 2000; Dolman 2002, 1–11, 86–112; Hille 2009; Johnson-Freese 2017, 56–75; Klein 2019, 96–123; Marino 2020; Sevastopulo and Hille 2021). If theory is a guide, the "virtues of bipolarity" in the international space order with two space superpowers may turn out to be a force for stability (Waltz 1979, 168; Mearsheimer 2001, 335).

Drawing on neoclassical realist frameworks in IR that give place of eminence to states and their interests, this chapter probes the shape, dynamics, and significance of the resulting alignments in the contemporary space domain. The approach is realist because, at its core, it is about understanding how states conceptualize international threats and opportunities, bridge interactions between the external environment and domestic constraints, and ponder alignments in their own interests in the evolving, uncertain, and unclear trajectories of the international space order (Lobell, Ripsman, and Taliaferro 2009, 5; Ripsman, Taliaferro, and Lobell 2016, 2–11). To the best of my knowledge, this is the first such effort of its kind, giving us an opportunity to reflect on issues of theoretical, historical, and policy interest. A central goal of this essay is to use the neoclassical realist framing to trace and map the emerging alignments in the space domain, and to build an understanding of what they mean and signify to the states involved, especially the two leading poles.

The remainder of this essay proceeds in three parts. The first part turns to some principal IR works to frame the analytics, logic, and dynamics of alliances in the space domain. My goal is to extract some general elements that drive state perceptions and decisions on alliances so that we have a lens with which to examine the emerging evidence. Both material and perceptual threats loom large in the space security landscape and give us a way to connect to an influential IR explanation—balance of threat—on the origins of alliances. The second part turns to tracing and mapping the evidence on threats and emerging alliances in the contemporary space domain in which states are the principal authoritative actors. It unbundles the swirl of threats they face in, through, and at the nexus of outer space activities. It then maps the evolution of US and China-led space alliances in chronological order, weaving together a narrative that comports with the theoretical constructs. To be clear, this is a work that aims to bring together the strands of history, politics, and policy, and I do not propose to "test" the derivations from existing works; rather I aim to see if they resonate at all in the evidence we can glean at this early stage. Third, the analysis gives us some takeaways. As the two poles seek to lead in outer space affairs, they should develop a better understanding of their allies' interests, what motivates them, and what the sum total of these interactions means for peaceful prospects in space all around.

BRINGING ALLIANCES INTO THE SPACE DOMAIN

There are many aspects of alliances that draw scholarly attention in interstate relations. Aside from what defines them, there are long-running debates about how alliances come about, hold together, perform, dissolve, and affect prospects for stability over time in peacetime and wartime and in different regions of the world (Liska 1962, 1968; Beres 1972; Ward 1982; Walt 1985; 1987; 2009; Christensen and Snyder 1990; Snyder 1990; 1997; Morrow 1991; Leeds, Long, and Mitchell 2000; Miller 2003, 2012; Weitsman 2004; 2014; Sprecher 2006; Pressman 2008; Mansoor 2016; Cha 2016; Kim 2016; Rynning and Schmitt 2018; Izumikawa 2018; 2020; Poast 2019; Henry 2020, 2022; Crawford 2021). Some of the "fundamental issues of alliances—their capability aggregation purpose, balancing and bandwagoning behaviors, and management functions" may be relevant to the contemporary space domain (Weitsman 2004, 3).

But we are at the early stages of trying to assess what, if anything, all this means in practice to the interactions of self-interested states in the international space order. For that reason, rather than any kind of an exhaustive review, my modest goal here is to extract some strands in the voluminous literature on alliances that can frame our understanding of how, whether, and why they are emerging in the space domain. I scan some key works with a set of questions in mind: What might indicate an alliance in the given complexities of the domain? Are threats the primary reason for the emergence of alliances in the space competition today. If so, how do we unbundle the threats the two leading contenders face? If not, what else might matter?

Conceptualizing Space Alliances

Their protean nature makes precise definitions of alliances hard (Kann 1976; Ward 1982, 3–10; Wilkins 2012, 56–72; Snyder 1997, 1–16). Further, extending their analysis into the unfolding tendrils of the new space race is also hard because the foundational dual-use technologies cut across a wide assortment of agreements in the civilian, commercial, and military realms no matter who happens to be developing them (Johnson-Freese 2007, 6–7; Pekkanen and Kallender-Umezu 2010, 2, 21, 223–224; Tyson and Lang 2018, 20–21). It is fiction to think that any space-related agreement among states today is motivated purely by either economic or military considerations alone, that it can be easily distinguished as being merely defensive in nature, or that it can be divorced from other strands of the bipolar contest in the international system.

In this chapter I build on Stephen Walt's definition that an "alliance (or alignment) is a formal (or informal) commitment for security cooperation between two or more states, intended to augment each member's power, security, and/or influence. Although the precise arrangements embodied in different alliances vary enormously, the essential element is a commitment for mutual support against some external actor(s) . . . these arrangements affect both the capabilities that national leaders can expect to draw up and the opposition they must prepare to face" (Walt 2009, 86). While some question the broad emphasis on "security cooperation" it is a necessary conflation in a domain underpinned by a dual-use technology (Walt 1987, 1; Rynning and Schmitt 2018, 653).

To my mind, these broad considerations help capture the actual alliance patterns we see emerging in the space domain today, as indicated by cross-cutting formal or informal, military or non-military, bilateral or multilateral agreements among states that are designed to ensure some level of commitment, exchange of benefits, and mutual security against other states (Weitsman 2004, 27; Nye 2009, 70; Taliaferro 2019, 17; Izumikawa 2020, 15; Rapp-Hooper 2020, 7; Cha 2016, 185–219). With this lens, prospects for new space alliances are as important to focus on as older ones that can be organically repurposed or nested in a wide range of settings.

Some Explanations for Alignments in the Space Domain

There are many explanations for why states might set up, seek, and keep alignments in the space domain. Just to be clear up front: I draw together a few explanations that, to me, seem the best tailored to the space domain nested in the great power competition today, that are centered on dual-use capabilities of material interest to states, and that go across the balancing behavior of both leader and follower states in an anarchic system. I caution against overtheorizing because "no abstract criterion can supply reliable guidance in either making or analyzing alignments without reference to concrete conditions and conflicts, and to particular objectives in matters of security, stability, and status" (Liska 1962, 26).

One straightforward explanation comes from traditional balance of power theories in which the basic idea is that no one state, or coalition of states, dominates the scene (Morgenthau 1948, 222; Waltz 1979, 116–28; Paul 2004, 4–11). Here checking and balancing is at work (Schweller 2016); it follows that leading contenders would seek to balance the other driven by concerns with their relative (great power) standing. The relational logic between alliances and balance of power is simple enough: "Put affirmatively, states enter into alliances with one another in order to supplement each other's capability. Put negatively, an alliance is a means of reducing the impact of antagonistic power, perceived as pressure which threatens one's independence" (Liska 1962, 26). We should expect to see both internal balancing by all states through efforts at increasing space capabilities and external balancing through alliances that serve to aggregate capabilities for one side (Morrow 1991).

A second explanation is one that supplements—not displaces—the emphasis on capabilities with also one on a balance of threat (Walt 1987, 17–49). The higher the threat to one state's space security posed by a belligerent state—provoked, say, by the development of dual-use space capabilities and demonstrations of their offensive uses in and through space—the more likely states will balance against it by coming together. More precisely, "An imbalance of threat occurs when the most threatening state or coalition is significantly more dangerous than the second most threatening state or coalition" (Walt 1987, 265, Figure 1). But the very emphasis on threats forces attention on other stimuli by which domestic decision-makers—operating under their own colliding or consensual sets of beliefs, incentives, and constraints—"correctly" perceive them (Schweller 2004, 168–81). Aggregate power, geographic proximity, offensive capability, and aggressiveness of intentions also resonate in present policy debates about space security (Walt 1987, 21–26). Geographic proximity to the source of belligerence, along with perceived aggression, may make a leading state capitalize on the strategic concerns of other states in the region to rally them to a like-minded coalition.

A third explanation, that also supplements the basic emphasis on capabilities, centers on the basic premise that the "economics of producing war continue to matter greatly [and] wealth remains an essential prerequisite for war" (Caverley 2018, 305). The expectation of economic benefits or resource exchanges, which makes one side more capable in the aggregate, may trigger efforts at balancing those capabilities though not in predicable ways. States of all stripes have an interest in materially advancing their economic standing and positioning their nations in the evolving space frontiers through alliances, triggering all kinds of hard and soft balancing prospects (Pape 2005). Industrial capacity and technology underpin national power, and leading industrial states are generally identical with great powers; if a change in industrial rank likely leads to a corresponding change in the hierarchy of power, states should look for opportunities to link economically with allies to reap joint gains in and through space (Morgenthau 1948, 136–41; Brawley 2004, 78–81).

This is critical for capability aggregation models in practice, which need to rethink the non-military and exchange aspects of alliances (Kim 2016, 5, 14–21, 28–48; Poast 2019, 6–7). In particular, explicit trade and investment links that tie in domestic constituencies makes the alliance useful, concrete, and credible to the participants and rival coalitions; as well, alliance-specific gains from trade may be higher among space allies, especially in a bipolar world, and turn out to be a boon also to the political-military side of their relations (Gowa 1994, 78, 121; Long and Leeds 2006; Poast 2012). Preemptively redirecting economic gains toward the alliance also helps to minimize the repercussions of security externalities (Long and Leeds 2006, 434–35). Follower states are incentivized to stay with the side through which they can partake of the spoils of innovation on Earth, in the outer space void, or on celestial bodies. Leading states may also be incentivized to align since no state is self-sufficient in the geophysics of the space domain. As relations develop over time, they can optimize their net benefits by exchanging the resources needed for space security with their allies including "access to geostrategically significant locations" (Izumikawa 2020, 14–16), such as the physical advantages of geography for ground stations and launch sites, or assets in cislunar space or on celestial bodies, for example.

How well, if at all, do these ideas resonate in the emerging realities of alignments in the space domain? This presents an opportunity to contribute to a core debate identified by neoclassical realists, and germane to the space domain today: how and whether threatened states balance in the ways commonly predicted, and what that reflects about their alignment choices (Ripsman, Taliaferro, and Lobell 2016, 140–46; Schweller 2016). It also presents an opportunity to anchor these long-standing IR analytics in the dividing realities of the contemporary space domain.

STATES AND EMERGING ALLIANCES IN THE SPACE DOMAIN

With these conceptual building blocks, figuring out the prospects for alliances in the contemporary space race is the task at hand. I begin with a brief overview of its principal actors, and what I judge to be the principal threats the race presents at this historical stage. Drawing on these building blocks, I then turn to probing the shape and reasons for the emerging alignments we observe.

The Primacy of States

Importantly, in this second space race as in the old one, states remain the privileged actors and their strategies, policies, and decisions will shape the ways space alliances unfold in the foreseeable future (Lake 2008; Pekkanen 2019, 92). The principles of the foundational 1967 Outer Space Treaty (OST) further reinforce the role of states as the authoritative decision-makers and supervisors of space activities, whether at the international or national level (Masson-Zwaan and Hofmann 2019, 9; Lyall and Larsen 2018, 28–33; von der Dunk 2020, 3–6). Commercial players and their cutting-edge innovations today share the space stage with public actors; in the long run historical perspective, both personal initiatives and private funding have long been an integral part of the space story (Weinzierl and Sarang 2021; MacDonald 2017).

But it is states that will back, consume, and anchor many of the emerging new space technologies and services given their uncertain prospects in the marketplace. The role of states is going to be further reinforced as great power competition extends unambiguously to strategic technologies, including for space. Among those seen as most likely to be at the "center of gravity for space leadership" in such competition are space transportation and logistics, power for space systems, and space manufacturing and resource extraction (Butow et al. 2020, 7).

The United States has already responded to China's economic progress, and the new consensus in Washington is that a more "muscular industrial policy" is essential for safeguarding US preeminence (Economist 2022). The same goal has also driven the United States toward "technological decoupling," that is reducing the flow of technology products, services, and inputs to and from China on its own and, where possible, with other private and public actors around the world (Bateman 2022, 9; Tobita 2022). But just as technonationalism is rising visibly to the fore in the United States, China is competing back. China is seen as a "techno-security" state, a concept broadly understood as an innovation-centered, security-maximizing regime that prioritizes the development of technologies and defense capabilities for national security (Cheung 2022, 2–14). For Chinese leadership, technology is indisputably critical to national security, and space is marked as a "commanding height in strategic competition" (Pollpeter, this volume).

As both the United States and China strategize about how best to defend their interests and persuade their allies around the world in the space domain, they also have to grapple with the intertwined forces unfurling in the space domain today: democratization (rising number of new states), commercialization (unprecedented technologies often led by companies), and militarization morphing into open weaponization (implicating arms races in great power rivalry) (Zhang 2005; Baiocchi and Wesler 2015; Pekkanen 2019; Masson-Zwaan 2019). Further complications arise from the deepening nexus of the space domain with other technology frontiers such as cyber, AI, and quantum, with which we are also just beginning to grapple for purposes of strategy, policy, and governance (Martinez, this volume; Raska and Davis, this volume; Pekkanen 2016; Pekkanen, Aoki, and Mittleman 2022). There are opportunities and threats in this multifaceted tapestry for all states seeking advantages and probing alignments.

Unbundling the Swirl of Threats

It is threats that draw policy attention in space security today, and that may also help account for the increased state interest and spending. I draw together what I see as the principal threats swirling in, through, and at the nexus of civilian, commercial, and military space. I make no claims that the threats I identify are exhaustive, or that some matter definitively more than others; I see them more as specific and diffuse swirls—sometimes illuminated, other times not—in the tapestry of national and alliance decision-making. I assess that states face at least five interrelated threats in a world returned to great power competition between the United States and China, which together amplify discord and frustrate strategy and governance for space activities (Moltz 2014; Townsend 2020; Townsend, this volume); they also complicate prospects for alliances in the space domain. I further assess that these threats begin with orbital debris and stretch to well beyond geosynchronous orbits from Earth in ways that implicate both military and economic security. There are good reasons why they are especially concerning for the great power underpinnings of the United States in the bipolar contest.

First, orbital debris threatens the critical satellite infrastructure in its path. Orbital debris refers to discarded boosters, satellite fragments, and leftover and defunct pieces from human space ventures that zoom around in Earth orbits. US and European estimates suggest there are 23,000–36,500 pieces of debris larger than 10 cm, 500,000–100,000 pieces between 1 and 10 cm, and over 100–130 million pieces greater than 1 mm (NASA n.d.; Liou 2020; ESA 2022). About 8,000–10,400 metric tons of orbital debris is already circling the planet and can enable a runaway chain reaction of collision and more debris called the Kessler syndrome. Regardless of the estimates, the threat is this: Orbital debris moves faster than a speeding bullet (8–10 km/s), and can be lethal to anything in its path—humans, their space assets, and operations (Amos 2021; Etkind and McGuinness 2021).

Our twenty-first century way of life is critically dependent on space assets in a fragile environment, which cannot repair or renew itself. At present, there are 5,465–6,800 known operational satellites in space (UCS 2022; ESA 2022); and if mega-constellations of commercial satellites stay the course that number is projected to go upward of 100,000 by the end of the decade (Lawrence et al. 2022, 428). The loss of satellites up there can affect the factual knowledge down here of interest to decision-makers charged with protecting economic, enviornmental, and national security on land and the oceans (Pekkanen, Aoki, and Mittleman 2022). It can devastate our commercial, banking, and financial businesses. It can render useless our ability to see, navigate, broadcast, and digitally connect across borders in peace and war time. It can also destroy the basis for nuclear deterrence, upon which depends the security of the United States and its allies (Finch and Steene 2011; Krepon 2013).

The second threat is anti-satellite (ASAT) targeting and testing, such as from missiles with the potential to add to the debris. Whether such tests are meant to signal elite military space capabilities that deter rivals is debatable; what is more immediately clear is that they threaten all space missions with the specter of even more perilous debris orbiting around. In 2007, China used a ground-based direct-ascent missile to take out its own aging weather satellite (Covault 2007; Kahn 2007; Chow 2017). This event created an estimated 3,400 pieces of debris that will be around for several decades before decaying. Despite the international outrage and condemnation of the Chinese test, other states followed suit. The United States in 2008 (Wolf 2008), India in 2019 (Times of India 2019) and Russia in 2021 (Moscow Times 2021) also demonstrated capabilities to generate space debris.

The normalization of deliberate escalatory behavior by spacefaring countries not only adds to the volume, spread, and lethality of the debris cloud (Tellis 2019), it also introduces uncertainty about the legal and normative basis for constraining offensive state behavior in space and at a time in which respect for international law and diplomacy has declined (Israel 2014; Burns and Thomas-Greenfield 2020). These conditions are likely to continue in the current geopolitical flux, inviting others to similarly acquire or advance ASAT capabilities, whether kinetic or non-kinetic (Harrison et al. 2022, 2–7). They also pose credible risks for the commercial mega-constellation satellites that may become legitimate military targets in ground wars (Reuters 2022).

A third threat comes from the fact that technology-centered solutions to orbital debris are themselves a problem. Ninety-five percent of space technologies are dual use, meaning they can serve both civilian and military purposes (Johnson-Freese 2007, 6–7, 30–34). This means that dealing with space debris is as much a national security issue as it is a technical one, whether we are dealing with human or autonomous missions (Pekkanen 2018; Townsend 2020, 31–35; Miller 2021, 1–2). To think of debris circling the Earth as just an obstacle in the path of such missions is naive. As all outer space activities are deeply rooted in the geopolitics on Earth, the hidden challenge of the debris is the weaponization of space technologies meant to clean it up.

The ambiguities of dual-use technologies also mean that counterspace capabilities can be couched in commercial and government proclamations of making space operations safe, sustainable, and servicable (Pekkanen 2020). This has spurred what can best be described as a counterspace race, involving both old and new space entrepreneurs. Spacecraft ostensibly intended for orbital debris and other kinds of servicing can also degrade, damage, disable, or destroy rival satellites and spacecraft. This can affect civilian, commercial, and military assets in a non-discriminatory manner, with grave consequences for a target country's society, economy, and defense.

Orbital debris, along with clean-up technologies, poses a non-discriminatory threat to all spacefaring countries, but it is most immediately threatening for the United States. This is because the United States accounts for over 60 percent of all known operational satellites today, the bulk of them commercial (UCS 2022); this dependence is likely to increase if mega-constellations, led by US companies, stay the course. While there are reports that China is aiming for a mega-constellation with around 13,000 national satellites to enable an internet network (Jones 2021), current estimates suggest that it only has a total of around 541 satellites.

There is no doubt that all stakeholders would lose in the event of a debris catastrophe, whether it comes about accidentally (collisions or blow-ups, say) or deliberately (kinetic); but there is also no doubt the collateral damage may be worthwhile for a rival because it would deal a far more crippling blow to the more heavily space-dependent United States. This is the United States' Achilles heel, and both its allies and rivals know it (Griggs 2018). This fact also explains the expanding allied emphasis on Space Domain Awareness (SDA), knowledge of the space environment in ways that allow the US military to "'understand potential adversaries on orbit, their capabilities, their weapons, their operations and intentions'" (Erwin 2022b). If attribution is indeed going to be a military mission, then non-kinetic threats will likely become the next frontier—jamming, lasers, rendezvous proximity operations, cyberattacks, for example (Sokolski 2022; Livingstone and Lewis, 2016). The nexus of a digitized critical space infrastructure that is vulnerable to cyberattacks will be especially challenging as satellite-based commercial internet platforms go into place through mega-constellations.

Fourth, there is no getting away from the fact that all these strands are colored by what military leaders see as the historical inevitability of great power competition in a new warfighting domain (Hille 2009). One threat assessment sums it up: "Beijing is working to match or exceed US capabilities in space to gain the military, economic, and prestige benefits that Washington has accrued from space leadership" (ODNI 2022, 8). As the United States has designated China a peer competitor bar none, their national rivalries now extend to military, civilian, and commercial space activities in all orbital regimes, near to and far from Earth (USGOV 2017; 2022; USSF 2020, 14; DIA 2022). The United States, in short, must prepare for conflict that extends or originates in space, in ways that make it less meaningful to talk about space war distinct from terrestrial war; rather, we are looking at a future where it will most likely be "'an extension of traditional armed conflict into the space domain of human endeavor'" (Cronk 2021). This involves matters well beyond just the protection of critical satellite infrastructure that fuel US global preeminence.

Among them is countering advanced space weapons that negate US ballistic missile defenses worldwide. China's reported test of a new nuclear-capable hypersonic missile—a "spacecraft" not a missile, the Chinese foreign ministry claimed—raises concerns about US capabilities for defending against and deterring rivals on a global basis (Sevastopulo and Hille 2021; Sevastopulo 2021). The dual-use nature of competing technologies also raises concerns about the intentions behind military and science "experiments" such as those conducted by the equally secretive US and Chinese spaceplanes. The crewless US X-37B landed after a record 908 days on orbit in its sixth mission, and carried also for the first time a service module for additional experiments (Erwin 2022c); meanwhile, a Chinese reusable spaceplane has demonstrated that it can eject objects potentially capable of proximity operations (Jones 2022). When a US company performs a feat that is supposed to herald a new era of commercial servicing for aging spacecraft in geosynchronous orbit with its robotic Mission Extension Vehicles (MEV), which may, as it happens, also be seen as a potential solution for space debris, the same logic can be attributed to other technology demonstrations (Chang 2020). China has used its space debris mitigation satellite to shift one of its defunct satellites in geosynchronous orbit into a higher-than-usual graveyard orbit, a feat which may also well be billed as just another technology demonstration and not an offensive capability (Jones 2022).

Another ripening US-China rivalry involves positioning for the cislunar regime, the combined Earth-Moon two body gravitational system (USSF 2020, 6). China's impressive feat of landing on the far side of the moon, and reported proclamations, whether hyperbolic or not, that it seeks to establish a US$10 trillion "space economic zone" between the Earth and the moon by 2050 threaten US primacy and leadership in outer space affairs (Cao 2019; Jones 2020). In this vast region, first mover advantages across an integrated range of activities—locating and developing satellites for communication, positioning, and navigation; setting up gateways, habitats, labs, and settlements; exploiting space resources on the moon, asteroids, and other celestial bodies; and so on—will determine whose rules matter and who ultimately governs (Erwin 2020).

Finally, economic threats are intimately connected to space technology leadership. The expanding policy emphasis on decoupling, noted above, has turned the hopeful paradigm of economic interdependence on its head. As aptly noted, technology matters deeply to the bipolar contestation because, on one side, "the US government has come to see technological interdependence with China as a major threat to American security, prosperity, and values. Washington fears that Beijing can leverage technological linkages to steal secrets, spread disinformation, surveil dissidents, hold US infrastructure hostage, and leap ahead in economic competition, among other threats"—themes that are asserted outright by political leadership and are the impetus behind the Wolf Amendment that largely bars space collaboration between the two countries (Foust 2019; O'Connor 2021; Bateman 2022, 9, 35–36). China has also learned about fragility and dependence, and sees US laws and policies causing " 'targeted decoupling [from the West] of Chinese products, technology, industries and regions' " as a realistic threat, already restricting access to strategic technologies such as advanced semiconductor chips; as far as China is concerned the bipolar contest has "entered a long-term phase" (Jiang 2022).

The recognition of a long game is especially pertinent to space, and states will continue to loom large out there in the foreseeable future, given the realities of the space economy today. The fact is that, while visions of lunarscape may dance in our heads, the commercial state of play reveals sobering gaps between revenues and rhetoric. The global space economy was estimated to be around US$370 billion in 2021, comprising commercial space revenues, government procurement, and other government spending (Euroconsult 2022). It is the commercial side that dominates the picture at around 75 percent of the total, with government procurement at 16 percent (divided evenly between civil and defense clients), and another 9 percent from other government clients.

Some signs about these economic realities are certainly encouraging. According to some reports, the global pandemic appears not to have affected the prospects for continued growth in the global space economy too much, again dominated by the commercial sector which increased its revenues by about 6 percent; notably, despite ups and downs, higher spending on both military and civil space programs by some governments may also have boosted growth, such as the estimated 18 percent increase in spending in the United States and 23 percent increase in China (Werner 2021; Space Foundation 2022). Given present trajectories of private funding, technology innovations, and increasing public-sector interest, the global space industry is projected to generate revenues of around US$1 trillion by 2040 (Morgan Stanley 2020).

However, although commercial segments such as Earth observation, Space Situational Awareness (SSA), space logistics, and other technology demonstration missions draw excited attention, they remain at around 8 percent of the total global space market. Put another way, at present, the satellite industry accounts for well over 70 percent of the global space economy including satellite manufacturing, ground equipment, and satellite services (Bryce Tech 2022). Launch vehicle innovations, such as reusability pioneered by Blue Origin and SpaceX, draw headline news; but the launch market itself was estimated to be just US$5.7 billion in 2021 (relative to the total satellite industry revenues of US$279 billion). Similarly, while there is much interest surrounding an in-space economy, including commercial space stations, the fact is that the bulk of products and services remain focused on earthly uses (Foust 2022c; Weinzierl and Sarang 2021).

While the business case may be tenuous, perceptions have charged forward. There appears to be "palpable sense" that we have already entered a commercial "orbital age," the next industrial revolution led by technologies that are commercializing space; and while there may be skepticism about it, the United States is being called on to prepare to lead or to follow China (Vice 2022). In other words, the balance of power in space in the future will be affected by responses (or not) to the shifting balance of power between these two leading contenders around us today. It matters how the leading contenders strategize. As China's leadership observes, "A new round of scientific and technological revolution and industrial transformation is well under way, and a significant shift is taking place in the international balance of power, presenting China with new strategic opportunities in pursuing development" (Xi 2022, 21).

Mapping the Bipolarization of Space Alliances

One set of responses to the swirl of threats has come in the form of alliances, with the United States trying to externally balance China's space power and vice versa. For the United States, "A key component of China's strategy is to displace the US as the leading power in space and lure US allies and partners away from US-led space initiatives, through its Belt and Road initiative and plans for an Earth Moon Economic Zone" (Butow et al. 2020, 11). China's leadership marks manned spaceflight, lunar and Martian exploration, and satellite navigation as core technologies amid emerging strategic industries; and while it eschews the language of alliances perhaps because they can be sees as the divisive "erection of 'fences and barriers,'" it is nevertheless "committed to promoting a new type of international relations, deepening and expanding global partnerships . . . and broadening the convergence of interests with other countries" (Xi 2022, 7, 53–54). By whatever name they call their external balancing, there is little question that both the United States and China are competing to lead and head up allied ventures that expand activities in cislunar space and allow control of critical chokepoints because the thinking is:

> As space activities expand beyond geosynchronous orbit, the first nation to establish transportation infrastructure and logistics capabilities serving GEO and cislunar space will have superior ability to exercise control of cislunar space and in particular the Lagrange points and the resources of the Moon. Lunar resources, including hydrogen/oxygen for propellant that enable cheaper mobility for civil, commercial and national security applications, are key for access to asteroid resources and Mars, and to enable overall space commercial development. (Butow et al. 2020, 11)

As noted previously, the space economy at present suggests the profitability of commercial developments in cislunar space is a long way off, and the success of one mission—no matter how spectacular such as China landing on the far side of the moon or, more recently, the US Artemis I spacecraft entering the lunar sphere of gravitational influence (Cheshier 2022)—is just that, one mission and not a trend. Further, in this cloudy future, figuring out actionable items that confer lasting military control and advantages need very careful thinkthrough for purposes of space security (Erwin 2019; Pekkanen 2022a).

All that said, the tug and pull of threats noted above is leading the United States and China to be wary of each other in ways that cut across the civilian, commercial, and military space realms. One indication of this is that the United States is no longer seen as an uncontested unipolar power in space and is having to fortify its alliances to balance the challenge posed by China's expanding side in the space domain (Pekkanen 2022b). Some analysts have already marked the significance of, for example, what these trajectories mean in the context of the Belt and Road Space Information Corridor that promises benefits from Earth observation (EO) and position, navigation, and timing (PNT) space assets spread across stakeholders in Asia, Europe, and Africa (Pollpeter, this volume). Others have marked what fragmented and contested emerging cleavages mean for space resources exploitation (Krolikowski and Elvis, this volume). Some analysts believe that in the foreseeable future space cooperation is likely to proceed in two blocs, one led by the United States and the other by China (Wu, this volume).

To add to and distinguish from this body of knowledge, I draw attention to how the bipolarity in the international space order is also extending to the tussle over space stations and, looking ahead, the role they may play in the positioning of moon bases. We have some understanding of what space alliances may look like and how they might work with the United States in the lead, and I provide a brief historical overview of its activities related to the International Space Station (ISS). This contextualizes what the United States is building on and what China is aiming at. Each, today, has visions of leadership about the future of space stations and celestial body bases; and their quest for allies is deepening the bipolarity we observe. Where possible, I weave in the theoretical constructs raised at the outset, remaining attuned to how and whether the narratives of balancing, threats, and exchanges manifest in practice for states leading or pondering alignments.

Space Alliance Politics in the Past

The imagination of space stations is not new. They have a history that crystallized in the early twentieth century and emerged in popular culture prior to becoming a concept widely advocated by spaceflight theoreticians: "base camp to the stars" (Launius 2003, 1–51, 7; Baker 2007, 1–19). Nor is great power rivalry over them new (Burrows 1998, 142–46). Eventually, they materialized in the earlier technology endeavors—more orbital labs than permanent space stations—of the United States and the USSR that crisscrossed civilian and military efforts, and led to the notable Russian achievement of the world's first space station in 1971 (Launius 2003, 53–54; Baker 2007, 15, 21–25; Ivanovich 2008, 48–59). As the US-Soviet bipolar geopolitical rivalry began to dissipate in the 1990s, space stations took on a more collaborative hue. Russia's Mir station operated from 1986 to 2001 as the world's first modular station that enabled human habitation; and it hosted successive US shuttle docking and astronaut exchanges through the Shuttle-Mir program between 1995 and 1998 (Uri 2021a; 2021b; Launius 2003, 244–245, Appendix 8).

Nowhere has this collaborative narrative been more celebrated than in the case of the ISS, seen as the largest international civil cooperation program to date (Cross 2019, 1418). Led by the United States, the domestic policy path to the ISS was more protracted, negotiated, and winding than is widely appreciated. After all, what do you do when you have been to the moon and back? In the post-Apollo era, the race was done and won, there was no national emergency, no "technological challenge as threatening as an old-fashioned war," no uncompromising objective that had to be met with an enemy in mind; further, there appeared to be little top-level political consensus on the purpose and direction of national space policy, hard to get a sitting president to even say space station much less endorse it outright in public (McCurdy 1990, 25, 34–35, 56–62).

The technology missions emerged slowly, trying to build on unused Apollo hardware, and were always marked by competing priorities that had to get through budgetary, policy, and political gatekeepers. These included: Skylab, the United States' first space station, launched in 1973 and abandoned in 1974, which crashed back to Earth in 1979; the space shuttle transportation system, which meanwhile tried to get off the Earth and finally did so in April 1981; the European Spacelab module that flew aboard the shuttle from 1983 to 1998 but was not a US space station; and the curious case of Freedom station, thought of as the successor to Skylab, that became a program of perpetual design well into the 1990s and was redirected to the ISS as US astronauts began to train on the Russian Mir, signaling a new era of international cooperation (Shayler 2001, xiii–xv, 297–333; Launius 2003, 111–41: Neal 2014; MacDonald 2017, 195–99).

Technology is only one part of the story, however. The ideological heart of US leadership in the 1980s, meaning famously that of the then president, was focused on winning the bipolar contest with the Soviets, including in space (USGOV 1984; Stares 1985, 225–29; McCurdy 1990, 161; Launius 2003, 120–21). The Strategic Defence Initiative (SDI, aka Star Wars) that drew attention to ballistic missile defense research and development was as much a part of the national space tapestry as visions of US "technological leadership" that took shape and were trumpeted in public for the benefit of both domestic and international audiences (USGOV 1984a; 1984b). When it finally came in 1984, the presidential directive to NASA to develop a "permanently manned space station and to do it within a decade," also laid out a mandate for NASA to invite participation by allies who shared similar goals about peaceful, economic, and scientific gains in space and could help "meet . . . challenges and share in their benefits" (USGOV 1984b).

There was no question, though, that the United States would lead. But the international pathways to bringing allies on board was a long and arduous process; it also cut across US presidents more or less enthusiastic about space activities, field centers more or less dubious about international partnerships, and the national security establishment always concerned with the military implications of foreign entanglements in space ventures (McCurdy 1990, 99–107, 197–203; Longsdon 1998). It took considerable time and diplomacy to determine the degree and nature of international involvement (e.g., joint engineering? mere use of facilities?), to figure out how costs and gains would be distributed, to persuade possible allies—some of them skeptical of collaboration and in favor of autonomous capabilities—of the "what" and "why" of the space station concept (Kuzminski 2023).

Mirroring the interests of a wide variety of US stakeholders, European and Japanese players too were watchful of safegaurding their own accumulated material knowledge and industrial advantages. At the end of many studies of hardware contributions and mission requirements by the potential allies, the general concept of a "distributed architecture" for the space station gained ground as the basis for international cooperation among the United States, Canada, Japan, and Europe; but that did not subsequently stop tough rounds of negotiations in the 1980s and 1990s, including when a major new actor, the Russian Federation, was added to the mix (Longsdon 1998, 12). Their expectations for the give-and-take of technology element contributions, for example, to what became the ISS are detailed in the four bilateral agreements that NASA signed with each of these players (NASA 1998). These frameworks also raised broader issues of territorial control for sovereign states interested in building allied architectures in space (Stuart 2009, 13). The successful inclusion of a diminished Russia—whose predecessor at one time was the principal source of geopolitical rivalry for the United States—is a powerful reminder of the importance of national interests, the fluidity of great power status, and the changeability of alignments in the international space order.

Contemporary Alliances Politics in the Space Domain

The United States is once again facing a singularly prominent contender—this time China. China has risen; it has intensifying geopolitical influence, expanding dual-use capabilities in space, and a demonstrable will to lead in space affairs. While the United States has, to varying degrees, brought all the threats enumerated earlier to wrap Chinese space activities in a cloak of negativity—orbital debris, kinetic ASAT testing, dual-use technologies, warfighting domain, industrial primacy—China has pushed back. When the US Secretary of Defense released the "Tenets of Responsible Behavior in Space" with calls for, among other things, behaving with due regard for others, limiting debris, and avoiding harmful interference China questioned whether that could be taken seriously from a power that was, from its point of view, building a space force, thwarting arms control, and seeking military dominance in space (USDOD 2021; Global Times 2022).

From the perspective of fostering peaceful prospects in outer space, neither side appears particularly responsible to the other. Nor can either side take it for granted that it can get to, use, and move about in space free from threats of disruption, whether accidental, deliberate, or other. In this environment, any space activities related to space stations that can be construed as augmenting an alliance is taken as aimed at the other. These elements are gathering force at time when the physical life-cycle of the aging US-led ISS nears its end, and is not expected to function beyond the 2030s. In fact, preemptive plans to deorbit the ISS are underway (Foust 2022b). The jostling for what comes next and is led by whom—the United States or China—is the beating heart of bipolarity in the present space order.

THE UNITED STATES AND ITS "ALLIES"

Having shepherd the ISS, the United States comes to the new bipolar contest with preexisting networks, technology pathways, and diplomatic clout in leading space alliances. For the post-ISS era, commercialization is an important theme. The United States has been championing the commercial utilization and academic research opportunities of the ISS (ISS National Laboratory n.d.). It is also supportive of private sector space stations to ensure there is an uninterrupted "American-led commercial economy in low-Earth orbit" (NASA 2021).

There are some notable commercial projects by US companies—Orbital Reef space station led by Blue Origin and Sierra Space; Starlab from Voyager Space (and its operating company, Nanoracks) and Lockheed Martin; and private astronaut missions to the ISS and its own space station by Axiom Space (Foust 2022c). But there is a big gap between vision and profits for all such business ventures relative to, as discussed earlier, the terrestrial space economy. Where space stations will go commercially no one can say with certainty, but they will likely continue to attract popular and political attention.

Meanwhile the United States is also working on a "human-tended" space station orbiting the moon, Gateway, which is a critical supporting component of NASA's Artemis mission (Dunbar 2022). The US Artemis mission is aimed at building an ecosystem for deep space exploration, with a base on the moon that enables human boots on Mars (NASA 2020b). Practically, it is about finding and using critical resources that sustain human presence and enable long-term exploration; as well, it is about learning to live and operate on other celestial bodies through innovations and teamwork.

The mission is certainly about scientific discovery, economic benefits, and inspiration; but it is also unquestionably about US leadership of a "global alliance" that works together to learn and innovate technologies for the benefit of all (Dunbar n.d.). As they did with the ISS, international partners such as Europe, Canada, and Japan will work to provide capabilities (e.g. external robotics, additional habitation, habitation, refueling) to support and sustain the Gateway space station (Dunbar 2022). Commercial partners include SpaceX, which is building on its track record for delivery to the ISS and is contracted to deliver cargo and other supplies to Gateway.

To advance the Artemis mission, the United States came up with the Artemis Accords, putting itself in a leading diplomatic position with other spacefaring powers (USDOS 2022a). It also gave itself interpretive and diplomatic clout by grounding the accords in the provisions of the OST. The express purpose of the Artemis Accords is to "establish a common vision via a practical set of principles, guidelines, and best practices to enhance the governance" of civil exploration and use of outer space (NASA 2020a, Section 1). The principles are meant to be pragmatic and, in the implementation of the provisions of the OST and other relevant international instruments focused on Artemis program activities, meant also to "establish a political understanding regarding mutually beneficial practices for the future exploration and use of outer space" (NASA 2020a, preamble). The vision of the accords has resonated widely, appealing, as intended, to international and commercial partners interested in building and sustaining space utilization. The number of signatories has risen from the original eight in 2020 to twenty-three at the close of 2022 (NASA 2020b; USDOS 2022b).

The US leadership of Gateway, and the Artemis mission overall, is likely to be intertwined with military space architectures. This was true of supportive activities by NASA and the US Department of Defense with respect to the ISS. A more recent Memorandum of Understanding (MOU) between NASA and the US Space Force indicates, protecting and defending US national interests in cislunar space and beyond will require "new collaborations" for safety and security (NASA 2020c). It is foreseeable that manned commercial and civilian space stations, and what they are meant to support especially on the lunar surface, will themselves require force protection and security in a competitive bipolar international order (Davenport 2021). SDA will expand well beyond Earth orbits, and calls for a Cislunar Highway Patrol System (CHPS) that "'supports civil and commercial efforts in the cislunar domain'" are already at the conceptual stage (Erwin 2022a). It is not easy to divorce these trajectories from the way the United States is also spearheading closer space defense collaborations with key military partners in Europe and the Asia-Pacific, who supposedly share uniform perceptions of some threats involving the space domain (USDOD 2022; Park 2022; Roh 2022).

CHINA AND ITS "SIDES"

While China does not have a history of an international collaborative project such as the ISS, it has a functional crewed space station, the Tiangong (Jones 2022). China's space station is up and running at a time when the ISS is thought of as having "'good years left'" (Foust 2022a). This means specifically that there could be a space station gap in the near future for the United States. Intertwined with this possibility are the more diffuse national security concerns about falling behind in frontier technologies, which has galvanized a muscular industrial policy response in the United States and also alerted China to the merits of self-reliance as noted above. Space might well be the case that can invigorate even newer thinking on alliances in China's intellectual and policy circles (Zhang 2012).

China's feats are undoubtedly impressive, and it has been able to stick to a plan of action for its manned space program, which dates back to Project 921 in 1992 (Lin 2017; Johnson-Freese, 2018; Lu 2021). While this does not mean that everything has proceeded smoothly or without criticism, the speed and determination with which China moved on the space station project is noteworthy. China went from space labs to a space station and from unmanned to manned spaceflight missions. Its space station has already moved beyond construction to modular expansion and onto the first stages of scientific and technological applications and development (Jones 2022; Xinhua 2022). China has already landed on the near and far side of the moon, engaged in complex sample return missions, and may have plans to complete a manned lunar outpost around 2030 (China Daily 2022).

China's technological inroads make its political leadership in the space domain not just attractive but highly credible (State Council Information Office 2022). Along with scientific and astronaut collaboration with space agencies from Europe, Russia, and Pakistan, China has used the auspices of the United Nations Office for Outer Space Affairs (UNOOSA) to embed "cooperative projects from members states of UN with interest" in its space station (Lu 2021, 12–13). In 2019, its UN program "Access to Space for All" awarded projects involving India, Peru, Mexico, Saudi Arabia, as well as Japan and European Space Agency countries considered formal ISS allies (Chang 2022). China's all-weather partner, Pakistan, has an eye on Chinese space technologies to help monitor and respond to its recurring earthquake disasters and to send its own astronauts into space (Bokhari 2019). The UAE, a signatory state on the Artemis Accords, also signed an agreement with China to land a rover on the moon (Nasir 2022).

Since March 2021, when they signed an MOU, China's partnership with Russia on the International Lunar Research Station (ILRS) has drawn a great deal of global policy attention (CNSA-ROSCOSMOS 2021; Mahshie 2022). It is cocooned in their uniform geopolitical stance. Referring to themselves as the sides in a joint statement in February 2022, China and Russia pointed to the rapid and profound transformation in the world order, proclaimed there were "no limits" and "no forbidden" areas for their collaboration, and asserted that their "bilateral strategic cooperation" was not aimed at others (Russian Federation 2022). This framing includes the space domain—and by extension the development of the ILRS that is seen widely as a counterpoint to the Artemis mission. Neither China nor Russia are signatories to the Artemis Accords, and their MOU is indicative of a closer space alliance between the two. The ILRS, building cumulatively on Chinese and Russian technology, is to proceed in three phases from reconnaissance to construction to utilization. While the ILRS is envisioned as a moon base, it is intended to focus on "multidisciplinary scientific research activities on the lunar surface or in lunar orbit" (Xinhua 2021). The ILRS seeks other mission partners as it cuts across issues of science, technology, law, and policy (CNSA-ROSCOSMOS 2021).

The "long yet complicated" space relations between China and Russia alerts us to possible obstacles ahead in their cooperative ventures (Hines 2021). But as with China's space station, there are reasons why the ILRS might still be a magnet for other spacefaring countries. China brings considerable diplomatic and technological heft of its own to the bipolar politics of the international space order. It has worked to anchor three of its major satellites systems—a "Spatial Information Corridor" comprising remote sensing, communication and broadcasting, and PNT capabilities—in countries along its high-profile Belt-and-Road around the world; and, in doing so, it has emphasized their needs for building up capacity and synergizing developments strategies (Jiang 2018). It has showcased applications especially for its operational BeiDou system, which has entered the mass market, with over 80 percent of smart phones in China in 2021 supporting its positioning function; beyond that, China's Beidou aims to be the "world's BeiDou" as it demonstrates its practical utility in transportation (e.g., vehicle monitoring, port construction and operations), precision agriculture, meteorology, disaster management, and also space station missions (Lu 2022, 8–17, 18; Larsen, this volume).

Further, through its leadership of the Asia Pacific Space Cooperation Organization (APSCO) formally since 2008, China has assiduously cultivated partners, networks, and platforms with developing countries in the broader Asia-Pacific region, and raised awareness of the potential of its space technologies and services for their capacity building purposes (APSCO n.d.). This is the ecosystem that China can leverage as it expands beyond its partnerships with Pakistan and Russia noted above to other countries as well, such as in Europe, West Asia, and the Middle East, with their own interests in lunar and deep space exploration (Bo 2021; Nereim 2022).

CONCLUDING REFLECTIONS

The United States and China are engaged in balance of power politics in the space domain. Relative to every other spacefaring country, the industrial scale and ambition of their space ventures traverse civilian, commercial, and military realities in ways that put them in a global league of their own. The United States has competed before in a bipolar contest and comes to its second space race with experiential learning and capabilities that make it an attractive alliance leader. China, having been named the lead competitor outright, is competing across the full spectrum of technologies and partnerships on its side that are also embedded in, and benefit from, its stewardship of infrastructure projects as well as regional and international organizations.

Each of them is responding to a swirl of material and ideational threats to its great power standing and leadership in the space domain, and one indication of their external balancing is evident in the ways they are tussling over allies in the case of space stations and, looking ahead, cislunar space. The emerging evidence suggests that their actions and reactions are reinforcing a bipolarization of alliances in, through, and at the nexus of space. This bipolarization relates to present space stations in Earth, projected space stations in lunar orbits, and also to bases on the moon and other celestial bodies in the foreseeable future.

While the threats go some distance in explaining what the United States and China are doing, there are other takeaways in the evidence that suggest they should act with great restraint in leading space alliances. First, threats motivate some follower states some of the time, but it is the prospect of exchanges in their developmental interests that appears more important in keeping them aligned. Even formal military pact allies of the United States, for example, are engaged in some economic or scientific way with China's space station. Russia, on China's side today, has been a successful ISS partner for the past few decades.

Second, it is uncertain whether support for warfighting alliances in the space domain outright is going to resonate widely. Trying to turn the kind of bipolar space security cooperation we see more broadly into outright warfighting cooperation may not be a winning alliance strategy for the leading states at this stage. This is not just because follower states may disagree about the unbundled threats all states face, but because those are not the only threats they face. They also see threats internal to the two leading poles that make space alliances with just one or the other dubious—political instability, demagoguery, hyper polarization, protestation, changeability, wavering, overreach, for instance. In other words, neither leading pole is all attractive all the time no matter how shiny their technologies on display.

Third, as both internal and external capabilities will continue to matter in space operations, alliances are likely to harden as the nature of the bipolar contest comes into sharper focus. Domestic technologies and innovations will be center stage in the contestation. But congruence from follower states and international audiences cannot be taken for granted. This means the two poles will have to spend far greater resources on the diplomacy of alliances to augment their space security and influence.

ACKNOWLEDGMENTS

For their thoughtful comments, I thank Iain Henry, Lincoln Hines, Yasuhiro Izumikawa, Beth Kier, Tongfi Kim, Frank Kuzminski, Brett Ashley Leeds, Howard McCurdy, Jon Mercer, Robert Pekkanen, Sophia Pekkanen, Jeff Taliaferro, and Øystein Tunsjø.

REFERENCES

Allison, Graham. 2017. *Destined for War: Can America and China Escape Thucydides's Trap?* New York: Houghton Mifflin Harcourt.

Allison, Graham. 2021. "The Great Rivalry: China vs. The US In the 21st Century." Belfer Center for Science and International Affairs, Harvard Kennedy School. https://www.belfercenter. org/publication/great-rivalry-china-vs-us-21st-century.

Amos, Jonathan. 2021. "Russian Anti-Satellite Missile Draws Condemnation: Analysis." *BBC News.* November 16, 2021. https://www.bbc.com/news/science-environment-59299101.

APSCO (Asia-Pacific Space Cooperation Organization). n.d. "About APSCO." http://www. apsco.int/html/comp1/content/WhatisAPSCO/2018-06-06/33-144-1.shtml.

Baiocchi, David, and Wesler, William, IV. 2015. "The Democratization of Space: New Actors Need New Rules." *Foreign Affairs* 94, no. 3: 98–104.

Baker, Philip. 2007. *The Story of Manned Space Stations: An Introduction.* Chichester, UK: Springer-Praxis.

Bateman, Jon. 2022. "US-China Technological 'Decoupling': A Strategy and Policy Framework." Carnegie Endowment for International Peace. https://carnegieendowment. org/files/Bateman_US-China_Decoupling_final.pdf.

Beres, Louis René. 1972. "Bipolarity, Multipolarity, and the Reliability of Alliance Commitments." *The Western Political Quarterly*, 25, no. 4: 702–10.

Bokhari, Farhan. 2019. "Pakistani Astronaut to Board Chinese Rocket in Race with India," *Nikkei Asia*. July 29. https://asia.nikkei.com/Politics/International-relations/Pakistani-astronaut-to-board-Chinese-rocket-in-race-with-India.

Brands, Hal, and Michael Beckley. 2021. "Washington is Preparing for the Wrong War with China." *Foreign Affairs*, December 16. https://www.foreignaffairs.com/articles/china/2021-12-16/washington-preparing-wrong-war-china.

Brands, Hal, and John Lewis Gaddis. 2021. "The New Cold War: America, China, and the Echoes of History." *Foreign Affairs* 100, no. 6: 10–20.

Brawley, Mark R. 2004. "The Political Economy of Balance of Power Theory," in *Balance of Power: Theory and Practice in the 21st Century*, edited by T.V. Paul, James J. Wirtz, and Michel Fortmann, 76–99. Stanford, CA: Stanford University Press.

Bryce Tech. 2022. "SIA: State of the Satellite Industry Report 2022." https://brycetech.com/reports/report-documents/SIA_SSIR_2022.pdf.

Burns, William J., and Linda Thomas-Greenfield. 2020. "The Transformation of Diplomacy: How to Save the State Department." *Foreign Affairs* 99, no. 6: 100–111. https://www.foreignaffairs.com/articles/united-states/2020-09-23/diplomacy-transformation.

Burrows, William E. 1998. *This New Ocean: The Story of the First Space Age*. New York: Modern Library.

Butow, Steven J, Thomas Cooley, Eric Felt, and Joel B. Mozer. 2020. "State of the Space Industrial Base 2020: A Time for Action to Sustain US Economic & Military Leadership in Space (Summary Report)." Department of Defense (USSF-DIU-AFRL). https://aerospace.csis.org/wp-content/uploads/2020/07/State-of-the-Space-Industrial-Base-2020-Report_July-2020_FINAL.pdf.

Cao, Siqi. 2019. "China Mulls $10 Trillion Earth-Moon Economic Zone." *Global Times*. November 1, 2019. https://www.globaltimes.cn/content/1168698.shtml.

Caverley, Jonathan D. 2018. "The Economics of War and Peace." In *The Oxford Handbook of International Security*, edited by Alexandra Gheciu and William C. Wohlforth, 304–18. New York: Oxford University Press.

Cha, Victor D. 2016. *Powerplay: The Origins of the American Alliance System in Asia*. Princeton, NJ: Princeton University Press.

Chang, Kenneth. 2020. "An Orbital Rendezvous Demonstrates a Space Junk Solution." *New York Times*. February 26, 2020. https://www.nytimes.com/2020/02/26/science/mev-1-northrop-grumman-space-junk.html?searchResultPosition=1.

Chang, Kenneth. 2022. "Why Some Scientists Choose China's Space Station for Research." *New York Times*. December 12, 2022. https://www.nytimes.com/2022/12/12/science/tiangong-science-physics.html.

Cheshier, Leah. 2022. "Artemis I—Flight Day Five: Orion Enters Lunar Sphere of Influence Ahead of Lunar Flyby." NASA. https://blogs.nasa.gov/artemis/2022/11/20/artemis-i-flight-day-five-orion-enters-lunar-sphere-of-influence-ahead-of-lunar-flyby/.

Cheung, Tai Ming. 2022. *Innovate to Dominate: The Rise of the Chinese Techno-Security State*. Ithaca, NY: Cornell University Press.

China Daily. 2022. "China to Complete Lunar Outpost by 2028." *China Daily*. November 22, 2022. https://global.chinadaily.com.cn/a/202211/22/WS637c8877a31049175432b3ea.html.

Chow, Brian G. 2017. "China's Well-Crafted Counterspace Strategy." *SpaceNews*. July 10, 2017. https://spacenews.com/op-ed-chinas-well-crafted-counterspace-strategy/.

Christensen, Thomas J., and Jack Snyder. 1990. "Chain Gangs and Passed Bucks: Predicting Alliance Patterns in Multipolarity." *International Organization* 44, no. 2: 137–68.

Christensen, Thomas J. 2015. *The China Challenge: Shaping the Choices of a Rising Power.* New York: W. W. Norton & Company.

CNSA-ROSCOSMOS. 2021. "International Lunar Research Station—Guide for Partnership (V1.0)." Technical Presentations Made at the Committee on the Peaceful Uses of Outer Space, 64th Session (August 30, 2021), UNOOSA. https://www.unoosa.org/documents/pdf/copuos/2021/AM_3._China_ILRS_Guide_for_Partnership_V1.0Presented_by_Ms.Hui_JIANG.pdf.

Covault, Craig. 2007. "Chinese Test Anti-Satellite Weapon." *Aviation Week & Space Technology.* January 17, 2007. https://spaceref.com/uncategorized/chinese-test-anti-satellite-weapon/.

Crawford, Timothy W. 2021. *The Power to Divide: Wedge Strategies in Great Power Competition.* Ithaca, NY: Cornell University Press.

Cronk, Terri Moon. 2021. "Space-Based Capabilities Critical to US National Security, DOD Officials Say." *DOD News.* US Department of Defense. https://www.defense.gov/News/News-Stories/Article/Article/2629675/space-based-capabilities-critical-to-us-national-security-dod-officials-say/.

Cross, Mai'a K. Davis. 2019. "The Social Construction of the Space Race: Then and Now." *International Affairs* 95, no. 6: 1403–21.

Davenport, Christian. 2021. "Tensions with Russia Are Now Spilling into Space, Complicating International Space Station Partnership." *The Washington Post.* December 21, 2021. https://www.washingtonpost.com/technology/2021/12/21/us-russia-space-station-tension/.

DIA (US Defense Intelligence Agency). 2022. "Challenges to Security in Space: Space Reliance in an Era of Competition and Expansion." https://www.dia.mil/Portals/110/Documents/News/Military_Power_Publications/Challenges_Security_Space_2022.pdf.

Dolman, Everett C. 2002. *Astropolitik: Classical Geopolitics in the Space Age.* New York: Frank Cass.

Dunbar, Brian. 2022. "Gateway." Media Resources, NASA. https://www.nasa.gov/gateway/overview.

Dunbar, Brian. n.d. "Artemis." NASA, Specials. https://www.nasa.gov/specials/artemis/.

Economist. 2022. "Joe Biden's Industrial Policy Is Big, Bold and Fraught with Difficulty." *The Economist.* September 13, 2022. https://www.economist.com/united-states/2022/09/13/joe-bidens-industrial-policy-is-big-bold-and-fraught-with-difficulty.

Erwin, Sandra. 2019. "Congressional Panel Looks at National Security Implications of China's Space Ambitions." *SpaceNews.* April 25, 2019. https://spacenews.com/congressional-panel-looks-at-national-security-implications-of-chinas-space-ambitions/.

Erwin, Sandra. 2020. "US Military Eyes a Role in the Great Power Competition for Lunar Resources." *SpaceNews.* August 20, 2020. https://spacenews.com/u-s-military-eyes-a-role-in-the-great-power-competition-for-lunar-resources/.

Erwin, Sandra. 2022a. "Industry Proposals Sought for 'Cislunar Highway Patrol' Satellite." *SpaceNews.* March 21, 2022. https://spacenews.com/industry-proposals-sought-for-cislunar-highway-patrol-satellite/.

Erwin, Sandra. 2022b. "Private Industry Aims to Fill Demand for Space Threat Intelligence." *SpaceNews.* September 18, 2022. https://spacenews.com/private-industry-aims-to-fill-demand-for-space-threat-intelligence/.

Erwin, Sandra. 2022c. "X-37b Spaceplane Completes Its Sixth Mission, Lands after Nearly 30 Months in Orbit." *SpaceNews*. November 12, 2022. https://spacenews.com/x-37b-space-plane-completes-its-sixth-mission-lands-after-nearly-30-months-in-orbit/.

ESA, (European Space Agency). 2022. "Space Debris by the Numbers." https://www.esa.int/Space_Safety/Space_Debris/Space_debris_by_the_numbers.

Etkind, Marc, and Jackie McGuinness. 2021. "NASA Administrator Statement on Russian ASAT Test." Press Release 21-156, NASA. https://www.nasa.gov/press-release/nasa-administrator-statement-on-russian-asat-test.

Euroconsult. 2022. "Euroconsult Estimates that the Global Space Economy Totaled $370 Billion in 2021." https://www.euroconsult-ec.com/press-release/euroconsult-estimates-that-the-global-space-economy-totaled-370-billion-in-2021/.

Finch, James, and Shawn Steene. 2011. "Finding Space in Deterrence: Toward a General Framework for 'Space Deterrence.'" *Strategic Studies Quarterly* 5, no. 4: 10–17.

Foot, Rosemary, and Andrew Walter. 2011. *China, the United States, and Global Order*. New York: Cambridge University Press.

Foust, Jeff. 2019. "Defanging the Wolf Amendment." *The Space Review*. June 3, 2019. https://www.newsweek.com/nasa-welcomes-china-space-travel-unifying-force-us-ban-1588704.

Foust, Jeff. 2022a. "Hard Choices Facing Commercial Space Stations." *SpaceNews*. October 19, 2022. https://spacenews.com/foust-forward-hard-choices-facing-commercial-space-stations/.

Foust, Jeff. 2022b. "NASA Asks Industry for Input on ISS Deorbit Capabilities." *SpaceNews*. August 20, 2022. https://spacenews.com/nasa-asks-industry-for-input-on-iss-deorbit-capabilities/.

Foust, Jeff. 2022c. "Roscosmos Head Revises Comments About Quitting ISS after 2024" *SpaceNews*. July 31, 2022. https://spacenews.com/roscosmos-head-revises-comments-about-quitting-iss-after-2024/.

Friedberg, Aaron L. 2011. *A Contest for Supremacy: China, America, and the Struggle for Mastery in Asia*. New York: W.W. Norton & Company.

Global Times. 2022. "US in No Position to Mention 'Responsible Behavior' in Space as Pentagon Doc a Grave Threat to Peace, Security: Chinese FM." *Global Times*. September 7, 2022. https://www.globaltimes.cn/page/202209/1274879.shtml.

Gowa, Joanne. 1994. *Allies, Adversaries, and International Trade*. Princeton, NJ: Princeton University Press.

Griggs, Mary Beth. 2018. "Trump's Space Force Aims to Create 'American Dominance in Space' by 2020." *Popular Mechanics*. August 9, 2018. https://www.popsci.com/space-force-2020/.

Harrison, Todd, Kaitlyn Johnson, Makena Young, Nicholas Wood, and Alyssa Goessler. 2022. "Space Threat Assessment 2022." Center for Strategic & International Studies (CSIS), Washington, DC. https://csis-website-prod.s3.amazonaws.com/s3fs-public/publication/220404_Harrison_SpaceThreatAssessment2022.pdf?K4A9o_D9NmYG2Gv98PxNigLxS4oYpHRa.

Henry, Iain D. 2020. "What Allies Want: Reconsidering Loyalty, Reliability and Alliance Interdependence." *International Security*, 44, no. 4: 45–83.

Henry, Iain D. 2022. *Reliability and Alliance Interdependence: The United States and Its Allies in Asia, 1949–1969*. Ithaca, NY: Cornell University Press.

Hille, Kathrin. 2009. "China General Sees Military Space Race," *Financial Times*. November 9, 2009. https://www.ft.com/content/9be4fa1c-c8a1-11de-8f9d-00144feabdc0.

Hines, R. Lincoln. 2021. "Houston, We Might Have a Problem: Russia's ASAT Test and the Limits of China-Russia Space Cooperation." Modern War Institute. https://mwi.usma.edu/houston-we-might-have-a-problem-russias-asat-test-and-the-limits-of-china-russia-space-cooperation/.

Hyten, Lt. Col. John E. 2000. "A Sea of Peace or a Theater of War: Dealing with the Inevitable Conflict in Space." ACDIS Occasional Paper, Program in Arms Control, Disarmament, and International Security, University of Illinois at Urbana-Champaign.

Israel, Brian. 2014. "Treaty Stasis?" American Journal of International Law Unbound 108: 63–69. https://www.cambridge.org/core/journals/american-journal-of-international-law/article/treaty-stasis/EC004CDD39BDF638E02435E9CDFA049C.

ISS National Laboratory. n.d. "About: History and Timeline of the ISS." ISS National Laboratory, Center for the Advancement of Science in Space. https://www.issnationallab.org/about/iss-timeline/.

Ivanovich, Grujica S. 2008. Salyut—the First Space Station: Triumph and Tragedy. Chichester, UK: Springer-Praxis.

Izumikawa, Yasuhiro. 2018. "Binding Strategies in Alliance Politics: The Soviet-Japanese-US Diplomatic Tug of War in the Mid-1950s." International Studies Quarterly 62, no. 1: 108–20.

Izumikawa, Yasuhiro. 2020. "Network Connections and the Emergence of the Hub-and Spokes Alliance System in East Asia." International Security 45, no. 2: 7–50.

Jiang, Hui. 2018 (30 Jan). "The Spatial Information Corridor Contributes to Unispace+50." Technical Presentations made at the Scientific and Technical Subcommittee, 55th Session. https://www.unoosa.org/documents/pdf/copuos/stsc/2018/tech-08E.pdf.

Jiang, Yaling. 2022. "China State Think Tank Sees 'Targeted Decoupling' in Supply Chains with the West as a Top Risk for 2022 Amid Rising Tensions." South China Morning Post. January 14, 2022. https://www.scmp.com/tech/policy/article/3163447/china-state-think-tank-sees-targeted-decoupling-supply-chains-west-top.

Johnson-Freese, Joan. 2007. Space as a Strategic Asset. New York: Columbia University Press.

Johnson-Freese, Joan. 2017. Space Warfare in the 21st Century: Arming the Heavens. New York: Routledge.

Johnson-Freese, Joan. 2018. "China's Space Station: Persistence Pays Off." Georgetown Journal of International Affairs. May 28, 2018. https://gjia.georgetown.edu/2018/05/28/china-space-persistence-pays-off/.

Jones, Andrew. 2020. "From a Farside First to Cislunar Dominance: China Appears to Want to Establish 'Space Economic Zone' Worth Trillions." SpaceNews. February 15, 2020. https://spacenews.com/from-a-farside-first-to-cislunar-dominance-china-appears-to-want-to-establish-space-economic-zone-worth-trillions/.

Jones, Andrew 2021. "China Is Developing Plans for a 13,000 -Satellite Megaconstellation." SpaceNews. April 21, 2021. https://spacenews.com/china-is-developing-plans-for-a-13000-satellite-communications-megaconstellation/.

Jones, Andrew. 2022. "China's Mystery Spaceplane Releases Object into Orbit." SpaceNews. November 2, 2022. https://spacenews.com/chinas-mystery-spaceplane-releases-object-into-orbit/.

Jones, Andrew. 2022. "China Is Considering Expanding Its Tiangong Space Station." SpaceNews. December 7, 2022. https://spacenews.com/china-is-considering-expanding-its-tiangong-space-station/.

Jones, Andrew. 2022. "China's Shijian-21 Towed Dead Satellite to a High Graveyard Orbit." *SpaceNews*. January 27, 2022. https://spacenews.com/chinas-shijian-21-spacecraft-docked-with-and-towed-a-dead-satellite/.

Kahn, Joseph. 2007. "China Confirms Test of Anti-Satellite Weapon." *New York Times*. January 23, 2007. https://www.nytimes.com/2007/01/23/world/asia/23cnd-china.html?searchRes ultPosition=2.

Kann, Robert A. 1976. "Alliances versus Ententes." *World Politics* 28, no. 4: 611–21.

Kim, Tongfi. 2016. *The Supply Side of Security: A Market Theory of Military Alliances*. Stanford, CA: Stanford University Press.

Klein, John J. 2019. *Understanding Space Strategy: The Art of War in Space*. London and New York: Routledge.

Krepon, Michael. 2013. "Space and Nuclear Deterrence." *The Space Review*. September 16, 2013. https://www.thespacereview.com/article/2367/1.

Kuzminski, Frank J. 2023. "A Certain Idea of Space: How Leaders Shape Military Space Posture in Europe." PhD diss., University of Washington.

Lake, David A. 2008. "The State and International Relations." In *The Oxford Handbook of International Relations*, edited by Christian Reus-Smit and Duncan Snidal, 41–61. New York: Oxford University Press.

Launius, Roger D. 2003. *Space Stations: Base Camps to the Stars*. Old Saybrook, CT: Konecky & Konecky.

Lawrence, Andy, Meredith L. Rawls, Moriba Jah, et al. 2022. "The Case for Space Environmentalism." *Nature Astronomy* 6: 428–35. https://www.nature.com/articles/s41 550-022-01655-6.

Leeds, Brett Ashley, Andrew G. Long, and Sara McLaughlin Mitchell. 2000. "Reevaluating Alliance Reliability: Specific Threats, Specific Promises." *The Journal of Conflict Resolution* 44, no. 5: 686–99.

Lin, Xiqiang. 2017 (14 Jun). "The Latest Progress, Future Planning and International Cooperation of China's Human Space Program." Technical Presentations made at the Committee on the Peaceful Uses of Outer Space, 60th Session, UNOOSA. https://www.uno osa.org/documents/pdf/copuos/2017/copuos2017tech29E.pdf.

Lind, Jennifer. 2023. *Half-Vicious: China's Rise, Authoritarian Adaptation, and the Balance of Power*. Book manuscript.

Liou, J.C. 2020. "Risks from Orbital Debris and Space Situational Awareness." 2nd IAA Conference on Space Situational Awareness, Washington DC. https://ntrs.nasa.gov/citati ons/20200000450.

Liska, George. 1962. *Nations in Alliance: The Limits of Interdependence*. Baltimore, MD: Johns Hopkins University Press.

Liska, George. 1968. *Alliances and the Third World*. The Washington Center of Foreign Policy Research, School of Advanced International Studies. Baltimore, MD: Johns Hopkins University Press.

Livingstone, David, and Patricia Lewis. 2016 (Sep). "Space, the Final Frontier for Cybersecurity?" Research Paper, International Security Department, Chatham House, The Royal Institute of International Affairs, 1–44. https://www.chathamhouse.org/sites/defa ult/files/publications/research/2016-09-22-space-final-frontier-cybersecurity-livingstone-lewis.pdf.

Lobell, Steven E., Norrin M. Ripsman, and Jeffrey W. Taliaferro, eds. 2009. *Neoclassical Realism, The State, and Foreign Policy*. New York: Cambridge University Press.

Long, Andrew G., and Brett Ashley Leeds. 2006. "Trading for Security: Military Alliances and Economic Agreements." *Journal of Peace Research* 43, no. 4: 433–51.

Longsdon, John M. 1998 (Nov). "Together in Orbit: The Origins of International Participation in the Space Station." Monographs in Aerospace History, NASA History Division, Office of Policy and Plans, NASA, Washington, DC.

Lu, Xiaochun. 2022. "Beidou Navigation Satellite System Application Cases Sharing." Technical Presentations made at the Committee on the Peaceful Uses of Outer Space, 65th Session, UNOOSA, 1–19. https://www.unoosa.org/documents/pdf/copuos/2022/1._China_2022-0531-BeiDou_Navigation_Satellite_System_Application_Cases_Sharing_for_COPUOS.pdf.

Lu, Yaofeng. 2021. "Progress and International Cooperation: China Manned Space Program." Technical Presentations made at the Committee on the Peaceful Uses of Outer Space, 64th Session, UNOOSA. https://www.unoosa.org/documents/pdf/copuos/2021/CMSA_Lu_Yaofeng_Progress_and_International_Cooperation_China_Manned_Space_Program.pdf).

Lyall, Francis, and Paul B. Larsen. 2018. *Space Law: A Treatise.* 2nd ed. New York: Routledge.

MacDonald, Alexander. 2017. *The Long Space Age: The Economic Origins of Space Exploration.* New Haven, CT: Yale University Press.

Maher, Richard. 2018. "Bipolarity and the Future of US-China Relations." *Political Science Quarterly* 133, no. 3: 497–525.

Mahshie, Abraham. 2022. "Space Force Can Only 'Mitigate' China-Russia Space Cooperation." *Air Force Magazine.* May 24, 2022. https://www.airforcemag.com/space-force-can-only-mitigate-china-russia-space-cooperation/.

Mansoor, Peter R. 2016. "Conclusion: Alliances and Coalitions in the Twenty-First Century." In *Grand Strategy and Military Alliances*, edited by Peter R. Mansoor and Williamson Murray, 376–81. New York: Cambridge University Press.

Marino, Ben. 2020. "China and the US: The Arms Race in Space." *Financial Times.* August 27, 2020. https://www.ft.com/video/80b1eb31-6cbc-422d-865b-29686dc9b235.

Masson-Zwaan, Tanja. 2019. "New States in Space." *American Journal of International Law Unbound* 113: 98–102. https://www.cambridge.org/core/journals/american-journal-of-international-law/article/new-states-in-space/E68383DE71B60A711EE1E4578CA303A8.

Masson-Zwaan, Tanja, and Mahulena Hofmann. 2019. *Introduction to Space Law (Fourth Edition).* The Netherlands: Wolters Kluwer.

McCurdy, Howard E. 1990. *The Space Station Decision.* Baltimore, MD: The Johns Hopkins University Press.

McMahan, Tracy. n.d. "From Dream to Reality: Marshall Space Flight Center' Role in Developing Space Stations." Marshall History, NASA. https://www.nasa.gov/centers/marshall/history/stations.html.

Mearsheimer, John J. 2001. *The Tragedy of Great Power Politics.* New York: W. W. Norton & Company.

Mearsheimer, John J. 2021. "The Inevitable Rivalry: America, China, and the Tragedy of Great-Power Politics." *Foreign Affairs* 100, no. 6: 48–58.

Medeiros, Evan S. 2019. "The Changing Fundamentals of US-China Relations." *The Washington Quarterly* (Fall): 93–119.

Miller, Gregory D. 2003. "Hypotheses on Reputation: Alliance Choices and the Shadow of the Past." *Security Studies* 12, no. 3: 40–78.

Miller, Gregory D. 2012. *The Shadow of the Past: Reputation and Military Alliances Before the First World War.* Ithaca, NY: Cornell University Press.

Miller, Gregory D. 2021. "Deterrence by Debris: The Downside to Cleaning up Space." *Space Policy* 58: 1–6. https://doi.org/10.1016/j.spacepol.2021.101447.

Moltz, James Clay. 2014. *Crowded Orbits: Conflict and Cooperation in Space*. New York: Columbia University Press.

Morgenthau, Hans J. 1948. *Politics among Nations: The Struggle for Power and Peace*. 6th ed. New York: Alfred A. Knopf.

Morrow, James D. 1991. "Alliances and Asymmetry: An Alternative to the Capability Aggregation Model of Alliances." *American Journal of Political Science* 35, no. 4: 905–33.

Moscow Times. 2021. "Russia Confirms Space Weapon Test, Dismisses 'Hypocritcal' US Concerns." *The Moscow Times*. November 16, 2021. https://www.themoscowtimes.com/2021/11/16/russia-unveils-exhaust-fume-perfume-in-honor-of-checkmate-stealth-jet-a75578.

NASA (National Aeronautics and Space Administration). 1998. "Partners Sign ISS Agreements." https://www.nasa.gov/mission_pages/station/structure/elements/partners_agreement.html.

NASA (National Aeronautics and Space Administration). 2020a. "The Artemis Accords: Principles for Cooperation in the Civil Exploration and Use of the Moon, Mars, Comets, and Asteroids for Peaceful Purposes." https://www.nasa.gov/specials/artemis-accords/img/Artemis-Accords-signed-13Oct2020.pdf.

NASA (National Aeronautics and Space Administration). 2020b. "NASA, International Partners Advance Cooperation with First Signings of Artemis Accords" Press Release 20–097. https://www.nasa.gov/press-release/nasa-international-partners-advance-cooperation-with-first-signings-of-artemis-accords.

NASA (National Aeronautics and Space Administration). 2020c. "Memorandum of Understanding between the National Aeronautics and Space Administration and the United States Space Force." https://www.nasa.gov/sites/default/files/atoms/files/nasa_ussf_mou_21_sep_20.pdf.

NASA (National Aeronautics and Space Administration). 2021. "NASA Selects Companies to Develop Commercial Destinations in Space" Press Release 21–164. https://www.nasa.gov/press-release/nasa-selects-companies-to-develop-commercial-destinations-in-space.

NASA (National Aeronautics and Space Administration). n.d. "NASA Orbital Debris Program Office: Frequently Asked Questions." Astromaterials Research & Exploration Science. https://orbitaldebris.jsc.nasa.gov/faq/.

Nasir, Sarwat. 2022. "China to Help UAE Land Rover on Moon's Surface." *The National*. September 16, 2022. https://www.thenationalnews.com/uae/uae-in-space/2022/09/16/china-to-help-uae-land-rover-on-moons-surface/.

Neal, Valerie. 2014. "Skylab Is Falling!" Stories, National Air and Space Museum https://airandspace.si.edu/stories/editorial/skylab-falling.

Nereim, Vivian. 2022. "China to Cooperate with Gulf Nations on Nuclear Energy and Space, Xi Says." *The New York Times*. December 9. https://www.nytimes.com/2022/12/09/world/middleeast/china-saudi-arabia-gulf-summit.html.

Nye, Joseph S. Jr. 2009. *Understanding International Conflicts: An Introduction to Theory and History* 7th ed. New York: Pearson Longman.

O'Connor, Tom. 2021. "NASA Hails China Space Travel as 'Unifying Force,' But U.S. Law Bans Alliance," *Newsweek*, May 5, 2021. https://www.newsweek.com/nasa-welcomes-china-space-travel-unifying-force-us-ban-1588704.

ODNI (US Office of the Director of National Intelligence). 2022. "Annual Threat Assessment of the US Intelligence Community." Reports & Publications. https://www.dni.gov/files/ODNI/documents/assessments/ATA-2022-Unclassified-Report.pdf.

Pape, Robert Anthony. 2005. "Soft Balancing against the United States." *International Security* 30, no. 1: 7–45.

Park, Si-soo. 2022. "Biden Vows to Expand Space Cooperation with South Korea, Japan." *SpaceNews*. May 23, 2022. https://spacenews.com/biden-vows-to-expand-space-cooperation-with-south-korea-japan/.

Paul, T. V. 2004. "Introduction: The Enduring Axioms of Balance of Power Theory and Their Contemporary Relevance." In *Balance of Power: Theory and Practice in the 21st Century*, edited by T.V. Paul, James J. Wirtz, and Michel Fortmann, 1–25. Stanford, CA: Stanford University Press.

Pekkanen, Saadia M. 2016. "China Leads the Quantum Race While the West Plays Catch Up." *Forbes*. September 30, 2016. https://www.forbes.com/sites/saadiampekkanen/2016/09/30/china-leads-the-quantum-race-while-the-west-plays-catch-up/#1f98d8eb5928.

Pekkanen, Saadia M. 2017. "China's Ambitions Fly High: 'One Belt, One Road' to Extend into Space." *Forbes*. May 26, 2017. https://www.forbes.com/sites/saadiampekkanen/2017/05/26/chinas-ambitions-fly-high-one-belt-one-road-to-extend-into-space/?sh=1934062a4c0c.

Pekkanen, Saadia M. 2018. "Why Space Debris Cleanup Might Be a National Security Threat." *The Conversation*. November 13, 2018. https://theconversation.com/why-space-debris-cleanup-might-be-a-national-security-threat-105816.

Pekkanen, Saadia M. 2019. "Governing the New Space Race." *American Journal of International Law Unbound* 113: 92–97. https://www.cambridge.org/core/journals/american-journal-of-international-law/article/governing-the-new-space-race/14BD9B37A7A15A8E225A5355BB29E51B.

Pekkanen, Saadia M. 2020. "Thank You for Your Service: The Security Implications of Japan's Counterspace Capabilities." *Texas National Security Review*, Policy Roundtable, edited by Jonathan D. Caverley and Peter Dombrowski, 70–89, October 1, 2020. athttps://tnsr.org/roundtable/policy-roundtable-the-future-of-japanese-security-and-defense/.

Pekkanen, Saadia M. 2021. "Cautionary Remarks on the Emerging Bipolarity of Space Alliances: A Japanese Perspective." In *The New Space Age: Beyond Global Order*. Perry World House, University of Pennsylvania. https://global.upenn.edu/sites/default/files/perry-world-house/Pekkanen_SpaceWorkshop.pdf.

Pekkanen, Saadia M. 2022a. "The Promise and Peril of Satellite Imagery." *Seattle Times*. August 26, 2022. https://www.seattletimes.com/opinion/zooming-in-on-the-promise-and-peril-of-satellite-imagery/.

Pekkanen, Saadia M. 2022b. "Geopolitics Goes into Orbit with the US and China's Space Ambitions." *East Asia Forum*. December 7, 2022. https://www.eastasiaforum.org/2022/12/07/geopolitics-goes-into-orbit-with-the-us-and-chinas-space-ambitions/.

Pekkanen, Saadia M., and Paul Kallender-Umezu. 2010. *In Defense of Japan: From the Market to the Military in Space Policy*. Stanford: Stanford University Press.

Pekkanen, Saadia M., Setsuko Aoki, and John Mittleman. 2022. "Small Satellites, Big Data: Uncovering the Invisible in Maritime Security." *International Security* 47, no. 2: 177–216. https://doi.org/10.1162/isec_a_00445.

Poast, Paul. 2012. "Does Issue Linkage Work? Evidence from European Alliance Negotiation, 1860–1945." *International Organization*, 66, no. 2: 277–310.

Poast, Paul. 2019. *Arguing About Alliances: The Art of Agreement in Military-Pact Negotiations*. New York: Cornell University Press.

Pollpeter, Kevin. 2020. "China's Space Program: Making China Strong, Rich, and Respected." *Asia Policy*, 15, no. 2: 12–18.

Pollpeter, Kevin, Timothy Ditter, Anthony Miller, and Brian Waidelich. 2020. "China's Space Narrative: Examining the Portrayal of the US-China Relationship in Chinese Sources and Its Implications for the United States." Washington, DC: China Aerospace Studies Institute (CASI).   https://www.airuniversity.af.edu/Portals/10/CASI/Conference-2020/CASI%20 Conference%20China%20Space%20Narrative.pdf?ver=FG0Q8Wm2DypB4FaZDWu NTQ%3D%3D.

Pressman, Jeremy. 2008. *Warring Friends: Alliance Restraint in International Politics*. New York: Cornell University Press.

Rapkin, David P, William R. Thompson and Jon A. Christopherson. 1979. "Bipolarity and Bipolarization in the Cold War Era: Conceptualization, Measurement, and Validation." *Journal of Conflict Resolution*, 23, no. 22: 261–95.

Rapp-Hooper, Mira. 2020. *Shields of the Republic: The Triumph and Peril of America's Alliances*. Cambridge, MA: Harvard University Press.

Reuters. 2022. "Russia Warns West: We Can Target Your Commercial Satellites." *Reuters*. October 27, 2022. https://www.reuters.com/world/russia-says-wests-commercial-satellites-could-be-targets-2022-10-27/.

Ripsman, Norrin M., Jeffrey W. Taliaferro, and Steven E. Lobell. 2016. *Neoclassical Realist Theory of International Politics*. New York: Oxford University Press.

Roh, Suk-jo. 2022. "US to Launch Regional Space Force Command in Korea." *The Chosunilbo*. November 28, 2022. https://english.chosun.com/site/data/html_dir/2022/11/28/2022112801 299.html.

Russian Federation. 2022. "Joint Statement of the Russian Federation and the People's Republic of China on the International Relations Entering a New Era and The Global Sustainable Development." President of Russia, Kremlin. http://en.kremlin.ru/supplement/5770.

Rynning, Sten, and Olivier Schmitt. 2018. "Alliances." In *The Oxford Handbook of International Security*, edited by Alexandra Gheciu and William C. Wohlforth, 653–67. New York: Oxford University Press.

Schrogl, Kai-Uwe, and Christina Giannopapa. 2020. "Europe in Space: Partner, Competitor, and Model for Asia." *Asia Policy* 15, no. 2: 50–56.

Schweller, Randall L. 2004. "Unanswered Threats: A Neoclassical Realist Theory of Underbalancing." *International Security* 29, no. 2: 159–201.

Schweller, Randall L. 2016 (May). "The Balance of Power in World Politics." Oxford Research Encyclopedias. https://doi.org/10.1093/acrefore/9780190228637.013.119.

Sevastopulo, Demetri. 2021. "China Conducted Two Hypersonic Weapons Tests This Summer." *Financial Times*. October 20, 2021. https://www.ft.com/content/c7139a23-1271-43ae-975b-9b632330130b.

Sevastopulo, Demetri, and Kathrin Hille. 2021. "China Tests New Space Capability with Hypersonic Missile." *Financial Times*. October 16, 2021. https://www.ft.com/content/ba0a3 cde-719b-4040-93cb-a486e1f843fb?s.

Shayler, David J. 2001. *Skylab: America's Space Station*. Chichester, UK: Springer-Praxis.

Shifrinson, Joshua. 2020. "The Rise of China, Balance of Power Theory and US National Security: Reasons for Optimism." *The Journal of Strategic Studies* 43, no. 2: 175–216.

Shirk, Susan L. 2008. *China: Fragile Superpower*. New York: Oxford University Press.

Shirk, Susan L. 2022. *Overreach: How China Derailed Its Peaceful Rise*. New York: Oxford University Press.

Snyder, Glenn H. 1990. "Alliance Theory: A Neorealist First Cut." *Journal of International Affairs* 44, no. 1: 103–23.

Snyder, Glenn H. 1997. *Alliance Politics*. Ithaca, NY: Cornell University Press.

Sokolski, Henry. 2022. "A China-US War in Space: The After-Action Report." *Bulletin of the Atomic Scientists*. January 17, 2022. https://thebulletin.org/premium/2022-01/a-china-us-war-in-space-the-after-action-report/.

Space Foundation. 2022. "The Space Report 2022 Q2 Showing Growth of Global Space Economy." Space Foundation. https://www.spacefoundation.org/2022/07/27/the-space rep ort-2022-q2/.

Sprecher, Christopher. 2006. "Alliances, Armed Conflict, and Cooperation: Theoretical Approaches and Empirical Evidence." *Journal of Peace Research* 43, no. 4: 363–69.

Stanley, Morgan. 2020 (24 Jul). "Space: Investing in the Final Frontier." Morgan Stanley Research. https://www.morganstanley.com/ideas/investing-in-space.

State Council Information Office (People's Republic of China). 2022. "China's Space Program: A 2021 Perspective." White Paper, The State Council, The People's Republic of China. https://english.www.gov.cn/archive/whitepaper/202201/28/content_WS61f35b3dc6d09c94e48a4 67a.html.

Stuart, Jill. 2009. "Unbundling Sovereignty, Territory and the State in Outer Space: Two Approaches." In *Securing Outer Space*, edited by Natalie Bormann and Michael Sheehan, 8–23. New York: Routledge.

Taliaferro, Jeffrey W. 2019. *Defending Frenemies: Alliance Politics and Nuclear Nonproliferation in US Foreign Policy*. New York: Oxford University Press.

Tellis, Ashley J. 2019. "India's ASAT Test: An Incomplete Success." Carnegie Endowment for International Peace. https://carnegieendowment.org/2019/04/15/india-s-asat-test-incompl ete-success-pub-78884.

Times of India. 2019. "'Mission Shakti' and ASAT Missile Test: All You Need to Know." *The Times of India*. March 21, 2019. https://timesofindia.indiatimes.com/india/mission-shakti-and-a-sat-missile-test-all-you-need-to-know/articleshowprint/68594586.cms.

Tobita, Rintaro. 2022. "US Pushes Japan and Other Allies to Join China Chip Curbs." *Nikkei Asia*. November 1, 2022. https://asia.nikkei.com/Politics/International-relations/US-pus hes-Japan-and-other-allies-to-join-China-chip-curbs.

Townsend, Brad. 2020. *Security and Stability in the New Space Age: The Orbital Security Dilemma*. New York: Routledge.

Tunsjø, Øystein. 2018a. *The Return of Bipolarity in World Politics: China, the United States, and Geostructural Realism*. New York: Columbia University Press.

Tunsjø, Øystein. 2018b. "Another Long Peace?" *The National Interest*. https://nationalinterest.org/feature/another-long-peace-33726.

Tyson, Neil deGrasse, and Avis Lang. 2018. *Accessory to War: The Unspoken Alliance between Astrophysics and the Military*. New York: W. W. Norton & Company.

UCS, (Union of Concerned Scientists). 2022 [2005]. "UCS Satellite Database." Latest data update by UCS, May 1, 2022 (first posted 2005). https://www.ucsusa.org/resources/satellite-database.

Uri, John. 2021. "50 Years Ago: Launch of Salyut, the World's First Space Station." NASA Johnson Space Center, NASA History. https://www.nasa.gov/feature/50-years-ago-launch-of-salyut-the-world-s-first-space-station.

Uri, John. 2021a. "35 Years Ago: Launch of Mir Space Station's First Module." NASA History, NASA Johnson Space Center. https://www.nasa.gov/feature/35-years-ago-launch-of-mir-space-station-s-first-module.

Uri, John. 2021b. "20 Years Ago: Space Station Mir Reenters Earth's Atmosphere." NASA History, NASA Johnson Space Center. https://www.nasa.gov/feature/20-years-ago-space-station-mir-reenters-earth-s-atmosphere.

USDOD (US Department of Defense). 2021. "Tenets of Responsible Behavior in Space." Memorandum for Secretaries of the Military Departments, Secretary of Defense, USDOD. https://media.defense.gov/2021/Jul/23/2002809598/-1/-1/0/TENETS-OF-RESPONSIBLE-BEHAVIOR-IN-SPACE.PDF.

USDOD (US Department of Defense). 2022. "DOD and Partners Release Combined Space Operations Vision 2031." Release, USDOD. https://www.defense.gov/News/Releases/Release/Article/2941594/dod-and-partners-release-combined-space-operations-vision-2031/.

USDOS (US Department of State). 2022a. "International Cooperation in Nasa's Artemis I Program." Office of the Spokesperson, Fact Sheet. https://www.state.gov/international-cooperation-in-nasas-artemis-i-program/.

USDOS (US Department of State). 2022b. "Nigeria and Rwanda: First African Nations Sign the Artemis Accords." Media Note, Office of the Spokesperson. https://www.state.gov/nigeria-and-rwanda-first-african-nations-sign-the-artemis-accords/.

USGOV (US Government). 1984a. "Address to the Nation and Other Countries on United States - Soviet Relations." Archives, Major Presidential Speeches—First Term: 1981–1984, Ronald Reagan Presidential Library & Museum. https://www.reaganlibrary.gov/archives/speech/address-nation-and-other-countries-united-states-soviet-relations.

USGOV (US Government). 1984b. "Address before a Joint Session of the Congress on the State of the Union - January 1984." Archives, Major Presidential Speeches—First Term: 1981–1984, Ronald Reagan Presidential Library & Museum. https://www.reaganlibrary.gov/archives/speech/address-joint-session-congress-state-union-january-1984.

USGOV (US Government [The White House]). 2017. "National Security Strategy of the United States of America." https://trumpwhitehouse.archives.gov/wp-content/uploads/2017/12/NSS-Final-12-18-2017-0905-2.pdf.

USGOV (US Government [The White House]). 2022. "National Security Strategy." https://www.whitehouse.gov/wp-content/uploads/2022/10/Biden-Harris-Administrations-National-Security-Strategy-10.2022.pdf.

USSF (United States Space Force). 2020. "Space Capstone Publication: Spacepower—Doctrine for Space Forces." Headquarters United States Space Force. https://www.spaceforce.mil/Portals/1/Space%20Capstone%20Publication_10%20Aug%202020.pdf.

Vice, Tom. 2022. "The Most Significant Industrial Revolution in History Is Underway in Space and the US Must Lead It." *The Washington Post*. July 13, 2022. https://www.washingtonpost.com/creativegroup/sierra-space/the-most-significant-industrial-revolution-in-history-is-underway-in-space-and-the-u-s-must-lead-it/.

von der Dunk, Frans G. 2020. *Advanced Introduction to Space Law*. Cheltenham, UK; Northampton, MA: Edward Elgar Publishing.

Walt, Stephen M. 1985. "Alliance Formation and the Balance of World Power." *International Security* 9, no. 4: 3–43.

Walt, Stephen M. 1987. *The Origins of Alliances*. Ithaca: Cornell University Press.

Walt, Stephen M. 2009. "Alliances in a Unipolar World." *World Politics* 61, no. 1: 86–120.

Waltz, Kenneth N. 1979. *Theory of International Politics*. Long Grove, IL: Waveland Press.

Ward, Michael Don. 1982. *Research Gaps in Alliance Dynamics*. Monograph Series in World Affairs. Vol. 19, Book 1. Denver: University of Denver.

Weinzierl, Matthew and Mehak Sarang. 2021. "The Commercial Space Age Is Here." *Harvard Business Review*. February 12, 2021. https://hbr.org/2021/02/the-commercial-space-age-is-here.

Weitsman, Patricia A. 2004. *Dangerous Alliances: Proponents of Peace, Weapons of War*. Stanford, CA: Stanford University Press.

Weitsman, Patricia A. 2014. *Waging War: Alliances, Coalitions, and Institutions of Interstate Violence*. Stanford, CA: Stanford University Press.

Werner, Debra. 2021. "Global Space Economy Swells in Spite of the Pandemic." *SpaceNews*. August 23, 2021. https://spacenews.com/space-report-2021-space-symposium/.

Westad, Odd Arne. 2019. "The Sources of Chinese Conduct: Are Washington and Beijing Fighting a New Cold War?" *Foreign Affairs* 98, no. 5: 86–95.

Wilkins, Thomas S. 2012. "'Alignment,' Not 'Alliance'—The Shifting Paradigm of International Security Cooperation: Toward a Conceptual Taxonomy of Alignment." *Review of International Studies* 38, no. 1: 53–76.

Wolf, Jim. 2008. "US Shot Raises Tensions and Worries over Satellites." *Reuters*. February 21, 2008. https://www.reuters.com/article/us-satellite-intercept-vulnerability-idUSN2144210520080222.

Xi, Jinping. 2022 (16 Oct). "Hold High the Great Banner of Socialism with Chinese Characteristics and Strive in Unity to Build a Modern Socialist Country in All Respects." Report to the 20th National Congress of the Communist Party of China, Ministry of Foreign Affairs of the People's Republic of China. https://www.fmprc.gov.cn/eng/zxxx_662805/202210/t20221025_10791908.html.

Xinhua. 2021. "China, Russia Ink Accord on Building Scientific Research Station on Moon." *Xinhuanet*. March 9, 2021. http://www.xinhuanet.com/english/2021-03/09/c_139797869.htm.

Xinhua. 2022. "China's Space Station Tiangong Enters New Phase of Application, Development." *China Daily*. December 10, 2022. https://www.chinadaily.com.cn/a/202212/10/WS639449e9a31057c47eba3c08.html.

Zhang, Feng. 2012. "China's New Thinking on Alliances." *Survival* 54, no. 5: 129–48.

Zhang, Hui. 2005. "The US Weaponization of Space: Chinese Perspectives." Presentation at NPRI Conference, Full Spectrum Dominance: The Impending Weaponization of Space, Warrenton, Virginia, May 16–17. https://www.belfercenter.org/sites/default/files/legacy/files/NPRI_Dominance_zhanghui.pdf.

Zhao, Lei. 2022. "Xi: China Open to Space Exchanges, Cooperation." *China Daily*. November 22, 2022. https://www.chinadaily.com.cn/a/202211/22/WS637c039aa31049175432b0d5.html.

Zhao, Suisheng. 2022. "The US-China Rivalry in the Emerging Bipolar World: Hostility, Alignment, and Power Balance." *Journal of Contemporary China* 31, no. 134: 169–85.

Zhou, Bo. 2021. "In Afghanistan, China Is Ready to Step into the Void." *New York Times*. August 20, 2021. https://www.nytimes.com/2021/08/20/opinion/china-afghanistan-taliban.html.

CHAPTER 12

....

DETERRING ATTACKS ON
SPACE SYSTEMS

....

FORREST E. MORGAN

SINCE the 1991 Gulf War, the military forces of developed nations have become increasingly dependent on support from orbital assets. This is especially true of Western states, as they typically conduct expeditionary operations, making them highly reliant on satellites for support in important areas ranging from environmental monitoring and communications to intelligence, surveillance, reconnaissance, and precision targeting. As a result, potential adversaries are developing counterspace capabilities in hopes of reducing the effectiveness of Western military forces in war.

Responding to this emerging threat, military leaders, defense analysts, and space systems developers have sought ways to defend space-based capabilities. Such efforts, however, have met only limited success because orbital space is an offense-dominant environment—that is to say, it is easier to attack satellites and their supporting infrastructure than it is to defend those assets. Offense dominance challenges are even more prevalent in another national security field, that involving nuclear weapons. Since it has been so difficult to develop effective defenses against salvos of nuclear-armed missiles, states have relied instead on threatening nuclear counterstrikes to deter potential adversaries from attacking. With this in mind, thoughtful people have asked whether states can also rely on deterrence to discourage potential adversaries from attacking in space.

This chapter explores that question. It begins with a brief review of the history of national security space operations to understand why space systems, which have not been attacked in any significant way before, are being increasingly threatened today. Next it explains the concept of deterrence, which first drew public attention early in the Cold War when US leaders threatened nuclear retaliation to discourage the USSR from invading Western Europe. As the Cold War progressed, academics and security analysts studied deterrence in depth, gaining a richer and more nuanced understanding of the dynamics that result in deterrence success or failure. The product of these decades of study is a substantial literature on deterrence.

This chapter summarizes the most relevant points of this literature and applies insights gained from it to the question of deterrence in space. It finds that strategies to deter attack on national security space systems face several difficult challenges, which pose serious risks that deterrence in space will fail should a terrestrial conflict erupt between near peer competitors that are spacefaring nations. Yet, the future of deterrence in space may not be as bleak as these findings would suggest. Emerging trends in space lift, the proliferation of commercial satellites, and international networking extend the potential of dampening the effects of offense dominance in space, making orbital assets less lucrative as targets before and during conflicts and thereby bolstering deterrence in in that domain (see Whitman-Cobb, this volume). Meanwhile, growing international dependence on space and concern about the dangers of orbital debris are strengthening a taboo against space warfare. Taken together, these trends offer opportunities for shifting from platform-centric deterrence strategies to mixed strategies incorporating network-centric resilience measures to deny benefits to potential attackers and diplomatic, economic, and potentially military measures to punish them. The chapter closes on the hopeful note that, if such trends continue, national space infrastructures could evolve into something resembling an international global utility, one from which all nations derive greater benefit in preserving and protecting than in attacking. In such a future, there would be powerful incentives for states to behave responsibly in space.

How Space Became Both a Force Multiplier and an Achilles Heel

The space age began with the USSR's October 1957 launch of Sputnik, the first artificial satellite to orbit the Earth. People with memories of this era tend to recall the intense competition between that country and the United States to achieve various "firsts" in space: the first satellite, the first human in orbit, the first spacecraft to orbit the moon, and especially, the first country to put humans on the moon and return them safely to Earth. This competition was an important aspect of the Cold War, with Moscow trying to show the world that Marxist-Leninism was a scientific movement that would dominate the future and Washington determined to demonstrate that free-market capitalism was the superior engine for economic success and scientific achievement. But while this very public contest was underway, an equally intense competition was taking place beyond public view.

Space Support to Nuclear Missions

National security space programs on both sides of the Iron Curtain began with the development of systems to enhance the superpowers' nuclear warfighting capabilities.

In both defense establishments, the initial interest in space focused on a desire to develop intercontinental ballistic missiles. This was especially true of the USSR. Lacking a force of intercontinental bombers with which to deliver nuclear weapons, Premier Josef Stalin felt vulnerable to American nuclear threats (MacDougall 1985, 46–55). President Dwight D. Eisenhower, while also interested in missiles, wanted to develop reconnaissance satellites to collect strategic intelligence on the USSR. Facing a hostile nuclear power with a closed society and a vast, impenetrable interior, he feared surprise attack and wanted a means of monitoring Soviet missile developments and collecting information on the Soviet military and industrial complex in order to do nuclear targeting in the event of war (MacDougall 1985, 115–118; Schriever 1998, 14). The United States orbited its first successful photo-reconnaissance satellite, developed in a highly classified program codenamed CORONA (publicly called Discoverer and described as biomedical research), in August 1960. This was the beginning of what would become a steady series of US strategic reconnaissance missions (Day 1998, 51–55). The Soviets protested these overflights vehemently until they orbited their own successful reconnaissance satellite, Zenit 2 (publicly called Kosmos 4), in April 1962 (Gorin 1998, 165–66).

Over the next two decades, both countries developed a wide range of space capabilities to support their nuclear deterrence and warfighting missions. Space-based photo-reconnaissance was followed by weather satellites to support mission planning. Photo-reconnaissance platforms were supplemented by satellites with sensors for collecting data from other portions of the energy spectrum. Communications satellites were orbited to provide survivable command and control of nuclear forces operating around the globe. Navigation satellites were developed to support ballistic missile submarines and nuclear-armed surface vessels. By the early 1970s, the United States was operating a satellite early warning system to detect missile launches and nuclear detonations in the atmosphere and space, and the USSR was in the process of developing a system with comparable capabilities (Peebles 1997, 32–55).

The early years of national security space operations were marked by tension and threats, but the superpowers eventually settled into a grudging forbearance of each other's military and intelligence activities in that domain. While several factors led to this arrangement, two are prominent. First, political dynamics between Washington, Beijing, and Moscow toward the end of the Vietnam War led to a temporary thaw in East-West relations known as détente. Taking advantage of this development, the superpowers reached several key arms control agreements, including the Strategic Arms Limitations Treaty, signed in May 1972. Compliance verification was a temporary obstacle in these negotiations, because Soviet leaders objected to on-site inspections. So the parties agreed that each side would use "national technical means (NTMs)"—a euphemism for reconnaissance satellites, which neither side openly admitted having—as a way to verify the other party's compliance. They further agreed that neither signatory would interfere with the other's NTMs of verification, thereby formally accepting the overflight of reconnaissance satellites (Stares 1987, 145).

Second, and perhaps more importantly, by the early 1970s, both superpowers realized that they had built such large nuclear arsenals and diversified delivery systems that neither could strike the other without receiving a devastating counterstrike in return. In essence, they found themselves in a condition of mutual-assured destruction (MAD). Given this circumstance, maintaining stability in the nuclear stalemate became a principal concern, because avoiding nuclear war had become a matter of national survival. As a result, each side avoided taking actions that it thought the other side might interpret as the beginning of, or preparation for, a surprise attack, for fear of prompting the other side to launch a preemptive attack in an effort to reduce the damage it might otherwise receive. Because each side's national security space capabilities had become an integral part of its nuclear warfighting infrastructure, it had a strong incentive to allow the other side to operate in space without interference. This relative freedom from the threat of attack in space, along with the recently signed treaties, led some observers in the West to believe that space had become a sanctuary from war. Sadly, they were mistaken (Buono 2020; Buono and Bateman, this volume).

Growing Support to Conventional Military Operations

By the mid-1970s, developments were emerging that increased the risk that space systems would be attacked should war occur between the superpowers. While the majority of space systems in both camps were still devoted to supporting nuclear operations, each side had also begun using its space capabilities to support conventional military operations. Military leaders had discovered that weather satellites, developed to support strategic photo-reconnaissance mission planning, could also provide valuable information for planning conventional military missions, whether on land, on sea, or in the air. Communication satellites developed to support nuclear command-and-control could also provide long-haul connectivity to conventional forces beyond the range of terrestrial radio. Navigation satellites developed to guide nuclear-armed ships were also providing guidance to conventional naval combatants. All of these developments created incentives for the belligerents to attack space capabilities should a conventional conflict occur. Incentives which were stronger for the Soviets, since US forces would probably be fighting in Europe or Asia where they would be more reliant on space support. As a result, in 1975 the Soviets began testing ground-based lasers, temporarily blinding three US satellites in multiple incidents, and the following year, they resumed testing their co-orbital anti-satellite (ASAT) weapon, a system they had begun developing in the late 1960s, but put on hold at the onset of détente (Stares 1985, 143–146, 262). Now, with détente eroding, President Gerald Ford, just before leaving office in January 1977, responded to these developments by ordering the US Department of Defense to begin developing its own conventional ASAT weapon. This effort would eventually reach fruition as an air-launched, direct-ascent, kinetic-kill ASAT missile with one successful test in 1985 (Moorman 1998, 171).

Space support to conventional operations accelerated during the last decade of the Cold War. Both sides increasingly used communications and weather satellites to support conventional military operations. More significantly, both sides began developing new navigation satellite systems—the USSR with its Global Navigation Satellite System (GLONASS) and the United States with its Global Positioning System (GPS)—with plans to use them to support conventional warfighting as well as nuclear operations. Both of these systems achieved initial operational capability to provide limited support to terrestrial forces by the early 1990s. Conversely, reconnaissance satellites, at least on the US side, remained firmly under control of the intelligence agencies, which tasked them almost exclusively for "national strategic" missions: those in support of national decision making, nuclear deterrence, and nuclear warfighting (Burrows 1986, 199–224). However, change was in the wind. Under President Ronald Reagan, US military space forces were reorganized to better support conventional military operations. Air Force Space Command stood up in 1982, followed by Navy Space Command in 1983, US Space Command in 1985, and Army Space Command in 1988. Similarly, the USSR reorganized its Missile Forces Space Troops and Anti-Missile and Anti-Space Defense Troops several times during this era in efforts to find the best way to support both conventional and nuclear warfighting missions.

Space Support and Western Conventional Military Dominance

The threshold event, in terms of space support to conventional military operations, was the First Gulf War in 1991. As the US-led coalition deployed forces to fight Iraq, President George H. W. Bush and Secretary of Defense Dick Cheney directed the US space and intelligence communities to make every possible effort to break down classification barriers in order to provide all necessary space support to those forces (Hall 2006, 16). Satellite imagery, once reserved for national strategic missions, was provided to show conventional force commanders Iraqi force dispositions and movements (Keaney and Cohen 1995, 162–63). Military communications satellites, mainly designed to support command-and-control of nuclear forces, were moved and reconfigured to provide an unprecedented volume of bandwidth to conventional warfighters. And when that capacity was fully subscribed, the Department of Defense leased channels on commercial satellites to provide even more (Winnefield, Niblack, and Johnson 1994, 204–13). Even data from strategic missile warning satellites were brought to bear. Air Force Space command and US Space Command quickly set up direct communications links to deliver missile warning reports from a fixed ground station in the United States to theater users, providing warning of SCUD missile attacks (Keaney and Cohen 1995, 242–43). Most significantly, GPS, with an initial operational capability provided by sixteen of the planned twenty-four satellites on orbit, provided coalition ground forces sufficient navigational support to enable the now famous "hail Mary" maneuver: the flanking movement across open desert that ultimately routed Iraq's frontline forces (Winnefield, Niblack, and Johnson 1994, 203–204). In sum, space support to conventional forces was a large part of how the Western coalition managed to quickly defeat the world's fourth largest army at a cost of only 345 combat fatalities and 1,000 wounded (National Army Museum n.d.).

While the Gulf War provided a dramatic demonstration of what conventional military forces could achieve with space support, it was only a foretaste of what was to come. In July 1995, GPS reached full operational capability enabling a whole new class of precision weapons using GPS data to guide them to their targets. Moreover, as advanced, space-enabled command-and-control systems were developed to integrate near real-time intelligence, surveillance, and reconnaissance information with GPS data, a new generation of network-centric warfare concepts emerged, propelling Western forces toward a transformation in conventional warfighting effectiveness, one which they repeatedly demonstrated in the post–Cold War era in conflicts from the Balkans to the Middle East to South Asia (Shimko 2010, 191–72).

Space: A Force Multiplier and an Achilles Heel

These dramatic increases in capability have made space a force multiplier, enabling states with access to space support to reduce the sizes of their military forces, pleasing political leaders and citizens alike. However, they have also called attention to how much Western forces benefit from space support and have come to rely on it. This dependence has not been overlooked by potential adversaries. After observing the coalition's performance in the Gulf War, China set out to modernize its military forces and update its doctrine with a focus on countering the West's space-enabled advantages. Chinese military doctrine now views space superiority, the ability to use space while denying adversaries the ability to do the same, as a key component of what it calls "informatized war" (DIA 2019, 14). Likewise, Russia sees space as both a key enabler of the West's advanced military capabilities and its Achilles heel (DIA 2019, 24). Consequently, both states are developing kinetic counterspace capabilities, such as co-orbital systems and ground-based, direct-ascent ASAT missiles, and a wide variety of non-kinetic counterspace capabilities, such as jammers, lasers, and cyber weapons, to offset the West's perceived advantages by interfering with or destroying satellites (DIA 2019, 20–21, 28–29; Weeden and Sampson 2019, 1-1-2-21).

Western defense officials have followed these developments with concern. To mitigate the threats they present, they have tasked security analysts and system developers to devise tactics and capabilities to defeat them. However, such tasks are hard to fulfill, due to the physics of orbital space and the nature of the systems that operate there. Satellites are fragile pieces of equipment that travel on predictable paths at extremely high speeds, making them very limited in their ability to maneuver. Unlike in war on land, there are no geographical features in space to provide cover. Satellites can be attacked with explosive devices or by kinetic impact—given the speeds at which they orbit, contact with objects of even very small mass can have catastrophically destructive effects. The attacks may come from other satellites whose orbits are calculated to bring them close to (or on a collision course with) their targets, or they can be carried out using terrestrial weapons located in the countries over which they pass. And satellites are not only vulnerable to explosive and kinetic attack; they can be attacked by directed-energy weapons, such as lasers; the communication links connecting them to terrestrial users and other satellites can be jammed; and they and their supporting infrastructure have varying degrees of vulnerability to cyberattack. Finally, lacking any other counterspace weapon—or wishing to make a dramatic statement—a nuclear-armed adversary in extremis could attack orbital assets by detonating a nuclear weapon in or near space. The net result of all of these conditions and vulnerabilities is that orbital space is an offense-dominant environment. It is easier to attack systems operating there than it is to defend them (Wright, Grego, and Gronlund 2005, 5–18).

Given the historical precedent of resorting to threats of retaliation to discourage enemy attack in another offense-dominant warfighting domain, that involving nuclear weapons, thoughtful people have asked whether deterrence might be a viable strategy to protect a state's national security space capabilities. Allow us to explore that question.

DETERRENCE IN THEORY AND IN SPACE

Deterrence is as old as human existence. From time immemorial people have threatened punishment to discourage aggressive behavior and have fielded armies and built defenses to deny potential attackers expectations of easy victory. But formal thinking about deterrence only emerged in the twentieth century when the development of air power gave states the ability to threaten punishing costs on potential attackers by bombing population and industrial centers deep in their homelands (Quester 1986, 1–5). Deterrence thinking crystalized in the Cold War, and deterrence became a strategic end in itself when the nuclear capabilities of the opposing camps made the potential costs of deterrence failure horrific.

Deterrence was the central pillar of Western strategic thought from the late 1940s until the end of the Cold War. As that perilous chapter of history unfolded, analysts developed an increasingly complex body of theory explaining how deterrence works and used it to advise policy makers on strategies for posturing forces and managing the West's tense relationship with Moscow. This section draws from this literature and from more recent publications to summarize the fundamentals of deterrence and apply it to the realm of national security space operations.

The Fundamentals of Deterrence

The logic of deterrence is based on a fundamental principle of rational decision-making: cost-benefit analysis. To deter an opponent from taking some action, one threatens to respond in a way that would raise the opponent's expectation of resultant costs, reduce his or her expectation of resultant benefits, or both, so that the opponent calculates that the costs would outweigh the benefits and decides not to act. While this is a simple relationship, the first complication for strategy-making is that neither side can precisely calculate the actual costs and benefits of confrontations and conflicts in advance. Therefore, the deterrer fashions a threat that he or she hopes will be persuasive then the opponent must decide whether to defy that threat and proceed with the prohibited action based on an estimation of whether the *probable costs* of doing so would exceed the *probable benefits*.

To illustrate this logic, let us turn to a historical event mentioned in this chapter's introduction. In the early years of the Cold War, the USSR postured large numbers of armored and mechanized forces in Eastern Europe. This communicated a threat of aggression to the United States and its European allies. Because the alliance could not afford to raise conventional forces in Western Europe in sufficient numbers to offset the Soviet threat, US leaders threatened retribution with massive retaliation at a time and in a place of their choosing—which implied they would inflict massive costs with a nuclear attack on the Soviet homeland—should Soviet forces invade. Presumably, Josef Stalin weighed the probable of costs and benefits and decided not to act, having concluded the expected costs of nuclear retaliation would exceed the expected benefits of invading Western Europe (Freedman 1983, 76–90).

While this example is instructive, it does not adequately express the critical importance of threat credibility. For deterrence to be effective, the deterrer must convince the opponent that he or she has both the capability and the resolve to carry out the threat if the opponent takes the prohibited action. In other words, the threat must be credible (Boulding 1963, 224–34). In the forgoing example, Moscow had good reason to believe the US threat of massive retaliation was credible in response to a Soviet invasion of Western Europe. The United States clearly had the capability to inflict heavy costs on the Soviet homeland with its nuclear-armed bombers. Soviet leaders likely believed Washington had the resolve to do so as well. The United States had fought two world wars in Europe's defense earlier in the century and had used atomic bombs on another opponent less than ten years before threatening Moscow. However, almost immediately after the Eisenhower administration announced the doctrine of massive retaliation, Western scholars and military leaders began questioning the credibility of threatening such retribution in response to any but the most serious of Soviet attacks, such as a major nuclear attack or a full-scale invasion of Western Europe. The United States clearly had the capability to retaliate in response to lesser attacks, but they questioned whether US leaders would have the resolve (Kissinger 1957; Osgood 1957; Taylor 1960).

Resolve, or national will, is a complex phenomenon that depends on many factors, including the personalities and strengths of character of the leaders involved. But setting aside the idiosyncrasies of specific leaders, we can identify several prominent elements an opponent would likely consider when assessing the credibility of a deterrent threat. First, it would consider what stakes the deterrer has in the issue. States are less willing to risk great amounts of blood and treasure over issues in which they have only limited stakes than if major interests are threatened. The opponent would also weigh what it perceives to be the balance of interests—that is, how its stakes compare to what it believes are the deterrer's. Not only does that influence its perception of whether the deterrer really considers the issue worth fighting for, it colors the opponent's judgment of how committed each side truly is—i.e., which would more likely back down in a confrontation and how long and hard each side would fight should war occur (George and Simons 1994, 15, 281–82). Stakes and the balance of interests also factor heavily in other considerations, such as whether the deterrer can gain and maintain support for its actions from domestic constituencies and international partners. Much of that support also depends on whether the threatened retribution is perceived to be sufficiently proportionate to the opponent's aggression to be a morally justifiable response (Shue 1989, 23–24). Finally, national leaders consider the consequences of the deterrer carrying out its threats. If striking an opponent in retaliation would result in a costly, escalating war, or if the opponent can strike back in some way that would inflict serious costs on the deterrer, the opponent might doubt the deterrer is really willing to suffer those consequences. The deterrer's allies might doubt it too, if it is promising to fulfill extended deterrence commitments on their behalf (Wirtz 2018, 64–66; Miller 2021b).

Finally, an important point that analysts and policymakers sometimes overlook is that, for deterrence via the threat of punishment to be effective, not only does the threat have to be credible, but the *assurance* that the opponent *will not be punished* if he or she does not attack has to be credible, too. That reassurance does not necessarily have to be explicitly stated—indeed, often it is not—but the opponent must feel reasonably safe in not attacking, or there is no motive for restraint. In fact, if the deterrer's statements or behavior causes the opponent to conclude that punishment will be administered regardless of whether he or she attacks, that opponent might choose to attack preemptively in an effort to defend itself or limit the damage the deterrer can inflict (Schelling 1966, 4).

In sum, for deterrence to be effective, the deterrer must be able to make credible threats and assurances. The opponent must expect aggression to be punished, but punishment to be withheld in return for restraint.

Thus far we have discussed strategies designed to deter opponents from undertaking aggressive actions by threatening to impose costs on them in retribution—in other words, *punishment strategies*. However, there is another family of strategies designed to deter aggression by persuading opponents that one can defend against their attacks (or take counteroffensive actions) effectively enough to deny them the benefits of their aggression. These are called *denial strategies* (Snyder 1959).

As the difficulties of deterring limited aggression via threats of nuclear punishment became increasingly evident, scholars and security analysts turned their attention to prospects of deterrence by denial. In 1983 John Mearsheimer published a landmark study arguing that, to more reliably deter an aggressive conventional adversary, one needs to posture forces in ways that convince the opponent that a blitzkrieg-type attack would be defeated, or at least, defended against effectively enough that the opponent risks getting bogged down in a costly war of attrition. Once the opponent realizes that prospects of achieving a quick fait accompli are off the table, he or she is forced to weigh the increased probability of paying long-term costs against the diminished probability of enjoying the benefits of the aggression (Mearsheimer 1983, 28–30). Deterrence via threats of denial would be more credible and more reliable than threats of punishment alone, assuming the deterrer could posture sufficient force to be persuasive. While Mearsheimer's conclusions were based on the qualitative analysis of a limited number of historical cases, a considerable body subsequent work, some of it involving statistical analyses of larger numbers of cases, has provided support for the contention that strategies based on denial are more effective than those based on threats of punishment for deterring conventional attack (Huth 1988, 85–148; Huth and Russett 1988, 29–45; Rhodes 2000, 221–53; Petersen 2006; Gerson 2009, 32–48). These findings are instructive when assessing prospects for deterring attacks in space.

Deterring an adversary from attacking space systems would require the deterrer to issue potent and credible threats of punishment, denial, or some combination of both. While logically viable, making deterrent threats sufficiently powerful and believable to deter attacks in space would be difficult, regardless of how the strategy is fashioned.

Punishment-Based Deterrence in Space

Threats of punishment for attacks on space systems face unique challenges in terms of potency and credibility. The approach that most readily comes to mind entails threats of retribution against the opponent's satellites—the old "if you shoot ours, we'll shoot yours" model. Some observers have likened this to MAD in space, especially given risks that debris created by the shootout might cause a chain reaction wiping out large numbers of untargeted satellites (Gunasekara 2012, 2–36). However, such an analogy is faulty. Nuclear MAD held millions of human lives at risk, creating a visceral incentive for mutual restraint; space reprisal threatens no lives directly, so such a threat would probably lack sufficient potency to deter a serious opponent. In fact, given the disproportionate degree to which Western forces depend on space support, enemy leaders might welcome a game of satellite tit-for-tat, or even a mass destruction of space capabilities. Complicating matters, an adversary might well begin with nondestructive attacks, those that do not create debris or justify a costly punitive response.

With these problems in mind, some analysts have suggested that Western leaders should threaten to punish space aggressors with conventional military attacks in the terrestrial environment (Astorino-Courtois 2017, 4). Indeed, the West has substantial capability, mainly through the use of conventional air power, to punish other international actors and has done so on numerous occasions. Yet, powerful as these capabilities are, it may be difficult to make conventional threats potent enough to deter aggression against space systems. Unlike nuclear attacks, conventional forces generally cannot inflict great costs in a short period. Given sufficient time, conventional forces can impose terrible costs—indeed, they may even be comparable to those of limited nuclear attacks—but the costs are cumulative and take time. Aggressive leaders tend to be risk-acceptant optimists; as prospect theory would suggest, they tend to discount expectations of future cost when they see prospects of obtaining benefits in the near term (Kahneman and Tversky 1979, 263–91; Dawes 1988, 40–44; March 1994, 28). That is to say, they tend to believe that they will be able to withstand conventional punishment long enough to achieve their objectives.

Complicating matters, efforts to make threats of conventional punishment dire enough to deter attacks in space could undermine their credibility. For instance, threats to inflict carnage on enemy civilians in retribution for attacks on uninhabited platforms orbiting in space might not be believed. Carrying out such punishment would result in serious moral and political costs for the threatener (Miller 2021b). Credibility may be further weakened when there is no clear, logical relationship between the misbehavior and the threatened punishment. In a confrontation before the onset of war, threats to bomb targets in an adversary's capital or other major cities in response to an attack in space might be doubted, given the dubious linkage, escalation risks, and probable casualties and collateral damage that such a response would entail.

Conversely, threats to respond with punitive strikes against ASAT launchers, ground-based directed-energy weapons, or other portions of the adversary's counterspace architecture, such as tracking systems or command-and-control nodes, would have better linkage in that they are more clearly relatable to the act to be deterred. However, these threats might also be doubted in many scenarios because such targets would likely be outside the area in which the limited conflict would be fought. Even if believed, the threats might lack potency, given the resilience of dispersed networks and the difficulty of finding and destroying mobile weapon systems. Moreover, an adversary might not attach a high cost to the prospective loss of ASAT infrastructure if it believed it could inflict severe and irreparable damage on its enemy's space assets before effective counterstrikes could be carried out.

Denial-Based Deterrence in Space

Efforts to deter would-be aggressors by persuading them that they can be denied the benefits of attacking space capabilities also face serious challenges. Potential adversaries' writings and counterspace system developments indicate they would be highly motivated to attack space systems supporting Western military forces in a time of war (Harrison et al. 2021). These actors understand the importance of space support to Western forces and how difficult it is to defend space assets. That being said, satellites are not completely defenseless—some of them have passive defenses, such as electromagnetic pulse (EMP) shielding, radio frequency (RF) filters, and shuttered optics that make them somewhat more resilient to non-kinetic attacks. But these features contribute little to deterrence. Unlike visible forces and fortifications in the terrestrial environment, passive defenses on satellites are not observable in ways that are likely to convince adversaries that their attacks would not be effective. In fact, some defenses may need to be concealed in order to remain viable, thus virtually eliminating the deterrent value of their existence. Consequently, the challenge will be to find ways to reduce the prospective benefits of attacking friendly space systems that are demonstrable to potential enemies without undermining their effectiveness. Several approaches are possible, but all of them suffer certain limitations.

One option is to develop more active ways to defend satellites via such capabilities as enhanced maneuverability or onboard active defenses. Enhancing satellite maneuverability for defensive purposes would require improving propulsion systems on satellites so they could evade vehicles that attempt to attack them. However, as previously discussed, the extent to which enhanced maneuverability is possible is constrained by orbital mechanics. Today's satellites, once separated from the rocket boosters used to place them on station, can do little more than effect marginal changes in velocity (delta-V), because their maneuvering thrusters are designed only for orbit adjustment and attitude control. Making satellites capable of anything resembling evasive maneuvers would require adding more powerful propulsion systems to them or keeping rocket boosters attached during their operational missions. Both of these approaches present technical challenges and would add mass and, therefore, cost to the satellite. Satellite owners would have to weigh these costs against the limited benefits that capabilities for defensive maneuver might offer. Moreover, it would be difficult for even a highly maneuverable satellite to evade a direct-ascent ASAT missile, given its short flight time, and the speed-of-light strikes of non-kinetic weapons make evasion impossible, except in efforts to confuse enemy tracking before shots are fired.

Alternatively, one can envisage fitting out satellites with onboard active defenses, such as short-range kinetic or directed-energy weapons designed to disable or destroy other space vehicles that come into close proximity, or even developing escort satellites with such capabilities. But these ideas, while attractive in principle, would all require advances in space situational awareness; current capabilities are designed to support maintaining a catalog of orbital objects, but are inadequate for detecting, characterizing, and targeting (or evading) threats approaching those objects (Baird 2013, 58–61). Developing tactical space situational awareness and onboard satellite defenses would add substantial cost to each mission on which they are flown. Moreover, adding any new onboard capabilities, active or passive, would be a long-term solution at best, as they could not be retrofitted to platforms already in orbit; rather, they could only be installed on new satellites. Replacing operational satellites before they fail would almost certainly be unaffordable, so fully upgrading the existing orbital infrastructure would be at least a decade-long project even if the technology were available today. Escort satellites also face significant affordability challenges, as each of them could defend only one satellite at a time and could operate in only a single orbital plane, due, once again, to the rigid constraints that orbital physics impose on satellite maneuver.

Mixed Strategies for Deterrence in Space.

So far, this chapter has examined the challenges of punishment-based and denial-based strategies for deterrence in space as separate avenues. While such an approach is appropriate for concept exploration, actual strategy making is rarely so segregated.

Strategists typically attempt to weave together multiple, mutually supporting lines of effort to achieving their objectives. Applying this mindset to deterrence in space would entail developing policies and systems aimed at manipulating both side of prospective adversaries' cost-benefit calculations simultaneously, combining threats of punishment with demonstrated capabilities of denial.

On the punishment side, a mixed strategy would require communicating threats to impose costs in several dimensions—diplomatic and economic as well as military—on any state that initiates an attack on space systems. The foundation and central pillar of such a strategy might be a coordinated policy, perhaps expressed as a joint declaration or formal agreement among concerned states, explicitly condemning attacks on space systems. The intent would be to reinforce already emerging international taboos against space warfare. Although the United States, Russia, China, and India have all experimented with capabilities to destroy satellites, no state has yet attempted a destructive attack on another state's orbital assets. Now, more than sixty years into the space age, every additional year that passes without an attack in space persuades more citizens, business interests, and governments around the world that space warfare can be avoided and, due to the negative effects it could have on the operating environment shared by all spacefaring nations, ought to be prohibited. Ideally, aggressive states would be put on notice that violation of this taboo would be met with unified international condemnation, economic sanction, and where viable and appropriate, combined military action. Unfortunately, to date there does not appear to be sufficient consensus in the international community to present a unified front against aggression in space; rather, international concern has only found expression in pleas for states to abstain from space weaponization (UN 2018). Absent this unity, taboos will have little if any deterrent force.

The denial side of a mixed strategy would focus on persuading potential adversaries that the probability of obtaining sufficient benefit from attacking space assets would not be high enough to make it worth suffering the costs of international censure and retribution. Ideally, concerned states would pursue multiple avenues to make their vulnerable space systems more resilient and defendable, thereby demonstrating tangible capabilities to deny potential adversaries the benefits of attacking in space. Unfortunately, efforts to develop satellite defenses have seen limited success to date for reasons stated above. However, efforts to make space capabilities more resilient to attack may hold more promise.

Potential approaches for making space systems more resilient—and thereby reducing the potential benefits of an adversary attacking them—include dispersing the capabilities they provide across a larger number of platforms and placing redundant capabilities on orbit. Historically, many national security space missions have been hosted on platforms that support multiple payloads and users. This has created plum targets of concentrated capability. Similarly, some missions, such as imagery collection, have required satellites that are large, expensive, and easily detected, tracked, and targeted. Distributing these capabilities more broadly and adding depth via redundancy could reduce the benefits a prospective attacker would reap from any individual attack, forcing it to choose between not attacking or increasing the volume of its attacks along with the attendant risks of retribution.

Another way of reducing a potential attacker's prospective benefit would be to demonstrate that any orbital assets destroyed could be rapidly replaced during a conflict. "Rapid replenishment," as this capability is sometimes called, has long been a goal of Western leaders and space officials (United States Senate Hearings 1984, 3,568). Unfortunately, achieving it has always been beyond reach due to the high cost of space lift and the long lead times required for the design and manufacture of satellites and boosters.

In fact, costs, lead times, and orbital mechanics have been the principal factors hindering all efforts to make space systems more resilient and defendable. As a result, efforts to deter attacks in space remain likely to fail in a serious confrontation between near-peer competitors, even if mixed deterrence strategies are used. This is increasingly troubling as the military forces of developed nations become ever more dependent on support from space. Space systems would likely be among the first assets belligerents target at the brink of war. Strengthening deterrence against attacks on these systems would bolster general deterrence in a crisis, because potential belligerents would be less likely to attack in terrestrial domains if their adversaries were receiving non-degraded space support. But the current vulnerability of orbital assets makes deterrence failure more likely, and this raises serious first-strike stability concerns (Morgan 2010).

EMERGING TRENDS OFFER HOPE FOR BOLSTERING DETERRENCE IN SPACE

Despite the challenges that appear to make deterrence in space so fragile, new developments in commercial space lift and satellite constellation architecture, along with trends in system networking, offer hope that space systems will be more resilient with each passing year. If this hope is fulfilled, attacking in space will offer ever-decreasing benefits and deterrence will be bolstered.

One of these trends is the emergence of the commercial space lift industry. For most of the space age, building rockets and putting satellites in orbit were the exclusive purview of state agencies. This was largely because the enormous costs and high risks of such endeavors made commercial enterprises reluctant to enter these markets. However, policy changes in the United States and Europe in the late 1980s and 1990s, as well as the Russian Space Agency, Roscosmos, entering the commercial market after the breakup of the USSR, created conditions that spurred the emergence of a competitive commercial space lift industry. This trend has already begun to shorten launch timelines and bring down lift costs, and it will likely accelerate in the future, making rapid replenishment more feasible (Jones 2018).

An even more significant development is the recent explosion in the number of commercial satellites put in orbit. This trend first became evident in the late 1990s with the launch of several constellations of commercial communications satellites into low-earth orbit. It accelerated dramatically starting around 2015 as earth observation satellite companies began orbiting large constellations of tiny "cubesats," satellites consisting of cube-shaped modules measuring as small as 10 cm on a side. Some of these constellations are composed of over a hundred satellites. They sweep through low earth orbit photographing large swaths of the earth's surface multiple times a day (Anderson 2019).

These developments offer prospects of revolutionizing not only communications and earth observation, but weather monitoring and navigation as well. And this is only a foretaste of what might be on the horizon. Space launch entrepreneurs have embarked on plans to orbit constellations of thousands of small communications satellites to provide global internet coverage (Crist 2021). While some observers have lamented the orbital congestion and traffic management problems such swarms of satellites will create, they offer untold possibilities for making national security space capabilities more robust and resilient.

Historically, military and intelligence space capabilities were hosted almost exclusively on government owned and operated platforms. However, when military communications satellites were unable to meet coalition demands in the First Gulf War and the US military began leasing commercial bandwidth to fill the gap, a new trend of supplementing government-owned resources with commercial capabilities was begun. This trend has grown substantially in the years since, expanding from communications to imagery and other forms of data collection, and it will only accelerate in the future. Skeptics may complain that commercial assets are not hardened or built to military specifications, making them more vulnerable to enemy action and natural failure. But that is platform-centric thinking. When a military or intelligence mission is being supported by hundreds or thousands of satellites, what does it matter if the enemy can degrade or disable a few tens or scores of them (Morin and Wilson 2020)? And in terms of deterrence, that is the crucial question a potential aggressor would have to consider when deciding whether to attack in space: Would the probable benefit of doing so, in terms of degrading its adversary's warfighting capabilities, justify the probable cost it would pay in terms of international retribution? In sum, space strategists need to move beyond thinking in twentieth-century, platform-centric terms and shift to a twenty-first century, network-centric, capabilities-based perspective.

Greater reliance on commercial space capabilities will also bolster deterrence in other ways. Most commercial space service providers do not serve one user, or even one nation, alone. They have multiple customers around the globe—the same communications and earth observation constellations that support the military and intelligence missions of one nation will likely be contracted by other government and civilian clients around the world. This increases the probability that a state that attacks these assets would be subject to international censure, punishment, and potentially even a broader conflict. In fact, both sides of future terrestrial conflicts could discover they are receiving support from the same commercial space systems, making it impossible to attack those assets without degrading their own missions.

From Deterrence to Responsible Behavior in Space

Despite the inherent weakness of strategies to deter attacks in space to date, there is an ever growing list of reasons to be hopeful that spacefaring nations will act responsibly in the future. Historically, punishment-based deterrence strategies have not had much chance of discouraging a committed aggressor who believes attacking space capabilities would improve its chances of winning, or at least surviving, a serious conflict with a peer or near peer adversary. It is too difficult for an individual nation to make credible threats potent enough to deter attacks on uninhabited robotic spacecraft when the benefits of doing so appear so appealing. At the same time, prospects for reducing the benefits of attacking in space have been hindered by the fragility of space systems, deficiencies in space situational awareness, the difficulty of defending satellites, and the tyranny of orbital mechanics.

Yet, several trends suggest there will be growing pressure on all states to abstain from attacking in space. First, the commercialization of space support and the proliferation of large, networked constellations of small satellites are making these services both more resilient—thereby, lessening offense-dominance in the space domain and reducing prospective benefits of attacking there—and internationally interdependent, thereby increasing the probability that doing so would result in serious diplomatic, economic, and, potentially, military costs. Second, international concern about the dangers of orbital debris will intensify as more large constellations go into orbit. Not only will this increase political pressure on states to not act in ways that wreck the environment, it will make them increasingly concerned that doing so would endanger their own satellites and others providing them commercial services (Miller 2021a). Finally, with the emergence of space tourism and an increasing number of states doing human space exploration, the growing human presence in space will only intensify these concerns. All of these trends make it likely that, in the future, states will be more willing to enter into international agreements, such as arms control treaties, "rules of the road," and transparency and confidence-building measures, to stabilize the space domain and govern the behavior of states there.

Ultimately, as multinational commercial space services proliferate, today's national space infrastructures could evolve into something resembling an international global utility, one from which all nations derive greater benefit in preserving and protecting than in attacking. As this occurs, disincentives for attacking in space will become ever more intense, and the taboo against doing so will become stronger and more widely held in the international community, ideally, approaching universal acceptance. If that happens, national security concerns could evolve from thinking in terms of deterrence in space to simply promoting responsible behavior in that domain.

REFERENCES

Anderson, Stephen G. 2019. "Cubesats: The Smallest Big Thing in Remote Sensing Sciences." *SPIE*. The International Society for Optics and Photonics. July 1, 2019. https://spie.org/news/spie-professional-magazine-archive/2019-july/cubesats.

Astorino-Courtois, Allison. 2017. "Space and U.S. Deterrence: A Virtual Think Tank (ViTTa) Report." Produced in Support of the Strategic Multilayer Assessment (SMA) Office (Joint Staff, J39).

Baird, Mark A. 2013. "Maintaining Space Situational Awareness and Taking It to the Next Level." *Air and Space Power Journal* (Sep–Oct): 50–72.

Boulding, Kenneth E. 1963. "Towards a Pure Theory of Threat Systems." *The American Economic Review* 53, no. 2: 424–34.

Buono, Stephen. 2020. "Sanctuary or Battlefield." *Perspectives on History*. July 15, 2020. https://www.historians.org/publications-and-directories/perspectives-on-history/summer-2020/sanctuary-or-battlefield-fighting-for-the-soul-of-american-space-policy.

Burrows, William E. 1986. *Deep Black: Space Espionage and National Security*. New York: Random House.

Crist, Ry. 2021. "Starlink Explained: Everything You Should Know about Elon Musk's Satellite Internet Venture." *C|Net*. August 24, 2021. https://www.cnet.com/home/internet/starlink-satellite-internet-explained/.

Day, Dewayne A. 1998. "The Development and Improvement of the CORONA Satellite." In *Eye in the Sky: The Story of the CORONA Spy Satellites*, edited by Dewayne A. Day, John M. Logsdon, and Brian Latell, 48–85. Washington, DC: Smithsonian Institution.

Dawes, Robin M. 1988. *Rational Choice in an Uncertain World*. Fort Worth, TX.: Harcourt Brace.

DIA (Defense Intelligence Agency). 2019. *Security Challenges in Space*. Washington, DC.

Freedman, Lawrence. 1983. *The Evolution of Nuclear Strategy*. Studies in International Security. London: Palgrave Macmillan.

George, Alexander L., and William E. Simons. 1994. *The Limits of Coercive Diplomacy*. 2nd ed. Boulder, CO: Westview Press.

Gerson, Michael S. 2009. "Conventional Deterrence in the Second Nuclear Age." *Parameters* (Autumn): 32–48.

Gorin, Peter A. 1998. "Zenit: The Soviet Response to CORONA." In *Eye in the Sky: The Story of the CORONA Spy Satellites*, edited by Dewayne A. Day, John M. Logsdon, and Brian Latell, 157–70. Washington, DC: Smithsonian Institution.

Gunasekara, Surya Gablin. 2012. "Mutually Assured Destruction: Space Weapons, Orbital Debris, and the Deterrence Theory for Environmental Sustainability." *Air and Space Law* 37 (January): 2–36.

Hall, R. Cargill. 2006. *Military Space and National Policy: Record and Interpretation, National Space Policy and Its Interaction with the U.S. Military Space Program*. Washington, DC: George C. Marshall Institute.

Harrison, Todd, Kaitlyn Johnson, Joe Moye, Makena Young. 2021. *Space Threat Assessment 2021*. Washington, DC: Center for Strategic & International Studies.

Huth, Paul. 1988. *Extended Deterrence and the Prevention of War*. New Haven, CT: Yale University Press.

Huth, Paul, and Bruce Russett. 1988. "Deterrence Failure and Crisis Escalation." *International Studies Quarterly* 32, no. 1: 29–45.

Jones, Harry W. 2018. "The Recent Large Reduction in Space Launch Cost." 48th International Conference on Environmental Systems, July 8–12, 2018, Albuquerque, New Mexico. https://ttu-ir.tdl.org/bitstream/handle/2346/74082/ICES_2018_81.pdf.

Kahneman, Daniel, and Amos Tversky 1979. "Prospect Theory: An Analysis of Decision under Risk." *Econometrica* 47, no. 2: 263–91.

Keaney, Thomas A., and Eliot A. Cohen. 1995. *Revolution in Warfare?: Air Power in the Persian Gulf War*. Annapolis, MD: Naval Institute Press.

Kissinger, Henry. 1957. *Nuclear Weapons and Foreign Policy*. New York: Council on Foreign Relations.

MacDougall, Walter A. 1985. *The Heavens and the Earth: A Political History of the Space Age*. Baltimore, MD: Johns Hopkins University Press.

March, James G. 1994. *A Primer on Decision Making*. New York: Free Press.

Mearsheimer, John J. 1983. *Conventional Deterrence*. Ithaca, NY: Cornell University Press.

Miller, Gregory D. 2021a. "Deterrence by Debris: The Downside of Cleaning Up Space." *Space Policy* 58: 101447.

Miller, Gregory D. 2021b. "Preventing War with a Warfighting Domain: Nuclear Deterrence Lessons for Space." *Astropolitics* 19, no. 3. DOI: 10.1080/14777622.2021.1994338.

Moorman, Thomas S. "The Air Force in Space, Its Past and Future." In *The U.S. Air Force in Space: 1945 to the 21st Century*, edited by Cargill Hall and Jacob Neufeld, 169–75. Proceedings of the Air Force Historical Foundation Symposium, Andrews AFB, Maryland, September 21-22, 1995. Washington, DC: USAF History and Museums Program.

Morgan, Forrest E. 2010. *Deterrence and First-Strike Stability in Space: A Preliminary Assessment*. Santa Monica, CA: RAND Corporation.

Morin, Jamie, and Robert S. Wilson. 2020. "Leveraging Commercial Space for National Security." Aerospace Corporation Center for Space Policy and Strategy. https://aerospace.org/sites/default/files/2020-11/Morin-Wilson_Leveraging_20201113.pdf https://aerospace.org/sites/default/files/2020-11/Morin-Wilson_Leveraging_20201113.pdf.

National Army Museum. n.d. "Gulf War." London. https://www.nam.ac.uk/explore/gulf-war.

Osgood, Robert. 1957. *Limited War: The Challenge to American Security*. Chicago, IL: University of Chicago Press.

Peebles, Curtis. 1997. *High Frontier: The United States Air Force and the Military Space Program*. Washington, DC: Air Force History and Museums Program.

Petersen, Michael. 2006. "The Perils of Conventional Deterrence by Punishment." *War on the Rocks*. https://warontherocks.com/2016/11/the-perils-of-conventional-deterrence-by-punishment/.

Quester, George H. 1986. *Deterrence Before Hiroshima: The Airpower Background of Modern Strategy*. London: Routledge.

Rhodes, Edward. 2000. "Conventional Deterrence." *Comparative Strategy* 19, no. 3: 221–53.

Schelling, Thomas C. 1966. *Arms and Influence*. New Haven, CT: Yale University Press.

Schriever, Bernard A. 1998. "Military Space Activities: Recollections and Observations." In *The U.S. Air Force in Space: 1945 to the 21st Century*, edited by Cargill Hall and Jacob Neufeld, 11–18. Proceedings of the Air Force Historical Foundation Symposium, Andrews AFB, Maryland, September 21–22, 1995. Washington, DC: USAF History and Museums Program.

Shimko, Keith L. 2010. *The Iraq Wars and America's Military Revolution*. Cambridge: Cambridge University Press.

Shue, Henry. 1989. *Nuclear Deterrence and Moral Restraint: Critical Choices for American Strategy*. Cambridge: Cambridge University Press.

Snyder, Glenn H. 1959. *Deterrence by Denial and Punishment*. Princeton, NJ: Center of International Studies, Princeton University.

Stares, Paul B. 1985. *The Militarization of Space: U.S. Policy, 1945–1984*. Ithaca, NY: Cornell University Press.

Stares, Paul B. 1987. *Space and National Security*. Washington, DC: The Brookings Institution.

Taylor, Maxwell D. 1960. *The Uncertain Trumpet*. New York: Harper and Row.

UN (United Nations Meeting Coverage). 2018. "Raising Alarm over Possible Space Wars, First Committee Delegates Explore Ways to Build New Order for Preventing Celestial Conflict, Confrontation." First Committee, Seventy-third Session, 16th & 17th Meetings (AM & PM) GA/DIS/3609, October 24, 2018. https://www.un.org/press/en/2018/gadis3609.doc.htm.

United States Senate Hearings. 1984. "Department of Defense Authorization for Appropriations for Fiscal Year 1985." Committee on Armed Services, March 6–May 4. Washington, DC: Government Printing Office.

Weeden, Brian and Victoria Sampson. 2019. *Global Counterspace Capabilities: An Open Source Assessment*. Washington, DC: Secure World Foundation.

Winnefield, James A., Preston Niblack, and Dana J. Johnson. 1994. *A League of Airmen: U.S. Air Power in the Gulf War*. Santa Monica, CA: RAND Corporation.

Wirtz, James J. 2018. "How Does Nuclear Deterrence Differ from Conventional Deterrence," *Strategic Studies Quarterly* (Winter): 58–75.

Wright, David, Laura Grego, and Lisbeth Gronlund. 2005. *The Physics of Space Security: A Reference Manual*. Cambridge, MA: American Academy of Sciences.

CHAPTER 13

ARMS CONTROL AND THE MYTH OF PEACEFUL USES IN OUTER SPACE

JESSICA WEST

THE concept of peace has been fundamental to the development of the global governance of outer space. The Outer Space Treaty (OST), which sets out the governing principles for outer space, opens by recognizing "the common interest of all mankind in the progress of the exploration and use of outer space for peaceful purposes," (United Nations 1967). Described by US President Lyndon B. Johnson as "the most important arms control development since the Limited Test Ban Treaty of 1963" (Johnson 1966), it is commonly referred to as a non-armament treaty, alongside its predecessor the Antarctic Treaty. Yet this peaceful image of outer space governance is difficult to reconcile with the escalation of rhetorical drumbeats of space as a "warfighting domain" (Smith 2017) and weapons tests in outer space (Tass 2021).

Despite early proclamations of success, arms control has been one of the most intractable challenges of space governance. It is true that Article IV bans the orbiting, placement, or stationing of nuclear weapons and other weapons of mass destruction in space, including on the moon and other celestial bodies. However, the treaty is largely silent on the placement or use of conventional weapons or other types of force, and on how exactly peace in outer space is to be maintained. Efforts to address this silence have been many. The prevention of an arms race in outer space, PAROS, has been on the United Nations' (UN) agenda since 1978, and at least three groups of governmental experts (GGE) have tried to advance it since the 1990s. Since 1981, various treaty proposals to restrict the placement and use of weapons in outer space have been tabled. Processes to develop transparency and confidence-building measures (TCBMs) and rules of the road have also been initiated. However, so far, no efforts since the OST have succeeded.

The most common explanation for the seeming intractability of arms control efforts related to outer space is that the technical challenges associated with arms control—in particular creating definitions and verifying dual-use capabilities—are simply too difficult (Ford 2020b). Others blame lack of political will (Meyer 2016). Such explanations are not convincing. As anti-arms-control advocate and space-power theorist Colin Grey long argued, the unique geography of outer space does not make it unique in military strategy (Klein 2021).

Freedom—specifically, freedom of action—is a core principle of the OST that has almost never been qualified by restrictions (Saunders 2021). Military space strategy has been strongly influenced by the governing principles of sea/naval power (Bowen 2020). Naval power projects military force beyond land, epitomizing notions of freedom, command, and control (Gray 1994). Naval force has also, notoriously, remained outside of strategic arms control initiatives. Yet even in the United States, where resistance to arms control is perhaps strongest, since 2010, national policy has stipulated that arms control proposals will be considered "if they are equitable, effectively verifiable, and enhance the national security of the United States and its allies" (President of the United States, Barak Obama 2010).

The concept of peaceful purpose offers another possible answer. Notions of peace are deeply entwined with the development and demonstration of the principle of freedom in space. Drawing on theory of political myth, I contend that the failure to restrict weapon use in space is a consequence of an abiding myth of the peacefulness of outer space. Labeling peace in outer space a myth does not mean that it is untrue. But myths hide as much as they reveal. I argue that this myth has served to legitimize military uses of space and camouflage weapons programs, stymying efforts at arms control. While there is some evidence to suggest that this emphasis on the peaceful use of outer space has made the deployment of weapons in space taboo for most, it is also true that a general belief in this myth has permitted some space actors to engage in military competition, cloaked by a fog of peace.

This chapter proceeds with an overview of the scope of space arms control literature before turning to theory of political myth, and its relative absence from international relations (IR) scholarship. Reflecting on the role of myth in our collective understandings of outer space past and present, I draw parallels between scholars who emphasize similar contradictions and myth-making related to equality and freedom in outer space; my own argument situates the intractability of space arms control in what I describe as the myth of peace in outer space. Turning to the roots and evolution of this myth, I situate it in the "space for peace" sentiment that marked rhetoric of the early space age. As with the principle of equality, the concept of peace is embedded in the primacy of freedom, which I argue serves to camouflage rather than restrict military activities in outer space.

The chapter then identifies a series of effects of this myth on space governance broadly and arms control in particular including gaps in rules related to military activities in outer space, protracted disagreements about the aims and means of potential new arms control restrictions, efforts to mask the development and testing of weapons in outer space as peaceful, and the growing blur of war and peace in space. Ending with consideration of a new political process to identify norms of responsible behavior in outer space, I conclude that the solution is not technical, nor even purely political. Arms control helps to perpetuate the myth of peace in outer space. Making this reality requires reclaiming the concept of peace and re-imagining what a peaceful future in outer space might be.

Myth and International Relations

This chapter adopts a novel approach to the treatment of arms control in outer space by situating it in the context of political myth. It builds on my shorter work at Project Ploughshares that seeks to unravel the ways in which our collective concepts and stories about space—such as space as peaceful—work to mask complex realities (West 2021b).

While some scholars have denounced the relevance or desirability of arms control measures in outer space (Gray 1992; Dolman 2012; Pavelec 2012), voices calling for new arms control measures are growing (Grego 2021; Samson and Weeden 2020). But progress requires understanding the nature of the gap. Some point to inadequacy of the existing legal framework (Henderson 2020). The nature of space technology is another focus, with some claiming that it has outstripped law (Beer 1985) and others pointing to the offensive nature of space capabilities that create a strong security dilemma (Townsend 2020). National security policies that prioritize deterrence are another culprit (Koplow 2019). The picture is further complicated by the deep linkages between arms control in space and security dynamics on Earth (Silverstein, Porras, and Borrie 2020).

In turn, scholars have identified creative ways to mobilize existing treaty and customary international law to fill in these gaps (Koplow 2009; Murphy 2019). Emphasis on environmental preservation is emerging as a significant theme (Su 2013). Meanwhile Clay Moltz argues that the goals of arms control in outer space have been too grand, and instead urges more modest proposals (Moltz 2002; 2006) These themes increasingly overlap amid growing calls to prioritize a ban on debris generating anti-satellite tests. Drawing on the past example of the Limited Test Ban Treaty that barred nuclear explosions in the oceans, the atmosphere, and outer space, this proposal prioritizes shared interests in environmental sustainability in outer space (Samson and Weeden 2022; Arbatov 2019; Su 2013) as well as the potential humanitarian consequences of debris damage to critical infrastructure and services essential to civilians (International Committee of the Red Cross 2021). While more modest arms control restrictions that might mitigate some of the most harmful and indiscriminate impacts of the use of weapons in space are welcome, the underlying resistance to arms control in space runs deeper.

By shifting focus to the role of myth, I build on the sentiment of experts, such as former Canadian diplomat Paul Meyer, who argue that the problem is not purely technical, but also political (Meyer 2020). Yet, the intractability of the arms control question in outer space runs deeper than a lack of political will. Drawing on constructivist arguments about the role of political discourse, Columba Peoples (2011) argues that the ongoing arms control gap is a result of the growing securitization of outer space, whereby even non-military uses of space are positioned as essential to national security. Complimenting this attention to the broader set of political ideas and discourse within which arms control is situated, I add an understanding of the role that the nebulous concept of peace plays in masking and legitimizing an ongoing military buildup aimed at outer space. I do this by situating the concept of peace in outer space as myth.

Myths underpin much modern knowledge, including IR. But myth has received little academic treatment by IR scholars. Where it has been considered, it is usually by way of "myth busting" to reveal the beliefs and narratives core to the field as wrong (de Guevara 2016b). Examples include such common beliefs as the notion of an "international community" (de Guevara 2016a). Another example: the narrative that links the peace of Westphalia in 1648 with the emergence of the current international system of states is a foundational myth of IR, which is based on "a past that is largely imaginary" (Osiander 2001, 251). Citing a range of popular myths in IR that claim to both explain and predict everything from "empires" to the "clash of civilizations" and the "end of history," Cynthia Weber argues that myths represent apparent truths and present perspective as objective (Weber 2005).

But myths are also deeply political. Building on the work of German philosopher Hans Blumenburg, Chiara Bottici situates myth in the realm of the imagination, which she argues makes the world possible by transcending differences between real and fictitious (Bottici 2007, 223). She defines political myth as "the work on a common narrative by which the members of a social group make significance of their political experiences and deeds" (Bottici 2007, 179). Such myths shape the political conditions in which the group operates (de Guevara 2016b, 21). Reflecting on this work, Meili Steel argues that we should "see politics as a struggle for people's imaginations in which myth always plays a distinctive but variable role" (Steele 2010, 1141).

Central to this understanding of political myth is the duality of the work *of* myth, and work *on* myth, which Bottici borrows from Blumenburg. The concept of work *on* myth shows that myth is not static, not a single narrative: "it is a process of continual work on a basic narrative pattern that changes with the circumstances" (Bottici and Challand 2006, 318).

In turn, the political work *of* myths "tell us who we are and what we should be concerned with, and they provide blueprints for arguments about policy choices" (Leira and de Carvalho 2018, 222). But this form of knowing can also hinder investigation (Flood 2002) and allow misconceptions to persist.

Myths are not necessarily *untrue,* but they almost always oversimplify. While they promote and construct knowledge, they also "exclude and misconstruct" (Leira and de Carvalho 2018). By making stories simple, they "combine and mediate contradictory realities" (Mathieu 2020, 341). This is particularly true in the arena of public policy, where Dvora Yanow argues that public agencies use myths to shift attention away from competing but equally valued societal principles, especially where they would undermine the unspoken goals of the agency. She writes that "policy myths . . . fill silences in discourse about public policy matters. Yet these myths also facilitate the tacit understanding of and communication about verboten goals" (Yanow 1992, 399). It is here where I situate the myth of peacefulness in outer space, arguing that it has served to create a fog of peace that reconciles and conceals a reality of military competition and arms racing.

Although this argument offers a unique perspective on the technical challenges and debates about arms control in outer space, the latter is no stranger to myth. From Artemis to Guwak, space has long been a source of myth making and human understanding of the world. With the dawn of the contemporary space age, France's *Le Figaro* declared that the myth of space had become reality (Harford 1997). Before Sputnik-1 became the first artificial satellite to orbit the Earth in 1957, outer space was viewed as a tabula rasa "unbounded and undefined in law or politics" (Jessup and Taubenfeld 1959, 364). All stories seemed possible. But this blankness too, was myth; space was already a place of human knowledge and experience (Mitchell et al. 2020). Instead, the age of spaceflight unleashed a new age of myth-making that overwrote the old ones.

Examining the history of the OST, Cristian van Eijk exposes the prominence of what he calls three dominance myths—"that space is without history, without victims, and without rules"—which he argues helped to erase the contributions of the global south to space governance (van Eijk 2022, 28). Indeed, what was claimed as a legal and political void in space was quickly filled with the ideas and power structures that dominated the Cold War (Westad 2007; Craven 2019). In addition to silencing the global south, many of the myths about new empires and civilization's end that emerged at this time helped to legitimize and mobilize military activities in outer space. For example, US media characterized the launch of Sputnik as a sign that a new dark empire (the USSR) was on the ascendant, as evil as the Japanese empire that had bombed Pearl Harbor and made necessary the development of the atomic bomb (Divine 1993, 37). Fear of this new enemy fueled an arms race, which Lyndon Johnson described as "a race for survival" (McDougall 1997, 8). The notion of outer space as the "ultimate high ground" is another myth that has informed and shaped military space strategy (Bowen 2020).

As Yanow argues, such simplified myths about the space age have obscured tensions and contradictions behind key concept and principles. For example, the principle of sovereign equality in space—the idea that all sovereign states are formally equal—masks and even legitimizes fundamental inequality among states in outer space (Saunders 2021). To this point, van Eijk (2022) insists that the OST is based on two opposing values, namely freedom and equality. My assessment adds peace as a third. Jinyuan Su writes that while the principle of peaceful purposes is "agreed upon among states in principle" it is "disputed in substance" (Su 2010, 81). I argue that this practical ambiguity helps to serve political myth.

The following is an examination of both the work on, and the work of, the myth that outer space is a peaceful domain, rooted in the slogan "space for peace." Similar to critiques of the principle of sovereign equality, this peaceful ideal has served to legitimize the principle of freedom of action in outer space and the free overflight of objects over the Earth, which was institutionalized in the UN Committee on the Peaceful Use of Outer Space (COPUOS) and the OST.

Work on the concept of peaceful purpose has continued to provide the political foundation for global activities in outer space. In doing so, it has served to reconcile tensions between peaceful and military activities in outer space, creating a "fog of peace" that not only legitimizes military activities but also provides a moral high ground, which is too often used to divert attention from a build-up of weapons and an arms race in outer space. And so, the myth that peace already exists hinders the adoption of meaningful arms control measures. Without additional work on myth to redefine what peace in outer space means, technological solutions to arms control will be insufficient.

FREEDOM OF SPACE AND THE MYTH OF PEACEFUL PURPOSES

The concept of peaceful purposes has a long and complex history that predates the OST (Buono and Bateman, this volume; Pekkanen and Blount, this volume). Closely linked to the principle of "freedom of space," it has been entwined with military activities and objectives, serving to both legitimize and camouflage them.

The principle of freedom of space was established in practice with the successful launch on October 4, 1957, of Sputnik-1, which orbited the Earth freely and without protest from other states. But the demonstration of this freedom was closely linked to concepts of peace. Sputnik was launched under the auspices of the scientific community to coincide with the International Geophysical Year (IGY). Claiming to promote "peaceful co-existence," the USSR called Sputnik a "success for all mankind" (Shreve 2003). But in fact the Soviet government used the Sputnik satellite program to also test inter-continental ballistic missile technologies; subsequent "civilian" space efforts in the USSR likewise satisfied military interests (Harford 1997, 123).

The United States also made a show of peaceful purpose. Following a 1955 report of the Technological Capabilities Panel at the Science Advisory Committee, "space for peace" became a mantra of US space policy under President Eisenhower, linking freedom of space for all to peaceful use (Tabuchi 2020). In this case, the freedom to employ military satellites, particularly military reconnaissance satellites that could be used for arms control verification, was closely linked with peaceful purpose because the satellites were not seen to pose an offensive threat. But this marriage of convenience was largely intended for public display.

The US rocket and missile capabilities that formed the basis for space launch vehicles were developed under the auspices of the army, navy, and air force. Both the army and air force had satellite programs to develop reconnaissance capabilities long before the launch of Sputnik (Divine 1993, 11–25). However, the cloak of peaceful use was on view at the first US satellite launch, which also coincided with the IGY. Under Project Vanguard, the US Department of Defense was charged with providing the rocketry to launch a "scientific satellite" into orbit, with development by the National Science Foundation

(National Security Council Planning Board 1955). Released National Reconnaissance Office records show that not only did Project Vanguard replace established efforts to develop military reconnaissance satellites with a "scientific" payload, but the Vanguard rocket was selected over the army's more reliable Juno rocket, which was closely linked to the military's ICBM program, so that the launch would appear more "civilian" (Perry 1973). During this time, military leaders were directed not to discuss military applications of space technology (Hall 1998).

This "space for peace" project has thus been seen as a dual-use space program to launch a civilian scientific satellite that established the principle of freedom of space and unimpeded overflight of Earth so that military satellites might follow (Spires 1998). Such description does not deny the genuine desire for peace in outer space of many at this time, but instead acknowledges the complex political and technical experiences that shaped the emergence of human activities in outer space, including the quest for peace.

These were echoed internationally as "space for peace" emerged as a "universal norm" (Tabuchi 2020, 25). Indeed, the mantle of peacefulness became a mark of international prestige and leadership in space. The National Aeronautics and Space Administration (NASA) was created in 1958 to preserve US leadership in space science and technology and its applications "to the conduct of peaceful activities" (National Aeronautics and Space Act 1958). The USSR also employed the language of peaceful and scientific uses when describing its developing space program, although some at the time considered the words "duplicitous" (Spires 1998).

This aspirational focus on peace shaped the international governance of outer space even while it enveloped and shrouded military activities. Despite the significant involvement of military units in the development of space launch and satellite capabilities, both the United States and the USSR made a series of proposals that space should be used "exclusively" for "peaceful purposes." In January 1958, after the launch of the first US satellite, President Dwight Eisenhower proposed "to solve what I consider to be the most important problem which faces the world today," suggesting that the United States and USSR agree to *only* use space for peaceful purposes. The Soviets responded with a proposal that space be under the control of the United Nations, that a ban be placed on military uses, and that an international program for banning rockets be set up (McDougall 1997, 179). Still, in 1958 preliminary US domestic space policy acknowledged that "international arrangements on uses of outer space for peaceful purposes will have to take into account possible non-peaceful applications in determining the net advantage to U. S. security" (National Security Council 1958).

But the principle of the peaceful use of outer space had captured the world's imagination. In 1958 the UN General Assembly (UNGA) adopted Resolution 1348 (XIII), which declared that the activities and resources of outer space must be engaged for peaceful purpose (United Nations General Assembly 1958), and established COPUOS. Based on a recognition of "the common interest of mankind in outer space" and "the common aim that outer space should be used for peaceful purposes," COPUOS was mandated to negotiate an international treaty that would lay out the broad principles of how outer space would be used, and by whom.

At this time, many states—including those connected to the Non-Aligned Movement—were eager to limit space activities to *exclusively* peaceful uses (Saunders 2021). Not until 1963 did the United States make public at the UN First Committee its long-held policy that defined "peaceful uses" as "non-aggressive" and "beneficial" (United States 1962). This interpretation embraced the passive use of military satellites. "Peaceful purposes" thus emerged as a euphemism for what it did *not* exclude, namely military use.

Nor did peaceful purposes seem to preclude the testing of weapons in space. The United States conducted the first nuclear detonations in space in 1958 (Defense Nuclear Agency 1958). In 1959 the US Bold Orion program, which was testing the feasibility of air-launched ballistic missiles, conducted a flight test that targeted a point in space very close to the US Explorer-I satellite and demonstrated the ability of ballistic missiles to intercept satellites (Weeden 2014). In 1963, the USSR began tests of a co-orbital anti-satellite (ASAT) system, designed to approach a satellite target from orbit (Grego 2012).

Negotiations of the OST concluded in 1966 and the treaty was ratified in 1967. Peace is at the heart of the treaty, but the concept of peaceful purposes is not defined. Some argue that the OST provides "a general legal basis for the peaceful uses of outer space" (United Nations 2002, Forward). However, the only explicit non-armament provision is found in Article IV, which preserved the moon and other celestial bodies "exclusively for peaceful purposes" and banned the placement, installation, or stationing of nuclear weapons or other weapons of mass destruction in orbit. Moreover, while Article III stipulated that states must conduct activities in space in accordance with international law, "in the interest of maintaining international peace and security," it also referenced the UN Charter, quietly expressing the idea that outer space may also be a site of military self-defense, blurring peace with war (Craven 2019). In effect, peace did not refer to the nature of capabilities in space or their *use*, but to the end *purpose* or *objective*. In a Machiavellian twist, the means of space activities were justified by their ends. This twist is evident in the military undertones of the race to the moon (McDougall 1997, 8).

A similar undertone is evident today in China's 2022 White Paper describing its space activities as striving to both "facilitate global consensus on our shared responsibility in utilizing outer space for peaceful purposes" and to "protect China's national rights and interests, and build up its overall strength" (State Council Information Office of the People's Republic of China 2022). Likewise, under the umbrella of the principle of "freedom of use of space" the joint release of the "Combined Space Operations Vision 2031" by the United States with Australia, Canada, France, Germany, New Zealand, and the United Kingdom (UK) asserts that military capabilities are important both to freedom of space and to peaceful space domain, and that potentially aggressive capabilities may be needed to protect these values (United States Department of Defense 2022).

By justifying and camouflaging military activities behind a veil of peace, the principle of peaceful uses not only allowed a growing array of military space applications to flourish but also made the imposition of control and restrictions on military activities in space more difficult.

THE LACK OF GOVERNANCE OF MILITARY ACTIVITIES IN OUTER SPACE

Arms control agreements for other domains allow the peaceful use of technology while restricting harmful or military use. No such agreement covers activities in space. There is little to restrict military or even "non-peaceful" uses of space (Grunert 2021). Instead, military activities have been situated as both peaceful *and* beyond the scope of rules that govern peaceful use.

Take, for example, the International Telecommunication Union (ITU), which co-ordinates international radio-communication services and the use of the shared radiofrequency spectrum by non-military operators. Article 48 of the ITU constitution gives states "their entire freedom with regard to military radio installations." Similarly, the 1972 Registration Convention, which is intended to create transparency in space by identifying and maintaining an international register of launched objects in accord with Article VIII of the OST, is in practice poorly applied to military activities. Few satellites are registered as having a military function; information on the few that are reveals little about actual uses and capabilities (Jakhu, Jasani, and McDowell 2018).

This lack of governance of military activities is most evident at COPUOS. While military space applications have been included within the scope of peaceful use, a narrow definition of "peaceful" keeps any discussion of specific military activities or potential *non-peaceful* uses of space off limits (Froehlich, Seffinga, and Qiu 2020). For example, during negotiation of the voluntary rules for the long-term sustainability of outer space that were adopted in 2019, several proposed rules for activities that overlap with military capabilities were left out, such as any use of lasers (Chair, Committee on the Peaceful Uses of Outer Space 2018). Even the discussion of possible dual-use capabilities is taboo at COPUOS.

Concerns related to the military uses of space are handled by the UN First Committee, which is responsible for disarmament and international security, and by the Conference on Disarmament (CD), the single UN body tasked with negotiation of international arms control agreements. But there, too, the myth of the peaceful use of outer space has served to impede effective restrictions on military activities.

THE PROTRACTED STATUS OF SPACE ARMS CONTROL NEGOTIATIONS

Gaps in the operationalization of the spirit of arms control and peaceful purposes that informs the OST were formally recognized at the First Special UNGA Session devoted to disarmament in 1978. It concluded that additional measures were needed to "prevent an arms race in outer space" (PAROS) (United Nations General Assembly 1978).

PAROS has been a formal agenda item of the UNGA since 1981, used to pursue measures that would ban or otherwise restrict the development, testing, or deployment of space-related conventional weapons. Thus far such measures have not reached fruition.

Instead, differences over priorities and methods of arms control have created opposing blocs of states (West and Azcarate Ortega 2022). This stalemate has been reinforced by political dysfunction that has left the CD paralyzed since 1996 (Meyer 2021b).

Although not the whole story, these political fault lines must be considered in any comprehensive understanding of current arms control dynamics in outer space and are themselves indicative of the underlying tensions and contradictions that belie notions of peace and arms control in space.

Weapons in Space versus Weapons Aimed at Space

The first two UNGA resolutions on PAROS, adopted in 1981, aimed at competing problems, which have obstructed agreement since. The Soviet-led resolution "Conclusion of a Treaty on the Prohibition of the Stationing of Weapons of Any Kind in Outer Space" called on the CD to negotiate a treaty based on a draft submitted by the USSR (United Nations General Assembly 1981a). Led by Western states, the resolution "Prevention of an Arms Race in Outer Space" called for the CD to establish an ad hoc working group to negotiate an "effective and verifiable agreement" to prohibit ASAT systems (United Nations General Assembly 1981b). The division of the international community into two camps, one concerned with *space-based* weapons (often referred to as the weaponization of outer space) and the other Earth-based ASAT weapons *aimed at space* continues today.

Numerous draft treaties that deal with the weaponization of space have been proposed yet have largely ignored the challenge of Earth-based ASATs. In 1981 the USSR submitted the "Draft Treaty on the Prohibition of the Stationing of Weapons of any Kind in Outer Space" to the UN Secretary-General; it called for states "not to place in orbit around the earth objects carrying weapons of any kind, install such weapons on celestial bodies, or station such weapons in outer space in any other manner" (Stojak 2002, 26). The draft made no mention of Earth-based ASAT systems, even though the United States and the USSR had been engaged bilaterally on such a ban (York 1983).

A 1983 version of this draft included language on the use of force, or threat of use of force, against space objects that would, in theory, encompass threats from Earth-based weapons but not their development or testing. This language is repeated in the draft "Prevention of the Placement of Weapons in Outer Space, the Threat or Use of Force against Outer Space Objects" presented to the CD by Russia and China in 2008 and updated in 2014; it remains the primary arms control instrument currently on the table at the UN, but faces ongoing objections from a large group of states, in part because it does not adequately respond to what many see as an active ASAT arms race (West 2021a).

One driver of efforts to prioritize a ban on weapons in space is concern about the possible deployment of space-based interceptors for ballistic missile defense purposes, which Russia and China in particular fear would neutralize their nuclear deterrents (Silverstein, Porras, and Borrie 2020). Although such defense systems remain hypothetical, the concern remains, highlighting linkages between arms control in space and security dynamics on Earth.

A UN GGE convened in 2018–2019 to study practical measures to advance a possible treaty on PAROS identified a number of obstacles to a weapons ban, including technical challenges related to definitions, verification of space weapons, and difficulties associated with technology that is either dual-use or can be repurposed (Nigeria on behalf of the African Group 2019).

A New Treaty versus Existing International Law

Some states are pushing for an additional arms control treaty specifically related to outer space because they believe that existing international law does not sufficiently prevent an arms race in outer space. However, other states oppose not only the proposed content of a new treaty, but the need for any treaty at all. They argue that existing law already provides "an equitable, practical, balanced and extensive legal system for ensuring the use of outer space for peaceful purposes" (Conference on Disarmament 1994). Instead, these states advocate voluntary TCBMs.

Numerous TCBM initiatives have met with limited practical success. In 1993 a UN GGE produced a study of the applicability of TCBMs in outer space "to avoid conflicts based on misperceptions and mistrust" (United Nations Secretary-General 1994). Although it concluded that most states remain primarily concerned with the placement of weapons in outer space, it also recommended additional TCBMs related to dual-use capabilities, technical measures to facilitate confidence in space activities, the use of existing mechanisms to provide alerts in case of accidents, and consideration of proposals for "rules of the road" in space. But there was no follow-up.

A 2013 UN GGE report on TCBMs recommended information exchange on space policies and goals and on orbital information and natural space hazards, risk reduction notifications prior to scheduled maneuvers on orbit, and voluntary visits to launch sites and control centers (United Nations General Assembly 2013). Discussions on practical implementation of these recommendations are stalled at the UN Disarmament Commission.

One of the only initiatives to be taken up from these two reports has been the development of voluntary "rules of the road" for space activities. But this pursuit has created further division in the arms control debate.

Controlling Hardware or Behavior?

The focus on TCBMs in space is the result of a preference for voluntary rather than legal measures, as well as efforts that focus on *behaviors* rather than weapons or *hardware*. The desired products are codes of conduct or rules of the road.

European Union (EU) member states drafted a voluntary Code of Conduct for Outer Space Activities in 2008. In 2014, following international consultations, the EU released an updated version. Among its principles was a commitment to "refrain from any action which brings about, directly or indirectly, damage, or destruction, of space objects unless such action is justified" (European Union 2014, Para 51). Multilateral discussion on the draft code subsequently failed. Some states objected to holding the talks beyond the mandate of the UN. There were also substantive concerns related primarily to the use of force and the right to self-defense in outer space (Blount 2018).

Voluntary measures related to PAROS include a Russian-led resolution at the UNGA to promote political declarations not to be the first to place weapons in outer space, also known as "no first placement." According to Russian reports, thirty states have made such a declaration. Opponents discount these claims, however, because they fail to define "space weapons" and cannot be verified (West 2021a).

Since 2020 the UK has sponsored a new initiative "Reducing Space Threats through Norms, Rules and Principles of Responsible Behaviours" through the UNGA's First Committee. Seeking to restart stalled discussions on PAROS, it is focused on the behaviors that drive conflict, rather than specific hardware capabilities. The UK first called on states to characterize activities "that could be considered responsible, irresponsible or threatening" and to share ideas on developing norms of responsible behavior. More than thirty states submitted input to the UN Secretary-General (United Nations Secretary-General 2021). Then, in 2021 the UNGA adopted a resolution to continue this work through an Open-Ended Working Group (OEWG) (United Nations General Assembly 2021); more than 70 states participated in the discussions. Yet, despite three weeks of substantial meetings in 2022 and 2023, the OEWG was unable to agree to any sort of final documentation, blocked largely by Russian objections to the very premise of the discussion (Hitchens 2023).

Overall these cleavages provide some credence to arguments that arms control is not technically feasible (Ford 2020b). But technical challenges require technical solutions, many of which have been proposed in the past, including means of verifying an arms control agreement. An International Satellite Monitoring Agency was first detailed by France in 1978. In 1987, Canada presented a PAXSAT concept that used satellites to monitor and verify the absence of weapons in space. And in 1988, Russia proposed an International Space Inspectorate (Gasparini Alves 1991). The abundance of space situational awareness data today—some from commercial sources—makes technical solutions more feasible than ever. And not only for technical problems. Technical solutions to the political challenges of negotiating a new treaty have also been pitched, such as the adoption of an additional protocol to the OST (Meyer 2021a).

Instead, there is a deeper problem at play. As suggested by references to arms control measures in space as "hypocrisy" and "snake oil" (Ford 2020a), there is not only deep resistance to but also suspicion of efforts to constrain military uses of or the deployment of weapons in outer space. Indeed, the protracted nature of the debate points to fundamental differences over not only the solutions to arms control in space, but the nature of the problem itself.

These differences, while clearly political, are rooted in the concept of peaceful purposes that underpins efforts to prevent and arms race in outer space. A working paper tabled by Canada at the CD in 1986 noted persistent conflicting interpretations by member states of "peaceful purposes," including one that involved no military use (Canada 1986). How can there be a fruitful discussion when there is not even agreement on basic terms? Yet these differences are a direct result of the way in which the concept of peaceful uses of outer space emerged as a myth that helped to reconcile commitments to peace with military activities.

Forty years and many weapons tests later, the PAROS debate continues, unresolved. And military activities in space also continue, camouflaged by a cloak of peace.

Peace as Camouflage for Weapons

Despite lack of practical progress on arms control in outer space, there is some evidence that the spirit of peaceful purposes has encouraged self-restraint in the development and deployment of weapons in outer space, even possibly a taboo (Harrison 2020). Yet this restraint, insofar as it exists, may have less to do with a desire to preserve peace than what Clay Moltz has argued is a general belief that space is too important for war (Moltz 2008).

Despite the peaceful rhetoric of the OST, and the decades of political wrangling on PAROS, there is a long history of developing and testing weapons systems in and for space (Grego 2012). Indeed, the first weapons tests in space involved a series of nuclear detonations in 1958, less than a year after the first satellite entered orbit (Defense Nuclear Agency 1958). Annual assessments of global counterspace capabilities published by the Secure World Foundation indicate that the development, testing, and even deployment of possible weapons in space, and of weapons that target objects in space, are ramping up (Weeden and Samson 2023). The shift to warfighting in space found in policies and strategies among a growing number of national military organizations also speaks against the idea that such a taboo has gained general acceptance (West 2022).

As previously discussed, arms control efforts related to outer space are conducted under the mandate of PAROS. But like peaceful purposes, PAROS is a reflection of the mythical function of notions of peace in outer space, which legitimize and camouflage military activities and interests.

Indeed, the *prevention* in PAROS is a misnomer that suggests that there is only a need to control a possible future and not a present situation in which weapons continue to be developed. A UNIDIR report calls PAROS outdated, arguing that an arms race that reaches into outer space is *already* under way (Silverstein, Porras, and Borrie 2020). Indeed, PAROS was outdated from its birth.

PAROS became a focus of the UN in the late 1970s and early 1980s, a period that saw a simmering ASAT race between the United States and the USSR. This race prompted the two superpowers to begin bilateral arms control discussions on banning or otherwise restricting the use of such weapons. These talks failed, partly because of the practical challenges of arms control outlined above, but largely because of the geopolitical rift caused by the Soviet invasion of Afghanistan (York 1983).

The reality of this arms race was obscured when space-based strike weapons became the focus of PAROS following the Soviet-led resolution in 1981 and the subsequent series of proposed treaties aimed at the non-weaponization of outer space. This focus also obscured a growing weapons capability *in* space.

From the 1960s until 1985, the USSR operated a fractional orbital bombardment system (FOBS), to deliver nuclear weapons from orbit. This system arguably violated the one arms control restriction in the OST: not to orbit nuclear weapons in space. Historians note that, rather than call the OST into question, the United States permitted FOBS to exist, citing a variety of technical reasons, including that the system wasn't "in" space and was not "tested" (Siddiqi 2000).

When is a weapon not a weapon? When the world chooses to believe only in the legitimate activities on display and not the military buildup taking place behind the scenes. It's exceedingly difficult to control weapons that no one admits to having.

The USSR never admitted that it was conducting satellite intercept tests for the roughly two decades that its ASAT program existed. It referred instead to satellites that "carry scientific equipment to continue research in outer space" (Leitenberg 1984, 31). This pattern has been repeated time and time again—and not only by Russia. China's first demonstration in 2007 of a kinetic anti-satellite weapon—which intercepted one of its own aging weather satellites—was described as a "scientific experiment," with the claim that "China all along upholds the peaceful use of outer space and opposes weaponization and arms race in outer space" (*Space War* 2007).

But the US ASAT demonstration in 2008 produced the most elaborate theater of peace. During Operation Burnt Frost, a de-orbiting US satellite was intercepted and destroyed; the claim was that this action saved Earth from ecological danger (Greenemeier 2008). In 2020, Russia released a projectile from another object in orbit, as part of what it described as a benign "satellite servicing" experiment (West 2020).

There are other cases in which weapons systems have been presented as peaceful. The US "Star Wars" program—a ballistic missile defense system based on a layer of interceptors in space—is a prime example. Advocates for a treaty that bans space weapons like to target just this sort of program. Yet, US President Reagan presented the system as "purely defensive, peaceful technology" that would help to free the world of nuclear weapons (Weinraub 1986).

The practice of using camouflage to disguise weapons systems might be waning. Following its destructive Mission Shakti ASAT test in 2019, India openly boasted that it had joined an "exclusive group of space faring nations" with a demonstrated ASAT capability. However, India also claimed that the test fulfilled a "responsibility to defend the country's interests in outer space," while insisting that "India has no intention of entering an arms race in outer space" and that "space must only be used for peaceful purposes" (Government of India 2019). This juxtaposition of contradictory perspectives only makes sense in the context of the prevailing myth of the peaceful use of space, in which the ends justify the means. Certainly, India's boastfulness reflects the growing intensity in warfighting rhetoric by space actors, who justify "defensive militarization" in the pursuit of peace (Craven 2019).

WAR (AND PEACE) IN SPACE

Elsewhere I have written that the shift to military organization, planning, and capabilities specifically aimed at warfighting in outer space threatens to destroy the fragile peace that has been sustained by the OST's ability to balance opposing factors (West 2022). A closer examination of this development suggests that the myth of peaceful purposes continues to function as a means of reconciling military activities with peaceful ends, thus evading efforts at arms control.

The United States established its position that outer space is an operational domain of warfighting in 2020, with the creation of the Space Force as the sixth branch of its armed forces. US space power is designed to target "an adversary's space and counterspace capabilities, reducing the effectiveness and lethality of adversary forces across all domains" with the intent to "neutralize adversary space missions before they can be employed against friendly forces" (United States Space Force 2020, 36). Yet, the space power doctrine also acknowledges the maintenance of peace as the purpose of space under international law (United States Space Force 2020, 17).

Within the last decade, Russia has created its Aerospace Forces. In 2021, Russia conducted a destructive ASAT test that targeted a defunct Soviet-era intelligence satellite. Russia admitted that "we have successfully tested a cutting-edge system of the future. It hit an old satellite with precision worthy of a goldsmith." The act was justified as part of a "routine activity to strengthen the nation's defenses" in response to US military activities (Tass 2021).

China has established the Strategic Support Force, which integrates space, cyberspace, and electronic warfighting components for what it describes as "informationized" warfare (State Council Information Office 2019). China has stated that "we will not attack unless we are attacked, but we will surely counterattack if attacked" (State Council Information Office 2019).

The UK, France, Italy, and Germany host military space commands. France refers to an operational framework for "self-defense" in space (The French Ministry for the Armed Forces 2019, 9). Japan's Air-Self-Defense Force contains the Space Operations Squadron. India has constructed a tri-force Defence Space Agency.

In 2019, NATO formally declared space an "operational domain," although it has resisted direct references to "warfighting." Secretary-General Jens Stoltenberg has stated that NATO would not "weaponize" space (Banks 2019). Instead, the focus is on "collective defense" as expressed in Article 5 of its founding treaty.

All of these space actors seem to ascribe to a strategy that incorporates "active defense," which extends beyond traditional protection measures to include actions against a threat as it materializes (Harrison, Johnson, and Young 2021, 36). And so even warfighting in space is being seen as a way to preserve peacefulness and stymie calls for restrictions.

Norms of Behavior: A Path Forward?

The UK-led initiative on PAROS aimed to restart stalled discussions on arms control in outer space by focusing on the development of norms of "responsible behavior" in outer space (United Nations General Assembly 2021). To overcome technical divisions that have plagued arms control debates in the past, this process focused on identifying and characterizing different types of behavior as threatening, irresponsible, or responsible. The intent to create agreed rules of behavior that, when applied, will prevent the escalation of conflict through accidents, miscommunication, and miscalculation, and to consider how such understandings might contribute to a legally binding agreement.

But the potential impact of the initiative goes further than this. By shifting the focus from weapons and even purposes to the *effects* of behaviors and activities in outer space, it begins to strip away the peaceful camouflage that has protected weapons from arms control efforts for decades. While some states view any effort to characterize the nature of behaviors in space as subjective, subjectivity is, in fact, what makes this process valuable, as it requires that the international community pass judgment on what is peaceful, or responsible, and what is not.

Yet one result of a focus on behaviors that the many weapons systems currently being developed for use against space systems will likely remain intact. A possible outcome is that this this work on norms will not in fact reign in the growing drive to the use of weapons in space, but rather make warfighting activities there safer, adding to the density of the fog of peace in space.

Moreover, existing norms related to outer space governance, such as those for debris mitigation and the long-term sustainability of the space environment, are not sufficiently observed. COPUOS, for example, has adopted debris mitigation guidelines; Article 4 calls for states to "avoid intentional destruction and other harmful activities" (UN Committee on the Peaceful Uses of Outer Space 2010). Yet Russia's destructive ASAT test in November 2021 created a cloud of thousands of pieces of debris (US Space Command Public Affairs Office 2021). This action calls into question the ability of norms to rein in harmful military behavior, particularly when actions are characterized as peaceful or defensive.

Related to the growing support for behavioral approaches to security and arms control in outer space, momentum is also growing for a ban on kinetic ASAT testing, similar to the 1963 Partial Test Ban Treaty that barred nuclear explosions in the ocean, the atmosphere, and outer space (Outer Space Institute 2021). In the context of the OEWG process, the United States initiated a growing, voluntary moratorium on destructive tests of direct-ascent ASAT weapons as a concrete example of a norm of behavior (United

Nations General Assembly 2022). Echoing concerns with the behavioral approach of the OEWG, China objects on the basis that such effort to not address the development and possession of such weapons themselves (Zhen 2023).

Nonetheless, such modest and practical arms control initiatives that prevent the use of the most destabilizing activities in space and the use of weapons systems that cause indiscriminate harm such as kinetic ASATs (see Morgan, this volume; Townsend, this volume) are valuable and deserve support. In the short term, they can also help to stabilize the growing tension between the principles of peace and freedom that is at the heart of the myth of peace in outer space.

Yet the continued standoff between approaches to PAROS that hobbled the OEWG suggests that many states do not desire any restrictions related to outer space whatsoever. It is increasingly clear that while technical solutions to the politics and practicalities of arms control in space are necessary, they are insufficient without also tackling the political myth that military activities are inherently peaceful.

Conclusion: Mobilizing Work on Myth

For a long time, I viewed the proclivity to hide and deny aggressive military uses of space as a sign of the strength of the principle of peaceful purposes. But now I fear that the murky definition of "peace" is cynically and consciously used to conceal violence. The meaning of "the peaceful use of outer space" has been stretched to the point that the term has lost almost all value. And this elasticity of meaning has been harmful, effectively concealing weapons programs and blocking effective arms control measures.

It is more than fifty years too late to try to ban military uses of space. Instead, we must reclaim the integrity of the concept of peace.

This chapter has elucidated the role of the myth of peace in outer space in stymying arms control efforts. But the ongoing process of arms control itself—the enduring if elusive promise that an arms race can still be prevented—also helps to perpetuate the political functions of that myth. As Jinyuan Su argues regarding the interpretation of peaceful use in outer space as "non-aggressive," it is not sufficient for the vision of peace that is at the heart of the OST (Su 2010). Instead, Columba Peoples insists that arms control itself must be reconceptualized to emphasize "Controlling the Means of Violence." Doing this involves a transformatory politics that promotes a culture of peace (Peoples 2011). This can be done in part by doing work *on* myth.

Myths are not static; they are created, promoted, and worked on. In short, myths and the politics that underpin them can be resisted, reclaimed, and change (see examples in Lincoln 2014). My contribution to this remaking has been to reveal the fractures that are embedded in the concept of peace in outer space yet camouflaged by the political work of myth. But more work is needed. The myth of peace must be wrested from military narratives. This is far from easy. Militarism is among the most pernicious of political myths (Millar 2016)

Civil society voices are positioned to tackle this resistance to and work on myth. Beyond the space community, there is scope to work in concert with organizations such as the Women's League for International Peace and Freedom (WILPF), which promote non-military, feminist approaches to peace. There is also opportunity to join cause with many states in the global south that have maintained a long-standing opposition not only to the weaponization of outer space, but to its rampant militarization.

At the heart of this process is a re-imagining of the future of peace in outer space. Such re-imagining is essential as activity on the moon expands. Although the OST strictly forbids military activity of any kind on the moon, we have seen firsthand the effects that a foggy notion of peace can have.

The fog of peace can hide the buildup of non-peaceful activities until the moment that catastrophe strikes. And when that fog is dispelled, we may find that we have been groping our way across a battlefield all along.

References

Arbatov, Alexey. 2019. "Arms Control in Outer Space: The Russian Angle, and a Possible Way Forward." *Bulletin of the Atomic Scientists* 75, no. 4: 151–61. https://doi.org/10.1080/00963 402.2019.1628475.

Banks, Martin. 2019. "NATO Names Space as an 'Operational Domain,' but without Plans to Weaponize It." *Defense News*. November 20, 2019. https://www.defensenews.com/smr/ nato-2020-defined/2019/11/20/nato-names-space-as-an-operational-domain-but-without-plans-to-weaponize-it/.

Beer, Thomas. 1985. "Contemporary Security Policy in Outer Space—Military Technology vs. International Law." *Arms Control* 6, no. 2: 183–202. https://doi.org/10.1080/0144038850 8403821.

Blount, P.J. 2018. *Sorting out Self-Defense in Space: Understanding the Conflicting Views on Self-Defense in the EU Code of Conduct.* Monograph Series IV. Conflicts in Space and the Rule of Law. Montreal: McGill University Institute of Air and Space Law.

Bottici, Chiara. 2007. *A Philosophy of Political Myth.* Cambridge: Cambridge University Press. https://doi.org/10.1017/CBO9780511498626.

Bottici, Chiara, and Benoît Challand. 2006. "Rethinking Political Myth: The Clash of Civilizations as a Self-Fulfilling Prophecy." *European Journal of Social Theory* 9, no. 3: 315–36. https://doi.org/10.1177/1368431006065715.

Bowen, Bleddyn E. 2020. *War in Space: Strategy, Spacepower, Geopolitics.* Edinburgh: Edinburgh University Press.

Canada. 1986. "Terminology Relevant to Arms Control and Outer Space CD/OS/WP.15." Working Paper. Conference on Disarmament. https://undocs.org/pdf?symbol=en/CD/716.

Chair, Committee on the Peaceful Uses of Outer Space. 2018. "Draft Guidelines for the Long-Term Sustainability of Outer Space Activities A/AC.105/C.1/L.367." Working Paper by the Chair of the Working Group on the Long-term Sustainability of Outer Space Activities. United Nations. https://www.unoosa.org/res/oosadoc/data/documents/2019/aac_105c_1l/ aac_105c_1l_367_0_html/V1804974.pdf.

Conference on Disarmament. 1994. "Report of the Ad Hoc Committee on Prevention of an Arms Race in Outer Space CD/1271." United Nations. https://undocs.org/CD/1271.

Craven, Matt. 2019. "'Other Spaces': Constructing the Legal Architecture of a Cold War Commons and the Scientific-Technical Imaginary of Outer Space." *European Journal of International Law* 30, no. 2: 547–72. https://doi.org/10.1093/ejil/chz024.

Defense Nuclear Agency. 1958. "Operation Argus." https://apps.dtic.mil/sti/pdfs/ADA122 341.pdf.

Divine, Robert A. 1993. *The Sputnik Challenge*. New York: Oxford University Press.

Dolman, Everett Carl. 2012. "New Frontiers, Old Realities." *Strategic Studies Quarterly* 6, no. 1: 78–97.

European Union. 2014. "EU Proposal for an International Space Code of Conduct, Draft." European External Action Service—European Commission. March 31, 2014. https://eeas. europa.eu/topics/disarmament-non-proliferation-and-arms-export-control/14715/eu-proposal-international-space-code-conduct-draft_en.

Flood, Christopher. 2002. *Political Myth: A Theoretical Introduction*. Theorists of Myth. New York; London: Routledge.

Ford, Christopher A. 2020a. "Whither Arms Control in Outer Space? Space Threats, Space Hypocrisy, and the Hope of Space Norms." Presented at the Center For Strategic and International Studies Webinar on "Threats, Challenges, and Opportunities in Space," Zoom, April 6. https://2017-2021.state.gov/whither-arms-control-in-outer-space-space-threats-space-hypocrisy-and-the-hope-of-space-norms/index.html.

Ford, Christopher A. 2020b. "Arms Control in Outer Space: History and Prospects." Arms Control and International Security Papers. 1, no. 12. Office of the Undersecretary of Arms Control and International Security.

Froehlich, Annette, Vincent Seffinga, and Ruiyan Qiu. 2020. *The United Nations and Space Security: Conflicting Mandates between UN COPUOS and the CD*. Vol. 21. Studies in Space Policy. Cham: Springer International Publishing. https://doi.org/10.1007/978-3-030-06025-1_1.

Gasparini Alves, Péricles. 1991. *Prevention of an Arms Race in Outer Space: A Guide to the Discussions in the Conference on Disarmament*. UNIDIR/91/79. New York: United Nations.

Government of India. 2019. "Frequently Asked Questions on Mission Shakti, India's Anti-Satellite Missile Test Conducted on 27 March, 2019." Press Release, Government of India. https://www.mea.gov.in/press-releases.htm?dtl/31179/Frequently_Asked_Questions_on_Mission_Shakti_Indias_AntiSatellite_Missile_test_conducted_on_27_March_2019.

Gray, Colin S. 1992. *House of Cards: Why Arms Control Must Fail*. Cornell Studies in Security Affairs. Ithaca, NY: Cornell University Press.

Gray, Colin S. 1994. "Sea Power: The Great Enabler." *Naval War College Review* 47, no. 1: 18–27.

Greenemeier, Larry. 2008. "U.S. Set to Destroy Crippled Satellite Before It Contaminates the Atmosphere—Scientific American." *Scientific American*. February 15, 2008. https://www.sci entificamerican.com/article/destroy-crippled-satellite/.

Grego, Laura. 2012. "A History of Anti-Satellite Programs." Union of Concerned Scientists. https://www.ucsusa.org/sites/default/files/2019-09/a-history-of-ASAT-programs_lo-res.pdf.

Grego, Laura. 2021. "The Case for Space Arms Control." In *Commercial and Military Uses of Outer Space*, edited by Melissa de Zwart and Stacey Henderson, 81–95. Issues in Space. Singapore: Springer Singapore. https://doi.org/10.1007/978-981-15-8924-9_7.

Grunert, Jeremy. 2021. "The 'Peaceful Use' of Outer Space?" *War on the Rocks*. June 22, 2021. https://warontherocks.com/2021/06/outer-space-the-peaceful-use-of-a-warfighting-domain/.

Guevara, Berit Bliesemann de. 2016a. "Introduction: Myth and Narrative in International Politics." In *Myth and Narrative in International Politics*, edited by Berit Bliesemann de Guevara, 1–11. London: Palgrave Macmillan UK. https://doi.org/10.1057/978-1-137-53752-2_1.

Guevara, Berit Bliesemann de. 2016b. "Myth in International Politics: Ideological Delusion and Necessary Fiction." In *Myth and Narrative in International Politics*, edited by Berit Bliesemann de Guevara, 15–46. London: Palgrave Macmillan UK. https://doi.org/10.1057/978-1-137-53752-2_2.

Hall, R. Cargill. 1998. "Civil-Military Relations in America's Early Space Program." In *The U.S. Air Force in Space: 1945 to the Twenty-First Century*, edited by R. Cargill Hall and Jacob Neufeld, 19–33. Washington DC: USAF History and Museums Program. https://doi.org/10.21236/ADA442852.

Harford, James. 1997. *Korolev: How One Man Masterminded the Soviet Drive to Beat America to the Moon*. New York: Wiley.

Harrison, Todd. 2020. "International Perspectives on Space Weapons." Aerospace Security Project. Center for Strategic and International Studies. https://aerospace.csis.org/wp-content/uploads/2020/05/Harrison_IntlPerspectivesSpaceWeapons-compressed.pdf.

Harrison, Todd, Kaitlyn Johnson, and Makena Young. 2021. "Defense against the Dark Arts in Space: Protecting Space Systems from Counterspace Weapons." Aerospace Security Project. Center for Strategic and International Studies.

Henderson, Stacey. 2020. "Arms Control and Space Security." In *Handbook of Space Security: Policies, Applications and Programs*, edited by Kai-Uwe Schrogl, 95–110. Cham: Springer International Publishing. https://doi.org/10.1007/978-3-030-23210-8_135.

Hitchens, Theresa. 2023. "Russia Spikes UN Effort on Norms to Reduce Space Threats." *Breaking Defense*. https://breakingdefense.com/2023/09/russia-spikes-un-effort-on-norms-to-reduce-space-threats/.

International Committee of the Red Cross. 2021. "The Potential Human Cost of the Use of Weapons in Outer Space and the Protection Afforded by International Humanitarian Law." Position paper submitted by the International Committee of the Red Cross to the Secretary-General of the United Nations on the issues outlined in General Assembly Resolution 75/36. https://front.un-arm.org/wp-content/uploads/2021/04/icrc-position-paper-unsg-on-resolution-A-75-36-final-eng.pdf.

Jakhu, Ram S., Bhupendra Jasani, and Jonathan C. McDowell. 2018. "Critical Issues Related to Registration of Space Objects and Transparency of Space Activities." *Acta Astronautica* 143 (February): 406–20. https://doi.org/10.1016/j.actaastro.2017.11.042.

Jessup, Philip C., and Howard J. Taubenfeld. 1959. "Outer Space, Antarctica, and the United Nations." *International Organization* 13, no. 3: 363–79. https://doi.org/10.1017/S0020818300009000.

Johnson, Lyndon. *Statement by the President Announcing the Reaching of Agreement on an Outer Space Treaty, 8 December 1966. Public Papers of the Presidents of the United State.* https://quod.lib.umich.edu/p/ppotpus/4731549.1966.002/815?rgn=full+text;view=image.

Klein, John J. 2021. "Some Lessons on Spacepower from Colin Gray." *Naval War College Review* 74, no. 1: Article 7.

Koplow, David. 2009. "ASAT-Isfaction: Customary International Law and the Regulation of Anti-Satellite Weapons." *Georgetown Law Faculty Publications and Other Works*. January. https://scholarship.law.georgetown.edu/facpub/453.

Koplow, David A. 2019. "Deterrence as the MacGuffin: The Case for Arms Control in Outer Space." *SSRN Electronic Journal*. https://doi.org/10.2139/ssrn.3436311.

Leira, Halvard, and Benjamin de Carvalho. 2018. "The Function of Myths in International Relations: Discipline and Identity." In *The SAGE Handbook of the History, Sociology and Philosophy of International Relations*, edited by Andreas Gofas, Inanna Hamati-Ataya, and Nicholas Onuf, 222–35. N.p.: SAGE.

Leitenberg, Milton. 1984. "Studies of Military R&D and Weapons Development." Center for International and Security Studies University of Maryland. https://man.fas.org/eprint/lei tenberg/index.html.

Lincoln, Bruce. 2014. *Discourse and the Construction of Society: Comparative Studies of Myth, Ritual, and Classification*. New York: Oxford University Press. https://doi.org/10.1093/acp rof:oso/9780199372362.001.0001.

Mathieu, Xavier. 2020. "Sovereign Myths in International Relations: Sovereignty as Equality and the Reproduction of Eurocentric Blindness." *Journal of International Political Theory* 16, no. 3: 339–60. https://doi.org/10.1177/1755088218814072.

McDougall, Walter A. 1997. *The Heavens and the Earth: A Political History of the Space Age*. Paperback ed. Johns Hopkins. Baltimore, MD: Johns Hopkins University Press.

Meyer, Paul. 2016. "Dark Forces Awaken: The Prospects for Cooperative Space Security." *The Nonproliferation Review* 23, no. 3–4: 495–503. https://doi.org/10.1080/10736700.2016.1268750.

Meyer, Paul. 2020. "Arms Control in Outer Space: Mission Impossible or Unrealized Potential?" https://www.cgai.ca/arms_control_in_outer_space_mission_impossible_or_u nrealized_potential.

Meyer, Paul. 2021a. "Could an Optional Protocol Be the Way to Stop the Weaponization of Outer Space?" *International Journal: Canada's Journal of Global Policy Analysis*. (June): DOI:002070202110205. https://doi.org/10.1177/00207020211020521.

Meyer, Paul. 2021b. "Does the Conference of Disarmament Have a Future?" *Journal for Peace and Nuclear Disarmament* (October) 1–8: https://doi.org/10.1080/25751654.2021.1993632.

Millar, Katharine M. 2016. "Mutually Implicated Myths: The Democratic Control of the Armed Forces and Militarism." In *Myth and Narrative in International Politics*, edited by Berit Bliesemann de Guevara, 173–91. London: Palgrave Macmillan UK. https://doi.org/10.1057/978-1-137-53752-2_9.

Mitchell, A., S. Wright, S. Suchet-Pearson, K. Lloyd, L. Burarrwanga, R. Ganambarr, M. Ganambarr-Stubbs, B. Ganambarr, D. Maymuru, and R. Maymuru. 2020. "Dukarr Lakarama: Listening to Guwak, Talking Back to Space Colonization." *Political Geography* 81 (August): 102218. https://doi.org/10.1016/j.polgeo.2020.102218.

Moltz, James Clay. 2002. "Breaking the Deadlock on Space Arms Control." *Arms Control Today*. April 2002. https://www.armscontrol.org/act/2002-04/features/breaking-deadlock-space-arms-control.

Moltz, James Clay. 2006. "Preventing Conflict in Space: Cooperative Engagement as a Possible U.S. Strategy." *Astropolitics* 4, no. 2: 121–29. https://doi.org/10.1080/14777620600910563.

Moltz, James Clay. 2008. *The Politics of Space Security: Strategic Restraint and the Pursuit of National Interests*. Stanford, CA: Stanford Security Studies.

Murphy, Jeffrey. 2019. "The Cold Vacuum of Arms Control in Outer Space: Can Existing Law Make Some Anti-Satellite Weapons Illegal?" *Cleveland State Law Review* 68, no. 1: 125.

"National Aeronautics and Space Act." 1958. National Archives and Records Administration, Washington, DC. https://history.nasa.gov/spaceact.html.

National Security Council. 1958. "NSC 5814/1 Preliminary U.S. Policy on Outer Space." Aerospace Corporation. https://aerospace.org/sites/default/files/policy_archives/NSC-5814-1%20Space%20Policy%20Aug58.pdf.

National Security Council Planning Board. 1955. May 20. NSC 5520. "Draft Statement of Policy on U.S. Scientific Satellite Program General Considerations." Dwight D. Eisenhower Presidential Library and Museum.

Nigeria on Behalf of the African Group. 2019. "Recommendations to Promote the Practical Implementation of Transparency and Confidence-Building Measures in Outer Space Activities with the Goal of Preventing an Arms Race in Outer Space, in Accordance with the Recommendations Set out in the Report of the Group of Governmental Experts on Transparency and Confidence-Building Measures in Outer Space Activities A/CN.10/2019/WP.1." Disarmament Commission. https://digitallibrary.un.org/record/3801525/files/A_CN-10_2019_WP-1-EN.pdf.

Osiander, Andreas. 2001. "Sovereignty, International Relations, and the Westphalian Myth." *International Organization* 55, no. 2: 251–87.

Outer Space Institute. 2021. "International Open Letter on Kinetic Anti-Satellite Testing." Outer Space Institute. http://outerspaceinstitute.ca/docs/OSI_International_Open_Letter_ASATs_PUBLIC.pdf.

Pavelec, Sterling Michael. 2012. "The Inevitability of the Weaponization of Space: Technological Constructivism Versus Determinism." *Astropolitics* 10, no. 1: 39–48. https://doi.org/10.1080/14777622.2012.647392.

Peoples, Columba. 2011. "The Securitization of Outer Space: Challenges for Arms Control." *Contemporary Security Policy* 32, no. 1: 76–98. https://doi.org/10.1080/13523260.2011.556846.

Perry, Robert. 1973. "A History of Satellite Reconnaissance." Vol. I. National Reconnaissance Organization. https://www.nro.gov/Portals/65/documents/foia/docs/hosr/hosr-vol1.pdf.

President of the United States, Barak Obama. 2010. "National Space Policy of the United States of America." The White House. https://history.nasa.gov/national_space_policy_6-28-10.pdf.

Samson, Victoria, and Brian Weeden. 2020. "Enhancing Space Security: Time for Legally Binding Measures." *Arms Control Today*. December 2020. https://www.armscontrol.org/act/2020-12/features/enhancing-space-security-time-legally-binding-measures.

Samson, Victoria, and Brian Weeden. 2022. "It's Time for a Global Ban on Destructive Antisatellite Testing." *Scientific American*. January 14, 2022. https://www.scientificamerican.com/article/its-time-for-a-global-ban-on-destructive-antisatellite-testing/.

Saunders, Melanie K. 2021. "Conference Diplomacy as the Machinery for Manufacturing Consent: PAX Americana and the Case of the Outer Space Treaty and the World Trade Organization." *Melbourn Journal of International Law* 22, no. 1: 1–34.

Shreve, Bradley G. 2003. "The US, the USSR, and Space Exploration, 1957–1963." *International Journal on World Peace* 20, no. 2: 67–83.

Siddiqi, Asif A. 2000. "The Soviet Fractional Orbital Bombardment Systems (FOBS): A Short Technical History." *Quest: The History of Spaceflight Quarterly* 7, no. 4: 22–32.

Silverstein, Benjamin, Daniel Porras, and John Borrie. 2020. "Alternative Approaches and Indicators for the Prevention of an Arms Race in Outer Space." 5. Space Dossier. UNIDIR.

Smith, Marcia. 2017. "Top Air Force Officials: Space Now Is a Warfighting Domain." SpacePolicyOnline.com. May 17, 2017. https://spacepolicyonline.com/news/top-air-force-officials-space-now-is-a-warfighting-domain/.

Space War. 2007. "China Says Anti Satellite Test Did Not Break Rules." February 12, 2007. https://www.spacewar.com/reports/China_Says_Anti_Satellite_Test_Did_Not_Break_Rules_999.html.

Spires, David N. 1998. "The Air Force and Military Space Missions: The Critical Years, 1957–1971." In *The U.S. Air Force in Space: 1945 to the Twenty-First Century*, edited by R. Cargill Hall and Jacob Neufeld, 33–46. Washington DC: USAF History and Museums Program. https://doi.org/10.21236/ADA442852.

State Council Information Office. 2019. *China's National Defense in the New Era*.

State Council Information Office of the People's Republic of China. 2022. "China's Space Program: A 2021 Perspective." http://www.cnsa.gov.cn/english/n6465652/n6465653/c6813088/content.html.

Steele, Meili. 2010. "Review Essay: The Importance of Myth for Political Philosophy (Under Consideration: Chiara Bottici's *A Philosophy of Political Myth*)." *Philosophy & Social Criticism* 36, no. 9: 1137–41. https://doi.org/10.1177/0191453710379033.

Stojak, Lucy. 2002. "The Non-Weaponization of Outer Space." International Security Research and Outreach Programme International Security Bureau, Department of Foreign Affairs and International Trade Canada. https://www.international.gc.ca/arms-armes/assets/pdfs/stojak2002.pdf.

Su, Jinyuan. 2010. "The 'Peaceful Purposes' Principle in Outer Space and the Russia-China PPWT Proposal." SSRN Scholarly Paper ID 1662224. Rochester, NY: Social Science Research Network. https://papers.ssrn.com/abstract=1662224.

Su, Jinyuan. 2013. "The Environmental Dimension of Space Arms Control." SSRN Scholarly Paper ID 2285298. Rochester, NY: Social Science Research Network. https://papers.ssrn.com/abstract=2285298.

Tabuchi, Yumi. 2020. "Project Vanguard and Ike's 'Space for Peace.'" *Nanzan Review of American Studies* 42: 23–42.

Tass, Sergey. 2021. "New Russian System Being Tested Hit Old Satellite with 'Goldsmith's Precision'—Shoigu." *TASS Russian News Agency*. November 16, 2021. https://tass.com/science/1362219.

The French Ministry for the Armed Forces. 2019. "Space Defence Strategy." Report of the "Space" Working Group.

Townsend, Brad. 2020. "Strategic Choice and the Orbital Security Dilemma." *Strategic Studies Quarterly* (Spring): 27.

UN Committee on the Peaceful Uses of Outer Space. 2010. "Space Debris Mitigation Guidelines of the Committee on the Peaceful Uses of Outer Space." UN Office of Outer Space Affairs.

United Nations. 1967. Treaty on Principles Governing the Activities of States in the Exploration and Use of Outer Space, including the Moon and Other Celestial Bodies.

United Nations. 2002. *United Nations Treaties and Principles on Outer Space*. New York: United Nations.

United Nations General Assembly. 1958. "Question of the Peaceful Use of Outer Space, RES 1348 (XIII)." United Nations. https://www.unoosa.org/oosa/oosadoc/data/resolutions/1958/general_assembly_13th_session/res_1348_xiii.html.

United Nations General Assembly. 1978. "Resolutions and Decision Adopted by the General Assembly during Its Tenth Special Session, Supplement No.4 (A/S-10/4)." United Nations. https://www.un.org/disarmament/wp-content/uploads/2017/05/A-S10-4.pdf.

United Nations General Assembly. 1981a. "Conclusion of a Treaty on the Prohibition of the Stationing of Weapons of Any Kind in Outer Space, A/RES/36/99." United Nations. https://digitallibrary.un.org/record/27062?ln=en#record-files-collapse-header.

United Nations General Assembly. 1981b. "Prevention of an Arms Race in Outer Space A/RES/ 36/97C." United Nations. https://www.unoosa.org/oosa/oosadoc/data/resolutions/1981/ general_assembly_36th_session/res_3697c.html.

United Nations General Assembly. 2013. "Report of the Group of Governmental Experts on Transparency and Confidence-Building Measures in Outer Space Activities A/68/189." United Nations. https://www.un.org/ga/search/view_doc.asp?symbol=A/68/189.

United Nations General Assembly. 2020. "Reducing Space Threats through Norms, Rules and Principles of Responsible Behaviours: Resolution." United Nations. https://digitallibrary. un.org/record/3893851?ln=en.

United Nations General Assembly. 2021. "Prevention of an Arms Race in Outer Space: Reducing Space Threats through Norms, Rules and Principles of Responsible Behaviours A/ RES/76/231." https://digitallibrary.un.org/record/3952870/files/A_RES_76_231-EN.pdf.

United Nations General Assembly. 2022. "Destructive Direct-Ascent Anti-Missile Testing A/ RES/77/41." https://digitallibrary.un.org/record/3996915?ln=en.

United Nations Secretary-General. 1994. *Study on the Application of Confidence-Building Measures in Outer Space A/48/305.* Disarmament Study Series. New York: United Nations. https://doi.org/10.18356/f24a0a1e-en.

United Nations Secretary-General. 2021. "Reducing Space Threats through Norms, Rules and Principles of Responsible Behaviours." United Nations Disarmament Yearbook. United Nations Office for Disarmament Affairs. https://doi.org/10.18356/9789210056700c009.

United States. 1962. *International Cooperation in the Peaceful Uses of Outer Space.* New York: United Nations.

United States Department of Defense. 2022. "Combined Space Operations Vision 2031." https:// media.defense.gov/2022/Feb/22/2002942522/-1/-1/0/CSPO-VISION-2031.PDF.

United States Space Force. 2020. "Spacepower: Doctrine for Space Forces." Space Capstone Publication. https://www.spaceforce.mil/Portals/1/Space%20Capstone%20Publication_ 10%20Aug%202020.pdf.

US Space Command Public Affairs Office. 2021. "Russian Direct-Ascent Anti-Satellite Missile Test Creates Significant, Long-Lasting Space Debris." United States Space Command, Department of Defense. November 15, 2021. https://www.spacecom.mil/News/Article-Disp lay/Article/2842957/russian-direct-ascent-anti-satellite-missile-test-creates-significant- long-last/.

van Eijk, Cristian. 2022. "Unstealing the Sky: Third World Equity in the Orbital Commons." *Air and Space Law* 47, no. 1: 25–34. https://kluwerlawonline.com/journalarticle/Air+and+ Space+Law/47.1/AILA2022002.

Weber, Cynthia. 2005. *International Relations Theory: A Critical Introduction.* 2nd ed. London; New York: Routledge.

Weeden, Brian. 2014. *Through a Glass Darkly: Chinese, American, and Russian Anti-Satellite Testing in Space.* Washington DC: Secure World Foundation. https://swfound.org/media/ 167224/through_a_glass_darkly_march2014.pdf.

Weeden, Brian, and Victoria Samson. 2023. *Global Counterspace Capabilities.* Washington DC: Secure World Foundation. https://swfound.org/media/207567/swf_global_counterspace_c apabilities_2023_v2.pdf.

Weinraub, Bernard. 1986. "Reagan Terms 'Star Wars' Peaceful Project Like Radar." *New York Times.* October 18, 1986, sec. World. https://www.nytimes.com/1986/10/18/world/reagan- terms-star-wars-peaceful-project-like-radar.html.

West, Jessica. 2020. "Did Russia Test a Weapon in Space?" *Project Ploughshares* (blog). https://ploughshares.ca/pl_publications/did-russia-test-a-weapon-in-space/.

West, Jessica. 2021a. "Outer Space." *First Committee Monitor* 19, no. 5: 27–29.

West, Jessica. 2021b. "Outer Space: Cloaked by a Fog of Peace." *Ploughshares Monitor*. https://ploughshares.ca/2021/09/outer-space-cloaked-by-a-fog-of-peace/.

West, Jessica. 2022. "From Peaceful Uses to Warfighting: The Dangers of the New Military Era in Space." In *Military Space Ethics*, edited by Nikki Coleman, 269–86. Havant, UK: Howgate Publishing.

West, Jessica, and Almudena Azcarate Ortega. 2022. *Space Dossier 7: Norms for Outer Space: A Small Step or a Giant Leap for Policymaking?* Geneva: United Nations Institute for Disarmament Research. https://unidir.org/sites/default/files/2022-04/UNIDIR-Space_Dossier_7.pdf.

Westad, Odd Arne. 2007. *The Global Cold War: Third World Interventions and the Making of Our Times*. 1st paperback ed. Cambridge; New York: Cambridge University Press.

Yanow, Dvora. 1992. "Silences in Public Policy Discourse: Organizational and Policy Myths." *Journal of Public Administration Research and Theory* 2, no. 4: 399–423.

York, Herbert F. 1983. "Bilateral Negotiations and the Arms Race." *Scientific American* 249, no. 4: 149–61.

Zhen, Liu. 2023. "China Slams U.S. Call to Ban Anti-Satellite Missile Tests as 'Fake Arms Control.'" *South China Morning Post*. https://www.scmp.com/news/china/diplomacy/article/3232073/china-slams-us-call-ban-anti-satellite-missile-tests-fake-arms-control.

CHAPTER 14

ETHICS IN SPACE SECURITY

Virtue and the Future of Cosmopolitanism

KOJI TACHIBANA

INTRODUCTION

ETHICS has power to guide us in a specific direction. Unlike laws, ethics regulates our behaviors not through penalties for violations but by cultivating our minds to pursue good and avoid evil. This is true not only at the individual level but also the national and international levels such as for refugee issues, international disputes, and security issues in space. This chapter investigates why space security calls for an appropriate ethical underpinning and which ethics is most appropriate to realize security in space.

First, I present the difficulty in defining the notion of space security. Space security, which has traditionally been understood as a part of national security, has recently expanded to include other security issues such as human, economic, and environmental. However, this conceptual expansion makes it difficult to precisely define space security. In the next section, I explain that, to realize such space security, we need a shared understanding of the idea of peaceful uses of space, which is widely accepted as the focal meaning of space security. Although nations have adopted various legally non-binding soft law instruments for realizing this idea, they furtively tend not to follow such instruments if they do not deem it to be in their national interests. Therefore, to realize space security, we must share a certain ethics that dissuades countries from taking advantage of loopholes and makes them understand that the idea is worthy of willing compliance.

The chapter then goes on to scrutinize which ethics is most appropriate to realize the idea of peaceful use in space. First, I suggest two roles of ethics in international relations (IR) theory: as a ground moral theory (deontology, utilitarianism, and virtue ethics) and as a moral view (skepticism, state moralism, and cosmopolitanism). Then, I identify two conditions that ethics must satisfy to realize international peace and security in space: caring for the interests of other people and states, and evaluating values based on multiple ambiguous criteria. I argue that, as a moral view, cosmopolitanism satisfies the conditions most. I next discuss which type of ground moral theory enables cosmopolitanism to realize the peaceful uses of space and thereby contribute most to space security. Examining the major forms, I argue that the cosmopolitanism in question must be normative rather than descriptive, moral rather than institutional, and virtue ethics-based rather than deontology-based or utilitarianism-based. I then demonstrate that this sort of cosmopolitanism can regulate nations' behaviors by considering the case of space resources as an example. I conclude that, if ethics can make up for what the law lacks, nations and space agencies must promote space education to cultivate a cosmopolitan virtue.

ON SPACE SECURITY

Space Security as National Security

In the twentieth century, space activities were related primarily to national or state security, the core of which was addressed by military means, combined with diplomatic and political strategies. As became evident during the Cold War, space activities are a means of gaining technological and military superiority, including air superiority, over other countries. John F. Kennedy's 1960 presidential campaign illustrated this. He spoke of a "missile gap" to emphasize that the Soviet Union's superiority in the space race threatened US national security, claiming that US space technologies needed to be reinforced for national security. The National Aeronautics and Space Administration (NASA) Apollo program began following his election. Historically speaking, therefore, space activities, military power, and national security are closely connected.

After the Cold War, international cooperation became more prominent. A symbolic example of such cooperation is the International Space Station (ISS) maintained and operated by fifteen countries, including the United States and Russia. Underlying this peaceful tone, however, a military strategy for national security has continued to exist: the US Space Force was formed in 2019 and the UK Space Command in 2021. Even Japan, which does not officially have a military, has been militarized since the Basic Space Law was implemented in 2008 (Pekkanen 2021) and established the Space Operation Squadron for security purposes in 2020. The bond between space activities and national security remains strong in many countries. Therefore, it is natural that the notion of space security has been understood as a part of national security achieved by military means (Aoki 2012; Sheehan 2015; Freeland and Gruttner 2021).

Expansion of the Concept of Space Security

The scope of space security has gradually been expanded beyond the military to areas including environmental, economic, and human securities. Concerning environmental security, the Outer Space Treaty (OST) of 1967 stipulates that space exploration must be conducted in such a way as to avoid harmful contamination of space (Art. IX). This stipulation has become more relevant because the space environment is at risk of contamination by various space debris, such as abandoned rockets, disused satellites, and other refuse left by space activities. In January 2007, for example, China destroyed satellite FY-1C to test the ability of anti-satellite (ASAT) weapons. This military experiment produced about 2,000 pieces of trackable space debris at altitudes in range of the orbits of the ISS and many information-gathering satellites (IGSs). As the ISS and IGSs were at risk of collision with the debris, China's experiment drew international condemnation, which encouraged the United Nations Committee on the Peaceful Uses of Outer Space (COPUOS) to adopt legally non-binding guidelines for space debris mitigation in February 2007. Although China announced that it would not further conduct any such experiments, similar events continue to occur such as the United States' (unofficial) ASAT test in 2008 and the India's ASAT test in 2019. Recently, Russia's ASAT experiment on November 15, 2021, also created more than 1,500 pieces of trackable debris and required crews aboard the ISS to shelter in capsules (BBC 2021). These experiments show that space activities motivated by national security concerns can harm the space environment, which may constrain the possibilities for further space activities.

The participation of private companies in space activities calls for the implementation of measures to ensure economic security in space. The end of the Cold War made it more difficult for the space superpowers to allocate a budget to their space agencies. So, they welcomed the participation of private companies. Space can provide great business opportunities to the private sector, because market projections are increasing to trillions of US dollars. At present, thousands of satellites belonging to various private companies are in operation to provide communication, weather information, and other services. Some enterprises even transport astronauts to the ISS and provide space travel for billionaires. Upcoming space businesses include active debris removal, the development of vehicles for exploring the moon and Mars, and the mining and use of space resources. Although private companies are interested in such business, the OST might not be able to support such interests well because Article II obviously says that celestial bodies are not subject to appropriation, while no articles stipulate any regulations on resources acquired in space. Therefore, it is assumed that private operators can legitimately claim ownership of such resources by conducting their activities in accordance with their respective domestic laws (IISL 2015). Accordingly, the earlier a country established its laws regarding space resources, the easier it is for companies in that country to acquire space resources. At present, four countries have enacted such domestic laws: the United States (Public Law 114-90 of 2015), Luxembourg (Law of 20 July 2017), the United Arab Emirates (UAE) (Federal Law No. 12 of 2019), and Japan (Act No. 83 of 2021).

The concept of human security in general was first proposed by the United Nations Development Programme (1994, 22), which advocates (1) shifting the focus of security from the state to the "ordinary people," (2) recognizing the "protection from the threat of disease, hunger, unemployment, crime, social conflict, political repression and environmental hazards" as aspects of security, and (3) building a secure society that improves people's quality of life. As Amartya Sen (2003a) emphasizes, national security "concentrates primarily on safeguarding the integrity and robustness of the state and thus has only an indirect connection with the security of the human beings who live in these states." The expanded notion of space security must address the ideal of human security, although what exactly is at stake regarding human security in space must be further determined (Sheehan 2015; Martinez 2020; Borowitz, this volume).

Definition of Space Security

The expansion of the concept of space security raises problems in defining it. While scholars widely agree that the notion has been and should be thus expanded, there is no consensus on its definition. There are at least four considerations in the difficulty of defining it, which stem from space security's transcendence of terrestrial national boundaries. The first consideration is that the progress of space activities produces three aspects of space security: outer space for terrestrial security, security in outer space, and terrestrial security from outer space such as asteroids (Sheehan 2015).

The second consideration concerns multilateralism in governance (Antoni 2020). Under the Cold War structure, solely the two space superpowers of the United States and the USSR were responsible for maintaining space security. With progress in space activities, an increasing number of countries have to participate in space security consultations. Furthermore, considering the recent diversification in space activities, international non-governmental organizations (NGOs) and delegates of private industries may have to be involved in these discussions.

The third consideration in defining space security is that the relationship between national and space securities remains unclear. The expansion of the concept of space security does not necessarily imply that national security will no longer retain a central role in space security issues. For example, Johnson-Freese (2018) argues that national security is still at the core of space security issues, which should be addressed primarily through a military approach. However, even he admits that the notion of space security has not been articulated clearly enough to determine the state's responsibilities in space, saying that the United States "expects other countries to behave as responsible actors, but it has yet to define what that means".

The fourth consideration is the conceptual distinction between space security and other concepts such as space safety and space sustainability (Martinez 2020; Pelton, Sgobba, and Trujillo 2020). They seem to be closely related to each other because they commonly concern global issues. Therefore, to provide a distinctive definition of space security, it should be described to which extent it differs from these concepts. These four considerations make it difficult to define space security, allowing different entities to interpret the concept differently based on their focuses and perspectives.

Peaceful Uses, Soft Laws, and Ethical Underpinnings

The Ambiguity of Peaceful Uses

Despite the conceptual ambiguity of the expanded notion of space security, it seems possible to identify its focal meaning as the peaceful uses of space (Antoni 2020; Blount 2021; Johnson-Freese 2018). An explicit statement regarding "peaceful uses" and "peaceful purposes" can be found in Articles III and IV of the OST, which say, "States Parties to the Treaty shall carry on activities in the exploration and use outer space, . . . in the interest of maintaining international peace and security" and "[t]he Moon and other celestial bodies shall be used by all States Parties to the Treaty exclusively for peaceful purposes." These statements seem to naturally lead us to assume space security as the uses of space for peaceful purposes. However, the following sentence in Article IV causes confusion about and dents our confidence in the concepts of peaceful uses and purposes: "[t]he use of military personnel for scientific research or for any other peaceful purposes shall not be prohibited."

We can posit three reasons the notion of the peaceful uses of space is so confusingly characterized. First, it is almost impossible to sufficiently distinguish between peaceful and non-peaceful space activities. Peace is generally considered to be the opposite concept of war, but military power has been used in both peacetime and war-related activities. For example, although many military satellites can target enemy bases, they may be considered to be used for peaceful activities if they merely monitor the military movements of other countries and the intelligence gathered is exclusively used to suppress any disturbing movements or prevent significant conflicts.[1]

Second, many space technologies are capable of dual uses. The end of the Cold War blurred the boundaries between the military, scientific, and commercial uses of space (Sheehan 2015). The above-mentioned military satellites can also be used to collect weather and atmosphere information to anticipate global issues like natural disasters and global warming. Conversely, non-military scientific crafts can also be used for military purposes. For example, JAXA's robotic spacecraft, *Hayabusa*, was the first in the world to successfully collect a sample of material from a small near-Earth asteroid. However, as this robotic spacecraft technology could also be applied as ASATs, such scientific achievements might not be regarded as purely scientific and peaceful activities (Pekkanenn 2020; 2021).

Third, strategies intended for peaceful purposes might result in non-peaceful events. Just as the preliminary military mobilization of European countries triggered World

---

[1] To solve this ambiguity, some propose the "aggressive" and "non-aggressive (or passive)" interpretation and other introduce the "non-military" and "military" interpretation (Masson-Zwaan and Hofmann 2019, chap. 2, note 12).

War I (Herz 1950), it is quite possible for actions mutually intended to be peaceful to lead to a security dilemma, resulting in a violent conflict. A space race between space powers, such as the United States, Russia, and China, could evolve into non-peaceful relations.

The concept of peaceful use and purposes is thus ambiguous. Although every state agrees with the idea, they are unlikely to agree on a more detailed description of what it entails because such descriptions might restrict their free activities in space that increases or maintains their national interests. The more specifically it is descried and the more actors get involved, the more difficult it becomes to obtain consensus from the international community and enact a legally binding instrument such as a treaty. This can result in the COPUOS being stuck because it adopts a consensus-based decisions making process that requires the members of the committee "to reach agreement in its work without need for voting" (A/AC.105/PV.2) (UNCOPUOS 1962, 4–5).[2] Because of this difficulty, existing international legal frameworks, including the United Nations Charter and the OST, remain inadequate to prevent an arms race in space and to achieve peaceful uses (Tronchetti 2012). Under the current vague descriptions of peaceful uses and purposes, nations have a certain discretion to decide whether an action or policy is peaceful or not.

Soft Law Approach

Scholars propose that instruments advocating the peaceful uses of outer space should be understood not as legally binding hard law but non-binding soft law (Ferrazzani 2012; Tronchetti 2012; Johnson-Freese 2018; Blount 2021; Freeland and Gruttner 2021). Soft law is a general term that covers various forms of legally non-binding instruments, including "principles, norms, standards or other statements of expected behavior in the form of recommendations, charters, terms of reference, guidelines, [and] codes of conduct" (Ferrazzani 2012). Such instruments usually contain both basic guidelines and transparency and confidence-building measures (TCBMs) (Tronchetti 2012). They are used in various fields of space activity and function in three ways: as substitutes for treaties by harmonizing national laws or developing an international regime; as purely technical guidelines; or as *lex ferenda* that declare the desirable norms for IR (Aoki 2012).

However, different soft law instruments have different reasons for adopting the soft law approach. For example, instruments comprising technical guidelines describe such guidelines relatively clearly, but they are formed as soft law instruments because technical updates frequently occur. Such updates must be reflected in the guidelines, but treaties and other hard law instruments cannot be rapidly revised due to the procedural complexity of amending them.

---

[2] However, it should be noted that this procedure is not wholeheartedly approved of. Some delegations question the validity of consensus, saying that "consensus should not be identified with unanimity or used to block general agreements" (UNCOPUOS 1996, 31).

Instruments concerning the peaceful uses of space are formed in soft law for a different reason than that of technical guidelines. As such documents are highly concerned with international politics, in which each country has its own space agenda, policy, and strategy, it is difficult to create descriptions that satisfy the needs and aims of every country. Instead, countries reach an agreement in support of the idea of peaceful use, leaving its descriptions and criteria vague. Examples of such soft law instruments include the International Charter on Space and Major Disasters (2000), the Hague Code of Conduct Against Ballistic Missile Proliferation (2002), space debris mitigation guidelines of the Scientific and Technical Subcommittee of the Committee on the Peaceful Uses of Outer Space (2007), and the (revised version of) International Code of Conduct for Outer Space Activities (2010). Although these instruments include sections that describe principles and general measures, their descriptions of peaceful use still contain certain ambiguities. For example, the International Code of Conduct (2010), which makes it possible to significantly enhance space security, remains ambiguous in the absence of definitions for several key terms and the possible endorsement of the proliferation of ASATs (Tronchetti 2012).

Ethical Underpinnings

Soft law instruments do not enable the legal punishment of nations for failing to follow the guidelines or regulations contained therein. Due to this limitation, countries tend to follow a soft law instrument only if they "deem [it] to be in their national interest" (Tronchetti 2012). They may also adopt a hypocritical attitude, such as taking advantage of a loophole and claiming to have followed a regulation verbally, while not following it in spirit (Ferrazzani 2012). Therefore, to actualize the idea of peaceful use as soft law, something must underpin the idea to dissuade countries from taking advantage of loopholes and make them understand that the peaceful use of space has intrinsic value that makes it worthy of willing compliance.

Some scholars expect ethic or a sense of humanity to play a role in such underpinning: Ferrazzani (2012), for example, observes that soft law instruments contain "quasi ethical values"; Blount (2021) argues that "security and safety in the space domain are maintained less by recourse to legal precepts and more by a need for coordinated multilateralism, which is supported by an underlying supranational ethic"; and Freeland and Gruttner (2021) propose that "we must remain conscious of, and continue to hold onto, the fundamental sentiment of 'humanity' that underpins space law in order to avoid inconceivable scenarios." Humanity and ethic, which are discussed in ethics, differ from law in that they regulate people's behavior not through penalties for violations but by cultivating their mind to pursue good and avoid evil. Accordingly, as some scholars assert, it may be reasonable to expect the idea of the peaceful uses of space to be substantiated by a shared humanistic ethic.

However, it should be noted that sharing a certain ethic does not imply that the shared values realize the peaceful use envisioned. For example, if nations shared a Hobbesian ethic—"war of all against all *(bellum omnium contra omnes)*"—they would fall into a state of violence (Hobbes, 1647, *præfatio*); if they shared Thrasymachus's ethical view as expressed in Plato's *Republic*—"justice is nothing but the advantage of the stronger (εἶναι τὸ δίκαιον οὐκ ἄλλο τι ἢ τὸ τοῦ κρείττονος συμφέρον)"—they would endorse or reinforce the national order with the strongest countries taking the most resources (Plato 2003, 338c2–3). As these situations are not what we expect as peaceful states, countries sharing a certain ethic is not sufficient for them to reach a desirable understanding of peaceful use. To achieve this effect, therefore, it must be scrutinized what sort of ethic should be shared.

ETHICS IN INTERNATIONAL RELATIONS

Two Roles of Ethics in IR Theory

Ethics has the power to guide behaviors in a specific direction. This is true not only at the individual level but also the national level. Whether one is religious or non-religious, an individual with a certain ethic is motivated to act in alignment with such ethic, and a state that adopts a particular ethic is motivated to employ policies not in conflict with their ethical beliefs. Laws on abortion and marriage are examples of policies influenced by such beliefs.

Compared to the cases in individual and domestic politics, the role of ethics is less visible in IR because of a weaker global consensus on values and the complexity in decision-making. However, ethics still plays a significant role there. Some further argue that global security is "the highest good—the end—of ethics" (Burke, Lee-Koo, and McDonald 2014, 6). The three major moral theories in IR theory are: deontology, which defines rightness of an action as consistency with the moral laws; utilitarianism, which identifies it with the greatest happiness of the greatest number of people; and virtue ethics, which focuses on a person's character rather than such universal principles as moral laws or the sum of happiness (Burke, Lee-Koo, and McDonald 2014; Ney and Welch 2016).

Against the background of these theories, Ney and Welch (2016, 29) propose "three views on the role of morality" in IR theory: skepticism, cosmopolitanism, and state moralism (see also Beitz 2005). Skepticism, also called political realism, casts doubt on the very existence of moral norms. According to skeptics, it is always right to prioritize national interests because no norms should be followed to the detriment of national interests. Cosmopolitanism is the opposite of skepticism. Cosmopolitans belittle the existence of national borders and, accordingly, the institution of the state. They believe that borders and institutions cause inequality among people, arguing first and foremost that every individual should be treated equally by everyone regardless of their nation or culture (Pogge 2008, chap. 7). The third view is state moralism, also called the morality of states. This position falls somewhere between skepticism and cosmopolitanism, recognizing both the institution of the state and the moral norms that states should follow. State moralists believe that state sovereignty is the most essential norm and, therefore, that it is wrong to interfere beyond their borders with other states even if this would maximize their own national interests.

The relationship between theory and view in ethics is not straightforward. This has confused scholars. For example, in the case of cosmopolitanism, Beitz (2005, 18) has complained that "cosmopolitanism is not a complete moral conception: it leaves open too many questions. An indication of this is that both utilitarianism and a globalized contractualism count as cosmopolitan theories. . . . These areas of theoretical indeterminacy mean that a wide range of normative positions might count as cosmopolitan." However, such confusion will disappear if we remember that the relationship need not be one-to-one. Although skepticism is an exception because it denies the very existence of moral norms and thereby is not committed to the theory of either deontology or utilitarianism, state moralism and cosmopolitanism can be grounded in either theory. For example, two countries could adopt the same state-moralistic view for different reasons: one country might respect state sovereignty for a utilitarian reason, believing that such respect would increase overall welfare, whereas the other may do so for a deontic reason, believing such respect to be a moral obligation to the autonomy of other states. Although these two countries would act similarly in most cases, they might make different decisions in others. Imagine a case, for instance, where a legitimate democratic process established a new government that supported terrorism. The utilitarian country might violate the sovereignty of that state in the belief that respecting its sovereignty would not contribute to or may even deteriorate international welfare in the long run. In contrast, the deontic country would continue to respect the state's sovereignty even if it harmed international society, believing this to be their moral duty.[3]

And thus ethics takes a twofold position in IR theory, namely, moral theory and moral view. Moral view prescribes how to behave in international society, whereas moral theory provides the theoretical background for that moral view. Although the association between moral view and moral theory is not one-to-one, the prescriptions of each view are restricted or regulated by its ground theory. Therefore, to determine which ethic would best achieve the peaceful uses of space, we must identify which combination of theory and view would be most appropriate for achieving it. I shall examine moral views in the next two subsections and theories in the following section.

Two Conditions for Space Security

We can identify two conditions for an ethic that substantiates the concept of peaceful uses of space. The first condition concerns a nation's care for the interests of other people

---

[3] The case of cosmopolitanism will be examined in the subsection on Deontology, Utilitarianism, and Virtue Ethics.

and states, which can contradict prioritizing its own national interests. Article I of the OST says that every space activity "shall be carried out for the benefit and in the interests of all countries, irrespective of their degree of economic or scientific development, and shall be the province of all mankind." It remains unclear what the benefit of all countries and the province of all mankind are. These ambiguities are said to "constitute an obstacle for treaty-making" (Aoki 2012). However, the general idea of this article and its relevance to peaceful uses is clear, as international peace and security cannot be maintained without care for the interests of others. Therefore, an appropriate ethic must help soft law approaches to implement the idea through care for others as the province of all humankind to maintain international peace and security.

The second condition concerns the ability of value evaluation that makes appropriate decisions based on multiple ambiguous criteria. The principle of the peaceful uses of space is not a hard law instrument consisting of clearly defined statements from which the correct decision can be deduced. Rather, as a soft law instrument, it is made up of vague statements so that it can reflects multiple evaluative criteria, including not only scientific and military criteria but also human, economic, and environmental ones. However, this vagueness makes room for allowing nations to interpret soft law instruments arbitrarily. For example, an overemphasis on economic and commercial values "challenges the core principle of the 'peaceful purposes' doctrine that underpins the current international legal regulation of outer space" (Freeland and Gruttner 2021). Therefore, the ethic required must guide us to judge and act in a non-deductive but appropriate manner.

Cosmopolitanism as a Desirable Moral View for Space Security

Which moral view would then most satisfy the two conditions for the ethic appropriate to space security? Skepticism is likely to satisfy the second condition, value evaluation, well. Because it involves no moral rules to follow in deducing decisions, it enables the flexible comparison and weighing of various values to prioritize national interests. In contrast, skepticism cannot meet the first condition because it encourages the consideration only of its own interests and thus fails to consider the quality of life of people in other countries.

State moralism does not adequately meet the first condition because it encourages states to consider other states' interests as long as they do not infringe on its own national sovereignty. Accordingly, it is possible that even if the people of a neighboring country were struggling to make ends meet, the country in question may not intervene to the extent needed because it respects the neighboring country's self-determination. It is also possible that even if an action favorable to a country's own national interests would decrease other countries' interests, they could keep taking that position if it would not infringe on the national sovereignty of other countries. If it were justifiable in light of international laws, the country would also believe that other states should not infringe on its national self-determination. These imaginary situations suggest such an overemphasis on national security negatively impacts global security (Freeland and Gruttner 2021). State moralism may therefore not satisfy the first condition well. Its satisfaction of the second condition depends on which moral theory is adopted.

Cosmopolitanism satisfies the first condition most adequately because this view does not only attach no importance to the borders or institution of the state but also emphasizes the interests of other countries and their inhabitants equally to a given country's own. As with state moralism, however, whether this view satisfies the second condition depends on which moral theory is adopted. Cosmopolitanism thus seems to be the view most likely to support the idea of the peaceful uses of space. It should be noted, however, that I am not presenting this argument as a decisive one. As many existing countries adopt state moralism, it is worth considering how state moralism realizes space security. Here, I argue that cosmopolitanism theoretically satisfies the first condition better than state moralism. Still, whether cosmopolitanism does so depends on the moral theory that grounds it; therefore, we must investigate which type of cosmopolitanism would most satisfy the conditions.

COSMOPOLITANISM AND SPACE SECURITY

A Brief History of Cosmopolitanism

The political ideology of cosmopolitanism dates back to the ancient Greek philosopher Diogenes the Cynic. When asked where he came from, he replied, "*cosmopolitēs* (a citizen of the world)," indicating that no nation could define him (Diogenis Laertii 1964, VI. 63. 3).[4] Later, Stoicism contributed to the propagation of cosmopolitanism to some extent. In the eighteenth century, social events such as the French Revolution and the *Déclaration des Droits de l'Homme et du Citoyen de 1789* inherited cosmopolitanism while Immanuel Kant and Jeremy Bentham also defended it (Kleingeld and Brown 2019). In particular, in his discussion of *jus inter gentes* and *jus cosmopoliticum*, Kant (1795) laid the foundation for modern cosmopolitanism by showing the potential for an international order based on a union of nations.

Since the twentieth century, various forms of cosmopolitanism have been proposed: moral, economic, political, institutional, cultural, rooted, situated, Christian, discrepant, feministic, liberal, socialistic, and so on (Bernstein 2011; Kleingeld and Brown

---

[4] It is noteworthy that Mozi (468–376 BC), an ancient Chinese philosopher, also proposes a similar idea "universal love (兼愛)," saying that: "Partiality should be replaced by universality. . . . If men were to regard the states of others as they regard their own, then who would raise up his state to attack the state of another? . . . If men were to regard the families of others as they regard their own, then who would raise up his family to overthrow that of another?" (Mozi 2003, 42).

2019). David Harvey calls these "adjectival cosmopolitanisms" and describes the status quo as follows:

> Unfortunately, cosmopolitanism has been constructed from such a variety of standpoints as to often confuse rather than clarify political-economic and cultural-scientific agendas. It has acquired so many nuances and meanings as to make it impossible to identify any central current of thing and theorizing, apart from a generalized opposition to the supposed parochialisms that derive from extreme allegiances to nation, race, ethnicity, and religious identity. (Harvey 2009, 78–79)

Martha Nussbaum (2019, chap. 6) also states that cosmopolitanism is basically "a comprehensive ethical doctrine" but that "the term 'cosmopolitanism' is now too vague to be useful." We cannot completely examine such a diverse range of cosmopolitanisms here. Instead, I shall introduce three significant perspectives on cosmopolitanism related to our present question and identify which form of cosmopolitanism best satisfies the two above-mentioned conditions.

Normative or Descriptive Cosmopolitanism

The first perspective on cosmopolitanism distinguishes between descriptive and normative views (Beck 2006). To present a view as normative is to recommend it as right or assert that it should be agreed upon, adopted, or conducted, whereas to present it as descriptive is to assert that, in fact, it has occurred in reality. As descriptiveness and normativity are not mutually exclusive, some scholars take both, arguing that globalization or "cosmopolitanization" is in fact advancing in such areas as communications and economics and proposing to weaken the role of national borders (Beck 2006, 17–18; Singer 2016, chaps. 4–5). However, it remains open what kind of relationship descriptive and normative cosmopolitanisms may have with each other. For example, Hume's law would indicate that the former does not imply the latter (Hume 1739–1740, III-1-1). A more moderate position would admit that the former supports the latter to some extent but argue that different grounds are required to fully justify the normativity of the latter.

As a matter of fact, then, to what extent has globalization advanced in space? Human space exploration has gradually changed ideologies on various terrestrial borders. Symbolic examples of such change include the international cooperation required to operate the ISS, the figures of multinational astronauts and cosmonauts working and living together onboard, and the anecdotes of these astronauts and cosmonauts. For example, Koichi Wakata, a JAXA astronaut, reports that he "believe[s] that the farther away humankind goes from the Earth, the stronger the bond as humanity will be. Rather than being a person from a certain country, you become an 'inhabitant of the Earth'" (Osaka 2019, 40). These examples demonstrate rising views about cosmopolitanization in space.

However, one could assert that such examples are not sufficient to claim descriptive cosmopolitanism. Nations work together because their national interests coincide, but once their interests are in conflict, their activities may diverge. For example, considering the forthcoming end of the operation of the ISS, the future IR situation might not remain as cooperative: Russia and China have started to work on their own moon and deep space exploration programs, while the United States has launched the Artemis program. This divergence might lead to the end of "the long and stable relationship of space cooperation between these two countries [the United States and Russia]" (Boley and Byers 2020). Therefore, at present, it is reasonable to say that even though the world is currently heading toward cosmopolitanism in space, the normative aspect of cosmopolitanism should primarily be focused because such descriptive situation remains unstable and normativity in space is of concern here.

Moral or Institutional Cosmopolitanism

The second perspective concerns the nature of cosmopolitanism. As shown in earlier, cosmopolitanism takes too many forms to be sorted out. However, in the context of this paper, moral cosmopolitanism is preferable because we seek an *ethical* norm that can realize space security. Moral cosmopolitanism "hold[s] that all human beings are morally important and must be properly taken into account in practical deliberations about any actions (especially lawmaking and policymaking) that may significantly affect anyone's vital, fundamental, or otherwise important interests" (Bernstein 2011, 711). Accordingly, it stands "opposed to any view that limits the scope of justification to the members of particular types of groups, whether identified by shared political values, communal histories, or ethnic characteristics" (Beitz 2005, 17). Following this position, therefore, a space policy is morally wrong if it considers only the interests of a particular country or people or disregards the disadvantages suffered by other countries or people. If such a policy does not violate any international laws or treaties, it is legally permissible but would be ethically unacceptable under moral cosmopolitanism.

Moral cosmopolitanism is often compared to institutional cosmopolitanism, which claims that national borders should be abolished. Although moral cosmopolitanism holds that we should help those who are unable to live a worthwhile life due to borders, ethnic conflicts, and war, it does not necessarily claim that we should dismantle states' current political institutions to help such people. In this sense, moral cosmopolitanism can also be labeled as a "mild" position (Caney 2001). This view would be satisfied with existing institutions if people in distress could be adequately assisted through donations and the activities of NGOs such as the Red Cross and Oxfam. Although moral cosmopolitanism can endorse institutional and other forms of cosmopolitanism if donations and NGOs' activities are insufficient, its basic position concerns our ethical attitude toward the world.

Deontology, Utilitarianism, and Virtue Ethics

As explored earlier, a given moral view like cosmopolitanism has the potential to be grounded in various moral theories such as deontology, utilitarianism, and virtue ethics. Since each theory is recognized as a possible basis for cosmopolitanism, it should be examined which theory can form the most appropriate basis of normative moral cosmopolitanism for space security.

Deontology has long been recognized as an anticipated ground theory of cosmopolitanism. It defines the morality of an action not according to its consequences but by its consistency with the moral laws universally and equally applicable to every human being. Typical examples of such laws include "do not treat people only as a means to an end" and "do not lie." Hence, policies that exploit or deceive people are considered morally wrong. Based on such a deontic viewpoint, cosmopolitan policies are morally right because they equally respect all people. Onora O'Neill (2000, chaps. 9–10), a Kantian cosmopolitan philosopher and politician, advocates a moderate institutional cosmopolitanism that makes boundaries "porous" to carry out cosmopolitan actions.

Utilitarianism is the other well-known theory of cosmopolitanism. This theory provides a threefold formalization of moral rightness: an action or policy is morally right if (1) its consequences (2) produce the welfare or utility (3) to the greatest extent and of as many people as possible (Sen and Williams 1982). As this theory considers all people's welfare equally, it is similar to deontology in respect of the impartiality of people (Shapcott 2010). Following such a utilitarian principle, one can make a cosmopolitan claim like "if it is in our power to prevent something very bad from happening, without thereby sacrificing anything morally significant, we ought, morally, to do it" (Singer 1972, 231). Using the moral imperative of "ought," based not in a Kantian notion of duty but in utilitarian sum-ranking, utilitarianism can position a cosmopolitan action not as a supererogation but as an obligation.

The third theory that can ground cosmopolitanism is virtue ethics. In contrast to deontology and utilitarianism, it focuses on a person as a criterion of right and wrong. Aristotle (1984, 1107a1–2), the originator of virtue ethics, puts this focus as follows: rightness is "determined by reason and in the way in which the man of practical wisdom would determine it (ὡρισμένη λόγῳ καὶ ᾧ ἂν ὁ φρόνιμος ὁρίσειεν)." Virtue ethicists do not think that the moral rightness of an action can be deduced from such abstract rules as those adopted by deontology and utilitarianism. Instead, such a rightness must be determined individually, considering the specific contexts in which the action in question is situated. Virtues as personal character traits make it possible for people to consider a given context and determine the appropriate action.

Major virtuous character traits, including "justice, honesty, charity, courage, practical wisdom, generosity, [and] loyalty," work not as external rules but as internal action-guidance in light of human flourishing (Hursthouse 1999, 34ff.). Aristotle (1984, 1104b13–16) explains this by saying that virtue involves pleasure and pain, which can be well understood as likes and dislikes (Urmson 1988, 26–27). Once we acquire the trait of charity, for example, we behave charitably not because we *ought* to be charitable but because we *delight* in being charitable. Therefore, charitable people prefer to help those suffering in distant countries than to maximize their national interests. Because such preferences occur *effortlessly* for charitable people, legally binding regulations are not needed to lead them to act peacefully.

Virtues can be in conflict with each other, depending on the situations. *Phronēsis* (practical wisdom), a higher-ordered virtue, can mediate such conflicts. Imagine a dilemma case of infidelity, in which one's loyalty to a best friend is not consistent with generosity to that friend's partner, but both loyalty and generosity are morally required. There is no general and universal rule to resolve this sort of issue. We must individually decide, taking into account the context, relationships, and any other relevant factors. A *phronimos*, a person of practical wisdom, handles such situations in light of (and to achieve) *eudaimonia*, the life worth living as a human being or, in short, human flourishing.

Virtue ethicists propose how virtues can ground cosmopolitanism in several ways. Costa (2016) emphasizes the corrective role of cosmopolitan virtue in IR theory: Cosmopolitan virtues could correct the harmful tendencies that people and states may fall into in IR, such as egoistic national interests, extreme patriotism, and conspiracy theories. Since cosmopolitan virtues in this role can work with whatever view they currently hold, skepticism or state moralism, they can improve the situations. Accordingly, such virtues "can count as virtues even if they do not always translate into the most effective policies" (Costa 2016). Van Hooft (2007) lists the nine cosmopolitan virtues, including hope, courage, and compassion. He argues that these virtues are required for cultivating the mind of global citizenship, based on which people can truly recognize the humanity of others and, accordingly, have concern for distant people. Moreover, others argue that aesthetic sensitivity and respect for others' lives should be considered in the age of New Space. They present examples of space colonization to imagine the possibility to build commercial and residential facilities on the moon: this would produce gigantic scientific and economic value but also damage the lunar environment or exploit some people's livelihoods. Although we may tend toward advancing this development project, virtue ethicists criticize such space colonization because it exhibits insensitivity to the environmental and aesthetic value of the universe untouched by humans (Sparrow, 2015); or, because such colonization lacks compassion for the lives of people sacrificed for the rest of humanity (Tachibana 2020).

Virtue Ethics-Based Cosmopolitanism

Virtue ethics is the most desirable moral theory to ground normative moral cosmopolitanism in space because, as discussed below, virtue ethics-based cosmopolitanism best satisfies the two conditions outlined above: to care for the interests of other people and states, and to make appropriate decisions based on multiple ambiguous criteria. And does so to a greater extent than rival theories.

First, virtue ethics-based cosmopolitanism can satisfy the first condition more than the other theory-based forms of cosmopolitanism because only virtue ethics identifies human flourishing as a moral requirement. Take a hypothetical case of space resources as an example. Appealing to the so-called Lockean proviso, one might justify the first-come-first-served approach in the following way: pioneers, such as private companies, from developed countries have the right to privately possess space resources, "at least where there is enough, and as good, left in common for others" (Locke 1988, 2nd Tr., §27). Both deontology and utilitarianism can endorse the proviso if the distribution of goods in such conditions does not infringe on their principles in that such distribution can satisfy the condition of the impartiality of people. However, from the virtue ethical point of view, the distribution of goods is not the only issue to be considered. Following Aristotelian tradition, Amartya Sen (1987, 3) mentions the ethical origins of economics and argues that economic distribution cannot be morally correct if it does not contribute to "achieving 'the good for man.'" An appropriately equal distribution of goods might not be enough to enable some people to flourish for reasons such as physical disabilities or chronic diseases. What should be equally distributed are not goods but the conditions to flourish in life (Sen 1982, chap. 16; 2003b). This idea can be crystallized into the capabilities approach, which lists the central human capabilities that society must bestow on everyone for them to be able to flourish (Nussbaum 2000; 2019, chap. 7). This broadly Aristotelian virtue-ethical viewpoint enlightens us to regard space resource issues, such as first-come-first-served attitudes toward property and the possible methods of distribution, not merely as issues of economic security but also as issues of human security.

Virtue ethics-based cosmopolitanism also satisfies the second condition more than the other theories-based cosmopolitanisms. Deontology and utilitarianism adopt abstract and universal principles, respectively, so their implications for the peaceful uses of space can be described as follows:

> Deontology: An action based on a set of soft law instruments is suitable for the peaceful uses of space if and only if it is in accordance with the moral laws.

> Utilitarianism: An action based on a set of soft law instruments is suitable for the peaceful uses of space if and only if it contributes to maximizing the welfare of the greatest number of people.[5]

Both formulations might seem to provide good criteria to ensure the peaceful uses of space. First, deontology thus formulated would prevent nations from lying to other nations to advance their own space strategies or treating other nations only as a means to their own ends. However, even if the nation does not lie or treat others only as a means, their behavior might not be peaceful because, for example, a nation's honest space

---

[5] Strictly, if we follow Singer's understanding of utilitarianism, this principle extends beyond persons to a broader range of morally considerable beings.

operation for the benefit of allied countries can cause military tension. We may add other moral laws to justify such behavior as peaceful. However, this never forms sufficient moral rules that can determine every parameter of the peaceful uses in space in every possible case.

Utilitarianism also encounters difficulty. Following utilitarian criteria, a nation's action would be justified if the action achieved the greatest welfare for the greatest number of people by sacrificing a small number of individuals. However, we do not think such an action would be peaceful. Rather, we would consider choosing another more peaceful option that might not maximize welfare but would not sacrifice anyone. Artistic activities in space may be an example of such peaceful actions. The maximization of welfare is a feature worthy of consideration but is neither a necessary nor a sufficient condition for peaceful uses of space.

Being different from deontology and utilitarianism, virtue ethics formulates the concept of the peaceful uses of space as follows:

> Virtue ethics: An action based on a set of soft law instruments is suitable for the peaceful uses of space if and only if it is what a virtuous agent would perform or suggest in this (and comparable) circumstances.

This formulation shows that, by appealing to or acquiring desirable character traits of a virtuous agent, we can take the particular context into account and, accordingly, form an appropriate judgment on the basis of ambiguous descriptions provided by soft law instruments. Following virtue ethics, various evaluation criteria do not work as decisive or authoritative rules but as values worthy of consideration. Therefore, if the situation requires a nation to lie to another nation or not to maximize total welfare and if such actions would be what a virtuous agent would perform in this situation, then they can be justified as peaceful.

On Space Resources

Let us examine the case of space resources from the viewpoint of virtue ethics-based cosmopolitanism. As shown at the beginning of the chapter, the lack of descriptions about the dealing of space resources in the OST or other international laws enable nations to give private operators legitimate ownership of such resources once they have established the related domestic laws. The international community might not accept such possibility because, by exploiting first-mover advantages, these enactments eventually endorse a first-come-first-served approach (Boley and Byers 2020). In this regard, an egalitarian alternative would be the Moon Agreement (1979) ratified by eighteen countries and signed by four. Article XI of this agreement declares that "natural resources [of the moon] are the common heritage of mankind" and, accordingly, international society must "establish an international regime, including appropriate procedures, to govern the exploitation of the natural resources of the moon as such exploitation is about to become feasible." It does not permit such resources to be claimed as anyone's property, or at least, to be freely exploited by particular nations or private operator for their own interests but recommends space resources mining to be governed by an international body.[6]

However, first-movers would not be pleased with the agreement because it conflicts with their national interests to promote the commercial exploitation of space resources. Indeed, the four countries that enacted domestic laws and other space faring nations such as Russia and China have not ratified or signed this agreement. In this respect, the US government clearly expresses its attitude toward this issue in an executive order issued on space resources in April 2020 (White House 2020), stating that "Americans should have the right to engage in commercial exploration, recovery, and use of resources in outer space, consistent with applicable law" and declares promotion of the establishment of "joint statements and bilateral and multilateral arrangements . . . for the public and private recovery and use of space resources." Such establishment is the Artemis Accords concluded among eight states in October 2020. Section 10 of the accords declares that the extraction of space resources is not subject to national appropriation and that such extraction is consistent with the OST and other international laws. As of December 2023, the number of signatories of this accords has reached thirty-three countries and one island territory, including the four first-mover countries and some who participate in the ISS, such as Canada, the United Kingdom, Germany, France, and Italy.

Both the Moon Agreement and the Artemis Accords can be legitimately consistent with the OST because the OST says nothing about the space resources mining. Therefore, in principle, each nation can commit itself to either position (or reject both) for a different reason to legal consistency. What reason, then, makes countries choose the instrument that they chose? The States Parties to the Moon Agreement consist mostly of developing countries that have yet to have space capabilities, whereas the Signatories to the Artemis Accords predominantly consist of the four first-movers and other space faring countries. This contrast suggests that each country chooses the side that maximizes their own national interests under the mask of righteous words.

This behavioral principle may especially apply to Japan. Two congressmen who drafted Japan's Space Resources Law state that "one objective of the law is to promote formulating international rules. . . . It is very important for Japan to play a leading role in the formulation by establishing domestic laws, in order to prevent the interests of developing countries that are yet to have the capabilities of space exploitation from being harmed by the unregulated exploitation that first-movers may conduct" (Kobayashi and Ohno 2021). This statement itself is unquestionably righteous. It aligns with Japan's strategy that aims at "reinforc[ing] the image of Japan carrying on with peaceful intentions for both domestic and international audiences" (Pekkanen 2021).

---

[6] This part of the agreement can be interpreted in a different way as it states that "natural resources in place" cannot become property of anyone (Art. XI, 3). If the *natural* resources can be interpreted as unmined, one can claim ownership once the resources are mined and separated from their origin.

It remains to be seen what Japan will actually do. However, its most likely courses of action are to play "a leading role" in following the accords and contributing to making it a fait accompli or to continue its exploitation activities, justifying them for the reason that they are not "unregulated exploitation" because they follow both Japan's domestic law and the accords. Both these behaviors would be logically consistent with the wording of the congressmen's statement.

If such actions were taken, however, developing countries in space would not consider Japan to be truthful. Rather, they would think that Japan adopted a hypocritical attitude and exploited a loophole. They would also assume that Japan's "peaceful image" strategy contained something deceitful. At the end, they might conclude that the accords will not redistribute economic resources in their favor but instead consolidate the existing resource allocation structure (see Bull 2012, chap. 12).[7,8]

A similar state of affairs has already unfolded in the form of a confrontation between nations with space capabilities and those without, regarding the extent to which the notion of the peaceful uses of space permits military activities (Friman 2005). As Blount (2021) points out, "[w]hile all of these actors [namely, the United States, Russia, China, and India] give lip service to the need to keep space secure, none seems to be willing to truly engage in substantive talks on maintaining multilateral space security and, instead, opt to entrench themselves within their own national interests." It will not be surprising if a similar situation would arise in the context of space resources problems.

What is at work here is precisely the same politics as is at work on Earth: the justification and maximization of states' own interests based on state moralism. What is missing is an awareness of certain considerations, such as whether exploiting space resources is *a good way of living as humans* in space, whether damaging space environments is bereft of *aesthetic sensitivity*, and whether a hypocritical attitude is *truthful* to other countries. State-moralistic nations would govern space without or dismissing such considerations, but such governance would be less peaceful than the governance of nations aware of these considerations—and it is cosmopolitan virtues that make such awareness possible.

---

[7] The other three first-movers may be less equivocal than Japan in this respect. Luxembourg overtly aims to be a leading space industrial country in Europe by positioning itself "as a pioneer in the exploration and utilisation of space resources" (Luxembourg Space Agency 2019). The UAE declares to "promote the UAE's regional and international presence in the space sector" (UAE 2021). As mentioned above, the United States officially expresses its economically hegemonistic attitude in the executive order and the Artemis Accords. However, their profound intentions regarding national security and other issues remain unclear, so further cautious study will be required.

[8] The Hague Working Group (2019) published a report that may help to mediate the Moon Agreement and the Artemis Accords. This report suggests they could be consistent by proposing that it not only appreciates the economical use of space resources and the contributions of pioneer operators (§ 4.2.e, 4.2.k), but also proposes a concrete framework of international regimes that the agreement requires (§18) (Kozuka 2021). It should be noted in this respect that Australia, Mexico, and Netherlands ratified the agreement and signed the accords, and France signed both.

CONCLUSION

Historians identify three factors that led to the Age of Exploration or Discovery in Europe: advances in science and technology, such as the development of shipbuilding and the introduction of the compass from Arabia or China, the need to explore the open seas to compensate for the loss of economic hegemony in the Mediterranean, and legal circumstances that allow such avaricious exploration. Being backed up by papal's rescripts, the kings of European countries such as the Portuguese Empire and the Spanish Empire financially supported sailors and legally authorized those who found "new" lands to exploit resources privately. It is not difficult to observe similarities between that age and the present age. Our age of space exploration also seems to be driven forward by three similar factors: technological advancements sufficient to explore deep space, economic opportunities that may bring the nation immense profits, and unilateral legalizations that justify explorations and exploitations by private operators.[9] We must learn from history to avoid replicating the Age of Exploration. What we must discover in space is not resources but the future of humanity.

Virtue ethics-based cosmopolitanism is the most suitable framework for discovering this future. Cultivating cosmopolitan virtues, we can appreciate the idea of the peaceful uses of space vaguely described in soft law instruments and, accordingly, avoid exploiting loopholes in these instruments. Such cosmopolitan virtues should be helpful even to state moralists and skeptics because virtues can play a corrective role. If a state moralist wishes to maximize their own national interests, virtues will warn them against doing so excessively. Thus, virtue ethics-based cosmopolitanism is relevant to everyone who is responsible for realizing space security.

As any student of history can prognosticate, the future of space security must be ominous if the cosmopolitan mindset does not percolate through nations. These less-cosmopolitan nations would still cooperate to the extent that they actually do so under the current international framework. They may even develop some soft law instruments to realize the peaceful uses of space. However, insofar as they keep state-moralistic or skeptic minds, they would pursue their own interests in a cunning way. Such equivocal behaviors would increase international tensions. Finally, the second age of exploration, demarcación, or serious conflict in space, would be inevitable in the future.

Education will play a crucial role in avoiding such a dire future and realizing peace in space, as it does more generally in approaches toward ethics which focus upon the virtue of agents and their capabilities in complex situations. As Sen (2003a) discerns regarding human security, space security also "demands ethical force and political recognition." This force and recognition will rely on people's and nations' understanding of the intrinsic value of the peace in space. Nations and space agencies have promoted

---

[9] An important difference from the Age of Exploration is that the Space Age of Exploration does not (probably) have religious purposes such as missionary activities.

space education to convey the joys of space sciences and technologies. However, space education must focus more on cultivating cosmopolitanism in people's minds. Space agencies have broadcasted the international cooperation of astronauts and cosmonauts living and working in the ISS. As mentioned earlier, this cooperation indeed contributes to promoting cosmopolitanism, but it is not enough. We should also encourage people to consider what actions have been taken by nations and organizations such as the COPUOS to secure space, why many countries are still pursuing their national interests, and what else must be done to establish the peace in space. These considerations will demonstrate why a cosmopolitan mindset is required.

In particular, the space sector should emphasize the value of the fact that, unlike Earth, space has no borders. Due to the long and complex history on Earth, we can hardly remove national, cultural, and institutional borders that have divided people and caused conflicts. These borders have prevented the adoption of cosmopolitanism on Earth and labeled it as idealism. In space, however, such borders do not exist. Space education must emphasize the value of space as a descriptively cosmopolitan region. At the same time, it is also important to emphasize that space does not have any border *so far*. Space may come to have borders if we behave as we have on Earth. Therefore, space education must convey that we must not make the same mistakes as we have on Earth but make every effort to maintain the precious value of the lack of borders in space.

The word *cosmopolitēs* (literally, space-citizen) was spoken by Diogenes 2500 years ago. At present, perhaps in a way very different to what Diogenes imagined, we have the opportunity to substantially realize cosmopolitanism for the first time in human history. We need the virtue of hope to believe we can do this and the virtue of courage to put it into practice.

Acknowledgments

I wish to express my gratitude to Anthony Milligan, Soichiro Kozuka, Saadia M. Pekkanen, and P.J. Blount for their comments on the penultimate version of this paper.

References

Antoni, Ntorina. 2020. "Definition and Status of Space Security." In *Handbook of Space Security: Policies, Applications and Program*, edited by Kai-Uwe Schrogl, 9–33. 2nd ed. Cham, Switzerland: Springer.

Aoki, Setsuko. 2012. "The Function of' Soft Law' in the Development of International Space Law." In *Soft Law in Outer Space: The function of non-binding norms in international space law*, edited by Armgard Marboe, 57–86. Wien: Böhlau Verlag.

Aristotle. 1984. *Nicomachean Ethics*. Translated by Sir David Ross. In *The Complete Works of Aristotle*, edited by Jonathan Barnes, 1729–1867. Revised Oxford Translation. 2 vols. Princeton, NJ: Princeton University Press.

BBC News. 2021. "Russian Anti-Satellite Missile Test Draws Condemnation." https://www.bbc. com/news/science-environment-59299101.

Beck, Ulrich. 2006. *The Cosmopolitan Vision*. Translated by Ciaran Cronin. Cambridge: Polity Press.

Beitz, Charles R. 2005. "Cosmopolitanism and Global Justice." *The Journal of Ethics* 9: 11–27.

Bernstein, Alyssa R. 2011. "Moral Cosmopolitanism." In *Encyclopedia of Global Justice*, edited by Deen K. Chatterjee, 711–17. Cham, Switzerland: Springer.

Blount, P.J. 2021. "Peaceful Purposes for the Benefit of All Mankind: The Ethical Foundation of Space Security." In *War and Peace in Outer Space: Law, Policy, and Ethics*, edited by Cassandra Steer and Matthew Hersch, 109–22. New York: Oxford University Press.

Boley, Aaron, and Michael Byers. 2020. "U.S. Policy Puts the Safe Development of Space at Risk." *Science* 370, no. 6513: 174–75.

Bull, Hadley. 2012. *The Anarchical Society: A Study of Order in World Politics*. With Forewords by Andrew Hurrell and Stanley Hoffman. 4th ed. New York: Columbia University Press.

Burke, Anthony, Katrina Lee-Koo, and Matt McDonald. 2014. *Ethics and Global Security: A Cosmopolitan Approach*. London: Routledge.

Caney, Simon. 2001. "International Distributive Justice." *Political Studies* 49: 974–94.

Costa, M. Victoria. 2016. "Cosmopolitanism as a Corrective Virtue." *Ethical Theory and Moral Practice* 19, no. 4: 999–1013.

Diogenis Laertii. 1964. *Vitae Philosophorum*. 2 vols. Edited by H. S. Long. Oxford: Clarendon Press.

Ferrazzani, Marco. 2012. "Soft Law in Space Activities—An Updated View." In *Soft Law in Outer Space: The Function of Non-Binding Norms in International Space Law*, edited by Armgard Marboe, 99–118. Wien: Böhlau Verlag.

Freeland, Steven, and Elise Gruttner. 2021. "Outer Space Security." In *The Oxford Handbook of the International Law and Global Security*, edited by Robin Geiß and Nils Melzer, 679–96. Oxford: Oxford University Press.

Friman, Johanna. 2005. "War and Peace in Outer Space: A Review of the Legality of the Weaponization of Outer Space in the Light of the Prohibition on Non-Peaceful Purposes." *Finnish Yearbook of International Law* 16: 285–312.

Hague Working Group (The Hague International Space Resources Governance Working Group). 2019. "Building Blocks for the Development of an International Framework for the Governance of Space Resource Activities." https://www.universiteitleiden.nl/binaries/cont ent/assets/rechtsgeleerdheid/instituut-voor-publiekrecht/lucht--en-ruimterecht/space-resources/final-bb.pdf.

Harvey, David. 2009. *Cosmopolitanism and the Geographies of Freedom*. New York: Columbia University Press.

Herz, John H. 1950. "Idealist Internationalism and the Security Dilemma." *World Politics* 2, no. 2: 157–80.

Hobbes, Thomas. 1647. *De cive*. Amsterodami: Apud Ludovicum Elzevirium.

Hume, David 1739-1740. *A Treatise of Human Nature: Being an Attempt to Introduce the Experimental Method of Reasoning into Moral Subjects*. 3 Vols. London.

Hursthouse, Rosalind. 1999. *On Virtue Ethics*. Oxford: Oxford University Press.

IISL (International Institute of Space Law). 2015. "Position Paper on Space Resource Mining." http://iislweb.space/wp-content/uploads/2020/01/SpaceResourceMining.pdf.

Johnson-Freese, Joan. 2018. "Space and National Security." In *The Oxford Handbook of U.S. National Security*, edited by Derek S. Reveron, Nikolas K. Gvosdev, and John A. Cloud, 435–52. Oxford: Oxford University Press.

Kant, Immanuel. 1795 [1912/23]. "Zum ewigen Frieden. Ein philosophischer Entwurf von Immanuel Kant." In *Kant's gesammelte Schriften*, 341–86. Herausgegeben von der Königlich Preußischen Akademie der Wissenschaften, Band VIII. Berlin: Georg Reimer/De Gruyter.

Kleingeld, Pauline, and Eric Brown. 2019. "Cosmopolitanism." *Stanford Encyclopedia of Philosophy*. https://plato.stanford.edu/entries/cosmopolitanism/.

Kobayashi, Takayuki, and Keitaro Ohno. 2021. "The Background, Aim, and Contents of Space Resources Law." *New Business Law* 1203: 74–80. (In Japanese.)

Kozuka, Soichiro. 2021. "International Significances of Japan's Space Resources Law." *New Business Law* 1203: 80–82. (In Japanese.)

Locke, John. 1988. *Two Treatises of Government*. Edited by Peter Laslett. Cambridge: Cambridge University Press.

Luxembourg Space Agency. 2019. "Spaceresources.lu Initiative." https://space-agency.public.lu/en/space-resources/the-initiative.html.

Martinez, Peter. 2020. "Space Sustainability." In *Handbook of Space Security: Policies, Applications and Programs*, edited by Kai-Uwe Schrogl, 319–40. 2nd ed. Cham, Switzerland: Springer.

Masson-Zwaan, Tanja, and Mafulena Hofmann. 2019. *Introduction to Space Law* (Fourth Edition). Alphen aan den Rijn, Netherlands: Wolters Kluwer.

Mozi. 2003. *MOZI: Basic Writings*. Translated by Burton Watson. New York: Columbia University Press.

Ney, Joseph S. Jr., and David A. Welch. 2016. *Understanding Global Conflict and Cooperation: An Introduction to Theory and History*. 10th ed. London: Person.

Nussbaum, Martha. 2000. *Women and Human Development: The Capabilities Approach*. Cambridge: Cambridge University Press.

Nussbaum, Martha. 2019. *The Cosmopolitan Tradition: A Noble but Flawed Ideal*. Cambridge, MA: Belknap Press.

O'Neill, Onora. 2000. *Bounds of Justice*. Cambridge: Cambridge University Press.

Osaka, Takuro. 2019. "The Cosmology of Light: From the Origin of Life to the Cosmos—Light Art by Takuro Osaka." PhD Program in Empowerment Informatics, School of Integrative and Global Majors, University of Tsukuba.

Pekkanen, Saadia M. 2020. "Thank You for Your Service: The Security Implications of Japan's Counterspace Capabilities." *Policy Roundtable: The Future of Japanese Security and Defense*. https://tnsr.org/roundtable/policy-roundtable-the-future-of-japanese-security-and-defense/#essay5.

Pekkanen, Saadia M. 2021. "Neoclassical Realism in Japan's Space Security." In *The Oxford Handbook of Japanese Politics*, edited by Robert J. Pekkanen and Saadia M. Pekkanen, 763–90. Oxford: Oxford University Press.

Pelton, Joe, Tommaso Sgobba, and Maite Trujillo. 2020. "Space Safety." In *Handbook of Space Security: Policies, Applications and Programs*, edited by Kai-Uwe Schrogl, 265–98. 2nd ed. Cham, Switzerland: Springer.

Plato. 2003. *Platonis Rempublicam*. Edited by S. R. Slings. Oxford: Oxford University Press.

Pogge, Thomas. 2008. *World Poverty and Human Rights*. 2nd ed. London: Polity.

Sen, Amartya. 1982. *Choice, Welfare and Measurement*. Oxford: Basil Blackwell.

Sen, Amartya. 1987. *On Ethics and Economics*. Oxford: Blackwell Publishing.

Sen, Amartya. 2003a. "Development, Rights and Human Security." In *Human Security Now*, edited by Commission on Human Security, 8–9. New York: Commission on Human Security.

Sen, Amartya. 2003b. "Social Choice Theory and Justice" In *Constructions of Practical Reason: Interviews on Moral and Political Philosophy*, edited by Herlinde Pauer-Studer, 148–78. California: Stanford University Press.

Sen, Amartya, and Bernard Williams. 1982. "Introduction: Utilitarianism and Beyond." In *Utilitarianism and Beyond*, edited by Amartya Sen and Bernard Williams, 1–22. Cambridge: Cambridge University Press.

Shapcott, Richard. 2010. *International Ethics: A Critical Introduction*. Cambridge: Polity Press.

Sheehan, Michael. 2015. "Defining Space Security." In *Handbook of Space Security: Policies, Applications and Programs*, edited by Kai-Uwe Schrogl, P. L. Hays, J. Robinson, D. Moura, C. Giannopapa, 7–21. Cham, Switzerland: Springer.

Singer, Peter. 1972. "Famine, Affluence, and Morality." *Philosophy and Public Affairs* 1, no. 3: 229–43.

Singer, Peter. 2016. *One World Now: The Ethics of Globalization*. New Haven, CT: Yale University Press.

Sparrow, Robert. 2015. "Terraforming, Vandalism and Virtue Ethics." In *Commercial Space Exploration: Ethics, Policy, and Governance*, edited by Jai Galliot, 161–78. Surrey, UK: Ashgate.

Tachibana, Koji. 2020. "Virtue Ethics and the Value of Saving Humanity " In *Human Enhancements for Space Missions: Lunar, Martian, and Future Missions to the Outer Planets*, edited by Konrad Szocik, 169–81. Cham, Switzerland: Springer.

Tronchetti, Fabio. 2012. "A Soft Law Approach to Prevent the Weaponisation of Outer Space." In *Soft Law in Outer Space: The Function of Non-Binding Norms in International Space Law*, edited by Armgard Marboe, 361–86. Wien: Böhlau Verlag.

UAE (The United Arab Emirates). 2021. "UAE National Space Strategy 2030." https://u.ae/en/about-the-uae/strategies-initiatives-and-awards/federal-governments-strategies-and-plans/national-space-strategy-2030.

UNCOPUOS (The United Nations Committee on the Peaceful Uses of Outer Space). 1962. "Report of the Committee on the Peaceful Uses of Outer Space (A/5181)." https://digitallibrary.un.org/record/844041.

UNCOPUOS (The United Nations Committee on the Peaceful Uses of Outer Space). 1996. "Report of the Committee on the Peaceful Uses of Outer Space (A/51/20)." www.unoosa.org/pdf/gadocs/A_51_20E.pdf.

United Nations Development Programme. 1994. *Human Development Report 1994*. Oxford: Oxford University Press.

Urmson, James Opie. 1988. *Aristotle's Ethics*. Oxford: Blackwell.

van Hooft, Stan. (2007). "Cosmopolitanism as Virtue." *Journal of Global Ethics* 3, no. 3: 303–15.

White House 2020. "Encouraging International Support for the Recovery and Use of Space Resources." https://www.federalregister.gov/documents/2020/04/10/2020-07800/encouraging-international-support-for-the-recovery-and-use-of-space-resources.

PART III

STATECRAFT AND STRATEGY

CHAPTER 15

....

US NATIONAL SECURITY INTERESTS IN SPACE

....

SCOTT PACE

INTRODUCTION

....

OVER the past sixty-plus years, since the first satellite was launched by the USSR, space activities have transitioned from experimental and symbolic to routine and critical to the global economy, international security, and public safety. Space assets today are integral parts of multiple critical infrastructures, such as communications, energy, emergency services, and transportation. Given the importance of space assets, a dilemma exists for the United States and other spacefaring states in that the shared domain of space is not subject to sovereign control. Aside from the practical difficulties of controlling regions beyond the Earth, there are also legal barriers. The 1967 Outer Space Treaty (OST) specifically states that "outer space is not subject to national appropriation by claim of sovereignty, by means of use or occupation, or by any other means" (OST, Art. II). Like other shared domains, such as the high seas, the polar regions, and arguably cyberspace, space is a domain in which state and non-state actors interact beyond national borders. Given their increasing dependence on space activities, how can states protect their interests in the space domain without sovereign control?

There is extensive literature on how space power should be defined and understood from the Cold War period through today (Klein 2020). Unsurprisingly, space security discussions tend to focus on technical possibilities, military strategy, doctrine, and arms control as opposed to more general discussions of international relations (IR) theory applied to how nations interact regarding space interests. As a result, the standard language of IR theory, such as realism, structural realism, and constructivism, is not often found in space writings (Pfaltzgraff 2011) Writings on space are typically concerned with advocacy for desired policies, programs, and budgets as opposed to the academic foundations of the positions advocated.

This chapter briefly reviews the current US approach to space security, including national policy statements and actions such as the creation of the United States Space Force (USSF), the formulation of space power doctrine, and the shaping of the international space environment. In all areas of US space activity, international relations have a prominent role in which states can be adversaries, allies, partners, suppliers, and customers. In seeking to understand and explain these relationships, different theories can and should be applied in different situations depending on how well their underlying assumptions align with practice. While realist theory describes the geopolitical competition between the United States, Russia, and China in the space domain, a fuller understanding of the US approach to space security activities requires a mixture of theories. Such a mixed, pragmatic approach is commonly referred to as "eclectic theorizing" in IR literature, and frames the discussion below (Katzenstein and Sil 2008; Sil and Katzenstein 2010).

IR Perspectives on US Space Security

US space activities have evolved greatly from their Cold War origins. Beginning with strategic reconnaissance and competition to influence world opinion, the United States developed advanced technical capabilities in support of its security, economic, and diplomatic interests. A clear separation between civil space programs, such as the National Aeronautics and Space Administration's (NASA) human space exploration efforts, and intelligence activities, such as the then-classified CORONA satellite reconnaissance program, was intentionally made. This distinction between "white world" and "black world" programs was a deliberate choice to advance US diplomatic interests, which required openness, and security interests, which required secrecy. Both efforts were built on the same material foundations of the US industrial base, workforce, and infrastructure. The US response to Soviet military and space actions can be most easily explained by the imperatives of structural realism. The realist response was a defensive one however, seeking to counter the impacts of Soviet capabilities rather than to deprive the Soviets of those capabilities or decisively subdue the USSR.

As in the past, US space activities today cannot be understood in isolation but should be seen in the context of broad US interests—diplomatic, intelligence, military, and economic. The United States does not have a single space program, but rather a diverse space enterprise with distinct government agencies, private industries, academic and non-profit actors, and non-government organizations. The challenge for US policymakers is to create and implement national policies and strategies that align disparate space activities such that they are mutually supporting and not contrary to overarching US national interests. In a colloquial metaphor, the task is to ensure the energy of space activities creates thrust in a desired direction and not merely Brownian motion.

The US space enterprise can be thought of as comprising a portfolio of activities. As with financial portfolios, some elements are high risk, high payoff while others are lower risk, but lower payoff, and resources are allocated accordingly. In the military sector, which reflects realist thinking, the United States has stood up a dedicated military service, the USSF, and reestablished the US Space Command. In the civil sector, reflecting ideas of complex interdependence, NASA's Artemis Program seeks to return humans to Moon, with commercial and international partners. Commercially, US space industries are experiencing dynamic growth with record launch rates, large satellite constellations, and new space-based information services. Internationally, in line with constructivist viewpoints, the United States is engaged in promoting norms of responsible behavior and the long-term sustainability of space activities in bilateral and multilateral fora. Constructivism can particularly appropriate to understanding multilateral institutions with participants, sometimes including nongovernmental organizations (NGOs), of widely varying space capacities and their own complex relationships.

KEY CONTEMPORARY TRAJECTORIES

The US approach to space security has been and continues to be shaped by a few key trends or trajectories. The space domain has changed dramatically over the past two decades, becoming much more globalized (as measured by the number of states participating) and democratized (i.e., rising number of non-state actors) as technical and economic barriers to entry decline. Estimates for the size of global space economy vary widely from under $200 billion to almost half-a-trillion dollars (Crane 2020). The largest revenue sectors are not the manufacture and launching of satellites themselves, but the space-enabled data and services they provide such as communication, navigation, and remote sensing. The growing global dependency on space-enabled services has not, however, been matched by measures to provide greater assurance as to the availability and resiliency of those services against intentional interference.

Much as the United Kingdom rose to power as a seafaring nation, the United States is a "spacefaring nation," both benefiting from and reliant on the capability to operate in space. How states choose to navigate and shape this shared domain is an important issue with limited precedents in other domains. International maritime law developed over hundreds of years and applies distinct norms to different regions such as the high seas, exclusive economic zones, and territorial seas. International aviation law developed more rapidly, but with the clarity of sovereign control over national air spaces and well-defined air navigation regions. The Antarctic Treaty System covers a specific geographic region and sovereign claims are only placed in abeyance—not ruled out. In several of these shared domains, specifically the oceans, cyberspace, and the Antarctic, China pursues its national interests regardless of international legal obligations (notably the South China Sea) and there is no reason to believe a priori that space will be different. The behaviors of problematic powers, like China and Russia, and smaller powers such as North Korea and Iran, therefore need to be considered in protecting US national interests in space activities.

Capabilities to destroy, degrade, or otherwise interfere with space assets are known as counterspace capabilities. Counterspace capabilities may employ a range of techniques and effects, from destructive kinetic strikes to reversible jamming, and be employed from the ground or in-space against space-based targets (United States Defense Intelligence Agency 2019). Both the USSR and the United States developed and demonstrated anti-satellite (ASAT) weapons during the Cold War. Neither state engaged in widespread operational deployment of weapons in space.

After the end of the Cold War, there was a lull in ASAT testing from 1995 to 2005 as shown in Figure 15.1 from the NGO Secure World Foundation (Secure World Foundation 2020). The most visible of these tests was the 2007 Chinese ASAT test in which they destroyed one of their own satellites and in the process generated tens of thousands of pieces of debris which remain a hazard to this day. The United States does not officially recognize the 2008 intercept of USA-193 as an ASAT test. The event was known as "Operation Burnt Frost" and used a re-purposed SM-3 Aegis missile to intercept a decaying US military satellite in space claiming that the re-entering satellite posed a potential hazard to persons on the ground (Johnson 2021).

Military threats to the United States can be categorized as those of "revisionist powers" such as China and Russia, "rogue states" such as Iran and North Korea, and non-state terrorist threats (United States Department of Defense 2018). The US military tends to be an expeditionary force that operates away from the homeland. In doing so, it benefits from and is more reliant on space capabilities than states that are operating on the periphery of their own homelands. Russia and China recognize this asymmetric reliance and have built counterspace capabilities to hold US space assets at risk and thus reduce the benefits the United States may derive from them. Iran and North Korea

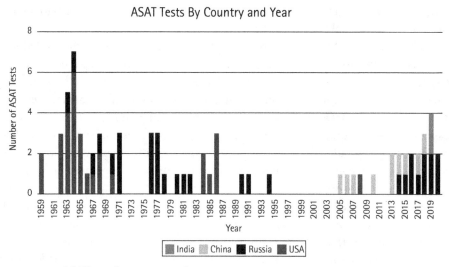

FIGURE 15.1 ASAT tests by country and year.

Source: Courtesy Secure World Foundation.

do not have significant space capabilities and may be less constrained in attacking US space assets, e.g., high-altitude nuclear bursts that would indiscriminately harm all satellites, not just US ones. Non-state actors are not a threat in space, but cyber and terrorist attacks are possible against ground stations and terrestrial control networks and personnel.

US National Space Policy

After a twenty-five-year hiatus, President Trump reconstituted the National Space Council (NSpC) in 2017 (Trump 2017). As a policy-making body within the White House, like the National Security Council and the Domestic Policy Council, the NSpC was responsible for all sectors of US space activity: national security, civil, and commercial. A primary purpose of the council was to integrate and oversee US space policies so as to advance US national interests. This meant resolving internal US government policy conflicts regarding space and ensuring that space activities were aligned with national interests—not just those of the performing agencies or affected communities. During the Trump administration, the NSpC oversaw new initiatives to return Americans to the moon, streamline the regulation of commercial space activities, create a new armed service for space, and update overall national space policy.

President Biden subsequently decided in 2021 to maintain the NSpC, which is chaired by the vice president (Bender 2021). This decision, along with decisions to maintain the NASA Artemis program to land the next American astronauts on the moon and endorse the USSF, represents bipartisan agreement on major space policy decisions in an otherwise polarized political environment. Other areas of ongoing consensus on space matters concern the threat posed by Chinese and Russian counterspace capabilities and continued rejection of Chinese and Russian space-related arms control proposals.

National space policy does not change automatically with changes in presidential administrations. Presidential policies and executive orders remain in force unless and until a subsequent president decides to change them. US space policy issues are traditionally nonpartisan with rare exceptions, such as claims of a missile gap in the 1960 presidential election or the Strategic Defense Initiative during the Reagan administration. Support has remained stable for peaceful overflight and, since the OST entered into force, the ban on sovereign claims to celestial bodies and placement of weapons of mass destruction in space. Over time national space policies tend to grow in length as they retain foundational provisions and add new topics, such as space traffic management, radiofrequency spectrum management, and workforce education.

One example of space policy shifting significantly between administrations concerns space arms control. The Reagan administration set down criteria that any arms control measures would have to be "verifiable and equitable" (Office of the Press Secretary 1982). The George W. Bush administration's 2006 National Space Policy rejected arms control measures without condition, stating that:

The United States will oppose the development of new legal regimes or other restrictions that seek to prohibit or limit U.S. access to or use of space. Proposed arms control agreements or restrictions must not impair the rights of the United States to conduct research, development, testing, and operations or other activities in space for U.S. national interests." (United States 2006).

The United States came under international criticism for this flat rejection of arms control, which seemed to bar even the potential for discussion. The Obama administration's space policy reverted to the earlier formulation: "The United States will consider proposals and concepts for arms control measures if they are equitable, effectively verifiable, and enhance the national security of the United States and its allies" (United States 2010). The Trump administration continued this same language in its 2020 National Space Policy (United States 2020). Thus presidential policy was changed but later returned to a previous formulation. Each change or restatement required specific presidential direction and did not occur automatically with changes in administrations.

The first principle of the 2020 National Space Policy is that "It is the shared interest of all nations to act responsibly in space to ensure the safety, stability, security, and long-term sustainability of space activities" (United States 2020). This principle is woven into guidelines for each space sector. Specifically for the national security sector, the United States will "deter hostilities, demonstrate responsible behaviors, and, if necessary, defeat aggression and protect United States interests in space through:

- Robust space domain awareness of all activities in space with the ability to characterize and attribute potentially threatening behavior;
- Communicating to competitors which space activities the United States considers undesirable or irresponsible, while promoting, demonstrating, and communicating responsible norms of behavior;
- Assured, credible, and demonstrable responses to defend vital national interests in space;
- Resilient space-enabled missions that reduce the impact or deny the effectiveness of adversaries' actions; and
- Synchronized diplomatic, information, military, and economic strategies that:
  o Deter adversaries and other actors from conducting activities that may threaten the peaceful use of space by the United States, its allies, and partners; and
  o Compel and impose costs on adversaries to cease behaviors that threaten the peaceful use of space by the United States, its allies, and partners." (United States 2020).

The five elements of deterrence require the acquisition of particular space capabilities. In order to perform attribution, the United States needs space domain awareness. In order to signal to adversaries, the existence of norms of behavior can indicate where changes or violations detrimental to security or spaceflight safety occur. Responses to changes or violations may in turn be communicated by words (e.g., diplomatic exchanges) or actions (e.g., changes in force readiness). Of course, in order for deterrence to have a real effect on the thinking of an adversary, the United States must have credible capabilities and not just strong words.

Readers of Thomas Schelling will recognize the first three bullets as corresponding to the classic elements of deterrence: attribution, signaling, credibility (Schelling 1966; see also Morgan, this volume). The latter two points are also related to deterrence, with resilience contributing the denial of attack objectives and cost imposition representing retaliation. Resilience is also important to crisis stability and mitigating incentives for a first strike in the space domain. Retaliation need not be in-kind and may range from sending a stern démarche, imposing economic sanctions, to the considered threat or use of nuclear weapons. Of special relevance to space, cost-imposition may be cross-domain and not limited to space. The National Space Policy specifically states: "The United States will develop strategies, capabilities, and options to respond to any purposeful interference with or attack on the space systems of the United States or its allies . . . . Such strategies, capabilities, and options will allow for a deliberate response at a time, place, manner, and domain of its choosing" (United States 2020).

Creation of the USSF

For the United States, national security uses of space began with the launch of reconnaissance satellites to gain intelligence on the USSR and avoid risky (and illegal) aerial overflights. Other applications such as weather prediction, communications, and missile warning soon followed. The first human space launchers were re-purposed Intermediate Range Ballistic Missiles (IRBMs) (Redstone) and Intercontinental Ballistic Missiles (ICBMs) (Atlas, Titan). The early military uses of space were typically highly classified and associated with strategic intelligence and nuclear missions. Over time, space systems became used more widely across the US national security community and with Operations Desert Shield and Desert Storm in 1991 came into public prominence. Operation Desert Storm was often termed the "first space war," not because there was conflict in space but because space systems were widely acknowledged as an advantage for the United States in the war's military operations. While only a small fraction of the munitions used relied on precision guidance from the Global Positioning System (GPS), commercial GPS receivers were widely used by US forces. Warnings of Scud tactical missile launches were relayed from satellites, and communication and weather services relied on satellites.

Space-based information and services were used by all US Armed Forces, but as the Department of Defense (DoD) executive agent for space, the air force had the bulk of responsibility for acquiring and operating space systems. While the air force had always sought to be the primary service for space, it also faced organizational and cultural tensions in balancing responsibility for space systems with traditional air force platforms such as fighters, bombers, and transports. Beginning in the Cold War, successive generations of air force and DoD leadership sought to better integrate air and space activities within the air force. They recognized the military importance of space and they understood that space has unique characteristics; however, their efforts to link air and space operations across an "Aerospace Force" met with internal resistance. After several decades of effort, however, space systems were not prioritized commensurate with aircraft, space personnel were not promoted commensurate with non-space personnel, and multiple space organizations, programs, and offices led to a lack of clear accountability for the space domain.

Congress had become increasingly concerned with US national security space in the post–Cold War period, holding hearings and creating special commissions. In January 2001, the congressionally mandated Commission to Assess National Security Space Management and Organization delivered a report in which it warned of a potential "Space Pearl Harbor" and called for consolidation and strengthening of space organizations within the DoD and the intelligence community (Commission to Assess United States National Security Space Management and Organization 2011). As the commission's chair was Donald Rumsfeld, expectations arose after he was nominated and confirmed as the new secretary of defense in the George W. Bush administration that the commission's recommendations would be implemented. Eight months later, however, the September 11 attacks on New York and Washington occurred and attention shifted to the Middle East and terrorism, not space.

During the Bush and Obama administrations, the pace of Russian and Chinese ASAT testing picked up. Russian and China reorganized their own armed forces to focus more directly on space, with the Russian Aerospace Defense Forces being established in 2015 and the creation of the People's Liberation Army Strategic Support Forces (PLASSF) in 2016. The Obama administration opposed officially calling space a "war-fighting domain" but did propose funding to improve the resilience of space systems to a range of attacks, including cyber. The Trump administration decided to recognize space as a war-fighting domain and quickly issued a space strategy that called for a "whole-of-government" approach to US leadership in space, in close partnership with the private sector and allies. The strategy emphasized four pillars: "transform to more resilient space architectures"; "strengthen deterrence and warfighting options"; "improve foundational capabilities, structures, and processes"; and "foster conducive domestic and international environments" (White House 2018). Each of these goals could also be found in the 2001 Rumsfeld Commission Report.

The combination of Chinese and Russian actions to hold US assets at risk, the recognition of space as a war-fighting domain and not as a sanctuary, and dimmed prospects for arms control, increased administration and congressional interest in space security. In a larger context, the return of what could be termed great power rivalry, with Russian annexation of Crimea, Chinese challenges in the South China Sea, and cyberattacks from both, all added to a sense of urgency for long-standing national security reforms.

In the 2017 National Defense Authorization Act, Section 1616, the director of the Office of Management and Budget (OMB) was asked to make recommendations to "strengthen the leadership, management, and organization of DoD with respect to the national security space activities of the Department" (Office of Management and

Budget, 2017). While also reminiscent of the Rumsfeld Commission recommendations on space reorganization with the DoD, the OMB recommendations went further in defining four options:

- Create a separate military space service;
- Create a "space corps" within the Air Force;
- Create a space version of Special Operations Command (SOCOM), a combatant command that also has major acquisition authorities;
- Create a space version of the Missile Defense Agency (MDA), which would acquire space capabilities for use by all armed services.

Departments of the armed services, led by civilian service secretaries, are responsible for performing "organize, train, and equip" activities and provide forces which are assigned to military-led operational Combatant Commands, which may have regional or theater (United States European Command, or USEUCOM) responsibilities or functional (e.g., United States Transportation Command, or USTRANSCOM) responsibilities. A United States Space Command (USSPACECOM) had been created in 1985 but was merged with United States Strategic Command (USSTRATCOM) in 2002 after the events of September 11. Space responsibilities were transferred to USSTRATCOM, which also had responsibilities for nuclear and cyber missions. In August 2019, USSPACECOM was reactivated with a mission to "conduct operations in, from, and to space to deter conflict, and if necessary, defeat aggression, deliver space combat power for the Joint/Combined force, and defend US vital interests with allies and partners." (United States Department of Defense 2021).

At a meeting of the NSpC on June 18, 2018, President Trump directed the DoD and the Joint Staff to create a "Space Force" as a separate military service dedicated to space (Loverro 2018). In effect, the president rejected the MDA and SOCOM models in favor of either a fully separate "Department of the Space Force" that would be equivalent to the other service departments, or a "Space Force" that would be a separate armed service within the existing Department of the Air Force, much as the Marine Corps is within the Department of the Navy. Over the next few months, the administration settled on the latter approach, which was essentially the same as prior bipartisan proposals for a "Space Corps" in the House of Representatives. On December 19, 2019, President Trump signed the 2020 National Defense Authorization Act, which had passed Congress with bipartisan support, creating the USSF. This was the first creation of a new US military service since the creation of the Air Force in 1947.

Space Power Doctrine

US military doctrine has been developed for every type of military activity, with space being no exception (United States Joint Staff 2000). Doctrine is developed by each service and for joint and combined arms operations. For joint space operations, Joint

Publication 3-14 *Space Operations* describes military space capabilities and how they relate to joint capabilities as well as the command and control of joint space operations (United States Joint Staff 2020). While retaining continuity with previous versions, the latest version of this joint publication included the reestablishment of USSPACECOM as well as conforming with national space policy.

With the creation of the USSF, one of the first actions was to create military doctrine for the new military service. *SPACEPOWER: Doctrine for Space Forces* was released in June 2020 and defined space power as a form of military power distinct from other domains, such as land, sea, or air power. It did not try to blend air and space power into a single "aerospace" construct but stressed the importance of being integrated with other forms of military power (United States Space Force 2020). In turn, military space power is a component of larger national space power, which includes economic and diplomatic forms of power. As described in USSF doctrine:

> For example, military spacepower enables a nation to protect and defend space-based sources of economic power while advances in commercial space technology make military space operations more effective and lethal. At the same time, military and economic power generate a robust backdrop for diplomacy, which leverages space activities to communicate with and influence other actors. Space-based information collection strengthens diplomatic instruments by providing reliable methods to verify international agreements and treaties. Because the components of national spacepower are mutually reinforcing, they must be developed and coordinated for a nation to realize the full strategic benefits of national spacepower. (United States Space Force 2020, 14).

This view of space power is also consistent with the role of the NSpC as a high-level means of integrating space activities across different space sectors (i.e., national security, economic, and civil) and resolving conflicts among competing policy interests. With this larger context in mind, the cornerstone responsibilities of military space forces are to preserve:

- "Freedom of Action—Unfettered access to and freedom to operate in space is a vital national interest; it is the ability to accomplish all four components of national power—diplomatic, information, military, and economic—of a nation's implicit or explicit space strategy. Military space forces fundamentally exist to protect, defend, and preserve this freedom of action.
- Enable Joint Lethality and Effectiveness—Space capabilities strengthen operations in the other domains of warfare and reinforce every Joint function—the US does not project or employ power without space. At the same time, military space forces must rely on military operations in the other domains to protect and defend space freedom of action. Military space forces operate as part of the closely integrated Joint Force across the entire conflict continuum in support of the full range of military operations.

- Provide Independent Options—A central tenet of military space power is the ability to independently achieve strategic effects. In this capacity, military space power is more than an adjunct to landpower, seapower, airpower, and cyberpower. Across the conflict continuum, military spacepower provides national leadership with independent military options that advance the nation's prosperity and security. Military space forces achieve national objectives by projecting power in, from, to space." (United States Space Force 2020, 29)

SHAPING THE SPACE ENVIRONMENT

At the risk of alliteration, the purposes of behavioral norms in space can be summarized as "safety, security, stability, and long-term sustainability"—with civil and military interests in safety, a military concern with security and stability, and all space sectors interested in the long-term sustainability of space activities. The purpose of norms is not just to be safe and responsible (although those are good things) but also to ensure effective signaling as part of a deterrence strategy to restrain adversary behavior. For threatening or actively hostile activities, particularly in space, signaling is a key part of a compellence strategy to change adversary behavior. Again, given the difficulty of defending satellites and space assets generally, signaling will need to be part of cross-domain operations (e.g., cyber, terrestrial forces) in which understood norms of behavior will be crucial.

The United States has held bilateral space security dialogues with Russia to discuss how to improve communications and reduce the risks of misunderstandings (United States Department of State 2020). The United States has had civil space dialogues with China, but not a dedicated space security exchange. A US-China Civil Space Dialogue was established through the US-China Strategic and Economic Dialogue in 2015 (United States Department of State 2020). While focused bilateral and multilateral space security discussions are important, the large amount of civil and commercial space activities, and the dual-use nature of space technologies and operations, argue for a "whole of government" approach defining space norms of behavior. This means including NASA and the Departments of Commerce and Transportation, along with State and Defense, in discussions with Russia and China.

Civil and commercial space activities may offer the best near-term opportunities to shape behavior in space operations. NASA has been leading the Artemis Accords which consist of a set of "principles for cooperation in the civil exploration and use of the Moon, Mars, Comets, and Asteroids for Peaceful Purposes" (NASA 2021). These principles are based on existing international law and thus do not represent any fundamentally new legal concept. However, bringing them together does provide a common vision for space exploration and development. Among the key elements of the Artemis Accords are the need for mutually agreed upon "safety zones" to avoid conflicts in extracting space resources, protection of historical sites (such as the Apollo lunar landing sites), and mitigating the creation of harmful space debris. As of this writing (July 2021), there are twelve signatories: the United States, the United Kingdom, the United Arab Emirates, Ukraine, New Zealand, Luxembourg, the Republic of Korea, Japan, Italy, Canada, Brazil, and Australia (NASA 2021).

Progress has been made in the discussion of guidelines for the long-term sustainability of space activities (LTSSA) in the United Nations (UN) Committee on the Peaceful Uses of Outer Space (COPUOS). The committee adopted twenty-one voluntary non-binding guidelines by consensus in June 2019 (United Nations Office for Outer Space Affairs 2021). These guidelines dealt with topics such as policy and regulatory frameworks for space activities, safety of space operations, capacity building, and international cooperation, and followed a process in which subject matter experts first proposed ideas and best practices already known to the space community and then sought international understanding and acceptance. This process was similar to the process leading to the adoption of UN guidelines for the mitigation of orbital debris (United Nations Office for Outer Space Affairs 2019) and reflected a constructive perspective shared by many of the participants.

The growth of orbital debris, along with deployment of large constellations of hundreds, if not thousands of satellites, has focused attention on space traffic management—how can collisions between objects in space be avoided? Answering this question typically consists of three parts: (1) creating better knowledge of all the objects that exist in space; (2) mitigating the creation of new debris; and (3) reducing the amount of debris already in space. The United States has a system capable of finding and tracking objects in space, begun initially for national security reasons during the Cold War (see Townsend, this volume). However, the legacy space surveillance and tracking system of ground-based electro-optical and radar sensors is increasingly challenged in keeping up with the growth of space objects of all kinds. The United States led the development of orbital debris mitigation guidelines, which have been broadly accepted by the international community but are unevenly implemented. Finally, the United States and a few other countries (e.g., Japan) have developed capabilities for active debris removal, but legal, economic, and policy questions make it uncertain as to how such capabilities can be employed.

In order to comprehensively address space traffic management, the United States issued its first national policy on this topic, Space Policy Directive 3 (United States 2018). The president directed the Department of Commerce to take over responsibility from the DoD for providing basic space situational awareness data to civil and commercial users. Commerce would do this through the creation of a "open architecture data repository," which could accommodate commercial as well as government data sources on space objects and space environmental conditions. This shift in responsibility would then allow DoD to focus on military needs using classified information and encourage use of more agile commercial data sources (as compared to legacy government systems). The United States has a large number of bilateral agreements to share space situational awareness information and to help countries interpret the data and receive notification of potential collisions. In addition, the Federal Communications Commission is also updating orbital debris mitigation conditions for US-licensed communications satellites (Federal Communications Commission 2020). The United States encourages the adoption of similar satellite regulatory practices in other countries.

While the United States is pursuing diplomatic approaches to ensure a safer, more secure, stable, and sustainable space environment, seeking to amend or replace existing space treaties is not one of them. As noted earlier, the United States is open to considering arms control proposals that meet three key and clearly defined criteria but does not see a need for new space treaties or for renegotiating existing ones that provide the existing legal regime for space. Similarly, the United States has not endorsed proposals for new transnational authorities for space governance, e.g., space traffic management. Space is already considered a broadly permissive environment with few constraints on what the United States, or any other state, may do. This also reflects a skepticism of potential constraints on US freedom of action in space and the difficult of reaching a binding legal agreement that could be successfully ratified by the US Senate.

It is sometimes asserted that space is a "global commons" similar to the high seas. Since space is not subject to "national appropriation by claim of sovereignty, by means of use or occupation, or by any other means" per the OST, some policy and legal experts assert that outer space must therefore be a res communis or global commons (Goehring 2021). This argument rests on the concept of regions beyond national sovereignty being the "common heritage of mankind" as found in the UN Convention on the Law of the Sea (UNCLOS) and the 1979 Moon Agreement (United Nations 1984). The United States did not ratify either agreement, although it does recognize the navigation portions of UNCLOS as customary (and thus binding) international law. The Trump administration issued an Executive Order specifically stating that space is not a global commons and that the 1979 Moon Agreement would not be considered as a basis of customary international law (Trump 2020).

The United States participated in the development of the 1979 Moon Agreement, but ultimately, along with other spacefaring states, choose not to sign it, largely due to differences over how space resources would be governed. Similar questions over deep seabed resources led to the United States not signing UNCLOS but accepting the navigation provisions. Those who support open access to and use of outer space for peaceful purposes are drawn to the "permissive" aspect of the global commons term. To others, the term commons raises the potential for constraints being imposed on space activities as a commons is necessarily governed by multiple parties. Ambiguity in the definition of global commons, not just in space, but in environmental applications as well, has led multiple US administrations to avoid the term in legally binding agreements. One way to think of the situation is that a global commons is not a default condition that results from the lack of sovereignty but something that must be positively agreed to by states, as was the case with the definition of the high seas in UNCLOS.

In contrast to the 1979 Moon Agreement or the "common heritage of mankind" concept of a global commons, the US approach to ensuring a conducive space environment contains multiple elements. These include transparent publication of space policies and strategies, promoting best regulatory practices and industry-led standards, developing voluntary international guidelines, making space situational awareness information widely available, and creating opportunities for civil, commercial, and military space cooperation. The NSpC provides a strong integrative function to ensure diplomatic, security, and economic activities are mutually supportive and aligned across diverse implementation mechanisms. The United States has not sought to create a "one size fits all" solution to space governance issues, whether that be a global space agency, a single space traffic management authority, or an expansion of existing international space treaties.

The NSpC published *A New Era for Deep Space Exploration and Development* in 2020 to provide a larger rationale and context for the Trump administration's space policy directives (National Space Council 2020). The document focused on civil and commercial efforts such as the commercialization of Low Earth Orbit, returning to the moon to stay, and extending a human presence to Mars. These efforts are not just space projects but part of the pursuit of wider national interests (National Space Council 2020). This vision recognizes that space activities will include countries that do not share US values and may have interests in competition with those of the United States and its allies. The task for the United States is to pursue its own interests and those of its allies while persuading likeminded nations, and deter, dissuade, or compel, if necessary, potential adversaries to respect those interests.

Closing Observations

In the next few decades, it is unlikely that there will be a major war with China or Russia as long as nuclear and regional conventional deterrence remains robust. It is also unlikely that there will be a comprehensive update to the OST, a global space agency, or single global space traffic management authority, a reduction in the reliance of the US military and economy on space, or vital national interests separate from the Earth. US freedom of action in space, however, is a vital national interest and the United States can be expected to protect this interest without reservation. Given these realities, and the diversity of space activities, this chapter suggests that analytical eclecticism is a pragmatic way to frame theoretical understanding of the US approach to international space security.

In line with realist frameworks, the United States built space capabilities to counter Soviet power in a variety of military and diplomatic forms. Similarly, China's actions as an adversary on military, economic, and diplomatic fronts have supported a realist approach to China in all areas, including space cooperation. Overall, today, the United States seeks to deter conflict among major powers, enhance regional stability, and ensure an international environment conducive to US values and interests—including in space. In doing so, the US approach to space can be characterized as one of defensive realism. US space forces are focused on delivering capabilities to terrestrial forces and ensuring freedom of action in space rather than comprehensive command of the space domain for its own sake. In terms of geopolitical theory, US space operations are inherently global and US interests are terrestrially focused. Thus, US military space doctrine is more akin to that of a coastal and littoral navy than a blue water navy seeking to defend or interdict widely separated strategic locations.

While realism characterizes US space behavior with respect to adversaries, the lens of complex interdependence characterizes US space behavior with allies and friends. The conditions of complex interdependence apply to traditional allies and partners such as Japan, Canada, and members of the European Space Agency. With the Artemis Program, these traditional allies and partners are joined by new partners such as the United Arab Emirates, Australia, New Zealand, and the Republic of Korea. Space cooperation is just one element of multiple issues that characterize US relations with these countries, but such cooperation is symbolic of overall positive ties. While many space partners are part of military alliances with the United States, military force does not dominate the agenda of issues between them. Interactions occur through a multiplicity of channels, including civil society.

Relationships with allies and partners are also key to the US approach to shaping norms of behavior in space. Sometimes termed coalitions of the like-minded, these relationships can be seen as expressions of constructivism in how they work within international organizations (e.g., COPUOS), within industry groups such as standards bodies, and within NGOs. Persons within these groups typically share common goals or ideals, such as the use of space technology for the needs of developing countries, reducing the risk of war in space, reducing the threat of orbital debris, and promoting space exploration generally. Constructivist behavior is most obvious in the interaction of states, NGOs, and industry in shaping the guidelines for the LTSSA within COPUOS. Constructivism can also explain patterns in less visible, specialized debates such as space traffic management, planetary defense (protecting the Earth from asteroid strikes), planetary protection (protecting the Earth and other celestial bodies from biological contamination), and governance of the extraction of non-terrestrial materials.

It is likely that space globalization and democratization will continue with an ever more capable private space sector, and that the United States will lead the development of new norms of behavior in space to improve space stability. These norms will be developed in a variety of forums with China and the United States as active participants finding areas of agreement. Space is an area of potential conflict with China as a result of linkages to terrestrial conflicts such as Taiwan and the South China Sea. Space, the moon, and other celestial bodies are not inherently areas of conflict unless China makes them so.

The United States approach to adversaries, allies and friends, and international organizations is best understood as a *stratégie mélange* in which hard calculations of military and economic power are mixed with US values and shared social relationships. To be sure, this is not unique to US international relations, which have historically contained mixtures of hard and soft power, of calculation and sentiment. The United States has historically maintained both open civil space activities and classified military and intelligence space activities. The mixed approach of the United States with its space programs had value after Sputnik as a contrast to the USSR. Today, the increased diversity of space actors continues to support a mixed approach for the United States in cooperating and competing with other states.

If, in the decades ahead, economically sustainable space settlements become a reality, the United States will need to decide whether they constitute vital national interests. If so, US national security strategies, national space policies, and military forces will adapt to deter and defend them against intentional threats. At the same time, US diplomats will seek out like-minded countries, with their own interests at stake, to ensure a stable environment for those settlements. The United States will remain committed to ensuring activities in the space domain are for peaceful purposes as described under existing international law. However, what mix of approaches it will take to ensuring space is used for peaceful purposes will likely change with changes in technology and the scope and scale of national interests. To be sure, IR theorists will have rich new material for studying the behavior of states as they expand into environments beyond the Earth.

References

Bender, Bryan. 2021. "Biden to Renew National Space Council." *Politico*. March 29, 2021. Accessed at https://www.politico.com/newsletters/morning-defense/2021/03/29/scoop-biden-to-renew-national-space-council-794316.

Crane, Keith W. 2020. *Measuring the Space Economy: Estimating the Value of Economic Activities in and for Space*. Washington, DC: Institute for Defense Analyses.

Goehring, John S. 2021. "Why Isn't Outer Space a Global Commons?" *Journal of National Security Law and Policy* 11: 573–90 (June 3). https://jnslp.com/2021/06/03/why-isnt-outer-space-a-global-commons/.

Johnson, Nicholas L. 2021. "Operation Burnt Frost: A View from Inside." *Space Policy* 56; 1–5. https://doi.org/10.1016/j.spacepol.2021.101411.

Katzenstein, Peter J., and Rudra Sil. 2008. "Eclectic Theorizing in the Study and Practice of International Relations." In *Oxford Handbook of International Relations*, edited by Christian Reus-Schmitt and Duncan Snidal, 109–30. Oxford: Oxford University Press.

Klein, John J. 2020. *Understanding Space Strategy: The Art of War in Space*. New York: Routledge.

Loverro, Douglas. 2018. "Why the United States needs a Space Force," *Space News*. June 25, 2018.

Pfaltzgraff, Robert L. 2011. "International Relations Theory and Spacepower." In *Toward a Theory of Spacepower: Selected Essays*, edited by Charles D. Lutes and Peter L. Hays, 37–56. Washington, DC: National Defense University Press.

Schelling, Thomas C. 1966. *Arms and Influence*. New Haven, CT: Yale University Press.

Secure World Foundation. 2020. "SWF Releases Updated Compilation of Anti-satellite Testing in Space." June 30, 2020. https://swfound.org/news/all-news/2020/06/swf-releases-updated-compilation-of-anti-satellite-testing-in-space/.

Sil, Rudra, and Peter J. Katzenstein. 2010. "Analytic Eclecticism in the Study of World Politics: Reconfiguring Problems and Mechanisms across Research Traditions." *Perspectives on Politics* 8, no. 2: 411–31.

Official Statements, Directives, and Reports

Commission to Assess United States National Security Space Management and Organization. 2011. January 11. "Report of the Commission to Assess United States National Security Space Management and Organization." Washington, DC.

Federal Communications Commission. 2020. "FCC Updates Satellite Orbital Debris Mitigation Rules." Press Release, April 23, 2020. https://docs.fcc.gov/public/attachments/DOC-363947A1.pdf.

NASA. 2021. "The Artemis Accords." https://www.nasa.gov/specials/artemis-accords/index.html.

National Space Council. 2020. July 23. "A New Era for Deep Space Exploration and Development." Washington, DC.

Office of Management and Budget. 2017. December 17. "OMB Report on the Leadership, Management, and Organization of the Department of Defense's Space Activities." Washington, DC.

Office of the Press Secretary. 1982. July 4. "Fact Sheet Outlining United States Space Policy." Ronald Reagan Presidential Library. http://www.reagan.utexas.edu/archives/speeches/1982/70482b.htm.

Trump, Donald J. 2020. "Encouraging International Support for the Recovery and Use of Space Resources. Executive Order 13914, April 6, 2020." *Federal Register* 85, no. 70: 20381–82.

Trump, Donald J. 2017. "Reviving the National Space Council. Executive Order 13803, June 30, 2017." *Federal Register* 82, no. 129: 31429.

United Nations. 1967. "Treaty on Principles Governing the Activities of States in the Exploration and Use of Outer Space, including the Moon and Other Celestial Bodies." Entry into Force, October 10, 1967. https://www.unoosa.org/oosa/en/ourwork/spacelaw/treaties/outerspacetreaty.html.

United Nations. 1984. "Agreement Governing the Activities of States on the Moon and Other Celestial Bodies." Entry into Force, July 11, 1984. https://www.unoosa.org/oosa/en/ourwork/spacelaw/treaties/moon-agreement.html.

United Nations Office for Outer Space Affairs. 2019 *Space Debris Mitigation Guidelines of the Committee on the Peaceful Uses of Outer Space*. United Nations Publications. Vienna, Austria.

United Nations Office for Outer Space Affairs. 2021. "Long-term Sustainability of Space Activities." https://www.unoosa.org/oosa/en/ourwork/topics/long-term-sustainability-of-outer-space-activities.html.

United States. 2006. August 31. *US National Space Policy*. Office of the Press Secretary. Washington, DC.

United States. 2010. June 28. *National Space Policy of the United States of America*. Executive Office of the President. Washington, DC.

United States. 2018. June 18. "Space Policy Directive-3, National Space Traffic Management Policy." Washington, DC.

United States. 2020. December 9. *National Space Policy of the United States of America*. Executive Office of the President. Washington, DC.

United States, The Defense Intelligence Agency. 2019. *Challenges to Security in Space*. Defense Intelligence Agency. Washington, DC.

United States, The Department of Defense. 2018. *National Defense Strategy*. Department of Defense. Washington, DC.

United States, The Department of Defense. 2021. *US Space Command Mission*. https://www.spacecom.mil/Mission/.

United States, The Department of State. 2020. "Briefing with Assistant Secretary for International Security and Nonproliferation Dr. Christopher A. Ford on the US-Russia Space Security Exchange, Via Teleconference, July 24, 2020." https://2017-2021.state.gov/briefing-with-assistant-secretary-for-international-security-and-nonproliferation-dr-christopher-a-ford-on-the-u-s-russia-space-security-exchange/index.html.

United States, The Joint Staff. 2000. *Joint Warfare of the Armed Forces of the United States Joint Publication 1*. Department of Defense. Washington, DC.

United States, The Joint Staff. 2020. *Space Operations Joint Publication 3–14*. April 10, 2018. Incorporating Change 1, October 26, 2020. Department of Defense. Washington, DC.

United States Space Force. 2020. *SPACEPOWER: Doctrine for Space Forces*. Washington, DC.

White House. 2018. "President Donald J. Trump is Unveiling an America First National Space Strategy." Fact Sheet. https://trumpwhitehouse.archives.gov/briefings-statements/president-donald-j-trump-unveiling-america-first-national-space-strategy/.

CHAPTER 16

NEOCLASSICAL REALISM AS A FRAMEWORK FOR UNDERSTANDING CHINA'S RISE AS A SPACE POWER

KEVIN POLLPETER

IN October 2017, Chinese leader Xi Jinping stated that China had "stood up, became rich, and is becoming strong." In 2010, China overtook Japan to become the second largest economy in the world and its defense budget is now the second largest behind the United States. China's rising economic and military power has led to an increased presence in Asia and globally. China's rise as a world power is also reflected in its rise as a space power. As China has expanded globally, it has also established a more prominent position in space. Prior to 2000, China did not figure prominently as a space power. It conducted few launches and trailed other powers in the number of satellites in orbit. China's space technologies were also much inferior to those of the leading space powers in terms of both capability and reliability.

Since approximately 2000, however, China has made important progress across a broad range of space technologies, including launchers, satellites, lunar exploration, and human spaceflight technologies. China is now a leader in space launches and has the second largest number of satellites in orbit behind the United States. It has conducted robotic missions to the moon and Mars and its space station is now fully operational at a time when the International Space Station is nearing the end of its service life. China has developed a space-based command, control, communications, computers, intelligence, surveillance, and reconnaissance (C4ISR) system composed of remote sensing, navigation, and communications satellites to better project power and is building a robust suite of counterspace capabilities that include direct ascent kinetic kill vehicles (KKVs), directed energy, electronic warfare, cyber, and co-orbital satellite systems to deny space capabilities to adversaries. China now has the ambition to transform itself from a "major space power to a strong space power" with the intent to be on par with and eventually surpass the United States (Liu and Su 2014).

This chapter examines China's competitive activities as a space power through the lens of international relations (IR) theory. It takes a neoclassical realist approach that posits that China's space program over the long term has conformed to realist models of behavior even if over the short term intervening factors may have inhibited China's response to relative changes in space power. It argues that China's search for space security is rooted in a techno-nationalist strategic culture that conditions it to think and act in realist terms that emphasize competition, conflict, and the balance of power. This realist mindset has been an important influence in shaping the People's Republic of China (PRC) leadership's thinking on how it approaches IR, including its approach to space. This mindset tends to emphasize threats to security and the need for balance against potential adversaries.

This chapter argues that the primary motivation for China's space program has been national security. It finds that China's space program is inherently tied to the PRC leadership's view of the international security situation and that China's build up of military space capabilities cannot be divorced from the leadership's view of the need to protect it from international security threats, particularly those perceived as coming from the United States. It also argues, however, that China's rise as a major space power was decades in the making. Although the PRC leadership since the 1950s realized the importance of space to their country's security, China lacked the technology and know-how to compete with the United States and USSR. It was not until 2015 that the PRC officially announced that space was central to maintaining their country's security, calling it "a commanding height in strategic competition" and one of four "critical security domains" in its 2015 defense white paper.

USING IR THEORY TO EXPLAIN CHINA'S RISE AS A SPACE POWER: THE CASE FOR NEOCLASSICAL REALISM

Neoclassical realism is a theoretical approach based on the realist school of IR theory. According to realism, the primary concern of states is to "seek to ensure their survival" (Waltz 1979, 91). But states operate in an anarchic international environment in which there is no authority above the state. The anarchic nature of the international system creates a lack of trust among states and a self-help situation in which states would rather rely on themselves for their own security rather than on other states. Within this system, states that "do not help themselves or do so less effectively than others, will fail to prosper and will lay themselves open to dangers" (118).

A defining characteristic of realism is balance of power theory (Waltz 1979, 117). According to realism, an increase in one state's power will result in other states increasing their capabilities in an attempt to balance the power of other states. Balancing can create security dilemmas and arms races as each state responds to increases in power by the other state. As a result, states seek to reduce their dependency on others while at the same time increasing the dependency of others on their own state (Viotti and Kauppi, 68–69). Realism also predicts that this balancing behavior will result in states tending to imitate each other (68–69; Waltz 1979, 128; Layne 1993, 15).

Neoclassical realism builds upon the structural influence of Waltz's anarchic system and its balance of power theory by taking into account internal factors. It seeks "to explain why, how, and under what conditions the internal characteristics of states—the extractive and mobilization capacity of politico-military institutions, the influence of domestic societal actors and interest groups, the degree of state autonomy from society, and the level of elite or societal cohesion—intervene between the leaders' assessment of international threats and opportunities and the actual diplomatic, military and foreign economic policies those leaders pursue" (Lobell, Ripsman, and Taliaferro 2009, 4).

Consequently, neoclassical realism posits that although states over the long term may generally conform to realist models, i.e., balancing behavior, in the short term intervening factors may inhibit a state's ability to respond to relative changes in power (Lobell, Ripsman, and Taliaferro 2009, 4). As Fareed Zakaria writes, "It is a truism that in the long run, increasingly wealthy nations will have increasing worldwide influence. But the nature of their rise, the time frame in which it occurs, the areas and issues that become flash points—all these specific matters remain uncertain" (Zakaria 1998, 12). Based on this, the role of internal forces that govern the accumulation and mobilization of wealth and its application to power requires a more inclusive theory of IR that takes into account the interactive nature of the external and internal forces that affect decision-making. This article is among the first to apply neoclassical realist frameworks to the space domain (Pekkanen 2022; Pekkanen, this volume).

CHINA: A REALIST POWER

China has been described as the one power that "has seen the fewest changes in its basic philosophy of international relations between the Cold War and post–Cold War era" (Khan 2018, 4). Since the 1950s, every Chinese leader since Mao Zedong has viewed their country as existing in a fundamentally dangerous world, which required China to approach IR with a realist strategic culture that stresses maintaining a balance of power with potential adversaries (Keohane 1986, 158–203; Khan 2018, 37; Christensen 1996, 37).

China's strategic culture takes a zero-sum view of world affairs which assumes that war is inevitable and a central issue for the state (Johnston 1995, 62). It assumes that China's adversaries are "rapacious or threatening in nature" and that China must acquire military capabilities that can deny the enemy the ability to act according to its will (212, 249).

China's realist strategic culture is reflected in its approach to technology development. A defining characteristic of China's view of technology and its relation to national security is techno-nationalism. Samuels writes that techno-nationalism informs a country's approach to its industrial structure, the role of foreign technology, and economic growth (Samuels 1994, 68). He defines the term "as the belief that technology is a fundamental element in national security, that it must be indigenized, diffused, and nurtured in order to make a nation rich and strong" (x).

Techno-nationalism focuses on a number of characteristics that correspond to the realist framework of balancing and self-help. It treats technology as a primary component of national power that can determine the fate of a nation. States must compete with other states in certain technologies or develop new technologies that can surpass or disrupt existing technologies. As a result, states adopting a techno-nationalist approach attempt to reduce their dependence on other states for technology and seek the capability to independently develop technologies.

China's techno-nationalist approach to science and technology (S&T) is best summarized by Mao Zedong who stated that "Whatever the enemy has, we must have. Whatever the enemy does not have we must also have." More recently, China's adherence to techno-nationalism has given rise to what Tai Ming Cheung calls a "techno-security state" defined as an "innovation-centered, security-maximizing regime that prioritizes the building of technological, security, and defense capabilities to meet expansive national security requirements based on heightened threat perceptions and the powerful influence of domestic security coalitions" (Cheung 2022, 2–3). Cheung argues that PRC security policy has exhibited elements of a techno-security state since the founding of the PRC in 1949, but that PRC leader Xi Jinping has accelerated and expanded the adoption of techno-security state policies since coming to power in 2012 (2–3).

REALISM, TECHNO-NATIONALISM, AND CHINA'S SPACE PROGRAM

The PRC desire to maintain a balance of power with its adversaries in space technologies has been evident since nearly the founding of the PRC in 1949. These efforts initially focused on ballistic missiles but the need to broaden China's space capabilities gained more impetus due to two "shocks" to the Chinese Communist Party: the 1991 Gulf War and the 1999 bombing of the PRC embassy in Belgrade. Both events not only demonstrated the importance of space to the ability of modern militaries to achieve rapid dominance they also highlighted the vulnerability of China to military threat and intimidation from an advanced military like that of the United States. Nevertheless, it would take more than fifty years from the founding of the PRC space program in 1956 to reach a point where China considered itself as having emerged into the ranks of the major space powers.

EARLY EFFORTS: 1956–1989

China's space program was established in 1956 as a response to the need to develop ballistic missiles for its nuclear weapons program. China's initial efforts at developing space technologies were first the result of a recognition that China needed to compete with the United States and the USSR in strategic technologies. Declaring that "the future of the nuclear program would determine the destiny of the state," Mao focused on nuclear weapons, satellites, and the ballistic missiles needed to launch them in what would become known as the "two bombs and one satellite" program (Lewis and Xue 1988, 121). The impetus for the development of ballistic missiles was related to US nuclear threats and the inability of China to effectively threaten the United States. According to Lewis and Hua, "the Chinese leadership understood that only long-range ballistic missiles could strike the homeland of the United States, Beijing's enemy and a nation that had repeatedly threatened China with nuclear attack" (Lewis and Hua 1992, 7).

There was, however, a large gap between the recognition of need and China's ability to achieve the security it sought. The PRC space program faced a lack of technological know-how, poor work conditions, and political turmoil. China was a poor country that had just emerged from a destructive civil war and had fought the United States to a standstill on the Korean peninsula just three years earlier. Moreover, the low technological state of its defense industrial base was worsened by the destructive policies of the Great Leap Forward from 1958 to 1962 and the Cultural Revolution from 1966 to 1976 that caused mass starvation and sent China into societal chaos.

At the beginning of the program, China lacked the factories to produce the materials for ballistic missiles and possessed none of the infrastructure to conduct research and development (R&D), such as wind tunnels, engine test sites, and launch sites (Chang 1995, 208). The low technological state of the defense industry challenged China's techno-nationalist leanings. But China's leaders recognized that Soviet assistance would have to play a critical role (Lewis and Xue, 63). The USSR transferred R-1, R-2, and R-11F ballistic missiles to China that were improved variants of the German V-2 used during World War II in addition to blueprints and "technical documents for manufacturing, testing, and launching" (Chang 1995, 214).

China's techno-nationalist inclinations of going it alone, however, were made a necessity in 1960 when the USSR ceased its technological assistance to China after relations between the two countries ruptured over differences in ideology, Soviet concerns over what was considered Chinese adventurism in regard to Taiwan, and Chinese concerns over perceived Soviet intentions to subordinate China to Soviet influence in Asia (Luthi 2008, 92–113, 150–56). This action further isolated China from the international community and cut off its only dependable access to foreign technology and knowhow.

Despite these immense challenges, China was able to successfully launch its first ballistic missile in 1960, with deployments beginning in 1961, but achieved only qualified success in developing more capable missiles. The development of the DF-5, an intercontinental ballistic missile (ICBM) that could strike parts of the continental United States, began in 1966 but missiles were not deployed until 1981. Even then, numbers were small and came nowhere near the thousands of ICBMs deployed by the United States and the USSR. The United States, for example, fielded its first ICBM in 1959 and fielded nearly two thousand in the 1960s and 1970s, including submarine-launched ballistic missiles (NSA 2006).

China also began work on developing satellite technologies during this time. China's first satellite, the Dongfanghong-1 (DFH-1/East is Red-1), launched on April 24, 1970, was a direct response to the launch of Sputnik by the USSR in 1957. The DFH-1 was technologically similar to Sputnik but was technologically inferior to the satellites being launched by the USSR and the United States at that time in 1970. Although the DFH-1 was a simple satellite, it indicated an intent to develop a space program with a broader set of capabilities. In October and November 1965, the defense industry and military conducted a forty-two-day meeting to discuss the development of that first satellite and the supporting infrastructure that would need to be created to make it a success. That meeting also determined that the DFH-1 would be used as the foundation to build other types of satellites, including earth observation, weather, and communication satellites. (Kulacki and Lewis 2009, 14)

As a result, the time period between 1956 and 1989 was paradoxically a time of both great accomplishment and modest outcomes for China's space program. China's fledgling defense industry was able to overcome significant hurdles to achieve initial success in ballistic missiles, space launch vehicles, and satellites, but faced greater challenges in reaching technological parity with the United States and USSR and in operationalizing these capabilities. China had developed a nuclear deterrent that could threaten the continental United States, but its small inventory raised questions over the ultimate effectiveness of that deterrent. Its performance in space launch and satellite technologies was even less impressive. From 1970 to 1989, China had successfully launched just nineteen satellites on as many rockets. After its launch of the DFH-1 in 1970, China was only able to conduct four more successful launches during the 1970s, and although the pace of launches increased in the 1980s it paled in comparison to the United States and the USSR, which were frequently launching 10–15 rockets annually during this time.

Moreover, the satellites that would be launched in the decades that followed would be technologically inferior to those launched by the USSR and the United States. Most satellites launched during this time were the *Recoverable* series of remote sensing satellites that returned their film payload by returning to the Earth rather than transmitting their images back to Earth digitally. Moreover, China did not launch its first communications satellite until 1984 and its first weather satellite until 1988, accomplishments achieved by the United States in 1962 and 1960, respectively.

SHOCKS TO THE SYSTEM: THE 1990S

While China was able to overcome technological inexperience, international isolation, and political chaos to achieve several high-profile successes, one other factor held China back. Although many in the military and defense industry recognized the benefits of space capabilities, the utility of space in advancing PRC interests was not widely agreed upon within the PRC government. Space was viewed by many as offering too few benefits at too high a cost for a poor country like China. For example, some of China's military and defense experts had recommended the development of a PRC counterpart to a Global Positioning System (GPS) as early as 1982 but were only able to garner funding for low-level research (China Newsweek 2010). Human spaceflight was similarly stalled. Proponents had been advocating for a human spaceflight space program as early as 1987, and even though research on related technologies was being conducted, the approval to send astronauts into space remained elusive (China Space News 2003, P34). Both projects were viewed by many as too expensive and beyond China's engineering capabilities. In the case of satellite navigation, many wondered why China needed to develop a system when they could use GPS for free. Nevertheless, both projects would be approved in the early 1990s. What accounted for this change in perspective?

This change in attitudes toward its space program appears to have been driven by two factors. The first was an initial determination that the People's Liberation Army (PLA) needed to develop a warfighting force capable of defending PRC territory, and later its expanding global interest. This included the development of space based C4ISR capabilities to enable long-range precision strikes to defend China's interests far from its coastal waters, as well as counterspace capabilities that can threaten and degrade an adversary's space assets. The second was a widespread belief among PRC military strategists that the United States plays a destabilizing role in world affairs and that it restricts China's rise as a world and space power. As a result, many PLA officers concluded that China must develop space and counterspace capabilities to deter the United States from interfering with its rise.

The requirement for the PLA to develop a warfighting force capable of defending PRC interests, including in outer space, was the result of a long process of research that began with analysis of the performance of the US military since the First Gulf War in 1991. PRC analysts described this war as the first "space war" because of the US military's use of GPS, communication, and reconnaissance satellites (Shen et al. 2007, 46). According to PRC analysts, US reliance on space only increased in subsequent operations. During Operation Iraqi Freedom, nearly 80 percent of long-haul communications were carried over commercial satellites. GPS, still experimental during the 1991 Gulf War, began to be fully enmeshed in US military operations. During the Gulf War, just 8 percent of the munitions used during Desert Storm were precision guided. This increased to 35 percent in the Kosovo War, to 60 percent in Operation Enduring Freedom, and 68 percent in Operation Iraqi Freedom. PRC authors concluded from these observations that modern war required the use of space and that this necessitated the ability to defend space-based assets (Zhou and Liu 2006, 36).

The 1995 bombing of the PRC embassy in Belgrade served as a second shock that would further harden attitudes toward the United States. Although the United States called the bombing accidental, it was widely perceived as intentional in China, where it generated large protests and caused concern within the PRC leadership. China's leadership decided to refrain from taking immediate action in a meeting convened immediately after the event and instead decided on a long-term response that would fundamentally affect the course of its weapons development. The PRC would concentrate on building strategic conventional weapons capable of deterring the United States by striking at US military weakness (Cheung 2022, 182). Specifically, the PLA was called on to develop weapons that that could "look far, shoot far, and shoot accurately" and pose an asymmetric threat to the US military (Zhang 2011, 163). The resulting program was called the New High Technology Project or 995 Program after the month and year (May 1995) of the embassy bombing.

The 995 Program had a profound impact on weapons development resulting in a massive increase in defense R&D spending between 1999 and 2009 that was more than the total spending on R&D during the previous fifty years. Commenting on the 995 Program in 2012, retired Major General Yao Youzhi, stated that the PLA "should be grateful to the Americans" for providing the rationale for increased defense spending, indicating that its progress in weapons development would not have occurred if the Belgrade bombing had not taken place (Cheung 2022, 182–83).

Both the First Gulf War and the 1999 embassy bombing had a profound doctrinal and technological effect on the PLA that resulted in the elevation of space as a military domain, making it a central component of PLA warfighting. At the time of the First Gulf War, the PLA was a large and low-tech military that planned to leverage China's large population and low technological base in a "People's War" approach that emphasized the use of large numbers of troops and unsophisticated technology to overwhelm an opponent. The defeat of the Iraqi military, which had been using similar doctrine, command and control structure, and weapons as the PLA generated concern that the PLA was unprepared to successfully defend China in a war against a high-tech opponent like the United States.

This conclusion began a process in the PLA that sought to understand the nature of modern war and the steps that would be needed to be taken by the PLA to prevail in a military conflict with an advanced military. PRC military research was prolific and identified several overarching factors that the PLA would need to address to make itself into a modern fighting force (Finkelstein 2007, 71–72). The research, motivated by the First Gulf War as well as by US military operations in the Balkans, Iraq, and Afghanistan, would move the PLA away from its focus on massed formations to a concept of operations that would take information superiority, defined as the ability to use information and deny information to an adversary, as the primary factor in winning modern war. In the words of one group of authors, "If information technology is the vanguard of the new technological revolution, then information warfare will be the core of the new military revolution" (Pollpeter 2010, 195)

This research was heavily influenced by the US military concept of "network-centric" warfare that envisioned achieving an information advantage that would enable a shift from attrition warfare to a faster and more effective warfighting style characterized by speed of command. PRC analysts concluded that the ability to collect, process, and transmit information as well as the ability to deny those capabilities to an adversary are essential factors for success on the modern battlefield and the precondition for achieving supremacy in the air, at sea, and on the ground (Peng and Yao 2001, 358). As a result, these analysts concluded that the PLA must give up prosecuting "wars of annihilation" and instead prioritize strikes against key C4ISR nodes in an attempt to paralyze the enemy.

The need for the PLA to evolve from a force focused on mass to a force focused on information was apparent in the increasing amount of attention devoted to outer space in PLA writings. Characterizations of the role of space in future military operations moved from treating space as a mere extension of air power to viewing space as an indispensable and independent domain. Based on their study of US military operations, PRC analysts assessed that 70–90 percent of the US military's intelligence was gathered through space technologies and that 80 percent of its communications went through satellites (Pollpeter et al. 2019, 56).

PLA analysts concluded that space had become so vital to fighting modern war that no military could do without it and that the center of gravity in military operations had transitioned to outer space. PLA analysts argued two findings from these conclusions. First, the use of space was a force multiplier for the US military that enabled it to achieve decisive victories and needed to be emulated. Second, the US military's reliance on space exposed it to vulnerabilities that, if properly exploited by the PLA, could severely degrade US military performance (Jiang and Wang 2013, 14). They argued that space operations could play a critical role in the PLA's asymmetric strategy against the United States (as required by the 995 Program) in two ways: by enabling long-range precision strikes against land, air, and naval targets and in denying adversaries the use of their own space assets.

Based on this analysis, PLA analysts would make the often repeated statement that "whoever controls space will control the Earth" and that outer space is the new high ground of military operations. They argued that the goal of space operations is to achieve space superiority, defined as "ensuring one's ability to fully use space while at the same time limiting, weakening, and destroying an adversary's space forces" (Jiang and Wang 2013, 6). PLA analysts described space-based C4ISR systems as a critical part of a modern military sensor-to-shooter network through the application of reconnaissance, meteorology, missile early warning, communication, and navigation capabilities that can help monitor the activities of potential adversaries, enable communication between friendly units, and provide positioning, navigation, and timing data.

Counterspace operations, on the other hand, were intended to deny, degrade, disable, or destroy an opposing side's space capabilities. This can include attacks against ground and space based space assets through the use of kinetic and non-kinetic means. Counterspace operations not only include offensive and defensive operations in space against an adversary's space forces, but also air, ground, and naval operations against space assets (Jiang and Wang 2013, 6).

PRC Assessments of US Military Views of Space

In addition to their study of US military operations, PRC analysts concluded that the United States was attempting to build technologies, concepts, and organizations to dominate space (Zhao 2001, 50; Wei, Qin, and Liu 2002, 4). PLA analysis of the US military's intentions in space focused on the proposal and eventual establishment of the US military's Space Force, the development of space technologies by the US military, and the publication of a US military doctrine and strategy, which have been perceived as evidence that the United States is determined to develop offensive counterspace capabilities that would inhibit China's access to space. According to the PRC Ministry of Defense, "It is known to all that the US, in pursuit of space hegemony, has formed the Space Force, spent enormous amounts of money on enhancing space combat readiness and unilaterally initiated an arms race in the space" (Li 2020).

PRC analysts, for example, noted that *Joint Vision 2010*, published by the US military's Joint Chiefs of Staff in 1996, contained references to space operations, which they concluded was evidence that the United States was intent on both achieving space superiority and developing a space force (Zhu and Zhang 2005, 8). PRC writers analyzing another document, the 1997 *Global Engagement: A Vision of the 21st Century Air Force*, focused on the US Air Force's commitment to transition from being an air force to an air and space force, concluding that it was the first time that the United States had officially declared an intention to establish a space force (Tang 2001, 20). PRC articles reviewing the US Space Command's *Vision 2020*, wrote that the report described the US military as "very dependent on space capabilities" and "even more dependent on space capabilities by 2020" and as advocating for the ability to control space (Li et al. 2005, 631–35; Xiong et al. 2005, 26). PRC researchers analyzing the 2006 US National Space Policy asserted that the document expressed the intention to use any and all necessary means to ensure US security, including denying adversaries access to space. In light of these conclusions, PLA researchers concluded that China must develop its own capabilities to deter the United States from attacking PRC space assets and to preserve its own access to space (Bao 2007).

PRC analysts also focused on the US military's Schriever space wargames as evidence that the United States is attempting to dominate space. According to a 2005 PRC article, the Schriever series of war games demonstrates that "space warfare is not far away" and concluded that China "must develop a new national security concept that places space security within national security strategy" (Xiong et al. 2005, 28). Other authors asserted that the Schriever war games illustrate US willingness to develop space weapons and that China must prepare for an arms race in space (Yuan 2001, 28). Other PRC sources viewed the war games as a deterrence measure by the United States taken to try to prevent China from developing its own space weapons (Teng 2007).

PRC analysts also cite US testing of counterspace and missile defense related technologies as evidence that China must develop its own counterspace technologies (China News Agency 2007; Hong 2008). According to one report, the United States "has spared no efforts" in its development of space weapons (China News Agency 2007). PRC analysts cite the 1985 launch of a direct ascent anti-satellite (ASAT) missile that destroyed a US satellite and the October 1997 test of the MIRACL laser against a US defunct weather satellite as evidence that the United States possesses an extant ASAT capability. More recently, PRC analysts describe the X-37B Orbital Test Vehicle as a "weapon without rival" and emphasized that the X-37B can "strike any location on earth within two hours" (Zhao 2010).

2015: FROM ANALYSIS TO OPERATIONAL RELEVANCE

The analysis of PLA researchers did not automatically result in changes in the PLA's approach to warfare or to space operations, however. Indeed, the analysis that began after the First Gulf War did not appear to reach its culmination until 2015—a nearly thirty-year process. Although the importance of space to future PLA warfighting was identified early on, it was just one element in what would become a comprehensive overhaul of the PLA. The PLA concept of operations would undergo several iterations that would reflect an increasing emphasis on the role of information technology. In 1993 the PLA changed its concept of operations from "local wars under modern conditions" to "local wars under modern, high-tech conditions." This change in the understanding of war would also place a greater emphasis on joint operations, defined as two or more services participating in an operation under a single command. This requirement would not become codified into PLA regulations until 1999. These new regulations saw operations as occurring across five domains: air, land, sea, and increasingly outer space and cyberspace.

The new regulations were followed in 2004 by a change in the PLA's characterization of war from "local wars under modern, high-tech conditions" to "local wars under informatized conditions." This new designation emphasized even more the importance of information to winning modern wars. In the same year, evidence emerged that the PRC considered space an important area of military competition when the PLA was given its "New Historic Missions" (Mulvenon 2009; Hartnett 2008). In addition to protecting PRC interests in the traditional domains of the land, air, and sea, the New Historic Missions expanded PLA responsibilities to protecting PRC interests in outer space. According to one *Liberation Army Daily* editorial on the New Historical Missions, "the struggle for space supremacy and the acceleration of space weaponry development will have a significant effect on China's security and development. Creating a space 'shield' has become an inevitable requirement that must be met in order to maintain national security" (Liberation Army Daily 2006).

But even with the new regulations and concepts of operations, enacting meaningful change was difficult for the PLA. Breaking down the barriers between the services to enable true jointness faced much resistance from the services themselves who did not want to give up responsibilities and the authority to command their own forces for the sake of a more powerful joint force. As a result, reforming the PLA, and integrating space more fully into PLA operations, stalled until Xi Jinping took power in 2012.

Xi took many measures to change the PLA, including breaking the service fiefdoms that prevented real operational reform. These reforms began in 2015 and introduced new operational concepts and reorganized the command-and-control structure to make it more suited for joint operations. Importantly, the reforms established the Strategic Support Force to train, equip, and operate the PLA's space, cyber, and electronic warfare forces, establishing for the first time an operational space command of its own.

The importance attached to space in these reforms would be presaged in PLA writings after Xi took power in 2012. According to the 2013 *Study of Space Operations*, a textbook published by the PLA's top think-tank, the Academy of Military Science (AMS), "Whoever is the strongman of military space will be the ruler of the battlefield; whoever has the advantage of space has the power of the initiative; having 'space' support enables victory, lacking 'space' ensures defeat" (Jiang and Wen 2013, 1). Similarly, the authors of the 2013 *Science of Military Strategy*, also published by AMS, concluded that space is the new high ground, that without space superiority, one is at a disadvantage in all other domains, and that space would form a "new triad" of deterrence along with nuclear and cyber deterrence (Shou 2013, 73).

More importantly, official PRC government documents beginning in 2015 made official the growing importance of space to the PLA. The PRC's 2015 defense white paper called outer space "a commanding height in international strategic competition" and stated that "threats from such new security domains as outer space and cyberspace will be dealt with to maintain the common security of the world community" and designated outer space one of four critical security domains along with the nuclear, maritime, and cyber domains.

Technological Progress

While the PLA struggled with reform in the 1990s and 2000s, technological progress began to show results. Although the PRC's space program progress was slow and, in some cases, stalled in the 1990s, the massive injection of funding for defense R&D that resulted from the 995 Program appears to have jumpstarted space-related R&D. Space also became a prominent feature of civilian R&D plans. The 2006–2020 Medium and

Long-term Plan for Science and Technology Development, for example, included sixteen megaprojects, three of which were space related. These included human spaceflight and lunar exploration, the establishment of a high-resolution earth observation system, and satellite navigation. In 2011, the Twelfth Five-year Plan governing the period 2011–2015, designated space as one of China's seven strategic emerging industries that permitted it to receive preferential policy treatment and funding. (USBC 2013, 4). Space was also prioritized for development under the 2015 "Made in China 2025" plan (MIIT 2016).

With this focus, the program made tremendous progress. In the 1990s, PRC launchers were unreliable and China had just a few satellites in orbit. Today, the PRC has more than 500 satellites in orbit, and the reliability of its space launch vehicles is at international standards. The PRC is also launching more rockets and satellites than at any other time in its history. In the period 2012–2022 China conducted 274 space launches,192 of which were conducted since 2017 (Global Times 2022).

Not surprisingly, the PRC now has the second largest number of satellites in orbit. According to information collected by the Union of Concerned Scientists, 5,465 satellites were in orbit on April 30, 2022. Of these, 3,433 were US, 541 were PRC, and 172 were Russian. Since 2000, the PRC has launched more than 20 new types of satellites. Moreover, many of these systems play a role in the "informatized" force that the PLA seeks to employ. China now has a global satellite navigation system comparable to the US GPS, Beidou, that provides positioning and navigation to the PLA and enables PLA forces to conduct precision strike. According to the US Space Force, the PRC how has 229 remote sensing satellites—the second most behind the United States—that can be used to identify, track, and target an adversary military. In order to better connect its forces, the PRC has 48 communication satellites that allow disparate forces to communicate and for over-the-horizon targeting (Lerch 2022).

The PRC is also developing a number of counterspace and counterspace-related technologies that will enable it to carry out operations to deny adversaries the use of space. Most prominently, a PRC test of a KKV in 2007 destroyed a retired FY-1C meteorological satellite. PRC counterspace and counterspace-related testing has expanded since then to include co-orbital satellites, directed energy weapons, jammers, and cyber weapons in what appears to be an effort to develop capabilities to threaten satellites from the ground to geosynchronous orbit. According to the Director of National Intelligence, "the PLA has an operational ground-based antisatellite (ASAT) missile intended to target low-Earth-orbit satellites, and China probably intends to pursue additional ASAT weapons capable of destroying satellites up to geosynchronous orbit" (Coats 2019, 17). The PLA is also expected to deploy a ground-based laser system for use against satellites in LEO by 2020 (Shanahan, 2019) In 2018, cyber security company Symantec revealed that attacks coming from Chinese IP addresses had targeted a satellite communications operator and a geospatial imaging and mapping organization (Symantec 2018). In January 2022, a PRC Shijian-21 satellite moved a derelict Beidou satellite to a graveyard orbit that was widely assumed to have counterspace implications (Lerch 2022).

SPACE DIPLOMACY

As the PRC's space program has grown in strength, the PRC has also been more willing to use its space program as one element of its foreign policy that is designed to re-fashion the international system by lessening US influence and making it more suited to serving China's interests (Xi 2017). Paralleling the PRC's overall foreign policy mes-sage of "building a community of shared future for mankind," China's space diplo-macy advocates the building of "a shared vision for humanity in space" that emphasizes China's role in promoting the peaceful uses of space, international space cooperation, and the advancement of humankind, while downplaying the national security aspects of its space program.

The PRC has stated that it is open to a variety of international cooperative efforts, including hosting astronauts and experiments, building modules for inclusion on the space station, and launching resupply missions. The *People's Daily* states that opening up China's space station to all UN member countries is described as "an important symbol" of its transitioning from independent development to international cooperation as well as a demonstration of China's self-confidence and openness (Sina 2019). According to Xinhua, China's space station belongs to China and the world, and China is committed to opening the space station to all countries so that "cooperation, mutual benefit, and win-win bloom in space" (Zhang 2018).

The PRC's "shared vision" framework is also evident in China's Belt and Road Space Information Corridor, an element of China's Belt and Road Initiative (BRI), an effort involving more than seventy countries spanning Asia, Europe, and Africa. The PRC has signed at least ninety-eight space-related agreements with thirty countries and three international organizations, including twenty-three agreements with eleven coun-tries involved in the BRI for space-related cooperative activities (Feng 2017). The PRC advertises that the Space Information Corridor will provide space-based earth obser-vation, communications and broadcasting, and navigation and positioning to member countries. The PRC expects the Space Information Corridor to eventually cover Southeast Asia, South Asia, Western Asia, Central Asia, Africa, Oceania, and Central and Eastern Europe (State Council 2016).

The PRC's narrative stressing the peaceful uses of space is also evident in its stance on space arms control. The PRC stresses that it "always adheres to the principle of the peaceful use of outer space and opposes the weaponization of space and an arms race in space and guarantees that its space activities benefit the whole of mankind." It maintains that "outer space is [the] common heritage of all mankind, and the benefits of space de-velopment should be enjoyed by all," and that "for any country, to maximize the military and security value of outer space, or even seek to place weapons there, would yield no benefit to the security of its own or the world" (Wu 2014).

Before China's 2007 ASAT test, PRC policy was widely regarded as unconditionally opposed to all types of ASAT weapons. According to China's 2005 white paper on arms control and disarmament: "Taking weapons into outer space will lead to an arms race there and make it a new arena for military confrontation. Such a prospect is not in the interest of any country." The white paper noted that "China has all along stood for peaceful use of outer space" and that "the existing international legal instruments on outer space cannot effectively prevent weaponization of and an arms race in outer space." The white paper also urged the international community to "take effective preventive measures, negotiate and conclude relevant international legal instrument to prohibit deployment of weapons in outer space and the threat or use of force against objects in outer space so as to ensure that outer space is used purely for peaceful purposes" (Ministry of Foreign Affairs of the Peoples Republic of China 2005).

China has continued to maintain this stance since the 2007 ASAT test and has, jointly with Russia, proposed draft treaty language on space arms control at the UN Conference on Disarmament. Despite this effort, China and Russia have opposed a space code of conduct proposed by the European Union that would establish non-binding guidelines for space activities, including those related to offensive counterspace activities.

THE PRC AS A SPACE POWER

The PRC is a space power contending with the leading world space powers. Although the PRC is still not the equal of the United States, it has made substantial progress since 2000. China's rise as a space power can be attributed to the PRC leadership's perceived need to maintain a balance of power with the United States in military space technologies. One important takeaway from this chapter is that a country's approach to space can be inherently tied to earthly matters. The PRC's leadership views the United States as an existential threat that required the development of space capabilities to both balance against and offset the US military's technological advantage. The PRC's response to competing with the United States is not purely military, however. As its space power has grown, the PRC has also begun using space as a diplomatic tool to differentiate itself from the United States as a more inclusive and equitable superpower.

The use of neoclassical realism to explain China's rise as a space power can demonstrate its utility in bridging the gap between constructivist approaches that emphasize ideational factors and realist approaches that emphasize material factors to account for state actions. This chapter, for example, does not discount the role of historical and political factors in shaping China's approaches to international competition, but argues instead that these historical and political factors have shaped China's leadership to act in ways that conform to realist IR theory.

The use of neoclassical realism can also account for the different interpretations of PRC intent in regard to its space program. The debate in the 1990s and 2000s over the type of international actor that China would become shaped the debate of how the United States should respond to the rise of China's space program, with those using a more constructivist approach arguing for engagement and cooperation as a way to mitigate the potential competitive aspects of China's space program and those taking a realist approach arguing for a policy of containment as a way to deny China the means to compete with the United States. Neoclassical realism, with its emphasis on long-term responses to threats, appears to suggest that debate over the policy challenges of responding to a rising power are the result of intervening factors that delay the material responses of the rising power even if the intention to challenge the status quo power may have been made much earlier. This delay between a state's intention and its ability to carry out its intentions creates a period of uncertainty over the true direction of a state's response to the status quo power that results in a policy debate over the ability of the status quo power to shape the end state of its relationship with the rising power.

Harvard University's Graham Allison has written that whether the United States and China can avoid the Thucydides Trap—the notion that when a rising power threatens to displace a ruling one, the most likely outcome is war—is the defining question for the world today (Allison 2015). This analysis of the PRC response to the United States in space indicates that a realist dynamic does exist between the two countries that will make it difficult to escape the Thucydides Trap. It suggests that the two countries may be entering a security dilemma defined as "the means by which a state tries to increase its security decrease[s] the security of others" (Jervis 1978, 169). This new dynamic will likely increase the chances of armed conflict between the two countries as efforts to develop "defensive" capabilities are viewed as inherently offensive by the other side (170).

References

Allison, Graham. 2015. "The Thucydides Trap: Are the U.S. and China Headed for War?" *The Atlantic*. September 24, 2015. http://belfercenter.ksg.harvard.edu/publication/25783/thucydides_trap.html.

Bao, Shixu. 2007. "Dominance in Space." *Beijing Review*. March 21, 2007.

Chang, Iris. 1995. *Threat of the Silkworm*. New York, NY: BasicBooks.

Cheung, Tai Ming. 2022. *Innovate to Dominate: The Rise of the Chinese Techno-Security State*. Ithaca, NY: Cornell University Press.

China News Agency. 2007. "Space Arms Race Driven by US is Worrying, Says Chinese Military Expert." October 10, 2007.

China Newsweek. 2010. "Tanmi zhongguo beidou daohang weixing: zuigao jimi dao minyong lishi 20 nian" [Exploring China's Beidou Navigation Satellite: From Highest Secret to Civilian Use in 20 Years]. December 30, 2010. http://www.sina.com.cn.

China Space News. 2003. "Zuigaoceng lingdao paiban." [The Highest Leader Has the Final Say]. October 16, 2013.

Christensen, Thomas J. 1996. "Chinese Realpolitik." *Foreign Affairs* 75, no. 5: 37–52.

Coats, Dan R. 2019. "Statement for the Record: 2019 Worldwide Threat Assessment of the U.S. Intelligence Community to the Senate Select Committee on Intelligence." Office of the Director of National Intelligence. January 29. https://www.dni.gov/files/ODNI/documents/2019-ATA-SFR---SSCI.pdf.

Feng, Hua. 2017. "Space Cooperation Expands China's Belt and Road 'Circle of Friends.'" *People's Daily*. May 14, 2017. http://en.people.cn/n3/2017/0514/ c90000-9215306.html.

Finkelstein, David. 2007. In *Right-Sizing the People's Liberation Army: Exploring the Contours of China's Military*, edited by Roy Kamphausen and Andrew Scobell, 69–140. Carlisle, PA: U.S. Army War College.

Hartnett, Daniel. 2014. "The "New Historic Missions": Reflections on Hu Jintao's Military Legacy." *In Assessing the People's Liberation Army in the Hu Jintao Era*, edited by Roy Kamphausen, David Lai, and Travis Tanner, 31–80. Carlisle, PA: U.S. Army War College.

Hong, Yuan. 2008. "US Ulterior Motives in Destroying Satellite with Missile." *Beijing News*. February 22, 2008.

Global Times. 2022. "China Eyes Manned Moon Explorations, Mars Sample Retrieval: 20th CPC Congress Delegate." October 22, 2022. https://www.globaltimes.cn/page/202210/1277691.shtml.

"How Many and Where Were the Nukes?".National Security Archive. August 18, 2006. https://nsarchive2.gwu.edu/NSAEBB/NSAEBB197/index.htm.

Jervis, Robert. 1978. "Cooperation Under the Security Dilemma." *World Politics* 30, no. 2 (January): 167–214.

Jiang, Lianju, and Wang Liwen, eds. 2013. *Kongjian zuozhanxue jiaocheng* [Textbook for the Study of Space Operations]. Beijing: Military Science Publishing House.

Johnston, Alastair Iain. 1995. *Cultural Realism: Strategic Culture and Grand Strategy in Chinese History*. Princeton, NJ: Princeton University Press.

Keohane, Robert O. 1986. "Theory of World Politics: Structural Realism and Beyond." In *Neorealism and Its Critics*, edited by Robert O. Keohane, 158–204. New York: Columbia University Press.

Khan, Sulmaan Wasif. 2018. *Haunted by Chaos: China's Grand Strategy from Mao Zedong to Xi Jinping*. Cambridge: Harvard University Press.

Kulacki, Gregory and Jeffrey Lewis. 2009. *A Place for One's Mat: China's Space Program, 1956–2003*. Cambridge, MA: American Academy of Arts and Sciences.

Layne, Christopher. 1993. "The Unipolar Illusion: Why New Great Powers Will Rise," *International Security* 17, no. 4 (Spring): 5–51.

Lerch, Ron. 2022. "The Space Domain: Emerging Factors and Threats." Space Force. https://www.ssc.spaceforce.mil/Portals/3/20220516%20Threat%20Baseline_AATS_1.pdf.

Lewis, John Wilson, and Hua Di. 1992. "China's Ballistic Missile Programs: Technologies, Strategies, Goals." *International Security* 17, no. 2 (Fall): 5–40.

Lewis, John Wilson, and Xue Litai. 1988. *China Builds the Bomb*. Stanford, CA: Stanford University Press.

Li, Jiayao. 2020. "Defense Ministry's Regular Press Conference on Feb. 28." *China Military Online*. March 1, 2020. http://eng.mod.gov.cn/news/2020-03/01/content_4861321.htm.

Li Yong, Wang Xiao, Yi Ming, and Wang Long. 2005. "Countermeasure Technology and Threats Against Space-based Photoelectric Imaging and Remote Sensing Device." *Infrared and Laser Engineering* 34, no. 6: 631–35, 640.

Liu, Fei, and Su Dong, "Zhongguo hangtian keji jituan gongsi longzhong zhaokai 2012 niandu gongzuo huiyi." [China Aerospace Science and Technology Corporation Opening of the 2012 Work Conference]. January 20, 2012. http://www.gov.cn/gzdt/2012-01/20/content_2049966.htm.

Lobell, Steven E. , Norrin M. Ripsman, and Jeffrey W. Taliaferro. 2009. "Introduction: Neoclassical Realism, the State and Foreign Policy." In *Neoclassical Realism, the State, and Foreign Policy*, edited by Steven E. Lobell, Norrin M. Ripsman and Jeffrey W. Taliaferro, 1–41. Cambridge: Cambridge University Press.

Luthi, Lorenz M. 2008. *The Sino-Soviet Split: Cold War in the Communist World.* Princeton, NJ: Princeton University Press.

MIIT (Ministry of Industry and Information Technology). 2016. "<Zhongguo zhizao 2025> jieshizhi: jiaokuai tuidong hangtian zhuangbei fazhan." ["Made in China 2025" Explained: Accelerate the Promotion of Space Equipment." May 12, 2016. http://www.miit.gov.cn/n11293472/n11295193/n11298598/16619995.html.

Ministry of Foreign Affairs of the Peoples Republic of China. 2005. "China's Endeavors for Arms Control, Disarmament and Non-Proliferation."White Paper. September 1, 2005. https://www.fmprc.gov.cn/mfa_eng/wjb_663304/zzjg_663340/jks_665232/jkxw_665234/200509/t20050901_599120.html.

Mulvenon, James. 2009. "Chairman Hu and the PLA's 'New Historic Missions,'" *China Leadership Monitor* no. 27 (Winter): 1–11.

Peng, Guangqian, and Yao Youzhi. 2001. *Zhanlue xue.* [The Science of Strategy]. Beijing: Military Sciences Press.

Pekkanen, Saadia M. 2020. "Neoclassical Realism in Japan's Space Security," In *The Oxford Handbook of Japanese Politics*, edited by Robert J. Pekkanen and Saadia M. Pekkanen, 763–90. New York: Oxford University Press.

Pollpeter, Kevin. 2010. "Towards an Integrative C4ISR System: Informationization and Joint Operations in the People's Liberation Army." In *The PLA at Home and Abroad: Assessing the Operational Capabilities of China's Military*, edited by Roy Kamphausen, David Lai, and Andrew Scobell, 193–235..Carlisle, PA: Strategic Studies Institute.

Pollpeter, Kevin, Timothy Ditter, Anthony Miller, and Brian Waidelich. 2019. "China's Space Narrative: Examining the Portrayal of the US-China Space Relationship in Chinese Sources and Its Implications for the United States." China Aerospace Studies Institute/CNA. https://www.airuniversity.af.edu/Portals/10/CASI/Conference-2020/CASI%20Conference%20China%20Space%20Narrative.pdf?ver=FGoQ8Wm2DypB4FaZDWuNTQ%3d%3d.

Samuels, Richard. 1994. *Rich Nation Strong Army.* Ithaca, NY: Cornell University Press.

Shanahan, Patrick M. 2019. "Remarks by Acting Secretary Shanahan at the 35th Space Symposium, Colorado Springs, Colorado." https://dod.defense.gov/News/Transcripts/Transcript-View/Article/1809882/remarks-by-acting-secretary-shanahan-at-the-35th-spacesymposium-colorado-sprin/.

Shen, Silu, Feng Shuxing, Wang Jia, and Li Yadong. 2007. "Qianxi junshi hangtian renwu zhihui juece." [Research on the Command Decision-making in Military Space Mission]. *Zhihui zhuangbei jishu xueyuan xuebao* [*Journal of the Academy of Equipment Command and Technology*] 18, no. 1: 146–50.

Sina. 2019. "Tong yitian! Tanyue, zairen liangda hagntian gongcheng jieyou da xiaoxi." [On the Same Day! The Lunar Exploration and Human Spaceflight Programs Have Big News]. June 13, 2019. https://tech.sina.cn/d/tk/2019-06-13/detail-ihvhiqay5447820. d.html?vt=4&cid=38718.

Shou, Xiaosong. 2013. *Zhanlue xue* [Science of Military Strategy]. Beijing: Military Science Press.

State Council Information Office of the People's Republic of China. 2016. China's Space Activities in 2016. https://www.scio.gov.cn/zfbps/32832/ Document/1537024/1537024.htm.

Symantec. 2018. "Thrip: Espionage Group Hits Satellite, Telecoms, and Defense Companies." June 19, 2018. https://www.symantec.com/blogs/threat-intelligence/thrip-hits-satellite-telecoms-defense-targets.

Tang, Baodong. 2001. "Meijun jiji zhunbei taikong zuozhan." [The US Military Actively Prepares for Space Operations], *Xiandai Junshi* [Conmilit].

Teng, Jianqun. 2007. "Thoughts Arising from the U.S. Military's Space Exercise." *Liberation Army Daily*. February 1.

US-China Business Council (USBC). 2013. "China's Strategic Emerging Industries: Policy, Implementation, Challenges, and Recommendations." https://www.uschina.org/sites/defa ult/files/sei-report.pdf.

Viotti, Paul R., and Mark V. Kauppi. 1987. *International Relations Theory: Realism, Pluralism. Globalism, and Beyond*. Needham Heights, MA: Viacom.

Waltz, Kenneth N. 1979. *Theory of International Politics*. Long Grove, IL: Waveland Press.

Wei, Qiyong, Qin Zhijin, and Liu Erxun. 2002. "Qianxi 2020 nianqian meijun zhanlue zhongdian de zhuanbian—cong zhuangbei fazhan kan meijunshi zhanlue zhongdian keneng de bianhua." [Analysis of the Change of U.S. Military Strategy Before 2020—View on the Transformation of the Emphases of U.S. Military Strategy]. *Daodan yu hangtian yunzai jishu* [*Missile and Space Vehicles*] 50, no. 4: 1–4.

Wu, Haitao. 2014. "Remarks by H.E. Ambassador WU Haitao at the Space Security Conference 2014," United Nations Conference on Disarmament, March 19, http://www.china-un.ch/ eng/dbtyw/cjjk_1/cjthsm/t1140194.htm.

Xi, Jinping. 2017. "Work Together to Build a Community of Shared Future for Mankind." Xinhua. January 18. 2017http://www.xinhuanet.com/english/2017-01/19/c_135994707.htm.

Xiong, Xiaolong, Li Ronggang, You Dade, Zhang Shiliao, "Duoqu zhi taikongquan." [Seizing Space Supremacy]. *Feihang daodan* [Winged Missile Journal]. October.

Yuan, Jun. 2001. "Meiguo taikong zhanlue yu taikongzhan yanxi." [The US Military's Space Strategy and Space Wargames]. *Zhongguo hangtian*. [Aerospace China]. July.

Zakaria, Fareed. 1998. *From Wealth to Power: The Unusual Origins of America's World Role*. Princeton, NJ: Princeton University Press.

Zhang, Ying. "Xinhua guoji shiping: rang kaifang gongying linian zhangying taikong." [Xinhua International Commentary: Let Openness and Win-Win Bloom in Space]. Xinhua. May 29, 2018. http://www.xinhuanet.com/world/2018- 05/29/c_1122907625.htm.

Zhao, Chu. "Taikong zhan: tiaozhan, zhongdian yu duice." [Space Warfare: Challenge, Key Points, and Response]. *Guoji zhanwang* [Global Military Reports]. May 1, 2001.

Zhou, Lei, and Liu Hao. 2006. January. "Tianji xinxi xitong jidui haijun hangkong zhuangbei de yingxiang." [Space-based Information Systems and Their Influence on Naval Aviation]. *Feihang Daodan* [Winged Missiles].

Zhu, Naibo, and Zhang Li. 2005. December. "Meijun xinxi xitong yitihua jianshe ji qishi." [Integrated Building of U.S. Forces Information System and Enlightenment].

CHAPTER 17

....

RUSSIA'S INTEGRATED STATECRAFT IN THE SPACE DOMAIN

....

FLORIAN VIDAL

INTRODUCTION: WHAT DRIVES THE RUSSIAN SPACE STRATEGY? A NEW POLITICAL NARRATIVE

....

FOR two decades, Russian foreign policy has sought to rebuild its power on the international scene (Stoner 2021). This strategy directly affects both the post-Soviet space and former areas of Soviet influence, including the Middle East. This trajectory reflects a neorealist perspective of the return of Russia as a prominent actor in international relations at the beginning of the twenty-first century (Khan Afridi and Jibran 2018; Romanova 2012). As Laruelle and Radvanyi (2019) remind us, Russia has had to process global geopolitical shifts over the past three decades while continually evaluating its own identity, development trajectory, and role in the international arena. Russia has long maintained that "tools and tactics by which major powers pursue and uphold their dominant regional positions depend on the level of external pressure" (Götz 2016, 302). Echoing this dramatic shift, Russia—under Vladimir Putin—has reinstated such instruments of power including in the space domain (Vidal 2021). This chapter engages with the historical context of Russia's space program and seeks to chart how contemporary and future policy will address space security.

Space has a unique place in the Russian national narrative. During the Cold War, the USSR financed sizeable military and civilian space programs. As a matter of pride, Russian authorities have sought to preserve the competitive gap in space activities. Russian space strategy is guided by "three clusters of factors—power, ideas and domestic influences" (Götz and McFarlane 2019, 714). Together, these factors shape Moscow's actions on the international stage. If the quest for prestige and status is a driver of Russian foreign policy, then space policy remains an important vector of this quest. Russian space policy also serves as an instrument for reaffirming Russia's sovereignty and internal power. It is an effective communication channel visible to the Russian public. To reaffirm autonomy in the space domain, Russia intends to redeploy space infrastructure within its territory to develop a new national narrative surrounding space activities (Vidal 2021). The point for Russia is not only to break with an industrial and geographic organization inherited from the USSR but also to become self-reliant. The gradual shift from the Baikonur Cosmodrome in Kazakhstan to the newly built Vostochny Cosmodrome in Eastern Siberia demonstrates this political narrative perfectly.

The power of this narrative echoes public perception of the Soviet space odyssey. In April 2021, sixty years after Yuri Gagarin's flight, an opinion poll indicated that 91 percent of Russians concluded that Russia needs to play a part in space exploration while 75 percent of them did not want budget cuts on space programs (Vciom 2021). Russian authorities, therefore, rely on a public opinion that is nostalgic for a Soviet scientific legacy (Gerovitch 2015; Kohonen 2009). The Soviet space program is one of the highest technological achievements of the past century. In recent years, Russian space activities, however, indicate a military turn on the part of Moscow, which curtails efforts to further develop a credible commercial space sector. This posture echoes the militarization of the elite under Vladimir Putin and the rise of a militocracy paradigm (Rivera and Werning Rivera 2018). Additionally, Federal Order No. 379 issued on September 28, 2021, by the Federal Security Service (FSB) regarding the restriction of information dissemination related to "the field of defense, military and technical activities of the Russian Federation" is another signal of this shift (Federal Security Service 2021).

Contemporary Russia is attempting to renew its status with an ambitious space policy, which is conditioned by two critical Soviet legacies: management of the industrial apparatus and the application of military doctrine. In moving forward with this policy, Russia may struggle to contend with its long-standing space competitor, the United States, and the fast-growing newcomer, China. Given the fact that space ambitions are intertwined with and underpinned by the Russian regime, what role does Russia intend to play in the space security order in light of new space competition?

With this question in mind, this chapter first examines the key drivers that shape Russia's space policy. The nature and components of the country's space strategy remain critical for global stability, especially because the Russian Ministry of Defense (Minoborony) has a leading role in the upkeep of the space program and the conduct of its activities. Space strategy is influenced by the implications of the collapse of the USSR, with its negative impact on the ecosystem of the Russian space sector and by the formation of an ideological foundation drawing on Soviet mythology. In light of this, this chapter next aims to depict the nature of the military components of the space program and military influence on its development. Finally, this chapter seeks to analyze the political and strategic role of space within the context of Russian objectives in the international arena.

ANALYTICAL DRIVERS OF RUSSIA'S SPACE POLICY

The Systemic Driver: Russia's Return to Great Power Competition

Under Putin, Russia began to re-engage in global activism, allowing it to position itself as an alternative to Western states as an international partner, in an effort to balance the influence of these states. To take up this international posture, Russia adopted "transactional, flexible, adaptable, non-ideological, and asymmetric approaches to Great Power competition" (Herd 2021, 1). Russia's stance on the international stage appears opportunistic and designed to maximize leverage while minimizing costs. To achieve these goals, Stronski (2019) highlights, "Moscow boasts an agile and skilled diplomatic establishment and lacks ethical constraints in pursuit of its objectives." This broader context and diplomatic stance also applies to the space sector.

In the early 2000s, the Russian government pursued a new course in rebuilding its space program. The political decision to reinvest in the space domain was motivated by two key drivers: first, the recognition of the military vulnerabilities that Russia faced and, second, the recognition of the country's space program as one of the few remaining elements of its international prestige (Moltz 2019). Among the priorities laid down, Putin plugged the gaps in Russia's military constellations and backed a new ambitious space program (e.g., Vostochny Cosmodrome, Angary family rocket).

The Domestic Driver: The Failure of Restructuring

Since the end of the Cold War, the Russian space program has remained in the shadow of the golden age of Soviet engineers and scientists, led by Korolev, who built the substance still to be found in the country's space industry. At its heyday, eight hundred thousand people worked in the Soviet space sector, but the number of employees has shrunk sharply in a trend that has been maintained (Harford 1997; Vidal 2021). In the meantime, Moltz highlights that the USSR's collapse "led to the selling off of many Russian space technologies" (2019, 19).

Despite the crippling institutional arrangement of Russian space governance, industrial and technological components still rely on simple but reliable Soviet made spacecraft and rockets (Harford 1997). The Putin regime built on this legacy in order to maintain a narrative directed toward its domestic audience with regard to the scientific and political influence of Russia as global power (Gerovitch 2015; Siddiqi 2010).

Without major technological breakthroughs and pioneering policy, the nation's space strategy skillfully sustains an organization inherited from the past, despite all institutional shortcomings.

The Ideological Driver: Deterrence and Autarky

Combining systemic and domestic drivers, Russia pursues ambitious space governance through a powerful and deep-rooted ideological stance. First, Russian power bases its space policy on dissuasion of Western powers, an ideological opposition that is built on the legacy of the Cold War. This stance feeds the narrative of a temporal continuity with the previous period that was indelibly marked with the opposition between the USSR and the United States. In Russia, the concept of strategic deterrence assumes a broader definition than the Western concept of deterrence. It includes deterrent instruments that are offensive and defensive; nuclear and non-nuclear, military and non-military in nature (Ven Bruusgaard 2016). The space domain is therefore fully integrated in the deterrence policy maintained by Russia.

In addition, Russia has fostered, since the Bolshevik period, the idea of autarky in its economic sense (Dohan 1976). This ideological posture gained a new dimension in 2014 after the implementation of the first economic sanctions following the annexation of Crimea by Russia. Autarky finds ramifications in the macroeconomic and financial realm of the country as a way to reduce external vulnerabilities due to the increasing pressure of Western sanctions (Milesi-Ferretti 2022). In other words, autarky is a systemic reaction to the country's concerns about the assumption of external intervention (Laruelle and Radvanyi 2019). Ultimately, Russian space industry is on a trajectory of economic and technological autarky to ensure that it remains an independent power.

NATURE AND COMPONENTS OF THE RUSSIAN SPACE PROGRAM: THE WIDENING DEFENSE GRIP

This section sets out the principal elements of the Russian space program, examining the role of state institutions, technologies, and contextual realities in the drive to make Russia autonomous in space.

Russian Space Policy: A State Comprehensive Vision

After the end of the Cold War and the break-up of the USSR, the space program encountered serious difficulties in sustaining intense activities in the field. After a deep economic depression and the loss of two decades, Russia regained some capabilities starting in the early 2010s. To proceed with a renewal of its space policy, the Russian government unveiled a few key state documents to support this shift:

- Strategy for Development of Russian Space Activities until 2030 and beyond (adopted in 2012, and updated in 2021)
- Strategic Development of State Space Corporation Roscosmos until 2025 and until 2030 (adopted in 2017)

The first of these documents underlined the need to ensure Russian cosmonautics operated at an international level and Russia would be entrenched as one of the top three global space powers by 2030. The first document was updated in January 2021 to adjust to the expansion of low Earth orbit (LEO) satellite constellations and to improve Russian access to outer space. The second document noted that "the state interests of the Russian Federation require a significant expansion of the range of products and services to ensure defense, socio-economic development, science and international cooperation" (Roscosmos 2017). These federal government policy documents remain sufficiently unclear and imprecise with regard to implementation of broad policy objectives. Despite this vagueness, the Russian state stands by its political and financial commitments to support space ambitions linked to the country's international status. Indeed, this state strategy includes significant financial subsidies to bear the costs of "financing the Russian government's attempts to ensure Russia's global space leadership, as well as its state-run scientific and defense space programs" (Luzin 2021b). To this end, Russian authorities have relied on critical plans to drive renewal of the country's space program.

In the 2010s, the Russian government focused on three large-scale projects: manufacture of the Angara launch vehicle, construction of the new spaceport at Vostochny, and the return of Russian cosmonauts to space (Goble 2021). With federal support, these three core projects reflect the vertical vision of the Russian space policy, which mirrors the vertical power that the Putin regime has developed over the last decades (Monaghan 2012; Golts 2018). Regarding the development of the space sector, all strategic decisions are determined from the top of the Russian state. Once decided, federal agencies and administrative bodies implement them. The Russian federal agency, Roscosmos, is in this respect the primary receptacle of this state policy.

Roscosmos: The Comet's Tail of the Soviet Era

In 2015, the establishment of Roscosmos, a state corporation, was designed to fulfill three core missions: regulation of the industry (both legally and technically); distribution of orders and resources of the industry; and authorized representation of the owner (the Russian state) in most enterprises of the space industry including mainly federal enterprises, institutions, and joint-stock companies with a predominant state share. As Skvortsov rightly noted, "these functions are almost constantly in conflict with each other" (2018). Being both the owner's representative and the customer, Roscosmos must think in terms of both profitability and business value, on the one hand, and cost minimization and performance maximization, on the other hand. This split position makes the effectiveness of the space industry's management model unsustainable in the long term.

The totalizing dimension of Roscosmos, an element inherent in its creation, aimed to close the gaps in a sector that had been unable to reform itself since the 1990s. In the meantime, Russia's space industry has managed to preserve most of the technological potential of the Soviet space industry. Although the Russian agency benefits from relatively stable funding, it upgraded Soviet-era relics like the Soyuz rocket instead of accelerating the development of a new rocket (Zak 2020a). From this legacy, Roscosmos intends to build on "a model that would allow it to put in place civil and military space programs with confidence" (Luzin 2020b). To achieve this, the federal agency began to implement specialized holdings, organized within its structures, but separated according to their functions: satellites, missiles, science, and ground infrastructures.

Even if the Russian space sector is fully capable of executing all state-funded tasks in space exploration, the range of these tasks has diminished significantly after the end of the Cold War. As Kohonen recalls "the Soviet space industry was born within the military industrial complex but the space program was never merely a military program" (2009, 115). Nevertheless, most Soviet space development remained under the supervision of the Ministry of Defense and the Military-Industrial Commission until the collapse of the Soviet regime (Harford 1997). This lack of initial clarification mirrors today's crisis of governance in Russia's space industry. The present priority of the country's program is preserving its inherited capabilities, which prevents it from developing to its true potential. Insufficient motivation and lack of vision on the part of federal authorities are factors of this limited use of the space industry capacity, but major space projects are now being cultivated by Ministry of Defense orders (Egorov 2018; Luzin 2020b). This situation reflects the failure to establish a strong private sector in this industrial field, as exemplified by the industrial setback of the promising company KosmoKurs, which planned to send tourists into space (RIA Novosti 2021). This imbalance is due to the character of the Russian model for space development, which posits a dominant role for the government (Moltz 2019). Thanks in part to Putin's rule, which retains absolute political control over the process, space commercialization and innovation wholly remain within a state-centric pattern. Since 2000, this trend confers most commercial space flights to the Russian federal agency.

As part of its initial mission, Roscosmos tried to improve the situation, while supporting private space startups to grow in the national space ecosystem. For this purpose, a venture fund in partnership with other Russian national institutes of economic development was created under the guidelines of President Putin. The projected fund was shaped for forming public-private synergies. Yet, it had little impact on the national space industry, as it fails to solve any of the industry's intrinsic issues (Egorov 2018). Even more astonishingly, in the absence of a diversified business model, dependence on foreign revenues for the past two decades has created unsustainable conditions for the Russian space sector. The termination of a long-term contract with the National Aeronautics and Space Administration (NASA) in 2020 is a clear demonstration of these volatile conditions. To compound this, the poor economic environment for commercial space activities does not attract Russian investors (Berger 2021a). The looming end of major international cooperation projects (i.e., Atlas rocket launch program; the International Space Station program) will further dry up Roscosmos's profits. Unable to effectively reform the space industry, Roscosmos has failed in its mission to date, namely the establishment of a competitive civil space sector. More notably, Putin expressed his dissatisfaction regarding Roscosmos's performance in September 2021. He underlined the failure to fulfill directives on long-term objectives in the space arena (Berger 2021b). As a result, the Russian government plans severe budget cuts through 2024. To sum up, the agency did not bring financial and scientific success as initially expected.

In addition, Roscosmos's governance is questionable. For instance, Dmitry Rogozin, who ran the federal body from 2018 to 2022, was previously Russian ambassador to NATO (2008–2011). Since Crimea's annexation by Russia in 2014, Rogozin had also been under Western sanctions. The Russian space community remained skeptical about the appointment of a non-expert in the field, and Rogozin was subject to significant criticism. His constant media bluster to compete with US tycoons such as Elon Musk did not hide financial scandals and loss of confidence due to repeated failures (Mirovalev 2021; Misnik 2021). Aside from these short-term considerations in leadership, Roscosmos's attempts to rectify the situation mostly target the consequences of the current industrial crisis: poor work performance, poor reliability of manufactured goods, and low levels of technological development.

A Restricted Policy: Endemic Burdens and External Drivers

Considering the stated ambition to maintain Russia as an autonomous stakeholder in the space field, Russian authorities have to deal with structural and comprehensive hurdles connected to unresolved systemic economic issues that the country has faced for several decades. Among them, bureaucratic red tape and widespread corruption cripple the space sector, meanwhile the ongoing trajectory is embedded in this deteriorating process.

While relying on Soviet space technologies, this legacy includes a darker side, which critically affects the state's ability to revitalize its space policy. This heavy burden comprises several factors: industrial obsolescence, demographic aging, and decline of innovation capacities (Aliberti and Lisitsyna 2019). Regarding human resources, Luzin stresses three entangled curses—low labor productivity, high costs, and scarce human capital—that cripple the Russian space industry (2020b). The same can be seen in the old industrial infrastructure, which is inadequate to meet fast-growing global space competition.

Although federal authorities do not seek to invest further resources, the structural depressive cycle is called to follow this downward trajectory. In return, endemic burdens will become harder to bear for the space industry. More specifically, geopolitical conditions since 2014 following Crimea's annexation have created further critical conditions. The implementation of Western economic and financial sanctions has struck, as Luzin argues, "a blow to the country's capabilities in the production of high-tech weapons and military equipment and in manufacturing civilian products" (2020c). Overall, the defense sector bears a much higher cost than any other economic segment from this sanction regime. For instance, Russia's "import substitution" (*Importozameschenie*) policy is unable to replace most electronic components for manufacturing GLONASS satellites and may entirely rely on Russian components after 2026 (Luzin 2020c; 2021a), critically slowing down satellite modernization programs. In a broader perspective, the supply of defense technologies, military equipment, and dual-use products (e.g., microelectronics) are critical to the advancement of the Russian space program. Unequivocally, this industrial isolation undermines the sustainability of the Russian space field in the long run. And last but not least, declining revenues from Western partners weaken Russian companies in the face of the country's economic instability.

The Centrality and the Indisputable Role of the Ministry of Defense

The military component of the Russian space program is an essential pillar of the strategic autonomy envisioned by the federal authorities. For this purpose, the Ministry of Defense (Minoborony) established in 2015 the Space Forces, a separate branch within the Air and Space Forces (VKS). The Space Forces' activities cover a large spectrum: space situational awareness, satellite launch and operations, space infrastructure maintenance, and early warning of ballistic missile threats (Ministry of Defense of the Russian Federation 2015).

Aside from military space activities, Minoborony also works to maintain the civil space sector with critical investments, such as in new launch vehicle tests. A genuine legacy of the Soviet era, the ministry serves as a central organization in the launch of investment programs but also of innovation programs (Vidal 2021). More specifically, the ministry defines space strategy jointly with Roscosmos. Their competition in the control of strategic space infrastructure assets points to the increasing ministry influence in the space program (2021). In this battle for influence, Putin could arbitrate in favor of the ministry, while Roscosmos is crippled with chronic debts. Although space programs in the civilian sector are experiencing notorious difficulties, Russia seems to be able to hold on to substantial military capabilities in this field.

In that respect, Minoborony demonstrates its vital role in the expansion of the Russian space sector. Most notably, it is actively involved in validation of the Federal Space Program (FKP) budget. As part of its budget, it can also encompass a space component. For instance, the ten-year state armament program (*gosudarstvennaia programma vooruzheniia*, also called GPV 2027), related to all military purchases until 2027 by the ministry, encompasses the development of defense systems to protect Russian satellites.

The ministry's orders and operations regarding satellites are becoming ever more prominent. Its significance permeates space activity and boosts innovation in the sector.

Among the 169 satellites in orbit, over 100 are dedicated to military activities or are dual use (UCS 2022). In particular, the program encompasses the expansion of a constellation of 10 geostationary Earth orbit (GEO) and highly elliptical orbit (HEO) satellites to integrate the Tundra early-warning system—as part of the integrated satellite system (EKS) *Kupol* to track ballistic missile launches. Consisting of 5 satellites as of now, the system, once complete, will provide constant coverage of all potential missile launch areas (Zak 2021c). In addition, the Russian global navigation system GLONASS operates under Minoborony control (see Larsen, this volume). All in all, the principal purpose of upgrading the satellite constellation is to meet Russia's military objectives in consolidating its deterrence posture from space.

Regarding the upcoming launches of the Angara-A5 rocket, the Khrunichev Space Center contracted with Minoborony for mass production of this heavy launcher. As it is under the full control of the Plesetsk Cosmodrome, it has planned new launches over the next few years. To go further, the ministry has a catalyzing function for innovative schemes. Under its supervision, a long-term project led by the company KB Arsenal is underway since the beginning of the twenty-first century. Based in St Petersburg, this project is developing a transport and energy module (TEM), a large space tug propelled by electric engines and powered by a nuclear source (Zak 2020b). Furthermore, Rosatom—the Russian State Nuclear Energy Corporation—has acknowledged that it will contribute to the design of this space tug together with Roscosmos. However, this bold project highlights uncertainties as its costs have constantly increased since 2012, and there is no clear timetable and course of action for flight testing.

Hence, while the Russian Ministry of Defense acts as a technology and funding provider of space activities, the numerous programs shaped by the ministry confirm the influence and dependence of Roscosmos in defining critical space achievements in the future. In other words, this key stakeholder is "a pillar for both the Russian space program architecture and its financial support" (Vidal 2021).

MILITARY DIMENSION AND TECHNOLOGICAL DEVELOPMENT

In light of the role played by the Ministry of Defense noted above, this section takes a closer look at key elements of Russia's military space realities.

Space Domain in Military Doctrine: The Art of the Grey Zone

As Podvig argues, "the space forces' mission is defined in a way that calls for action only in response to a threat 'in space and from space'" (2021, 35). In other words, the primary mission of Russia's space forces is defensive by nature, but does not exclude offensive operations in space, for which the space forces rely on an advanced warfare approach. Against a backdrop of multidimensional warfare, Russian military doctrine comprehends the importance of information-driven modern technologies, which incorporate long-range precision strike platforms as well as offensive cyber capabilities. As a result, the Russian vision of modern warfare is evolving toward non-contact warfare (*beskontaknaya voenna*). As Lavrov rightly underscores, "Russian military strategists see the trajectory of modern warfare being dominated by the struggle to achieve information dominance as a prerequisite to military victory" (2017).

In this respect, the Russian army believes that the struggle for information dominance begins before conflict erupts. Then, once conflict has begun, information dominance is used to subdue an opponent's decision-making "by either denying the adversary's ability to utilize space-enabled information or by corrupting that information to mislead an adversary into making decisions contrary to their military objectives" (Lavrov 2017). Indeed, the role of space in conflict is critical for providing key information for leading military operations on the ground as well as denying the adversary's ability to act.

In a broader perspective, as noted earlier, Russian military doctrine emphasizes a concept of deterrence that is wider than just the nuclear deterrence implemented during the Cold War. In a shifting paradigm, deterrence should be understood as strategic, to include concepts such as new generation warfare (Bowen 2020). Consequently, it involves not only nuclear weapons, but also strategic conventional weapons, and non-military measures in which space plays a part (Meshcheryakov, Kaïralapov, and Sinikov 2021). For instance, the ongoing modernization of the GLONASS navigation system stands as a critical effort to more efficiently support military operations in the context of the deployment of high-precision weapons. Considering Russian military investment in electronic warfare (EW), this is intended to mitigate US space-based capabilities. During the late 1990s and early 2000s, Russia's GLONASS satellite system had atrophied to a mere seven satellites, not enough for effective military application. For example, in the first Chechnyan war from 1994 to 1996, Russian pilots and ground forces came, in part, to rely upon western-based GPS navigation systems (Lavrov 2017).

In order to renew its doctrine, the Russian army defined a critical approach to space: the art of the grey zone. As Davis explains, grey zone activities fall just below the level of outright aggression (2021; Raska and Davis, this volume). In this respect, Russia intends to improve its military space capabilities in jamming and radio intelligence as well as capabilities against ground-based space infrastructure. Overall, the objective is to prevent its adversaries using their space-related infrastructure (Luzin 2020a). Russia may plan to employ soft-kill capabilities that disable, deny, or damage (3D concept) a satellite, rather than physically destroy it, which would imply further political and security consequences (Davis 2021). Consequently, the practice of grey zone activities involves avoiding direct confrontation with its adversaries. In the next decades, the expansion of satellite megaconstellations will widen opportunities for grey zone practices that Russia may exploit.

Counterspace Technologies: State of Play

To implement its military doctrine in space, Russia has advanced a variety of counterspace-technologies enabling it to hold a strategic position. The goal is to preserve the power balance in that field. The Ministry of Defense works on three critical systems: anti-satellite (ASAT) missiles, disruptive systems against space and ground infrastructures, and electronic and cyber counter-space technologies.

ASAT Missiles: A Controversial System in Complete Operation

Among the space military capabilities that Russia appears to be exploring, a land-based anti-satellite system is critical for space security architectures. Whereas the Soviets had already worked on direct-ascent ASAT weapons in the 1980s, the ongoing system is designed to destroy or incapacitate satellites. A program to accomplish these goals started in 2009, with the Russian company Almaz-Antey principal developer of the *Nudol* interceptor system. Launched from the Plesetsk Cosmodrome, the Ministry of Defense has tested *PL19 Nudol* numerous times against simulated targets since 2014 (Panda 2021; SWF 2020).

In November 2021, this ASAT system demonstrated its ability to destroy the Soviet-era satellite Kosmos-1408—launched in 1982 (Interfax 2021). This was the first time a Russian strike was directed against a live satellite target, the destruction of which generated a debris cloud that significantly contributed to a degraded environment in LEO. However, this system does not appear to have the capability to threaten targets beyond LEO (SWF 2022). In a broader context, Russia is not alone in developing and testing such weapons. China (2007), the United States (2008) and India (2019) conducted similar destructive tests against their own satellites. It is indisputable that such a military system endangers space activities and the Russian demonstration points to a pressing need to address this type of operation.

An Extensive Toolkit for Disrupting Space and Ground Infrastructures

Over the past several years, Russian military space programs have displayed wide-ranging disruptive and innovative tools. These include non-kinetic physical counterspace weapons, which bring together several components able to cause destructive effects on satellites or ground systems without making physical contact. For instance, lasers can be used to temporarily dazzle or permanently blind the sensors on satellites, and higher-powered lasers can cause components to overheat. With regard to the latter issue, there is no doubt that "Russia is developing, or intending to develop, high power space-based laser weapons" (SWF 2022, 16). In this field, Russia intends to maintain a variety of non-kinetic counterspace technologies such as the Peresvet laser system. This system has been, at first sight, designed to be a mobile trailer-mounted laser system, however, Minoborony plans to put Peresvet on an airborne carrier. The Peresvet laser system will be the second airborne laser system, following Sokol-Echelon, as announced in 2016 (Harrison et al. 2021).

Inspector satellites are another instrument Russia began to deploy in 2013. As rendezvous proximity operation satellites advance, that led by Kosmos-2543 demonstrated significant capabilities from Russian space forces. The probe positioned itself in a trajectory that allowed it to stalk a US spy satellite (USA 245). As a reminder, the probe was originally propelled by another Russian satellite called Kosmos-2542 in December 2019 (Zak 2021a). Although the Kosmos-2543 test is unique, Grush suggests that the object "may be more insidious than just another inspector satellite" (2020). Such developments illustrate the thin line that grey zone activities imply. According to Podvig, such activities indicate that "Russia has an active program or several programs to develop a capability to approach and inspect orbital objects" (2021, 42).

Electronic and Cyber Counterspace Technologies

For Russian military forces, electronic counterspace technologies have the advantage of targeting the electromagnetic spectrum through which space systems transmit and receive data. In concrete terms, this allows jamming devices to interfere with communications to or from satellites by generating noise in the same radio frequency band. One key area for priority development is Moscow's use of space to increase its EW capabilities, such as jamming enemy satellites and communications (Hendrickx 2020). According to McDermott, "this is rooted in the belief the wars of the future will witness a concerted effort to deny effective communications to enemy forces by targeting space-based assets" (2020a).

Recent development programs include the Tirada-2, a mobile jamming system that may suppress space communications. The Bylina-MM, a ground-based mobile system with a focus on jamming satellite communication channels, is another EW system in development. Bylina includes an automated system that can recognize assets and determine how to attack them. Finally, Russia also reportedly has two radar jammers—Krasukha-2 and Krasukha-4—which may be capable of interfering with radar reconnaissance satellites (Harrison, Johnson, and Young 2021).

Another hybrid warfare tactic that Russian military forces could deploy into space might be cyber counter-technologies. Doing so has the advantage of diluting the responsibility of the entity responsible for its use. Indeed, accurate and timely attribution of cyberattacks can be difficult because attackers can use a variety of methods to conceal their identity, such as using hijacked servers to launch an attack (Harrison, Johnson, and Young 2021). In that case, cyberattacks target the data, and the systems that use, transmit, and control the flow of data.

SPACE AS AN INTEGRATED OBJECT OF RUSSIA'S GEOPOLITICAL AND STRATEGIC AMBITIONS

Finally, it is helpful to also understand the role that space plays in Russia's broader standing and objectives in the international system.

The Multidimensional Integration of the Defense System

As previously mentioned, Russian military doctrine is intertwined to respond to the multifaceted challenges introduced by modern warfare. The concept is to design an integrated defense, particularly with aerospace defense forces. The integration of the Russian military infrastructure allows dealing with the threat of an enemy as a system (Bowen 2020).

In this overall idea of an integrated defense system, Russian military theorists acknowledge that the implementation of network-centric capabilities in Russian military forces will encompass a change in the stance of the military leadership at all levels (Kiselev 2017). First, this new integrated system is shaped to form an automated infrastructure and to operate in a single information space. As Revaitis observes, Russia tested in Syria "the capabilities of network-centric warfare by conducting a joint air-space-navy operation" (2020, 15). To put it another way, Russian military operations in the Middle East since 2015 provide a theatre to show this modernization, which also comprises further developing modern means of surveillance and reconnaissance to fill the modernized telecommunications networks. It also means populating the armed forces with "sufficient numbers of high-precision weapons" (McDermott 2020b). Consequently, innovation of the defense system is a prerequisite for the comprehensive modernization of the Russian army and directly influences military space programs.

The Russian political and military leadership has performed a central role in promoting innovation, overriding institutional conservatism, and increasing the responsiveness of the extensive defense sector bureaucracy since sweeping military reforms were set in motion in 2008. The basic principle for supporting innovation in the Russian defense sector has been entrenched "in the traditional, centralized state-driven top-down model, albeit with some adjustments" (Zysk 2021, 14). From a double emulation, of the United States and China, the civil-military integration allows connecting the commercial, scientific, and technological dimensions (Zysk 2021). Advanced technological development programs allowed an incremental change, leading to a gradual evolution in the character of Russian warfare. The incorporation of new technologies from the Fourth Industrial Revolution—known as 4IR technologies (artificial intelligence, robotics, etc.)—changes the architecture of defense and shifts it to a complete and multidimensional integration model. This evolution constitutes a strategic and operational improvement to the existing Russian defense infrastructure.

Indeed, this infrastructure transformation responds to the need to improve Russian intelligence, surveillance, and reconnaissance (ISR) capabilities, critical in the defense space program, which capitalizes on the Soviet legacy. Russian authorities are mostly building on old programs from the USSR, including a positioning, navigation, and timing (PNT) system, robust communications, and ISR satellites. As McDermott notes, "an integrated communications model is gradually becoming a more realistic prospect for the Russian military" (2020b), which contains a plan to entirely digitize the mobile command post in the near future. Moscow's military exploitation of space is rooted in its wider drive to strengthen Russian ISR capabilities in support of military activities.

Specifically, the Russian military space program involves technical developments, which seek to increase the accuracy and targeting of conventional precision strikes.

Toward a Strategic Nexus: The Case of the Arctic Region

During the Cold War, the Arctic gained a strategic dimension in which the USSR and the United States pursued their military confrontation. The USSR established airbases, radar stations, and anti-aircraft batteries to protect its northern flank. During this time, the North Pole was considered the shortest route for their strategic weapons (Aliyev 2019). After the Cold War and the crisis years, Russia's approach to the Arctic became firmly rooted in its overarching national security objectives. Russia hosts over 80 percent of its sea-based nuclear capabilities along the Kola Peninsula, next to the Barents sea. The Arctic plays a central role in Russia's strategic deterrence posture, while Minoborony retains a large influence in structuring and organizing Russian presence in the polar region. The growing significance of this area in the last decades all fits together with the space program backed by the ministry. While Moscow supports large development plans in the Arctic, including the Northern Sea Route (NSR), Russia's military buildup in the Arctic along its northern border is consistent with its national security doctrine and defense strategy (Hersman, Brewer, and Simon 2021).

Since the mid-2000s, the new Arctic strategy supported by the Russian authorities is based once again on the Soviet legacy. Echoing the space field, the Artic follows a similar track in which Soviet infrastructure allows for military redeployment. As a result, Russia has reactivated over fifty Soviet-era military bases in the Arctic, including ten radar stations and thirteen airbases (Hersman, Brewer, and Simon 2021). The Plesetsk Cosmodrome remains a critical piece of infrastructure that relies jointly on Arctic and space policies. This Russian spaceport, established in 1957, was used to place mainly military satellites into polar orbit during the Soviet era.

In that framework, the Plesetsk Cosmodrome, located in Mirny, Arkhangelsk Oblast, is mainly dedicated to launching military satellites. However, this Russian spaceport also provides a strategic pillar for Russia's geopolitical ambitions (Vidal 2021). All combined, the modernization of military infrastructure (naval, aerospace, land) in the Arctic region is a priority of the Russian government. The significance of this ground infrastructure is far-reaching in maintaining the advancement of the space program. Among those programs, launching and testing of the new launcher vehicle, Angara, at the Plesetsk Cosmodrome is central. In a transitional regime and waiting for the entry into operation of the Vostochny Cosmodrome, the Arctic spaceport was modernized in 2014 and bridges the infrastructure gap to meet the specifications for the commissioning of new launchers (Zak 2020c).

The same strategic ground infrastructure also allows the Russian Ministry of Defense to pursue the completion of military satellite constellations. Among diverse satellite programs, GLONASS remains a priority. Russian forces are proceeding in progressive replacement of the older generation GLONASS-M with new navigation satellites

GLONASS-K (Luzin 2021a). Other satellites have also been tested, often for military purposes. In September 2021, the Soyuz rocket sent a classified payload into orbit—the first Razbeg imaging satellite, also known as Kosmos-2551. The spacecraft was initially supposed to be in a near-polar orbit for reconnaissance purposes but aborted to adjust its orbit (Zak 2021b). The failed spy satellite was finally de-orbited and crashed back to Earth on October 20, 2021 (Wall 2021). In fact, the main advantage of sending spacecraft into orbit from the Arctic region relates to the polar orbit. This is because, over time, the Earth "rotates underneath the spacecraft and allows the entire planet to be visible" (Howell 2021).

Finally, Russia's efforts to improve its anti-access/area-denial systems and monitoring and surveillance capabilities increase interoperability between the Arctic region and space. For instance, the new Orion-3 UAV program is part of this security trend. This UAV can be equipped with a satellite terminal, which will allow the vehicle to be controlled and to receive information from anywhere in the world (Dmitrak 2021). With regard to the Arctic region, this new UAV is able to sustain monitoring operations of the NSR and bolster an integrated security approach in the northernmost area.

Moving Away from the United States, toward a Chinese Orbit

Since the 1990s, the relationship between the United States and Russia in the space sector has been commercial. For two decades, the Russian federal space agency sold seats to NASA to send US astronauts to the International Space Station (ISS). In 2020, this business partnership came to an end, while practical cooperation continues, such as scientific exchanges and cooperation on the ISS. The end of the contractual relationship opens new challenges and opportunities for the Russian space program, as ways must be found to support Roscosmos's ambitions.

Among the alternatives, Russia is moving closer to China, which appears to be a cornerstone of this strategic renewal (see Pekkanen, this volume). The rapprochement between Russia and China in the space domain covers multiple layers: diplomatic, scientific, industrial, and military. On the diplomatic side, Moscow and Beijing jointly coordinate their bilateral channel to work on a treaty on the Prevention of an Arms Race in Outer Space (PAROS). In 2014, they submitted a new draft Treaty on the Prevention of the Placement of Weapons in Outer Space, the Threat or Use of Force against Outer Space Objects (PPWT). Under the auspices of United Nations (UN) institutions, they introduced Sino-Russian draft provisions, explicitly Article II of the PPWT, "not to place any weapons in outer space" (United Nations 2014). Both countries have advocated a common vision on the peaceful uses of space, including a feasible approach for the international community to prevent the weaponization of an arms race in outer space in a legally binding form.

However, Russia and China voted against a resolution introduced by the United Kingdom in December 2020 that seeks to establish "norms, rules and principles of responsible behaviors" in space, which passed at the UN General Assembly with 164 countries in favor (Bowman and Thompson 2021). While this normative framework could reduce the chances for dangerous miscalculation, both countries continue to work separately on ground-based ASAT missile capability. Furthermore, Russia is helping China's efforts to build an early-warning system, which is part of the ever-expanding "strategic partnership" (Vidal 2021). The system includes a space-based echelon, which comprises satellites that can detect launches of ballistic missiles from the territory of any state in real time. In this respect, the shared vision of Russian- and Chinese space policies and further military integration challenge Western countries. In practical terms, Russian support in developing an early-warning system in China will result in coverage of a large territory from the Arctic to South-East Asia.

The civil scientific and technical Sino-Russian cooperation program also reinforces mutual benefits. Under the guidance of Roscosmos and the China National Space Administration (CNSA), this program includes six sections with working subgroups. Among the cooperation items, both sides agreed to commit to establishing a joint lunar and deep-space data center. Although it is limited to technical cooperation, this five-year agreement includes special materials development, collaboration in satellite systems, Earth remote sensing, and space debris research (Jones 2019). Overall, this bilateral cooperation has afforded Russia the possibility of pursuing the type of ambitious scientific space voyages that the country is no longer able to afford (Kramer and Lee Myers 2021). One of the emblematic projects relates to the moon: Moscow and Beijing are coordinating a series of lunar missions aimed at building a permanent research base on the south pole of the moon by 2030 (Roscosmos 2021). Although there is no clear schedule to implement such a project, Moscow's participation remains questionable with dried up funds.

Finally, while under economic sanctions and without legal access to European and US space technologies, Moscow may rely upon the supply of microelectronics from China (Gorenburg 2020). The country is trying to minimize purchases made out of necessity to avoid technological dependence. Thus, Sino-Russian cooperation in outer space is unlikely to go beyond targeted and largely symbolic collaboration (Luzin 2020d). As Lukin brings to light, the assertive new foreign policy conducted by China may restrict the further deepening of this partnership (2021).

CONCLUSION: RUSSIA, A TROUBLEMAKER IN THE PEACEFUL USE OF OUTER SPACE?

The apparent military turn of space activities, taken by Russian authorities, needs to be understood in its historical and contemporary context. First, the origins of the Soviet space program were of a military nature. To put it another way, what we are observing today is a return to the basics. Moscow's space posture reflects the principal foreign policy trend that has taken shape in the last decade—further decoupling from the West. In the context of the Russian invasion of Ukraine, the relationships between Russian and Western powers crossed the point of no return, putting an end to the post–Cold War period. The emerging geopolitical transformations will directly affect space security architectures. But so far, the future of Russia's position in outer space is entirely open, and it is unclear whether Russia will pursue responsible conduct or dive toward becoming a pirate state.

If the prediction of Roscosmos's former chief Rogozin that future wars will happen in space is accurate, Russia might enter the space competition between major powers for military-technology superiority (Misnik 2021). There is also the possibility of a Russian grey zone strategy, which will ultimately undermine "strengthening regulatory arrangements and establishing norms of responsible behaviour" (Davis 2021). Given these possibilities, the question is: Does Russia want to be a normative power or a disruptive power in space security? Although this remains an open question, Moscow intends to prevent a forceful confrontation in outer space. In recent years, Russian diplomats have expressed their support for shaping tailored practices that can prevent a military confrontation in outer space (Ivanov 2020). As some observers have reminded us, Russia has expressed an interest in limiting the use of force in space (Podvig 2021).

To build an architecture for sustaining space security, a diplomatic encounter should be undertaken between NATO countries and Russia, while recognizing that the participation of China is henceforth essential. Clearly, though, future space security architectures will remain heavily affected by the deteriorating international context . Despite all that, the introduction of UN Resolution 75/36 into the General Assembly in December 2020 is a starting point in designing a global space security body (United Nations 2020). However, structural discrepancies persist between the United States and Russia. While the United States, with the support of its allies, prioritizes the ASAT threat for space-based objects, Russia focuses on ballistic missile defense and "the potential orbiting of weapons in outer space, including those that could strike objects on Earth" (West and Vyse 2022, 16). In a world driven by great power confrontation, Russia carefully conceived and implemented military capabilities to reinforce space deterrence in a similar way to nuclear deterrence in the past.

References

Aliberti, Marco, and Ksenia Lisitsyna. 2019. *Russia's Posture in Space: Prospects for Europe.* Cham, Switzerland: Springer.

Aliyev, Nurlan. 2019. "Russia's Military Capabilities in the Arctic." International Centre for Defence and Security. June 25, 2019. https://icds.ee/en/russias-military-capabilities-in-the-arctic/.

Berger, Eric. 2021a. "Russia's Space Chief Wishes His Oligarchs Invested In Space Like Branson and Musk." *Ars Technica*. July 13, 2021. https://arstechnica.com/science/2021/07/russias-space-chief-wishes-his-oligarchs-invested-in-space-like-branson-and-musk/.

Berger, Eric. 2021b. "Putin Slashes Russia's Space Budget and Says He Expects Better Results." *Ars Technica*. October 8, 2021. https://arstechnica.com/science/2021/10/putin-slashes-russias-space-budget-and-says-he-expects-better-results/.

Bowen, Andrew. 2020. "Russian Armed Forces: Military Doctrine and Strategy." Congressional Research Service. https://sgp.fas.org/crs/row/IF11625.pdf.

Bowman, Bradley, and Jared Thompson. 2021. "Russia and China Seek to Tie America's Hands in Space." *Foreign Policy*. March 31, 2021. https://foreignpolicy.com/2021/03/31/russia-china-space-war-treaty-demilitarization-satellites/.

Davis, Malcom. 2021. "The Commercial Advantage in Space's Grey Zone." *The Strategist*. June 16, 2021. https://www.aspistrategist.org.au/the-commercial-advantage-in-spaces-grey-zone/.

Dohan Michael. 1976. "The Economic Origins of Soviet Autarky 1927/28 -1934." *Slavic Review* 35, no. 4: 603–35. https://doi.org/10.2307/2495654.

Dmitrak, Natalya. 2021. "Uzhe Pyat Let V Nebe. Kakovui Vozmozhnosti I Perspektivui Rossiĭskogo Bespilotnika *Orion*." *TASS*. October 11, 2021. https://tass.ru/armiya-i-opk/12610939.

Egorov, Vitali. 2018. "Commercial Alternatives: The Issues and Challenges of the Russian Space Industry—Part III." *Spacewatch Global*. March 26, 2018. https://spacewatch.global/2018/03/commercial-alternatives-issues-challenges-russian-space-industry-part-iii/.

Federal Security Service of the Russian Federation. 2021. Prikaz Federal'noĭ sluzhbȳ bezopasnosti Rossiĭskoĭ Federatsii ot 28.09.2021 № 379. *Rossijkaya Gazeta*. October 1, 2021. https://rg.ru/2021/10/01/fsb-prikaz379-site-dok.html.

Gerovitch, Slava. 2015. *Soviet Space Mythologies: Public Images, Private Memories, and the Making of a Cultural Identity*. Pittsburgh, PA: University of Pittsburgh Press.

Goble, Paul. 2021. "For Russians, Space Program Measures Status of Putin's Authoritarian Modernization." *Eurasia Daily Monitor* 18, no. 113 (July). https://jamestown.org/program/for-russians-space-program-measures-status-of-putins-authoritarian-modernization/.

Golts, Aleksandr. 2018. "Determinants of Russian Foreign Policy: Realpolitik, Militarism and the Vertical of Power." DGAPKompakt 19: 9–12.

Gorenburg, Dmitry. 2020. "An Emerging Strategic Partnership: Trends in Russia-China Military Cooperation." Marshall Center, *Security Insights* 54. https://www.marshallcenter.org/en/publications/security-insights/emerging-strategic-partnership-trends-russia-china-military-cooperation-0.

Götz, Elias. 2016. "Neorealism and Russia's Ukraine Policy, 1991–Present." *Contemporary Politics* 22, no. 3: 301–23. http://dx.doi.org/10.1080/13569775.2016.1201312.

Götz, Elias, and Neil MacFarlane. 2019. "Russia's Role In World Politics: Power, Ideas, and Domestic Influences." *International Politics* 56: 713–25. https://doi.org/10.1057/s41311-018-0162-0.

Grush, Loren. 2020. "Russia Just Tested Satellite-Destroying Tech in Space, US Space Command Claims." *The Verge*. July 23, 2020. https://www.theverge.com/2020/7/23/21335506/russia-anti-satellite-weapon-test-kosmos-2543.

Harford, James. 1997. *Korolev: How One Man Masterminded the Soviet Drive to Beat America to the Moon*. New York: John Wiley & Sons.

Harrison, Todd, Kaitlyn Johnson, and Makena Young. 2021. *Defense against the Dark Arts in Space. Protecting Space Systems from Counterspace Weapons*. Washington, DC: Center for Strategic and International Studies.

Harrison, Todd, Kaitlyn Johnson, Joe Moye, and Makena Young. 2021. *Space Threat Assessment 2021*. Washington, DC: Center for Strategic and International Studies.

Hendrickx, Bart. 2020. "Russia Gears Up For Electronic Warfare In Space." *The Space Review*. October 26, 2020. https://www.thespacereview.com/article/4056/1.

Herd, Graeme. 2021. "Russian Space Systems And The Risk Of Weaponizing Space." In *Russia's Global Reach. A Security and Statecraft Assessment*, edited by Graeme Herd, 1–8. Garmisch-Partenkirchen: The Marshall Center.

Hersman, Rebecca, Eric Brewer, and Maxwell Simon. 2021. "Strategic Stability and Competition in the Arctic." *CSIS Briefs*. January 6, 2021. https://www.csis.org/analysis/deep-dive-debrief-strategic-stability-and-competition-arctic.

Howell, Elizabeth. 2021. "Russian Soyuz Rocket Sends Classified Military Payload to Orbit." *Space.com*. September 11, 2021. https://www.space.com/russian-soyuz-rocket-launches-classified-payload.

Interfax. 2021. "Voennȳe RF Podtverdili, Chto Sbili Sovetskiĭ Sputnik V Khode Ispȳtanii." *Interfax*. November 16, 2021. https://www.interfax.ru/russia/803293.

Ivanov, Vladimir. 2020. "O Slezhenii Za Kosmicheskoĭ Obstanovkoĭ Rasskazal Nachal'nik Gts RKO." *Nezavisimoe*. March 15, 2020. https://nvo.ng.ru/nvo/2020-03-15/100_space_150320.html.

Jones, Andrew. 2019. "China, Russia to Cooperate on Lunar Orbiter, Landing Missions." *SpaceNews*. September 9, 2019. https://spacenews.com/china-russia-to-cooperate-on-lunar-orbiter-landing-missions/.

Khan Afridi, Manzoor, and Ali Jibran. 2018. "Russian Response to Syrian Crisis: A Neorealist Perspective." *Strategic Studies* 38, 2: 56–70.

Kiselev, Valery. 2017. "K Kakim Voĭnam Neobkhodimo Gotovit' Vooruzhenneȳ Silȳ Rosssii." *Voennaya Mysl'*, no. 3: 37–46.

Kohonen, Iina. 2009. "The Space Race and Soviet Utopian Thinking." *The Sociological Review* 57, no. 1: 114–31.

Kramer, Andrew, and Steven Lee Myers. 2021. "Russia, Once a Space Superpower, Turns to China for Missions." *New York Times*. June 15, 2021. https://www.nytimes.com/2021/06/15/world/asia/china-russia-space.html.

Laruelle, Marlène, and Jean Radvanyi. 2019. *Understanding Russia: The Challenges of Transformation*. Lanham, MD: Rowman & Littlefield.

Lavrov, Anton. 2017. "Russia's GLONASS Satellite Constellation." *Moscow Defense Brief* no. 4. https://bmpd.livejournal.com/2845443.html?comments.

Lukin, Alexander. 2021. "Have We Passed the Peak of Sino-Russian Rapprochement?" *The Washington Quarterly* 44, no.3: 34–46. https://doi.org/10.1080/0163660X.2021.1970904.

Luzin, Pavel. 2020a. "Russia Is Behind in Military Space Capabilities, but that Only Drives its Appetite." *Defense News*. April 2, 2020. https://www.defensenews.com/opinion/commentary/2020/04/02/russia-is-behind-in-military-space-capabilities-but-that-only-drives-its-appetite/.

Luzin, Pavel. 2020b. "Endless Rumbles Of Roscosmos Reform." *Riddle*. August 26, 2020. https://www.ridl.io/en/endless-rumbles-of-roscosmos-reform/.

Luzin, Pavel. 2020c. "Sanctions and the Russian Defence Industry." *Riddle*. October 30, 2020. https://www.ridl.io/en/sanctions-and-the-russian-defence-industry/.

Luzin, Pavel. 2020d. "In Search of New Partners in Space." *Riddle*. December 11, 2020. https://www.ridl.io/en/in-search-of-new-partners-in-space/.

Luzin, Pavel. 2021a. "GLONASS Program for 2021–2030." *Eurasia Daily Monitor* 18, no. 12 (January). https://jamestown.org/program/glonass-program-for-2021-2030/.

Luzin, Pavel. 2021b. "Russian Astronautics: A Fresh Start." *Riddle*. July 7, 2021. https://www.ridl.io/en/russian-astronautics-a-fresh-start/.

McDermott; Roger. 2020a. "Russia's Military Exploitation of Outer Space." *Eurasia Daily Monitor* 17, no. 47 (April). https://jamestown.org/program/russias-military-exploitation-of-outer-space/.

McDermott; Roger. 2020b. "Tracing Russia's Path to Network-Centric Military Capability." *Eurasia Daily Monitor*. December 9, 2020. https://jamestown.org/program/tracing-russias-path-to-network-centric-military-capability/.

Meshcheryakov, S.D., M.T. Kaĭralapov, and A.A. Sinikov. 2021. "Vozdushno-Kosmicheskie Silў V Strategicheskom Sderzhivanii: Neobkhodimost' I Dostatochnost'." *Voennaya Mysl'* no. 11: 22–28.

Milesi-Ferretti, Gian Maria. 2022. "Russia's External Position: Does Financial Autarky Protect Against Sanctions?" *Brookings Institution*. March 3, 2022. https://www.brookings.edu/blog/up-front/2022/03/03/russias-external-position-does-financial-autarky-protect-against-sanctions/.

Ministry of Defense of the Russian Federation. 2015. "Novii Vid Booruzhennykh Syl RF—Vozdushno-kosmicheskie Sily – Pristupil K Neseniyu Boevogo Dezhurstva po Vozdushno-kosmicheskoĭ Oborone." Minoborony Rossi. August 3. https://z.mil.ru/spec_mil_oper/news/more.htm?id=12047166@egNews.

Mirovalev, Mansur. 2021. "The Oligarch Behind Russia's Failing Space Program." *WhoWhatWhy*. September 9, 2021. https://whowhatwhy.org/politics/international/the-oligarch-behind-russias-failing-space-program/.

Misnik, Lidiya. 2021. "«Voĭna Budushchego Nachnet-Sya V Kosmose». Bol'shoe Interv'yu Dmitriya Rogozina." *Gazeta*. August 29, 2021. https://www.gazeta.ru/politics/2021/08/29_a_13928414.shtml?updated.

Moltz, James Clay. 2019. "The Changing Dynamics of Twenty-First-Century Space Power." *Journal of Strategic Security* 12, no. 1: 15–43.

Monaghan, Andrew. 2012. "The *Vertikal*: Power and Authority in Russia." *International Affairs* 88, no. 1: 1–16. https://doi.org/10.1111/j.1468-2346.2012.01053.x.

Panda, Ankit. 2021. "The Dangerous Fallout of Russia's Anti-Satellite Missile Test." Carnegie. November 17, 2021. https://carnegieendowment.org/2021/11/17/dangerous-fallout-of-russia-s-anti-satellite-missile-test-pub-85804.

Podvig, Pavel. 2021. "Russian Space Systems and the Risk of Weaponizing Space." In *Advanced Military Technology in Russia. Capabilities and Implications*, edited by Samuel Bendett et al., 34–46. London: The Royal Institute of International Affairs.

Revaitis, Algirdas. 2020. "Russian Perception of its Network-Centric Warfare Capabilities in Syria." *Journal of Baltic Security* 6, no. 1: 1–18. https://doi.org/10.2478/jobs-2020-0003.

Ria Novosti. 2021. "V Rossii Zakruivaet-Sya Kompaniya, Planirovavshaya Razvivat Kosmicheskiĭ Turizm." *Ria Novosti*. April 6, 2021. https://ria.ru/20210406/kompaniya-1604377528.html.

Rivera, David W., and Sharon Werning Rivera. 2018. "The Militarization of the Russian Elite under Putin." *Problems of Post-Communism* 65, no. 4: 221–32. https://doi.org/10.1080/10758216.2017.1295812.

Romanova, Tatiana. 2012. "Neoclassical Realism and Today's Russia." *Russia in Global Affairs* 3. https://eng.globalaffairs.ru/articles/neoclassical-realism-and-todays-russia/.

Roscosmos. 2017. "Roskosmos. Obsuzhdenie Strategii Razvitiya Goskorporatsii." Roscosmos Corporation. March 31, 2017. https://www.roscosmos.ru/23380/.

Roscosmos. 2021. "Rossiya I Kitaĭ Podpisali Memorandum O Sozdanii Lunnoĭ Stantsii." Roscosmos Corporation. March 9, 2021. https://www.roscosmos.ru/30248/.

Siddiqi, Asif A. 2010. *The Red Rockets' Glare: Spaceflight and the Soviet Imagination, 1857–1957.* New York: Cambridge University Press.

Skvortsov, Vadim. 2018. "Chto Ne Tak V Kosmicheskoj Strategii Rossii." Vc.ru. July 20, 2018. https://vc.ru/future/42276-chto-ne-tak-v-kosmicheskoy-strategii-rossii.

Stoner, Kathryn. 2021. *Russia Resurrected: Its Power and Purpose in a New Global Order.* New York: Oxford University Press.

Stronski, Paul. 2019. "Late to the Party: Russia's Return to Africa." Carnegie Endowment for International Peace. October 16, 2019. https://carnegieendowment.org/2019/10/16/late-to-party-russia-s-return-to-africa-pub-80056.

SWF. 2020. June 30. "SWF Releases Updated Compilation of Anti-satellite Testing in Space." Secure World Foundation.

SWF. 2022. April. *Global Counterspace Capabilities: An Open Assessment.* Secure World Foundation.

UCS. 2022. "UCS Satellite Database." Union of Concerned Scientists. Last updated January 1, 2022. https://www.ucsusa.org/resources/satellite-database.

United Nations. 2014. "Draft Treaty on the Prevention of the Placement of Weapons in Outer Space, the Threat or Use of Force against Outer Space Objects." Conference on Disarmament, June 12, 2014. https://undocs.org/pdf?symbol=en/CD/1985.

United Nations. 2020. "Reducing Space Threats Through Norms, Rules and Principles of Responsible Behaviours." UN Resolution 75/36, General Assembly, December 16, 2020. https://digitallibrary.un.org/record/3895440?ln=en.

Vciom. 2021. "Den Kosmonavtiki." *Vciom Novosti.* April 12, 2021. https://wciom.ru/analytical-reviews/analiticheskii-obzor/den-kosmonavtiki.

Ven Bruusgaard, Kristin. 2016. "Russian Strategic Deterrence." *Survival: Global Politics and Strategy* 58, no. 4: 7–26. https://doi.org/10.1080/00396338.2016.1207945.

Vidal, Florian. 2021. *Russia's Space Policy: The Path of Decline?* Paris: French Institute of International Relations.

Wall, Mike. 2021. "Failed Russian Spy Satellite Falls to Earth in Brilliant Fireball." Space.com. October 20, 2021. https://www.space.com/russian-spy-satellite-kosmos-2551-fireball-video.

West, Jessica, and Lauren Vyse. 2022. *Arms Control in Outer Space: Status, Timeline and Analysis.* Waterloo, Ontario: Project Ploughshares.

Zak, Anatoly. 2020a. "Everything You Need to Know about Russia's (Possibly Fictional) Super Heavy Rocket." *Popular Mechanics.* February 3, 2020. https://www.popularmechanics.com/space/rockets/a30705512/yenisei-rocket-russia/.

Zak, Anatoly. 2020b. "Russia Reveals a Formidable Nuclear-Powered Space Tug." Russianspaceweb.com. Last modified August 25, 2021. https://www.russianspaceweb.com/tem.html.

Zak, Anatoly. 2020c. "Angara Launch Complex in Plesetsk." Russianspaceweb.com. Last modified December 21, 2020. http://www.russianspaceweb.com/plesetsk_angara.html.

Zak, Anatoly. 2021a. "Soyuz-2-1v Launches a Possible Military Inspector Satellite." Russianspaceweb.com. Last modified August 25, 2021. http://www.russianspaceweb.com/cosmos-2542.html#2021.

Zak, Anatoly. 2021b. "Soyuz-2-1v Rocket Launches Military Payload." Russianspaceweb.com. Last modified October 20, 2021. http://russianspaceweb.com/emka2.html.

Zak, Anatoly. 2021c. "Russia Launches a Missile-Detection Satellite." Russianspaceweb.com. Last modified November 28, 2021. http://russianspaceweb.com/eks5.html.

Zysk, Katerina. 2021. "Military R&D, Innovation and Breakthrough Technologies." In *Advanced Military Technology in Russia: Capabilities and Implications*, edited by Samuel Bendett et al., 11–22. London: The Royal Institute of International Affairs.

CHAPTER 18

JAPAN'S GRAND STRATEGY IN OUTER SPACE

SAADIA M. PEKKANEN

THIS essay illuminates Japan's grand strategy in outer space affairs. Reflecting cross-cutting definitions and approaches, grand strategy is adapted here to refer to all the diverse means by which a state produces prosperity and security for national ends in a strategic domain (Balzacq, Dombrowski, and Reich 2019, 5–9, citing Posen, 6; Wirtz 2009, 13–15, 20–25; Ripsman 2019, 290–93; Balzacq and Krebs 2021, 1–6). The conceptual lens of grand strategy has already emerged in some major historical and international relations works on Japan's foreign and security policies (Samuels 2007; Kawasaki 2012; Michishita and Samuels 2012; Oros 2017; Paine 2017; Michishita 2022; Hughes 2022a; Green 2022). It has also been integrated in works on technology and innovation, which highlight a range of material and ideational elements that can affect prospects for state power, interests, and standing in international politics over time (Samuels 1994; Ripsman and Kovac 2021, 213–14; Fischer, Gilli, and Gilli 2021; Cantelmo and Kreps 2021).

I extend the concept of grand strategy specifically to Japanese statecraft in the contemporary space domain, which is marked by a rising number of spacefaring countries, unprecedented commercial trends, and a slide toward weaponization (Pekkanen 2019). Both established and emerging powers are responding to the threats, challenges, opportunities, and uncertainties brought about by these deeply intertwined realities. The question is how they are doing so. The focus here is on how Japan is responding to the promise and perils of the new space realities and whether grand strategy analytics and its own historical patterns give us a coherent way to conceptualize Japan's broader conduct in the contemporary space domain. Balancing, bandwagoning, hedging, buck-passing, integrating, or being reactive, isolationist, internationalist, and neutral, for example, are responses that do not, to my mind, quite capture what Japan is doing across the board in the unfurling space realities today (Calder 1988; Heginbotham and Samuels 2002; Lind 2004; Samuels 2007; Matsuda 2012; Sahashi 2017; Koga 2018; Liff 2019; Midford 2020, 2022; Michishita 2022; Green 2022). We need a new way to see

Japan's grand strategy to produce prosperity and security in its own interests in the contested and competitive politics of outer space. I assess that the Japanese state is doing that by proactive positioning on all fronts in the space domain—economic, military, diplomatic.

The remainder of this essay is in three parts. First, to frame the narrative, I draw together elements of grand strategy thinking that comports with my understanding of both the Japanese state and the realities of the space domain. Second, within that domain, I turn to the evidence, showing how Japan's all-fronts proactive positioning plays out in its foreign relations in practice. Third, I end with some takeaways for what allies, rivals, and others concerned with stability in the international relations of space may expect from the Japanese state in the years ahead.

GRAND STRATEGY AND THE JAPANESE STATE IN THE SPACE DOMAIN

In this section, I bring distinct but isolated sets of scholarship into an interdisciplinary conversation with one another—grand strategy, Japan, and space security. My goal is to extract some connections between the grand strategy works and the conduct of the Japanese state in the contemporary space domain.

A good place to begin is with the meaning of grand strategy, which has long been a "complex and multilayered thing" in theoretical and analytical works on the subject (Kennedy 1991, 4). Grand strategy can mean different things to different people, such as whether a military-centric conceptualization—aptly put as the "obsession with the battlefield"—is or is not even the proper scope for thinking about grand strategy over time and domains (Murray and Grimsley 1994, 4; Martel 2015, 24–27; Milevski 2016, 1–12; Balzacq, Dombrowski, and Reich 2019, 5–6). Some say grand strategy is defined as the "theory, or logic, that binds a country's highest interests to its daily interactions with the world" (Brands 2012, 3). Doing grand strategy means that states are not simply reacting to every little dot that may blossom or erupt but operating under some "intellectual architecture" that guides them in always uncertain and sometimes dangerous times (Brands 2014, 1, 3). Others opine it is the intermingling of military and nonmilitary elements to preserve and enhance a nation's long-term interests, done in such a way that the state manages to align its boundless aspirations with its limited capabilities whether in wartime or peacetime (Kennedy 1991, 5; Gaddis 2018, 21).

Grand strategy is not invented all at once, and a long learning process may well be necessary to survive and outlive others; those who did both historically for long stretches of time improvised strategic responses to a wide variety of threats drawing on their reservoir of military expertise, intelligence, and diplomacy as appropriate (Luttwak 2009, 11–14). In the long sweep of its history, Japan too improvised and adapted in tune with external competition and threats (Green 2022, 16–44). Aside from scope and applicability, there are also questions about the continuing analytical and practical utility of the idea of grand strategy (Milevski 2016, 143–53; Brands and Feaver 2021, 561–71). Mindful therefore of its frailties in meaning and practice, we need to cast a very pragmatic eye on its prospects in the space domain because

> grand strategy is an inherently difficult endeavor that will tax the abilities of even the most capacious leader. It requires a holistic view of interests, threats, and re- sources, as well as an understanding of the multidimensional yet finite nature of power. Grand strategy demands the ability to make sense of a multitude of com- plicated and confusing international events, and an awareness of how a country's responses to these events may complement or contradict one another. Doing grand strategy also necessitates the vision to link today's policies to a country's highest and most enduring interests, and the willingness to make hard decisions about priorities and trade-offs. In sum, grand strategy is not simply a struggle against one enemy or another; it is a fight against the complexity, disorder, and distraction that inevi- tably clutter the global scene. It is bound to be an exacting task, one full of potential pitfalls. (Brands 2012, 10–11)

The real-world chaos and complexity captured in this framing should be kept firmly in mind in the unfolding great-power competition in the international order today in which all states have to strategize (Brands, Feaver, and Inboden 2023). This competition also matters in the contemporary space domain in which Japan is seeking to position. There is no easy way to describe the domain, but I assess that decision-makers have to pay attention to three deeply intertwined military and nonmilitary trends that echo the grand strategy debates noted above (Baiocchi and Wesler 2015; Pekkanen 2019; Masson-Zwaan 2019).

One is *democratization*, which means space activities are expanding to a growing number of states and non-state actors spread all around the world. The rising number of participants, and their varied interests, complicates the prospects for building con- sensus on the underlying rules and principles about how to behave and engage in space. Another trend, *commercialization*, links the historic involvement of private actors and individuals in outer space activities to the present ambitions of a whole new genera- tion of entrepreneurs intent on profiting in commercial markets all the way to off-world settlements. It draws attention to the unprecedented innovations that promise great prosperity, but also to how these developments test and pinpoint controversies in ex- isting principles for safe, sustainable, and secure operations in space. A final significant trend also with deep roots in the past, *militarization*, layers in challenges because of the underlying dual-use nature of space technologies that have historically cut across com- mercial and military realms. This duality poses new challenges for peaceful prospects in outer space, given the intensifying geopolitical rivalries that are moving things toward space *weaponization*, and the incentives for states to shift the balances of space power in their favor to gain relative advantages over their rivals.

Even established spacefaring countries find it challenging to understand, much less respond, to these intermingled realities in the space domain. Officially, for most of the postwar period Japan had normative and constitutional constraints that were meant to restrict the military use of space. But Japan today is one of the world's preeminent space-faring countries, with significant depth spanning civilian, commercial, and military space technologies. Many analysts, myself included, have covered these developments and their significance for Japan's standing in the space domain and, from there, the direction of its space security policies (Oros 2007; Pekkanen and Kallender-Umezu 2010; 2011; Moltz 2012, 43–69; Martin 2015; 2021: Kallender 2016; Kallender and Hughes 2019; Fatton 2020; Pekkanen 2020; 2021b; 2022). Japan has full spectrum capabilities in liquid and solid-fuel rockets, satellites and spacecraft, and deep space probes with counterspace capabilities that can travel billions of miles to and from Earth. Here, I certainly keep an eye on these dual-use capabilities as they are an integral part of Japan's space security narrative over time, but I fold them into the broader analytical challenge of using a grand strategy lens to understand its responses.

There have been visible transformations in Japan's state apparatus to better deal with the many trends unfurling in outer space affairs. These transformations are layered in with long-evolving institutional changes that have fortified top-down cabinet-level policy-making and greater prime ministerial power, which in reality should be thought of as more punctuated than linear in their progression in domestic politics (Krauss and Pekkanen 2011, 226–59; Shinoda 2022; Mulgan 2022) Among the most noted changes is the new institutional apparatus for national security decision-making. A decade-long search for a "control tower" to reinforce, above all, the political leadership of the prime minister's office in foreign and security policy-making led to the creation of the first-ever National Security Council (NSC) in late 2013 (Fukushima and Samuels 2018, 782; Liff 2018, 259–67). With it came also the creation of the country's first National Security Strategy, an "authoritative Cabinet-promulgated document," which now infuses a whole-of-government approach to Japan's foreign and defense affairs (Liff 2018, 265). As well there followed in 2014 a National Security Secretariat in the Cabinet Secretariat to administer and coordinate all inter-agency processes to fortify the new changes.

Importantly, Japan's institutional innovations in the space domain predate these broader changes in the country's foreign and defense policy-making processes. Today, Japan has acquired a space policy-making structure that allows for more coherent national level strategizing than ever before in its postwar history (Aoki 2009; 2011; Suzuki 2015; Fukushima 2017; Takada 2019, 3; Pekkanen, Aoki, and Takatori n.d.). The enactment of the Basic Space Act in 2008 elevated national space policy to a strategic priority, charging the state with the responsibility for promoting systematic and comprehensive measures to advance Japan's space development and use. It also set up the Strategic Headquarters for National Space Policy (Strategic Headquarters) under the Cabinet, chaired by the prime minister with all ministers of state. The Strategic Headquarters acquires advice from a Committee on National Space Policy, coordinates with the National Space Policy Secretariat, and interacts across virtually all ministries and other government agencies such as the Japan Aerospace Exploration Agency (JAXA). It is this state apparatus that is under the spotlight for positioning Japan in the emerging space-related technology frontiers, military realities, and diplomatic interactions.

While the Japanese state is prominent and now has the institutional capacity to set space policy and act in coordinated ways at the highest national levels, this does not mean it is omnipotent, coherent, or effective. One look at the coordination necessary across ministries and agencies, with their own long-standing competences, jurisdictions, and networks should make us circumspect about any such sweeping claims. Among the principal ones involved in the new institutional apparatus for space policy are: the Ministry of Foreign Affairs (MOFA) for international relations; the Ministry of Defense (MOD) for national security and defense; the Ministry of Environment for greenhouse gas observations; the Ministry of Land, Infrastructure, Transport and Tourism (MLIT) for meteorological satellites; the Ministry of Internal Affairs and Communication (MIC) for communications and broadcast; the Ministry of Education, Culture, Sports, Science and Technology (MEXT) for science and technology development; the Ministry of Economy, Trade and Industry (METI) for space industry promotion; the Cabinet Secretariat with the Cabinet Intelligence and Research Office (CIRO) overseeing the Cabinet Satellite Intelligence Center (CSICE) responsible for the information-gathering satellites; and the Cabinet Office overseeing the Quasi-Zenith Satellite System (QZSS), a regional positioning service.

But it is not just the tangible institutional architecture that matters. Focusing on it alone leads to a predictable focus on intra-bureaucratic clashes over jurisdictional lines that divide decision-makers. There are also I believe ideas that unite them, particularly in the face of a slowly building but increasingly uniform understanding of external threats involving the space domain—kinetic and non-kinetic, accidental and deliberate, regional and global (Pekkanen 2022c, 769–71; Pekkanen, this volume). We need to factor in a set of perceptual and ideational elements that influence the responses of space-focused decision-makers, and which have long been noted by Japan scholars in different contexts and over time. Having learned from and contributed to this body of knowledge, I assess there is consistency and continuity to Japanese responses, best characterized as deeply developmental and historically realist (Johnson 1982, 305–24; Samuels 1994; 2007, 7–8, 15–18; Green 1995; Pyle 2007, 41–65; Pempel 2013, 193–97; Pekkanen 2003; 2022; Martin 2021; Govella 2021; Noble 2022; Iida 2022). A certain swirl of elements from these works is germane to my interpretations of Japan's responses related to space activities—developmentalism, industrial policy, competitiveness, power attentiveness, pragmatism, adaptation, autonomy, security-economic linkages, technonationalism, nurturance, diffusion, indigenization, emulation, innovation, for instance.

Building on these material and ideational foundations, I claim that the Japanese state is engaged in proactive positioning on "all fronts" in the space domain. The essence of Japan's grand strategy in outer space comes from the word "kakuhōmen," which I take to be every direction, all quarters. This is what it means in practice: At all times, in every way, by whatever processes necessary and in any forum available, the Japanese state's all-fronts vision keeps it attentive to locking in specific national advantages, big or small, concrete or nebulous. Whenever possible, with whomever is willing, Japan seeks these advantages and remains sensibly attuned to the fact that some will work out over time and others will not. From its actions, we can see that it never dwells, constantly prunes, is consistently aware, and always adapts. It is not omniscient, nor is it impervious to mistakes or poor judgment. It is just watchful of any and all openings that keep its national interests positioned at the cutting edge of developments in the space frontiers, whether those happen to be economic, military, or diplomatic. The Japanese state is not so much sprinting in some finite space race as it is proactively positioning in an unbounded marathon. On that field, it matters less who is first and what was won and more whether Japan is present.

JAPAN'S ALL-FRONTS GRAND STRATEGY IN PRACTICE

Japan may not have named its grand strategy, but every instrument of its national power is proactively positioning on all fronts in, through, and at the nexus of the space domain. This is evident in the country's foreign space relations. Whether in ways or through means that are big or small, deep or shallow, concrete or rhetorical, going back decades or starting now, around us on Earth or aimed at celestial bodies, Japanese statecraft is attentive to all kinds of geoeconomic and geopolitical opportunities with a broad sweep of partners that may serve its national interests. Just how and when they may, in fact, serve national ends may not be clear to the varied decision-makers, but Japan is positioned to be advantaged if and when they do. Not primacy, but presence.

I am mindful that there is a real danger to imputing grand strategy constructs especially in retrospect, and to downplaying the uncertainties and ambiguities that always roil decisions and choices in the thick of things (Murray 2011, 9–11, 21–25). For that reason, while I provide some historical context for each of the economic, military, and diplomatic fronts, I seek to specifically illuminate the more recent or emerging dots within them that reflect decisions aimed at unfolding frontiers—that is, trade and industrial policies aligned, investments made, technologies showcased, markets opened, budgets shaken, projects initiated, missions undertaken, exercises held, instruments signed, declarations made, and so on. Taken together, they are reasonable indicators for how proactive positioning plays out in an all-fronts grand strategy, especially when, as in the space domain, the pathways are uncharted, outcomes are uncertain, and international structural change is the order of the day.

Economic and Technological Front

Japan's interest in proactive positioning at the economic and technological nexus of space is intimately tied to its experiences, culture, and history. As it has confronted wave after wave of technological change over time, its highest priority has always been to remain positioned at whatever that frontier happens to be (Pekkanen 2003, 213). Aside

from situational imperatives, such as those in postwar Japan that reduced it to an economic rubble, this priority also reflects deeply embedded ideas about the role of states
and, of particular interest here, the strategic and ideological uses of technologies, their
interlinkages between civilian and military applications, and the ways their autonomy,
diffusion, and nurturance advances national security (Johnson 1982, 307–8; Samuels
1994, x, 1–56, 337–41). This is the backdrop to a more specific priority of interest today,
space, in which economic and security realities have reinforced the role of the state.

As in other countries, there is also a consensus in Japan that space activities promise
both prosperity and security in a dual-use industry, and that Japanese business and defense stakeholders cannot afford to "miss the opportunities that space offers" (Aoki 2017
[for quote]; Keidanren 2022). Prosperity certainly beckons. The global space industry
is estimated to be around US$370 billion and projected to go to US$1 trillion by 2040
(Euroconsult 2022; Morgan Stanley 2020). But despite decades of efforts at breaking
into global commercial markets, the comparative reality and international prospects are
sobering for Japan. In 2019, the overall sales of Japan's space industry were estimated at
just over US$3 billion; and the activities of the industry's pillars, rockets and satellites,
still remain numerically small relative to global competitors (SJAC 2021, 1; 2022b, 42, 44,
Fig. 6, Fig. 7, Fig. 8, Fig. 9). The industry as a whole is not export driven, and over 95 percent of its demand is generated domestically, with JAXA, other government and public
organizations, as well as satellite communication and broadcasting entities accounting
for roughly two-thirds of the final demand (SJAC 2021, 7–8, Fig. 2, Fig. 2.1; 2022a, 12).

Whether market prospects for Japan will brighten anytime soon remains to be seen.
Meanwhile, as evidenced in an expanding space-focused law and policy framework, the
Japanese state remains as attentive as ever to the nature, direction, and speed of techno-
logical change and what it means for Japan's standing in the international space order.
Beyond the 2008 Basic Space Act, Japan has enacted a Space Activities Act, a Remote
Sensing Data Act, and a Space Resources Act (CO n.d.; Aoki 2017; Pekkanen, Aoki, and
Takatori n.d.). Its latest revisions to the country's Basic Space Plan also shows its awareness of recent conditions that require a priority focus on both economic and national
security, and the ecosystem necessary for continued advancement of space technologies
that cut across civilian, commercial, and military uses (CO 2022). Japan has long marked
the "space industry as a vector for technology development and for international technology cooperation" (Selding 2010). It remains vigilant about competitiveness, but the
industrial policy of its leading economic ministry, METI, is "being harnessed to the
task of protecting strategically vital industrial capacities even if the effect on economic
growth is minimal or even negative" (Noble 2022, 370). The rise of China and the return
of industrial policy, including in the United States and Europe, only legitimates Japan's
focus on fortifying the national space industrial base as part and parcel of its broader attentiveness to economic diplomacy (Solis 2020).

These realities suggest that while the Japanese state is certainly interested in commercial gains and market shares, those are not the only thing it is interested in. Its proactive positioning, on both domestic and international fronts, is driven also by the belief
that spillovers and innovations in the space industry are critical to preserving Japan's

industrial future. JAXA's New Enterprise Promotion Department has been rebranded as the Business Development and Industrial Relations Department; it has officially conceptualized the importance of "spin-off" (linking aerospace technology out to other) and "spin-in" (having non-aerospace technologies linked back in) in its institutional mission for the development, expansion, and utilization of space (JAXA 2022). With one of the smallest space budgets among its global peers over the postwar period, Japan has, compared to its past, recently set a record new space budget at over US$4 billion for space activities (Park 2021). Building on its long-evolving foundational technologies, the budget signals another way Japan is proactively positioning itself in some of the most critical emerging frontiers in space.

Japan is moving to double its space markets by the 2030s, seeking to support concrete new businesses beyond just the hardware of rockets and satellites to those also poised to at the nexus of software frontiers and satellite data that map all human activities on the planet (Nikkei Asia 2017; Pekkanen, Aoki, and Mittleman 2022). Japanese companies at the forefronts of small satellites and big data, such as Axelspace, are prized by the space policy establishment for innovating what may well become a new critical infrastructure for humanity (Axelspace 2022). As such businesses search for use cases for the mountains of data collected, they raise profound questions about the stability and security of all states (Pekkanen 2022a). This includes Japan, where the government is keen on the small satellites frontier but also seeks to screen the leakage of important national data related to military and national security. It is potentially an area where Japan may position itself in the looming global governance challenges.

Positioning Japanese hardware worldwide nevertheless remains a priority item for the whole of the government and is consistent with the long trajectory of Japan's efforts to indigenize space technologies. One endeavor stretches back decades, and eventually became the US-led International Space Station (ISS). Along with the governments of Canada, Russia, and those of the European Space Agency, Japan signed a bilateral agreement with the National Aeronautics and Space Administration (NASA) to provide specific space stations elements, such as a multipurpose experiment module and cargo delivery to and from the station (NASA 1998a; 1998b). Working with foreign space agencies that already had manned space technology, Japan emphasized that it had "absorbed this knowledge, sublimated it, and materialized it" in its own contributions to the ISS (JAXA n.d.).

With those building blocks, Japan is positioned now to move to the post-ISS age, in which the United States is seeking to shape cislunar space, and human and space exploration therein, with principles and innovations empowered by its partners (see Pekkanen, this volume). Japan has signed both the US-led Artemis Accords and the Civil Lunar Gateway Agreement (Foust 2020; 2021). This time around, it is not playing catch-up but is proactively positioning its technologies, such as landers and rovers, as well as its own human capital, in the wide sweep of resulting US missions (JAXA 2021; Nikkei Asia 2022a). One of its leading lunar companies, ispace, has transacted the world's first commercial contract of space resources, to acquire and sell lunar regolith to NASA (Schierholz and Finch 2020; ispace 2022); and the Japanese government has issued its first license in November 2022 under the Space Resources Act enabling ispace to do so (Pekkanen, Aoki, and Takatori n.d.). Japanese astronauts have already been on private SpaceX rockets to the ISS and, if things stay their course, Japan has ensured that at least one will land on the lunar surface (Kyodo 2021; 2022).

With its experiential and technological base, Japan is already also a credible partner with emerging spacefaring countries. Many of these countries are keen to design and launch near-Earth or deep-space missions that work for their national interests, priorities, and budgets (Chang 2022). Among the most important partners is the United Arab Emirates (UAE), with whom JAXA began cooperation on a satellite in 2013 prior to the formation of that country's space agency in 2014. As JAXA put it when they formalized a cooperation agreement, "both agencies intend to develop a mutually beneficial relationship by utilizing technologies and human resources for space exploration and utilization JAXA have accumulated for a long time," including its Kibo segment on the ISS (JAXA 2016). Australia also draws attention in Japan's portfolio, and the two countries have signaled a partnership that will drive their space industries forward (DISR 2020a; 2020b). Like the UAE, Japan has a collaborative history with Australia that predates the formation of its space agency in 2018. Aside from experiments going back to the 1990s, Australia has long been involved with Japan's high-profile Hayabusa mission. It has collaborated both in the first mission that launched in 2003 and the second that launched in 2014 (SpaceNews Staff 2010; Jones 2020).

Japan's investments and partnerships like these in future space technologies is considered necessary by the country's top political leadership for Japan to remain, as it is now, "'a future independent space power'" (Associated Press 2020). Japan continues to cultivate opportunities and partners carefully over time, and always with an eye on all fronts to positioning its own technologies and services worldwide that serve its manifold interests. These are themes that emerge also in the context of military space realities, particularly with the United States, as well as space diplomacy that criss-crosses multilateral and regional affairs.

Military and Defense Front

It is fiction to think that proactive positioning for dual-use space capabilities can remain restricted to civilian or commercial purposes. Nowhere is this more evident than in the context of Japan's relations with the United States, still marked as one of the most important bilateral relationships, bar none (Krauss 2022). Expectations for the role of space in the bilateral relationship have come a long way from the era in which, at one time, economic friction seemed to overwhelm all their interactions. Among the most well-known disputes related to market opening in Japan was a specific one about procurement contracts for satellites and components, which fell under the controversial US Super 301 provisions of the 1988 Trade Law (Hershey 1990; Reuters 1990). Even as they sought to ensure the competitiveness of their home firms by leveling the market access playing fields in such disputes, both governments nevertheless remained wedded to their military alliance. Over time, security concerns, rather than economic friction, have come to take on greater importance in their bilateral interactions (Krauss 2022, 827).

The US-Japan Security Treaty, revised in 1960, is a high-profile component of their evolving military space realities today. The United States has marked space as a "distinct warfighting domain," requiring new responses, capabilities, and expertise in a "new strategic environment" (USDOD 2020, 1). There is certainly uniformity of views in both countries on kinetic and non-kinetic threats that can disrupt principles of the "right of access to space and freedom of navigation in space" (Sheehan 2015, 9; Pekkanen 2022, 769–71). That said, the United States is relatively much more dependent on space assets, accounting already for over 60 percent of all operating satellites today—an asymmetric dependence likely to grow with US-led mega constellations going into place (UCS 2022). This disproportionate reliance also affects the US military which, in its own words, "will continue to depend on space to project power and to respond rapidly to crises worldwide to a greater extent than potential adversaries" (USDOD 2020, 4). This is concerning to the United States and presumably also its allies such as Japan who may also not be as reliant on space assets for territorial defense but are dependent on US extended deterrence (Suzuki 2013, 106; Griggs 2018). Article V of their treaty explicitly "recognizes that an armed attack against either Party in the territories of Japan would be dangerous to its own peace and safety and declares that it would act to meet the common danger" in line with established legal and policy frameworks (MOFA 1960).

Japan, today, is capitalizing on the space security agenda with a more vigilant United States in the great power competition today and so reshaping prospects for what their alliance can do in outer space where space assets can be legitimate targets in wartime (Pekkanen 2015c; Reuters 2022). But given that the Japanese military is relatively not as dependent on space, what it means for the two allies to "act" in meeting the "common danger" requires scrutiny in the space domain. Just because it is operating under a formal military pact, shares threat perceptions, and supports military space proclamations does not mean that Japan is any the less guarded about the industrial and economic trajectory of its space activities writ large. In fact, in my judgment, it is more accurate to think of a whole-of-alliance reality between the two countries in which Japan is not a junior partner but a proactive positioner of its human and technology interests in the alliance. If, as US political leaders assert, "Space cooperation is a critical component of [the] alliance . . . [and extends] across commercial, civil, and security sectors . . . [and if] Japan's contributions will advance scientific knowledge and protect . . . brave astronauts" then they should adjust for scenarios to include Japanese astronauts who may one day walk alongside US ones on the moon (Etkind and McGuinness 2022).

Further, Japan is empowered to position both its advanced dual-use capabilities and its human capital in the alliance because of its "security renaissance" (Oros 2017). A threatening regional security environment, eroding domestic pacifism, ever more supportive law and policies from revamped national security policy-making processes, all facilitate Japan's new military space positioning. What once seemed controversial now seems not just possible but necessary in defense of Japan.

In June 2011, the US-Japan Security Consultative Committee voiced concerns, among other things, about "evolving threats" such as to outer space where they shared interests, and the importance of ensuring the "protection of and access to space" and "the resilience of critical infrastructure, including the security of information and space systems" (MOFA 2011, 2, 6 [for quotes], 9). Even then, the joint statement was specific about the ways the bilateral space security partnership might be deepened, pinpointing space situational awareness (SSA), satellite navigation, space-based maritime domain awareness (MDA), and utilization of dual-use sensors as target areas for cooperation. In 2012, those foci were deepened at the highest political levels of space diplomacy when their leadership declared "sustainability, stability, and free access to and use of space vital to our national interests" and specifically reinforced the multiple benefits of regional navigation (interoperability between GPS and QZSS), satellite-based observation, and SSA (MOFA 2012).

Japan's proactive positioning on these fronts is showing up concretely in the context of their military alliance. By 2013, Japan had an unclassified SSA agreement with the United States and was reportedly moving to a classified one as well (McLeary and Hitchens 2019). In 2020, reportedly a first, the US military paid for a payload to be carried on Japan's QZSS (Hitchens 2020). This gives content to interoperability, as the payloads will allow Japan's QZSS to enhance geostationary SSA capabilities in the Eurasian theatre and facilitate US resilience in its Space Surveillance Network that tracks operational satellites and space debris. Japan's ever keener threat awareness of anti-satellite (ASAT) attacks, cyberattacks, and jamming in the space domain will deepen its interest in strengthening strategic early warning capacities, and in doing so through more active alignment with the United States (Lal et al. 2018, 20–22, 24, Table 2-1). Aside from agreements on sensor technologies with the US Space Force, Japan is also positioning its military personnel in space operations by placing them in US Space Command (Erwin 2021). Japan started its first Space Operations Squadron to monitor debris and suspicious satellites, expanded to a second squadron to monitor also electromagnetic interference, and continues training with the US military to operate in the space domain (MOD 2020; JIJI 2020a; Dominguez 2022).

Japan is in a volatile region with rapidly expanding military expenditures and where the U.S. is strengthening alliances in the space domain (Sato 2020; Moriyasu 2022; Roh 2022). The country faces provocative actions from both China and Russia and also has territorial disputes with both (Reuters 2021; Nikkei Asia 2022b). As well, Japan is now threatened by a near constant barrage of diverse North Korean missiles, including potential ICBM firings, all of which trigger J-Alert emergency broadcasting systems for the public at large (Johnson 2022). That the defense policy establishment has named the risks and threats from China, Russia, and North Korea outright is significant (NSC 2022, 8–10; NSS 2022, 4–5). That Japan's famously pacifist public is beginning to do the same is even more so. Over time, all these security challenges have seeped into the sentiments of the Japanese people, heightening their sensitivity to military conflict and increasing poor impressions of regional actors (Hadano 2022). Japan still has its pacifist constitution, with the war-renouncing Article 9. But today the Japanese public is not so much averse to constitutional change as it is sensitive to the actual specifics of such proposals, meaning their contents and their proposers, as well as the domestic and international contexts (McElwain 2022a, 37). Polls over time suggest that while the public may be only a little less disagreeable on the issue of amending Article 9 in some ways, it is much more agreed on amending the constitution to enumerate the government's obligations and powers in states of emergencies (McElwain 2022b, 323–24, Table 21.1).

The steady drumbeat of missile launches and territorial incursions erodes the country's pacifism, creating an opening for the national security establishment to be more transparent about Japan's military capabilities, defensive and offensive, including those at the nexus of space. This was already foreseeable with the passage of the 2008 Basic Space Law, which legitimized space technology pathways and postures in line with international legal interpretations—"non-aggressive" as opposed to the much higher, and unrealistic, bar of "non-military" for a dual-use technology (Pekkanen and Kallender-Umezu 2010, 251). Today, while ongoing debates caution that we should be wary of projecting any kind of linear progression, Japan has largely shed pacifist constraints on its defense and security postures (Berger 1993; Oros 2008; 2017; Hughes 2022a; 2022b; Smith 2019; 2022).

Some loosened constraints matter outright for enabling its grand strategy on the military space front, interweaving them also with the narratives in the economic front discussed above and diplomatic one that follows. With an eye on increasing corporate participation in the lucrative international arms market, Japan's first-ever National Security Strategy served as the basis, in April 2014, for the relaxation of the principles on the ban of arms exports that dated back to 1967; in light of the Ukraine war, these principles may reportedly be further revised to allow for the export of lethal weapons (Liff 2018, 264–65; Pryor 2016; Kyodo 2022). That strategy also cleared the path for the July 2014 Cabinet Decision that reinterpreted the constitution to recognize Japan's right, however limited, to collective self-defense; in practice, this means that Japan could aid an ally under attack or respond in cases justified by international law (Nippon.com 2014). These changes, in my view, do not signify that Japan will invade or attack in the space domain. Rather I foresee that these conditions give Japan's defense and foreign policy establishment the latitude to more determinedly signal deterrence by demonstration of acquired capabilities.

To a significant extent Japan has already done just this in the space domain. But the security implications of its demonstrated kinetic and non-kinetic space capabilities have been little understood and never officially or transparently communicated. All that may change in the years ahead. Japan is set to increase its defense budget to 2 percent by 2027; it had been under the 1 percent guideline since 1976 (Nikkei Staff 2022). There does not appear to be much political blowback to a key plank of this new budget, namely acquiring counterstrike capabilities to attack rival missile launch sites and other targets. Instead, the real hitch on the horizon appears to be how to pay for all this as the Liberal Democratic Party is cautious about raising taxes to pay for defense spending. Nor is there likely to be much controversy about actuating the country's long-standing Ballistic Missile Defense (BMD) cooperation with the United States so that it may do what it is meant to do: guard against such incoming missiles in defense of Japan. In fact, consistent with MOD's proclamations in 2013, BMD can now also extend realistically to "limited attack" on the source of those launches (Pekkanen 2015a, 224). If MOD can own and operate national security satellites in support of its terrestrial operations involving BMD, it can also move to defend them through disruptive or offensive actions, such as those targeting "command-and-control capabilities of opponents through the electromagnetic spectrum" (Aoki 2009, 387; Dominguez 2022 [for quote]). Further, interceptors built for BMD can demonstrably be reconfigured to serve as an ASAT weapon to target and destroy orbiting satellites (Johnson-Freese 2007, 7, 101, 107; Grego 2011, 2–3, Table 2; Pekkanen and Kallender-Umezu 2010, 192–93).

Qualitatively, Japan is a formidable military space power. It is continuously and proactively positioning its technologies and interests in the counterspace race, which it knows can adversely affect the great power underpinnings of its formal ally. Just as we single out space powers who present solid-fuel ballistic missile capabilities in the guise of civilian rockets, Japan's *Epsilon* too should be marked not as an operational weapon of war but as a potential strategic weapon for deterrence and coercive diplomacy (Pekkanen and Kallender-Umezu 2010, 128–129; Pekkanen 2015b). Japan's counterpace capabilities are advanced, and their development stretches discursively over decades. These include assets for performing rendezvous proximity operations that were tested in plain sight in 1997 and long-duration spacecraft that can shoot bullets into asteroids in the name of sample-return science missions tested in 2019 (Pekkanen 2020).

Along with the loosened policy constraints, these pre-existing capabilities can enable Japan to extend collective self-defense more explicitly to space and its ally, something it already recognizes for cyberspace (Bartlett 2022, 792). Just what circumstances or cases in the space nexus would "constitute an armed attack for the purposes of Article V of the US-Japan Security Treaty," and what Japan could bring to the alliance in such a scenario and whether that would serve its enduring interests is something to keep an eye on in its all-fronts positioning on the military front (MOD 2019). Now that Article V protections have been officially extended to space as well, the next frontier to watch for are disruptive and offensive operations as "joint responses to serious threats to, from and within space" (MOFA 2022 [for quote]; Miki and Shigeta 2023).

Regional and Global Diplomatic Front

Japan has a long history of entering, adapting to, and even exiting from numerous international organizations in world politics, but the overall assessment is that the country's policies toward them remain relatively understudied (Lipscy and Tamaki 2022). It does not come as a surprise, then, that Japan's space diplomacy in regional and international settings also draws less scholarly and policy attention (Pekkanen 2023). Little remarked, the diplomacy has been channeled over decades through organized multilateral forums; as it was set in motion, it could not always have been crystal clear how and whether its tendrils would aid the country's proactive positioning in the economic and security fronts. Today, as the space policy-making apparatus continues to coalesce under national political leadership, this diplomatic portfolio is proving useful for positioning Japanese interests in a bipolar international space order, and in embedding Japanese space technologies based on shared understanding of their uses to emerging spacefaring countries.

On the regional front, which gets the bulk of its diplomatic attention, Japan has operated its space affairs independently for close to thirty years. Japan's interactions have been anchored in the multilateral Asia-Pacific Regional Space Agency Forum (APRSAF), an institutionalized forum dating back to 1993 that Japan set up, designed, and whose evolution it still leads (APRSAF n.d.). Analysts have put APRSAF in comparative and regional contexts, analyzing what it suggests for rivalry, influence, leadership, capacity-building, governance, and collaboration (Suzuki 2013 Moltz 2016; Jakhu and Pelton 2017; Pekkanen 2021a; Yan 2021; Yoshimatsu 2021). There are also the historical turns in Japan's foreign relations in the early 1990s that are relevant to its birth and mission. APRSAF came about in an era when Japan, looking beyond the confines of US-led security coalitions in the post–Cold War world, found itself isolated among its neighbors, and began its own journey toward a more sustained kind of regional security multilateralism (Midford 2018, 2022). I see that broader momentum also shaping the course and contents of APRSAF because the foundational technology it seeks to govern and disseminate is dual use, with unavoidable implications for security as noted above. Japan has worked quietly and patiently over decades to make APRSAF a hub for diplomatic reassurance and geoeconomic advantage and to influence projection in cross-regional and global forums. This painstaking diplomacy may well have been a way " 'to give other countries a sense of security' " (JIJI 2020b).

Under the leadership of MEXT and JAXA, with their concerted focus on science and technology, APRSAF has turned out to be a wide and inclusive forum for space security and safety. MEXT once described APRSAF as a "place for discussing concrete international cooperative projects in the Asia Pacific region for the development of space technology and applications for the future" (MEXT 2006). Its messaging and work obviously resonate worldwide as indicated by the rise of participants over time (MEXT 2021, 190). In 2019, APRSAF claimed participation from 844 organizations from 52 countries and regions and 32 international organizations. While APRSAF's principles were clarified in 2012, the core vision has not really changed: implementing space agencies would continue to collaborate keeping in mind the goal that "APRSAF aims to promote and expand peaceful uses of space activities and their applications for socio-economic development in Asia and the Pacific" (APRSAF 2012). With this aim, APRSAF's consensual, dialogic, voluntary, and solution-focused institutional design reinforces positive perceptions about Japan in the space domain—that Japan is putting its dual-use space technologies in the service of regional socio-economic security writ large and not as a basis to reemerge as a threat to its neighbors (Midford 2022, 701).

APRSAF's longstanding rubric gives Japan a decided advantage in proactively positioning its technologies, experience, and networks in the region. This is important at a time that Japan is pursuing a different geoeconomic strategy in the Asia-Pacific:

the international order, which aided Japan's rise, is under stress, and China's rise has reshaped economic prospects across Asia (Katada 2020, 25–26). As Japan seeks to shape the new space realities in the face of these changes, APRSAF has allowed it to engage in and out of the region from Southeast Asia to South Asia and the Middle East to Oceania and beyond. One prominent mode of engagement is the MEXT and JAXA partnerships with different countries to carry out a high-profile annual conference. The co-hosts help rotate the location of the conference out of Japan, which have been held in, for example, Mongolia, Malaysia, Korea, Thailand, Australia, Indonesia, India, Vietnam, Singapore, and the Philippines. Doing so allows higher on-the-ground visibility for APRSAF dialogues and activities. MEXT calls it the "largest space-related conference in the Asia-Pacific region" that aims to promote space utilization in collaborative ways (MEXT 2020).

There are also other domestic players who have long been involved in Japan's international engagements. JAXA's partnership with the Japan International Cooperation Agency (JICA) is especially noteworthy. JICA was established in 1974 but locates its roots in technical cooperation projects going back to 1954 (JICA n.d.). Its present global agenda stretches across every conceivable aspect of socioeconomic development, including science and technology cooperation on global issues. In recipient countries, the enumerated agenda items are a candidate for Japan's assistance, such as its technical cooperation, its Official Development Assistance (ODA) loans, or grant aid. As it happens, JICA's thematic portfolio chimes well with efforts to restructure APRSAF's working groups activities in line with the Nagoya Vision in 2019. The resulting working group names are geared toward themes of socioeconomic and sustainable development: Satellite Applications for Societal Benefit, Enhancement of Space Capability, Space Education for All, Space Frontier, and Space Policy and Law (APRSAF 2021). In April 2014, JAXA and JICA signed a partnership agreement that would synergize their "hand in hand" approach to regional and global problem-solving in line with their expertise, including prominently the promotion of space-related systems and utilization of space technologies (JAXA 2014; Suzuki 2014, 10–12).

APRSAF's newly established Space Policy and Law Working Group (SPLWG) also helps to draw a direct line to one aspect of Japan's global space diplomacy. SPLWG was established with the understanding that space technology and space policy and law are "inseparable pairs" in outer space affairs. Its purpose is to enhance capacity building in space policy and law, and to raise awareness of and policy options for common regional issues. Importantly, SPLWG seeks to interject the collective regional voice at cross-regional and global levels, particularly related to the sustainable, safe, and stable use of outer space that is of paramount concern to civilian, commercial, and military stakeholders worldwide. Although it was established in 2021, SPLWG gives Japan an opportunity to lead and shape the making of a like-minded diplomatic community, one that can be a basis for soft and allied influence across and beyond the regional setting. The building blocks for its formation have gone in slowly over time.

In 2017, at the APRSAF-24 annual meeting, there was a first-ever special session on space policy with officials from Malaysia, Thailand, Indonesia, Vietnam, India, and Korea showcasing new national developments and prospects for joint cooperation; the official from Japan made it clear also that one mode for capacity building in emerging spacefaring countries lay in "using Japan's space asset[s]" such as the deployment of Philippine microsat from ISS/Kibo (APRSAF 2017; Saeki 2017). The Joint Statement that came out of APRSAF-24 also stressed the importance of "high-level meetings" among space policy stakeholders, regular interactions that could lead to shared understanding of "common issues and interests in our region" (APRSAF 2017).

This diplomatic platform has allowed APRSAF to reach out worldwide. In fact, SPLWG traces its efforts back to a cross-regional initiative with the European Space Policy Institute (ESPI). In 2018, APRSAF and ESPI held the first Inter-Regional Space Policy Dialogue with the thematic focus of socio-economic development for countries in the Asia-Pacific region with significant interests in advancing full-scale (APRSAF 2018). They followed that up with a second dialogue that plugged space policy practitioners from both regions into an ESPI workshop, as well as at a side event at the sixty-second session of the United Nations Conference on Peaceful Uses of Outer Space (COPUOS) (APRSAF 2019; ESPI 2019). It was the space policy practitioners who proposed the launch of the National Space Legislation Initiative (NLSI) at the annual meeting in 2019 (Kuriyama et al. 2020, 6; APRSAF 2019, 1–2).

The diplomatic advantage for Japan is that in speaking to mutual national interests it is also tethering a regional community to international space law—and so laying the groundwork for an allied regional bloc that, over time, is more likely to share an understanding of responsible behavior in space that is consistent with international standards and norms (APRSAF 2019, 1–2; Kuriyama et al. 2020, 19–24; Pekkanen 2022b). At a time of greater congestion and contestation in space activities, including the threat of space debris, the APRSAF community is endeavoring to find not just technological solutions but also legal and policy pathways forward for the sustainable utilization of outer space. The principles of the foundational Outer Space Treaty, through implementation and interpretation, help guide state behavior and shape state practice as technologies shift, circumstances change, and new opportunities beckon. Already the NLSI participating states have submitted a first-ever joint report to COPUOS that is expected to contribute to a UN resolution on the peaceful exploration of outer space (APRSAF 2021).

Japan's independent maneuvering through APRSAF also makes its alignment with US moves to advance national security norms for responsible behavior in space highly credible. The new US commitment to not conduct destructive, direct-ascent ASAT testing has been folded into Japan's broader regional to global diplomatic agenda (USGOV 2022). In the context of the UN Conference on Disarmament, Japan has announced to the global community it too is joining the US commitment to ensure the "peaceful, safe, stable, secure and sustainable environment" for future generations (GOJ 2022). As well, it has thrown its diplomatic weight behind the UK-led resolution in the UN General Assembly on reducing space threats through norms, rules, and principles of responsible behavior (UNGA 2020; MOFA 2020).

Concluding Remarks

If grand strategy is the logic that purposefully structures a state's economic, political, and diplomatic activities, Japan is executing it in the space domain. This framing gives us a different way to see Japan's reemergence and reengagement with a changing world order in which the United States is seen as a declining power and China a rising one. Japan is historically attuned to working through opportunities and living through threats as world orders shift. In all the complexity and disorder that clutter the contemporary space domain, Japan is engaged in proactive positioning. Through whatever means, processes, and forums available, the Japanese state's all-fronts vision keeps it attentive to locking in specific national advantages. The path is not straightforward, and the point is not whether the advantages materialize. After all, no one knows what might turn out to be a gain or turn into a flop that resurrects as a benefit; sometimes also the positioning is for results no one may live to see.

Japan's proactive positioning is activated by a rising and increasingly uniform awareness among decision-makers of what the underlying space technology is and just what it can do for Japan in the tumultuous world order today. The full force of Japan's statecraft, perhaps more coordinated and coherent than ever before in its postwar history, is being proactively structured to steer through that tumult. Where, with whom, and how Japan is positioning in the international space order reflects that proactivism on many fronts.

On the economic and technological front, Japan is keenly interested in ensuring its firms are positioned to capture gains, market shares, and spillovers in lucrative commercial markets such as those centered on small satellites and big data more immediately and space stations further out. On the military and defense front, under the rubric of their formal alliance, Japan shares US concerns about the nature of evolving threats and the importance of SDA for the safety and security of space assets. Japan has positioned both its sensor technologies as well as its personnel in the sprawling and spreading space defense architecture centered on its ally's capabilities. With changes in its legal frameworks, as well as Article V protections of the mutual security pact extended to space, it is poised to move into counterspace weapons and to rethink its disruptive and offensive actions in, through, and at the nexus of space. On the regional and global diplomatic front, Japan has kept the door open to new and old players, allies, and rivals. It has independently led the soft and informal APRSAF for over three decades, all the while gathering networks, accumulating experiences, and stressing technology development and utilization. Its science and technology diplomacy has reassured neighbors that Japan's advanced dual-use capabilities are not a threat but can also be transposed to servicing their concrete economic and security interests. On the global normative and rule-making plane, Japan has also increasingly moved in concert with partners from Europe, Oceania, and the United States. Like them, Japan too stresses the importance of responsible behavior in outer space linked to international peace and security.

Grand strategies live in the real world, in which at any time little is certain and all is fluid. With that understanding Japan is bringing its own historic ways of navigating changes in the international system to outer space. Japan is already a prominent and competent space actor, with an industrial base that has targeted, developed, and tested some of the most advanced dual-use space technologies in plain sight over the postwar period. Importantly, Japan's varied actors were able to do this despite low budgets, scattered activities, and prohibitive normative and constitutional constraints. Given the substantive political changes that distinguish the new Japan from its postwar past, the opportunity now arises to see where Japan is headed in the space domain.

Of some things we can be sure. Japan is not playing catch-up and it is not a junior partner to anyone. Just as it did in different contexts and earlier times, the Japanese state continues to strive in the international space order so that Japan may endure, unbroken, with constant presence on all fronts.

Acknowledgments

For their comments, I thank Hal Brands, Peter Feaver, Mike Green, Saori Katada, Seunghyun Kim, Ellis Krauss, Andrew Oros, Robert Pekkanen, Sophia Pekkanen, and T. J. Pempel.

References

Aoki, Setsuko. 2009. "Current Status and Recent Developments in Japan's National Space Law and Its Relevance to Pacific Rim Space Law and Activities." *Journal of Space Law* 35, no. 2: 363–38.

Aoki, Setsuko. 2011. "The National Space Law of Japan: Basic Space Law and the Space Activities Act in the Making." 6th Eilene M. Galloway Symposium on Critical Issues in Space Law, 1 December 2011, Cosmos Club, Washington D.C. http://www.iislweb.org/docs/2011_gallo way/Aoki.pdf.

Aoki, Setsuko. 2017. "New Law Aims to Expand Japan's Space Business." *Nippon.Com.* March 3, 2017. https://www.nippon.com/en/currents/d00294/.

APRSAF (Asia-Pacific Regional Space Agency Forum). 2012. "Principles of APRSAF." https://www.aprsaf.org/about/pdf/Principles.pdf.

APRSAF (Asia-Pacific Regional Space Agency Forum). 2017. "Joint Statement of the 24th Session of the Asia-Pacific Regional Space Agency Forum (Bengaluru, India)." APRSAF. https://aprsaf.org/annual_meetings/aprsaf24/pdf/joint_statement/Joint%20Statement.pdf.

APRSAF (Asia-Pacific Regional Space Agency Forum). 2017. "APRSAF-24: Special Session for Space Policy (Space Policy Session)." APRSAF. https://aprsaf.org/annual_meetings/aprsa f24/pdf/program/SapcePolicySessionConceptPaper.pdf.

APRSAF (Asia-Pacific Regional Space Agency Forum). 2018. "APRSAF-ESPI Jointly Held "Inter-Regional Space Policy Dialogue." APRSAF. https://www.aprsaf.org/initiatives/new_efforts/space_policy/espi.php.

APRSAF (Asia-Pacific Regional Space Agency Forum). 2019. "The 2nd Inter-Regional Space Policy Dialogue—Asia Pacific and Europe." APRSAF. https://www.aprsaf.org/initiatives/new_efforts/space_policy/espi_2nd.php.

APRSAF (Asia-Pacific Regional Space Agency Forum). 2019. "Joint Statement: Record of the 26th Asia-Pacific Regional Space Agency Forum (Nagoya, Japan)." APRSAF. https://aprsaf. org/annual_meetings/aprsaf26/pdf/outcome_documents/Joint_Statement.pdf.

APRSAF (Asia-Pacific Regional Space Agency Forum). 2021. "Charter of APRSAF Working Group (New Formation from APRSAF-27)." APRSAF, APRSAF/EC/4/2021. https://www. aprsaf.org/working_groups/about/pdf/Charter_WG.pdf.

APRSAF (Asia-Pacific Regional Space Agency Forum). 2021. "National Space Legislation Initiative Activity Report." NLSI Study Group, APRSAF. https://www.aprsaf.org/initiatives/ national_space_legislation/pdf/AP27_PPT_presentation_for_NSLI_report.pdf.

APRSAF (Asia-Pacific Regional Space Agency Forum). n.d. APRSAF Official Website. https:// www.aprsaf.org/.

Asahi_Shimbun. 2020. "Basic Rule for Space Squadron: Space Cannot Be a 'Battleground' (Editorial)." http://www.asahi.com/ajw/articles/13388301.

Associated Press. 2020. "Japan to Boost Space Cooperation with U.S. In Revised Policy." *The Asahi Shimbun.* June 30, 2020. https://www.asahi.com/ajw/articles/13502173.

Axelspace. 2022. "Yuya Nakamura, Ceo of Axelspace Wins the Ministry of Economy, Trade and Industry Award at the 22nd Japan Venture Awards." News, *Axelspace,* December 9, 2022. https://www.axelspace.com/news/japanventureawards/.

Baiocchi, David, and William Wesler IV. 2015. "The Democratization of Space: New Actors Need New Rules." *Foreign Affairs,* 94, no. 3: 98–104.

Balzacq, Theirry, Peter Dombrowski, and Simon Reich. 2019. "Introduction: Comparing Grand Strategies in the Modern World." In *Comparative Grand Strategy: A Framework and Cases,* edited Theirry Balzacq, Peter Dombrowski, and Simon Reich, 1–22. New York: Oxford University Press.

Balzacq, Theirry, and Ronald R. Krebs. 2021. "The Enduring Appeal of Grand Strategy." In *The Oxford Handbook of Grand Strategy,* edited by Thierry Balzacq and Ronald R. Krebs, 1–21. New York: Oxford University Press, 2021.

Bartlett, Benjamin. 2022. "Cybersecurity in Japan." In *The Oxford Handbook of Japanese Politics,* edited by Robert J. Pekkanen and Saadia M. Pekkanen, 791–808. New York: Oxford University Press, 2022.

Berger, Thomas U. 1993. "From Sword to Chrysanthemum: Japan's Culture of Anti-Militarism." *International Security* 17, no. 4: 119–50.

Brands, Hal. 2012. "The Promise and Pitfalls of Grand Strategy." Strategic Studies Institute (SSI), External Research Associates Program Monograph 548. Carlisle Barracks, PA: U.S. Army War College, 1–67. https://press.armywarcollege.edu/cgi/viewcontent.cgi?article= 1547&context=monographs.

Brands, Hal. 2014. *What Good Is Grand Strategy? Power and Purpose in American Statecraft from Harry S. Truman to George W. Bush.* Ithaca, NY: Cornell University Press.

Brands, Hal, and Peter Feaver. 2021. "Getting Grand Strategy Right." In *The Oxford Handbook of Grand Strategy,* edited by Thierry Balzacq and Ronald R. Krebs, 559–74 New York: Oxford University Press, 2021.

Brands, Hal, Peter Feaver, and William Inboden. 2023. "Stress Testing American Grand Strategy II: Critical Assumptions and Great-Power Rivalry." Report, American Enterprise Institute (AEI), Washington, DC, 1–38.

Calder, Kent E. 1988. "Japanese Foreign Economic Policy Formation: Explaining the Reactive State." *World Politics* 40, no. 4: 517–41.

Cantelmo, Robert G., and Sarah E Kreps. 2021. "Grand Strategy and Technological Futures." In *The Oxford Handbook of Grand Strategy*, edited by Thierry Balzacq and Ronald R. Krebs, 706–20. New York: Oxford University Press, 2021.

Chang, Kenneth. 2022. "Why Some Scientists Choose China's Space Station for Research." *New York Times*. December 12, 2022. https://www.nytimes.com/2022/12/12/science/tiangong-science-physics.html.

CO (Cabinet Office, Government of Japan). 2022. "Uchū Kihon Keikaku Kōteihyō Kaitei Ni Muketa Jyūten Jikō No Pointo (Gaiyō) [Priority Items of the Revised Process Chart of the Basic Space Plan (Synopsis)]." Tokyo. https://www8.cao.go.jp/space/plan/plan2/kaitei_f yo4/juten_gaiyo.pdf.

DISR (Department of Industry, Science and Resources, Australia). 2020. "Australia and Japan Strengthen Space Collaborations." News. https://www.industry.gov.au/news/australia-and-japan-strengthen-space-collaborations.

Dominguez, Gabriel. 2022. "As Space Race Escalates, Japan Bolsters Defense Capabilities in New Domains." *The Japan Times*. January 6, 2022. https://www.japantimes.co.jp/news/2022/01/06/national/japan-space-defense/.

Erwin, Sandra. 2021. "Japanese Military Strengthens Ties with U.S. Space Command." *Spacenews*. April 1, 2021. https://spacenews.com/japanese-military-strengthens-ties-with-u-s-space-command/.

ESPI (European Space Policy Institute). 2019. "ESPI-APRSAF Workshop, Inter-Regional Space Policy Dialogue between Asia-Pacific and Europe." https://www.espi.or.at/events/espi-aprsaf-workshop-inter-regional-space-policy-dialogue-between-asia-pacific-and-europe-15-06-2019/.

Etkind, Marc, and Jackie McGuinness. 2022. "NASA, Japan Announce Gateway Contributions, Space Station Extension." Release 22-118. https://www.nasa.gov/press-release/nasa-japan-announce-gateway-contributions-space-station-extension.

Euroconsult. 2022. "Euroconsult Estimates That the Global Space Economy Totaled $370 Billion in 2021." https://www.euroconsult-ec.com/press-release/euroconsult-estimates-that-the-global-space-economy-totaled-370-billion-in-2021/.

Fatton, Lionel. 2020. "Japan's Space Program: Shifting Away from 'Non-Offensive' Purposes?" *Notes de l'Ifri: Asie.visions* 115: 1–36.

Fischer, Sophie-Charlotte, Andrea Gilli, and Mauro Gilli. 2021. "Technological Change and Grand Strategy." In *The Oxford Handbook of Grand Strategy*, edited by Thierry Balzacq and Ronald R. Krebs, 221–38. New York: Oxford University Press, 2021.

Foust, Jeff. 2020. "Eight Countries Sign Artemis Accords." *Spacenews*. October13, 2020. https://spacenews.com/eight-countries-sign-artemis-accords/.

Foust, Jeff. 2021. "NASA and Japan Finalize Gateway Agreement." *Spacenews*. January 13, 2020. https://spacenews.com/nasa-and-japan-finalize-gateway-agreement/.

Fukushima, Mayumi, and Richard J. Samuels. 2018. "Japan's National Security Council: Filling the Whole of Government?" *International Affairs* 94, no. 4: 773–90.

Fukushima, Yasuhito. 2017. "Nihon No Bōei Uchū Riyō: Uchū Kihon Hō Seiritsu Zengo Keizokuse to Henka [Japan's Use of Space for Defense: Continuity and Change before and after the Basic Space Law]." Briefing Memo, National Institute of Defense Studies (NIDS), March 2017, 1–6. http://www.nids.mod.go.jp/publication/briefing/pdf/17/201703.pdf.

Gaddis, John Lewis. 2018. *On Grand Strategy*. New York: Penguin Press.

GOJ (Government of Japan). 2022. "Statement Delivered by Ambassador Ichiro Ogaswara of the Delegation of Japan to the Conference on Disarmament." Second Session of the

Open-Ended Working Group on Reducing Space Threats through Norms, Rules and Principles of Responsible Behaviours. https://documents.unoda.org/wp-content/uploads/2022/09/Japan-statement-at-second-session-OEWG-space_22.pdf.

Govella, Kristi. 2021. "The Adaptation of Japanese Economic Statecraft: Trade, Aid, and Technology." *World Trade Review* 20, no. 2: 186–202.

Green, Michael J. 1995. *Arming Japan: Defense Production, Alliance Politics, and the Postwar Search for Autonomy*. New York: Columbia University Press.

Green, Michael J. 2001. *Japan's Reluctant Realism: Foreign Policy Challenges in an Era of Uncertain Power*. New York: Palgrave.

Green, Michael J. 2022. *Line of Advantage: Japan's Grand Strategy in the Era of Abe Shinzō*. New York: Columbia University Press.

Grego, Laura. 2011. "The Anti-Satellite Capability of the Phased Adaptive Approach Missile Defense System." Public Interest Report, Federation of American Scientists (Winter): 1–6. https://fas.org/pubs/pir/2011winter/2011Winter-Anti-Satellite.pdf.

Griggs, Mary Beth. 2018. "Trump's Space Force Aims to Create 'American Dominance in Space' by 2020." *Popular Mechanics*. August 9, 2018. https://www.popsci.com/space-force-2020/.

Hadano, Tsukasa. 2022. "Majority of Chinese Think Taiwan Strait Conflict Is Likely: Poll." *Nikkei Asia*. December 1, 2022. https://asia.nikkei.com/Politics/International-relations/Majority-of-Chinese-think-Taiwan-Strait-conflict-is-likely-poll.

Hershey, Robert D. Jr. 1990. "A Basic Pact on Satellites with Japan." *New York Times*. April 4, 1990. https://www.nytimes.com/1990/04/04/business/a-basic-pact-on-satellites-with-japan.html.

Hitchens, Theresa. 2020. "Air Force Funds Hosted Payloads on Japan Sats." *Breaking Defense*. February 19, 2020. https://breakingdefense.com/2020/02/air-force-funds-hosted-payloads-on-japan-sats/.

Hughes, Christopher W. 2022a. *Japan as a Global Military Power: New Capabilities, Alliance Integration, Bilateralism-Plus*. New York: Cambridge University Press.

Hughes, Christopher W. 2022b. "Remilitarization in Japan." In *The Oxford Handbook of Japanese Politics*, edited by Robert J. Pekkanen and Saadia M. Pekkanen, 681–700. New York: Oxford University Press, 2022.

Iida, Keisuke. 2022. "Linkages between Security and Economics in Japan." In *The Oxford Handbook of Japanese Politics*, edited by Robert J. Pekkanen and Saadia M. Pekkanen, 663–78. New York: Oxford University Press, 2022.

ispace. 2022. "Ispace Receives Interim Payment on Lunar Regolith Transfer Contract." Press Release. https://ispace-inc.com/news-en/?p=3696.

Jakhu, Ram S and Joseph N. Pelton. 2017. "Global Space Governance from Regional Perspectives." In *Global Space Governance: An International Study*, edited by Ram S. Jakhu and Joseph N. Pelton, 65–86. Cham, Switzerland: Springer.

JAXA (Japan Aerospace Exploration Agency). 2014. "Signing of Partnership Agreement between JAXA and JICA." Press Release. https://global.jaxa.jp/press/2014/04/20140423_jica.html.

JAXA (Japan Aerospace Exploration Agency). 2016. "JAXA and Uaesa Sign a Cooperation Agreement." Press Release. https://global.jaxa.jp/press/2016/03/20160322_uaesa.html.

JAXA (Japan Aerospace Exploration Agency). 2021. "Data Acquisition on the Lunar Surface with a Transformable Lunar Robot, Assisting Development of the Crewed Pressurized Rover." Press Release. https://global.jaxa.jp/press/2021/05/20210527-1_e.html.

JAXA (Japan Aerospace Exploration Agency). 2022. "Business Relations and Industrial Relations Department: Our Mission." https://aerospacebiz.jaxa.jp/en/about/.

JAXA (Japan Aerospace Exploration Agency). n.d. "International Space Station (ISS) and Japanese Experiment Module 'Kibo.'" https://global.jaxa.jp/projects/iss_human/kibo/.

JICA (Japan International Cooperation Agency). n.d. JICA Official Website. https://www.jica.go.jp/index.html.

JIJI. 2020a. "Japan Launches New Squadron to Step up Defense in Outer Space." *The Japan Times*. May 18, 2020. https://www.japantimes.co.jp/news/2020/05/18/national/sdf-launches-space-operations-unit/.

JIJI. 2020b "One Month into His Tenure, Suga Eager to Achieve Results." *The Japan Times*. October 17, 2020. https://www.japantimes.co.jp/news/2020/10/17/national/politics-diplomacy/one-month-into-tenure-yoshihide-suga/?utm_source=piano&utm_medium=email&utm_campaign=72&pnespid=a9dukBu_dCkAfiSk49.sB5Oto41gbGxQ6aIKRA.

Johnson, Chalmers. 1982. *MITI and the Japanese Miracle: The Growth of Industrial Policy, 1925–1975*. Stanford, CA: Stanford University Press.

Johnson, Jesse. 2022. "North Korean ICBM Launch That Triggered Alert May Have Failed In-Flight." *The Japan Times*. November 3, 2022. https://www.japantimes.co.jp/news/2022/11/03/national/north-korea-missile-j-alert/.

Johnson, Jesse, and Gabriel Dominguez. 2023. "U.S. To Boost Military Capabilities in Japan and Step up Cooperation amid China Worries." *The Japan Times*. January 12, 2023. https://www.japantimes.co.jp/news/2023/01/12/national/politics-diplomacy/us-japan-two-plus-two-23/.

Johnson-Freese, Joan. 2007. *Space as a Strategic Asset*. New York: Columbia University Press.

Jones, Andrew. 2020. "Hayabusa2 Delivers Asteroid Sample to Earth after Six-Year Voyage." *Spacenews*. December 5, 2020. https://spacenews.com/hayabusa2-delivers-asteroid-samples-to-earth-after-six-year-voyage/.

Kallender, Paul. 2016. "Japan's New Dual-Use Space Policy: The Long Road to the 21st Century." *Notes de l"Ifrie: Asie.visions* 88: 1–37.

Kallender, Paul, and Christopher W. Hughes. 2019. "Hiding in Plain Sight? Japan's Militarization of Space and Challenges to the Yoshida Doctrine." *Asian Security* 15, no. 2: 180–204.

Katada, Saori N. 2020. *Japan's New Regional Reality: Geoeconomic Strategy in the Asia-Pacific*. New York: Columbia University Press.

Kawasaki, Tsuyoshi. 2012. "The Rising Sun Was No Jackal: Japanese Grand Strategy, the Tripartite Pact, and Alliance Formation Theory." In *The Challenge of Grand Strategy: The Great Powers and the Broken Balance Between the World Wars*, edited by Jeffrey W. Taliaferro, Norrin M. Ripsman, and Steven E. Lobell, 224–45. New York: Cambridge University Press.

Keidanren (Japan Business Federation). 2022. "Uchū Kihon Keikaku No Jikkō Ni Muketa Teigen [a Proposal for the Implementation of the Basic Space Plan]." Tokyo, Keidanren, 1–10. https://www.keidanren.or.jp/policy/2022/068_honbun.pdf.

Kennedy, Paul. 1991. "Grand Strategy in War and Peace: Toward a Broader Definition." In *Grand Strategies in War and Peace*, edited by Paul Kennedy, 1–7. New Haven, CT: Yale University Press.

Koga, Kei. 2018. "The Concept of 'Hedging' Revisited: The Case of Japan's Foreign Policy Strategy in East Asia's Power Shift." *International Studies Review* 20, no. 4: 633–60.

Krauss, Ellis S., and Robert J. Pekkanen. 2011. *The Rise and Fall of Japan's LDP*. Ithaca, NY: Cornell University Press.

Krauss, Ellis S. 2022. "Japan-US Relations: The Most Important Bilateral Relationship in the World." In *The Oxford Handbook of Japanese Politics*, edited by Robert J. Pekkanen and Saadia M. Pekkanen, 811–31. New York: Oxford University Press.

Kuriyama, Ikuko, Koichi Kikuchi, Takashi Iwai, and Yoko Kagiwada. 2020. "A Regional Initiative for Studying the Status of National Space Laws." Presentation at IAC-20-E7.5.10, International Astronautical Federation (IAC) 2020 Congress, October 12–14, 2020. https://www.aprsaf.org/initiatives/national_space_legislation/pdf/Publications_IAC2 020_PPT.pdf.

Kyodo. 2020b. "Japan and the U.S. Agree to Boost Defense Cooperation in Outer Space." *The Japan Times.* August 27, 2020. https://www.japantimes.co.jp/news/2020/08/27/national/ abe-meets-u-s-space-force-chief/.

Kyodo. 2021. "Japan's Hoshide, Others Head to Space Station Aboard SpaceX Rocket." *Nikkei Asia.* April 23, 2021. https://asia.nikkei.com/Business/Science/Japan-s-Hoshide-others-head-to-space-station-aboard-SpaceX-rocket.

Kyodo. 2022. "Japan Considers Revising Strict Rules to Allow Export of Lethal Weapons." *The Japan Times.* November 18, 2022. https://www.japantimes.co.jp/news/2022/11/18/national/ lethal-weapons-exports/.

Kyodo. 2022. "Japan and the U.S. To Cooperate on Future Moon Landing by Japanese Astronaut." *The Japan Times.* May 19, 2022. https://www.japantimes.co.jp/news/2022/05/19/ national/japan-us-cooperate-moon-landing/.

Lal, Bhavya, Asha Balakrishnan, Becaja M. Caldwell, Reina S Buenconsejo, and Sara A Carioscia. 2018. "Global Trends in Space Situational Awareness (SSA) and Space Traffic Management." IDA Science & Technology Policy Institute, IDA Document D-9074. Washington, DC, The Institute for Defense Analyses (IDA).

Liff, Adam P. 2018. "Japan's National Security Council: Policy Coordination and Political Power." *Japanese Studies* 38, no. 2: 253–79.

Liff, Adam P. 2019. "Unambivalent Alignment: Japan's China Strategy, the US Alliance, and the 'Hedging' Fallacy." *International relations of the Asia-Pacific* 19, no. 3: 453–91.

Lind, Jennifer M. 2004. "Pacifism or Passing the Buck? Testing Theories of Japanese Security Policy." *International Security* 29, no. 1: 92–121.

Lipscy, Phillip Y., and Nobuhiko Tamaki. 2022. "Japan and International Organizations." In *The Oxford Handbook of Japanese Politics*, edited by Robert J. Pekkanen and Saadia M. Pekkanen, 515–34. New York: Oxford University Press.

Luttwak, Edward N. 2009. *The Grand Strategy of the Byzantine Empire.* Cambridge, MA: The Belknap Press of Harvard University Press.

Martel, William C. 2015. *Grand Strategy in Theory and Practice: The Need for an Effective American Foreign Policy.* New York: Cambridge University Press.

Martin, Deirdre. 2015. "Militarizing Space: Evaluating Competing Explanations." Paper Presented at the ISA Annual Conference, New Orleans, February 19, 2015.

Martin, Deirdre Quinn. 2021. "Quiet Acquisition: The Politics of Justification in Military Capability Trajectories." PhD diss., Department of Political Science, University of California Berkeley.

Masson-Zwaan, Tanja. 2019. "New States in Space," *American Journal of International Law Unbound* 113: 98–102. https://www.cambridge.org/core/journals/american-journal-of-international-law/article/new-states-in-space/E68383DE71B60A711EE1E4578CA303A8.

Matsuda, Yasuhiro. 2012. "Engagement and Hedging: Japan's Strategy Toward China." *The SAIS Review of International Affairs* 32, no. 2: 109–19.

McElwain, Kenneth Mori. 2022. "The Japanese Constitution." In *The Oxford Handbook of Japanese Politics*, edited by Robert J. Pekkanen and Saadia M. Pekkanen, 23–40. New York: Oxford University Press.

McElwain, Kenneth Mori. 2022. "Constitutional Revision in the 2021 Election." In *Japan Decides 2021: The Japanese General Election*, edited by Robert J. Pekkanen, Seven R. Reed, and Daniel M. Smith, 319–31. Cham, Switzerland: Palgrave.

McLeary, Paul, and Theresa Hitchens. 2019. "US, Japan to Ink Hosted Payload Pact to Monitor Sats." *Breaking Defense*. August 5, 2019. https://breakingdefense.com/2019/08/us-japan-to-ink-hosted-payload-pact-to-monitor-sats/.

MEXT (Ministry of Education, Culture, Sports, Science and Technology, Japan). 2006. "White Paper on Science and Technology." Section 3.2.2.8. https://www.mext.go.jp/en/publication/whitepaper/title03/detail03/sdetail03/sdetail03/1372929.htm.

MEXT (Ministry of Education, Culture, Sports, Science and Technology, Japan). 2020. "Mext Minister Makes Opening Remarks at APRSAF Online 2020." https://www.mext.go.jp/en/news/topics/detail/mext_00037.html.

MEXT (Ministry of Education, Culture, Sports, Science and Technology, Japan). 2021. "Kagaku Gijutsu Inobēshon Hakusho [White Paper on Science, Technology, and Innovation]." https://www.mext.go.jp/b_menu/hakusho/html/hpaa202101/1421221_00023.html.

Michishita, Narushige. 2022. "Japan's Grand Strategy for a Free and Open Indo-Pacific." In *The Oxford Handbook of Japanese Politics*, edited by Robert J. Pekkanen and Saadia M. Pekkanen, 493–513. New York: Oxford University Press.

Michishita, Narushige, and Richard J. Samuels. 2012. "Hugging and Hedging: Japanese Grand Strategy in the Twenty-First Century." In *Worldviews of Aspiring Powers: Domestic Foreign Policy Debates in China, India, Iran, Japan, and Russia*, 146–80. New York: Oxford University Press.

Midford, Paul. 2018. "Decentering from the U.S. in Regional Security Multilateralism: Japan's 1991 Pivot." *The Pacific Review* 31, no. 4: 441–59.

Midford, Paul. 2020. *Overcoming Isolationism: Japan's Leadership in East Asian Security Multilateralism*. Stanford: Stanford University Press.

Midford, Paul. 2022. "Global and Regional Security Multilateralism in Japan's Foreign Policy." In *The Oxford Handbook of Japanese Politics*, edited by Robert J. Pekkanen and Saadia M. Pekkanen, 701–21. New York: Oxford University Press.

Miki, Rieko, and Shunsuke Shigeta. 2023. "U.S. Poised to Extend Japan Security Umbrella into Space." *Nikkei Asia*. January 9, 2023. https://asia.nikkei.com/Politics/International-relations/U.S.-poised-to-extend-Japan-security-umbrella-into-space.

Milevski, Lukas. 2016. *The Evolution of Modern Grand Strategic Thought*. New York: Oxford University Press.

MOD (Ministry of Defense, Japan). 2019. "Joint Statement of the Security Consultative Committee." https://www.mod.go.jp/en/d_act/us/docs/201904_js.html.

MOD (Ministry of Defense, Japan). 2020a. "Uchū Sakusentai No Shinpen Ni Tsuite [on the Formation of the Space Operations Squadron]." News Release. https://www.mod.go.jp/asdf/news/release/2020/0518/.

MOD (Ministry of Defense, Japan). 2020b. "Uchū Sakusentai Shinboru Maaku Ni Tsuite [on the Emblem of the Space Operations Squadron]." News Release. https://www.mod.go.jp/asdf/news/release/2020/0731/#.

MOFA (Ministry of Foreign Affairs, Japan). 1960. "Treaty of Mutual Cooperation and Security between Japan and the United States of America." https://www.mofa.go.jp/region/n-america/us/q&a/ref/1.html.

MOFA (Ministry of Foreign Affairs, Japan). 2011. "Joint Statement of the Security Consultative Committee—toward a Deeper and Broader U.S.-Japan Alliance: Building on 50 Years of

Partnership—by Secretary of State Clinton, Secretary of Defense Gates, Minister for Foreign Affairs Matsumoto, and Minister of Defense Kitazawa." https://www.mofa.go.jp/region/n-america/us/security/pdfs/joint1106_01.pdf.

MOFA (Ministry of Foreign Affairs). 2012. "Fact Sheet: U.S.-Japan Cooperative Initiatives." https://www.mofa.go.jp/region/n-america/us/pmv1204/pdfs/Fact_Sheet_en.pdf.MOFA (Ministry of Foreign Affairs, Japan). 2020. "Uchū Kūkan ni Okeru Sekinin Aru Kōdō ni Kan Sur Ketsugian no Kokurensōkai Honkaigi no Saitaku [Adoption of the Draft Resolution on Responsible Behavior in Outer Space in the Plenary Meeting of the UN General Assembly]." https://www.mofa.go.jp/mofaj/press/release/press24_000058.html.

MOFA (Ministry of Foreign Affairs, Japan. 2022. "Joint Statement of the Security Consultative Committee ("2+2")." https://www.mofa.go.jp/files/100284739.pdf.

Moltz, James Clay. 2012. *Asia's Space Race: National Motivations, Regional Rivalries, and International Risks*. New York: Columbia University Press.

Moltz, James Clay. 2016. "Asian Space Rivalry and Cooperative Institutions: Mind the Gap." In *Asian Designs: Governance in the Contemporary World Order*, edited by Saadia M. Pekkanen, 116–34. Ithaca, NY: Cornell University Press.

Moriyasu, Ken. 2022. "'Geopolitical Powder Keg' Asia Jacks up Global Military Spending." *Nikkei Asia*. April 25, 2022. https://asia.nikkei.com/Politics/International-relations/Indo-Pacific/Geopolitical-powder-keg-Asia-jacks-up-global-military-spending.

Mulgan, Aurelia George. 2022. "The Role of the Prime Minister in Japan." In *The Oxford Handbook of Japanese Politics*, edited by Robert J. Pekkanen and Saadia M. Pekkanen, 57–73. New York: Oxford University Press.

Murray, Williamson. 2011. "Thoughts on Grand Strategy." In *The Shaping of Grand Strategy: Policy, Diplomacy, and War*, edited by Williamson Murray, Richard Hart Heinrich, and James Lacey, 1–33. New York: Cambridge University Press.

Murray, Williamson, and Mark Grimsley. 1994. "Introduction: On Strategy." In *The Making of Strategy: Rulers, States, and War*, edited by Williamson Murray, MacGregor Knox, and Alvin Bernstein, 1–23. New York: Cambridge University Press.

NASA (National Aeronautics and Space Administration). 1998a "International Space Station: Space Station Assembly—Partners Sign ISS Agreements." https://www.nasa.gov/mission_pages/station/structure/elements/partners_agreement.html.

NASA (National Aeronautics and Space Administration). 1998b. "NASA-Japan Agreement: Memorandum of Understanding between the National Aeronautics and Space Administration of the United States of America and the Government of Japan Concerning Cooperation on the Civil International Space Station." https://www.nasa.gov/mission_pages/station/structure/elements/nasa_japan.html.

Nikkei Asia. 2017. "Japan Aims to Double Its Space Market to $21bn by 2030s." *Nikkei Asia*. May 12, 2017. https://asia.nikkei.com/Economy/Japan-aims-to-double-its-space-market-to-21bn-by-2030s.

Nikkei Asia. 2022a. "Honda to Join Lunar Rover Project by JAXA." *Nikkei Asia*. September16, 2022. https://asia.nikkei.com/Business/Aerospace-Defense/Honda-to-join-lunar-rover-project-by-JAXA.

Nikkei Asia. 2022b. "Japan's Defense White Paper Sounds Alarm over China-Russia Ties." *Nikkei Asia*. July 27, 2022. https://asia.nikkei.com/Opinion/The-Nikkei-View/Japan-s-defense-white-paper-sounds-alarm-over-China-Russia-ties.

Nikkei Staff. 2022. "Japan Set to Increase Defense Budget 2% of Gdp in 2027." *Nikkei Asia*. November 28, 2022. https://asia.nikkei.com/Politics/Japan-set-to-increase-defense-budget-to-2-of-GDP-in-2027#.

Nippon.com. 2014. "Shūdanteki Jieiken Kōshi O Gentei Yōnin - Kakugi Kettei [Limited Recognition of the Right to Collective Self-Defense—Cabinet Decision]." Nippon.com. https://www.nippon.com/ja/features/h00062/.

Noble, Gregory W. 2022. "METI's Miraculous Comeback and the Uncertain Future of Japanese Industrial Policy." In *The Oxford Handbook of Japanese Politics*, edited by Robert J. Pekkanen and Saadia M. Pekkanen, 353–75. New York: Oxford University Press.

NSC (National Security Council, Japan). 2022. "Kokka Anzen Hoshō Senryaku Ni Tsuite." Cabinet Decision, MOD. https://www.mod.go.jp/j/approach/agenda/guideline/pdf/security_strategy.pdf.

NSS (National Security Secretariat, Cabinet Secretariat, Japan). 2022. "Kokka Anzen Hoshō Senryaku (Gaiyō) [National Security Strategy (Synopsis)]." MOD. https://www.mod.go.jp/j/approach/agenda/guideline/pdf/security_strategy_outline.pdf.

Oros, Andrew L. 2007. "Explaining Japan's Tortured Course to Surveillance Satellites." *Review of Policy Research* 24, no. 1: 29–48.

Oros, Andrew L. 2008. *Normalizing Japan: Politics, Identity, and the Evolution of Security Practice*. Stanford, CA: Stanford University Press.

Oros, Andrew L. 2017. *Japan's Security Renaissance: New Policies and Politics for the Twenty-First Century*. New York: Columbia University Press.

Paine, S. C. M. 2017. *The Japanese Empire: Grand Strategy from the Meiji Restoration to the Pacific War*. New York: Cambridge University Press.

Park, Si-soo. 2021. "Japan Budgets a Record $4.14 Billion for Space Activities." *Spacenews*. March 9, 2021. https://spacenews.com/japan-budgets-a-record-4-14-billion-for-space-activities/.

Pekkanen, Saadia M. 2003. *Picking Winners? From Technology Catch-up to the Space Race in Japan*. Stanford, CA: Stanford University Press.

Pekkanen, Saadia M. 2015a. "Japan's Ballistic Missile Defense and 'Proactive Pacifism.'" In *Regional Missile Defense from a Global Perspective*, edited by Peter Dombrowski and Catherine Kelleher, 217–37, Stanford, CA: Stanford University Press.

Pekkanen, Saadia M. 2015b. "All Eyes on China, but Japan May Be the Space Power to Watch." *Forbes*. May 30. https://www.forbes.com/sites/saadiampekkanen/2015/05/30/all-eyes-on-china-but-japan-may-be-the-space-power-to-watch/#780f92374a8f.

Pekkanen, Saadia M. 2015c. "U.S.-Japan Military Space Alliance Promises to Grow in 'New Ways.'" *Forbes*. October 27, 2015. https://www.forbes.com/sites/saadiampekkanen/2015/10/27/u-s-japan-military-space-alliance-promises-to-grow-in-new-ways/#1708792b7d5d.

Pekkanen, Saadia M. 2019. "Governing the New Space Race." *American Journal of International Law Unbound* 113, 92–97. https://doi.org/10.1017/aju.2019.16.

Pekkanen, Saadia M. 2020. "Thank You for Your Service: The Security Implications of Japan's Counterspace Capabilities." *Texas National Security Review*, Policy Roundtable, October 1, 2020: 70–89. https://tnsr.org/roundtable/policy-roundtable-the-future-of-japanese-security-and-defense/.

Pekkanen, Saadia M. 2021a. "China, Japan, and the Governance of Space: Prospects for Competition and Cooperation." *International relations of the Asia-Pacific* 21, no. 1: 37–64.

Pekkanen, Saadia M. 2021b. "Japan's Space Defence Policy Charts Its Own Course." *East Asia Forum*. https://www.eastasiaforum.org/.

Pekkanen, Saadia M. 2022a. "The Promise and Peril of Satellite Imagery." *The Seattle Times*. August 26, 2022. https://www.seattletimes.com/opinion/zooming-in-on-the-promise-and-peril-of-satellite-imagery/.

Pekkanen, Saadia M. 2022b. "Developing State Practice for the Governance of Space Resources." In Governing the Global Commons: Challenges and Opportunities for US-Japan Cooperation, edited by Kristi Govella. Policy Paper, German Marshall Fund, 35–38. https://www.gmfus.org/sites/default/files/2022-12/Govella%20et%20al%20%20-%20US%20Japan%20cooperation%20-%20paper%20-%20web.pdf.

Pekkanen, Saadia M. 2022c. "Neoclassical Realism in Japan's Space Security." In The Oxford Handbook of Japanese Politics, edited by Robert J. Pekkanen and Saadia M. Pekkanen, 763–90. New York: Oxford University Press.

Pekkanen, Saadia M. 2023. "Japan's Space Diplomacy in a World of Great Power Competition." The Hague Journal of Diplomacy, 18, no. 2-3: 282–316.

Pekkanen, Saadia M., and Paul Kallender-Umezu. 2010. In Defense of Japan: From the Market to the Military in Space Policy. Stanford, CA: Stanford University Press.

Pekkanen, Saadia M., and Paul Kallender-Umezu. 2011. "National Security in Japan's Space Policy." In Japan in Decline: Fact or Fiction?, edited by Purnendra Jain and Brad Williams, 92–109. Kent, UK: Global Oriental.

Pekkanen, Saadia M., Setsuko Aoki, and John Mittleman. 2022. "Small Satellites, Big Data: Uncovering the Invisible in Maritime Security." International Security 47, no. 2: 177–216. https://doi.org/10.1162/isec_a_00445.

Pekkanen, Saadia M., Setsuko Aoki, and Yumiko Takatori. n.d. "Japan in the New Lunar Space Race." August 17, 2023. Available online: https://doi.org/10.1016/j.spacepol.2023.101577.

Pempel, T. J. 2013. "Conclusion: The Uneasy Dance of Economics and Security." In The Economy-Security Nexus in Northeast Asia, edited by T. J. Pempel, 189–206. New York: Oxford University Press.

Pryor, Cystal. 2016. "Japan: Revising Arms Export Regulation." Worldecr. May 23, 2016 https://www.worldecr.com/archive/japan-revising-arms-export-regulation/.

Pyle, Kenneth B. 2007. Japan Rising: The Resurgence of Japanese Power and Purpose. New York: PublicAffairs.

Reuters. 1990. "Talks on Satellites Stalled." New York Times. March 15, 1990. https://www.nytimes.com/1990/03/15/business/talks-on-satellites-stalled.html?searchResultPosition=3.

Reuters. 2021. "China, Russia Navy Ships Jointly Sail through Japan Strait." Reuters. October 19, 2021. https://www.reuters.com/world/asia-pacific/china-russia-navy-ships-jointly-sail-through-japan-strait-2021-10-19/.

Reuters. 2022. "Russia Warns West: We Can Target Your Commercial Satellites." Reuters. October 27, 2022. https://www.reuters.com/world/russia-says-wests-commercial-satellites-could-be-targets-2022-10-27/.

Ripsman, Norrin M. 2019. "The Emerging Sub-Field of Comparative Grand Strategy." In Comparative Grand Strategy: A Framework and Cases, edited by Thierry Balzacq, Peter Dombrowski, and Simon Reich, 284–302. New York: Oxford University Press.

Ripsman, Norrin, and Igor Kovac. 2021. "Material Sources of Grand Strategy." In The Oxford Handbook of Grand Strategy, edited by Thierry Balzacq and Ronald R. Krebs, 205–20. New York: Oxford University Press.

Roh, Suk-jo. 2022. "U.S. To Launch Regional Space Force Command in Korea." The Chosunilbo. November 28, 2022. https://english.chosun.com/site/data/html_dir/2022/11/28/2022112801299.html.

Saeki, Koji. 2017. "Paradigm Change in Space and Corresponding Policy." APRSAF-24. https://aprsaf.org/annual_meetings/aprsaf24/data/day17/SpacePolicy5_Japan.pdf.

Sahashi, Ryo. 2017. "Japan's Strategic Hedging under Trump," *East Asia Forum*. https://www.eastasiaforum.org/2017/06/06/japans-strategic-hedging-under-trump/.

Samuels, Richard J. 1994. *"Rich Nation, Strong Army": National Security and the Technological Transformation of Japan*. Ithaca, NY: Cornell University Press.

Samuels, Richard J. 2007. *Securing Japan: Tokyo's Grand Strategy and the Future of East Asia*. Ithaca, NY: Cornell University Press.

Sato, Taro. 2020. "The Case for Japan-U.S. Space Cooperation in the Indo-Pacific." *The Japan Times*. June 21, 2020. https://www.japantimes.co.jp/opinion/2020/06/21/commentary/japan-commentary/case-japan-u-s-space-cooperation-indo-pacific/.

Schierholz, Stephanie, and Josh Finch. 2020. "NASA Selects Companies to Collect Lunar Resources for Artemis Demonstrations." Release 20-118, NASA. https://www.nasa.gov/press-release/nasa-selects-companies-to-collect-lunar-resources-for-artemis-demonstrations.

Selding, Peter B. de. 2010. "Japanese Government Seeks to Reorient Space Spending." *SpaceNews*. September 28, 2010. https://spacenews.com/japanese-government-seeks-reorient-space-spending/.

Sheehan, Michael. 2015. "Defining Space Security." In *Handbook of Space Security: Policies, Applications and Programs*, edited by Kai-Uwe Schrogl, Peter L. Hays, Jana Robinson, Denis Moura, and Christina Giannopapa, 7–21. Vol. 1. New York: Springer Reference.

Shinoda, Tomohito. 2022. "The Policy-making Process in Japan." In *The Oxford Handbook of Japanese Politics*, edited by Robert J. Pekkanen and Saadia M. Pekkanen, 245–62. New York: Oxford University Press.

SJAC (Society of Japanese Aerospace Companies). 2021. "Japanese Space Industry: Annual Survey Report—Fiscal Year 2019 Results." Tokyo, SJAC, 1–33. https://www.sjac.or.jp/english/pdf/publication/JapaneseSpaceIndustryAnnualSurveyReport_FY2019.pdf.

SJAC (Society of Japanese Aerospace Companies). 2022a. "2021 Uchū Kiki Sangyō Jittai Chōsa Hōkokushō: Gaiyō [Report on the Survey of the State of the Japanese Space Industry: Synopsis]." No. 819, 1–20. https://www.sjac.or.jp/pdf/data/5_R3_uchu.pdf.

SJAC (Society of Japanese Aerospace Companies). 2022b. "Sekai No Uchū Sangyō Dōkō [Trends in the Global Space Industry]." Tokyo, SJAC, 38–46. https://www.sjac.or.jp/pdf/publication/backnumber/202209/20220905.pdf.

Smith, Sheila A. 2019. *Japan Rearmed: The Politics of Military Power*. Cambridge, MA: Harvard University Press.

Smith, Sheila A. 2022. "How Japan Is Doubling Down on Its Military Power," Council on Foreign Relations, https://www.cfr.org/article/how-japan-doubling-down-its-military-power.

Solis, Mireya. 2020 "The Underappreciated Power: Japan after Abe." *Foreign Affairs* 99, no. 6 123–32.

SpaceNews Staff. 2010. "Hayabusa: Mission Accomplished," *Spacenews*. November 30, 2010. https://spacenews.com/hayabusa-mission-accomplished/.

Stanley, Morgan. 2020. "Space: Investing in the Final Frontier," Morgan Stanley Research. https://www.morganstanley.com/ideas/investing-in-space.

Suzuki, Akiko. 2014. "APRSAF Activity in the Asia-Pacific Regiona for the Next Decade." 57th Session of the Committee on the Peaceful Uses of Outer Space, Vienna, June 11–20, 2014, 1–13. https://www.unoosa.org/pdf/pres/copuos2014/tech-15.pdf.

Suzuki, Kazuto. 2013. "The Contest for Leadership in East Asia: Japanese and Chinese Approaches to Outer Space." *Space Policy* 29: 99–106.

Suzuki, Kazuto. 2015. "Space Security in Japan." In *Handbook of Space Security: Policies, Applications, Programs*, edited by Kai-Uwe Schrogl, Peter L. Hays, Jana Robinson, Denis Moura, and Christina Giannopapa, 397–412. New York: Springer Reference.

Takada, Shuzo. 2019. "Space Policy of Japan." Cabinet Office, National Space Policy Secretariat, Tokyo, Japan.

Tani, Shotaro. 2017. "The 'Final Frontier' Is Now the Next Place of Business." *Nikkei Asia*. January 27, 2017. https://asia.nikkei.com/Economy/The-final-frontier-is-now-the-next-place-of-business3.

Tateshita, Yumiko. 2022. "Progress Report on Aprsaf's Initiatives for Enhancing Space Policy and Law Capacity in the Asia-Pacific Region." 65th session of the Committee on the Peaceful Uses of Outer Space, June 2, 2022, 1–16. https://www.unoosa.org/documents/pdf/copuos/2022/1._Japan_TateshitaLSC_Tech-presen_final_4.pdf.

UCS (Union of Concerned Scientists). 2022 [2005] "UCS Satellite Database." Last updated May 1, 2022. https://www.ucsusa.org/resources/satellite-database.

USDOD (US Department of Defense). 2020. "Defense Space Strategy: Summary." https://media.defense.gov/2020/Jun/17/2002317391/-1/-1/1/2020_DEFENSE_SPACE_STRATEGY_SUMMARY.PDF?fbclid=IwAR2TYXPZVQm00-ybSXM3UHOYK-sRsdlvaETKChf1raiGaFMYR64QkMxu_90.

UNGA (United Nations General Assembly). 2020. "Resolution Adopted by the General Assembly on 7 December 2020: 75/36 Reducing Space Threats through Norms, Rules and Principles of Responsible Behaviours." Seventy-Fifth session, Agenda item 101a, A/RES/75/36. https://digitallibrary.un.org/record/3895440.

USGOV (US Government [The White House]). 2022. "Fact Sheet: Vice President Harris Advances National Security Norms in Space." Statements and Releases. https://www.whitehouse.gov/briefing-room/statements-releases/2022/04/18/fact-sheet-vice-president-harris-advances-national-security-norms-in-space/.

Wirtz, James J. 2009. "Space and Grand Strategy." In *Space and Defense Policy*, edited by Damon Coletta and Frances T. Pilch, 13–26. New York: Routledge.

Yan, Yongliang. 2021. "Capacity Building in Regional Space Cooperation: Asia-Pacific Space Cooperation Organization." *Advances in Space Research* 67, no. 1: 597–616.

Yoshimatsu, Hidetaka. 2021. "Japan's International Engagements in Outer Space." *Australian Outlook*. June 15, 2021. https://www.internationalaffairs.org.au/australianoutlook/japans-international-engagements-in-outer-space/.

CHAPTER 19

....

INDIA'S SPACE PROGRAM

Its Evolution and Future Trajectory

....

RAJESWARI PILLAI RAJAGOPALAN AND
ŠUMIT GANGULY

INTRODUCTION

....

INDIA'S space program has come a long way since it started in the early 1960s. Though a poor country, India's leaders had always emphasized the need for India to remain at the forefront of technological developments. Thus, India developed a relatively large and complex civilian nuclear program that emphasized the development of an indigenous atomic technology base. Similarly, India also stressed developing supercomputing facilities. Seen in this light, it is not a surprise that India also established an indigenous space program. However, unlike other areas of high technology, the space program has been a resounding success. India's civilian nuclear sector, despite advances, is still struggling, forcing India to continue to seek external support. Similarly, India's supercomputing abilities, despite its early promise, have faltered, with barely a couple of supercomputers in the top 500 (Banerjee 2020; Dutt 2021). By contrast, India's space program is considered a success, both in terms of its size and its technological achievements.

One of the most noteworthy developments has been that though initially focusing largely on civilian needs, India's space program has also expanded to cater to growing military and security requirements. Changes in regional security dynamics, especially in its neighborhood, provided an important context for pushing India in this direction, as did global security developments. Within India's Indo-Pacific neighborhood, China's advancing space prowess, especially its sizeable inventory of counterspace capabilities, has had a considerable influence on India's changing approach to space. The recognition within the Indian security policy community that ignoring the growing Chinese space capabilities can have negative consequences for its national security is increasingly driving the Indian shift on space security. Also, developments in the larger global space are an important factor driving the shifts in the Indian approach to both space security and broader global non-proliferation efforts. A key aspect of the change in the Indian position involves shifting from an ethical and principled position of objection to space militarization to one that is driven by pragmatism and national security requirements. This Indian recognition of new security compulsions has made its approach to space security a lot more pragmatic and nuanced. India's position has evolved a great deal from the 1970s and 1980s when it was one of the most vehement critics of the military space programs of both the United States and the USSR. Also, as the requirement for space capacity has increased, India has opened the space sector to private sector participation, albeit in a limited manner, to achieve the capability mix required to meet its growing space demands.

This remainder of the chapter is set up as follows. The first section traces the evolution of India's space program starting from the 1960s. The second section describes India's key achievements in the space sector that have shaped its overall space profile. The third section examines the drivers that are shifting India's space program, from a development orientation to one with a greater focus on space security, which include changing threat perceptions within the space domain and the shifting global balance of power. The subsequent section outlines India's responses to changing space conditions, specifically, policy, institutional, technological, and commercial. The final section looks at the emerging contours of India's space program and possible implications for India's peaceful space pursuit.

EVOLUTION OF INDIA'S SPACE PROGRAM

Today, India is, without question, a space power to be reckoned with. It has successfully placed a vehicle on the moon (Carter 2019), an orbiter around Mars (Amos 2019), and despite delays, is planning a manned space mission in 2024 (PTI 2022). The program, which also launches satellites for advanced industrial countries on a commercial basis ("ISRO Launches 10th Satellite . . . " 2018), had quite modest beginnings (Jha 2017). Its genesis can be traced back to 1962 with the creation of the Thumba Equatorial Rocket Launching Station (TERLS) in the southern Indian state of Kerala. The choice of this fishing village stemmed from its proximity to the electrojet, an earth-circling current associated with the magnetic equator (McElheny 1965, 1487–89).

The Indian space program—started at a time when much of the country was still mired in dire poverty—benefited from three distinct sources. At the outset, under Prime Minister Nehru the country had embarked on a quest for technological autonomy (Nayar 1983). To that end, even prior to its independence in 1947, it had started civilian atomic research (Anderson 2010). The country's leadership, especially under Nehru, had believed that the harnessing of a range of scientific and technological processes was critical to ending India's economic backwardness (Tyabji 2007, 130–36).

The program also significantly benefited from the visionary outlook of the first director of the Indian Space Research Organisation (ISRO), Vikram Sarabhai. The scion of a wealthy family from the state of Gujarat, Sarabhai, a physicist trained at Cambridge, had spelled out a vision for space exploration shortly after the inception of the organization. Finally, thanks to the efforts of Sarabhai, and another visionary and entrepreneurial scientist, Homi Jehangir Bhabha, another Cambridge-trained physicist, who had worked under Lord Earnest Rutherford, the nascent Indian space program also benefited considerably from a range of foreign collaboration. Three countries, the United States, the USSR, and France, in particular, played vital roles in boosting the fledgling space program. Finally, the country also benefited from critical assistance from the United Nations (UN).

As early as 1961, Sarabhai, who had already established himself as an authority on cosmic ray research, traveled to the United States where he met with two key individuals, Wilmot Averill and Arnold Frutkin, who were in charge of the National Aeronautics and Space Administration's (NASA) Office of International Programs. At this meeting, Sarabhai proposed the creation of a space research station in India. Bereft of the appropriate technology, he sought material assistance from NASA while offering a possible locale and scientific manpower (Siddiqi 2015, 420–51). Fortunately for Sarabhai, NASA had a mandate to extend international collaboration and so his plea received a sympathetic hearing from his US interlocutors. In part, the welcome reaction from his US counterparts, stemmed from Cold War considerations: the United States was keen on limiting possible Soviet involvement in the promotion of science and technology in the developing world (Siddiqi 2015, 430).

Sarabhai's efforts were successful. The United States proved willing to help but suggested that for such collaboration to prove fruitful India would need to create a single, nodal agency with which NASA could cooperate. With the support of Bhabha and with Nehru's imprimatur, in February 1962, India set up the Indian National Committee for Space Research (INSCOSPAR). Sarabhai was appointed as the first director of this organization (Siddiqi 2015, 432). Along with Sarabhai, three other scientists, K. R. Ramanathan, M. G. K. Menon, and A. P. Mitra, were also appointed as members of the organization. With the creation of this entity, the next task that confronted Bhabha and Sarabhai involved the selection of a suitable site for the rocket launching station. To that end, Sarabhai invited a set of US scientists to advise him and the Indian government on the choice of an appropriate site. One of the US scientists, Laurence J. Cahill Jr., who was interested in cosmic ray research wanted to run an experiment at the geomagnetic equator. Accordingly, his Indian counterparts sought a location in southern India. After taking into account local conditions, including the inevitable dislocation of native inhabitants of the area, they chose a fishing village, Thumba, in the southern state of Kerala (Siddiqi 2015, 436).

The next task, of course, involved the training of Indian scientists in the fundamentals of rocketry. To that end, a selected group of talented Indians were sent to a NASA facility at Wallops Island, Virginia. After obtaining suitable training in rocket launches, they returned to Kerala to carry out the first space launch. As agreed upon earlier, NASA provided the rocket technology as well as some technical assistance in the form of key personnel who came to India. After some initial technical and organizational hitches, given the rudimentary state of the newly created facility, a Nike-Apache rocket was successfully launched from Thumba on November 21, 1963 (Siddiqi 2015, 440). India's space program had now formally been inaugurated.

The next endeavor involved the development of a satellite instructional television experiment (SITE). Initially, the US Department of State had been chary of cooperating with India on this project because it had turned down a request to place Voice of America (VOA) transmitters in the country. However, Frutkin, aware of the geographic advantages that India offered, asked Sarabhai to make a request for US technological assistance. Sarabhai, keen on developing India's nascent space program, readily agreed.

Accordingly, he requested the use of an Applications Technology Satellite (ATS) for a year to conduct a SITE in India's villages. To that end, the Indian Department of Atomic Energy and NASA signed an agreement for a SITE experiment in 1966 (Raman 1997, 215–26). In time, this project proved to be highly successful. Using NASA's experimental communications satellite, ATS 6, educational television programs for farmers and students were broadcast to two thousand four hundred villages in six states for the duration of a year (Tefft 1988, 33–42).

Even as the United States had proven to be the principal contributor to the inception and development of the Indian space program, the USSR, France, and the UN also made important contributions in these early years. The Soviets, quite understandably, were keen to offer assistance because the United States had been involved with the program from the outset. The French contribution was idiosyncratic: an Indian scientist, Praful Bhavsar, had worked with a noted French astrophysicist, Jacques Blamont, who had, in turn, been responsible for the development of a French rocket, the Veronique (Siddiqi 2015, 437).

Subsequently in 1964, Blamont provided three Centaure rockets carrying sodium ejectors. These were successfully launched and enabled Indian scientific personnel to gain further experience. Later Sarabhai purchased the license to manufacture the Centaure Rockets and also the more powerful Dragon (Blamont 2015, 5).

LANDMARK DEVELOPMENTS

The next major development was the launch of the Indian National Satellite System (INSAT). This was made possible through ISRO's collaboration with NASA. To facilitate this collaboration, Sarabhai created the National Study Group for Satellite Communications (NASCOM). Its remit was to coordinate the activities of a range of ministries including education, health, communication and information, and broadcasting. With this entity in place, Indian scientists made a creditable performance at the first UN Space Conference held in Vienna, Austria, in 1968 where they presented a variety of technical papers. Subsequently, a group of Indian engineers traveled to the United States to learn about satellite technology. This enabled them to acquire sufficient technical knowledge to lay the foundations of INSAT (Chitnis 2015, 29). The initial purpose of INSAT technology was to beam television programs designed to aid Indian agriculture.

To that end, in mid-1968, the government set a seventeen-member committee composed of both scientists and engineers at the Space Science and Technology Center at Thumba to conduct a preliminary feasibility study. Initially, the committee had concluded that the satellite would be built with foreign collaboration. However, they had not anticipated the possible reluctance of advanced industrial states to transfer such technology. Some initial negotiations with NASA to borrow the ATS-6 gave rise to optimism about such collaboration. However, in the end these discussions proved unfruitful. Nevertheless, Sarabhai was undaunted and in 1970 he announced plans for an Indian National Satellite at the Bombay National Electronics Conference. Unfortunately, bureaucratic politics hampered his visionary endeavor. Neither the Post and Telegraphs Department nor the Ministry of Defence expressed much interest in the development of satellite telecommunications. Worse still, in December 1971 Sarabhai met an untimely death.

In January 1972, the Government of India appointed Satish Dhawan, another space scientist, to head the country's space program. Dhawan had previous experience in aeronautics having had worked at the state-owned firm Hindustan Aeronautics Limited (HAL) and was also familiar with Soviet aerospace technology. Along with Dhawan's appointment came the creation of a Department of Space (DoS). Dhawan successfully persuaded Indian Prime Minister Indira Gandhi to locate the entity in the southern city of Bangalore (later Bengaluru).

Dhawan proved to be an energetic proponent of India's space program. Cognizant that he could not terminate the SITE program without seriously jeopardizing India's relationship with NASA, he decided to make SITE a success. In the meanwhile, the government showed scant interest in INSAT owing to fiscal constraints. Once SITE succeeded, however, INSAT was revived, with the Ministry of Telecommunications awakening to the possibilities of satellite technologies (Srinivasan, 1997). Thereafter, the United States and the European Space Agency helped launch a series of INSAT satellites. One of the first INSAT satellites, INSAT-IB, made national television broadcasting possible: signals relayed by the satellite could reach the most remote villages enabling 60–75 percent of the population to watch television (Teftt 1988, 39).

The next major development was the successful pursuit of a Satellite Launch Vehicle, the SLV-3. Again, Sarabhai was at the forefront of this effort as early as 1970. At this point, the goal was a relatively modest endeavor: to launch a satellite vehicle of 10 kilograms into low earth orbit. The task of developing this vehicle was assigned to a young India-trained engineer, A. P. J. Kalam. Fortunately for Kalam, he had the support of senior scientist-bureaucrats who gave him considerable leeway to pursue this project. Notable among them was Bhrahm Prakash, who had become the director of the Vikram Sarabhai Space Centre.

It took a team, that Kalam assembled, seven years to accomplish this particular mission. In the end, the SLV-3 was a four-stage solid propulsive vehicle. Its lift-off weight was 17 tonnes and its total length was 22 meters. It was designed to launch a 35 kilogram satellite into a low earth elliptical orbit. Eventually, the vehicle was launched in August 1979 from the Sriharikota Range in the central Indian state of Andhra Pradesh. This initial effort, unfortunately, failed at the launch stage owing to some technical design flaws. Despite the lapse, the engineers managed to detect the likely sources of malfunction and set about to work on a second launch. This successful launch came about on July 18, 1980. The fourth stage of the rocket successfully placed the Rohini satellite into low earth orbit (Kalam 2015, 118–23) and India successfully mastered the launch of satellite technology.

This launch laid the foundations of subsequent developments in the space program including the pursuit of the Augmented Satellite Launch Vehicle (ASLV) and the Polar Satellite Launch Vehicle (PSLV). The ASLV program was designed to launch a number of satellites, the Stretched Rohini Satellite Series (SROSS). The four satellites in this series carried payloads to study gamma rays and conduct studies of the upper atmosphere. With the development of the PSLV, the organization could now place 1,000 kilogram remote sensing satellites into the Sun Synchronous Polar Orbit (SSPO).

By the 1970s, ISRO had entered the arena of remote sensing. This led to the launch of the Bhaskara-I and Bhaskara-II satellites. These, in turn, led to the Indian Remote Sensing program designed to foster the National Natural Resources Management System (NNRMS). The NNRMS was focused on developing a national inventory of natural resources. Subsequently, the ISRO went on to develop high-resolution imagery satellites and also improved its remote sensing capabilities with the development of the Synthetic Aperture Radar (SAR), at a much later date (Nagendra 2016, 38–45).

It took India into the late 1980s to launch its first ASLV. Unfortunately, the initial two efforts were failures. However, the two subsequent launches proved to be successful. The next effort that was mounted was the more powerful Polar Satellite Launch Vehicle (PSLV). Once again, the initial launch in September 1993 proved to be a fizzle. Subsequently, however, there were fifteen consecutive successful launches placing thirty satellites fourteen of which were Indian and sixteen foreign into a range of orbits (Noronha 2009).

THE LAST TWO DECADES: A NEW PHASE IN INDIA'S SPACE PROGRAM

In the new millennium, India's space program saw its share of both setbacks and achievements. One of the principal failures was its initial effort to place a geosynchronous satellite launch vehicle, the GSLV-D3, into orbit in April 2010. After an apparently successful lift-off, the rocket lost altitude shortly after third stage ignition after having reached a height of 87 miles and a speed of around 11,000 miles per hour. This was a significant setback for the organization as this launch had been designed to make it self-reliant in launching heavy satellite payloads (Butterworth-Hayes 2010, 34). The program, continued to face problems, as a second launch in December of 2010 also failed (Noronha 2012).

Later, in January 2018, the Indian space program reached a milestone of sorts. On January 11, the ISRO launched its hundredth satellite along with thirty others from the Sriharikota space launch center in the state of Andhra Pradesh. This development came in the wake of a series of other achievements over the past several years. For example, in 2008 India had launched its first unmanned lunar space probe, Chandrayaan-1. The subsequent attempt to ensure the soft landing of an unmanned vehicle on the moon proved to be, at best, a partial success. Though the mission, Chandrayaan-2, launched in September 2019, did succeed in reaching the moon, it did a hard landing into its surface. ISRO scientists, however, insisted that the mission was not a complete failure even though the Vikram lander (named after Vikram Sarabhai) failed to properly deploy (Koksal 2019).

Later in 2014, it had successfully launched the Mars Orbiter Mission, the Mangalyaan, at a cost that was at least ten times lower than that of a comparable US project. This mission, by all accounts, has proven to be a significant success. Launched in September 2013, it reached Martian orbit in 2014. Initially, the device was expected to have a life of six months. However, seven years later, it was still in orbit around Mars and transmitting vital data ("ISRO's Mars Orbiter . . ." 2021). And in 2016, the ISRO had successfully tested the Reusable Launch Vehicle-Technology Demonstrator (RLV-TD), which again had been built on a shoestring budget (Indo Asian News Service 2018). This device, about 6.5 meters in length, could be likened to a miniature version of NASA's space shuttle. A booster rocket carried the RLV 56 kilometers above Earth, past the upper limits for aircraft and weather balloons. After the booster rocket detached, the RLV traveled through the mesosphere before reaching an altitude of 65 kilometers (Gearin 2016).

In the next section we turn to a discussion of the recent shift in the space program and policy, which has emphasized questions of space security.

INDIA'S APPROACH TO SPACE SECURITY
FROM THE 2000S

India had for long approached space security from a doctrinaire perspective or a sanctuary school of thought, reiterating the peaceful and civilian use of space and voicing strong opposition to the militarization and weaponization of space. India, therefore, was vehemently opposed to the US Strategic Defense Initiative program, efforts at developing ballistic missile defenses (BMD), and the repeated anti-satellite (ASAT) tests by the US and the USSR (Subbarao 1989, 560–78). Of course, at the time, India did not possess the wherewithal to acquire any of these capabilities, and hence its logic was clear. However, since the 2000s, India's approach to outer space has been undergoing significant changes. This has corresponded with India becoming a more visible and influential player in Asian and global politics, which has influenced its attitudes and approaches to space security. An important shift in its position on these issues involves a move from one based on morality and principles to one that is guided by pragmatic national security considerations. India had traditionally been a vehement critic of space militarization, emphasizing that outer space should be used only for peaceful purposes. More recently, however, India's rhetoric has softened because adherence to these prior commitments were impinging on its national interests. In the next section, we turn to a discussion of how external factors, most notably changing threat perceptions, have altered the course of India's space program.

THE DRIVERS OF INDIA'S RECENT APPROACH TO SPACE SECURITY

This section discusses a set of factors that have affected India's newer approaches to space security that draw on standard IR analytics, namely threat perceptions and balance of power. States are expected to respond to changes in their security circumstances. Though these responses may not be instantaneous, the expectation is that states that wish to survive and prosper will need to pay attention to changes in the security conditions that they face. Moreover, we should also expect that states would prioritize security concerns over other demands. These can be seen in India's space behavior, in terms of how its focus has shifted over the last decade.

Changing Threat Perceptions

Perceptions of growing threats from Pakistan and, more recently, China have led to shifts in India's space program. Though India's space program always included some security considerations, this has become much more pronounced because of the development of Pakistani and Chinese capabilities. This can be traced to two sources: the growth of Pakistan's missile capabilities and then China's efforts to weaponize space.

Though India was the first to develop surface-to-surface ballistic missiles in the subcontinent, Pakistan quickly caught up with India through collaboration with China, North Korea, and Iran. It developed a number of short- and medium-range missiles, some of them using variations of the old Soviet-origin SCUD missiles, in collaboration with North Korea. The best known of these is the Ghauri medium-range missile (Center for Strategic and International Studies n.d). Probably as a consequence of the delays in the development in its indigenous missile capabilities, Pakistan sought to buy some missiles from China, such as the M-9 and M-11 (Cirincione, Wolfsthal, and Rajkumar,

2005). These developments induced India to seek BMD. The pursuit of India's BMD goes to the mid-1990s, a short while after news of Pakistan's M-9 and M-11 missiles became public (Rajagopalan 2005, 606). India pursued indigenous development of BMD systems but also sought such systems from a variety of sources including Israel and Russia.

After the South Asian nuclear tests in 1998, as the nuclear forces of both countries expanded, Indian concerns became even greater because its nuclear doctrine and no first use posture required its national command authority to survive a possible Pakistani nuclear strike (Ganguly 2014, 373–82; Rajagopalan 2017). India's pursuit of BMD also led to a drastic change in its approach toward arms control in this arena. Thus, when the United States under President George W. Bush walked out of the Anti-Ballistic Missile (ABM) Treaty in 2001, India was one of the few countries that did not criticize the US decision (Ministry of External Affairs 2001; Rajagopalan 2011). India's tacit support for the US withdrawal from the ABM treaty was even more surprising because India had traditionally strongly objected to any effort to expand the arms race into outer space and was vigorously opposed to previous US missile defense efforts such as the Strategic Defense Initiative (SDI) (Strategic Digest 1985, cited in Tellis 2006). The change in India's attitude becomes less surprising when seen against the backdrop of India's own security concerns about Pakistan's missiles. India's shift on the ABM treaty was also significant because it, along with India's earlier refusal to accede to the Comprehensive Test Ban Treaty (CTBT), were indicators of a fundamental Indian re-evaluation of the relationship between its national security and arms control (Rajagopalan and Biswas 2016).

By the late 2000s, China's growing power, with technological prowess in outer space, and its growing ambitions led to further changes in India's threat perceptions with regard to outer space. In particular, China's first successful ASAT test in January 2007 was a rude wake up call to India, leading it to further reconsider its interests on outer space security. Yet China's ASAT test was only the tip of the spear, because its growing space capabilities as well as its competition with the United States led to the development of a variety of counterspace technologies including ground-based lasers, directed energy weapons, cyber warfare capabilities, and Rendezvous Proximity and On-Orbit Satellite Servicing (OOSS) technologies (Weeden and Samson 2021; Harrison et al. 2021).

Further, while most militaries around the world use space for a number of passive military activities including intelligence, surveillance, and reconnaissance (ISR) missions, a 2019 report by the US Defense Intelligence Agency (DIA), "Challenges to Security in Space," stated that China had developed fairly advanced space surveillance capabilities that are "capable of searching, tracking, and characterizing satellites in all earth orbits" (Defense Intelligence Agency 2019). That these capabilities can be used for effective counterspace operations has been a growing concern to India, among others.

China's institutional innovation in creating the People's Liberation Army Strategic Support Force (PLASSF) is particularly significant because it indicates that China sees outer space as playing an increasingly important role in modern warfare (Costello and McReynolds 2018). The establishment of the PLASSF is notable from several angles, the most important being the integration of the army's outer space, cyber space, and electronic warfare, making it a more potent force to deal with. While almost all of these were developed to counter the United States, there was little doubt that these could easily be deployed against India given India's own growing presence in space.

The Shifting Global Balance of Power

Growing tensions with a rising and more assertive China has also sped India's space program along. For one, the growing tensions have reduced the likelihood of progress in international arms control. This has affected the outer space regime too, because the existing space regime has become increasingly incapable of managing contemporary requirements. These new challenges include a spike in the number as well as diversity of stakeholders, space debris, counterspace weapons, arms races, small satellites, and large satellite constellations.

Over the last decade, international recognition of these problems has led to a number of efforts to come up with new mechanisms to supplement the few existing Cold War agreements. For example, a proposal on the Prevention of Arms Race in Outer Space (PAROS) has been around for more than three decades, but the Conference on Disarmament (CD), the traditional venue for space security and arms control issues, has yet to hold a productive session on it (see West, this volume). There have been other efforts as well, including the China-Russia sponsored draft Treaty on the Prevention of the Placement of Weapons in Outer Space, the Threat or Use of Force against Outer Space Objects (PPWT), originally proposed in 2008 (with a revised text introduced in 2014); the 2010 EU-initiated International Code of Conduct for Outer Space Activities (ICoC), the UN Group of Governmental Experts (GGE) on Transparency and Confidence Building Measures (TCBMs) in 2013, and the 2018–2019 GGE on Further Effective Measures for the Prevention of an Arms Race in Outer Space. Given the prevailing international security climate, it is unlikely that any of these efforts will be successful because of the lack of consensus among great powers, which has been a significant impediment.

These growing problems affect all space programs and not just India's. In the absence of successful multilateral efforts, national space programs that are uncoordinated internationally face the danger of leading to deliberate or unintended damages. For example, the problem of international space debris affects satellites of all nations as does the problem of uncontrolled re-entry, such as the recent Chinese re-entry event (NASA 2019; China Manned Space 2021; Wattles 2021). The absence of international coordination has encouraged countries including India to develop their space programs without adequate international regulation and governance. A more direct effect has been on the increasing focus on security applications of space technology. The growing tensions and the expansion of terrestrial conflicts to outer space has forced India to increase its own investment in such technologies and innovations.

Thus, as noted earlier, India developed its own ASAT capability and has expanded utilization of space assets for military services. Some of this is relatively benign, such as space-based communications including GSAT-6 and GSAT-7A communication satellites. In addition, India has also expanded the use of space-based surveillance satellites including RISAT-1 for a variety of purposes, including counterterrorism. Many of these are dual-use satellites but India also has a few purely security-oriented satellites. India has not yet launched space-based early warning systems, unlike the United States and the USSR during the Cold War period. Though there are no publicly known plans for such systems, it is quite possible that India will eventually develop these, especially considering that India's no first use doctrine requires survivability of the National Command Authority, which can be aided by early warning of enemy missile launches.

Increasing global competition also has another effect, which is a nascent space race between China and the others, that is very reminiscent of the space race between the United States and the USSR during the early Cold War. This has led to a heightened salience of space achievements such as interplanetary and deep space explorations. A good example of this is the ongoing race for Mars as well as the establishment of a new international space station. While India has not been at the forefront of this, India's political leaders have also recognized the need to stay in the race. This has meant greater investment in India's lunar mission, Mars probes, and human space missions. In addition, this has also led to international collaboration with India's strategic partners such as France, Japan, and the United States on these issues. (Rajagopalan 2018, 465–70)

Another consequence of the increasingly uncertain political climate is that India has become much more open to international collaboration, especially with its new strategic partners. Though India benefited from international collaboration in the early stages of its space program, these had declined substantially since the 1980s because of international technology control regimes. (Rajagopalan 2018, 465–79) India's international partners were no longer willing to collaborate with an India that was considered a proliferation risk, while India itself became a lot more wary about such cooperation because of its distrust of its former partners, specifically the United States. A concrete instance of this is India's keenness to develop cryogenic engine technologies in the late 1980s in order to have more efficient launches and large payload launch capability. While Russia was willing to supply the cryogenic engine technology to India, the United States prevented that transfer from taking place arguing that it was a violation of Missile Technology Control Regime (MTCR) norms (Chengappa 1993).

However, in the last decade, India's space collaborations have dramatically increased. This is a consequence of the willingness of others to now cooperate with India largely because of India's status as a potential counterweight to China. Equally importantly, India has also become more open to such collaborations, though admittedly, this change has been slow in coming, and there is still residual suspicion in the Indian space establishment about many of its current partners. The Indian space establishment has bad memories of international sanctions and continuing bitterness on this front still limits Indian openness to international collaboration. Nevertheless, the changing international political dynamics is slowly eroding such suspicions. Consequently, India is now collaborating with France, the United States, Japan, and Australia (White House 2021; Rajagopalan 2021a; Ministry of External Affairs 2018).

INDIA'S SPACE SECURITY RESPONSES

India has responded in a number of ways to the changing security conditions. On the one hand, there have been policy changes that shifted India's stand on the positions that it had previously taken on outer space issues. These changes in India's diplomatic stance were also accompanied domestically by institutional changes to deal with emerging security concerns. Further, there were also changes to India's technological focus as well as its engagements with industrial and commercial sectors to increase India's space competitiveness and capacities in space.

Policy Responses

China's ASAT test in 2007 had an important influence on India's space policy debate. The shift in India's approach to space is a gradual one but it is in alignment with the broader shift evident in India's approach to global security and norms. That India is a now a member of all the global export control regimes with the exception of the Nuclear Suppliers Group (NSG) is an indicator of this change. India's approach to space security and the broader global non-proliferation efforts is a reflection of the rapidly changing security environment in India's neighborhood and advancements in the larger global space. India has traveled a great distance from the 1970s and 1980s when New Delhi was one of the most vocal, high-pitched critics of the United States' SDI and the ASAT tests conducted by both the United States and the USSR (Strategic Digest 1985, cited in Tellis 2006).

The Chinese ASAT test triggered a new debate within India on how to protect its assets in space. Surprisingly, there was a unanimous view across the board, from the political leadership to the scientific and military bureaucracy, in calling for a fresh approach, including the need for developing appropriate deterrence measures against China ("India Says Chinese Anti-Satellite Program a Global Threat" 2010). On multiple occasions, leaders highlighted the threat from China, with then Defence Minister Pranab Mukherjee clearly stating that "There are also new set of challenges which China poses such as the strategic challenge as China develops its capabilities in outer space . . . We would need to develop more sophisticated ways of dealing with these new challenges posed by China" (Mukerjee 2008; Menon 2010; Rao 2010).

Institutional Responses

In terms of an institutional response, India moved to establish an aerospace tri-service command headed by the Indian Air Force. Following the Chinese ASAT test, debates about India's space policy gained momentum. It quickly set up an Integrated Space Cell under the headquarters of the Integrated Defence Staff within the Ministry of Defence in 2008. This was an important step in bringing about better integration among the different departments and ministries—the DoS, the Ministry of Defence, and the armed forces—in order to create a more coordinated and synchronized approach to space. According to the Ministry of Defence, the rationale for the new cell was to generate options in response to "offensive counter space systems like anti-satellite weaponry, new classes of heavy-lift and small boosters and an improved array of Military Space Systems . . . in our neighbourhood" (Ministry of Defence 2008).

More than a decade later, after India's ASAT test in March 2019, it took the next steps to further institutionalize its space policy architecture. In 2019, the government established a tri-service Defence Space Agency (DSA), as an interim institutional measure before setting up a full-fledged aerospace command (Rajagopalan 2013). The DSA is responsible for space security policies and strategies while the government has also set up a Defence Space Research Organisation (DSRO), an institution akin to the Defence Research and Development Organisation (DRDO), tasked with research and development of the capabilities required for the Indian armed forces to execute strategies formulated by the DSA ("India Creates Defense Space Research Agency . . . " 2019; Rajagopalan 2019). The DSA, based in Bangalore, will house around 200 personnel, all sourced through the existing Defence Imagery Processing and Analysis Centre, New Delhi, and the Defence Satellite Control Centre, Bhopal (Prasad 2020). The Indian Navy also proactively established a new office called the Assistant Chief of Naval Staff Communications, Space and Network Centric Operations (ACNSCSNCO) in June 2012, tasked with oversight and management of space-based military capabilities for the Indian Navy. This office was established so as to make a switch from a "platform-centric Navy" to a "network-enabled Navy" (Rajat Pandit 2012).

Technological Responses

Along with gradual changes in India's approach to space policy and institutional changes, India's space program began to develop deeper military characteristics. One of the first indicators of this was when India launched its first dedicated military satellite, GSAT-7, for the Indian Navy in August 2013 (Lele 2013). The satellite was tasked with augmenting India's space-based maritime communications and electronic intelligence and overall enhancement of India's maritime security apparatus (Singh 2019). The satellite will aid India's ability to monitor the waters of both the Arabian Sea and the Bay of Bengal region. This was seen as particularly important in the context of the changing strategic dynamics in the Indian Ocean Region. Prior to the GSAT-7 launch, the Indian Navy relied on Inmarsat, a United Kingdom satellite telecommunication enterprise that offers communication services to ships.

India launched a second dedicated military satellite, the GSAT-6, in August 2015 (Ramesh 2018). Like GSAT-7, GSAT-6 is also tasked with secure communications for the Indian military. Further, ISRO launched the GSAT-7A satellite in December 2018 in an effort to meet the growing communication requirements for the Indian Air Force and the Indian Army. This satellite was primarily for the Indian Air Force, but the army will receive 30 percent of its capacity (Ramesh 2018). In April 2019, the ISRO launched EMISAT (Electro-Magnetic Intelligence Satellite), a satellite jointly manufactured by ISRO and DRDO (Kumar 2019). The satellite has been developed for the Indian Armed Forces with the purpose of strengthening their ability to track and intercept enemy radars by sensing electromagnetic rays they emit.

India also appears to have quickly recognized that arms control was unlikely to lead to any fruitful conclusion on issues such as ASAT and that it would have to consider deterrence as a key element in dealing with China's technological developments. This led to India's own ASAT test in March 2019. India's ASAT demonstration was a direct consequence of the changing space environment where India calculated that inaction could leave it vulnerable in an important national security technology realm. Nevertheless, questions were raised on the sufficiency of the ASAT test in producing effective deterrence against China. In fact, following the Indian ASAT, Ashley Tellis, a noted US defense analyst, argued that India's demonstration of its ASAT capability "will only exacerbate the rivalry between the two countries," and that India should "prepare for a long-term space competition" (Tellis 2019). Given the intensifying security dynamics in space and on Earth, India plans to augment its counterspace capabilities beyond ASAT weapons. According to Director General Satheesh Reddy, the DRDO is "working on a number of technologies like DEWs (directed-energy weapons), lasers, electromagnetic pulse (EMP) and co-orbital weapons etc." While clarifying that these are political decisions, Reddy added that "space has gained importance in the military domain. The best way to ensure security is to have deterrence" (Pandit 2019).

Another Indian space initiative is its navigation system, the Indian Regional Navigation Satellite System (IRNSS) or NAVIC. Though a smaller version of the US GPS with a coverage of just 1,500 kilometers around its neighborhood, it also has military utility. The constellation, with 7 satellites, provides a positional accuracy of 20 meters in its primary area around the borders. To provide a context, the US GPS Signal-in-Space (SIS) accuracy using appropriate GPS receivers receive a horizontal accuracy of 3 meters or better and vertical accuracy of 5 meters (U.S. Government 2020).

NAVIC offers two kinds of services—Standard Positioning Service (SPS) for the general public and Restricted Service (RS) meant for military and other government agencies. In relation to GPS and China's Beidou navigation systems, this is a small move, but it is still capable of aiding terrestrial navigation, disaster management, and vehicle tracking, as well as providing an autonomous navigation system to the Indian military.

Commercial and Industry Response

Finally, another response has been in terms of the changing role of the space industry in India's space agenda. Space technologies are increasingly being developed by private actors, and this phenomenon has spread from Western capitalist societies to India.

Though not as large as the US or Chinese private space sector, India's private space sector—largely based around Bangalore and Hyderabad—has grown in the last decade. India's space establishment has been slow to acknowledge these changes, but this appears to be changing with the establishment of the Indian National Space Promotion and Authorization Centre (IN-SPACe) and NewSpace India Limited (NSIL, the commercial wing of the ISRO), which will both help create a level playing field for private companies and enable them to play a more determining role in India's space growth (Ramesh 2018). IN-SPACe's role as bridging agency between the ISRO and the private sector could change the nature of engagement between the two.

This change is the result of both the availability of the private space sector but also the growing demands that ISRO alone is not able to manage. Smaller start-up private sector actors tend to be far more nimble and effective in developing niche technologies than the ISRO has been. Along with this, the ISRO has also now licensed one of its traditional launch vehicles, the PSLV, to be manufactured and operated by the private sector. In the most recent decision, the DoS plans to transfer the manufacturing of two of its rockets— the Geosynchronous Satellite Launch Vehicle (GSLV) MK III and the Small Satellite Launch Vehicle (SSLV)—entirely to its industry partners (PTI 2021). Three industry bids have been received so far to in response to NSIL's request for proposals (RFP). The three bids to develop the rockets are from Hindustan Aeronautics Limited (HAL)-Larsen and Toubro, Bharat Electronics Limited-Adani-Bharat Earth Movers Limited, and Bharat Heavy Electricals Limited (PTI 2021). Given that these industries have had a history of working with the ISRO in the past, mostly in the form of supplying components and systems, the chances of this experiment succeeding are quite high. Given ISRO's capacity gaps, engaging the private sector is the most practical route for India to step up its space competitiveness.

Thus, the Indian space program has evolved considerably to respond to the changing space security dynamics in India's Indo-Pacific neighborhood and beyond. India has recognized that ignoring the advanced military space programs of countries like China with a growing inventory of counterspace capabilities could be detrimental to its own national security. Thus, it has had to alter and shift away from its decades-old position of peaceful uses of space to one which focuses on deterrence as an important aspect of its approach to space. India's ASAT test in March 2019 was a demonstration of this new policy approach, driven by national security considerations and, more specifically, the requirements of an emergent deterrent strategy.

CONCLUSIONS

The Indian space program has had its share of setbacks and failures. Nevertheless, on balance, it has demonstrated that a space program could be viable in a relatively poor country. Moreover, for a program that has an annual budget of around $2 billion, its accomplishments have been substantial (Goh 2019). From its humble beginnings at

Thumba, the program has become multifaceted and has made India a space power of some consequence. The pioneers of the Indian space program had not envisioned major space exploratory or interplanetary missions such as the Chandrayaan or Mangalyaan but the Indian program has evolved to encompass these areas. These have also allowed India to get a seat at the high table where global space rules are formulated. While the interplanetary missions are civilian focused and generally strengthened India's space profile, India has had to also respond to changes in the space security domain.

China's repeated ASAT tests and its development, testing, and deployment of a range of counterspace capabilities have had negative consequences on India's ability to protect its space assets, in addition to having broader military, security, and economic implications. Given the large-scale dependence of Indian society, economy, and military on space assets, any disruption or destruction of its space assets will have repercussions that will be felt across multiple sectors. The end result is an Indian space program that is large, complex, and broad enough to encompass both civilian and security purposes. The growing space security orientation would suggest a rebalancing of India's priorities. While India will continue to seek to exploit space for developmental purposes, it will also emphasize the utility of outer space for its security.

This shifting Indian space orientation as well as the increasingly uncertain international political climate suggest that India will become more engaged with like-minded partners in the space security domain, leading to greater collaborations with strategic partners such as the United States, France, Japan, and Australia. India has already strengthened its space engagements with each of the Quad countries but the possibility of a Quad space network in the coming years is real, because each of the Quad countries remain concerned about space security threats from China and/or Russia (Rajagopalan 2021b). The Quad leaders in their joint statements in the last couple of years have highlighted space governance as an important agenda (Rajagopalan 2021c). This is an important shift for India since it traditionally sided with G-21 countries on space governance matters that emphasized legally binding verifiable mechanisms. Other than India, the remaining three Quad countries have preferred voluntary political agreements such as TCBMs. Therefore, India's commitment to consult and work with the Quad countries on space governance is a recognition of the enormity of the space security challenges New Delhi is confronted with.

References

Amos, Jonathan. 2019. "Why India's Mars Mission is so Cheap—And Thrilling." BBC.com. March 24, 2019. https://www.bbc.com/news/science-environment-29341850.

Anderson, Robert S. 2010. *Nucleus and Nation: Scientists, International Networks and Power in India.* Chicago, IL: University of Chicago Press.

Banerjee, Prasid. 2020. "India's Supercomputing Abilities, Despite Early Promise, Has Faltered, with Barely a Couple of Supercomputers in the Top 500." *Live Mint.* November 18, 2020. https://www.livemint.com/technology/gadgets/india-now-has-two-of-the-top-100-most-powerful-supercomputers-in-the-world-11605616784315.html.

Blamont, Jacques. 2015. "Starting the Indian Space Program." In *From Fishing Hamlet to Red Planet: India's Space Journey*, edited by P. V. Manoranjan Rao, B. N. Suresh and V. P. Balagangadharan, 5. New Delhi: Harper Collins.

Butterworth-Hayes, Phil. 2010. "Critical Times for India's Space Program." *Aerospace America* (October): 34.

Carter, Jamie. 2019. "First China, Then Israel—and Now India is Landing on the Moon." *TechRadar*. March 27, 2019. https://www.techradar.com/news/first-china-then-israel-now-india-is-landing-on-the-moon-in-2019.

Center for Strategic and International Studies. n.d. "Ghauri (Hatf 5)." CSIS Missile Defense Project. https://missilethreat.csis.org/missile/hatf-5/.

Chengappa, Raj. 1993. "US Blocks Critical Cryogenic Deal, Forces India to Indigenise." *India Today*. August 15, 1993. https://www.indiatoday.in/magazine/science-and-technology/story/19930815-us-blocks-critical-cryogenic-deal-forces-india-to-indigenise-811389-1993-08-15.

China Manned Space. 2021. "The Debris of the Last Stage of the Long March-5B Y2 Carrier Rocket Reentered the Atmosphere." Press Release. May 9, 2021. http://en.cmse.gov.cn/news/202105/t20210509_47890.html.

Chitnis, E.V. 2015. "Early ISRO: 1961–1971." In *From Fishing Hamlet to Red Planet: India's Space Journey*, edited by P. V. Manoranjan Rao, B. N. Suresh and V. P. Balagangadharan, 29. New Delhi: Harper Collins.

Cirincione, Joseph, Jon B. Wolfsthal, and Miriam Rajkumar. 2005. "Pakistan." In *Deadly Arsenals: Nuclear, Biological, and Chemical Threats*, edited by Cirincione, Joseph, Jon B. Wolfsthal, and Miriam Rajkumar, 239–58. Washington DC: Carnegie Endowment for International Peace. http://www.jstor.org/stable/j.ctt6wpkbk.16.

Costello, John, and Joe McReynolds. 2018. "China's Strategic Support Force: A Force for a New Era." *China Strategic Perspectives*, no. 13: 35–40. https://ndupress.ndu.edu/Portals/68/Documents/stratperspective/china/china-perspectives_13.pdf.

Defense Intelligence Agency. 2019. "Challenges to Security in Space." Defense Intelligence Agency. https://www.dia.mil/Portals/27/Documents/News/Military%20Power%20Publications/Space_Threat_V14_020119_sm.pdf.

Dutt, Anonna. 2021. "India Adds Another Supercomputer at Mohali under National Mission." *Hindustan Times*. November 18, 2021. https://www.hindustantimes.com/india-news/india-adds-another-supercomputer-under-national-mission-101635922198527.html.

Ganguly, Sumit. 2014. "India's Pursuit of Ballistic Missile Defense." *The Non-proliferation Review* 21, no. 3–4: 373–82.

Gearin, Conor. 2016. "India's Space Place." *New Scientist*. May 28, 2016.

Goh, Deyana. 2019. "ISRO's 2019-20 Budget Increases by 15.6 percent to US 1.88billion." *SpaceTech*, October 31. https://www.spacetechasia.com/isros-2019-20-budget-increases-by-15-6-to-us1-88b/.

Harrison, Todd, Kaitlyn Johnson, Joe Moye, and Makena Young. 2021. "Space Threat Assessment 2021." Washington DC: Center for Strategic and International Studies. https://csis-website-prod.s3.amazonaws.com/s3fs-public/publication/210331_Harrison_SpaceThreatAssessment2021.pdf?gVYhCn79enGCOZtcQnA6MLkeKlcwqqks.

"ISRO Launches 10th Satellite: A Look at Space Agency's Ten Achievements." 2018. *Hindustan Times*. January 12, 2018.

"India Creates Defense Space Research Agency, Plans July War Game Simulation." 2019. *Space Daily*. June 13. http://www.spacedaily.com/reports/India_creates_Defense_Space_Research_Agency_plans_July_war_game_simulation_999.html.

"India Says Chinese Anti-Satellite Program a Global Threat." 2010. *Space Daily*. April 12, 2010. www.spacedaily.com.

Indo Asian News Service. 2018. "India to Launch 31 Satellites Including 28 from 6 Other Countries." *Hindustan Times*. January 20, 2018. https://tech.hindustantimes.com/tech/news/india-to-launch-31-satellites-including-28-from-6-other-countries-story-spbUFe9gQzA2ezVQ8P3IcP.html.

"ISRO's Mars Orbiter Was Made for Mission Life of Six Months in Orbit Completed Seven Years This Month." 2021. *FirstPost*. September 27, 2021. https://www.firstpost.com/tech/science/isros-mars-orbiter-was-made-for-mission-life-of-six-months-completed-seven-years-in-orbit-this-month-10001781.html.

Jha, Martand. 2017. "Genesis of the Space Program: How a 'Non-Aligned' India Negotiated the Space Race." *Outlook*. October 3, 2017.

Kalam, A. P. J. 2015. "India's First Launch Vehicle." In *From Fishing Hamlet to Red Planet: India's Space Journey*, edited by P. V. Manoranjan Rao, B. N. Suresh and V. P. Balagangadharan, 118–23. New Delhi: Harper Collins.

Koksal, Ilker. 2019. "Chandrayaan 2: India's Moon Mission—A Failure or Not." *Forbes.com*. September 20, 2019. https://www.forbes.com/sites/ilkerkoksal/2019/09/20/chandrayaan-2-indias-moon-mission-a-failure-or-not/?sh=13ba2b156ada.

Kumar, Chetan. 2019. "Days after A-SAT, EMISAT Adds to India's Defence Capability." *Times of India*, April 1. https://timesofindia.indiatimes.com/india/days-after-a-sat-emisat-add-to-indias-defence-capability/articleshow/68669542.cms.

Lele, Ajey. 2013. "Commentary | GSAT-7: India's Strategic Satellite." *Space News*. September 9. https://spacenews.com/37142gsat-7-indias-strategic-satellite/.

Lele, Ajey. 2015. "GSAT-6: India's Second Military Satellite Launched." *IDSA Comment*, Institute for Defence Studies and Analyses. August 31, 2015. https://idsa.in/idsacomments/GSAT6IndiasSecondMilitarySatelliteLaunched_alele_310815.

McElheny, Victor K. 1965. "India's Nascent Space Program." *Science* 149, no. 3691: 1487–89.

Menon, Shivshankar. 2010. "Address by NSA at the 9th IISS Asia Security Summit." Transcript of Lecture Delivered at the 9th IISS Asia Security Summit, June 5, 2010. *Strategic Digest* 40, no. 7 (July): 766.

Ministry of Defence. 2008. "Special Cell Set Up to Counter Growing Threat to Space Assets." Press Release. June 10, 2008. http://www.pib.nic.in/newsite/erelcontent.aspx?relid=39503.

Ministry of External Affairs. 2001. "The Minister of External Affairs had a Telephonic Conversation This Afternoon with U.S. National Security Adviser, Dr. Condoleezza Rice." Press Release. May 2, 2001. https://www.mea.gov.in/press-releases.htm?dtl/10732/.The_Minister_of_External_Affairs_had_a_telephonic_conversation_this_afternoon_with_US_National_Security_Adviser_Dr_Condoleezza_Rice.

Ministry of External Affairs. 2018. "India-France Joint Vision for Space Cooperation." Press Release. March 10, 2018. https://mea.gov.in/bilateral-documents.htm?dtl/29597/IndiaFrance+Joint+Vision+for+Space+Cooperation+New+Delhi+10+March+2018.

Mukherjee, Pranab. 2008. "Address by Mr. Pranab Mukherjee, Hon'ble Minister for External Affairs at National Defence College, New Delhi, 3rd November 2008—India's Security Challenges and Foreign Policy Imperatives." Transcript of Lecture Delivered at National Defence College, New Delhi, November 3, 2008. https://mea.gov.in/Speeches-Statements.htm?dtl/1767/Address+by+Mr+Pranab+Muk.

Nagendra, Narayan Prasad. 2016. "Diversification of the Indian Space Programme in the Past Decade: Perspectives on Implications and Challenges." *Space Policy* 36: 38–45.

NASA. 2019. "NASA Administrator Statement on Chinese Rocket Debris." Press Release. May 9, 2021. https://www.nasa.gov/press-release/nasa-administrator-statement-on-chinese-rocket-debris.

Nayar, Baldev Raj. 1983. *India's Quest for Technological Independence.* New Delhi: Lancers.

Noronha, Joseph. 2009. "Life Begins at 40." *SP Aviation.* November 1, 2009.

Noronha, Joseph. 2012. "Year of Reckoning." *SP Aviation.* July 27, 2012.

Pandit, Rajat. 2012. "Navy Creates New Post to Harness Space-Based Capabilities." *Times of India.* June 3. https://timesofindia.indiatimes.com/india/navy-creates-new-post-to-harness-space-based-capabilities/articleshow/13774463.cms.

Pandit, Rajat. 2019. "Satellite-Killer Not a One-off, India Working on Star Wars Armoury," *Times of India,* April 7. https://timesofindia.indiatimes.com/india/satellite-killer-not-a-one-off-india-working-on-star-wars-armoury/articleshow/68758674.cms.

Prasad, Narayan. 2020. "What Does India's Space Budget for 2020 Tell Us?" *The Wire.* February 6, 2020. https://science.thewire.in/spaceflight/department-of-space-newspace-nsil-isro-gaganyaan-budget-2020-dsa-dsro-pslv-production/.

PTI. 2021. "Indian Industry to Produce Two More Entire Rockets, GSLV-Mk III and SSLV, Says DoS." *Economic Times.* September 19. https://economictimes.indiatimes.com/news/india/indian-industry-to-produce-two-more-entire-rockets-gslv-mk-iii-and-sslv-says-dos/articleshow/86338837.cms?from=mdr.

PTI. 2022. "Gaganyaan Mission Can't Happen This Year or Next Year, Focus Fully on Safety Aspects: ISRO Chief." *Times of India.* June 30. https://timesofindia.indiatimes.com/india/gaganyaan-mission-cant-happen-this-year-or-next-year-focus-fully-on-safety-aspects-isro-chief/articleshow/92579979.cms?utm_source=twitter.com&utm_medium=social&utm_campaign=TOIDesktop.

Rajagopalan, Rajesh. 2005. "India: Largest Democracy and Smallest Debate?" *Contemporary Security Policy* 26, no. 3: 606.

Rajagopalan, Rajeswari Pillai. 2019. "A First: India to Launch First Simulated Space Warfare Exercise." *The Diplomat.* June 12, 2019. https://thediplomat.com/2019/06/a-first-india-to-launch-first-simulated-space-warfare-exercise/.

Rajagopalan, Rajeswari Pillai. 2011. "India's Changing Policy on Space Militarization: The Impact of China's ASAT Test." *India Review* 10, no. 4 (October–December): 354–78.

Rajagopalan, Rajeswari Pillai. 2013. "Synergies in Space: The Case for an Indian Aerospace Command." *Observer Research Foundation Issue Brief* No. 59 (October). https://www.orfonline.org/wp-content/uploads/2013/10/IssueBrief_59.pdf.

Rajagopalan, Rajeswari Pillai. 2017. "Strategic Implications of India's Ballistic Missile Defense." Unedited Working Paper for the FAS Project on Nuclear Dynamics in a Multipolar Strategic BMD World, May 8, 2017. https://uploads.fas.org/media/ Strategic-Implications-of-India%E2%80%99s-Ballistic-Missile-Defense.pdf.

Rajagopalan, Rajeswari Pillai. 2018. "India's Space Ambitions and Capabilities." In *The Oxford Handbook of India's National Security,* edited by Sumit Ganguly, Manjeet Pardesi, and Nicolas Blarel, 465–70. New Delhi: Oxford University Press.

Rajagopalan, Rajeswari Pillai. 2019. "India's Emerging Space Assets and Nuclear-Weapons Capabilities." *The Non-proliferation Review* 26, no. 5–6: 465–79.

Rajagopalan, Rajeswari Pillai. 2021a. "India-France Agree on Space Security Dialogue." *The Diplomat*. September 3, 2021. https://thediplomat.com/2021/09/india-france-agree-on-space-security-dialogue/.

Rajagopalan, Rajeswari Pillai. 2021b. "India's Space Cooperation with the US—and the Quad—Intensifies." *The Diplomat*. March 29, 2021. https://thediplomat.com/2021/03/indias-space-cooperation-with-the-us-and-the-quad-intensifies/.

Rajagopalan, Rajeswari Pillai. 2021c. "The Quad Commits to Regulating Space." *The Diplomat*. October 1, 2021. https://thediplomat.com/2021/10/the-quad-commits-to-regulating-space/.

Rajagopalan, Rajeswari Pillai, and Biswas, Arka. 2016. "Locating India within the Global Non-Proliferation Architecture: Prospects, Challenges and Opportunities." October. https://www.orfonline.org/wpcontent/uploads/2016/08/ORF_Monograph_NonProliferation.pdf.

Ramesh, Sandhya. 2018. "ISRO to Launch Advanced GSAT-7A Satellite for IAF and Army Today." *The Print*. December 18. https://theprint.in/science/isro-to-launch-advanced-gsat-7a-satellite-for-iaf-and-army-today/165548/.

Rao, Nirupama. 2010. "Address by Foreign Secretary at Harvard on 'India's Global Role.'" Transcript of Lecture Delivered at Harvard University, September 20, 2010. https://www.mea.gov.in/Speeches-Statements.htm?dtl/741/.

Rao, Rahul. 2021. "India's Human Spaceflight Plans Coming Together Despite Delays." *Space.com*. June 17, 2021. https://www.space.com/india-human-spaceflight-plans-gaganyaan.

Siddiqi, Asif A. 2015. "Science, Geography, and Nation: The Global Creation of Thumba," *History and Technology* 31, no. 4: 420–51.

Singh, Surendra. 2019. "Isro to Build 2nd Dedicated Satellite for Navy to Interlink Warships, Aircraft." *Times of India*. July 21. https://timesofindia.indiatimes.com/india/isro-to-build-2nd-dedicated-satellite-for-navy-to-interlink-warships-aircraft/articleshow/70310935.cms.

Srinivasan, Raman. 1997. "No Free Launch: Designing the Indian National Satellite." In *Beyond the Ionosphere: The Development of Satellite Communications*, edited by J. B. Andrew, 215–26. Washington, DC: National Aeronautics and Space Administration.

Subbarao, M V. 1989. "India and Star Wars." *The Indian Journal of Political Science* 50, no. 4: 560–78. http://www.jstor.org/stable/41855457.

Strategic Digest. 1985. "India Opposes SDI." *Strategic Digest* 15, no. 10 (October): 1304.

Tefft, Shiela. 1988. "The Chariot of Indra." *Air and Space* (May): 33–42.

Tellis, Ashley. 2006. "The Evolution of US-Indian Ties: Missile Defense in an Emerging Strategic Relationship." *International Security* 30, no. 4: 114.

Tellis, Ashley. 2019. "India's ASAT Test: An Incomplete Success." Carnegie Endowment for International Peace. April 15. https://carnegieendowment.org/2019/04/15/india-s-asat-test-incomplete-success-pub-78884.

Tyabji, Nasir. 2007. Jawaharlal Nehru and Science and Technology." *Contemporary Perspectives* 1, no. 1: 130–36.

US Government. 2020. "Global Positioning System Standard Positioning Service Performance Standard." https://www.gps.gov/technical/ps/2020-SPS-performance-standard.pdf.

Wattles, Jackie. 2021. "NASA Criticizes China's Handling of Rocket Re-entry as Debris Lands Near Maldives." *CNN Business*. May 9, 2021. https://edition.cnn.com/2021/05/08/app-international-edition/china-space-debris-long-march-rocket-reentry-scn/index.html.

Weeden, Brian, and Samson, Victoria. 2021. "Global Counterspace Capabilities: An Open Source Assessment." Washington DC: Secure World Foundation. https://swfound.org/media/207162/swf_global_counterspace_capabilities_2021.pdf.

White House. 2021. "Joint Statement from Quad Leaders." Press Release. September 24, 2021. https://www.whitehouse.gov/briefing-room/statements-releases/2021/09/24/joint-statem ent-from-quad-leaders/.

White House. 2021. "U.S.-India Joint Leaders' Statement: A Partnership for Global Good." Press Release. September 24, 2021. https://www.whitehouse.gov/briefing-room/statements-releases/2021/09/24/u-s-india-joint-leaders-statement-a-partnership-for-global-good/.

CHAPTER 20

FRENCH SPACE SECURITY IN HISTORICAL PERSPECTIVE

Balancing Strategic Autonomy and Cooperation

XAVIER PASCO

SPACE has always been a domain of choice for any observer interested in under-standing the nature of policy-making in the field of big tech governmental programs with a heavy strategic impact on international relations and world security issues. At first blush, space programs may look like a symbol of humanity's quest for discoveries and exploration. The moon programs of the 1960s, the International Space Station, or even scientific probes developed from the outset of the space era, seem to tes-tify how much space has lived on in a dynamic of its own, fed by genuine scientific prowess and candid dreams for the future of humankind. However, a slightly more attentive look at the history of space policies worldwide leads to the adoption of a more prosaic view. Briefly summarized, most often space accomplishments have been linked to security-oriented political visions, national security thinking, and strategic interests. These types of interests have regularly impregnated high-level decisions with a regular ability to make political sense from (sometimes complex) technological capacities which in turn usually gain governmental support when they serve a political vision.

It is helpful to recall the very early role given to Earth observation (EO) from space (including early warning or electronic intelligence satellites) at a time when two blocs were in the process of establishing mutual coexistence rules in the nuclear age. These programs have perfectly illustrated the connection between innovative space technologies and the strategic frameworks that make them politically meaningful at a given moment in time. The nature of such a connection has of course constantly evolved given the various political requirements and constraints over the years. But while those sorts of connections and their profound meaning will differ from one period to another or from one country to another, they have been a major factor influencing the making of space policies worldwide.

I have long had passionate discussions and differences of perception along those lines with John Logsdon, the well-known space historian and a good personal friend for several decades. In an op-ed published almost twenty-five years ago, Professor Logsdon questioned the reality of such explanations, which he felt put too much emphasis on purely strategic, top-down decision mechanisms for explaining space policy-making. Indeed, the importance given to the mechanisms of political decisions and the way technological and political fields interact in the design of a public policy remains a widely debated issue. The relations between the different stakeholders are obviously key to understanding the meaning of any space policy-making process. However, the historical and cultural contexts of a given time period also play an essential role. Early space policies were the result of the post-war period and the emerging Cold War. This explains the usual regalian character of those policies (along with the dominant public origin of the budgets involved). The Apollo decision of the early 1960s, but also the major space orientations of the last few decades, whether the space station or the return to the moon, contain a part of the culture and political reading of the domestic and international environment of the time. This influence can certainly be evaluated, but it mostly transcends institutional affiliations. In this sense, space policies can hardly be isolated from larger paradigmatic views that provide a common cultural and political background to the communities involved in their making.

At the very least, John Logsdon questioned even the notion of "strategy" when it comes to space policy-making in the United States. For him, few people think in terms as large as I do (Logsdon 1997), assuming my French nationality would reflect more familiarity with a political culture of an administratively centralized state than an exact assessment of the reality in other political systems. Commenting on Logsdon's position, some authors believe that this "inclination to see the U.S. space policy as an uncoordinated, yet highly successful linkage of the output of a plurality of organizations should come as no surprise. The view that the US political system has no strategic centre capable of elite led decision making is an old and powerful element in the central liberal discourse of American political ideology." Which leads them to assert: "These nostrums are in fact, key parts of the US theory of political pluralism, which represents America's own distinctive contribution to modern liberalism" (Lawrence and Hansson 1998).

Again, the point is that differences in political cultures must certainly be acknowledged and factored in for a deep understanding of public policy mechanisms, in this case space policy-making. And indeed, various dynamics contribute to the complexity of decisions made on big high-tech enterprises such as space programs. Many expectations, interests or even fears exist in the communities involved in such programs, whether they are policy oriented (be they national executive and legislative or local powers) or industrial (with the big tech giants and nowadays a new generation of small or larger start-ups). Communities of users, governmental (specifically military) or growingly commercial have also their proper reading of the "general interest." Such a mosaic of perceptions and interests must be considered, and their respective strategies can be easily accepted as a structuring feature of any public big space decision. Incidentally, it would also be misleading to consider that such diverse influences do not play any role in countries like France. While John Logsdon is too much a fine "connoisseur" of the French system to take this view himself, more imprudent observers may be led to overly caricature a political system that remains equally complex and diversified.

However, while keeping these aspects in mind, the history of space programs can hardly be seen as a primary result from a chaotic process from which long-term strategic thinking would play such a minor role. More accurately, decision-making in the space domain may result from various mixes of state "realism" (i.e., calculated positioning at the highest levels of states resting upon perceptions of the nation's "strategic" interest at a given time), with more "liberal"-oriented processes (involving notably inner competition between core institutional interests) as well as with additional interactions between a larger circle of players involving industry, other economic and social stakeholders, and media or lobbying groups for example. These latest so-called "pluralist" or "constructivist" theories emerged in the 1960s (Dahl 1961), questioning the role given by some authors to the political-administrative elites in decision making processes (Wright-Mills 1956), reclaiming them from a Weberian tradition. Although one can segment these approaches into many subcategories, this three-level reading grid can help us better understand national decisions regarding space programs and also help assess their evolution and rationale.

In this vein, a more recent and promising concept may be borrowed from French political scientists Bruno Jobert and Pierre Muller who introduced the notion of "referential" as a representation of the role and place of a sector in a society at a given time (Jobert and Muller 1987). According to these authors, public policy-making also consists in maintaining some form of social cohesion by avoiding the rise of only sectoral policies and ensuring or maintaining the link between global and sector-related views and issues. This link may largely contribute to create common "referentials": "This global/sectoral relationship [called RGS] can only be transformed into an object of public intervention according to the image that the actors concerned have of it. It is this representation of the RGS, which is called a public policy referential, which designates the set of standards or reference images, according to which the States' intervention criteria and the objectives of the public policy in question are defined" (Muller 1994).

The objective of this chapter is to better assess the evolution of French space policy in the security and defense domain and better understand its motivations. The "public policy referential" described above will be used as a guiding concept for this study. The first part will be devoted to setting the historical scene that has presided over the founding years of the French space programs. This part will provide a particular view on the first institutional and industrial arrangements that have marked the space military effort over the years. The second part will focus on the consolidation of military space programs in France during the 1970s and the 1980s. It will underline the impact of the international strategic context on domestic decisions made in a country possessing its own nuclear arsenal, a key element of the development of military satellites in France. But it will also introduce the new European dimension as a complicating factor for setting a national course over these years. The final section will try to show how the national and European sides have tended to reconcile through a subtle balance between autonomy and cooperation that I consider a key feature that can help explain French military decision in the field of military space over time to the present.

THE FOUNDING YEARS (1958–1961)

Since the beginnings of the space age, France has traditionally been the most active space country in Europe. The third national space power, having orbited its own satellite after the USSR and the United States in 1965, France has been quick to endorse the role of a key medium power. The post–Second World War Gaullist years were years of national affirmation on the world stage, with an accent put on the strategic autonomy. These were also years of national reinforcement inside the political and administrative systems. As is well known, the role of the president would be largely overhauled with the advent of the "Fifth Constitution" adopted in 1958, giving a first signal of an increasingly embodied republic, light years away from a parliamentary fourth republic, which had run out of political leadership and resources. It also signaled new beginnings for more powerful institutions in charge of supporting this new national vision.

This was illustrated in 1958 and 1961 with the successive creation of the Directorate of Military Applications in the Atomic Energy Commissariat and of the National Center for Space Studies (Centre national d'Etudes Spatiales, CNES), two brand new institutions that would spearhead the entry of France into modern times. In this respect, space was deliberately placed on an equal footing with atomic energy and would be given a long-term agenda and the necessary resources to fulfill it. One can only be struck by the parallel perceptions that dominated the administrative actions for reinforcing space and nuclear efforts in those first years. Nuclear and space efforts were quickly conceived in parallel while Prime Minister Michel Debré was declaring in front of the national assembly that "a country's potential for scientific and technical progress has become one of the decisive assets for the international influence of a people and a nation" (Moulin 2017). Interestingly enough, the French prime minister delivered this message in May 1961, the very same month of President Kennedy's moon speech in front of the US Congress.

These successive political decisions laid the groundwork for a coordinated and centralized industrial effort capable of developing rockets with strategic capabilities as well as "satellite-launch" (called Lance-satellites at the time) systems in the aftermath of the International Geophysical Year. It led to the creation in September 1959 of the SEREB (Société pour l'étude et la réalisation des engins balistiques). This first "space company" materialized the political vision of a unified national industry through a unique front desk in charge of all research and development efforts in the field of ballistic missile and space launch systems (Moulin 2017, 107–45).

These seminal years have largely tainted the French effort and contributed to making it highly specific. Analysis of these first years reveals how much the international context has contributed to development at the highest levels of a state, marked by largely shared perceptions of the strategic importance of developing autonomous rocket capabilities. The post-war "Gaullist" view was that a world structured around two dominant geo-political actors should act as a strong incentive for France to find its own role and narrative. This political posture clearly helped propel powerful internal institutions and industries which would grow their proper strategies and cultures. Classical "political-administrative elites" have played a key role in the building of the whole French space institutional and industrial complex. A few names stand out (such as Pierre Guillaumat or Louis Bonte among others), who have had a decisive influence in organizing the French space effort and its supporting industry. A few other names might be added to complete what one calls the aeronautics and space elite of the time. In this context, common references and views have supported a rather unified vision at the highest levels of the republic for initiating French space programs and perhaps more importantly, its underlying principles until today.

By developing a large missile and space industry, France has obviously nurtured a space culture of its own, embodied in institutions like CNES or industries like Matra, (then Matra Marconi Space, composing today parts of Airbus Defense and Space and Thales Alenia Space) or Aerospatiale (first transformed into EADS, then becoming ArianeGroup, the builder of today Ariane launchers). This has had obvious consequences, especially in making a nascent national effort coexist with the necessity of engaging new cooperation efforts at a wider European level. Over the years, efforts by French industry to better "Europeanize" its investments and capabilities, as well as its ever-growing export-oriented strategy, particularly in the field of satellite manufacturing, have contributed to put Europe at the top of the national agenda.

STRATEGIC AUTONOMY AS A MAIN DRIVER OF FRENCH MILITARY SPACE (1975–1995)

In parallel, the history suggests how closely the development of a space industry in France has been also linked to the national priority of developing a nuclear deterrence force. As already mentioned, SEREB undertook the bulk of the activity surrounding ballistic missiles and space launchers, prefiguring a long-standing industrial arrangement that has lasted until today with its long-time successor, ArianeGroup. This company has remained the sole producer of missiles and space rockets with a few first-rank contractors mostly scattered around les Mureaux (a small city west of Paris) where ArianeGroup's headquarters is located. Obviously, successive directors have shared the view of a sacred duty to maintain a deterrence force, and the simple fact that SEREB and its successors had to develop a ballistic missile force made this industry a very peculiar one. This link and the synergies created between missile and space launch activities also explain how much France quickly became the main supporter in Europe of strong and autonomous access to space. National strategic autonomy rests on the industrial ability of France to master its own deterrence capability, implying the consolidation of a tool that would find in space adventure a necessary complement.

But beyond this sole functional link, the status of nuclear power has made France more rapidly receptive to key space applications than others medium powers. The fact that space has been structured by the political cycles of the 20th Century and more particularly by the confrontation between the two superpowers has been well-documented. Even before the launch of Sputnik in October 1957, the United States had launched the WS-177 L program, namely the Discoverer/Corona program destined to overfly the USSR. and to capture images of supposed advances in the field of ballistic missiles (Stares 1985, 38–58). The Soviet authorities have not delayed too long, and spy satellites have ended up being considered on both sides as critical elements of the new mutual deterrence. Those systems were conversely accepted as key "national technical means" in some of the most prominent disarmament texts of the time, such as the SALT-1 treaty (Stares 1985, 165; Richelson 1990, 110–12).

France, at its pace and with its resources, was no exception and paid attention early on to military EO satellites. Decided on in 1977, a first series of civilian EO satellites, the SPOT (Satellite probatoire d'observation de la terre) family has paved the way for a militarily dedicated series, the HELIOS family. The decision to develop such new capabilities was made in 1986, at the time the first SPOT-1 satellite was launched. On the military side, the very first interest emerged as early as in 1977 with a precursor project, SAMRO, destined to provide France with a first nuclear targeting capability. However, the project lacked the clear mission statement needed to justify the very high-resolution capabilities planned. It also suffered from other priorities in the field of military telecommunication satellites (with the launch of the Syracuse program) and was dropped in 1982.

A renewed interest in such capabilities arose in the middle of the 1980s. President Reagan's Strategic Defense Initiative (SDI) was in full swing, showing new perspectives in the use of space for strategic purposes. On its side, Germany was announcing its decision to get equipped with radar satellites to better monitor zones of interest in Central Europe. (Heisbourg and Pasco 2011, 38). This German position sounded like the end of hopes for cooperation on a common program that had been cherished by the French authorities since the early 1980s. This new global strategic situation led to the revival of the SAMRO project in 1985 and transformed it into the new highly protected HELIOS program destined to serve the highest national political authorities. The goal was simply to make France the third power to access fully independent space intelligence means.

This quest for autonomy was in this case the apparent dominant factor of decision-making. It can be noted here that the deterrence-related dimension of French strategic thinking at this time could not logically be shared by other European member states. For this particular reason, initial reflections on the SAMRO and then Helios program remained reserved to domestic thinking only. At times, this typical connection between a state-of-the-art space technology and a political project that makes it meaningful may be more complex than it may appear. For French authorities, European cooperation had also become largely recognized as a reference framework. The push for building a deeper European autonomy was part of the French political project. Promoting multilateral cooperation for HELIOS was presenting a number of long-term advantages both politically and industrially. At the occasion of the first HELIOS satellite launch in 1995, Charles Bigot, then Arianespace CEO declared "the great pride of the Company [Arianespace] in launching for the first time a European defence satellite" (Heisbourg and Pasco 2011, 41). From a policy-level standpoint, this was a unique opportunity to showcase France as an example to follow in front of mostly undecided Europeans when it came to security and military matters. Additionally, any European cooperation perspective in the military domain would convey the natural idea of French prominence. This general sense of French leadership rapidly set the tone of bilateral European relationships in the field of military space cooperation. The proximity between nuclear deterrence and military use of space would after all make this reading relevant and relatively easy to convey and get accepted.

But again, history shows that this cooperation also had more prosaic motivations. France had to find financial support for a costly military satellite program. At the time, the cost was established at around 10 billion French Francs (€2.12 billion) in 2020 purchasing power. While the French discourse sounded very "national" at times, paradoxically one of the key goals had always been to open the project to cooperation as much as possible. France needed all financial support it could receive for the program while it could provide a national rationale to its conception and its management.

A cooperation agreement was signed on September 27, 1987, between France, Italy, and Spain, with France keeping the bulk of the program and 79 percent of financing, while Italy and Spain contributed respectively to 14 percent and 7 percent of Helios 1. Most importantly, this agreement resulted in shared industrial roles, with the Franco-British firm Matra Marconi Space the lead integrator and companies like Alenia, Datamat, Telespazio, Vitrociset, and Crisa completing the European team. Engaging European industry for the first time on military cooperation was a significant step for the promoters of a nascent European-wide industry. The stakes were high for economic and financial circles and well worth bending the usual rules and practices. Obviously, this whole enterprise could be seen as an experiment. It had to devise an agreement between countries about image sharing while pictures from space were essentially still a very scarce resource. These difficulties have been only slowly resolved and they have had a direct impact on the successor program, Helios 2 (Heisbourg and Pasco 2011, 43–49).

For France, these efforts were without precedent, as they were designed to reconcile the highest requirements for national autonomy with a need for European cooperation that France itself was calling for. The ambition of the idea was noted in a document of the Western European Union (WEU) from 1996: "The novelty and successes of the Helios 1 programme are not due solely to the fact that three European countries, France, Italy and Spain, agreed to cooperate on the first European space programme for defence purposes, or because some thirty firms from those countries worked together closely on the development of the two satellites and ground facilities. What really differentiates Helios 1 from other programmes carried out in cooperation and makes the venture particularly distinctive is the fact that the participating countries also share the in-orbit operation of the satellite." The report goes on, quoting the one of the directors of the French procurement agency (Délégation Générale pour l'Armement, DGA) for whom the Helios program was "an entirely new departure for a security and defence system and for our defence headquarters and services that are the users of such systems" (Lenzer 1996, 8).

A SEMINAL PERIOD THAT HELPED SET THE SCENE FOR AUTONOMY AND COOPERATION IN MILITARY SPACE

This historical diversion through the Helios program and its evolution is informative about the variety of objectives and interests leading a medium power to invest in space security and defense. By providing a first real experience, the Helios program, with all its limitations, has contributed to a greater realism and probably also to a greater maturity of future multilateral montages. In the first place, the role taken by industry and its ever-growing "Europeanization" has helped forged new intergovernmental discussions at the European level. This trend toward a greater Europeanization of the industry has obviously added complexity to the national narrative, and it must certainly be considered as having been a key factor in the increasingly balanced strategy sought by France between autonomy and cooperation as years passed. Today, five countries are partners in the latest military EO program, CSO (Composante Spatiale Optique) and despite initial difficulties, a necessary balance between defense and industrial interests had to be found in order to keep it on track. In addition to France, Belgium, Germany, Italy, Sweden, and Switzerland have contributed. The German contribution directly allowed the construction of a third satellite in the series with, in exchange, an access to imagery for the three satellites. As an aside, here again, the bi-national Airbus Group was instrumental in conceiving a widely scoped scheme that would fit both governmental and industrial interests. The intergovernmental agreement was also linked to non-space industrial arrangements between Airbus Group, Dassault Aviation, and Finmeccanica that would position Germany as the European leader in the field of Medium Altitude Long Endurance Unmanned Aerial Vehicle (MALE UAV).

More generally, it can be argued that contemporary French decisions in military space policy-making cannot be viewed in isolation from their European and industrial backgrounds. Constrained by limited available budgets for the last twenty years but also by the rising number of foreign military operations, the French program, more than others, has chosen to focus on hard military needs, including most notably intelligence, surveillance, and reconnaissance (ISR) programs, or core telecommunications programs, leaving some other parts of defense needs (such as additional telecommunication capabilities, or even precision, navigation, and timing, PNT, programs such as Galileo) possibly covered by commercial players or fully cooperative European programs. For the French military, choosing non-national military-owned programs to cover military functions was not a given. But lessons learnt from early cooperation in some of the most traditionally "regalian" programs helped them sort out their priorities and possibly delegate to industrial so-called trusted actors some of the support missions that are expected to play a growing role in military operations. New ways of sharing space capabilities have been envisioned. This has been the case for Syracuse IV, the last generation satellite for military telecommunications with a first satellite launched in October 2021. While not really based on a public-private partnership, this program has inaugurated a new relationship between the military and industry. In this case, Airbus and Thales Alenia Space have been allowed to commercialize excess capacity, that is, any not used by French defense. This rather innovative arrangement has been used to lower contractual burdens and, in a sense, looks to be a precursor of future bolder partnerships. In this case, it is even envisioned that military procurement may receive some repayment in the case of oversold capacities, as defined in the contract.

This illustrates quite well the new dependencies French authorities are willing to accept vis-à-vis commercial players on even some of the core military capabilities. For several years already, similar schemes involving "trusted actors" have also been suggested for future observation and data collection programs. This certainly remains today a remote target that will need fine tuning and that will have to consider pros and cons of yet to be proven solutions. However, arguably, this kind of calculation may also apply to wider and more open European cooperation and could indeed represent the basis for a new French space security policy.

THE NARROW PATH TOWARD A NEW STRATEGY FOR A NEW SPACE SECURITY: COMBINING NATIONAL AND EUROPEAN POSITIONING (FROM 2008 TO TODAY)

In 2008, the "Defense and Security White Book" (in French, "Défense et Sécurité Nationale. Le livre Blanc") published under the Sarkozy presidency was the first official document to really consider space as part and parcel of the French global defense apparatus. By putting space systems at the heart of a "fifth strategic function" (knowledge and anticipation), this 2008 publication explicitly acknowledged the usefulness of space systems for theatre-level operations beyond a sole high-level strategic role. Here, this white book was also drawing heavily from a document published one year before by Ministry of Defense: "Let Us Make More Space for Our Defense." In introductory remarks to this 2007 document, Defense Minister Michèle Alliot-Marie insisted that "space assets play a critical role, as demonstrated during recent conflicts. Such assets enable the countries that possess them to assert their strategic influence on the international scene and to significantly enhance their efficiency during military operations," thus confirming the shift toward a more theater-oriented space architecture (French Ministry of Defense 2007).

At a doctrinal level, this new analysis would have important consequences. It was implying that satellites were de facto about to gain a new military status, transitioning from intelligence-oriented assets to more active systems taking a direct part in operations. All this would make them possible legitimate targets in case of crisis. It was acknowledged in 2007 that "the increasing number of space-based military assets could encourage the emergence of in-orbit offensive assets such as standby mini or microsatellites that may be activated, on demand, to intercept, damage or even destroy other space-based systems" (French Ministry of Defence 2007, 17). In France, as for many other space powers, the Chinese ASAT test performed on January 11, 2007, had reinforced the view of the importance of space assets and the need for stronger protectives measures. China was already hailed as the future strategic peer competitor by the United States themselves. This colored this international event with a special strategic significance. The US intercept in February 2008 as well as the Cosmos-Iridium collision almost exactly one year later finally brought space security to the forefront. This would mean for France a rather radical change in the way military institutions had approached space until then. From an environment mostly structured by strategic intelligence needs, space would possibly become a theatre of conflicts, with all that means in terms of capabilities, preparedness, and organizational arrangements.

Military institutions would have to learn quickly and within a few years. They first had to evolve from a strict linkage with a deterrence policy to a more operational posture, making use of satellites in an ever-growing number of external operations. Now they also would have to organize the protection of their space assets, in other terms get ready to fight in space. Consequently, this led to the creation in 2008 of a first Joint Space Command whose main function would be to coordinate the use of military systems by the armed forces. From an institutional point of view this was no small step, and it would have effects on the global perception of the role given to space inside the entire military institution. From then on, inner institutional perceptions and roles would progressively change, with soon-to-come new approaches regarding threats and associated protection measures to deal with them.

A 2013 updated version of the "Defense and Security White Book" (in French, "Livre Blanc, défense et sécurité nationale") already confirmed this increased role for space. But a new "Strategic Review of Defense and National Security" ordered by President Macron in 2017 (Strategic Review of Defense and National Security 2017) would be even more explicit, stating that "outer space is also a domain of strategic and military rivalry" and is "a domain of confrontation where some states can be tempted to use force to deny access or threaten to damage orbiting systems" (45). Hence, "In outer space, our dependence on capabilities that are vulnerable today must lead us to enhance their protection and, by working in close cooperation with our American and European allies, to increase redundancy where necessary" (71).

With Arnaud Danjean, a right-wing member of the European parliament and former military analyst, as lead author the report insisted on the need to find what was called a "balanced operational cooperation." Space was identified as a good candidate for such a balanced strategy: "Lastly, in order to secure our military space assets, French forces will have to continue working in partnership with those Nations with assessment and action capabilities in outer space." What would this mean precisely? "The aim of the operational partnerships and cooperative efforts established by France, particularly in Europe, is to facilitate joint operational engagements, and thus ultimately to enhance our relative operational autonomy by bringing in additional or complementary assets. Such partnerships also provide other benefits, in terms of legitimacy and acceptability of operations that France seeks to carry out. Lastly, they create or strengthen existing ties that rely on the proper recognition of respective security priorities by each party. To this end, on the basis of an early assessment, cooperative projects must reflect a sufficient convergence of political wills and military needs in terms of calendars and capabilities. From a capacity standpoint, they must contribute to making operations sustainable and ultimately deliver savings (costs, equipment volumes, maintenance, numbers of deployed personnel, etc.) when compared to a strictly national approach" (Strategic Review of Defense and National Security 2017, 76–77).

Some areas in space have quickly appeared as good examples for such favorable cost/benefits ratios (Hzorensky and Bataille, this volume). As early as 2007, the surveillance of space was conceived the perfect candidate for a win-win situation: "Rather than create a purely national capability we would prefer a European cooperation project, which could lead to the creation of a system for use by the international community. In order to achieve this goal, we must simultaneously: Introduce a credible national surveillance capability for low earth orbit satellites, thus opening the door to a cooperative venture among European nations (GRAVES system: from a technology demonstrator to an operational system); Contribute effectively to the definition of a dual requirement aimed at identifying objects liable to cause damage to launchers or satellites. In this respect, the Ministry of Defence takes a keen interest in the initiative launched by European Space Agency (ESA) in December 2005 to develop a Space Situational Awareness (SSA) prototype to be submitted to the member States for a decision at the next ESA ministerial council meeting" (French Ministry of Defense 2007, 17).

This position could then hardly be seen as a surprise. In the first place, for France as for many other countries in the world, the notion of sovereignty in the field of space surveillance has historically been nuanced by long-standing relationships with the United States, for long the sole data provider in the field. Still active today, this relationship has taught us how such a well-designed cooperative process could be technically fruitful. However, the operational use of an autonomous asset, starting from 2005 with the GRAVES radar, was seen as an imperative "ultimately to enhance our relative operational autonomy by bringing in additional or complementary assets" in accordance with the principle of "balanced operational cooperation" that was mentioned in the 2017 document.

The Space Surveillance and Tracking consortium of countries launched by the European Commission in 2014 had to be an important piece of this global cooperative strategy. Composed today of the national agencies of some seven European Union (EU) Member States, this consortium is intended to mutualize existing national assets, whether civilian or military, and provide a few services to operators via the EU Satellite Centre (EU SatCen) based in Torrejon, close to Madrid in Spain. Early difficulties in reaching agreements on the sharing of limited EU budgets as well as about EU's role in defining the governance and the data policy of the system did not prevent European Union Space Surveillance and Tracking (EUSST) from achieving a genuine operational level that makes it a real service provider to key operators.

THE 2019 FRENCH "SPACE DEFENSE STRATEGY"

But such cooperation should not be confused with a substitution for national space surveillance programs. The new French "Space Defense Strategy" published in 2019 has almost theorized the coexistence of autonomy and cooperation in national space policy thinking. In line with the 2017 "National Security and Defense Review" already mentioned, the 2019 "Space Defense Strategy" confirmed that "France's GRAVES radar is an essential component of its space surveillance system. Its renovation in 2022 will extend its working life and improve its effectiveness. . . . Forming the basis for our low Earth orbit SST architecture, the post-GRAVES capability will be a national asset." Simply, the document notes that it "may be strengthened by bilateral cooperation with Germany or draw on the EUSST initiative (though it has not given full satisfaction to date) or some other European financing arrangement such as the European Defence Fund or EDIDP" (French Ministry for the Armed Forces 2019, 46). In other terms, while such developments are being clearly reaffirmed by France as the perfect example of a purely national domain, it may possibly benefit from non-sovereign and even non-military capabilities, for example as developed by the EU.

Beyond this sole example, the general tone of the 2019 document as well as the accompanying political speeches have given the impression that a dual strategy of autonomy and cooperation had been fully integrated. The "Space Defence Strategy" acknowledges that "there are possibilities for cooperation on space operations with the UK, along with the United States and other partner countries" (French Ministry for the Armed Forces 2019, 32); it adds that "the US is also a key ally for our military space operations" (34). Minister Florence Parly, in a speech announcing the new French military strategy in space, has made these trajectories a prominent national product. Echoing the document's introduction, which states that "French actors in both the public and the private sector must guard against more recent threats, such as the proliferation of space debris, jamming, blinding and directed-energy weapons" (9), she noted that "our allies and our adversaries have been militarizing space. . . . Our first responsibility is to protect our space capabilities. They are essential to our operations, they are essential to the functioning of our economy and of our society" (Parly 2019). Insisting on the sovereign right of "self-defense", her speech also highlighted the rather innovative concept of "active defense" (also developed in the strategy itself):

> This is why I have decided to launch a new armament program called "Mastering space." Just that. It will comprise two parts: surveillance and active defence. Our first responsibility is to protect our capabilities in space. . . . We have to watch our satellites more and better. . . . Once equipped with these new surveillance capabilities, we will be able to organize our active defence. And here I want to be precise: Active defence has nothing to do with an offensive strategy, it is rather about self-defence. It is about, when a hostile act has been detected, characterized and attributed, responding to it in an adapted and proportionate way, in compliance with the international law.

This is where a political signal may also have been sent on purpose. The point is to recall that deterring adversaries from attacking assets considered as critical to the nation is not an uncommon policy for France. It may even be a claim for the specificity of the strategic positioning of France in the field of space, at both international and European levels. Addressing space security by declaring the existence of possible "red lines" is meant to establish a clear distinction between a French "space defense" policy and the security-only oriented approach as privileged by the European partners.

This can appear fully coherent with the dual approach of space security as de facto historically endorsed by France in the European context. But beyond that dimension only, contemporaneous political speech on space in France speaks volumes about a specific strategic culture and history. It clearly reminds us of the historical link mentioned above between national nuclear destiny and the early roots of the development of national military space programs. This close historical association between the two domains exists in other countries, for example in the United States. It explains the common reference in this country to the notion of "space deterrence," as sometimes mentioned in public official documents or in expert works (Pasco 2021, 110–11).

However, in the case of France, this notion of deterrence remains exclusively linked to the nuclear posture, where no room for any decision sharing may exist. The wording used in the space domain differs slightly with an accent on the notion of "discouragement," making sure that no confusion can be made with a nuclear deterrence posture. The French strategy rather elects to "discourage and thwart action by any ill-intentioned third party." More precisely "[military space operations] . . . span various passive and active measures relating to prevention, taking a comprehensive approach (diplomatic, media, economic, legal, etc.); the resilience of all space assets; the defence in space of our space assets" all this being meant for "preserv[ing] freedom of access to and action in space" (French Ministry for the Armed Forces 2019, 38).

Of course, the situation in space may be considered as differing widely from the highly codified nuclear deterrence environment. Nuclear strategies are based on mutually clear perceptions of "red lines" and unambiguous rules, behaviors, and procedural steps be-tween possible adversaries equipped with nuclear weapons. The dynamics of the space environment make it hardly comparable to the nuclear strategic domain. Space surveil-lance systems are far from guaranteeing a global picture that would be precise enough to attribute responsibilities to any catastrophic event in space. More largely, by evidently signaling its intent to avoid the usage of a nuclear deterrence-based rhetoric, this spe-cific approach can also be viewed as leaving by principle a door open to more widely shared (and possibly discussed) space security options. Beyond the sole need to curb the feeling that France may *in-fine* intensify the militarization of space, the message is also that a pragmatic path may be to couple such protective measures with more efficient col-lective security mechanisms, discussed internationally and acceptable to all.

The influence of the complex dynamics of space activity worldwide as well as the European environment cannot be ignored in current French decision-making. National government decisions cannot set the tone alone anymore given the interaction of many communities or interests and larger uncertainties in managing collective space security. This interdependence, as well as reliance on space systems, including in the European context, had rendered a reshaping of the French space defense strategy necessary. It has also made it more complex and necessarily more permeable to its environment. By mentioning at times the influence of outside dynamics, such as the emergence of the NewSpace domain (Klein and Boensch, this volume), the French strategy makes no se-cret of the importance of this new framework. Paradoxically, these new uncertainties have translated in this case into some sort of doctrinal flexibility that both legitimates an apparently harsher military stance and calls at the same time for collective security issues to be inscribed as a priority on the international agenda.

AUTONOMY AND COOPERATION: A SPECIFICALLY FRENCH "REFERENTIAL" FOR YESTERDAY AND TOMORROW?

What lessons can be learned from this very brief history of the French approach to space defense and security? Mostly, it shows how much this approach has always been struc-tured through a combination of autonomy and cooperation, reflecting in passing the composite nature of interests at stake in France and in Europe. Both realism and con-structivism could be taken as convincing explanatory schemes when it comes to French military space policy-making. A look at recent orientations amply demonstrates the key role played by the collective perception of the global environment and how much it can orient the dynamics and feed the influences in the process. The European dimension, at all periods, has played a major role in orienting and delineating the reflections of the national military communities. More largely, institutional actors have constantly been in contact with other interest groups (such as industry, European institutions, other EU Member State representatives, or even the media to start with). They also have witnessed more recently, like others, developments worldwide that they do not control. After all, in democracies fortunately, policies are being modeled by those interactions and cannot be reduced to the expression of homogeneous visions stemming from the sole institutional elites. If only because of the rapid evolution of technologies and economic strategies, such a vision would appear simplistic to say the least.

However, it would certainly be equally simplistic to see in these constant and mutually influential interactions the sign of a complete absence of organization, and ultimately a lack of meaning in the decisions taken and the strategies put in place. In France indeed, the need for finding a balance between autonomy and cooperation in space, and most notably in military space, may also have resulted in a shared view by all the stakeholders of global objectives mostly derived from the post-war period. These common goals have been able to capture most of the sectoral and institutional objectives in a commonly defined "referential" or public policy line. It seems to have passed the test of time. This has been mostly the result of the firm early space policy attachment to the nuclear deterrence strategy put in place on the eve of the Gaullist years. But acquiring a strategic nuclear force never meant giving up the idea of building a stronger political and industrial Europe. The presence of these parallel objectives could be noticed very early on in finding ways to mutualize investments in other domains. Sharing views and capabilities in space for advancing the cause of Europe has been a strong political objective. This dual approach has certainly formed a common reference, which has proved instrumental for all communities and has become a largely shared framework for advancing French thinking about the military uses of space.

In this regard, the French Space Defense Strategy published in 2019 is perfectly in line with these early times. At least, it cannot be seen as disconnected from this historical strategic framework. It advocates on the one hand the need for autonomy (some could call it sovereignty) in defense of strictly national assets. In this respect, it simply extends the implicit reference to the Gaullist years which has been long accepted by the main national stakeholders and continues to be a prime reference of national public debate. But it also reiterates the importance of enlarged cooperation, notably at the European level, keeping alive the same dual-track policy that has been implemented since the founding years.

For these reasons, while many may have considered references in the French strategy to "active defense" or lasers as possibly opening a Pandora's box, these orientations as seen from France do not prevent a parallel effort of consultation and cooperation. On the contrary, they may even call for them in a more urgent way. At the risk of appearing provocative, the new "Space Defense Strategy" does reflect the same sense of political pragmatism advocated in the first years of the nuclear deterrence force. It continues the tradition of a strong national stance, while it may also be used to call for opening discussions and for inventing possible new (and more efficient) cooperation schemes, not only in Europe but also internationally. Whether this posture will be successful or not remains to be seen. But, at least, this approach, rather traditional in its conception, may well sound like the new common "referential" of military space policy-making that will be used in France for the years to come.

REFERENCES

Dahl, Robert. 1961. *Who Governs? Democracy and Power in an American City*. New Haven, CT: Yale University Press.

French Ministry for the Armed Forces. 2017. "Strategic Review of Defence and National Security." https://cd-geneve.delegfrance.org/Strategic-review-of-Defence-and-national-security-2017.

French Ministry for the Armed Forces. 2019. "Space Defence Strategy, Report of the Space Working Group." Paris, DICOD. https://www.vie-publique.fr/sites/default/files/rapport/pdf/194000642.pdf.

French Ministry of Defense. 2007. "Let us Make More for Our Defence: Strategic auidelines for a Space Defence Policy in France and in Europe." Paris. DICoD. https://aerospace.org/sites/default/files/policy_archives/France%20MOD%20Space%20Defense%20Feb07.pdf.

French Ministry of Defense. 2008. "Défense et Sécurité Nationale. Le livre Blanc." Paris, Odile Jacob. https://www.vie-publique.fr/sites/default/files/rapport/pdf/084000341.pdf.

French Ministry of Defense. 2013. "Livre Blanc, défense et sécurité nationale." Paris, Direction de l'information légale et administrative. https://fr.calameo.com/read/000331627d6f04ea4fe0e.

Heisbourg, François, and Xavier Pasco. 2011. *Espace militaire, L'Europe entre coopération et souveraineté*. Paris: Editions Choiseul.

Jobert, Bruno, and Pierre Muller. 1987. *L'Etat en action, Politiques publiques et corporatismes*. Paris: Presses Universitaires de France.

Lawrence, Philip, and Anders Hansson. 1998. "American space Hegemony: Accident or Design?" *Space Policy* 14: 1–3.

Lenzer, Christian (rapporteur). 1996. *WEU and Helios 2*. Assembly of the Western European Union, Technical and Aerospace Committee Document 1525, 41st Ordinary Session (2nd Part), Paris. aei.pitt.edu/53681/1/B0944.pdf.

Logsdon, John, 1997. "Is There a U.S. Strategy for Space?" *Space News* 8, no. 35: n.p.

Moulin, Hervé. 2017. *La construction d'une politique spatiale en France, Entre indépendance nationale et dynamiques européennes, 1945–1975*. Paris: Beauchesne.

Muller, Pierre. 1994. *Les politiques publiques*, 26. Paris: Presses Universitaires de France.

Pasco, Xavier. 2021. "Space Security in the 21st Century: A French View." In *Space and Missile Wars: What Awaits?*, edited by Henry D. Sokolski. 97–26. Arlington, VA: Nonproliferation Policy Education Center.

Parly, Florence. 2019. *Déclaration de Mme Florence Parly, ministre des armées, sur la stratégie spatiale de défense, à la Base aérienne 942 de Lyon le 25 juillet 2019, Ministry of Armed Force*. 25 July 2019. https://www.vie-publique.fr/discours/268578-florence-parly-25072019-strategie-spatiale-de-defense.

Richelson, Jeffrey T. 1990. *America's Secret Eyes in Space: The U.S. Keyhole Spy Satellite Program*. New York: Harper & Row.

Stares, Paul B. 1985. *The Militarization of Space, U.S. Policy, 1945–1984*, Ithaca, NY: Cornell University Press.

Wright-Mills, C. *The Power Elite*. 1956. New York: Oxford University Press.

....

CHAPTER 21

UK SPACE POLICY

A Quest for Coherence

....

MARK HILBORNE

THE government of the United Kingdom (UK) has only very recently begun formulating its position on the space domain. Until this point, national space policy was a significant gap in UK strategic thinking. As it publishes its strategy, it has become clear that the UK is transitioning from a reliance on integration with and reliance upon, in particular, the United States and the Five Eyes alliance, and moving toward establishing sovereign capabilities in space, driven by new opportunities in the space economy along with the realization of the importance of space from a security perspective. What has emerged is a space policy that seeks to at once address concerns over the security of its own space assets and critical national infrastructure that depends on space, and its role within its principal alliances, while also serving the growing economic and societal benefits that derive from space. Simultaneously the UK is seeking a greater voice in the international governance of space as a means to enhance its diplomatic leverage. To accomplish this, the UK government has sought a cross-sector approach to space policy in which these divergent aims are reconciled. The UK government will not be able to replicate the full spectrum of space capabilities upon which it relies, yet it is able to contribute in specific ways to the systems of allies and partners. It must therefore target key areas that will deliver the maximum military, scientific, and commercial return on investment.

The 2021 Integrated Review of Security, Defence, Development and Foreign Policy made the first significant inclusion of space in any such a UK policy document. As befits an integrated review, it provided a wide perspective of the UK's security, including in the space domain, encompassing economic prosperity, diplomacy, and security. The term integrated in this document refers to the cross-governmental approach, encompassing civil, commercial, and military sectors, but also the UK's allies and partners, which remains a constant from earlier decades. With the review, space gained recognition as a domain in its own right.

The ensuing National Space Strategy and Defence Space Strategy of 2021 and 2022 both maintained the same thrust. Space security was framed in the wider context, protecting national interests in and through space but, more widely, supporting tech-nological development and delivering economic benefits for the population of the UK. Even the Defence Space Strategy notes the importance of diplomatic efforts in framing aspects of space governance. Similarly the recent Joint Doctrine Publication 0-40, "UK Space Power," (Ministry of Defence 2022c) though focused on the operational level, notes that the four instruments of national power (diplomatic, information, military, and economic) are needed to achieve wider government aims. This broader perspective fits within the current drive for multi-domain integration and shows a nuanced under-standing as to how space can support national interests.

Within developing policy sits a clear goal of protect and defend—this is reiterated numerous times in policy documents. This is based upon some sound thinking on the nature of space power, but the way in which this would be manifest requires further de-velopment. Concepts such as deterrence in space are only given a short discussion at the end of JDP 0-40, and these require greater analysis.

History

Despite a fairly minimal presence in space since the beginning of the space era, the UK was in fact an early entrant into the domain. The country can claim to be the first to op-erate a satellite after the two Cold War belligerents, with the successful placement into orbit of the Ariel I satellite in 1962. An effort to bring prominent German scientists to the UK who had direct experience in Nazi Germany's aerospace efforts also aided the development of a number of rocket and missile projects in the 1950s and 1960s. These included the Blue Streak Intermediate Range Ballistic Missile (IRBM), the Black Knight launch vehicle/re-entry test vehicle, and the proposed Black Prince which would have combined the two previous vehicles into a multistage launcher capable of deploying medium-sized payloads into orbit. The latter goal was achieved with the BLACK ARROW program, which successfully launched the UK's Prospero satellite in 1971. To date, this remains the only launch of a UK satellite by a UK launch vehicle.

While there was significant promise in these programs, soon after the launch of Prospero, the UK government ended the funding for space projects. Subsequent UK satellite launches were to be handled by US rockets. This set a long-standing dynamic for UK space development, leading to a reduction of domestic expertise and reliance on allies for various elements of its space endeavors. The Blue Streak missile was later repurposed to become the first stage of the Europa rocket, developed by the European Launcher Development Organisation (ELDO), precursor to the European Space Agency (ESA). This served to further shift expertise out of the UK.

Currently the UK has a singular domestically developed sovereign space-based capability—the Skynet satellite communication system. This was developed in the 1960s, allowing the UK to become the third nation to have a sovereign satellite com-munication (SATCOM) system (Mitchell 2019). When Skynet 1 was launched in 1969, it was the first military satellite in geostationary orbit. This capability continued until the mid-1970s, when the cancellation of Skynet 3 meant that the UK became reliant on US and NATO allies for its SATCOMs. The lack of indigenous capability proved highly problematic during the Falkland's conflict, and this spurred the introduction of the Skynet 4 series. The program is currently running version 5, with Skynet 6 planned to launch in 2025 on a Falcon 9 rocket (Henry 2020 and Airbus 2022).

In addition to space-based capabilities, there are important ground-based elements operated by the UK. Principal among these is RAF Fylingdales. It was designed as part of the US ballistic missile warning system and thus is not a space surveillance system. Nonetheless this capability is inherent in the design, and it is capable of generating useful space data, coordinated at the Space Operations Coordination Centre at RAF High Wycombe. While this can be used by the UK, it cannot be shared, so it is limited as a sovereign source of space data. Importantly, however, it does enable the UK to receive data from the US Space Fence, which is the most capable space surveillance system currently. Thus Fylingdales adds to the standing of the UK, enabling it to access an incredibly valuable resource.

While key government initiatives and programs have been traditionally somewhat limited in scope, scale, and number, the strength of the commercial space sector is notable in contrast. The UK has long been regarded as a center of entrepreneurial activity, and this is reflected in the commercial space sector. The UK is home to the third highest number of "unicorn" start-ups, and the most per one million of population (Future SST Markets Research: Final Report 2020). The UK space sector includes a diverse range of companies, covering both the manufacture of satellites, or components thereof, as well as services from space, and markets such as insurance of space assets.

Perhaps most notable among these is Surrey Satellites, which is a leader in the manufacture of small satellites (smallsats). It builds and operates satellites for a number of operators, notably the UK Ministry of Defence (MoD) (CARBONITE 2 satellite), the Canadian Department of National Defence (SAPPHIRE) and the Nigerian government (NigeriaSat-2 and NX satellites). Other companies include Oxford Space Systems, developing low-cost antennas and structures suitable for smaller satellites; Reaction Engines, developing a hypersonic propulsion system; and Skyrora and SpacePort Cornwall, both developing vertical and horizontal space launch capabilities for the UK.

Thus, while there are clearly pockets of expertise and excellence, UK space strategy has historically not invested directly in space capabilities, but rather relied extensively on allies for both specific capabilities and expertise. This represented fairly good value for the UK, due to minimal expenditure with continued access, but nevertheless, in terms of strategy and doctrine, space was a void. The commercial sector is now driving a much more dynamic space sector, and this has been laterally recognized by the government as an opportunity, a driver for growth, and a way of stimulating the high-technology sector more widely. Yet despite the ingenuity that has been demonstrated from within the private sector, the UK still has some way to go before it consolidates a coherent space strategy.

SPACE EMERGES

The importance of space has gradually been crystalizing within the UK government since 2010. It is then that organizational and policy changes can start to be tracked, demonstrating the realization that space confers military, economic, and diplomatic power. This realization regarding all three factors developed in parallel, and thus the fairly holistic vision of space began to evolve.

This first notable change is the creation of the UK Space Agency (UKSA) in 2010 ("UK Space Agency Launched in London" 2010). The agency replaced the British National Space Centre (BNSC), while taking closer control over budgets and policy of the UK's civilian space activities. Previously, these had been generated by a partnership of government departments and science funding councils, but with the UKSA, these were drawn together under a single managerial structure. This was an important step in generating coherent oversight.

Doctrinal and conceptual thinking had begun adding space into the vocabulary just prior to this. The Future Air and Space Operating Concept 2008 and 2009 starting to introduce space as a military function (Ministry of Defence 2008; 2009). Previously titled the FAOC, adding space was significant, primarily as this document represents the thoughts of the Chief of the Air Staff (CAS), and so represented a key shift in thinking from the leadership. This then led to the UK Military Space Primer, published by the MoD (Ministry of Defence 2010). This was the first formal conceptual publication devoted to space. It served to establish a basic understanding of space and establish a space lexicon in the MoD. The RAF's AP 3000 single service doctrine also encompassed concepts on the nature of space power.

As single service doctrine was replaced by joint doctrine, the Joint Doctrine Publication (JDP) 0-30 UK Air and Space Doctrine, both 2013 and 2017 editions, included sections on space as the title suggests. In 2014, the UK's first National Space Security Policy (NSSP) was released, followed by the first National Space Policy (NSP) in 2015.

These documents sowed the seeds for more overarching policy outputs, starting with the 2021 Integrated Review of Security, Defence, Development and Foreign Policy—*Global Britain in a Competitive Age*—which made the first significant inclusion of space in any such a UK policy document (the 2010 Strategic Defence and Security Review merely mentioned the need for a National Space Policy, recognizing the UK's increasing dependence on space). As befits an integrated review, the view of space covers a wide spectrum, encompassing economic prosperity, diplomacy, and security. This was a significant and positive development, indicating the growing importance that the space domain has in helping attain policy objectives in these key areas. While there is not much that was new or unexpected in the review, space became recognized as a domain of operations alongside land, air, maritime, and cyber—an important step in itself.

The term integrated in this document refers both to the cross-governmental approach, encompassing civil, commercial, and military sectors, but also to the UK's allies and partners, which is consistent with earlier decades. The recognition that a cross-government strategy is required is an important step and will be critical in unlocking the potential of the UK in space. Platforms and technologies operating in space are very frequently dual use, and this is true across the whole spectrum of space activities: launch, the satellites themselves and their tracking, even the data and imagery that is generated by these. This creates a blurring of sectors, making military, commercial, and civilian increasingly hard to distinguish, and driving the need for a coherent approach.

The referral to the importance of allies in the space domain is a clear recognition of the limitations the UK still faces in the space domain. While the review outlines a desire to increase the UK's sovereign capabilities, there will be a continued need for and a reliance on allies. This is likely to increase as a level of resilience in space is pursued as competitors develop more robust counterspace capabilities. Even states that command a full suite of space capabilities, such as the United States, increasingly seek collaboration with capable allies. Furthermore, the review highlights the need to engage with key alliances and security structures, such as NATO and the Combined Space Operations (CSpO) initiative, as well as NASA and the European, Canadian, Australian, and Japanese space agencies.

Beyond the security factors the review makes a strong case for economic elements as well. The value of the space sector to the UK economy is set out, and its value as a driver for future scientific research and how it might act as an engine for further growth are also recognized.

Particularly noteworthy, the review also addresses the diplomatic and governance aspect of space. This is of central importance for space security generally, but is also a mechanism for "global Britain" to extend its influence. This is an area in which the UK had already made some important contributions, giving greater weight to the review's goals. Within the Conference on Disarmament in Geneva, the UK had tabled a draft resolution on responsible behaviors in space, which was adopted in November 2020. The international diplomatic sphere is an area where the UK has a useful degree of leverage, and strengthening governance in space will benefit its increasing stake and voice in the domain.

Critically, with the integrated review, space as a domain became normalized, taking its place alongside the other traditional domains and cyber. Furthermore, it sets out a broad vision for UK space policy, one that is integrated across sectors and with allies and partners.

National Space Strategy

The integrated review was followed by the first National Space Strategy (NSS) in September 2021 (HM Government 2021). While, the integrated review was focused on defense and security from a broad perspective, the NSS was focused on space from a broad perspective. It provided an ambitious declaration of the UK's future role in the delivery of space capability.

In tandem with the review, it revealed a growing awareness among policy and decision makers that space is not merely a lucrative industrial sector that is militarily important, it is also an increasingly useful instrument of statecraft and geoeconomic influence (Sheldon 2021, 9). The document sought to balance the competing requirements of industrial, civil, military, and government needs in space. Being so broad, perhaps inevitably, the document drew criticism that it was shallow in terms of detail, with few specifics (Suess 2021).

Although the strategy provided an accurate assessment of UK capabilities at the time, the forward-looking aspects were quite vague. More positively, there was a clear effort to link the civilian, commercial, and defense aspects of UK space activities. There are centers of expertise in all these areas in the UK, and pooling these as much as possible is critical to maximize efficiency. This is increasingly the case with dual-use technology. Thus the NSS reiterates the wide-ranging theme that has become a dominant strain in UK space policy-making.

There was not much that was innovative or new in the NSS however. It documented prior achievements well, but there was less detail about the future, in particular those aspects pertaining to defense. In particular there were no details about increased expenditure.

The visions and goals, as set out in the document, pertain to growing and leveling up the UK's space economy, promoting the values of global Britain, leading pioneering discovery, protecting national interests in and through space, and, finally, using space to deliver for UK citizens and the world. These are to be achieved by a number of "pillars" which involve, among other things, building both trading and global partnerships and leading in areas such as diplomacy and space regulation. Once again this points to a wide perspective in how the government views the space sector, though notably, there was not much information pertaining to defense and security in the NSS.

DEFENSE SPACE STRATEGY

The focus on defense in and from space fell to the Defence Space Strategy (DSS), released in February 2022 (Ministry of Defence 2022a). While the previous documents had an integrated focus, a separate defense space strategy leant specific emphasis on the military and security aspect of space.

The DSS is similar to the previous documents in that it sets out a broad set of guidelines for the UK's goals in space, but again concrete specifics were lacking. It did provide a fairly clear idea of spending allocation however, for the previously agreed extra £1.4 billion (over 10 years, as set out in the March 2021 Defence Command Paper, see Ministry of Defence 2022b) for space being apportioned according to "capability themes":

- Satellite Communications (SATCOM): Skynet 6 has been given an extra £60 million on top of its core budget of £5 billion
- Intelligence, Surveillance, and Reconnaissance (ISR): £970 million
- Space Control: £145 million
- Space Command and Control: £135 million
- Space Domain Awareness (SDA): £85 million

This does not however represent a significant investment, given the cost of many of the technologies involved, and the ten-year time spread. France, with a similar sized economy, planned to spend approximately half the ten-year UK figure in 2022 alone— £646 million (Machi 2021). As might be expected, the UK figure pales in comparison with that of the United States.

Of these themes, the Skynet SATCOM system is clearly the largest, and is considered the first priority in the DSS. As noted above, this remains the sole domestically developed sovereign space-based capability. Developing SATCOM to handle greater data throughput is clearly a core requirement, enabling this system to integrate with systems in other domains, as well as those in space.

While being allocated a very small amount of the budget, SDA is nonetheless considered the second priority. The objective is to enhance the UK's ability "to detect, track, characterize and attribute objects in space and build agility into our space Command and Control mechanisms and decision making." As I have maintained in other research, SDA adds broad capabilities and is key to defending UK economic and security interests, while also enabling the UK to seize commercial and diplomatic opportunities offered by space (Hilborne and Presley 2020). This capability can be less expensive than others, particularly if ground-based elements are relied upon, and thus the smaller budgetary allocation may well be appropriate. A key benefit of this capability is that it will ultimately enable the UK to provide data to allies, as opposed to being merely a beneficiary. This will enhance its standing within alliance structures, in addition to wider efforts such as international discourse on space sustainability.

ISR is listed as a third priority, though it received the second highest amount of the budgetary allocation. Described in the paper as "those elements of Earth Observation (EO) primarily utilised by Defence and Intelligence" which might be Earth-facing or space-facing, it is recognized as a dual-use system, enabling both civilian and military end users. The key element of this is the ISTARI Programme, a multi-satellite system to support greater global surveillance and intelligence for military operations, as well as MINERVA, an associated data transport system that acts as a digital spine for integration with other space systems as well as with land, air, sea, and cyber technologies. The satellite will be based on the Surrey Satellite Technology Ltd (SSTL) Carbonite + platform, itself a derivation of the satellites developed for the RAF Carbonite 2 programs using commercial off-the-shelf (COTS) technologies ("UK Orders First Defence Satellite for Minerva Programme" 2022). The combination of these systems is similar in concept to the US National Defense Space Architecture (NDSA), though the US system will be much larger, consisting of many hundreds of satellites (Lopez 2021). Alongside this there is a program to deliver a laser communication system to transmit data from space to earth at very high speeds.

Much like building sovereign SDA capabilities, creating a military ISR system will also allow the UK to be a contributing nation in terms of building a wider space sensing capability, with similar intelligence, military, and potentially diplomatic rewards.

The next priority is command and control. The DSS defines this as a comprehensive understanding of data that has been drawn from multiple sources, that will then "enable balanced, risk-aware decision-making, exploitation of opportunities and control of activities through space." Within this sit three key elements. First is developing the UK Space Command and evolving it into a well-organized joint command. Second is to enhance the Space Operations Centre (SpOC), while also establishing a National Space Operations Centre that will serve civilian and commercial requirements. The final element is a Training Needs Analysis to establish how to most effectively grow and nurture domestic expertise. It is here that the idea of a Space Academy is also presented, which may develop into a critical hub of thinking in the space domain (it has not yet been made clear how this will be established and whether it would be a single institution).

The final priority is that of space control, for which £145 million is being allocated. The DSS describes protecting and defending the UK's interests in the space domain, deterring hostile acts, and ensuring sufficient resilience in the face of hostile acts. These will include exploring "carefully calibrated effects to assure our access to, and operational independence in, space."

This language chimes with a resonating theme in the DSS—that of protect and defend. This theme introduces some important questions regarding how to achieve this, and the nature of deterrence in space. How these concepts are viewed and framed in UK defense policy will be discussed later in the paper, but in the DSS, there is not much indication as to how concepts like deterrence in space would function. I have argued that standard concepts of deterrence do not function effectively in space. How the MoD defines deterrence will be critical (Hilborne 2019).

The final items in terms of priorities are position, navigation and timing (PNT) and Launch. While only given a very short description—and no budgetary input—PNT is recognized as being critical to military activity and highly vulnerable to disruption. Gone however are the aspirations that were expressed by the government for a sovereign PNT system after the UK's exit from the Galileo program. Such a sovereign capability would have cost billions and starved other important streams of development. Instead, the DSS focuses on developing and securing a resilient PNT capability.

Launch too is seen as a necessary step in terms of resilience. However, the DSS notes that this will be developed with the UKSA and commercial companies and that the UK will continue to rely on allies and partners.

On the diplomatic aspect, the DSS is forthright. It notes the close coordination between the Foreign, Commonwealth and Development Office (FCDO), who have been at the forefront within international forums on space policy. It was a UK initiative that produced the UN General Assembly Resolution on Reducing Space Threats through Norms, Rules and Principles of Responsible Behaviours, which gained very strong support in the initial and subsequent resolutions (Hitchens 2021a; 2021b). These soft-power efforts are seen as inextricably linked to hard power, as they can reduce threats and stabilize behavior in the space domain.

Overall, the DSS provides a balanced view of space, and there are a number of positive points, as it begins the process of establishing UK space policy, specifically in terms of defense and security. There was a robust message that the UK would take an active role in military space and that it will deter hostile acts and ensure sufficient resilience.

The wider contributions of industry and commercial companies are acknowledged, as are those of allies and partners. These underpin the "Own-Collaborate-Access" framework, and there is a clear recognition that the value of space is a key aspect of national power, and it is a domain that is increasingly contested. But space is also framed in the wider context, of security writ large: military, but also economic and diplomatic.

However, there were omissions. There were specifics missing—how the UK can best integrate its capabilities into those of its key allies was not fully clear. The UK is constrained by a limited budget, and this needs to be used efficiently. Specific schedules and objectives were not defined.

Furthermore, the DSS does not refer to "space power" (though this is mentioned in passing when noting the mission of UK Space Command). This is a complex term that needs specific framing, and the DSS would have been an ideal opportunity to do so. The terms "to deter" and deterrence are in the DSS, but how the former can be achieved and what deterrence means in the space domain are not examined. What the UK capabilities would be in this regard are not described beyond "carefully calibrated effects," but these seem likely to be "sub threshold" reversible or temporary effects, such as dazzling, jamming, or spoofing an opponent's satellite, as opposed to hard-kill weapons, such as DA-ASATs. There is then much to be clarified.

Joint Doctrine Publication (JDP) 0-40, UK Space Power

Some of the conceptual points that were lacking in the DSS were covered in the subsequent Joint Doctrine Publication 0-40 "UK Space Power" (Ministry of Defence 2022c). This is an operational-level doctrine that sits alongside the other key domains' doctrines. Previously, space was covered doctrinally as part of JDP 0-30, "UK Air and Space Doctrine." With JDP 0-40, space gains recognition as a separate domain of military operation. It outlines many key elements, such as the roles of space power and its employment, while also setting out definitions for space power; concepts such as deterrence are discussed, though these are quite limited.

JDP 0-40 makes some useful practical observations, such as the infrastructural elements of space operations (the ground segment, the space segment, and the link segment), as well as aspects of the physical environment, such as orbital mechanics and space weather. The characteristics of space power are also outlined. Advantages are noted as perspective—that is the high vantage point of space; access—the ability to overfly other sovereign states; persistence—the ability to overcome the impermanence of air platforms; and versatility—the ability of a single platform to use a variety of sensors and provide services to multiple users simultaneously. Limitations of space power are: cost—space is inherently expensive; vulnerability—the result of weak signals and lack of protection; predictability—orbital paths remain fixed; limited responsiveness—the ability to launch and reconstitute space assets; and orbital congestion—while space is vast, desired orbits or not, and orbital slots are quickly becoming increasingly scarce.

JDP 0-40 defines space power itself as: "exerting influence in, from, or through, space" (Ministry of Defence 2022c, 4). Once again though, a wide view is taken, as it notes that the UK government pursues its goals by leveraging the four instruments of national power (diplomatic, information, military, and economic) needed to achieve wider government aims. It also maintains the view that space is interconnected with the other four operational domains. So while a specific doctrine publication, the wider themes identified in the NSS and DSS are all present: "UK space power is inherently integrated, containing military, civil and commercial elements" (Ministry of Defence 2022c, 4).

This equates well with longer-established definitions. For instance, Lupton argued in 1988 that space power is an element of national power analogous to air, sea, and land power. It therefore possesses elements of national power that enable a nation to exert influence through use of a particular medium, in this case space. He notes that the purpose of this may be purely military, but also nonmilitary. Additionally, all elements of national power "embody not just military forces but civilian capabilities as well." (Lupton 1988, 4). Through this, Lupton defines space power as "the ability of a nation to exploit the space environment in pursuit of national goals and purposes and includes the entire astronautical capabilities of the nation." (4). This echoes the broader perspective that UK space policy incorporates.

A decade later, Johnson, Pace, and Gabbard stated that "spacepower is connected to other forms of national power such as economic strength, scientific capabilities, and international leadership." (Johnson, Pace, and Gabbard 1998, 8). Similarly, in 1999, James Oberg argued that it is "the combination of technology, demographic, economic, industrial, military, national will, and other factors that contribute to the coercive and persuasive ability of a country to politically influence the actions of other states and other kinds of players, or to otherwise achieve national goals through space activity" (Oberg 1999).

More recent research expands these ideas slightly further by explicitly incorporating diplomatic capabilities. Lutes in 2008 argues that "spacepower both contributes to and is supported by other forms of power: diplomatic, informational, military, and economic, among others" (Lutes 2008, 67). Similarly in 2012 Al-Rodhan defined space power as a function of seven state capacities, identified as "social and health issues, domestic politics, economics, the environment, science and human potential, military and security issues, and international diplomacy" (Al-Rodhan 2012). Thus the doctrinal definition of space power in JDP 0-40 and indeed in wider policy mirrors this wider view as expressed in the literature.

One of the last sections in JDP 0-40 is devoted to deterrence, which states that space threats are increasing, raising the need to deter hostile action. The document adopts the NATO definition, which states that deterrence is "the convincing of a potential aggressor that the consequences of coercion or armed conflict would outweigh the potential gains. This requires the maintenance of a credible military capability and strategy with the clear political will to act." (Ministry of Defence 2022c, 82).

Reiterating the broad conception of space, deterrence in space is cast very much in a multi-domain light, noting that "deterrence in, through or using space capabilities is not an independent activity but must form part of the wider strategy." (Ministry of Defence 2022c, 82). Supporting ideas put forth in the Multi-Domain Integration, as laid out in Joint Concept Note 1/20: Multi-Domain Integration (Ministry of Defence 2020, 1/20), deterrence is viewed as "a whole-of-government activity to which Defence contributes" (Ministry of Defence 2022c, 82).

While this develops the concept, it does not give concrete details as to how this might function. The mechanisms of deterrence are difficult to operationalize in space due to a number of factors. Key concepts of traditional deterrence were established in a very specific time and with a very specific weapons system—the Cold War and nuclear weapons. These concepts also had at their heart striking back at the enemy. Striking back in space is hugely complicated due to the physical realities of the space domain. It presents a potential "own-goal" for the deterring state, by creating increased space-debris.

As James Lewis argues, a conceptual core of deterrence is that only the threat of a truly destructive form of retaliation has a deterrent effect, and such a threat can only be credibly made in response to an attack that involves the use of force and poses an existential threat or threatens serious harm to national interests. In so doing, it sets the threshold below which deterrence cannot function. While Lewis was writing on the cyber realm, this logic can be applied to the space domain as well. Attacks on space assets do not pose existential threats or immense harm to vital interests, and so are potentially not deterrable (Lewis 2013).

Furthermore, a key element of deterrence is communication—known as one of the three "C's" (capability, credibility, and communication). This was much more straightforward in principle during the Cold War, with a simpler bilateral axis of communications, combined with sustained direct and indirect diplomatic engagement with rivals. Such communication currently is much more complex. A state must now communicate its deterrent posture to a diverse set of potential opponents in the space domain, and this therefore becomes much harder to calibrate. The interaction and signaling that characterized the decades of the Cold War are no longer present in many of these relationships. Understanding how potential adversaries interpret and respond to threats will be profoundly more difficult.

A further difficulty in applying concepts of deterrence in space is the issue of discrimination and attribution. The intentions of spacefaring states are inherently difficult to judge, and the rules about what is permissible in space are vague. This creates the opportunity for tactics that might be described as gray zone to amplify the haziness. Partially for this reason, it seems far more likely that the kind of attacks that will predominate the in space domain are those that dazzle, jam, spoof, or manipulate satellites or their signals. Attribution of these is difficult if not often impossible, and in such an environment the mechanics of deterrence become much harder to operationalize. Among other things, a clear communication posture is compromised.

The traditional categories of deterrence—either by punishment or denial—when applied to space might appear easier if concepts such as Cross Domain Deterrence or Multi-Domain Deterrence are considered, and this is very much the framework that features in UK strategic thinking. In such a framework, retaliation for an attack on space assets is not limited to a response in kind, and thus space deterrence is no longer limited to space. This approach intuitively sounds a more nuanced and therefore more effective form of deterrence.

An example of this might be that in response to an attack on one state's satellites, the counterattack is against the relevant ground segment, or command and control facility of the attacking country and its space infrastructure. This may meet calculations of proportionality, but it nonetheless may be perceived as escalatory, in that the counterattack would likely occur on the other state's sovereign territory. Different domains will be characterized by different sensitivities. This would create more complexity and increased potential for misperception and miscalculation, and thus escalation.

Dual-use capabilities and the increasing use of space systems in conventional operations will also create further intricacies. The former will manifest itself with the greater presence of commercial actors—and their contracts with government—and the increased use of COTS designs in military assets. Distinction between these systems will be harder, as many satellites could be used for military or non-military purposes, and rules of engagement will incorporate commercial space assets used for military purposes.

In parallel, states increasingly rely on space assets for conventional operations, as opposed to their more strategic orientation during the Cold War. This creates added impetus to interfere with or target a state's satellites in order to undermine its military capabilities in a conflict. If it was perceived that the attacking state might gain an advantage, then the benefits would outweigh the risk in such a calculation (Harrison et al. 2017).

There is still the danger that this can become entangled with strategically orientated satellites as well. For instance, the United States doesn't operate discrete communication satellites for nuclear forces. Both the older Milstar satellites and their replacement—the Advanced Extremely High Frequency (AEHF) satellites—are for both nuclear and "high priority" non-nuclear users. An attack for conventional or operational purposes might be misconstrued as a deliberate attack on nuclear command and control, creating destabilizing and potentially escalatory forces (Hilborne 2019).

The document notes that the UK's deterrence posture remains enshrined in NATO through Article 5 of the North Atlantic Treaty, which refers to resilience as a key element of deterrence. It points out that "NATO resilience is predicated on three pillars of activity:

- layered resilience allowing aggression to be withstood;
- a mutually supporting integrated force to provide options to political leaders; and
- the ability to project stability through activities such as military dialogue, capacity building and operations." (Ministry of Defence 2022c, 88).

Whether or not resilience is a part of deterrence is a point of debate that needs illuminating in JDP 0-40, and UK space policy more widely. Measures in space that would enhance resiliency would include spreading capabilities over constellations of smaller satellites, rather than relying on single large satellites, or distributing information flows via the platforms of allies. Both can dilute threats and reduce the possibility of a catastrophic loss of capability (see Mureşan and Georgescu 2015). The ability to replenish space assets quickly means capabilities can be reconstituted, and this could lead to space contributing to stability rather than being a source of instability. Where possible, transferring some capabilities to other platforms in other domains—for instance, to very long endurance, very high-altitude UAVs—might be a useful method of aiding resiliency as well.

While these measures do not conform to concepts of deterrence as developed during the Cold War, they would nonetheless affect an opponent's cost-benefit calculus, ensuring that the benefits are more difficult to achieve. JDP 0-40, among other UK space policy documents, does not draw this distinction, and it is a key point of space security that requires greater attention and understanding. So while protect and defend is a central theme in JDP 0-40, and within this, the operation of deterrence, the intricacies that will present themselves in this domain need greater exploration.

Conclusions

As UK space security policy continues to be formulated, it is clear that the UK government is seeking a cross-sector approach that seeks to address security in a wide context. Policy outputs and institutional changes all have as their objectives securing the UK's valuable space assets and its space dependent critical national infrastructure, while also fortifying its position within alliance structures and serving the wider economic and societal benefits that are brought by the space sector. This has been expressed consistently in the main policy documents produced by the UK in recent years. Since the first recognition of space as a military function in the Future Air and Space Operating Concepts of 2008 and 2009, the UK government has kept a wide view of the importance of the space domain, and of space security. With the 2021 Integrated Review of Security, Defence, Development and Foreign Policy, space was included for the first time in any such UK policy document, and space as a domain became normalized, taking its place alongside the other traditional domains and cyber. This has been amplified in both the National Space Strategy, and the Defence Space Strategy, and even the operational doctrine JDP 0-40 notes the need for a broad view of how national advantage can be developed in and through space. Consistent with this is the international leadership demonstrated by the UK in the UN as it drove the General Assembly Resolution on Reducing Space Threats through Norms, Rules and Principles of Responsible Behaviours.

While the UK government will not be able to replicate the full spectrum of space capabilities upon which it relies, it seeks to contribute individual capabilities to the systems of allies and partners. In order to do so, policy can be expected to focus on key areas that will deliver the maximum military, scientific, and commercial return on investment.

REFERENCES

Airbus. 2022. "SKYNET 6A Satellite Passes Critical Design Review." July 13. https://airbus-ds-gs.com/2022/07/13/skynet-6a-satellite-passes-critical-design-review/.

Al-Rodhan, N. R. F. 2012. "Space Power and Meta-Geopolitics." In *An Analysis of Space Power, Security and Governance* (First Edition), edited by Nayef R. F. Al-Rodhan, 18–43. St Antony's Series. London: Palgrave Macmillan.

Harrison, Todd, Zack Cooper, Kaitlyn Johnson, and Thomas G. Roberts. 2017. *Escalation and Deterrence in the Second Space Age*. Washington DC: Center for Strategic and International Studies.

Henry, Caleb. 2020. "British Military Finalizes Skynet-6A Contract with Airbus." *Spacenews.com*. https://spacenews.com/british-military-finalizes-skynet-6a-contract-with-airbus/.

Hilborne, Mark, "The Limits of Space Deterrence." Conference Paper Delivered at the Space Operations Summit, London, May 28, 2019.

Hilborne, Mark, and Mark Presley. 2020. "Towards a UK Space Surveillance Policy." The Policy Institute. https://www.kcl.ac.uk/dsd/assets/towards-a-uk-space-surveillance-policy-final.pdf.

Hitchens, T. 2021a. "Exclusive: UK Pushes New UN Accord on Military Space Norms. The US Intends to Support the British Effort." Breaking Defense. https://breakingdefense.com/2021/09/exclusive-uk-pushes-new-un-accord-on-military-space-norms/.

Hitchens, T. 2021b. "UN Committee Votes 'Yes' On UK-US-Backed Space Rules Group." Breaking Defense. https://breakingdefense.com/2021/11/un-committee-votes-yes-on-uk-us-backed-space-rules-group/.

HM Government. 2021. "National Space Strategy." https://www.gov.uk/government/publications/national-space-strategy.

Johnson, D. J., S. Pace, and B. Gabbard. 1998. *Space: Emerging Options for National Power*. Santa Monica: RAND Corporation.

Lewis, James A. 2013. *Reconsidering Deterrence in Cyberspace*. Washington, DC: Center for Strategic and International Studies,

Lopez, Todd C. 2021. "'Warfighter Council' Guides Capability Development for Space Development Agency." *DOD News*.

Lupton, David E. 1988. *Space Warfare*. Montgomery, AL: Air University Press.

Lutes, C. D. 2008. "Spacepower in the 21st Century." *Joint Force Quarterly* 49: 66–72.

Machi, Vivienne. 2021. "Next-gen Tech Investments, Platform Upgrades Lead France's 2022 Defense Budget." *DefenseNews*. https://www.defensenews.com/global/europe/2021/09/22/next-gen-tech-investments-platform-upgrades-lead-frances-2022-defense-budget/

#:~:text=Furthermore%2C%20the%20French%20military%20plans%20to%20spend%20
€646,weapon%20aboard%20a%20warship%20at%20sea%20next%20year.

Ministry of Defence. 2008; 2009. *Future Air and Space Operating Concept*. 2008 and 2009 eds.

Ministry of Defence. 2010. "The UK Military Space Primer." https://www.gov.uk/government/ publications/the-uk-military-space-primer.

Ministry of Defence. 2020. "Joint Concept Note 1/20: Multi-Domain Integration, DCDC." https://assets.publishing.service.gov.uk/government/uploads/system/uploads/attachme nt_data/file/950789/20201112-JCN_1_20_MDI.PDF.

Ministry of Defence. 2022a. *Defence Space Strategy, Operationalising the Space Domain*. https:// assets.publishing.service.gov.uk/government/uploads/system/uploads/attachment_data/ file/1051456/20220120-UK_Defence_Space_Strategy_Feb_22.pdf.

Ministry of Defence. 2022b. "Defence Command Paper, Defence in a Competitive Age." https://assets.publishing.service.gov.uk/government/uploads/system/uploads/attachme nt_data/file/974661/CP411_-Defence_Command_Plan.pdf.

Ministry of Defence. 2022c. "Joint Doctrine Publication 0-40. UK Space Power." https://assets. publishing.service.gov.uk/government/uploads/system/uploads/attachment_data/file/1101 450/20220831-JDP_0_40_UK_Space_Power_web.pdf.

Mitchell, Keith. 2019. "Skynet: The Real Communication Satellite System." *The National Archives*. October 24, 2019.

Mureşan, Liviu, and Alexandru Georgescu. 2015. "The Road to Resilience in 2050." *The RUSI Journal* 160: 6.

Oberg, James E., 1999. *Space Power Theory*. Colorado Springs, CO: US Air Force Academy.

Presley, Mark, Stuart Eves, and Dorn. 2020. "Future SST Markets Research: Final Report." https://assets.publishing.service.gov.uk/government/uploads/system/uploads/attachme nt_data/file/917909/MAP_Analytica_-_UKSA_Future_Markets_Research_-_Final_Rep ort_Pub.pdf.

Sheldon, John B. 2021. *Britain and the Geopolitics of Space Technology: Safeguarding Long-Term Space Interests in an Era of Great Power Competition*. Policy Exchange, London.

Suess, J. 2021. "The First UK National Space Strategy." *RUSI*.

"UK Orders First Defence Satellite for Minerva Programme." 2022. *Airforce Technology*. April 5, 2022. https://www.airforce-technology.com/news/uk-satellite-order-minerva/.

"UK Space Agency Launched in London." 2010. *Telegraph*. March 23, 2010. https://web.archive. org/web/20100326140837/http://www.telegraph.co.uk/science/space/7505184/UK-Space-Agency-launched-in-London.html.

CHAPTER 22

THE EUROPEAN UNION'S DEEPENING ENGAGEMENT IN SPACE SECURITY

Hedging through Strategic Autonomy

MATHIEU BATAILLE AND TOMAS HROZENSKY

INTRODUCTION

THE European Union (EU) approved the creation of its first formal space program in a milestone legislation, the EU Space Programme Regulation adopted in 2021 (European Union 2021a). With this document, the EU committed its highest budget on space activities ever and expanded its already noticeable presence in the space domain with new activities that indicate a clear reinforcement of space security themes.

This follows an evolution that has transformed the place of space in EU policy-making, moving from a minor policy domain with some potential socio-economic benefits to a much larger sector of strategic importance. In this regard, this chapter will analyze the increasing recognition of the security and strategic dimensions of space for the EU. These dimensions focus on two aspects: (1) supporting European security and defense actors on Earth through indigenous space infrastructure, and (2) protecting European space assets in orbit.

These concerns can be seen in the components of the Space Programme (Galileo, Copernicus, SSA, GOVSATCOM), which all have a security dimension, as well as in the myriad of other activities in space surveillance and tracking (the EU SST Partnership), international transparency and confidence-building measures (e.g., the 3SOS Initiative), space traffic management (various parallel research projects), or civil-military synergies (the Action plan on synergies between civil, defence and space industries published in 2021).

Moreover, the intentional connection between space and security topics has also increased in EU narrative. Thus, the EU Space Programme Regulation notes that: "Space technology, data and services have become indispensable in the daily lives of Europeans and play an essential role in preserving many strategic interests . . . To achieve the objectives of freedom of action, independence and security, it is essential that the Union benefits from an autonomous access to space and is able to use it safely" (European Union 2021a, 1). Similarly, political statements of high-level political representatives of the EU, both at the level of European Commission (COM) and at the level of Member States in the Council of the EU, confirm this perception, arguing that "space has a direct impact on our geopolitical goal of strategic autonomy" (Michel 2021) or that "space is an enabler of security and defence" and "investing in space is about investing in technological sovereignty" (Breton 2020). Finally, space is now part of the broader strategic posture of the EU, as can be demonstrated by the integration of this domain into EU's policies and strategies on foreign policy (2016 Global Strategy for the EU's Foreign and Security Policy) and security (2020 EU Security Union Strategy). This trend is now growing further as the development of space capabilities is being fostered through actual EU funding instruments and cooperation frameworks for security and defense (European Defence Fund (EDF), Permanent Structured Cooperation (PESCO)).

In this chapter, we address how and why the EU, particularly through COM initiatives, is moving down this pathway. Our argument is that the EU is driven internally by the concept of "strategic autonomy" in specific response to the evolving international context, and that the decision to pursue this autonomy reflects hedging behavior. By hedging, we mean an "insurance policy" or a "risk management strategy" (Haacke 2019, 381) that aims at protecting the interests of a political entity in a context of uncertainty, where the circumstances in which the actor is moving can change over time.

This chapter is divided as follows. First, we set out a brief overview of the relevant space actors and provide some details on general EU efforts toward strategic autonomy. Second, we turn to the hedging literature. We argue that hedging is the rationale behind EU strategic autonomy efforts, in which space security activities are a growing element. Third, we show how this quest for strategic autonomy takes shape in practice, through a review of the capabilities and policy efforts pursued by the EU. Fourth, the conclusion will provide a summary of the argument as well as implications for international relations (IR) theories, space policy, and peaceful prospects in outer space.

EU IN SPACE: MULTIPLE INSTITUTIONAL ACTORS AND A PERVASIVE SECURITY DIMENSION

The Management of Space Activities in the EU: A Complex Landscape

The EU is a rather unique political actor, different from states and with specific characteristics. In the space sector, it acts in parallel with the space engagement of its

Member States and two other major Europe-based international organizations—the European Space Agency (ESA) and the European Organisation for the Exploitation of Meteorological Satellites (EUMETSAT). ESA and EUMETSAT memberships partly overlap but do not fully match EU membership. While the Commission might generally be seen as the entity representing EU (space) interests, it is not the only decision-maker in the EU institutional setting and can be constrained, in particular, by the will of Member States. The different actors and their roles in EU space-related legislative, policy-making, and implementation processes are summarized below:

- **European Commission (COM):** responsible for the overall implementation of the EU Space Programme, primarily through its Directorate-General on Defence Industry and Space (DG DEFIS), formally set up in 2019. The Commission also proposes new legislation appropriating financial resources on space and pursues additional initiatives outside the Space Programme envelope.
- **Council of the European Union (Council):** body representing the 27 EU Member States, one of the two co-legislators (co-approving the general framework and budget for EU space engagement). It meets in different formats at the level of ministers of EU Member States.
- **European Parliament (EP):** the second legislative body in the EU (co-approving the general framework and budget for EU space engagement) which represents EU citizens through directly elected representatives.
- **European External Action Service (EEAS):** the EU's diplomatic arm, presenting and furthering its position on the international stage. Within the EEAS, the Unit SecDefPol.5 is the main office in charge of space affairs.
- Two primary operational agencies: the **European Union Agency for the Space Programme (EUSPA)** managing the exploitation, commercialization, and user uptake of data provided in particular by Galileo and Copernicus, and serving as the front desk of the EU SST Partnership and the **European Union Satellite Centre (SatCen)** providing satellite imagery and analysis for the EU and its Member States.

A concrete example will help explain the importance of these different actors and of interinstitutional negotiations. While the initial proposal of COM for the 2021–2027 EU Space Programme was of €14.2 billion in June 2018, the final budget, which was approved in April 2021, was ultimately reduced to €13.2 billion, primarily as a result of Member States' decisions.

While the European Commission has been the driving force in spearheading many EU space activities, the interest and active involvement of EU Member States (e.g., through legislative approval or actual technical implementation, such as in the EU SST) has been instrumental in rolling these initiatives out and sustaining them. This growing activism can be explained in part by the growing importance of the notion of strategic autonomy, which today plays a central role in defining EU presence in space.

STRATEGIC AUTONOMY: A UBIQUITOUS BUT IMPRECISE CONCEPT

What is Strategic Autonomy?

While originally designed to explain the efforts of Europeans in developing a joint security and defense policy, the "strategic autonomy" concept is being increasingly leveraged by EU officials to support their initiatives in a broad range of domains, including space. It is worth noting that the notion has not been developed by IR scholars, but by policymakers and think tanks. Therefore, it has been elaborated with a "practical" objective in mind rather than an "analytical" one. Moreover, this concept is currently almost exclusively used in the context of the EU and has gained limited international recognition in the academic literature. These specificities explain why its definition remains unclear. To better grasp it, several elements must be considered.

First, "strategic autonomy" is not synonymous with "autarky" in which Europe would rely exclusively on its own resources. By enhancing strategic autonomy, the EU and its Member States aim at reducing (but not forgoing) their dependence on third states and at being free to decide when they want to cooperate with partners outside of the EU. Overall, efforts to ensure European strategic autonomy can be understood as the search for "freedom from external control" (Howorth 2019, 2).

Moreover, strategic autonomy is a multidimensional concept. To be fully autonomous, Europe needs to enhance its capacities in several domains. Progress in three dimensions is usually deemed necessary to reach strategic autonomy: the *political* dimension, i.e., "the capacity to take security policy decisions and act upon them"; the *operational* dimension, i.e., "the capacity, based on the necessary institutional framework and the required capabilities, to independently plan for and conduct civilian and/or military operations"; and the *industrial* dimension, i.e., "the capacity to develop and build the capabilities required to attain operational autonomy" (Kempin and Kunz 2017, 10). A fourth dimension is sometimes added, the *institutional* one, i.e., "the availability of the necessary governance structures, in order to prepare for and administer the decisions that are taken at the political level" (Zandee et al. 2020, 9).

Finally, the nature of strategic autonomy is debated: while some authors consider autonomy as an absolute concept (an actor either *is* or *is not* autonomous) (Howorth 2019), others conceptualize it as akin to a spectrum (actors have a degree of autonomy, they are *more* or *less* autonomous) (Fiott 2018).

There is thus some agreement on the meaning and components of strategic autonomy but no common definition is shared by all stakeholders and interpretations of the concept vary (e.g., from one Member State to the other), which is problematic given the increasing pervasiveness of the term in European debate. In the case of the space domain, strategic autonomy is usually mentioned as a driver of specific activities (e.g., initiatives on launchers, development of a European satcom constellation, etc.). A more comprehensive definition was recently proposed, taking into account the various stages of space operations: "A strategically autonomous actor is one that can design, develop, launch and operate space systems without hindrance" (Fiott 2020, 19).

Why Does Europe Want Strategic Autonomy?

Beyond the definitional work, an important consideration is that the concept of "strategic autonomy" has mainly been constructed in relation to the United States. The latter is the primary ally of European states and the main purveyor of Europe's defense, especially through NATO. Europe remains heavily dependent on US capabilities and will to act in case of conflict. For instance, in Libya in 2011, even though aerial strikes were conducted by European armies, most of the fuel and ISR capabilities were provided by the United States (Quintana, quoted in Fiott 2021). The initial motivation to enhance the strategic autonomy of Europe was therefore to decrease dependence on the United States in the security and defense fields, so that Europe can act whenever its interests are at stake. This raises another understanding of strategic autonomy, which sees as a primary objective the reinforcement of the transatlantic relationship through greater burden-sharing between allies across the Atlantic. With time, demands for enhanced strategic autonomy have moved beyond sheer defense toward other essential domains for EU interests, including space. The fact that the desire for more strategic autonomy is primarily a tool in the EU-US relationship has a few consequences.

On the one hand, the promotion of European strategic autonomy does not stem from a threat-based narrative that would call for such autonomy to be developed as a necessity to withstand a vital security threat. The EU's objective is not to prepare for a war with the United States (or any other country) but rather to develop its own capabilities to better serve its own interests as well as to fare better in the global economic and scientific competition. For instance, the decision not to develop counterspace capabilities can, among other motivations, be understood as willingness from the EU to show that it does not have "adversaries" in space. This is particularly the case when calls for greater strategic autonomy are made for domains such as space, quantum, or access to critical raw materials.

On the other hand, this behavior is not pursued to benefit from great power competition. Indeed, the EU is not playing one great power (China) against the other (the United States) to reap additional benefits. It rather aims at enhancing its autonomy through the development of selected capabilities (such as space ones) to be able to keep its freedom and reduce the leverage that the United States (or other emerging actors) could use on it in the current tense international context.

Therefore, the decision of the EU to strengthen its strategic autonomy in the space domain cannot be explained by traditional balance-of-power theory, as it follows neither a "balancing" nor a "bandwagoning" approach. Consistent with its mandate, COM action can be interpreted as an attempt to protect the "European interest" in space, in all its dimensions (in particular economic and security-related), and to keep all options open.

In this regard, the EU's quest for strategic autonomy in space should be considered as an example of strategic hedging behavior, that is, a kind of "insurance policy" (Tessman and Wolfe 2011, 216) that would protect the EU should drastic changes in the conditions shaping the international environment occur.

Deciphering the Rationale Behind the EU's Drive for Strategic Autonomy

We now turn to deciphering the rationale for the increasing involvement of the EU in space security efforts. This rationale is the consequence of both internal and external factors. This chapter will analyze the latter: it will consider that the path taken by EU space activities is a specific response to the evolving international context. In that sense, it will be argued that EU's quest for strategic autonomy in space and its consequences in terms of capability development result from a strategic hedging behavior.

As mentioned above, a strategic hedging behavior is an "insurance policy" or, in other words, a "risk management strategy" (Haacke 2019, 381) that aims at protecting the interests of a political entity in a context of uncertainty, where circumstances can change over time. To reach this objective, the hedging behavior implies both competitive and integrating mechanisms (Art 2004) as well as ambiguity on a state's positioning toward major powers (Koga 2018; Haacke 2019). Similarly, the EU quest for strategic autonomy in space does not have a confrontational stance but mixes competitive and cooperative elements. For instance, Galileo's signals, as well as images from Copernicus' Sentinel satellites, are available for free to all actors around the world (cooperative element). However, the use of some of their services, in particular those related to security matters (e.g., Galileo's Public Regulated Service (PRS); Copernicus Security Service) are mostly dedicated to European authorities (competitive element), but are also allowed to third parties under specific agreements (integrative element).

The concept of "hedging" has been developed in the past decades as a third way between the "balancing" and "bandwagoning" behaviors traditionally identified by balance-of-power theory. However, the lack of clarity in the definition of the concept has led to several conceptions of what hedging means. This chapter will mostly use the framework proposed by Brock Tessman in two articles (Tessman and Wolfe 2011; Tessman 2012) to demonstrate why the search for EU strategic autonomy in space can qualify as hedging behavior.

When is Strategic Hedging Behavior Employed?

There is consensus among scholars that hedging behavior is more prevalent in situations of strategic uncertainty, in particular in a context of power transition (Jackson 2014; Koga 2018; Haacke 2019). More precisely, according to Tessman, hedging is a "core strategy" carried out by second-tier actors in a unipolar deconcentrating system, i.e., "countries (with the exception of the system leader) that enjoy major power or regional power status" (Tessman 2012, 194). The current international system can be considered as such, due to the evolving balance of power between the United States and China; and EU development of space capabilities for security purposes would be one of the means deployed by European actors to cope with the new global context.

Furthermore, if we focus exclusively on the space domain, the characterization of this domain as a "unipolar deconcentrating system" also applies. Indeed, the United States is far ahead of other space actors, be it in terms of resources spent, military capabilities, or diversity of their applications. Moreover, the country masters the most advanced technologies in the field. As such, the United States is a hegemon in space, and the gap is such that other political entities (Russia, China, and Europe) must be considered second-tier actors. The system is thus unipolar. However, despite the importance of this gap, the rapidly growing space activity of the rest of the world, in particular China and, to a lesser extent, Europe and other new entrants, reduces the relative power of the United States. For instance, in the past few years, both China and Europe have reached operational capability for their GNSS constellations, therefore reducing their dependence on GPS. Regarding Earth observation, the Copernicus program is the biggest provider of data in the world, and China has launched multiple and technology-diversified systems over the past years. Finally, China is the country that has conducted the most launches each year between 2018 and 2021. Therefore, although the global space sector remains unipolar, it is currently undergoing a process of deconcentration. This is a favorable context for the adoption of strategic hedging behavior by other actors in the system.

What Constitutes Strategic Hedging Behavior?

Moving from the context generating a hedging strategy to the content of such a behavior, Tessman distinguishes two different types of behaviors: Type A hedging consists of improving "the long-term ability of the hedging state to compete successfully during a potential militarized dispute with the system leader . . . while consciously avoiding any sort of provocation that might spark a military confrontation in the short term" (Tessman 2012, 204); Type B hedging consists of the implementation of "actions that address the potential loss of public goods or subsidies currently provided by the system leader" (Tessman 2012, 205). The rationale behind the EU's increasing involvement in space can be interpreted as the second type of hedging identified by Tessman, which is conducted through several actions: diversifying providers, finding ways to decrease reliance on the goods or subsidies themselves, or developing independent provision capabilities.

The last one in particular is at the core of the efforts initiated by COM. Indeed, EU authorities and Member States have been reliant on several space technologies to conduct their security activities, both on Earth and in space. For instance, satellite navigation signals are crucial to conduct (military) operations, while space situational awareness (SSA) data are essential to protect European satellites orbiting Earth. For many years, these services have been provided as a public good by the United States, that is, for free and on a non-discriminatory basis (at least for European partners). However, this reliance on an external actor, which could halt provision of the service at any time if it serves its interest, has been considered as too risky by European stakeholders, even more in the context of a cooler transatlantic relationship. On the other hand, they did not accept the option of no longer relying on the provided goods per se (i.e., navigation signals and SSA data). Therefore, to continue benefitting from them, the EU has decided to decrease its reliance on *US-provided* public goods by developing its own capabilities in an autonomous manner through Galileo (and its PRS signal) and the EU SST initiative. This motivation was already clearly expressed by the Commission in 2002 (quoted in Giegerich 2007, 496):

> It is crucial for Europe and the world as a whole to have a choice and not remain dependent on the current monopoly of the American GPS system . . . the EU wishes to develop, with Galileo, a system over which it has control and which meets the need for accuracy, reliability and security . . . There is no question of coming into conflict with the United States which is and will remain our ally, but simply a question of putting an end to a situation of dependence. If the EU finds it necessary to undertake a security mission that the US does not consider to be in its interest, it [the EU] will be impotent unless it has satellite navigation technology that is now indispensable.

A second criterion helps to identify strategic hedging. As explained above, the decision to hedge is a third way between "balancing" and "bandwagoning". Therefore, to be labeled as hedging behavior, an activity cannot be attributed to a balancing behavior in the sense of the balance-of-power theory, that is, either internal balancing (strengthen one's own defense capabilities) or external balancing (creation of alliances ostensibly directed at the hegemon) (Tessman and Wolfe 2011). This qualification does not correspond to European space efforts. Indeed, although European initiatives in defense could be characterized as internal balancing because they lead to a military build-up, the situation is different in the space context.

One major explanation is that the development of dual-use capabilities, which have both civil and military applications, is at the core of EU initiatives in space. For instance, Galileo's PRS will be used for military purposes, but will also benefit other authorized entities such as fire brigades or health services. Moreover, contrary to other GNSS programs in the world, Galileo is fully managed by civil organizations. The same can be said for Copernicus' Sentinel satellites and the Security Service provided by the program, for which armed forces represent only a (limited) share of the users, others being civil agencies. Therefore, European initiatives in space do not intend to develop capabilities that are purely military. They rather aim at enhancing the means of both the EU and its Member States, so that they can efficiently tackle both external *and* internal challenges, for defense or non-military security purposes.

Another characteristic of "hedging" in IR is that it is a *strategic* behavior. To reach this status, the issue area at stake has to be recognized as strategic by decision-makers at the highest level of the political entity conducting the hedging strategy, and the coordination of the behavior must be subject to centralized oversight, for instance through the creation of a dedicated entity (Tessman 2012). In other words, hedging is "a purposive strategy of risk management by the leadership" (Haacke 2019, 395). In this context, it has already been mentioned that the strategic dimension of space has gained prominence in EU strategic publications over the years, and that speeches by high-level EU officials in the past years have consistently reiterated the strategic importance of space for the security and autonomy of Europe (Breton 2020; 2021), even considering it a "frontline" of EU strategic autonomy (Borrell 2021). In 2019, the creation, for the first time, of a Directorate-General for Defence Industry and Space within the European Commission has also underlined the importance of these domains for EU authorities. This institutionalization of the management of space issues is also in line with Tessman's requirement for an organization coordinating and overseeing the "implementation" of the strategic hedging behavior.

Finally, strategic hedging behavior must "involve observable domestic or international cost(s) to the hedging state, including but not . . . limited to acceptance of significant economic inefficiencies or diplomatic backlash" (Tessman and Wolfe 2011, 220). EU officials are willing to suffer such costs to see their projects move forward. First, the Space Programme represents a financial cost for the EU budget (€13.2 billion for 2021–2027). In addition, the history of Galileo demonstrates the determination of EU officials to pursue their objectives in space despite the negative impact that they may have in the short term. Indeed, the willingness of the EU to develop its own GNSS created economic and security-related concerns in the United States and a strong backlash from the US administration at the beginning of the 2000s.

This led the two sides to lengthy and complicated negotiations over technical and political components of the program, which finally concluded with an agreement in 2004 (Giegerich 2007). One of the results of this agreement was greater interoperability between GPS and Galileo, showing that, even though hedging displays a competitive aspect (willingness of the EU to pursue Galileo even if it displeases US partners), it also encompasses integrative mechanisms (close cooperation being necessary for interoperability). Moreover, the beginnings of Galileo displayed a number of financial inefficiencies, in part due to the failure of the framework originally decided on (a public-private agreement) and the transformation of the project into a fully institutional program in 2007. Overall, between 1994 and 2020, an estimated €13 billion were spent on Galileo (Villafranca-Izquierdo 2021). However, despite the rise in costs and the governance issues as well as diplomatic frictions, the Commission and EU Member States decided to continue moving forward with their project of a European GNSS, due to the perception of this project as essential for European actors.

To sum up, all EU space initiatives encompass a prominent security dimension and take place in a unipolar deconcentrating system, which is the type of system most conducive to hedging strategies by second-tier actors. Moreover, they pass the four filters identified by Tessman to qualify the behavior of a political entity as a "strategic hedging" behavior. This hedging strategy has concrete effects in terms of EU space capabilities and policy efforts, which will be discussed in the next section.

CHARACTERISTICS OF EU ENGAGEMENT IN SPACE SECURITY

The unique fundamental characteristics of the EU as well as its desire to ensure its strategic autonomy for hedging purposes profoundly shape EU action in space security matters. In a historical perspective, it can be observed that the EU has gradually increased its involvement in security and defense-related aspects of space activities, with an acceleration in recent years, and that this dimension has taken a more prominent role. On the other hand, in some other specific themes related to space security, the EU has not yet acted.

Evolution of the Content of EU Space Activities

Early exploratory efforts at EU space engagement emerged in the late 1970s and early 1980s, when the EP adopted its first space-related resolutions, underscoring the benefits Europe could derive from space activities (telecommunications, Earth observation, and scientific research), industrial opportunities and positive effects on European autonomy (Reillon 2017). In the late 1980s and 1990s, COM issued several communications, which confirmed a focus on space applications, including also satellite navigation. Beyond the EP and COM, the Council also began addressing the importance of EU engagement in space.

Most notably, developments in the 1990s gave birth to two flagship programs on satellite navigation (Galileo and EGNOS) and Earth observation (Copernicus). The rationale for both programs focused largely on the socio-economic benefits enabled by them. Although the security and strategic dimensions have been recognized and subsequently pursued soon from the onset, for instance with the development of Galileo's PRS for authorized users or the addition of the word "Security" to the former name of Copernicus—Global Monitoring for Environment and Security, they were not an overarching driver. However, some experts (Darnis, Pasco, and Wohrer 2020) argue that negotiations on these programs (in particular for Galileo) and broader political developments in the 1990s spurred the trend of securitization of space in Europe. As an example, during the conflicts in the former Yugoslavia in the 1990s, US authorities denied European actors access to US satellite capabilities' data on conflict regions (Klimburg-Witjes 2021).

In the 2000s, the formalization of EU and ESA relations included policy efforts attempting to define a high-level European space policy. Beyond socio-economic aspects, the new European Space Policy of 2007 recognized space as a strategic asset for European independence and security and called for increased synergies between civil and defense space programs (Commission of the European Communities 2007). A year later, the Space Council, a body gathering ministers from both EU and ESA Member States, adopted a resolution noting that "space infrastructure security" had become a growing concern.

The 2010s witnessed an acceleration of these trends. In the policies on space adopted at the EU level during this decade (European Commission 2011; European Commission 2016), European institutions continued the approach focusing on space applications and their socio-economic benefits; however, security themes gradually developed into far more substantial components of EU space policy than before (and with an expanded spectrum of applications, such as space surveillance or secure communications). The security dimension could also be found in repeated calls for maintaining European autonomy in accessing and using space.

This can be documented by the 2016 Joint EU-ESA "Shared Vision and Goals for the Future of Europe in Space," one of the latest strategic documents on space. This identified the need for a European capacity to protect space infrastructure as a foundation of the objective: "To ensure European autonomy in accessing and using space in a safe and secure environment". One additional element of autonomy, specifically technological non-dependence, has become increasingly present in EU space policy-making, to respond to the major reliance on non-European lines of supply for important space technologies.

In parallel with deepening the security components of its space policy, the EU also developed a comprehensive defense and security policy framework in the 2010s. In this context, several initiatives were introduced, such as the European Defence Fund and the Permanent Structured Cooperation. Over the years, space has become an integral part of these initiatives, and synergies are being encouraged (for instance with the release by the Commission of an Action plan on synergies between civil, defense, and space industries in February 2021). Several projects aimed at enhancing EU space defense capabilities are now ongoing, with a rather limited, but increasing, budget (Bataille and Messina 2020). They are the few exceptions to the otherwise duality-oriented position of the EU when it comes to the development of space capabilities.

Current Status

In this section, we provide an overview of what the EU does and does not do in space security, expanding on the main points set out in Table 22.1.

What the EU "Does" in Space Security

The two long-term EU flagship programs, Galileo/EGNOS and Copernicus, offer the EU a high level of autonomy, by providing different types of essential capabilities, such as observing Earth, protecting infrastructure, sustaining digital networks, or ensuring the security of trade routes (Fiott 2020). To this end, these programs are specifically designed to include services for authorized national or EU users tasked with security or defense-related missions:

- Within Galileo, the PRS shall provide more precise and secure navigation signals for authorized governmental users (e.g., border control, civil protection authorities, emergency responders, etc.). As of September 2023, the PRS has not yet reached full operational capability across the EU.
- Within Copernicus, the Security Service provides information in response to Europe's security challenges, improving border and maritime surveillance and support for EU external action.

While the Galileo program remains under civil control (as does Copernicus), recent initiatives indicate a growing interest from military actors of EU Member States in a greater uptake of Galileo for military missions. Moreover, the security and defense potential of Galileo in Europe is well recognized both at EU and national levels (Fiott 2020). While some Member States benefit from autonomous national capabilities, including military, in Earth observation and satellite communications, this is not the case for satellite navigation. Therefore, the use of Galileo will reinforce the strategic autonomy and, thus, the hedging potential of the EU and its Member States.

The recent addition of GOVSATCOM (originally conceived in 2013) to the EU Space Programme continues the trend of supporting security-related missions with EU space capabilities. This initiative aims to ensure the availability of reliable, secure, and cost-effective governmental satellite communications services for EU and national public authorities managing critical missions and infrastructure (European

---

Table 22.1. What the EU Does and Does Not Do in Space Security

What the EU "does" in space security	What the EU "does not do" in space security
• Ownership of strategic space assets providing essential capabilities and services for security and defense-related purposes and fostering European strategic autonomy • Pursuit of indigenous capabilities to protect European space infrastructures • Promotion of space sustainability in international space fora	• Implementation of a *dedicated* military space program • Development of indigenous counterspace capabilities • Limited autonomy across the space technology supply chain

Union 2021a). As of 2023, a final system architecture for GOVSATCOM has not yet been decided. This decision may be impacted by the emerging "Secure Connectivity Initiative" that is currently in conceptual stages. This project, spearheaded by the COM, became an official EU space program in March 2023 following the adoption of the Regulation establishing the Union Secure Connectivity Programme (IRIS^2/IRSS) (European Union 2023).

With regard to EU space capabilities, the case of SatCen is also relevant. SatCen has long been the only agency of the EU capable of creating an indigenous intelligence capability (Robinson and Romancov 2014). However, beyond Copernicus satellites, SatCen needs to rely considerably on commercial providers, including for sensitive needs, such as very-high-resolution optical or radar imagery.

The substantial public investments into EU space assets and a growing reliance of Europe on space services create high stakes for the EU to protect its space assets against possible risks (Moranta et al. 2018). Responding to this need, in 2014, COM and five EU Member States stood up an EU space surveillance and tracking capability in the form of the EU SST Support Framework (which became the EU SST Partnership in 2022 and involves 15 participating states as of September 2023).

Based on an intergovernmental model of pooling the national capabilities of participating countries (see Pasco, this volume), the EU SST has developed operational services for satellite operators to assist them in protecting their space assets. The EU SST employs a dual-use model, in which participating countries contribute with sensors mostly owned and operated by their militaries.

In the EU Space Programme (2021 onward), the EU SST is envisioned as evolving into a more ambitious initiative (with increased funding for research and development activities, and possible new services). Nevertheless, it is expected that ownership and operation of SST assets (e.g., optical telescopes, radars, laser ranging stations) will remain national in the future, limiting the perspectives for an actual EU-owned/operated SST infrastructure.

It is important to note that EU SST capabilities currently do not allow for full European autonomy in space situational awareness in relevant orbital regimes (low and geosynchronous) and European actors need to rely on US data. The anticipated long-term evolution foresees major enhancement of European capabilities (Faucher, Peldszus, and Gravier 2019) with the objective to increase the level of autonomy (in particular vis-à-vis US data). However, achieving full autonomy across all orbits will remain a challenging task if investment does not increase substantially.

Beyond the pursuit of space capabilities, the EU also engages in multilateral space platforms, in particular on the topics of space sustainability and security. Overall, the EU approach to international space matters is best encapsulated by the following EU statement from the 2021 session of the Scientific and Technical Subcommittee of UNCOPUOS (European Union 2021b, 1):

> The EU and its Member States strongly promote the preservation of a safe, secure and sustainable space environment . . . , the peaceful use of outer space on an equitable

and mutually acceptable basis . . . and the need to ensure responsible behaviour in outer space in the framework of the UN.

The first major EU initiative was the International Code of Conduct for Outer Space Activities (ICoC), a non-binding code of behavior in space (Johnson 2014), which was ultimately unsuccessful. In the following years, the EU continued to advocate for voluntary international guidelines. While the status of an international organization limits the scope of EU involvement in other platforms such as UNCOPUOS or the Conference on Disarmament, the EU regularly addresses these fora, with statements calling for responsible behavior in space (European Union 2018). To promote the need for sustainable space operations, the EEAS launched the Safety, Security, and Sustainability of Outer Space (3SOS) public diplomacy initiative in 2019.

What the EU "Does Not Do" in Space Security

As already noted, EU activities in space security are also marked by significant particularities, which are observable when comparing the EU to other global space powers. The first of these differences is the absence of a space program dedicated to military activities, although an EU Space Strategy for Security and Defence was released in March 2023 (European Commission and High Representative of the Union for Foreign Affairs and Security Policy 2023). In addition, contrary to other space powers, EU engagement in space remains "civil" in terms of overall ownership and oversight of programs. Although the dual-use aspect is strongly embedded in EU space engagement, and EU space initiatives also support defense actors, military space operations per se are in the remit of EU Member States. Similarly, some space technologies critical for the conduct of military operations on Earth (very-high-resolution Earth observation data, signal intelligence, early warning or global secured satcom networks) are currently missing at the EU level. Some EU Member States have developed these capabilities nationally, but the EU does not automatically have an unrestricted access to them.

While different forms of counterspace capabilities or technologies and systems suspected as such have been pursued and developed by four other space powers (the United States, Russia, China, and India), open-source resources suggest no activity on this issue at the EU level. In addition, the available data suggest counterspace capabilities are not pursued by EU Member States in their national programs either. This situation reinforces the argument according to which EU space security initiatives are not part of a threat-based narrative.

Given that peaceful uses of outer space, international collaboration, and responsible behavior in space are foundational principles of both the EU and its members, it can be anticipated that denying the use of space capabilities by potential "adversaries" will attract only marginal interest. Even though the EU does not pursue the major deterrence potential associated with counterspace capabilities, its increased efforts in SST in recent years could be perceived as a contributing factor to deterrence, by generating enhanced situational awareness in orbit.

The last of the identified limitations, the lack of supply chain autonomy, has a more profound impact, as it shines a spotlight on EU freedom of action; and it could be argued this applies to Europe at large and not just the EU. Despite a wide array of capabilities, Europe fails to reach the same level of autonomy as its international partners or competitors and still needs to externally source certain components (mostly electronic), materials, and technologies not available within Europe (Aliberti, Hrozensky, and Bataille 2020).

This situation stands in contrast with the increasing EU ambitions in international politics and in the space sector. From a "harder" security standpoint, limited autonomous capabilities to produce space technologies could be a potential weakness, reducing EU freedom of action in a situation where access to foreign sources of supply would be denied. The recognition of the issue of technological dependence has led to the launch of multiple initiatives (e.g., joint EU-EDA-ESA initiative on "Critical Space Technologies for European Non-dependence") and the level of dependence has been reduced. This was not least motivated by the growing political interest in developing autonomous space capabilities, which are increasingly recognized as having a profound impact on overall European strategic autonomy.

This summary of EU engagement in space security shows that EU actions in the space domain can be interpreted through the theory of strategic hedging behavior. The synthesis of the sections above is set out in Table 22.2, giving us concrete connections between the theoretical framework and EU activities related to space security.

CONCLUSION

The EU, particularly through the various initiatives of COM, is expanding its outreach in space. An important element is that most, if not all, of the EU space initiatives have a security dimension, either on Earth or in space. This dimension has been present from the onset of EU endeavors (e.g., it was already one of the rationales behind the flagship programs Galileo and Copernicus), but its significance has grown over time, with the diversification of EU space projects (e.g., GOVSATCOM and EU SST), and the increasing integration of space in defense initiatives such as EDF and PESCO.

These efforts are related to the will of the EU to enhance its overall strategic autonomy, including both *in* and *through* space, as emphasized in EU discourse in the past five years. This quest for EU strategic autonomy in space can be interpreted as hedging behavior aimed at managing the risks induced by the evolution of the international context, including of the global space domain. In that context, the development of its own capabilities by the EU is not about preparing for confrontation with a designated adversary but rather reducing its reliance on external partners.

The adoption of hedging behavior by an organization that does not possess all the prerogatives of a state and the EU's turn toward space security raise questions and open perspectives for further research.

Table 22.2. Summary of EU Engagement in Space Security

Hedging criterion (according to Tessman)	Translation into EU space initiatives
Does behavior improve the ability of the actor to cope without public goods or subsidies that are currently being provided to it by the system leader (Type B hedging)?	EU programs reduce reliance on data and services provided by the US government (e.g., GPS signals, SSA data) through the development of capabilities owned and operated by European actors (e.g., Galileo PRS, Copernicus Security Service, EU SST services).
Does behavior avoid direct confrontation of the system leader via external or internal balancing?	EU space efforts focus on the development of dual-use capabilities that can indeed be useful for military, but also (and primarily) for civil purposes. Moreover, even if space is integrated in EU defence initiatives, the decision not to develop (yet) a military space program or counterspace capabilities limits the extent of European military build-up.
Is behavior strategic in the sense that it is developed, funded, and coordinated at the highest levels of government? Does it involve an issue area that has been explicitly recognized as of major national security interest by the highest levels of government in the relevant state?	Space is funded through a dedicated line of the EU budget, agreed by COM, Member States, and the European Parliament. Space has been labeled as a strategic area in EU officials' speeches and EU publications, and the creation of DG DEFIS has allowed coordination and centralization of the space initiatives that embody the hedging behavior.
Does behavior involve observable domestic and/ or international cost(s) to the hedging state, including but not limited to acceptance of significant economic inefficiencies or diplomatic backlash?	The EU Space Programme represents a considerable financial burden which, though reduced following the COVID-19 crisis, has been maintained at its highest level ever. Moreover, the EU accepted suffering diplomatic costs with its US ally, as well as financial inefficiencies, at the beginning of its flagship program Galileo.

First, "strategic hedging is designed to primarily reflect the national interest, as defined by the highest levels of governing authority" (Tessman 2012, 209). In the context of the EU, hedging behavior would thus reflect a "European interest". Yet, even though the Commission is supposed to represent this "European interest" (which may explain its proactive role and its adoption of a hedging strategy), we can question whether the latter really exists or is acknowledged by the various stakeholders involved in EU processes (in particular by Member States). Moreover, if the Commission is undoubtedly a key player, the variety of actors and the weight of Member States in the EU institutional framework makes the identification of the "highest levels of governing authority" a difficult task.

Second, this chapter focused on the external factors affecting EU initiatives in space. Therefore, the hedging strategy adopted by the EU in and through space is seen as a response to the evolution of the international context that would threaten the conditions under which space is used for security and defense purposes. However, on top of this rationale, the complexity of the EU setup makes it very likely that some internal elements provide a complementary explanation to the recent activism of COM. All EU stakeholders have their own interests, therefore turf battles and principal/agent problems are likely to take place (in particular between COM and Member States with advanced space programs, such as France, Germany, or Italy). In that context, the growing emphasis on the strategic and security aspects of space could be seen as a securitization strategy of COM to convince Member States to grant it more responsibilities and funding in space matters.

Finally, the increasing focus of the EU on space security matters could be troubling from the perspective of ensuring the use of space for peaceful purposes. However, the EU is at the forefront of discussions on responsible behavior in space and long-term space safety and sustainability. Therefore, the fact that the EU is addressing security issues will not increase tensions, as it will likely continue to focus on the promotion of norms and rules when it addresses an external (non-EU) audience. But the possession of autonomous security capabilities could play a role in increasing the credibility of the EU and, thus, strengthening its voice on the international stage.

DISCLAIMER

The views and opinions expressed are those of the authors and do not necessarily reflect the official position of ESPI.

REFERENCES

Aliberti, Marco, Tomas Hrozensky, and Mathieu Bataille. 2020. *European Space Strategy in a Global Context*. ESPI Report 75. Vienna: European Space Policy Institute. https://espi.or.at/downloads/send/2-public-espi-reports/548-european-space-strategy-in-a-global-context-full-report.

Art, Robert J. 2004. "Europe Hedges Its Security Bets." In *Balance of Power: Theory and Practice in the 21st Century*, edited by T. V. Paul, James J. Wirtz, and Michel Fortmann, 179–213. Stanford, CA: Stanford University Press

Bataille, Mathieu, and Valentine Messina. 2020. *Europe, Space and Defence: From "Space for Defence" to "Defence of Space."* ESPI Report 75. Vienna: European Space Policy Institute. https://espi.or.at/publications/espi-public-reports/send/2-public-espi-reports/502-europe-space-and-defence.

Borrell, Josep. 2021. "Space: Space: Remarks by the High Representative/Vice-President Josep Borrell at the 13th European Space Conference." https://eeas.europa.eu/headquarters/headquarters-homepage/91401/space-remarks-high-representativevice-president-josep-borrell-13th-european-space-conference_en.

Breton, Thierry. 2020. "12th Annual Space Conference—Closing Speech by Commissioner Thierry Breton." https://ec.europa.eu/commission/commissioners/2019-2024/uropa/announcements/12th-annual-space-conference-closing-speech_en.

Breton, Thierry. 2021. "Speech by Commissioner Thierry Breton at the 13th European Space Conference." https://ec.europa.eu/commission/commissioners/2019-2024/uropa/announ cements/speech-commissioner-thierry-breton-13th-european-space-conference_en.

Commission of the European Communities. 2007. "Communication From the Commission to the Council and the European Parliament: European Space Policy." https://eur-lex.europa. eu/LexUriServ/LexUriServ.do?uri=COM:2007:0212:FIN:en:PDF.

Darnis, Jean-Pierre, Xavier Pasco, and Paul Wohrer. 2020. *Space and the Future of Europe as a Global Actor: EO as a Key Security Aspect*. Rome: Istituto Affari Internazionali. https://www. iai.it/en/pubblicazioni/space-and-future-europe-global-actor-eo-key-security-aspect.

European Commission. 2011. "Communication from the Commission to the Council, the European Parliament, the European Economic and Social Committee and the Committee of the Regions: Towards a Space Strategy for the European Union that Benefits its Citizens." https://eur-lex.europa.eu/legal-content/EN/TXT/PDF/?uri=CELEX:52011DC0 152&from=EN.

European Commission. 2016. "Communication from the Commission to the Council, the European Parliament, the European Economic and Social Committee and the Committee of the Regions: Space Strategy for Europe." https://eur-lex.europa.eu/legal-content/EN/TXT/ PDF/?uri=CELEX:52016DC0705&from=EN.

European Commission and High Representative of the Union for Foreign Affairs and Security Policy. 2023. "Joint Communication to the European Parliament and the Council: European Union Space Strategy for Security and Defence." https://ec.europa.eu/transparency/docume nts-register/detail?ref=JOIN(2023)9&lang=en

European Union. 2018. "Statement on the Occasion of the UNISPACE + 50—High Level Segment of the United Nations Committee on the Peaceful Uses of Outer Space." https:// www.unoosa.org/documents/pdf/copuos/2018/hls/01_03E.pdf.

European Union. 2021a. "Regulation (EU) 2021/696 of the European Parliament and of the Council of 28 April 2021 Establishing the Union Space Programme and the European Union Agency for the Space Programme and repealing Regulations (EU) No 912/2010, (EU) No 1285/2013 and (EU) No 377/2014 and Decision No 541/2014/EU." https://eur-lex.europa.eu/ legal-content/EN/TXT/PDF/?uri=CELEX:32021R0696&from=EN.

European Union. 2021b. "Statement on the occasion of the fifty-eighth session of the Scientific and Technical Sub-Committee of the United Nations Committee of the Peaceful Uses of Outer Space." https://www.unoosa.org/documents/pdf/copuos/stsc/2021/statements/2021- 04-19-AM-Item03-03-7EUE.pdf.

European Union. 2023. "Regulation (EU) 2023/588 of the European Parliament and of the Council of 15 March 2023 establishing the Union Secure Connectivity Programme for the pe- riod 2023–2027." https://eur-lex.europa.eu/legal-content/EN/TXT/PDF/?uri=CELEX:320 23R0588&qid=1695060684852.

Faucher, Pascal, Regina Peldszus, and Amélie Gravier. 2019. "Operational Space Surveillance and Tracking in Europe." *First International Orbital Debris Conference*. https://www.hou. usra.edu/meetings/orbitaldebris2019/orbital2019paper/pdf/6165.pdf.

Fiott, Daniel. 2018. "Strategic Autonomy: Towards 'European Sovereignty' in Defence?" Brief Issue. *European Union Institute for Security Studies* no. 18 (November). https://www. iss.europa.eu/content/strategic-autonomy-towards-%E2%80%98european-sovereig nty%E2%80%99-defence.

Fiott, Daniel. 2020. *The European Space Sector as an Enabler of EU Strategic Autonomy*. In- Depth Analysis requested by the Security and Defence (SEDE) Subcommittee, European

Parliament.   https://www.europarl.europa.eu/RegData/etudes/IDAN/2020/653620/
EXPO_IDA(2020)653620_EN.pdf.

Fiott, Daniel. 2021. "European Defence and the Demands of Strategic Autonomy." In *The Future of European Strategy in a Changing Geopolitical Environment: Challenges and Prospects*, edited by Michiel Foulon and Jack Thompson, 19–21. The Hague: The Hague Centre for Strategic Studies. https://hcss.nl/report/european-defence-and-demands-of-strategic-autonomy/.

Giegerich, Bastian. 2007. "Navigating Differences: Transatlantic Negotiations over Galileo." *Cambridge Review of International Affairs* 20, no. 3: 491–508. https://doi.org/10.1080/095575 70701574196.

Haacke, Jürgen. 2019. "The Concept of Hedging and its Application to Southeast Asia: A Critique and a Proposal for a Modified Conceptual and Methodological Framework." *International Relations of the Asia-Pacific* 19, no. 3: 375–417. https://doi.org/10.1093/irap/lcz010.

Howorth, Jolyon. 2019. "Autonomy and Strategy: What Should Europe Want?" Security Policy Brief, no. 110 (April). Egmont Institute. http://www.jstor.com/stable/resrep21390

Jackson, Van. 2014. "Power, Trust, and Network Complexity: Three Logics of Hedging in Asian Security." *International Relations of the Asia-Pacific* 14, no 3: 331–56. https://doi.org/10.1093/irap/lcu005.

Johnson, Christopher. 2014. "Draft International Code of Conduct for Outer Space Activities Fact Sheet." Secure World Foundation. https://swfound.org/media/166384/swf_draft_international_code_of_conduct_for_outer_space_activities_fact_sheet_february_2 014.pdf.

Kempin, Ronja, and Barbara Kunz. December 2017. "France, Germany and the Quest for European Strategic Autonomy: France-German Defence Cooperation in a New Era." Notes du Cerfa, no. 140. Ifri. https://www.ifri.org/sites/default/files/atoms/files/ndc_141_kempin_kunz_france_germany_european_strategic_autonomy_dec_2017.pdf.

Klimburg-Witjes Nina. 2021. "Shifting Articulations of Space Security: Boundary Work in European Space Policy Making." *European Security*. https://doi.org/10.1080/09662 839.2021.1890039.

Koga, Kei. 2018. "The Concept of 'Hedging' Revisited: The Case of Japan's Foreign Policy Strategy in East Asia's Power Shift." *International Studies Review* 20, no. 4: 633–60. https://doi.org/10.1093/isr/vix059.

Michel, Charles. 2021. "Space Action at the Heart of European Strategic Autonomy—Speech by President Charles Michel at the 13th European Space Conference." European Council. https://www.consilium.europa.eu/en/press/press-releases/2021/01/12/space-action-at-the-heart-of-european-strategic-autonomy-speech-by-president-charles-michel-at-the-13th-european-space-conference/.

Moranta, Sebastien, Giulia Pavesi, Lisa Perrichon, Serge Plattard, and Martin Sarret. 2018. *Security in Outer Space: Rising Stakes for Europe*. ESPI Report 64. Vienna: European Space Policy Institute. https://espi.or.at/downloads/send/2-public-espi-reports/371-security-in-outer-space-rising-stakes-for-europe.

Reillon, Vincent. 2017. *European Space Policy: Historical Perspective, Specific Aspects and Key Challenges*. European Parliamentary Research Service.https://www.europarl.europa.eu/RegData/etudes/IDAN/2017/595917/EPRS_IDA(2017)595917_EN.pdf.

Robinson, Jana, and Michael Romancov. 2014. "The European Union and Space: Opportunities and Risks." Non-proliferation Papers. No. 37 (January). Stockholm International Peace Research Institute. https://www.sipri.org/sites/default/files/EUNPC_no-37-1.pdf.

Tessman, Brock F. 2012. "System Structure and State Strategy: Adding Hedging to the Menu." *Security Studies* 21, no. 2: 192–231. https://doi.org/10.1080/09636412.2012.679203.

Tessman, Brock F., and Wojtek Wolfe. 2011. "Great Powers and Strategic Hedging: The Case of Chinese Energy Security Strategy." *International Studies Review* 13, no. 2: 214–40. https://doi.org/10.1111/j.1468-2486.2011.01022.x.

Villafranca-Izquierdo, Lou. March 2021. "La gouvernance de Galileo, laboratoire de la politique spatiale européenne." Note d'analyse du GRIP. Groupe de recherche et d'information sur la paix et la sécurité.

Zandee, Dick, Bob Deen, Kimberley Kruijver, and Adája Stoetman. 2020. "European Strategic Autonomy in Security and Defence: Now the Going Gets Tough, it's Time to Get Going." Clingendael Report. Clingendael Institute.

CHAPTER 23

PERSPECTIVES ON MEMBERSHIP IN THE SPACE CLUB IN WEST ASIA

Israel and the UAE

DEGANIT PAIKOWSKY

INTRODUCTION

TRADITIONALLY, West Asian countries were not active players in global space activity. But a transformation is underway, and we identify greater state interest in advancing national space activity in many of the region's countries. This trend should be viewed in a larger context. Over the last three decades, space technology and knowledge based on information from space gradually became fundamental to achieving military power and economic prosperity on Earth. From national security and commercial perspectives, possessing national technological capacity in space technology has tremendous potential to provide stability, security, and strategic leverage over others. In this chapter, we ask: What are the driving forces for advancing space strategies in West Asia and how is space activity securitized by different actors? To answer these questions, the cases of Israel, an established spacefaring nation, and the UAE, an emerging spacefaring nation, will be discussed through the theoretical lens of membership in clubs, such as the space club.

West Asia is part of the larger area of the Middle East. There is no one definition of the identity of the countries included under this region. For simplicity, following OECD guidelines, the countries this chapter refers to as part of West Asia are Bahrain, Iraq, Israel, Jordan, Kuwait, Lebanon, Oman, Qatar, Saudi Arabia, Syria, UAE (United Arab Emirates), and Yemen. It should be noted that Iran, which is taking steps toward space capabilities is not considered an integral part of West Asia. Therefore it is not addressed

Table 23.1. Israel and the UAE—Selected Socio-demographic Parameters

	Israel	UAE
Total area	21,937 sq km	83,600 sq km
Population	8,787,045	9,856,612 (July 2021 est.)
GDP per capita	$38,300* (2020 est.)	$67,100* (2019 est.)
GDP Composition	Agriculture: 2.4% (2017 est.) Industry: 26.5% (2017 est.) Services: 69.5% (2017 est.)	Agriculture: 0.9% (2017 est.) Industry: 49.8% (2017 est.) Services: 49.2% (2017 est.)
Military Expenditure	4.8% of GDP (2020 est.)	6% of GDP (2020 est.)

Note: * 2017 US dollars.
Source: Data was retrieved from the CIA Factbook website.

directly in this chapter. Nevertheless, Iran's shifts of power and especially the way it challenges global and regional orders impact the securitization of space in the region.

The methodological rationale for comparing Israel and the UAE in the broader region is that the two countries have similar characteristics but different preferences and space policies. The purpose of the comparison is not to produce rules or generalizations. Instead, the comparison attempts to highlight the variation between these countries and to elucidate different perceptions and behavioral patterns regarding space and space security. Israel and the UAE were selected because of their vast interest in space compared to other countries in the region, impacting the richness of available data. Additionally, the two countries are similar in many characteristics (see Table 23.1). They also share interests and ambitions about space, but overall, their approach to space securitization and membership in the space club is different, as will be elaborated.

This chapter comprises four sections. The first discusses the role of technological clubs in international relations and the motivations of medium-sized and small countries to seek indigenous technological capability even on a limited scale and, based on that capability, to gain access to clubs. This section builds on earlier and diverse work to develop the underlying parameters of this chapter. The changing concept and role of the space club in the past versus current world politics are presented in the second section. I present space activity in West Asia, discuss the two case studies of Israel and the UAE, and compare and analyze them according to the model of the space club in the third section. The fourth and final section highlights insights and conclusions.

TECHNOLOGICAL CLUBS IN INTERNATIONAL RELATIONS

In different eras in history, expertise in certain technological areas is "identified as an indicator of power and symbol of high standing. Usually, acquiring and developing this expertise requires massive investments of resources and large-scale national efforts. Despite the difficulties, risks, and high costs, or because of them, nations that aspire to power and high standing often invest valuable resources and efforts in acquiring it. The nations that have succeeded in this task are recognized by many as an elite group—a club." In this context, decision-makers and state officials often emphasize the political aspect of their country's accomplishments, justifying national efforts to acquire such qualities by arguing for membership in the club (Paikowsky 2017, 1).

The most important body of literature dealing with technological clubs and their role in world politics is Institutional Design Theory (IDT). IDT scholars define international institutions as explicit public arrangements that prescribe, proscribe, and authorize behavior (Koremenos, Lipson, and Snidal 2001, 762). They examine and analyze the wide variance across different kinds of institutional arrangements, arguing that their variation is rooted in rational design considerations. Among the criteria they use to classify institutions are the exclusivity of the membership, scope of issues covered, centralization of management, hard/soft rules for controlling the institution, and the flexibility and formality of the institutional arrangement (Abbott et al. 2000; Abbott and Sindal 2000; Kahler 2010; Koremenos, Lipson, and Snidal 2001; Pekkanen 2016).

International organizations (IOs) (Finnemore 1993; Katzenstien, Keohane, and Krasner 1998; Keohane 1981; Pekkanen 2016) and international regimes (Hass 1980; Jervis 1982; Krasner 1983) are usually formed to coordinate behavior among several countries regarding a certain issue area. Security communities are integrated groups of states designed to settle disputes and conflicts among their members using peaceful means (Deutch et al. 1957; Adler and Barnett 1981). The primary characteristics differentiating technological clubs from these institutions are their purpose and role. Clubs are exclusive political institutions that separate a small number of countries from the rest of the world (Paikowsky 2017; Stephen and Stephen 2020). In this context, technological clubs exemplify the means and symbols of power of a specific issue-area and reflect shifts of power in the international system.

In general, IOs, regimes, security communities, and clubs are based on a broad consensus regarding shared ideas and perceptions. Nevertheless, IOs, regimes, and security communities derive their authority, power, legitimacy, and effectiveness from the target population's widest possible adherence and participation, i.e., they are based on broad accessibility. Conversely, as elite groups, clubs must preserve a wide and clear gap between the haves and have-nots. Their exclusivity and appeal in terms of power, standing, and esteem remain only by keeping their gates closed. By producing a distinction between powerful and less powerful nations, clubs, formal or informal, serve as structural expressions of the distribution and shifts of power. In that sense, membership rules define both club members and non-members (Koremenos, Lipson, and Snidal 2001, 784). Through clubs, states absorb the actions and characteristics exhibited by great powers and what it takes to be one. States use club membership to project power and standing and claim privileges such as influence over world governance. Therefore, clubs play an important role in global governance (Paikowsky 2017, 215–17).

In technological clubs, the basis for the separation between the haves and have-nots is that members have acquired exclusive and unique capabilities that others do not have but are widely accepted as force multipliers or as currencies of power and high standing (Paikowsky 2017). The dynamic through which technological clubs emerge includes several steps. First, the great powers develop and project unique skills and capabilities as benchmarks for competition over power and high standing. Second, other countries acknowledge these skills' tangible and intangible strategic values. These capabilities make identifying the stronger, higher-status players easier and distinguish them from weaker states. Third, to maintain their power and status or achieve the power and position they aspire to, both medium-sized and emerging powers seek these capabilities and membership in the superior group. The great powers oppose fast technological proliferation because it might erode their superiority. Therefore, to guarantee their strategic advantages, they impose restrictions on the flow of technology and know-how and provide only limited cooperation. As a result of this process, the group of haves remains small and exclusive—a club (Paikowsky 2017, 39–42).

Motivations to Develop Indigenous Technological Capacity and Gain Access to Technological Clubs

Scholars of interstate power relations, power shifts, and international institutions give attention to technology and great power parity. Nevertheless, explaining why and tracing the processes and practices explaining how states interact over means and symbols of power is lacking especially considering small countries. Distinguished realist scholars emphasized the need to develop and acquire technology as a component of hard power and military strength in a self-reliant, cost-effective manner, aligning with other states to preserve relative power and deter potential threats (Morgenthau 1967; Deutsch 1978). Others developed these principles further, focusing on the structure of power distribution as the explanatory mechanism of state behavior in developing or acquiring technologies (Waltz 1979). Nevertheless, these accounts still lack explanations for the kind of power provided, how power conception is constructed, and how it changes over time. In other words, what are the factors that make the international community attribute more power to certain qualities than they do to other qualities, and how do they securitize these qualities? Furthermore, why join international institutions related to technological capabilities of this kind?

Answers to such questions are often found in the works of constructivist scholars who investigate how the dynamics of knowledge diffusion and learning socialize states to perceive certain qualities as more powerful and threatening than others, attribute values to those who develop such qualities and define them as an exclusive and powerful group. They reason that norms and conventions shape states' goals, perceptions of their interests, and the means they use to achieve those goals. Additionally, these norms and conventions have a more significant impact than external threats or demands by domestic groups (Finnemore 1996; Katzenstein 1996; Wendt 1999). Such meaning and significance may be achieved through epistemic communities that coordinate or structure international politics by implementing expectations and values in the policy process (Adler and Hass 1992; Adler 1992; 2004; 2019). Therefore, one can conclude that states operate according to collective expectations of the proper behavior of actors with a given identity (Florini 1996; Paikowsky 2017). Thus, the proliferation of high-technology weaponry, for example, is strongly associated with its socially constructed meaning (Eyre and Suchman 1966).

In dialogue with these theoretical scholarships, and to comprehensively grasp states' motivations to embark on indigenous technological development, I suggest using the perspective of analytical eclecticism (Katzenstein and Sil 2008). Analytical eclecticism is premised on a pragmatic foundation and allows trespassing across theoretical scholarships. Based on that, both tangible and intangible elements ranging from threat-based or security-minded considerations to aspirational objectives motivate states in their decisions.

Extrapolating from this, scholars of Institutional Power Shift Theory (IPST) conclude that states not only understand that international institutions matter (Koremenos Lipson, and Snidal 2001), but they use club institutions and club membership to further their own goals (Frankenbach, Kruck, and Zangl 2021). IPST scholars view obtaining membership in clubs and the associated privileges as central goals of emerging powers (Kahler 2013; Kruck and Zangl 2019; 2020; Lipscy 2017; Zangl et al. 2016). Membership in clubs is often costly, but it signals (Koremenos, Lipson, and Snidal 2001, 784) that one is cut above non-members. Medium-sized and small countries that perceive themselves as powerful, or wish to become powerful, seek to emulate the leading powers: their objective in developing indigenous technological capacity is not global leadership. They look to use technological advancement and club membership to leapfrog development stages for a stronger economy and military empowerment, which they aspire to translate into a demonstration of a power shift entailing them a higher status and greater influence on the international system and on their future. Therefore, they often choose to engage in technological development, even on a limited scale that obviously does not allow them full independence, just to prove their ability and by that to earn the powerful countries' attention, upgrade their overall international standing, and gain material goods (Paikowsky 2017, 215–17).

THE SPACE CLUB IN WORLD POLITICS

Since the beginning of the space age, the space club has been a significant international institution in power politics. State officials, the media, and the public referred to a space club when discussing international space technology and exploration activity. Different countries claimed membership in the elite space club.

This section builds on the theoretical and empirical findings of a previous study of mine on the power of the space club in world politics (Paikowsky 2017). It outlines the changing concept of the space club in world politics and the motivations of countries to develop space capacities and securitize space through the prism of membership in the space club.

It should be noted that the space club was and still is an informal institution. There is no formal organization or association with dedicated regulations, an admissions committee, or any central management that separates the haves from have-nots in the field of space. In the absence of a formal process to become a member of the space club, bilateral and multilateral cooperation with existing club members is an essential practice by which newcomers earn club membership. Club membership provides tangible and intangible benefits. Among the valuable privileges is cooperation with other space-faring nations, including transferring technology and know-how. Additionally, the space club fulfills an essential role in organizing the stratification of power and status in the international system.

The Emergence of the Space Club and Motivations to Join the Space Club

The politics of space in the Cold War mainly focused on the race between the two superpowers, who promoted space accomplishments as a means of power and competence, symbolizing high standing and national pride. In their actions, they socialized other countries to perceive expertise in space as one of the significant indicators for being a great power. Hence, countries that perceived themselves as great powers and those that aspired to become one wanted to master space technology. At the same time, for strategic reasons, each of the superpowers, separately, closely monitored cooperation in the field of space and imposed severe restrictions on the spread and transfer of space technology and know-how. As a result, only a handful of countries were able to develop and demonstrate indigenous technological expertise in space. The international community acknowledged the countries that succeeded as an elite group—the space club. By their actions, the superpowers took upon themselves the role of the club's gatekeepers.

The borderline between club members and non-members should be drawn to include states that demonstrate indigenous space capability and exclude those that don't. Nevertheless, countries involved in space research and technology differ in their investments and capabilities. Therefore, a pyramid-shaped model is the most suitable to describe the hierarchical structure of the space club, in which club membership costs and benefits are unequal. The basis of the pyramid is wide and contains a large number of actors relative to the number of actors on the highest level. At the bottom, costs and benefits are much lower than on higher levels of the pyramid. Because the space club is not a formal institution, it has a fluid and dynamic structure. The levels of membership of the space club pyramid change according to progress in technology and changes in geopolitics.

In general, space capability is open to all, and acquiring it is mostly dependent on the political will of a country's leaders. Club members attempting to prevent a country from acquiring the necessary capabilities may impose restrictions and difficulties on it, such as refusing to sell needed materials, implementing export controls to this country, and so forth. Trying to ban efforts to acquire a technological capability completely is nevertheless impossible. And yet, this does not mean that every country that demonstrates that it developed space capability automatically becomes a club member. Joining the space club is usually done in three stages. First, by a public demonstration of space capability or expertise, such as indigenously launching a satellite into orbit or sending a significant space exploration mission to the moon or Mars. Second, by a formal statement in which leaders and state officials characterize the event as "joining the space club." Other club members acknowledge the newcomer's membership in the third and final stage. In practice, they welcome the new country into the club by entering into joint ventures and sharing knowledge and technology with it.

Membership in the space club provides different functions to different types of countries. For the superpowers, the space club was, and still is, an important arena in which they exercised their leadership, interacted, and competed with one another in a civilized manner. For medium-sized or regional powers, membership meant they were cut above ordinary states, allowing them to identify their status compared to larger and more powerful countries. In the hands of the weak or small, club membership was a tool to gain empowerment, get attention, and be placed in a higher category of capability and power than the one to which they belonged.

Countries with strong incentives to achieve and project power enhance international standing, national esteem, and pride are more likely to adopt ambitious strategies for their space activity and prefer the development of indigenous capability. By contrast, low incentives of these kinds result in a more moderate approach to space and even in a decision not to "join the club." These countries are more likely to adopt a strategy of purchasing space services and products from other nations. One way or the other, joining the space club is a legitimate, rational, and significant consideration explaining decision-making and national preferences in space technology and exploration.

Current Status of the Space Club

In the years following the end of the Cold War, the space club continued to be a competitive informal club based primarily on technological capability. However, in the last decade, global space activity experienced rapid growth in the number of countries involved in national space activity. Additionally, technological and economic developments, especially the growth in commercial activities to develop launch capabilities and flying cargo and humans to low earth orbit (LEO) and beyond, threaten the space club's value. This process shakes the pyramid's structure and changes the borderline between members and non-members.

To preserve the exclusivity and uniqueness of the space club and their membership in it, established spacefaring nations must expand and upgrade their space programs in new directions. Therefore, the future of the space club depends on the willingness of its leading members to preserve its small size by redesigning a higher barrier between the haves and have-nots and by focusing on capabilities, which the private sector will not develop by itself due to their costs and lack of commercial efficiency.

Observing current great power dynamics in global space activity, one can agree that a national space program remains a means of power and statehood to a large extent. Furthermore, many established and emerging spacefaring states still securitize membership in the space club as a way of advancing national security and prosperity. Therefore, it is unlikely that the space club will cease to exist in the near future.

In this context, established and emerging spacefaring nations have already taken several directions to redesign and raise the bar for access to the space club: Human missions to the moon and later on to Mars; longer-distance journeys deep into the solar system and beyond; the development of super-heavy launch capability; the development of practices and mechanisms toward a cis-lunar economy including the extraction and production of materials in space; the development and deployment of Space Situational Awareness systems and Global Navigation Space Systems (GNSS); and even the development and deployment of space weapons including anti-satellite systems (ASATs). These directions generally involve complex and sophisticated scientific and technological high-risk projects, which demand long-term national commitments and the allocation of extensive resources. Together or separately, these activities set new boundaries to the space club, which most countries are unable or uninterested in crossing. In recent years, the number of West Asian countries involved in space dramatically expanded. However, only a few of them follow in some of these directions. The next section provides an overview of space activity in the region.

SPACE ACTIVITY IN WEST ASIA

In general, West Asian countries acknowledged space expertise and membership in the space club as a means of power. However, differences exist in how they transformed this understanding into actual preferences and priorities regarding their level of space activity or the lack thereof. For many years, space activity in West Asia was limited, and Israel was the only spacefaring nation with an indigenous space capacity. Many countries focused only on the procurement of satellite communication services. For example, in 1976, the Arab League initiated ArabSat to provide satellite communication services to the Arab world. Its first satellite was launched in 1985. ArabSat, the leading satellite services provider in the Arab world, operates from Saudi Arabia, its largest partner (ArabSat 2021).

Over the last two decades, the international system at large has experienced shifts of power. For example, the rise of new global powers, such as China and India, and the decline of established powers, such as the United States and Russia. Power shifts also took place within West Asia or on its margins. For example, Iran's rise as a regional power and the decline of Syria, Iraq, and to some extent Egypt under the events of the Arab Spring. Moreover, West Asia is significantly affected by megatrends such as global climate changes, which bring about desertification, shortages of water, and natural disasters. Together with the shifts of global and regional power, these challenge the existing regional order and the power and standing of the region's countries.

In this context, several West Asian countries decided to take advantage of the growing global space market and became more active in space for civil, commercial, and military purposes. The motivations for greater involvement in space activity range from national needs to exploit space for development, environmental sustainability, economic prosperity, and national security. The most active among them are the UAE, Saudi Arabia, and Turkey. In 2015, Turkey stated that developing an independent capability to build its own satellites is strategically important. Over time, it will contribute to the Turkish economy (de-Selding 2015). Saudi Arabia has also taken steps to upgrade and expand its capabilities. They all seek to develop indigenous scientific and technological capacities. However, they suffer from a shortage of scientific-human infrastructure for research and development in the space field. For this reason, they focus on developing national infrastructures, including the human capacity needed for national space programs.

These countries are motivated by a diverse mix of tangible considerations ranging from economic prosperity, development, and national security concerns. For example, on the international level, current global climate changes call for reducing the overall global use of fossil energy sources. This trend threatens the economic stability of the region and of specific countries that traditionally depended on oil for their economy. Indeed, some of the region's countries look to reduce economic vulnerability from the dependence on revenues from oil and its products by developing modern and diverse economies. National space programs and national space ecosystems fit well with this strategy. Another threat-based consideration is the growing instability in the region due to concrete attacks on national infrastructure by terrorist militias, which have taken place in recent years. Data gathering from space can assist in mitigating these threats. Additionally, more intangible aspirational motivations of intra-Arab competition and greater influence in the region also affect decisions to advance science and technology in the field of space (Gozansky 2019). Nevertheless, Israel remains the only country capable of launching satellites into space so far. Most countries of the region still pursue only limited activity in space (see Table 23.2).

Table 23.2. Space Activity in West Asia—Selected Parameters

Country	Space Agency	First Indigenous Satellite	First Owned Satellite	National Astronaut	COPUOS Membership	Signatory to the Outer Space Treaty
Bahrain	2014				2017	2019
Iraq			2014 Tigrisat		1977	1969
Israel	1983	1988 Ofeq-1		2003	2015	1967
Jordan		2018 JY1-SAT			2012	1968
Kuwait		2021 QMR-KWT				1972
Lebanon					1959	1969
Oman					2015	
Qatar			2013 Es'hail 1		2015	2012
Saudi Arabia	2018	2000 SaudiSat1	1985 ArabSat-1A	1985	2001	1976
Syria	2014			1987	1980	1968
Turkey	2018	2003 Bilsat1	1994 TurkSat 1B		1977	1968
UAE	2014	2009 DubaiSat	2000 Thuraya 1	2019	2015	2000

Source: United Nations Office of Outer Space Affairs

Israel's Space Program

Israel's national space effort dates to the early 1980s; its primary motivation for being in space was to satisfy national security needs of early warning, deterrence, and self-reliance in advanced technologies. Israel's national space activities include a defense program (established in 1981 under the Ministry of Defense) and a civilian program led by Israel's Space Agency (ISA), created in 1983 and operating under the Ministry of Science, Technology, and Innovation. This section builds on former works by the author (Paikowsky 2011; 2017; Paikowsky, Azoulay, and Ben Israel 2020; Paikowsky and Azoulay 2020).

In 1988, Israel launched the Ofeq-1 satellite on an Israeli launcher. Ofeq would go on to become a line with increasingly advanced earth observation capabilities. Israel's national satellites are primarily for remote sensing and communications. The country also has an indigenous launch capability to LEO provided by the Shavit family of launchers. Israel launches its satellites westward—opposite the rotation of the Earth—because of its geo-strategic location. Launching eastward presents a strategic threat of firing a projectile in the direction of hostile states east of Israel, risking that parts might fall onto their territory. The decision to launch westward results in an approximately 30 percent loss in launch efficiency. Therefore, Israel's space industry specialized in developing lightweight satellites to minimize the load on the launcher.

In the 1990s, Israeli industries began to develop commercial platforms, such as the Amos communication satellite series, EROS remote-sensing electro-optical series, subsystems, and other equipment. In 2010, to reach greater industrial scale and competitiveness in the growing world space market, Israel expanded its focus to include civilian applications and scientific activity (Paikowsky and Levi 2010). So far, only modest resources have been allocated to these activities. Nevertheless, over the last decade, a commercial ecosystem has evolved. It includes a variety of companies that provide diverse services and products.

Originally, Israel's space industry was based on its defense industries. Israel Aerospace Industries (IAI) group is the main contractor in many space projects, including assembling Ofeq, Amos, and Eros satellites and developing the Dror-1 communications satellite. Rafael Advanced Defense Systems' propulsion department is the main propulsion systems supplier for Israel's space projects, while Elbit's El-op develops electro-optical payloads. Nevertheless, in 2019, both Rafael and Elbit each separately announced their decision to enter the nanosatellite systems market (Azulai 2019; Fastcompany.com 2020).

There are several providers of commercial space services in Israel; one of them is Gilat Satcom, a prominent provider of telecommunication solutions specializing in global mobile satellite services. ISI (ImageSat International) is a commercial provider of satellite imagery and analysis services using the EROS series. SpaceCom is a commercial provider of satellites communications services to Africa, Europe, Asia, and the Middle East.

Following the defense-related space advances and subsequent commercial and civil space enterprises, a community of space start-ups has emerged in Israel over the past ten years. The activities of several start-up companies, such as SpacePharma, NSLcom, Effective Space Solutions (purchased by Astroscale), StemRad, ASTERRA-Utilis, Helios, and others, are noteworthy.

Israel's space ecosystem also builds on strong academia: the aerospace engineering faculty and the Asher Space Research Institute (ASRI) at the Technion, the Ben-Gurion University remote sensing laboratory, the School of Physics and Astronomy, and the newly established center for small satellites at Tel Aviv University, the Weizmann Institute of Science, and the Hebrew University of Jerusalem.

In 2008, Israel's space industrial base suffered instability exemplified by a reduction in the ongoing production of satellites and satellite systems. Additionally, orders outside of Israel were small, and the local budget was not enough to meet future needs (Getz et al. 2008). As a result, Israel's space community has undergone a long and comprehensive process, reevaluating its goals, objectives, and policies. In 2009–2010 a presidential task force envisioned a greater commercial scale for Israel's space industry. The resulting programs and policy led to an increase in the allocations of funds to the ISA budget and grants for start-ups and research in the civilian space fields (ISA's grants are distributed through Israel's Innovation Authority). Nevertheless, the increase in the ISA budget was only a small portion of the original amount recommended by the task force (Paikowsky 2017, 165).

In 2012–2015, another team that overlooked Israel's civil space policy operated under the National Council for Research and Development. A third team was formed after the loss of the Amos-6 communications satellite on the SpaceX launch pad in September 2016. This committee focused on communication satellites and provided its recommendations in December 2016. Its report called for a multi-year national plan focusing mainly on Israeli firms' full development and construction of four communications satellites. To increase the overall competitiveness of Israeli space firms in the global market, the report recommended prioritizing the development of products and services in areas where Israel has a potential advantage, such as remote sensing and space cybersecurity (Government of the State of Israel 2016).

As part of the Israel space program's expansion to include civil space activities, the ISA developed a community outreach and education office that funds and directs public educational programs for children and youth. Among the educational projects that have evolved is the Herzliya Science Center Space Lab. Since 2014, this project has launched more than ten nanosatellites built by high school students.

In the last decade, an important non-governmental initiative was the Beresheet Moon lander by SpaceIL. It was launched aboard a SpaceX Falcon-9 launcher in February 2019. Several weeks later, it successfully entered lunar orbit. While Beresheet crash-landed on the lunar surface on April 11, 2019, it nevertheless achieved most of its objectives. In 2021, it was announced that SpaceIL continues with a second mission, the Beresheet-2, planned to be launched in the mear future (Trabelsi 2021).

ISA prioritizes collaboration with other space agencies. The motivation for international cooperation stems from the aspiration to capitalize on Israel's relative strengths, especially in miniaturization; create synergy between Israeli institutions and industry and their peers in partner countries; provide business opportunities; and upgrade foreign relations between partner countries. ISA's major counterparts are NASA, European Space Agency (ESA), National Center for Space Studies (CNES) of France, German Aerospace Center (DLR), the Italian Space Agency (ASI), and the Indian Space Research Organization (ISRO). In 2021, following the 2020 Abraham Accords, ISA signed an agreement with the UAE space agency (Bell 2021).

Israel also supports multilateral activities and initiatives toward the peaceful uses of outer space. In 2015, Israel was voted in as a regular member of the United Nations (UN) Committee on the Peaceful Uses of Outer Space (COPUOS 2020). In 2017, Israel was voted to serve on the six-member Steering Bureau of COPUOS. Israel participated in the open-ended consultations held by the European Union regarding an International Space Code of Conduct. The code was discussed for several years, but the process was not completed. Israel also supported the UN Guidelines on the Long-Term Sustainability of Outer Space (LTS), which were adopted in 2019.

The UAE Space Program

The UAE space program is considered the most advanced and ambitious among the Arab countries. Nevertheless, the UAE's space capacity is still in the making; its early space activity dates to the 1990s. But it was only in 2014 that the UAE established its space agency, currently the leading force of the nation's space activity. The agency collaborates with the Mohammed Bin Rashid Space Centre (MBRSC), a government of Dubai entity that serves as an incubation chamber for building local capacity in space technology. MBRSC leads the technological development of the UAE satellite program. The UAE is investing in developing and expanding national infrastructure and capacities, especially but not limited to human capital, to attract Government to Government (G2G) collaborations and corporations. The long-term goal is to achieve a sustainable and competitive local space industrial base (Blount and Amara 2020).

In 2014, the UAE chose Mars as its starting mission (Al Rashedi, Al Shamsi, and Al Hosani 2020, 624). Many emerging spacefaring nations rely on the space capabilities of other countries or commercial providers for their early steps in space. The Emirates Mars Mission (EMM), to study Mars's atmosphere and climate, signals that the UAE is different. The motivation driving the EMM is to "fundamentally redirect a nation's trajectory. Through its design and execution, the EMM pursues a UAE future in which its economy diversifies from traditional activity, including oil and finance, and inspires a generation towards scientific and entrepreneurial careers. This is a mission for national development before it is a mission of science." Another driving force for the EMM is regional leadership (Steenmans et al. 2019).

In July 2020, the EMM Hope research probe was successfully launched from Japan. The mission advanced a diplomatic track for UAE's leadership and efforts in enhancing regional and global prosperity and well-being. In a national context, the mission focused on public outreach and succeeded in changing perceptions regarding careers in science and promoting new fields of studies in local universities. At the international level, UAE signaled that it is developing the scientific and technological capacities needed to support its leadership position in the region, aiming for greater prosperity (Steenmans et al. 2019).

Aside from the EMM, the UAE launched into space several satellites. DubaiSat-1 and DubaiSat-2 were developed with counterparts in South Korea and were launched in 2009 and 2013, respectively. KhalifaSat, the first remote sensing satellite designed and developed by the UAE, was launched from Japan in 2018. The YahSat-1 and YahSat-2 communications satellites were launched in 2011 and 2012, respectively. In 2017, a nanosatellite, Nayif-1, was developed by the MBRSC in collaboration with educational institutions (UAE Government Portal n.d.).

In 2016, the UAE announced the establishment of a space research center affiliated with the UAE University at Al Ain called the National Space Science Technology Centre (NSSTC). The NSSTC is responsible for constructing and operating a Hyperspectral Earth Observation Satellite (Blount and Amara 2020).

One of the main industry players in the UAE is Yahsat, a satellite telecommunications provider based in Abu Dhabi. With its three geosynchronous satellites, Yahsat offers a variety of military, civil, and commercial satellite communications solutions across the region. Yahsat also owns Thuraya, a UAE mobile satellite communications company (Blount and Amara 2020). Overall, the UAE looks to create an attractive environment for the space industry (Al Rashedi, Al Shamsi, and Al Hosani 2020, 626). The UAE cooperates with leading spacefaring nations and foreign companies to accomplish these ambitious endeavors. For example, the UAE has invested in Virgin Galactic because it looks to advance space tourism activity from its territory.

On the defense side, the UAE also purchased two advanced satellites for military purposes (Falcon Eye) from French companies. The first satellite was lost in July 2019, when the Vega launcher crashed a few minutes after launch (Doffman 2019). A year later, in December 2020, the second Flacon Eye high-resolution remote sensing satellite was successfully launched into space (Meed 2020).

In 2016, the UAE space agency launched a National Space Policy. The UAE's vision regarding space is to become a leader and a hub in this field for the region and more globally. The policy is aligned with the UAE government's ambitions and higher interests, as reflected in the national agenda of the UAE Vision 2021 and Centennial 2071. "The latter aims to enhance the role of the space sector and, thereby, make the UAE among the best countries in the world with a stable and diverse economy providing for current and upcoming Emirati generations. This entails the transition toward a knowledge-based economy centered on innovation, high-level education, and increasing national expertise and qualifications" (Al Rashedi, Al Shamsi, and Al Hosani 2020, 624).

In 2019, the UAE published its National Space Strategy 2030, which is aligned with the UN's seventeen sustainable development goals (SDGs-2030) and the COPUOS LTS (Robinson 2020, 364). In December 2019, the National Space Law was approved and implemented. This sets the regulatory basis for space activities in the UAE. The policy goal underpinning the law is to create a legal framework to support the country's ambitions of becoming a leading player in the global space sector (Blount and Amara 2020). It covers the organization and objectives of space projects undertaken by the country, including peaceful space exploration and the safe use of space technologies. The law is unique in the fact that it "addresses new and complex concepts, such as the right to own resources found in space and organizing manned space travel and other commercial activities, such as asteroid mining" (Al Rashedi, Al Shamsi, and Al Hosani 2020, 624). The UAE is the third country in the world, after the United States and Luxembourg, to have specific requirements in its national legal framework on the exploitation and utilization of space resources (Blount and Amara 2020).

The UAE Space Agency cooperates or has MOUs with several international and regional space agencies, among them the United States, France, China, India, Japan, South

Korea, Italy, Germany, Kazakhstan, Saudi Arabia, Egypt, Bahrain, Luxembourg, the UK, and Russia (Al Rashedi, Al Shamsi, and Al Hosani 2020, 633; Blount and Amara 2020). As stated earlier, in October 2021, under the overarching 2020 Abraham Accords, it signed an agreement with the Israel Space Agency. Through its agreement with China, the UAE takes part in the Belt and Road Initiative. Consequentially it enjoys services, such as BeiDou Satellite Navigation System, satellite communications, and remote sensing (Hui 2018).

The UAE also drives regional collaboration in the space field. In 2019, it launched the Arab Space Collaboration Group, which includes partnerships between the UAE and ten other countries. The primary objective is to share knowledge and initiate joint projects to advance the region's space industry. The UAE Space Agency chairs the group. Dr. Al Ahbabi, the then director-general of the UAE Space Agency, said: "Space is all about cooperation" (Nasir 2019).

The UAE is seeking a central role in multilateral processes and dialogues regarding the future use of space for global development. For example, it hosted the first High-Level Forum (HLF) in Dubai in November 2016, co-organized by the United Nations Office of Outer Space Affairs (UNOOSA) and the government of the United Arab Emirates. It resulted in the Dubai Declaration, which recommended the forum continue to serve as a platform for the space community to exchange views on connecting the four pillars of the UNISPACE + 50 and Space2030 and to encourage collaboration with the UN Office of Outer Space Affairs (Al Rashedi, Al Shamsi, and Al Hosani 2020, 627). In 2021, the UAE also hosted in Dubai the International Astronautical Federation's IAC2021.

FINAL NOTES ON SPACE ACTIVITY IN WEST ASIA AND ON MEMBERSHIP IN THE SPACE CLUB

In this chapter, I analyzed space activity in West Asia. I compared Israel, an established spacefaring nation, and the UAE, an emerging spacefaring nation, through the lens of a space club. This examination strengthened our understanding regarding the significance of expectations and aspirations in strategic considerations of emerging powers and even small countries to develop space capacities and determine the focus and intensity of their activity, or the lack thereof. The evidence provided supports the argument that global and regional governmental space activity is explainable with the framework of technological clubs.

Additionally, the evidence exemplifies the significant change the space club has undergone in recent years. Space is now more accessible and affordable. This reality enables more countries, some of which are not only new to space but are considered emerging nations in general, to play an ambitious role in the space club. The examination teaches us that tangible, pragmatic considerations are prerequisites in the realm of space but are inadequate in explaining national science and technology decision-making and the setting of policy priorities. Political will and aspirational motivations are important. Membership in the space club provides an important added value of political power.

Israel and the UAE have the most advanced space ecosystems in West Asia. Each of the two ecosystems contains several dozen government, industry, academia, and civil society entities that facilitate and contribute to the national space economy. Additionally, they both have definite needs for the use of space application services. Nevertheless, as outlined here, each country adopted different policies and performed a different set of space activities. Consequently, their membership in the space club is based on different achievements and expertise, exemplifying different motivations.

The UAE appears to have recognized the unique benefits that space club membership provides and adopted an integrative strategy of cooptation to be included in the club. The UAE based its membership on ambitious space exploration missions in collaboration with established spacefaring nations. For the UAE, membership in the space club signals that it is a cut above other countries in the region. It also signals to established spacefaring nations that it aspires to a leadership role.

As rather a newcomer to the space club, the UAE securitizes space and membership in the space club from a broad national security approach. The UAE's goal is to reach a high position in the international system as a regional power whose influence on regional and perhaps on global affairs is significant. That's why the UAE attributes great value to becoming an acknowledged spacefaring nation and ambitiously insists on an indigenous space capacity. To advance in that direction, it moves on two vectors that complement each other. In the first one, the UAE's goal is to use its space program for tangible goods such as national development, economic diversification and prosperity, environmental sustainability, and national security, which mainly answer threat-based considerations. Along the second vector, the UAE uses highly visible space missions that strive for a great deal of exposure and recognition as a meaningful contributor to space exploration. These activities are set to answer more aspirational motivations.

In the space community, the UAE uses its voice regarding space security to support stability and sustainability in the space environment, which exemplifies an approach focused on space safety (Antoni 2020). This is consistent with its National Space Policy, which emphasizes the importance of international cooperation and the importance of adherence to international norms (Blount and Amara 2020).

Israel, by contrast, was and still is, motivated by much more pragmatic threat-based considerations. Israel sees special significance in providing national space expertise to keep it safe and secure at modest costs. For Israel, membership in the space club is a significant strategy to deal with the country's security challenges. Membership in the space club is a means to project power in a non-aggressive way, strengthen diplomatic ties, and upgrade the overall posture of the country. It is not an end. Hence, space security was primarily associated with using space for national security and defense.

However, the recent expansion of Israel's space ecosystem demanded change in its orientation toward space security and sustainability. Israel now attributes greater attention to securing the space environment for peaceful uses. This interest extends beyond security needs; should outer space become inaccessible and unsafe, this will negatively impact Israel's national and commercial space activities.

In this context, Israel's current approach to space security may be described as threefold: first promoting a robust and diversified space sector that provides for Israel's national security needs; second protecting and safeguarding Israel's space assets, systems, and capabilities; third, maintaining a safe and sustainable space environment for all users (Paikowsky, Azoulay, and Ben Israel 2020). However, the contemporary expansion of global space activities, especially toward a future cis-lunar economy, puts Israel at a crossroads. Its narrative regarding space focuses on exploiting space to mitigate threat-based national security considerations. Nevertheless, regionally and globally, sustaining its lofty role in the space club means it has to play a more central and active role in economic and diplomatic space activities.

In summary, the differences between the two countries regarding their motivations and accompanying strategies for space are not only in technical expertise and know-how. The differences between them are also in the role they perceive themselves playing in world politics and in their aspirations. In the UAE, the space program and membership in the space club serve as a source of political power for international standing, regional influence, and national esteem. The space program allows the UAE to project an image of an ambitious and advanced regional power and link itself with strong and developed spacefaring nations through collaborations. Conversely, Israel developed its space program out of a deep sense of threat and aspirations for becoming a power. It continues to pursue expertise in space for pragmatic reasons.

Considering these two different approaches to the securitization of space and the fact that many countries in West Asia are interested in a greater presence in space, the UAE and Israel may find common ground to advance space activity in the region. Over the last decade, the United States began to disengage from its overall involvement in the region and prefers modest involvement. This development may demand greater engagement and collaboration in regional affairs to sustain stability and achieve prosperity. Despite the rather different path each country took on its way to space, both Israel and the UAE share a rather similar approach to the idea of using space for peaceful purposes in the region and in space—advancing science and technology for development, prosperity, stability, and security. Therefore, the space scientific projects both Israel and the UAE pursue separately could serve as fertile ground for this kind of collaboration and perhaps a regional "space club."

References

Abbott, K. W., R. Keohane, A. Moravcsik, A. Slaughter, and D. Snidal. 2000. "The Concept of Legalization." *International Organization* 54, no. 3: 401–19.

Abbott, K. W., and D. Snidal. 2000. "Hard and Soft Law in International Governance." *International Organization* 54, no. 3: 421–56.

Adler, E., and M. Barnett (eds.). 1981. *Security Communities.* Cambridge: Cambridge University Press.

Adler, E. 1992. "The Emergence of Cooperation: National Epistemic Communities and the International Evolution of the Idea of Nuclear Arms Control." *International Organizations* 46, no. 1: 101–45.

Adler, E. 2004. *Communitarian International Relations: The Epistemic Foundation of International Relations.* London: Routledge.

Adler, E. 2019. *World Ordering: A Social Theory of Cognitive Evolution.* Cambridge: Cambridge University Press.

Adler, E., and P. M. Hass. 1992. "Conclusion: Epistemic Communities, World Order, and the Creation of International Policy Coordination." *International Organization* 46, no. 1: 373–74.

Al Rashedi, N., F. Al Shamsi, and H. Al Hosani. 2020. "UAE Approach to Space and Security." In *Handbook of Space Security*, edited by K. Schrogl, 622–52. New York: Springer.

Antoni, N. 2020. "Definition and Status of Space Security." in In *Handbook of Space Security*, edited by K. Schrogl, 9–34. New York: Springer.

ArabSat. 2021. https://www.arabsat.com/english/about.

Azulai, R. 2019. "Rafael Develops Nano Surveillance Satellites." *Globes.co.il.* April 7, 2019. https://en.globes.co.il/en/article-rafael-enters-spy-satellite-market-1001281341.

Bell, J. 2021. "Israel Signs Landmark Agreement on Space Cooperation, Planetary Research." *Al Arabia News.* October 21, 2021. https://english.alarabiya.net/News/middle-east/2021/10/21/UAE-Israel-sign-landmark-agreement-on-space-cooperation-planetary-research.

Blount, P. J., and M. Amara. 2020. "UAE-Brief." SPARC. https://www.sparc.uw.edu/uae/.

de Selding, P. B. 2015. "Construction of Turksat's 1st Domestic Satellite Now Underway." *Space News.* April 21, 2015, 2–15. spacenews.com/construction-of-turksats-1st-domestic-satellite-now-underway/.

Deutsch, K., S. Burrell, R. Kann Jr., and M. Lee. 1957. *Political Community and the North Atlantic Area: International Organization in the Light of Historical Experience.* Princeton, NJ: Princeton University Press.

Deutsch, K. 1978. *The Analysis of International Relations.* 2nd ed. New Jersey: Prentice-Hall.

Doffman, Z. 2019. "Crashed UAE Military Spay Satellite Raises Possibility of Enemy Cyberattack." *Forbes.* July 12, 2019.https://www.forbes.com/sites/zakdoffman/2019/07/12/did-an-iranian-cyberattack-force-a-military-spy-satellite-to-drop-from-the-sky/?sh=61b243a353b0.

Eyre, D., and M. Suchman. 1996. "Status, Norms and the Proliferation of Conventional Weapons: An Institutional Theory Approach." In *The Culture of National Security: Norms and Identity in World Politics*, edited by P. Katzenstein, 79–113. New York: Columbia University Press.

Fastcompany.com. 2020. March 10. "The World's 50 Most Innovative Companies." https://www.fastcompany.com/90457907/space-most-innovative-companies-2020.

Finnemore, M. 1993. "International Organizations as Teachers of Norms: The United Nations Educational, Scientific, and Cultural Organization and Science Policy." *International Organization* 47, no. 4: 565–97. https://doi.org/10.1017/S0020818300028101.

Finnemore, M. 1996. *National Interests in International Society.* Ithaca, NY: Cornell University Press.

Florini, A. 1996. "The Evolution of International Norms." *International Studies Quarterly* 40, no. 3: 365–66. https://doi.org/10.2307/2600716.

Frankenbach, Patrick, Andreas Kruck, and Bernhard Zangl. 2021. "India's Recognition as a Nuclear Power: A Case of Strategic Cooptation." *Contemporary Security Policy*. https://doi.org/10.1080/13523260.2021.1920117.

Getz, D., A. Katzman, B. Zalmanowitz, D. Paikowsky, V. Sega, and Y. Even Zohar. 2008. *The Impact of the Space Industry on Israel's Economy*. Haifa: Samuel Neaman Institute for Advanced Studies in Science and Technology, The Technion.

Government of the State of Israel, Ministry of Science and Technology. 2016. "Space Committee Report." (In Hebrew.) https://www.gov.il/he/departments/news/most_news20161220.

Gozansky, Y. 2019. "Shooting for the Stars: The Arab 'Space Club.'" *INSS Insight*. June 16, 2019. https://www.inss.org.il/publication/shooting-stars-arab-space-club/.

Hass, E. R. 1980. "Why Collaborate? Issue-Linkage and International Regimes." *World Politics* 32, no. 3: 357–405.

Hui J. 2018. "The Spatial Information Corridor Contributes to UNISPACE+50." http://www.unoosa.org/documents/pdf/copuos/stsc/2018/tech-08E.pdf.

Jervis, R. 1982. "Security Regimes." *International Organization* 36, no. 2: 357–78.

Kahler, M. 2010. "Regional Institutions in an Era of Globalization and Crisis: Asia in Comparative Perspective." Paper Prepared for Delivery at the 2010 Annual Meeting of the American Political Science Association, 2–5 September 2010, Washington DC.

Kahler, M. 2013. "Rising Powers and Global Governance: Negotiating Change in a Resilient Status Quo." *International Affairs* 89: 711–29. https://doi.org/10.1111/1468-2346.12041

Katzenstein, P. (ed.). 1996. *The Culture of National Security: Norms and Identity in World Politics*. Columbia: Columbia University Press.

Katzenstein, P., R. Keohane, and S. Krasner. 1998. "International Organization and the Study of World Politics." *International Organization* 52, no. 4: 645–85.

Katzenstein, P., and R. Sil. 2008. "Eclectic Theorizing in the Study and Practice of International Relations." In *Oxford Handbook of International Relations*, edited by C. Reus-Smit and D. Snidal, 109–30. Oxford: Oxford University Press.

Keohane, R. 1989. *International Institutions and State Power*. Boulder, CO: Westview Press.

Koremenos, K., C. Lipson, and D. Snidal. 2001. "The Rational Design of International Institutions." *International Organizations* 55, no. 4: 761–99.

Krasner, S. (ed.). 1983. *International Regimes*. Ithaca, NY: Cornell University Press.

Kruck, A., and B. Zangl. 2019. "Trading Privileges For Support: The Strategic Cooptation of Emerging Powers into International Institutions." *International Theory* 11, no. 3: 318–43. https://doi.org/10.1017/S1752971919000101

Kruck, A., and B. Zangl. 2020. "The Adjustment of International Institutions to Global Power Shifts: A Framework for Analysis." *Global Policy* 11, no. 3: 5–16.

Lipscy, P. Y. (2017). Renegotiating the World Order: Institutional Change in International Relations. Cambridge: Cambridge University Press.

Meed. 2020. "UAE Launches Defense Satellites." *Aerospace Technology*. December 11, 2020. https://www.aerospace-technology.com/comment/uae-defence-satellite/.

Morgenthau, H. 1967. *Politics among Nations*. 4th ed. New York: Alfred Knopf.

Nasir, S. 2019. "UAE Launches Arab Space Collaboration Group." Khaleej Times. March 18, 2019. https://www.khaleejtimes.com/uae/uae-launches-arab-space-collaboration-group.

Paikowsky, D. 2011. "From the Shavit-2 to Ofeq-1—A History of the Israeli Space Effort." *Quest* 18, no. 4: 4–12.

Paikowsky, D. 2017. *The Power of the Space Club*. Cambridge: Cambridge University Press.

Paikowsky D., and T. Azoulay. 2020. "SPARC Brief—Israel." Space Policy and Research Center (SPARC) Washington University. https://www.sparc.uw.edu/israel/.

Paikowsky, D., T. Azoulay, and I. Ben Israel. 2020. "Israel's Approach to Space Security and Sustainability." In *Handbook of Space Security—Policies, Applications and Programs*, edited by K. U. Schrogl, 589–600. 2nd Ed. Switzerland: Springer.

Paikowsky, D., and R. Levi. 2010. *Space as a National Project—An Israeli Space Program for a Sustainable Israeli Space Industry, Presidential Taskforce for Space Activity Final Report*. Jerusalem: Israel Ministry of Science and Technology.

Pekkanen, M. S. 2016. "Introduction: Agents of Design." In *Governance in the Contemporary World Order*, edited by Saadia M. Pekkanen, 1–32. Ithaca, NY: Cornell University Press .

Robinson, J. 2020. "Space Security Policies and Strategies of States: An Introduction." In *Handbook of Space Security*, edited by K. Schrogl, 359–66. New York: Springer.

Schrogl KU. (ed.) 2020. *Handbook of Space Security—Policies, Applications and Programs*. 2nd Ed. Switzerland: Springer.

Space Watch Middle East. 2019. "UAE Space Agency Signs MoU with Virgin Galactic for al Ain Operations." https://spacewatch.global/2019/03/uae-space-agency-signs-mou-with-virgin-galactic-for-al-ain-operations/.

Steenmans, I., J. C. Mauduit, J. Chataway, and N. Morisetti. 2019. *Emirates Mars Mission: A Mission to a Transformative Future—A Transformative Value Analyses Report for the Mohammed Bin Rashid Space Center*. London: University College London. https://www.ucl.ac.uk/steapp/sites/steapp/files/emirates_mars_mission_report.pdf.

Stephen, M. D., and K. Stephen. 2020. "The Integration of Emerging Powers into Club Institutions: China and the Arctic Council." *Global Policy* 11, no. S 3: 51–60. https://doi.org/10.1111/1758-5899.12834.

Trabelsi, N.. 2021. "SpaceIL Raises $70 Million for Beresheet 2 Moonshot." Globes. https://en.globes.co.il/en/article-spaceil-raises-70m-for-beresheet-2-moonshot-1001377673.

UAE Government Portal. n.d. "Space Science and Technology." https://u.ae/en/about-the-uae/science-and-technology/key-sectors-in-science-and-technology/space-science-and-technology.

Waltz, K., 1979. *Theory of International Politics*, New York: McGraw-Hill.Wendt, A. 1999. *Social Theory of International Politics*. Cambridge: Cambridge University Press.

Zangl, B., F. Heußner, A. Kruck, and X. Lanzendörfer. 2016. "Imperfect Adaptation: How the WTO and the IMF Adjust to Shifting Power Distributions among Their Members." *The Review of International Organizations* 11, no. 2: 171–96. https://doi.org/10.1007/s11558-016-9246-z.

CHAPTER 24

MILITARY SPACE STRATEGIES AND AFRICAN REALISM

Egypt, South Africa, and Nigeria

SAMUEL OYEWOLE

INTRODUCTION

STUDIES on space strategies, and their military dimensions, are dominated by the experiences and perspectives of the leading space powers, some of which are covered in this volume, such as the United States, the Soviet Union/Russia, Europe (especially the United Kingdom, France, Italy, and Germany), Japan, China, and recently India, Israel, and few other countries (Al-Rodhan 2012; Bormann and Sheehan 2009; Bowen 2020; Burger and Bordacchini 2019; Dawson 2017; Hays 2011; Sadeh 2013; Schrogl 2015; Pekkanen 2022). Amid these, African experiences and perspectives on space strategies, and the military-security dimension particularly, are among the least heard in extant literature. This is considerably connected to the recency and marginality of space capabilities of the African countries in the global context and limited attention for the subject in the region.

Although the origin of modern space research and development in the continent can be traced to the eighteenth century, given some of the activities of visiting and settler scientists and engineers in South Africa, the first satellite owned and operated by an African state was only orbited in 1998, which was forty-one years into the space age (Dubow 2019; Oyewole 2022a). Despite the growing space policy priority and investment of African states in the last three decades, the continent accounted for less than 1 percent of the annual total of global space spending between 2018 and 2020 (Space in Africa 2021a). Africa equally owned or operated less than 1 percent of all recorded satellites ever orbited (UCS 2021). Without an inventory of orbital launcher/ship, long range missile, and other anti-satellite weapons, Africa and its leading powers have little or no capabilities that are required to conduct offensive or defensive operations in and through space.

Despite the forgoing, the growing potential and development of Africa in space and related security should not be ignored or underestimated. Although the region currently has limited capacity to operate in or through space, many African states have developed some capabilities to extract space support to advance their civil (research and development), commercial, and military interests. African governments and investors have established and operated close to a hundred ground facilities as well as co/sponsored and co/operated 57 satellites over the last 2 decades (Oyewole, 2023). Moreover, no fewer than 125 satellites that are expected to be launched before 2025 are in different stages of development across 23 African countries (Space in Africa 2021b). The continent spent more on space programs than Latin America, the Caribbean, and Oceania combined in both 2019 and 2020 (Space in Africa 2021a). The revenue of the space industry, which was made up of 283 companies in 31 countries, across the continent was also projected to rise from US$7.37 billion in 2019 to US$10.24 billion by 2024 (Space in Africa 2021b; 2021c).

It is against this background that relevant (human and material) resources and conversion capacities (institutions and programs) have been developed in Africa to gain space support for the development and security aspirations of the peoples and governments of the region. In most cases, African space strategies have been motivated by the desire to promote the socio-economic interests of the affected governments and populations. Accordingly, studies on space in Africa predominantly focus on space institutions, policies, programs, and resources and their contributions to national, regional and human development (Abiodun 2017; Froehlich 2019a; 2019b; Gottschalk 2010). The growing resort to space strategies in Africa is also motivated by human security (Adebola and Adebola 2015; Amusan and Oyewole 2022; Froehlich and Siebrits 2019; Oyewole 2017) and, in some cases, military security (Oyewole 2020a; Froehlich, Ringas, and Wilson 2020).

The objective of this chapter is to examine the development and rationales for military-security dimensions of space strategies of African states, and the implications. With that purpose in mind, this chapter interrogates African security realities and ideational values in the development and rationales for military space strategies and capabilities of Egypt, South Africa, and Nigeria. Accordingly, this chapter is further divided into four sections, following this introduction. The first section operationalizes the concept of military space strategies and contextualizes it in the framework of African realism. The second section examines the development of African space strategies, with emphasis on military dimension. The third section interrogates the development and rationales for the military space strategies in the aforementioned countries just before the concluding fourth section.

MILITARY SPACE STRATEGIES IN AFRICAN REALISM

Space strategy is a carefully designed and meticulously implemented plan to prioritize, sponsor, develop, manage, coordinate, and integrate disparate space activities across civil, commercial, and security sectors. Military space strategy is an aspect of space security strategies sponsored by the state and managed by the armed forces to advance national defense, security, and power projection (see Bowen 2020; Dawson 2017; Klein 2019; Mowthorpe 2004; Sadeh 2013; Wright 2020). It traditionally entails a program of action that is primarily designed to defend a state from external aggression and project its power in the international system. The purpose of such program can be further extended to support enforcement of internal law and order and management of disasters. Accordingly, military space strategy can be described as the development and acquisition of space capabilities by and/or for the armed forces and their application toward advancing defense, security, disaster management and power projection.

African realism is a proposed fusion of Africanism and realism as a theoretical framework to better understand the realities of the African international system, including the military-security of its space strategies. As shown in both this volume and extant literature, realism is a dominant theory in international relations (IR) and by extension the foremost framework of understanding space politics and policy and their military-security dimension (Dawson 2017; Goswami and Garretson 2020; Sadeh 2013; Sheehan 2007). Although this chapter acknowledges the unique position of realism in any attempt to understand the military-security dimension of space strategies, it cannot ignore the uniqueness of Africanism in understanding the regional context of the subject matter. Accordingly, this chapter observes that none of these perspectives can provide sufficient understanding of the realities of the African international system, and particularly the connectivity between space strategies and military-security in the continent, in their isolation.

Africanism is an anti/post-colonial perspective that emerged from African studies with the aim of researching and reconstructing the colonial bestowed narrative of the continent. This perspective considered realism and its positions on state-centrism, self-centered interest, self-help, struggle for survival and power, security dilemmas, and the anarchical international system as *unAfrican* (Ogunnubi and Oyewole 2020a). Africanism is largely cynical of a state-centric order, given that Africa's international system is made up of colonial imposed state structures, which remain alien and contested in many considerations. As such, many Africanists often prefer to support non-state actors, especially primordial publics and organizations as well as (local and regional) non-governmental and intergovernmental organizations, which are actively involved in cooperation, competition and/or conflict with the state (Cornelissen, Cheru, and Shaw 2015; Nnoli 2006).

The philosophical foundation of Africanism is built on the ideations of equality, justice, solidarity, brotherhood, collectivism, consensus, cooperation, regionalism, integration, and unity (Abegunrin 2009; Falola and Essien 2014). These are against realist notions of the state as a selfish actor in a struggle for survival, which is only guarantee with the pursuit of power that is bound to create a security dilemma, in IR. The Africanist framework further prioritizes human security above the military dominated security interest of the realists. Against this background, Africanism is the antithesis to space militarization and weaponization. Instead, it considers space as a frontier to advance African aspiration for scientific equality and justice, socio-economic development, and shared and collective benefits through solidarity, brotherhood, cooperation, and regionalism (Froehlich 2019a; 2019b; Gottschalk, Waswa, and Oyewole 2018; Oyewole 2022a; 2017).

Based on the foregoing, the military-security dimension of space strategies is only compatible with the principles of Africanism, when: (1) it is motivated by the desire to place Africa in a better position globally, that is, to close the research, development, and security gaps between the region and the rest of the world and enhance the dignity of its people; (2) it is organized on the bases of collectivism, solidarity, cooperation, and regionalism; (3) it produces shared benefits and promotes equality, welfare, and justice. However, while the civil space programs in Africa are increasingly driving close to these ideations, the military-security dimensions are far off. Although they can be argued to be enhancing the position of the region globally, military space programs in African are dominantly state based. Moreover, their contribution to the shared benefits, equality, welfare, justice, and dignity of the populations of the region is debatable.

Against this background, realism is required to understand the growing state-centric trend of military-security dimension of space strategies in Africa. However, realism has a tendency to overestimate the inherent statist, selfish, survival, power, and status driven aspects of African space strategies, while underestimating their strength for cooperation, solidarity, regionalism, and shared benefits. Equally, Africanism has a tendency to underestimate some realist aspects of African space strategies, while overestimating the ideational dimension. Accordingly, this chapter considers African realism, a proposition that combines elements of Africanism with realism, as a better and potentially balanced theoretical perspective to understand the subject.

African realism is premised on the assumption that Africa's IR feature a complex arrangement of cooperation, competition, and conflict between and among state and non-state actors that operate within and outside the territorial confines of the region. In this case, the interest of the state is to promote both development and security in human and state-centric terms, in a proportional arrangement that is sensitive to the unique need of concerned actors and the given context. This interest recognizes the importance of military and other aspects of national security as well as all the available frontiers to pursue them, without overemphasizing these in the general framework of state policy priorities. Moreover, the competition for power and occasional conflict among (leading) African states is mixed with genuine desire for regional leadership, emancipation, consensus, collectivism, and cooperation as well as solidarity, brotherhood, and support for one another (Adebajo 2006; 2010; Amusan and Oyewole 2017; Ogunnubi 2013; Oyewole and Ogunnubi 2020b; Oyewole 2020b; 2021a).

It is against this background that African realism assumes that space is a domain for African states to advance the development and security aspirations of their peoples and governments in cooperation, competition, and conflict between and among state and non-state actors that operate within and outside the territorial confines of the region. Inasmuch as Africanism promotes cooperation, realism promotes competition that can degenerate into conflict. Yet, conflict, especially among states, is often resolved before degenerating to armed conflict in the framework of African realism. Most armed conflicts are therefore between state and non-state forces. In this case, military power, and particularly the military-security dimension of space strategy is essential to maintain territorial integrity, suppress insurrection, protect lives and properties, defend critical infrastructure, manage disasters, and support fellow

African countries with inadequate capacities in crisis situations (Oyewole 2020b). The conception of the military-security dimension of space strategy in the framework of African realism is currently limited to space support for military and strategic operations that advance national and regional interests, which are defined as defense, security, and power projection (Oyewole 2020a; 2022a; Froehlich and Siebrits 2019; Froehlich, Ringas, and Wilson 2020; Gottschalk, Waswa, and Oyewole 2018).

AFRICAN SPACE STRATEGIES AND MILITARY-SECURITY BACKGROUND

The development of African space strategies traditionally has its origin in the art and practices of astrology, cosmology, and divining by pre-colonial African societies. Except in the case of Egypt, modern scientific space research and development in Africa took off during the colonial era. This was the case in South Africa, which has attracted European scientists and investments since the eighteenth century (Dubow 2019; Oyewole 2022a), and Algeria from 1890s. Despite the wave of independence between the 1940s and 1980s, Western powers pursued their space strategies with investment in civil and military infrastructure across the region, as evident in South Africa, Algeria, Nigeria, Kenya, DR Congo, and Libya (Froehlich and Siebrits 2019; Oyewole 2017). From the 1950s, the first wave of African space strategies emerged, which were mostly militarized with an emphasis on space, missile, and nuclear triad capabilities. As this chapter will show later, Egypt, South Africa, and later Libya were prominent players in this consideration, before domestic and international pressure affected their pursuits between the 1970s and early 2000s (Oyewole 2020a).

With enduring interests of and collaborations with foreign powers, the second wave of African space strategies emerged in the 1990s, with civil dominated programs. Since this period, Africa has witnessed an influx of Western dominated foreign civil/research and commercial space actors, which provide satellite services and start-up support for local capacity building. Non-Western powers, such as China, Russia, and India, have also influenced African space strategies. On these bases, Africa has developed civil and commercial dominated space programs, which feature some thirty space agencies, three hundred space companies, fifty-seven satellites, and over one hundred ground facilities as of early 2023 (Space in Africa 2021a; Froehlich and Siebrits 2019; Oyewole 2017; 2020a; 2023).

Since the 2010s, there has been a renewed trend of military-security interests and programs in African space strategies. At least some military space capabilities and strategies can be found in six African countries, notably Algeria, Egypt, Libya (until recently), Morocco, Nigeria, and South Africa. Although some of these countries had earlier pursued missile or launcher capabilities, with potential convertibility for offensive operation in space, African military space strategies and capabilities are predominantly passive and defensive: they are largely limited to extraction of space support for military operations and strategies in their immediate region. Accordingly, Table 24.1 shows African satellites, ground facilities, and related institutions, that were designed

Table 24.1. African Military Space Programs: Notable Assets, Institutions, Operations and Status

Countries	Military/Dual-use Satellites	Civilian Satellites: known/suspected to be used for military and strategic ends	Ground Facilities: for military space programs	Military Space Institutions	Known/Suspected Space Supported Military and Strategic Operations	Comments on Status of the Military Space Program
Algeria	None	AlSat-1 (2002–2010), Alsat-2A (2010), Alsat-1B (2016), Alsat-2B (2016), Alsat-1N (2016)	Rocket launch site, Hammaguir and Sounding rocket launch site, Béchar	Unspecified	Border monitoring with Morocco and Libya	No overt use, but capable of passive and defensive space support for military and strategic interests
Egypt	Tiba-1 (2019) EgyptSat-A (2019)	EgyptSat-1 (2007–2011) EgyptSat-2 (2014–2015); Nilesat 201 (2010) and Nilesat 301 (2022)	Ballistic missile test and launch facility, Jabal Hamzah	Unknown military command work closely with Egyptian Space Agency, and Nilesat	Communication and ISR for strategic decisions and military preparedness or operation in Mediterranean Sea, Red Sea, River Nile with emphasis on Ethiopian Dam, border with Israel and Libya, and against insurgents in Sinai and beyond.	Unfulfilled pursuit of defensive and possible offensive capabilities in space (in the 1960s); passive and defensive military space support (since 1970s), driven by internal and external strategic demands
Libya	–	–	Sounding rocket launch site, Tawiwa	–	–	Unfulfilled pursuit of potentially offensive space capabilities (until 2000s)

Morocco	Mohammed VI-A (2017), Mohammed VI-B (2018)	—	Military satellite control station, near Salé's airport, Rabat	Unspecified	ISR over Spain and Algeria, & Polisario Front	Passive and defensive military space support, driven by internal and external strategic ends
Nigeria	Delsat-1 (2023)	NigeriaSat-2 (2011), NigeriaSat-X (2011), Nigcomsat-1R (2011)	Defence Space Administration, Abuja and affiliated centers.	Defence Space Administration (2014) and affiliated centers; in collaboration with civil and commercial institutions	ISR and communication support in the wars against Boko Haram insurgents in the Lake Chad region; piracy in the Gulf of Guinea; armed bandits, smugglers and kidnappers across Nigeria; peacekeeping/ enforcement in Mali, Sudan, and Central Africa Republic, etc.	Passive and defensive military space support, driven by internal and external strategic demands
South Africa	Condor-E2 (2014)	ZaCube-2 (2018), MDASat-1 A, B and C constellation (2022), EOS-Sat-1 (2023)	Overberg Test Range, near Arniston	Department of Defence; Air Force; in collaboration with civil and commercial institutions	ISR for maritime and regional situation awareness and security, and peacekeeping, as evident in the DR Congo	Capable of offensive operation in space (1980s); passive and defensive military space support (since 1990s), driven by internal and external strategic demands

Source: Data extracted from Oyewole (2020a) with author's extension.

and employed for military or dual purposes, and associated operations in the last two decades.

Many other African countries have displayed an interest and potential to pursue military space strategies. Beyond the six countries that dominate the discussion of this section, over twenty other African countries have active civil space programs that could be employed or advanced for military purposes. Eight of these countries, namely Angola, DR Congo, Ethiopia, Ghana, Kenya, Rwanda, Sudan, Tunisia, Uganda, and Zimbabwe, have sponsored and operated at least a satellite. Amid these, Angola, DR Congo, Ethiopia, Kenya, and Sudan are leading African military powers that have the potential to pursue military space strategies for regional power and status. Equally, Ghana, Rwanda, and Tunisia as well as Cameroon, Cote D'Ivoire, Senegal, Uganda, and Zimbabwe have similar potential to boost their regional power, prestige, and status. Some of these countries have the potential to pursue a military space program as a strategic option to balance rival powers, manage internal security crises, and support military power projection.

EMPIRICAL EVIDENCE OF AFRICAN REALISM IN MILITARY SPACE STRATEGIES

This section takes a closer look at some of the military-security developments and strategies of three key countries noted in Table 24.1, namely Egypt, South Africa, and Nigeria.

Egypt

The military-dimension of Egyptian space strategy can be considered in two phases, which were born out of realism and cross-cutting idealism in national security and foreign affairs. The first phase is between the 1950s and 1970s. Following the rise of Israel and the defeat of the Arab forces in 1948, the Egyptian military led a successful political revolution in 1952 and subsequently pursued socio-economic transformation and military modernization. This period was shaped by the realism of the security dilemma in the Middle East, arising from Arab-Israeli conflict and East-West geopolitics, and Egypt's status as a regional power (Eilam, 2014; Kienle 2022; Springborg et al. 2021). The invasion of Egypt by Israel, France, and the United Kingdom in 1956 further heightened threats to the country's security (Hahn 1991). Moreover, multiple idealisms shaped Egypt's national interests during this period. Although pan-Arabism was prominent, non-alignment and pan-Africanism were also apparent. Egypt wanted to register Arab presence in space and add space to its credentials as a leading power in the Middle East, Africa, and the Third World. Its commitment to Africa was equally evident in its extensive military support and contributions to supplies and training of ground and air forces in Algeria, Libya, Nigeria, Somalia, and Sudan between the 1950s and 1960s (SIPRI 2021; Oyewole 2021).

Between the 1950s and 1970s, Egypt pursued a space strategy and other dimensions of power (air, land, sea, and nuclear capabilities) to boost its military effectiveness and international status. With the support of German engineers, Egypt built a single stage rocket with capacity range of 600 kilometers and 1,000 kilogram payload in 1963, and was developing an Explorer-type satellite of 5–10 kilogram and a 2 or 3 stage rocket to launch it into orbit in 1964–1965 (Pirards 1991). Although the satellite project was supposed to be a scientific instrument, the space program was generally driven by military and strategic interests. The rocket program was largely managed by the Missile Command of the Egyptian armed forces, which had 4,000 personnel in 1970 and was independent of the army and the air force. This program supported the development of 100 missiles as of 1970 (IISS 1965–1970). With the pace of its development in the 1960s, Egypt had the potential to develop satellite and missile capabilities for passive and active space militarization respectively. However, the 1960s and 1970s witnessed both internal and external dynamics that halted the pursuit and actualization of Egyptian military interests in space.

The pressure from Israel, the United States, and European powers forced Germany and other foreign partners to cease support for Egyptian space program in the 1960s. The defeat of Arab forces by Israel in the 1967 Six-Day War, the war of attrition between 1967 and 1970, and the Ramadan/Yom Kippur War of 1973 further undermined the country's military modernization, including space-related programs (Pirards 1991; Kienle 2022; Said 2004; Siniver 2013). Amid these, Egypt saw a regime change in 1970 and subsequently normalized relations with Western powers and embraced the diplomatic solutions that produced the 1979 peace treaty with Israel (Springborg et al. 2021). These de-escalated tensions in the region and deemphasized the military space program in the country. Accordingly, Egypt halted its then aggressive pursuit of space, missile, and nuclear weapons capabilities. This trend paved the way for the transition of Egypt's space strategy from military to socio-economic oriented interests.

Between the late 1970s and early 2000s, Egypt prioritized regional cooperation and socio-economic interests in space. It established a center for remote sensing in 1973 and the National Authority for Remote Sensing and Space Sciences (NARSS) in 1994. It became one of the formative members and a shareholder of the Arab Satellite Communications Organisation (Arabsat), which was established in 1976 and sponsored and operated twenty satellites between 1985 and 2019 (Oyewole 2020a). In 1989, Egypt also launched Nilesat, a public-private satellite communication company, which has since sponsored five satellites for telecommunications, including Nilesat-101 (1998), Nilesat-102 (2003), Nilesat-103 (2005), Nilesat-201 (2010), and Nilesat-301 (2022). However, the global war against terrorism re-militarized the post–Cold War order, changed the balance of power in the Middle East, and repurposed Arab countries to confront local and transnational threats (Kienle 2022; Springborg et al. 2021). This is critical for Egypt, as a US ally that has struggled with militant Islamist movements for decades, and as an Arab power in a turbulent regional order. Moreover, US intervention in the region further showcased the importance of space support in modern warfare and encouraged many countries to modernize their forces.

Military interest in space capabilities was renewed in Egypt in the early 2000s. The desire for a high-resolution satellite led Egypt to sponsor Egypt-Sat-1 and 2 (2007–2011 and 2014–2015) built by Ukraine and Russia respectively. Although these satellites were primarily managed by the NARSS, they provided services for the military and for government institutions (Shay 2015). In 2019, the Egyptian Space Agency (ESA) was established to coordinate disparate space research and development in the country. The same year, the orbital assets of the country was expanded with the addition of two locally built earth observatory (EO) satellites (NarssCube-1&2) for scientific demonstration and two dual-use satellites (Tiba-1 and EgyptSat-A). The EgyptSat-A (or MisrSat-2) is a US$100 million high-resolution EO satellite jointly developed by the NARSS and Russian engineers and launched by the latter on February 21, 2019, as a follow-up to and advancement on the failed EgyptSat-2 (Spacewatch Global 2019). In 2016, Egypt signed an arms deal worth US$1.2 billion with France, which includes US$300 million for a TIBA-1 satellite that was jointly built by Airbus Defence and Space (ADS) and Thales Alenia Space (TAS) for military and civil communications, and launched in October 2019 (Oyewole 2020a). Furthermore, Egypt's scientific demonstration EO satellites Horus 1&2 were launched in March 2023. The Egyptian military has also partnered with Nilesat for satellite supported communication.

Egyptian owned and operated satellites, among other space assets, have supported the military and strategic interests of the country in the insurgent-threatened Sinai Peninsula and beyond; in the blue economy and maritime governance in the Mediterranean Sea and beyond; along the River Nile with the contested Ethiopian Dam; in the Red Sea threatened by the Somali pirates; along the borders with Libya with transnational terrorism and other crimes; on the sensitive frontiers with Israel and Palestine; and for general regional situation awareness in Africa and the Middle East. These indicate the security realities that underscore the Egyptian passive military space strategy. However, these have not undermined Egyptian socio-economic and regional interests in space. Most space assets and activities in Egypt in the last two decades are under the control of civil and commercial entities, which the military silently work with to gain space supported command and control via computers, communications, intelligence, surveillance and reconnaissance (C4ISR). Moreover, in February 2019, Egypt won the bid to host the headquarters of the African Space Agency (ASA) and allocated US$10 million in support. These among others are indications of the level of Afrocentric realism in the Egyptian military space strategy.

South Africa

The military-security dimension of South Africa's space strategy can be examined in two phases, which are rooted in the realism and idealism of its national politics, security, and foreign policies. The first phase is between the 1950s and early 1990s. This period was shaped by the apartheid regime, a system of racial discrimination through which the majority of the population (Black Africans) were segregated and subjugated to the political and economic control of the White minority (Beinart and Dubow 1995; Guelke 2005). Moreover, the regime maintained a colonial grip over Namibia until 1990, supported the Portuguese colonial wars against African nationalist movements of 1960s and early 1970s, sponsored a puppet White minority regime in Rhodesia (now Zimbabwe) between 1965 and 1980, and intervened militarily in post-colonial African countries, prominently Angola and Mozambique between 1975 and 1990. Between the 1950s and early 1990s, the apartheid regime confronted the resistance of African nationalists internally and externally. The struggle also gained the support of post-colonial African states and other Third World Countries, the Soviet Union, Cuba, and the communist bloc (Anderson and Bell 2019; Jaster 1989). Hence, the military dimension of South Africa's space strategy until the early 1990s was motivated by the Afrikaners' racial conception of Africanism, with White minority domination of the Black majority, and the security realism of the apartheid regime (Oyewole 2022a).

The apartheid regime developed land, sea, air, space, and nuclear capabilities to advance its defense, security, power projection and international prestige. As of 1970, for instance, South Africa and Rhodesia had 240 and 48 combat aircraft respectively, when only 6 independent sub-Saharan African countries possessed such capabilities with an aggregate of 142 combat aircraft (IISS 1970). As of the late 1980s, the apartheid regime also developed 6 nuclear bombs, which no other African countries have developed (Albright and Stricker 2016; van Wyk 2014). In this context, South Africa pursued military space strategy. In 1963, South Africa banned civilian rocket flights, which started in 1947, and made it an exclusive military program. With the support of France and Israel, South Africa developed missile capabilities, which were also planned to advance orbital launch capabilities. As of the 1980s, South Africa developed intermediate range, single-stage ballistic missiles (known as RSA-1 and 2) with a warhead mass of 1,500 kilograms and trajectories of 1,100–1,900 kilometers. Prior to 1990, the regime was considering the development of a military satellite for ISR and RSA-3 missiles, a version of the Israeli Jerico-2 missile that was converted into the *Shavit* space launcher, with a similar conversion plan (Gottchalk 2010; Oyewole 2022a; van Wyk 2014). These had the potential to catapult South Africa into an active military space program before they were cancelled.

In the late 1980s and early 1990s, the apartheid regime came under local and international pressure, even from its allies in the West, to embrace multiracial democracy. This period witnessed a radical change in South Africa's national politics and defense, security, and foreign policies (Cock and Mckenzie 1998; Guelke 2005). The transitional rollback of racial-based socio-economic discrimination and segregation, dialogue with African nationalist movements, concessions in the form of state pardons for imprisoned nationalists, and inclusive governance all paved the way for the first multiracial election and a majoritarian democracy. This development was well received by post-colonial African states and their allies in the developing world, which transformed South Africa from their adversary to a friendly and sister nation. This period also marked the end of the Cold War and the collapse of the Soviet Union and communism. Accordingly, these social, political, and economic changes neutralized some of the leading threats to the internal and military security of South Africa. This development gave the transition and early post-apartheid regimes sufficient basis to demilitarize South Africa, as evidenced by the reduction in the defense budget, downsizing of the military, unilateral destruction of existing nuclear weapons and some essential capabilities to reproduce them, and cancellation of military space program (Albright and Stricker 2016; Oyewole 2022b; Stapleton 2010).

From the late 1990s, South Africa's scientific, foreign, security, and defense policies came in line with African realism. The post-apartheid regime saw the need to balance the development and security interests of South Africa, which is closely aligned with the interests of the region, which are designed and pursued in cooperation and competition with other nations (Cawthra 1997; Cock and Mckenzie 1998). Accordingly, South Africa's post-apartheid space strategy and its military dimension aim to unlock and advance national development potential, status, power capabilities, and prestige, as well as regional pride, leadership, innovation, and solutions. The operationalization of the strategy started with civil to commercial programs. In 1999, South Africa became the first African country to produce a satellite locally and the second after Egypt to own an orbital asset. The South African National Space Agency (SANSA) was established in 2010 to coordinate disparate space activities, which significantly involved state-owned centers, higher institutions, private entities, and non-governmental organizations (NGOs) (Oyewole 2022a). As of early 2023, South Africa has orbited twelve satellites, eleven of which were locally designed and developed by research institutions and spinoff companies with the support of the government, for technological demonstration, EO, agricultural support, and maritime situation awareness.

Post-apartheid South Africa's interests in a military space strategy started to gain momentum in 2005, leading to a secret deal with Russia in May 2006 for the design and development of a spy satellite for the country. The deal was uncovered in January 2014 and the satellite, Condor-E2, was launched in December of that year (Oyewole 2020a). This became an African first owned and operated reconnaissance satellite, which put the region on the global map of military space players. The internal and regional security demands of the country necessitated this project and associated military strategy. Military space capabilities are relevant to supporting South Africa's interests in the blue economy and maritime governance and security in the southwestern Indian Ocean, southeastern Atlantic Ocean, and Antarctic Ocean as well as in regional situation awareness, security strategies, and international peacekeeping. Accordingly, the South African military has benefited from space support in combating illegal, unreported, and unregulated (IUU) fishing, piracy, and other maritime crimes, as well as peacekeeping in Congo (Oyewole 2022a). Apart from Condor-E2, South African military and strategic planners have equally used satellite slots and data (such as SPOT 6 and 7) procured by the government from foreign commercial entities and locally produced satellites, such as ZaCub-2. Moreover, in January 2022, South Africa deployed a constellation of high-resolution nanosatellites for Maritime Domain Awareness, MDASat-1 A, B, and C (Campbell 2022).

South Africa's military space strategy has received mixed reactions from other leading African countries, as Egypt, Nigeria and Morocco have also stepped up their capabilities. However, all these countries maintained friendly relations and varying degrees of co-operation and commitment to regionalism, without conflicting military interests, in space. South Africa is one of the forty-five members of the Regional African Satellite Communication Organisation (RASCOM) that was established in 1992, and one of the sponsors of the African Resource Management (ARM) satellite constellation that was established in 2003. The country was instrumental to the involvement of African countries, such as Botswana, Ghana, Kenya, Madagascar, Mauritius, Mozambique, Namibia, and Zambia in the multinational Square Kilometre Array (SKA). It was a leading advocate of the African Very Long Baseline Interferometer Network (AVN), ASA and other regional space programs. Its multinational space companies operate across Africa, and its institutions and facilities are open to other Africans for training and capacity building (Oyewole 2022a). These, among others, are indications that the military-security dimension of South Africa's space strategy is pursued in alignment with its socio-economic interests in space, as well as the mutual enhancement of national competitiveness and regional cooperation.

Nigeria

The military-security dimension of Nigeria's space strategy is born out of its national politics, and foreign, defense, and security policies. The program started in 2010s, although its origin can be traced to 1970s, when Nigeria made a passionate advocacy for African nuclear and space programs without significant actions. Following the military intervention in 1966 and the subsequent thirty months of civil war that ended in 1970, Nigerian politics became militarized and its foreign policy was radically transformed to advance nationalist and Africanist agendas (Imobighe and Ali 2012; Osaghae 2011). Considered a regional power, Nigeria announced its space interest to other African countries in 1970, with the hope of registering the presence of the region in the global map of nuclear and space powers and responding to the regional threats of apartheid South Africa and neo/colonial forces (Abiodun 2017; Adeniji 2000; Akinyede and Boroffice 2013; Oyewole 2022a). Nevertheless, political instability and inadequate commitments and capabilities affected the actualization of this interest in the 1970s and 1980s.

From the mid-1990s, Nigeria began to actualize its interests in space with a civil program, starting with the establishment of the National Centre for Remote Sensing (NCRS) in 1995 and the National Space Research and Development Agency (NSRDA) in 1999. Ever since then, close to twenty new NSRDA and autonomous centers have been established in Nigeria to further advance different aspects of research and development for civil space program. The commercial program commenced with the establishment of state-owned Geo-Apps Plus Limited in 2003 and Nigeria Communication Satellite (NIGCOMSAT) Limited in 2004 (Abiodun 2017; Akinyede and Boroffice 2013; Oyewole

2022a). While civil and commercial interests are dominant in Nigeria's space strategy between the 1990s and 2000s, it has created room for military interests. Even without a coherent military space strategy, the Nigerian government and armed forces are not oblivious to the prospects of space support. The leadership role of the Nigerian military in regional peacekeeping and peace-enforcement operations in Liberia and Sierra Leone between the 1990s and early 2000s involved space-supported communication for command and control, as satellite devices shrank the distance between the foreign theatres and the home front (Adeshina 2002; Oyewole 2022a). Nevertheless, Nigeria's interests in and commitments to developing passive military space strategy only became clearly and coherently known to the public in 2014.

On October 9, 2014, Nigeria announced the establishment of the Defence Space Agency as an autonomous entity in the Ministry of Defence, which was later renamed the Defence Space Administration (DSA) by an act of parliament in 2016 and approved by the president on February 3, 2017. The institution has responsibility for developing and maintaining satellite inventories for military intelligence, surveillance and reconnaissance (ISR), communication and navigation, orbital launch capabilities, and cyber operations, among others. Affiliated to the DSA are the Space Innovation and Development Centre (SIDC), Defence Earth Observation Centre (DEOC), Defence Satellite Communication Centre (DSCC), Defence Cyber Operation Centre (DCOC), and Defence Space School (FRN, 2016). However, not all of these centers have become fully operational. More than five years after its formation, therefore, the DSA remains considerably dependent on state-owned civil and commercial space entities, despite its growing capacity and capabilities. The institution is running on a low budget by global standards, having only received approximately US$45 million in budget allocations between 2017 and 2021 (Oyewole 2022a). Although this is impressive by African standards, the funding is lower than the known investment made by South Africa, Egypt, and Morocco on military and dual-use space capabilities, especially high-resolution and/or radar satellites, with little or no known formal institutional framework.

Nigeria became the first African country to institutionalize its military space program with establishment of DSA in 2014. This development coincided with the publicity of the covertly developed and the eventual launch of South African military satellite in the same year. Some observers are already concerned that Africa is heading for space race, and this may be taking a military dimension (Gottschalk, Waswa, and Oyewole 2018; Oyewole 2020a). As of early 2022, however, no other African country has established a definite and publicly known institutional framework for the military-security dimension of space strategy. Nevertheless, if the trend in African civil space strategies is anything go by, more countries in the region are expected to establish dedicated military institutions for this purpose in the near future. In 1999, when Nigeria established the NSRDA to coordinate its disparate civil space programs, it was the first African agency of its kind. Similar agencies were established by Algeria (2002), South Africa (2010), Kenya (2017), Egypt (2019), Rwanda (2020), and many more countries thereafter. These are indications of the competitive nature of African space strategies, which have not necessarily undermined the desire for cooperation or fueled major confrontation and conflict among space nations in the region.

Beyond status and prestige, the military dimension of Nigeria's space strategy was born out of the security realities of the country. The protracted campaign of terror by Boko Haram in Nigeria and its neighbors in the Lake Chad region was at its peak in 2014 and 2015, when it was recognized as the deadliest terrorist group globally. The group made global headlines and attracted condemnation from across the world following the abduction of 276 female students in north-eastern Nigeria in 2014. It started the territorial conquest of the Lake Chad region in 2012, declared an Islamic Caliphate with headquarters in Gwoza in August 2014, and was in control of 20,000 square miles of Nigerian territory, which spread across 23 Local Government Areas (LGAs) in Adamawa, Borno, and Yobe states as of early 2015. As of 2020, the crisis was reported to have resulted in the death of more than 200,000 people, while approximately 100,000 were kidnapped or missing, over 2 million were displaced, and property worth 2 trillion naira was destroyed (Oriola, Onuoha, and Oyewole 2021). In response, Nigeria deployed 3,000 troops into the troubled region in 2011, and raised their strength to 8,000 in 2013, 20,000 in 2014, 25,000 in 2015 and 50,000 in 2017, with significant decline in the campaign of terror, recovery of lost territory and hostages, and stabilization of the region since 2016 (Onuoha and Oyewole 2018). Nigeria is also faced with other security challenges, such as armed banditry, kidnapping, smuggling, and maritime piracy, as well as demands on its military contribution to hegemonic stability in Africa. These among others have compelled Nigeria to improve its military capabilities, including the space component.

Until 2023, when the first Nigerian military satellite Delsat-1 was launched, it has employed the country's civil and commercial space assets to advance tactical and strategic interests through space supported ISR and communication. Nigeria had earlier sponsored six satellites: two for communication, two for EO, and two for technological demonstration. In addition, Nigeria is currently funding the development of no fewer than five satellites, including two for communication and three high-resolution ones for EO, one of which is planned for technological demonstration (Oyewole 2022a). In 2023, the military has also announced plan to launch four more satellites to create a constellation of five satellites to be utilized for military reconnaissance purposes (Oyewole, 2023). The Nigerian government and military also receive space support from foreign commercial service providers and partners or friendly countries, including positioning and navigation satellites. In 2016, the Nigerian Air Force (NAF) initiated a research and development collaboration with the NSRDA and the DSA to produce guided missiles, which has been inducted into the service to boost the force's air power.

Nigeria's space capabilities have been utilized to various degrees to support military campaigns against Boko Haram and other Islamist insurgencies in the Lake Chad region, maritime robbery and piracy in the Gulf of Guinea, armed banditry in the northern region, smuggling along the borders, and kidnapping across the country, as well as regional peacekeeping and enforcement operations in Mali, Sudan, and the Central Africa Republic, among others. In this manner, space strategy has featured in advancing the military-security dimension of Nigeria's national and regional interests.

Nigerian satellite imagery and communications have considerably supported military and strategic planning and responses to insurrections, transnational threats, and natural disasters within and outside the country. These have contributed to Nigeria's status, competitiveness, and power projection, especially in Africa, without undermining the socio-economic interests of the country, and the desire for cooperation and regionalism in space.

Nigeria has considerably balanced its commitments to Africanism with its security realities. It managed to support Guinea-Bissau, Liberia, Mali, Niger, and Sudan militarily, and in some cases with space capabilities, even with its challenging internal security situation. Nigeria's support for cooperation and regionalism is also evident in its membership of RASCOM and sponsorship of the ARM satellite constellation. Its advocacy for ASA was also backed by an unsuccessful bid to host its headquarters, which was won by Egypt. Nigeria has hosted, managed, and sponsored the African Regional Centre for Space Science and Technology Education-English (ARCSSTE-E) for the United Nations Office of Outer Space Affairs (UNOOSA) since 1998 and the Institute of Space Science and Engineering (ISSE) for the African University of Science and Technology (AUST) since 2015. Nigeria has also provided free satellite imagery to support early warning and disaster management to many countries in Africa and beyond in the last two decades (Oyewole 2022a). These among others are indications of cooperation among competition, as expected of the military-security dimension of space strategy in the framework of African realism.

CONCLUSION

Africa investment in space has grown in the last twenty-five years, reflecting its increasing priority by countries in the region. Although civil and commercial dimensions have dominated the landscape of African space programs, the military dimension is also becoming increasingly noticeable. While active military space programs in the continent remain largely limited in quality and quantity, especially on the global scale, a growing number of African countries have the potential to purse a passive military space strategy. This also means that the space capabilities and utilities of these countries are likely to improve with time. These have the potential to contribute to the strategic capabilities, military operational efficacy, power and status, regional brotherhood/cooperation, and hegemonic currency of African countries. These have made African realism a considerable framework of understanding this emerging regional trend.

As evident with the selected cases in this chapter, the desire for a military space strategy to improve strategic capabilities, operational efficiency, international status, regional leadership, and competitiveness among African states has not undermined their desire for collaboration, regionalism, and brotherhood. However, more African countries may develop interests in military space strategy, which may create a more competitive situation. Other potential candidates for military space interests and capabilities in Africa are Angola, DR Congo, Ethiopia, Ghana, Kenya, Rwanda, Sudan, Tunisia, Uganda, and Zimbabwe with at least a satellite in orbit. Equally, Cameroon, Cote D'Ivoire, and Senegal, have the potential to join the list. In any case, Africanist desire for brotherhood, cooperation, and regionalism will continue to balance and crisscross realist desire for competition, power, status, and national interest as a driving force in African and by extension space politics.

Yet, there are concerns that military space strategies can undermine civil and commercial dimensions of space programs, affecting their research and development potential and transparency, international support, human rights, democracy, regional cooperation, and peace in Africa. Accordingly, effective and transparent management of military interests, capabilities, and utilities in African space strategies are essential to enhance peace, security, and development prospects in the region.

REFERENCES

Abegunrin, Olayiwola. 2009. *Africa in Global Politics in the Twenty-First Century: A Pan African Perspective*. London: Palgrave Macmillan.

Abiodun, Adigun Ade. 2017. *Nigeria's Space Journey: Understanding Its Past, Reshaping Its Future*. Abuja: African Space Foundation.

Adebajo, Adekeye. 2006. *Prophets of Africa's Renaissance: Nigeria and South Africa as Regional Hegemons*. Lagos: Nigerian Institute of International Affairs.

Adebajo, Adekeye. 2010. *The Curse of Berlin: Africa after the Cold War*. Scottsville: University of KwaZulu-Natal Press.

Adebola, Olufunke, and Simon Adebola. 2015. "Space-Enabled Systems for Food Security in Africa." In *Handbook of Space Security: Policies, Applications and Programs*, edited by Kai-Uwe Schrogl et al., 759–78. New York: Springer.

Adeniji, O. 2000. *Essays on Nigerian Foreign Policy Governance and International Security*. Ibadan, Nigeria: Dokun Publishing House.

Adeshina, R. A. 2002. *The Reversed Victory: The Story of Nigerian Military Intervention in Sierra Leone*. Ibadan, Nigeria: Heinemann Educational Books.

Akinyede, J. O., and R. A. Boroffice. 2013. *Nigeria's Quest in Space*. Ile-Ife, Nigeria: Obafemi Awolowo University Press.

Albright, David, and Andrea Stricker. 2016. *Revisiting South Africa's Nuclear Weapons Program: Its History, Dismantlement, and Lessons for Today*. Washington, DC: Institute for Science and International Security (ISIS) Press.

Al-Rodhan, Nayef R. F. 2012. *Meta-geopolitics of Outer Space: An Analysis of Space Power, Security and Governance*. London; New York: Palgrave Macmillan.

Amusan, Lere, and Samuel Oyewole. 2017. "The Quest for Hegemony and the Future of African Solutions to African Development Problems: Lessons from Headways in African Security Sector." *Journal of Asian and African Studies* 52, no. 1: 21–33.

Amusan, Lere, and Samuel Oyewole. 2022. "Precision Agriculture and the Prospects of Space Strategy for Food Security in Africa." *African Journal of Science, Technology, Innovation and Development*. DOI: 10.1080/20421338.2022.2090224.

Anderson, Noel, and Mark S. Bell. 2019. "The Limits of Regional Power: South Africa's Security Strategy, 1975–1989." *Journal of Strategic Studies*. DOI: 10.1080/01402390.2019.1695123.

Beinart, William, and Saul Dubow, eds. 1995. *Segregation and Apartheid in Twentieth-Century South Africa*. London; New York: Routledge.

Bormann, Natalie, and Michael Sheehan, eds. 2009. *Securing Outer Space*. London; New York: Routledge.

Bowen, Bleddyn E. 2020. *War in Space: Strategy, Spacepower, Geopolitics*. Edinburgh: Edinburgh University Press Ltd.

Burger, Edward, and Giulia Bordacchini, eds. 2019. *Yearbook on Space Policy 2017: Security in Outer Space: Rising Stakes for Civilian Space Programs*. Geneva: Springer.

Campbell, Rebecca. 2022. South Africa Has Just Deployed Its First Truly Operational Satellites. *Engineering News*. February 4, 2022.

Cawthra, Gavin. 1997. *Securing South Africa's Democracy: Defence, Development, and Security in Transition*. London: Macmillan Press Ltd.

Cock, Jacklyn, and Penny Mckenzie, eds. 1998. *From Defence to Development: Redirecting Military Resources in South Africa*. Claremont, South Africa: David Philip Publishers (Pty) Ltd.

Cornelissen, Scarlett, Fantu Cheru, and Timothy Shaw, eds. 2015. *Africa and International Relations in the 21st Century*. New York: Palgrave Macmillan

Dawson, Linda. 2017. *The Politics and Perils of Space Exploration Who Will Compete, Who Will Dominate?* Cham, Switzerland: Springer.

Dubow, S. 2019. "200 Years of Astronomy in South Africa: From the Royal Observatory to the 'Big Bang' of the Square Kilometre Array." *Journal of Southern African Studies*. 45, no. 4: 663–87.

Eilam, Ehud. 2014. *The Next War between Israel and Egypt: Examining a High-intensity War between Two of the Strongest Militaries in the Middle East*. London: Vallentine Mitchell.

Falola, Toyin, and Kwame Essien, eds. 2014. *Pan-Africanism, and the Politics of African Citizenship and Identity*. New York: Routledge.

FRN (Federal Republic of Nigeria). 2016. *Defence Space Administration Act, 2016*. Abuja: FRN.

Froehlich, Annette, ed. 2019a. *Embedding Space in African Society: The United Nations Sustainable Development Goals 2030 Supported by Space Applications*. Cham, Switzerland: Springer.

Froehlich, Annette, ed. 2019b. *Integrated Space for African Society: Legal and Policy Implementation of Space in African Countries*. Cham, Switzerland: Springer.

Froehlich, Annette, and A. Siebrits. 2019. *Space Supporting Africa: A Primary Needs Approach and Africa's Emerging Space Middle Powers*. Cham, Switzerland: Springer.

Froehlich, Annette, Nicolas Ringas, and James Wilson. 2020. *Space Supporting Africa*. Vol. 3. *Security, Peace, and Development through Efficient Governance Supported by Space Applications*. Cham, Switzerland: Springer.

Goswami, Namrata, and Peter A. Garretson, 2020. *Scramble for the Skies: The Great Power Competition to Control the Resources of Outer Space*. Lanham, MD: Lexington Books.

Gottschalk, Keith. 2010. "South Africa's Space Program." *Astropolitics* 8, no. 1: 35–48.

Gottschalk, Keith, Peter Waswa, and Samuel Oyewole. 2018. "The African Space Race." *Filling Space*. September 28, 2018.

Guelke, Adrian. 2005. *Rethinking the Rise and Fall of Apartheid: South Africa and World Politics*. New York: Palgrave Macmillan.

Hahn, Peter L. 1991. *The United States, Great Britain, and Egypt, 1945–1956: Strategy and Diplomacy in the Early Cold War*. Chapel Hill: University of North Carolina Press.

IISS. 1965–1970. *Military Balance*. London: IISS (International Institute of Strategic Studies).

Imobighe, T. A., and W. O. Ali, eds. 2012. *Perspectives on Nigeria's National and External Relations*. Ibadan, Nigeria: University Press.

Jaster, Robert Scott. 1989. *The Defence of White Power: South Africa's Foreign Policy under Pressure*. New York: Palgrave Macmillan.

Kienle, Eberhard. 2022. *Egypt: A Fragile Power*. New York: Routledge.

Klein, John J., 2019. *Understanding Space Strategy: The Art of War in Space*. New York: Routledge.

Mowthorpe, Matthew. 2004. *The Militarization and Weaponization of Space*. Lanham, MD: Lexington Books.

Nnoli, Okwudiba. 2006. *National Security in Africa: A Radical New Perspective*. Enugu, Nigeria: Pan African Centre for Research on Peace and Conflict Resolution (PACREP).

Ogunnubi, Olusola. 2013. "Hegemonic Order and Regional Stability in sub-Saharan Africa: A Comparative Study of Nigeria and South Africa." PhD Diss., University of KwaZulu-Natal, South Africa.

Ogunnubi, Olusola, and Samuel Oyewole, 2020. "Africanism, Power Politics and International Relations in Africa." In *Power Politics in Africa: Nigeria and South Africa in Comparative Perspective*, edited by Olusola Ogunnubi and Samuel Oyewole, 1–7. Newcastle, UK: Cambridge Scholars Publishing.

Onuoha, Freedom, and Samuel Oyewole. 2018. *Anatomy of Boko Haram: The Rise and Decline of a Violent Group in Nigeria*. Doha, Qatar: Al Jazeera Centre for Studies.

Oriola, Temitope, Freedom C. Onuoha, and Samuel Oyewole, eds. 2021. *Boko Haram's Campaign of Terror in Nigeria: Contexts, Dimensions and Emerging Trajectories*. London: Routledge.

Osaghae, Eghosa. 2011. *The Crippled Giant: Nigeria since Independence*. Ibadan, Nigeria: John Archers Ltd.

Oyewole, Samuel. 2017. "Space Research and Development in Africa." *Astropolitics* 15, no. 2: 185–208.

Oyewole, Samuel. 2020a. "The Quest for Space Capabilities and Military Security in Africa." *South African Journal of International Affairs* 27, no. 2: 147–72.

Oyewole, Samuel. 2020b. "Military Capabilities of Regional Powers in Africa: Nigeria and South Africa in Comparative Perspective." In *Power Politics in Africa: Nigeria and South Africa in Comparative Perspective*, edited by Olusola Ogunnubi and Samuel Oyewole, 57–85. Newcastle, UK: Cambridge Scholars Publishing.

Oyewole, Samuel. 2021. "Air Power Capabilities and Applications of African Regional Powers." Presentation at the (British) Royal Air Force Museum Conference on New Thinking in Air Power, September 16.

Oyewole, Samuel. 2022a. "Assessing the Contribution of Space Policy to Development and Security in Nigeria and South Africa." PhD Diss., Department of Political Studies and International Relations, North-West University, South Africa.

Oyewole, Samuel. 2022b. "Defence and Security Policy of South Africa." In *Readings in Defence, Security and Strategic Studies*, edited by Freedom C. Onuoha, Gerald E. Ezirim, and Chris M. A. Kwaja, 124–135. Nsukka: University of Nigeria Press.

Oyewole, Samuel. 2023. "The African Orbital Journey in Space Age: From Spectator to Participant." *Vanguardia Dossier* 88, no. 15: 72–75.

Oyewole, Samuel, and Olusola Ogunnubi. 2020. "Concluding Thought: An Afrocentric Perspective on Regionalism, Hegemony and Geopolitics." In *Power Politics in Africa: Nigeria and South Africa in Comparative Perspective*, edited by Olusola Ogunnubi and Samuel Oyewole, 254–62. Newcastle, UK: Cambridge Scholars Publishing.

Pekkanen, Saadia M. 2022. "Neoclassical Realism in Japan's Space Security." In *The Oxford Handbook of Japanese Politics*, edited by Robert J. Pekkanen and Saadia M. Pekkanen, 763–90. New York: Oxford University Press.

Pirards, Theo. 1991. "German Rockets in Africa: The Explosive Heritage of Peenemunde." *Acta Astronautica* 40, no. 12: 885–98.

Sadeh, Eligar, ed. 2013. *Space Strategy in the 21st Century*. New York: Routledge.

Said, Rushdi. 2004. *Science and Politics in Egypt: A Life's Journey*. Cairo: The American University in Cairo Press.

Schrogl, Kai-Uwe et al., eds. 2015. *Handbook of Space Security: Policies, Applications and Programs*. New York: Springer.

Shay, Shaul. 2015. Egypt Wishes to Join the "Space Club." *Israel Defense*. December 23, 2015.

Sheehan, Michael. 2007. *The International Politics of Space*. New York: Routledge.

Siniver, Asaf (ed). 2013. *The Yom Kippur War: Politics, Legacy, Diplomacy*. New York: Oxford University Press.

SIPRI. 2021. SIPRI Arms Transfers Database. http://www.sipri.org/contents/armstrad/at_data.html.

Space in Africa. 2021a. March. "Global Space Budget: A Country-Level Analysis." Lagos.

Space in Africa. 2021b. July 6. "African Space Industry Revenue to Surpass USD 10.24 billion by 2024 Despite Covid-19 Setback."

Space in Africa. 2021c. July 20. "A Review of 283 Upstream and Downstream Companies in the African Space and Satellite Industry."

Spacewatch Global. 2019. "Egypt's EgyptsatA Successfully Launched by Russia Despite Slight Launch Issue.

Springborg, Robert, Amr Adly, Anthony Gorman, Tamir Moustafa, Aisha Saad, Naomi Sakr, and Sarah Smierciak, eds. 2021. *Routledge Handbook on Contemporary Egypt*. New York: Routledge.

Stapleton, Timothy J. 2010. *A Military History of South Africa: From the Dutch-Khoi Wars to the End of Apartheid*. Santa Barbara, CA: Praeger.

UCS (Union of Concerned Scientists). 2021. Satellite Database. https://www.ucsusa.org/resources/satellite-database.

van Wyk, Jo-Ansie. 2014a. "Apartheid South Africa's Nuclear Weapons Program and Its Impact on Southern Africa." *Austral: Brazilian Journal of Strategy & International Relations* 3, no. 6: 119–40.

Wright, John C. 2020. *Deep Space Warfare: Military Strategy Beyond Orbit*. Jefferson: McFarland & Company.

CHAPTER 25

SPACE SECURITY FROM LATIN AMERICAN PERSPECTIVES

OLAVO DE O. BITTENCOURT NETO AND
JAIRO BECERRA

REGIONAL ASSESSMENTS

STATES consider space security concerns based on their national interests. Due to diverse factors such as geography, culture, economy, and technological advancements, regional partners usually share common perspectives. To emerging spacefaring nations such as those of Latin America, space security has particular relevance, since they tend to over rely on a small selection of space assets. Such limited space infrastructure is of relevance to the economic, political, and social development of nations of the region. Consequently, strategic decisions related to space activities are approached by Latin American governments with regard to secure and sustainable access to outer space.

Latin America was first recognized as a regional block in the mid-nineteenth century, during the international conference "Initiative of America: Idea for a Federal Congress of the Republics." Since then, several relevant cooperative initiatives have been undertaken by those nations, through a wide scope of agreements and institutions (Lambert 1979). Today, Latin America comprises 20 sovereign nations and 14 dependent territories in South, Central, and North America and the Caribbean, encompassing a vast region of approximately 19,197,000 km² home to more than 652 million people. Nations therein share cultural and historical links, including a colonial past, mostly of Portuguese, Spanish, and French origin (Williamson 2009).

As we discuss in this chapter, despite its local particularities and different economic development levels, Latin American people share a similar history and a joint future (Prado and Pellegrino 2021). Common expectations and demands are experienced by

Latin American nations, as far as space activities are concerned, in their pursuit of sustainable development. Similar burdens are generally faced in that regard, including budget constraints and limited access to strategic technology due to trade barriers. Space activities remain in large part quite expensive, and access to related technology is often the subject of political and legal constraints by major spacefaring nations. Therefore, international space cooperation has been recognized in Latin America as an important tool to secure access to space-related services and data.

MULTIFACETED VIEWS ON SPACE SECURITY

Space services are managed to address Latin American demands, supporting local policies and regulatory initiatives. Throughout the region, space infrastructure is imperative for providing strategic data for economic activities, land occupation, weather observation, frontier monitoring, and environmental protection. Additionally, space capabilities interconnect business and people in an area of dissimilar human occupation. Therefore, considerations of space security are certain to influence policymakers throughout the region on regulatory and cooperative initiatives (Winter 2007).

As far as space security is concerned, Latin America represents an important regional example with regard to related efforts by emerging spacefaring nations. Although a shared vision on space security is still being developed in the region, it is reasonable to argue that the secure and sustainable access to and use of outer space is of relevance to the whole international community.

Due to the inherent relevance of space activities to the sustainable development of every Latin American nation, space security is increasingly being acknowledged as a relevant topic in domestic and international agendas. While addressing space security in Brazil, José Monserrat Filho, one of Latin America's most renowned space policy experts, asserted that it is "more advisable, useful, and forward-looking to define space security not according to the interest of only one or some individual countries but according to the interests of all countries, of all the international community, and of all humankind. In the century of the greatest challenges to the survival of [the] human species and our common planet, this seems to be the most effective, fair, and responsible approach to space security" (Monserrat Filho 2015). Such a broad perspective on space security can be observed throughout Latin America, in general terms.

Latin American space initiatives have been intrinsically linked with the progress of space exploration at a global level. In the early days of the space age, the region absorbed Cold War considerations in relation to the exploration and use of outer space, within the so-called space race involving the global superpowers the United States and the USSR. The constant evolution of space technology and the slow but certain development of an important space economy would later play a relevant part in the different national space policies throughout the region. Nowadays, global power dynamics can be felt

throughout the region, with increasing participation of China in international cooperation agreements.

US influence in Latin America since World War II cannot be ignored, due to its significant impact on shaping strategic policies throughout the region for a wide range of
topics. Nevertheless, it is worth considering the impact of the Non-Aligned Movement
(NAM) (Colombia 2022), which includes twenty-seven Latin American and Caribbean
nations (Waybackmachine 2022). Such movements shaped and molded a general
policy of regional independence based on neutrality, thus leading to space security
considerations related to access to space, access to space data, or claims over the geostationary orbit segment by certain equatorial states.

Consequently, Latin American perspectives regarding space security have reflected,
in general, broad concerns over a certain set of issues: freedom of outer space; peaceful
exploration and use of outer space; and access to strategic satellite-based services, most
importantly those related to telecommunication, remote sensing, and data transfer and
processing. In the opinion of the nations of the region, those areas of concern should be
addressed by a fair and inclusive international framework.

ENGAGEMENT IN INTERNATIONAL AND REGIONAL ORGANIZATIONS

Latin American nations have participated actively in legal and political space-related
multilateral forums such as the United Nations (UN) Committee on the Peaceful Uses
of Outer Space (COPUOS), where they have defended their local interests. As early as
1963, the Brazilian delegate Geraldo de Carvalho acted as the committee's rapporteur,
collaborating with the drafting of the Declaration of Legal Principles Governing the
Activities of States in the Exploration and Use of Outer Space (United Nations 1963).
Even then, at the beginning of the space age, a time when international debate was in-
tensively driven by the geopolitical clash between the United States and the USSR, the
major Latin American considerations regarding space security were already being
presented to the global audience in a consistent manner.

Since those earlier COPUOS sessions, Latin American participation therein has
only increased. Argentina, Brazil, and Mexico took part of its first meeting, when it was
still an ad hoc committee. Chile and Venezuela joined in 1963. Colombia and Ecuador
would only become members in 1977, due to their national claims over the segments
of geostationary orbit above their territories. This was a major concern for those nations for decades, combined with access to outer space. Uruguay joined in 1980. Cuba,
Nicaragua, and Peru became members in 1994, just before enactment of the 1996
Declaration on International Cooperation in the Exploration and Use of Outer Space
for the Benefit and in the Interest of All States, Taking into Particular Consideration
the Needs of Developing Nations. Bolivia finally joined in 2007, during a new wave of

space development in the region, supported by an ideological position of certain states regarding the need to safeguard independent access to outer space. Costa Rica joined in 2012, Paraguay in 2018, Dominican Republic in 2019, and Panama in 2021, reflecting their recent space activities (United Nations 2022). Therefore, COPUOS is marked by diplomatic representation from Latin American countries, which have participated consistently in international debates regarding peaceful exploration and use of outer space.

Bender (1995) addressed, in an appropriate synthesis, Latin American strategic policy perspectives since 1945 based on those nations' capacity to generate technological development and to promote its interests in the international level, including access to and use of outer space. The author considered that major global actors, by classifying Latin American nations as "less developed States and developing States," could imply a differentiation with respect to their competencies and rights over their national territories. Accordingly, it might be considered that the most vulnerable nations would suffer a greater burden in protecting their own interests, while those more developed could participate on a more equal footing vis-à-vis spacefaring nations. As Bender notes "It must be remembered that although the terms Less Developing Countries and Developing Countries have been used to suggest two distinct groups of competition, this characterization is far from accurate" (253). This complex scenario has influenced the region's policies regarding space activities and their applications, and consequently the Latin American relationship with space security.

Broadly speaking, local considerations have been marked by concerns regarding autonomy in space technology, access to strategic space services, and active participation in multilateral forums to support their national interests.

In that regard, reference should be made to a major legal and political concern supported since the 1970s by certain Latin American nations, notably Colombia and Ecuador, regarding sovereignty over geostationary segments above their national territory. Their position denounced a growing interest over the use of outer space, as shared by many developing nations, which did not have the capabilities or economic and technical resources to promote advanced space activities. The general fear was that Latin American countries could be losing their technological and legal opportunity to claim and assure possible sovereign rights over outer space in relation to the major spacefaring nations, thus being neglected in the space arena (Becerra 2014). An intense diplomatic campaign in favor of this position thus ensued in the 1970s and 1980s, not only at the UN but also in bilateral relations throughout the Latin American region, producing a relevant impact in the discussions on the uses of outer space. Although such a claim would eventually fail to be recognized internationally, it serves to prove how nations such as Colombia have been active and concerned about multilateral discussions involving outer space since the early stages.

The development of technological capacities to perform strategic space activities is an important Latin American space security worry, one which has led to many instances of international cooperation. Partnerships with major spacefaring nations have always been recognized as means to an end, thus providing access by Latin American nations to sensitive technology. Reference should be made to the development by the United

States of their rural satellite program in 1980, which was conceived by the US Agency for International Development (USAID) to provide necessary capabilities in the field of satellite communications for developing nations. The initiative favored the development of a trusting environment among Latin American nations regarding benefits from international cooperation on remote sensing, without abandoning their national goal of securing autonomous access to outer space (Weerakoon 1990).

Nowadays, remote sensing technology is of major relevance to Latin American nations, as recognized by the UN Food and Agriculture Organization (FAO): "much of the sustainable future of Latin America and the Caribbean depends on the recovery and protection of their forests, the recovery of habitats, the restoration of the land and the sustainable use of those resources that have not yet been degraded" (Durango et al. 2019, 31).

The UN Economic Commission for Latin America and the Caribbean (ECLAC/CEPAL) has for decades sought to promote space development in the region. Accordingly, it has helped to organize multilateral meetings at the regional level to promote space capabilities, such as the Fourth Plenary Meeting of Latin American Remote Sensing Specialists, held in Santiago, Chile in 1984.

ECLAC/CEPAL also contributed to the organization of a space experts' meeting in Argentina in 1985, with the support of the Organization of American States (OAS), where the following reports were presented: "Telecommunications through Satellites: A Sphere of Horizontal Cooperation in the Peaceful Uses of Outer Space" and "Intergovernmental and Non-governmental Scientific Bodies, Global and Regional" (United Nations 1986). The event contributed to the establishment of a fundamental basis for deeper regional space collaboration.

Another early space cooperative endeavor occurred in 1986, when Intelsat launched the Project Share program as a preliminary experiment to provide space-related basic knowledge to developing countries (Weerakoon 1990). The project attested, with its great reception in Latin America, a growing interest from developing nations in obtaining autonomous capabilities to conduct their local space projects.

International space cooperation initiatives may also be identified in different instances, such as Latin American participation in the verification of the Strategic Arms Limitation Talks (SALT) agreements (Center for Nonproliferation Studies 1972), regarding nuclear weapons limitations. Indeed, reference should be made to the initiative of non-aligned nations (Ministerio de Relaciones Exteriores 2022), an international grouping which the vast majority of Latin American nations were part of and which provided third party verification of such agreements.

Additionally, Latin America has maintained an active participation regarding debates on effective measures for the prevention of an arms race in outer space at the UN Conference on Disarmament, in Geneva. An ad hoc committee was established therein in 1985, to identify and examine relevant issues such as legal protection of satellites, nuclear power systems in space, and various confidence-building measures. In 2017, the UN created a Group of Governmental Experts to consider and make recommendations on substantial elements of an international legally binding instrument on the prevention of an arms race in outer space (Resolution A/RES/72/250). Experts from Latin America participated in the discussions, representing Argentina, Brazil, and Chile. At its first meeting, the group selected as its chair the Brazilian Ambassador Guilherme de Aguiar Patriota. A final report came out in 2019, examining also the Latin American positions toward the maintenance of international peace and security and preserving conditions for international cooperation in the peaceful exploration and use of outer space (United Nations 2019).

Regarding the international legal framework concerning the peaceful exploration and use of outer space, Latin American nations have recorded relevant contributions, as attested by different regulatory proposals included in UN international instruments (Jasentuliyana 1999). Since the early stages of the space age, regional players have been engaged in space activities, promoting benefits not only locally but also globally, and incorporating the perspectives of less developed countries. These themes have influenced Latin American participation in the development of legal instruments related to space security, including the recently approved COPUOS Guidelines for the Long-term Sustainability of Outer Space Activities (United Nations 2019).

ASSESSING COUNTRY CASES

Latin American nations have addressed space security concerns in their national space programs and projects, reflecting their local concerns and perspectives. The assessment of certain examples may provide relevant information regarding domestic endeavors therein.

Throughout the region, successive local governments have acknowledged the importance of developing national space programs as well as the strategic relevance of international cooperation to secure sustainable and equitable access to outer space. Usually, certain topics have received specific attention in local initiatives, such as the peaceful uses of outer space, the preservation of the space environment, regional space development, compliance with international agreements, and access to strategic space data and services in order to increase regional capabilities. Those assessments are instrumental in the furtherance of space security as an international agenda.

As far as national space activities are concerned, from the mid-1990s onward Latin America nations have arguably been divided into three distinct groups:

- A first leading group, composed of Argentina, Brazil, and subsequently Chile, with their own national developments in the space sector;
- A second group, made of countries which intend to develop national programs despite local restraints, while having intensive political and legal engagement at the international level, such as Colombia, Mexico, Venezuela, Peru, Uruguay, and Ecuador; and

- A third group, composed of the remaining Latin American nations, with no particular interest in the matter or lacking economic and/or technical resources to carry on space activities, thus being relegated to the sphere of influence of other major spacefaring nations.

In the remainder of this section, we consider prospects for current regional developments through more detailed assessments of Argentina, Brazil, and Colombia. Despite their geographic, social, and political differences, these three countries provide concrete examples regarding space security initiatives in Latin America. As already noted, Argentina and Brazil are considered regional space leaders, having developed their national capacities for autonomous access to outer space for decades. Their technological leadership is recognized throughout Latin America. Beyond these two prominent spacefaring nations, other countries of the region have developed initiatives to support their own space programs but have not been able to effectively realize them due to economic and political restraints, as well as insufficient comprehension of related matters by policymakers. We therefore include Colombia in order to provide a broader perspective on the region, and as a representative of countries that may not be considered regional space leaders but that nevertheless have legitimate concerns regarding space security.

Brazil

A regional emerging spacefaring nation, Brazil is of fundamental relevance to this study due to its long-standing space program and wide range of space activities and capabilities. This review of Brazilian considerations regarding space security provides a general understanding of Latin American perspectives, as well as of regional cooperative endeavors (Petrônio 2002).

The Brazilian space program has a long history, always being guided by national demands. The program encompasses different initiatives, including the development of artificial satellites, launching vehicles, and launching centers. Space cooperation agreements have been accorded by Brazil with a wide range of partners, including from Latin America (Bittencourt Neto 2011).

Brazil has undertaken relevant space activities through various projects and initiatives. As early as 1950, the Aerospace Technology Command (CTA) was created, as part of the Ministry of Defence. The Institute for Space Research (currently National Institute of Space Research, INPE) emerged in 1969, with headquarters in São José dos Campos. A few years later, the Brazilian Commission of Space Activities (COBAE) was established, to coordinate and monitor the implementation of the national space program. Under COBAE, the Complete Brazilian Space Mission (MECB) was envisioned, involving the development of national space objects, launching centers, and launching vehicles. Finally, in 1994, the Brazilian Space Agency (Agência Espacial Brasileira,

AEB) was created, as the civilian national authority responsible for developing and implementing the national space program (Petrônio 2002).

Brazilian space assets are diversified. Special reference should be made to the Alcantara Launching Center (Centro de Lançamento de Alcântara, CLA), Brazil's most important space port. Established in 1983, CLA is located in a privileged geographical region, near the equator line. Thus, the launching center facilitates more efficient launch to equatorial and polar orbits, adopting trajectory parameters that do not traverse inhabited areas or foreign airspace (Paubel 2002).

Brazil has produced or assembled a wide range of space objects, mostly at the Institute for Space Activities (Instituto Nacional de Pesquisas Espaciais, INPE). Related south-south partnerships have been developed, notably with China, in accordance with the longstanding China-Brazil Earth Resources Satellites Program (De Oliveira 2009).

Regarding Brazilian launch vehicles, despite budgetary and technical constraints, projects have been developed for decades, leading to successful sounding rockets (Paubel 2002). Progress has also been identified regarding a launching vehicle designed for micro satellites, through partnership with Germany, which attests to Brazilian technological and scientific expertise.

AEB was constituted by Law 8.854, of February 10, 1994, with the mission of improving coordination of the Brazilian space program. A civilian entity headquartered in Brasília, the nation's capital, it coordinates the efforts of INPE with those of the Aerospace Technical Center (Centro Técnico Aeroespacial, CTA). Since its conception, subsequent regulations were enacted, restructuring its organization chart and structure.

The AEB has stressed the peaceful nature of the national space program (Costa Filho 2002), following the provisions of the Federal Constitution of 1988. Brazil has been part of important regional disarmament agreements, for instance the Treaty of Tlatelolco (1967), which bans nuclear weapons in Latin America and the Caribbean.

The National Program for Development of Space Activities (Programa Nacional de Desenvolvimento das Atividades Espaciais, PNDAE), established by Decree 1.332, of December 8, 1994, outlines the goals and objectives of the Brazilian space program. As such, the document provides clarification regarding the national perspective on space security. Additionally, the National Program of Space Activities (Programa Nacional de Atividades Espaciais, PNAE), a periodically reviewed instrument, has been enacted to plan and promote the PNDAE (Brennan and Vichi 2011).

Brazilian space policy is based on the advancement of local resources toward development of autonomous space capabilities designed to address national demands. International cooperation, including efforts on the regional level, is considered one of the means to such an end. The following specific objectives are identified in Brazilian space policy:

- The promotion of technical and scientific capabilities to support space autonomy, in order to advance solution of local problems;
- The development of space systems (for instance, remote sensing systems), capable of providing applicable space services and data. In this context, reference should

be made to the Canberra Declaration of 2019, by the Group on Earth Observation, which acknowledges the importance of remote sensing to space security, as does the Brazilian regulatory framework;

- National capacity building to participate and gain competitivity in space-related markets. Indeed, Brazil has been able to support a competitive aerospace industry with global participation. The major national aerospace champion is EMBRAER, supported by other industry representatives involved with launching vehicles, electronics, and compounds. Consequently, Brazil has participated in relevant international efforts, and is widely appraised as a Latin America space leader (Presidência da República 1994).

In the planning and implementation of Brazilian national space initiatives, the following guidelines are to be observed, as provided by local regulation:

(1) Prioritizing applying space technology to address national problems: the resources allocated to the development of Brazilian space activities should be concentrated on initiatives aimed at finding solutions to local demands or regarded as of interest to the nation as a whole. In principle, a relevant difference can be identified when compared to, for instance, the National Aeronautics and Space Act (United States of America 1958), which encompasses a more humanitarian perspective regarding the advancement of human knowledge, involving the Earth's atmosphere and outer space;

(2) Focus on major projects: based on national experience, it is considered that progress in the space sector is more significant, and better appreciated by the public, when advanced through large mobilizing programs, which concentrate efforts on clear, consistent, and worthy objectives, and which impose scientific and technological challenges on the entities responsible for their performance. To overcome constraints and improve coordination between national entities involved with the national space program, Brazil has developed the National System for Development of Space Activities (Sistema Nacional de Desenvolvimento das Atividades Espaciais, SINDAE), through Decree 1.953, of July 10, 1996. Interoperability in space activities was later addressed by Decree 10.046, of October 9, 2019, regarding governance and information exchange at the federal level;

(3) Pursue end results: space-related governmental initiatives must guarantee that results produce concrete benefits for Brazilian society. As far as data is concerned, the document provides that "in general, this guideline implies significant efforts of data analysis and processing and the non-development of technologies for this purpose, as well as the non-establishment and operation of appropriate structures. It also implies efforts at technological diffusion";

(4) Careful consideration of public expenditures: government spending should be allocated to address relevant goals, thus following the public administration principle of efficacy, as observed by many other nations. Additionally, selected projects should be deemed cost-effective;

(5) Promote international cooperation: in the context of international cooperation, the adoption of international standards to facilitate cooperative efforts is considered. By the same token, a special relationship is to be developed with nations facing similar demands, without losing sight of the fact that cooperation must respond to the interests of Brazil in the first place. Therefore, it must be clear which benefits an international cooperative initiative could provide to Brazil for the fulfilment of its policy objectives; and

(6) Promote the participation of the private sector: the active participation of local private industry is encouraged, as a mechanism to foster national development and innovative technological advances.

The following guidelines are also included in the Brazilian Space Policy, but involve more specific elements than those explained above: optimize the use of resources; capacity building for strategic technologies; pragmatism in the design of new space systems; support for scientific activities; emphasis on space applications; coherence between autonomous programs; and, finally, reconciling technological objectives with scientific and application objectives and dual-use technologies.

Reference should be made to the suggestions offered by José Montserrat Filho for Brazil to achieve long-term success in outer space (Monserrat Filho 2010): AEB must consolidate itself as the agency responsible for national space policy and effective coordination of the system of all national space institutions; the Brazilian space program should achieve its sustainable development and implementation with the timely transfer of budgetary resources, so as to achieve the objective of making space activities a national priority; and greater public awareness needs to be obtained about program end results, particularly in the National Congress and in the framework of a stronger public policy.

Brazilian space legal framework is composed of a vast array of legislative instruments, encompassing laws, decrees, directives, and related norms. At the time of writing, Brazil still does not have a specific law regulating national space activities. In accordance with Article 22, X, of the 1988 Brazilian Constitution, such topics are subject to federal exclusive jurisdiction (Bittencourt and Freire e Almeida 2021). On the other hand, the AEB has enacted several administrative edicts regulating launching activities taking place on Brazilian territory, resulting in a fragmented regulatory framework.

Argentina

Another Latin America emerging spacefaring nation, Argentina's space development program reflects perspectives arguably similar to those of Brazil. Indeed, attention is reserved to the development of national capabilities designed to access and process space data and in realization of the general space security concern of sovereign management of sensitive information.

Over the years, Argentina has sought national space developments through many different initiatives. In 1960, it established the National Commission for Space Research (Comisión Nacional de Investigaciones Espaciales, CNIE), affiliated to the Argentinian Air Force. In the 1970s, there was the Condor program for the development of space launching vehicles. Finally, in the early 1990s, the Argentinian government created the National Commission for Space Activities (Comisión Nacional de Actividades Espaciales, CONAE) (Republic of Argentina 1991).

The Argentinian Space Development Plan is overseen by CONAE. Established as the de facto national space agency, CONAE was created by Decree 995 of 1991 as an administrative autarchy somewhat similar to AEB. As far as the body's administration and budget are concerned, they remain under direct control of the Presidency of the Republic. CONAE acts in the areas of its competence at the scientific, technical, industrial, commercial, administrative, and financial levels, both in the public and private sectors (Faramiñán Gilbert 1997).

CONAE's main function is to "understand, design, execute, control, manage and administer projects and undertakings in space matters" (Republic of Argentina 1991). This is realized through the preparation and execution of the National Space Plan for the Use and Exploitation of Space Science and Technology for Peaceful Purposes.

Reference is made to Law 25,467 of 2001 (Argentine Congress 2001), which establishes the National System of Science, Technology, and Innovation. The instrument allows CONAE to develop harmonization and optimization of the whole national system, toward the promotion of related activities, including those related to space.

The Argentinian National Space Plan encompasses relevant space security features, such as access to space, space exploration for peaceful purposes, space education, and capacity-building and the nation's insertion into the international space community (Government of Argentina 2021). Much of this is generally similar to the Brazilian Space Program. Anyway, a clear focus on the development of capabilities related to space data access and processing is observed, highlighting a major space security concern, i.e., space information management.

The Argentinian National Space Plan includes the following:

(1) Space Information Use and Management: covering a broad spectrum of the "use, distribution and management" of "primary and value-added" data to solve the needs and requests of Argentina regarding this type of information;

(2) Data receiving and Control of Satellites and Launching Vehicles: related to space data control, involving systems for data receiving and processing;

(3) Satellite Systems: supporting expertise in satellite system design, assembly and operation, whether autonomously or in cooperation with other nations and international organizations;

(4) Space Access: development of the Satellite Injector Program for Light Payloads (Programa de Inyector Satelital Para Cargas Útiles Livianas, ISCUL), and all related components;

(5) Integration, Testing, and Qualification: development of the entire cycle for the production and operation of locally manufactured launcher and satellite systems;

(6) Peaceful Uses and Exploration of Outer Space: collaboration with programs for the exploration and use of outer space in interplanetary missions at an international level, through the manufacture of parts for the missions and the construction of monitoring stations in Argentine territory;

(7) Education and Capacity-Building: development of projects to promote the necessary technical skills in space sciences; and

(8) National Relationship and International Introduction: plans for the dissemination of space activities' end-results and their benefits to the public and private sector, promoting international cooperation.

In the Argentinian National Space Plan, special attention is reserved for remote sensing, designed to provide applied solutions for local communities. Accordingly, remote sensing activities are envisioned as means to address social needs, promising easily accessible, processed data to be distributed among various interested parties, divided by sectors, namely: water, land cover, atmosphere and climate, agriculture and forestry, fishing, mining, energy, health, emergencies, land use planning and integrity, and, finally, national security.

Colombia

Unlike Brazil and Argentina, Colombia's space activities are still at an early stage of planning and execution. Since many other Latin American nations are arguably at the same level of space development, the Colombian case is of relevance to the present study.

Colombia has enacted regulations to promote space development at the level of the so-called Conpes or public policy documents. In particular, Conpes 3585 of 2009 provided for the consolidation of national policy on geographic information and data infrastructure (ICDE) as well as remote sensing capabilities (DNP 2009). The fundamental document regarding national space policy is Conpes 3983 of 2020, which is the space development policy designed to develop enabling conditions for the promotion of national competitiveness (Colombia) (DNP 2020). Conpes 3983 represents the most recent space policy directive at the domestic level; it aims to cover the topic with greater attention to detail, thus encouraging projects in both public and private sectors.

In accordance with Conpes 3983, space development is to be pursued by Colombia in accordance with different initiatives, designed to increase national capabilities in the sector. Business projects are particularly desired, to generate value and increased productivity (DNP 2020). As far as space security is concerned, the document provides the national goal of Colombia obtaining autonomous access to outer space. At the international level, it is established that Colombia shall support the peaceful uses of outer space, exercising relevant influence on important issues.

Due to various developments and rates of progress involving public policies regarding the space sector in recent years, Colombia has recognized the need to promote initiatives toward implementation of space technology and services to develop its public and especially private sectors.

Colombia has been focused on trying to install space telecommunications systems and acquiring remote sensing data, without having a clear policy fostering a comprehensive strategy at all levels. The main barriers preventing the development of a policy framework for the support of space activities have been acknowledged as follows:

> First, there is no long-term strategic vision for the space sector that identifies potentialities and improves human capital. The main policy initiatives on space issues in the country have focused on the acquisition of satellites to meet specific needs in terms of communications and satellite images, without a clear strategy; second, given the lack of information on this sector, the entry barriers to private initiative concerning space projects in the country have not been measured, and; third, there is a weak institutional framework that does not allow the articulation of different instances and actors towards a common goal. (DNP 2020)

Colombia has progressively implemented space policies in a rationalized context that has changed over time to reflect social demands. Up to now, no substantive and coordinated set of achievements has been materialized. In one way or another, only relative and residual progress has been observed, mostly at the international level.

Three specific objectives are identified therein to create enabling conditions in space activities, in accordance with certain lines of action (DNP 2020):

(1) Foster the establishment of a long-term space development policy: identifying the need to have a set of legal, political, technical, and economic strategies that could provide for a sustainable space program. Nevertheless, it is acknowledged that there is a risk that certain projects may eventually be abandoned due to unforeseen factors, as observed with the National Earth Observation Plan (Plan Nacional de Observación de la Tierra, PNOT);

(2) Promote enabling conditions for the private space sector, thus contributing to further productivity, diversification, and sophistication of the country's production system: removing obstacles to the development of private initiatives in the space sector, including deficient technical capacity, insufficient knowledge of the sector's particularities, lack of adequate regulation protecting the interests of the private sector or insufficient cooperation, and interaction with the public sector;

(3) Support more efficient public expenditures on satellite services: achieving better articulation between actors and entities involved in the space sector in the search for greater fluidity of competences and actions aimed at strengthening the space sector in Colombia.

Composing a set of interrelated directives, the importance of autonomous development of the national space sector at the public and private level is acknowledged in the document. Access to space is addressed within the framework of applicable international treaties, allowing the consideration of current concerns such as space sustainability, license and authorization of national space activities, registration of national space objects, as well as international liability for damages caused by space objects.

Currently the most relevant space policy development ordinance in Colombia, Conpes 3983 attempts to address the space sector in its entirety. By establishing deadlines and setting clear goals, the document intends to encourage governmental bodies to conclude their respective analysis of space-related aspects in expedited form. The overarching purpose is to achieve compliance with policy objectives, although some are recognized as more straightforward than others. Eventually, a new document may be enacted in the future, providing a threshold for further developments in the field.

FUTURE REGIONAL PERSPECTIVES

During the past few years, several factors have contributed to increased space initiatives throughout Latin America: the adoption of UN General Assembly resolutions that have laid the foundations for a framework advancing trust and international cooperation; the development of international cooperation agreements between different nations of the region for the implementation of space programs and technology transfer; space sector technological advancements increasing the number of states with the capacity to develop space activities and systems at lower cost; further understanding of the strategic advantages of space activities for developing nations, such as remote sensing and telecommunications, introducing the space sector into the public agenda of many countries of the region (United Nations 2022); and the increase of participation of the private sector in the development of space activities, diversifying and popularizing the industry, with wide-ranging effects even for developing nations (European Space Policy Institute 2018).

Such continuous process has led to the current scenario where almost all Latin American nations have some level of space activity. Nevertheless, a shared regional perspective on space security is still to come about, due to different political, social, and economic factors at play.

As there are, increasingly, similar perspectives on space security, space activities, and regional coordination benefits, initiatives toward the development of a space agency for Latin America have recently gained momentum. Such actions are considered relevant for better addressing common problems and shared concerns, acknowledging cultural and historical bonds, and also promoting access to sensitive technology. Related projects require, inevitably, relevant political effort to align interests and share burdens. A regional space agency, as for instance the European Space Agency (ESA), would most certainly require the enactment of international agreements in order to constitute a new international organization. Archer (2001) explains that international organizations are generally perceived as formal and continuous structures created by agreement between members of at least two sovereign states, with the purpose of following a common objective. A regional space agency would further advance Latin America space cooperation, providing greater opportunity for concerted action. Any initiative in that direction could be based upon previous collaborative efforts in the region. Many space-related agreements have been accorded between Latin American nations, involving different space activities.

Several Latin American nations have established national space programs to address domestic interests and local demands. Although commonly distinct in structure and budget, those efforts may eventually be deemed complementary in scope. Common benefits ranging from a greater multilateral coordination are evident in relation to strategic space activities, including remote sensing, telecommunication, position, navigation, and timing.

Latin American mechanisms of political and economic coordination are, as a matter of fact, abundant and may provide illustrative examples. Since the independence movements of the nineteenth century, important inter-American integration instances may be identified: the Centro-American Common Market (MCCA, part of the Central American Organization); the Caribbean Community (CARICOM); the Latin American Free Trade Association (ALALC); the Latin American Integration Association (ALADI); the Andean Community of Nations (CAN); and the Common Market of the South (MERCOSUR). Varying in scope and results, those initiatives attest to the existence of common interests throughout the region, as well observed by Casella (1996).

The idea of a regional space agency has been addressed by a number of Americas Space Conferences (Conferencias Espaciais de las Américas, CEAs). Organized since the 1990s, the CEAS are envisioned as enabling mechanisms for fostering space cooperation between American nations. With UN support, the CEAS have arranged events which considered the benefits of a Latin American space cooperation, thus creating a regional mechanism for integration of space initiatives toward common goals and needs.

The idea was specifically promoted by Chile during the Fourth CEA, and later included in the Declaration of Cartagena de Indias (2002). At the following CEA, held at Quito, Ecuador, in 2006, the further development of national space agencies was considered as an important enabler of a regional space agency. The Declaration of San Francisco de Quito, of 2006, included a specific plan of action for advancing political coordination regarding space activities.

Latin American nations have, individually or as groups, supported the development of a regional space agency at different multilateral forums. For example, the Mexican delegation supported such a course of action during the Fifty-Second COPUOS session (1997). Chile and Argentina also endorsed similar projects in official statements and before the press.

An initiative worthy of mention involved the Union of South American Nations (UNASUR), constituted by the Treaty of Brasilia of May 23, 2008. With headquarters at Quito, Ecuador, UNASUR incorporates several ministerial councils, including the South American Defence Council (SADC). On the occasion of UNASUR's First Extraordinary Meeting of the SADC, on November 10–11, 2011, the Second Lima Declaration was agreed, including the proposal that member states should study the feasibility of creating a South American Space Agency; the constitution of a working group to that end was also suggested. Nevertheless, the project did not advance, perhaps due to the fact that UNASUR itself has lost political relevance across the region.

More recently, the project of establishing a regional space agency has once again gained traction, this time under the Community of Latin American and Caribbean States (CELAC). Accorded in 2010 and formally constituted one year later, the CELAC is a regional international organization devoted to furthering cooperation among Latin America and the Caribbean nations, advancing a common agenda regarding shared concerns. Currently, CELAC has thirty-three member-states, including most South American nations.

During the Sixth CELAC Summit, on September 18, 2021, the Constitutive Agreement of the Latin America and Caribbean Space Agency ("Agencia Latinoamericana y Caribeña del Espacio, ALCE) was signed, establishing an international organization designed to coordinate space cooperation among nations of the region, toward peaceful uses of space. ALCE, which will be headquartered in Mexico, emerged based on a previous joint declaration regarding the constitution of a regional space cooperation mechanism, signed in 2020 by Argentina, Mexico, Bolivia, Ecuador, Paraguay, Honduras, and Costa Rica.

In accordance with its constitutional act, the ALCE will be an international organization devoted to the coordination of exploration, research, space technology, and related applications, contributing to complete and sustainable development of the region vis-à-vis space activities, for the benefit of Latin American and Caribbean nations. The organization is envisioned as capable of advancing joint satellite remote sensing capabilities for agriculture, natural disasters, homeland security, oceanography, meteorology, exploitation of natural resources, urbanism, and cartography. By promoting the improvement of communication between local satellite systems, the member nations intend to address common natural threats and vulnerabilities, which have specific relevance in the fight against climate change. Whether ALCE will effectively come into fruition remains an open question. Certainly, various political and economic factors will affect the future steps undertaken by the different Latin American nations. Nevertheless, the identification of common interests and shared perspectives, as far as space activities are concerned, is of great relevance to space security in the region.

In our opinion, space security in Latin America currently revolves around a certain set of concerns. First, it is pursued throughout the region as a comprehensive and coordinated access to strategic space services and data, considered as fundamental tools for the sustainable development of each and every nation of the region. Such a perspective is connected with discussions regarding freedom of outer space, as well as peaceful exploration and use of outer space.

Second, Latin American nations seek the steady improvement of national technical and human capabilities to fully operate in outer space, in order to design and promote space activities designed to meet local demands. One may observe a utilitarian approach in relation to space capabilities. Autonomy in the space sector is also often desired. Here, concerns over the long-term sustainability of outer space are acknowledged, including space debris, space traffic management, and space situational awareness.

Finally, further international cooperation and coordination in outer space is desired. Bilateral, regional, and global partnerships are envisioned as means to an end, capable of providing access to strategic technologies and space-related services. Originally, those partnerships involved the United States and occasionally, European nations. Nowadays, other players have entered the equation, such as China. Additionally, Latin American nations seek to participate in the major multilateral debates involving space activities, presenting their perspectives in different multilateral space policy forums.

A common, shared Latin American perspective on space security may be deemed as a work in progress. Nevertheless, similar national concerns and local demands could drive the nations of the region toward further cooperative space endeavors and initiatives. However vast and various Latin America may be, the future of space activities throughout the region faces a similar set of challenges, as far as security is concerned.

Concluding Remarks

In a world increasingly dependent on space activities and infrastructure, space security represents a global concern. National and multilateral initiatives toward space governance, considering the sustainability of space activities, are seen in many regions. Latin America is no stranger to this, with domestic frameworks and international cooperation agreements focusing on the development of peaceful and secure space activities, thus addressing national interests.

Latin American nations have addressed space security in their domestic space programs and space-related legislation, acknowledging local interests while sharing common concerns. Space activities are currently widely recognized as fundamental assets for the development of all states. Latin American nations recognize the strategic value of space infrastructure and a shared interest in securing autonomy in the space sector. Nevertheless, most nations of the region over rely on a limited set of space objects to address their local demands. For this reason, Latin America has relevant concerns over contemporary issues in space security, in particular dangers to the sustainable and peaceful uses of outer space.

In various multilateral venues, including the UN, Latin American states have presented their concerns over militarization and weaponization of outer space. Indeed, if outer space eventually becomes a theater of war, as advocated by certain military powers, severe constraints on regular space activities would be experienced across the globe. Since Latin American nations acknowledge the importance of space infrastructure for their sustainable development, conflicts in outer space are deemed particularly dangerous. For that reason, many delegations of the region have presented their voices internationally against an arms race in outer space, as records of the UN Disarmament Commission certainly testify.

One may identify, as a relevant feature in Latin American space policy, the growing reliance on international cooperation agreements to gain access to strategic space data and services. Through different programs, joint action and collaboration has been instituted, within the framework of applicable multilateral space law treaties.

In parallel, the enactment of domestic policy frameworks for the development of space activities has been identified in several Latin American nations, notably in emerging spacefaring nations such as Brazil and Argentina. Those regulations often stipulate a public body responsible for providing and monitoring the performance of a national space program, designed to address local needs in accordance with the international legal framework. A ripple effect throughout the region may be observed, since those regulatory instruments may be deemed as relevant examples by other Latin American nations, when considering their space policy mechanisms.

Common interests and a joint future justify further regional space cooperation among Latin American nations, eventually leading to the constitution of new institutions, such as a regional space agency. Multilateralism reduces coordination costs and supports more effective solutions. As political and economic contingencies affect the development of national space programs in the region, the many challenges should not be taken for granted. However, considerations on space security are certain to influence policymakers throughout the region on regulatory and cooperative initiatives.

REFERENCES

AmbaSat. 2021. "Build Your Own Satellite and Have It Launched into Space." *AmbaSat.com.* https://ambasat.com/ambasat-2/ambasat-1/.

Archer, Clive. 2001. *International Organizations.* 3rd ed. London: Routledge.

Arevalo-Yepes, C., and S. Ospina, eds. 2016. *Global Perspectives on Regional Cooperation in Space: Policies, Governance and Legal Tools.* Paris: IAA.

Becerra, Jairo. 2014. *El principio de libertad en el derecho espacial.* Bogotá: Universidad Católica de Colombia.

Bender, R.. 1995. *Utrecht Studies in Air and Space Law. Space Transport liability. National and International Aspects.* Vol. 15. Zuidpoolsingel: Kluwer Law International.

Bittencourt Neto, Olavo de O. 2011. *Direito Espacial Contemporâneo.* Curitiba, Brasil: Juruá.

Bittencourt Neto, Olavo de O., and Daniel Freire e Almeida. 2021. "Brazilian Space Law." In *Oxford Research Encyclopedias, Planetary Science,* edited by Peter Read. Oxford: Oxford University Press. https://doi.org/10.1093/acrefore/9780190647926.013.213.

Brennan, Louis, and Alessandra Vecchi. 2011. *The Business of Space, the Next Frontier of International Competition.* New York: Palgrave Macmillan.

Casella, Paulo Borba. 1996. *Mercosul: Exigências e Perspectivas.* São Paulo, Brazil: LTr.

Casella, P. B. 2009. *Direito Internacional dos Espaços.* São Paulo, Brazil: Atlas.

Center for Nonproliferation Studies. 1972. "Interim agreement between the United States of America and the Union of Soviet Socialist Republics on certain measures with respect to the limitation of strategic offensive arms (Salt I)." https://media.nti.org/documents/salt_1.pdf.

Colombia. Ministerio de Relaciones Exteriores. 2022. "Movimiento de los Países No Alineados (NOAL)." https://www.cancilleria.gov.co/international/multilateral/consensus/non-aligned.

Costa Filho, E. 2002. *Política espacial Brasileira*. Rio de Janeiro: Revan.

De Oliveira, Fabíola. 2009. *Brasil-China—20 Anos de Cooperação Espacial: CBERS—O Satélite da Parceria Estratégica*. São Carlos, Brazil: Cubo.

DNP, 2009. "Conpes 3585, Consolidación de la política nacional de información geográfica y la infraestrutura colombiana de datos espaciales." Colombia: Consejo Nacional de Política Económica y Social de la República de Colombia; Departamento Nacional de Planeación. https://www.igac.gov.co/sites/igac.gov.co/files/normograma/conpes_3585_de_2009.pdf.

DNP. 2020. "Conpes 3983, Política de desarrollo espacial: condiciones habilitantes para el impulso de la competitividad nacional." Colombia: Consejo Nacional de Política Económica y Social de la República de Colombia; Departamento Nacional de Planeación. https://colab oracion.dnp.gov.co/CDT/Conpes/Econ%C3%B3micos/3983.pdf.

Durango, Sandra, Leidi Sierra, Marcela Quintero, Erwan Sachet, Paula Paz, Mayesse Da Silva, Jefferson Valencia, and Jean Francois Le Coq. 2019 "Estado y perspectivas de los recursos naturales y los ecosistemas en América Latina y el Caribe (ALC)." Santiago de Chile: FAO. http://www.fao.org/3/ca5507es/ca5507es.pdf.

European Space Policy Institute. ESPI. 2018. *The Rise of Private Actors in the Space Sector*. Vienna: European Space Policy Institute. https://espi.or.at/publications/espi-public-repo rts/category/2-public-espi-reports.

Faramiñán Gilbert, Juan Manuel de. 1997. "Argentine" *in* AAVV (dir. S. Courteix). In *Le Cadre Institutionnel des Activités Spatiales des États*. Paris: Ed. A. Pédone.

Gobierno de Argentina. 2021. "Plan Espacial Nacional. Cursos de Acción." https://www.argent ina.gob.ar/ciencia/conae/plan-espacial/cursos-de-accion.

Group on Earth Observations. GEO. 2019. "Canberra Declaration." Canberra. https://www. earthobservations.org/documents/geo16/MS%204.2_Canberra_Declaration.pdf.

Jasentuliyana, Nandasiri. 1999. *International Space Law and the United Nations*. Boston: Kluwer Law International.

Lambert, Jacques. 1979. *América Latina*. São Paulo, Brazil: Universidade de São Paulo.

López, Andrés, Paulo Pascuini, and Adrián Ramos. 2019. "Economía del espacio y desarrollo: el caso argentino." *Revista Iberoamericana de Ciencia, Tecnología y Sociedad* 14, no. 40: 111–33. https://www.redalyc.org/jatsRepo/924/92459230004/html/index.html.

Monserrat Filho, José. 2007. *Direito e política na era espacial*. Rio de Janeiro, Brazil: VieiraandLent.

Monserrat Filho, José. 2010. "Regulation of Space Activities in Brazil." In *National Regulation of Space Activities*, edited by Ram Jakhu, 61–80. Heidelberg; London; New York: Springer Dordrecht.

Monserrat Filho, José. 2015. "Brazilian Perspective on Space Security." In *Handbook of Space Security*, edited Kai-Uwe Schrogl et al., 469–91. Heidelberg; London; New York: Springer Dordrecht.

Nossin, Jan. 2022 *Aplicaciones de la Teledetección en Proyectos de Desarrollo*. Madrid: Spanish Geographic Association. http://tig.age-geografia.es//docs/IX_2/Nossim_1.PDF.

Paubel, E. F. C. 2002. *Propulsão e controle de veículos aeroespaciais: Uma introdução*. Florianópolisl: UFSC.

Petrônio, Noronha de Souza. 2002. "Histórico do Programa Espacial Brasileiro. Curso Introdutório em Tecnologia de Satélites. Unidade 1/Parte 1.4/Versão 1.0." São José dos Campos: INPE. http://mtc-m21c.sid.inpe.br/col/sid.inpe.br/mtc-m21c/2019/08.22.14.06/doc/140_Historico%20do%20Programa%20Espacial%20Brasileiro_P1.4_v1_2002.pdf.

Prado, Maria Ligia, and Gabriela Pellegrino. 2021. *História da América Latina*. São Paulo, Brazil: Contexto.

Presidência da República Casa Civil Subchefia para Assuntos Jurídicos. 1994. "Decreto N° 1.332, Aprova a atualização da Política de Desenvolvimento das Atividades Espaciais—PNDAE." http://www.planalto.gov.br/ccivil_03/decreto/1990-1994/d1332.htm.

Presidência da República Casa Civil Subchefia para Assuntos Jurídicos. 2019. "Decreto N° 10.046, dispõe sobre a governança no compartilhamento de dados no âmbito da administração pública federal e institui o Cadastro Base do Cidadão e o Comitê Central de Governança de Dados." http://www.planalto.gov.br/ccivil_03/_Ato2019-2022/2019/Decreto/D10046.htm.

United States of America. 1958. "National Aeronautics and Space Act of 1958, Public Law 85-568."

United Nations. 1963. Office for Outer Space Affairs OOSA. A/5549/Add.1. Report of the Committee on the Peaceful Uses of Outer Space, Addendum. COPUOS 5th session. 1963. https://www.unoosa.org/pdf/gadocs/A_5549E_and_A_5549Add1E.pdf.

United Nations. 1986. "Actividades espaciales de las Naciones Unidas y las organizaciones internacionales. Examen de las actividades y los recursos de las Naciones Unidas, sus organismos especializados y otras organizaciones internacionales competentes en la esfera de la utilización del espacio ultraterrestre con fines pacíficos." A/AC.105/358. New York: Naciones Unidas. https://digitallibrary.un.org/record/113419/files/A_AC.105_358-ES.pdf.

United Nations, 2019. "Report of the Conference of Disarmament, 2019 Session." https://digitallibrary.un.org/record/3828992.

United Nations. 2020. "Status of International Agreements Relating to Activities in Outer Space as of 1 January 2020." https://www.unoosa.org/documents/pdf/spacelaw/treatystatus/TreatiesStatus-2020E.pdf.

United Nations. 2021. "Bilateral and Multilateral Agreements Governing Space Activities." *Office for Outer Space Affairs*. https://www.unoosa.org/oosa/en/ourwork/spacelaw/nationalspacelaw/bi-multi-lateral-agreements.html.

United Nations. 2022. "OOSA. Committee on the Peaceful Uses of Outer Space: Membership Evolution." https://www.unoosa.org/oosa/en/ourwork/copuos/members/evolution.html.

United Nations. 2022. "Documents and Resolutions Database." *Office for Outer Space Affairs*. https://www.unoosa.org/oosa/documents-and-resolutions/search.jspx.

Waybackmachine. 2022. Página web de archivo de los países no alineados NOAL. https://web.archive.org/web/20060516173149/http://www.nam.gov.za/.

Weerakoon, W.T. 1990. "Use of Satellite Communication for Technology Development and Transfer in Developing Countries." In *Space Commercialization: Satellite Technology. Progress in Astronautics and Aeronautics*, edited by F. Shahrokhi, N. Jasentuliyana, and N. Tarabzouni, 117–31. Washington, DC: American Institute of Aeronautics and Astronautics.

Williamson, Edwin. 2009. *The Penguin History of Latin America*. London: Penguin.

Winter, Othon Cabo, et al (eds.) 2007. *A Conquista do Espaço—do Sputnik à Missão Centenário*. Brasília, Brazil: Agência Espacial Brasileira.

CHAPTER 26

....

SOUTHEAST ASIA SPACE SECURITY AND STRATEGY

Development, Drivers, and Dynamics

....

PRASHANTH PARAMESWARAN

INTRODUCTION

....

OVER the past few years, key countries in Southeast Asia have been looking to increase their investments in space technologies and accompanying capabilities. While developments in this domain may still be in their early stages, they deserve emphasis given Southeast Asia's aggregate importance as the world's fifth-largest economy sitting aside some of its strategic sea lanes and home to the hub of institutional development in the Asia-Pacific region, as well as the reality that the region contains a mix of middle and smaller powers that are already beginning to play pivotal roles on their own as well as within the broader context of trends around cooperation and competition emerging regionally and globally.

This chapter examines the evolution of the intentions and capabilities of Southeast Asian states, the underlying security and strategic imperatives behind them, as well as the mix of progress and limitations thus far in the space domain at the domestic, subregional, regional, and global levels. Drawing on a mix of conversations with officials and other stakeholders familiar with ongoing developments as well as existing secondary sources, it seeks to examine the development, drivers, and dynamics inherent in Southeast Asia's space domain, drawing insights on not just their existing and future capabilities, but also dynamics of competition and cooperation between them, their interactions with external partners and potential future directions, and implications for the evolving security landscape of the subregion and beyond.

The chapter makes three main arguments. First, the increasing pursuit of space capabilities by a wider range of Southeast Asian states over the past few years needs to be understood in the wider context of the multi-decade long thinking in this domain, which can be roughly divided into three phases based on observed dynamics both within the region and in the wider Asia-Pacific and global context. Second, while there are many drivers motivating Southeast Asian states, four major ones can be identified based on both what is in the public domain as well as privately held beliefs among policymakers: technological diffusion; rising commercial opportunities; intra-regional competition among Southeast Asian countries; and a more sobering wider regional and global geopolitical environment. Third, while the development of Southeast Asian space capabilities to date may not be as advanced as that of other more advanced space players in Asia, the experiences so far nonetheless reveal some significant and relevant insights into the mix of progress and limitations in the domestic, subregional, and wider regional and global layers of dynamics.

The chapter adopts the approach of analytical eclecticism, which allows for a more comprehensive and granular appreciation of the diversity of Southeast Asia's approaches to space thinking and practice and their underlying foundations (Sil and Katzenstein 2010). As such, while it acknowledges the role of states, the primacy of national interests and the role of relative power and competition in the regional and global realm as realist theories of international relations would suggest, it also clearly specifies the importance of pressures from non-state actors, economic cooperation and identity development within regional institutions that are typically emphasized more in other theoretical traditions in international relations including liberalism and constructivism. The approach also allows for the nesting of Southeast Asia as a region within the wider Indo-Pacific and global context, subject to broader trends including technological diffusion, competitive power dynamics, and growing linkages between wider political, economic, and security developments, in addition to domestic factors such as imperatives tied to economic development or national security.

To account for the range of approaches across the eleven countries in one of the world's most diverse regions, each of the aforementioned core sections will mention cases in point within Southeast Asia to provide support for general arguments being advanced, with a view to touching on as much of the region as possible and covering both mainland and maritime Southeast Asia. This will help identify pockets of evidence emerging on the thinking and practice in the region, however nascent this might be in some cases relative to more advanced examples in other parts of Asia. The examples will elaborate on some of the words and actions with a focus on nation states and governments, though they will also touch on non-governmental spheres such as commerce to the extent that these are tied to state activities. Where relevant, examples will also seek to make note of ongoing and potential plans being undertaken by states in Southeast Asia, gleaned from their actions as well as insights from primary and secondary sources utilized for the chapter.

The chapter is divided into four sections. The first section traces the evolution of Southeast Asian space thinking and capabilities over time, adopting a phased approach based on the observed behaviors of individual countries as well as broader regional and global trends out to the acceleration of this trend in recent years. The second section examines the drivers behind the increased pursuit of space capabilities by Southeast

Asian states, noting the comprehensive considerations that go into intentions and capabilities. The third section delves into some of the dynamics evident in the region as well as within some of the key Southeast Asian countries in the space domain, examining the domestic, subregional, regional, and global domains. The fourth section offers conclusions, limitations, and considerations for future work.

DEVELOPMENT OF SOUTHEAST ASIA SPACE THINKING AND PRACTICE

Southeast Asian countries began developing their space capabilities in the 1960s in a context where the region was divided by the Cold War—as captured by the founding of the Association of Southeast Asian Nations (ASEAN) in 1967, which initially only included four countries (Indonesia, Malaysia, Philippines, and Thailand) and was viewed by those outside of it as an anti-communist bloc (Parameswaran 2022; Ngoei 2019). In maritime Southeast Asia, Indonesia, the region's largest economy, established the first national space agencies among Southeast Asian countries back in 1963 named the National Institute of Aeronautics and Space (LAPAN), which led it to subsequently become one of the first developing countries to possess a domestic satellite operational capability by the 1970s (Wiryosumarto 1999). There were occasional milestones in other parts of the region as well, with a case in point being the Philippines' development of a laser-guided rocket program in the 1970s despite the absence of a coherent institutional framework for collaboration across government (Francisco 2016).

Meanwhile, in mainland Southeast Asia, Thailand, the region's second-largest economy, began developing the region's first Ground Receiving Station at Lad Krabang, Bangkok, in 1982, which made the country an early distribution hub for satellite data (Thongchai 2010; Ongsomwang 2000). Vietnam notched a regional achievement still echoed today, becoming the first Southeast Asian country to put a man in space in 1980 via the Soviet Union's Interkosmos program. That development came just a few years after the country had been reunified following the withdrawal of US military forces from the country and the end of the Vietnam War that had dominated attention in Southeast Asia previously. Elsewhere in mainland Southeast Asia, capabilities remained quite basic and limited to specific applications, including satellite meteorology in the case of Myanmar.

The end of the Cold War, from the 1990s out to the early 2000s, saw a greater attention paid to space by a wider set of Southeast Asian countries as the world shifted away from a bipolar system and governments became increasingly responsible for addressing a wider swathe of non-traditional security challenges across the board (Alagappa 2003; Liow and Emmers 2006; Ang 2019). As bigger Southeast Asian economies became more developed, space initiatives began to become a more comprehensive part of wider development objectives in countries such as Indonesia and Thailand (Wiryosumarto 1999).

Meanwhile, other Southeast Asian counties also joined in. For instance, while Vietnam was the first Southeast Asian country to put a man in space, it was only in 2006 that the government established the Space Technology Institute within the Vietnam Academy of Science and Technology. Malaysia began to build out its space program beyond a limited focus on remote sensing in the 1970s and 1980s, with the establishment of a dedicated space agency first accomplished in 2002, while the Philippines began to take more steps in the direction of developing telecommunications satellites even as overall space-related activities continued to be distributed across many different agencies within the country.

Space cooperation began to take place at the subregional and wider regional levels as well. For instance, as ASEAN expanded to add the remaining mainland Southeast Asian countries to form the ten-member grouping it is today, it also expanded its focus out to a three-pillared community—comprising the political-security, economic, and sociocultural domains—and touched on aspects of space too (Acharya 2001). This began with the ASEAN Expert Group on Remote Sensing (AEGRS) in 1993 which was then subsequently upgraded to the Subcommittee on Space Technology and Applications (SCOSA) under the ASEAN Committee on Science, Technology, and Innovation (COSTI) in 1997. This evolution took place amid a series of other developments as well, including the evolution of the ASEAN Regional Forum (ARF).

Regionally, as wider Asia-Pacific space powers began setting up groupings of their own, Southeast Asian countries also began to be involved in the emerging institutional patchwork. For instance, the initial Asia-Pacific Workshop on Multilateral Cooperation in Space Technology and Applications was held in Beijing in 1992 and evolved into the Asia-Pacific Space Convention (APSCO), which, when signed in October 2005, included both Indonesia and Thailand (APSCO 2011; Pekkanen 2021a). Southeast Asian countries also continued to engage with the Japan-led Asia-Pacific Regional Space Agency Forum (APRSAF) that began in 1993; indeed, in the 2000s, four different Southeast Asian countries had paid host to meetings that originally began with Japan—Malaysia (2001), Thailand (2004), Indonesia (2006), and Vietnam (2008)—and eventually all Southeast Asian nations had joined the grouping (Thongchai 2010).

The 2010s and 2020s have seen a more pronounced interest in space from a greater number of Southeast Asian countries. These included some relatively smaller and less developed ones amid the increasing intersections between space and the growing responsibilities of Southeast Asian governments across areas such as promoting sustainability, providing technological innovations to their populations, and responding to advances around them and in the wider region and world.

In maritime Southeast Asia, Singapore's space capabilities, which had been in development since the 1990s, became more visible starting in the 2010s, with the founding of the Office for Space Technology and Industry (OSTIn) in 2013 and the launch of over a dozen satellites in under a decade (Economic Development Board n.d.). And in mainland Southeast Asia, tiny, landlocked Laos saw a much-delayed satellite project it had begun considering in the 2000s finally kick off following the securing of financing and launch help from China, with its first telecommunications satellite LaoSat1 taking off from a launchpad in Sichuan in November 2015 (Vientiane Times 2015). Separately, following an effort to build Myanmar's own satellite system with assistance from countries like Japan, Vice-President Myint Swe signaled greater interest in establishing a dedicated national space agency, along with attendant space legislation and regulations, noting that subcommittees would subsequently be formed to explore the idea in subsequent years to develop these capabilities (Spacewatch Asia Pacific 2018).

Subregional cooperation also began to become more widespread and structured. As a case in point, the Brunei-Indonesia-Malaysia-Philippines East Asia Growth Area (BIMP-EAGA), established in 1994 to promote economic development among the four participating countries, has seen a greater interest in space cooperation as part of a wider set of priorities. Thus far, manifestations of this have focused around elements of the space economy such as satellite connectivity and digital transformation (BIMP-EAGA Facilitation Center 2021). Within ASEAN, work on space also began to be articulated more clearly, with goals, priority areas, and objectives. For instance, within SCOSA, key priority areas from 2016 to 2025 had been focused on three areas: geoinformatics, satellites, and space technology applications, which included disaster risk reduction, agriculture, and surveying and mapping (ASTNET n.d.). The ARF also began to serve more as one of several venues for conversations around space security issues such as space hazards and promoting transparency and confidence-building, even as the ASEAN Defense Ministers' Meeting (ADMM) evolved to have more of a primus inter pares status within ASEAN security-related discussions (Teo 2016; Searight 2018).

Having discerned three phases in the development of Southeast Asia space capabilities, it is clear that the last few years, while contextually linked to previous periods, have nonetheless seen an acceleration in capabilities by a wider range of countries. That being established, the chapter now turns to the various drivers powering the more recent acceleration in the development of capabilities.

Drivers Behind the Accelerated Pursuit of Southeast Asia Space Capabilities

The first driver of the acceleration in the development of capabilities by Southeast Asian states is rising technological diffusion. The proliferation of space technologies over the past few decades has accelerated the democratization of the space sector, with greater involvement by a larger number of developing countries beyond just major powers (Rajagopalan 2021). Southeast Asia has not been immune to this driver. As with other subregions, governments have grown to recognize the link between outer space and terrestrial technological functions, including telecommunications, satellite-based navigation systems, weather forecasting, and security needs such as intelligence, reconnaissance, and surveillance (Garrity and Husar 2021). The extent of attention to the technological aspect is reflected in ASEAN cooperative objectives meant for regional guidance into the 2020s, which references technological applications including those related to "Remote Sensing (RS), Global Navigation Satellite System (GNSS), Geographic Information System (GIS), satellite meteorology, space education and research, communication, environmental and natural resource management, and development planning." (ASTNET n.d.).

Myanmar's foray into space, which had seen progress in the 2010s, was initially powered significantly by this driver, even though the contested nature of civil-military dynamics in the country has often led to a focus that is dominated by the potential security implications of such a pursuit. In particular, the Ministry of Transport and Communications saw the development of satellites as being key to achieving its initial goal that 95 percent of the population could utilize broadband connectivity by 2022, along with providing e-government services including e-banking out in far-flung areas of the country and facilitating better communications in the advent of a natural disaster, such as those that the country had been prone to in the past (Myanmar Times 2019).

Similarly, Brunei's space ambitions have been seen partly through this technological prism, with the government and companies viewing space as part of a holistic focus on Industry 4.0 (or Fourth Industrial Revolution or 4IR)—a shorthand for the set of rapid significant changes to technology and related industries and processes in the twenty-first century due to a confluence of developments including interconnectivity and automation (Schwab 2017). As such, initiatives both at home and abroad tend to be focused not just on narrower endeavors such as satellite development but around building partnerships to evolve the info-communication ecosystem across a whole range of areas including data centers, internet-of-things services, and halal logistics (ACCESSWIRE 2021).

The second driver is rising commercial opportunities. Southeast Asian countries are increasingly becoming aware of the opportunities that lie in the so-called space economy—a catchall term, which, per one comprehensive definition of the concept, can be said to include an upstream sector (focused on fields such as research and development, manufacturing and launch); a downstream sector (around space infrastructure and "down to earth" products and services relying on satellite data and signals to function); and activities derived from space-derived activities but are not dependent on it to function (like technology transfers from the space sector to automotive or medical sectors) (OECD Space Forum 2021). The promise of the resultant commercial opportunities has also become increasingly clear over time in a trend that is set to continue and is accelerated by the growing role of a larger number of private sector players beyond governments: by one count, the economic potential of the industry was set to more than double from the late 2010s to upward of one trillion dollars by 2040 (Morgan Stanley 2021).

Cambodia's space journey is a case in point. Prime Minister Hun Sen's publicized ambition to launch a Cambodia-owned satellite in December 2016, delivered during the launching ceremony of the building of the Ministry of Posts and Communications, explicitly noted the important and urgent need for involvement by the private sector, after initial government forays in the early 2010s did not translate into reality, in part due to funding issues (Sok Chan 2016). Similarly, in maritime Southeast Asia, Singapore has prioritized commercial opportunities in the development of its own ecosystem, drawing on its status as a regional hub and advanced technological capabilities. Beyond Singapore's national space agency, OSTIn, Singapore's space system integrates academia, startups, and other industry groups carrying out a range of activities, including satellite manufacturing; provision of satellite-based services; development of new space technologies to advance national priorities such as on aviation, maritime, and climate; and boosting the talent pool in science, technology, engineering, and mathematics (STEM) fields (Lim 2013; AWS 2021).

A third driver is subregional competition within Southeast Asia. Whether it is in the pursuit of military modernization writ large or the quest for specific capabilities such as submarines, Southeast Asian states have tended to be motivated as much if not more by regional competitiveness among each other—a variation of the keeping up with the Joneses phenomenon—rather than solely by extraregional threats (Parameswaran 2021; Koh 2018; Laksmana 2018). This regional competition is further reinforced by the development of space capabilities by larger powers in the wider Asia-Pacific region, such as China, India, and Japan, since this enables these bigger powers to further extend their reach via collaboration in subregions like Southeast Asia, and concurrently also increases the pursuit of proliferating opportunities for Southeast Asian states to diversify their linkages with a wider range of powers to achieve their own national objectives (Goswami 2021).

A case in point is Malaysia. In a clear illustration of the importance of regional competitiveness in overall strategy, the goals set out in the country's National Space Policy (NSP) 2030, which was launched in 2019 and promoted by the Malaysian Space Agency (MYSA), focused not just on areas such as boosting the country's GDP or job creation, but also targets like making the space sector among the top three in research and development in Southeast Asia, alongside rebalancing the country's suite of space technologies to become majority-self-reliant by that year (Bernama 2021). Malaysia is far from alone in this respect in Southeast Asia. For instance, like MYSA, the Vietnam National Space Center (VNSC) has also previously noted that the country's increasing investments in outer space and the commensurate development plans had been partly motivated by a quest to "become one of the leading countries in the region in this field" (Vietnam National Space Center 2017). Vietnam's last defense white paper released in December 2019 also made note of sobering regional realities, framing the space domain as being part of the product of the Fourth Industrial Revolution, which "is exerting impacts on all aspects of social life on a global scale," including the advance of modern weapons and equipment deemed to have "basically transformed military organizations and ways of warfighting." (Ministry of National Defense 2019; author conversation, November 2021).

The fourth driver is wider regional and global geopolitical competition and its effects on space. While space may be a relatively new security domain, it is also where uncertainty has increased for Southeast Asian states over the past few years due to a confluence of events, including their increasing vulnerability to anti-satellite systems amid their growing reliance on space-related capabilities, the absence of clear rules internationally amid challenges to the so-called rules-based order as well as intensifying global competition between the United States and China. The potential second-order effects of these developments on the Indo-Pacific in general and Southeast Asia in particular are already in evidence as well, whether it be in China's attempts to fold in bilateral cooperation with Southeast Asian states under the umbrella of its Belt and Road Initiative Space Information Corridor (or Space Silk Road), US efforts to build outer space-related cooperation with select regional states as part of developing a network of strategic and comprehensive partnerships in its wider Indo-Pacific strategy, or Japan's continued efforts to play a role in shaping the evolution of space-related regional institutions (Parameswaran 2014; Spacewatch Asia Pacific 2018; Pekkanen 2021b).

Some Southeast Asian countries themselves have begun publicly speaking out about the privately held beliefs among officials about how this driver has factored into ongoing decisions, despite the sensitivities in doing so. For instance, in 2019, LAPAN's chairman Thomas Djamaluddin noted plainly that Indonesia's dependence on international satellites was a vulnerability that needed to be urgently addressed given changing international geopolitics. "If there is a problem in international relations, it is better we have the capability to make satellites, along with a launcher," he told *Nikkei Asian Review* in an interview (Obe 2019).

International geopolitical factors also played a role in the acceleration of efforts to set up the Philippine Space Agency after years of consideration. This applied both in terms of the need to develop its own capabilities for defense given the dual nature of some of the capabilities being considered as well as advancing the broader thrust of President Rodrigo Duterte's "independent foreign policy," which sought to reduce the dependence of the Philippines on its alliance with the United States. "The drive to create an independent space program fits with President Rodrigo Duterte's goal of developing an independent foreign policy and self-reliant defense capability," Rogel Mari Sese said in 2016, in his capacity at the time as program leader at the National SPACE Development Program that was working to establish the space agency (Sese 2016). "The current geopolitical and economic situation obliges the Philippines to ensure that it will have an independent space program that also cooperates with current and future partners in the Asia-Pacific region and beyond," he added.

Having established the role of the four discrete drivers in powering the recent acceleration in the development of space-related capabilities by a range of Southeast Asian countries, the next section endeavors to examine the dynamics in these cases, looking at the domestic, subregional, regional, and global realms.

Dynamics at the Domestic, Regional, and Global Levels

As more Southeast Asian countries have become interested in space due to the aforementioned drivers and have begun developing their own capabilities, a range of dynamics have become clearer at the domestic and subregional as well as global and regional levels. Each of these realms have revealed their own mix of opportunities and challenges over the past few years as countries have been met with progress as well as limitations.

Domestically, the activity is a mix of commercial, civil, and military domains, with varying degrees of emphasis and integration. On the one hand, this has held out opportunities for Southeast Asian states, some of which have been able to leverage well despite constraints. For instance, while Singapore may lack the physical space for some activities and has to manage sensitivities among its neighbors about initiatives in the security domain, it has nonetheless leveraged its strengths as a global financial hub and intellectual center along with its cutting-edge defense technological prowess to integrate the commercial, civil, and defense aspects of space (Teo 2021). Singapore's domestic space ecosystem, built around the three pillars of innovation, capabilities, and partnerships, includes the development of satellites by its top universities, advancing applications in the defense domain as well as regional security thinking, and encouraging the growth of startups through institutions such as its Office for Space Technology and Industry (OSTIn) (Economic Development Board n.d.). Singapore has also used its convening power to highlight its concerns in the security realm. For instance, at the Third Singapore Defense Technology Summit in 2021, Singapore Defense Minister Ng Eng Hen warned of a "contest for dominance, if not supremacy, in space," noting that "space can become a militarized zone and strategic miscalculations and inadvertent escalations can ensue" (Ng 2021).

At the same time, advances in the domestic domain also come with their share of challenges. In some Southeast Asian countries, the development of an institutional and legal architecture around space has often lagged the actual activities undertaken. A case in point in this respect is the Philippines. Despite repeated calls for the creation of a dedicated space agency by experts to facilitate streamlining and funding, the country went decades without one even as aspects of space research and development, including the development of small-scale satellites and the training of experts, continued on via various agencies including the Department of Science and Technology (DoST). This gap between inadequate structure and ongoing activity finally began to be bridged when President Rodrigo Duterte signed the Philippine Space Act into law in August 2019, creating the Philippine Space Agency (PhilSA) (Republic Act of the Philippines 2019).

Subregionally, the dynamics among Southeast Asian states comprises a range of bilateral, minilateral, and ASEAN-wide interactions, each with their own realities. On the positive side of the ledger, subregional cooperation can afford an avenue for countries to promote positive-sum behavior and even sometimes manage their differences. For instance, since the 2010s in particular, Thailand has seen the development of its Thailand Earth Observation Satellite (THEOS) as having the potential to help manage aspects of ties with other fellow mainland Southeast Asian states including Cambodia and Laos, whether it be updated mapping that can feed into decisions on borders, surveying areas that are key for shared tourism revenues, or highlighting disaster-prone areas increasingly important in the Mekong subregion (Pakorn Apaphant 2020). While differences remain, from bilateral issues such as the Thailand-Cambodia Preah Vihear temple dispute to uncertainties about China's role in the subregion, space has nonetheless provided an avenue for collaboration (Author conversation, December 2021).

Yet the subregional domain can also pose its own challenges, particularly when it extends further out to include a larger number of countries in the ASEAN context. Despite the presence of institutions within ASEAN such as SCOSA, the reality is that structural limitations, including differences in capabilities between Southeast Asian states and ASEAN's own institutional constraints more widely, has thus far restricted priority areas to more basic applications of space technology such as geoinformatics and satellites for disaster risk reduction, agriculture, and surveying, rather than more ambitious initiatives that could include technology transfer or joint development (ASTNET n.d.; Parameswaran 2022; Natalegawa 2018; Haacke 2003; Ba 2009). Additionally, at least thus far, unlike some other domains where alternative, extra-ASEAN institutional development has spurred internal collaboration, outer space has not fallen into this category and ASEAN-level institutional engagement on space continues to be proceeding much more gradually relative to bilateral engagement between individual ASEAN states and key major powers (Rafikasari, Sumarlan, and Swastanto 2020). For instance, while SCOSA has engaged in informal dialogues with other regional bodies such as APRSAF, this pales in comparison to the bilateral work that Tokyo has been undertaking with individual Southeast Asian countries (Pekkanen 2021b).

The regional and global domain holds out opportunities for Southeast Asian states, which some have been able to leverage quite well. A notable example in this regard is Vietnam. As part of an offshoot of its omnidirectional foreign policy that prioritizes looser alignments, Vietnam has engaged with a diverse array of partners to develop various aspects of its capabilities, centered around the VNSC (Chapman 2017). Over the past decade, Vietnam has signed formal agreements regarding space technology cooperation with countries such as Russia, Belgium, India, and France, facilitating cooperation in areas including satellites, remote sensing, data processing, and information and broadcasting (UNOOSA 2020). It has also pursued more specific lines of collaboration with a wider array of powers, be it Japan in helping strengthen human resource development or the United States when it comes to civil space dialogue and coordination for challenges such as climate change (Vietnam National Space Center 2017; White House 2021).

On the other hand, this realm is also not without its share of limitations. Indonesia's efforts to leverage international partnerships to build domestic infrastructure such as its own spaceport and a satellite manufacturing facility by 2045—the centennial anniversary of its independence—is a case in point. LAPAN has sought partnerships leveraging ideas such as a potential location in Biak as the first non-military equatorial spaceport in the Pacific, recognizing that a collaborative approach could help both make the case for a larger facility to allow greater latitude in launch intensity and frequency without the reliance of overseas facilities and provide commensurate financing that has been difficult to find domestically (Rayda 2021). Yet despite offering this project to countries such as China, India, Japan, and South Korea along with companies such as SpaceX, this has run into what an official described as a "chicken and egg scenario," where greater financing commitments would be needed to facilitate regional uptake, but a certain amount of regional uptake would also be needed to rationalize that financing (Author conversation, December 2021). While it is certainly still early days and there are alternatives, it illustrates some of the challenges in this domain and could delay Indonesia's more ambitious initial timelines for its space ambitions (Rayda 2021).

CONCLUSION

The argument advanced in this chapter, and the sections on the developments, drivers, and dynamics of Southeast Asian space capabilities, suggest certain conclusions, along with limitations as well as opportunities for future studies. In terms of conclusions, first, though the pursuit of space capabilities by Southeast Asian states certainly did not progress in a strictly linear trajectory but in an uneven fashion, one can nonetheless detect multiple phases in the evolution across decades, out to the most recent period where we have seen an acceleration in this across the widest range of countries. Certain realities have proved enduring even amid ongoing shifts, including the search for solutions by governments to address wide-ranging and evolving challenges, the level of national economic development that facilitated investments in domains such as space, and the foreign alignments that Southeast Asian states were able to leverage at various points in their history in order to further their own national interests.

Second, the increased pursuit of space-related capabilities by Southeast Asian countries over the past few years has been driven by a comprehensive confluence of economic, political, and security factors, with the mix between these drivers varying across them and all of them speaking to the subregion's connectivity with the rest of the Asia-Pacific out to the broader international stage. While some of these may be more widespread globally, such as the intensification of technological diffusion and the increased clarity of commercial opportunities, others, such as the competitive context among Southeast Asian states and a sobering geopolitical picture for smaller countries relative to the great powers from the "inside out," are more region-specific.

Third, the complex dynamics underway in the region in this space suggest that the outlook for the development of capabilities is likely to be mixed and uneven. It is certainly clear that the aggregate amount of activity in the space domain has increased over the past few years, and that some countries have been able to make progress in their objectives, be it in terms of developing a commercial space ecosystem at home or fashioning a series of relationships abroad to reinforce existing capabilities. Yet the range of capabilities of most of the Southeast Asian countries to date is still quite limited relative to the more advanced countries in the Asia-Pacific such as China and Japan. And they have faced a series of challenges in doing so that are structural in nature, including the lag between space-related activity and the level of institutional and legal development; the institutional constraints of ASEAN as an institution; and a competitive regional environment that can complicate plans to leverage certain strategic advantages.

Fourth, the trajectory of these ongoing dynamics deserves careful watching to assess their impact on peaceful purposes in and through space in the region and globally. While the space capabilities of Southeast Asian states may still be in their initial stages relatively speaking, the mix of competitive dynamics and lingering differences between these countries and among external powers with a presence in Southeast Asia, coupled with constraints from the lack of institutional and legal development, means that space domain will not be immune from how countries manage peace and conflict between them. This is especially the case if the space capabilities of countries become more extensively integrated into the advancement of national security imperatives such as the active management of territorial and maritime disputes, or if they become nested within the broader context of intensified geopolitical competition between external powers in the wider Indo-Pacific region.

These conclusions do add value to the existing literature in terms of understanding the origin, evolution, and future prospects of the space ambitions of Southeast Asian states and where the overall level of activity in the subregion stands. That said, at the same time, they are also not without their share of limitations, which also suggest some significant areas worthy of further exploration. This is particularly the case with respect to the examination of more past, detailed cases of inflection points in Southeast Asia space dynamics; the disaggregation of Southeast Asian states as actors down to the individual interests within specific agencies; and more granular examinations of the intersection between wider conversations on regional and global challenges and the evolving space ambitions of Southeast Asian states.

First, since only a portion of this chapter has necessarily been devoted to the broad sweep of Southeast Asia space dynamics over time, it has not focused squarely on some specific inflection points in the earlier stages of its evolution, be it regional reactions to Indonesia's setting up of LAPAN or internal debates within ASEAN about how to evolve space dynamics in the 2000s. A closer examination of the dynamics in these episodes could sieve out more detailed insights into how Southeast Asian states evolved their perceptions of each other and sought to shape an agenda for the content of their cooperation before more contemporary realities, such as increasing US-China competition and the fraying of the rules-based order, came to pass. This would place an even greater focus on intraregional dynamics in a more longitudinal and specific fashion.

Second, while the argument has been cognizant of the various policy agencies within each of the Southeast Asian countries and the interests within them, its breadth has naturally not been able to do full justice to the granularities in this respect. A more in-depth examination of the changing mix of ASEAN perspectives among a single institution—such as a designated state agency—or interagency competition across a few case studies, can better illustrate how a "Southeast Asia view" on space dynamics can in fact belie the more complex convergences and divergences that existed and the highly contingent nature of eventual outcomes that resulted. This is particularly salient in more recent decades, when there have been debates about how to distribute space-related responsibilities, whether or not to adopt new legislation and what to include, and who should fill key positions in new or existing institutions in order to advance certain agenda items.

Third and finally, though this chapter has sought to tell the evolving story of Southeast Asia's space capabilities around the wider set of regional and global challenges generally speaking, the scope has limited a broader, deeper exploration of this aspect in a way that fully appreciates the intersecting nature of these dynamics. A greater focus on this could help more fully situate the space ambitions of Southeast Asian states in a way that is more heavily weighted toward the broader international conversation around certain areas, such as the peaceful uses of outer space, the management of challenges such as space debris, and the absence of a clear set of rules. This could pave the way for an examination of Southeast Asia space dynamics around a specific theme or how regional and global trends can come to dominate ties in certain periods.

REFERENCES

ACCESSWIRE. 2021. "Angkasa-X Plans to Set Up a Satellite Connected Borneo Island." July 7, 2021. https://www.accesswire.com/654383/Angkasa-X-Plans-to-Set-up-a-Satellite-Connected-Borneo-Island.

Acharya, Amitav. 2001. *Constructing a Security Community in Southeast Asia: ASEAN and the Problem of Regional Order*. London; New York: Routledge.

Alagappa, Muthiah, ed. 2003. *Asian Security Order: Instrumental and Normative Features* Stanford, CA: Stanford University Press.

Ang, Cheng Guan. 2019. *Southeast Asia after the Cold War: A Contemporary History*. Singapore: National University of Singapore Press.

ASEAN Science & Technology Network (ASTNET). n.d. "ASEAN Sub-Committee on Space Technology and Applications." https://astnet.asean.org/sub-committee-on-space-technology-and-applications-scosa/.

Asia-Pacific Space Cooperation Organization. 2011. "Role of the Asia-Pacific Space Cooperation Organization in the Asia-Pacific Region." https://www.un-spider.org/sites/default/files/Session5_Role_of_APSCO_in_Space_Cooperation_in_the_Asia_Pacific_Region.pdf.

AWS Public Sector Blog Team. 2021. "AWS and OSTIn Sign Statement of Strategic Intent to Expand Singapore's Emerging Space and Technology Environment." Amazon Web Services. November 30, 2021. https://aws.amazon.com/blogs/publicsector/aws-ostin-sign-statement-of-strategic-intent-expand-singapores-emerging-space-technology-environment/.

Ba, Alice. 2009. *[Re]negotiating East and Southeast Asia: Region, Regionalism and the Association of Southeast Asian Nations*. Stanford, CA: Stanford University Press.

Bernama. 2021. "MYSA Eyes RM 3.2 billion GDP Contribution from Space Sector Via NSP 2030." *New Straits Times*. April 21, 2021. https://www.nst.com.my/business/2021/04/684158/mysa-eyes-rm32-bil-gdp-contribution-space-sector-nsp-2030.

BIMP-EAGA Facilitation Center. 2021. "Low Earth Orbit Satellites Could Usher in BIMP-EAGA's Space Economy." August 18, 2021. https://bimp-eaga.asia/article/low-earth-orbit-satellites-could-usher-bimp-eagas-space-economy.

Chapman, Nicholas. 2017. "Mechanisms of Vietnam's Multidirectional Foreign Policy." *Journal of Current Southeast Asian Affairs* 36, no. 2: 31–69.

Economic Development Board. n.d. "Introducing OSTIN." https://www.edb.gov.sg/content/dam/edb-en/our-industries/aerospace/OSTIn-brochure.pdf.

Francisco, Mikael Angelo. 2016. "Why the Philippines Needs a National Space AGENCY." GMA News Online. October 9, 2016. https://www.gmanetwork.com/news/scitech/science/584375/why-the-philippines-needs-a-national-space-agency/story/.

Garrity, John, and Arndt Husar. 2021. "Digital Connectivity and Low Earth Orbit Satellite Constellations: Opportunities for Asia and the Pacific." ADB Sustainable Development Working Paper Series No. 76. April 2021. https://www.adb.org/sites/default/files/publication/696521/sdwp-076-digital-connectivity-low-earth-orbit-satellite.pdf.

Goswami, Namrata. 2021. "Status of Existing and Emerging Asia-Pacific Space Powers Capabilities." NAPSNet Special Reports. August 20, 2021.

Haacke, Jurgen. 2003. *ASEAN's Diplomatic and Security Culture: Origins, Development and Prospects* London; New York: RoutledgeCurzon.

Koh, Collin Swee Lean. 2018. "Viewing Maritime Forces Modernization in the Asia-Pacific in Perspective." *Maritime Issues.*

Kyaw Soe Htet. 2019. "Myanmar's Very Own Satellite Now in Orbit." *Myanmar Times.* August 8, 2019. https://www.mmtimes.com/news/myanmars-very-own-satellite-now-orbit.html.

Laksmana, Evan. 2018. "Is Southeast Asia's Military Modernization Driven by China? It's Not that Simple." *GlobalAsia* 13, no. 1.

Lim, Kevin. 2013. "Singapore Plots Economic Lift-Off with Satellites, Spacecraft." Reuters. July 23, 2013. https://www.reuters.com/article/singapore-satellites/singapore-plots-economic-lift-off-with-satellites-spacecraft-idINL4N0FN0V920130723.

Liow, Joseph Chinyong, and Ralf Emmers, eds. 2006. *Order and Security in Southeast Asia: Essays in the Memory of Michael Leifer.* London; New York: Routledge.

Ministry of National Defense. 2019. *2019 Viet Nam National Defense.* Vietnam: National Political Publishing House.

Morgan Stanley. 2001. "A New Space Economy on the Edge of Liftoff." February 1, 2021. https://www.morganstanley.com/Themes/global-space-economy.

Natalegawa, Marty. 2018. *Does ASEAN Matter? A View from Within.* Singapore: ISEAS Yusof Ishak Institute.

Ng, Eng Hen. 2021. "Welcome Address by Minister for Defense Dr Ng Eng Hen at the 3rd Singapore Defense Technology Summit." MINDEF Singapore. October 12, 2021. https://www.mindef.gov.sg/web/portal/mindef/news-and-events/latest-releases/article-detail/2021/October/12oct21_speech.

Ngoei, Wen-Qing. 2019. *Arc of Containment: Britain, the United States and Anticommunism in Southeast Asia.* Ithaca; London: Cornell University Press.

Obe, Mitsuru. 2019. "Philippines, Malaysia and Indonesia Bet on Space as Growth Engine." *Nikkei Asian Review.* December 2, 2019. https://asia.nikkei.com/Business/Aerospace-Defense/Philippines-Malaysia-and-Indonesia-bet-on-space-as-growth-engine.

Ongsomwang, Suwit. 2000. "Remote Sensing and GIS Activities in Thailand." https://www.researchgate.net/publication/242269757_REMOTE_SENSING_AND_GIS_ACTIVITIES_IN_THAILAND.

Organization for Economic Co-operation and Development (OECD) Space Forum. 2020. "Measuring the Economic Impact of the Space Sector: Key Indicators and Options to Improve Data." Background Paper for the G20 Space Economy Leaders' Meeting (Space20), October 7, 2020. https://www.oecd.org/sti/inno/space-forum/measuring-economic-impact-space-sector.pdf.

Parameswaran, Prashanth. 2021. "COVID-19 and Asia's Security Landscape." In *Asia-Pacific Regional Security Assessment 2021*, edited by IISS, 205–215. Routledge: Singapore.

Parameswaran, Prashanth. 2022. *Elusive Balances: Shaping U.S.-Southeast Asia Strategy*. Singapore: Palgrave.

Parameswaran, Prashanth. 2014. "Explaining US Strategic Partnership in the Asia-Pacific Region: Origins, Developments and Prospects." *Contemporary Southeast Asia* 36, no. 2 (August): 262–89.

Pekkanen, Saadia M. 2021a. "China, Japan and the Governance of Space: Prospects for Competition and Cooperation." *International Relations of the Asia-Pacific* 21, no. 1 (January): 37–64.

Pekkanen, Saadia M. 2021b. "Japan's Space Defense Policy Charts its Own Course." *East Asia Forum*. January 18, 2021. https://www.eastasiaforum.org/2021/01/18/japans-space-defence-policy-charts-its-own-course/.

Rafikasari, Astri, Sutrimo Sumarlan, and Yoedhi Swastanto. 2020. "Challenges and Opportunities in Strengthening ASEAN Space Technology Cooperation." *The Indonesian Journal of Southeast Asian Studies* 3, no. 2 (January): 173–87.

Rajagopalan, Rajeswari Pillai. 2021. "Rules-Based Order in Outer Space." *Asialink*. February 22, 2021. https://asialink.unimelb.edu.au/insights/rules-based-order-in-outer-space.

Rayda, Nivell. "Spaceport Will Bring More Benefits than Risks, Says Indonesian Space Agency as Papuans Divided Over Project." *Channel NewsAsia*. March 18, 2021. https://www.channelnewsasia.com/asia/indonesia-biak-papua-spaceport-spacex-elon-musk-launchpad-rocket-259016.

Republic Act of the Philippines. 2019. "REPUBLIC ACT No. 11363 or Philippines Space Act." https://philsa.gov.ph/philippine-space-act/.

Schwab, Klaus. 2017. *The Fourth Industrial Revolution*. New York: Crown Business.

Searight, Amy. 2018. "Strengths, Challenges of ASEAN-Led Security Forum." *The Straits Times*. October 27, 2018. https://www.straitstimes.com/opinion/strengths-challenges-of-asean-led-security-forum.

Sese, Rogel Mari. 2016. "Q and A: Will a Space Agency Jump-Start the Philippines' Space Program?" *World Politics Review*. November 3, 2016. https://www.worldpoliticsreview.com/will-a-space-agency-jump-start-the-philippines-space-program/.

Sil, Rudra, and Peter J. Katzenstein. 2010. *Beyond Paradigms: Analytic Eclecticism in the Study of World Politics*. London: Palgrave.

Sok Chan. 2016. "PM Wants Fast Data Satellite." *Khmer Times*. December 16, 2016. https://www.khmertimeskh.com/63110/pm-wants-fast-data-satellite/.

Spacewatch Asia Pacific. 2018. "Cambodia and China Great Wall Industry Corp Sign Agreement for Belt and Road Communications Satellite." https://spacewatch.global/2018/01/cambodia-signs-china-great-wall-industry-corp-belt-road-communications-satellite/.

Spacewatch Asia Pacific. 2018. "Myanmar Mulling Space Agency Earth Observation Small Satellite with Japanese Assistance." https://spacewatch.global/2018/09/myanmar-mulling-space-agency-earth-observation-small-satellite-with-japanese-assistance/.

Teo, Chee Hean. 2021. "Reach for the Stars—Strengthening Our Innovation, Capabilities and Partnerships." Speech at the Global Space & Technology Convention, June 7, 2021.

Teo, Joseph. 2016. "Statement on Behalf of the Association of Southeast Asian Nations by Mr Joseph Teo, Deputy Permanent Representative of the Republic of Singapore to the United Nations on the First Committee Thematic Debate on Outer Space (Disarmament Aspects)." October 19, 2016. https://www.un.org/disarmament/wp-content/uploads/2016/10/19-Oct-ASEAN-OuterSpace.pdf.

Thongchai, Charuppat (APRSAF). 2010. "Interview with Dr. Thongchai Charuppat, Advisor, Geo-Informatics and Space Technology Development Agency (GISTDA)." Interview published at Asia-Pacific Regional Space Agency Forum. APRSAF, January 27, 2010. https://aprsaf.org/interviews/interviews_2010/40.php.

Pakorn Apaphant. 2020. "Thailand's Potential in Space Industry: Conversation with Geoinformation and Space Technology Development Agency's Dr. Pakorn Apaphant." Interview by Thailand Today. September 2, 2020. https://www.youtube.com/watch?v=w7cE 8zDoqV8.

United Nations Office for Outer Space Affairs (UNOOSA). 2020. "The Space Economy Initiative." Kick-Off Webinar Summary Report. June 15, 2020. https://www.unoosa.org/oosa/en/ourwork/topics/space-economy/index.html.

Vientiane Times. 2015. "Laos Launches its First Satellite." November 23, 2015. https://www.nationthailand.com/international/30273543.

Vietnam National Space Center. 2017. "Recent Development and Implementation Plan 2017–2022 of Vietnam Space Center Project." https://vnsc.org.vn/en/news-events/recent-development-and-implementation-plan-2017-2022-of-vietnam-space-center-project/.

White House. 2021. "Fact Sheet: Strengthening the U.S.-Vietnam Comprehensive Partnership." August 25, 2021. https://www.whitehouse.gov/briefing-room/statements-releases/2021/08/25/fact-sheet-strengthening-the-u-s-vietnam-comprehensive-partnership/.

Wiryosumarto, H. 1999. "Indonesia's Space Activities." Proceedings of the Euro-Asia Space Week on Cooperation in Space—"Where East and West Finally Meet." November 23–27, 1998.

CHAPTER 27

THE DYNAMICS OF SOUTH KOREA'S SPACE TRAJECTORIES

SU-MI LEE AND HANBEOM JEONG

JUNE 21, 2022, was "a monumental moment" in South Korea's space development (Park S. 2022c). After successfully sending its homegrown rocket KSLV-2, or Nuri, into orbit from the Naro Space Center in Goheung located on the southwestern tip of the Korean peninsula, South Korea became the seventh country to join the exclusive group of spacefaring countries, including Russia, the United States, France, China, Japan, and India, that are capable of building a rocket carrying a satellite weighing more than 1 ton. This triumph did not come at the first trial. On October 21, 2021, South Korea (officially, the Republic of Korea, ROK) launched its three-stage Nuri rocket that carried a 1.5-ton dummy payload to test if it could carry and send a satellite into orbit 600–800 km above the Earth (Bloomberg 2021; Choe 2021). The mission to push its payload into orbit was incomplete because the third stage of the rocket burned out sooner than expected (Choe 2021). A couple of months later, the Korea Aerospace Research Institute (KARI), the lead developer, revealed that the drop in pressure in the three-stage oxidizer tank caused the shutdown of the engine prematurely, and it would seek to devise ways to mitigate the errors (Public Relations of the KARI 2021). With its arduous efforts, in June 2022, KSLV-2 successfully placed a performance test satellite into low Earth orbit and deployed four satellites (Park S. 2022c; Lee 2022d). In May 2023, Nuri put a primary payload, NEXTSat-2, as well as seven CubeSat into orbit (Wall 2023).

The Nuri project is one of many ambitious space developments Seoul has announced in recent years. In late February 2021, South Korea pledged over US$550 million for its space programs that involved sixteen government bodies. Several weeks later it revealed its plan to send its own moon lander with its own launch vehicle by 2030 (Stangarone 2021). A few days after the Biden-Moon summit in May 2021 that terminated the 1979 Memorandum of Understanding (MOU), which had restricted South Korea's missile capability, it became the tenth member of NASA's moon-exploration coalition, the

Artemis program. Seoul also announced its plan to establish its own satellite system, the Korean Positioning System (KPS), that it hopes to complete by 2035; it would cost the country US$3.56 billion (An 2020, 36; Park 2021a). In late August of 2021, South Korea announced that it would launch its first lunar orbiter, the Korea Pathfinder Lunar Orbiter (KPLO), in 2022; it is currently scheduled to be launched on August 1, 2022. In the Biden-Yoon summit in May 2022, Washington reaffirmed its support for South Korea's ambitious KPS project (Ministry of Foreign Affairs of the Republic of Korea 2022). Then, in the following month, South Korea successfully launched its first three-stage rocket with four small satellites into orbit on its own. In December 2022, in its Fourth Space Development Promotion Plan, the South Korean government announced its ambitious plan to land on the moon by 2032 and on Mars by 2045 (Lee 2022a).

While South Korea is one of the top countries with the most advanced technology, it is considered a late bloomer in the realm of space (Choe 2021). As the minister of Science and Information and Communication Technology (ICT) proclaimed after the successful recent Nuri launch, "this is a milestone we achieved nearly 30 years after the country launched its first sounding rocket in June 1993" (Park S. 2022c).

What accounts for South Korea's endeavor in space development? To answer this question, we review the history of South Korea's space programs, highlighting major milestones and government policies. Then, taking the realist approach to analyze the drivers behind South Korea's space development, we show how South Korea's desire to develop space programs is attributed to its security concerns about the threats from North Korea. We uncover how distrust in the anarchical international system leads South Korea to pursue self-reliance while signing into space cooperation with the United States to strengthen and expand the scope of its existing ROK-US security alliance. We also discuss the economic considerations behind South Korea's space endeavor. This chapter ends with a projection of the future trajectory of South Korea's space development.

Overview of Historical and Contemporary Trajectories

In the 1970s, the South Korean government recognized the potential economic and security benefits of developing a space program. However, as the timeline in Table 27.1 indicates, it was in the 1980s when the government released the official plan, the 1985 Long-Term Plan for the Development of Science and Technology toward the 2000s, that prepared the country for serious space development (An 2020, 34). In 1986, it established the Astronomy and Space Science Institute as an affiliate of the Korea Electronics and Telecommunications Research Institute (Hwang 2021b). In the following year, the South Korean government passed the Aerospace industry Development and Promotion Act of 1987. This act allocated a significant amount of budget to space programs and

Table 27.1. Timeline: Major Events in South Korea's Space Development

	Milestones	Government Policy
1980s	1986: Establishment of the Astronomy and Space Science Institute 1989: Establishment of the Korea Aerospace Research Institute (KARI)	1985: Long-Term Plan for the Development of Science and Technology toward the 2000s 1987: Aerospace industry Development and Promotion Act
1990s	1999: First multipurpose satellites KOMPSAT1 (Arirang-1)	1996: National Space Development Plan
2000s	2001: Joining the Missile Technology Control Regime (MTCR) 2004: Collaboration agreement with Russia 2006: Launch of KOMPSAT-2 (Arirang-2) 2008: First Korean astronaut into space	2005: Space Development Promotion Act
2010s	2013: First research satellite STSAT-2C 2015: First satellite developed by private sector, KOMPSAT-3A (Arirang-3A)	2012: Revision to the 1979 MOU (missile range) 2017: Revision to the 1979 MOU (payload) 2018: Third Basic Plan for 2018–2022
2020s	2020: First military communications satellite, ANASIS-II 2021: CAS500-1, a mid-sized satellite 2021: Establishment of a Space Operations Center under the ROK's Air force 2022: First bilateral agreement on a joint space policy with the United States 2022: Launch of KSLV-2, Nuri, with the first indigenously built rocket	2020: Revision to the 1979 MOU (fuel type) 2021: Termination of the 1979 MOU 2021: Joining the Artemis Accords 2022: Fourth Basic Plan for 2023-2027

provided legal frameworks for KARI, which was established to be in charge of aerospace development in 1989 (An 2020, 34–35). Since then, KARI has played an indispensable role in South Korea's space development. In the beginning, collaborating with the United Kingdom and the United States, KARI focused on acquiring technology to develop its own satellites. Such efforts resulted in the successful launch of South Korea's first artificial satellite, KITsat-1 (Korean Institute of Technology Satellite) from Guiana in 1992 (Moltz 2012).

While continuing with its satellite development, in the 1990s, KARI's focus shifted to developing rockets. KARI built solid-fueled rockets that successfully reached the altitude of 180 kilometers; however, South Korea's effort to build carrier rockets came to a halt due to the 1979 Memorandum of Understanding—the missile guidelines or missile note—agreed upon between South Korea and the United States, which limited the missile range to 180 kilometers and payload to 1,000 pounds and allowed only liquid fuels for a missile (Kim 2010, 519). To reinforce its space development efforts, in 1996, Seoul issued the National Space Development Plan that aimed to help it become a space power. It proposed South Korea would focus on developing satellites and acquiring indigenous launch capability (Wan 2010, 5). As the first step, it prescribed that South Korea would begin developing and placing KSLV-1 that would carry an indigenously developed satellite into orbit (An 2020, 35). In 1999, Korea launched its first multipurpose satellite KOMPSAT1, or Arirang-1.

Seoul joined the Missile Technology Control Regime (MTCR) in 2001, hoping to acquire technology to build a booster. After its negotiation with Washington failed due to Washington's "concerns over rocket technology proliferation," Seoul signed an agreement with Moscow in 2004 that the latter would provide the former with a liquid-fuel first stage booster that would carry Seoul's solid-fuel second stage booster and satellite (Wan 2010, 6; Moltz 2012). The 2001 revision to the 1979 MOU extended the missile range from 180 kilometers to 300 kilometers. With the launch of Arirang-2 (KOMPSAT-2), in 2006, South Korea became the seventh country in the world to possess a 1m-class, high-resolution satellite (Hanwha 2021). Thanks to South Korea's collaboration with Russia, it celebrated its first Korean astronaut sent into space in 2008 (Moltz 2012). The successful decade was possible probably because of the South Korean government's proactive policy. In 2005, South Korea announced the Space Development Promotion Act that mandated the government to "devise a basic program every five years that would promote space development and manage space objects" (Wan 2010, 5). The 2005 Act helped structure and promote basic and comprehensive plans for space development in South Korea (United Nations Office for Outer Space Affairs 2005). The latest plan, "Third Basic Plan for 2018–2022," announced in February 2018, "sought to execute space development that would improve public safety and quality of life" (An 2020, 35).

The 2010s witnessed more progress in South Korea's space program. Although their 2009 and 2010 launches were not successful, South Korea's collaboration with Russia placed its first research satellite STSAT-2C, weighing 100 kilograms, into orbit in 2013 with its first launch vehicle, KSLV-1 (Moltz 2012; Hanwha 2021). The KOMPSAT-3A (Arirang-3A), the first satellite developed by the private sector in South Korea, was launched from the Yasny launch base in Russia on March 26, 2015 (Kang 2015). Other welcome news in the 2010s was a series of revisions to the 1979 missile guidelines. The 2012 revision extended the range of a ballistic missile from 300 kilometers to 800 kilometers and changed the payload limit to 500 kilograms; the 2017 revision eliminated the limit on the payload (Lee 2021, 72–73).

Drastic changes marked the 2020s. Hyungjun Ahn, the team leader of Research Policy Team II of the National Space Policy Research Center at the Science and Technology Policy Institute (STEPI), identifies two inflection points in the history of South Korea's space development (Cho 2021). The first inflection point occurred in 2005 when the Space Development Promotion Act was enacted; the second inflection point occurred in 2021, when a series of important developments took place (Cho 2021). On July 20, 2020, South Korea's first military communications satellite carried by a Falcon 9 rocket of SpaceX was sent to space from the Kennedy Space Center in

Florida (Smith 2021). A week later, thanks to another revision to the 1979 bilateral agreement, South Korea was allowed to build solid-fueled rockets for space activities (Choe 2021). In March 2021, KARI launched CAS500-1, a mid-sized satellite, which can be developed quickly at a lower cost and, thus, very competitive in the global market (KARI 2021).

The Biden-Moon summit in May 2021 concluded with the termination of the 1979 missile guidelines. A few days later, South Korea signed the Artemis Accords, becoming the tenth member of the Artemis moon exploration program, led by NASA. On August 27, 2021, South Korea's Air Force and the US Space Force (USSF) announced that they would institute a consultative body in charge of assisting the two countries' cooperation on space policy and missile defense. They also agreed to carry out US-led joint military drills to fortify US defense capabilities in outer space (Lee 2021, 74). A couple of weeks later, South Korea's government announced that it would expend 687 billion won (US$593 million) from 2022 through 2027 to help domestic aerospace companies successfully launch their business in the global space market by sharing state-owned space launch vehicle technologies with them (Park 2021c). In late September 2021, South Korea's air force established a space operations center that was tasked with devising space policies for its armed forces, facilitating cooperation with domestic and international partners such as the USSF, and coordinating the activities of various entities involved in space policies (Park 2021d). A few weeks later, the chief of USSF General John W. "Jay" Raymond called for further military cooperation between South Korea and the United States in space (Park 2021e). The first Nuri launch in October 2021 was not successful; yet, it was a celebratory event that boosted South Korea's confidence in space technology.

In late April 2022, the United States and South Korea reached the first bilateral agreement on a joint space policy that would strengthen their capabilities to confront growing space security threats (Park S. 2022b). This agreement was born of the Space Cooperation Working Group session held on April 25, 2022, that reaffirmed both parties' commitment to space cooperation. The two countries were committed to "sharing intelligence about the space domain, nurturing space experts through training and exercises, and enhancing interoperability for combined space operations" (Park S. 2022b). South Korea's space budget for 2022 was set at US$619 million. Although much less than that of other spacefaring countries such as India, Japan, and China, it was 15 percent more than the amount the government initially requested, which rarely happens (Park S. 2022a). On June 21, 2022, South Korea successfully launched KSLV-2 that carried four small satellites into orbit successfully (Lee 2022b).

The list of South Korea's achievements in outer space seems shorter than its comparable counterparts; nonetheless, it is impressive, given the constraints it has been under in developing space technology for almost the entire thirty-year period (Pasligh 2021). To project the trajectory of South Korea's space development over the next thirty years, one must understand the impetus behind South Korea's space development in the past thirty years.

DRIVERS BEHIND SOUTH KOREA'S SPACE DEVELOPMENT

The primary drivers behind South Korea's space development are rooted in its desire to survive. More specifically, national security and economic concerns are at the forefront of South Korea's space development. On one hand, the South Korean government seeks to develop space programs on its own or to cooperate with other countries to counter North Korea's threats in the anarchical international system. On the other hand, its efforts to expand its space programs are driven by its desire to grow economic power and ensure economic security.

National Security Concerns: Self-reliance

From the realists' point of view, a state's capability is a better predictor of its behavior than its intent because no one can be certain about the state's intention (International Relations 2006, 231; Mearsheimer 2007, 73). States have a number of reasons to hide their true intentions behind their policy. Even if there were a way to access their intentions, such intentions would not render consequential information because their intentions do not always result in an intended policy or outcome (Morgenthau 1978). Thus, to predict other states' behavior, one is forced to "assume the worst about the intentions of other states" and assess their capabilities while competing with them for power for its survival (Mearsheimer 2007, 75).

North Korea's continual display of its military might and its constant threats remain the primary impetus behind South Korea's desire to maintain and expand its military capabilities using space (Jeong S. 2021). All countries observed during the Gulf War, later dubbed the First Space War, how the US forces utilized space (more specifically satellites) to "enhance force capability through precision guidance, positioning, accurate surveillance" (Kim 2010, 516). The use of space has become a crucial part of national security in any country that is capable of space development as it enables "intelligence-gathering, position, navigation, and timing (PNT) capacities, communication, and surveillance" (Samson 2014, 13). In the case of South Korea, the use of space helps address an imminent security concern: North Korea.

As North Korea expands its nuclear and missile capabilities, South Korea's need to protect itself from its neighbor's missile attacks grows. Seoul has realized that for its protection, it could not rely on US forces in South Korea, which could be withdrawn at any time. The pursuit of South Korea's missile technology, which is essential to space development, dates back to the early 1970s when the administration of Chung Hee Park attempted to develop its own ballistic missile and nuclear technologies, preparing itself for a possible withdrawal of US forces (Kim 2010, 519). South Korea built its own missile, White Bear (NHK-1), and successfully tested it. However, worrying that South Korea's missile technology would provoke and lead to an arms race between North Korea and South Korea, Washington blocked the deployment of the missile, promising it would transfer its own missile technology to Seoul (Choe 2021; Kim 2010, 519). Shortly after, the two countries signed the 1979 MOU, which restricted South Korea from developing space launch rockets on its own. Lack of functioning launch technology forced South Korea to rely on other countries for sending its satellites and other space objects into orbit and, thus, lose its autonomy by having to disclose to others sensitive information such as payload types (e.g., confidential payloads) and launch schedules (Seo, Bae, and Yeung 2021). Such a vulnerable position was very unsettling for South Korea, which was aware it could not solely rely on any other state for launch vehicles.

Former US President Trump's threat to withdraw troops from South Korea revived this very concern among South Koreans and reminded them of the necessity of self-reliance to protect themselves from North Korea (Choe 2021). Opportunely, the Biden-Moon summit on May 21, 2021, removed the 1979 bilateral agreement. Right after the summit, Prime Minister Sye-Kyun Chung of South Korea expressed on Twitter that with the removal of the missile guidelines, South Korea has achieved "secure complete missile sovereignty [for the first time] in 42 years" (Kim 2021a). Symbolically, the termination of the 1979 missile guidelines was significant ("missile sovereignty"); however, more importantly and practically, it was significant because it removed all the restrictions that had barred South Korea from developing its own launch vehicle with confidential payloads for over forty years (Lee 2021, 74). The termination of the 1979 MOU enables the country to keep the mission of space objects confidential and launch satellites to any range and at any time, to be less dependent on other countries' space technology, and to proactively assess and monitor North Korea's threat level (Choe 2021). It would also facilitate meaningful space cooperation between South Korea and other spacefaring countries as the former would not have to solely rely on the latter for launch vehicles.

After the Biden-Moon summit, Defense Minister Wook Suh announced a plan to mass-produce tactical ground-based missiles that could destroy underground artillery bases in North Korea by 2025 (Park 2021d). Seoul also announced its plan to acquire new submarine-launched ballistic missiles (SLBMs) designed to protect the country from North Korea's nuclear-powered submarines (Jeong S. 2021). Minister Suh also spoke about building an Iron-Dome interceptor system against North Korean artillery in 2021 (Jeong S. 2021). Two months after the summit, Seoul placed its first military communications satellite, carried by a SpaceX Falcon 9 rocket, into orbit, which is expected to serve as its "eyes and ears" in space (Choe 2021).

These developments did not sit well with North Korea, which understands the military application of space technology, as Pyongyang itself was able to successfully test three intercontinental ballistic missiles (ICBMs) in 2017 only after it put satellite space vehicles into orbit (Choe 2021). As recently as September 2021, North Korea claimed it had tested an advanced hypersonic missile (DW News 2021); given that hypersonic missiles cannot be easily intercepted by any current missile defense system operated by the South Korean military (Yoon 2021), South Korea's effort to utilize space and strengthen its defense system will continue. South Korea perceives its presence and activity in space as its only guarantor of survival in the space age (Hwang 2021a). On January 3, 2022, the Joint Chiefs of Staff of South Korea announced that it had established the Military Space Branch as a dedicated organization to lead the development of military space power (Yonhap News 2022). The Military Space Branch of the Joint Chiefs of Staff "oversees military and space-related tasks, such as establishing a space strategy based on the land, sea, and air jointness, establishing a concept for joint space operation, and establishing a joint space operation execution system in connection with each operational command" (Yonhap News 2022).

National Security Concerns: Through the Alliance

South Korea and the United States have considered each other an ally for decades. Upon the signing of the 1953 Mutual Defense Treaty, the two countries formed the ROK-US alliance. Although the end of the Cold War changed the strategic importance of the alliance, the mismatched strategic goals of the two allies necessitated redefining the nature of the alliance (Lee 2021, 73), and discussion on the transition of wartime operational control (OPCON) and special measures agreement (SMA) negotiations on defense cost-sharing heated up both sides, military cooperation between the two countries has remained ironclad. According to the 2020 survey conducted among Koreans by the Chicago Council on Global Affairs, 87 percent of the respondents who knew a great deal about the bitter negotiations on the SMA still supported the ROK-US alliance. The same survey also reports that 83 percent of the respondents were confident that the United States would defend South Korea if it was attacked by North Korea (Friedhoff 2020). To South Korea, the ROK-US alliance serves as a backbone of its defense capabilities against North Korea.

In recent years, Washington's active engagement with Seoul on a variety of space programs has accelerated the pace of South Korea's space development. Although cooperation between Seoul and Washington in civil space issues was instituted with the 2015 Space Policy Dialogue, the series of new developments that took place in the past few years expanded formal cooperation and talks on space developments concerning national and international security between the two countries. The timing of Washington's enthusiastic assistance seems to coincide with the growing friction between the United States and China. Although Seoul and Washington have built and maintained an ironclad friendship over the years, it seems Washington's main interest in Seoul materialized when there was a security concern in the Northeastern Asian region (Wan 2010, 13). More importantly, as Daniel Pinkston (2009) once said, "[South Korea]'s alliance with the United States has both driven and constrained its space program" (9).

As China's influence grew in many domains including the economy, military, and space, it has destabilized the status quo in the region as well as the world and transformed its cooperative relations with the United States into competitive (Pollpeter et al. 2020, 7). Tensions between the United States and China have been palpably displayed over issues such as "territorial disputes in the South and East China Seas; Chinese cyberwarfare to destabilize the US and other liberal democracies; authoritarian attempts to crack down on dissent in Hong Kong or to brutally repress the ethnic and religious identities of local communities in Xinjiang and Tibet; and competition for dominance in the high technology sector and in space exploration" (Martin 2021; Nilsson-Wright and Jie 2021, 3). In the realm of outer space, the tension between the United States and China was already high since the United States had barred China from joining the International Space Station (ISS) project (Poulssen 2016, 20). The United States passed the Department of Defense and Full-Year Continuing Appropriations Act of 2011, which prohibited NASA from using any funds for projects involving China, and this act heightened China's resentment of the United States. Some argue that the establishment of the USSF under the US Air Force as one of the six branches of the US military in 2019 set up a Cold-War style space race between the United States and China (Markovich, Chatzky, and Siripurapu 2020).

As the country with the second highest number of satellites in orbit, China boasts comprehensive space capabilities equipped with "direct ascent kinetic kill vehicles (KKVs), directed energy, electronic warfare, cyber, and co-orbital satellite systems" (Pollpeter et al. 2020, 7). Although Beijing appears to hope its space programs and activities would help grow its political, economic, and military power, its primary motivation behind space development seems to be national security. This did not go unnoticed by Washington. The US Department of Defense report published on September 1, 2020, warned about China's ongoing development and improvement of ASAT (anti-satellite) weapons technology that could destroy space objects in low and high orbits (Erwin 2020). Although China may justify its development/improvement of ASAT technology on the grounds that it would be used to remove its decommissioned satellites or to defend its assets in space, Washington is forced to assume the worst about China's intention behind its effort to improve ASAT technology and consider it a threat to US space assets as well as its military efficacy, because the United States relies heavily on space technology for its military operations (Stokes et al. 2020). "Should Washington fail to maintain its dominance in its space technology and capabilities, its military capabilities and efficacy on Earth would also be significantly undermined" (Lee 2021, 78).

Washington's concern was explicitly expressed by former US Vice President Mike Pence when he stated that "the United States and China are in a new space race 'with even higher stakes' than the space race between the United States and the Soviet Union, and that China has an 'ambition to seize the lunar strategic high ground and become the world's preeminent spacefaring nation'" (Pollpeter et al. 2020, 7). China's announcement of its first collaboration with Russia on a space project, the International Lunar Research Station, further heightened the stakes and worsened tension and friction between the two countries. Stressing that the International Lunar Research Station will be accessible to any interested countries, China seems to aim to establish international space governance with support from developing countries by asserting its leadership, establishing new norms and principles, and ultimately reshaping the world order (Nilsson-Wright and Jie 2021, 3). Thus, Washington would not be overreacting if it considered Beijing a revisionist power that opposes US values and interests (Pollpeter et al. 2020, 7). As

US-China relations become more competitive, Washington's status as a hegemon has been challenged and undermined. This state of affairs appeared to impel Washington to mobilize its allies against Beijing by expanding and redefining the scope of its alliance with its partners (Martin 2021).

In recent years, Washington's efforts to isolate Beijing that involved Seoul include proposals to form trilateral relations with South Korea and Japan and the Quadrilateral Security Dialogue (QUAD) with South Korea, Japan, India, and Australia, both of which South Korea carefully declined to join. It is not coincidental that the first two political leaders whom the Biden administration invited to the White House were from Japan and South Korea (Kim 2021a). Washington inviting South Korea to join the NASA-led Artemis program and terminating the 1979 bilateral missile agreement seem part of its scheme to confront and contain China and Russia in space and maintain its command of space by expanding the scope of the ROK-US alliance and facilitating South Korea's space technology development to its advantage.

Notably, South Korea collaborated with Russia in the early 2000s when its negotiations with the United States failed. Washington was well aware that Seoul could work with Russia again and strengthen its ties with Russia if Washington did not bring Seoul into its space program. More importantly, the United States might have realized that losing South Korea to Russia or China would minimize its influence in the East Asian region (Wan 2010, 15). Thus, from Washington's point of view, assisting South Korea with its space program was a step toward forming multilateral coalitions to contain China and Russia and consolidate the US foothold in the Indo-Pacific region.

This dynamic between the United States and China places South Korea between a rock and a hard place. For the past few decades, South Korea has been a strong ally of the United States in the region while maintaining mutually beneficial economic relations with China. Any South Korean is familiar with the "US for security and China for economy" mantra; it means South Korea cooperates with the United States for national security and collaborates with China for economic development. To be sure, it does not intend to suggest South Korea *should* work with either side for national security or economic development; rather, it describes the current state of affairs. The mantra captures the uncomfortable position of South Korea, between the two great powers.

South Korea expects that states' uncertainty about the others' intentions will lead to a security dilemma and, eventually, to an arms race in space, which threatens international security. To mitigate the possibility of misperception of others' intentions and discourage irresponsible behavior, South Korea thinks transparency and confidence-building through space situational awareness should be practiced (Republic of Korea 2021). Yet, Seoul does not consider any particular state a threat or potential threat in space at the moment. Thus, its primary concerns about space security are more about risks caused by crashes and collisions of space objects than threats posed by other space powers. Accordingly, to maintain space security, the South Korean government focuses on preparing for and preventing the fallout of such risks by collaborating with other countries rather than confronting or neutralizing other space powers. Nevertheless, as a security partner of the United States, South Korea is under pressure to join the US effort to confront China, which has been its economic partner for decades.

Since the end of the Korean war, the United States had been an irreplaceable ally to South Korea in building national power. Simply, Washington was Seoul's sole partner in restoring and building its national security and economy (Snyder 2012; Stangarone 2013, 54). The collapse of the Cold War changed this state of affairs, and its aftermath was evident in the East Asia region: an unprecedented neoliberal regionalism replaced the realist competition under the US hegemonic leadership. Yet, such reciprocal benefits of regional cooperation led by Washington ended by the early 2010s when East Asia returned to a bipolar system (Kupchan 2022). The rival of the United States was China whose status had risen thanks to economic globalization that grew its manufacturing industry exponentially. China was a revisionist power that menaced US hegemonic status, opposing its values and interests in East Asia. Unfortunately, as a country that developed and maintained mutually beneficial relations with both the United States and China, South Korea has found itself in a precarious position, blunting backlashes from the friction between the two great powers.

The ROK-US exclusive military cooperation continued while the United States was no longer South Korea's primary economic partner, though Washington was still a co-operative economic partner of South Korea, which shared the values and profits from the partnership. South Korean political leaders heavily depended on aid and preferen-tial tariffs from the United States to maintain political offices. However, as the South Korean economic capacity grew and international integration was expedited, China became South Korea's primary economic partner (Cheong 2006). The close interde-pendent relations between the two East Asian countries have deepened as neoliberal in-ternational order was consolidated in their countries since the 1990s. Both South Korea and China prioritized economic development as their primary goal and undertook ne-oliberal reforms and integration of domestic economic systems. This brought the two countries together and hardened the interdependence of their economies. As a result, South Korea, once a net importing country, has transformed itself into a net exporting country, and all the while China has been the largest trade partner to South Korea.

South Korea's economy relies heavily on trade with China. Many South Korean busi-ness companies directly or indirectly profit from exporting services and products to China; most South Koreans and businesses benefit from goods imported from China. Since China is the largest market for South Korean companies and the largest supply source of production parts, any downshift in the two countries' economic partnership would result in immeasurable damages to businesses in both countries; consumers in South Korea would suffer from a shortage of goods and, thus, high prices. The 2021 urea solution crisis in South Korea attests to the vulnerability of South Korea's economy to China's policy. It also shows how China could be an invaluable partner that could help South Korea with many critical economic issues. As China imposed export restrictions on urea to address its own power crisis, South Korea, which relied on China for more than 97 percent of its urea, faced an unforeseen shortage of urea solutions needed to re-duce emissions from factories and vehicles using diesel, including commercial trucks and public buses. Predicting an imminent stoppage of diesel vehicles and factory operations, South Korean experts warned about a major transportation and logistics crisis (Korean Herald 2021). However, after successful negotiations between Beijing and Seoul, the former agreed to expedite the shipment of urea to the latter, preventing a disruption in public transportation and the supply chain in South Korea (Korean Herald 2021).

As China's share in South Korea's economy has increased, China's effort to interfere with South Korea's politics has also grown. The so-called 2016 THAAD (Terminal High Altitude Area Defense) crisis in South Korea demonstrates how China uses its influence over South Korea's economy for its political agenda and how vulnerable South Korea's economy is to the China factor. As a retaliation to the disposition of the THAAD missile system in Seongju, South Korea, in 2016, Beijing banned Chinese group tours to Korea and K-culture (Korean entertainment, music, TV dramas, and movies) in China. This political action taken by the Chinese leadership resulted in a devastating loss to South Korea's tourism industry, particularly the Myeong-dong Special Tourist Zone in Seoul (Kim and Lee 2020). As of 2022, such restrictions are still in place, continuing to cause considerable financial losses in South Korea's tourism industry.

More important than the economic considerations, South Korea cannot overlook China's political leverage over North Korean issues. China's position on denuclearization is on the Korean peninsula, not North Korea; it does not directly criticize North Korea. China's motive behind its engagement in the Six-Party talks seems to be mainly to keep the United States out of the East Asian region. Nonetheless, as North Korea's only ally and patron (Lee 2020), China plays a critical role in penetrating North Korea and tempering its hostile behavior. Thus, to take advantage of Beijing's close relations with Pyongyang, it is in Seoul's best interest to maintain its mutually beneficial relations with Beijing.

However, in a similar vein, the ROK-US alliance is a lifeline for South Korea in countering North Korea. While South Korea is fully committed to the alliance that has expanded to outer space, the purpose of the alliance remains unchanged for South Korea: confronting North Korea, not China. If its space cooperation with the United States puts South Korea under pressure to directly confront China in space, considering the severely detrimental consequences that such anti-China policies might bring to its economy, South Korea is unlikely to follow the United States' lead to confront China. However, if its space cooperation with the United States offers a better measure to prepare South Korea against the threats from North Korea, South Korea might move its position closer to the US side. Such an approach seems to be favored by the new administration of South Korea that supported the US declaration on banning ASAT missile tests in April 2022 (Lee 2022c). Notably, it appears to contradict its position stated in the 2021 Republic of Korea's National Report on the UNGA Resolution A/RES/75/36 where it defines space threats as follows:

> We could find that some try to define space threats based on the capability itself such as kinetic, non-kinetic, electronic, and cyber capabilities. Use, demonstration, or

testing of those capabilities could threaten others. On the other hand, threats could be defined based on the intention of certain actions or activities to the space system and people, and the ROK Government preliminarily sees threat in that point of view. The ROK Government believes that any activities intended to destroy, damage, deny, disturb, or degrade space assets of other States should be deemed as a threat. (Republic of Korea 2021, 3)

This contradiction could have resulted from the change in the administration. Nonetheless, South Korea's public support of the US initiative could be seen as the new administration's deliberate way to set a precedent for dealing with the two great powers. If Washington could help South Korea develop a surveillance system in space that would monitor and check North Korea through space cooperation, Seoul might as well support Washington's cause in return.

To maintain the ROK-US alliance expansion to space, South Korea is under pressure to deal with another regional player: Japan. Washington's wish to have South Korea collaborate with Japan puts South Korea in an uncomfortable position. From a geopolitical perspective, Japan is a major partner of South Korea. Although the Empire of Japan annexed the Korean peninsula in 1910 and tried to wipe out Korean culture, language, and history, Japan has been a core economic partner of South Korea as the latter grew its economy. Given this backdrop, the United States has sought to establish a tri-alliance with South Korea and Japan in East Asia, planning a hub-and-spoke model to organize it. However, until the issues pertaining to Japanese Military Sexual Slavery (known as "Comfort Women") are resolved, military cooperation between South Korea and Japan is a highly sensitive, controversial subject, which would not sit well with the public in South Korea. Japan's denial and justification of the invasion of the Korean peninsula have undermined its trustworthiness among Koreans and hindered any future-oriented cooperation between them from being developed and implemented. Recent extreme conservatives' swing at Japanese politics reinforced antagonism between them, making tri-alliance a remote possibility.

In the Biden-Moon summit in May 2021, Washington emphasized the need for cooperation between South Korea and Japan; Seoul's response to the suggestion was lukewarm. Such a response is expected, given distrust, antipathy, and wariness toward Japanese militarism existing among South Koreans. While it has joined the Artemis program of which Japan is one of the eight founding members, Seoul would likely remain hesitant about joining bilateral or trilateral military cooperation with Tokyo, including space cooperation, as long as Tokyo does not change its attitude on past affairs with South Korea (Kwon, Seo, and Bae 2022). Like the case with China, Seoul may consider collaborating with Japan if doing so is a prerequisite to maintaining the ROK-US alliance that aims to counter North Korea. Unlike the case with China, Japan seems to have little role in mitigating North Korea's threats. Moreover, it seems feasible for South Korea to support US objectives and maintain the ROK-US alliance without getting directly involved with Japan—at least for now.

Economic Concerns: Market and Security

The use of space is crucial not only for a country's national security but also for its economic security. Not only does space provide a lucrative opportunity for spacefaring countries (Kim 2010, 515), it also becomes another arena for competition. Space creates and expands commercial ventures for the space industry to explore and exploit (Stangarone 2021); the number of profitable space developments include the global 6G network (BBC 2020), space mining (Park 2021b), space travel (Weinzierl and Sarang 2021), 3D bioprinting (Sims 2021), space-based solar power, and space waste collectors (Park H. 2022). As one of the most technologically advanced countries in communication, South Korea currently focuses on building and maintaining a 6G communications satellite network and its own navigation system, the Korean Positioning System (KPS), similar to the US Global Positioning System (GPS) (Clarke, Lee, and Woolnough 2021; Stangarone 2021). According to Minister Hye-sook Lim of South Korea's Science and ICT Ministry, these systems are not merely about fast data communication anywhere on Earth (the land, the sea, and the air) but are used to help operate urban air mobility, drones, and self-driving services more accurately (Bloomberg 2021; Stangarone 2021). More importantly, 6G will enable rapid data transmission between objects, which is central for self-driving cars and urban air traffic (e.g., drones) to function effectively, efficiently, and precisely (Jeong E. H. 2021, 13). South Korea has pledged 4 trillion won (over US$3 billion) to develop and establish the KPS (Kim 2021b).

During the Biden-Moon summit in May 2021, both countries confirmed their commitment to cooperation on both GPS and South Korea's planned KPS (National Coordination Office for Space-Based Positioning, Navigation, and Timing 2021). This commitment was reaffirmed at the Biden-Yoon summit in May 2022. The KPS will render ultra-precise information on PNT, which enhances the functionality and productivity of devices using urban air mobility and autonomous driving technologies in the future lucrative industry (Kim 2021b). These commercial opportunities will encourage the involvement and investment of the private sector in space development in South Korea, where the government still remains the primary initiator/coordinator of space programs.

At the same time, while denying the moon and other celestial bodies are the common heritage of mankind, some spacefaring states have sought to exploit natural resources such as precious metals and minerals in space. A US Executive Order was signed in April 2020 that allowed exploration, recovery, and use of resources in space for commercial purposes (Executive Office of the President 2020). Russia plans to install a permanent lunar station that could help extract helium from the moon and China hoped to mine asteroids to extract rare minerals, while Luxembourg passed a legal framework that would protect property rights over space resources (Kamboj 2020). "Canada, Australia, and the United Arab Emirates" seemed supportive of this stance on space resources (Sheetz 2020). The current state of space politics seems to subscribe to the realist worldview; "like early common law that gave property rights to those who were there first," it seems "whatever one grabs in space becomes her/his possessions" (Lee and Jeong 2020).

As Scott Pace, the Executive Secretary of the National Space Council, puts it, "as with past frontiers, it is those who show up, not those who stay home, who create the rules and establish international norms that create stability and deter tragedies" (Pace 2016). Although it is a late bloomer in space development, South Korea does not intend to stay home, watching space and its resources be claimed by other countries.

CONCLUSION

In the short thirty-year history of space development, the main driver behind South Korea's space programs lies in the aftermath of the Korean war that ended without a peace agreement in 1953: national security. With neighboring North Korea constantly threatening to use nuclear missiles, South Korea has sought a way to monitor North Korea's movement and mitigate any threat, if possible, without relying heavily on other countries' space technology. South Korea's efforts to develop missiles date to the 1970s, when the Park administration realized it needed to strengthen its own defense system against North Korea in case of the withdrawal of US troops from South Korea. Such efforts were tempered by the 1979 MOU that constrained South Korea's development of missile technology. The still-classified bilateral agreement was signed between South Korea and the United States due to the latter's concerns about a potential arms race between the two Koreas, delaying the progress of Seoul's space development. After multiple revisions to the 1979 missile guidelines over the years, the Biden-Moon summit in May 2021 did away with the forty-two-year-old agreement. Since then, the South Korean government has announced a series of new space projects, and discussions on ROK-US space cooperation have proliferated.

South Korea's space cooperation with the United States presented two decisive moments. It offered an opportunity for the two countries to set aside differences (e.g., issues on the transition of wartime OPCON and SMA negotiations on defense cost-sharing) and revamp and strengthen the seventy-year-old ROK-US alliance by redefining its nature and expanding it to space. It also forced South Korea to walk a tightrope between the two great powers, China and the United States (Lee 2021, 81). As competition for dominance over outer space further intensifies tensions already existing between the two great powers, this balancing between them has created a bipolar system in space where one side consists of the United States and its former allies from the Cold War era alliance and the other side includes China, which extends its Belt and Road Initiative to the realm of space to secure its own power. For now, the US side maintains its dominance in outer space, but there is no guarantee that this status quo will continue (Pekkanen 2021, 2). South Korea appears to be recruited to join the US-led alliance in space against the China camp. This put South Korea between a rock and a hard place, given China is capable of severely hurting South Korea's economy. However, South Korea's main concern with space development is national security. Thus, as long as its space cooperation with the United States could effectively prepare the country to withstand North Korea's threats, South Korea appears to be willing to move closer to the US camp. The ROK-US Summit held in May 2022 reaffirmed their commitment to space cooperation as an extension of their existing alliance (Ministry of Foreign Affairs of the Republic of Korea 2022). However, against Washington's wishes, Seoul would not likely collaborate with Tokyo directly for any project pertaining to military or security due to its unresolved issues with Japan.

The emphasis on national security does not mean that South Korea's space endeavor is solely driven by its security concerns. Seoul has developed a number of space programs to venture into a new lucrative market, hoping to dominate the new cutting-edge technology domain. Among them are 6G and KPS, which are essential technologies for urban air mobility and autonomous driving in that future lucrative industry. Economic drivers also concern economic security to ensure South Korea's place in outer space.

South Korea's preoccupation with national security should not overshadow its commitment to the peaceful use of space. Article 1 of the 2005 Space Development Promotion Act indicates that South Korea's space development, first and foremost, aims "to facilitate the peaceful use and scientific exploration of outer space" (Republic of Korea 2021, 1). By supporting the US initiative on banning ASAT missile tests, the South Korean government reaffirmed its commitment to the peaceful use of outer space proposed by United Nations (UN) General Assembly Resolution 75/36 on "reducing space threats through norms, rules, and principles of responsible behaviors" and pledged to continue to develop norms for the peaceful and sustainable use of space (Lee 2022c). Such commitments are also observed in *Korea's New Challenge: The Third Space Development Promotion Basic Plan* circulated in 2018 by joint ministries in which the South Korean government pledges to keep outer space a safe domain for everybody through space cooperation by resolving global issues and international space security. In the report, the South Korean government pledges to work with the UN Committee on the Peaceful uses of Outer Space (COPUOS), UN Global Environment Outlook (GEO), the Organization for Economic Co-operation and Development (OECD), Space Forum, and the International Astronautical Congress (IAC) to address global issues. Seoul also emphasizes that, through space situational awareness, it would work with other space powers as well as COPUOS, the Inter-agency Space Debris Coordination Committee (IADC), the World Meteorological Organization (WMO), and the International Civil Aviation Organization (ICAO) and exchange information on space conditions such as space debris removal and detection/projection of potential collisions between space objects (Joint Ministries 2018, 45). The same sentiments are echoed in *The First Basic Plan for Space Risk Preparedness* (2014–2023) published in 2021 by the joint ministries (Joint Ministries 2021, 22).

As a late bloomer in the realm of space, South Korea is presented with various options and routes to grow its space program. That said, one thing is very clear. As former ROK President Moon expressed, the country's primary objective in pursuing space development is to build a defense system via space technology to preserve and ensure peace (DW News 2021). Seoul also hopes to take advantage of the uncharted lucrative sphere.

How it will accomplish its objectives in space development while not being swayed by political conditions remains South Korea's greatest challenge in the coming years.

ACKNOWLEDGMENTS

Su-Mi Lee thanks the Korea Foundation for its generous support for the research via the KF Field Research Fellowship.

REFERENCES

An, Hyoung Joon. 2020. "South Korea's Space Program: Activities and Ambitions." *Asia Policy* 15, no. 2: 34–42.

BBC. 2020. "China Sends 'World's First 6G' Test Satellite Into Orbit." *BBC*. November 7, 2020. https://www.bbc.com/news/av/world-asia-china-54852131.

Bloomberg. 2021. "South Korea Seeks to Move Up Its Spot in Global Space Race." *Bloomberg*. July 15, 2021. https://www.bloomberg.com/news/articles/2021-07-14/south-korea-seeks-to-move-up-its-spot-in-global-space-race.

Cheong, Young-rok. 2006. "Impact of China on South Korea's Economy." In *Dynamic Forces on the Korean Peninsula: Strategic & Economic Implications*, edited by James M. Lister, 61–81. Washington, DC: The Korea Economic Institute of America. http://www.keia.org/sites/defa ult/files/publications/09.Cheong.pdf.

Cho, Seung Hwan. 2021. "기술개발 중심의 우주개발 정책, 이제는 안보와 외교,경제 고려 해야." ("Space Development Policy Centered on Technology Development, Now Consider Security, Diplomacy and Economy.") *Donga Science*. September 8, 2021. https://m.dongascie nce.com/news.php?idx=49216.

Choe, Sang-hun. 2021. "South Korea's First Homemade Rocket Lifts Off but Is 'One Step Short.'" *New York Times*. October 21, 2021. https://www.nytimes.com/2021/10/21/world/asia/south-korea-rocket.html.

Clarke, Carrington, Sookyoung Lee, and Mitch Denman Woolnough. 2021. "Asia is in the Midst of a Space Race, but It's Not Just About Exploration. It's Also a Military Flex." *Australian Broadcasting Corporation*. October 21, 2021. https://www.abc.net.au/news/2021-10-22/korea-china-india-space-race-military-flex/100547832.

DW News. 2021. "South Korea Space Rocket Test Prompts Fear of Arms Race with North." *DW News*. October 21, 2021. https://www.dw.com/en/south-korea-space-rocket-test-prompts-fear-of-arms-race-with-north/a-59572929.

Erwin, Sandra. 2020. "Pentagon Report: China Amassing Arsenal of Anti-satellite Weapons," *Spacenews*, September 1, 2020. https://spacenews.com/pentagon-report-china-amassing-arsenal-of-anti-satellite-weapons/.

Executive Office of the President. 2020. "Executive Order 13914: Encouraging International Support for the Recovery and Use of Space Resources." White House. April 6, 2020. https://www.federalregister.gov/documents/2020/04/10/2020-07800/encouraging-international-support-for-the-recovery-and-use-of-space-resources.

Friedhoff, Karl. 2020. "Troop Withdrawal Likely to Undermine South Korean Public Support for Alliance with United States." The Chicago Council on Global Affairs. August 2020.

https://www.thechicagocouncil.org/sites/default/files/2020-12/2020_sma_korea_brief_0.pdf.

Hanwha. 2021. "Korea is Reaching New Heights as a Player in the Global Space Race." Hanwha. November 25, 2021. https://www.hanwha.com/en/news_and_media/stories/innovations/korea-is-reaching-new-heights-as-a-player-in-the-global-space-race.html.

Hwang, Jeong Ah. 2021a. "국가우주전략이없다." (No National Space Strategy.) *Hankookilbo*. March 23, 2021. https://www.hankookilbo.com/News/Read/Print/A2021032209460002654.

Hwang, Jeong-ah. 2021b. "눈앞에 다가온 K스페이스 시대." (The Era of K-space is Approaching.) *Hankookilbo*. July 12, 2021. https://www.hankookilbo.com/News/Read/Print/A2021071209460000573.

International Relations. 2006. "Conversations in International Relations: Interview with John J. Mearsheimer (Part II)." *International Relations* 20, no. 2: 231–43.

Jeong, Eui Hoon. 2021. "우주를 줄게: 재사용 로켓의 선물." (I'll Give You the Universe: Reusable Rocket's Gift.) Eugene Investment & Securities. April 19, 2021. https://www.eugenefn.com/comm/vkdlfekdns.do?msgId=375758.

Jeong, Sarah. 2021. "South Korea's Defense Capabilities and Acquisition Programs." Wilson Center. August 31, 2021. https://www.wilsoncenter.org/blog-post/south-koreas-defense-capabilities-and-acquisition-programs.

Joint Ministries. 2018. "대한민국의 새로운 도전: 제 3차 우주개발 진흥 기본계획." (Korea's New Challenge: The Third Space Development Promotion Basic Plan.) 관계부처 합동 (Joint Ministries). February 2018.

Joint Ministries. 2021. "제 1차 우주위험대비 기본계획 (2014-2023): 2021년도 시행계획안." (The First Basic Plan for Space Risk Preparedness (2014–2023): The 2021 Action Plan Draft.) 관계부처 합동 (Joint Ministries). January 2021.

Kamboj, Megha. 2020. "Outer Space: A Victim of Power Competition?" JURIST. Jun. 1, 2020. https://www.jurist.org/commentary/2020/06/megha-kamboj-outerspace-power-competition/.

Kang, Tae-jun. 2015. "South Korea's Quest to Be a Major Space Power." *The Diplomat*. March 27, 2015. https://thediplomat.com/2015/03/south-koreas-quest-to-be-a-major-space-power/.

KARI. 2021. "Compact Advanced Satellite 500." KARI. June 25, 2021. https://www.kari.re.kr/eng/sub03_03_03.do.

Kim, Bong Soo. 2021b. "[아시아초대석] 우주개발, 시스템 정비해 제대로 일 벌일 때." ([Asia Invitation Seat] About Space Development, System Maintenance and Work Are Done Properly.) *Asia Economics*. December 6, 2021. www.asiae.co.kr/news/print.htm?idxno=2021120614063969441&udt=1.

Kim, Hyejin, and Jungmin Lee. 2020. "The Economic Costs of Diplomatic Conflict." Bank of Korea (BOK) Working Paper. November 26, 2020. https://www.bok.or.kr/eng/bbs/B0000268/view.do?nttId=10061415&menuNo=400067&searchWrd=economic+costs+of+diplomatic+c&searchCnd=1&sdate=&edate=&pageIndex=1.

Kim, Sang-Min. 2021a. "U.S. Lifts Missile Limits on South Korea." Arms Control Association. June 2021. https://www.armscontrol.org/act/2021-06/news/us-lifts-missile-limits-south-korea.

Kim, Tae-Hyung. 2010. "South Korea's Space Policy and Its National Security Implications." *The Korean Journal of Defense Analysis* 22, no. 4: 515–29.

Korean Herald. 2021. "China to Ship 18,700 tons of Urea to South Korea." *Korean Herald*. November 10, 2021. www.koreaherald.com/common/newsprint.php?ud=20211110000741.

Kupchan, Cliff. 2022. "Bipolarity is Back: Why It Matters." *The Washington Quarterly*. February 2, 2022. https://www.eurasiagroup.net/live-post/bipolarity-is-back-why-it-matters.

Kwon Hyuk-chul, Young-ji Seo, and Ji-hyun Bae. 2022. "Seoul Denies Reports of US Request for S. Korea to Hold Military Drills with Japan." *Hankyoreh*. May 20, 2022. https://english.hani.co.kr/arti/english_edition/e_international/1043693.html.

Lee, Chung Min. 2020. "South Korea Is Caught Between China and the United States." Carnegie Endowment for International Peace. October 21, 2020. https://carnegieendowment.org/2020/10/21/south-korea-is-caught-between-china-and-united-states-pub-83019.

Lee, Jung-ho. 2022a. "Fourth Space Development Promotion Plan: Unmanned Landing on the Moon in 2032, on Mars in 2045." *The Kyunghyang Shinmun*. December 22, 2022. http://english.khan.co.kr/khan_art_view.html?artid=202212221752047&code=710100#.

Lee, Keun-young. 2022b. " Successful Nuri Launch Writes New History of S. Korea In Space." *Hankyoreh*. June 21, 2022. https://english.hani.co.kr/arti/PRINT/1047937.html.

Lee, Su-Mi. 2021. "South Korea's Space Program and Its Implication." *The Korean Journal of Security Affairs* 26, no. 2: 69–88.

Lee, Su-Mi, and Hanbeom Jeong. 2020. "Cooperation in Outer Space: Need vs. Willingness." *The Korean Journal of Security Affairs* 25, no. 2: 26–44.

Lee, Young-tae. 2022c. "정부 '美 '인공위성 요격 미사일 시험 금지 선언' '환영' . . . '중·러 압박.'" (Government Welcomes the U.S. Declaration on Banning ASAT Missile Tests . . . Pressure on China and Russia.) *Newspim*. April 21, 2022. https://www.newspim.com/news/view/20220421001029.

Lee, Youngwan. 2022d. "Nuri's Second Mini-satellite into Space: KAIST-developed Cube Satellites Send Signals to Ground Stations." *Chosun Ilbo*. July 2, 2022. https://www.chosun.com/economy/science/2022/07/02/X3IFII22PVHIVM3ZQ6QG3RV2IQ/.

Markovich, Steven J., Andrew Chatzky, and Anshu Siripurapu. 2020. "Space Exploration and U.S. Competitiveness." Council on Foreign Relations. June 10, 2020. https://www.cfr.org/backgrounder/space-exploration-and-us-competitiveness.

Martin, Peter. 2021. "Biden's Asia Czar Says Era of Engagement with China Is Over." *Bloomberg*. May 26, 2021. https://www.bloomberg.com/news/articles/2021-05-26/biden-s-asia-czar-says-era-of-engagement-with-xi-s-china-is-over?sref=EWvigcvl.

Mearsheimer, John J. 2007. "Structural Realism." In *International Relations Theories: Discipline and Diversity*, edited by Tim Dunne, Millja Kurki, and Steve Smith, 71–86. New York: Oxford University Press.

Ministry of Foreign Affairs of the Republic of Korea. 2022. "ROK-US Leaders' Joint Statement." Ministry News. May 22, 2022. https://www.mofa.go.kr/eng/brd/m_5674/view.do?seq=320722&page=1.

Moltz, James Clay. 2012. "The KSLV I Launch and South Korea's Space Strategy." Council on Foreign Relations. October 17, 2012. https://www.cfr.org/report/kslv-i-launch-and-south-koreas-space-strategy.

Morgenthau, Hans J. 1978. *Politics Among Nations: The Struggle for Power and Peace*. 5th ed. New York: Alfred A. Knopf.

National Coordination Office for Space-Based Positioning, Navigation, and Timing. 2021. "Joint Statement by the United States of America and the Republic of Korea on Civil Global Navigation Satellite Systems Cooperation." U.S. Space Force. May 2021. https://www.gps.gov/policy/cooperation/korea/2021-joint-statement/.

Nilsson-Wright, John, and Yu Jie. 2021. *South Korean Foreign Policy Innovation amid Sino-US Rivalry: Strategic Partnerships and Managed Ambiguity*. London: Chatham House.

Pace, Scott. 2016. "Space Cooperation among Order-Building Power." *Space Policy* 36: 24–27.

Park, Hohyeon. 2022. "정부 주도 우주정책 폐지해야...우주청으로 최소화 필요." (Government-led Space Policy Must Be Abolished . . . Need to Be Minimized by the Space Agency.) *Sedaily*. March 25, 2022. https://www.sedaily.com/News/NewsView/NewsPrint?Nid=263K10PVA0.

Park, Si-soo. 2021a. "With Artemis Accords on the Table, South Korea, U.S. to Widen Cooperation in Space Exploration, Security." *Spacenews*. May 25, 2021. https://spacenews.com/with-artemis-accords-a-done-deal-south-korea-u-s-to-widen-cooperation-in-space-exploration-security/.

Park, Si-soo. 2021b. "South Korea Touts Artemis Accords as a Way to Settle International Space Issues." *Spacenews*. August 19, 2021. https://spacenews.com/south-korea-touts-artemis-accords-as-a-way-to-settle-international-space-issues/.

Park, Si-soo. 2021c. "South Korea to Spend $593 Million on Public-To-Private Transfer of Rocket Technologies." *Spacenews*. September 8, 2021. https://spacenews.com/south-korea-to-spend-593-million-on-public-to-private-transfer-of-rocket-technologies/.

Park, Si-soo. 2021d. "South Korea's Air Force Opens Space Ops Center." *Spacenews*. October 4, 2021. https://spacenews.com/south-korean-air-force-opens-space-center/.

Park, Si-soo. 2021e. "'We Go Together': US Space Force Chief Seeks Deeper Space Cooperation with South Korea." *Spacenews*. October 18, 2021. https://spacenews.com/we-go-together-us-space-force-chief-seeks-deeper-space-cooperation-with-south-korea/.

Park, Si-soo. 2022a. "South Korea's Double-digit Space Budget Boost." *Spacenews*. April 21, 2022. https://spacenews.com/south-koreas-double-digit-space-budget-boost/.

Park, Si-soo. 2022b. "U.S., South Korea Agree to Cooperate on Space Situational Awareness for Military Purposes." *Spacenews*. April 26, 2022. https://spacenews.com/u-s-south-korea-agree-to-cooperate-on-space-situational-awareness-for-military-purposes/.

Park, Si-soo. 2022c. "South Korea Rocket Puts Satellites in Orbit for the First Time in Second Flight." *Spacenews*. June 21, 2022. https://spacenews.com/south-korean-rocket-puts-satellites-in-orbit-for-the-first-time-in-second-flight/.

Pasligh, Hendrik. 2021. "South Korean Space Diplomacy Reaches for the Stars." East Asia Forum. August 31, 2021. https://www.eastasiaforum.org/2021/08/31/south-korean-space-diplomacy-reaches-for-the-stars/.

Pekkanen, Saadia M. 2021. "Cautionary Remarks on the Emerging Bipolarity of Space Alliances: A Japanese Perspective." In *The New Space Age: Beyond Global Order*, edited by Julia Ciocca, Rachel Hulvey, and Christina Ruhl, 1–6. Philadelphia, PA: Perry World House. https://global.upenn.edu/sites/default/files/perry-world-house/Pekkanen_SpaceWorkshop.pdf.

Pinkston, Daniel. 2009. "Space Cadets: The Korean Peninsula's Rocket Competition." *Jane's Intelligence Review* 21, no. 9: 8–13.

Pollpeter, Kevin, Timothy Ditter, Anthony Miller, and Brian Waidelich. 2020. *China's Space Narrative: Examining The Portrayal Of The Us-China Space Relationship In Chinese Sources And Its Implications For The United States*. Montgomery, AL: The China Aerospace Studies Institute.

Poulssen, Jesper. 2016. "Rivals and Cooperation in Outer Space: The Politics Surrounding Rivals and (non-)Cooperation Regarding Space." Master's thesis, University of Leiden.

Public Relations. 2021. "누리호 조사위원회 결과 보도자료." (Nuriho Investigation Committee Results Press Release.) Korea Aerospace Research Institute. December 29, 2021. https://www.kari.re.kr/cop/bbs/BBSMSTR_000000000011/selectBoardArticle.do?nttId=8128&kind=&mno=sitemap_02&pageIndex=1&searchCnd=&searchWrd=.

Republic of Korea. 2021. "Republic of Korea's National Report on the UNGA Resolution A/RES/75/36." Report of the Secretary-General on Reducing Space Threats through Norms, Rules and Principles of Responsible Behaviors (2021). United Nations Office for Disarmament Affairs. May 3, 2021. https://front.un-arm.org/wp-content/uploads/2021/05/210503-National-Submission-Republic-of-Korea_75_36.pdf.

Samson, Victoria. 2014. "Space Technology Cooperation and Its Effects on National Security and International Stability." In *Space Technology Development: Effects on National Security and International Stability*, edited by Jiyoung Park, 10–32. Seoul, Korea: Asan Report. http://en.asaninst.org/contents/space-technology-development-effects-on-national-security-and-international-stability/.

Seo, Yoonjung, Gawon Bae, and Jessie Yeung. 2021. "South Korea Fails to Put Dummy Satellite into Orbit." CNN. October 21, 2021. https://www.cnn.com/2021/10/21/asia/south-korea-nuri-rocket-launch-intl-hnk-scn/index.html.

Sheetz, Michael. 2020. "Trump Wants More Countries to Join US Policy Approach to Space Resources, Lunar Mining." CNBC. April 6, 2020. https://www.cnbc.com/2020/04/06/trump-executive-order-on-us-space-resources-and-mining-policy.html.

Sims, Josh. 2021. "Why Astronauts are Printing Organs in Space." *BBC*. June 1, 2021. https://www.bbc.com/future/article/20210601-how-transplant-organs-might-be-printed-in-outer-space.

Smith, Josh. 2021. "From Spy Satellites to Mobile Networks, S. Korea Pins Space Hopes on New Rocket." *Reuters*. October 14, 2021. https://www.reuters.com/world/asia-pacific/spy-satellites-mobile-networks-skorea-hopes-new-rocket-gets-space-programme-off-2021-10-15/.

Snyder, Scott. 2012. *The US-South Korea Alliance: Meeting New Security Challenges*. Boulder, CO: Lynne Rienner Publishers.

Stangarone, Troy. 2013. "The US-South Korea Economic Relationship." *Education About Asia* 18, no. 3: 53–55.

Stangarone, Troy. 2021. "South Korea Moves Closer to Launching Its First Lunar Orbiter." *The Diplomat*. September 4, 2021. https://thediplomat.com/2021/09/south-korea-moves-closer-to-launching-its-first-lunar-orbiter/.

Stokes, Mark, Gabriel Alvarado, Emily Weinstein, and Ian Easton. 2020. "China's Space and Counterspace Capabilities and Activities." Project 2049 Institute. https://www.uscc.gov/sites/default/files/2020-05/China_Space_and_Counterspace_Activities.pdf.

United Nations Office for Outer Space Affairs. 2005. "Space Development Promotion Act." Selected Examples of National Laws Governing Space Activities: Republic of Korea. May 31, 2005. https://www.unoosa.org/oosa/en/ourwork/spacelaw/nationalspacelaw/republic_of_korea/space_development_promotions_actE.html.

Wall, Mike. 2023. "South Korea's Homegrown Nuri Rocket Launches 8 Satellites on 3rd-ever Mission (Photo)." *Space.com*. May 26, 2023. https://www.space.com/south-korea-nuri-rocket-launch-may-2023.

Wan, Stephanie. 2010. "U.S.-South Korean Space Cooperation: A Background on South Korea's Space Program, America's Geopolitical Influences, and Future Areas for Strategic Collaboration." The Secure World Foundation. September 2010. https://swfound.org/media/205872/us-korean_space_cooperation_final_sept_2010.pdf.

Weinzierl, Matt, and Mehak Sarang. 2021. "The Commercial Space Age is Here." *Harvard Business Review*. February 12, 2021. https://hbr.org/2021/02/the-commercial-space-age-is-here.

Yonhap News. 2022. "합참, 군사우주과 신설… 합동우주작전 수행체계 정립 등 임무." (Joint Chiefs of Staff Establishes Military and Space Division... Missions such as Establishment of

Joint Space Operation Execution System.) *Yonhap News*. January 3, 2022. https://m.donga science.com/news.php?idx=51427.

Yoon, Sukjoon. 2021 "Like It or Not, the South Korea-US Alliance is Changing." *The Diplomat*. August 27, 2021. https://thediplomat.com/2021/08/like-it-or-not-the-south-korea-us-allia nce-is-changing/.

CHAPTER 28

FROM PASSIVE TO ACTIVE SPACE POWERS

Australia and Aotearoa New Zealand

MATTHEW STUBBS AND DESISLAVA GANCHEVA

INTRODUCTION

IN this chapter, we examine the space security situation in New Zealand and Australia. As small and middle powers, respectively, in the Pacific, it might be expected that these two countries would have relatively little to contribute to the global space security picture. That expectation would be mistaken. As we will demonstrate, both New Zealand and Australia are significant space players, and they are in the process of redefining their interests in space security, moving from being passive users of space services to becoming contributors of space capabilities, building alliances, and contributing to space security dialogues.

This reflects the changing strategic environment in the Indo-Pacific region. Australia sees the Indo-Pacific region as "in the midst of the most consequential strategic realignment since the Second World War" (Department of Defence 2020a). The rise of geopolitical competition between China and the US in the Indo-Pacific region has sharpened regional states' focus on their own strategic vulnerability and need to modernize their military toolkit. Further, Space 2.0 has created commercial opportunities and states and their corporations want to capture a share of the global space economy. Such strategic and economic drivers have been crucial to Australia and New Zealand's calculus in becoming active players in the space domain.

While it might be tempting to see this move to active space participation as reflecting merely a neorealist turn, in our view the picture is more complex. In the second section of this chapter, we set out our theoretical approach to the space security perspectives of Australia and New Zealand. While there is strong evidence of neorealism in both Australia and New Zealand as seen by activities amounting to external balancing (and, in Australia's case, also internal balancing), we argue that other perspectives (including cosmopolitanism and neoliberalism) are also relevant to both nations' approaches. In this chapter we adopt an eclectic theorization approach, seeking to draw insights from a range of analytical traditions in order to capture the richness and complexity of current Australian and New Zealand practices in respect of space security.

In the third section, we begin by examining Australia's lengthy history as a space power, charting the growth of its aspirations in terms of sovereign space capability and the growth of its commercial space sector. The fourth section examines the emergence of space as a strategic consideration in New Zealand. In the fifth section, we examine both countries' engagement with multilateral space security dialogues. In the sixth section, we examine how Australia and New Zealand approach the issue of peaceful purposes. Finally, the seventh section reflects on the drivers of the evolution that we catalogue, and looks to the future, identifying several topics that are likely to be significant for the countries' engagement in space security matters going forward.

POLITICAL AND ECONOMIC DRIVERS OF AUSTRALIAN AND NEW ZEALAND SPACE SECURITY PERSPECTIVES

We locate ourselves in the tradition of eclectic theorizing identified by Peter Katzenstein and Rudra Sil, and our chapter deliberately draws on "eclectic modes of scholarship that trespass deliberately across competing research traditions with the intention of defining and exploring substantive problems in original, creative ways" (Katzenstein and Sil 2008, 126). We therefore seek to derive insights, where appropriate, from disparate international relations traditions including cosmopolitanism, neoliberalism, and neorealism.

We also find a mixture of economic and strategic drivers at play. We acknowledge the connection between economy and security, as Retter et al. (2021, 4) have observed: "[i]n the globally interconnected and interdependent world, the economy is intimately connected with both national and international security." However, the pursuit of economic growth can be a primarily domestic, rather than international, phenomenon, as Katzenstein (1976, 2) has noted, "economic policies result at least as much from the constraints of domestic structures as from the functional logic inherent in international effects." For example, we see that sometimes the primary driver of support for a domestic space industry is a matter of seeking to promote job-creation to derive domestic electoral advantage, yet at other times the same action can also be undertaken with a view to pursuing international strategic advantage.

There is no doubt that strategic perspectives and concerns are important motivators for the approaches to space security taken by Australia and New Zealand. Our analysis here shows Australia and New Zealand are responding to the threat posed by the increasing counter-space capabilities of strategic adversaries and also provides evidence of both countries seeking to guard against the potential for conflict.

There are also important economic drivers behind both countries' increasing investment in the space sector. Australia and New Zealand seek to increase their market share in the rapidly growing global space economy. Further, investment in the space sector is seen by both countries as promoting the growth of high-tech industry, creating jobs, and investing in technologies that have broader economic applications. The Australian Civil Space Strategy claims that between direct and spill-over benefits, all Australian market sectors are positively influenced by space capabilities (Australian Space Agency 2019, 6). This is supplemented by a prediction by the Review of Australia's Space Industry Capability that the "next generation" of high-tech jobs in Australia will have a dependence on these services, making investment in space crucial for the future of Australia's economy (Expert Reference Group 2018, 6).

Just as there are a mixture of economic and strategic drivers at play in the approaches to space security by both countries examined in this chapter, so we see a range of theoretical perspectives being relevant without any being dominant.

Outer space perhaps uniquely lends itself to cosmopolitan perspectives (see e.g., Schmidt 2022), because issues arising in space inherently transcend territorial boundaries, and space activities are dependent on international partnerships. Numerous policy statements from both Australia and New Zealand reflect a cosmopolitan approach. However, there is also no doubt that both countries are seeking to encourage the development of their own space industries, confounding any complete acceptance of cosmopolitanism.

Equally, there is much to suggest a neoliberal approach by both countries to outer space. To the extent that they have sought to promote cooperation between states in lieu of the pursuit of narrow self-interest, both Australia and New Zealand can be seen as embracing a neoliberal ideal (see e.g., Jervis 1999). This perspective is clear in both countries' extensive engagement in multilateral space security dialogues. However, neoliberalism sits somewhat awkwardly with the undoubted extent to which both countries have pursued means of government incentivization to stimulate the private space industry.

There is also considerable relevance of realism. This is particularly apparent in the defense space policy statements of both Australia and New Zealand, which make clear the threats to both countries from self-interested foreign actors in terms consistent with classic realism (see e.g., Fabian 2019). From a neorealist perspective (see e.g., Waltz 1979), in the approaches taken to respond to these threats we see in New Zealand considerable evidence of external balancing through reliance on alliances, while Australia is pursuing both internal balancing (through enhancing its sovereign capabilities) as well as external balancing (through extensive alliance building).

Ultimately, in our view, there are a complex mixture of influences on the approaches taken by both Australia and New Zealand to space security, which defy the adoption of any particular framework of analysis (whether neoliberalism or neorealism, cosmopolitanism or capitalism) as offering a comprehensive explanation for both countries' space policy. Instead, we see, through the lens of eclectic theorizing, the possibility of drawing insights from a range of traditions that can assist our understanding of the real-world conduct of Australia and New Zealand in defining their space security strategies.

AUSTRALIA'S JOURNEY IN CIVIL AND MILITARY SPACE

Australia's story in space began at the start of the space age in the late 1950s, with the establishment of a space launch facility at Woomera Rocket Range as well as tracking stations across the country. Australia's geography puts it in a unique position to provide Southern Hemisphere orbital coverage, and its vast landmass with low electro-magnetic pollution and clear skies make it a perfect location for space-tracking ground stations, telescopes, radars, and satellite communications.

During the early space age, Australia participated in a range of rocket testing programs and the Woomera Rocket Range played a pivotal role (Dougherty 2017b). Woomera went on to be used for the testing of several hundred UK (United Kingdom), Australian, European, and US sounding rockets. Australia was one of the first nations to launch its own satellite into space from its national territory: Weapons Research Establishment Satellite-1 or WRESAT, which was launched in 1967 on board a US Redstone rocket donated to Australia (DSTG, n.d.). By 1969, Australia hosted the largest number of tracking facilities outside the United States (Dougherty 2017a). Australia also became a founding member of the International Telecommunications Satellite (INTELSAT) consortium, established in 1964 to provide a global satellite tele-communications network.

There was no central government policy driving Australia's early involvement in space, and in the absence of a defined national space policy, Australia subsequently fell behind its allies in undertaking space activities. It was not until the Space Activities Act 1998 (Cth) that Australia passed national space legislation. The act instituted a "comprehensive regulatory framework for space activities in Australia" that was intended to attract investment but also ensure Australia met its international obligations under the United Nations Space Treaties (Dougherty 2017a, 3). No domestic commercial launch capability in fact resulted.

The lack of policy interest changed with the onset of Space 2.0, the rapid transformation of the space sector and the growing involvement of small and medium Australian enterprises in the global space industry. The Turnbull government came to reconsider Australian space engagement and the failure of Australia to capture a larger share of the global space industry (Bryce 2017). In mid-2017, the government announced the Review of Australia's Space Industry Capability which was undertaken by an Expert Reference Group (ERG) chaired by Dr Megan Clark AC. One of the review's key recommendations was the establishment of a space agency. In September 2017, the government announced the establishment of the Australian Space Agency during the International Astronautical Congress in South Australia.

The review and the government's response was a turning point for Australia's role in the space sector. It was followed by the passage of much needed amendments to the Space Activities Act 1998 (Cth), which is now known as the Space (Launches and Returns) Act 2018 (Cth). The establishment of the Australian Space Agency and reform of Australia's national space legislation has now put Australia on a path to meaningful growth in its space sector.

Space Agency Establishment and Achievements

The Australian Space Agency commenced operation on July 1, 2018, as a division within the Department of Industry, Innovation and Science. It soon released its charter (Australian Space Agency 2018), which indicated that: "The Agency's purpose is to transform and grow a globally respected Australian space industry that lifts the broader economy, inspires and improves the lives of Australians—underpinned by strong international and national engagement. The Agency is intended to embody the ambitious national space agenda that Australia had previously lacked and seek to establish Australia as a global space actor."

In 2019, the agency released "Advancing Space: Australian Civil Space Strategy 2019-2028," the first of its kind for Australia. Notably, this is a civil strategy with domestic economic motivations at its heart, although strategic concerns are also visible. The strategy is built on four strategic space pillars: open the door internationally; develop national capability in areas of competitive advantage; ensure safety and national interest are addressed; and inspire and improve the lives of all Australians. It also makes clear that meeting Australia's international obligations and supporting a rules-based order are central to achieving this vision (Australian Space Agency 2019, 4)—highlighting a cosmopolitan, neoliberal vision. It sets the foundation for growth in the space sector by laying out a phased investment in National Civil Space Priorities for Australia and sets a timetable for regulatory reform to enable launch to space from Australia and the foundations for human space flight from Australia (4).

In 2022, Australia made a number of financial commitments to grow the space sector, including: a AUS$32.3 million co-investment in spaceport or launch sites across Australia; AUS$32.5 million to procure and provide spaceflights for Australian technology to be launched into space; a framework for human spaceflight in Australia; a commitment to put an Australian astronaut in space; and AUS$52 million to create a manufacturing and test hub to produce launch vehicles and satellites. The Australian Space Agency will also develop a Space Strategic Update (Department of Industry, Science, Energy and Resources 2022). In its 2022 budget, Australia announced AUS$1.16 billion in funding (up to 2038) for a national space mission (National Space Mission for Earth Observation) designed to "strengthen our sovereign capability as well as grow the sector and create hundreds of new jobs" as well as to "make Australia more self-sufficient when it comes to critical Earth Observation data" (Price 2022). This demonstrates Australia's desire to move from being a consumer of space capabilities to being an active contributor through the development of sovereign earth observation capabilities.

The principal driver for these developments is the pursuit of economic opportunities, but there is also considerable evidence of a strategic desire to increase sovereign capabilities.

Australia's Defense Space Involvement and Space Policy

The Australian Defence Force's (ADF) uptake of space capabilities has, until recently, been driven more by operational necessity than concerted policy commitments. In 2003, Optus C-1, the world's largest hybrid commercial and military communications satellite, was launched. It provides the Department of Defence with satellite communications over Australia and in the Asia-Pacific region (Hill 2003). The ADF's ability to control the military payload of Optus C-1, and the more recently launched Intelsat-22 (in the Indian Ocean region), has highlighted the benefits of having sovereign control over satellite communications, when compared to relying on infrastructure controlled by other nations such as the US Wideband Global SATCOM program in which Australia is a partner.

The 2016 Defence White Paper was a turning point for Australia's journey in space. It identified six key drivers shaping Australia's security environment, including the emergence of new complex, non-geographic threats, such as the threats in cyberspace and space (Department of Defence 2016, 40–41, 51). The white paper highlighted the ADF's reliance on space-based capabilities to support a modern, networked military on operations, as well as the fact that potential adversaries are developing counter-space capabilities.

The Defence White Paper (and its accompanying Integrated Investment Plan) sought to invest about AUS$10 billion into strengthening Defence's space surveillance and space situational awareness capabilities to ensure the security of its space-enabled assets. It also acknowledged that limiting militarization in space will require international cooperation to establish and manage a rules-based system—"a prospect that does not seem likely in the immediate future" (Department of Defence 2016, 53). Here, the harsh tone of neorealism is unmistakable—the prospect of neoliberal or cosmopolitan solutions was expressly excluded and in their place a large investment (for a middle power) in internal balancing was chosen instead.

Defence Strategic Update and Force Structure Plan of 2020

In 2020, the Defence Strategic Update (DSU) and Force Structure Plan reassessed and adjusted defense policies and investments in response to the changing strategic environment. The strategic update positions Australia to be "able—and understood as willing—to deploy military power to shape our environment, deter actions against our interests and, when required, respond with military force" (Department of Defence 2020a, 6).

In relation to space, the government committed to significantly increase investment in Defence's space capabilities, including plans for a network of satellites to provide a sovereign communications network and an enhanced space control program. The government also committed to continue investment in space situational awareness. The total investments are approximately AUS$7 billion over the next decade (Department of Defence 2020a, 39). Further, the DSU commits to acquiring a sovereign space-based imagery capability to enhance coverage of the Indo-Pacific region (Department of Defence 2020a, 40).

In July 2020, the then Minister for Defence outlined three key facets of the government's space policy. First, enhancing sovereign capabilities to assure ADF access to space—this includes the capability acquisitions listed above as well as the creation of a Space Domain within the Royal Australian Air Force. Second, deepening cooperative relationships with key international partners and allies, such as the Combined Space Operations Initiative (CSpO). Third, developing technologies locally to protect Australian space assets and offering opportunities to export these capabilities to international partners (Reynolds 2020). Here we see again a mixture of driving forces—economic (in developing a domestic space industry) and neorealist (in the internal balancing of enhancing sovereign capability and the external balancing of alliances such as CSpO).

These policy statements marked a turning point, being the first time the government announced plans to "enhance Australian Defence Force space control capabilities to counter emerging space threats to Australia's free use of the space domain" (Department of Defence 2020b, 63). In July 2021, the Government provided more clarity on this capability through a media release from new Defence Minister Peter Dutton, which stated that "A Space Electronic Warfare capability, as part of the Australian Defence Force's approach to space control, seeks to detect and deter attempts to interfere with, or attack, our use of the space domain" (Dutton 2021).

In 2022, Defence established its Space Command. Space Command elevates and expands the previously created Space Domain and will involve members of all forces combining to better achieve Australia's strategic space objectives and assure Australia's access to space. To this end, Space Command will develop strategic space plans and policies and a resilient and effective space architecture in close collaboration with Australia's allies (Air Force 2022).

The securitization of space goes beyond the realm of defense. In 2020 and 2021, Australia passed national security legislation aimed at securing Australian critical infrastructure and resources. The space sector is specifically featured in the majority of these reforms. The Security of Critical Infrastructure Act 2018 (Cth) was amended to specifically include the space sector as one of eleven critical infrastructure sectors that it seeks to protect. Accordingly, satellite terminals, ground stations, or future space infrastructure can now be regarded as "critical infrastructure" under Australian law

---

Table 28.1. National Security Legislative and Policy Amendments in Australia and Their Relevance to the Australian Space Sector.

Security Legislation Amendment (Critical Infrastructure) Act 2021	Adds "space technology" to sectors to which the Security of Critical Infrastructure Act 2018 applies (Department of Home Affairs 2021b).
Telecommunications and Other Legislation Act 2017 (Cth) (known as the Telecommunication Security Sector Reforms)	Amends the Telecommunications Act 1997 to establish a security obligation on carriers to do their best to protect networks and facilities from unauthorized access and interference—including a requirement to maintain "competent supervision" and "effective control" over telecommunications networks and facilities owned or operated by them (Department of Home Affairs 2021c).
"Blueprint for Critical Technologies" and "The Action Plan for Critical Technologies"	"Transportation, robotics and space" is identified as one of the nine technologies that are "current and emerging technologies that have been identified as having a significant impact on our national interest (economic prosperity, national security and social cohesion)" (Department of the Prime Minister and Cabinet 2021a and 2021b).

(Department of Home Affairs 2021a). Space was also announced as one of six National Manufacturing Priorities under the AUS$1.3 billion Modern Manufacturing Initiative announced in October 2020, which was followed up by the release of the Space National Manufacturing Priority Road Map (Department of Industry, Science, Energy and Resources 2021). The space sector has thus been given due consideration and inclusion in recognition of the important role that such capabilities play for Australia's national security interests. Table 28.1 provides a summary of some pieces of policy and legislation that have recently been introduced, which apply to the space sector.

Thus far, we see Australia pursuing a predominantly economic motivation in its civil space policy and a predominantly neorealist security motivation in its defense space policy. The picture becomes even more complex once its concurrent diplomatic efforts are taken into account, as they will be in the fifth section. First, however, the next section addresses New Zealand's space security policies.

NEW ZEALAND AS A SPACE POWER

New Zealand is a comparatively new player in outer space. While it does not have the history of space engagement that Australia does, in the past decade New Zealand has publicly embraced commercial space activities, become a significant player in the space launch market, and has come to articulate security interests in respect of outer space.

A number of key developments for New Zealand occurred in 2016. First, the New Zealand Space Agency was established. Second, New Zealand became a member of the United Nations (UN) Committee on the Peaceful uses of Outer Space (COPUOS) (General Assembly 2016, 32). Third, it promulgated its first domestic space legislation, which became law the following year as the Outer Space and High-Altitude Activities Act 2017 (NZ) (Ministry of Business, Innovation & Employment, n.d.) Fourth, it concluded a Technology Safeguards Agreement (TSA) with the United States. Fifth, it commenced the formal steps in its domestic law to become a party to the Registration Convention, which it did on January 23, 2018. Sixth, it undertook important regulatory preparations for its first commercial space launch, signing a contract with Rocket Lab on September 17, 2016, which cleared the way for the launch of a test rocket from the Mahia Peninsula on May 25, 2017 (Joyce 2016). We examine Rocket Lab and New Zealand's domestic launch capability in more detail below.

In many ways, these developments were motivated more by the desire to establish an effective commercial space industry than they were by any security considerations. Equally, however, even in these ostensibly commercially focused activities, the strategic significance of outer space was clear in the actions of the government of New Zealand.

New Zealand as a COPUOS member

In its statement to the Fourth Committee of the UN General Assembly regarding joining COPUOS, New Zealand noted both motivations. First, it explained that it "takes its responsibilities as a country hosting space launches extremely seriously" and wished to "enable the development of a space industry in New Zealand, while ensuring its safe, secure and responsible operation." Second, it stated that it "relies on assured access to space-based systems to support its economic prosperity and maintain public safety. We have a clear interest in working with international partners to promote the responsible and peaceful use of space" (Ministry of Foreign Affairs and Trade 2016). The statement by New Zealand at the fifty-ninth COPUOS session in 2016 reiterated both these points, adding that "a rules based approach to the responsible use of space by all nations is ultimately necessary to ensure that access to and use of space can be maintained for all" (Ministry of Foreign Affairs and Trade 2016).

New Zealand's articulation of the strategic significance of outer space is also reflected in the much quieter process a year earlier in 2015 when it formally became part of the Combined Space Operations initiative (CSpO) (Neas 2020), a matter we address below. These statements by New Zealand in the context of its joining COPUOS mix the economic with the strategic, in a similar way to Australian statements considered earlier.

Outer Space and High-Altitude Activities Act 2017 (NZ)

New Zealand maintains a strong commercial focus in space and has stated that "The establishment of a New Zealand-based space industry is strongly aligned with the Government's Business Growth Agenda" (Foreign Affairs, Defence and Trade Committee 2016, 1).

The Outer Space and High-Altitude Activities Act 2017 (NZ) addresses the various permits required to undertake activities relevant to outer space. In practice, the primary clients launching from New Zealand have been from the United States. Given the bilateral relationship has not been without its challenges over the years, particularly in respect of nuclear matters, this is a significant strategic engagement between the two states.

Technology Safeguards Agreement (2016)

In 2016, New Zealand concluded a TSA with the United States, to "facilitate the development of a New Zealand-based space industry that is internationally credible, well-connected and competitive" (Foreign Affairs, Defence and Trade Committee 2016, 1). The TSA is "consistent with New Zealand's firm commitment to countering the proliferation of weapons of mass destruction and their means of delivery" (New Zealand 2016, 2). But non-proliferation was accompanied by a harder-edged motivation as well: "Without the TSA, New Zealand based space operators will not be given access to the US technology they require . . . Similarly, US payloads will not be approved for transfer to New Zealand" (New Zealand 2016, 3).

At what price did the TSA get New Zealand access to US rocket launch technology? Some of the restrictions accepted by New Zealand are unavoidable, given the fact that rockets and launch vehicles appear on the US Munitions List (22 CFR § 121.1) and are thus subject to the United States' highly restrictive Arms Export Control laws (22 USC § 2778). Accordingly, the TSA requires the preparation of Technology Transfer Control Plans (Art. 4(4)), and New Zealand agrees to "prevent unescorted or unmonitored access" by New Zealand representatives (Art. 4(2)) and ensure that US participants "retain control" of (Art. 4(3)) US launch vehicles, spacecraft, related equipment, and/or technical data, as well as the "segregated areas" for storing US technology, which it is required to establish and place under US control (Art. 4(3)). New Zealand further undertakes to prevent re-transfer of US material and information (Art. 5(2)).

While those restrictions are an unavoidable cost of doing business with the United States, New Zealand also "assures" the United States that it "will not develop or acquire" any Missile Technology Control Regime (MCTR) Category I rocket systems "without prior consultation" with the United States" (Art. 3(1)). Notwithstanding that consultation is a low barrier, this is in our view an unreasonable restriction on the development of New Zealand's sovereign space capabilities. It is one thing to accept limitations on US technology, but quite another to accept unrelated restrictions on the development of technology in New Zealand.

The practical effect of the US international trade in arms regulations noted above is that US rocket technology can only be used and controlled by US companies. Accordingly, the now-prominent New Zealand space start-up Rocket Lab in 2013 became a subsidiary of a US parent company, Rocket Lab USA. In part, this was a business decision because of the availability of capital and customers in the United States. But it was also rendered almost inevitable by US export controls. As Rocket Lab founder Peter Beck has acknowledged, one of the reasons for establishing Rocket Lab USA as the parent company in 2013 was that "the launch vehicle is a U.S. launch vehicle, so there's a lot of legal reasons why we need to be a U.S. company" (Botsford End 2015).

New Zealand did, however, secure one concession in its TSA—the United States is required to provide "a written statement of the function of each US spacecraft with sufficient information . . . to determine whether a launch would be consistent with the laws, regulations and policies" of New Zealand. This provision ensures that New Zealand is able to comply with its own policies, and in particular the New Zealand Nuclear Free Zone, Disarmament, and Arms Control Act 1987 (NZ).

New Zealand's Strategic Policy Position Regarding Space

New Zealand has made a number of public policy statements relevant to space security in the defense context. As the 2019 Defence Capability Plan put it, space-based systems "are a prerequisite to maintaining a professional, combat capable and flexible force" (New Zealand 2019, 131). Noting that New Zealand does not have its own space-based defense infrastructure (26), the policy articulates two principal foci. First, striking a multilateralist tone, it indicates that: "A rules-based approach to the responsible and peaceful use of space by all nations is ultimately necessary to ensure that access to and use of space can be maintained" (19). Second, however, the policy articulates cooperation with key allies (a form of external balancing) as essential: "Defence also supports the promotion of New Zealand's interests through its engagement on space issues with the Combined Space Operations initiative . . . As New Zealand's Defence partners move towards closer interoperability in space, Defence must ensure it has the right people with the right expertise to contribute" (38).

This is perhaps an inevitable approach for a small power, but it nonetheless displays a considerable maturity—recognizing its strategic dependence on outer space, and its dependence on allies in providing it with access to space, while pursuing multilateral means to advance space security.

In 2022, the New Zealand Space Agency released a consultation paper for a New Zealand space policy (New Zealand Space Agency 2022). The foreword by Stuart Nash, Minister for Economic and Regional Development, speaks to both economic and security considerations. Thus, he lauds New Zealand's "journey to becoming a space faring country" and highlights that "In 2018/19, our space sector contributed $1.69 billion to our national economy and supported 12,000 jobs" (1). Further, he explains that: "Space is also becoming more crowded and complex, and making sure it is used sustainably is a global challenge. As a small nation, we have an interest in having a strong international rules-based system that ensures space is used responsibly and peacefully" (1).

The consultation paper identifies five cross-cutting government interests in space, being: economic, national security, international, safe and secure regulation, and environmental. Of the national security interest, the document indicates that "Space technologies protect and advance New Zealand's national security interests," particularly highlighting space contributions to maritime domain awareness and support for New Zealand Defence Force operations (7), of which it later highlights humanitarian assistance and disaster relief (HADR) and stability and support operations (14–15). On the international interest, the document notes that "New Zealand promotes the responsible use of space internationally."

The consultation paper outlines New Zealand's national security objectives in space as, among others, to: (1) "use space assets to protect and advance New Zealand's national security and economic interests," (2) "manage the broad range of security risks in space," and (3) "collaborate with international space and security partners to pursue New Zealand's national security and economic interests" (13). It specifically identifies threats including "irresponsible space activities that cause debris" and "malicious interference with our critical infrastructure" (13) as well as remote and physical interference with space systems (16). The consultation paper also highlights the importance of "Defence space cooperation" with international partners to "ensure our national security space operations promote a secure, stable, safe, peaceful, and operationally sustainable space domain."

New Zealand's international policy objectives in respect of space are said to include: (1) "advocating for effective international rules, norms and standards," (2) "partnering with like-minded launch states," and (3) "collaborating internationally to increase New Zealand's influence and capabilities" (23).

New Zealand's strategic policy approach to space thus incorporates at least three key positions. First, it emphasizes the multilateral options for promoting space security, a cosmopolitan approach to building international regulation (consistent with a neoliberal account, as well as an external balancing strategy consistent within a neorealist approach). Second, it seeks to have the economic benefits of its space industry, even if they come at some cost, as the New Zealand-US TSA arguably did, placing particular emphasis on New Zealand's space launch capability (consistently with a neorealist account). Third, it recognizes that the access to space capabilities that it needs for defense will come as part of broader strategic alliances with key allies, rather than through its own capabilities. Compared with Australia, New Zealand's approach is more reliant on external balancing, as New Zealand is not in a position to make the investments in sovereign capability to match Australia's internal balancing strategies.

New Zealand and Australian Multilateral Engagement on Space

Australia was an inaugural member of COPUOS from 1958, and New Zealand has been a member since 2016. Both have been contributors to multilateral space security dialogues in a variety of contexts. In this section we examine a sample of their more recent multilateral space security engagement.

General Assembly Resolutions 75/36 and 76/231

Australia was one of the sponsors of the UK-led process leading to UN General Assembly Resolution 75/36 "Reducing Space Threats through Norms, Rules and Principles of Responsible Behaviours." This apparently anodyne resolution—chiefly asking states to "reach a common understanding of how best to act to reduce threats to space systems" and "share their ideas on the further development and implementation of norms, rules and principles of responsible behaviours"—saw votes against it from China and Russia and an abstention from India. Whatever might be the merits of that debate, both Australia and New Zealand (along with China, India, Russia, and others) have responded to the invitation to transmit their ideas to the UN Secretary-General.

Australia commenced by articulating an expressly security focused goal: "Threats—or the perception of threats—against space systems contribute to geopolitical instability and insecurity. It is thus vital to reduce these threats by articulating and maintaining responsible behaviours in relation to space systems" (Australia 2022, 1). Australia added that this "would also facilitate certainty and stability necessary to encourage investment in and growth of the commercial space sector" (1). It seems significant to us that security was the first matter raised and commercial uses of space the second.

Australia then suggested ten proposed principles. Some of the principles refer to threats that Australia shares with all nations. They express a concern for preserving access to space, including avoidance of debris and promoting transparency and predictability. These are matters that would have a great impact on small and middle powers, which are consumers of space services. Other proposed principles reflect the perspective of a middle power seeking to develop and safeguard its own space capabilities. Thus, Australia seeks clarity around rendezvous and proximity operations and clarification of how classic principles such as due regard might apply to non-kinetic interference with space systems.

New Zealand similarly indicated that it "is strongly committed to the peaceful, safe, stable, secure and sustainable use of outer space" (New Zealand 2021, 2). New Zealand highlighted that "all countries have a strong national and collective interest in ensuring the safe, responsible and peaceful use of outer space" (2). This multilateralist perspective fits the interests of a small power.

In these statements, both Australia and New Zealand demonstrate a mature understanding of threats to space security. Both are proactively engaging in multilateral dialogues to pursue opportunities to enhance space security in a manner that is consistent with the approaches of their key allies Canada, the UK, and the United States. Notably, however, neither state is actively pursuing new treaty proposals. Indeed, Australia has been very clear in its rejection of the Russia-China proposal for a treaty on the Prevention of the Placement of Weapons in Outer Space, the Threat or Use of Force Against Outer Space Objects (PPWT), as well as its rejection of no first placement initiatives (Mansfield 2018, 3).

Australia was one of the sponsors of General Assembly Resolution 76/231 "Reducing Space Threats through Norms, Rules and Principles of Responsible Behaviours" of December 2021, which established an Open-Ended Working Group on this topic to report to the General Assembly in 2023 (again, over the negative votes of China and Russia and with India abstaining) (United Nations, 2021). One of the functions of that working group is to "Make recommendations on possible norms, rules and principles of responsible behaviours relating to threats by States to space systems"—creating the possibility that this initiative will be the locus of important developments on space security in the coming years, to which both Australia and New Zealand will be contributors.

Artemis Accords

A key development in 2020–2021 for both Australia and New Zealand was their becoming signatories to the Artemis Accords. This is significant for a number of reasons. First, it explicitly links both countries to the space program of the United States. Second, it shows that both countries accept that space law is most likely to be developed through means other than the development of new multilateral treaties. Third, it indicates particular views as to the interpretation and application of the Outer Space Treaty (OST), as the Artemis Accords do advance previous understandings of the law in areas including the legality of obtaining title to space resources through extraction and the legality of declaring limited safety zones around space resource utilization facilities.

Statements made by both countries upon signature indicate some important policy perspectives. New Zealand made three key points: "we take responsibilities of kaitiakitanga [guardianship] of the space environment seriously," that the accords respond to the "need for additional rules or standards to ensure the conservation and long-term sustainability" of space activities, and that "Space exploration not only increases our knowledge of our planet and universe and encourages research, science and innovation, it also provides economic opportunities for New Zealand" (Mahuta and Nash 2021). Australia made a similarly cosmopolitan observation that it was "establishing vital principles that will create a safe, peaceful, and prosperous future in space for all of humanity to enjoy," but also focused on commercial opportunities: "Given Australia's capabilities in space communications, robotics and automation, Earth observation, space medicine as well as capabilities in the resources sector, Australia is ready to contribute its best ideas and knowhow to support the future of space exploration" (Australian Space Agency 2020c).

Combined Space Operations Initiative (CSpO)

Both New Zealand and Australia are also part of the Combined Space Operations Initiative (CSpO). Established in 2014 with Australia, Canada, the UK, and the United States as original parties, CSpo has grown to include New Zealand (2015), Germany

(2019), and France (2020). The body serves as an important locus for cooperation in space security, which is given particular operational focus through its members' involvement in the Combined Space Operations Centre (CSpOC). Although CSpO is not a public-facing activity, its Principles Board has nonetheless made statements regarding space threats, including condemning Russia's November 2021 anti-satellite (ASAT) test as "dangerous destructive testing" which risks "damaging space objects, and threatens the security of current and future space explorers" (Defence Connect 2021).

Peaceful Purposes

Australia and New Zealand frequently commit to the exploration and use of outer space for peaceful purposes in accordance with the requirement under art IV of the OST that the moon and other celestial bodies are to be used exclusively for peaceful purposes. Notwithstanding its rather cosmopolitan attractions, though, for the most part the frequent invocation of "peaceful purposes" is something of a mantra—a phenomenon which is true globally, not just for Australia and New Zealand.

Australia, which is committed to developing significant sovereign military space security capabilities, regards such activities as consistent with its peaceful purposes obligations. Australia's 2013 Satellite Utilisation Policy provides the clearest indication of its approach to peaceful purposes. Principle 4 is that Australia will "Contribute to a stable space environment," which is explained to mean that "Australia will continue to support rules-based international access to the space environment; promoting peaceful, safe and responsible activities in space" (DIISRTE 2013, 13). The policy goes on to identify a range of relevant commitments, including that Australia will support "international regulatory frameworks applicable to space" and also "appropriate international space arms control and transparency and confidence-building measures." Similar approaches to the peaceful purposes obligation can be seen in Australia's response to General Assembly resolution 75/36 (Australia 2022) and in the statement of Dr Megan Clark AC upon signature of the Artemis Accords (Department of Industry, Science, Energy and Resources 2020). While the peaceful purposes obligation does not apply to the void space where satellites are located in any event (Cheng 2000), what is more important is that Australia views peaceful purposes through the lens of space sustainability and treats it as requiring compliance with the other norms of space law (and international law more generally), not as imposing some different obligation. As with most states, Australia also treats peaceful purposes as requiring non-aggressive, rather than non-military, use of celestial bodies (ADDP 2016, [1.24]).

Similarly, New Zealand has noted that "all countries have a strong national and collective interest in ensuring the safe, responsible and peaceful use of outer space" and it has identified the "collective interest . . . to ensure the safe and secure access to and use of space, and a space environment that is sustainable, peaceful, and free from conflict" (New Zealand 2021, 2). Again, here peaceful purposes is invoked in the context of space sustainability, absence of conflict, and preservation of the rules-based order.

These views regarding peaceful purposes have some of the hallmarks of cosmopolitan and neoliberal approaches as befitting small and middle powers, although there is also more than a touch of realism in adopting an approach to peaceful purposes that also permits a quite extensive range of activities by the state. Perhaps the most important lesson from these perspectives, though, is that Australia and New Zealand see their peaceful purposes obligations as inherent in compliance with their other obligations in respect of non-aggressive uses of outer space consistent with the goal of space sustainability and not as imposing some broader or free-standing restriction on space activities.

REFLECTIONS ON DRIVERS, FUTURE OPPORTUNITIES, AND CHALLENGES

We end with some final reflections on present and future trends and challenges.

Drivers

Ultimately, in this analysis we have seen evidence of motivations from a range of intellectual traditions. The move to active participation in space through Australia's drive to develop sovereign capabilities (and New Zealand's existing launch capabilities) are clear examples of internal balancing consistent with a neorealist approach, and both countries engage in external balancing through alliances. However, both Australia and New Zealand also conceive of outer space in the context of the preservation of the applicable international normative regime, which is consistent with cosmopolitan and neoliberal accounts. There is also evidence of space security being viewed through a domestic economic lens, which sits outside of these theoretically driven approaches altogether.

In addition to this evidence of the relevance of a number of different drivers impacting Australian and New Zealand approaches to space security, we have also seen some divergence of perspectives within nations. This is clearest with Australia, where Defence appears to be taking a neorealist perspective, the Australian Space Agency pursuing economic goals, and multilateral engagement (led by the Department of Foreign Affairs and Trade) being consistent with cosmopolitan and neoliberal accounts. Although this may seem incoherent, instead we see it as reflecting the complexity of drivers of space security engagement—and justifying our choice of eclectic theorization as a paradigm through which to examine the movement of both Australia and New Zealand in the direction of active, instead of merely passive, engagement in space.

Australian Alliance Building

The AUKUS partnership between Australia, the UK, and the United States (announced on September 16, 2021) could also have important consequences for Australia's space future. Enrico Palermo, Head of the Australian Space Agency, has noted the potential for "even greater trade and collaboration across the space sector in the near future" as a result (*The Guardian*, 2021). While this statement appears commercially focused, that increased strategic collaborations in space are under consideration is illustrated by the joint statement issued at the annual Australia-US meeting of Foreign and Defence Ministers (AUSMIN) on September 16, 2021, which indicated that: "The United States and Australia recognize the importance of establishing shared capabilities in Space Domain Awareness, Space Command and Control, Satellite Communications, and Positioning, Navigation, and Timing" (Department of State 2021). While it remains unclear exactly how AUKUS will impact on Australia's space security in the future, there is considerable potential for AUKUS to create enhanced opportunities for Australia in a variety of space contexts.

Further, Australia is a member of the Quadrilateral Security Dialogue (Quad) along with India, Japan, and the United States. On September 24, 2021, the Quad Leaders issued a joint statement that specifically highlighted agreement on heightened space cooperation: "In space we will identify new collaboration opportunities and share satellite data for peaceful purposes . . . We will also consult on rules, norms, guidelines and principles for ensuring the sustainable use of outer space" (White House 2021a).

At the same time as making this statement, the Quad established a Space Working Group (White House 2021b). While it has yet to be seen what this body achieves, the promise of enhanced space cooperation amongst the four Quad nations is an interesting one. Through both AUKUS and the Quad, Australia is poised to enter a new era of enhanced space security partnerships, constituting a powerful external balancing strategy.

Australian TSA Negotiation

We have earlier addressed the restrictive nature of certain provisions of the New Zealand-US TSA. There is also a questionable restrictive provision to be found in the UK-US TSA. The UK undertakes to "Not use funds obtained from Launch Activities for programs for the acquisition, development, production, testing, deployment, or use of rocket or unmanned aerial vehicle systems" (Art 3(1)(e)). We see no reason why any nation should be prevented from using the funds from launch activities to develop their own space industries. This provision, and the related provision found in the TSA concluded by New Zealand requiring consultation before domestic capabilities are developed, is an example of overreach by the United States—well beyond any measure that could be seen as necessary to protect US technology.

Australia is in negotiations with the United States for a TSA (Porter 2021). It is to be hoped that in it there will be no provisions equivalent to the two unfavorable provisions noted above. While there are inevitable limits required by United States domestic legislation, there is scope for Australia as a senior ally and member of the AUKUS partnership to secure a better deal than both New Zealand and the UK in their TSAs.

CONCLUSION

In this chapter, we have examined the space security situation in New Zealand and Australia. It has been a story of considerable development in the past decade, with both countries developing increasingly sophisticated understandings of the strategic importance of space to them, and the opportunities they have to enhance their space security situation.

Domestically, both countries have been encouraging the growth of their commercial space sectors. Interestingly, despite Australia's longer history of involvement in space, New Zealand proved to be more agile, and it has developed an effective launch capability. In order to secure this launch market, New Zealand had to accept a TSA with the United States, which imposes some restrictions on its space activities. Australia is currently negotiating a TSA, and as it is an important ally to the United States, we hope the conditions of the negotiations are more favorable than those endured by New Zealand and the UK. Both Australia and New Zealand have established space agencies and both have national space legislation regulating and licensing commercial space activities. The commercial space industry in both countries is booming. In this perspective on space, we can see internal balancing at play, as well as some domestically focused economic drivers.

As would be expected of small and middle powers, promoting multilateral engagement is important for both countries. Both are members of COPUOS and have been supporters of the process that has led to the establishment of the Open-Ended Working Group on Reducing Space Threats through Norms, Rules and Principles of Responsible Behaviours. While both countries have expressed quite altruistic perspectives in this respect at times, New Zealand has also described its motivation in terms of *kaitiakitanga*, a Māori word conveying an obligation of guardianship over the outer space environment. Australia and New Zealand recognize their potentially influential role in respect of space security at the UN and in other multilateral forums, and they both recognize that they have vital national security interests in the space domain, reflecting cosmopolitan and neoliberal accounts.

Australia and New Zealand are customers of a range of space-based services. However, both have displayed an increasing awareness of the vulnerability this creates. For a middle power such as Australia, one available solution is to develop sovereign capability—something Australia is dramatically expanding its focus on, as a form of internal balancing. As a smaller power, New Zealand lacks the resources to be able to make such a large investment in sovereign space capability. As a result, it has looked (as has Australia) to its allies, seeing cooperation and interoperability in space as essential means of meeting its space security needs, as a form of external balancing. There are some important cooperative relationships shared by both countries, including being signatories to the Artemis Accords and members of CSpO. Australia has additional new partnerships, however, through AUKUS and the Quad, both of which have the potential to have significant positive impacts on Australia's space security situation into the future.

Australia and New Zealand have had a positive impact on space security, exceeding that which might be expected from nations of their size. They are players in multilateral space diplomacy, consumers of space-based services, and have rapidly developing space industries. Both nations are active in regional architectures with key partners and allies, which provide a level of protection around their access to space-based services. Australia is additionally developing sovereign space capability in satellite communications, imaging, and space control. Although New Zealand and Australia remain exposed to significant space security threats, they have both been taking practical and effective steps to mitigate those threats and take advantage of the opportunities (commercial and strategic) available to them. The drivers of these actions are complex, and we have argued that eclectic theorization offers the best explanation for the range of factors which have motivated Australia and New Zealand in their journeys toward more active participation in space.

References

"Agreement between the Government of New Zealand and the Government of the United States of America on Technology Safeguards Associated with United States Participation in Space Launches from New Zealand." Signed June 16, 2016, entered into force December 12, 2016, NZTS 2016/14 ("TSA").

"Agreement in the form of an Exchange of Notes between the Government of the United Kingdom of Great Britain and Northern Ireland and the Government of the United States of America on Technology Safeguards associated with United States Participation in Space Launches from the United Kingdom." Signed 16 June 2020.

Air Force. 2022. "Defence Space Command." https://www.airforce.gov.au/our-mission/defence-space-command.

Australia. 2022. "Australian Submission to the Report of the Secretary-General on Resolution 75/36 on Reducing Space Threats through Norms, Rules and Principles of Responsible Behaviours." https://front.un-arm.org/wp-content/uploads/2021/05/Australian-Submission-to-the-report-on-Resolution-75-36-final.pdf.

Australian Defence Doctrine Publication (ADDP) 2016. "Operational Employment of Space." No. 3.18. 2nd ed.

Australian Space Agency. 2018. Australian Space Agency Charter. 18-COM12765. Canberra: Australian Government.

Australian Space Agency. 2019. Advancing Space: Australian Civil Space Strategy 2019–2028. ISBN 978-1-925050-93-6. Canberra: Commonwealth of Australia.

Australian Space Agency. 2020a. *Advancing Space: Communications Technologies and Services Roadmap 2021–2030*. ISBN 978-1-922125-80-4. Adelaide: Australian Space Agency.

Australian Space Agency. 2020b. *State of Space Report: January 1, 2018–June 30, 2019*. Canberra: Commonwealth of Australia.

Australian Space Agency. 2020c. "Australia Signs NASA's Artemis Accords." Media Release. Department of Industry, Science, Energy and Resources. October 14, 2020. https://www.industry.gov.au/news/australia-signs-nasas-artemis-accords.

Australian Space Agency. 2021. "Moon to Mars initiative: Launching Australian industry to space." Department of Industry, Science, Energy and Resources. February 16, 2021. https://www.industry.gov.au/news/moon-to-mars-initiative-launching-australian-industry-to-space.

Botsford End, Rae. 2015. "Rocket Lab: The Electron, the Rutherford and Why Peter Beck Started it in the First Place." *SpaceFlight Insider*. May 2, 2015. https://www.spaceflightinsider.com/missions/commercial/rocket-lab-electron-rutherford-peter-beck-started-first-place/.

Bryce Space and Technology, 2017. "Global Space Industry Dynamics." Bryce Space and Technology. https://brycetech.com/reports/report-documents/Global_Space_Industry_Dynamics_2017.pdf.

Cheng, Bin. 2000. "Properly Speaking, Only Celestial Bodies Have Been Reserved for Use Exclusively for Peaceful (Non . . . Military) Purposes, but Not Outer Void Space." *International Law Studies* 75: 81–117.

Defence Connect. 2021. "CSpO Members Condemn Russia's Anti-satellite Missile Test." *Defence Connect*. December 9, 2021. https://www.defenceconnect.com.au/key-enablers/9226-cspo-members-condemn-russia-s-anti-satellite-missile-test.

Defence Science and Technology Group (DSTG). n.d. "WRESAT—WEAPONS RESEARCH ESTABLISHMENT SATELLITE." https://www.dst.defence.gov.au/innovation/wresat-%E2%80%94-weapons-research-establishment-satellite?msclkid=52109886c87d11ec88678494f105703a.

Department of Defence. 2016. *2016 Defence White Paper*. ISBN 978-0-9941680-5-4. Canberra: Commonwealth of Australia.

Department of Defence. 2020a. *Defence Strategic Update*. Commonwealth of Australia.

Department of Defence. 2020b. *Force Structure Plan*. Commonwealth of Australia.

Department of Home Affairs. 2021a. "Protecting Critical Infrastructure and Systems of National Significance." June 1, 2021. https://www.homeaffairs.gov.au/reports-and-publications/submissions-and-discussion-papers/protecting-critical-infrastructure-systems.

Department of Home Affairs. 2021b. "Security of Critical Infrastructure Act 2018." December 10, 2021. https://www.homeaffairs.gov.au/about-us/our-portfolios/national-security/security-coordination/security-of-critical-infrastructure-act-2018.

Department of Home Affairs. 2021c. "Telecommunications sector security reforms." November 5, 2021. https://www.homeaffairs.gov.au/nat-security/Pages/telecommunications-sector-security-reforms.aspx.

DIISRTE (Department of Industry, Innovation, Science, Research and Tertiary Education). 2013. *Australia's Satellite Utilisation Policy*. DIISRTE 12/257. Canberra: Commonwealth of Australia.

Department of Industry, Science, Energy and Resources. 2022. "Keeping Australia's Space Sector Soaring." https://www.industry.gov.au/news/keeping-australias-space-sector-soaring.

Department of Industry, Science, Energy and Resources. 2020. "Australia Signs NASA's Artemis Accords." October 14, 2020. https://www.industry.gov.au/news/australia-signs-nasas-artemis-accords.

Department of State. "Joint Statement on Australia—US Ministerial Consultations (AUSMIN) 2021." https://www.state.gov/joint-statement-on-australia-u-s-ministerial-consultations-ausmin-2021/.

Department of the Prime Minister and Cabinet. 2021a. *Blueprint for Critical Technologies: The Australian Government's Framework for Capitalising on Critical Technologies to Drive a Technologically-Advanced, Future-Ready Nation.* ISBN 978-1-925364-81-1. Canberra: Commonwealth of Australia.

Department of the Prime Minister and Cabinet. 2021b. *The Action Plan for Critical Technologies.* Canberra: Commonwealth of Australia.

Dougherty, Kerrie. 2017a. *Australia in Space: A History of a Nation's Involvement.* Hindmarsh: ATF Press.

Dougherty, Kerrie. 2017b. "Lost in Space: Australia Dwindled from Space Leader To Also-Ran in 50 Years." *The Conversation.* September 22, 2017. https://theconversation.com/lost-in-space-australia-dwindled-from-space-leader-to-also-ran-in-50-years-83310.

Dutton, Peter. 2021. "Defence Explores Options for Space Electronic Warfare." Media release. Department of Defence. July 29, 2021. https://www.minister.defence.gov.au/minister/peter-dutton/media-releases/defence-explores-options-space-electronic-warfare.

Expert Reference Group. 2018. *Review of Australia's Space Industry Capability.* Canberra: Department of Industry, Science, Energy and Resources.

Fabian, Christopher David. 2019. *A Neoclassical Realist's Analysis of Sino-U.S. Space Policy.* Grand Forks: ProQuest Dissertations Publishing.

General Assembly. 2016. *International Cooperation in the Peaceful Uses of Outer Space.* Resolution 71/90. UN Doc A/RES/71/90.

Hill, Robert. 2003. "New Era of Defence Communications Launched into Space." Media release. Defence Ministers & Parliamentary Secretary. June 12, 2003. https://parlinfo.aph.gov.au/parlInfo/download/media/pressrel/S7N96/upload_binary/s7n962.pdf;fileType=application%2Fpdf#search=%22media/pressrel/S7N96%22.

Jervis, Robert. 1999. "Realism, Neoliberalism, and Cooperation: Understanding the Debate." *International Security* 42, no. 24: 1.

Joyce, Steven. 2016. "Govt Signs Contract Authorising Rocket Lab Launches." Media Release. New Zealand Government. September 17, 2016. https://www.beehive.govt.nz/release/govt-signs-contract-authorising-rocket-lab-launches.

Katzenstein, Peter J. 1976. "International Relations and Domestic Structures: Foreign Economic Policies of Advanced Industrial States." International Organization 1, no. 30: 1.

Katzenstein, Peter, and Rudra Sil. 2008. "Eclectic Theorising in the Study and Practice of international Relations." In *The Oxford Handbook of International Relations,* edited by Christian Reus-Smit and Duncan Snidal, 109. New York: Oxford University Press.

Mahuta, Nanaia, and Stuart Nash. 2021. "Space Exploration Soars with Artemis Accords." Media Release. New Zealand Government. June 1, 2021. https://www.beehive.govt.nz/release/space-exploration-soars-artemis-accords.

Mansfield, Sally. 2018. "Statement by H.E. Sally Mansfield, Ambassador and Permanent Representative of Australia to the United Nations, Geneva." https://www.un.org/disarmament/wp-content/uploads/2018/11/statement-by-australia-os.pdf.

Ministry of Business, Innovation & Employment. n.d. "Outer Space and High-Altitude Activities Regulatory System." https://www.mbie.govt.nz/cross-government-functions/reg ulatory-stewardship/regulatory-systems/outer-space-and-high-altitude-activities-regulat ory-system/.

Ministry of Foreign Affairs and Trade. 2016. "Membership of the Committee on the Peaceful Uses of Outer Space. https://www.mfat.govt.nz/en/media-and-resources/membership-of-the-committee-on-the-peaceful-uses-of-outer-space/.

Neas, Ollie. 2020. "Revealed: New Zealand's Role in the New American War-Fighting Frontier—Space." *The Spinoff*. January 14, 2020. https://thespinoff.co.nz/society/14-01-2020/revealed-new-zealands-role-in-the-new-american-war-fighting-frontier-space.

New Zealand. 2016. "National Interest Analysis—Technology Safeguards Agreement." https://www.parliament.nz/resource/en-NZ/00DBSCH_ITR_69357_1/a547a574617eef61024dd d01b00c797a1f01229a.

New Zealand. 2019. *Defence Capability Plan 2019*. ISBN 978-0-478-27899-6. Wellington: Ministry of Defence.

New Zealand. 2021. "Norms, Rules and Principles of Responsible Behaviours in Space: New Zealand Contribution."

New Zealand Space Agency. 2022. "New Zealand Space Policy Review Consultation." https://www.mbie.govt.nz/have-your-say/new-zealand-space-policy-review.

Porter, Christian. 2021. "New Measures to Help Grow Australia's Civil Space Sector." Media release. Ministers for the Department of Industry, Science, Energy and Resources. July 1, 2021. https://www.minister.industry.gov.au/ministers/porter/media-releases/new-measu res-help-grow-australias-civil-space-sector.

Price, Melissa. 2022. "Australia's First National Space Mission Central to Budget 2022–23." Media release. https://www.minister.industry.gov.au/ministers/price/media-releases/aus tralias-first-national-space-mission-central-budget-2022-23.

Retter, Lucia, et al. 2021. *Relationships between the Economy and National Security*. Cambridge: RAND Europe.

Reynolds, Linda. 2020. "Defence in Space: Securing the New Frontier." Media release. Department of Defence. July 28, 2020. https://www.minister.defence.gov.au/statements/2020-07-28/defence-space-securing-new-frontier.

Schmidt, Nikola. 2022.*Governance of Emerging Space Challenges: The Benefits of a Responsible Cosmopolitan State Policy*. New York: Springer.

The Guardian. 2021. "Aukus Pact to Deepen Australia, US Collaboration on Space Technology." October 7, 2021. https://www.theguardian.com/science/2021/oct/07/aukus-pact-to-deepen-australia-us-collaboration-on-space-technology.

United Nations. 2021. "Reducing Space Threats through Norms, Rules and Principles of Responsible Behaviours." First Committee, General Assembly. UN Doc A/C.1/76/L.52.

Waltz, Kenneth N. 1979. *Theory of International Politics*. Reading: Addison-Wesley.

White House. 2021a. "Joint Statement from Quad Leaders." https://www.whitehouse.gov/brief ing-room/statements-releases/2021/09/24/joint-statement-from-quad-leaders/.

White House. 2021b. "Fact Sheet: Quad Leaders' Summit." https://www.whitehouse.gov/brief ing-room/statements-releases/2021/09/24/fact-sheet-quad-leaders-summit/.

PART IV

....

STRATEGIC IMPLICATIONS OF CAPABILITIES

....

PART IV

STRATEGIC
IMPLICATIONS OF
CASUALTIES

CHAPTER 29

ANTI-SATELLITE AND SPACE WEAPONS

Risks and Paths to Peace

LAURA GREGO

INTRODUCTION

SATELLITES have from their earliest days been important strategic assets. Given this importance both the United States and the USSR in the Cold War era pursued means to counter them, and indeed a number of anti-satellite systems were developed and some were fielded. However, satellites performed many stabilizing functions, including establishing secure bilateral communications and providing early warning of ballistic missile launches, and it did not appear to serve anyone's interests to make the space environment especially hostile (Johnson and Rodvold 1993; Podvig 2001; Moltz 2019). Nuclear arms control treaties provided protections for spy satellites that could verify these agreements, through the provisions of non-interference with "national technical means." Much of the anxiety over space weapons and anti-satellite (ASAT) weapons was overblown, no state attacked the others' satellites or fielded space-based weapons, and the era was one of relative restraint.

What has changed? One change is that the strategic uses of space has grown and expanded. Space-based sensors support not just early warning of ballistic missile launch but are an essential component of US efforts to build strategic missile defenses and the United States periodically considers putting missile defense interceptors in space. While the physics is not favorable, international law does not forbid the stationing in space of weapons (except for weapons of mass destruction), either aimed at other space objects, including long-range ballistic missiles as they traverse space, or at terrestrial targets (Aoki, this volume). Such "bolts from the blue" ground-attack weapons would be very threatening and destabilizing as they could support the distant application of force to negate time-sensitive targets, including the part of a state's strategic deterrent dependent on nuclear-armed ballistic missiles, including mobile missiles. While no state has yet fielded either space-based interceptors or ground-attack weapons, the possibility that they might in the future is an important consideration, given no agreements to limit them are in place.

Looking to the yet more distant future, as space technology matures and becomes cheaper, states are also looking beyond the near-earth environment to securing their future access to potential resources on celestial bodies such as asteroids and the earth's moon. Currently, scores of missions to the moon and cislunar space over the next decade are planned by more than a dozen states, many to map the moon's resources (Johnson 2022).

An additional important shift is that in recent decades, military satellite systems have become critically important beyond strategic functions. Satellites form the backbone of modern militaries and provide an efficient way for states to get services such as intelligence, surveillance, and reconnaissance; navigation and timing signals; and secure, high-volume, and long-distance communications (Hays and Wirtz, this volume). This is especially important for an actor, such as the United States, that has or aspires to have a global military footprint. Former vice chairman of the Joint Chiefs of Staff and former commander of US Strategic Command and Air Force Space Command General John Hyten emphasized the importance of space to national security: "Space is critical to everything we do" (Erwin 2021).

Space-derived capabilities are important even for powers that at least at present act more regionally. China, in its 2015 defense white paper, acknowledged that "Outer space has become a commanding height in international strategic competition" (State Council of the People's Republic of China 2015) and recognizing that space would be crucial to success in informatized local conflicts, created the People's Liberation Army's Strategic Support Force that year to take over much of China's military space efforts (Pollpeter, Chase, and Hegenbotham 2017).

In Russia's military doctrine, military outer space operations are framed more as a risk posed by others than an opportunity for it to exploit. A central strategy for deterring and preventing conflict is to "resist attempts by some states or group of states to achieve military superiority through the deployment of strategic missile defense systems, the placement of weapons in outer space or the deployment of strategic non-nuclear high-precision weapon systems" (Russian Federation 2014). This is consistent with the US Defense Intelligence Agency assessment that "Russia has concluded that gaining and maintaining supremacy in space has a decisive impact on the outcome of future conflicts" and that Russia "believes that having the military capabilities to counter space operations will deter aggression by space-enabled adversaries and enable Russia to control escalation of conflict if deterrence fails" (DIA 2017, 36). Additionally, these same space services are also deeply embedded in economic activity, and the loss of such services could be economically crippling to modern, connected economies, adding yet another strategic concern.

Another important change is the complexity of the environment. While space in the past was the preserve of a small number of well-resourced states, many more states, non-governmental, and commercial entities are now spacefaring. While the United States continues to field the most satellites, both in number and in mass (a proxy for capability), China now owns more satellites than the long-time second most important space power, Russia, and continues to launch satellites at a formidable clip (Union of Concerned Scientists 2023). Around ten states can launch satellites independently (depending how this capability is counted), and launch can be secured from numerous commercial launch providers. Scores of states own and operate satellites, and while the number of satellites had been growing incrementally over the previous decades, in the last few years the satellite population has been increasing very rapidly, due in large part to commercial satellites. Commercially owned satellites can be important strategically, as they often provide capacity to states, including for national security purposes. Thus while the proliferation of space actors makes the environment more complex, it can also provide stability, as states can increase the robustness of their satellite services by buying them commercially or engaging in alliances.

However, while satellites are extremely valuable assets, they are also inherently vulnerable to interference and disablement. This includes weapons stationed in space. The high cost of space launch (around US$15,000 per kilogram to low earth orbit) (Roberts 2020) ensures that few satellites will carry extra mass in the form of armor or protection. The communication channels between the satellite and control station must balance ease of connectivity for multiple users with protection from interference of those channels, and satellite operations may be highly networked and vulnerable to cyber intrusion and attack (Livingstone and Lewis 2016). Satellites cannot retreat to safe spaces; they travel on repeated, predictable orbits and many pass repeatedly over large areas of the globe, territory friendly and unfriendly. Many tactics can be used to interfere with or disable an adversary's space capabilities, with a range of technical sophistication and effectiveness. In general, it is much more difficult to defend space assets than to attack them.

Given these realities, states dependent on space increasingly see space as a sphere to be dominated and defended. Their potential adversaries see space dependence of powerful states as a weakness to exploit. As the United States, China, Russia, and other states deepen their investments in space for national security purposes, they also continue to develop ASAT weapons and associated technologies to protect their space capabilities and deny them to others. While the advantage is generally to the offense technologically, how far those advantages extend in time and other circumstances, and whether the advantage will be decisive, will depend on the context and resources available and on what escalation risks are tolerable.

However, seeking increased security through the development and accumulation of space weapons and ASAT weapons may drive reactions which ultimately may create less security overall. For example, leaving actors to pursue space and ASAT weapons without constraint will assuredly increase the number of threats everyone faces. As threats proliferate, resources must be spent to increase the robustness of space systems, and in the absence of shared understandings about intentions around these technologies, mistakes and miscalculations will surely be made. In the case of the United States, preoccupation with achieving superiority and dominance has kept it from pursuing diplomatic strategies that might have shaped the space environment more favorably for all.

To illustrate these points, this chapter will first consider the relative advantages of space offense and defense and the motivations states have for pursuing ASAT and space weapons technologies. It will then look more closely at the technologies themselves and what their attributes imply about their usefulness and the offense-defense balance. The final section discusses in more detail the cases of the United States, China, and Russia as well as prospects for shaping this environment to better favor chances for peace and stability.

ASAT Weapons, Space Superiority, and the Offense-Defense Balance

In the complex and insecure space environment, states seek to secure their interests tied to space and seek ASAT weapons for a number of reasons.

First, given space's crucial role for powerful and technically advanced states, potential adversaries seek ways to negate or offset these advantages by attacking the relatively vulnerable space link. For example, they may jam communications satellites that relay command and control to forward-based attacking drones or damage the sensors of reconnaissance satellites that provide battle assessments. While the most aggressive and indiscriminate ASAT weapons can hinder the use of large numbers of satellites, most conceivable attacks will instead impose costs and slow down a well-resourced adversary rather than stop it in its tracks. This is especially true over longer timescales during which replacement assets can be fielded or other means to provide services can be recruited. Thus, against a well-resourced adversary, ASAT attacks are in practice likely to be more useful on short timescales.

However, prevailing in rapid and decisive attacks appears to be a central concern of military planners (see e.g., Kofman 2020 for a discussion of US perspectives; DIA 2017, 22 for an assessment of Russian perspectives). This is one reason why an actor like the United States, which is very space-dependent but also has many more resources to work with, still worries about retaining decisive control over the space environment and worries about attacks even from less technically advanced states. However, the concern about losing important space assets in the opening moments of a crisis can increase "use it or lose it" pressure and the incentive to go first in a crisis.

Second, states seek ASAT and space-based weapons to try to create security for their own space assets, by using them as an element of deterrence or by using them as satellite defenders (see Morgan, this volume). However, deterrence predicated on "like for like" attacks is not a considered a strong strategy among actors with varying levels of space dependence. And defensive weapons for satellites sound better in theory than in practice. They might be useful under certain conditions but would require comprehensive ability to monitor the space environment and react quickly. Given the characteristically vast distances between satellites, at least one bodyguard would need to be assigned to each important satellite. This would rapidly become too expensive except for the most important systems. While they may provide protection under a limited number of scenarios for a limited number of satellites, they cannot provide confidence in the survivability of those satellites (see e.g., Butt 2008). Such defensive weapons, of course, may look like offensive weapons to others. They would need to carry enough fuel and sufficient guidance capability to maneuver to intercept incoming weapons; this would also provide them the capability to serve as offensive weapons in their own right.

To actually control access to space by others, as is implied by phrases like "space superiority" and "space dominance," would require the ability to do a number of very challenging tasks. That actor would need to be able to field ASAT weapons systems that could effectively identify and target threatening satellites, potentially many of them, then interfere, damage, or destroy them in a way that does not impair its own use of space, that is, without creating so much debris or radiation that space is too dangerous or expensive to use. Additionally, it would likely need a way to discourage or prevent its adversaries from launching satellites or ground-based ASAT missiles, which would be both technically very challenging and very provocative.

A weapons system that could effectively stop ground-launched ASAT weapons or space launches would be exorbitantly expensive to build, extremely destabilizing, and likely easy to counter as it was being assembled. Given orbital dynamics, space-based weapons systems that are meant to destroy time-sensitive targets such as ballistic missiles or space-launch vehicles would require a large constellation of orbiting weapons in order to have one in the right place at the right time. For example, to theoretically stop one missile launch, these systems require hundreds of orbiting weapons and would cost tens to hundreds of billions of dollars (National Academy of Sciences 2012, 58–62). A similar sized system would be needed to stop a satellite launch. However, if the "defensive" constellation is missing a few weapons because the adversary has targeted them, the attacker can simply time the launch during those gaps in coverage. Thus such a defensive system is itself vulnerable to attack and disablement and will not create a lasting advantage.

Third, states seek ASAT weapons as a way to discourage or deter other states from developing threatening postures such as dominance of the space environment or seeking unilateral strategic advantage of other types in the first place. Because, as mentioned, space-based weapons are themselves vulnerable to attack, a potential adversary can make them less attractive options by simply demonstrating the ability to hold them at risk. This is a motivation for China and Russia, who are both concerned about the potential US pursuit of space-based missile defense systems and space-based ground-attack weapons, to test ASAT weapons in a way that shows destructive capability.

Other rationales for developing ASAT weapons include less strategic reasons, such as not wanting to be left behind technologically, wanting to accrue prestige, and to secure a seat at the decision- making table.

Space is often regarded as offense-dominant, in that satellites are relatively vulnerable to interference and destruction, even to an "asymmetric" attack from less-powerful adversaries wielding less-sophisticated and less expensive weapons. It is worth looking at that assertion with care, as it has important nuances and exceptions: as noted above, the advantages are likely to be bounded in important ways. For example, while it may be relatively easy to hold a given satellite or a few of them at risk, denying an actor the benefits derived from space-based capabilities entirely is very much harder to do. For example, the US Global Positioning System (GPS) has a number of attributes that make it difficult to target as a system, including anti-jamming technology, redundancy, a high altitude, and the ability for its services to degrade gradually rather than catastrophically as satellites are lost (Wright, Grego, and Gronlund 2005, 165). Additionally, the effects of an attack can be blunted if that actor has access to needed capabilities from commercial providers or allies, or can supplement with ground-based capabilities, at least on a regional basis. The attack's effects might be temporally bound, as well, if the defender has the ability to launch new satellites rapidly to replenish those that were lost.

INTERFERING WITH SATELLITES: OVERVIEW

To better illustrate the strategic challenges posed by ASAT weapons as well as the possible solutions to these challenges, it is useful to look at some of their specific characteristics. Interference with satellites can range from temporary or reversible effects to the permanent disabling or destruction of the satellite. Their effects may be apparent right away, or it might be difficult for the attacker to assess the effectiveness of the attack. They may be relatively technically unsophisticated and within reach of non-spacefaring actors or may be on the cutting edge of technology and only used by the most capable states. They may be stealthy or relatively easily attributable. They may be precisely targeted or indiscriminate, endangering many satellites for example, by creating long lasting, dangerous space debris or crippling radiation fields. They may be bespoke to the weapons mission or draw on dual-use technology.

First, it is important to note that while spacefaring nations have an inherent ability to develop effective ASAT weapons, no state can expect to have a monopoly on them. Advanced spacefaring nations have the ability to place objects in orbit, many of them to geosynchronous altitude; to track objects in space; and to develop homing interceptors (though not all have done so). They could develop systems to attack satellites in geosynchronous orbits as well as low earth orbits (LEOs). They could also deploy ASAT weapons relatively quickly in response to the deployment of ASAT weapons by another country.

And although their options will be limited relative to those of spacefaring nations, less technically sophisticated countries can hold at risk satellites in LEO, which can be reached by ground-based ASAT weapons using missiles that are much less capable than the launchers needed to put those satellites in orbit. Countries with short- or medium-range missiles can reach satellites in LEO at an altitude of roughly half the range of the missile, though the technology to damage a satellite once there would require more sophistication; they would not necessarily have the ability to develop homing interceptors.

Temporary and Reversible Interference

States may choose to interrupt an adversary's satellite services in a temporary and reversible way as it may seem minimally risky and escalatory, given no permanent damage to the satellite is done and the effects are often not just temporally limited but geographically limited.

Satellites are commonly reported to be subject to temporary and reversible interference, such as electronic interference with their communication systems (jamming) and laser interference with imaging sensors (dazzling or blinding). Jamming of satellite communications to ground-based receivers is called "downlink" jamming. For example, an adversary on the ground could field a radio transmitter at the same frequency as a GPS signal, which can overwhelm local GPS receivers and deny an adversary the ability to navigate, or the transmitter could be designed to send out fake, "spoofed," GPS signals with inserted errors. For example, Russia reportedly routinely spoofs GPS signals around important Russian personnel and strategic sites, as well as in combat zones (C4ADS 2019). This kind of jamming is geographically limited to at the very most the line of sight of the jammer, and while tactically useful, is not actually interference with the satellite or space system itself. An adversary need not be spacefaring nor especially technologically advanced to attempt a downlink jamming attack.

Perhaps more serious is the jamming the "uplink," a communications signal from a ground station to the satellite, a necessary channel to provide command and control of the satellite. To do this successfully, the attacker must be within the satellite receiver's footprint and transmitting at the correct frequency. High-value satellites can be designed so their command and control channels to be resistant to such attacks. However, the use of anti-jamming techniques can significantly reduce a satellite's communication capabilities—such as the amount of information it can transmit. And jamming non-military satellites can still be problematic for the US military because it relies on dual-use commercial satellites for a significant portion of its satellite communications needs (Thompson 2010).

Earth-observing satellites may be interfered with temporarily (dazzled) by ground or space-based lasers. The sensor would be overwhelmed or "dazzled" by the bright light, much as the human eye could be overwhelmed by a flashlight pointed at it. However, especially for high-resolution reconnaissance satellites, the area on the ground that can be "defended" by any one dazzling laser is fairly small and interference is limited to the short period of time that the satellites' optics are viewing the location of the laser, and so only effectively work on territory controlled by the attacker, making it more of a defense of sensitive sites. (Of course, it can also draw attention to that site.) At sufficiently high powers, and if the satellite cannot protect itself with a shutter or other mechanism, the sensor could suffer permanent damage in a "blinding" attack. However, it will be difficult for the attacker to know whether a blinding attack was successful or not, as there won't be an observable sign of damage, limiting its usefulness.

These types of activities provide temporary, localized denial of satellite-based services such as navigation or intelligence gathering. They are not especially complex or expensive and are likely to be widely held. They also permit identifying the author of such interference. Jammers and dazzlers can be localized providing attribution in peacetime and perhaps targeting and destruction in battle conditions. The United States fields a jamming system called the Counter Communications System which is deployed globally to provide uplink jamming capability against geostationary communications satellites. Russia is developing a mobile laser system known as Peresvet that appears to be designed to dazzle imagined sensors and protect mobile missiles from being imaged. The United States military reports that Russia and China regularly target US satellites with dazzling, jamming, and cyber-attacks (Rogin 2021).

While interfering with satellites in this way is counter to international regulations, for example, the International Telecommunication Union (ITU) which regulates satellite use of the electromagnetic spectrum, clearly has rules against jamming (International Telecommunication Union 2020, 15.1) the frequency with which these activities appear to happen suggest that they are well below the threshold for initiation of hostilities. However, an organized and widespread set of jamming and dazzling attacks might not be treated with the same light touch.

A more sophisticated adversary might try to gain control of the satellite using cyber-attacks, though this will be a more effective strategy against relatively unprotected civilian satellites than against sensitive national security satellites, for which significant protections will have been taken. Cyber-attacks are likely to be less easily attributable than electromagnetic attacks like jamming and dazzling.

Disablement and Damage

To destroy a satellite or permanently alter its functionality is a step further in sophistication and in escalation. They are more escalatory not only because they cause permanent damage, but because many of these technologies create indiscriminate follow-on effects.

For example, early ASAT weapon programs (such as the US Mudflap and Thor programs) relied on nuclear explosions in space. The x-rays released by the explosion of a nuclear ASAT weapon used in LEO would destroy unshielded satellites in in the line of sight of the explosion, and the explosion would generate a persistent radiation environment that would last months to years and would slowly damage unshielded satellites in LEO. While high-altitude satellites would not be directly affected by the explosion, this radiation environment could also make it more difficult for them to communicate with ground stations. The Partial Test Ban Treaty and the obvious drawbacks of damaging the space environment ended this practice. Because it would make parts of space difficult to impossible to use, it is assumed that spacefaring states would be self-deterred from considering such weapons. But given that the technologies required to mount such a destructive and indiscriminate attack consist of the ability to produce a nuclear weapon and launch it on a relatively short-ranged missile, this remains a concern, especially given a state such as North Korea could mount such an attack and also has no satellites of its own to be concerned about.

As technical sophistication improved the ability to control spacecraft, the USSR tested a weapon that would be launched into the same orbit as its target and propel shrapnel toward it when it got close enough. The United States tested an airplane-launched small missile that destroyed its target with the force of impact. This latter "hit to kill" or "kinetic kill" technology eventually became the central technology of US ballistic missile defenses: ground-launched missiles that would aim to destroy long-range ballistic missiles as they traversed the same part of the LEO where satellites orbit. Today, the United States, China, India, and Russia have demonstrated the use of ground-based kinetic kill weapons to destroy satellites. Satellites in LEO can be attacked by kinetic-kill ASATs carried on short- and medium-range missiles launched from the ground, though more powerful missiles allow a longer reach and more flexible targeting options. ASAT weapons stationed on the ground or in LEO can be designed to reach targets at higher altitudes in a matter of hours (Wright and Grego 2002).

While these types of weapons have the military advantage of decisively destroying the satellite in a quickly verifiable way, they have the serious disadvantage of creating potentially enormous amounts of dangerous debris that might persist in space for months or decades and create indiscriminate hazards. China's ASAT test in 2007 that generated thousands of pieces of debris which would last for decades generated a large amount of public and private international criticism. China has continued to test the system but against missile targets that would assure little debris would be produced. India learned this lesson and tested its similar weapon at a relatively low altitude in 2019, to reduce the lifetime of the debris produced.

The destruction of one large satellite could potentially double the amount of debris in LEO (Wright 2007); the destruction of many satellites would make areas of space possibly too risky and expensive to use. For this reason, it is assumed that states would be self-deterred from using them, that they are weapons of last resort. However, the United States possesses a large reserve of this capability in the guise of its ballistic missile defense program, with forty-four interceptors that could reach all of LEO, and in the near future, scores more interceptors with similar capability, potentially hundreds counting the improved interceptors for regional systems in partner systems in Europe and East Asia (Grego 2011). Following China's test in 2007 and India's in 2019, Russia tested its own missile-launched destructive ASAT weapon in 2021.

Because of the drawbacks of this kind of weapon, states are also pursuing other ways to decisively and verifiably hold satellites at risk in ways that do not generate debris. The cutting-edge technology in this regard is equipping satellites with the ability to closely approach an adversary's satellite without that satellite's cooperation, usually referred to as proximity operations or rendezvous technology (Pekkanen 2020; Weeden and Samson 2021). This technology has obvious beneficial uses, such as the inspection, repair, or refueling of satellites; the capture and deorbiting of defunct satellites to avoid them creating debris; or the building of large structures. It can also be used for less benign purposes such as espionage, including signals interception. Or it can permit getting close enough to an adversary's satellite to disable it without creating debris, for example, with a high-powered microwave attack on its electronics, setting it spinning unpredictably or impairing its sensor. It may be possible to minimize the size and observable characteristics of these weapons to increase their stealth and perhaps create "space mines" that are difficult to detect and attribute.

Mitigation Strategies

Given the reality of satellite vulnerability, states are choosing different strategies to safeguard their interests. Some choose various strategies of deterrence (Morgan, this volume). This might include deterrence by threat of retaliation, though given how unevenly held space capabilities are, it is likely that the retaliation may not be in kind. And given the difficulty of timely attribution for some types of attacks, retaliatory threats may not be persuasive.

Another strategy is to deter attacks by lowering the benefit an attack might bring. Satellite systems can be made robustly, to be resistant to many kinds of interference and to be able to perform their missions even if a few satellites are lost. A space actor can take steps to reduce a given satellite's vulnerability, such as hardening satellite components to radiation or debris, including anti-jamming techniques on communications channels, building redundant ground stations, developing the capability to quickly replace satellites with on-orbit spares or rapidly launched replacements, and distributing the task of a single satellite among clusters of smaller satellites. Thus, satellite systems can be intentionally designed to be less vulnerable than the individual satellites in the system.

Even in the face of loss of an entire satellite system, with proper planning the satellite system's mission may be performed, even if provisionally, by other means. For example, air- and ground-based back-up systems can provide some of the militarily relevant, time-urgent capabilities that would be lost if the satellite system was disrupted or destroyed. A space actor may seek to integrate their space capabilities more closely with allies so that they can draw on each other's systems in the face of an attack.

As discussed above, states may also seek defensive weapons that could defeat certain types of ASAT attack. For example, in the wake of having one of its sensitive national security satellites shadowed by a Russian satellite, France announced that it would explore building on-orbit defensive weapons to counter such threats (Trevithick 2019).

Given the relative fragility of individual satellites, it may be surprising that states have not pursued more arms control measures to limit the availability of ASAT technologies. During the Cold War, the United States and the USSR considered ASAT weapon bans, and agreed on protections for certain satellites in the guise of banning interference with "national technical means" of verifying compliance with important arms control agreements, which was largely understood to mean an agreement not to interfere with each other's intelligence satellites.

The plethora of ways to interfere with a satellite has been a contributing reason for the dearth of such agreements. The China-Russia draft Prevention of the Placement of Weapons in Outer Space Treaty (PPWT) provides a definition for space-based weapons, but omitted a definition of ASAT weapons, instead limiting behavior, in which states shall "not resort to the threat or use of force against outer space objects of States" (Russian Federation and People's Republic of China 2014; see West, this volume; Zhou and Wang, this volume).

This omission is a point of criticism from the United States, which argued that the treaty was not very useful if it did not cover the development of ground-based ASAT weapons. However, from another point of view, any comprehensive definition of ASAT weapons would capture strategic missile defenses of the type that the United States fields and plans to continue fielding, because of their innate ASAT capabilities. The inclusion of such a definition would almost certainly lead to the same result—little interest from the United States.

The United States, Russia, and China

Given the importance of space and the US advantages in technical sophistication and economic resources, there has been a strain of thought in the Pentagon that the United States could dominate and control space, perhaps indefinitely, especially after the dissolution of the USSR. In 2004, the US Undersecretary of the Air Force and director of the National Reconnaissance Office Peter Teets described space in this way: "Today, space power represents a decisive, asymmetric advantage for the US government and, in particular, for military and intelligence organizations" (Teets 2004). The same year, the US Air Force Counterspace Operations Doctrine made clear that the US goal was not only to preserve its own advantage but to "be prepared to deprive an adversary of the benefits of space capabilities" and that space superiority should be sought and "ensures the freedom to operate in the space medium while denying the same to an adversary" (USAF 2004). The operating descriptions for the US military approach to space has reliably been "superiority" and "dominance."

The George W. Bush National Space Policy declared that space capabilities are vital to the US national interests, and that the United States would "take those actions necessary to protect its space capabilities; respond to interference; and deny, if necessary, adversaries the use of space capabilities hostile to U.S. national interests" (Bush 2006). Bush's Commander of Air Force Space Command put it more succinctly: "Space Superiority is the future of warfare. We cannot win a war without controlling the high ground, and the high ground is space" (Lord 2005). Shortly after China destroyed a satellite in its 2007 ASAT test, the United States followed suit by destroying a failed national security satellite with a missile defense interceptor, claiming it was necessary for public safety.

The Obama National Space Policy avoided language that invoked dominance and superiority, stating that "will employ a variety of measures to help assure the use of space for all responsible parties, and, consistent with the inherent right of self-defense, deter others from interference and attack, defend our space systems and contribute to the defense of allied space systems, and, if deterrence fails, defeat efforts to attack them," and planned to use tools such as international agreements and increased space situational awareness to augment stability (Obama 2010).

While China's test of an ASAT weapon against its own LEO satellite in 2007 created great concern, another watershed moment came in 2013, with China's test of a high-altitude suborbital missile, reportedly to tens of thousands of kilometers altitude. Such a missile could be used to propel the hit-to-kill weapon it tested in 2007 to altitudes the United States largely considered insulated from such threats by their distance (Weeden and Samson 2021). A number of the most important national security satellites operate at high altitudes, out of easy reach of ground-based missiles, including the GPS navigation constellation in medium earth orbits and the missile warning satellites in geosynchronous orbits. US decision makers renewed attention to strategies of resilience and robustness in military space systems and began speaking of space as a "warfighting domain." As General John W. Raymond, then Commander of US Air Force Space Command testified in 2017, "For decades, United States has enjoyed unimpeded freedom of action in the space domain [but] in the not too distant future, near-peer competitors will have the ability to hold every U.S. space asset in every orbital regime at risk" (Raymond 2017).

In 2019, the Trump administration doubled down on the narrow military approach to achieving security, and established the US Space Force, a new branch of the US Air Force focused on training and equipping military space forces and a doctrine to employ lethal force "in, from, and to space" (US Space Force 2020). That this approach is winning the day is borne out not only by rhetoric but by interest and investments in space control technology, and by a historical resistance to engaging in diplomatic initiatives to limit ASAT weapons and space weapons. That the United States believed that it would be able to protect its satellites is supported by the its continuing to invest in large, expensive satellites to provide capability rather than transitioning to a more robust, distributed system, though this can also be partially explained by bureaucratic inflexibility and that some missions cannot be adequately performed by smaller satellites. This approach does appear to be giving way, as the Pentagon is currently developing a number of small-satellite LEO constellations that would among other things provide communications and missile tracking capability.

The orbital regime of concern is also expanding. US space doctrine states that "commercial investments and new technologies have the potential to expand the reach of vital National space interests to the cislunar regime and beyond in the near future" (US Space Force 2020).

The United States decentered the dominance rhetoric and did not openly pursue ASAT weapons, aside from a system designed to interfere with adversary communications. "Space supremacy implies that one side could conduct operations with relative impunity while denying space domain freedom of action to an adversary. Space supremacy is not always desirable, or attainable against a peer adversary, and should not be the unconditional goal of military spacepower" (US Space Force 2020). However, the United States has also declined to consider limits on space and ASAT weapons and has developed technologies that are suitable for ASAT purposes, including sophisticated proximity operations satellites operating in LEO as well as geosynchronous orbits. It also fields dozens of missile defense interceptors, which can be repurposed as ASATs in LEOs, and maintains interest in space-based missile defense systems, which could be used against satellites in any orbit. The United States also fields the most comprehensive space surveillance system, a necessary component of targeting others' satellites. Given its role as the main provider of this information, it confers the greatest ability to identify threats and bad behavior, and to perhaps conceal its own.

Given ASAT weapons are much more effective as offenses rather than defenses, the development of ASAT weapons by a state such as the United States is likely to indicate the interest in the ability to effectively "control" or "dominate" space by restricting others' access to it, rather than keeping its satellites safe. However, despite strong US Space Force rhetoric, the United States is also exploring other, soft power, ways to secure its interests. Recently, the United States has been cultivating closer cooperation with allies in the military space domain to increase resiliency to threats (Ackerman 2021). The Biden Administration Space Priorities Framework states that "U.S. national security space operations will continue to comply with applicable international law and demonstrate leadership in both the responsible use of space and stewardship of the space environment" (United States 2021). This includes efforts to ban intentional destruction of satellites in orbit, which would create large amounts of debris (Hitchens 2021), starting with gathering support for voluntary moratoria on destructive direct-ascent ASAT tests. Such a move protects the space environment though it does little to hinder US ASAT capabilities, some of which are tested in its missile defense program and others that do not create debris.

The United States faces potential adversaries, Russia and China, which depend less on satellites than it does, and so ASAT weapons provide it relatively less advantage. Given this reality, the fact that the United States has historically declined to engage in international efforts to limit ASAT weapons indicates that it may not be convinced this imbalance will be the case in the future, may not want to limit its freedom of action, or that it does not believe there is an arms control regime that it would benefit from.

At the same time, attempting a strategy of dominance is technically and economically not practical. While recognizing that it cannot obtain assured security unilaterally, the United States seems to be seeking a strategy to get enough power to secure its interests. However, declining to engage in negotiated constraints on ASAT weapons has ensured that there are no legal and normative constraints on conduct in space and on particularly dangerous technologies, including debris-producing weapons. Such constraints could augment stability in crises, avoid incentives for a space arms race, and provide guardrails to preserve the space environment. However, instead, ASAT weapons have proliferated to more states and have grown in number and sophistication.

China and Russia have continued to develop and test a full complement of ASAT weapons relevant technologies (Weeden and Samson 2021; Harrison 2021). Both have tested ground-based missile ASAT weapons against satellites and are testing and using satellite proximity operations in sometimes provocative ways, shadowing other satellites closely and launching multiple subjects. The United States claims that its satellites experience hacking, jamming, and dazzling attacks daily from China and Russia (Rogin 2021).

China and Russia have multiple and evolving reasons for their ASAT programs. For China in particular, the desire not to be left behind technologically has been an important driver. For example, China's test of an ASAT weapon in 2007 was interpreted by some analysts not so much as a deliberate strategic message to the United States and other potential adversaries but rather as a natural milestone of a technical program begun in the 1980s as "part of an imperative to keep pace with the United States and others" (Kulacki and Lewis 2008). The hit-to-kill technology demonstrated is one that the United States had pioneered in the 1980s and first successfully tested against a ballistic missile in 1984 and against a satellite in 1985 and subsequently began to incorporate into its missile defense program.

Chinese and Russian ASAT programs are designed to deter the United States from seeking unilateral advantage, by demonstrating the ability to counter their space assets, including space weapons or weapons-supporting satellites. The Russian Federation military doctrine identifies a main task "to resist attempts by some states or group of states to achieve military superiority through the deployment of strategic missile defence systems, the placement of weapons in outer space or the deployment of strategic non-nuclear high-precision weapon systems" (Russia 2014).

The 2013 Science of Military Strategy, an authoritative text published by the Chinese Academy of Military Science, describes China's counterspace strategy in a deterrence framework, to pressure adversaries not to initiate space warfare and to "conduct limited space warfare operations as a warning or a reprimand to stop an opponent from recklessly escalating the level of space hostilities." Further, it suggests "In the space domain, China's bottom line is, as always, the principle of 'if you don't attack me, I won't attack you'" (Kulacki 2019).

The development of ASAT weapons may also serve to deter the United States from even pursuing space weapons programs that China and Russia find especially threatening. Russia and China have for decades expressed serious concern about the possibility that the United States might pursue space-based ballistic missile defenses which could degrade their nuclear deterrents. Russia and especially China (with its relatively smaller nuclear forces) have an interest in preventing the United States from believing it could mount a decisive pre-emptive attack, enabled by the substantial US nuclear arsenal, the ability to conduct precision conventional strikes (enabled by space assets) on key nuclear command and control capabilities, and an effective missile defense that could deal with any remaining nuclear forces. China and Russia demonstrating their capability to destroy such space-based interceptors may be intended to deter the United States from attempting to build such a system in the first place. This is consistent with the central diplomatic effort China and Russia have jointly made for space security, the draft PPWT submitted to the United Nations Conference on Disarmament, the central proposal of which would ban weapons from space.

The preferred diplomatic approach of Russia and China, the negotiation of a legally binding instrument under the auspices of the United Nations, differs in substance and process from the preferred approach of the United States, to create politically binding norms under the aegis of "responsible behavior." It remains to be seen if these differences can be bridged (see Zhou and Wang, this volume).

Risks

Recent decades have seen the United States making extensive use of space to project power globally and attempting to secure those interests with a strategy of maintaining superiority by developing some ASAT weapons and technologies to hold other states' assets at risk. It has resisted efforts to establish negotiated constraints and instead privileged its freedom of action and pursuit of superiority in space. China and Russia have developed and tested a robust array of ASAT weapons that could be used to counter existing and proposed US systems and, especially China, increased investments in space assets to support national security goals.

Absent any constraint, this is likely to both result in an arms race dynamic, with pursuit of more numerous and more sophisticated ASAT and space weapons given the perception that they may be useful in some circumstances, and the investment of resources in satellite systems to make them more robust to attack. This dynamic not only wastes resources, it risks the health of the space environment by contamination with debris from weapons test and use. It also generates the risk of miscalculation and generating or exacerbating terrestrial conflicts, given how little experience states have with warfare in space (Grego 2020). There has been little shared understanding about intentions around these technologies, and there are few robust ways to resolve misunderstandings about space activities in a timely manner.

Misperception around intentions can be a destabilizing factor, as can misunderstandings and lack of clarity about legal norms and how existing international law applies in space. The Outer Space Treaty, the fundamental legal document governing space, provides consultation mechanisms to engage states around activities that might interfere with the peaceful use of outer space, but no state has yet invoked them. And given the lack of precedent, states may have differing interpretations of how serious different types of interference are and what appropriate reactions might be, and this could be quite dangerous. For example, on March 2, 2022, amid reports that Russian satellite control centers had been hacked in the opening days of the Russian invasion of Ukraine, the head of the Russian space agency and former prime minister, Dmitry Rogozin, was reported as warning that cyber-attacks on the satellites would be "actually a casus belli, a cause for war" (Reuters 2022).

CONCLUSION

Despite an early advantage, the United States cannot realistically maintain security in space through use of force, if dominance is to mean assured access to space and the ability to deny it to others given the relative ease of offense versus defense in space. An approach of increasing resilience in space systems by increasing their robustness and increasing cooperation with allies is likely to be more promising.

Given these risks, and an increasing awareness of them, it is possible that they can be curbed using a number of approaches. Transparency and confidence building measures can help address some dangers of misperception and misunderstanding. Legal and normative constraints on conduct in space and on particularly dangerous technologies, including hit-to-kill missiles could augment stability in crises, curtail incentives to arms race, and provide guardrails to preserve the space environment.

At the same time, attempts to create constraints will eventually need to address the underlying security concerns to be effective. For example, it will be difficult to limit ASAT weapons without limiting space weapons technologies that have the (at least perceived) potential of conferring large strategic advantages, such as space-based missile defenses and ground-attack weapons. For these reasons, these issues will need to be addressed in the context of larger strategic stability and arms control processes, which given current conditions, may not happen for quite some time. But it is crucial that it does, given the risks posed to the space environment and to all people of confrontation among powerful, nuclear-armed states.

REFERENCES

Ackerman, Robert K. 2021. "U.S. Space Force Gathers International Allies." Signal. https://www.afcea.org/content/us-space-force-gathers-international-allies.

Bush, George W. 2006. "U.S. National Space Policy." https://csps.aerospace.org/sites/default/files/2021-08/Natl%20Space%20Policy%20fact%20sheet%2031Aug06.pdf.

Butt, Yousaf. 2008. "Can Space Weapons Protect US Satellites?" *Bulletin of the Atomic Scientists.* July 22, 2008. https://thebulletin.org/2008/07/can-space-weapons-protect-u-s-satellites/.

C4ADS. 2019. "Above Us Only Stars: Exposing GPS Spoofing in Russia and Syria." https://www.c4reports.org/aboveusonlystars.

Defense Intelligence Agency. 2017. "Russia Military Power." https://www.dia.mil/Portals/110/Images/News/Military_Powers_Publications/Russia_Military_Power_Report_2017.pdf.

Erwin, Sandra. 2021. "Hyten: U.S. Space Force Is 'on Solid Ground' Despite Speculation." Space News. January 24, 2021. https://spacenews.com/hyten-u-s-space-force-is-on-solid-ground-despite-speculation/.

Grego, Laura. 2011. "The Anti-Satellite Capability of the Phased Adaptive Approach Missile Defense System." Federation of American Scientists Public Interest Report. Winter 2011. https://pubs.fas.org/pir/2011winter/2011Winter-Anti-Satellite.pdf.

Grego, Laura. 2020. "Outer Space and Crisis Risk." In *War and Peace in Outer Space: Law, Policy, and Ethics*, 263–84, edited by Cassandra Steer and Matthew Hersch. New York: Oxford University Press.

Harrison, Todd, Kaitlyn Johnson, Joe Moye, and Makena Young. 2021. "CSIS Aerospace Security Project." March 31, 2021. https://www.csis.org/analysis/space-threat-assessm ent-2021.

Hitchens, Theresa. 2021. "Biden Administration to Propose New Global Norms for Military Space." Breaking Defense. December 1, 2021. https://breakingdefense.com/2021/12/biden-administration-to-propose-new-global-norms-for-military-space/.

International Telecommunication Union, 2020. Radio Regulations 2020. https://www.itu.int/hub/publication/r-reg-rr-2020/.

Johnson, Kaitlyn. 2022. "Fly Me To The Moon: Worldwide Cislunar and Lunar Missions." Center for Strategic and International Studies. https://www.csis.org/analysis/fly-me-moon-worldwide-cislunar-and-lunar-missions.

Johnson, N.L., and D.M. Rodvold. 1993. *Europe and Asia in Space, 1993–1994.* Colorado Springs, CO: Kaman Sciences Corp.

Kofman, Michael. 2020. "Getting the Fait Accompli Problem Right In U.S. Strategy." *War on the Rocks.* November 3, 2020. https://warontherocks.com/2020/11/getting-the-fait-accom pli-problem-right-in-u-s-strategy/.

Kulacki, Gregory. 2019. "The US Congress Needs Facts, Not Hyperbole, on China's Space Program." *The Diplomat.* November 21, 2019. https://thediplomat.com/2019/11/the-us-congr ess-needs-facts-not-hyperbole-on-chinas-space-program/.

Kulacki, Gregory, and Lewis, Jeffrey. 2008. "Understanding China's Antisatellite Test." *The Nonproliferation Review* 15, no. 2: 335–47.

Livingstone, David, and Patricia Lewis. 2016. "Space, the Final Frontier for Cybersecurity?" Chatham House. https://www.chathamhouse.org/sites/default/files/publications/research/2016-09-22-space-final-frontier-cybersecurity-livingstone-lewis.pdf.

Lord, Lance W., General. 2005 "Space Superiority." *High Frontier.* Winter 2005. https://www.law.upenn.edu/live/files/7841-genlnclrdspcsuperpdf.

Moltz, James Clay. 2019. *The Politics of Space Security.* Stanford, CA: Stanford University Press.

National Academy of Sciences. 2012. Making Sense of Missile Defense.

Obama, Barack. 2010. "The National Space Policy of the United States of America." https://obamawhitehouse.archives.gov/sites/default/files/national_space_policy_6-28-10.pdf.

Pekkanen, Saadia. 2020. "Thank You for Your Service: The Security Implications of Japan's Counterspace Capabilities." Policy Roundtable: *The Future of Japanese Security and Defense.* Texas National Security Review. https://tnsr.org/roundtable/policy-roundtable-the-future-of-japanese-security-and-defense/#essay5

Podvig, P., ed. 2001. *Russian Strategic Nuclear Forces.* Cambridge, MA: MIT Press.

Pollpeter, Kevin L., Michael S. Chase, and Eric Heginbotham. 2017. "The Creation of the PLA Strategic Support Force and its Implications for Chinese Military Space Operations." RAND Corporation.

Raymond. 2017. Statement of General John W. Raymond Commander, Air Force Space Command to House Armed Services Committee on Fiscal Year 2018 Priorities and Posture of the National Security Space, May 19, 2017. Enterprisehttps://docs.house.gov/meetings/AS/AS29/20170519/105974/HHRG-115-AS29-Wstate-RaymondJ-20170519.pdf.

Reuters. 2022. "Russia Space Agency Head Says Satellite Hacking Would Justify War-Report." March 2, 2022. https://www.reuters.com/world/russia-space-agency-head-says-satellite-hacking-would-justify-war-report-2022-03-02/.

Russian Federation. 2014. "The Military Doctrine of the Russian Federation." https://rusmil sec.files.wordpress.com/2021/08/mildoc_rf_2014_eng.pdf.

Roberts, Thomas G. 2020. "Space Launch to Low Earth Orbit: How Much Does It Cost?" Center for Strategic and International Studies. https://aerospace.csis.org/data/space-lau nch-to-low-earth-orbit-how-much-does-it-cost/.

Rogin, Josh. 2021. "Opinion: A Shadow War in Space Is Heating Up Fast." *Washington Post*. November 30, 2021. https://www.washingtonpost.com/opinions/2021/11/30/space-race-china-david-thompson/.

Russian Federation and People's Republic of China. 2014. "Draft Treaty on the Prevention of the Placement of Weapons in Outer Space, the Threat or Use of Force against Outer Space Objects." https://www.reachingcriticalwill.org/images/documents/Disarmament-fora/cd/2014/documents/PPWT2014.pdf.

The State Council of the People's Republic of China. 2015. "China's Military Strategy." http://english.www.gov.cn/archive/white_paper/2015/05/27/content_281475115610833.htm.

Teets, Hon. Peter B. 2004. "Space in the Twenty-First Century." *Air and Space Power Journal*. Summer 2004. https://www.airuniversity.af.edu/Portals/10/ASPJ/journals/Volume-18_Is sue-1-4/sum04.pdf.

Thompson, Loren. 2010. "Lack of Protected Satellite Communications Could Mean Defeat for Joint Force in Future War." Lexington Institute. https://www.lexingtoninstitute.org/lack-of-protected-satellite-communications-could-mean-defeat-for-joint-force-in-future-war/.

Trevithick, Joseph. 2019. "The French Have Plans for a Constellation of Laser-Armed Miniature Satellites." *The Drive*. July 26, 2019. https://www.thedrive.com/the-war-zone/29152/the-fre nch-have-plans-for-a-constellation-of-laser-armed-miniature-satellites.

Union of Concerned Scientists. 2023. UCS Satellite Database, v. January 1, 2023. http://ucsusa.org/satellites.

United States. 2021. "United States Space Priorities Framework." United States White House. https://www.whitehouse.gov/wp-content/uploads/2021/12/United-States-Space-Priorities-Framework-_-December-1-2021.pdf.

United States Air Force. Counterspace Operations. 2004. "Air Force Doctrine Document 2-2.1." https://irp.fas.org/doddir/usaf/afdd2_2-1.pdf.

United States Space Force Headquarters. 2020. "Space Capstone Publication: Spacepower, Doctrine for Space Forces." https://www.spaceforce.mil/Portals/1/Space%20Capstone%20 Publication_10%20Aug%202020.pdf.

Weeden, Brian, and Victoria Samson, eds. 2021. "Global Counterspace Capabilities: An Open Source Assessment." Secure World Foundation. https://swfound.org/counterspace/.

Wright, David. 2007. "Space Debris." Physics Today 60, no. 10: 35. https://physicstoday.scitat ion.org/doi/10.1063/1.2800252.

Wright, David, and Laura Grego. 2002. "Anti-Satellite Capabilities of Planned US Missile Defence Systems." *Disarmament Diplomacy*. 68.

Wright, David, Laura Grego, and Lisbeth Gronlund. 2005. "The Physics of Space Security: A Reference Manual." American Academy of Arts and Sciences. https://www.amacad.org/publication/physics-space-security-reference-manual.

....

CHAPTER 30

THE GREATEST
TRANSFORMATION

How Cyber Is Defining Security in the Space Domain

....

LARRY F. MARTINEZ

INTRODUCTION

....

THIS chapter is about what happens when earthbound cyberspace conflict merges into outer space as the "high ground" battlefield for twenty-first century global dominance. Cyber's role in defining outer space security is a remarkable story that persistently flashes ever more prominently onto the radar screens of science-challenged social and mainstream media. To address dismissive "fake news" social media trolling, it is important to note the definitional starting point underlying this analysis: "Cyber" is electronic communication between billions of inter-connected devices (or, the internet of things, IoT), whose operation is determined by software code. Cyber "security" is the effort to deter deployment of unauthorized software code manipulations intended to disrupt the operation of billions of devices and networks crucial for vital societal or security infrastructures.

Cyber is a story of growing commercial momentum and increasing disinformation, as analytically opaque as the trillions of lines of code running this digitizing planet. For behind the headlines of "Stuxnet" in 2009 or the North Korean attack paralyzing Sony's networks in 2014 or the stomach-lurching rollercoaster ride of Game Station stocks in 2021, and the Russian attack against ViaSat in the opening day of the February 2022 invasion of Ukraine, lurks the on-going story about the greatest transformation of world power since the development of the atomic bomb in the late 1940s. "In short, cyber is transforming 'Space Force' visions of an outer space 'high ground' battlefield of kinetic weaponry into one where projections of stealthy cyber power reorder the logic determining planetary power configurations and outer space governance" (Blount 2019, 1–14).

This chapter will first assess the challenges cyberspace has presented to the international community and the state and suggest five factors that underly these challenges. After that assessment, this chapter's analysis will proceed in five major sections. The first section will examine cybersecurity as a factor of international systemic change. The second section will focus on the fundamental contradictions about cybersecurity that obfuscate and politicize efforts to develop comprehensive systemic governance responses to cyber vulnerabilities. The third section outlines cyber as a growing factor of planetary power and the doctrinal vacuum perpetuating disjointed responses to vulnerabilities that politicize efforts to coordinate governance. The fourth section focuses specifically on the securitization of cyber governance for both terrestrial as well as space-based domains. Finally, a concluding fifth section points to the role of cyber as a systemic factor of change and where paradigmatic shifts may lead as cyber increasingly defines the battlefield for planetary power. Let's now turn to the first section's

What Has Changed? Five Factors to Consider

"The unleashed power of the atom," lamented Albert Einstein in 1946, "has changed everything save our modes of thinking, and thus we drift toward unparalleled catastrophe" (Krauss 2013). It is sobering to consider that development of the atomic bomb and eventually thermonuclear weapons was accomplished in a much shorter timespan than the strategic doctrines and legal agreements guiding their use, control, and proliferation. Analogously, the world today finds itself at a "modes of thinking" tipping point with respect to cyber weaponry and conflict much closer to Einstein's in 1946 than the 1995 decision to indefinitely extend the Non-Proliferation Treaty. While atomic weapons fundamentally transformed world politics during the late-twentieth century, cyber is already posing far-reaching challenges to strategic doctrine and international governance in the twenty-first because, in contrast to nuclear weapons, cyber weapons are usable and are proving their usability every day (NATO 2017. Will "unparalleled catastrophe" be the result in a cumulative failure to adapt "modes of thinking"? Five factors outlined below illustrate the difficulty the international community is encountering in developing a strategic doctrine for the use, control, and proliferation of cyber weaponry on earth as in space.

Cyber Security's Commercial Clout

First, cyber security (in terms of both attacks and defenses) is fueling exponential market growth for state and especially non-state commercial firms (both legal and criminal). Malware and ransomware are today fueling a dramatic growth of an increasingly lucrative market, that saw a 130 percent growth in ransomware attacks in 2020, with global losses to governmental and commercial sectors estimated to exceed USD$6 trillion annually, with a ransomware attack taking place every eleven seconds (Cook 2021). Crypto currency markets act to facilitate cyber security market growth as they currently amass more than USD$3 trillion in digital assets, decentralized finance, and non-fungible tokens (Ossinger 2021). In sum, the commercial cyber security market is achieving worldwide commercial clout that outstrips financial and budgetary resources of most governmental cyber safeguard agencies.

Physics of Electromagnetism and the Attribution Dilemma

Second, earth-space telemetry and satellites have since their inception been victims of electromagnetic interference and intentional disruption. Solar eruptions, cosmic radiation, as well as human-generated radio spectrum "jamming" and satellite software "hacks" continue to challenge technology designers and system operators, while at the same intensifying uncertainty attributes failure faults to natural causes or intentional attacks. In 2010, Intelsat's network operators struggled to regain control of their Galaxy 15 geostationary satellite after a solar storm zapped its receivers off-line. The nicknamed "zombie" satellite then began an uncontrolled drift in the geostationary orbit that required adjacent satellites to move to safer orbital positions. Going through the equinox shadow period drained the onboard batteries that re-booted Galaxy 15's operating system resulting in restoration of the satellite's receiver and station keeping control (Choi 2010). In contrast to Galaxy 15, an intentional software intervention is blamed for the solar disruption to the joint US-Germany-UK "Rosat" x-ray astronomy satellite in 1998. Experts have identified evidence showing that Russia manipulated the NASA Goddard Space Flight Center computer code controlling Rosat, directing the satellite to over-expose its highly sensitive star tracker sensors to direct sunlight, resulting in loss of satellite navigational control (Baylon 2014, 7–13).

Integration of Space Systems into the Internet of Things

Third, the 1998 Rosat incident underlines how space systems are only as secure as their ground-based telemetry segment. To paraphrase the common adage, "a (cyber security) chain is only as strong as its weakest link," where that vulnerable link today is the all-pervasive IoT. In previous eras, ground-space telemetry segments were highly isolated. Telemetry sent commands to the satellite's on-board operating systems using forms of digital modulation. Meanwhile, the satellite payload would provide its remote sensing scans or communications relay services to earthbound users usually through separate networks of earth stations using analog modulation techniques. The advent of internet-based digital networking services in the 1990s promoted the evolution toward integrated digitized satellite services eroding the protective wall of incompatibility between satellites and their ground segments. The network isolation of earth segments further eroded in the explosion of web-based services where satellites such as those in the large constellations are directly connected through millions of earth stations directly into the internet's IP (internet protocol) space.

Combined with the commercial focus on selling billions of IP-connected cameras, phones, media appliances, personal computing appliances and the like, by the second decade of the twenty-first century a largely unregulated myriad of billions of IP devices now formed what is called the IoT, into which satellites and their ground segments now find themselves intimately connected. The vast majority of IoT devices have little or no security built into their firmware, due to the intense profit maximizing drive of the global suppliers seeking to reduce user inconveniences often associated with higher grades of cyber security. In sum, do you really want that Echo device in your bedroom? On a higher plane, the business models of large constellations systems such as Starlink or OneWeb are premised on their complete networked integration as internet service providers' inter-connecting myriads of non-regulated and insecure IP-connected devices, each which presents a soft target vector to cyber attackers.

Cyber as Disrupter of Global Power Hierarchies

Fourth, outer space, once a region shielded from earthbound conflict by its gravitational inaccessibility and legal status as a demilitarized zone under international treaties, is now losing those distinctions that had previously favored the major space powers—most notably the United States and Russia—and the other technologically advanced states with launch and satellite capabilities—including China, and Japan as well as the spacefaring countries in Europe. Today, the traditional space powers are encountering an increasingly crowded and competitive space jurisdictional environment, dominated by a growing tier of emerging spacefaring countries, encompassing the UAE, Israel, Iran, South Korea, North Korea, and over a hundred other countries operating satellite systems. They are joined by an growing realm of commercial firms seeking to expand their offerings of launching and satellite services for increasing numbers of governmental and commercial users of cyber-vulnerable information networks. In short, cyber conflict is disruptive of long-standing power hierarchies, as *asymmetrical* warfare, where a small force can disrupt a large one, making cyber the defining security challenge for not only outer space but planetary power configurations in all domains: land, sea, air, space, and cyberspace.

Cyber Conflict as Asymmetrical Warfare

Fifth, finally, and perhaps most crucially, while the atomic bomb was extremely difficult to develop even for highly technologically adept countries during the Cold War and afterward, the integration of space-based cyber capabilities into terrestrial internet infrastructures is wide open to the rapidly expanding roster of state and commercial actors seeking to exploit software vulnerabilities in the pursuit of strategic and profit goals (United Nations Test Ban Treaty 1963). Outer space, once a region in the 1960s–1970s shielded by its distance from earth and set aside as a demilitarized zone by international treaties, is now in the twenty-first century losing those distinctions that previously confirmed the privileged status of the leading space powers.

Today, the United States, Russia, Europe, China, Japan, India—and a lower tier of spacefaring countries, including Brazil, Israel, Iran, South Korea, North Korea, and over one hundred others operating satellite systems—are facing a transformed outer space operating environment they no longer monopolize. Especially for the United States, as the world's most powerful military power, a cyber-conflicted outer space reveals the Achilles vulnerability of US power characterized as *asymmetrical* warfare, a battlefield where a small force can move a large one. As cyber militarizes the world, including the "high ground" of outer space, cyberconflict on earth is now cyberconflict in space.

THE CONUNDRUM ABOUT CYBERSECURITY

This second section identifies the inherent technology-policy conundrum encountered in efforts to establish global governance of digital information systems that any user of credit cards will recognize—why did the system fail? While credit cards provide travelers with a convenience unimaginable to traveler check veterans only decades earlier, their use and fraudulent misuse through security compromises pose fundamental policy impasses that require governments to closely coordinate highly sensitive policies affecting their most powerful financial institutions. Space-based internet systems linking billions of users and devices pose a policy challenge of a fallible yet powerful technology that is already refocusing efforts to extend twenty-first century strategic governance.

Joining death, taxes, and Covid, there is one more absolute given in an uncertain and unforgiving world: The technological inevitability that software will fail. Even for safety focused applications as tested and verified as those designed for commercial passenger aircraft, aviation incidents in 2018 and 2019 faulting the Boeing 737 Max's MCAS artificial intelligence (AI) avionics tragically verify software's fallibility (Klotz 2021, 1–2). Meanwhile, aviation is now joined by auto and truck manufacturers as they and their governments speed toward an electric vehicle (EV) future, attracting customers with vehicles featuring increasingly sophisticated autonomous navigational capabilities.

Increasingly autonomous AI-directed vehicles navigating the land, sea, air, and space realms become, in essence, the largest and most latency-intolerant IoT devices requiring an almost unimaginable expansion of inter-vehicle data links. The accelerating shift to IoT raises the specter of crucial societal sectors becoming completely dependent on the reliability of sensors, software, and data networks, in addition to their designed hardness to resist cyber-attacks. Iranian nuclear engineers during the 2010 Stuxnet cyber-attack, were in a real-time software crisis analogous to 737 Max pilots attempting to wrestle control back from rogue computers (Kushner 2013, 1–3). Cybersecurity, in the broadest sense of the term, presents itself as perhaps the most salient yet contradictory issue affecting on-going technological deployments not only in the aviation, transportation, and space sectors, but in other ultra-crucial societal sectors such as healthcare and finance. Today, the entire planet is facing a Stuxnet or 737 Max future.

(Cyber) Security in Space

As noted above, space systems are, as all terrestrial data-reliant systems, vulnerable to external and internal electromagnetic threats. While there are a multitude of external threats including kinetic devices—prompting growing concerns for the physical security of spacecraft and space situational awareness (SSA)—the external cyber threats under discussion here are those posed by entities attempting to incapacitate spacecraft using electromagnetic means. Internal cyber threats are those exploiting software vulnerabilities (Fritz 2013, 21–50).

External Threats

High-power electromagnetic waves (e.g., electromagnetic pulse, EMP) pose a direct threat to terrestrial and space-based microprocessor controlled devices. But the long-lasting ramifications are especially crucial for those operating as sensitive spacecraft scientific and optical sensors, antennas, on-board computers, and other payload components beyond the reach of earthbound maintenance and replacement. At one extreme are the electromagnetic pulses emanating from terrestrial, atmospheric, or exo-atmospheric atomic explosions or directed energy beam weapons designed to overwhelm satellites' protective shielding or system electronics "hardening." At a lower power level but nonetheless capable of incapacitating a satellite is the use of radio frequency "jamming" where clandestine transmitters "capture" a satellite's receivers rendering it useless to the intended operators. In sum, while external electromagnetic disruptions do pose existential threats to space systems operations, their purview lies largely outside this chapter's focus on software-related assaults against space systems (Fritz 2013, 21–50).

Internal Threats

Spacecraft have evolved in synch with information and communication technologies (ICTs) from their *analog* origins to become, in essence, orbiting *digital* computer systems. While satellites from the very beginning of the space age employed analog payloads, their control technologies and telemetry were analog/digital. While satellites into the 1990s relied on analog techniques for information relay among earth-bound analog network providers, the control over satellite functions was accomplished through highly secure telemetry links digitally "piggybacking" on analog pathways between large earth stations and the satellites. Significantly, the analog "payload"—the actual profit-generating communications services including TV, voice, and other services—was technologically dissimilar from the digital telemetry pathways used for controlling the satellites.

As noted above, the shift to all-digital satellites that began in the 1990s accelerated not only satellites' ability to provide in-orbit telecommunications switching and internet services, but also exposed satellite-based networks to the enormous cyber-vulnerabilities that internet connectivity poses to all terrestrial networked systems. This represents a fundamental technological shift from analog modulation techniques (i.e., amplitude modulation or frequency modulation, among others) for relaying voice, sound, or video, with geostationary satellites in the 1960s–1990s that were most often configured as "bent pipes," where the satellite transparently retransmitted back to earth what they received. In other words, the communications payload of a satellite (as regulated by the ITU and national telecommunications regulators) was technologically distinct in an electronic and regulatory sense from the physical engineering platform of the satellite itself as launched and placed into orbit as per launching state treaty stipulations under purview of the United Nations (UN) Committee on Peaceful Uses of Outer Space (COPUOS).

More significantly in a governance sense, the legal jurisdictional arrangement between COPUOS and the International Telecommunication Union (ITU) was developed by UN member countries to closely fit the technological configurations of the first generations of "analog" space telecommunications systems in the 1960s. While the COPUOS proposed legal instruments specifying state obligations regarding broad issues of outer space exploration, militarization, use, ownership, and liability, the ITU extended its longstanding role as radio spectrum regulator to encompass space satellites and their orbits.

Going forward decades later into a digital era of internet-connected satellite large constellations challenges the "technological fit" of the existing COPUOS-ITU governance regime. Instead of highly secure analog governmental space systems, the COPUOS-ITU regime is attempting to adapt jurisdictional contours to effectively address the cyber issues posed by commercial satellite systems providing highly vulnerable internet connectivity among billions of users and devices. Quantum entanglement notwithstanding, the stark fact is that amid the millions of lines of code, thousands of satellites could be disabled by changing a single bit from "1" to a "0" for a battery-charging parameter in their operating firmware (Fritz 2013, 21–50). Unprecedented capabilities promised by migration of cyber into the quantum realm will further intensify the disruptive effects of dynamic technological change into the space governance regime (Seffers 2020, 18–20).

THE RISE OF CYBER AS A FACTOR OF PLANETARY COERCIVE POWER

This third section examines how technology in the form of cyber is becoming a prime disruptive force behind not only economic upheavals, but more fundamentally as a factor reconfiguring systemic power thereby threatening the essential legitimacy of the post-Westphalian nation-state itself as "the" core element of the international system as postulated by international relations (IR) theorists (Demchak and Dombrowski 2011, 36–39). IR theory seeks to develop analytical frameworks that attempt to identify and assess factors changing the configurations of strategic, economic, and political power resulting from states, international organizations, and transnational corporations pursuing courses of action perceived to promote their survival in an anarchic self-help international system. In the 1950s, international analysts developed new methodologies and theoretical paradigms for assessing the disruptive role played by proliferating nuclear weapons to otherwise conventional systemic configurations of power previously dominated by battleships, tanks, and aircraft. Atomic weapons and missile delivery systems required a fundamental rethinking of deterrence and the logic of armed engagement and warfare. Seeking the most effective use of conventional weapons was once a winning strategy, abruptly it became clear in the 1950s–1960s that use of nuclear weapons ensured annihilation. Today, that factor of change is cyber.

To perhaps paraphrase the obvious, "cyber security has the world's attention." Amid a global pandemic, cyber continues to claim its priority as a key topic in big power summit meetings, alongside reports of cyber-attacks temporarily shutting down nuclear processing facilities and motorists forced to queue at gas stations in panic pumping as a cyber "ransomware" assault paralyzed oil distribution infrastructure. (Bergamasco et al. 2020) Meanwhile, cryptocurrency prices rise and fall in cadence with social media–fed rumors roiling world financial markets, also now vulnerable to spasms of social media–generated market gyrations affecting public trust in the reliable operation of institutional regulation of stock markets and currencies. Meanwhile on October 5, 2021, Facebook, Instagram, and WhatsApp disappeared from their billions of users' screens due to a Facebook self-generated software error. Perhaps the most insidious threat to democratic processes stems from the business model driving the privacy and trust threatening actions of Big Tech, namely the Surveillance Capitalism Model which sells users' online behaviors to advertisers through porous online platforms such as Facebook or Google (Zuboff 2019, 3–24). While cyber in its terrestrial manifestations is certainly grabbing headlines, it is also disrupting long-held views about the security of outer space systems, as large constellations of communications satellite deploy vulnerable internet connectivity to additional billions of subscribers (Batey 2021, 34–35).

Twenty-first century IR scholars find themselves confronting cyber in a setting eerily similar to their strategizing twentieth-century predecessors following the atomic bombardments of Hiroshima and Nagasaki in World War II. While atomic, and later, thermonuclear weapons fundamentally shifted configurations of strategic power in the aftermath of World War II, strategic thinking about coercive power struggled to keep pace with technological innovations in weapons, delivery systems, and civil defense. The enormous destructive power of atomic weapons realigned not only the power topographies of the international system but also required a rethinking of pre-existing theoretical frameworks premised on the conventional "hard shell" reifications of the sovereign nation-state as the international system's prime actor (Kello 2017, 23–80).

Just as the development of nuclear weapons in the 1950s launched an extensive effort to understand how the characteristics of these weapons transformed international security and governance, this must now be pursued for cyber. For example, preexisting notions of deterrence developed initially for conventional weapons were no longer valid as deterrence doctrines for atomic weapons. For the first time perhaps in human history, strategic war planners and theorists were confronting the unique and contradictory situation where to use the means of deterrence, i.e., atomic weapons, meant losing the war through mutually assured destruction (MAD), negating the very goal of deploying the atomic deterrence forces in the first place. Analogously, as Kaplan points out, to use a cyber weapon may mean losing it as its greatest power may lie in its invisibility, again a far cry from conventional weapons deterrence doctrine (Kaplan 2016, 39–56).

Theorizing Space and Cyber as Strategic Factors of International Power

Beginning with the German development of the V-2 rocket in World War II, there has always existed an awareness on the part of the world's military establishments of the enormous strategic advantage inherent in the ability to control and exploit the "high ground" of outer space. Historians credit the Cuban Missile Crisis in 1962 with instilling a "close call" sobriety between the superpowers for controlling nuclear weapons outside their national territories. Desiring to limit the proliferation of nuclear weapons that would diminish superpower dominance, both the Soviet Union and the United States backed a series of treaties that banned the deployments of nuclear weapons in Antarctica, the deep seabed, and outer space (Antarctic Treaty System 1959).

In 1999, the US Department of Defense as part of its efforts to raise public and congressional awareness about space warfare commissioned studies focusing on military implications of outer space exploitation (Oberg 1999). Their investigative approaches emphasized that outer space is an increasingly crucial domain for international security that is fundamentally different than simply an extension of the strategic competition to control airspace. Coming some sixteen years after pronouncement of US President Ronald Reagan's proposed Strategic Defense Initiative (SDI), advocates of "space power theory" argued for greater doctrinal attention be focused on post–Cold War outer space as the new "high ground" in the struggle for worldwide security. Other studies emphasized the Pentagon's focus on achieving "The Doctrine of Space Superiority," stipulating that "[d]eceiving the satellite may be the best of all strategies [as compared to kinetic disruption destruction] as the operator is unaware of the deception and continues to act based on false information." At the turn of the millennium, military strategic research was already showing how the cyber-attack vector of outer space may outstrip more traditional "high ground" strategizing (Handberg 2000, 189–249).

Today, the question about cyber's implications for disrupting governance of the international system in general, and the space domain in particular, is raising a much more epistemological query for the IR discipline (Harris 2014, 69–82). In short, cyber is disrupting not only the way foreign policymakers perceive and think about the international system, it is also altering the very discourse that seeks to clarify the relationship between perceptions and kinetic realities. The very "virtualness" of cyber is its securitization, i.e., the reality of cyber is the discourse about it (Blount 2019, 79–93).

SECURITIZATION OF CYBER IN THE INTERNATIONAL SYSTEM

This fourth section will now amplify the discussions begun in the previous two, examining how the conundrum and contradictions of cyber (the first section) intensify the doctrinal challenge as states and commercial firms attempt to tackle cyber's role as a factor of coercive power (the second section). This section outlines an analytical approach that examines the securitization of cyber as a power factor. Securitization identifies the epistemological and methodological barriers to operationalizing discourse about how cyber operates as a factor of coercive power along a wide continuum of interventions and disruptions, adding to the intrinsic difficulty in defining how it is redefining outer space security and its governance. In short, the massive clout of the Big Tech sector militates this analysis toward an approach that encompasses that financial heft. Given these epistemological questions (i.e., how to isolate cyber as a causal factor of change), a "securitization" analytical framework offers powerful insights largely unavailable using more traditional strategic doctrine approaches utilized for earlier kinetic battlefields (Blount 2019, 16–78).

To paraphrase theoretical discourse for "securitized" resources, "securitization" examines the "complex social construction" of "cyber security" as a factor that continues to influence "competing conceptions and transformations of discourse and practice." In other words, securitization can be fundamentally understood as a sociological narrative that explains the "social construction" of key factor(s) disrupting the conventional views of security (Al-Kharusi 2019, 48–64). Carrying the discussion forward, the dual-sided military-civilian nature of internet infrastructures means that cyber's "social construction" is one also dominated by a market-economics *commercialization* discourse (Manz 2021, 18–23).

In Table 30.1, the narrative of markets incorporates a "transaction cost economics" theoretical perspective offering powerful analytical insights about governance authority and legitimacy, where institutional and governance competencies are defined by (information) transaction costs (Williamson 1996, 50–52). A market comes into existence where high internal transaction costs compel less-expensive external purchases. Coase's theory of the firm is illustrated by the decision-making calculus of a would-be novice homebuilder who could buy externally all the materials and labor to build a house, but where those high transaction costs dictate hiring a general contractor for whom those

Table 30.1. Cyber as a Factor of Planetary Power			
Military-Technological	Economic	Political	Cultural
Narrative of Capacity and Resiliency	Narrative of Markets	Narrative of Power	Narrative of Norms

transactions are performed internally (Williamson 1996, 219–49). "Disintermediation" is the shifting of cost parameters to favor direct external transactions. Travel agents were disintermediated by the internet when airline passengers could buy tickets directly from airlines on their smartphones. History is replete with far-reaching examples of new technologies shifting market narratives that fundamentally disrupt long-standing systemic power relationships and legitimation narratives. (The university readership of this chapter will recognize a similar market narrative shift as the Covid pandemic moved classroom instruction into virtual spaces, challenging the "educational" narrative validating massive campus expenditures in office buildings, dormitories, and recreation centers.) In essence, the greatest transformation in planetary power is taking place as cyber continues to increasingly supplant (disintermediate) kinetic military weaponry as a more cost-effective modality for projecting coercive power.

Assessing the Social Construction of Cyber as a Disintermediating Factor of Planetary Power

Cyber may be viewed as a factor affecting the technological/military, economic, political, and cultural configurations power, depicted in Table 30.1.

Disintermediation of Governance

A securitization analytical approach based on transaction cost theory offers powerful insights about how narratives or discourse create power realities. For example, an economic "market" narrative about communication satellites highlights their role in the Cold War's "disintermediation" of the East-West ideological competition following Sputnik in 1957, explained in a narrative utilizing information transaction costs.

Just as Gutenberg's printing press radically reduced information transaction costs that resulted in a fifteenth-century information revolution and consequent armed struggle over governance narratives (i.e., the Thirty Years' War), today an analogous securitization process is taking place in the form of the twenty-first century's World Wide Web and ubiquitous space-based communication systems (Man 2002, 13–19). Reminiscent of Gutenberg's disruption of information transaction costs, communication satellites disintermediated the Soviet state's traditional role in controlling transborder flows of ideas and service-based commerce, entertainment, and services. By the late 1980s, millions of satellite receiver dishes obviated states' attempts to control information flows and protect domestic broadcasting monopolies, thereby disintermediating the Soviet Union's narrative for state legitimacy.

Today's internet and networked communication satellites are bypassing previously high information transaction costs that formerly shielded countries and societies thereby disintermediating narratives legitimizing nation-state governance. Just as their fifteenth-century counterparts, twenty-first century elite institutions and states are attempting to maintain their influence over systemic narratives in the face of an over-whelming social media disruption of conventional discourse controls and institutions. With disintermediation narratives in mind, we can now turn to cyber's disruption of outer space governance brought about by its ability to erode the high transaction costs narrative that formerly justified a primarily kinetic discourse for outer space militarization.

Securitization of Cyber

In short, *cyber is disintermediating outer space security due to its lower transaction costs.* As the preceding analyses demonstrate, the radical reductions in technological trans-action costs fueled by the internet communications revolution have resulted in the deployment of thousands of commercial large constellation satellites that are transforming narratives formerly justifying a discourse of state-centric outer space security. In the face of trillion-dollar cyber-attack industrial sectors, kinetic space weapons are the battleships of World War II whose role was supplanted by the more nimble and cost-effective projections of power offered by aircraft carriers. The cost comparisons are shocking. Compared to the millions or billions of dollars required to launch and op-erate anti-satellite weapon systems, governmental and commercial cyber security establishments jealously safeguard their store of "zero day exploits" that can incapacitate an orbiting space asset in a matter of seconds for "a fistful of dollars," as the Rosat inci-dent demonstrates, thereby confirming widespread discourse about the "Wild West" of space governance (Martinez 2015, 1–3).

The extremely low information transaction costs in IP packet-switched network architectures portends a future where complete societal or global infrastructures, de-pendent on space-based data relay, navigation, remote sensing, reconnaissance, and target identification, will be vulnerable to widespread paralysis or loss of function due to their vulnerability to the factors listed above. The simple fact is that electromagnetic interference and intentional hacking pose transaction costs far below those required for kinetic space weapons. The once exclusive "Space Club" is now open to the cyber street's hackers (Paikowsky 2017, 76–95). The market transaction costs narrative also points to the market attractiveness of non-cyber securitization as well. Intentional space de-bris deployment at certain orbital altitudes used by certain classes of security-crucial space systems may be already on planning documents for states with more modest space capabilities. A readily available and competitively priced commercial rocket costing a few million dollars could economically deposit enough space debris at crucial orbital altitudes to incapacitate satellites worth billions of dollars. This transformation of the outer space operating environment will increasingly be subject to the narratives of capacity and power.

Securitization of Outer Space Governance

As the transaction cost analysis shows, the mechanisms of governance with respect to cyber take on several narratives as shown in Table 30.1. While the technological view is depicted by a narrative of capacity, the economic, political, and cultural power configurations are demarcated by narratives of markets, power, and norms, respectively. While the claim of the state to control the technological sphere has been decentralized (i.e., disintermediated) by the packet-switched network architecture of the internet and social media, a narrative shift is evident to reestablish the primacy of state control through employment of the market, power, and norms narratives. This is very evident in the current policy debates taking place in many parts of the globe over anti-competitive business practices (market narrative), electoral misinformation campaigns (power narrative), and the worldwide cultural debate (norms narrative). A prime example of this turmoil is evident when one examines the narratives surrounding cryptocurrencies (e.g., Bitcoin or Blockchain). While it is beyond the scope of this chapter to definitively analyze the controversies or narratives over "crypto," they nonetheless exemplify a securitization counter-narrative about state-mandated central bank control over national currencies. Cumulatively, even the crypto narratives share a cyber security focus as they appeal to widespread mistrust of governmental attempts to justify an enhanced state role and presence in what were conventionally regulated economic and societal sectors as the internet initially deployed in the 1990s.

Similarly in the space domain, the rapid expansion of non-state actors into a burgeoning commercial space sector challenges traditional policy spheres monopolized by states through the "hard" law space treaties. Here too, the information transaction cost disintermediation threatens state functions and jurisdictional legitimacy. Perhaps the greatest threat facing the continuing sustainability of the space sector is that posed by space debris. The enormous information transaction costs to assess and devise mitigation strategies have already disintermediated most individual state roles in favor of "soft" law voluntary collaborations exemplified by the private Space Data Association (SDA) or what is becoming one of the most crucial yet least known non-governmental organizations regulating space software security—the Consultative Committee for Space Data Systems (CCSDS). "Hard" law approaches with written treaties compelling the sharing of what many state and non-state entities consider proprietary information about satellite launches and orbits also threaten to reveal national security establishments' space radar detection and SSA capabilities. AI is already reducing the information transaction costs that justify state-endorsed mechanisms such as the SDA, placing increased attention on other narrative attempts, especially the economic market narrative, to maintain a state role in space and cyber security.

Topography Discourse of Cyberspace: Mapping the Cyberwar "High Ground" Battlefield

A RAND Corporation 2009 study characterizes the on-going ambiguity about cyber as follows:

> Cyberspace is its own medium with its own rules. Cyber attacks, for instance, are enabled not through the generation of force but by the exploitation of the enemy's vulnerabilities. Permanent effects are hard to produce. The medium is fraught with ambiguities about who attacked and why, about what they achieved and whether they can do so again. Something that works today may not work tomorrow (indeed, precisely because it did work today). Thus, deterrence and war fighting tenets established in other media do not necessarily translate reliably into cyberspace. Such tenets must be rethought. (Fritz 2013

As such, the geography of traditional military-strategic domains (i.e., "Air-Land-Sea-Space") do not present a tight discursive fit to the "virtual" cyber domain. Instead of real-world geographical mapping, a technology map of the cyber domain is represented by the Open Systems Interconnect (OSI) model of information network hierarchies (Blount 2019).

The Open Systems Interconnect Network Model

Terminology about cyber has created a spatiality of "uploads" and "downloads" embodied in the OSI model's "topography" that differentiates the technological discourse securitizing cyber outlined in Table 30.2 (IISL 2017, 1–3).

Beginning at the bottom level of "physical" connections, the OSI model discourse moves progressively "up" to higher levels of "1s" and "0s" inter-connections until we arrive at the seventh level which accommodates the actual software applications (such as

Table 30.2. Open Systems Interconnect (OSI) Model (ITU)

Layer	Function	Example
7	Application	Satellite battery charging app
6	Presentation	Translate network data to app
5	Session	Software dialogues between computers
4	Transport	Software error control
3	Network	Transferring data packets between network nodes
2	Data Link	Protocols controlling interconnections
1	Physical	The physical medium (wires, optical fibers, connectors)

the web browser you are currently using to read this) that can be perceived with human senses.

Layers 6–7: Hacking

The application and presentation layers are the actual aspects of the virtual experience that are perceivable by human beings and their senses. Software applications that perform or engage human beings with social media, video games, banking accounts, e-books, etc., are all examples of the wide variety of online experiences that the online applications provide users. As the vast majority of the applications are commercially provided, they are also occupying the least regulated layers of the network hierarchy.

Layers 3–5: Cyberconflict

Network, transport, and session layers constitute the normally "invisible" functions of network software protocols that provide the interfaces for the billions of data bytes to be transmitted in a secure fashion between devices connected to networks.

Layers 1–2: Cyberwar

The physical and data link layers are specifications for the physical connectors, electrical power provision, and wiring specifications that provide the physical infrastructure. Interference or disruption of these layers would constitute the closest approximation to kinetic weapon destruction of physical infrastructure.

Both the Rosat and Stuxnet cyber incidents exemplify the multidimensionality of attack vectors, where the initial breaching of the facilities' physical plants themselves (layers 1–2) constitute the disabling of security measures most approximate to an armed intervention in conventional warfare terms. Each incursion also apparently gained access to their targeted devices through network connections (layers 3–5), culminating in the operational disruption accomplished through manipulations of the operating software itself (layers 6–7). Rosat's attacker repositioned the satellite to over-expose the navigational sensors, while Stuxnet directed the Siemens centrifuge controllers to overspin their devices to destruction.

While the OSI Model characterizes much of the *technological* discourse about cyber, its operationalization as a theoretical framework requires an intensified focus on significant evolutionary aspects of cyber's discourse for *market and power* securitization. As Professor Debora Spar in her book, *Ruling the Waves: From the Compass to the Internet, A History of Business and Politics along the Technological Frontier*, points out:

> In fact, it is precisely the lack of established regulation that makes the technological frontier so political. In order for commerce to grow in any uncharted territory there need to be rules. Not regulation necessarily, or even governments—just rules. There need to be property rights, for example, and some sense of contracts. In higher technology areas, there need to be rules for intellectual property (who owns the operating system? Under what terms?) and provisions for standardization (how do different products work together? Which technical platform

becomes the norm?). Without such rules, commerce may still emerge, but it will not flourish. There may be bursts of commercial activity and a handful of pioneers who cherish life on the edge, but wide-scale commerce will remain elusive. This is a powerful lesson of history and tragedy that still affects large swaths of the global economy. Without rules, and particularly without rules of property and exchange, markets simply will not grow. Just look at Russia in the 1990s, or some of Africa's more chaotic regions. A similar dynamic prevails along the technological frontier. New markets need new rules if they are to flourish, and their creation is a distinctly political act. (Spar 2001)

Simply put, it is the lack of a comprehensive global governance narrative with respect to the IoT that politicizes disjointed efforts to enhance space cybersecurity. However, the accelerating vulnerability of vital societal sectors and functions on space-based systems will wring regulatory reform out of pure necessity to avert systemic collapse. As such, cyber security will increasingly serve as the factor compelling far-reaching recalibrations of planetary governance with unknown ramifications for configurations of global power.

CYBER AS A SYSTEMIC FACTOR OF CHANGE

While the fourth section investigated how cyber securitizes discourse space governance, this fifth and concluding section now turns to examine how cyber acts as an agent of change compelling discourse about (1) the traditional role of the state as the central actor in space security; and more specific theoretical frameworks defining (2) the demarcation of "peaceful uses" between those cyber applications ostensibly for defensive purposes and those employed to project coercive force; and finally, elements of IR deterrence theory explaining (3) state approaches to space security as an increasingly crucial element of overall state security.

Cyber as a Technological Disrupter to the Role of the State

From Hacking to Cyberwar

Acknowledging that computer data systems crash all the time, the problem of attribution (i.e., assigning the cause or perpetrator of a data system failure), is a central facet to analyzing the stages or ranges of cyber-conflict from malicious hacking to strategic cyberwar. Systems analysts, strategic planners, and legal experts have proposed a variety of typologies. Susan Brenner's 2009 book, *Cyberthreat: The Emerging Fault Lines of the Nation State*, focuses her typologies on the legal categories of "Cybercrime," "Cyberterrorism," and "Cyberwarfare," exemplifying the evolving state of discourse about cyber security and its governance (or lack thereof) (Brenner 2009, 8–12).

Cyber as a Factor Promoting Cooperation and Conflict

The first satellite launches in 1957 and 1958 signaled that governments were, for the first time, able to sustain a technological and later, human-military, presence in outer space. In contrast to today's highly commercialized telecommunications industrial sector, governments were the entities launching satellites and conducting outer space activities during the birthing of the highly cooperative outer space COPUOS-ITU governance regime into the 1970s. As commercial firms began exploiting declining transaction costs of space access, regulatory control, and market expansion, commercial market competition eroded the tight congruence between the COPUOS mechanisms for developing outer space international law and the ITU's jurisdictional boundaries. In short, the commercialization and privatization of outer space activities beginning in the 1970s increasingly required states in the COPUOS-ITU regime to undertake regulatory and legal initiatives in order to accommodate the new commercial space and telecommunications actors within a barely functioning international legal framework as exemplified by the minimal accessions to the 1979 Moon Treaty.

Outer space, or to be more precise, use of the outer space environment, is governed by two sets of rules: (1) the rules governing outer space *as a place* (primarily COPUOS) and (2) the rules governing *electromagnetic outer space* (primarily ITU), i.e., the use of radio frequencies used to communicate and command space vehicles and satellites. As such, the jurisdictions of the two regimes overlap with regard to radio frequency regulations pertaining to outer space vehicles. Outer space, it is important to note, exists as a physical *place*, i.e., the physical space beyond the earth and its atmosphere, and as *electromagnetic outer space*, i.e., the radio frequency communications pathways that interconnect space vehicles as they traverse through physical outer space. The shift to "soft" international law exemplified by the 2019 Long Term Sustainability Guidelines and the 2020 Artemis Accords are attempts to bridge the widening gaps between a government-centered COPUOS-ITU regime and the exploding realms of commercial space activity exemplified by the large constellations, space mining, and space tourism.

Cyber Governance as a Factor in Space Security

The crucial link between cyber governance and space security was the focus of a 2016 ITU "Symposium on Interference Free Spectrum for Satellites," where the "cyber risks to satellites and other space-based assets" were discussed among governmental and commercial representatives. Effective and comprehensive cyber governance of the radio spectrum and management of orbital resources plays a crucial role in creating a hybrid "hard" and "soft" law legal environment that effectively assigns accountability and global enforcement jurisdictions and mechanisms. However, as cybersecurity analyst Carolyn Baylon emphasized, "commercial satellite operators themselves need to exercise greater transparency in reporting violations of international rules respecting the electromagnetic security of satellites" (Baylon 2016, 7–13). Mirroring the trans-Atlantic discourse over the application of the European Union's General Data Protection Regulation (GDPR), a comprehensive regime appears chimerical, especially in light of fundamental disagreements over large constellations and space debris governance. As one may paraphrase China's 2021 note to the United Nations about Starlink's space debris threat to its crewed space station, "it's a mess."

Concluding Observations: Toward Planetary Governance of Space Security

What is the bottom line? This chapter urges the reader to "follow the money." Using a market narrative, this chapter has argued that cyber is disintermediating outer space governance institutions and processes that are themselves reeling from their encounters with a rapidly commercializing space marketplace that transplants terrestrial cyber market clout and security vulnerabilities into outer space. Cyber security challenges long-standing Westphalian state-centric paradigms premised upon assumptions about kinetic battlefields between governmental opponents. Instead, the international community is confronting an OSI layered 3-D chessboard of commercial and governmental entities wielding cyber-weapons and firewalls where advantage accrues to the stealthy intruder whose presence is never known, in dramatic contrast to traditional doctrines for kinetic weapons deterrence premised on highly visible displays of credibility-enhancing destructive force.

Meanwhile, UN-based treaties and intergovernmental organizations, (i.e., the UNCOPOUS-ITU regime) founded upon archaic pre-internet institutional and technological factors, are becoming less relevant to on-going planetary regime evolution premised upon efforts to forge narratives for merging "cyber" and "space" battlefields and governance domains. Prime evidence is the process in COPUOS that adopted the Long-Tern Sustainability (LTS) Guidelines in June 2019. Most telling is the fact that the proposed LTS Guidelines that failed to gain COPUOS consensus approval were predominately those addressing space-based cyber operations (Martinez 2018, 2–3).

Outer Space and Cyberspace: Twenty-First Century Battlefields for Planetary Power

Cyber is a factor of power whose strategic doctrine is evolving. Cyber magnifies the intrinsically disintermediative narratives that politicize conventional terrestrial governance, but combined with the governance gaps inherent in the COPUOS-ITU outer space regime, the disintermediation of governance in space is all the more acute. In a military sense, outer space satellites, whose missions are defined by their ability to function as reliable parts of telecommunications networks, and were once thought to be beyond the reach of terrestrial conflict, are now facing the threat of cyberwar on three fronts: (1) cyberwar against the physical integrity and functioning of the satellite; (2) cyberwar against the software integrity and functioning of the satellite; and (3) cyberwar against the space region occupied by the satellite. In sum, cyber poses the greatest transformation to space and global security since the development of atomic weapons.

This is well known. In 2010, General James Cartwright, vice-chairman of the US Department of Defense Joint Chiefs of Staff, underlined in a speech the growing recognition that "outer space and cyberspace *together* constitute a unique technologically created domain that will be a focus for international strategic conflict and politics during the 21st Century" (Martinez 2010). According to Cartwright, strategic doctrine and war fighting are quickly moving into a combined space-cyberspace domain whether for force projection through unmanned vehicles on earth or space-aware satellites, including directed beam weapons. Technologically and commercially, the trend toward seamless network integration of internet capabilities into space satellite systems creates globe-encompassing space-based infrastructures for both military and civilian navigation, reconnaissance, data communications, broadcasting, and financial and banking functions, among a myriad of other services with dual-use military and civilian applications. Most crucially, Cartwright pointed out that "the growing military presence in outer space is also identifying cyber's security challenge to long-standing jurisdictional and institutional roles traditionally assigned to discourse about state sovereignty" (Martinez 2010). Increasingly, cyber's growing vulnerability to disruption, whether intentional or accidental is fueling its salience as a factor militarizing outer space and its governance. Perhaps the naming of the Pentagon's newest command, the "Space Force," was a bit premature. As this chapter has argued, cyber defines the space security domain as one dominated by a worldwide struggle to control 1s and 0s. Whether planetary politics become a "positive-sum" or "zero-sum" game depends on that struggle's outcome (Martinez 2010).

References

Al-Kharusi, Lamya. 2019. "The Making of 'Energy Security' in Oman: Tracing Discourses and Practices." PhD Diss., Kings College, London.

Antarctic Treaty System. 1959. The Antarctic Treaty. 12 U.S.T. 794, T.I.A.S. No. 4780, 402 U.N.T.S. 71. https://www.ats.aq/e/antarctictreaty.html.

Batey, Angus. 2021. "How To Tackle The Space Sector's Cyber Challenge." *Aviation Week*. July 26, 2021. https://aviationweek.com/defense-space/space/how-tackle-space-sectors-cyber-challenge#.

Baylon, Carolyn. 2014. "Challenges at the Intersection of Cyber Security and Space Security: Country and Institution Perspectives." Chatham House Research Paper, December 2014.

Baylon, Carolyn. 2016. "Interference-Free Spectrum for Satellites." Presentation at ITU Satellite Symposium on June 14, 2016, Geneva.

Bergamasco, Federico, Roberto Cassar, Rada Povpova, and Benjamyn I. Scott. 2020. *Cybersecurity: Key Legal Considerations for the Aviation and Space Sectors*. Alphen aan den Rijn: Kluwer Law International B.V.

Blount, P. J. 2019. *Reprogramming the World: Cyberspace and the Geography of Global Order*. Bristol: E-International Relations Publishing.

Brenner, S. 2009. *Cyberthreat: The Emerging Fault Lines of the Nation State*. Oxford: Oxford University Press.

Cook, Sam. 2021. "2018–2021 Ransomware Statistics and Facts." Comparitech. https://www.comparitech.com/antivirus/ransomware-statistics/.

Demchak, Chris, and Peter Dombrowski. 2011. "Rise of the Cybered Westphalian Age." *Strategic Studies Quarterly* 5, no. 1: 32–61.

Choi, Charles Q. 2010). "Attempt to Shut Down Zombie Satellite Galaxy 15 Fails." *Space.com*. https://www.space.com/8344-attempt-shut-zombie-satellite-galaxy-15-fails.html.

Fritz, Jason. 2013. "Satellite Hacking: A Guide for the Perplexed." *Culture Mandala: Bulletin of the Centre for East-West Cultural and Economic Studies* 10, no. 1: 21–50.

Handberg, Roger. 2000. *Seeking New World Vistas: The Militarization of Space*. Westport: Prager.

Harris, Shane. 2014. *@War: The Rise of the Military-Internet Complex*. New York: Houghton, Mifflin, Harcourt.

IISL (International Institute of Space Law) Cyberspace Working Group. 2017. "What is the Technical Architecture of Cyberspace?" University of Cologne Institute for Air and Space Law.

International Telecommunication Union (ITU). Symposium on Interference-Free Spectrum for Satellites, June 13–14, 2016, Geneva. https://www.itu.int/en/ITU-R/space/Presentations/Harmful%20Interference%20to%20Space%20Services_Ciccorossi.pdf.

Kaplan, Fred. 2016. *Dark Territory: The Secret History of Cyber War*. New York: Simon and Schuster.

Kello, Lucas. 2017. *The Virtual Weapon and International Order*. New Haven: Yale University Press.

Klotz, Irene. 2021. "Boeing's Space Taxi Faces Another Lengthy Delay." *Aviation Week and Space Technology*. August 25, 2021. https://aviationweek.com/defense-space/space/boeings-space-taxi-faces-another-lengthy-delay.

Krauss, Lawrence M. "Deafness at Doomsday." *New York Times*. January 15, 2013. (https://www.nytimes.com/2013/01/16/opinion/deafness-at-doomsday.html.

Kushner, David. 2013. "The Real Story of Stuxnet." *IEEE Spectrum*. February 26, 2013. https://spectrum.ieee.org/the-real-story-of-stuxnet.

Man, John. 2002. *The Gutenberg Revolution*. London: Bantam.

Manz, Barry. 2021. "EW Goes Commercial . . . From Space." *Journal of Electronic Dominance*. February 2021:44(2) p. 18.

Martinez, Larry. 2010. Author's notes at University of Nebraska Third Annual Space and Cyber Conference, hosted by CSIS and ABILA, FCBA, New America Foundation, Newseum, Washington, DC, September 9–10, 2010.

Martinez, Larry. 2015. "The Hard or Soft Law of 'Gravity.'" IAC-15-E7.3.4-x29542. IISL Colloquium, Jerusalem.

Martinez, Peter. 2018. "Development of an International Compendium Of Guidelines For The Long-Term Sustainability of Outer Space Activities." *Space Policy* 43: 13–17.

NATO Cooperative Cyber Defence Centre of Excellence. 2017. *Tallin Manual 2.0 on the International Law Applicable to Cyber Warfare*. Cambridge: Cambridge University Press.

Oberg, James, and Brian Sullivan. 1999. "Space Power Theory." Introductions by Colin S. Gray and Howell M. Estes III. Colorado Springs, CO: US Air Force Academy. OCLC 41145918. https://en.wikipedia.org/wiki/James_Oberg.

Ossinger, Joanna. 2021. "The World's Cryptocurrency Is Now Worth More Than \$3 Trillion." *Time*, November 8, 2021. https://time.com/6115300/cryptocurrency-value-3-trillion/.

Paikowsky, Deganit. 2017. *The Power of the Space Club*. Cambridge: Cambridge University Press.

Seffers, George I. 2020. "DARPA's Quantum Quest May Leapfrog Modern Computers." *Signal*, June 2020, 74:10: 18–20.

Spar, Deborah. 2001. *Ruling the Waves: From the Compass to the internet, A History of Business and Politics along the Technological Frontier*. New York: Harcourt.

United Nations. *Test Ban Treaty of 1963*, https://2009-2017.state.gov/t/avc/trty/199116.htm (accessed September 26, 2021).

Williamson, Oliver. 1996. *The Mechanisms of Governance*. Oxford: Oxford University Press.

Zuboff, Shoshana. 2019. *The Age of Surveillance Capitalism: The Fight for a Human Future at the Frontier of Power*. New York: Public Affairs.

CHAPTER 31

THE "AI WAVE" IN SPACE OPERATIONS

Implications for Future Warfare

MICHAEL RASKA AND MALCOLM DAVIS

THE *Star Wars* movie series has captivated audiences for generations with images of futuristic galactic warfare. From the Imperial Stormtroopers carrying heavy blaster rifles to Anakin Skywalker's iconic blue lightsaber and the many fighting spaceships featuring hyperdrives and laser cannons, including Han Solo's Millennium Falcon, the Star Wars universe imagined space-like smart weapons and interplanetary conflicts. In the real world, the ideas of humanoid robots, laser weapons, space operations, and counter-space weapons are increasingly becoming a reality, gradually reshaping the direction and character of warfare. Indeed, the convergence of advanced novel technologies—such as artificial intelligence (AI) systems, robotics, additive manufacturing (or 3D printing), quantum computing, directed energy, and other "disruptive" technologies, defined under the commercial umbrella of the Fourth Industrial Revolution (4IR)—promise new and potentially significant opportunities for defense applications and, in turn, for increasing one's military edge over potential rivals. These increasingly rely on assured access to new domains, notably the space domain, as part of an evolving multi-domain operations concepts and open the possibility that new types of military capabilities and operations will occur in this domain (McCall 2021). The same transformation is relevant to the cyber domain and operations across the electromagnetic spectrum.

Much of the current debate arguably portrays the "next-frontier" technologies as synonymous with a "discontinuous" or "disruptive" military innovation in the character and conduct of warfare—from the "industrial-age" toward "information-age warfare" and now increasingly toward "automation-age warfare" (Raska 2020). For example, advanced sensor technologies such as hyperspectral imagery, computational photography, and compact sensor design aim to improve target detection, recognition, and tracking capabilities and overcome traditional line-of-sight interference (Freitas et al. 2018). Advanced materials such as composites, ceramics, and nanomaterials with adaptive properties will make military equipment lighter but more resistant to the environment (Burnett et al. 2018). Emerging photonics technologies, including high-power lasers and optoelectronic devices, may provide new levels of secure communications based on quantum computing and quantum cryptography (IISS 2019).

For modern militaries, the application of emerging technologies such as machine-learning algorithms to diverse problems promises to provide unprecedented capabilities in terms of speed of information processing, automation for a mix of crewed and autonomous weapons platforms and surveillance systems, and ultimately, command and control (C2) decision-making (Horowitz 2018; Cummings 2017). Military organizations aim to increasingly utilize AI algorithms to process multiple data streams that provide situational awareness and intelligence of the operational environment and cyber support to enable future operations. While these are only early versions of emerging capabilities that are likely to advance considerably between now and 2040, the actual use of AI-enabled systems reflects the pace of defense innovation and the urgency to incorporate the value of AI and machine learning into military capabilities, both of which are likely to increase as more AI-enabled systems are deployed. Consequently, the diffusion of AI systems is seen as having profound implications for how militaries adopt new technologies, for how on an operational level militaries adapt to and apply new technologies, and for our understanding of the future battlespace.

In this context, emerging technologies are also increasingly integrated with the space domain, which is seen as vital for implementing novel operational and organizational concepts such as Multi-Domain Operations (MDO)—a US concept emerging from the 2018 US National Defense Strategy. For example, the US Army Training and Doctrine Command defines MDO as "how the US Army, as part of the joint force, can counter and defeat a near-peer adversary capable of contesting the US in all domains, in both competition and armed conflict. As part of the joint and multinational teaming, the concept describes how the US ground forces may deter adversaries and defeat highly capable near-peer enemies in the 2025–2050 timeframe" (Feickert 2021). The US Air Force defines the concept in terms of command and control across multiple domains—emphasizing the coordinated execution of authority and direction to gain, fuse, and exploit information from any source to integrate planning and synchronize the execution of MDOs in time, space and purpose to meet the commander's objectives (Grest and Heren 2019).

Rather than be seen purely as a service-specific concept for the US Army or US Air Force, MDO seeks to enhance "integration of military forces across the operational domains—land, maritime, air space and cyber—through a combination of organisational reform and emerging technology" (Spears 2019). As this chapter argues, space and cyberspace as new domains of military rivalries are vital elements of this MDO approach but are also central to an emerging AI Wave in warfare. In particular, the confluence of disruptive technologies and innovative thinking on how new domains will impact future warfare contributes toward a new phase in defense and military innovation, namely the AI-driven Revolution in Military Affairs (AI-RMA) or AI Wave. In turn, the strategic importance of the space domain in this concept demands that critical systems are protected. New missions such as space control and new organizations such as space forces are emerging in the face of growing counter-space threats developed by peer adversaries. This may represent the potential of real change as disruptive and emerging technologies propel a new AI-RMA forward, which may occur more rapidly than previous information technology (IT) driven RMAs.

In this chapter, we examine these realities. In the twenty-first century, the evolution of space capabilities is set to become transformative in several ways that could accelerate the introduction of an AI Wave and reinforce the concept of MDOs. This represents the latest step in a long development of space capabilities from the earliest years of the space age to future military capabilities that embrace an AI Wave. Space is becoming an ever more critical domain that provides the foundation for other military capabilities and transformational systems that can radically reshape the character and conduct of future warfare.

THE AI WAVE: STRATEGIC COMPETITION FOR EMERGING TECHNOLOGIES

Driven mainly by quantum leaps in information technologies, the trajectory of "disruptive" defense and military innovation narratives and debates have been defined in the context of an IT-driven Revolution in Military Affairs (IT-RMA), which has progressed through at least five stages: (1) the initial conceptual discovery of the Military-Technical Revolution by Soviet strategic thinkers in the early 1980s; (2) the conceptual adaptation, modification, and integration in the US strategic thought during the early 1990s; (3) the technophilic RMA debate during the mid-to-late 1990s; (4) a shift to the broader "defense transformation" and its partial empirical investigation in the early 2000s; and (5) critical reversal questioning the disruptive narrative from 2005 onward (Gray 2006; Raska 2016). Since the mid-2010s, however, with the accelerating diffusion of novel technologies such as AI and autonomous systems, one could argue that a new AI-RMA—or the sixth RMA wave—has emerged (Raska 2021).

The new "AI-enabled" defense innovation wave differs from the past IT-led waves in several ways. First, the diffusion of AI-related defense and military innovation proceeds at a much faster pace, through multiple paths and patterns, notably through the accelerating geostrategic competition between great powers—the United States, China, and to a lesser degree Russia. Strategic competitions between great powers are not new; they have been deeply rooted in history—from the Athenian and Spartan grand strategies during the Peloponnesian War in the third century BCE to the bipolar divide of the Cold War during the second half of the twentieth century. However, the character of the emerging strategic competition differs from analogies of previous strategic competitions. In the twenty-first century, strategic competitions are more complex and diverse, reflecting multiple competitions under different or overlapping sets of rules in which long-term economic interdependencies coexist with core strategic challenges (Lee 2016).

However, technological innovation is portrayed as a central source of international influence and national power in a contest over future supremacy—generating economic competitiveness, political legitimacy, and military power (Mahnken 2012). Specifically, for the first time in decades, the United States faces a strategic peer competitor, China, capable of pursuing and implementing its own AI-driven military modernization. In this regard, the question is not whether the AI-RMA wave is "the one" that will bring about a fundamental discontinuity in warfare, and if so, how and why? Instead, it is whether the US AI-RMA can be nullified—or at least weakened—by corresponding Chinese or Russian AI-RMAs. In other words, the margins of technological superiority between great powers are effectively narrowing, accelerating the strategic necessity for more disruptive defense and military innovation.

Second, contrary to previous decades, which, admittedly, utilized *some* dual-use technologies to develop major weapons platforms and systems, the current AI-enabled wave differs in the magnitude and impact of commercial technological innovation as the source of military innovation (Raska 2021). Large military-industrial primes are no longer the only drivers of technological innovation; instead, advanced technologies with a dual-use potential are being developed in the commercial sectors and then being "spun on" to military applications. In this context, the diffusion of emerging technologies, including 3D printing, nanotechnology, space and space-like capabilities, AI, and drones, are not confined solely to the great powers (Hammes 2016). The diffusion of AI-enabled sensors and autonomous weapon systems is also reflected in defense trajectories of select advanced small states and middle powers such as Singapore, South Korea, Israel, and others. These have the potential to develop niche emerging technologies to advance their defense capabilities and economic competitiveness, political influence, and status in the international arena (Barsade and Horowitz 2018).

Third, the diffusion of autonomous and AI-enabled autonomous weapons systems, coupled with novel operational constructs and force structures, challenge the direction and character of human involvement in future warfare—in which algorithms and data may shape human decision-making and future combat is envisioned in the use of Lethal Autonomous Weapons Systems (LAWS). Advanced militaries are selectively experimenting with varying technologies that use data analytics to enable automation in warfare, and these technologies are increasingly permeating future warfare experimentation and capability development programs (Jensen and Pashkewitz 2019). In the United States, for example, select priority research and development areas focus on the development of AI-systems and autonomous weapons in various human-machine type collaborations, i.e., AI-enabled early warning systems and command and control networks, space and electronic warfare systems, cyber capabilities, lethal autonomous weapons systems, and others.

Taken together, the convergence of the three drivers—strategic competition, dual-use emerging technological innovation, and changing character of human-machine interactions in warfare—propel a new set of conditions that define the AI-RMA wave.

Its diffusion trajectory inherently also poses new challenges and questions concerning strategic stability, alliance relationships, arms control, ethics and governance, and ultimately, the conduct of combat operations (Stanley-Lockman 2021a). International normative debates on the role of AI systems in the use of force, for example, increasingly focus on the diffusion of LAWS and the ability of states to conform to principles of international humanitarian law. As technological advancements move from science fiction to technical realities, states also have different views on whether the introduction of LAWS would defy or reinforce international legal principles. Facing the contending legal and ethical implications of military AI applications, military establishments increasingly recognize the need to address questions related to safety, ethics, and governance, including the space domain, which is crucial to building trust in new capabilities, managing risk escalation, and revitalizing arms control. The critical question is whether existing norms and governance mechanisms will prevent militaries from moving into a new phase of "automation warfare" in which algorithms will enable the control and actions of robotic weapons capable of selecting and engaging targets without human control. Indeed, there are growing tensions among different expert communities on whether militaries should focus their ethics efforts narrowly on LAWS or, more broadly, on the gamut of AI-enabled systems (Stanley-Lockman 2021b).

APPLICATION OF THE "AI WAVE" IN SPACE OPERATIONS

This section discusses the evolution and spread of AI Wave in space operations.

The Evolution of Space Power and Space Capabilities

The emergence of an AI Wave in space operations will see the role and significance of the space domain grow as more terrestrial military systems become interdependent with space systems. Rather than merely a secondary, supporting adjunct to traditional air, sea, and land domains, space is now emerging as of equal importance to these terrestrial domains. Crucially, the importance of space capabilities inherently raises the prospect that it will become a warfighting domain in any future conflict.

Space has certainly been militarized since the dawn of the space age in the 1960s, with early US and Soviet satellites providing intelligence, surveillance, and reconnaissance (ISR), satellite communications and, most importantly, nuclear command and control (NC2) and missile early warning services (see Buono and Bateman, this volume). These were essential to ensuring a stable nuclear balance. The 1970s and 1980s saw the development of satellite navigation as a new role for space, with the US Global Positioning System (GPS) vital for military operations but also becoming essential for a wide range of services for civil use, including banking systems, supply chains, and financial trading. The role of the space domain expanded in the 1990s to support a broader range of military and civil tasks. For example, space capabilities were a key component of coalition military operations during the 1991 First Gulf War, with GPS, intelligence collection satellites, and sophisticated digital satellite communications enabling a range of new military technologies. These included networked command and control of coalition forces during Operations Desert Storm and Desert Sabre best epitomized by the "Blue Force Tracker" capability used by coalition forces that clearly showed the location of friendly forces and reduced the risk of "blue on blue" engagements.

In the twenty-first century, space capabilities continue to expand in importance to enable networked MDOs and support new types of military capabilities, including supporting autonomous systems in the air, on land, and under the waves. For example, the positioning, navigation, and timing (PNT) services provided by global navigation satellite systems such as the US GPS, Europe's Galileo, as well as China's Beidou and Russia's Glonass are not just essential to the navigation or targeting of precision weapons. The timing signals generated by such satellites are vital in maintaining network-centric warfare, while advanced digital satellite communications allow for global military operations and long-range power projection. A good example is the control of armed unmanned autonomous vehicles such as Predator and Reaper drones over conflicts in Afghanistan controlled from ground facilities in Nevada via satellite systems.

The importance of space in warfare is growing, particularly as autonomous systems expand to become prolific over the future battlespace and become a critical component for future force structures of armed forces. As Western liberal democracies begin to acquire lethal autonomous weapons systems, their requirement to observe the principles of jus in bello and international humanitarian law in shaping rules of engagement when using autonomous systems to deliver lethal force will demand a human "on the loop" to give broad oversight and direction to an autonomous system, and in some cases, such as with the delivery of lethal effect, "in the loop" to allow direct control, or at the very least, authority to release a weapon (Davis 2020b). There is a need to balance an aspiration toward developing trusted autonomy for these systems, whereby humans stay in the loop, against a need for positive control depending on tactical and political requirements. Both demand resilient space capabilities for ensuring positive and survivable command and control, real-time battlespace awareness through a network of space and non-space based ISR platforms, as well as assured access to PNT services.

It certainly is conceivable that in the future, fully autonomous systems employing advanced AI could allow humans to go "off the loop," with machine intelligence making decisions about tactics and weapons employment. Such an approach would be inconsistent with current requirements set by Western democracies observing jus in bello and international humanitarian law. However, the approach taken by authoritarian states is a little less clear, and the development of autonomous systems that employ AI for tactical command and control without human control or oversight could potentially deliver tactical military advantage in the hands of a determined adversary (Davis 2019a).

The Small and the Many—The Rise of Small Satellites

The US Army's Multi-Domain Transformation Strategy (US Army 2021) released in 2021, argues that future wars will occur across all domains at long range, and at high speeds, both in terms of physical actions and movements, as well as in cognitive terms, which relates to the speed of decision making. It notes that "Artificial Intelligence, autonomy and robotics will continue to change the character of operational campaigns, resulting in a battlefield that is faster, more lethal and distributed." The pace of future operations in temporal and cognitive terms, together with the physical size and complexity of the future battlespace, demands greater integration of AI into traditionally human-controlled battle management and command and control processes. This AI-enabled command and control will place a greater emphasis on the sensor-end of the "sensor to shooter kill chain," employing large numbers of small satellite constellations and responsive space access to augment or reconstitute space capabilities in the face of emerging counter-space threats. Embracing these capabilities generates military advantages in terms of speed of decision-making and the fidelity of knowledge and awareness of the battlespace that simply could not be gained without investment in such technology, while creating a degree of insurance against adversaries gaining a lead. The requirement to maintain a comparative military-technological advantage over an opponent has been a constant throughout the history of warfare, from sword and spear to nuclear weapons to space warfare in the future. This will likely not change.

Satellites for military purposes have been traditionally large, complex, and expensive, each costing millions or even billions to develop and deploy. These continue to be pursued for the major US and allied defense projects. For example, the Australian Defence SATCOM System (ASDSS) to be acquired under Defence Project JP-9102 envisages the acquisition of four to five large satellites based in geosynchronous orbit (Yeo 2019). However, a key development since the 1990s has been the "small satellite" which, as the name suggests, is smaller and cheaper than traditional larger satellites. Yet smaller doesn't necessarily imply less capability, as advances in satellite technology and computing have meant that small satellite constellations, comprising a number of satellites working together toward a common operational requirement, such as the provision of maritime domain awareness, can become a viable alternative to a single larger satellite at a considerably lower cost. Small satellites also benefit from greater opportunity in taking advantage of rapid innovation cycles. Instead of a single large satellite with a life of twenty to thirty years and little or no means to update its capabilities once in orbit, a constellation of small satellites can be rapidly augmented with newer technology that enhances a nation's space capability more rapidly and provides more responsive provision of key tasks, such as maritime security roles (Pekkanen, Aoki, and Mittleman 2022).

Small satellites emphasize the "small, cheap and many" paradigm over the "large, expensive and few" approach of traditional space architectures. Their lower cost makes them affordable to a wider range of actors in a manner that democratizes access to space, particularly when matched by responsive space launch. The development of reusable launch vehicles reduces the cost of launching such satellites. In the 1980s and 1990s, each Space Shuttle launch would cost US$1.7 billion per launch, with a payload launched at US$65,400 per kilogram to orbit. In comparison, SpaceX's partly reusable Falcon 9 Heavy launch vehicle costs US$95 million per launch and can place a payload into orbit at US$1,500 per kilogram to orbit (Roberts 2020). The SpaceX Starship Super Heavy fully reusable launch vehicle (O'Callaghan 2022) will drop this cost further to around US$10 million per launch. With a launch capacity of 100 metric tons, the opportunity to launch large numbers of satellites very quickly becomes possible, especially with a fully reusable launch vehicle that can launch on a regular basis. This development is also aligned with the rapid growth of the commercial space sector that in many ways has overtaken traditional government-run space agencies, with SpaceX now launching US Air Force satellites on their partly reusable Falcon 9 rockets. In effect, space is getting cheaper and easier to access for more state and non-state participants. This development will lead to rapid growth in the global space economy from about US$350 billion to more than US$1 trillion by 2040, particularly with the growth of large satellite mega-constellations (Morgan Stanley 2020).

For the AI wave, this is a significant development. The proliferation and development of autonomous systems demand resilient command and control for global MDOs and enhanced battlespace awareness through large constellations of small satellites operating in low Earth orbit (LEO) and, in some cases, medium Earth orbit (MEO). The development of the small satellite concept combined with rapid, low-cost access to orbit facilitates a further innovation that reinforces the potential for the AI wave in space, in the form of satellite mega-constellations, made up of potentially tens of thousands of small satellites in LEO controlled by adaptive AI algorithms. These will also provide critical services to support an information-based society and economy. For example, SpaceX is deploying its Starlink mega-constellation to provide satellite-based internet, in effect a "broadband in the sky" while Amazon's Project Kuiper seeks to provide competition to the SpaceX Starlink service and is partnered with Arianespace, United Launch Alliance, and Blue Origin, also owned by Amazon owner Jeff Bezos (Grush 2022).

Exploiting Mega-Constellations in Future War

If military forces were to harness this technology in the form of a dedicated military mega-constellation, they could have assured high-speed satellite communications or potentially, pervasive and comprehensive earth observation from thousands of satellites in the LEO. If combined with traditional large communications satellites in the geostationary orbit (GEO) and higher-end reconnaissance satellites, in a "high-low mix" (Davis 2019b), the space domain becomes ever more important in terms of controlling advanced networked autonomous systems, and for understanding the battlespace to a high level of fidelity on a round-the-clock basis. This is not a possibility that is distant in the future. At the outset of the Russian invasion of Ukraine, SpaceX dispatched large numbers of portable ground terminals for Starlink to ensure access to the internet for Ukraine's government and military in the face of Russian attempts to jam satellites and bring down server infrastructure (Lerman and Zakrzewski 2022).

Military applications for mega-constellations might also include enabling a "military internet of things" to support advanced global logistics that would track critical components of military systems. Small satellite mega-constellations would be crucial in providing resilient digital information networks at a global range, with the large number of satellites enhancing resilience compared to total reliance on a small number of large satellites. The latter are more vulnerable to counter-space capabilities and have limited bandwidth to support operational demand. A mega-constellation is highly distributed and thus resilient against counter-space attacks and can be quickly augmented by additional satellites to enhance bandwidth. It is also easier to reconstitute lost capability if needed, in the face of an adversary counter-space attack, given the falling cost of launch and the potential for enhanced launch tempo of reusable launch vehicles.

Contested Space and Space Forces

While space is now recognized as an operational domain and not just an enabling adjunct to terrestrial operations, there is a growing risk that it will quickly become a warfighting domain given the growth of counter space or anti-satellite (ASAT) capabilities that are emerging in China and Russia, as well as India (Weeden and Samson 2021). Other states, such as Japan and Australia, are responding to the challenge of ASATs through developing defensive systems such as ground-based space electronic warfare to neutralize space-based threats. For example, Australia is pursuing an analysis of this capability under Defence Project 9358 (DEF-9358) with the aim to use "soft kill" technologies to disable rather than destroy an opponent's ASATs from the ground (Department of Defence (Australia) 2021). Japan is also establishing a similar capability, as it creates a second space defense unit (the first being tasked with space situational awareness) dedicated to monitoring electromagnetic threats to its satellites (Park Si-soo 2021). The establishment of this second space defense unit deepens Japan's ability to cooperate with its partners on space security challenges and reinforces an emerging trend in Western liberal democratic states responding to counterspace threats coming from authoritarian states, while not moving directly to the acquisition of ASATs. Meeting the challenge posed by emerging counter-space systems is one of the most significant aspects of an AI-RMA in the future and is explored below.

Assuring access to the space domain both in literal terms, that is, an ability for responsive space launch and accessing vital space capabilities to support terrestrial military operations, is critical. The growth of counter-space capabilities suggests that the space domain will quickly become one of direct military conflict in a future crisis as potential adversaries seek to deny US and allied access to space. The development of counter-space capabilities includes direct-ascent kinetic kill systems such as the Chinese SC-19 tested in January 2007 (Weeden 2010) and believed to be operationally deployed

(Department of Defense 2022) as well as the Russian Nudol (Davis 2021) last tested in November 2021 (Weeden and Samson 2021). China and Russia have also demonstrated co-orbital soft kill technologies and capabilities that would seek to damage, disable, or deny, but not destroy an opponent's satellites (DIA 2022). Finally, the potential for cyber-attack on satellites or ground stations controlling them, as well as uplink and downlink jamming, presents a third challenge for utilizing space as part of an MDO approach to warfare and by extension, supporting AI-RMA type forces, including autonomous systems (Austin, Wright, and Rajagopalan 2022).

With the growing importance of space capabilities and the emerging threat posed by counter-space technologies, it is little surprise that organizational change is occurring alongside more sophisticated thinking regarding the space domain. The establishment of the United States Space Force in 2018, a response to Chinese military reforms from 2015 onward that brought about the PLA Strategic Support Force (PLASSF), perceives the space domain as more than simply an enabler for terrestrial military operations, but a warfighting domain (United States Space Force 2020). The key question is how far does this evolution go, particularly when new types of military capability, as suggested by an AI Wave in space operations, are considered in the coming decades?

Firstly, in terms of space forces, the concept of a space force or some form of dedicated "space command" is now an emerging trend for many states, rather than simply a unique policy of the United States and the former Trump administration. The Biden administration has kept the US Space Force in place, and a debate is now emerging as to its future role and scope of its activities and mission (Davis 2020a). Nor is it likely that the US Space Force would be eliminated by any future administration, given China and Russia's rapidly growing challenge in space. The question to be addressed now is about the force's role as strategic and military operations in space intensify, particularly in relation to evolving counter-space capabilities (Bender 2021). The answer is likely to depend not just on actions in space, but the evolution of emerging military technologies on Earth, that if pursued, could create an AI-RMA in Space Operations. If the AI-RMA is to transform war on Earth, then how does a highly competitive and contested space domain, in which major powers have established a range of space and counter-space capabilities to support military operations on Earth, and potentially, space warfare activities in space, play a role in shaping this RMA?

The concept of a space force or space command should be seen as a critical step in organizational evolution that can contribute to new operational concepts, doctrines, and military strategy that addresses this issue. Rather than evolving separately from events on Earth, the concept of war in space is inherently linked to conflicts or wars on Earth, with space linked to geocentric operations (Bowen 2020), at least for the foreseeable future. According to Bowen, space operations are distinct and separate from terrestrial military developments. He challenges the validity of space as a "high ground" from which victory can be gained separately from military activities below. Bowen also perceives space as a "cosmic coastline" and argues that "space power and operations in orbit must be seen as primarily a supporting force or capability, not a direct war-winning capability or a scene dominated by spectacular battles." Bowen is correct to highlight the link between space power and terrestrial military forces, but his argument that "space is perceived as a secondary theatre, and not essential or pressing as terrestrial ones" is likely to be open to challenge, particularly as future military forces rely on emerging technologies in an AI-RMA to conduct MDOs (7). While certainly military forces can generate the use of force—fight a war as politics by other means—without space, their effectiveness is vastly reduced, particularly if their opponents can utilize space capabilities to enable and enhance their own effectiveness. The lessons of earlier military-technological revolutions and RMAs are clear in this regard. Iraq in 1991 had far less grasp of the battlespace, and a much-reduced ability for effective operational maneuvre, because it lacked effective space capabilities for communications, intelligence, surveillance, and reconnaissance, as well as PNT. In this sense, the space domain is of crucial strategic importance in war, and this importance will only grow in the coming years. Space is an operational domain, even if its primary role is *currently* an enabler for terrestrial military forces.

Other Western democracies recognize the risks posed by increasing astrostrategic competition and the challenge of assuring access to critical space capability. They are pursuing, if not an independent space force like the United States, then various forms of defense space commands. One example is Australia, which established its own Defence Space Command in February 2022. The Australian Defence Force (ADF) Defence Space Command (DSpC) sits within the Royal Australian Air Force (RAAF) and "will coordinate space support across multiple theatres and across all phases of conflict from peace to war and provide space forces and expertise to Joint Operations Command" (Department of Defence 2022). The move toward establishing DSpC within the RAAF follows a dramatic transformation of thinking within Australia's defense community about the role of the space domain, once considered merely an adjunct for enabling terrestrial military operations. With Australia overwhelmingly dependent on the United States and other allies to provide "upstream" capabilities, such as satellites and launch capability, there has been a marked shift in Australia's thinking on space. The 2020 Defence Strategic Update and its accompanying Force Structure Plan highlighted this change, with a significant investment of AUD$7 billion over ten years to acquire sovereign controlled space capability, enhance space domain awareness, and develop a space control capability (Department of Defence 2020). The 2022 Defence Space Strategy and the Space Power eManual reinforce the Australian perception of space as an operational domain (Department of Defence 2022). There is likely to be an increasing debate within Australian strategic policy circles about how rapidly an "operational domain" becomes a "warfighting domain" and whether in fact, the term "operational" can be sustained, especially given the United States official doctrine with regard to space as a "warfighting domain."

As the debate over the role of the space domain becomes more complex and, perhaps appropriately, more sophisticated in nature, there is more engagement between what might be considered traditional military-focused discussions on technology, capability, and space operations with other stakeholders, including space law and space regulation communities. The 1967 Outer Space Treaty still forms the basis of space law and sets a foundation for the development of new approaches to space law and regulation that will be better placed to manage a far more complex and multifaceted environment (Davis 2020a). One example of this process is the establishment of the Woomera Manual project by the University of Adelaide, which highlights the need for new thinking and new approaches to space security while recognizing much has changed since 1967 and seeking to find a way to manage the military use of space and prevent uncontrolled space weaponization. (University of Adelaide 2022) Likewise, the tabling of United Nations General Assembly Resolution 75-36 by the United Kingdom on establishing norms of responsible behavior in space has led to the establishment of an Open-Ended Working Group within the United Nations toward new approaches to regulatory and legal constraints on weaponization. The fact that the United States, and most of its allies, are supporting this important resolution, notably with the Biden administration announcing a ban on testing direct-ascent kinetic kill ASATs, highlights that the space domain is becoming more contested and congested and competitive. Efforts such as the Woomera Manual and the UN Open Ended Working Group on norms of responsible behavior in space sit comfortably alongside traditional approaches to space control with both complementary to the effort to respond to counterspace threats.

In summary, the implications of the AI wave on the emerging space domain are as follows: The space domain is emerging not just as a secondary theatre which merely enables terrestrial military success but as an operational domain that is crucial to the fighting ability of modern military forces engaging in joint and integrated operations across multiple domains. The recognition of space as a key domain of warfare, including in concepts such as MDOs, is firmly established. The growth of AI-enabled systems and technologies will depend more on space capabilities to function effectively, especially in the context of approaches to the use of autonomous systems consistent with the requirements of jus in bello that promotes discrimination, proportionality, and necessity under international humanitarian law. Our reliance on networks of sensors and shooters to rapidly assess and understand the future battlespace, and generate rapid precision effects, together with faster machine-enhanced battlespace management and command and control, lies at the heart of the AI-RMA. What is critical is turning data and information coming from sensors into knowledge and understanding of a tactical and operational environment rapidly enough to deliver precision effects in time and space across multiple domains in the future battlespace and generate dilemmas through MDOs that occur faster than an opponent's decision cycle. The space domain is critical in achieving this outcome in future conflicts, and yet, space is a highly contested domain, with the growth of adversary counter-space capabilities becoming ever more challenging to the ability of Western liberal democracies to assure access to space. Adversaries will increasingly seek to challenge the ability of Western liberal democracies to access space, aiming to disrupt or destroy "sensor to shooter" links, and to attack the information-based societies and economies that depend on space access. Space is an operational domain but is likely to quickly become a warfighting domain in future wars.

CHALLENGES AND LIMITATIONS

Integrating data streams and AI systems across different military platforms, including space systems and organizations, to transform computers from tools into problem-solving "thinking" machines will continue to present a range of complex technological, organizational, and operational challenges (Raska, Zysk, and Bowers 2022). These may include developing trustworthy algorithms that will enable these systems to better adapt to changes in their environment, learn from unanticipated tactics, and apply them on the battlefield. It would also call for designing ethical codes and safeguards for these thinking machines. Another challenge is that technological advances, especially in defense innovation, are a continuous, dynamic process: breakthroughs are always occurring. Their impact on military effectiveness and comparative advantage could be significant and hard to predict at their nascent stages. Moreover, such technologies and resulting capabilities rarely spread evenly across geopolitical lines.

Most importantly, however, the critical question is how much we can trust AI systems, particularly in safety-critical systems, including in the application of space technologies? As Missy Cummings warns, "history is replete with examples of how similar promises of operational readiness ended in costly system failures and these cases should serve as a cautionary tale" (Cummings 2021, 14). Furthermore, a growing field of research focuses on how to deceive AI systems into making wrong predictions by generating false data. Both state and non-state actors may use this so-called adversarial machine learning to deceive opposing sides, using incorrect data to generate wrong conclusions and, in doing so, alter the decision-making processes. The overall strategic impact of adversarial machine learning on international security might be even more disruptive than the technology itself (Danks 2020).

In this context, complex AI systems and data streams also need to be linked technologically, organizationally, and operationally. For many militaries, this is an ongoing challenge—in MDO conceptions, they must be able to effectively (in real-time) integrate AI-enabled sensor-to-shooter loops and data streams between the various services and platforms. This means effectively linking the diverse air force, army, navy, space and cyber battle management systems and data; command and control, communications and networks; ISR; electronic warfare; PNT; with precision munitions. While select AI systems may mitigate some of the challenges, the same systems create new problems related to ensuring trusted AI. Accordingly, one may argue that the direction and character of the MDOs, enabled through the space domain, will depend on corresponding strategic, organizational, and operational agility; particularly how AI technologies interact with current and emerging operational constructs and force structures.

The diffusion of emerging technologies poses new challenges on the level of human involvement in warfare, the need to alter traditional force structures and recruitment patterns, and in what domains force will be used. Modern militaries are developing their own and often diverse solutions to these issues. As in the past, their effectiveness will depend on many factors that are linked to the enduring principles of *strategy*—the ends, ways, and means to "convert" available defense resources into novel military capabilities and, in doing so, create and sustain operational competencies to tackle a wide range of contingencies. The main factors for successful implementation will not be technological innovations per se, but the combined effect of sustained funding, organizational expertise (i.e., sizeable and effective R&D bases, both military and commercial), and institutional agility to implement defense innovation (Cheung 2021).

Indeed, while emerging technologies are gradually becoming combat surrogates, the fundamental nature of warfare and strategy principles in defense innovation remain unchanged. War continues to be a contest of human wills for political ends, characterized by the realms of uncertainty and complexity, or what Prussian military theorist Carl von Clausewitz described back in the early nineteenth century as the "the fog of war." Advanced military technologies in the militarization of space brought by the AI-RMA also bring complexity and uncertainty to decision-making in warfare. Today's fog of war is in the uncertainties of data integrity and critical safeguards embedded in the various AI-enabled autonomous weapons systems. Moreover, the underlying patterns of defense innovation are also not changing. While many defense innovations such as AI systems are sourced from the products in the commercial arena, nearly every military innovation continues to spark a quest for a counter-innovation in a continuous cycle of technological challenge, conceptual response, and organizational adaptation. In short, nearly every military innovation is relative to the evolving capabilities of the opposing side and, almost always, temporary in duration.

At the same time, however, a military-technological tsunami is undeniably on the way that may defy previous revolutions in military affairs. Future warfare projections focus on the AI-wave—profound military-technological innovations, including the use of advanced fighter jets paired with a team of unmanned aerial vehicles, lethal autonomous weapons systems, hypersonic missiles, directed energy or laser weapons, and technologies relevant for competing in the space, cyber, and electromagnetic spectrum. While this viewpoint risks overhyping new technologies, it also shows that existing military bureaucracies and their traditional ways and means of warfare—weapons, tactics, training, acquisition, and operational approaches—may become rapidly obsolete, especially in a world where strategic vulnerabilities and dependencies co-exist across a range of factors, sectors, and countries.

In order to accelerate the development of the AI-RMA in space operations, modern militaries must learn to integrate multiple stakeholders and not just domains. The defense sector must better harness commercial-innovation technologies, including from space start-ups, while tapping into talent from academia and non-military sectors to meet strategic needs. Integrating operations in the space domain with established land, air, and sea domains will require new strategies and units, doctrinal revision to include new missions, new career paths, changing the curriculum of professional military education institutions, and revised training and experimentation. And herein lies the principal challenge for implementing the AI-RMA for space operations: developing holistic approaches to future warfare and embracing the natural complexity of an operational environment and novel technologies requires a new mindset—new ways of thinking and operating at every echelon of military organizations. The question is whether the traditional military mindsets can incorporate disruptive innovation paths, which embrace creativity and innovation and promote the rearrangement of existing rules in varying strategic cultures.

REFERENCES

Austin, Greg, Timothy Wright, and Rajeswari Pillai Rajagopalan. 2022. "Military Ambitions and Competition in Space: The Role of Alliances." IISS Research Paper. https://www.iiss.org/ blogs/research-paper/2022/02/military-ambitions-and-competition-in-space-the-role-of-alliances.

Barsade, Itai, and Michael Horowitz. 2018. "Artificial Intelligence beyond the Superpowers." *Bulletin of the Atomic Scientists.* August 16, 2018. https://thebulletin.org/2018/08/the-ai-arms-race-and-the-rest-of-the-world/.

Bender, Bryan. 2021. "What the Space Force Is, and Isn't?" *Politico.* March 2, 2021. https://www.politico.com/news/2021/02/03/space-force-explained-465799.

Bowen, Bleddyn. 2020, *War in Space—Strategy, Spacepower, Geopolitics.* Edinburgh: Edinburgh University Press.

Burnett, Mark, Paul Ashton, Andrew Hunt, et. al. 2018. "Advanced Materials and Manufacturing—Implications for Defence to 2040." Defence Science and Technology Group Report. Australia Department of Defence. https://www.dst.defence.gov.au/sites/defa ult/files/publications/documents/DST-Group-GD-1022.pdf.

Cheung, Tai Ming. 2021. "A Conceptual Framework of Defence Innovation." *Journal of Strategic Studies* 44, no. 6: 775–801. https://doi.org/10.1080/01402390.2021.1939689.

Cummings, Mary. 2017. "Artificial Intelligence and the Future of Warfare." Chatham House Research Paper. https://www.chathamhouse.org/sites/default/files/publications/research/ 2017-01-26-artificial-intelligence-future-warfare-cummings-final.pdf.

Cummings, Mary. 2021. "Rethinking the Maturity of Artificial Intelligence in Safety-Critical Settings." *AI Magazine* 42, no.1: 6–15. https://ojs.aaai.org/index.php/aimagazine/article/ view/7394.

Danks, David. 2020. "How Adversarial Attacks Could Destabilise Military AI Systems." *IEEE Spectrum.* February 26, 2020. https://spectrum.ieee.org/adversarial-attacks-and-ai-systems.

Davis, Malcolm. 2019a. "Strike on Saudi Oil Facilities Shows Need to Adapt to New Ways of Warfare." *ASPI Strategist.* September 18, 2019. https://www.aspistrategist.org.au/strike-on-saudi-oil-facilities-shows-need-to-adapt-to-new-ways-of-warfare/.

Davis, Malcolm. 2019b. "The Australian Defence Force and Contested Space." ASPI Report. https://www.aspi.org.au/report/australian-defence-force-and-contested-space.

Davis, Malcolm. 2020a. "Outdated Treaties Won't Stop the Rush to Control Resources in Space." *ASPI Strategist.* August 31, 2020, https://www.aspistrategist.org.au/outdated-treat ies-wont-stop-the-rush-to-control-resources-in-space/.

Davis, Malcolm. 2020b,. "Cheap Drones versus Expensive Tanks: A Battlefield Game-Changer?" *ASPI Strategist.* October 21, 2020. https://www.aspistrategist.org.au/cheap-dro nes-versus-expensive-tanks-a-battlefield-game-changer/.

Davis, Malcolm. 2021. "The Ramifications of Russia's Reckless Anti-Satellite Test." *ASPI Strategist*. November 18, 2021. https://www.aspistrategist.org.au/author/malcolm-davis/.

Department of Defence (Australia). 2021. "Defence explores options for Space Electronic Warfare."

Department of Defence (Australia). 2022. "Defence Space Command." https://www.airforce. gov.au/our-mission/defence-space-command.

Department of Defence (Australia). 2020. "Defence Strategic Update." https://www.defence. gov.au/about/publications/2020-defence-strategic-update.

Defense Intelligence Agency (DIA). 2022. "Challenges to Security in Space—Space Reliance in an Era of Competition and Expansion." Defence Intelligence Agency Report. https://www. dia.mil/Portals/110/Documents/News/Military_Power_Publications/Challenges_Security _Space_2022.pdf.

Department of Defence (United States). 2021. "Military and Security Developments Involving the People's Republic of China—Annual Report to Congress." Office of the Secretary of Defense. https://media.defense.gov/2021/Nov/03/2002885874/-1/-1/0/2021-CMPR-FINAL.PDF.

Feickert, Andrew. 2021. "Defense Primer: Army Multi-Domain Operations (MDO)." Congressional Research Service Brief. https://crsreports.congress.gov/product/pdf/IF/IF11409.

Freitas, Sara, Hugo Silva, José Almeida, and Eduardo Silva. 2018. "Hyperspectral Imaging for Real-Time Unmanned Aerial Vehicle Maritime Target Detection." *Journal of Intelligent and Robotic Systems*, no. 90: 551–70. https://doi.org/10.1007/s10846-017-0689-0.

Gray, Colin. 2006. *Strategy and History: Essays on Theory and Practice*. London: Routledge.

Grest, Heiner, and Henry Heren. 2019. "What is a Multi Domain Operation?" Conference Brief, Shaping NATO for Multi Domain Operations of the Future, October 8, 2019. https:// www.japcc.org/what-is-a-multi-domain-operation/.

Grush, Loren. "Amazon's Project Kuiper Books up to 83 Rockets to Launch its Internet Beaming Satellites." *The Verge*. April 5, 2022. https://www.theverge.com/2022/4/5/23010245/amazon-project-kuiper-megaconstellation-arianespace-ula-blue-origin.

Hammes, T.X. 2016. "Technologies Converge and Power Diffuses: The Evolution of Small, Smart, and Cheap Weapons." CATO Institute Policy Analysis. No. 786. https://www.cato. org/policy-analysis/technologies-converge-power-diffuses-evolution-small-smart-cheap-weapons.

Horowitz, Michael. 2018. "The Promise and Peril of Military Applications of Artificial Intelligence." *Bulletin of the Atomic Scientists*. April 23, 2018. https://thebulletin.org/2018/04/the-promise-and-peril-of-military-applications-of-artificial-intelligence/.

IISS (International Institute for Strategic Studies). 2019. "Quantum Computing and Defence." In *The Military Balance*, edited by ISSS, 18–20. London: Routledge.

Jensen, Benjamin, and John Pashkewitz. 2019. "Mosaic Warfare: Small and Scalable are Beautiful." *War on the Rocks*. December 23, 2019. https://warontherocks.com/2019/12/mosaic-warfare-small-and-scalable-are-beautiful/.

Lee, Chung Min. 2016. *Fault Lines in a Rising Asia*. Washington, DC: Carnegie Endowment for International Peace.

Lerman, Rachel, and Cat Zakrzewski. 2022. "Elon Musk's Starlink is Keeping Ukrainians Online When Traditional Internet Fails." *Washington Post*. March 19, 2022. https://www.was hingtonpost.com/technology/2022/03/19/elon-musk-ukraine-starlink/.

Mahnken, Thomas, ed. 2012. *Competitive Strategies for the 21st Century: Theory, History, and Practice*. Stanford, CA: Stanford University Press.

McCall, Stephen. 2021. "Space as a Warfighting Domain: Issues for Congress." Congressional Research Service Brief. https://crsreports.congress.gov/product/pdf/IF/IF11895.

Morgan Stanley. 2020. "Space: Investing in the Final Frontier." https://www.morganstanley.com/ideas/investing-in-space.

O'Callaghan, Jonathan. 2022. "SpaceX's Starship and NASA's SLS Could Supercharge Space Science." *Scientific American*. April 12, 2022. https://www.scientificamerican.com/article/spacexs-starship-and-nasas-sls-could-supercharge-space-science/.

Park Si-soo. 2021. "Japan to Launch 2nd Space Defense Unit to Protect Satellites from Electromagnetic Attack." *Space News*. November 15, 2021., https://spacenews.com/japan-to-launch-2nd-space-defense-unit-to-protect-satellites-from-electromagnetic-attack/.

Pekkanen, Saadia M., Setsuko Aoiki, and John Mittleman. 2022. "Small Satellites, Big Data: Uncovering the Invisible in Maritime Security." *International Security* 47, no. 2: 177–216. https://doi.org/10.1162/isec_a_00445.

Raska, Michael. 2016. *Military Innovation in Small States: Creating a Reverse Asymmetry*. New York: Routledge.

Raska, Michael. 2020. "Strategic Competition for Emerging Military Technologies: Comparative Paths and Patterns." *Prism—Journal of Complex Operations* 8, no. 3: 64–81. https://ndupress.ndu.edu/Portals/68/Documents/prism/prism_8-3/prism_8-3_Raska_64-81.pdf.

Raska, Michael. 2021. "The Sixth RMA Wave: Disruption in Military Affairs?" *Journal of Strategic Studies* 44, no. 4: 456–79. https://doi.org/10.1080/01402390.2020.1848818.

Raska, Michael, Katarzyna Zysk, and Ian Bowers (eds.). 2022. *Defence Innovation and the 4th Industrial Revolution Security Challenges, Emerging Technologies, and Military Implications*. New York: Routledge.

Roberts, Thomas. 2020. "Space Launch to Low earth Orbit: How Much Does It Cost?" Aerospace Security. Project of the Center for Strategic and International Studies. https://aerospace.csis.org/data/space-launch-to-low-earth-orbit-how-much-does-it-cost/.

Stanley-Lockman, Zoe. 2021(a). "Responsible and Ethical Military AI: Allies and Allied Perspectives." Center for Security and Emerging Technology Issue Brief. https://cset.georgetown.edu/publication/responsible-and-ethical-military-ai/.

Stanley-Lockman, Zoe. 2021(b). "Military AI Cooperation Toolbox: Modernizing Defence Science and Technology Partnerships for the Digital Age." Center for Security and Emerging Technology Issue Brief. https://cset.georgetown.edu/publication/military-ai-cooperation-toolbox/.

Spears, Will. 2019. "A Sailor's Take on Multi Domain Operations." *War on the Rocks*. May 21, 2019. https://warontherocks.com/2019/05/a-sailors-take-on-multi-domain-operations/.

US Army Chief of Staff. 2021. "Army Multi-Domain Transformation—Ready to Win in Competition and Conflict." https://www.army.mil/standto/archive/2021/04/23/.

United States Space Force. 2020. "Spacepower Doctrine for Space Forces." Space Capstone Publication. https://www.spaceforce.mil/Portals/1/Space%20Capstone%20Publication_10%20Aug%202020.pdf.

University of Adelaide, "The Woomera Manual." https://law.adelaide.edu.au/woomera/.

Weeden, Brian. 2010. "The 2007 Chinese Anti-Satellite Test—Fact Sheet." https://swfound.org/media/9550/chinese_asat_fact_sheet_updated_2012.pdf.

Weeden, Brian, and Victoria Samson, eds. 2021. *Global CounterSpace Capabilities—An Assessment*. Washington, DC: Secure World Foundation. https://swfound.org/media/207 162/swf_global_counterspace_capabilities_2021.pdf.

Yeo, Mike. 2019. "ADF to Acquire Next Generation Satellite Technology." *Asia Pacific Defence Reporter* 45, no. 6: 12. https://asiapacificdefencereporter.com/jp-9102-adf-to-acquire-next-generation-satellite-technology/.

CHAPTER 32

....

SECURITY DILEMMA, DEBRIS, AND THE FUTURE OF SPACE OPERATIONS

....

BRAD TOWNSEND

A key limiting factor on the utilization of Earth orbit and humanity's future access to and use of space is the ongoing generation of debris. This debris, defined as man-made objects—including fragments of satellites—in Earth orbit that are no longer functional is an issue that impacts all states equally as the physics of orbits does not respect national boundaries (IADC 2007, 6). That space has environmental limiting factors might be surprising since in general terms space is effectively infinite. However, Earth orbit, which is both the most useful portion of space and the gateway to anything beyond, is a relatively small and crowded region. The detritus of decades of human spaceflight is quickly building up and developing into a major hazard to the continued exploitation of space. As of 2021, the US Space Force satellite catalog was tracking more than 24,000 objects in orbit, of which more than half are debris. Each day dozens of these objects pass within a kilometer of each other generating a conjunction warning and the possibility that hundreds of more pieces of debris will be generated if they collide. These thousands of tracked objects include only those larger than 10 centimeters, which present a significant hazard to satellites; it excludes potentially hundreds of thousands of smaller objects that are too difficult to track (National Research Council 1995, 57). While the larger objects can easily destroy a satellite, the smaller and more difficult to track objects can still damage or disable one. This debris problem has significant implications for the future sustainability of Earth orbit as space becomes ever more critical to modern society. Debris generation, both accidental and intentional, will also become an increasingly central concern to spacefaring states as security competition expands into Earth orbit.

Satellites launched into all but the lowest orbits generally remain in orbit for decades or centuries unless active measures are taken to remove them. Each time a satellite is launched, both large and small pieces of unintentional debris are generated as expended boosters, bolts, and other necessary launch components are discarded. These incidental debris generated during the normal course of space operations are a hazard, but by themselves are manageable. It is when two larger objects, traveling at 8 kilometers per second collide, intentionally or unintentionally, that true danger arises. A single collision between two satellites can generate thousands of trackable pieces of debris that will gradually spread out to pollute that entire orbital altitude, threatening other satellites and potentially generating further debris. This cycle of debris generation could become self-sustaining as more satellites are launched, and more debris are generated, effectively making portions of Earth orbit unusable. The threat that debris pose to Earth orbit is a limiting factor on future space development and security, particularly as great power competition in space looks increasingly likely to lead to conflict within the domain.

Expanding security competition—in the traditional form of states seeking relative military and economic power over others—to the space domain holds new and uncertain risks. If security competition in the space domain leads to conflict it would be catastrophic for the long-term sustainability of space due to the high likelihood of significant debris generating events. Limiting security competition within the domain to avoid conflict is especially difficult since it would require cooperative action by all spacefaring states. Achieving multilateral cooperation in space is difficult since it is a borderless domain with significant strategic implications where technology is rapidly evolving and significant uncertainty exists about the intentions and capabilities of competing states.

Viewed through a realist international relations lens these conditions are ideal for security dilemma driven competition, and there are clear signs that a dilemma exists in space (Townsend 2020, 75–77). Security dilemmas, where one state's efforts to achieve security through the accumulation of power creates insecurity in neighboring states who accumulate power in response leading to an action-reaction cycle, are notoriously difficult to escape. In space, where borders do not exist so all states are neighbors preventing the localization of security issues, a multistate security dilemma exists, which further exacerbates the difficulties of defusing a dilemma (35–37). While escaping security dilemmas under these conditions is difficult, it is possible and necessary. This is especially true given the catastrophic consequences of uncontrolled debris generation if conflict does occur. The risk of debris generation ruining the space environment for all states means that the possibility exists for collective recognition that cooperation, or at least controlled competition, is desirable for all states.

The challenges of managing debris generation, its potential impact on security competition, and how debris can be mitigated or avoided entirely is the focus of this chapter. It will provide a brief overview of the growing issue of space debris, existing mitigation guidelines for limiting it, and discuss the impact that it may have on national security decision-making. The potential impact on decision-making is primarily viewed through a realist lens within the context of a security dilemma, though the impact and influence of liberal international relations themes such as the influence of international organizations and economic cooperation cannot be disregarded. To establish context for why debris generation can shape state behavior this chapter will first analyze the quantity of debris in orbit and the difficulty of tracking it. It will then discuss the possible mitigation and removal measures for debris generated in the course of normal space operations. The possibility of debris generated from the increasing weaponization of space and how that might shape state behavior is the focus of the final section of this chapter. The chapter concludes with recommendations for preserving Earth orbit for future space operations.

Debris Generation and Tracking

The increasing importance of space militarily and economically to states has made competition in space inevitable. Exactly how that competition will play out is unclear, but the reality of debris and their crucial role on the sustainability of Earth orbit will be a key contributing factor to shaping competition and security seeking behavior in space. How much importance the major spacefaring states place on the long-term sustainability of Earth orbit will determine the future of competition or cooperation in space. To understand how debris will impact that security competition between states it is first necessary to understand the challenges associated with debris mitigation and tracking. While international guidelines exist for how to mitigate debris, they remain simply guidelines, which states enforce domestically with varying levels of rigor. These guidelines also do nothing more than hint at a desire to limit the use of debris-generating weapons in orbit, at best an ineffectual effort to discourage their development. At the moment the United States has taken the lead in tracking debris, informing the world of potential debris generating collisions, and in leading the effort to develop effective guidelines for controlling incidental debris generation, as the rest of this section will demonstrate.

Using a combination of radar and telescopes, the United States maintains a catalog of objects in Earth orbit. As of 2021, this catalog was approaching 50,000 entries, of which nearly half are still active in orbit while the other half have reentered the atmosphere. These entries represent most of the objects in orbit bigger than 10 cm in diameter. There is no clear cut-off for this list, some objects larger in diameter than 10 cm remain undetected. Still, nearly all objects larger than 1 meter are actively tracked and cataloged by the United States, China, or Russia. These objects represent 60 years of space launch effort. The oldest object in orbit is the second US satellite ever launched, Vanguard 1. Placed into orbit just 5 months after Sputnik in 1958, it long ago ceased to function and can now be classified as debris. Vanguard 1 is joined by thousands of other satellites, rockets, and other objects as a cloud of debris circling the Earth that needs to be accounted for to ensure that active satellites do not collide with them.

Tracking space objects is not a simple task and not something that is done in real time for everything in orbit. The United States has the most extensive satellite tracking network, with both the US Space Force and the National Aeronautics and Space Administration (NASA) maintaining a small number of radars and telescopes that detect and catalog space objects. The radar sites are most effective for low Earth orbit (LEO, 200–1,600 kilometers), while powerful telescopes are used to track objects in higher orbits such as geosynchronous orbit (GEO, 36,000 kilometers) beyond the effective reach of radar (National Research Council 1995, 31–38). The radar sites work by establishing a virtual fence that detects and characterizes orbital objects as they pass over the monitoring site. When a satellite is launched, its initial orbital parameters are entered in the satellite catalog, and each time it passes over a tracking site, any small changes in its previous entry are updated. The predictability of objects in orbit makes it unnecessary to update every entry each time it passes over a site and makes it function- ally possible to maintain a catalog of objects in orbit and determine when two objects may collide.

Predictability of orbital elements also allows the US Space Force's Eighteenth Space Control Squadron, which maintains the US satellite catalog, to release notifications when conjunctions may occur. Conjunction notifications occur whenever two large space objects are predicted to pass within 1 kilometer of each other. If one or both of the objects are still active and the operator can be reached in time, then they can ma- neuver to avoid the potential collision risk; if not, the potential for a collision remains. Space Force lists dozens of possible conjunctions each day, and the vast majority of these are between objects which are no longer active. Even when one of the satellites is ac- tive, a collision can still occur. In 2009, an operational commercial satellite, Iridium 33, weighing 560 kg, collided with a defunct Russian satellite, Cosmos 2251, which weighed more than 900 kg (NASA 2009, 2). This was the first accidental hypervelocity collision of two intact satellites in history. It generated more than 1,800 pieces of new cataloged debris larger than 10 cm and likely thousands more that remain undetected and there- fore uncatalogued.

Accidental debris generation by the collision of two satellites is a significant debris generating event, but it has still only occurred once. More commonly, satellites or rocket bodies may fragment due to technical issues or malfunctions. NASA has cataloged more than 300 fragmentation events due to technical faults since the beginning of the space age (Ans-Meador et al. 2018, i). Causes vary for fragmentation events, but two examples are illustrative of the risks and challenges. In 2007, a Russian Briz-M upper stage exploded in LEO, almost certainly because of the remaining fuel on board, and generated more than 1,000 observed fragments. Of these fragments, only 102 were able to be accurately tracked and cataloged (4). A second example is the battery explosion aboard the Russian GEO satellite Ekran 2 in 1978. The event went undetected by the US optical space surveillance network and was only noted when the Russians admitted to it in 1992. At that point, the United States was able to identify and assign only four of the many pieces of debris generated by this event to its parent satellite (4–5). These two events are indicative of the challenges associated with tracking and detecting debris events, especially in higher orbits.

These two examples might give the impression that Russia is the only source for the generation of debris from technical issues or malfunctions. While Russian satellites ac- count for the majority of fragmentation events, the United States also has a relatively poor track record. For example, at least four Defense Meteorological Satellite Program (DMSP) satellites have fragmented due to technical anomalies (Ans-Meador et al. 2018, 583). The likely cause of each of these failures was an explosion of the onboard batteries, though that is uncertain since two of these anomalies occurred after the satellite was decommissioned and all fuel and batteries discharged. Whatever the cause these events generated between a few dozen and hundreds of pieces of debris that took the US Space Surveillance Network weeks to catalogue ("Recent Breakup of a DMSP Satellite" 2015). The break-up of these US satellites demonstrates how difficult it is to ascertain the exact cause of some break-ups, enabling engineers to mitigate the cause in future designs, since each of these break-ups occurred in the same class of satellite but under different conditions.

While explosions when propulsion systems fail during orbital maneuvers or as the result of residual fuel is the most common cause of fragmentation events, deliberate debris generation can also be devastating. The most infamous intentional debris-generating event is the 2007 destruction of the Chinese Fengyun 1C satellite during a Chinese anti-satellite (ASAT) weapons test. This test was the largest debris-generating event in history, creating an estimated 35,000 pieces of debris larger than 1 cm (NASA 2007, 2). This event by itself increased the quantity of debris on orbit by more than 15 percent, and because it occurred at a relatively high altitude of 850 kilometers, the debris will remain in orbit for decades to centuries. China's destruction of Fengyun 1C was not the first use of an ASAT, but it was the first to occur at such a high altitude and demonstrated that conflict that extends into space could be catastrophic for the safety and security of Earth orbit.

Orbital debris is a growing concern for future space operations, made worse by the complexity of tracking and cataloging the ever-growing quantity of debris in orbit. Incidental debris generation from normal operations is currently the largest generating source, but the increasing possibility of significant debris generation from conflict extending into space is a growing concern. As the destruction of Fengyun 1C demonstrated, even limited conflict in space that involves the use of ASATs would have catastrophic implications for future space utilization. Planning for methods to mitigate incidental debris while avoiding deliberate debris generation is an area of increasing focus in the governments of spacefaring nations and the international community.

Incidental Debris Mitigation and Removal

The incidental generation of debris during normal space operations is the largest source of debris creation. Various efforts to mitigate incidental debris have occurred and met differing levels of success and general acceptance. These efforts have not resulted in any binding international framework focused on limitation but rather in a patchwork of regulations from individual governments and a set of international space debris mitigation guidelines that are optional rather than mandatory. The impracticability of removing all but the largest debris and the borderless nature of Earth orbit means that failure by one state or actor to follow these guidelines poisons the space environment for all users. This section outlines the efforts to mitigate incidental debris generation and discusses several proposed approaches for successfully managing the problem.

Prior to the launch of the first satellites, knowledge of the near-Earth space environment was limited, and some experts feared that orbiting dust clouds or micrometeors would make spaceflight impractical. In 1946 Fred Whipple, an astronomer at the Harvard Observatory, predicted that 1 out of 25 spacecraft bound for the moon would be destroyed by meteoroids (Portree and Loftus 1999, 17). By the late 1960s, data from the first satellites and manned spacecraft demonstrated that the density of micrometeors was much lower than predicted. This led to decreased funding for research into micrometeorite impacts for several years. It was only in 1973 that a small team at NASA's Langley Research Center first became aware of the potential hazard posed by orbital debris and started studying it (Portree and Loftus 1999, 17). In 1974 this team presented a paper on the probability of collision with orbital debris, which determined that nearly 75 percent of objects in Earth orbit were debris produced by payloads or accidental on-orbit explosions (Brooks, Bess, and Gibson 1974). This paper triggered only limited additional study of the orbital debris problem by NASA and did not gain any real traction until 1976 when a NASA engineer, Donald Kessler, was asked to study the environmental risks of launching large solar power satellites into orbit (Portree and Loftus 1999, 21).

Kessler looked closely at the probability that debris could harm large space objects and determined that the risk was real and growing. Kessler's and other NASA engineer's investigation into the dangers of orbital debris over the next two years resulted in the publication of Kessler and Burton Cour-Palais's seminal paper in 1978 on the threat of debris growth in orbit. Kessler and Burton demonstrated that as the number of satellites in Earth orbit increases, the probability of collisions between satellites increases, which could produce fragments. These fragments would in turn increase the likelihood of further collisions leading to an active debris belt that endangered future space flight because the sources of debris exceeded the number of debris sinks, or natural removal paths (Kessler and Cour-Palais 1978, 2642–43). This idea of a self-sustaining debris cloud became known as the Kessler effect and led to increasing interest in studying the dangers of orbital debris.

Interest in orbital debris first penetrated the public consciousness in 1978 when a Soviet naval surveillance satellite, Cosmos 954, malfunctioned. The US military calculated that Cosmos 954 would reenter the Earth's atmosphere on January 23, 1978, with as much as 50 kg of enriched uranium on board but could not accurately determine where it would land (Cohen 1984, 79). The impending re-entry of nuclear material naturally gained international attention, and on January 24 the satellite entered the atmosphere over northern Canada, spreading radioactive debris over much of Canada's sparsely populated northwest. The Soviets determined that the malfunction aboard the satellite was likely the result of a collision with orbital debris. However, they could not be certain since the collision occurred when the satellite was outside their limited visibility zone for tracking space objects (Cohen 1984, 80). This incident gained attention at the highest levels of the US government, and early findings from Kessler's seminal paper on debris generation were used in testimony given to the US Senate by the NASA administrator on the Cosmos 954 incident (Portree and Loftus 1999, 26).

Research into understanding the sources of debris continued to develop over the next decade though it remained a relatively minor issue. Using optical sampling techniques, NASA discovered that the density of debris in orbit was much greater than originally thought (Portree and Loftus 1999, 44). NASA also found that old rocket boosters, particularly from US Delta rockets, regularly exploded in orbit, generating thousands of pieces of debris (Portree and Loftus 1999, 36). These explosions were caused by breaches in the fuel separation bulkheads between the fuel and oxidizer as the rocket expanded and contracted due to solar heating over time. The manufacturer quickly developed a fix for the problem by venting out the excess fuel on future Delta rockets, but mishaps with various rocket boosters continue to occur, significantly increasing the quantity of debris on orbit. The continued buildup of debris from regular space operations through the 1980s and from a 1985 ASAT test by the United States contributed to increased awareness of the debris problem.

This increased awareness eventually led to the development of early efforts to develop regulations that mitigated the generation of space debris. Developing policies for regulating debris generation naturally encountered resistance, even within NASA, as debris was still a minor problem, and any formal policy would likely result in increased costs (Portree and Loftus 1999, 29). The increased awareness of the debris problem finally generated concrete action when the US 1988 National Space Policy explicitly directed that "all space sectors will seek to minimize the creation of space debris. Design and operations of space tests, experiments and systems will strive to minimize or reduce accumulation of space debris consistent with mission requirements and cost effectiveness" ("Presidential Directive on National Space Policy" 1988, 4). Moving quickly, the US Department of Defense released its own internal policy on debris mitigation prior to the formal publication of the 1988 presidential policy, though it would be more than a decade before a government-wide policy would be issued (Portree and Loftus 1999, 55). The last sentence of the 1988 presidential policy also directed the establishment of a working group to provide recommendations for the implementation of the broad statement of policy on orbital debris quoted above. One of the key outcomes of this working group was that it encouraged the United States to "enter into discussion with other nations to coordinate debris minimization policies and practices" (Johnson 2014, 70). This guidance enabled debris experts from NASA to begin formally reaching out to counterparts in other nation's civil space agencies and eventually led to the establishment of the Inter-Agency Space Debris Coordination Committee (IADC) in 1993 (Johnson 2014, 71).

Shortly after the establishment of the IADC, the United Nations (UN) Committee on the Peaceful Uses of Outer Space (COPUOS) met for the first time to discuss the issue of space debris in 1994 (UN Office for Outer Space Affairs 2010, iii). COPUOS involvement in studying the debris problem had finally raised the issue to the highest official international space forum. However, it would still be years before accepted international guidelines were issued. While COPUOS continued to study the problem of debris in its annual sessions, informed by annual presentations from the IADC starting in 1997, the IADC continued to work on the publication of its own set of international guidelines (Johnson 2014, 71). The IADC, having grown to encompass eleven major spacefaring nations including China and Russia by 2000, finally published its first set of debris mitigation guidelines in 2002. These guidelines were an outgrowth of NASA safety standards for debris mitigation, which had also informed the United States' first national guidelines for orbital debris mitigation standard practices (ODMSP) published in 2001 (Liou 2019, 2).

The 2002 IADC guidelines identified two major protected orbital regions for special attention for debris mitigation. The first was the area of LEO out to an altitude of 2,000 kilometers, which encompassed a relatively small volume of space that is extremely crowded and useful for a variety of space missions. The second area of concern was GEO, which the IADC defined as the altitude of 35,786 kilometers above the equator plus or minus 200 kilometers and 15 degrees of inclination. GEO is the most valuable of Earth orbits because at this altitude objects fall around the Earth at the same rate that the Earth rotates, making them appear stationary with only minor perturbations relative to Earth's surface at the Equator. This phenomenon makes this orbit ideal for a variety of communications purposes, including television transmissions. Protecting these two orbital regimes for future exploitation is fundamental to preserving Earth orbit. To protect these two orbital regimes, the IADC guidelines focused on two broad categories of managing debris—mitigation and post-mission disposal—which varied depending on the orbit.

The IADC guidance for mitigating debris generation addressed two main areas of concern: limiting debris generation during normal operations and minimizing the potential for post-mission break-ups from stored energy (IADC 2007, 8). IADC guidance for limiting debris recognized that some debris generation during launch and in the course of normal operations was unavoidable and suggested taking all efforts to limit it without providing specific suggestions. Guidance for minimizing post-mission break-ups from stored energy, such as from the US Delta rockets mentioned earlier, was more specific. IADC recommended a variety of measures including depleting residual propellants, discharging battery systems, and safing reaction wheels. The guidance also encouraged spacecraft designers to "demonstrate, using failure mode and effects analysis . . . that there is no probable failure mode leading to accidental breakups" (IADC 2007, 8). These measures added up to little more than one page of general guidance for the most significant source of debris.

Guidance for post-mission disposal of spacecraft also varied depending on the orbit. Satellites and spacecraft in LEO orbit or passing through it in the course of their orbit are close enough to the Earth for disposal into the atmosphere to be the preferred method. IADC encouraged designers to establish disposal orbits that would result in re-entry within 25 years. This is not a simple task as a satellite in a purely circular orbit above 500 kilometers could remain in orbit for centuries. For spacecraft in GEO, retracing the 36,000 kilometers distance back to Earth requires an impractical amount of fuel, so another approach was needed. The IADC provided a simple calculation for boosting a

GEO satellite into a slightly higher altitude than nominal GEO, where orbital mechanics would ensure it would begin to drift relative to the Earth's surface and so no longer interfere with functional GEO satellites. Satellites in this so-called graveyard orbit just beyond GEO would remain in this orbit for hundreds of years until solar radiation pressure would again make them a threat to GEO. These satellites will eventually require active removal, though not for centuries.

The IADC guidelines proved to be extremely influential in shaping the discussion on orbital debris mitigation within the UN COPUOS forum. Since the IADC standards already represented a voluntary consensus among the most influential spacefaring nations, they were well received by COPUOS (United Nations 2010, iii). Despite the positive reception, it would still take nearly a decade for the final adoption of a set of voluntary standards, which largely mirrored the broad guidelines agreed to by the IADC. In 2010, after lengthy deliberation, the UN finally published these voluntary and largely qualitative guidelines. These high-level guidelines generated additional international recognition of the debris problem but only provided limited technical guidance on mitigation.

More detailed technical guidelines on debris mitigation were published a year after the UN standards by the International Organization for Standardization (ISO). ISO is a recognized international organization that publishes detailed voluntary international technical standards for a variety of topics from rolling bearings to metal alloys using expert advice from a variety of international stakeholders. The ISO guidance contained in ISO 24113, *Space Systems: Space Debris Mitigation Requirements*, built upon the general guidance provided by the IADC and UN guidelines to provide more detailed technical guidance for debris mitigation. This guidance remains voluntary unless codified and enforced in a specific nation's policy, but with its publication, a relatively complete framework for preventive debris mitigation in the course of normal space operations exists.

Despite the ISO, IADC, and UN standards providing guidance on preventing debris generation, a large and growing quantity of debris still exists in orbit. Even with the strict adherence to the various mitigation guidelines discussed above, the quantity of debris in orbit is increasing faster than the rate at which it reenters the atmosphere (Liou et al. 2013, 1). The obvious solution is some form of active debris removal; however, this is not an easy task. The large quantity of small debris in orbit between 5 mm, where it is large enough to penetrate debris shielding, and 10 cm, where it is actively tracked and can be avoided, represents the greatest risk to spacecraft. However, the hundreds of thousands of pieces of debris that fall into this range are impractical to remove, as is most of the slightly larger debris. The US Defense Advanced Research Projects Agency (DARPA) explored various strategies from using lasers and electromagnetic effects to large passive sweepers that would absorb smaller particles without success (Pulliam 2011, 32–37). For example, DARPA calculated that an approach relying on large passive debris-absorbers would require over 45,000 20-meter debris-absorbing spheres to begin having a measurable impact on removing smaller debris. Beyond the challenge of launching so many debris absorbers, if these passive systems encountered a larger object than they were designed to absorb, that object would likely fragment, generating even more debris (33). Therefore, the only remaining feasible approach to debris removal is to remove the largest objects, such as defunct satellites and rocket bodies, before they can fragment into smaller pieces while mitigating the generation of smaller debris through passive measures.

Analysis by the European Space Agency (ESA) debris office has demonstrated that removing as few as five large objects per year from the LEO environment could stabilize debris generation under ideal conditions (Virigili and Krag 2009, 4). The removal of these large objects would reduce the risk of fragmentation events from satellite collisions to the point where the debris environment would stabilize if nations strictly enforced passive debris mitigation guidelines. This low number is predicated on the assumption that no additional debris is added to the space environment and that future satellite launches adhere to end-of-mission disposal timelines. That level of absolute adherence to debris mitigation guidelines is not possible, especially as we move into an era of small satellite constellations numbering in the thousands. Without that strict adherence to mitigation guidelines, removing as few as five large objects each year will not be enough, and more satellites will have to be removed to achieve debris stability. The exact number is dependent on many factors, but the ESA analysis does demonstrate that active removal of large objects can be an effective strategy for stabilizing the debris environment.

Active de-orbiting of large objects is technically possible but no more commercially profitable than any other trash removal service without government support or regulation. In late 2020 the ESA and a Swiss company, ClearSpace SA, finalized the first contract to remove a piece of large debris from LEO (Parsonson, 2020). Under this contract, ClearSpace SA will use a specialized grappler (Figure 32.1) to capture a 112 kg Vega Secondary Payload Adapter (Vespa) left behind in high LEO. The grappler will then move the Vespa into a lower orbit, where it will quickly burn up in the atmosphere. This mission, planned for completion in 2025, will demonstrate a viable option for removing long-lived large pieces of debris, though this removal effort does not come cheaply. The mission will cost more than US$100 million, which is a steep price to pay for removing a single piece of debris.

A further complication with active debris removal is that the systems that can perform this task are inherently dual use. Using a debris removal platform, such as that developed by ClearSpace, as a weapon to capture and deorbit or damage active satellites requires only a change in intent, not in purpose. This dual-use nature would make the launch of large numbers of debris removal satellites by any single nation or the prepositioning of these platforms a highly suspect activity. Despite this perception risk, the active removal of large pieces of debris across all orbital regimes is an increasingly pressing need.

Funding large debris removal and following mitigation guidelines supports the common good but is a challenging multi-party problem where economic incentives encourage shirking responsibility. Orbital debris removal is at its core a classic tragedy of the commons problem. Inaction on debris mitigation leads to escalating

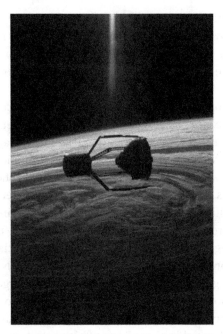

FIGURE 32.1 Specialized grappler designed to capture large orbital debris.

Source: Clearspace SA, 2021, used with permission.

costs in the form of damaged or destroyed satellites, additional debris shielding, and constellation redundancy. Since the technological challenges of large debris removal are difficult but solvable, debris removal and mitigation is a problem of incentives. One proposed approach to addressing this incentive problem is to institute an international orbital use fee structure (Rao, Burgess, and Kaffine 2020, 1). This approach is similar to the carbon tax currently unevenly applied globally to limit pollution, with some of the same issues. Another method is to create a global debris mitigation fund to which satellite operators would contribute on an equitable basis (Popova and Schaus 2018, 12). The challenge for both of these approaches is that they require a significant degree of international cooperation and some legal foundation for enforcement.

The 1967 Outer Space Treaty (OST) and the 1972 Liability Convention provide some legal basis for enforcing a large-scale international scheme for debris removal and mitigation. The OST is the oldest of a handful of international treaties, including the Liability Convention, which form the legal framework in space (see Aoki, this volume). All major spacefaring nations are signatories to the OST, which has no specific reference to debris generation. However, it does contain several useful provisions in Article 9 that can be interpreted as placing an obligation on signatories to protect the space environment (Popova and Schaus 2018, 6). The 1972 Liability Convention is more directly relevant to space debris. It places liability for damages on the state judged to be at fault for causing injury or damage to another space object (UN Liability Convention 1972, sec. 4). This section has not been tested though and suffers from a fault and attribution problem. If an active satellite collides with a derelict satellite of another nation, is it the fault of the derelict satellite that it has not reentered the atmosphere or the active satellite for failing to maneuver? A further complication is in the difficulty of assigning ownership to most smaller pieces of debris. In practice, the liability convention has proved difficult to apply, as demonstrated by the 2009 collision of the active Iridium 33 satellite and the derelict Russian Cosmos 2251 satellite. Even in this seemingly clear-cut case, a lack of tracking data of the actual collision and conflicting precollision data prevented its invocation (Listner 2012, 33). In sum, while a legal foundation for incentivizing debris removal and mitigation exists, it is difficult to apply in practice and remains untested.

Mitigating the generation of incidental debris created in the course of normal space operations and preventing the break-up of large satellites is critical for stabilizing the space environment. Small and medium-sized debris are the most significant threat to active satellites, but no effective means of actively removing them exists. The active removal of large debris coupled with strict adherence to debris mitigation guidelines developed by various international bodies will allow the continued exploitation of space with minimal disruption. This positive outlook for the space environment is challenged by the potential for active conflict to extend into space. Conflict extending into the space domain is very likely to result in significant debris-generating events that would dramatically destabilize the space environment.

DELIBERATE DEBRIS EVENTS

Just as satellites have become critical to the passage of information for civilian needs, they have also become essential to military operations, both in peacetime and during conflict. The ability to pass information through space and gather information from space is now essential to modern warfighting (see Hays and Wirtz, this volume). This military dependence on space naturally makes the domain ripe for future conflict. Any nation that can interfere or disrupt its adversary's ability to use space will gain a critical warfighting advantage. As a result, nations are anticipating that any future conflict will extend into space and so are reacting accordingly by creating dedicated military space services to defend their space assets and deter their adversaries. For the purposes of this chapter, the real danger of conflict is that it could quickly and dramatically increase the amount of debris in orbit unless states agree to limit the type and nature of weapons that they plan to use in these future conflicts.

The most dangerous debris generating event that could occur would be the indiscriminate use of debris generating ASAT weapons. The 2007 Chinese demonstration of a direct-ascent ASAT against the Fengyun 1C satellite created over four thousand pieces of trackable debris and thousands more too small to track. Since 2007, only a small fraction of this debris has de-orbited, and much of it will stay in Earth orbit for centuries. This single event in 2007 dramatically increased the total amount of trackable debris in orbit overnight. If a conflict were to occur that involved ASATs to achieve the operational aim of crippling an adversary satellite network, it would require the launching of dozens or even hundreds of missiles. Should such an event occur, the resulting destruction would dramatically increase the quantity of debris in orbit and likely damage many other satellites, potentially making certain orbits permanently unusable. Debris generated from such an attack would also damage the launching nation's own satellites over time, but for a critical window of weeks to months, the launching nation would possess a distinct military advantage.

China is not alone in possessing ground-based ASAT weapons either. The United States demonstrated an air-launched ASAT in 1985, and in a high-profile event in 2008, it destroyed a satellite using a ship-based missile originally intended for missile defense. More recently, India conducted a successful ASAT test in 2019, and Russia conducted multiple ASAT tests in 2020 and 2021, which culminated in the destruction of a defunct Russian satellite in November 2021. This Russian test was the largest debris generating event since the 2007 Chinese test. The debris from these various tests can quickly de-orbit if the target satellite is at an extremely low altitude, as in the case of the 2008 US event, or they can take centuries, as with the 2007 Chinese test (see Figure 32.2). The November 2021 Russian test occurred at 480 kilometers against a large defunct satellite and initial reports indicated over 1,500 pieces of trackable debris which would make it second only to the 2007 Chinese test. Given the altitude of the Russian test it is likely

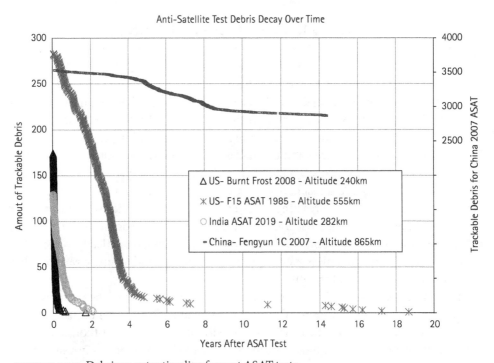

FIGURE 32.2 Debris re-entry timeline for past ASAT tests.

Source: Generated using data from Data Source Spacetrack.org (US Government).

the debris from this event could remain in orbit for up to 15 years jeopardizing an increasingly valuable LEO. Even if nations develop a method of disabling satellites using co-orbital systems, such as what the United States accused Russia of testing in 2020, the possibility of significant debris-generating events remains if conflict occurs in space (US Space Command Public Affairs Office 2020).

The demonstrated challenges of removing debris from orbit make warfare in space a delicate balance with operational, strategic, and organizational factors influencing how a nation might decide to fight within the domain. From a purely operational perspective, the short-term advantages to be gained from disabling or destroying an adversary's military satellites are enormous. Much like the civilian economy, military forces rely on space for a variety of generalized needs including communications, navigation, and precision timing. Militaries also use space for a number of national security unique needs as well, such as various forms of intelligence gathering and missile warning. These functions provide a critical warfighting and intelligence advantage that military forces and national decision-makers have come to rely upon. Suddenly removing these capabilities through the use of direct-ascent ASATs would be disruptive and disorienting as an adversary's ability to communicate, navigate, observe enemy actions, and use its own long-range weapons systems would be severely disrupted. This operational advantage would make the decision to ignore the long-term strategic impacts of the debris generation through the indiscriminate use of direct-ascent ASATs or other space weapons very attractive.

Long-term strategic concerns for the future viability of the space domain to support both national security uses and economic growth are limiting factors on space as a warfighting domain. Unlike the other terrestrial warfighting domains, kinetic means to disable or destroy adversary military systems have long-term environmental consequences. Senior military leaders are highly cognizant of the risks of debris generation and so must account for that in planning for any future conflict (Cohen 2021). Alternatives to debris-generating weapons could involve using electronic warfare or directed energy weapons to jam or damage adversary satellites in a manner that is either reversible or avoids the generation of thousands of small pieces of debris. The challenge with these methods is that your adversary can quickly recover their space asset or may be able to overcome the effects of jamming, so using a reversible or non-kinetic approach to space warfare is a less sure method of achieving military advantage. Further, where mistrust exists, two opposing states cannot be certain that the other will not choose to ignore the debris-generating aspects of kinetic weapons use in space, fueling dilemma-driven security seeking. For instance, China joined the IADC in 1993 and was aware of the debris challenge in orbit, yet its government still chose to conduct the destructive ASAT test against Fengyun 1C in 2007. Short-term national security concerns will undoubtedly weigh heavily against long-term debris mitigation concerns if no alternative exists to quickly destroy an adversary's satellites to achieve an immediate military advantage.

The perception of offense-dominance in the space domain also increases the possibility that direct-ascent ASATs will be used in significant numbers in a future conflict, at least in the near term. This perception results from the previous paradigm for satellite development and space launch, which until recently were extraordinarily expensive. This cost structure created an acquisition model, especially in the United States, where militaries launched as few highly capable satellites as possible to minimize cost. The result was a handful of exquisite and highly capable satellites performing military missions that terrestrial military forces had become dependent on for battlefield dominance. As long as space remained a relatively benign environment free from real threat, as it did from the end of the Cold War through to the 2010s, this developmental model worked. The recognition that the US military was highly dependent on space combined with the resurgence of Russia and the rise of China highlighted the vulnerabilities of this approach. These small numbers of exquisite satellites are very vulnerable to attack. So, if one side possesses direct-ascent ASATs and the other is dependent on a handful of large satellites for information gathering and transmission, then the domain is distinctly offense dominant. This offense-dominance encourages the further development and fielding of direct-ascent ASATs and other space weapons and opens up the possibility of a major space debris generating event should the space-capable great powers ever engage in even limited conflict.

As with most domains, the offense-defense balance in space is rapidly shifting as technology evolves and vulnerabilities are recognized and addressed. Commercial innovations in space launch and satellite development have shifted the paradigm for space systems away from singular highly capable platforms toward constellations of hundreds or thousands of satellites operating at much lower altitudes. Large satellite constellations change the dynamics of the offense-defense balance in interesting ways. First, the number of successful ASATs necessary to significantly degrade an adversary's ability to transmit and collect information from space has dramatically increased. Second, the much lower orbit common for many of these constellations has lowered the long-term consequences of ASAT use since the resulting debris will mostly re-enter in reasonable time frames. Conversely, crowded LEOs have raised the short-term consequences of ASAT use for satellites in this orbital regime by greatly increasing the possibility of debris collisions. Despite this shortened lifespan, an economically insensitive defender can still replace large numbers of satellites in a constellation relatively quickly, while an attacker relying on direct-ascent ASATs must launch hundreds of individual and expensive missiles to degrade that constellation. The apparent solution for the attacker is to shift away from ASATs toward the development of directed-energy weapons (DEWs), as the United States has accused both China and Russia of doing ("Challenges to Security in Space" 2019, 20–29). A DEW can be fired more than once and sequentially damage the satellites in a constellation as they pass overhead. The counter to this is to increase the altitude of the constellation allowing for more distance to disperse the energy generated by DEW's.

The likely result of this weapons development spiral is military constellations of satellites operating at high enough altitudes to be safely out of the range of DEW's yet in large enough numbers to make the use of direct-ascent ASATs economically and environmentally infeasible. This trend line will eventually put the defender in space at a distinct advantage, though newer and more capable classes of space weapons will constantly challenge this defensive advantage. However, for the next decade or more, as this arms race plays out, the threat of a major debris-generating event in space remains as the offense-defense balance continues to favor the attacker. This perception of offense dominance will only fuel security dilemma driven arming in orbit further exacerbating tensions between the United States, China, and Russia.

In addition to the long-term strategic consequences of conflict in space, organizational factors will also weigh heavily on the possibility of debris generating warfare in orbit. The space-focused military services within the major world powers are either extremely new or still in their nascent developmental stages. This will create a number of organizational incentives to pursue offensive military doctrines that are much more likely to be debris generating as they compete for resources within their respective nations (Posen 1986, 47–49). For instance, in the case of the US Space Force, its creation was highly political and initially strongly opposed by senior military leaders. Now, as the newest military service in the United States with relatively few personnel, operating in a new and uncertain environment, and with a substantially smaller budget relative to the other services, it must demonstrate its value in order to secure scarce resources and assure the policymakers that it is achieving its objective of protecting US and allied space assets. Offensive doctrines, which are more likely to end with the development of debris-generating weapons, have a higher likelihood of emerging in these situations—especially since few senior policymakers have any real knowledge of space or space warfare theory and so are unlikely to question the advice and analysis of their military space advisors.

It is impossible to predict if a large number of debris generating space weapons will be developed and deployed in a future conflict, but if this does occur, the impacts on the space domain will be catastrophic. Thus, the possibility of debris generation must have a significant influence on national policy. Whether this acts as a brake on security dilemma driven arms racing is less certain, especially as the perception of offense-dominance in space persists. Events outside the space domain will influence the degree to which cooperation is possible among the major spacefaring nations, though there is a recognition, based on various proposals for treaties banning weapons in space, that it is necessary. Avoiding a future that results in a major debris generating conflict requires concerted negotiations among the major spacefaring powers to find a common understanding of norms in space. While it is unreasonable to assume that some form of conflict will not extend into space, it is possible to establish norms of behavior and eventually arms control agreements that drive future conflict in space away from significant debris creation. As of 2021, there were no formal agreements in development that attempted to reconcile the issue of deliberate debris generation with the increasing possibility of future conflict extending into space. Absent an understanding of what form the laws of armed conflict will take in space, the future sustainability of Earth orbit is uncertain.

THE PROSPECTS FOR COOPERATION OR CONFLICT

Debris mitigation and removal are vital to the future sustainability of Earth orbit. Recognizing and understanding the degree of the problem is a challenge that has been largely overcome. In the last few decades, the publication of international standards and debris mitigation guidelines have been significant steps toward a sustainable space environment. Despite these positive steps, the launch of large satellite constellations will further stress the space environment and increase the possibility of incidental debris generation through collisions. Generally poor adherence to debris mitigation guidelines will further exacerbate this trend, as satellite operators do not fully adhere to existing guidelines and treat newer cheaper small satellites as disposable. This will incur a cost on the future exploitation of space, as debris continues to build more quickly than it is removed. If the current trend of debris generation is not mitigated by the active removal of significant numbers of defunct or disabled satellites combined with collision avoidance measures and strict adherence to debris mitigation guidelines, then many of the most useful Earth orbits may become unusable for future generations.

Security dilemma driven weaponization of space presents the most devastating potential future for the domain. With sustainability in orbit already challenged by commercial use, a conflict that involves the disabling or destruction of significant numbers of satellites to achieve military objectives could make the most valuable orbits unusable. The potential quantity of debris that could be generated if conflict involving kinetic ASAT weapons occurs is difficult to predict, but as the number of satellites used for national security purposes increases, so does the potential list of debris generating targets. The principal spacefaring nations are all party to various international debris mitigation guidelines, so at some level institutional knowledge of the threat that debris poses exists. However, this institutional understanding of the potential long-term debris problem will almost certainly be outweighed by the short-term national security need to deny an adversary the use of space during conflict.

Escaping the multi-state security dilemma and limiting future conflict in space is becoming increasingly difficult as tensions between the great spacefaring nations increase. The perception of offense dominance and the development of new and potentially game-changing classes of orbital weapons, such as China's testing of orbiting hypersonic weapons, are significant challenges to prospects for peace. These rapid unsettling technological developments are also an opportunity. As tensions increase, the motivation for overcoming organizational inertia and exploring opportunities for meaningful methods of mitigating arms racing also increases. A notable example of tentative steps in this direction is found in the recent announcement by the US Deputy Secretary of Defense in December 2021 at a meeting of the National Space Council that the United States would support a ban on debris generating ASAT weapons. This was a momentous announcement and represented a significant shift in US rhetoric that will hopefully be reciprocated. It is too early to predict if tentative steps toward establishing harder rules for behavior in space provide hope that conflict in the domain can be mitigated, if not entirely avoided, but at least there are positive signs.

Despite some encouraging signs, there are still significant challenges to ensuring the long-term sustainability of Earth orbit that must be overcome. Understanding the problem and developing internationally accepted debris mitigation guidelines are a positive first step. The next steps must involve elevating these guidelines to the level of international law and developing enforcement mechanisms for malign actors who choose not to adhere to them. As a complement to these guidelines, the accepted norms for the law of armed conflict must be updated to include avoiding the use of debris-generating weapons in orbit. All of these actions must be combined with better collision avoidance warning and response as well as a dedicated effort to remove large pieces of debris to ensure the sustainability of Earth orbit.

Sadly, complacency about the debris problem will most likely lead to inaction until the problem can no longer be ignored. The trigger for action will be, at best, the loss of multiple satellites in a short period of time due to collisions or debris strikes leading to loss of some critical global service, possibly a future space based internet. Alternatively, in a worst-case scenario, a limited war between two major space powers occurs which leads to the indiscriminate use of debris-generating weapons in orbit and the functional loss of various orbital regimes. Ultimately, the future sustainability of Earth orbit is uncertain and highly contingent on future events. If the increased debris mitigation actions mentioned here are taken, then the environment is sustainable; if not, or if conflict extends into orbit, then humanity will have to adapt to a future deprived of some or all of the benefits that exploitation of Earth orbit grants.

References

Ans-Meador, Phillip, John Opiela, Debra Shoots, and J. C. Liou. 2018. "History of On-Orbit Satellite Fragmentations 15th Edition." National Air and Space Administration, Orbital Debris Program Office.

Bastida Virgili, B., and H. Krag. 2009. "Strategies for Active Removal in LEO." Darmstadt, Germany: ESA.

Brooks, D. R., T. D. Bess, and G. G. Gibson. "Predicting the Probability that Earth-Orbiting Spacecraft Will Collide with Man-Made Objects in Space." Paper Presented at the International Astronautical Federation, 25th Congress, Amsterdam, Netherlands, September 1974.

"Challenges to Security in Space." 2019. Defense Intelligence Agency.

Cohen, Alexander F. 1984. "Cosmos 954 and the International Law of Satellite Accidents." *Yale Journal of International Law* 10, no. 78: 78–91.

Cohen, Rachel S. 2021. "For Military Superiority in Space, Start with Safety." Air Force Magazine. February 25, 2021. https://www.airforcemag.com/for-military-superiority-in-space-start-with-safety/.

IADC (Inter-Agency Space Debris Coordination Committee). 2007. "IADC Space Debris Mitigation Guidelines."

Johnson, Nicholas. 2014. "Origin of the Inter-Agency Space Debris Coordination Committee." NASA.

Kessler, Donald J., and Burton G. Cour-Palais. 1978. "Collision Frequency of Artificial Satellites: The Creation of a Debris Belt." *Journal of Geophysical Research* 83, no. A6: 2637–46.

Liou, J.C. "Orbital Debris Mitigation and U.S. Space Policy Directive-3." 2019. Paper Presented at the 56th Session of the Scientific and Technical Subcommittee to the Committee on the Peaceful Uses of Outer Space, United Nations, Vienna, Austria, February 11, 2019.

Liou, J. C., A. K. Anilkumar, B. Bastida Virgili, T. Hanada, H. Krag, H. Lewis, M. X. J. Raj, M. M. Rao, A. Rossi, and R. K. Sharma. 2013. "Stability of the Future LEO Environment—An IADC Comparison Study." Darmstadt, Germany: ESA. https://doi.org/10.13140/2.1.3595.6487.

Liou, J. C., A. K. Anilkumar, B. Bastida Virgili, T. Hanada, H. Krag, H. Lewis, M. X. J. Raj, M. M. Rao, A. Rossi, and R. K. Sharma. 2009. "The Collision of Iridium 33 and Cosmos 2251: The Space of Things to Come." Paper Presented at the 60th International Astronautical Congress, Daejeon, Republic of Korea, October 16, 2009.

Listner, Michael. 2012. "Iridium 33 and Cosmos 2251 Three Years Later: Where Are We Now?" *Space Review.* February 13, 2012. https://www.thespacereview.com/article/2023/1.

NASA (National Aeronautics and Space Administration). 2007. "Chinese Anti-Satellite Test Creates Most Severe Orbital Debris Cloud in History." *Orbital Debris Quarterly* 11, no. 2: 2–3.

NASA (National Aeronautics and Space Administration). 2009. "Satellite Collision Leaves Significant Debris Clouds." *Orbital Debris Quarterly* 13, no. 2: 1–2.

National Research Council, Committee on Space Debris. *Orbital Debris: A Technical Assessment.* Washington, DC: National Academy Press, 1995.

Parsonson, Andrew. 2020. "ESA Signs Contract for First Space Debris Removal Mission." *Space News.* December 2, 2020. https://spacenews.com/clearspace-contract-signed/.

Popova, Rada, and Volker Schaus. 2018. "The Legal Framework for Space Debris Remediation as a Tool for Sustainability in Outer Space." *Aerospace* 5, no. 55. .

Portree, David S., and Joseph P. Loftus. 1999. "Orbital Debris: A Chronology." NASA/TP-1999-208856. National Air and Space Administration.

Posen, Barry. *The Sources of Military Doctrine: France, Britain, and Germany between the World Wars.* Ithaca, NY; London: Cornell University Press, 1986.

"Presidential Directive on National Space Policy." 1988. The White House. February 11, 1988.

Pulliam, Wade. 2011. "Catcher's Mitt Final Report." Defense Advanced Research Projects Agency.

"Recent Breakup of a DMSP Satellite." 2015. *NASA Orbital Debris Quarterly* 19, no. 2: 1–2.

Rao, Akhil, Matthew Burgess, and Daniel Kaffine. "Orbital-Use Fees Could More than Quadruple the Value of the Space Industry." 2020. *Proceedings of the National Academy of Sciences of the United States of America* 117, no. 23.

Townsend, Brad R. 2020. *Security and Stability in the New Space Age, the Orbital Security Dilemma.* New York: Routledge Press.

United Nations. 2010. "Space Debris Mitigation Guidelines of the Committee on the Peaceful Uses of Outer Space." United Nations Office for Outer Space Affairs.

UN Liability Convention. 1972. "Convention on International Liability for Damage Caused by Space Objects." United Nations.

US Space Command Public Affairs Office. 2020. "Russia Conducts Space-Based Anti-Satellite Weapons Test." https://www.spacecom.mil/MEDIA/NEWS-ARTICLES/Article/2285098/russia-conducts-space-based-anti-satellite-weapons-test/.

CHAPTER 33

....

SPACE SUSTAINABILITY

Balanced Space Security Global Governance

....

WANG GUOYU

INTRODUCTION

THE international community comprehensively recognizes that global space governance (GSG) aims to preserve the long-term sustainability (LTS) of space activities.
Likewise, LTS should also be the paramount and terminal goal of space security global
governance, which is a significant component part of GSG. Only when the space environment is maintained and secured can a state enjoy the ability to conduct its space
activities free from harm, however, the space environment faces challenges from both
safety and security aspects. For instance, the United Nations (UN) Committee on the
Peaceful Uses of Outer Space (COPUOS) has stated that "The Earth's orbital space environment constitutes a finite resource that is being used by an increasing number of
States, international intergovernmental organizations, and non-governmental entities.
The proliferation of space debris, the increasing complexity of space operations, the
emergence of large constellations, and the increased risks of collision and interference
with the operation of space objects may affect the long-term sustainability of space activities" (UNCOPUOS 2019, Annex II para. 1). At the same time, "Outer space is seen
as becoming a new frontier of competition among major military powers" (Office for
Disarmament Affairs 2021), and "States largely refer to deliberate acts intended to interfere with, deny, disrupt, degrade, damage or destroy space systems"(Office for
Disarmament Affairs 2021) with "many of them expressing concern about space debris being one of the most significant threats to the space environment" (Office for
Disarmament Affairs 2021).

Pursuing a balanced space security global governance (SSGG) through space diplomacy is the most urgent goal for all countries to address amid these challenges to pave
the way toward space sustainability. Space sustainability must be achieved using a variety of different tools, including technical, legal, political, and diplomatic ones. This

chapter argues that core challenges to space sustainability are at the diplomatic level, and result from a variety of terms that lack clear definition in the discourse among states, which feeds the problem of misperceptions among the various actors within this context.

Misuse and/or the mixed-use of critical terms of art is one of the main obstacles preventing governments and civil society from achieving a common understanding concerning space security and global governance. Thus, this chapter first defines and categorizes the relevant key terms—including, space safety, space security, space sustainability, long-term sustainability, space environment safety and security—and analyzes their correlation to each other. Second, this chapter identifies the main challenges to space security with respect to preserving the space environment and sustainability. These challenges include misunderstanding, mistrust, and misperceptions at the strategic level among powers; the paradox between the need to maintain strategic stability and the needs for preserving space environment; the lack of effectively coordinative mechanisms regarding the avoidance of in-orbit collision; and uncertainties of the applicability of *lex lata*. Finally, the chapter provides recommendations for pursuing a balanced space security global governance. Three principles are proposed; comprehensiveness, equilibrium of interests, and self-restraint should be followed in international space rules making and security practices. This chapter identifies the essential elements and pillars for a balanced international solution regarding preserving the space environment and promoting the safety, security, and sustainability of space activities.

Recognition of the Terms of Space Security, Safety, and Sustainability

This section provides an overview of key concepts, their interrelationships, and divergences.

Space Security and Space Safety

The recognition of the distinction between the concepts of space security and space safety is not merely an academic issue but a critical element in confirming the proper international forum to deal with the relevant matters. The whole agenda of space diplomacy essentially relates to space safety and the safety of space activities (UNCOPUOS 2012). However, the blurring of the line between "space security" and "space safety" has become an obstacle to getting consensus on the appropriate forums and necessary measures to be taken by the international community to preserve or promote space security. For instance, during the COPUOS Long-term Sustainability Working Group (LTS WG) negotiations, when the Russian delegation proposed draft guidelines concerning active debris removal (ADR), some delegates opposed and held the position that ADR is a matter of space security and thus should be discussed in the Conference on Disarmament (CD) rather than in COPUOS. It has been general diplomatic practice that space security falls within the ambit of prevention of arms race in outer space (PAROS) or arms control in space and subsequently should be discussed in the First Committee of the United Nations General Assembly (UNGA) or the CD. In contrast, space safety is only relevant to dealing with risks during peaceful uses of outer space and thus should be discussed in COPUOS.

In addition, the translation of "space security" in different UN official languages might aggravate confusion brought by the distinction between "space security" and "space safety." For instance, these two terms share the exact same Chinese translation "外空安全", which brings more complexities for the accurate recognition of space security in China and in seeking a common understanding of the concept of space security between China and the other states. Translations are never produced in a cultural or political vacuum, nor can they be isolated from the context of the translations. The importance of emphasizing the differences between a source language and a target language and the cultural context of a translation is growing (Wang 2012).

There are some similarities among some Chinese and Western scholars regarding the connotation of space security; for instance, both recognize space security as an ability to keep space activities free from interference. Moltz argues that "we can define space security as the ability to place and operate assets outside the Earth's atmosphere without external interference, damage, or destruction" (Moltz 2011). This does not differentiate between challenges to space security that are caused by human activities and those caused by natural processes. Under this concept, issues like the avoidance of in-orbit collision and the management of space weather would be deemed space security matters. However, these issues are recognized as space safety matters and are mainly discussed in COPUOS or other civilian platforms. Therefore, this understanding of space security is not consistent with the diplomatic tradition or practice, although it reflects a significant understanding of space security.

This definition also does not reveal the close correlations between space security and space safety. In general, safety means "the condition of being protected from or unlikely to cause danger, risk, or injury" and security means "the state of being free from danger or threat" (Judy et al. 2013). In my presentations at the UNIDIR Space Security Conference in 2018 and at the Second Session of the Open-ended Working Group on Reducing Space Threats through Norms, Rules and Principles of Responsible Behaviours in 2022, space security was generally defined as being free from space threats and space safety was defined as referring to being free from space damage. The relation between space security and safety is depicted in Figure 33.1.

Taking this into account, this chapter argues that the basic characteristics of the relation between space security and space safety are as follows:

(1) Their scopes cross and overlap on a particular scale. It should not be directly taken as a relation between matters of arms control in space and peaceful use of

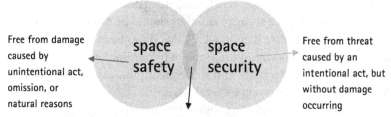

Free from damage caused by unintentional act, omission, or natural reasons

space safety

space security

Free from threat caused by an intentional act, but without damage occurring

Free from damage caused by an intentional act

FIGURE 33.1 Relations between space security and safety.

outer space or civil and commercial use of space, in that some space safety matters can also appropriately be discussed in terms of arms control, such as when they concern being free from damage caused by an intentional act.

(2) Space security and space safety exist in different dimensions; the main concerns are the status of the threat and the result of damage. Space security refers to the extent of national security and military concerns from a state's perspective. Space security is about how to handle effectively and respond to another state's space threats, interference, or even attack. From an international perspective or a perspective of space security global governance, space security is about how to avoid misunderstandings, misperceptions, or conflicts among states or how to avoid the escalation of disputes, disorder, and conflicts, which might cause irreversible damage to the space environment, provided that the disputes are unavoidable among some states. By contrast, space safety exists in a result-oriented dimension. It is about how to avoid damage, no matter whether caused by man-made or natural reasons, and how to mitigate the risks of damage occurring to the greatest extent practicable and feasible.

(3) Global space governance over a single issue could contain both space security and safety concerns. For instance, an anti-satellite (ASAT) test that generates a significant amount of space debris could be deemed a security matter since it proves the strategic deterrence capability of one state while generating a threat to its adversaries. It is also a matter of space safety since concerns being free from the damage caused by the generated space debris. In this regard, the governance of an ASAT test is always taken as a matter of arms control, but as a matter of fact, it is also a possible topic for discussion in COPUOS since it impacts safety. Likewise, people might not take the governance of mega-constellations as an arms control issue; however, it could also fall within the ambit of arms control or PAROS when there is evidence that this technology could be used for generating space threats, like maliciously approaching another state's space object or conducting other operations for a military purpose, which might bring misunderstanding, misperception, and tensions.

In conclusion, space safety should be defined as the maintenance of space assets and activities free from damage. The international community should determine the meaning of space security from both national and international perspectives. National space security is defined as the state of space assets, space activities, and space interests being free from threats or any other adverse effects made by other actors' deliberate behaviors—for instance, some unfriendly, provocative, and malicious space operations—along with the capability to take corresponding safeguards and responses. International space security has four lines of meaning: the first line refers to the state of being free from misunderstandings and misperception; the second line refers to the state of being free from conflicts; the third line refers to state of being related to involvement in comprehensive and intense conflicts, and it means trying to keep the conflicts on a small scale, among limited actors, and at a low intensity; and the fourth line refers to the state of being free from disorder conflicts which are already at high intensity. And when the fourth line becomes the international community's primary concern, it means there was a failure in maintaining the other three lines.

Space Sustainability, LTS, Space Environmental Safety, and Security

This section draws out the connections and meanings of space sustainability in the international context.

Space Sustainability

The chair of the COPUOS LTS of Outer Space Activities Working Group, Dr. Peter Martinez pointed out that "the word sustainability is derived from the Latin verb *sustinere* and is usually used in the context of being able to maintain an activity at a certain rate or level. Since the 1970s the concept of sustainability has been applied to human habitation and the equitable utilization of planet Earth and its resources" (Martinez 2018). It discloses two elements to define "sustainability": "maintain an activity at a certain rate or level" and "equitable utilization."

According to the Oxford Dictionary, "sustainable" also means "able to be upheld and defended" (Judy et al. 2013). A third element from an ethical perspective to define "sustainability" is self-restraint. Self-restraint could be taken as a subsequent requirement of the previous two elements, which means one is not supposed to always take full advantage of one's space rights, and space behavior should be justified from an ethical perspective, even if it is not expressly prohibited or restrained by international law. For instance, in the case of a mega-constellation, it is not prohibited by law for an actor to deploy thousands of small satellites in space; however, it might not be deemed a sustainable use if only a few slots and radio frequencies were left to others, even if its deployment does not lead to the saturation of the relevant orbit. If activity is still maintained at a specific rate or level, then it would not meet the elements of equitable utilization and self-restraint. Likewise, although ASAT testing is not prohibited by international law, the conduct of an ASAT test, which generates long-lived space debris, is still not consistent with the spirit of space sustainability. This is not only because it affects the existing and forthcoming space activities, but also due to the lack of necessary self-restraint.

Long-Term Sustainability of Space Activities (LTSSA)

According to the LTSWG Terms of References (ToR), "the Working Group will examine the long-term sustainability of outer space in the wide context of sustainable development of Earth" (UNCOPUOS 2011, para. 8). However, the ToR does not define the term LTS. Nonetheless, in the discussion of Expert Group D, there arose a need for greater clarity on the terminology of "long-term sustainability," particularly as it relates to the objectives and work-product of the LTSWG. As the Chinese expert on EG-D, I was responsible for drafting the "Terms and Definitions" for the EG-D Report with the assistance of Dr. Michael Mineiro. The draft states that:

> Because there is no universally accepted definition of sustainability, it is a concept that depends on the context and community in which it is used.
> The LTSWG, tasked with the LTS of outer space activities, generally considers the outer space physical environment within its scope, along with other elements like the regulatory, economic, operational, and political environment.
> The LTSWG is also advised to consider the principles applicable to outer space activities under international and applicable law while forming a consensus understanding of the LTS of outer space activity.
> Keeping all that in mind, the LTSWG should be cautious about the political consensus and practical concerns regarding the unduly prescribed scope of sustainability and seek an understanding of the term to warrant flexibility and evolution to fit the future needs of the space community.
> Noting the aforementioned, it is proposed that the long-term sustainability of outer space activities, within the context of the LTSWG, be defined as follows:
> The concept of the long-term sustainability of outer space activities recognizes that the use and exploration of outer space may result in negative impacts on the physical and operational outer space environment, mainly through the generation of space debris and increased possibilities of collision.
> The long-term sustainability of space activities requires that space actors consider their impact on the outer space environment and seek to manage their activities to mitigate and protect against the degradation of the physical and operational outer space environment.
> In the view of the LTS of outer space activities, space actors are encouraged to take notice of and strike a balance between different values related to the use, exploration, and exploitation of outer space. These include: peaceful use, free use, equal use, safe use, and efficient/effective use. (see Table 33.1)
> Long-term Sustainability of Outer Space Activities further requires that the use and exploration of outer space be inclusive, taking into account the interest of both current and future generations of mankind and the interest of developing countries. (Chinese Delegation 2012)

Table 33.1. Different Impacts of Space Activities and Sustainability on LTS

	Positive		Negative
Space sustainability and LTS of space activities	Peaceful use		Militarization, weaponization, battlefieldization, an arms race in space
	Equitable use		Unequitable use
	Safeguard safety	Avoid in-orbit collision	Risks led by in-orbit collision, break ups, long-term presence of space object
		Avoid break-ups	
		Avoid long-term presence of space object in orbit	
	Preserve security	Strategic understandings	Threat brought by strategic divergence, lack of TCBMs and other necessary channels of dialogue, mechanisms, differentiated legal interpretation to *lex lata* and even being unaware of each other's legal position. (For instance, State A takes one space behavior as legal but State B takes it as illegal and they are not aware of the other's legal point.)
		TCBMs, coordination, consultation, and other bilateral or multilateral mechanisms	
		Common recognition of *lex lata*	
	Effective use (low cost)		Ineffective use (high cost)

Space Environmental Safety and Security

First, space environment safety and security have inherent connections with space safety and security. Space environmental safety refers to the concerns that space be free from environmental damage and adverse changes caused by space activities—for instance as memorialized in Article IX of the Outer Space Treaty, which requires states to "conduct exploration of [space] so as to avoid [its] harmful contamination and also adverse changes in the environment of the Earth resulting from the introduction of extraterrestrial matter" (Treaty on Principles 1967). Space environmental safety falls within the ambit of space safety. The narrow sense of space environmental security also could be deemed as part of the concerns of space security, which means being free from the threat led by technically changing or destroying the space environment, for instance, "any technique for changing—through the deliberate manipulation of natural processes—the dynamics, composition or structure of the Earth, including its biota, lithosphere, hydrosphere, and atmosphere, or of outer space" (Convention on the Prohibition of

Military or Any Other Hostile Use of Environmental Modification Techniques 1978, Art. II). The broad sense of space environmental security is analogous to space security and safety in that "space environment" could be extended from the physical, natural world to a political and military one. In this sense, unfriendly, provocative, malicious space behavior may threaten an expectedly harmonized space environment, and any misunderstanding, misperception, miscalculation, or mistrust result in "damages" to the space environment.

Secondly, preserving space environment safety and security is one of the necessary means to maintaining LTS of space activities. LTS should be considered the highest priority goal for global space governance and the rule of law in space. The LTS goal requires, under space environment safety and security, not only being free from damage or threat, but also that active measures be taken to pursue a stable, balanced strategic, political, and legal environment in space.

Finally, as reflected by the title of this chapter, the following parts of this chapter will focus on the security aspects of preserving the space environment under space sustainability. Preserving the space environment could be a valuable tool to maintain space security. Any man-made threat to the space environment should be deemed a matter of space security and should be dealt with under the ambit of PAROS, arms control in outer space, or the governance of military space activities. Like those mentioned above, the space environment includes the physical and natural environment in space and the strategic, political, and legal environment in the space domain. Any divergence and conflicts in these non-physical aspects regarding space security would lead to adverse changes to the space environment. Therefore, space security and space environment are highly and tightly intertwined and interactive. The third part of this chapter addresses both the angles of physical and non-physical space environments.

Recognition of Challenges to Space Security with Respect to Preserving the Space Environment and Sustainability

This section sets out the principal challenges that intersect with space security and space environment and sustainability.

Misunderstanding, Mistrust, and Misperceptions at the Strategic Level among Powers

No matter whether from a historical or contemporary perspective, it is expected that states always try to maintain superiority and that states pursue strategic equilibrium with other states to reduce their sense of insecurity. This finds its expression in space but mixes with various mistrusts, misunderstandings, and misperceptions. US national space policy mentions "preserve and expand United States leadership," which might be deemed an ambition of space hegemony by foreign readers (White House 2020). China announced its "China dream" and "space power dream," likewise, which has been taken as the ambition of becoming an "international leader in space," or "China seeks to become a peer in technology and status of the United States in space" (US-China Economic and Security Review Commission 2019).

Such strategic divergence and mistrust will inevitably and subsequently bring more mutual blame and more profound mistrust and misperceptions. It combines with the contradiction brought by the US Wolf Amendment and other policies to isolate China in space, which indicates the high costs for the two countries to reach strategic understandings in space.

The United States publicly claims that "China and Russia present the greatest strategic threat due to their development, testing, and deployment of counter-space capabilities and their associated military doctrine for employment in conflict extending to space" (US Department of Defense 2020). In opposition, China stated that "It is the US that represents the top threat to security in outer space," no matter in terms of space strategy or action ("Chinese Foreign Ministry Spokesperson" 2022). "In terms of strategy, expressions like competition, adversaries, and threat are frequently used in the US National Space Strategy . . . In terms of actions, the US conducted rendezvous proximity operations or fly-overs that endangered other countries' satellites in orbit, tested offensive and defensive space capabilities, and interfered with normal space operations by other countries" (Permanent Mission of the People's Republic of China to the UN 2020). China criticizes the US declaration that space is a warfighting domain. However the United States holds that "Chinese and Russian military doctrines indicate that they view space as important to modern warfare and consider the use of counter-space capabilities as a means for reducing US, allied, and partner military effectiveness and for winning future wars. China and Russia have weaponized space as a way to deter and counter a possible US intervention during a regional military conflict" (US Department of Defense 2020).

The misunderstanding, mistrust, and misperceptions in space are the most dangerous challenge to space security, stability, and sustainability. The strategic divergence among the space powers and spacefaring countries is the fundamental reason for space operational contests. And it is also the main obstacle to seeking better coordination and cooperation among the powers.

The Paradox between the Need to Maintain Strategic Stability and the Need to Preserve the Space Environment

In general, from an objective perspective, strategic stability means the status deviating from war or military conflicts. However, from a subjective perspective, the connotation of strategic stability may vary due to the different stages and status with respect to the capability development of states. To an existing superpower, super priority might mean the most acceptable strategic stability and to the emerging superpowers, the more urgent and practical objective is to pursue and maintain strategic equilibrium and at least keep a safe and secure distance from the leader. Deterrence is always a tool that can be used to achieve these respective objectives, a concept that is deeply rooted in the nuclear domain but is not necessarily limited to this domain. This theory also applies to and is reflected in space practice.

Deterrence is central to the national security policy of all ages, which is achieved through, on most occasions, military measures (Mueller 2013). As far as I am concerned, from the perspective of game theory, deterrence is the tool of one party in a game to inflict perceptible, foreseeable costs or negative consequences on the other party, in order to pursue maximum benefits with minimum cost. Deterrence can be either an initiative threat or a responsive one. Then based on the perceptions of the category and extent of the deterrence inflicted by one on the other, the parties in the game would specify their respective follow-up measures and plans to gradually, pertinently, and systematically degrade and even eliminate the effects of the deterrence suffered.

However, the space capabilities and technologies that are effective in generating threat or strategic deterrence against adversaries always entail risks to the physical space environment, for instance, kinetic or non-kinetic ASAT capabilities. As to whether and to what extent these capabilities are conducive to maintaining strategic stability in space and the strategic stability in general is still to be observed.

Many states regard the possible development of various ASAT weapons, either deployed on-orbit or launched from systems deployed on the ground, in the air, or at sea, as a challenge to the security and sustainability of outer space and as a possible threat to international peace and security (Office for Disarmament Affairs 2021). Additionally, states have described various concepts for ASAT weapons that could be used to damage or destroy satellites directly, including, direct-ascent ASAT weapons; space-based anti-missile interceptors; co-orbital ASAT weapons that maneuver and approach a target; dual-use co-orbital systems include on-orbit serving and active debris removal; directed energy weapons including lasers, microwaves, and particle beams; electronic counterspace systems; cyber capabilities using software and network techniques to compromise, control, interfere, or destroy computer systems; and nuclear weapon detonations (Office for Disarmament Affairs 2021).

All these space military tools of a country represent a threat/deterrence to its rivals or adversaries. But the testing or use of some of these tools can generate space debris, including long-lived debris, in space, and damage the already congested space environment, for instance, kinetic ASAT tests. By contrast, "soft-killing" technologies, like jamming and spoofing, are less likely to be successful deterrents: "It is impossible to deter adversaries with invisible weapons" (Hitchens 2021).

Thus, paradoxically, the more effective and powerful the means for achieving strategic deterrence, superiority, or equilibrium, the riskier those means are to the space environment, and vice versa, the more destructive to the space environment a military space measure is, the more of a deterrent it is to an adversary.

On April 18, 2022, the United States committed to not conducting destructive, direct-ascent ASAT missile testing, and it further announced that "the United States seeks to establish this as a new international norm for responsible behavior in space" (White House 2022). This statement seems conducive to preserving the space environment, but it's also a game among space powers. ASAT capabilities are always the purview of relatively major powers (Mueller 2013). Therefore, it is still to be seen how other powers could be guaranteed maintenance of the current space strategic stability if they make a similar promise as the United States. This is critical to determining whether the "new international norm" would be endorsed by all in peace or lead to a new round of an arms race in space, in that if the door of the destructive, direct-ascent ASAT test were closed, other powers might positively seek alternative means to achieve the equivalent deterrence in space (Blount 2021).

The Lack of an Effectively Coordinative Mechanism Regarding the Avoidance of In-Orbit Collision

The space environment will not be able to bear a wait-and-see approach to identify the rules needed for predictability based on past liability outcomes. More incidents like the Iridium-Cosmos collision in 2009 will result in large portions of the orbital environment being unusable. Indeed, the trend toward developing very large constellations makes such collisions statistically more likely (Blount 2021). The risks of in-orbit collision are not only a matter of space safety or an unsettled legal issue, they also mean possible mistrust, misunderstanding, and misperception in certain circumstances.

In 2021, satellites in the Starlink constellation had two close encounters with the Chinese Space Station, and the Chinese Space Station implemented preventive collision avoidance control on July 1 and October 21 (Permanent Mission of China to the United Nations 2021). Due to the sensitiveness of the dates and the tensions between China and the United States in space and beyond, some speculation pointed out that the two approaches to avoiding collision have a particular political and military purpose beyond normal operations. The United States responded that "[i]n the specific instances cited in the note verbale from China to the Secretary-General, the United States Space Command did not estimate a significant probability of collision between the China Space Station and the referenced United States spacecraft" and that "[t]he United States is unaware of any contact or attempted contact by China with the United States Space Command, the operators of Starlink-1095 and Starlink-2305, or any other United States entity to share information or concerns about the stated incidents before the note verbale from China to the Secretary-General" (Permanent Mission of the United States of America to the United Nations 2022). Accordingly, China claimed that "after the incidents, China's competent authorities tried multiple times to reach the US side via e-mail but received no reply" (Ministry of Foreign Affairs of the People's Republic of China 2022).

No matter the facts of the case, this incident illustrates diplomatic debates, suspicion, and mistrust among the countries, partially caused by the lack of fixed, specific coordination mechanisms regarding avoiding in-orbit collisions. It shows the necessity and urgency of establishing bilateral or multilateral mechanisms in space traffic coordination, which is required by space safety concerns and the need to preserve the space environment from security perspectives.

Uncertainties of the Applicability of *Lex Lata* (Hard Law)

Another urgent and significant challenge to space security regarding preserving the space environment is the unclear applicability of international law, including space law (Wang and Li 2021). Complying with international law is the paramount guarantee of preventing space conflicts: stepping back, recognizing the legality of specific space behavior as the precondition for a state to conduct such behavior or take countermeasures against such behavior taken by its adversaries. In general, the threat of a space behavior and the subjective culpability of the mind of a particular space actor would be greater when the actors are fully aware of the illegality of this behavior than if they deem this behavior non-prohibited or lawful. Therefore, legal certainty is critical to maintaining space security. However, space behaviors closely related to space security, whether existing rules can apply and to what extent, still lack necessary and adequate international discussions, let alone common recognition. For instance, cyber interference with or attack against space systems, co-orbital operations (active debris removal, rendezvous proximity operation, approaching and accompanying flight), space self-defence, and space armed conflicts are all issues that lack legal clarity.

With respect to preserving the space environment from a space security aspect, it is not clear whether limiting the creation of space debris is an international obligation, whether the obligation of prior consultation applies in the scenario of space military contests, and how the due regard principle applies in the "grey area" between purely peacetime and wartime. The applicability of international space law in this grey area is still an unsettled issue.

Additionally, the applicability of general international law to space security matters is uncertain at best. For instance, could "environmental protection," as a customary international law (Statute of the International Court of Justice 1945, Art. 38(1)(b)), could apply in the space domain without any specific conditions? How do the Distinction Principle and Proportionality Principle in International Humanitarian Law (IHL) apply in space armed conflicts? There must be caution about discussing these matters since space has special characteristics. As space technologies are inherently dual use, with both civilian and military applications, it is especially challenging to configure an overarching architecture to govern space security activities (UNIDIR 2015). It's hard to tell whether a space object is for civilian or for military purposes, and the applicability of the Distinction Principle would be in question. The relevance of the Proportionality

Principle of IHL is also uncertain. Space war poses unique challenges since space debris is always an inevitable concomitant with space armed conflicts, and space debris could destroy any object nearby or in its trajectory without any discrimination, whether it is a civilian satellite or a military one (see Blount 2012).

States have not yet formally discussed the applicability of *lex lata* regarding space security issues. However, academia has preliminary debates in this regard, and no consensus has been achieved on some critical issues.

The Recommendations for Pursuing a Balanced Space Security Global Governance

Currently, space security is facing enormous challenges due to various technical, political, and legal reasons. In addition to the aforementioned challenges, the lack of transparency, inappropriate (official) statements and (academic) interpretation, and effects of geopolitical tensions all contribute to an unstable space environment. The divergence among countries regarding international space security governance is deeply rooted in the distinctions of culture and lack of common rationales or beliefs. It will continue to go nowhere if most of the national policies and international negotiations focus more on how to win a war than how to prevent space conflict. No matter which country proposes an international initiative on space security, the important standard should be to evaluate its value and feasibility to see whether it would be conducive to pursuing or maintaining stable space relations among powers and achieving strategic stability in space.

I argue three principles should be established to preserve strategic space stability, regarding space security or space environment governance respectively: comprehensiveness, equilibrium of interests, and self-restraint (Figure 33.2).

The comprehensiveness principle means that the international community needs a comprehensive solution rather than a proposal about a single issue, like placing weapons in space, testing certain ASAT weapons, or other military space behavior. All these concerns should be taken care of in a comprehensive solution because they interact with each other in the game of space security. Considering the precariousness of space security results from various reasons, such as the lack of strategic understandings, necessary mechanisms, and common recognition of *lex lata*, etc., an international initiative cannot be effective if it only reflects one of the above elements. States should positively work together on all of these matters in parallel. One small step in any of these fields might promote the process of the others. For instance, establishing a bilateral space traffic coordination mechanism might pave the way for achieving strategic understanding between two countries. This is another requirement of the comprehensiveness principle.

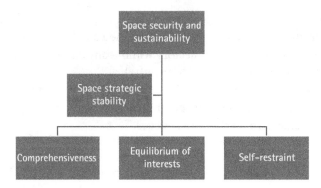

FIGURE 33.2 The principles to be established for strategic space stability.

The equilibrium of interests principle requires that any international solution for space governance reflect the appeals and interests of the relevant parties in a balanced way. International initiative in space security should not be taken as a tool to seek the superiority of one state and suppress its adversaries. Such an initiative would sooner or later be trapped in political debates and lead to nothing but high costs for the whole international community for such negotiations. The more comprehensive and compromised positions one initiative holds, the fewer the costs of the negotiation, and the more practical and effective the final solution would turn out to be.

The self-restraint principle is the subsequent requirement of the above two principles. But it applies to the formulation of international rules or solutions and every stage of security practices. Self-restraint requires all stakeholders to be appropriately and fairly engaged in space competition and contests in space security. One state should refrain from excessively provoking or threatening its adversaries, or taking other extreme actions, even if these behaviors are not expressly prohibited by international law. In any case, the actors in a space contest should do everything possible and practicable to avoid space (armed) conflict. When a conflict is inevitable or already occurring, each party in the conflict must prevent its escalation and try to keep the conflict on a small scale and at low intensity. If it fails again, then the actors have to put the deteriorated conflict in good legal order and try to ensure a controlled result; otherwise, this would be a disaster for the space environment, and is the last thing we would like to see.

To preserve the space environment and promote the safety, security, and sustainability of space activities, it is necessary and urgent to have a comprehensive and self-consistent international solution (see Figure 33.3). This solution should be an organic system with four pillars: strategic understandings, the establishment of mechanisms, recognition of *lex lata*, and new rules making. The solution should be guided by a well-recognized rationale—such as shared vision or shared understandings—take strategic space stability and long-term sustainability of space activities as an objective, enshrine basic principles—such as comprehensiveness, equilibrium of interests, and self-restraint—and consist of specific norms, mechanisms, and technical standards as its solid supports.

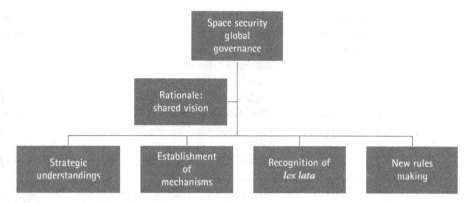

FIGURE 33.3 The four pillars for space security global governance.

All in all, there is still a long way to go to establish a new responsive international regime in the context of space security governance and PAROS. Space is becoming more and more congested, contested, and competitive, and even confrontational. Greater uncertainty and instability have been brought by the dual-use nature of space activities and the difficulties of space situational awareness (SSA) (France 2022). As a matter of fact, the fragile relations among powers bring more challenges than the fragility of space environment, and the dissymmetry of acknowledgement on key terms and applicability of *lex lata* among states are riskier than the lack of SSA. Therefore, the common recognition of these key factors should be the starting point to achieve a balanced SSGG. Only when states can better understand each other's conceptual and legal points of view is it possible for them to build mutual trust, establish practically coordinative mechanisms, and reach consensus on either non-legally binding or legally binding documents.

REFERENCES

Blount, P. J. 2012. "Targeting in Outer Space: Legal Aspects of Operational Military Actions in Space." *Harvard National Security Journal,* Online Edition, https://harvardnsj.org/2012/11/targeting-in-outer-space-legal-aspects-of-operational-military-actions-in-space/.

Blount, P. J. 2021. "Space Traffic Coordination: Developing a Framework for Safety and Security in Satellite Operations." *Space: Science & Technology.* https://spj.sciencemag.org/journals/space/2021/9830379/.

Chinese Foreign Ministry Spokesperson. 2022. "The US Has Been Weaving a Narrative about the So-called Threat Posed by China and Russia in Outer Space in an Attempt to Justify Its Own Military Buildup to Seek Space Hegemony." http://us.china-embassy.gov.cn/eng/zmgx/zxxx/202204/t20220414_10667671.htm.

Convention on the Prohibition of Military or Any Other Hostile Use of Environmental Modification Techniques. 1978.

France. 2022. "Current Context and Benefits of Establishing Norms of Responsible Behaviour."

Hitchens, Theresa. 2021. "Exclusive: Pentagon Poised to Unveil, Demonstrate Classified Space Weapon."

https://breakingdefense.com/2021/08/pentagon-posed-to-unveil-classified-space-weapon/
#:~:text=For%20years%2C%20Hyten%20has%20argued%20that%20it%20is,more%20ra
pid%20pace%20than%20some%20traditionalists%20find%20comfortable.

Martinez, Peter. 2018. "Development of an International Compendium of Guidelines for the Long-Term Sustainability of Outer Space Activities." *Space Policy* 43: 13–17.

Ministry of Foreign Affairs of the People's Republic of China. 2022. "Foreign Ministry Spokesperson Zhao Lijian's Regular Press Conference on February 10, 2022." https://www.fmprc.gov.cn/mfa_eng/xwfw_665399/s2510_665401/2511_665403/202202/t20220210_10640952.html.

Moltz, James Clay. 2011. *The Politics of Space Security: Strategic Restraint and the Pursuit of National Interests*. 2nd ed. Stanford, CA: Stanford University Press.

Mueller, Karl P. 2013. "The Absolute Weapon and the Ultimate High Ground: Why Nuclear Deterrence and Space Deterrence Are Strikingly Similar—Yet Profoundly Different." In *Anti-Satellite Weapons, Deterrence and Sino-American Space Relations*, edited by Michael Krepon and Julia Thompson, 41–60. Washingtown, DC: Stimson Center.

Judy Pearsall et al. 2013. *The New Oxford English-Chinese Dictionary*. 2nd ed. Shanghai: Shanghai Foreign Language Education Press.

Chinese Delegation (and Michael). August 6, 2012. Draft "Terms and Definitions" for EG-D Report. August 6, 2012.

Office for Disarmament Affairs. 2021. "Report of the Secretary-General on Reducing Space Threats through Norms, Rules, and Principles of Responsible Behaviors." U.N. Doc. A/76/77.

Permanent Mission of the People's Republic of China to the United Nations. 2020. "Document of the People's Republic of China pursuant to UNGA Resolution 75/36." http://un.china-mission.gov.cn/eng/chinaandun/disarmament_armscontrol/unga/202105/t20210501_9126875.htm.

Permanent Mission of China to the United Nations. 2021. Note Verbale Dated December 3, 2021, from the Permanent Mission of China to the United Nations (Vienna) addressed to the Secretary-General.

Permanent Mission of the United States of America to the United Nations. 2022. Note Verbale Dated January 28, 2022, from the Permanent Mission of the United States of America to the United Nations (Vienna) addressed to the Secretary-General.

Statute of the International Court of Justice. 1945.

Treaty on Principles Governing the Activities of States in the Exploration and Use of Outer Space, including the Moon and Other Celestial Bodies. *entered into force* 10 October 1967.

UNIDIR. 2015. Space Security Conference 2015: Underpinning Foundations of Space Security.

United Nations Committee on the Peaceful Uses of Outer Space. 2011. "Draft Report, Chapter II, Recommendations and Decisions." U.N. Doc. A/AC.105/L.281/Add.1.

United Nations Committee on the Peaceful Uses of Outer Space. 2012. "Long-term Sustainability of Activities in Outer Space: Working Paper Submitted by the Russian Federation." U.N. Doc. A/AC.105/2012/CRP.19.

United Nations Committee on the Peaceful Uses of Outer Space. 2019. "Report of the Committee on the Peaceful Uses of Outer Space." U.N. Doc. A/74/20.

US Department of Defense. 2020. "Department of Defense Releases Defense Space Strategy." https://www.defense.gov/News/Releases/Release/Article/2223539/department-of-defense-releases-defense-space-strategy/.

US-China Economic and Security Review Commission. 2019. *China's Pursuit of Space Power Status and Implications for the United States*. Staff Research Report.

Wang, Guoyu. 2012. "Comparison of Selected Space Law Terms of Art Used in Chinese and English Versions of the UN Space Treaties." *Journal of Space Law* 38, no. 2: 321–62.

Wang, Guoyu, and Li Chao. 2021. "Applicability of the Liability Convention for Private Spaceflight." *Space: Science & Technology*. Article 9860584. https://spj.sciencemag.org/journals/space/2021/9860584/.

White House. 2020. "Statement from the President on the National Space Policy." https://trumpwhitehouse.archives.gov/briefings-statements/statement-president-national-space-policy/.

White House. 2022. "Fact Sheet: Vice President Harris Advances National Security Norms in Space." https://www.whitehouse.gov/briefing-room/statements-releases/2022/04/18/fact-sheet-vice-president-harris-advances-national-security-norms-in-space/.

CHAPTER 34

....

NORM FORMATION AND SPACE TRAFFIC MANAGEMENT

....

P.J. BLOUNT

As a general rule, norms come from somewhere. In other words, norms do not spontaneously burst into existence, but rather they emerge through processes of iteration that lead to acceptance by the stakeholders concerned in a particular issue area. Norms have origins in discursive contestation, and they have a life cycle that can lead them to grow and flourish or to wither and die. This life cycle is complex, in particular within the international community, as it involves a variety of actors working in a variety of forums and pursuing a variety of interests and values. As a result, when norms finally do emerge they are more likely than not the product of multilateral efforts by a variety of actors in multivariate settings that facilitate the iteration and reiteration of a norm from its genesis until its acceptance.

The idea of a norm life cycle is particularly salient in examining emerging structures surrounding the concept of space traffic management (STM). At the moment, STM does not exist as a formal structure and better resembles a melange or stew of potential norms that may or may not rise to the top. At the moment, processes governing space traffic are ad hoc, non-formalized processes of coordination rather than more formal management structures. Though there has been much conjecture as to what attributes a functional and formalized STM system should possess, there is a need to understand the current normative structures and how these impact which norms may emerge from this "stew" of potential norms and how they might be ladled out. To this end, this chapter will explore the concept of STM through the perspective of the norm formation life cycle in order to present a better understanding of the dynamics surrounding emergent STM practices.

Specifically, this chapter will draw on Finnemore and Sikkink's theory of the norm life cycle and their claim that norms go through a life cycle in which they hit a "tipping point" followed by a "cascade" of acceptance. Within this context, this chapter will also employ Haas's notion of epistemic communities to discuss the discursive practices from which STM norms might be emerging. This chapter will then discuss the current state of norms in relation to space traffic coordination and the potential for the emergence of STM norms within the framework of the norm lifecycle. First, this chapter will proceed by scoping the analysis through a discussion of the theoretical frameworks of the norm life cycle and the notion of norm development through iterative discursive processes. Next, the chapter will turn to a discussion of the current state of space traffic norms with an emphasis on the norm of information sharing for space traffic coordination. Finally, it will turn its attention to potential practices that could indicate emerging norms of space traffic management, contextualized within the norm life cycle framework, and their future potential for development into accepted norms.

Normative Iteration

Norms are ill-defined things, and the term is often used to describe a variety of mechanisms that serve to impact the behavior of actors within a system. Herein, the concern is with norms in the international system. Within this context, there is a core division in the use of the term norm between the fields of international law and international relations. International law traditionally tends to use norm to indicate a provision of binding international law and often specifically customary international law. International relations practitioners and theorists, on the other hand, tend to adopt a more expansive meaning and employ the term to refer to principles that may not rise to the level of binding international law (see Zimmerman, Deitelhoff, and Lesch 2017, 693). For instance, the classic international relations definition offered by Finnemore and Sikkink is that norms are "shared ideas, expectations, and beliefs about appropriate behavior" (Finnemore and Sikkink 1998, 894). Herein the term will be used in the international relations sense as it gives a more comprehensive account of mechanisms that impact actors' behavior within a system or issue area. In essence, norms exist along a spectrum of rules or principles that have normative content but that can be more or less binding depending on the level of adoption and understandings surrounding the norm. Normative content, in turn, is the idea that some mechanisms or processes are imbued with some minimal power to affect the behavior of actors within a given system or issue area. For instance, technical standards are generally non-binding mechanisms, but broad acceptance of these standards can lead to them becoming expected practice among actors in a specific field. To this end, such standards contain normative content because they describe accepted behavior within a realm of activities and have "formal validity and cultural validation" through their recognition and adoption by stakeholders (Iommi 2020, 85). This broader definition allows for an understanding of norms at a variety of levels within a multilevel governance framework that defines acceptable behavior.

This idea that normative content occurs through different mechanisms at different levels in a governance framework implies that norms themselves can have mobility within a framework, from softer norms with less binding force to harder norms with more binding force. Norm formation then is an ongoing process in which normative content becomes more accepted through iteration within a system after its initial emergence. In the foundational article in the literature on norm formation, Finnemore and Sikkink articulate a three-stage life cycle through which norms emerge within the international community. The first stage in this process is norm emergence in which "norm entrepreneurs" push potential norms into the international community (Finnemore and Sikkink 1998, 896–901). The second stage is norm acceptance resulting in a "norm cascade" in which a critical mass of states accept norms (Finnemore and Sikkink 1998, 902–04). Finally, there is a stage of norm internalization wherein "norms acquire a taken-for-granted quality and are no longer a matter of broad public debate" (Finnemore and Sikkink 1998, 904–905). This model presents an excellent starting point for understanding norm emergence, but in an iterative process within a given system this model tends to treat norms as monolithic and ignores much of the nuance in the development of normative content as they are negotiated among actors. Norms themselves are not "static 'things.'" Their life cycle continues on past the internalization stage (Zimmerman, Deitelhoff, and Lesch 2017, 693), and they experience ongoing development through "interpretation, adjudication, contestation, dialogue, and compromise" (Iommi 2020, 97). Nevertheless, this three-stage model does broadly present a useful framework for understanding norm development.

Each of these stages is interesting in its own right, but in the context of space traffic management, it is fair to say that development is still very much in the norm emergence phase, which will be the focus of this chapter, though norm cascades may be on the horizon. In the norm emergence phase, Finnemore and Sikkink argue that norms "are actively built by agents having strong notions about appropriate or desirable behavior in their community" (Finnemore and Sikkink 1998, 896). These "agents" are "norm entrepreneurs" working through organizational platforms "from and through which they promote their norms" (899). Though Finnemore and Sikkink use examples of individual people being norm entrepreneurs, there is no reason why other types of entities cannot fulfill that role (see, e.g., Schünemann and Windwehr 2020, 3–4). Indeed, it is likely that in technical areas a variety of norm entrepreneurs may be engaging within a discursive space "to construct the rules and norms of the international system" (Cross 2013, 139). An example of this would be the process of internet standard adoption within the Internet Engineering Task Force (IETF), which takes place in a discursive process that seeks to achieve a norm cascade through "rough consensus" (Hoffman 2012; Alvestrand and Lie 2009).

To better understand the notion of norm entrepreneurs working within a discursive space, one can turn to Haas's notion of "epistemic communities" (Haas 1992). An epistemic community is a group of experts that function within a policy area and have technical expertise within that area (3). While an individual as a norm entrepreneur may exist for norms built solely around ethical content, for example Raphael Lemkin's pursuit of a ban on genocide, norms within highly technical content likely emerge within discursive spaces that allow for the participation of a variety of expert actors. Epistemic communities represent such a forum as "networks of knowledge-based experts" (2), and these experts can be "governmental or non-governmental, scientific or non-scientific" (Cross 2013, 147). Importantly, the cohesion of such groups can be variable (148–49), and they can themselves be places for discursive contestation over norms. Through such networks "the diffusion of new ideas and information can lead to new patterns of behavior" (Haas 1992, 3). These communities can directly "influence state interests" and "decision makers in one state may, in turn, influence the interests and behaviors in another state" resulting in "convergent state behavior" (4). Though Haas is concerned with "policy coordination" rather than norm formation, convergent behavior is a critical component of the above-mentioned concept of a norm cascade. More recent research on epistemic communities has suggested that they "are at the forefront of recognised trends towards transnational governance" (Cross 2013, 138). These communities seek to persuade states and nonstate actors thereby "shaping *governance* more broadly" (139).

Norms themselves "emerge in a highly contested normative space where they must compete with other norms and perceptions of interest" (Finnemore and Sikkink 1998, 897). The discursive space in which norms emerge is a melange or stew of actors, processes, forums, and narratives through which norm entrepreneurs seek to gain acceptance of a particular formulation of a norm and in which some actors may oppose the development of new norms. In issue areas that already exist within a complex of normative frameworks, norm building often occurs within spaces that give certain narratives more epistemic value than others. This epistemic value can come through the legitimacy bestowed through institutional processes or through the authority that gives an entity voice in a particular forum. While norms can emerge from single identifiable individuals as norm entrepreneurs, in established issue areas norms emerge from discursive interactions that negotiate the bounds and hardness of norms at multiple levels and in multiple interconnected forums.

More specifically, within the field of space governance we can observe institutions (such as the ITU), forums (such as the United Nations General Assembly and Committee on the Peaceful Uses of Outer Space and the Conference on Disarmament), as well as national level institutions and forums. There is also a diversity of actors that are all pushing and pursuing normative content based on their own interests and values. These include non-governmental organizations, commercial actors, and various epistemic communities. In this environment, norms tend to percolate in discursive spaces and gain legitimacy through reiteration in various forums indicating increasing acceptance at different levels of hardness. Norm entrepreneurs exist throughout these communities, and norm cascades may be better understood as a series of waves, as norms become accepted within different forums and at different levels within a governance framework. This iterative process means that norm internalization can also happen in an uneven manner across the discursive space as normative waves move across different actors. This is important in the space context as commercial, national, and international actors all play important roles in the discursive space of norm negotiation.

THE SPACE TRAFFIC MANAGEMENT AND NORM EMERGENCE

The process of norm formation is an ongoing one within the issue area of space traffic management. STM is a proposed concept for the management of on-orbit activities so as to prevent interference among spacecraft and other orbital objects and to prevent the degradation of the space environment. STM would necessarily consist of legal and technical mechanisms that would enable an institution to exert authority over the space environment to avoid harmful interference and debris creation (Blount 2019). Such a system is not currently extant, and at the moment such operations exist within a system that can be better described as space traffic coordination (Blount 2021). Space operators coordinate their activities on an ad hoc basis based on a variety of mechanisms that facilitate information sharing with regard to space situational awareness data. Though there is at present no formal system of STM, there is significant discourse within the international space community that recognizes STM as a critical concept to address the collective action problem of maintaining the orbital environment for future use in light of an increasing orbital population. At the same time, there is significant divergence among the actors within the space environment with regard to interests and values that results in a system wherein collective action is difficult to realize. The contemporary coordination process exists as a normative melange in which a variety of actors and processes interact within a number of forums. This means that STM presents an interesting example of a potential issue area in which the iterative process of the norm life cycle might be observed with the potential for norms to emerge and coalesce around common practices.

This section will first briefly present an overview of the actors that have the potential to behave as norm entrepreneurs and the forums in which these actors engage in normative discourse. It will then turn to a discussion of the current state of space traffic coordination and the extant normative mechanisms within that framework. This will help to illustrate how past norms have been constructed and the potential for new norms needed in order to transition from space traffic coordination to a normative framework for space traffic management.

Actors and Forums

Within the discursive space surrounding the potential development of STM there are a variety of actors. These include states, commercial actors, epistemic communities, and individuals, among others, all of which have the potential to serve as norm entrepreneurs. States are the traditional actors within the realm of space and major spacefaring states are concerned with preserving access to space for commercial, civil, and military programs. At the same time, for major spacefarers the interface of space with national security means that there is a cautiousness around adopting an STM system that could impact a state's freedom of action in the domain. Commercial actors, and specifically operators, are concerned with preserving their own investments in order to profit from their activities, meaning that they seek a balance between protection from risk, which STM could provide, with the potential for burdensome regulation, which such a system could impose. Epistemic communities are also forming in this issue area and are placing an emphasis on the preservation of the space environment. For instance, the International Astronautical Federation (IAF), the International Institute of Space Law (IISL), and the International Academy of Astronautics (IAA) recently completed a trilateral study on STM which is intended "to assist the decision-makers on national and international level, to promote the safe use of outer space" (IAF, IISL, and IAA 2022, 1). Finally, individuals or astro-environmentalists also play a role in advancing normative discussions within the community and within state, commercial, and epistemic communities (e.g., Jah and ten Eyck 2016).

These norm entrepreneurs are able to engage in a number of forums that create discursive space through which normative content can be advanced. Institutions at the international level serve as significant forums for states as do civil society actors that have observer status. The two most significant in this sphere are the United Nations (UN) Committee on the Peaceful Uses of Outer Space (COPUOS) and specifically its Scientific and Technical Subcommittee, which maintains STM as an agenda item, and the International Telecommunications Union (ITU), which provides formal mechanisms for coordinating space activities. State level institutions also play a role with civil and military policymaking processes and serve as sites for norm advancement and the development of interests and values within the context of national governments. Beyond formal institutions, numerous types of forums exist that foster discursive action by commercial or epistemic community actors. For example, the Space Data Association (SDA) is an industry group that fosters the exchange of space situational awareness information among industry actors, and IAF represents a forum wherein a number of types of actors may engage and discuss activities.

What can be seen here is that there is an active discourse on the norms and methods surrounding STM that spans actors as well as forums. While the establishment of a STM system that functions at the international level will require a norm cascade among states, smaller waves of normative development will need to come first. The IAF, IISL, and IAA trilateral study already mentioned is a good example of this dynamic. This interdisciplinary study provides "compelling insights and recommended behaviors over a comprehensive review of all dimensions and nuances of the STM challenge" (IAF, IISL, and IAA 2022, 2). Its central conclusion is that STM "will be difficult to execute without immediate changes in our [space environmental preservation] objectives and behavior" (2). This report includes the work of more than 130 individuals with wide representation from geographic regions, employers, and disciplines (21, appendix). It shows that there is coalescence around a number of recommendations with regard to STM that emerged from discursive dynamics of an epistemic community. Obviously, this report does not create norms, but it has significant potential to contribute to the building of normative content that can be transposed into other forums that do create norms.

Space Traffic Coordination

As stated above, STM does not currently exist and must be understood as a proposed future concept. At the same time, space operators at all levels have a need to ensure that their operations are safe and secure from interference in the orbital environment. Interference here is used in the generic sense to encompass the significant potential for unintentional interference in addition to intentional harmful interference. To accomplish this, actors must coordinate operations on an ad hoc basis, which requires operators to have access to actionable information about the orbital environment, so that they may plan their operations accordingly. This can be understood as space traffic coordination Within space traffic coordination there has been clear normative development around the notion of "information sharing," which enables such coordinative practices (Blount 2021, 3). This norm reflects the above-mentioned processes in that it has undergone continual development and refinement since it first emerged in the 1960s. This can be seen across a number of levels within the governance framework, and the norm is supported by both binding legal mechanisms and softer non-binding mechanisms containing normative content. This subsection will overview these mechanisms in order to show the contours of this multilevel norm and illustrate the current state of norm emergence within this sphere.

International Mechanisms

At the international level, there have been numerous mechanisms that support a norm of information sharing, and these date back to the emergence of governance in the early days of the space age. Indeed, the framework of international space law is significantly built around the concept of information sharing (Blount 2018). The Outer Space Treaty (OST), adopted in 1967, is a relatively permissive treaty with few prescriptive clauses. Rather the treaty emphasizes the notions of communication and cooperation throughout its text as a way for states to work together to ensure the peaceful uses of outer space. Numerous clauses throughout the treaty support different types of information sharing (specifically Art. V, Art. VIII, Art. IX, Art. X, Art. XI, and Art. XII; see Blount 2021, 4). The goal of these clauses is to reduce strategic risk among space actors by creating transparency within the space environment. While these clauses were initially targeted at reducing the potential for conflict within the space environment they serve as foundational norms for coordinative practices among states and their non-governmental actors. Article IX of the OST is illustrative: it requires, among other things, states to request bilateral consultations when they think their activities may cause harmful interference or when they think their activities may be harmfully interfered with by another state. This clause does not affirmatively ban harmful interference, nor does it require that states reach a resolution through the consultation process.

Instead, it requires that states coordinate in good faith with regard to resolving potential harmful interference. This requires information sharing in order to properly understand and resolve risk in such situations.

The Registration Convention of 1976 serves as a further basis for such information sharing. Building on the idea of a registry of space objects found in Article VIII of the OST, the Registration Convention requires states to register their spacecraft with an open access registry maintained by the United Nations (Art. III). Article IV of this treaty requires states to provide the following information when registering a spacecraft: "(a) Name of launching State or States (b) An appropriate designator of the space object or its registration number (c) Date and territory or location of launch (d) Basic orbital parameters, including (i) nodal period (ii) inclination (iii) apogee (iv) perigee (e) General function of the space object." This required information is quite basic, but it reinforces the normative basis for information sharing on space activities. The legal requirement for these minimum disclosures facilitates a database of satellites to which operators can turn to make assessments about potential interference. The usefulness of this database is limited in that it does not give a complete picture of the orbital environment because registration practices are uneven among states, updates to changed information are not consistently forthcoming, and this information does not give at present an even remotely real-time picture of the constantly evolving orbital environment. Nevertheless, these disclosures reinforce the norm of information sharing and transparency within the international system.

A final legal mechanism can be found in the coordination processes adopted by the ITU, the international body that pursues international coordination of the radiofrequency spectrum as a limited natural resource. Within this mandate is the coordination of radiofrequency spectrum used for space communications. The ITU Constitution clearly includes as one of the functions of the ITU to "effect allocation of bands of the radio-frequency spectrum, the allotment of radio frequencies and the registration of radio-frequency assignments and, for space services, of any associated orbital position in the geostationary-satellite orbit or of any associated characteristics of satellites in other orbits, in order to avoid harmful interference between radio stations of different countries" (Art. 1(2)(a)). This is a coordinative process in that the ITU does not grant or authorize the usage of specific frequencies but instead manages a registration system through which states can make known their future planned activities so that they can be coordinated with previously established operators to avoid interference. Specifically within the space context, this means that operators share not only the frequencies that they wish to employ but the orbital parameters as well. This information is critical to allowing operators to communicate and deconflict their space activities. This process though is for future services. Services that are already on-orbit, may use the ITU process to resolve issues of "harmful interference" as understood under the ITU's Radio Regulations (Art. 15). This type of interference is specific to radio frequency interference rather than physical interference and consists of a non-binding dispute resolution process (Oberst 2015). Nevertheless, the ITU framework presents the most robust and formalized information sharing regime with regard to space activities at the international level, but it can only deconflict operations before they are brought into service.

The international community has also adopted mechanisms that sit below the level of law but do contain normative content with regard to information sharing about space operations. These for the most part are concerned with the sustainability of the orbital environment. The first set of mechanisms are orbital debris guidelines, which have been adopted by both the Inter-Agency Debris Coordination Committee (IADC) and COPUOS (Inter-Agency Debris Coordination Committee 2007; United Nations Office for Outer Space Affairs 2010). These are non-binding mechanisms that contain normative content in relation to the limitation of orbital debris; both require that operators consult available data and design their missions accordingly so as to limit both debris creation from the activity and interference with other activities. These mechanisms do not set up formal information exchange frameworks, but rather they imply that information exchange is a necessary precursor to the limitation of debris creation.

The second non-binding mechanism of significance is the Long-Term Sustainability (LTS) guidelines that were adopted through the COPUOS process (United Nations Committee on the Peaceful Uses of Outer Space 2018). These guidelines are geared at the protection of the space environment for future operations and include numerous provisions that support the normative value of information sharing. Specifically, information sharing is explicit to the following guidelines:

> Guideline B.1: provide updated contact information and share information on space objects and orbital events.
> Guideline B.2: improve accuracy of orbital data on space objects and enhance the practice and utility of sharing orbital information on space objects.
> Guideline B.3: promote the collection, sharing, and dissemination of space debris monitoring information.
> Guideline B.4: perform conjunction assessment during all orbital phases of controlled flight.
> Guideline B.5: develop practical approaches for prelaunch conjunction assessment.

What can be seen through these various instruments is a constant evolution from the OST forward in the normative strength of information sharing, but also the growing support for more specific delineation of the information to be shared. Though the LTS guidelines are non-binding they increase the specificity of the information that needs to be shared in order to protect the viability of the space environment. This reflects the normative waves over time that mark the strengthening of the information sharing norm.

National Mechanisms

Processes at the state level also support the norm of information sharing. Under the OST, states are required to "authorize and continually supervise" their non-governmental actors (Art. VI). Authorization processes generally include a quantum of information to be shared with the authorizing state (Marboe and Hafner 2011). This enables the state to ensure that the operator is engaging in space activities in a responsible manner, but also allows the state to fulfill its international obligations with regard to information sharing as discussed above. A number of states have transposed debris mitigation guidelines into their domestic regulations and some states have begun the process of transposing the LTS guidelines into domestic regulation as well. This is significant as it does not simply pass these obligations on to commercial actors, but it provides support for the normative strength of these guidelines.

It is beyond the scope of this chapter to give a full account of these type of provisions that occur at the domestic level, but the case of the United States should be noted as it has been a leader in sharing data on the space environment. The US military is a dominant collector of space situational awareness data (or in the military's updated terminology space domain awareness data). The military collects and processes this data and shares it globally in a number of ways as authorized by law (10 U.S.C. § 2274; Chow 2011). The amount and quality of data shared depends on the receiving party, with the United States government and close allies able to receive a high-accuracy catalog of orbital data. Anyone, however, can access the still useful, but less accurate two-line element data. In addition to sharing the space situational awareness data, the US military processes this data to make determinations about potential on-orbit conjunctions, primarily to ensure the safe operations of its own assets, but it will directly (or indirectly in the case of operators in adversary nations) contact operators with conjunction data messages (CDM) if it calculates a potential on-orbit conjunction with an operational satellite. The CDM process is solely an information sharing process and the US military has no authority to require action from any operator. Such sharing, particularly by a national security actor, illustrates the strong support for the norm of information sharing.

In 2018, the executive branch in the United States adopted Space Policy Directive 3—National Space Traffic Management Policy. This is a policy document without binding force, but it does serve to set out the intent of how the United States will pursue its goals in the realm of space traffic management, which includes the support of the development of guidelines and standards at the international level (White House 2018, Sec. 1). The policy adopts the goal of moving the information sharing process (but not data collection process) away from the US military to the Department of Commerce. Further, it seeks to establish an "open architecture SSA data repository" so as "to facilitate greater data sharing with satellite operators and enable the commercial development of enhanced space safety services" (White House 2018, Sec. 5(a)(ii)). Such an architecture would be supported by standards and protocols that would allow for the integration of multiple sources of data. At the moment, this architecture has not been deployed as it will require authorization and appropriations from the US Congress, but the inclusion of this mechanism in the policy displays the criticality of information sharing to space traffic coordination and future management. It also displays strong support of the norm of information sharing.

Other Mechanisms

Beyond formalized structures within the international system and domestic legal systems, there are other actors and processes that contribute to the normative structures around information sharing. A prime example of this is SDA, mentioned above. This international consortium of commercial space operators facilitates the sharing of space situational awareness data among its members (Space Data Association n.d.). The goal of this consortium is to improve information sharing to protect commercial investment within the space domain.

In addition to SDA, there are a number of commercial entities that are pursuing the collection and sale of space situational awareness data as business models. These entities recognize the critical nature of this data to space operators and seek to create value added data products for these operators. While these companies may sit outside the normative scope of open information sharing, it is notable that Space Policy Directive 3 sees these companies as potential contributors to an open architecture data repository using "[m]easures to safeguard proprietary or sensitive data" (White House 2018, Sec. 5(a)(ii)). As a result, how commercial data from these entities gets treated within such an architecture will be an important node in understanding the limitations on information sharing for space traffic coordination processes. There are also interesting questions about the duties that might be owed by these companies. For instance, if a commercial data company were to predict an on-orbit collision that will not affect its customers, will it be under a duty to issue a CDM? Such questions illustrate the potential for normative growth within information sharing for space traffic coordination.

From Coordination to Management

The ad hoc processes of coordination supported by a norm of information sharing has thus far proven effective, but the system faces new pressures which could alter that dynamic. Specifically, new space architectures such as large constellations are placing new stress on the space environment by dramatically increasing the on-orbit population (IAF, IISL, and IAA 2022, 16–17). These constellations function as single systems that operate in an orbital shell around the Earth in order to provide continuous and low latency services to users. While these new architectures have potential to advance uses of low earth orbit, there is a need to ensure that the increased orbital population does not lead to orbital pollution or to interference with other operators. Coordination processes may not rise to the level needed in order to properly manage this new challenge. As an example, China has made a formal complaint about a close approach from a Starlink satellite (Grush 2021). Though there is controversy surrounding the actual risk level presented by this incident, such incidents will only become more probable as the orbital population increases.

STM has been put forward as a solution to the problems created by the increasing number of operators and satellites, but a significant amount of normative development is needed before such a system is possible. Core challenges to achieving this type of normative development result from the combination of the scale at which such a system needs to be able to function and the power dynamics that are involved with making management possible. The scale issue is that for STM to be effective it must be deployed globally and cover as many actors as possible. While states might take individual actions, such as the United States' Space Policy Directive 3, the multilateral nature of the space environment means that unilateral action by a single state will not be effective at effectuating STM. The issue of scale is linked to the power dynamics among the states engaged in space activities and in particular the three central actors of China, Russia, and the United States. These states have been reluctant to agree to new binding norms to govern space activities and to relinquish any of their own freedom of action in the strategic domain of space. While coordination places power to determine actions in the hands of the actors, management requires some shift in power to a centralized system that has decision-making authority. Within the current geopolitical system it is difficult to see how a transformation might take place that could facilitate a norm cascade toward STM among states.

Though states seem unlikely to undergo a shift toward normative development of an international management system, there are still opportunities for growth in this area. This could likely come from standardization processes surrounding the data, modeling algorithms, and eventually regulatory mechanisms (Blount 2019). STM is necessarily a complex of technical and regulatory mechanisms, but technical mechanisms are a necessary prerequisite to the adoption of regulation. In order to properly regulate the orbital environment, there must be both reliable data collected about that environment and reliable models made from that data to as accurately as possible predict the future state of the environment. This second point is important. Space situational awareness data does not give a real time picture of the orbital environment. Rather, it is a series of observations of orbital objects. As any particular object is observed repeatedly across time, the accumulated observations refine the accuracy of the information known about the object's orbital position. This data is then used to predict the future locations of that object within the environment. CDMs, then, are probabilistic predictions of collisions that might occur based on accumulated data. In a system of coordination, this means that the recipient of a CDM is able to weigh the risk that is posed to its space object and respond within its own bounds of risk tolerance through a cost benefit analysis. A management system, on the other hand, implies that some external authority is able to make that determination and compel action by a given actor. In order for such an authority to effectively manage the space traffic, it will need to rely on open, standardized, and transparent data that is processed using open, standardized, and transparent modeling. Legal mechanisms in turn must be based on a foundation of technical information.

Standardization is a mechanism through which normative content can be developed. Technical standards have become a significant mechanism for influencing the behavior of actors. These standards can flow from a variety of different sources (Gleason

2019), but technical standards are having increasing influence at the international level as seen through mechanisms such as the COPUOS Debris Mitigation Guidelines, the LTS guidelines, and the 2009 Safety Framework for Nuclear Power Source Applications in Outer Space (Blount Forthcoming). Indeed technical standards present significant benefits in moving governance forward while avoiding tricky political questions that hamper legal mechanisms. They also present avenues for epistemic communities to contribute as norm entrepreneurs as they bring the expert knowledge that is needed to craft acceptable guidelines. Technical mechanisms then present opportunities to develop normative instruments that can build the overall governance framework without requiring a full-bore norm cascade toward management mechanisms.

An example of where such guidelines could build STM practices would be technical guidelines and standards on collision avoidance. Such a mechanism would provide non-binding guidance on when action should be taken by an operator to avoid a potential collision in the orbital environment. Such a standard could be implemented by the operator on a voluntary basis, or it could be adopted at the national level to serve as guidance for the supervision functions of state authorities. Widespread acceptance of such a standard could lead to normative acceptance of what is proper behavior with regard to collision avoidance in the orbital environment and contribute to an understanding of what best practices are for the purposes of understanding fault within the space domain. In other words, norms can shape the "expectations" that actors have within the system (Gallagher and Docherty 2022, 229) As with similar mechanisms, such a standard could emerge from industry or an epistemic community, but could then be taken up by an institution such as the Scientific and Technical Subcommittee of COPUOS.

CONCLUSION

Norm formation takes time, especially in highly contested areas such as space that resist new top-level legal frameworks. With regard to STM, there seems to be an extensive amount of discourse, but the adoption of hard norms governing the area does not seem likely in the near term. At the same, these discursive practices surrounding the issue area and particularly within the epistemic communities involved are resulting in the development of normative content that can begin to build such future norms. As normative waves begin to emerge at lower levels they have the potential to become the building blocks that could lead to a norm cascade at higher levels within the governance framework. For STM, the real concern is one of time as many actors and operators within space are becoming increasingly concerned that without near-term action the orbital rush will result in irreparable damage to the space environment. Information sharing in this area shows the potential for acceptance of normative content, but the notion of management is fraught as states seek to preserve their freedom of action in the domain. Going forward STM will be of interest both for its practical effects for the preservation of the space environment and for the theoretical implications in the area of norm formation.

BIBLIOGRAPHY

10 U.S.C. § 2274.

Alvestrand, Harald, and Hakon Wium Lie. 2009. "Development of Core Internet Standards: The Work of IETF and W3C." In *Internet Governance: Infrastructure and Institutions*, edited by Lee A. Bygrave and Jon Bing, 126–46. Oxford: Oxford University Press.

Blount, P.J. 2018. "Innovating the Law: Fifty Years of the Outer Space Treaty." In *Innovation in Outer Space: International and African Legal Perspective*, edited by Mahulena Hofmann and P. J. Blount, 31–52. Baden-Baden: Nomos Verlagsgesellschaft mbH & Co. KG.

Blount, P.J. 2019. "Space Traffic Management: Standardizing On-Orbit Behavior." *American Journal of International Law Unbound* 113: 120–124.

Blount, P.J. 2021. "Space Traffic Coordination: Developing a Framework for Safety and Security in Satellite Operations." *Space: Science & Technology*. DOI: 10.34133/2021/9830379.

Blount, P.J. Forthcoming. "Technically Speaking: UNCOPUOS and the Technical Governance of Space," *Indian Review of Air and Space Law* .

Chow, Tiffany. 2011. "Space Situational Awareness Sharing Program: An SWF Issue Brief." Secure World Foundation. https://swfound.org/media/3584/ssa_sharing_program_issue_brief_nov2011.pdf.

Constitution of the International Telecommunication Union. 2018.

Convention on the Registration of Objects Launched into Outer Space. September 15, 1976.

Davis Cross, Mai'a K. 2013. "Rethinking Epistemic Communities Twenty Years Later." *Review of International Studies* 39, no. 1: 137–60.

Finnemore, Martha, and Kathryn Sikkink. 1998. "International Norm Dynamics and Political Change." *International Organization* 52, no. 4: 887–917.

Gallagher, Adrian, and Benedict Docherty. 2022. "What Role[s] do Expectations Play in Norm Dynamics?" *International Politics* 59, no. 2: 227–43.

Gleason, Michael P. 2019 *Establishing Space Traffic Management Standards, Guidelines, and Best Practices*. Washington, DC: Aerospace Corporation.

Grush, Lauren. 2021. "China Complains to UN after Maneuvering Its Space Station Away from SpaceX Starlink Satellites." *The Verge*. https://www.theverge.com/2021/12/28/22857035/china-spacex-starlink-tianhe-space-station-satellites-collisions.

Haas, Peter M. 1992. "Introduction: Epistemic Communities and International Policy Coordination." *International Organization* 46, no. 1: 1–35.

Hoffman, Paul, (ed.). 2012. "The Tao of IETF: A Novice's Guide to the Internet Engineering Task Force." https://www.ietf.org/tao.html.

IAF, IISL, and IAA. 2022. "Space Traffic Management Report: Executive Summary."

Inter-agency Space Debris Coordination Committee. 2007. "IADC Space Debris Mitigation Guidelines."

Iommi, Lucrecia Garcia. 2020. "Norm Internalisation Revisited: Norm Contestation and the Life of Norms at the Extreme of the Norm Cascade." *Global Constitutionalism* 9, no. 1: 76–116.

Jah, Moriba K., and Brian C. ten Eyck. 2016. "Academia's Role in Space Protection, Space Traffic Management & Orbital Debris Mitigation." *Room: The Space Journal* 8, no. 2: 82–85.

Marboe, Irmgard, and Florian Hafner. 2011. "Brief Overview over National Authorization Mechanisms in Implementation of the UN International Space Treaties." In *National Space Legislation in Europe: Issues of Authorisation of Private Space Activities in the Light of Developments in European Space Cooperation*, edited by Frans G. von der Dunk, 29–71. Leiden; Boston: Martinus Nijhoff.

Oberst, Gerry. 2015. "Dispute Resolution before the ITU: The Operator's Experience." In *Dispute Settlement in the Area of Space Communication*, edited by Mahulena Hofmann, 43–58. Baden-Baden, Germany: Nomos.

Radio Regulations. 2020.

Schünemann, Wolf Jürgen, and Jana Windwehr. 2020. "Towards a 'Gold Standard for the World'? The European General Data Protection Regulation between Supranational and National Norm Entrepreneurship." *Journal of European Integration* 43, no. 7: 859–74.

Space Data Association. n.d. https://www.space-data.org/sda/.

Treaty on Principles Governing the Activities of States in the Exploration and Use of Outer Space, Including the Moon and Other Celestial Bodies. October 10, 1967.

United Nations Committee on the Peaceful Uses of Outer Space. 2018. Guidelines for the Long-term Sustainability of Outer Space Activities. U.N. Doc. A/AC.105/2018/CRP.20.

United Nations Office of Outer Space Affairs. 2010. "Space Debris Mitigation Guidelines of the Committee on the Peaceful Uses of Outer Space." https:// www.unoosa.org/pdf/publicati ons/st_space_49E.pdf.

White House. 2018. "Space Policy Directive-3, National Space Traffic Management Policy."

Zimmerman, Lisbeth, Nicole Deitelhoff, and Max Lesch. 2017. "Unlocking the Agency of the Governed: Contestation and Norm Dynamics." *Third World Dynamics: A TWQ Journal* 2, no. 5: 691–708.

....

CHAPTER 35

SPACE RESOURCES AND PROSPECTS FOR CONTESTED GOVERNANCE

....

ALANNA KROLIKOWSKI AND MARTIN ELVIS

NATURAL resources found on celestial bodies, such as lunar regolith and asteroidal water, are growing more important to forthcoming space missions. Although actors are not yet actively exploiting space resources, several have designs to do so within the next half decade and more are likely to follow. Without new institutions to manage these activities, however, international disputes between such actors are already foreseeable. To address this governance gap, key spacefaring states are mounting efforts to create international rules for the exploitation of space resources. The international community is in the process of bifurcating into two coalitions, each pursuing its own approach to space resource governance. The first grouping, led by the United States, is creating permissive new institutions to support the near-term commercial exploitation of space resources. The second, a much larger and looser coalition comprising Russia, China, and numerous lesser spacefaring states, aims to gradually develop a binding multilateral agreement to govern space resources through the long-established United Nations (UN) Committee on the Peaceful Uses of Outer Space (COPUOS). While the two approaches are not entirely irreconcilable in principle, for now this cleavage portends the emergence of a contested and fragmented international regime for space resource exploitation.

The first part of this chapter introduces definitions, a typology, and the properties of space resources that shape their prospects for exploitation. The second section assesses the current state of governance structures for space resources, identifying the need for further institutional development. The third part analyzes states' different interests in space resource governance to explain the international community's bifurcation into these two camps, surveying the positions of key states and constituencies. The conclusion discusses prospects for regime development and implications for international relations and space development.

Space Resources: Definitions, Concepts, and Significance

Space resources are naturally occurring abiotic materials found on celestial bodies and having value to some actor, either in situ ("in place" at the point of extraction), in orbit, or once brought to Earth. Among the most important such substances are water, oxygen, iron, platinum group metals, thorium, helium 3, and regolith. However, because of the context-bound and situated nature of resources, it is helpful to broaden our conception of space resources to include not only tangible materials that can be recovered from celestial bodies but also other items of value derived from, or existing in, outer space. For instance, solar power harvested on the moon is a type of space resource.

Space resources can also consist of features, rather than materials. Consider for instance deep craters near the lunar poles. Untouched by sunlight, these formations sustain extremely cold temperatures, harboring water ice and solid forms of other materials that are otherwise volatile on the moon. It is not only these solid materials, but also the topographical features preserving their solid state, that bear value to actors. Moreover, the co-location of two or more resources can enhance their respective values. For instance, the lunar south pole features some of the moon's coldest cold traps in proximity to the so-called Peaks of Eternal Light, elevations that are almost continuously illuminated by the sun and therefore ideally suited to the placement of solar panels. The co-location of the trapped materials and a stable power supply makes the south pole a uniquely attractive destination for a range of missions. We call locations at which one or more resources exist in high concentrations "sites of interest." While such sites of interest exist on Mars and other distant destinations, in this chapter we confine our discussion to the moon and asteroids because these present the first targets of planned missions to exploit resources.

Humankind is just beginning to understand and exploit the solar system's wealth of natural resources beyond Earth. Efforts at conceptualizing space resources, characterizing their physical properties, and exploring how their exploitation could impact international relations are still preliminary. As of now, no actors are yet actively exploiting space resources on a large scale. But major space agencies have already undertaken missions to characterize them. And several space agencies and private companies have planned or active missions that will harvest space resources in one form or another within just a few years.

For now, much international activity in this domain consists of efforts to develop rules and institutions to govern the *future* exploitation of space resources. We define "governance" here as consisting of collective measures to address international problems that transcend the capacities of individual states to overcome, including in particular managing resources on celestial bodies beyond national jurisdictions (Weiss and Wilkinson 2014). In the realm of space resources, various efforts are already paving the way for an eventual international "regime," understood as a set of "principles, norms, rules, and decision-making procedures around which actor expectations converge in a given issue-area" (Krasner 1982, 185).

Though in its infancy, space resource governance deserves the attention of international relations specialists for several reasons. First, efforts at governing space resources are already contested, illustrating the potential for institution-building itself to become a source of international discord, a crucial but understudied dimension of global governance (Zürn 2018). Second, contestation over space resource governance consists of challenges to the "rules about the rules" for building institutions, including about which types of institutions should be empowered to make rules in the first place (Raymond 2019). The centrality of COPUOS to governing an emerging domain of space activity is under threat, in part due to the body's deficit of "performance legitimacy" or perceived effectiveness (Fioretos and Tallberg 2021, 106). Judging the gridlocked forum incapable of responding to new challenges posed by space resources, actors are creating new governance institutions that circumvent and could supplant COPUOS. The next few years will reveal whether COPUOS can adapt to remain a pillar institution or whether global space governance will fragment into multiple contending arrangements. Like many global regimes today, the regime governing space activities arguably sits at a crossroad between development and decline, its course portending the fate of institutions in comparable issue areas (Fioretos and Tallberg 2021).

A Typology of Space Resources

What makes a material or feature found on a celestial body a *resource*, i.e., value-bearing? The answer lies in its possible application in a space mission or business. In the context of a wide range of in-space activities, actors hope to eventually exploit space resources because doing so will limit the costly transport from Earth of materials, such as fuel. Moreover, some programs and missions aim specifically to assess and demonstrate the capacity for humans to dwell off Earth using local resources, known as in situ resource utilization (ISRU). So far, at least fourteen national space agencies have identified ISRU "as a needed capability for long-duration missions" to the moon, Mars, and deep space (Boley and Byers 2020).

Among the space resources likely to be exploited first are those involved in energy production. Water on asteroids could become propellant (Krolikowski and Elvis 2019). The Peaks of Eternal Light could host solar panels (Elvis, Milligan, and Krolikowski 2016). Lunar thorium and helium-3 could also be used to generate power (Elvis, Krolikowski, and Milligan 2021). Another group of resources could be used to build shelters or transports. Lunar or asteroidal water could sustain life on stations or bases. Lunar regolith could be processed into cement for building a habitat. A natural lunar tunnel forming a shield from radiation could be modified into a dwelling for astronauts. An asteroid, its orbit altered to bring it within reach of Earth and Mars, could ferry astronauts or equipment between them. Yet other resources bear unique value to

Table 35.1. Typology of Lunar Resources

Features		Materials	Scientific or Heritage Assets
Topographical features	Special locations	Thorium	Apollo landing sites
		Uranium	Other historical sites
Peaks of Eternal Light	33.1E, 0N	Rare Earth	
Cold traps	Sinus Medii	Elements	
Coldest traps	Lipskiy Crater	(REEs)	
Far-side smooth		Helium-3 (^{3}He)	
terrain areas		Iron	
Pits			

humankind for scientific or cultural reasons, such as the largest asteroids of each type or the Apollo landing sites. Finally, some resources, such as platinum-group metals extracted from asteroids, could find applications in existing or future industries on Earth. What counts as a resource will necessarily evolve with technology, missions, and business models. Because a given resource can have multiple applications, we categorize resources by form in Tables 35.1 and 35.2.

Over several decades, missions characterizing the moon and asteroids have revealed that many space resources are concentrated at only a handful of sites. Resources reachable with our current transportation technology and feasible to exploit are few and far from uniformly distributed. The moon features resource "hotspots" presenting high concentrations of desirable materials or significant features (Crawford 2015; Elvis, Krolikowski, and Milligan 2021) (see Table 35.2). Most of these sites are either few in number (perhaps a dozen or two), small in area (often a few kilometers across), or both. For example, most of the roughly one billion tons of water at the lunar poles lie in a few dozen cold traps some 5–50 kilometers across, while the Peaks of Eternal light near them are only 1 kilometer or so across (Elvis, Milligan, and Krolikowski, 2016). Helium-3 is also significantly more concentrated than was initially predicted (Kim et al. 2019).

Asteroidal resources are similarly concentrated in only a small fraction of all asteroids (Table 35.2) (Krolikowski and Elvis 2019). Large amounts of water or precious metals exist in only a tiny share of asteroids (Elvis 2014; Jedicke et al. 2015). Moreover, of the millions of asteroids in our solar system, only a minuscule portion approach Earth and fewer still are both resource-rich and on orbital trajectories that bring them within reach

Table 35.2. Typology of Asteroidal Resources

Features	Materials	Scientific or Heritage Assets
Low delta-v from Earth orbit	Platinum group metals	Largest asteroids
Potentially hazardous	Water	Unique asteroids (e.g. Kleopatra)
Potential Mars cyclers	Iron	

of today's rockets—perhaps a few dozen (Elvis 2014). And many of these will be infeasible to mine because of their structure, their motions, or other factors (Krolikowski and Elvis 2019). All in all, then, accessible asteroids bearing resources will be a truly precious few, even assuming significant improvements in prospecting and transportation technology.

The Growing Demand for Space Resources

Not only are space resources concentrated, but a growing number of actors is interested in them, portending crowding and interference at sites of interest. An anticipated "lunar renaissance," consisting in a flurry of international missions within the next decade, is under way. Many of these missions target a small number of resource-rich lunar destinations, possibly foreshadowing a similar trend in asteroid missions (Elvis, Krolikowski, and Milligan 2021). Over the next decade, at least six sovereign nations plan to land on the moon (see Table 35.3). NASA has ten missions approved as part of its Commercial Lunar Payloads Services program, roughly two per year to 2025, at least four of which will land near the south pole (Voosen, 2021). In addition, several private companies and the non-profit SpaceIL have stated intentions to visit the lunar surface. Table 35.3, listing recent and announced soft-landing missions, shows they are pooling around the south pole, where strategic resources are concentrated. A recent NASA study estimates that by 2026 at least twenty-two international missions will land in this resource-rich region (Swiney and Hernandez 2022).

These missions are precursors to more ambitious projects that will not only explore but also rely on local resources, including two planned bases at the moon's pole. The first such human-tended facility is part of the US Artemis Program, which aims to return humans to the moon "for long-term exploration and utilization" by 2025 (NASA 2020a). The south pole is "the ideal location for a future base camp given its potential access to ice and other mineral resources," NASA explains (NASA 2020c). The second base is the International Lunar Research Station, a Sino-Russian project expected in the 2030s. This human-tended facility will enable crews to undertake prolonged scientific experiments and gain experience living in off-Earth environments.

Further ahead, this early exploitation of space resources could be dwarfed by the demand from a larger in-space economy that might emerge within just two or three decades. The start could be space stations that purchase water harvested from asteroids or the moon. At least three private companies are already developing their own space stations to rent out to tourists, to research organizations, and to a proliferation of start-ups with plans to manufacture products in microgravity, ranging from novel optical fibers to human hearts (Elvis 2021). As such space stations and clienteles grow and multiply, the demand for space resources could leap upward.

Table 35.3. Recent and Planned Moon Landings

Organization	Primary country	Lander name	Earliest landing	Landing site
Sovereign, State				
CNSA	China	Chang'e 4	Landed, Jan 2019	Von Karman crater, Farside
		Chang'e 5	Landed, Dec 2020	near S. Pole;
		Chang'e 6	2024	Mons Rümker, Oceanus
		Chang'e 7	2024	Procellarum (sample return)
				TBD (sample return)
				S. Pole
ISRO	India	Chandrayaan-2	2019 Failed Sept 6	S. Pole region, near crater
+ JAXA	Japan	Chandrayaan-3	Landed Aug 2023	Manzinus C.
		LUPEX/SLIM	2024?	S. Pole region
JAXA	Japan	TBD	2022	
KARI/NASA	Korea	LUSEM	2024	Reiner Gamma
CSA	Canada	TBD	2026	
Roscosmos	Russia	Luna 25	NET 2022	Near S. Pole at Boguslavsky
Roscomos		Luna 27	2025?	crater;
& ESA				S. Pole-Aitken Basin
				S. Pole PSR water prospecting
ASA	Australia/US	TBD	NET 2026	Rover, NASA lander
NASA	US	Astrobotic, Intuitive Machines, Firefly, Masten	2022–2025	10 landers, as listed in the next section of this table
Commercial				
Astrobotic	US	Peregrine	2022	Lacus Mortis
		Griffin - VIPER	2023	Nobile Crater, near S. Pole
Masten	US	Xelene	2023	S. Pole
Intuitive Machines	US	Nova-C	2022	Vallis Schröteri
Firefly	US	Blue Ghost	2023	Mare Crisium
iSpace	Japan	HAKUTO-R M1	NET 2022	Near Lacus Mortis pit?
	UAE[a]	HAKUTO-R M2	2024	TBA
		HAKUTO-R M3	?	TBA
PTS	Germany	ALINA	2022?	Near Apollo 17?
Philanthropic, Non-profit				
SpaceIL	Israel	Beeresheet	2019 April	Mare Serenitatis
		Beeresheet2	11 failed	TBD (2 landers)
			NET 2025	

Notes: [a] UAE will supply a rover. "NET" means "no earlier than"; "TBA" means "to be announced"; "TBD" means "to be decided".

Source: Updated from (Elvis, Krolikowski, and Milligan 2021).

FORESEEABLE CHALLENGES:
INTERNATIONAL DISPUTES OVER SPACE
RESOURCES

Current characterizations of space resources suggest that in general they have five aspects with implications for how actors can exploit them. First, many space resources are *finite*, meaning they are easily exhausted. For example, once the limited quantities of exploitable lunar thorium are used up, they will no longer be available to anyone. Second, some space resources, though not exhaustible in the same sense, are *rival*, meaning that an actor's exploitation of them reduces others' ability to exploit them. For example, using a patch of smooth terrain on the moon's far side to install a radio telescope precludes other uses. Third, we can foresee that important space resources are likely to grow *scarce*, meaning that the demand for them will outstrip their supply. For instance, if an in-space propellant manufacturing industry emerges, a constraint on its growth could be the availability of accessible asteroidal water. Fourth, many space resources are *concentrated*, meaning that they are not widely distributed, but tend to exist in large quantities at small sites that are difficult for multiple actors to share or that could easily be captured by a single or few actor(s). Consider that extractable platinum will be found in a few large asteroids that rarely approach Earth. Fifth, many space resources are *excludable*, which means that an actor who develops the infrastructure to harvest such a resource can prevent others from accessing it. For example, an operator of solar panels on the moon could ensure that only actors who pay for the generated power receive it.

Because of these attributes, many space resources present significant *early-mover advantages*, meaning that the actors who exploit them first are likely to capture outsized gains relative to late comers. At a given site, a first mover could extract the overwhelming share of a finite resource or build infrastructure that allows them to control access to it. First-mover advantages could be especially pronounced in commercial exploitation. A given resource might be sufficient to sustain only one or two large extractive firms, especially if these firms must exploit resources at scale to cover high upfront technology development costs. Consider, for instance, the cost of developing robotic arms to extract asteroidal water or a press to produce bricks of lunar regolith. A first mover (or a small group of early movers) seizing the advantage of scale might enjoy economies that later entrants could not hope to match. Safe behind this natural barrier to competitors and reaping learning effects that further entrench their dominant position, early movers could become oligopolists or monopolists in a strategic industry of the future.

Left unmanaged, these attributes of space resources portend coordination challenges and disputes. As global experts have found, the "current lack of coordination mechanisms for lunar activities presents challenges to future missions and could lead to unintentional harmful interference, especially in light of the increased global interest in specific areas like the lunar south pole" (Moon Village Association 2021). Two scenarios by which even a small number of uncoordinated actors at a site of interest could stumble into a dispute are already foreseeable.

A "San Gimignano Towers" Race at the Peaks

The Peaks of Eternal Light are the prime destination for planned lunar missions (Table 35.3). Because these features are concentrated within a tiny area of about 1 square kilometer (Ross et al. 2023), the numerous missions destined for them face foreseeable interference problems (Elvis, Milligan, and Krolikowski 2016).

A particular challenge stems from the fact that towers erected to collect solar power at the peaks will cast long shadows. Even just two towers installed in this area would shadow each other at some point in the lunar day, the problem worsening as new towers are added. Shadowing will reduce the region effectively available for power generation to just a small fraction of the peaks area (Ross et al. 2023). To solve this problem, actors will be tempted to build taller towers. Increasing the elevation of a tower from 20 to 100 meters would yield a predicted 14-fold increase in output (Ross et al. 2023). While activity in the region is confined to small bases, the problem of shadowing interference will remain manageable. However, if actors attempt the extraction of water ice at scale, the problem could grow significant, demanding numerous towers at least 500 meters tall (Kornuta et al. 2019; Ross et al. 2023).

At that time, actors could be compelled to engage in a "San Gimignano" race to build taller and taller towers. In this medieval Tuscan town, dozens of towers were built by the Guelphs and their rivals, the Ghibellines, as each sought to outdo the other with the highest structure. On the moon, an analogous race for height and power would be costly for every participant, leaving all directly worse off, and could generate a construction boom that inflicts lasting environmental damage to the area. A coordination mechanism presents the most promising means to averting this challenge but has yet to be developed.

The First Mineable Asteroid

Most of the resources of the asteroids are tied up in the few largest ones, accessible only during short windows when they approach Earth (Elvis 2021; Jedicke et al. 2018). Within a decade, the asteroids making the best targets for private mining ventures will likely be discovered, launching a contest for who will exploit them. Given the governance deficit in this area, competing mining companies could engage in practices that are illegal on Earth, such as "claim jumping" or "rustling." Because no international regime exists to establish exclusive rights to minerals found on a celestial body, no actor could make an exclusive claim to mine an asteroid.

Absent any changes to this governance vacuum, two mining companies could plausibly send missions to the same small asteroid during the same brief orbital access period. The first mined asteroids will likely be only as large as a football stadium, some 100 meters across. Interference between two competitors targeting the same asteroid would be likely. Kicked-up debris or even a direct encounter could compromise either or both sides' equipment and threaten their entire investment. Either party could claim the other had inflicted harmful interference upon it, citing damages. As these operations would likely have different launching states, both bound by legal provisions on harmful interference, these harms would likely trigger international negotiations. However, without a common set of rules for resource activities, a basis upon which to resolve the dispute would prove elusive.

These two scenarios illustrate that governance mechanisms are needed to avert disputes at certain high-value sites within a mere decade or two. In the short term, actors might devise solutions to coordination problems at specific sites. However, the viability and legitimacy of such solutions ultimately depend on a larger governance framework that would define the nature and conditions of allowable space resource exploitation in the first place. Given foreseeable disputes, in the long term the need for a comprehensive international regime applicable across resource types and locations, grounded in a coherent set of general principles, and legitimate to a broad range of stakeholders is apparent.

The Status Quo of Space Resource Governance: Underdeveloped and Ambiguous

While a consensus has emerged that existing governance arrangements are insufficient to meet the coming challenges of space resource exploitation, the way forward remains uncertain. Insofar as states have agreed to international principles guiding their conduct toward space resources, these are found in the 1967 Outer Space Treaty (OST) (UNGA 1967; see Aoki this volume). Now a half-century old, this framework agreement was developed before commercial space resource exploitation was feasible. The document articulates only general principles for space activities writ large, leaving unspecified how these should apply to space resources, and remains silent on new questions arising from the emergence of private space companies in this area (von der Dunk 2018).

Three main provisions of the treaty are applicable to space resources, each requiring further development before it can serve as a basis upon which to create rules governing specific activities. The most important, Article II, forbids the "national appropriation" of celestial bodies (often understood as the claiming of sovereignty over them or their parts), but does not indicate whether *private* appropriation by commercial entities is allowable. A second provision, found in Article I, states that space exploration and use "shall be carried out for the benefit and in the interests of all countries," but there is as of yet no consensus on a specific mechanism or standard of benefit sharing. Article I also guarantees parties "free access" to celestial bodies but leaves unanswered the question of whether the large-scale recovery of materials for private use would violate this principle. Finally, Article IX creates an obligation for parties to act with "due regard" to the corresponding interests of other states and a duty to engage in consultations about space activities that could cause "potential harmful interference" with the activities of others. However, parties have yet to reach agreement on how this principle should be observed in practice.

Beyond the OST, the international community is divided on the relevance and status of the 1979 Moon Agreement. The agreement commits states to conducting space activities for the "common benefit of mankind," a provision whose interpretation has provoked a schism between major spacefaring states and developing countries. Because no major spacefaring state is a party to the agreement today, it is regarded as defunct, even though its principles are often invoked in international discussions of space resources.

Given these limitations, most states in COPUOS have recognized the need to develop additional governance mechanisms for space resources. In 2021, the body established a working group on space resources to explore the basis for a multilateral agreement. However, this entity will contend with a membership divided.

THE FUTURE OF SPACE RESOURCE GOVERNANCE: PLURAL AND CONTESTED

While all major spacefaring states maintain that any new governance framework for space resources should uphold the OST's principles, they disagree on how these should be developed into practical rules. States are coalescing into two groupings, each pursuing a distinct approach to building a regime. The first, led by the United States, is creating new voluntary "minilateral" mechanisms to support the near-term commercial exploitation of space resources. This approach, US advocates maintain, would not preclude the development of a broader multilateral agreement later. The second grouping, a larger and looser coalition comprising Russia, China, and numerous lesser spacefaring states, refuses to join the US-led process and instead aims to gradually develop a binding multilateral agreement in the long-established COPUOS forum.

States' divergent positions reflect in part the significant early-mover advantages that space resource exploitation presents. Those states with actors (agencies or firms) prepared to enter first, as early as within the next half decade, would benefit from a permissive regime that allows them to establish their dominant position as quickly as possible and with few constraints on their activities. In contrast, those sharing a stake in these common resources, but not prepared to exploit them first, would prefer a restrictive regime that delays the start of exploitation until their own capabilities have caught up to the leaders and that allows them to constrain the activities of early movers so as to minimize the latter's outsized capture of benefits. While a permissive regime would not necessarily leave late-entering states worse off than no regime, it would leave them less well off than early entrants, inflicting relative (though not necessarily absolute) losses.

The United States is arguably poised to benefit first and most from a permissive regime that facilitates commercial space resource exploitation: it has the world's most developed commercial space industry and was home to the first firms with the plans and capital to mine asteroids (though these ultimately failed). The main commercial space firms that would become eventual buyers of space resources, such as private operators of space stations, are also US-based. Moreover, in Artemis, the United States has a substantial national lunar exploration program that stands to benefit from the use of space resources in situ and from partnerships with commercial companies supplying space resources, such as water and regolith. In short, the United States has the most to gain from the quick adoption of rules that explicitly permit civil and commercial exploitation and the private appropriation of space resources.

It is hardly surprising, then, that the United States is spearheading the creation of new international arrangements that would facilitate and legitimize space resource exploitation in general and commercial exploitation in particular, thereby allowing it to entrench its early advantage in this area. The United States has taken steps to formalize international principles and establish rules of conduct toward space resources that would give private companies broad rights to harvest resources from celestial bodies and grant their activities protection from interference. In this endeavor, the United States is joined by other spacefaring states that expect to participate in the Artemis program and, in some cases, to establish their own beachheads in an emerging commercial space resource industry. As space law expert Christopher Johnson explains of the US position, "We're not going to wait to negotiate a treaty that we think is in our national interest . . . We believe we can go to the Moon and use resources there, so therefore we're going to go to the Moon and use resources there" (Grush 2020a).

In contrast to the Artemis partners, other major spacefaring states with far less developed commercial space companies will reap fewer benefits, if any, from the US-proposed arrangements and have opposed them to varying degrees. Russia and China among them, these states will likely be later entrants than the United States to any commercial exploitation business. They are joined by a wide range of lesser spacefaring powers and developing countries that recognize the promise of space resources but lack the capacity to exploit them for the foreseeable future. This loose collection of states seeks to uphold existing institutional arrangements and an interpretation of them that constrains rapid commercial exploitation, proposing instead incremental elaboration of the OST to support the gradual emergence of a more regulated industry. In advocating the consensus-seeking and thus often-paralyzed COPUOS as a forum for negotiating a complex international legal instrument, these states demand a process that would be inclusive and deliberative, but also slow, plodding, and likely to yield a more restrictive set of rules.

States' preferred outcomes reflect their perceived interests in space resource exploitation, which in turn depend on their overarching space policy goals and levels of national capacity. In the following section, we survey the positions and activities of key space-faring states related to space resource governance.

The United States and Its Artemis Partners

The most significant recent effort at developing a regime for governing space resources consists in the US-led Artemis Accords, a minilateral agreement between the United States and other countries on principles for the exploration and use of space resources. Hailed by advocates as no less than "a seminal development in the governance of a new age of space activities," the accords establish the foundations of a permissive space resource regime (Fidler 2020). Since 2020, the number of Artemis signatories joining the United States has climbed to twenty-eight, most of them US-aligned countries (see Table 35.4).

The main spacefaring states among the Artemis partners have the most to gain from quickly establishing a regime facilitating exploitation, and it is their companies that are poised to capture first-mover advantages in this emerging industry. The Artemis program is expected to require space resources to achieve some of its goals, such as establishing a lunar base. Moreover, several private ventures based in partner countries are already developing lunar mining technology, including Lunar Outpost and Masten Space Systems of the United States, ispace of Japan, and ispace Europe of Luxembourg. To kickstart their business and establish a precedent, in 2020 NASA awarded these companies the first-ever contracts for space resources, small awards "to collect space resources and transfer ownership to the agency" by 2024 (Schierholz and Finch 2020; Bridenstine 2020). Other signatories without significant capacity of their own are also drawn to the prospect of joining the Artemis program, to which signing the accords is a precondition (Boley and Byers 2020).

Supporting the emergence of a commercial exploitation industry has been a goal of US policy since 2015, when Congress passed legislation providing that a US citizen engaged in commercial recovery of a space resource shall be entitled to "possess, own, transport, use, and sell" it, subject to the OST (US Congress 2015; Blount and Robison 2016). Luxembourg, the United Arab Emirates, and Japan have since passed similar laws (Khalifa bin Zayed Al Nahyan 2019; Umeda 2021). Following an executive order to "encourage international support for the public and private recovery and use of" space resources, NASA developed a statement of "principles, guidelines, and best practices" for international partners to the Artemis program, forming the basis for the accords (NASA 2020b; Trump 2020).

The accords pave the way for commercial exploitation in several ways. Artemis signatories explicitly interpret the 1967 treaty as permitting the private appropriation of space resources, consistent with US and other national legislation to that effect (NASA 2020b, 4). Moreover, the partners agree to honor the principle of due regard and to refrain from creating "harmful interference" with each other's activities (NASA 2020b, 5). They also commit to developing "safety zones" around installations at sites of interest,

Table 35.4. Major International Agreements Addressing Space Resources

	1967 Outer Space Treaty	1979 Moon Agreement	2020 Artemis Accords
Mode	Multilateral, binding	Multilateral, binding	"Minilateral," non-binding statements of principles
Leading state	N/A	N/A	United States
Parties or signatories	110 states parties (with 89 additional signatories that have not ratified)	Armenia Australia Austria Belgium Chile Kazakhstan Kuwait Lebanon Mexico Morocco Netherlands Pakistan Peru Philippines Saudi Arabia Turkey Uruguay Venezuela	Argentina Australia Bahrain Brazil Canada Colombia Czech Republic Ecuador France Germany India Israel Italy Japan Luxembourg Mexico New Zealand Nigeria Poland Republic of Korea Romania Rwanda Saudi Arabia Singapore Spain Ukraine United Arab Emirates United Kingdom
Total number of parties or signatories	110 states parties	18 states parties	29 signatories

Table is current as of 22 September 2023.

Source: United Nations (n.d.); Kimball (2020); US Department of State, Office of the Spokesperson (2022); NASA (2023).

spaces within which "notification and coordination will be implemented to avoid harmful interference," taking the position that these are compatible with the OST's principle of free access (NASA 2020b, 5–6). Along with provisions encouraging transparency and registration, these measures are intended to avoid coordination failures and other disputes, such as a race at the Peaks and competing efforts to mine an asteroid.

They remain, however, controversial because some could be abused to effectively undermine other actors' free access to sites of interest (Elvis, Milligan, and Krolikowski 2016; Boley and Byers 2020).

The accords are voluntary agreements on principles, rather than binding legal instruments. However, by establishing a record of practice, the accords could influence future governance arrangements. Indeed, as NASA administrator Jim Bridenstine explained of the program to contract for regolith, "What we're trying to do is make sure that there is a norm of behavior that says that resources can be extracted and that we're doing it in a way that is in compliance with the Outer Space Treaty" (Boley and Byers 2020; Foust 2020). However, such a US-driven approach has consistently proven controversial, with experts challenging its legality and implications for sustainability and equity since at least the 2015 US act (Tronchetti 2015; De Man 2017).

Russia

The strongest resistance to the Artemis Accords has come from Russia, a country with plans to recover its status as an important lunar explorer, including through its research station with China. In contrast to the United States, however, Russia currently has no private firms expected to become suppliers to this program or to serve a commercial market for space resources.

The Russian government supports a restrictive regime to govern space resources. Russian officials argue that "universally recognized principles and standards of international space law" and the OST establish that the moon and other celestial bodies "cannot be subject to national appropriation in any way," making no allowance for materials extracted by private entities (Russia 2020a). The Artemis Accords and acts of national legislation that recognize private ownership of extracted resources are, in this view, incompatible with the treaty.

Russian critiques of the Artemis Accords often blur with opposition to the Artemis program itself, which Russia regards as US-led and hegemonic (Grush 2020b). Instead of the accords, the Russian government advocates for broadly multilateral and inclusive efforts at creating a binding international treaty for space resources within the UN system. Russian officials insist that the appropriate forum is COPUOS and stress the value of a "work framework that is fully non-discriminatory and totally devoid of claims to indisputable leadership" (Russia 2020b).

China

Ambitious plans for space exploration give China a significant stake in space resource governance. With several orbiters and rovers launched, Chang'e is the perhaps world's most active lunar program, intended to culminate in taikonaut landings and the research station with Russia in the 2030s. In 2020, Chang'e 5 made China only the third country to ever retrieve a lunar rock sample and the first to do so in over forty years. While China does not have major commercial firms poised to exploit space resources, it is home to a growing private space industry and the government has planned asteroid sample-return missions and reportedly studied the commercial potential of cislunar space.

The Chinese and Russian positions appear similar. US-imposed limits on any bilateral space cooperation with Chinese entities rule out the possibility of China joining the Artemis Accords. Like Russia, the Chinese government advocates a restrictive regime that is legally binding and UN-based. Chinese official media have criticized the Artemis Accords as hegemonic, citing a Russian expert likening the framework to a "space-based NATO" (Deng and Fan 2021). Instead, the Chinese government maintains, COPUOS is the appropriate forum for a broadly multilateral process that should give due regard to the interests of developing countries (China 2021).

India

With its own lunar program, India is an emerging space power that shares a direct stake in space resource governance and among the most recent signatories to the Artemis Accords. On its first mission, India's Chandrayaan program found evidence of water on the moon and its next mission will send a rover to study water traces and cold traps (ISRO 2022). Although Indian statements about space resource governance have been few, the country's long-standing commitment to UN-based processes and solidarity with developing countries suggested that it might prefer a COPUOS-based approach to space resource governance. In 2021, however, the Modi government signaled a new readiness to work with Washington on "setting new global norms to manage space, including rules for commercial competition" and a new liberalization of the sector to private companies (Mohan 2021). Amid this reorientation, in 2023 India formally joined the Artemis Accords (NASA 2023).

Minor Spacefaring States and Developing Countries

A large set of lesser spacefaring states and developing countries with smaller space programs, encompassing countries as diverse as Austria and Ethiopia, has advocated for a relatively restrictive regime for space resources. For the most part, these states have neither large civil programs nor private companies prepared to engage in near-term exploitation. Many advocate developing a legal regime for governing space resources through a multilateral process within COPUOS, starting with the working group (Austria et al. 2021). These states affirm the centrality of the OST and several stress the interests of developing countries in operationalizing the principles of equity and "common benefit." Many also advocate an expansive understanding of the "free access" principle at odds with proposals for safety zones or other forms of exclusion on celestial bodies.

Non-governmental Actors

Academic and other experts have contributed distinct perspectives on space resource governance, endorsing both permissive and restrictive regime elements. The most prominent is The Hague International Space Resources Governance Working Group, which aimed to define conceptual building blocks for a regime (Neto et al. 2020). International experts have also proposed the Vancouver Recommendations on Space Mining (Outer Space Institute 2020). And the Global Expert Group on Sustainable Lunar Activities convenes to consult on policy issues related to lunar missions (Moon Village Association 2021). These various contributions in general allow for the possibility of private appropriation and safety zones, but do not define what form implementing governance arrangements should take. In parallel to these initiatives, a growing chorus of experts is critical of plans for commercial exploitation, grounding their skepticism in environmental ethics and postcolonial theory (Tavares et al. 2021).

LONG-RUN IMPLICATIONS FOR SPACE SECURITY

Despite these various efforts at articulating a vision for space resource governance that would attract global support, a rift is forming between key state actors. The US-led Artemis coalition's stance is at odds with the Russian position, which finds a degree of support in China and numerous minor spacefaring states. Rather than abate, this schism is likely to grow more pronounced with the deterioration in Russia's relations with the United States and Europe resulting from the 2022 Russian invasion of Ukraine. If parallel efforts continue under the auspices of both Artemis and COPUOS, a plausible outcome is a fragmented and contested global landscape of institutions governing space resource exploitation.

A principal challenge to the development of space resource governance lies in states' vastly different levels of capacity and the early-mover advantages in exploitation. Most states are still developing basic space capabilities and thus have nothing to lose and perhaps something to gain from the slow global deliberation of a restrictive set of rules. The Artemis partners, however, would benefit most from an expeditious process and permissive rules. Rooted in fundamental differences, this cleavage will not be easily overcome, portending the fragmentation of COPUOS or even the larger international regime governing outer space affairs into two camps.

International cleavages may sharpen further as the value of the resources at stake comes into clearer view. Technological advances enabling new forms of access and recovery, alongside improved characterizations of resources, could either alleviate the scarcities we currently perceive in accessible space resources or bring new sites and materials within the sphere of competition between actors. In this respect, crucial enabling technologies will likely include efficient transportation systems, dexterous in-situ extraction tools, and advanced prospecting devices.

Finally, we can expect international competition and cooperation on space re-source issues to interact with developments on Earth in complex ways. Space-derived materials could either relieve terrestrial scarcities or bring gluts to terrestrial markets for important commodities, such as platinum. As the strategic value of cislunar space grows, governments may increase their support to commercial lunar resource ventures, backing their national champions. They could also establish public initiatives, such as long-term scientific missions to study sites of interest, for the sake of maintaining an active presence in these environments. In these respects, the politics of space resources, though contingent upon the physical distribution of materials and features on accessible celestial bodies, will remain intertwined with economic and security considerations on Earth.

REFERENCES

Austria, Belgium, Czech Republic, Finland, Germany, Greece, Poland, et al. 2021. "The Establishment of a Working Group on Potential Legal Models for Activities in Exploration, Exploitation and Utilization of Space Resources." A/AC.105/C.2/2021/CRP.22. Vienna, Austria: Committee on the Peaceful Uses of Outer Space (COPUOS), Legal Subcommittee.

Blount, P. J., and Christian J. Robison. 2016. "One Small Step: The Impact of the U.S. Commercial Space Launch Competitiveness Act of 2015 on the Exploitation of Resources in Outer Space." *North Carolina Journal of Law & Technology* 18: 160. https://heinonline.org/HOL/Page?handle=hein.journals/ncjl18&id=175&div=&collection=.

Boley, Aaron, and Michael Byers. 2020. "U.S. Policy Puts the Safe Development of Space at Risk." *Science* 370, no. 6513: 174–75. https://doi.org/10.1126/science.abd3402.

Bridenstine, Jim. 2020. "Space Resources Are the Key to Safe and Sustainable Lunar Exploration—Former NASA Administrator Jim Bridenstine." NASA Blogs. September 10, 2020. https://blogs.nasa.gov/bridenstine/2020/09/10/space-resources-are-the-key-to-safe-and-sustainable-lunar-exploration/.

China. 2021. "The Establishment of a Working Group on Potential Legal Models for Activities in Exploration, Exploitation and Utilization of Space Resources." A/AC.105/C.2/2021/CRP.18. Vienna, Austria: Committee on the Peaceful Uses of Outer Space (COPUOS), Legal Subcommittee.

Crawford, Ian A. 2015. "Lunar Resources: A Review." *Progress in Physical Geography* 39, no. 2: 137–67. https://doi.org/10.1177/0309133314567585.

De Man, Philip. 2017. "Luxembourg Law on Space Resources Rests on Contentious Relationship with International Framework." Working Paper No. 189. Leuven, Belgium: KU Leuven. https://ghum.kuleuven.be/ggs/publications/working_papers/2017/189deman.

Deng, Xiaoci, and Anqi Fan. 2021. "Exclusive: China, Russia to Sign New 5-Year Space Cooperation Program, Build Intl Lunar Station by 2035: Roscosmos." *Global Times*. December 9, 2021. https://www.globaltimes.cn/page/202112/1243731.shtml.

Dunk, Frans G. von der. 2018. "Asteroid Mining: International and National Legal Aspects." *Michigan State International Law Review* 26: 83. https://heinonline.org/HOL/Page?handle=hein.journals/mistjintl26&id=93&div=&collection=.

Elvis, Martin. 2014. "How Many Ore-Bearing Asteroids?" *Planetary and Space Science* 91: 20–26.

Elvis, Martin. 2021. *Asteroids: How Love, Fear, and Greed Will Determine Our Future in Space*. New Haven, CT: Yale University Press.

Elvis, Martin, Alanna Krolikowski, and Tony Milligan. 2021. "Concentrated Lunar Resources: Imminent Implications for Governance and Justice." *Philosophical Transactions of the Royal Society A: Mathematical, Physical and Engineering Sciences* 379, no. 2188: 1–21. https://doi.org/10.1098/rsta.2019.0563.

Elvis, Martin, Tony Milligan, and Alanna Krolikowski. 2016. "The Peaks of Eternal Light: A near-Term Property Issue on the Moon." *Space Policy* 38: 30–38. http://www.sciencedirect.com/science/article/pii/S0265964616300194.

Fidler, David P. 2020. "The Artemis Accords and the Next Generation of Outer Space Governance." Council on Foreign Relations. June 2, 2020. https://www.cfr.org/blog/artemis-accords-and-next-generation-outer-space-governance.

Fioretos, Orfeo, and Jonas Tallberg. 2021. "Politics and Theory of Global Governance." *International Theory* 13, no. 1: 99–111. https://doi.org/10.1017/S1752971920000408.

Foust, Jeff. 2020. "NASA Offers to Buy Lunar Samples to Set Space Resources Precedent." *SpaceNews*. September 10, 2020. https://spacenews.com/nasa-offers-to-buy-lunar-samples-to-set-space-resources-precedent/.

Grush, Loren. 2020a. "NASA Announces International Artemis Accords to Standardize How to Explore the Moon." *The Verge*. May 15, 2020. https://www.theverge.com/2020/5/15/21259946/nasa-artemis-accords-lunar-exploration-moon-outer-space-treaty.

Grush, Loren. 2020b. "Head of Russian Space Program Calls for More International Cooperation in NASA's Moon Plans." *The Verge*. October 12, 2020. https://www.theverge.com/2020/10/12/21512712/nasa-roscosmos-russia-dmitry-rogozin-artemis-moon-interntational-cooperation.

ISRO. 2022. "Chandrayaan 2." Indian Space Research Organisation (ISRO). 2022. https://www.isro.gov.in/chandrayaan2-home-0.

Jedicke, Robert, Mikael Granvik, Marco Micheli, Eileen Ryan, Timothy Spahr, and Donald K. Yeomans. 2015. "Surveys, Astrometric Follow-up, and Population Statistics." In *Asteroids IV*, edited by Patrick Michel, Francesca E. DeMeo, and William F. Bottke, 795–813. Tucson: University of Arizona Press.

Jedicke, Robert, Joel Sercel, Jeffrey Gillis-Davis, Karen J. Morenz, and Leslie Gertsch. 2018. "Availability and Delta-v Requirements for Delivering Water Extracted from Near-Earth Objects to Cis-Lunar Space." *Planetary and Space Science* 159: 28–42. https://doi.org/10.1016/j.pss.2018.04.005.

Khalifa bin Zayed Al Nahyan. 2019. "Federal Law No. (12) of 2019 on the Regulation of the Space Sector." United Arab Emirates. https://www.moj.gov.ae/assets/2020/Federal%20Law%20No%2012%20of%202019%20on%20THE%20REGULATION%20OF%20THE%20SPACE%20SECTOR.pdf.aspx.

Kim, Kyeong J., Christian Wöhler, Alexey A. Berezhnoy, Megha Bhatt, and Arne Grumpe. 2019. "Prospective 3He-Rich Landing Sites on the Moon." *Planetary and Space Science* 177: 104686. https://doi.org/10.1016/j.pss.2019.07.001.

Kimball, Daryl. 2020. "The Outer Space Treaty at a Glance." Arms Control Association. October 2020. https://www.armscontrol.org/factsheets/outerspace.

Kornuta, David, Angel Abbud-Madrid, Jared Atkinson, Jonathan Barr, Gary Barnhard, Dallas Bienhoff, Brad Blair, et al. 2019. "Commercial Lunar Propellant Architecture: A Collaborative Study of Lunar Propellant Production." *REACH* 13: 100026. https://doi.org/10.1016/j.reach.2019.100026.

Krasner, Stephen D. 1982. "Structural Causes and Regime Consequences: Regimes as Intervening Variables." *International Organization* 36, no. 2: 185–205. https://doi.org/10.1017/S0020818300018920.

Krolikowski, Alanna, and Martin Elvis. 2019. "Marking Policy for New Asteroid Activities: In Pursuit of Science, Settlement, Security, or Sales?" *Space Policy* 47: 7–17. https://doi.org/10.1016/j.spacepol.2018.04.005.

Mohan, C. Raja. 2021. "India's Space Program Inches Closer to America and the Quad." Foreign Policy (blog). October 13, 2021. https://foreignpolicy.com/2021/10/13/india-modi-space-program/.

Moon Village Association. 2021. "Report of the Moon Village Association on the Global Expert Group on Sustainable Lunar Activities." A/AC.105/C.1/2021/CRP.20. Vienna, Austria: Committee on the Peaceful Uses of Outer Space (COPUOS), Scientific and Technical Subcommittee.

NASA (U.S. National Aeronautics and Space Administration). 2023. "The Artemis Accords." NASA. https://www.nasa.gov/specials/artemis-accords/index.html.

NASA. 2020a. "Artemis Plan: NASA's Lunar Exploration Program Overview." Washington, DC: U.S. National Aeronautics and Space Administration (NASA). https://www.nasa.gov/sites/default/files/atoms/files/artemis_plan-20200921.pdf.

NASA. 2020b. "The Artemis Accords: Principles for Cooperation in the Civil Exploration and Use of the Moon, Mars, Comets, and Asteroids for Peaceful Purposes." U.S. National Aeronautics and Space Administration (NASA). https://www.nasa.gov/specials/artemis-accords/img/Artemis-Accords-signed-13Oct2020.pdf.

NASA (U.S. National Aeronautics and Space Administration). 2020c. "Lunar Living: NASA's Artemis Base Camp Concept." NASA. October 28, 2020. https://blogs.nasa.gov/artemis/2020/10/28/lunar-living-nasas-artemis-base-camp-concept/.

Neto, Olavo de Oliveira Bittencourt, Mahulena Hofmann, Tanja L. Masson-Zwaan, and Dimitra Stefoudi. 2020. *Building Blocks for the Development of an International Framework for the Governance of Space Resource Activities: A Commentary.* The Hague, The Netherlands: Eleven International Publishing. https://boeken.rechtsgebieden.boomportaal.nl/publicaties/9789462361218#152.

Outer Space Institute. 2020. "Vancouver Recommendations on Space Mining." Vancouver, Canada: Outer Space Institute. http://www.outerspaceinstitute.ca/docs/Vancouver_Recommendations_on_Space_Mining.pdf.

Raymond, Mark. 2019. *Social Practices of Rule-Making in World Politics.* New York: Oxford University Press.

Ross, Amia, Sephora Ruppert, Philipp Gläser, and Martin Elvis. 2023. "Towers on the Peaks of Eternal Light: Quantifying the Available Solar Power." Manuscript in preparation.

Russia. 2020a. "Comment by the Information and Press Department on the US President's Executive Order on Encouraging International Support for the Recovery and Use of Space Resources." 550-07-04–2020. Moscow, Russia: Ministry of Foreign Affairs of the Russian Federation.

Russia. 2020b. "Deputy Foreign Minister Sergey Ryabkov's Interview with the International Life Magazine, April 17, 2020." 592-20-04–2020. Moscow, Russia: Ministry of Foreign Affairs of the Russian Federation.

Schierholz, Stephanie, and Josh Finch. 2020. "NASA Selects Companies to Collect Lunar Resources for Artemis." NASA. December 3, 2020. http://www.nasa.gov/press-release/nasa-selects-companies-to-collect-lunar-resources-for-artemis-demonstrations.

Swiney, Gabriel, and Amanda Hernandez. 2022. "Lunar Landing and Operations Policy Analysis" U.S. National Aeronautics and Space Administration, Office of Technology, Policy, and Strategy. https://www.nasa.gov/sites/default/files/atoms/files/lunar_landing_and_operations_policy_analysis_final_report_24oct2022_tagged_0.pdf.

Tavares, Frank, Denise Buckner, Dana Burton, Jordan McKaig, Parvathy Prem, Eleni Ravanis, Natalie Trevino, et al. 2021. "Ethical Exploration and the Role of Planetary Protection in Disrupting Colonial Practices." *Bulletin of the AAS* 53, no. 4. https://doi.org/10.3847/25c2c feb.cdc2f798.

Tronchetti, Fabio. 2015. "The Space Resource Exploration and Utilization Act: A Move Forward or a Step Back?" *Space Policy* 34: 6–10. https://doi.org/10.1016/j.spacepol.2015.08.001.

Trump, Donald J. 2020. "Executive Order 13914 of April 6, 2020: Encouraging International Support for the Recovery and Use of Space Resources." Federal Register. https://www.fede ralregister.gov/documents/2020/04/10/2020-07800/encouraging-international-support-for-the-recovery-and-use-of-space-resources.

Umeda, Sayuri. 2021. "Japan: Space Resources Act Enacted." Global Legal Monitor. Library of Congress. https://www.loc.gov/item/global-legal-monitor/2021-09-15/japan-space-resour ces-act-enacted/.

UNGA. 1967. "Outer Space Treaty (Treaty on Principles Governing the Activities of States in the Exploration and Use of Outer Space, Including the Moon and Other Celestial Bodies)." United Nations General Assembly (UNGA). http://www.unoosa.org/oosa/en/ourwork/spacelaw/treaties/introouterspacetreaty.html.

United Nations. n.d. "2. Agreement Governing the Activities of States on the Moon and Other Celestial Bodies." United Nations Treaty Collection. https://treaties.un.org/pages/ViewDeta ils.aspx?src=TREATY&mtdsg_no=XXIV-2&chapter=24&clang=_en.

US Congress. 2015. U.S. Commercial Space Launch Competitiveness Act. Vol. 129 Stat. 704. https://www.congress.gov/114/plaws/publ90/PLAW-114publ90.pdf.

US Department of State, Office of the Spokesperson. 2022. "France Becomes Twentieth Nation to Sign the Artemis Accords." Washington, DC: U.S. Department of State. https://www.state.gov/france-becomes-twentieth-nation-to-sign-the-artemis-accords/.

Voosen, Paul. 2021. "The Coming Lunar Armada." *Science* 373, no. 6560: 1188–92. https://doi.org/10.1126/science.acx9028.

Weiss, Thomas G., and Rorden Wilkinson. 2014. "Rethinking Global Governance? Complexity, Authority, Power, Change." *International Studies Quarterly* 58, no. 1: 207–15. https://doi.org/10.1111/isqu.12082.

Zürn, Michael. 2018. *A Theory of Global Governance: Authority, Legitimacy, and Contestation.* Oxford: Oxford University Press.

CHAPTER 36

....

SPACE-BASED DATA AND HUMAN SECURITY

....

MARIEL BOROWITZ

INTRODUCTION

....

SPEAKING at the international seminar "Space Futures and Human Security" in 1997, the former secretary general of UNISPACE-82, Yash Pal, recounted the many new developments of the space age, but then challenged the audience to "tell me honestly if humans at large are more secure now than they used to be; are they happier?" His own conclusion was that things were "a wee bit" better, but that the improvements could have been much more significant. Asking the same question today—twenty-five years later— would likely result in a similar answer. This paper examines how the underlying power structures, particularly the dominance of national space programs, has limited the development and application of Earth observation technology to issues of human security, and how trends toward open data policies and commercial remote sensing are changing this dynamic.

Human security takes the individual, rather than the state, as the primary focus of security efforts. It includes ensuring humans have both "freedom from fear" and "freedom from want." The Human Development Report 1994 identified seven elements that comprise human security, including economic security, food security, health security, environmental security, personal security, community security, and political security (UNDP 1994).

Data gathered by Earth observing satellites clearly has the potential to contribute significantly to efforts to improve human security across its many dimensions, and many new and relevant applications have been developed. However, rather than provide a laundry list of programs and efforts, it is important to understand where—and why— this technology is not contributing as fully as it could be. To examine this issue, I first provide an overview of the current capabilities of Earth observation satellites and the applications of satellite data and applications to human security issues. How does the inherently global perspective of satellites align with the focus on the individual required by human security? How, or to what extent, can Earth observing technology be used to address human security issues?

I then focus on the actors involved in this area—particularly the entities that own Earth observing satellites and the resulting data and those who use and benefit from Earth observing satellite data. This framework highlights the important intersections between technological capability and traditional power structures, particularly the ways in which the state-centric nature of space activity affects the development and application of this technology to issues of human security.

Space activity is still largely dominated by states, which are concerned with national priorities, including national security, that may or may not align with human security efforts. Economic priorities have led to the growth of the commercial remote sensing sector, which introduces new and different incentives, albeit not necessarily ones that are better aligned to human security. Understanding the goals of these actors is important because the owners of the satellites set the agenda in terms of which technologies will be developed, what types of data will be collected, and what types of issues can most easily be addressed. The owners of these assets also set the rules regarding who may access the data.

While satellite owners play an important role, we must also consider those who access and use the data. There has been a global trend toward free and open provision of satellite data. Combined with increased prevalence of data analysis tools and training, this has helped to greatly expand the number and type of individuals and organizations that make use of satellite data. These changes in the user community create new centers of power that can generate knowledge and applications from satellite data better aligned with the needs of individuals. While these trends operate globally, there are persistent differences in the capabilities of actors in different nations around the world to access and utilize satellite data. This "digital divide" results in enduring disparities in the ability of individuals in different locations to contribute to human security.

Through an examination of these issues, this paper seeks to understand how Earth observing satellites are contributing to human security and the ways in which they are falling short. This analysis also points to changes in institutions and policies that would increase the contributions that space assets make to human security.

Human Security and the Role of State and Non-state Actors

The concept of human security seeks to emphasize the importance of security for the individual. As stated in the United Nations Development Program report that first popularized the concept: "In the final analysis, human security is a child who did not die, a disease that did not spread, a job that was not cut, an ethnic tension that did not explode into violence, a dissident who was not silenced." Rather than focusing on military interactions among states, it focuses on the many dimensions of security (e.g., economic, health, environmental) that directly impact individuals. However, it also recognizes that these concepts are interconnected. "Without peace, there may be no development. But without development, peace is threatened" (UNDP 1994). Just as conflict can result in negative impacts on individuals, challenges of human security (food insecurity, environmental change, etc.) can lead to instability and violence.

Human security not only centers the individual as the focus of security efforts, but also identifies the individual and other non-state organizations as security actors, able to influence and improve their own security (UNDP 1994). However, as the concept has developed and been adopted by international organizations and states, some have once again centered the state as the primary provider of human security. This debate about the role of actors at different levels—and particularly the role of state vs. non-state actors—has been central to the evolution of the concept of human security. Who decides what human security issues deserve attention and how these issues should be addressed? Who has the power to design and implement solutions to human security challenges? (Gjørv 2018).

Thomas and Tow (2002) argue that human security is particularly useful in transnational challenges, including identifying needs for humanitarian intervention. Under this conception, states can use the concept of human security to guide their actions. By contrast, Bellamy and McDonald (2002) see such a use of the concept as counter to the goals of human security, suggesting that it threatens to shift the focus back to a state-centric interpretation and prioritization of security, losing the essential focus on the individual. They identify a conflict between a focus on national security and one on human security—arguing that states are often the cause of human security challenges, making them poor candidates for addressing such issues.

Constructivist scholars, such as Martha Finnemore (1996), emphasize that national interest is influenced by international norms, which are themselves influenced by the preferences and actions of international organizations and other actors. Edward Newman (2001) argues that human security is best explained within this context: evolving transnational norms have given rise to this new concept of security. He argues that a multitude of actors—including civil society and commercial organizations—are contributing to this evolving concept on the international stage. Similarly, Yu-tai Tsai (2009) argues that with constructivism as a theoretical basis, we can focus on the shaping of knowledge in the international community, with conceptual understandings of human security being defined and shaped from the individual to society. This process could enable the realization of the concept of human security within the international community.

The human security concept illuminates a tension in the balance of power between the state and the society that operates both across and within nations. States with more resources may be able to set the priorities among human security issues—most likely in ways that align with their own national strategic goals. Similarly, individuals within states with more resources are likely to have an outsized influence on defining the human security agenda. This paper explores these issues within the context of the space sector. I look at the technical capabilities of Earth observing satellites and their ability to contribute to human security challenges. I then investigate the role of state and non-state actors in developing and applying these capabilities to understand how the agendas of satellite owners and satellite data users affect the application of satellite data to human security challenges.

Capabilities of Earth Observation Satellites and Human Security Applications

Satellites, by their nature, offer a global perspective, gathering data without consideration of political boundaries on the Earth. In addition to providing a great deal of data relevant to individual nations or regions, they offer a unique capability to collect comprehensive data relevant to areas not governed by a single nation, such as the oceans, the Arctic, and the Antarctic. They can collect data from visible or non-visible portions of the electromagnetic spectrum, and—with radar systems—they can collect information about the Earth at night and through clouds. Space technologies have been developed that measure minute differences in Earth's gravity, providing insight into resources below the surface.

While satellites typically capture large-scale geographic phenomena, rather than data on the scale of an individual, the global nature of the technology lends itself well to addressing challenges outside the realm of national politics and more aligned with those of human security. This can include large-scale transnational phenomena, such as climate change, regional droughts, or economic development. The norm of free overflight also means that satellites can be used to observe and identify developments within a nation that the observed state cannot efficiently observe, or would not disclose, on its own, such as illegal logging or ethnic violence. The relevance of Earth observing satellites to issues of human security are clear from the vast number of applications that have already been developed. While this paper will not attempt to comprehensively address all relevant applications, the following discussion provides illustrative examples.

As noted earlier, the Human Development Report 1994 identified seven elements that comprise human security: economic security, food security, health security, environmental security, personal security, community security, and political security (UNDP 1994). While other definitions have been proposed to align with various theoretical frameworks, the categories used in this founding document align well with an examination of practical applications and present a reasonable framework for thinking about the relevance of space technology to human security. This section looks at each in turn.

Economic Security: Assuring economic security requires that individuals have an assured basic income. Individuals lose economic security if they are unemployed, underemployed, or in a precarious employment position (UNDP 1994). While it is not possible to directly measure unemployment with satellites, "night lights" data collected by satellites has been used to estimate economic output, including changes over time (Gibson, Olivia, and Boe-Gibson 2020; Donaldson and Storeygard 2016). Analysis of landcover changes and settlement types based on satellite data have also been used to estimate the economic status of populations within a city or region (Bhaduri et al. 2019). As a whole, the field of economics has been steadily increasing its use of satellite data to better understand economic challenges (Florio and Morretta 2021).

Food Security: Food security requires that everyone has enough to eat—ready physical and economic access to food (UNDP 1994). This has long been an area in which satellite data has proven useful. Many applications have been developed that monitor agricultural development around the world (Nakalembe et al. 2021). Some applications use this data to provide information and services directly to farmers, overlapping with the goals of economic security above (Dash 2019). Others target decision-makers at the government level. For example, the US Agency for International Development has operated the Famine Early Warning System Network (FEWS NET) for more than thirty years. The system, developed in partnership with the National Aeronautics and Space Administration (NASA), makes extensive use of satellite data to identify droughts, flooding, and other environmental conditions that may lead to food insecurity, combines this information with other relevant data, and provides warnings to users around the world (Brown and Brickley 2012).

Health Security: Communicable diseases, including malaria, tuberculosis, and diarrheal diseases remain among the top ten causes of death in low-income countries (WHO 2019). (Although it is worth noting that deaths from these causes have decreased significantly over time.) Once again, this is an area in which applications based on satellite data have proliferated. Vector-borne diseases, such as malaria, are associated with environmental conditions in which disease vectors (mosquitos in the case of malaria) proliferate. Satellite data has been used to identify those conditions and provide advanced warning that can be used to target interventions. (Rogers et al. 2002). Satellite data has also been used to locate settlements in remote areas, assisting in providing medical services, including vaccinations (Barau et al. 2014). During the Ebola outbreak in 2014–2015, satellite data was critical for planning personnel deployment and identifying likely infection routes (Peckham and Sinha 2017).

Environmental Security: Humans require access to clean water, clean air, and a safe and clean environment. Pollution, severe weather, natural disasters, and climate-induced changes can threaten environmental security. Clearly this is an area in which Earth observing satellites—sometimes referred to as environmental satellites—have much to contribute. Satellite data is used to monitor water quality, air pollution, deforestation, desertification, ocean temperature, wildfires, drought, floods, landslides, hurricanes, biodiversity, and a host of other important environmental conditions (Wentz and Schabel 2000; Smith et al. 2020; Holloway, Jacob, and Miller 2018; Petrescu et al. 2018). In many cases, satellites provide a unique capability to monitor and understand these environmental phenomena, providing data that could not be collected as consistently or comprehensively with any other technology.

Personal Security: Personal security focuses on individuals' security from physical violence. Such violence can occur due to war, or it may be perpetrated by other groups or individuals within the state and related to issues such as crime, domestic abuse, child abuse, suicide, and drug use (UNDP 1994). Satellite data has long been used to provide reconnaissance and intelligence prior to and during warfare. While these assets may be used for planning and targeting attacks, improved reconnaissance and intelligence can also help to minimize the effects of war on non-combatant populations, as military leaders can more accurately locate military or industrial targets, rather than population centers. The transparency offered by reconnaissance satellites may also decrease the likelihood of conflict overall (Early and Gartzke 2021). Satellite imagery can also provide a level of transparency during conflict, allowing those outside the affected area to be aware of impacts (Casana and Laugier 2017). There is also ongoing research into whether satellite data can play a role in identifying areas at risk of crime (Wolfe and Mennis 2012).

Community Security: Community security involves avoiding incidences of ethnic violence or violence against indigenous peoples (UNDP 1994). Satellite data has been used to identify and raise awareness of Uighur "re-education" camps in China (Stern 2021). Research has also made use of satellite data to understand factors that contribute to the likelihood of ethnic violence (De Juan 2015; Rohner, Thoenig, and Zilibotti 2013).

Political Security: Finally, political security requires that individuals live in a society that honors their basic human rights. State repression, including human rights violations, is particularly prevalent during times of political instability. Political instability is also associated with a lack of freedom of the press (UNDP 1994). Satellite data can provide an important source of transparency, allowing the world to visualize and understand what is happening within a nation, even if activities are not publicly acknowledged. In addition to the case of the Uighur camps mentioned above, data has been used to monitor internal violence in Syria, Sudan, and other locations (Levinger 2009; Ri et al. 2019).

These examples clearly demonstrate that satellite data has broad applicability across the core concerns of human security. The global perspective of space-based systems lends itself well to an approach that seeks to look beyond the role of the state. This unique aspect of the space environment was recognized early in the space age. The preamble of the Treaty on Principles Governing the Activities of States in the Exploration and Use of Outer Space, including the Moon and Other Celestial Bodies (the Outer Space Treaty), which entered into force in 1967, states that the "exploration and use of outer space should be carried out for the benefit of all peoples irrespective of the degree of their economic or scientific development" (UN 1967). In 1999, the Vienna Declaration on Space and Human Development specifically called out the importance of using space applications for human security, including applications relevant to weather and climate forecasting; controlling infectious disease; and natural disaster mitigation, relief, and preventions (UN 1999).

It is also clear from these examples that space applications are much more prevalent in some areas of human security than others. This can be explained, in part, by differences in technical capabilities. Satellites are particularly well suited to directly address environmental security challenges, while economic security issues, for example, require more creative use of satellite data, often in combination with other data. However, some of the variation reflects purposeful differences in the types of satellite technologies and related applications that receive funding and support by satellite developers and owners. Therefore, I now turn to a discussion of the actors involved in satellite development and applications.

STATE AND NON-STATE ACTORS: SATELLITE OWNERS

As noted already, satellite owners "set the agenda," in a sense, by making decisions regarding which satellites will be built and what types of data they will collect. A multitude of design decisions determine the applications to which satellites are best aligned. Satellites can be placed in polar orbits, circling the Earth nearly perpendicular to the equator, to ensure they will provide full global coverage. Alternatively, less highly inclined satellites focus their coverage on equatorial zones of the Earth. Satellites placed in a geostationary orbit can continuously monitor a particular region, with only a handful of satellites needed to provide persistent global coverage.

Satellites can be optimized to provide high spatial resolution—making it possible to distinguish small objects on the ground. Very precise satellites are particularly valuable for surveillance and reconnaissance, while satellites with less precision are often sufficient for monitoring the types of large-scale changes associated with climate change. Satellites can collect data in different portions of the electromagnetic spectrum and may offer very high spectral or radiometric resolution, making it easier to determine the types of objects or materials on the ground. These choices affect whether satellites collect data about the Earth surface, as opposed to atmospheric conditions, soil moisture, or other aspects of the environment invisible to the naked eye. By adding additional satellites, developers may improve the temporal resolution of their constellation, making it possible to revisit the same location more frequently, and identify changes occurring on shorter timescales.

Advanced or unique technologies can be deployed on satellites—including radar technologies and gravity-monitoring technologies—that enable satellites to collect data about the Earth at night or in cloudy conditions, or even enable the collection of information about resources below the Earth's surface. And new technologies and capabilities will surely be developed in the future, allowing new applications. These design decisions—and the applications a satellite is optimized for—are made by the satellite owner. Thus, in an important way, the satellite owner "sets the agenda," determining which issues deserve attention. For this reason, it is important that we examine who owns the Earth observing satellites operating in orbit and seek to understand how these actors determine which satellites to build.

Distribution of Earth Observing Satellites by Owner

According to the Union of Concerned Scientists Satellite Database, as of September 2021 there were 4,550 operational satellites in orbit around the Earth. A review of the database shows that about a quarter of these, 1,028, are Earth observation satellites. About half of the Earth observation satellites in orbit are owned or operated by governments, while the other half are commercial. The number of government satellites is approximately evenly split between civil and military satellites. University developed satellites make up a small percentage of satellites on orbit (Figure 36.1; UCS 2021).

The owners and operators of these satellites come from 59 different countries (Figure 36.2). However, just a few of those play a particularly large role. China and the United States dominate in terms of government satellites, accounting for 35 percent and 20 percent of these satellites, respectively. Russia operates about 7 percent of government satellites currently in orbit. The European Space Agency (ESA), Japan, and India also have relatively large Earth observation programs. There are more than 100 entities operating commercial remote sensing satellites, but the vast majority of commercial satellites are developed in the United States (69 percent) and China (14 percent). France, Japan, the United Kingdom, and others host just a few such satellites (UCS 2021).

It is worth noting that simply looking at the number of satellites can be misleading—one large, advanced satellite may generate more or higher quality data than a constellation of one hundred simple satellites—and thus be much more capable of contributing

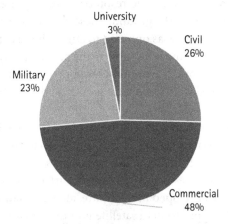

FIGURE 36.1 Earth observation satellites in orbit by owner-type, September 2021.

Source: UCS (2021).

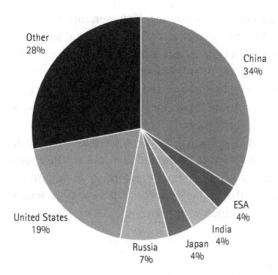

FIGURE 36.2 Government-owned earth observation satellites in orbit by nation, September 2021.

Source: UCS (2021).

to human security. However, these numbers are still useful as a first cut in understanding key actors in satellite Earth observations.

Next, to gain insight into how these satellite owners and operators affect the ability to address human security, we need to understand the process these entities use to determine which satellites to build (and the applications to which they will be best suited) and the policy governing access to data collected by these satellites. Within a state, Earth observation satellites are developed and operated by particular agencies, each with different missions, priorities, and development processes.

Military Satellites

In many of the states with the largest space programs, a significant portion of their Earth observation satellites are military systems. Specifically, in the United States, Japan, China, and Russia, at least half of all government Earth observation satellites are dedicated to military or intelligence missions. In India, military and intelligence missions make up about one third of national Earth observation systems. ESA is an outlier in this regard; its missions are exclusively civil in nature. This is due to the nature of the organization, which does not have a military mandate. European military and intelligence satellite missions are typically developed and owned by individual nations (UCS 2021).

These are systems developed by the military and used for military applications—directly contributing to the national security goals and strategic capabilities of the nations that own them. Nations with a large number of military space assets are much more able to leverage this technology for national security purposes, with significant imbalances in capabilities across nations. However, military and reconnaissance satellites are developed to achieve relatively narrow national security goals, utilizing high-resolution or radar imagery to detect military developments of potential adversaries or infrared sensors to detect missile launches. While some of these missions may contribute to personal security if they are used to help prevent war or to minimize collateral damage during war, for the most part these satellites are not designed to—and do not—contribute to human security goals.

Furthermore, the data collected by these satellites is typically classified and not made available to users outside of the military and intelligence communities, which further limits the ability of these systems to contribute to human security. This lack of access exacerbates imbalances between the state's ability to leverage space capabilities compared to that of individuals within society.

Civil Satellites

Approximately 260 Earth observation satellites on orbit, 25 percent of all Earth observation satellites, are owned and operated by civil government agencies. Like military satellites, as government owned satellites, these must be aligned with national priorities. However, the nations involved in these activities, the individuals and entities involved in mission selection, offer significantly more opportunities for involvement than military systems.

Many of the nations with the largest programs have multiple agencies involved in satellite development. For example, China, the United States, Russia, India, Japan, and Europe all have both space agencies and separate agencies that develop and operate meteorological satellites. The meteorological agencies typically prioritize continuity with respect to these operational assets, ensuring continuous weather-monitoring capabilities. These satellites play an important role in environmental security, providing critical data for forecasting hurricanes, floods, and other natural disasters. Data sharing from weather satellites is quite widespread across nations and is often freely available to all users (Borowitz 2017).

Most nations also have programs focused on scientific satellite development. These may incorporate direct input from the scientific community. For example, NASA periodically brings together the scientific community as part of a "decadal survey" to determine the highest priorities for Earth science missions in the next decade (Charo and Abdalati 2018). However, while this process is meant to ensure that scientists play the key role in mission prioritization, the results are still subject to political priorities, and differences in Earth science initiatives and funding are clear across different political administrations (Reardon et al. 2017).

Many other nations develop Earth observation strategies through a more government-centric process. ESA's Earth observation program aims to respond to "societal challenges such as food, water, energy, climate, and civil security." ESA also cooperates closely with the European Union on its Copernicus program, which aims to provide operational capabilities to monitor the Earth and provide data relevant to decision-makers. Central to the program is a "full, free, and open" data policy, which aims to support entrepreneurship and maximize socioeconomic benefits associated with space systems (Aschbacher 2017).

China's White Paper on Space Activities, released in 2016, noted the nation's rapid developments in Earth observation technology and committed to further developing satellites for observing the land, ocean, and atmosphere. The paper also included a discussion of key applications, including many that align with human security priorities, such as environmental protection, natural disaster prevention, climate change, and food security. It also planned to intensify services aimed at alleviating poverty and providing space information services for ethnic minority regions (China 2016). China has also committed to using satellite data to address issues relevant to human security through its Digital Belt and Road initiative, which leverages Earth observation data to support sustainable development in the region (Guo et al. 2018).

India's remote sensing program has also been application driven, with goals of both public good and economic development (Murthi 2018). Russia emphasizes the key applications to which its Earth observation satellites are designed to contribute, many of which align with human security issues, including farmland harvest and drought forecasts, fire and flood monitoring, pollution monitoring, and identification of illegal solid waste fields (Glavkosmos 2019). The first goal identified in Japan's Basic Plan on Space Policy, released in 2020, is "contributing to a wide range of national interests." This includes contributing to disaster management and national resilience, as well as contributing to solving global issues and achieving the United Nations sustainable development goals (Japan 2020).

While Japan's policy is particularly straightforward in this regard, all of these nations are pursuing human security goals only as they align with national interests. NASA's science-informed priorities are clearly impacted by national priorities and politics. China's Belt and Road Initiative is widely recognized as an effort to build soft power and influence within the region. The issues emphasized by India and Russia tend to be those particularly relevant to their own nation. This is not surprising, but as we think about the ability of satellites to contribute to human security, it is important to keep in mind that the technologies and applications prioritized and developed by states are filtered through the lens of national interest and national security.

While keeping in mind this fundamental limitation, it is important to acknowledge two trends that have improved the ability of Earth observation satellites to contribute to human security. First, the number of countries that operate civil Earth observation systems has increased significantly—to nearly forty as of 2021. This breadth of participation—including by many developing nations—means that a more diverse set of priorities (even if they are national priorities) are considered when developing these systems.

Even nations that do not operate their own Earth observation satellites may have a voice within international forums that deal with prioritizing and developing satellite applications. Involvement in international organizations such as the United Nations

Committee on the Peaceful Uses of Space, which has 95 members, or the Group on Earth Observations, which has 113 member countries, helps to ensure that the priorities of a diverse set of nations are discussed and considered. Compared to early in the space age, when space activities were limited to a handful of nations, increased participation results in applications relevant to a larger and more diverse set of individuals and makes a greater contribution to issues of human security.

Commercial Systems

Nearly half of all operational Earth observation satellites in orbit are designated as commercial, owned and operated by about fifty different entities spread across eighteen countries (UCS 2021). In some ways, the emergence of this commercial sector acts as a counterbalance to state-centric space activity, providing a venue by which alternative interests and priorities may be translated into space hardware and applications. However, just because commercial interests may differ from national interest (and even this may not be the case, as discussed below), this does not mean they will align with the human security priorities of individuals.

Many remote sensing companies espouse goals associated with benefitting humanity. For example, Planet, which operates more than a hundred Earth observation satellites, was founded with the goal of "using space to help life on Earth." Planet's mission is to "image all of Earth's landmass every day, and make global change visible, accessible, and actionable" (Planet 2021). The Chang Guang Satellite Technology Company in China, which operates twenty-seven Earth observation satellites and has plans to launch more than a hundred, states that its mission is "serving seven billion people on the globe with the remote sensing information product integrating sky, space and ground." Maxar maintains an Open Data program that enables the release of data and analytics in times of disaster to aid organizations working on the front lines (Maxar 2021b).

However, companies, by their nature, seek to prioritize revenue. Often, this means developing space systems that collect data most in demand by paying customers. For many companies, the primary customers are government defense and intelligence agencies. This may lead commercial entities to reflect the same national priorities expressed by states, and particularly by military and intelligence agencies. To the extent that these companies also serve non-governmental customers, these tend to be relatively narrow, with applications in areas such as finance (selling data to traders on Wall Street), or extractive industries, such as oil, gas, or mining. Unlike governments, these companies (and their non-governmental customers) have no obligation to use data in ways that serve taxpayers or the public at large. The goals of these customers are unlikely to align with the broad goals of human security.

Many companies are transparent about these dynamics. For example, Maxar, one of the leading commercial remote sensing companies in the United States, identifies defense and intelligence agencies in US and international governments as its "principal customers." It sees these agencies as a potential area for future growth, and notes "We seek to align our products and services with the U.S. Department of Defense's National Defense Strategy needs." It also has over 400 commercial customers in industries including "technology, telecom, transportation, mining, and oil and gas" (Maxar 2021a).

In addition to their influence as customers, governments also play an important role as regulators of commercial satellite remote sensing activities. Many nations limit the spatial resolution of imagery that companies may collect and sell. They may also have other limitations on the locations and/or customers to which these companies may sell their data. In some cases, limitations of one state can be overcome by purchasing data from a company based in another state, but, as a whole, national considerations still play an important role in what data is available and to whom, even in the commercial realm.

University and Other Systems

While there is significant talk about the increase in the number and type of users accessing space, for the most part we are seeing this in the expansion of the number of states involved in space activity and in the growth of the commercial industry. Civil society involvement in space programs is still quite limited. Of the 1,028 satellites in space, only about 30 are operated by non-governmental, non-commercial entities such as universities. Many of these are developed with a focus on providing hands-on experience for students, rather than collecting a particular type of data, and the capabilities of these satellites are typically limited. The development of satellites capable of conducting meaningful environmental missions is still largely beyond the capabilities of individuals and non-governmental organizations (NGOs).

State and Non-state Actors: Satellite Data Users

While satellites are still overwhelmingly developed and owned by state actors and by companies that seek to serve government and limited commercial customers, a number of trends have helped to make the population of satellite data users much more diverse. First, there has been a significant global trend toward open data policies for civil Earth observation satellites (Borowitz 2017). Combined with increasing data analysis capabilities and more widespread availability of training, this has made it much more practical for a wide range of actors to make use of satellite data. The increasing volume of data being made available by the growing commercial remote sensing sector further adds to these opportunities. As a whole, non-state actors today have access to more satellite data and more data analysis capability than ever before.

The breadth of engagement with satellite data is illustrated in some of the examples provided above. Academic use of satellite data is expanding beyond remote sensing specialists to become a common component of studies in the social sciences, such as economics (Florio and Morretta 2021). Many of the personal, community, and political security examples provided above were conducted by non-state actors. Use of satellite data for humanitarian and environmental monitoring by NGOs has become such a widespread phenomenon that there is a body of research devoted to understanding the impact of this "space-based activism" on international affairs (Rothe and Shim 2018; Larkin 2016; Van Wyk 2019).

In 2002, Karen Litfin (2002) called attention to the potential for NGOs to use satellite data to increase transparency, call attention to humanitarian or environmental issues, and disrupt state monopolies on information and interpretation with regard to these issues. Baker and Williamson (2006) highlighted the use of satellite data by the media, academics, and others for these purposes, as well. A recent publication by Lin-Greenberg and Milonopoulos (2021) provides evidence that disclosures of information from these non-governmental sources can indeed shift public opinion, providing information that has the power to contradict or reinforce government narratives.

However, there are limits to this trend. Rothe and Shim show that the vast majority of these non-state humanitarian and environmental monitoring efforts focus on issues in non-Western countries. While this may be due in part to biases within the nongovernmental organizations themselves (which are typically based in the Western world), Rothe and Shim highlight the importance of the "image complex" of satellite remote sensing. Highlighting the agenda setting role of satellite owners discussed above, they note that humanitarian entities typically have to work with imagery that has already been collected, rather than setting data collection priorities. Thus they are limited to focusing on regions in which larger customers, such as intelligence agencies, have prioritized data collection (Rothe and Shim 2018). Witjes and Olbrich (2017) further raise questions about the ability of these entities to contribute to transparency in an objective way.

Finally, while the involvement of non-state actors is increasing, it is not increasing equally, and significant inequities remain with regard to access and use of satellite data. Large, Western NGOs may be able to purchase large volumes of commercial satellite data, but this is not the case for many smaller organizations or for individuals. Mirroring broader issues in data equity seen beyond the space sector, it is those with more resources—in terms of funding, time, or technical capabilities—who will best be able to leverage satellite data, even when it is provided for free. This structural reality means that the democratization of satellite data—and its ability to allow non-state actors to play a significant role in prioritizing and addressing human security issues—is not without limits.

This dynamic is exacerbated by the digital divide: the capacity to access and work with satellite data is much lower in some nations than in others, due to limited access to reliable high-speed internet and other advanced technologies and infrastructure needed for data analysis. Therefore, in addition to the variation among individuals with different levels of resources and capabilities, there are systematic differences across nations that make it harder for the individuals living in these nations to access and use satellite data to address the human security issues that they identify as high priority.

REALIZING THE PROMISE OF SATELLITE DATA FOR HUMAN SECURITY

In 2022, just as in 1997, we see that although Earth observation satellites have made important contributions to the improvement of human security, there is much more that could be done. This is due, in part, to the power structures underlying the development of satellites and satellite applications. One of the key concepts underlying human security is that individuals are not only the appropriate focus of security efforts—they should also be active participants in defining and achieving human security goals.

Satellites provide global data relevant to a wide range of human security issues, including environmental security, food security, economic security, and personal, community, and political security. However, satellite development and operation remain out of reach for most individuals and NGOs. Instead, most Earth observation satellites are still owned either by states—which design and build systems to align with national priorities—or by commercial entities, which design their systems to meet the needs of their primary customers (who often happen to be states).

However, while the expansion in satellite ownership has been limited to new countries and commercial entities entering the sector, democratization of access to and use of satellite data has extended much farther. Due to trends in open data and decreasing costs for access to commercial data, as well as increasingly user-friendly data analysis tools and widely available training, use of satellite data has expanded rapidly. Researchers outside of the field of remote sensing are applying satellite data to their work. NGOs are using satellite data to analyze issues that they deem most important—issues that nations may have overlooked or chosen not to address. Entrepreneurs are using advanced data analysis techniques, including machine learning and artificial intelligence, to develop new products and services.

We have not reached the point where the average person on the street can access and use satellite data directly. However, with more and more researchers, companies, and non-profit organizations developing satellite applications, individuals have access to an increasing number of satellite applications. There has been a substantive improvement in the ability of satellite data to contribute to human security. Today, these contributions come not only through the use of these systems by governments, but also due to activities of non-state actors that leverage both government and commercial satellite data.

Moving forward, this trend is likely to continue, building on trends toward open access to government satellite data, increasing volumes of commercial remote sensing data, and increasing data analysis capabilities. While structural issues related to satellite ownership will continue, we may see some erosion of this effect as the user-base for this data grows. As more individuals start to make use of these applications and understand the potential of satellite data, they will be able to demand data, products, and services more tailored to their own needs. In this way, Earth observation satellites may evolve to be more responsive human security needs defined by individuals.

These are positive trends that should be encouraged and facilitated by those who wish to support the human security agenda. However, even those states that profess to support human security goals may be uneasy about the shift in power from the state to individuals that necessarily accompanies this trend. Initial activities in this direction—particularly the rise of satellite activism discussed above—suggest that states will have to adapt to these changes, as the growing number of actors in space makes strict national control over space data less and less feasible.

We must also be vigilant with regard to persistent inequities in the collection, access, and use of satellite data and its effect on the human security agenda. The number of actors in space—both state and non-state—will continue to rise, but just as we have seen already, these capabilities are not spread equally across nations or within them. Nations with more resources and technical capabilities will be able to garner more strategic benefits from space assets, and larger, more established NGOs will have an advantage over newer, smaller actors. Without clear recognition of this, there will be a warped view of human security that privileges the perspective of wealthy, typically Western, states and organizations, over those in the rest of the world. Ensuring that the trend toward democratization of space continues in such a way that access and use of space data becomes feasible for even those without significant resources is essential to fully realizing the goals of human security.

REFERENCES

Aschbacher, Josef. 2017. "ESA's Earth Observation Strategy and Copernicus." In *Satellite Earth Observations and Their Impact on Society and Policy*, edited by Masami Onoda and Oran R. Young, 81–86. Singapore: Springer.

Baker, John C., and Ray A. Williamson. 2006. "Satellite Imagery Activism: Sharpening the Focus on Tropical Deforestation." *Singapore Journal of Tropical Geography* 27, no. 1: 4–14.

Barau, Inuwa, Mahmud Zubairu, Michael N. Mwanza, and Vincent Y. Seaman. 2014. "Improving Polio Vaccination Coverage in Nigeria Through the use of Geographic Information System Technology." *The Journal of infectious diseases* 210, no. suppl_1: S102–S110.

Bellamy, Alex J., and Matt McDonald. 2002. "The Utility of Human Security': Which Humans? What Security? A Reply to Thomas & Tow." *Security Dialogue* 33, no. 3: 373–77.

Bhaduri, Budhendra L., Dalton Lunga, Jacob Arndt, Eric Weber, Amy Rose, and Robert Stewart. December 9–12, 2019. "Assessing Human Security with Remote Sensing and GeoAI." San Francisco, CA: AGU Fall Meeting Abstracts.

Borowitz, Mariel. 2017. *Open Space: The Global Effort for Open Access to Environmental Satellite Data*. Cambridge, MA: MIT Press.

Brown, Molly E., and Elizabeth B Brickley. 2012. "Evaluating the Use of Remote Sensing Data in the US Agency for International Development Famine Early Warning Systems Network." *Journal of Applied Remote Sensing* 6, no. 1: 063511.

Casana, Jesse, and Elise Jakoby Laugier. 2017. "Satellite Imagery-Based Monitoring of Archaeological Site Damage in the Syrian Civil War." *PloS one* 12, no. 11: e0188589.

Charo, Arthur, and Waleed Abdalati. 2018. "The 2017–2027 National Academies Decadal Survey for Earth Science and Applications from Space: An Overview of the Report." 42nd COSPAR Scientific Assembly 42: A3. 1-52-18.

China. 2016. White Paper on China's Space Activities. Information Office of the State Council. China.

Dash, Jadunandan. 2019. "Satellites and Crop Interventions." *Nature Sustainability* 2, no. 10: 903–904.

De Juan, Alexander. 2015. "Long-term Environmental Change and Geographical Patterns of Violence in Darfur, 2003–2005." *Political Geography* 45: 22–33.

Donaldson, Dave, and Adam Storeygard. 2016. "The View from Above: Applications of Satellite Data in Economics." *Journal of Economic Perspectives* 30, no. 4: 171–98.

Early, Bryan R., and Erik Gartzke. 2021. "Spying from Space: Reconnaissance Satellites and Interstate Disputes." *Journal of Conflict Resolution*. https://doi.org/10.1177/002200272 1995894.

Finnemore, Martha. 1996. "National Interests in International Society." In *National Interests in International Society*. Ithica, NY: Cornell University Press.

Florio, Massimo, and Valentina Morretta. 2021. "Earth Observation and Economic Studies: A Cross-fertilization Perspective." *Space Policy* 57: 101429.

Gibson, John, Susan Olivia, and Geua Boe-Gibson. 2020. "Night Lights in Economics: Sources and Uses." *Journal of Economic Surveys* 34, no. 5: 955–80.

Gjørv, Gunhild Hoogensen. 2018. "Human security." In *Routledge Handbook of Security Studies*, edited by Myriam Dunn Cavelty and Thierry Balzacq, 221–34. Milton Park, UK: Routledge.

Glavkosmos. 2019. "Earth Observation Data and Solutions." https://www.glavkosmos.com/en/earth-observation/.

Guo, Huadong, Jie Liu, Yubao Qiu, Massimo Menenti, Fang Chen, Paul F. Uhlir, Li Zhang, John van Genderen, Dong Liang, and Ishwaran Natarajan. 2018. "The Digital Belt and Road Program in Support of Regional Sustainability." *International Journal of Digital Earth* 11, no. 7: 657–69.

Holloway, Tracey, Daniel J. Jacob, and Daegan Miller. 2018. "Short History of NASA Applied Science Teams for Air Quality and Health." *Journal of Applied Remote Sensing* 12, no. 4: 042611.

Japan. 2020. Outline of the Basic Plan on Space Policy (Provisional Translation). National Space Policy Secretariat.

Larkin, Sean P. 2016. "The Age of Transparency: International Relations without Secrets." *Foreign Affairs* 95, no. 3: 136–46.

Levinger, Matthew. 2009. "Geographical Information Systems Technology as a Tool for Genocide Prevention: The Case of Darfur." *Space and Polity* 13, no. 1: 69–76.

Lin-Greenberg, Erik, and Theo Milonopoulos. 2021. "Private Eyes in the Sky: Emerging Technology and the Political Consequences of Eroding Government Secrecy." *Journal of Conflict Resolution*. https://doi.org/10.1177/0022002720987285.

Litfin, Karen T. 2002. "Public Eyes: Satellite Imagery, the Globalization of Transparency, and New Networks of Surveillance." In *Information Technologies and Global Politics: The Changing Scope of Power and Governance*, edited by James N. Rosenau and J. P. Singh, 65–88. Albany, NY: Suny Press.

Maxar. 2021a. "Annual Report on Form 10-K."

Maxar. 2021b. "Open Data Program." https://www.maxar.com/open-data.

Murthi, Kuppam Ramaiyer Sridhara. 2018. "New Paradigms for Commercial Benefits from India's Earth Observation Activities." *New Space* 6, no. 2: 117–24.

Nakalembe, Catherine, Inbal Becker-Reshef, Rogerio Bonifacio, Guangxiao Hu, Micheal Lawrence Humber, Christina Jade Justice, John Keniston, Kenneth Mwangi, Felix Rembold, and Shraddhanand Shukla. 2021. "A Review of Satellite-Based Global Agricultural Monitoring Systems Available for Africa." *Global Food Security* 29. https://doi.org/10.1016/j.gfs.2021.100543.

Newman, Edward. 2001. "Human Security and Constructivism." *International studies perspectives* 2, no. 3: 239–51.

Peckham, Robert, and Ria Sinha. 2017. "Satellites and the New War on Infection: Tracking Ebola in West Africa." *Geoforum* 80: 24–38.

Petrescu, Relly Victoria, Raffaella Aversa, Taher Abu-Lebdeh, Antonio Apicella, and Florian Ion Petrescu. 2018. "NASA Satellites Help Us to Quickly Detect Forest Fires." *American Journal of Engineering and Applied Sciences* 11, no. 1: 288–96.

Planet. 2021. "Company." https://www.planet.com/company/.

Reardon, Sara, Jeff Tollefson, Alexandra Witze, and Erin Ross. 2017. "Trump Budget Would Slash Science Programmes across Government." *Nature News* 546, no. 7656: 19.

Ri, Sayaka, Alden H Blair, Chang Jun Kim, and Rohini J Haar. 2019. "Attacks on Healthcare Facilities as an Indicator of Violence against Civilians in Syria: An Exploratory Analysis of Open-Source Data." *PloS one* 14, no. 6: e0217905.

Rogers, David J, Sarah E. Randolph, Robert W. Snow, and Simon I. Hay. 2002. "Satellite Imagery in the Study and Forecast of Malaria." *Nature* 415, no. 6872: 710–15.

Rohner, Dominic, Mathias Thoenig, and Fabrizio Zilibotti. 2013. "Seeds of Distrust: Conflict in Uganda." *Journal of Economic Growth* 18, no. 3: 217–52.

Rothe, Delf, and David Shim. 2018. "Sensing the Ground: On the Global Politics of Satellite-Based Activism." *Review of International Studies* 44, no. 3: 414–37.

Smith, WL, Qi Zhang, M. Shao, and E. Weisz. 2020. "Improved Severe Weather Forecasts Using LEO and GEO Satellite Soundings." *Journal of Atmospheric and Oceanic Technology* 37, no. 7: 1203–18.

Stern, Julia. 2021. "Genocide in China: Uighur Re-education Camps and International Response." *Immigration and Human Rights Law Review* 3, no. 1: 2.

Thomas, Nicholas, and William T Tow. 2002. "The Utility of Human Security: Sovereignty and Humanitarian Intervention." *Security Dialogue* 33, no. 2: 177–92.

Tsai, Yu-tai. 2009. "The Emergence of Human Security: A Constructivist View." *International Journal of Peace Studies* 14, no. 2: 19–33.

UCS. 2021. Union of Concerned Scientists Satellite Database. Updated September 1, 2021.

UN. 1967. Treaty on Principles Governing the Activities of States in the Exploration and Use of Outer Space, including the Moon and Other Celestial Bodies. United Nations.

UN. 1999. "Vienna Declaration on Space and Human Development." Report of the Third United Nations Conference on the Exploration and Peaceful Uses of Outer Space. 18 October 1999. Doc A/CONF.

UNDP. 1994. *Human Development Report 1994*. United Nations Development Program. New York: Oxford University Press.

Van Wyk, Jo-Ansie. 2019. "Pixels, Politics and Peace." *Journal of African Foreign Affairs* 6, no. 2: 31–50.

Wentz, Frank J., and Matthias Schabel. 2000. "Precise Climate Monitoring Using Complementary Satellite Data Sets." *Nature* 403, no. 6768: 414–16.

WHO. 2019. Global Health Estimates: The Top 10 Causes of Death.

Witjes, Nina, and Philipp Olbrich. 2017. "A Fragile Transparency: Satellite Imagery Analysis, Non-State Actors, and Visual Representations of Security." *Science and Public Policy* 44, no. 4: 524–34.

Wolfe, Mary K, and Jeremy Mennis. 2012. "Does Vegetation Encourage or Suppress Urban Crime? Evidence from Philadelphia, PA." *Landscape and Urban Planning* 108, nos. 2–4: 112–22.

CHAPTER 37

....

ENABLING NATIONAL
SECURITY THROUGH SPACE

Intelligence and Communications

....

PETER L. HAYS AND JAMES J. WIRTZ

ALTHOUGH the history and theory surrounding the use of military force in peace and war focuses on weapons and the troops that wield them in battle, there are two critical capabilities that must exist before militaries can play an effective role in matters of national security. In modern times, one of these capabilities is often referred to by the acronym ISR, which stands for intelligence, surveillance, and reconnaissance. To mount an effective defense, for example, it is necessary to have information about the number of troops and equipment possessed by the opponent (intelligence), information about whether those forces are undertaking preparations to launch an offensive (surveillance), and timely data about developments along potential avenues of attack (reconnaissance). For those contemplating an attack, ISR provides critical information about the location and status of the opponent's defenses, the terrain, weather, and military situation along avenues of advance, and the information needed to target weapons against enemy strongholds or to avoid the opponents' strengths and exploit their weaknesses instead. ISR is the starting point for officers and officials who want to follow the advice offered by the Chinese philosopher Sun-tzu: "know the enemy and know yourself; in a hundred battles you will never be in peril" (Sun-tzu and Griffith 1964, 84).

The second capability is an effective means of communication both within and among military units and between specific units and higher echelons of command. This "chain of command" generally terminates at a civil-military apex, the point at which politicians authorize, monitor, and in a general way guide military subordinates as they direct the forces under their command. Given the chaos and carnage of war, the vast distances covered, the limits of technology, and the impact of myriad extraneous factors, effective communications and the command and control that they enable can never be taken for granted (Grauer 2016). Drums, horns, flags, smoke signals, rockets, mirrors, telegraphs, radios, and most recently digital systems made possible by the information revolution—technologies that possess various ranges and data transmission rates—have been used to cut through the confusion and friction of war to enable military operations. In the nuclear age, reliable communications are especially critical when it comes to guaranteeing that political authorities can retain positive control (i.e., that weapons are *always* used following legitimate authorization) and negative control (i.e., that weapons are *never* used without legitimate authorization) over their nuclear arsenals (Wirtz and Larsen 2022).

Admittedly, as Sputnik, the first artificial satellite, was completing its initial orbit of the planet back in 1957, the potential for improved ISR or space-enabled communications was not the first military application that came to people's minds. Instead, observers quickly came to a terrifying realization: it now appeared possible to use a rocket to carry a nuclear warhead to attack targets at intercontinental ranges. To their minds, this new nuclear delivery system changed everything. Targets that would take bombers many hours of flight time to reach now could be attacked in under an hour by ballistic missiles.

An equally chilling observation soon followed: ISR and communication systems that were built to meet the threat posed by the relatively long flight times of bombers had been quickly rendered obsolete by the hypersonic speed of ballistic missiles. In other words, ballistic missiles could travel faster than the ISR and communications needed to alert defenses or to launch a retaliatory strike before it could be destroyed on the ground. Under these circumstances, it is no surprise that the Pearl Harbor Analogy informed US thinking about the importance of survivability when it came to nuclear deterrence (Schilling 1965).

Fortunately, the Dwight D. Eisenhower administration considered the full range of security implications created by this new access to space. Administration officials laid out comprehensive but secret plans to use space to deliver revolutionary ISR and communications capabilities that would provide the United States with decisive and enduring strategic advantages. These ISR, communication, and warning systems-of-systems would rely on space-based components; these capabilities would eventually provide a degree of situational awareness and command and control to officers and political authorities that was not even imagined when Sputnik shocked the world. These space-based and space enabled capabilities made possible everything from US-Soviet arms control during the Cold War, to holding targets at risk at global ranges using precision-guided conventional weapons, to providing relatively junior commanders with a "god's eye view" of the battlefield. The political, strategic, operational, and tactical effects of space assets are far reaching and continue to evolve as new technologies and applications are utilized in the "high terrain" of Earth orbit.

Exploiting space to enable terrestrial military operations entails more than just placing systems into orbit. The ISR and communications capabilities and the systems described in this chapter must be integrated into existing force structures, military doctrines, operations, and even logistical procedures before they can reach their full potential (Williamson and Wirtz 2021). Fully exploiting space capabilities also requires novel techniques and procedures, new types of training, and new career fields within existing organizational structures of the armed forces, or new career paths and new organizations. Most importantly, both defense civilians and officers engaged in traditional occupations must become familiar with the capabilities and limitations of these space assets before they can employ them most efficiently and effectively. Continuing effort with all these types of considerations is still a work in progress, so to speak, as new technologies and capabilities are integrated into the armed forces, the United States Space Force (USSF) continues to normalize its space operations, and the United States finds ways to mitigate the growing efficacy of Chinese and Russian space and counterspace capabilities. Indeed, space operations might be the most cost-effective way for the United States to counter Russia's and China's increasingly capable anti-access/ area denial systems and strategies.

To explore the impact of space-based capabilities on foreign and defense policies in general and US national security in particular, this chapter first examines the key issue that preoccupied governments on the eve of the space age. Specifically, what legal regime should govern outer space? The second section then describes the development and employment of space-based communications, ISR and related warning functions, and touches on navigation and environmental surveillance. It describes the space assets involved and how these systems shaped military tactics, operations, strategies, and national security policies. The third section identifies ongoing space developments that might affect the future impact of space-based assets on national security. The chapter concludes with a few recommendations and considerations for future research.

Is Satellite Overflight an Act of War?

Although the RAND Corporation's very first report in May 1946, "Preliminary Design of an Experimental World-Circling Spaceship," identified many important potential military missions for satellites including communications, attack assessment, weather monitoring, and strategic reconnaissance, few at that time considered developing those capabilities to be a priority. As the Cold War heated up, more terrestrial concerns, the Chinese civil war and the Korean War, for example, pushed space issues into the policy background.

The US approach to space changed early in the Eisenhower administration when it was determined that placing a reconnaissance satellite into orbit might provide a close look into an otherwise closed USSR. To realize this objective the United States not only needed to develop new technologies, it also had to create a more permissive legal regime for space than the regime that governed aviation. Washington wanted to establish a legal and policy framework that would legitimize satellite overflight, instead of treating an orbiting satellite as a violation of sovereign airspace and a potential act of war. Considerations surrounding the legal and policy regime for developing ISR satellites thus became the most important driver for US space policy at the opening of the space age. For decades, however, security restrictions obscured how these legal concerns led to US government efforts to hide its interest in using space for military and intelligence purposes.

In March 1954, the Eisenhower administration commissioned a secret Technological Capabilities Panel to study how the United States could use technology to reduce the threat of surprise attack; Eisenhower wanted the best minds in the country to find ways to avoid a nuclear Pearl Harbor. Key members of the panel strongly supported development of specialized aircraft and satellites for reconnaissance and gained Eisenhower's support for their most important recommendations. They briefed this initial concept for a national strategic reconnaissance program during a highly secret Oval Office meeting on November 24, 1954, that included the president, the secretaries of state and defense, and Department of Defense (DoD) and Central Intelligence Agency (CIA) officials. No official records of this meeting have been found, but it is clear that the president verbally authorized the CIA, with US Air Force support, to begin development of the U-2 high altitude reconnaissance aircraft. To support the president's goal of placing an ISR satellite into orbit, in March 1955 the Air Force consolidated its satellite design work and established specific requirements under the Weapons System (WS)-117L satellite program (Dienesch 2016).

In May 1955, the National Security Council developed a secret approach for establishing a favorable legal regime for operation of ISR satellites. This approach called for hiding satellite development behind the cloak of a civilian space program devoted to scientific activities, not intelligence gathering. DoD support to the US scientific satellite program would have to appear incidental; US space efforts would emphasize peaceful purposes and universal access to space for humankind. National Reconnaissance Office historian Cargill Hall summarized how the overarching goal of Eisenhower's space policy was put into practice: "The [civilian International Geophysical Year] scientific satellite program was clearly identified as a stalking horse to establish the precedent of overflight in space for the eventual operation of reconnaissance satellites" (Hall 1995). Secrets about the U-2 and WS-117L programs were initially so closely held by such a small group of officials that even senior officials in the Eisenhower administration did not realize the United States was racing into space and that the scientific space program provided a cover story to hide its secret and highest priority satellite and missile programs.

Despite the Eisenhower administration's careful planning to legitimize the operation of reconnaissance satellites, it was unprepared for the public response to the Soviet successes with Sputniks I and II on October 4 and November 3, 1957. Although the US public was alarmed by the Soviet's scientific achievement, witting officials inside the Eisenhower administration breathed a sigh of relief as Sputnik flew overhead. They had not intended that the Soviets be first to orbit a satellite, but urged that Washington raise no objections to this overflight and thereby helped establish a legal regime that favored US interests. A permissive space regime would give US space-based reconnaissance access to the closed USSR, while the Soviets would gain relatively less information by overflying the far more open United States. Nevertheless, it remained politically expedient to continue obscuring the origins and operation of space-based intelligence collection for decades; there was no need to alert the Soviets to potentially embarrassing overflights or to abandon the political high ground by emphasizing the military, not scientific, purposes behind the US space program. It is no coincidence that a civilian program under the National Aeronautics and Space Administration (NASA), not the US Air Force, soon took center stage as the public focus of US space efforts.

SPACE ENABLED SYSTEMS-OF-SYSTEMS

While the US public and the world focused on the exploits of NASA's early astronauts and the Kennedy administration's promise to put Americans on the moon by the end of the 1960s, the US government moved quickly to exploit the "high ground" of space for the purposes of immediate national security. Of primary importance were the efforts to bolster reconnaissance, early-warning, and command, control, and communication capabilities related to the US nuclear deterrent. The origins of the systems described here are part of a Cold War strategic context, which was global in scope, bi-polar in nature, and carried with it the risk of nuclear Armageddon.

SPACE-BASED ISR

By November 1958, work begun under the Air Force's WS-117L program grew to become three separate, secret, and high-priority satellite development efforts: photoreconnaissance via film return under the CIA's Corona program, photoreconnaissance via film readout return and signals intelligence under the Sentry/Samos program, and infrared detection of missile launches under the Missile Defense Alarm System (Midas) program. These efforts to develop operational ISR systems faced daunting technological challenges. The Corona satellite film return system was the most mature technology, yet between February 1959 and June 1960, it still suffered a string of 12 consecutive failures of various types before achieving its first successful film recovery in August 1960. Nevertheless, the efficacy of satellite photoreconnaissance was undeniable—the first successful film recovery from Discoverer 14 delivered 20 pounds of imagery, more than the combined 24 U-2 flights over the USSR (Ruffner 1995).

In response to the increasing importance of ISR satellites to US intelligence, the Kennedy administration moved to tighten the security around all US military space efforts. A classified DoD directive issued on March 23, 1962, known as the "blackout" directive prohibited advance notice and press coverage of all military space launches. It also forbade the use of the names of space programs such as Discoverer, Midas, and Samos. Military payloads on space vehicles would no longer be identified, and program names would be replaced by numbers. While this directive may have made it more difficult for the Soviets to distinguish between different types of US military space programs and rocket payloads, it also led to the wide divergence between public knowledge and perceptions of the NASA and DoD space programs that continues today.

The regime for ISR satellites also matured in important ways beginning in the 1960s. After orbiting their first ISR satellites, the Soviets stopped objecting to US satellite overflights, and the superpowers reached an informal modus vivendi that legitimized space-based reconnaissance and surveillance. Article XII of the 1972 Anti-Ballistic

Missile (ABM) Treaty contained the most important and formalized legitimization of ISR satellites in international law; it also is the first use of the euphemism national technical means of verification (NTM) in an international treaty. Before the ABM Treaty, most US-Soviet strategic arms control negotiations had broken down over the contentious issue of treaty verification. The United States consistently insisted on verification through on-site inspections, while the USSR consistently rejected inspectors on the ground inside their territory. By 1968, however, US policymakers had enough faith in the data gathering capabilities of their NTM (mainly ISR satellites) to agree to using space-based surveillance as a means of arms control verification. ISR satellites helped to establish a new type of arms control regime based on a "bridge" of trust between the superpowers.

The critical role of ISR satellites in enabling the first major superpower arms control negotiations, the 1969–1972 Strategic Arms Limitation Talks (SALT I), continued in almost every subsequent strategic arms control agreement. The language of Article XII of the ABM Treaty was repeated essentially verbatim in subsequent arms control treaties predicated on NTM verification including the 1972 Interim Agreement, the 1974 Threshold Test Ban Treaty, the 1976 Peaceful Nuclear Explosions Treaty, and the 1979 SALT II Treaty. Moreover, NTM remains important in the arms control treaties whose verification is also dependent on the breakthrough in onsite inspection reached at the end of the Cold War: the 1987 Intermediate-Range Nuclear Forces Treaty and the 1991 and 1993 Strategic Arms Reduction Treaties (START I and II), as well as more recent agreements such as New START.

Despite the critical importance of NTM in enabling the first strategic arms control agreements, ISR satellites had limitations that shaped the content of these agreements in fundamental ways. Restrictions in these agreements could only be as precise as could be "seen" by NTM. For instance, limits on underground nuclear testing were not included in the 1963 Limited Test Ban Treaty, partly because of difficulties in monitoring these types of tests using space-based sensors. By contrast, significant improvements in NTM capabilities led to differences in the units of limitation between the 1972 SALT I and 1979 SALT II Treaties. In 1972, NTM was asked to count very large immobile objects such as missile silos and large phased-array radars; by 1979, NTM was expected to distinguish between types of intercontinental-range ballistic missiles (ICBMs) and to count numbers of warheads. This fundamental interrelationship also drove the United States to improve the capabilities of its ISR satellites aggressively and to optimize these systems for arms control verification purposes, rather than specific military missions, throughout the remainder of the Cold War.

ISR in the Reconnaissance-Strike Complex

Coalition operations in Operation Desert Storm in 1991 mark the emergence of a Reconnaissance-Strike Complex (RSC), an inelegant translation of a concept first envisioned by the Soviet General Staff in the late 1970s that combines global ISR, microelectronics, and long-range precision-strike weapons. Former Air Force Chief of Staff Merrill McPeak labeled that conflict the "first space war" to describe the way space capabilities enhanced coalition operations. ISR capabilities are perhaps the most important of all those enabling the RSC because they allow comprehensive situational awareness including locating enemy targets, planning for ingress and egress routes, and assessing battle damage on targets attacked, thereby helping to identify those requiring additional strikes. When ISR capabilities include multispectral sensors such as real-time electro-optical imagery, radar imagery, infrared signatures, and signals intelligence, it becomes difficult for an enemy to hide any militarily significant activities. Whenever and wherever enemy forces are using radio communications or are in motion, they become visible and therefore targetable by the US RSC.

Table 37.1 shows how the US RSC has evolved over the last 20 years. During the 1991 Gulf War to eject Iraqi forces from Kuwait, only 8 percent of targets were struck with precision-guided munitions. Communication incompatibilities and other limitations meant that attack planning required an inflexible 72-hour cycle that provided limited capabilities to strike targets of opportunity and sometimes called for restriking targets already destroyed. By contrast, 30 years later, all time-critical-targets are struck using precision-guided munitions and most aircraft sorties launch without an assigned target. Through a process known as dynamic retasking, these aircraft can be sent to strike the most important target that emerges during their sortie. Table 37.2 describes the major space mission areas that contribute to the RSC including environmental warning; communications; missile warning; positioning, navigation, and timing; and ISR. It also shows the orbits in which most of the satellites operate and provides a listing of the satellite systems that support each mission area.

Today, China and Russia continue to develop significant space capabilities to establish their own RSC as well as capabilities to deny the US RSC (Pollpeter, this volume; Vidal, this volume). Access to or denial of these space capabilities could very well spell the difference between victory and defeat in modern great power conflicts. These space capabilities could be targeted preemptively or in first strikes because of their foundational importance in enabling almost all military operations. Moreover, disruption of US space capabilities is essential for China and Russia to execute their anti-access/area denial strategies.

Communications Satellites

In contrast to the regime for ISR satellites that was shaped by the actions of individual governments and informally regulated, the regime for communications satellites (comsats) was largely open, soon became commercialized, and is governed by a formalized system of international regulations. Developing military satellite communications (milsatcom) was not an initial priority. Today milsatcom is a fundamental enabler across all aspects of US RSC.

Table 37.1. Evolution of the Space–Enabled Reconnaissance–Strike Complex: The New US Way of War

Military Operation, Duration, and Megabits Per Second (Mbps) Data Delivered from Satellites to Deployed Brigade-Sized Units	Primary Types of Unguided and Precision-Guided Munitions (PGM) Used	Numbers and Percentages of Unguided and PGMs Used
Desert Storm, 1991: Kuwaiti Theater of Operations, 17 Days, 1 Mbps	Unguided Munitions: Multiple Types PGM: Tomahawk (Terrain Contour Matching); Paveway II (Laser), Maverick (Electro-Optical (EO) and Infrared (IR))	Unguided: 245,000 (92%) PGM: 20,450 (8%)
Allied Force, 1999: Serbia, 78 Days, 24.5 Mbps	Unguided Munitions: Multiple Types PGM: Paveway II (Laser), Joint Direct Attack Munition (JDAM) (Global Positioning System (GPS))	Unguided: 16,000 (68%) PGM: 7,700 (32%)
Enduring Freedom, 2001–2002: Afghanistan, 90 Days, 68.2 Mbps	Unguided Munitions: Wind-Corrected Munitions PGM: Multiple Types (Laser, EO/IR, GPS)	Unguided: 9,000 (41%) PGM: 13,000 (59%)
Iraqi Freedom, 2003: 29 Days, 51.1 Mbps	Unguided Munitions: Wind-Corrected Munitions PGM: Multiple Types (Laser, EO/IR, GPS)	Unguided: 9,251 (32%) PGM: 19,948 (68%)
Inherent Resolve (Counter ISIS and Worldwide Counterterrorism), 2014–2019, No Conventional Brigades Deployed	Unguided Munitions: None Reported PGM: Hellfire, Small Diameter Bomb, and Multiple Other Types including Remotely Piloted Vehicle (RPV) Delivered (Laser, EO/IR, GPS, Radar)	Unguided: None Reported PGM: Totals Not Reported (100%)

The US Advanced Research Projects Agency developed and launched Project Score, the United States' first comsat, which broadcast a recorded message from President Eisenhower in December 1958. NASA led subsequent early work to develop satcom capabilities, and this civilian and scientific effort became a major part of a significant public diplomacy campaign focused on satcom during the Kennedy administration. A public-private partnership, the Communications Satellite Corporation, was formed under the Communications Satellite Act of 1962; it launched Early Bird, the United

Table 37.2. Force Enhancement Missions, Primary Orbits, Major Systems

Environmental Monitoring	Communications	Positioning, Navigation, and Timing (PNT)	Missile Warning	Intelligence, Surveillance, and Reconnaissance (ISR)
Polar Low-Earth Orbit (LEO)	Geostationary Earth Orbit (GEO) and LEO	Semi-Synchronous Earth Orbit	Various	Various
Defense Meteorological Satellite Program (DMSP) ------------------ National Polar-Orbiting Operational Environmental Satellite System (NPOESS)*, Defense Weather Satellite System (DWSS)*, Weather System Follow-on Microwave (WSF-M)	Defense Satellite Communications System (DSCS) II, DSCS III, Ultra-High Frequency Follow-on (UFO), Milstar, Global Broadcast System (GBS), Iridium, commercial systems, Advanced Extremely High Frequency (AEHF), Wideband Global System (WGS), Mobile User Objective System (MUOS) ------------------ Transformational Communications System (TSAT)*, Enhanced Polar System	Global Positioning System (GPS) GPS II GPS IIR GPS IIR-M GPS IIF GPS III ------------------	Defense Support Program (DSP), GPS, Nuclear Detonation Detection System (NDS), Space-Based Infra-Red System (SBIRS), Space Tracking and Surveillance System (STSS) ------------------ Precision Tracking Space System (PTSS)*	Geospatial Intelligence (GEOINT) Satellites, Signals Intelligence (SIGINT) Satellites, Overhead Persistent Infrared (OPIR), Space Based Space Surveillance (SBSS), Geosynchronous Space Situational Awareness Program (GSSAP), commercial systems ------------------ ----- Future Imagery Architecture (FIA)*, Integrated Overhead SIGINT Architecture (IOSA), Space Radar*

Note: * programs-of-record that have been cancelled; systems below the dotted line are planned capabilities.

States' first dedicated comsat supporting international telecommunications, in April 1965 (Whalen 2010).

The Cuban Missile Crisis in October 1962 was the impetus behind new satcom efforts supporting national security. The hotline communications link between Moscow and Washington was initially established with land links in August 1963 and was augmented with both US and Soviet satcom links in 1978 (Klose 1978). The Defense

Communications Agency established the Worldwide Military Command and Control System in the early 1960s and in the 1970s added the Minimum Essential Emergency Communications Network as a subsystem of the Worldwide Military Command and Control System. The Minimum Essential Emergency Communications Network forms an important foundation for the current US nuclear command, control, and communications network for secure, high-fidelity, jam-resistant, and survivable communications links between the national command authorities and the strategic nuclear forces. Milsatcom systems, formerly the Defense Satellite Communications System, including Milstar and Advanced Extremely High Frequency satellites provide essential communications links for US nuclear forces.

Beginning in the 1980s, continuing evolution of concepts of operations and communications technology led the United States toward greater emphasis on interoperability, joint operations between the armed services, and direct support of the Joint Force with a common operational picture, even during tactical operations. Today, as shown in Table 37.2, the Joint Force is supported by a large and diverse network of dedicated milsatcom systems including the Wideband Global System and Mobile User Objective System; commercial satcom systems augment these dedicated capabilities. These milsatcom systems provide the links that tie together the RSC and enable seamless, real-time command and control of global joint operations. Current global operations of remotely piloted aircraft such as the Predator and Reaper systems illustrate these comprehensive communications linkages under a system known as remote split operations where takeoff and landings are controlled from overseas airfield locations and communication links for enroute aircraft control and mission data links are provided by both dedicated milsatcom systems and commercial satcom systems.

Missile Warning Satellites

Secret work to develop infrared sensors on Midas satellites to detect ballistic missile launches worldwide was part of the WS-117L effort begun in 1955. The first Midas satellite was launched in 1960, but the program suffered many setbacks including launch failures and problems with the infrared sensor until it was cancelled in 1966. The original concept called for many satellites in low Earth orbit (LEO) and was abandoned after it took more than a decade to develop this technology. In the late 1960s Program 461, a follow on to Midas, demonstrated the feasibility of infrared missile warning from LEO, but that program was also cancelled because the cost of orbiting the many LEO satellites needed to provide continuous global missile warning was prohibitive. Instead, in the late 1960s under Program 949, also known as the Defense Support Program, the Air Force developed a new and less expensive system that relied on large infrared telescopes placed on a few satellites in geostationary Earth orbit. Defense Support Program satellites were first launched in 1970 and the final Defense Support Program satellite (DSP-23) was launched in November 2007. Today, the United States' primary missile warning capabilities are provided by the Space-Based Infrared System first launched in May 2011.

It uses a staring sensor for simultaneous viewing of almost one third of the Earth, instead of the telescope sweeps on the Defense Support Program system that covers this same large area but only allows focus on individual sections every few seconds.

Global missile launch warning from space-based infrared sensors is the cornerstone of the US nuclear command, control, and communication system. Data from space affords the first indication of a potential attack and, when combined with data from long-range radars, provides dual phenomenology warning that gives high confidence that missile launch detections are valid, thereby giving more time for the selection of defense and response options. As missile warning sensor technology has improved, these systems have increasingly provided technical intelligence on a wider range of less intense infrared events including explosions, large fires, jet engine exhaust, and even small fires in cold environments. Both the United States and Russia have deployed extensive infrared satellite missile warning networks for decades. By contrast, the Chinese are only now beginning to deploy their first infrared missile warning satellites as a part of a major nuclear infrastructure improvement and modernization effort.

CURRENT SPACE SECURITY ISSUES AND CHALLENGES

The United States and other nations with space assets face looming challenges when it comes to maintaining space stability and deterring conflict. One set of challenges is linked to the basic attributes of satellites. Because satellites are generally quite fragile, travel on highly predictable orbital paths, and lack normal means of camouflage and concealment, most analysts believe space is a highly offense dominant domain, that is, it is far easier to attack than to defend in space. Several theories in the field of international relations contend that war is more likely when the offensive is dominant—especially if it is difficult to distinguish between offensive and defensive weapons. They argue that there are strong incentives for striking first in an offensive dominant setting should a conflict appear inevitable (Jervis 1978; Morgan 2010). When the offense is dominant, surprise attack is likely to be perceived as leading to large rewards compared to a situation in which defense is the dominant form of warfare.

Because space capabilities greatly enhance the efficacy of terrestrial forces, attacking these systems could provide significant advantages during a conflict. In addition, the speed of many potential types of attacks on space systems could create crisis instability since decision-makers—on all sides—would have very little time (perhaps only a handful of minutes) to decide what to do in the face of a sudden attack, creating a high risk of rapid escalation due to misunderstanding, miscommunication, and miscalculation. Widespread deployment of space-to-space and, especially, space-to-Earth weapons that would expand targeting options beyond just denying information flows from space would exacerbate many of these time pressures, challenges, and instabilities.

Another set of challenges flows from the offense dominant situation in space: Should active steps be taken to protect space assets? During the Cold War, Ashton Carter for instance, identified the "basic paradox of ASAT [anti-satellite] arms control" (Carter 1986, 68). While ASATs might hold at risk stabilizing space systems such as those that provide the hotline, missile warning, or NTM for arms control, Carter noted, they also reduce incentives to deploy potentially destabilizing space systems, especially those with space-to-Earth force applications. Carter's paradox, along with host of questions about how to handle the offense-defense balance in space or the tradeoffs between ASAT deployment and the overall desirability of ASAT arms control, remain to be resolved (Hays 2011).

More recent analyses consider a different set of issues related to the democratization of space and accelerating growth in the number of commercial satellites and their capabilities. These factors might be transforming space into a less offense dominant domain. Adversaries now confront greater challenges in attacking these proliferating systems. Attacks affect more users. The "entanglements" between commercial and military applications and systems can create unintended cascades of destruction and disruption as the loss of space resources produces unanticipated and unintended consequences (Townsend 2020). Others contend that while the democratization of space could increase stability by creating opportunities to support national security at lower costs and with highly distributed space architectures, this approach might violate principles in the laws of armed conflict that require states to separate military assets from civilian infrastructure (Koplow 2022).

These difficult challenges and dangerous strategic conditions seem ripe for enhanced political, legal, and governance approaches that might promote stability and decrease the likelihood of conflict. Nevertheless, there has been little progress in any of these areas for decades. Developing the Outer Space Treaty (OST) regime within ten years of Sputnik was a significant achievement, but the OST regime is woefully inadequate for addressing today's most troubling space security challenges, which includes the rapid growth in counterspace capabilities, acceleration of commercial space activities with greater military potential, and the ever-increasing danger of orbital debris. States seem to have little appetite for addressing these challenges in comprehensive ways and some even fear that reopening the OST regime would result in backsliding given today's divisive political environment.

Thus far, the United States has focused on the second-order issue of how it should organize to address these challenges. In August 2019, the United States reactivated the multi-Service United States Space Command and in December 2019 created its first new military service in more than seventy years by establishing the USSF (Pace, this volume) As these two organizations move forward, they will encounter several specific challenges in harnessing space assets to bolster national security. These challenges include developing appropriate doctrine and culture for the increasingly contested space domain, responding to counterspace threats, improving the process governing the acquisition of space capabilities, and accelerating the creation of wealth in and from space.

Improving Space Doctrine and Developing Space Culture

The USSF must develop the doctrine and culture needed to deal with the increasingly contested space domain. Simple, clear, and strongly held doctrine orients a military organization. Creation of the USSF as an independent military organization should accelerate the development of space doctrine and help move it beyond drawing simple analogies from maritime and air doctrine. As space doctrine matures, it will provide a foundation for the generation-long informal processes that will incubate a space-minded culture for the USSF.

Military doctrine is a formal set of beliefs that help translate national security strategies and policies into specific military objectives, develop the most effective and efficient military operations for accomplishing these objectives, and create appropriate military organizations, systems, and tactics for obtaining these objectives. Doctrine guides tactics and operations. Historian I. B. Holley (1974, 2) provided a more succinct definition of doctrine as "what is officially believed and taught about the best way to conduct military affairs." In practice, doctrine and organizations are usually inextricably woven together.

"Culture" is a more amorphous term that is centered on the social behavior and values of a group, how group members identify themselves, the contributions and achievements of the group, and the things that distinguish one group from another. Distinct military cultures arise from operational and social factors including shared concepts, values, behavior, and identity. Formal processes are seldom primary drivers in shaping culture. As a result, developing or changing the culture of a military organization is normally a generation-long process. In fact, it can be easier and quicker to create a new organization than to change the culture of an existing organization.

The greatest shortfall in current space doctrine is that it lacks anything like the simple, clear, and strongly held mantra that guided early airpower advocates: *airpower is inherently offensive, manifestly strategic, and therefore should be organized independently*. To address this shortfall, the USSF should first develop doctrine rooted in universally applicable fundamental principles, then doctrine for the space environment, and finally organizational doctrine specially adapted to space. This will help the USSF avoid one set of missteps the Air Force made in developing its space doctrine during the Cold War. The Air Force attempted to develop organizational doctrine without first promulgating a coherent environmental doctrine for space—an approach analogous to attempting to grow leaves without a supporting branch. Today, it is not clear that the range of fundamental and environmental space doctrine issues identified during the Cold War have been resolved. Recent US military space doctrine does provide more focus on the space environment and space operations, but the United States still lacks definitive answers to several key environmental questions related to doctrine, such as whether space is an inherently offensive domain with very large first mover advantages.

Because military personnel have little experience operating in outer space and no actual combat experience, the USSF finds itself in a rather difficult situation for developing doctrine. Sailors and pilots contributed to maritime and air doctrine, and they could find insights in their routine military operations at sea or in the air. By contrast, the USSF must explore different environments to look for ideas to help develop doctrine to deter and win space conflicts and, despite the logical shortcomings with this approach, explore what doctrine for operations at sea and in the air may have to offer for space. Promising concepts like command of the sea, command of the air, sea lines of communication, common routes, choke points, harbor access, concentration and dispersal, and parallel attack already have been appropriated into various strands of embryonic space theory. Ideas about lines of communications, common routes, and choke points have been applied directly onto the space domain. Other maritime and airpower concepts— harbor access and access to space, and command of the sea or air and space control— have been modified to contribute to an evolving space doctrine.

Adopting a more "littoral" perspective on military space operations, to borrow another term from the maritime realm, would help doctrine align more closely with current space operations, particularly for LEO or the "cosmic coastline," that is highly vulnerable to attack from Earth (Klein 2019; Bowen 2020). Later, it may become more appropriate to move toward Alfred Mahan and other blue-water maritime theorists as space capabilities mature, conflicts over space resources intensify, and the potential for large-scale, highly maneuverable space combat emerges in higher orbits and cislunar space (Hays 2020).

Reconsidering Lupton's Construct for Space Operations

Strategists interested in doctrine, space weapons, and organizational structures often refer to the four-part typology developed by Air Force Lieutenant Colonel David E. Lupton (1988) in his monograph, *On Space Warfare*, to organize their thoughts. Lupton's *sanctuary* concept posits that the most useful military applications of space are for systems that enhance strategic stability and facilitate strategic arms control. Satellites contribute to these critical functions by monitoring the strategic forces of potential enemies, reducing the likelihood of surprise attack, and providing NTM for arms control agreements. Because of the importance of the stabilizing functions performed by spacecraft, proponents of the sanctuary idea believe that space must be kept free of weapons, and they are especially concerned with prohibiting ASAT weapons that threaten spacecraft performing these vital functions.

The *survivability* concept focuses on improving the resilience of space systems. Like the sanctuary school, this school sees the ability of spacecraft to enhance stability as their most important function, but it also suggests that technological developments mean space can no longer be maintained as a sanctuary and emphasizes that space systems deployed to promote stability have significant ability to enhance the military effectiveness of terrestrial forces. This school emphasizes the idea that space systems are inherently less reliable, supportable, and survivable than are terrestrial forces, and must therefore specifically be designed and deployed in ways to make them more robust through defensive operations, reconstitution, and resilience through disaggregation, diversification, deception, protection, proliferation, and distribution. The survivability concept posits that passive defensive measures can be sufficient to enhance survivability and maintains that actions to counter ASAT weapons (referred to in US doctrine as defensive space control or defensive counterspace operations) should not be emphasized.

Control, Lupton's third concept holds that space should be thought of like other military theaters of operation where the primary military objective is to gain control over the domain. Control implies an ability to maintain one's freedom of action while denying freedom of action to adversaries. In the expanse of space, it is unlikely that one can exert control over large areas for extended times; control is more likely to be exercised over limited areas for specific times. Space strategists envision a scale of actions moving from temporary toward permanent effects that includes deception, disruption, denial, degradation, and destruction. The space control school posits that both offensive and defensive operations are important and likely to be conducted in space. The Air Force defines offensive counterspace operations as those "undertaken to negate an adversary's use of space capabilities, reducing the effectiveness of adversary forces in all domains" (Air Force Doctrine Publication 3-14 2021).

High Ground, Lupton's fourth concept holds that space clearly has the potential to be the decisive theater of combat operations. Reasoning by historical analogy, this school posits that space capabilities can be dominant just as holding the high ground is often the decisive factor in a land battle or as airpower often prevails over land and sea forces. Adherents to this image of space expect that future operations will dominate terrestrial forces. Lupton, along with many other analysts in the 1980s, linked the high ground school directly with the strategic defense initiative and the concept of space-based ballistic missile defense. The high ground school, however, encompasses more than legacy strategic debates over missile defense and envisions the emergence of multiple force application missions from space.

Table 37.3 expands on Lupton's concepts and provides brief descriptions of space system characteristics and potential employment strategies, likely combat missions for space forces operating in accordance with each of the schools, and the types of military organizations for space operations and advocacy usually desired by the proponents of each school. Several factors, including traditional military preferences for offensive doctrine in all domains, make it likely the USSF will accelerate the trend toward the control and high ground schools that has emerged over the past thirty or more years (Hays, 2020).

Blunting Counterspace Threats

The immediate operational challenge facing the USSF is to deter space conflict by blunting the growing counterspace threats the United States now faces. By describing space as a warfighting domain, the 2018 National Defense Strategy marks a fundamental

Table 37.3. Attributes of Military Space Doctrines

	Primary Value and Functions of Military Space Forces	Space System Characteristics and Employment Strategies	Conflict Missions of Space Forces	Appropriate Military Organization for Operations and Advocacy
Sanctuary	Enhance Strategic Stability Facilitate Arms Control	Limited Numbers Fragile Systems Vulnerable Orbits Optimized for NTMV	Limited	National Reconnaissance Office
Survivability	Above Functions Plus: Force Enhancement	Terrestrial Backups Commercial and International Augmentation	Force Enhancement Degrade Gracefully	Major Command or Combatant Command
Control	Control Space Significant Force Enhancement	Autonomous Control Attack Warning Sensors Less Vulnerable Orbits Hardening Redundancy Crosslinks Maneuver	Control Space Significant Force Enhancement Surveillance, Offensive and Defensive Counterspace	Combatant Command, Space Corps, or Space Force
High Ground	Above Functions Plus: Decisive Impact on Terrestrial Conflict Ballistic Missile Defense	Space Mission Assurance Defensive Operations Resilience Disaggregation Protection Distribution Proliferation Diversification Deception Reconstitution On-Orbit Spares 5Ds: Deception Disruption Denial Degradation Destruction Bodyguards and Convoys	Above Functions Plus: Decisive Space-to-Space and Space-to-Earth Force Application Ballistic Missile Defense	Space Corps or Space Force

shift away from legacy US perspectives on uncontested military space operations and the principals of free access and peaceful purposes enshrined in the 1967 OST. The United States' potential adversaries, particularly China and Russia, now view all aspects of space—including launch, on-orbit, up- and downlinks, and ground stations—as a "weak link" in US warfighting capabilities. Conversely, because US officials had long believed space to be a permissive environment, they did not make major investments in defensive capabilities for their space systems, even though almost all modern military operations have become increasingly reliant on space capabilities. These facts, coupled with renewed great power competition, have led adversaries to believe that by denying US space-enabled capabilities, they can gain strategic advantage over US response options—making those options less assured, less opportune, and less decisive. These assumptions can be destabilizing as adversaries may believe they can deter US entry into a conflict by threatening or attacking US space capabilities; these beliefs may even embolden them to employ a space attack as a "first salvo" in anti-access/area-denial strategies. This is a potentially dangerous situation that has moved past an inflection point, creating strategic disadvantages rather than the strategic advantages space traditionally provided the United States. The USSF must assess if current space strategy and systems are approaching a Clausewitzian culminating point where it becomes counterproductive to continue either offensive or defensive space operations in wartime.

Chinese and Russian development of space and counterspace capabilities is accelerating. The 2019 *Defense Intelligence Agency Challenges to Security in Space* report found that "Chinese and Russian military doctrines indicate that they view space as important to modern warfare and view counterspace capabilities as a means to reduce US and allied military effectiveness. Both reorganized their militaries in 2015, emphasizing the importance of space operations" (Executive Summary, III). Chinese and Russian counterspace weapon systems are designed to deny, degrade, disrupt, or destroy US military space systems, along with other civil, commercial, and international space capabilities upon which US national security relies. The 2019 *Worldwide Threat Assessment of the Intelligence Community* found "that commercial space services will continue to expand; countries—including U.S. adversaries and strategic competitors—will become more reliant on space services for civil and military needs, and China and Russia will field new counterspace weapons intended to target U.S. and allied space capabilities" (Coats 2019, 16).

Officials in Beijing and Moscow are clear that they intend to continue developing their own space capabilities while creating systems designed to counter the advantages provided by space-based systems to the United States. According to recent Chinese space strategy and doctrine, the People's Liberation Army (PLA) views space superiority, the ability to control the information sphere, and denying these advantages to adversaries as key components of conducting modern "informatized" wars. Russian military doctrine indicates that achieving warfighting supremacy in space will be a decisive factor in winning future conflicts. For example, Russia's 2014 Military Doctrine lists three space-enabled capabilities as main external military threats to Russia: "global strike," the "intention to station weapons in space," and "strategic non-nuclear precision weapons." In 2013, the Russian Duma officially recommended that Russia resume research and development of an airborne ASAT missile to "be able to intercept absolutely everything that flies from space." China and Russia are developing an array of increasingly sophisticated space capabilities, including dual-use systems in space, that could be applied to counterspace missions.

They appear to be training and equipping their military space forces to hold US and allied space services at risk, even as they push for international agreements on the non-weaponization of space. The PLA has an operational ground-based ASAT missile intended to target LEO satellites, and China probably intends to pursue additional ASAT weapons capable of destroying satellites up to geosynchronous Earth orbit. Russia is developing a similar ground-launched ASAT missile system for targeting LEO that is expected to be operational within the next several years. The Kremlin has also deployed a ground-based laser weapon, which is probably intended to blind or damage sensitive space-based optical sensors. Chinese and Russian proposals for international agreements on the non-weaponization of space do not address multiple issues connected to terrestrially based ASAT weapons development, which has allowed them to pursue space warfare capabilities while maintaining the position that space must remain weapons free. These challenges also highlight deficiencies in the current OST and raise questions about the continuing efficacy of this regime in addressing growing space security concerns.

In addition to growing kinetic and directed energy threats, the United States faces an even more pervasive global threat from electronic warfare systems and cyber capabilities capable of jamming and disrupting many space systems, particularly systems for satellite communications and navigation. Electronic warfare and cyber technology will continue to proliferate, and more advanced adversaries will continue to rapidly develop more sophisticated capabilities. The PLA routinely incorporates jamming and anti-jamming techniques against multiple communication, radar systems, and Global Positioning System (GPS) satellites in exercises. Russia acknowledges the deployment of radar-imagery jammers and is developing laser weapons designed to blind US intelligence and ballistic missile defense satellites.

Creation of the USSF should help the United States deal more effectively with growing counterspace threats by achieving more unity of effort. Of course, simply creating a new organization will not guarantee effectiveness. As with most issues, the devil is in the details regarding the USSF's ability to forge effective relationships with other national security space stakeholders as well as its success in setting appropriate requirements, justifying sufficient funding, and prioritizing the best ways to counter Chinese and Russian counterspace capabilities. Among the more difficult issues for the USSF will be prioritizing and balancing the three space mission assurance pillars of resilience, defensive operations, and reconstitution as well as determining the relative weight it should place on offensive and defensive measures to reduce the effectiveness of adversary counterspace capabilities. It is likely that the USSF will align more closely with the control school than the survivability school with respect to the need for offensive counterspace capabilities to enhance the survivability of US, allied, and commercial space systems.

Accelerating Creation of Wealth in and from Space

For at least two generations, the United States has been thinking seriously about long-term space exploration and exploitation challenges, the proper balance between this work and required near-term efforts, as well as the appropriate role of the military in these "flag follows trade" activities, but it has yet to reach consensus on the best approaches. In 1997, General Howell Estes, a commander of the original US Space Command, articulated a powerful vision for valuing space commerce above military space activity that is today an even more important consideration for the USSF:

> Today, more than ever, it is important that all Americans understand that our investment in space is rapidly growing and soon will be of such magnitude that it will be considered a vital interest—on par with how we value oil today. . . . Now while it might seem appropriate that I should be more concerned with military space, I must tell you that it is not the future of military space that is critical to the United States—it is the continued commercial development of space that will provide continued strength critical for our great country in the decades ahead. Military space, while important, will follow. Commercial space, as I said earlier, will become an economic center of gravity, in my opinion, in the future and as such will be a great source of strength for the United States and other nations in the world. As such, this strength will also become a weakness, a vulnerability. And it's here that the U.S. military will play an important role, for we will be expected to protect this new source of economic strength. (Hays 2002, 14)

The commercial space sector did not experience the explosive growth predicted by General Estes and others in the late 1990s, but it has shown steady growth and may be poised for much more rapid expansion today (Klein and Boensch, this volume).

The global space economy is currently valued at approximately US$400 billion, about 80 percent is commercial activity, and several forecasts predict it will grow to over US$1 trillion within the next 20 years. The increasingly significant role of billionaire "space barons" marks a major change in the economic environment for space. These actors control more wealth than many states, and they are pursuing long-term strategic objectives such as enabling billions to live and work in space and transforming humanity into a multi-planetary species. Such objectives may not align with the short-term profit motive of traditional economic actors and create novel opportunities and challenges for the US government, particularly with respect to how the government can best leverage the work of the space barons to improve security.

The role of the USSF in enabling and protecting space-based global utilities are key factors closely related to economic and commercial space considerations. Space-based global utilities provide basic services or public data, functions that are usually either highly regulated or freely provided by governments (Barowitz, this volume). Examples of space-based global utilities include weather data and GPS positioning and timing signals. Current US policy calls for these services to be provided as a public good without direct user fees. The importance of these space-based global utilities is growing, and they often constitute an embedded or enabling technology within many other systems. GPS timing signals, for example, provide a global "digital heartbeat" used to synchronize the "handshake" between telecommunications networks worldwide, locate and coordinate enhanced emergency responses, and deliver a location-time stamp for financial transactions. These examples indicate that space-based global utilities form a critical and expanding foundation of the modern global infrastructure for public services and commercial intercourse. There are, however, many questions about how global utilities should be perceived, the types and severity of threats these systems face, and how these threats might best be mitigated. Some analysts, primarily in the US military, believe that responding to threats to these systems requires increased space control efforts to provide protection. Other analysts note that civil and commercial satellite operators that provide global utilities are not clamoring for military protection and wonder if concerns about defenses and resiliency warrant the development of dedicated offensive military space control capabilities.

The USSF must address opportunities to create wealth in and from space; nevertheless, it is not evident that a military organization is the best way to focus on these concerns. As humanity continues to explore and increasingly harvest space resources, the fundamental values and economic models that underpin these activities are critical. The governments and commercial entities that are first to harvest space resources are likely to set important precedents that would play a major role in developing the governance structure for these space resources. Helping to set these precedents represents an enormous opportunity for the USSF, but it also raises serious issues about the relationship between military organizations and commercial activities.

CONCLUSION

As space becomes an increasingly contested domain, ISR and communications capabilities provided by space systems will remain critical for US national security. The USSF must aggressively pursue all appropriate measures to improve the resilience of these and other space capabilities that bolster US security. Work to develop better space doctrine, blunt counterspace threats, improve space acquisition, and accelerate creation of wealth in and from space will be key for advancing these efforts. Throughout, the United States must devote resources commensurate with the importance of space to its current and future security.

Several of the major issues requiring additional analysis and research relate to the appropriate scope of the USSF's focus over the near and long term. Some analysts believe that the USSF should aggressively pursue an expansive vision of its mission that emphasizes its role in enabling accelerated exploration and harvesting of space resources. They identify long-term strategic competition with China as the greatest challenge facing the United States and strongly argue that the USSF must focus primarily on this threat rather than focusing on securing US terrestrial military advantages over the short-term. Other analysts argue that a "space guard," structured similarly to the US Coast Guard, may be a more appropriate model given space as the ultimate frontier and the exploration, survey, safety, and constabulary functions likely to be needed in space. A final related issue for the USSF is its prospective role in developing and securing space-based solar power capabilities, technologies that hold the potential to reduce reliance on fossil fuels and their attendant climate change dangers.

Most importantly, it is clear that the policy, legal, and governance structures for space are underdeveloped. Leading space actors, including commercial space actors, must undertake a focused effort to extend and clarify these structures, while considering the best ways to make them more comprehensive, robust, and enforceable. Progress is needed to ensure that space continues to be primarily a peaceful domain that delivers benefits without devolving into a domain of instability and conflict. This work will not be quick or easy, but it must begin now.

DISCLAIMER

The views expressed in this chapter are solely those of the authors and do not necessarily reflect those of Falcon Research, George Washington University, any government, or any government agency.

REFERENCES

Air Force Doctrine Publication 3-14. 2021. "Counterspace Operations." Maxwell AFB: Air Force Doctrine Center.

Bowen, Bleddyn E. 2020. *War in Space: Strategy, Spacepower, Geopolitics*. Edinburgh: Edinburgh University Press.

Carter, Ashton B. 1986. "Satellites and Anti-Satellites: The Limits of the Possible." *International Security* 10, no.4: 46–98.

Coats, Daniel R. 2019. "Worldwide Threat Assessment of the US Intelligence Community." Statement for the Record, Senate Select Committee on Intelligence. https://hsdl.org/?view&did=829727.

Defense Intelligence Agency. 2019. "Challenges to Security in Space." https://apps/dtic/mil/sti/pdfs/AD1082341.pdf.

Dienesch, Robert M. 2016. *Eyeing the Red Storm: Eisenhower and the First Attempt to Build a Spy Satellite*. Lincoln: University of Nebraska Press.

Grauer, Ryan. 2016. *Commanding Military Power: Organizing for Victory and Defeat on the Battlefield*. Cambridge: Cambridge University Press.

Hall, R. Cargill. 1995. "Essay: Origins of U.S. Space Policy, Eisenhower, Open Skies, and Freedom of Space." In *Organizing for Exploration*, Vol. I. *Exploring the Unknown: Selected Documents in the History of the U.S. Civil Space Program*, edited by John M. Logsdon, 213–29. Washington: NASA History Office.

Hays, Peter L. 2002. *United States Military Space: Into the Twenty-First Century*. Colorado Springs, CO: Institute for National Security Studies, United States Air Force Academy.

Hays, Peter L. 2011. *Space and Security: A Reference Handbook*. Santa Barbara, CA: ABC-CLIO.

Hays, Peter L. 2020. "What Should the Space Force Do? Insights from Spacepower Analogies, Doctrine, and Culture." In *War and Peace in Outer Space: Law, Policy, and Ethics*, edited by Cassandra Steer and Matthew Hersch, 153–80. Oxford: Oxford University Press.

Holley, I. B., Jr. 1974. "An Enduring Challenge: The Problem of Air Force Doctrine." Harmon Memorial Lecture Series in Military History. USAF Academy.

Jervis, Robert. 1978. "Cooperation under the Security Dilemma," *World Politics* 30, no. 2: 167–214.

Klein, John J. 2019. *Understanding Space Strategy: The Art of War in Space.* New York: Routledge.

Klose, Kevin. 1978. "New U.S.-Soviet Hotline Replaces Fragile Land Lines With Satellites," *Washington Post.* January 17, 1978.

Koplow, David A. 2022. "Reverse Distinction: A U.S. Violation of the Law of Armed Conflict in Space." *Harvard Law School National Security Journal* 13, no. 1: 25–120.

Lupton, David E. 1988. *On Space Warfare: A Space Power Doctrine.* Maxwell AFB, AL: Air University Press.

Morgan, Forrest. 2010. *Deterrence and First-Strike Stability in Space: A Preliminary Assessment.* Santa Monica, CA: RAND.

Ruffner, Kevin C., ed. 1995. *CORONA: America's First Satellite Program.* Washington, DC: Central Intelligence Agency.

Schilling, Warner. 1965. "Surprise Attack, Death, and War: A Review," *The Journal of Conflict Resolution* 9, no. 1: 385–90.

Sun-tzu and Samuel B. Griffith. 1964. *The Art of War.* Oxford: Oxford University Press.

Townsend, Brad. 2020. "Strategic Choice and the Orbital Security Dilemma." *Strategic Studies Quarterly* 14, no. 1: 64–90.

Whalen, David J. 2010. "Communications Satellites: Making the Global Village Possible." Communications Satellite Short History. Washington: NASA History Office.

Williamson, Justin, and James J. Wirtz. 2021. "Hypersonic or Just Hype? Assessing the Russian Hypersonic Weapons Program." *Comparative Strategy.* 40, no.5: 468-81.

Wirtz, James J., and Jeffrey A. Larsen, eds. 2022. *U.S. Nuclear Command, Control, and Communications: History, Current Issues, and the Future.* Washington, DC: Georgetown University Press.

CHAPTER 38

....

THE STATE, DEVELOPMENT, AND HUMAN SECURITY IN SPACE

....

MOHAMED AMARA AND SAGEE GEETHA SETHU

INTRODUCTION

THE state plays the most crucial role in development, but this cannot be achieved without security. Here, security includes both military security as well as human security, thereby recognizing that human security is vital to ensuring peace and stability for all the nations of the world. In order to achieve such development and security, states need to strengthen themselves by focusing on capacity building, wherein investing in space technology is pivotal for their ability to contribute toward building space capacities for human security.

We argue that space sector investments have become tools for developmental purposes for many countries as states prioritize space as part of their national agenda so as to advance socio-economic and political security. Using the prism of international relations (IR), we argue that international cooperation on developments in space technologies are needed to achieve the developmental agendas of many emerging states around the world. This chapter explores the correlation between the three major components, namely the state, development, and human security, in the context of space. It endeavors to understand how states make decisions regarding the utilization of space technologies for ensuring human security as a means of development. We undertake case studies of four countries, namely the United Arab Emirates (UAE), South Africa, Indonesia, and Mexico. These countries broadly represent the Arab region, Africa, Southeast Asia, and the Americas and can be called emerging space countries, which have embarked on vigorous space advancement missions in the last decade or so.

To substantiate our arguments, the chapter will scrutinize the space policies and regulations of each of the countries so as to understand the key drivers that these countries take into consideration while adopting and pursuing space programs. It will be particularly relevant to see how far these emerging space nations have factored in human security during space policy-making and adoption of space laws and regulations. Furthermore, the privatization and commercialization of space in these countries will see an increased role of private entities in space activities and thereby lead to reduced funding by governments. It would mean that the developmental focus can shift from "public good" to "profit-oriented." This was a key concern even more than two decades ago, when the move toward commercialization of the space sector was seen as a paradigm shift from the security motive to the profit motive as the very purpose for which space activities were intended (Jasentuliyana and Karnik 1997). Although private actors play a significant role in the developmental process of a state, which may include the investments they make toward space projects that advance human well-being and security, the skepticism still exists. In spite of countries like UAE promoting commercialization of its space sector, we have yet to see if the "public good" element gets obliterated in the process.

The chapter will be broadly divided into four sections. The first section will provide a brief background to human security, examining the enlarged role of human security vis-à-vis space. The second section assesses the interface between space and IR, which explores how international cooperation becomes a tool for using space technologies for peaceful purposes. In the third section, the paper sets out the four chosen states, specifically, on a set of questions: which elements of human security are being pursued through space by states in these countries; why they are focused on some particular elements; and how states are engaging these goals, through their space law and policy as well as various space programs. In the final section, we compare and contrast these countries based on what they focus on vis-à-vis human security and how they seek to achieve the stated goals.

BACKGROUND

Understanding Human Security

The United Nations (UN) security agenda placed development and security of the individual at the center of the security spectrum and merged them in order to achieve international security (United Nations 2004). The various reports published by the UNDP reveal the development of human security and its scope and ambit. Defining the basic concept of security, the 1994 Human Development Report introduced new dimensions of human security, which equated security with humans and not territories, and with development and not arms (UNDP Report 1994). According to the report, human security is about "a child who did not die, a disease that did not spread, a job that was not cut, an ethnic tension that did not explode in violence, a dissident who was not silenced." It highlighted that human security is relevant to all nations, rich and poor, and though a few of the threats may slightly vary (e.g., hunger and disease in poorer countries and drugs and crime in rich nations), many threats, like environmental threats and job security, are common to all nations. The 1994 report identified four essential characteristics, namely, that human security is a *universal* concern, that its components are *interdependent*, that it is easier to *ensure through early prevention*, and that it is *people centered*. The report put forth seven categories of human security: economic, food, health, environmental, personal, community and political. These are the dimensions of human security that this chapter will rely on in the case studies.

Pursuant to the 2001 Human Development Report, the Commission on Human Security (CHS) was established and in its report stated that the aim of human security is "to protect the vital core of all human lives in ways that enhance human freedoms and human fulfilment" (CHS 2003). According to Sadako Ogata and Amartya Sen, human security is concerned with safeguarding and expanding vital freedoms of people, which require both shielding from threats as well as empowering people to take charge of their lives. This requires integrated policies that focus on people's survival, livelihood, and dignity (CHS 2003). The 2005 report by the UN Secretary General in the fifty-ninth session of the UN General Assembly specifically emphasized that security cannot be achieved without development and that conversely, development cannot be attained without security, and neither of these can be achieved without respect for human rights (UN Report 2005).

According to Hazel Smith (2005), both freedom from want and freedom from fear together form the twin fundamentals of human security. While "freedom from want" includes the right to food, shelter, and health education, "freedom from fear" includes the right to live a life without violence or political and religious repression, and freedom from fear of economic and natural disaster affecting life and livelihood. Human security also embraces access to positive freedoms, including the right to cultural identity, to make personal choices, and to take part in decision making at the individual and collective level. Human security is hence understood and interpreted broadly as encompassing not just territorial security through arms but also security through development of all people, including security in their homes, in their jobs, in their streets, in their communities, and in their environment (Mahbub ul Haq 1995; Ballin, Dijstelbloem, and de Goede 2020; Albert 2018). Human security principles are also at the core of the Sustainable Development goals the UN seeks to implement in the 2030 agenda through their human security approach. Thus, human security plays one of the most crucial roles in the development agenda of states, and using space technology will aid the states in advancing these multifaceted dimensions.

Understanding Human Security in the Realm of Space

The natural outcome of the importance placed on human security for development extends to the space realm. States utilize their existing and future resources, including space technology, toward the advancement of human security. The 1997 international seminar on Space Futures and Human Security, jointly organized by United Nations Office of the Outer Space Affairs (UNOOSA) and the Austrian government, brought together the world's leading experts, thinkers, and policymakers in space activities. They identified four aspects of human security (Jasentuliyana and Karnik 1997). First, environmental security, focusing on the use of space technologies in the area of natural resource management, environmental monitoring, and also matters relating to water pollution and hazardous wastes; second, economic security, dealing with food security and agricultural development as well as areas ranging from land-use planning to population growth and changing consumption patterns; third, social security, which includes communication infrastructures, tele-education, and the use of satellite disaster manage ment; and fourth, cultural security, which deals with the cultural effects of transnational satellite broadcasting, the globalization and commercialization of culture, and the role of space-based communications in spreading destructive ethnic prejudices as well as in safeguarding indigenous cultures.

For the purpose of investigating the four chosen countries, we adopt the seven parameters of human security as identified in the 1994 Human Development Report, namely economic security, food security, health security, environmental security, personal security, community security, and political security. These give a much more extensive list than the broad categories suggested by the space experts. However, it can be seen that, irrespective of the elements pursued by the states, they invariably seek international cooperation; this enhances prospects for IR with other states, whether with spacefaring or space-emerging nations. International cooperation has always been a top priority in the human security-development discourse (UNDP Report 1994; CHS 2003; Tadjbakhsh 2005; Alkire 2003; Fukuda-Parr and Messineo 2012). A brief discussion below on the IR perspective vis-à-vis space will help further this argument.

THROUGH THE PRISM OF THEORIES OF INTERNATIONAL RELATIONS

Space and IR is the study of exploration and exploitation of space for social, political, economic, and military purposes, and the consequences for relations between sovereign states in the international system (Roberts 1988). The dynamics of the space age have affected four major realms: international politics; the political role of science and scientists; the relationship of the state to technological change; and the political culture and values in nations of high technology (McDougall 1982). The study of space and IR is at the boundaries of two fields: science and technology, and IR (Roberts 1988). As early as 1988, the following were identified as the core issues in the field of space: (1) territorial imperatives, (2) technological change, (3) challenge and response, (4) the role of the state, (5) the militarization of space, (6) space and international law, (7) space and international political economy, and (8) war and space (Roberts 1988). All these issues were pertinent to the race-to-the top in space and particularly the arms-race by a few space-faring nations, particularly the United States and the Soviet Union.

Arguably, the issues in space and IR have gone beyond these core issues and IR in space has now moved toward maximum cooperation between countries for furthering the developmental agenda of the state. For example, the South African space policy includes cooperation with strategic nations in mutually beneficial and peaceful uses of outer space as one of the core guidelines. Likewise, one of the main purposes of UAE's National Space Policy is to stress the importance of international cooperation in the domain of outer space.

These policy trends are more oriented toward the liberal approach whereby, by increasing cooperation with other players, states avert conflicts and secure themselves from any war (see Whitman Cobb, this volume). These cooperation efforts are a step toward economic interdependence, which discourages states from conflict situations since they threaten each other's prosperity. Further, international institutions such as the International Monetary Fund (IMF) and the International Atomic Energy Agency (IAEA) are empowered to encourage cooperation among states, which will bring greater benefits to all concerned (Walt 1998). Liberalism therefore strongly advocates the promotion of international cooperation. This liberal approach counters the realism approach, whereby a state which is the single most powerful entity will ensure that their national security is intact and, toward this end, bolster their military capability in space. Edith Weeks argues that there is a shift from the realist interactions observed previously due to security concerns to a climate in which space law development on the international level has almost stagnated and domestic space law development is at the forefront. This reflects the global pattern during the time of a shift toward privatization and globalization since the 1990s. As a result, domestic policies within each state began to form dictating policy regarding commercial space activities (Weeks 2012).

We claim that states pursue varying elements of human security through the peaceful use of space technology, which requires increased international cooperation with many other states and actors. This includes both public as well as private participation. The case studies discussed in the next section substantiate these arguments and also illustrate which elements of human security are pursued by states and on what basis they decide to choose a particular element.

ANALYZING SPACE PROGRAMS

For the purpose of this paper, four countries have been identified, namely the UAE, Indonesia, Mexico, and South Africa. These are all space-emerging countries, chosen on the basis of even representation across the continents and their ability to represent the region, enhanced space strategies and advancement in space programs, adoption of space policies and laws which are contemporary and in line with international obligations, and increased focus on use of space technology for human security development. Human security emerges at the top of the developmental agenda of all these states. For example, the primary principle of the UAE's National Space Policy is "to enhance the lives of our citizens." To this end, the UAE space program and its activities will be used to enrich the country's knowledge about the universe and to continuously improve the lives of all UAE citizens.

In each of the case studies below, we elucidate and analyze the following parameters: what human security elements are being pursued, why these specific elements are being preferred, and how the state is pursuing them.

United Arab Emirates (UAE)

We begin with the UAE, which is steadily emerging as one of the most determined players in the new space realities.

As evident from its National Space Policy, the UAE's space activities seek to enhance education, scientific studies, and research, thereby contributing to the transfer of knowledge and technical skills and to the creation of local jobs. This will also help in providing better services, especially in the fields of telecommunications, broadcasting, navigation, weather, and climate monitoring, as well as in urban planning and other aspects of daily life that can benefit from space applications. Moreover, it is designed to promote a culture of innovation, particularly within the younger generations, and be a source of national pride and happiness for the UAE people and the region (UAE Space Policy 2016).

In alignment with its National Space Policy, space technology in UAE is used for the following purposes: supporting national security, disaster monitoring and response, humanitarian aid, key UAE industries, and generally the quality of life of its citizens. National security encompasses within itself the elements of human security, namely personal security and political security. Enhancing the level of security and protection of the national space capabilities (including cyber security) as well as promoting regional and international cooperation to mutually benefit and leverage the space capabilities of other allied countries, exchanging information to improve crisis management and recovery, and providing appropriate support to ensure business continuity ensures both the political security of the nation and the personal security of its citizens.

By identifying the existing national space capabilities, enhancing these existing capabilities, and developing new capabilities in the area of disaster and crisis monitoring, response systems, and supporting relief efforts during natural disasters at the national, regional, and global levels, the country safeguards environmental security, personal security, and community security. The UAE further intends to utilize space applications and technologies and develop national capabilities that support and promote the role of the UAE in international cooperation programs related to humanitarian aid. Moreover, the UAE space policy is meant to support business continuity, security, and safety at the national level and expand other opportunities for other key industrial sectors to benefit from space capabilities and identify available opportunities.

All space activities in the UAE, whether government or private, support and adhere to the primary principle, that is to enhance the quality of life of its citizens. To this end, relevant government authorities, academia, research and developments centers, and private entities in the space industry, with support and coordination from the UAE Space Agency, shall harness all opportunities, capabilities, services, and activities in the field of space, for the purpose of continuously improving the level of security, safety, and protection of the environment and public health; enhancing information support for public administration and policy-making; supporting initiatives that improve the quality of education; creating job opportunities; and raising the standard of living and services provided to UAE citizens and residents.

UAE's efforts to focus on the human security elements stems from the very purposes for which it adopted its national space policy, namely, to regulate and strengthen the space sector to focus on the state's priorities in accordance with the sustainability goals and to stress the importance of international cooperation in the domain of outer space. The country believes that space science and technology can contribute to the welfare of people and ultimately to achieving the goals set by UN-organized conferences to address the different aspects of economic and social development. The UAE's collaboration with the international space community will contribute to the realization of the UN goals and initiatives for sustainable development (UAE Space Policy 2016). Both space law and space policy focus on sustainability, thereby emphasizing the need for using space technologies for sustainable development (Sethu 2020).

Being a signatory to major international space treaties, the UAE is responsible for all the space activities that it undertakes. The UAE has signed and ratified the 1967 Outer Space Treaty, 1972 Liability Convention, 1975 Registration Convention, and 1968 Rescue Agreement. Moreover, it became the first country in the region to enact comprehensive national legislation, which incorporates the best practices from various space legislation across the world. The Space Sector Law (Federal Law No. 12 of 2019 on the Regulation of the Space Sector) resulted from the National Space Policy, the main goal of which is to build a strong and sustainable UAE space sector that supports and protects national interests and vital industries, contributes to the diversification and growth of the economy, boosts UAE specialized competencies, develops scientific and technological capabilities, engrains the culture of innovation and national pride, and strengthens the UAE's status and role, regionally and globally.

The Space Law aims to establish a legislative framework regulating the space sector so as to create an appropriate regulatory environment to achieve the objectives of the state's national space policy. This is for the purpose of stimulating investment and encouraging private and academic sector participation; supporting the implementation of the necessary safety, security, and environmental measures to enhance long-term stability and sustainability; and supporting the principle of transparency and the commitment of the state to implement the provisions of international conventions and treaties related to outer space and to which the state is a party.

It is also helpful to understand some specific programs. The establishment of the Thurayya Communications Company in 1997 marked the first step for UAE into the space sector and was followed by the establishment of the Al Yah Satellite Communication Company (Yahsat) a decade later in 2007. They strengthened their position when Yahsat acquired Thurayya in 2011. Meanwhile, in 2006, the Emirates Institution for Advanced Science and Technology (EIAST, renamed Mohamed Bin Rashid Space Centre, MBRSC) was established, furthering the commitment of the nation toward promoting scientific innovation and space technology advancement. Thereafter, in 2014 the UAE Space Agency was created as a federal agency pursuant to Federal Decree No. 1 of 2014, which is in line with UAE's National Innovation Strategy 2014, emphasizing the space sector as an innovation priority sector.

Within the country, MBRSC is the most important strategy partner of the Federal Space Agency. Along with the space agency, MBRSC is in charge of the Hope Probe exploration project, which reached Mars in 2021 and has been gathering information about the planet to share with the scientific community, the UAE Astronaut Programme, as well as an ambitious Mars 2117 vision to build human colonies on Mars by 2117. The center contributes to building a knowledge-based economy in the country and achieving sustainable development objectives. Moreover, its satellite program has led to the building and operation of earth observation satellites that offer imaging and data analysis services through the launch of satellites like DubaiSat-1, DubaiSat-2, and KhalifaSat. One of the main objectives of the center is to develop and innovate smart systems and applications that serve the community and decision makers in the UAE, thereby advancing human security.

Indonesia

Environmental security has been one of the prime concerns for Indonesia. Since the 1990s, the government had embarked on a mission of national development toward prosperity and justice for its people, with sustainable development and insight on the environment. The data collected through remote sensing from satellite operations, earth station operations, and satellite imagery are used in many sectors, such as forestry (forest inventory, fire detection), agriculture (crop yield assessment), transmigration (transmigration area preparation), geologic exploration (mineral, natural gas, and oil), marine and coastal management (mangrove, coral reef, oil spill monitoring, and hazard mitigation programs, etc.) (Kustiyo 1999).

Even during the COVID-19 pandemic and while dealing with other natural hazards, Indonesia has been able to use its space technologies to deal with unforeseen emergencies. For example, it has stepped up and applied geospatial techniques to generate "heatmaps" for those communities most vulnerable to the impacts of COVID-19 and other disasters. This mapping exercise has helped the country to identify the poorest people and their new needs, many of which remain excluded from social protection systems. National Institute of Aeronautics and Space's (LAPAN's) COVID-19 data hub, which combines statistics, crowdsourced data and mid-, high-, and very high-resolution satellite imagery, has performed risk assessment and visualization on the COVID-19 spread and helped the country be better prepared (Alisjahbana 2021).

We can therefore see that Indonesia focuses on environment security, food security, health security, and community security while using its space technologies. The question is why the state is focused on these elements.

One of the purposes of national space legislation is to optimize the implementation of space activities for the welfare of the nation, thereby securing human security. Furthering its space ambition, the Indonesian People's Consultative Assembly approved the 1993–1998 Guidelines of State Policy, which spelt out the Indonesian National Space Development Programme. The emphasis of this program was on the application of space technology for improving the welfare of its citizens, enhancing space science and technology, and human resources development (Mardianis 2014). Indonesian space legislation has specified that space activities are to be used for peaceful purposes by taking into account its national interest; security and safety; the development of science and technology; professional human resources on space activities; the reliability of space infrastructure; and the protection and management of the earth and space environment (Indonesian Space Act 2013, Arts. 7.2, 8; Kumar 2017) .

In Indonesia, satellite data has emerged as an important tool in understanding many environmental issues, such as disaster risk reduction, monitoring climate change, and water resource management, at a deeper level. Two of its homegrown satellites, used in research to mitigate natural disasters, were launched into orbit by India in 2015.

In fulfilling its international obligations, Indonesia has ratified the 1967 Outer Space Treaty, 1972 Liability Convention, 1975 Registration Convention, and 1968 Rescue Agreement (vide Indonesian Law No. 16 of 2002, Presidential Decree No. 20 of 1996, Presidential Decree No. 4 of 1999, Presidential Decree No. 5 of 1997 respectively). In order to comply with its international obligations, Indonesia promulgated the Indonesian Space Act No.21 of 2013. With 19 chapters and 105 articles, the 2013 act governs space activities that include space science, remote sensing, space technology capability, and launching and commercialization of space activities. The purpose of the act is to achieve self-reliance and improve the competitiveness of Indonesia in carrying out space activities; to ensure the sustainability of space activities for the benefit of present and future generations; to protect the state and its citizens from the negative impacts of space activities; and to optimize the implementation of international agreements for the national interest.

The act deals with the following aspects: space activities; competent authority; spaceport establishment and its operation; safety and security of space activities; mitigation of falling space objects and search and rescue of astronauts; registration of space objects; international cooperation; liability and indemnification; insurance, mortgage, and facility; environmental safety; financing; society engagement; and sanctions.

As per the 2013 act, "space activities" are to be carried by the Government Space Agency 'which is under and responsible to the president of Indonesia (Art. 38). Furthermore, other governmental institutions, local government, legal entities, and the community may carry out space activities in coordination with the Space Agency and in accordance with the laws (Art. 39). It is also mandated that commercial space activities may only be undertaken by a legal entity established under Indonesian Law and Foreign Enterprise (Art. 37 (1)).

Many of Indonesia's national law principles are in alignment with the Resolution adopted by the General Assembly on December 11, 2013 on Recommendations on national legislation relevant to the peaceful exploration of outer space (Mardianis 2014). Further, Government Regulation No. 11 of 2013, concerning remote sensing, provided for collecting and processing data, as well as storage, distribution, and usage of data and information dissemination. These activities produce primary data, processing data, and analysis information, which provides for effective resource surveys, environmental monitoring, and disaster prediction. This would improve people's welfare and also the nation's productivity (Diana and Ibrahim 2020).

Finally, it is important to know that Indonesia has had a space sector since 1963, marked by the establishment of the National Council for Aeronautics and Space (DEPANRI), and then continued by the creation of LAPAN, in the same year. LAPAN has had some success with developing research satellite technology, but it wants to make its mark in space flight by sending a homegrown rocket into orbit. Though it had to briefly halt its space activities until 1970 due its political situation, the country continued its activities broadly focusing on space applications. In support of space applications, the program geared up toward space science and technology, including R&D after 1980.

Indonesia's national space agency, LAPAN is responsible for managing its satellites, namely PALAPA satellites and LAPAN satellites. It currently operates six satellites (five on geostationary orbit and one in low Earth orbit) (Mardianis 2014). LAPAN and other space related agencies are now brought within the National Research and Innovation Agency (BRIN), thereby changing the focus to research and innovation and encouraging collaborations.

Mexico

The case of Mexico also illustrates a different mix of human security aspects related to space. Mexico's space sciences consist of space communications, earth observation, and natural disaster management. The MexSat satellite system is used primary for social help and disaster coverage, which includes support in disasters, telemedicine, distant learning, and early warning for disasters (Mendieta-Jimenez 2016). According to the Mexican National Development Plan, a space-based early warning system is to be set up for prevention, mitigation, and rapid response to national disasters, broadband infrastructure with new communication satellite technologies for capacity building, and space system based in satellite global navigation for modernization of transportation. The objective of the Mexican Space Agency (Agencia Espacial Mexicana, AEM) is to bring scientific, technological, and industrial development in aerospace to niche opportunities that allow the country to be competitive in the sector on an international scale and to generate more and better jobs, thereby ensuring economic and social security.

Mexico is adopting space technology for advancing human security by providing increased access to communication and the internet; creation of jobs; and disaster risk reduction. Furthermore, efforts are being made to democratize the space sector by using satellite applications that help reduce the digital divide and achieve greater well-being and social inclusion.

A number of factors drive the Mexican state to focus on these elements. Space technologies can be used to address problems related to agriculture, disasters due to natural phenomena, droughts, fires, security, environment, surveillance, and in the health sector. Moreover this sector had investments of around US$370 billion during 2020, and it is expected that in the coming years it will grow at a rate of 20 percent.

The long-term goal is to consolidate an innovation ecosystem for technology development based on societal applications and new business opportunities based on space technology, integrate Mexican institutions in international cooperation missions, position Mexico as a good actor in the international space community, and develop capabilities in a 12-year span to build 60 percent of a GEO system or its equivalent.

Like the other states, Mexico pursues its goals through law and policy. Being party to all the five major international space treaties, Mexico is at the forefront in space in the region. Apart from its international treaty obligations, the country proposes to bolster its commitments in two ways. First, to reinforce its international commitments through laws enacted by the Congress and second to participate actively in forums and organizations of the UN such as the Committee on the Peaceful Uses of Outer Space (COPOUS), Internaitonal Civil Aviation Organisation (ICAO), and International Telecommunication Union (ITU), with the purpose of generating proposals aimed at strengthening international law and providing security and safety (de Arellano 2016).

The national space policy has security, environmental security, and international cooperation as its main agenda. To this end, the Space Agency has also implemented an environmental sustainability policy to promote the development of space science and technology in coordination with the government departments responsible for this issue and achieve the rational use of natural resources and ensure long-term sustainability. Moreover, efforts are also made toward joint development of space-based solutions with social benefits.

An office for space known as the Comisión Nacional del Espacio Exterior (CONEE or National Space Commission) was created by presidential decree on August 31, 1962, and was attached to the Secretariat of Communications and Transport. It carried out experiments in rocketry, telecommunications, and atmospheric studies from 1962 to 1976 before the commission was dissolved in 1977. After a large gap, in 2005, a proposal for a space agency for Mexico was mooted and the AEM, a self-funded entity, was created. In 2010, the AEM, was approved by the president and Congress for purposes of increasing competitiveness and job creation as well as to open new spaces for the development of national entrepreneurs. Bringing economic stability to the country will ensure that they achieve economic security, one of the key aspects of human security.

Spearheading its commitment toward better cooperation internationally and in the region, the AEM has been to the forefront in bringing about the international convention establishing the Latin American and Caribbean Space Agency (ALCE).

Finally, in terms of specific programs, while trying to bring Mexico into the modern technological age, the Mexican government purchased a series of communications satellites to service the country, initially the Morelos 1 and 2, geostationary satellites operated between 1985 and 1998 to provide telephony, data, and television services, and then Solidaridad 1 and 2 operated from 1997. These satellites were eventually privatized and converted into the Satmex Satellite System. More recently, during the first decade of the twenty-first century, the Mexican Government acquired the MexSat constellation of geostationary satellites, comprised of the Morelos 3 satellite for fixed communications and the Bicentenario for mobile communications (Munoz 2019).

The ALCE, based in Mexico, coordinates cooperation in space technology, research, exploration, and related applications that contribute to and strengthen the comprehensive and sustainable development of a regional space program that will benefit the Latin American and Caribbean peoples. It will enhance the region's capabilities in Earth observation systems for use in agriculture, natural disasters (droughts, floods, fires, hurricanes), security and surveillance, oceanography, meteorology, exploration of natural resources, and urban intelligence and cartography. The agency will provide benefits such as improvements to satellite communication systems and the creation of maps of strengths, opportunities, threats, risks, and vulnerabilities, which are of particular importance for combating climate change.

The AEM use medium earth orbit for new communications faster bandwidths and technologies for speeding information transfer for early warning systems (Mendieta-Jimenez 2016). This is essential since Mexico faces yearly earthquakes, hurricanes, flooding, forest fires, drought, pollution, etc. In collaboration with the Thematic Network of the Space Science and Technology (RedCyTE) and National Council of Science and Technology (CONACYT), AEM has adopted the Orbit Plan, whose mission is to develop space technology favoring missions that have high societal impact. AEM and RedCyTE have entered into agreements to launch several projects that are essential for use in larger communities in Mexico. These include the use of the satellite infrastructure for linking remote communities and providing health, education, and communications; and developing new business for monitoring, communications, and location by satellite in the country.

Due to recurring earthquakes, special radio receivers are placed in schools, government offices, and TV and radio stations, which receive radio broadcast alerts providing early warning of imminent shaking. The system is designed to issue an alert that provides about one minute of warning before residents of Mexico City would begin to feel an earthquake. Since its inception in September 2017, the system issued a total of thirty-three alerts about earthquakes with estimated magnitudes of M6 or larger and seventy alerts for earthquakes with estimated magnitudes between M5 and M6 (Allen 2018). The use of satellite technologies helps a great deal toward putting the warning system in place.

South Africa

The South African state also uses the context of human security to make inroads into space. South Africa is increasingly reliant on space-based systems for a variety of services and applications, such as communications, navigation, meteorology, natural resource management, environmental monitoring, and disaster management. The 2008 National Space Policy recognizes that space systems provide vast socio-economic benefits by delivering information and services that protect lives and the environment, enhance prosperity and security, and stimulate scientific, industrial, and economic development.

The National Space Strategy identifies three key priority areas, namely, environmental resource management, to protect the environment and develop its resources in a sustainable manner; ensuring health safety and security of South Africa's communities; and stimulating innovation while leading to increased productivity and economic growth through commercialization. These address the human security elements of economic security, health security, environmental security, and community security.

A 2021 report by the World Economic Forum (Report of the World Economic Forum 2021) estimates that data collected from space could unlock US$2 billion a year in benefits for Africa. The report says satellites could address agricultural challenges by measuring crop health, improving water management by monitoring drought, and tracking tree cover for more sustainable forest management. In a continent where less than one-third of the population has access to broadband, more communication satellites could help people connect to the internet. South African startup Astrofica, which provides space consultancy services, supported the CubeSat program at Cape Peninsula University of Technology, which launched a constellation of maritime satellites for tracking ships along the southern African coast. The goal of the startup is to use the space industry to address Africa's challenges—from food security to national security (Bailey 2021).

The startup hopes to launch its first constellation of satellites by the end of 2022. This will provide decision makers with critical data sets in near real time. The company believes that the data will be used to monitor crop yield or track the use of fertilizers, as well as help governments with water management. Astrofica is looking for international collaborations to launch its first satellite on board a US SpaceX rocket, a Russian Soyuz rocket, or an Indian Polar Satellite Launch Vehicle.

The country is focused on these elements due to necessity. African countries are spending too much money acquiring agricultural data from international providers, which are not timely enough, although the company welcomes collaboration with foreign partners. A lot of South Africa's government departments are using satellite imagery to make decisions around certain policies. However, previously, different government departments would go to a service provider individually regarding various issues. Several package deals were negotiated for the whole of the government ensuring accessibility for all government departments to data (i.e., satellite imagery) to support evidence-based policies that address the socio-economic and environmental issues of the country.

South Africa is pursuing these goals though a number of ways. Space activities in South Africa are governed by the Space Affairs Act (No. 84 of 1993) which established the South African Council for Space Affairs. Pursuant to the act, the 2008 National Space Policy was laid down, providing an overarching guidance for the development of appropriate space capabilities and utilization of space systems applications to contribute to economic growth, reduction of poverty, and the creation of knowledge. This is to be carried out through support and promotion of relevant scientific research, capacity building, innovation, and industrial development, with the aim of utilizing space applications to contribute to the growth of the economy, poverty reduction, and knowledge creation. The policy also provides guidance to South African public and private sector stakeholders in the space arena, to inform South African participation in domestic and international space activities and promote improved coordination and co-operative governance.

SANSA, the South African National Space Agency, created in 2010, was set up to promote the use of space and strengthen cooperation in space-related activities while fostering research in space science, advancing scientific engineering through developing human capital, and supporting industrial development in space technologies. Adhering to its international obligations, South Africa is party to the Outer Space Treaty, Rescue Agreement, and Liability Convention.

In terms of some specific programs, South Africa developed the first domestic satellite in the continent, named Sunsat, in 1999. The Sunsat program had two main purposes: to train students in the technologies and sciences of spacecraft construction and to build a working satellite equipped with a high-performance Earth observation camera.

Since its inception in 2010, SANSA has produced a number of Earth observation and other data products for public use and for specific stakeholders. These include an informal settlement atlas, an annual country mosaic based on satellite images, a flood risk map that supports an early warning system, and a human settlements map layer that supports spatial planning and service delivery projects. The Earth Observation Programme has also maintained the online catalogue for data discovery and dissemination. SANSA also deployed a new HF radar at SANAE IV in Antarctica in 2014, as part of the global Super Dual Aurora Radar Network (SuperDARN), and recently completed the state-of-the-art Optical Space Research Laboratory (OSRL) at the South African Astronomical Observatory (SAAO) in Sutherland. This facility will provide crucial space science data to meet national and international obligations, raise the standard of South African research, and improve the understanding of the Earth's middle and upper atmosphere.

SANSA is involved in TT&C (telemetry, tracking, and command), operations, and data capture for SumbandilaSat, a weather microsatellite launched jointly by Stellenbosch University, SunSpace, and the Council for Scientific and Industrial Research (CSIR). SumbandilaSat has completed over 9,000 orbits, and SANSA has monitored in the region of 1,300 passes. The satellite produced good quality images, some of which have contributed to the European GMES program. It demonstrated capabilities important for the future of South Africa's space program.

There are also some commercial ventures. Dragonfly Aerospace, a private aerospace company, provides imaging systems for satellites and is now working on launching its own constellation, a system of satellites in orbit, which is far more powerful than a single satellite because they work together and combine the data. The company has nearly completed a 3,000 square meter satellite manufacturing facility in Stellenbosch, South Africa, with capacity to build up to 48 satellites per year with a mission to improve the lives of people around the world.

ANALYSIS AND CONCLUSION

The space policies, programs, and plans of these countries suggest the importance of three outcomes. First, strengthening IR is essential for enhancing space technology. Second, a major concern of all the four countries is to ensure human security. Third, countries have their own different priorities on which aspects of human security they have to focus on.

On the human security question, we drew attention to seven elements of security, namely, economic, food, health, environmental, personal, community, and political security. The countries studied have diverse priorities, and their choices of elements to pursue in human security are based on factors like demography, economic capability, environmental necessities, etc. The UAE's prime focus is to secure economic, environmental, personal, community, and political securities. Indonesia, a country prone to many natural disasters, has environmental and economic security at the top of its agenda. Mexico, on the other hand, has focused on job creation and disaster management, bringing economic, environmental, and personal security to the forefront. South Africa has taken up the mantle of ensuring food security for the African region and thereby prioritizing economic security over all others. However, it can also be noted that these countries are using space technologies for human security overall and hence fostering the development agenda.

All these countries are advancing their human security through international cooperation, which is a primary tool for fostering IR. There is cooperation at all levels in forming alliances, between space-emerging countries and spacefaring nations, between space-emerging countries and other space-emerging nations, between the governmental agencies of these countries, between government and private entities, as well as between private entities. Recently, AstroAgency of Scotland teamed up with UAE's private sector entity AzurX to gain market access and secure government contracts, which will help build spacecraft and satellites and thereby improve scientific research, telecoms, and internet connectivity (Nasir 2022). Also, NASA's MAVEN and the UAE Mars Mission Hope Probe are collaborating for greater scientific returns and data exchange.

The agendas of UAE's space programs are highly ambitious and the country's National Space Policy envisions this through its space future's goals and ambitions. It aims to diversify the economy and build a knowledge-based model that leverages technology and high-value-added activities. Therefore, the UAE strives to build, develop, and sustain an active, diversified, commercial space industry to become a regional and global leader in this field.

Indonesia has also been robust in its collaborative efforts with spacefaring countries like the United States (2012), Russia (2017), India (2019), and the European Union (2022). Establishing BRIN, the National Research and Innovation Agency, as an overarching super-governmental agency and bringing the space agencies within its ambit affirms the Indonesian diplomatic agenda that the use of space and space technology are for peaceful purposes, whereby the outputs will be used in agriculture, the environment and forestry, marine and fisheries as well as disaster management and reaction to emergencies (Handoko 2022). This ensures economic security, food security, health security, environmental security, and community security, five of the seven dimensions of human security.

Encouraging regional and international cooperation, Mexico has played a crucial role in having the ALCE signed by signed by eighteen Latin American and Caribbean countries, since it opened for signature on September 18, 2021. A framework agreement for cooperation signed in 2014 with French Space Agency CNES, the AEM has helped in dealing with issues related to the fight against climate change, including the adoption of the Mexico City Declaration in September 2015, which proved to be fundamental for taking into account the role of satellites during the preparation for COP21 (Diokh 2020).

Finally, in South Africa, SANSA has built strong international relationships through launch support with NASA, CNES, and the Indian Space Research Organisation (ISRO), among others, as well as through partnerships with organizations like Airbus Defence and Space (ADS) and Avanti Communications.

We analyzed the space policies and regulations of the UAE, Indonesia, Mexico, and South Africa focusing on the key drivers these countries pursued for adopting their space programs. The case studies identified human security as the principal element for investing in space technologies. Moreover, pursuing space programs encouraged and strengthened IR with both the spacefaring nations and the space-emerging nations, ushering in an era of socio-economic and political security for these countries, thereby ensuring "freedom from want" and "freedom from fear." We conclude that space technology cooperation between states results in improving IR and thereby helps the states to ensure that their human security goals are achieved, contributing to the development of their countries.

References

Alkire, S. 2003. "A Conceptual Framework for Human Security." Working Paper. CRISE, Department of International Development, University of Oxford.

Albert, I. O. 2018. "Nigeria's Security Challenges in Historical Perspectives." In , edited by A. Olukoju, O. Adesina, A. Adisoji, and S. Amusa, 2–14. Newcastle upon Tyne, UK: Cambridge Scholars Publishing.

Alisjahbana, A. S. 2021. "Keynote Speech at the 6th National Seminar on Aeronautics and Space Policy." Organised by LAPAN, September 15, 2021.

Allen, R. M., et al. 2018. "Lessons from Mexico's Earthquake Warning System." *EOS Newsletter*. September 17, 2018.

Bailey, S. 2021. "Why Africa is Sending More Satellites into Space." *CNN Business*. October 6, 2021.

CHS (Commission on Human Security). 2003. *Human Security Now: Protecting and Empowering People*. New York: UN Digital Library.

de Arellano, R. M. 2016. "Mexico Space Regulations." ICAO/UNOOSA Symposium.

Diana, S. R., and Ibrahim, I. M. 2020. "Intangible Economic Benefit of Remote Sensing Data in Indonesia." *International Journal of Research & Social Science* Special Issue 9, no. 7: 150–59.

Diokh, A. 2020. "All About the Mexican Space Agency." *Space Legal Issues*.

Fukuda-Parr, S., and C. Messineo. 2012. "Human Security." *Elgar Handbook of Civil War and Fragile States*, edited by G. K. Brown and A. Langer, 21–38. Cheltenham: Edward Elgar Publishing.

Handoko, L. T. 2022. "Led by BRIN, Indonesia's Space Program for Remote Sensing Expected to Improve." Opening Remarks by Head of BRIN Dr. L.T. Handoko at the Virtual Joint Workshop on Copernicus between BRIN and EU Copernicus on 16 March 2022.

Hirsch Ballin, E., H. Dijstelbloem, and P. de Goede. 2020. "The Extension of the Concept of Security." In *Security in an Interconnected World. Research for Policy*, edited by E. Hirsch Ballin, H. Dijstelbloem, and P. de Goede, 13–39. Cham: Springer.

Indonesian Law No. 16 of 2002.

Indonesian Presidential Decree No. 20 of 1996.

Indonesian Presidential Decree No. 4 of 1999.

Indonesian Presidential Decree No. 5 of 1997.

Jasentuliyana, N., and Karnik, K. 1997. "Space Futures and Human Security." *Space Policy* 13, no. 3: 257–64.

Kumar, A. 2017. "The Indonesian Space Act- Pristine Entrant in the Asia- Pacific Region." Paper Presented at the 60th IISL Colloquium on the Law of Outer Space. IAC-17, E7, 4, 9, x38352.

Kustiyo, T. M. 1999. "Remote Sensing Applications in Indonesia: Selected Papers on Remote Sensing, Space Science and Information Technology." In *Seminars of the United Nations Programme on Space Applications*. UNOOSAVol. 10, 39–44. New York: United Nations.

Mahbub ul Haq. 1995. *Reflections on Human Development*. New York: Oxford University Press.

Mardianis. 2014. The Indonesian Space Act No. 21/2013, 53rd Session of the UNCOPOUS Legal Subcommittee.

McDougall, W. A. 1982. "Technocracy and Statecraft in the Space Age—toward the History of a Saltation." *The American Historical Review* 87, no. 4: 1010–40.

Mendieta-Jimenez, F. J. 2016. *Development of the Space Sector in Mexico*. 67th IAC. Mexico: International Astronautical Federation.

Munoz, C. D. 2019. "Mexico's Path to Space." *Room Space Journal* 3, no. 21: 60–65.

Nasir, S. 2022. "Dubai's AzurX Teams up with Scotland's AstroAgency for Space Collaboration." *The National*. May 26, 2022.

Report of the World Economic Forum. 2021. "Unlocking the Potential of Earth Observation to Address Africa's Critical Challenges." World Economic Forum (weforum.org).

Roberts, D. 1988. "Space and International Relations." *Journal of Politics* 50, no. 4: 1075.

Sethu, S. G. 2020. "UAE's Entry into the Space League: Analysing the Legal Spectrum." Paper Presented at the Advances in Science and Engineering Technology International Conferences (ASET). IEEE.

Smith, H. 2005. *Hungry for Peace: International Security, Humanitarian Assistance and Social Change in North Korea*. Washington DC: United States Institute of Peace.

Tadjbakhsh, S. 2005. "Human Security: The Seven Challenges of Operationalizing the Concept." *Human Security: 60 Minutes to Convince*. Section SHS/FPH/PHS. Paris: UNESCO.

The Indonesian Space Act (No. 21 of 2013).

UNDP (United Nations Development Programme). 1994. *Human Development Report 1994*. New York: Oxford University Press.

UN Report. 2005. "In Larger Freedom: Towards Development, Security and Human Rights for All." A/59/2005/Add.3.

United Nations (UN). 2004. *A More Secure World: Our Shared Responsibility*. Report of the High-level Panel on Threats, Challenges and Change. New York: United Nations Foundation.

Walt, S. M. 1998. International Relations: One World, Many Theories. *Foreign Policy* 110: 29–46.

Weeks, E. 2012. *Outer Space Development, International Relations, and Space Law: A Method for Elucidating Seeds*. Newcastle upon Tyne, UK: Cambridge Scholars Publishing.

CHAPTER 39

GEOPOLITICS OF GLOBAL NAVIGATION SATELLITE SYSTEMS

PAUL B. LARSEN

INTRODUCTION

GNSS (Global Navigation Satellite Systems) is one of the most important technologies of the twenty-first century, comparable in geopolitics to the internet, both of which are of military origin. GNSS satellites provide basic positioning, navigation, and timing (PNT) information for the Earth as well as for satellites that encircle Earth in low Earth orbit (LEO). Each of the four GNSS—US Global Positioning System (GPS), Russian GLONASS, European Galileo, and Chinese Beidou—forms a global net from which they are able to serve everywhere, both on the Earth and in LEO.

GNSS is at a difficult geopolitical stage. It is a foundational part of the global economic and social infrastructure; its technology and magnitude of use are growing to the extent that society would have difficulty existing without it. Yet the weak GNSS web is easily disrupted by harmful interferences, and international law is inadequate to restrain states and criminals from interfering with its signals. Enforcement is weak because it is left to the individual states that compete with each other, while competition among states restrains them from bilateral or regional coordination. This chapter engages with how GNSS technology functions as a security driver in interstate relations and its effects on both cooperative and competitive processes among states.

GNSS BACKGROUND

At the outset, it is helpful to have an understanding of GNSS functions and context, as follows (Larsen 2021; UNOOSA 2016).

Technology: GNSS satellites are equipped with atomic clocks that measure time accurately and are synchronized with each other and with ground stations. Each satellite calculates and reports its own position, and thus are able to transmit accurate position and time to users. Each user must have at least four satellites within range in order to establish its position by GNSS. Satellites orbit in mid-Earth orbit (MEO) at approximately 12,000 miles above the surface of the earth. Each GNSS system consists of between 24 and 32 satellites. Each of those satellites emits a time signal accessed by the user.

The Three Segments of GNSS: The space segment consists of the orbiting satellites. Because they orbit in MEO they move faster than the Earth so each satellite passes over the same spot on Earth twice every day. Six satellites are always in the viewer's line of sight when viewed from the surface of the Earth. GNSS signals are weak, which makes it possible to jam or to substitute (spoof) signals by overwhelming them with stronger signals. The GNSS control segment consists of the master station as well as alternate control stations. It includes ground antennas and monitoring stations at the home state and around the Earth. The GNSS control segment contacts each satellite regularly to check and synchronize its atomic clock and its positioning information. Users must have an antenna to send signals to and receive signals from GNSS.

The Great Variety of Civilian Users: Civilization would suffer hugely from loss of GNSS. Civilian users constitute approximately 85 percent of all GNSS users. GPS is used most, nationally and internationally, because of its early introduction. It has constantly been updated. A 2019 survey of the US economy estimates that there would be a daily economic loss of US$1 billion if GPS were lost. Loss of other GNSS systems would wound economies around the world. Users include airlines and ships that navigate by use of GNSS. Alternative means of navigation are obsolete and no longer in use. Car drivers depend on GNSS to find their way. Driverless cars are operated by use of GNSS. Cell phones are required by the US Federal Communication Commission (FCC) to be equipped with GNSS so that users can be located in the event of an emergency. Farmers use GNSS for precision farming. Surveyors now rely on GNSS. Astronomers depend on GPS to synchronize receipt of data from outer space. Banks and stock exchanges use GPS to record the exact time that property rights are transferred. Satellites can navigate by GNSS in LEO without having to refer to a ground station. GNSS sensors are deposited in the oceans to measure the effects of climate change. When deposited on land the sensor can detect earthquakes. Global search and rescue is yet another function of GNSS.

Military Users: GNSS is part of virtually all aspects of military operations. However, military uses, many of which are classified, constitute only about 15 percent of all GNSS uses. Examples of military uses include armies identifying and moving soldiers toward military targets, establishment of targets for guided missiles, moving supplies to the front according to needs identified by GNSS, and reconnaissance. GPS satellites are equipped with sensors that can identify and report nuclear explosions.

Military Origins of GNSS: Except for the European Galileo, all the GNSS systems are of military origin. They are administered by national authorities that permit and enable civilian uses but view their GNSS as being primarily for military use. Despite the predominant civilian uses of GNSS, military oversight and management continues for national security reasons. State governments can only afford to maintain one GNSS system. The US military GPS originated in 1973 as a project of the Department of Defense (DoD). The Russian military authorities originated GLONASS during the same time period, but the system declined during the break-up of the USSR. The European GNSS operator, Galileo, was subsequently started in Europe by the European Space Agency (ESA). Galileo was built not only to strengthen the European space industry but for Europe to avoid depending on US, Russian, and Chinese military controlled GNSS. Chinese GNSS (Beidou) is also of military origin but is now operated by the China Space Administration (CNSA). It is dedicated to China's national security as well as to social and economic development. Beidou became globally operational in 2020.

Dual Use Tensions between Military and Civilian Users: GNSS is essentially dual use; its technology is an important element of both military and civilian activities. The dual nature of GNSS presents a threat to its military functions, which is countered by increasing encryption of military GNSS. Military authorities consider outer space a warfighting domain requiring military GNSS technology: GNSS is essential for guiding missiles. Interruption of GNSS signals is part of space warfare. But the versality of GNSS is a great benefit to civilian users enabling them to use highly developed military technology.

Dual use requires interagency coordination between military and civilian authorities. US GPS is coordinated by the interagency National Space-Based Positioning Navigation and Timing Executive Committee cochaired by the departments of defense and transportation, with participation of practically all the other government departments. The committee receives advice from the National Space-Based Positioning, Navigation and Timing Advisory Board, a federal committee of non-governmental GNSS experts serviced by its standing coordination office. The objective of the GNSS Committee is not only to coordinate US government military and civilian uses. It also serves as the forum for coordinating GNSS national and international policy interests with GNSS users around the world. US international activities are coordinated by the US Department of State with assistance from the technical experts of DoD, Department of Transportation (DOT) and others. The National Space-Based Positioning, Navigation and Timing Committee compares dual use problems of GPS with similar problems of the three other GNSS services—GLONASS, Galileo, and Beidou.

International differences: The most active and successful international coordination of international GNSS issues occurs in the International Committee on GNSS (ICG) of the United Nations (UN) Committee for the Peaceful Uses of Outer Space (COPUOS) (Larsen 2015; Mountin 2014). The ICG has established working groups on Compatibility and Interoperability, Enhancement of Performance of GNSS Services, Information Dissemination and Capacity Building, Reference Frames, Timing and Applications, and GNSS Compatibility and Spectrum. They have dealt with military/civil dual-use issues by simply leaving military uses outside of international regulation.

GNSS Competition among the United States, Russia, Europe Union, and China

This section describes the four GNSS systems emanating from the United States, Russia, the European Union (EU), and China. The development of GLONASS, Galileo, and Beidou may be viewed as a reaction to the US GNSS system. Russia and China found it difficult, if not impossible, to rely on what is in effect the US DoD for control of their military activities through use of US GPS. The European states also do not wish to be dependent on the United States. Therefore, each has developed its own fully global system. The four GNSS organizations differ significantly from each other.

GNSS are important to the great space powers, and each has established fully global systems even though logically one global navigation system would suffice to meet the needs of the entire world. But each of the superpowers wishes to have equal access to outer space in order to prevent domination by its competitors. GNSS is not only of military importance to the super space powers; it is fundamental for their national economies, because the superpowers compete with each other economically. GNSS systems exist not only for the important means of providing PNT information. They are also linked to and supportive of domestic and international surface trade activities. They support transportation of goods by rail, road, and air; international enterprises such as the new Chinese Trans-Siberian rail connections between Asia and Europe; and movements of goods under the improved North American Free Trade Agreement.

Subject to commitments made under international treaties, the individual GNSS systems are under the control of their national states. These states make the decisions to establish GNSS, and they finance, design, and launch the GNSS satellites into orbit. They build and operate GNSS control systems in their territories, and they make the system available for their national military authorities and civilian users. The individual states retain jurisdiction, control, and ownership over orbiting satellites registered in their countries pursuant to the Outer Space Treaty, Article VIII. If lost or turned into space debris, the satellites remain under the jurisdiction of the state of registry. Thus, in case of war, the state having jurisdiction can use its GNSS controls to restrict the use of its GNSS satellite to military uses for its military authorities. Fear of GNSS sole use by the military authorities is a strong reason and motivation for the multiple systems.

US Global Positioning System (GPS)

GPS offers global service. The first GPS satellite was launched by the US DoD in 1979. The service was originally intended solely for its military uses. Despite the vast expansion of civilian uses, DoD continues to operate and manage the GPS under US law, 19 U.S.C. 228(b). However civilian uses were authorized by President Regan in 1983 after a Korean Airliner strayed into Russian airspace and was shot down for violating Russian sovereign air space. The Korean pilots of the airliner could have avoided entry into Russian airspace if they had had access to GPS to determine their geographical location.

US GPS became fully operational in 1993. It contains at least twenty-four satellites and remains the most widely used GNSS service. It was the first global service to come online, it is free of charge for civilian uses and constantly serviced and updated. GPS access is built into virtually all PNT technology as GPS provides standard positioning service that is open to all users. Additionally, it provides encrypted precise positioning service that is only open to US military users, to civilian government users, and to foreign governments allied with the United States. GPS is an indispensable part of the military weaponry needed to guide missiles and many other known and secret military functions. GPS is generously funded by the US Congress for military purposes. It is unlikely that Congress would be willing to fund a purely civilian GPS as generously.

The US DOT views congressionally funded GPS as essential for regulation of air traffic. GPS is also essential for guidance of maritime traffic and for rail safety signals. Road traffic safety and traffic regulation is also dependent on GPS. Unmanned road, air, and space vehicles are guided by GPS. GPS is important for satellite remote sensing regulated by the National Ocean and Atmospheric Administration (NOAA) in the Department of Commerce (DOC). White House Policy Directive 13905 designated GPS a critical infrastructure in need of US government protection in 2020. The policy directive assigned GPS oversight functions to the DOC, but that has yet to be fully funded by Congress.

The mix of critical military and civilian uses is making it increasingly difficult to develop law and policy governing GPS. The US FCC—an independent federal agency that is not part of the executive branch—allocates and regulates scarce radio frequencies for GPS signals. GPS radio navigation signals have to be exclusive to be reliable; they must be free of outside radio interference. Commercial communication companies compete with GNSS for radio frequencies. FCC has recently favored these companies over GPS in allocation of radio frequencies, which is another source of friction (Federal Communications Commission 2020).

The many different demands on GPS as well as the variety of governmental uses make US GPS geopolitics difficult to manage. While GPS, by presidential policy decision, is made available for civilian uses, GPS policy is based on the assumption that GPS will remain under military control. The terms of civilian uses of the military GPS are coordinated by the interagency National Space-Based Positioning, Navigation and Timing Committee which is co-chaired by DoD and DOT. It includes a Civil GPS Service Interface Committee (CGSIC) that is seeking suggestions from the public for improvement of global GPS service. The CGSIC has established subcommittees on timing, information and surveying, mapping and geosciences.

GPS signals are compatible with the signals of GLONASS, Galileo, and Beidou. GPS is augmented for accuracy in the United States by the Wide Area Augmentation Service (WAAS). In Europe it is augmented by the European Geostationary Navigation Overlay

Service (EGNOS). Japanese and Indian regional navigations systems also augment local GPS.

The Russian GLONASS GNSS

GLONASS provides global services (About GLONASS n.d.; Karutin, Testoedoy, and Donchenko 2022). GLONASS and GPS were developed and became operational at the same time (1995). Both were developed by military authorities for military purposes. Both systems are essential ingredients of national military operations. Both systems orbit in MEO. Both were designed to have twenty-four orbiting satellites providing global service. Both are now available without charge for GNSS open services. GLONASS also provides a special high-grade service for military uses. GLONASS development declined in the Russian economic depression during the political changes of the 1990s, whereas GPS continued development and expansion during that time period. At the time of the Russian economic depression the leadership of GLONASS was transferred from the Russian military authorities to the civilian space agency Roscosmos, but it remains subject to Russian military uses. With the transfer to Roscosmos the development of GLONASS revived. GLONASS adopted a global system of differential correction and monitoring establishing integrity data and local correction data for greater accuracy. GLONASS provides open (free) access for civilian users but restricts higher quality signals to military and governmental users. GLONASS is financed through the Russian state budget. It is interoperable with the other GNSS services. The satellites have become increasingly more durable and now last up to seven years.

GLONASS provides an important complement to the other GNSS services. It establishes additional ways to acquire PNT assistance. GLONASS services comply with the international GNSS standards maintained by International Civil Aviation Organization (ICAO), International Maritime Organization (IMO), and COPUOS. Russia promotes commercial use of GLONASS. The Russian government requires cars with GNSS capability to have access to GLONASS. Major manufacturers of cellphones such as Samsung and Sony now include access to GLONASS in their cellphones.

Galileo GNSS

The European Galileo also provides global GNSS (Pont, Falcone, and Bautista 2022; European Space Agency 2021a; European GNSS Galileo Open Service Definition Document 2016). It is a civilian PNT service consisting of twenty-four operating satellites and, being non-military, would continue service if civilian service by the other GNSS services were discontinued for military reasons. It is financed and owned by the EU by virtue of EU Council Resolution 1321/2994 establishing the Galileo Supervisory Authority, now called the European Global Navigation Satellite Agency. Day-to-day operation is delegated to the ESA. The EU also established the European GNSS Agency for the purpose of marketing and promotion of Galileo services, which include: (1) basic free service; (2) regulated stronger and more precise commercial service that is also available free of charge; (3) an encrypted public regulated service for governmental uses; and (4) global search and rescue service that can inform victims that aid is coming. Galileo is interoperable with the other GNSS services and provides high quality service in conformity with international standards established by ICAO, IMO, and COPUOS. Galileo is coordinated with other GNSS services through the COPUOS International GNSS Committee (ICG) and other agreements so that users will receive virtually seamless GNSS service.

In 2018 the EU Commission mandated that all European smart cellphone receivers must be able to receive Galileo service. Consequently, all European computerized equipment now has access to Galileo. Galileo is the only non-US GNSS service that is allowed to provide service to non-governmental GNSS receivers in the United States pursuant to a 2018 decision of the FCC (UNOOSA 2016). Galileo is fully interoperable with the other GNSS services. If Galileo were to fail, the other GNSS systems would be available for global service. Galileo's management is particularly concerned with possible harmful interference with the radio navigation signals to and from Galileo satellites. In 2020 Galileo began to test open service navigation message authentications (OSNMA) of radio navigation signals confirming the authenticity of Galileo signals. Consequently, Galileo offers a special message authentication feature: message receivers can check the authenticity of GNSS information to verify the source of the incoming signal (European Space Agency 2021b). This feature, which is not part of the other three systems, will be available to all open (free) GNSS users. The European EGNOS augmentation service is now integrated into the Galileo service.

Chinese Beidou GNSS

The Chinese military authorities originated and designed Beidou (Yang 2022; BeiDou Navigation Satellite System n.d.). Beidou is financed by the Chinese government and remains an essential element of Chinese military equipment, although now administered by the Chinese National Space Agency (GNSA). The latest version of Beidou consists of twenty-four satellites in MEO. Five Beidou GNSS satellites are in geostationary orbit (GSO) in order to ensure system compatibility.

Beidou is available all over the globe. A basic unencrypted service is available free of charge to all civilian users. A more accurate encrypted service is available to the Chinese military and governmental services. The Beidou global service meets international standards established by ICAO, IMO, COPUOS, and other international organizations. Consequently, international computer equipment, including cellphones, now have built-in access to Beidou GNSS. Chinese authorities participate actively in international GNSS coordination of international integration. Beidou is now interoperable with the other three GNSS services and can be used as back-up service if other GNSS services fail. However, Beidou signals are not permitted for use in the United States for national security reasons. One of those reasons is that Beidou technology provides for two-way communication between the users and Beidou control. It can identify and track individual users in communication with Beidou. Like GPS and GLONASS, Beidou signals involve use of the code division multiple access principle for transmission of data. All satellites transmit on the same carrier frequency, but each satellite is assigned a different code.

INCREASING GNSS GEOPOLITICAL INSECURITY

The weak radio signals of GNSS tempt unfriendly states and criminals to jam or spoof them with stronger signals (Larsen 2021; Milner 2020). The result is signal interference and frustration of GNSS users. Sometimes interference may be intentionally caused by states intent on disrupting activities of an unfriendly states. Sometimes it may be caused by criminals who demand ransom for removal of the interference. Or it may be caused by a combination of governments and criminals. It may also be caused accidentally by solar radiation and flares (Mountin 2014).

Harmful interference is increasing and is causing concern about the reliability of GNSS. Particularly problematic are cyber-attacks on GNSS signals used to support infrastructures such as energy, health, environment, electricity, pipelines, air and shipping navigation, communication, disaster management, and banking.

There is now deep concern about the reliability of open civilian GNSS signals because they are not encrypted and so can be easily hijacked. Encryption of civilian GNSS is difficult because that would establish different legal relationships between the GNSS providers and GNSS users. Each user would then have to be identified in order to be permitted access to encrypted civilian signals. It could become difficult for GNSS providers to avoid legal liability for their signals.

A major GNSS insecurity problem is that military authorities consider outer space to be warfighting domain and space powers have plans seek to control space for national security reasons. Diversion of GNSS signals is one of the weapons in the arsenals of established military weaponry. Signal interference may be used in aggressive mode or it may be used in defensive mode as a legal right to deter increasing interference. The UN Charter allows defensive actions under Chapter 7, Article 51. Consequently use of interference for self-defense to deter interference may be a legal right (Mountin 2014).

Russia recently tested one of its anti-satellite missiles by destroying one of its own satellites in outer space generating more than 1,500 pieces of dangerous space debris, which endangered the International Space Station. When the United States protested because the addition of space debris would endanger many US satellites, Russia responded that it not only had the legal right to destroy its own property in outer space, but that it could use its anti-satellite weapons to destroy all US GPS satellites in order to blind all US

GPS-guided missiles (Cozzens 2021). Such an act by one space power against another space power could be construed to be an act of aggression and thus lead to UN action against Russia.

Cyber warfare consists of harmful interference with the digital signals of the enemy. All the space powers now have active cyber warfare capabilities for both defense and aggression (Erwin 2021). GNSS insecurity has risen due to hostile states using cyber technology to overpower weak GNSS signals. These interferences have both civilian and military consequences. Signal interference can occur either though jamming GNSS signals or by spoofing them. Signal jamming occurs when a hostile force obstructs a weak signal with a stronger signal. Signal spoofing is a different harmful interference, literally substituting GNSS signals with different signals containing a different message. Spoofing is more serious interference than jamming. Jamming merely eliminates the signals. Spoofing substitutes false signals, which may actually lead airplanes and ships to their destruction or mislead bank transfers and business deals. Both kinds of interferences have undermined public confidence in its reliance on GNSS as a pillar supporting modern societies.

Some of the interferences are caused by military authorities. Local police noticed in 2017 that GNSS signals in Norway had been jammed, and the Norwegian National Security Agency reported that the jamming originated in Russia (Danilov 2020). Russian spoofing of GNSS caused deviation of shipping in the Black Sea: between 2016 and 2018 10,000 spoofing events affecting 1,800 ships were reported (Milner 2020). War in the Middle East caused extensive jamming and spoofing of GNSS signals. Airline pilots reported that spoofing endangered access to airports (Carey 2019). Jamming and spoofing has also been reported in Asia (Milner 2020). These are just a few examples of cyber interference with GNSS. Encryption of GNSS signals is the obvious response to cyber harmful interference with GNSS. Military signals are already encrypted, and in response to these incidents military GNSS is in the process of becoming even more encrypted. However, 85 percent of GNSS signals are civilian signals, and they are not encrypted.

Considering the huge and varied volume of civilian GNSS users around the world, such as car drivers navigating by GNSS, it would be very difficult to organize encryption of civilian signals. The US DoD is in the process of installing the Military M-Code for greater protection of GPS from interference. The signals will be higher powered, the M-Code will have greater speed, and the encryption will be more sophisticated (Strout 2022). DoD is also developing an augmentary GPS named Navigation Technology Satellite-3 (NTS-3), which has advanced PNT capability and will become commercially available in 2023. NTS-3 will orbit in geostationary orbit and its signals will be jam-resistant (Larsen 2021; DiMassio 2021). How civilian service will be adjusted to the new technology is not yet known.

GNSS systems operated and subject to control by military authorities are particularly vulnerable during times of war and military confrontations. That creates uncertainty about its continued existence. Only one GNSS is not connected to the military operations, the European Galileo. That raises the possibility civilian Galileo may be the only global GNSS service available in times of war and military activities.

Jamming of civilian GNSS by civilians is a continuing problem. It is aggravated by commercial availability of inexpensive jammers that can be purchase for as little as US$200. An employee of a construction company bought a jamming devise in order to conceal his location from his employer while he took a break from his work. He activated the jammer near Newark International Airport with the result that he jammed the GPS navigation service at the airport, and it took a lot of time and detective work to discover the cause of this traffic disruption. Perhaps no one was more surprised than the construction employee who was only looking for a quiet break from work (Fisman and Sullivan 2013). Spoofing by civilians may be illustrated by a 2020 event when Falun Gong seized control of an Chinese TV signal in order to broadcast its own different message ("Jail for Falun Gong TV Hackers" 2002).

The space powers are aware that cyber-attacks, hijacking, jamming, and spoofing undermine the trustworthiness of GNSS signals. In response there are on-going strategic security dialogues. At this point in time, it is an open question whether states will agree to limit signal diversion or whether entirely different systems will emerge.

WAYS TO COUNTER INTERFERENCE VIOLATIONS OF GNSS

This section examines the range and institutional responses to harmful interference with GNSS signals.

Enforcement of Established GNSS International and National Regulations

GNSS military activities must be in compliance with the UN Charter: under Article 2, UN member states are required to refrain from using military GNSS to threaten or use force against other states. Under Chapter 7, the UN Security Council may take action against states that violate Article 2. Even so Article 51 allows states to use military GNSS to defend themselves. Self-defense has arisen as a legal right because of the increasing incidence of harmful interference with the GNSS (Mountin 2014).

The Outer Space Treaty (OST), 610 U.N.T.S. 205, regulates GNSS. Article I restricts the launch and performance of GNSS satellites in outer space to satellites serving the interests of all states. Article III requires GNSS satellites to comply with existing international law. Article IV specifically states that orbiting satellites may not to be used to facilitate use of weapons of mass destruction. Thus, military uses of GNSS raise the issue of whether GNSS is in violation of the OST's limit to peaceful uses.

In view of the extensive civilian uses of GNSS, the prevailing opinion is that GNSS does not violate OST Article IV. If the civilian uses were to be dropped and a purely military GNSS orbited, then the issue of peaceful use of outer space could arise to the extent that GNSS is used in outer space weaponry—for instance in guiding weaponry in LEOs. OST Article VI makes states internationally responsible for national GNSS activities in outer space, including those of non-governmental entities. Article VIII identifies GNSS satellites as being subject to the domestic laws and jurisdiction of the state in which they are registered. It thus identifies the state that is responsible for the activities of each GNSS satellite in orbit. Article IX regulates performance of GNSS satellites: they "shall conduct all their activities in outer space . . . with due regard for the corresponding interests of all other States Parties to the Treaty." States are obligated to enter into consultations if a state "has reason to believe that an activity or experiment planned by it or its nationals in outer space would cause harmful interference with activities of other States." These treaty obligations list legal remedies to interference with GNSS signals. Claims may be settled by parties themselves. Disputes can also be brought up in related UN international bodies such as COPUOS and the International Telecommunication Union (ITU).

Liability for GNSS is a special legal problem. OST Article VII makes procuring and launching states liable for damages caused by space debris of their GNSS satellites. However, the United States maintains that GPS cannot be liable for defective civilian GPS navigation signals because the signals are solicited and triggered by the operator seeking such information and they are free. In other words, the GNSS signals stem from the GNSS satellite and are not directed by the GNSS control station, which merely monitors the satellite. The damage may therefore not be sufficiently direct to impute liability of the GNSS operator. Galileo rejects potential liability in its 2021 Open Services Definition Document. The Chinese Beidou may however become liable because the information delivered to users can be controlled by the station of the GNSS operator. Military GNSS may be a special case of liability when military GNSS is used to guide a military missile to destroy a non-military target. Most of the states are now parties to the 1972 Liability Convention which provides for a special Claims Commission to decide the merits and amounts of individual claims.

GNSS operates by using radionavigation signals; thus the satellites are regulated by ITU treaties and regulations. ITU requires that radio frequencies and their related orbits must be registered in the ITU global International Frequency Register. The ITU will not register interfering radio frequencies in the register. GNSS signals, being unusually weak, are easily diverted by cyber-attacks from stronger signals. It is very easy for governments to interfere with the signals of enemy states and for criminal elements to hold GNSS signals hostage until ransom or other advantages are supplied by persons or companies dependent on use of GNSS. The ITU Constitution, Article 45, provides that states and individuals using radio frequencies may not use radio signals so as to interfere with the radio signals of member states or with signals or services of their authorized non-governmental entities. Thus cyber-attacks on signals violate Article 45. Virtually all states are members of the ITU and are parties to the ITU Constitution.

Harmful interference with GNSS signals may be caused by competing radio frequencies of private communication companies. ITU Radio Regulation i.169 defines harmful interference as interference which endangers the functioning of radio communication services. Radio navigation signal interferences are brought up in ITU conferences, and harmful interference may be resolved simply by redefinition of harmful interference with radio navigation. US domestic cyber security disputes are brought before and decided by the US FCC. Based on the ITU definition of harmful interference, the FCC allocated radio frequencies to a private communications company, Ligado Networks, uncomfortably close to allocated GPS radio frequencies. The US DoD strongly objected to Ligado's radio interference with the DoD-operated GPS signals. The FCC, which is not part of the US executive branch, asserted its freedom to make radio frequency allocation using the ITU definition. The FCC refused to measure harmful interference by a more refined definition advocated by DoD to avoid interference with its GPS signals. Thus the FCC decision favored Ligado. The dispute raises the question of whether the weak GNSS signals require stronger protection than ITU provides for radio communication companies (Federal Communications Commission 2020).

Cyber-attacks on GNSS by states may be met by countermeasures against offending states and by arms control among offending powers. That is difficult when cyber-attacks are caused by criminal elements, although intelligence services sometimes discover cooperation between the two sources of interference. Whereas harmful interference is illegal under the ITU Constitution Article 45, it is the obligation of individual states to enforce laws that protect signals from interference by criminals. In the United States the FCC enforces violations of the ITU Constitution. Jamming and spoofing GNSS signals are also criminal offenses under US law, 18 USC 1367, and are subject to criminal enforcement by the US Department of Justice.

GNSS International Services Mitigation of Harmful Interferences Problems in the COPUOS ICG

International coordination of GNSS began in 1999 with recommendations in UNISPACE III Resolution 54/68. Space powers like the United States are motivated by their national security policy concerns to abstain from direct bilateral contacts with other space powers regarding GNSS. For instance, the Wolf Amendment to NASA's 2011 Congressional Appropriation limits NASA's ability to deal directly with China. However all states, including the space powers, can and do participate in international discussions in CoPUOS where they can raise common concerns and adopt interference guidelines by consensus. One objective of the COPUOS ICG is use of GNSS to promote long-term space sustainability and to establish a special forum for contacts and cooperation among the existing GNSS services (Larsen 2015). National representatives to the ICG meetings tend to be technical GNSS experts, which promotes direct contacts among stakeholders. An over-all advantage of the ICG is bypassing restrictions on bilateral contacts such as the US Wolf Amendment's prohibition on direct US government contacts with China. The United States restricts location of GLONASS signal monitoring stations in the United States and Russia restricts location of GPS monitoring stations in Russia. However the United States and Russia both receive and share GNSS monitoring information within the framework of the ICG. This international sharing is essential for dependability of GPS, GLONASS, Galileo, and Beidou.

ICG Working Group on Compatibility and Interoperability.

National states tend to favor their national GNSS services. National GNSS services, with the exception of Galileo, serve vital national military purposes. However the four services also serve as global back-ups for each other. Compatibility and interoperability of the four services therefore have increased importance now that all the four GNSS systems are fully global. If one system were to be become paralyzed by harmful interference, or were to be preoccupied with military activities, then the world would be able to fall back on one of the other systems. Compatibility of all the GNSS services means that signals comply with ITU standards on harmful interference. Military and civilian GNSS services are separated from each other. Civilian signals are freely available and military signals are encrypted (UNOOSA 2015). All GNSS services now meet ICAO and IMO standards requiring all four GNSS services to be interoperable in order to be acceptable. These international standards thus become the standards for interoperability of GNSS navigation. International compatibility and interoperability guidelines also encourage all receivers to have access to all four GNSS systems thus precluding states mandating that receivers be limited to just one GNSS system. The Working Group on Compatibility and Interoperability facilitates international standards for GNSS services (UNOOSA 2019).

ICG Working Group on the Enhancement of Performance of GNSS Services

The focus of this working group is on ways to improve GNSS service. The operating interrelationships among the four GNSS services and elimination of conflicts are the group's major concern. The group's focus is on enhancement of interoperability among the four systems (UNOOSA 2019).

ICG Working Group on Information Dissemination and Capacity Building, Including GNSS Education and Training.

This working group is primarily involved with educating developing countries on the uses and advantages of the GNSS systems. Capacity training and education emanates from the regional UN centers for space science and technology. New educational opportunities continue to be created. The working group promotes training for capacity building in developing countries, promotes use of GNSS technologies, arranges regional workshops, and disseminates GNSS information (UNOOSA 2019).

ICG Working group on Reference Frames, Timing, and Application

The focus of this group is on surveying and timing reference systems. National surveying reference systems have in the past begun and stopped at national borders.

However GNSS now makes it possible to establish internationally coordinated reference frames for surveying. GNSS has become the foundation for the World Geodetic System based on the fact that the world is round and not flat. Thus land surveys are becoming more accurate. The working group is also concerned with uniform timing references for Coordinated Universal Time. The group is currently working on guidelines for improved transit antennas (UNOOSA 2019).

ICG Working Group on GNSS Compatibility and Spectrum

This group, assisted by the UNOOSA Secretariat, is preparing instruction on GNSS spectrum protection, interference and spectrum management, interference threats, in terference detection and mitigation, and interference challenges (UNOOSA 2019).

The GNSS Providers' Forum

GPS, GLONASS, Galileo, and Beidou as well as the GNSS augmenting services all manage similar problems and have much to learn from each other. Many of them also administer national military GNSS services that cannot be shared with other providers. Nevertheless, COPUOS decided in 2007 to establish a voluntary forum in which the GNSS providers meet to discuss common problems, such as spectrum management, and to promote interoperability and compatibility. The Providers' Forum is not designed to make policy but to share information among technical experts. All four global services as well as the related augmentation services participate in the Providers' Forum, which is supported by the UNOOSA Secretariat. As the forum is only intended for consultations, discussions tend to be freewheeling; participants talk about their individual practices, which may develop into GNSS-wide practices approximating soft law operating guidelines.

The GNSS Providers' Forum seeks to improve and facilitate open civilian radio signals. Basically, forum participants are in agreement on the following: (1) All GNSS signals and services should be compatible; civilian GNSS should be interoperable so to serve as many users as possible. (2) There should be maximum transparency of GNSS operations and signals so that manufacturers can build receivers that allow access to all four services. (3) Global monitoring is important for all the GNSS services to be accurate; all global services should be monitored for greater accuracy and dependability. (4) The GNSS radio spectrum should be made secure from harmful interference; the providers agree on enforcing domestic rules and regulations for protections against harmful interference. (5) The providers support the ICG work on compatibility and interoperability. The forum reports its activities and recommendations to the ICG. Thus the ICG can learn from the forum about the details of providing GNSS services.

Monitoring of Global GNSS Services for Accuracy

It is difficult for each GNSS provider to establish necessary global quality monitors of their own GNSS services. The decision of the ICG to provide necessary monitoring of all GNSS services, including signal management, for accuracy regardless of nationality is therefore an important benefit for all the services. Under the ICG monitoring arrangement, each ICG member volunteers to monitor its own performance as well as the observed performances of the other GNSS services. The national GNSS services have formed an international reporting network headquartered at NASA's Jet Propulsion Laboratory in California, which reports the monitoring observations to the ICG to be compiled in a common archive that is available for all ICG members.

Bilateral and Multilateral GNSS Problem Mitigation

Successful operation of each GNSS system requires cooperation among all of the GNSS systems. Most successful mitigation of GNSS problems occur in the COPUOS International GNSS Committee. Direct bilateral and multilateral cooperation among countries on mitigation is difficult because of geopolitical differences exemplified by the US Wolf Amendment. Each system needs to be monitored globally in order to maintain uniform and accurate global services. Thus GLONASS sought to establish monitoring stations in the United States. But the United States refused their presence within its territory for national security reasons. So monitoring had to be arranged though the ICG. Furthermore, it continues to be difficult for foreign GNSS systems to receive permission to send signals into the national space of other nations. That has been a particular problem in the United States where the FCC has consistently refused to permit the other three GNSS systems to send signals there. The FCC has finally permitted Galileo to send signals into US space, but with the restriction that it is only to provide service to non-governmental receivers. Nevertheless, most receivers are now equipped to access foreign GNSS systems.

Conclusion

The entire world depends on secure GNSS for all kinds of PNT activities. Better cyber security must be established for GNSS to be reliable. Practical operational security problems undermine dependance on GNSS to the extent that this valuable tool may become inoperative. Geopolitical differences among countries pose fundamental threats to GNSS signals. Space powers are competing for dominance of outer space. The military side, which is only 15 percent of GNSS use, tends to overshadow the civilian 85 percent of GNSS use.

It is a unique international accomplishment that all four GNSS systems are interoperable and that their GNSS experts can meet internationally to talk and learn about each other's services and technology in the ICG. They all suffer from harmful interference problems undermining dependability of GNSS. In the ICG they are able to share experiences, problems and talk about possible interference mitigation guidelines along the lines of COPUOS guidelines on space debris.

To facilitate collaboration in the years ahead in the present geopolitical competition, such guidelines should be approved by COPUOS and adopted by the UN General Assembly. The interference guidelines should be: (1) limited to GNSS; (2) recognize the OST Article IX obligation of states to cooperate and provide mutual assistance in mitigation of harmful interference; (3) express recognition of and respect for state sovereignty; (4) accept that GNSS is a necessary part of the global infrastructure; (5) acknowledge the advantage of GNSS free of jamming, spoofing, and other harmful interference; (6) express the urgency of stopping all jamming, spoofing, and other harmful interference; and (7) accept the burden on each state for enforcing prohibition of jamming, spoofing, and other harmful interference with civilian GNSS (Lyall and Larsen 2018; Jakhu 2010).

REFERENCES

About GLONASS. n.d. https://www.glonass-iac.ru/en/about_glonass/.

BeiDou Navigation Satellite System. n.d. http://en.beidou.gov.cn/.

Carey, Bill. 2019. "Aviation Groups Seek Action on Global Navigation Vulnerability." *Aviation Week and Space Technology*. https://aviationweek.com/air-transport/aviation-groups-seek-action-gnss-vulnerability.

Constitution of the International Telecommunication Union. 2015.

Convention on International Liability for Damage Caused by Space Objects. 1972.

Cozzens, Terry. 2021. "Russia Issues Threat to GPS Satellites." *GPS World*. https://www.gpsworld.com/russia-issues-threat-to-gps-satellites/.

Danilov, Peter B. 2020. "GPS Jamming Still Causing Problems in Finnmark." *High North News*. https://www.highnorthnews.com/en/gps-jamming-still-causing-problems-finnmark.

DiMassio, Joe. 2021. "Charting a New Course." *Aviation Week and Space Technology*. 58.

Erwin, Sandra. 2021. "U.S. Generals Planning for a Space War They See as All but Inevitable." *Space News*. https://spacenews.com/u-s-generals-planning-for-a-space-war-they-see-as-all-but-inevitable/.

European GNSS Galileo Open Service Definition Document. 2016. Issue 1.2. https://www.gsc-europa.eu/sites/default/files/Galileo_OS_SDD_V1.0_final.pdf.

European Space Agency. 2021a. "12 Things You Never Knew about Galileo Satellites." https://tinyurl.com/2p85xjcu.

European Space Agency. 2021b. "Galileo Open Service Navigation Message Authentication." https://gssc.esa.int/navipedia/index.php/Galileo_Open_Service_Navigation_Message_Authentication.

Federal Communications Commission. 2020. Order and Authorization in the Matter of Ligado. FCC 20-46. April 22, 2020.

Fisman, Raymond, and Tim Sullivan. 2013. "How GPS Transformed Trucking and Made the Open Road a Lot Less Open." *Wall Street Journal*. https://www.wsj.com/articles/BL-ATWORKB-1367.

Jakhu, Ram S. 2010. *National Regulation of Space Activities*. Dordrecht: Springer.

"Jail for Falun Gong TV Hackers." *CNN*. September 20, 2002. https://edition.cnn.com/2002/WORLD/asiapcf/east/09/20/china.falun.gong/.

Karutin, K., N. Testoedoy, and S. Donchenko. 2022. "Directions 2022: A New Epoch for GLONASS." *GPS World.* https://www.gpsworld.com/directions-2022-a-new-epoc-for-glon ass?/utm_source+Navigate%21+Weekly+GNSS+News&utm_medium+Newsletter&utm.

Larsen, Paul B. 2015. "International Regulation of Global Navigation Satellite Systems." *Journal of Air Law and Commerc* 80: 365–422.

Larsen, Paul B. 2021. "Will Harmful Interference Bring GPS Down?" *Journal of Air Law and Commerce* 86, no. 1: 3–66.

Lyall, Francis, and Paul B. Larsen. 2018. *Space Law: A Treatise.* 2nd ed. London: Routledge, Taylor & Francis Group.

Milner, Greg. 2020. "How Vulnerable is G.P.S.?" *The New Yorker.* https://www.newyorker.com/tech/annals-of-technology/how-vulnerable-is-gps.

Mountin, Sarah M. 2014. "The Legality and Implications of Intentional Interference with Commercial Communication Satellite Signals." *International Legal Studies* 90: 101.

Pont, G., M. Falcone, and M. M. Bautista. 2022. "Directions 2022: Galileo FOC, G2 on the Horizon." *GPS World.* www..gpsworld.com/directions-2022-galileo-fcc-g2=onthehorizon?/utm_source_Navigation%21=Weekly+GNSS+News&utm_medium+Newsletter&utm.

Strout, Nathan. 2022. "What will the U.S. Space Force Be Able To Do with Its New GPS III Variant?" *C4ISRNET.* https://www.c4isrnet.com/battlefield-tech/space/2022/01/09/what-will-the-us-space-force-be-able-to-do-with-its-new-gps-iii-variant/.

UNOOSA. 2016. *International Committee on Global Navigation Satellite Systems: The Way Forward.* New York: United Nations. https://www.unoosa.org/oosa/oosadoc/data/docume nts/2016/stspace/stspace67_0.html.

UNOOSA. 2019. "International Committee on Global Navigation Satellite Systems (ICG): Annual Meeting." https://www.unoosa.org/oosa/en/ourwork/icg/meetings/ICG-2019.html.

Yang, C. 2022. "Directions 2022: BDS Enters New Era of Global Services." *GPS World.* https://www.gpsworld.com?directions-2022-bds-enters-new-era-of-global-services/?utm_sou rce=Navigate%21+Weekly+GNSS+News&utm_medium=N.

CHAPTER 40

....

NEWSPACE AND NEW RISKS
IN SPACE SECURITY

....

JOHN J. KLEIN AND NICKOLAS J. BOENSCH

INTRODUCTION

....

COMMERCIAL space activities have expanded significantly in both volume and diversity, resulting in new capabilities and services that leverage commoditized, off-the-shelf technologies and lower barriers for market entry. Recent developments are contributing to a burgeoning space industry driven by entrepreneurial innovation and investment, advanced technology, and decreased costs. Governmental decision makers are seeking to leverage these commercial developments, which presents opportunities for gaining new capabilities using a faster, more responsive acquisition process. To promote greater efficiencies and augment national capabilities, many government leaders seek to utilize novel commercial technologies when promoting national security and economic activities.

NewSpace—the emerging commercial space ecosystem resulting from private investments and companies opening new or expanding existing markets—is playing a key role in this changing, global security landscape. Many security professionals anticipate that entrepreneurial interest and investment in space companies will lead to significant changes in civil, military, and commercial use of and access to space. Commercial space innovation is considered critical for developing emerging technologies and capabilities that can result in novel ways of operating and protecting national security interests extending into space. For this reason, many security professionals view NewSpace as essential for achieving a competitive advantage among rival states. While NewSpace companies are a source of innovation and benefit, some analysts have highlighted potential national security risks associated with these new capabilities and services. Despite the associated risks, governments have an opportunity to utilize emerging commercial space companies to achieve more strategic and political objectives, while spending less than they would have otherwise.

This chapter provides background on NewSpace and the growth in start-up space activity. Afterward, the chapter examines potential security risks associated with NewSpace companies and the novel capabilities involved. The chapter then provides a framework for better understanding and balancing the tradeoffs between of risks and net benefits to space security. Finally, the chapter assesses the potential role and contribution of NewSpace technologies in international relations and strategy.

Characterizing NewSpace Activities

During the mid-2000s, a new kind of space company emerged. Start-up entrepreneurs, some with impressive records of success, developed business plans and sought venture capital from investment firms and individual investors, with innovative NewSpace capabilities targeting new markets and seeking to expand existing ones. These so-called NewSpace companies are presently taking a leading role in space technological development by building the components, materials, ground infrastructure, and rockets that are deploying the next generation of spacecraft into space. In describing NewSpace, Joan Johnson-Freese says, "Companies that have become known as NewSpace actors are those largely financed by individuals operating with their own money and so are willing—and able—to take risks" (Johnson-Freese 2017, 138). Another type of NewSpace company includes those established contractors, manufacturers, and operators developing innovative capabilities and trailblazing new markets.

Start-up space companies, or those space companies that began as angel investor or venture capital-backed start-ups, raised US\$36.7 billion in investment from 2000 to 2020 (BryceTech 2021b; see Figure 40.1). The significant amount of private investment in the space industry is a relatively recent phenomenon, with 72 percent of investment taking place between 2015 and 2020. Globally, there are nearly 400 start-up space ventures that have received investment from over 1,200 investors. Over 50 percent of these companies are headquartered in the United States, 22 percent in Europe, and 8 percent in China (BryceTech 2021a). Growth in start-up space will, in part, be due to the growing international presence (see Figure 40.2). The past few years have experienced a surge in the number of non-US space start-ups obtaining financing. A report by BryceTech observes, "The next few years have the potential to transform the start-up space ecosystem" (BryceTech 2020).

Innovations in the commercial launch sector are improving access to space. The sector is currently developing multiple new launch vehicles across a range of payload classes—small to heavy lift (Klein 2019, 189). This development is international in scope, involves established and new launch providers, and is driven by both government and commercial demand to place satellites in orbit. Many commercial launch providers are investing in innovative technologies and processes to lower launch costs and increase competitiveness. Across industry, the launch price per kilogram decreased 34 percent from 2011 to 2020 (Satellite Industry Association 2021). Large and small launch vehicles

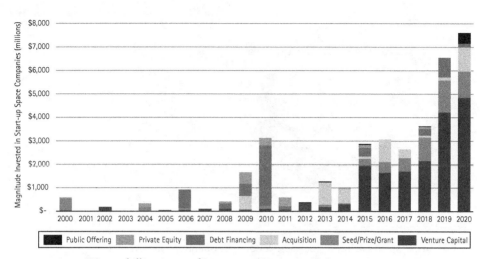

FIGURE 40.1 US$36.7 billion invested in start-up space companies, 2000–2020.

Source: BryceTech (2021a).

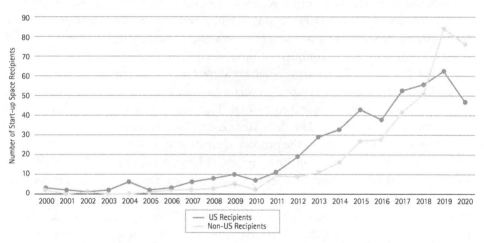

FIGURE 40.2 In 2020, 38% of companies receiving investment were based in the United States.

Source: BryceTech (2021a).

are also enabling increased access to space for smaller satellites through expanded rideshare initiatives.

The manufacturing and ground equipment sectors are also experiencing significant NewSpace driven developments. This includes miniaturization and modular satellites that are smaller, more sophisticated, and standardized for multiple missions to support on-demand production (Klein 2019, 191–92). Operators globally are launching small satellites for new remote sensing, communications, and other services (see Figure 40.3). Flexible, software-defined payloads aim to deliver speed and flexibility

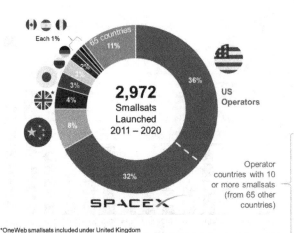

Operator Country	# of Smallsats
United States	2,027 (955 Starlink)
China	224
UK	129
Japan	82
Russia	83
Germany	49
Canada	29
Argentina	23
France	21
India	18
Australia	17
South Korea	17
Italy	16
Singapore	14
Spain	13
Israel	12
Finland	10

*OneWeb smallsats included under United Kingdom

FIGURE 40.3 Small satellites (smallsats, <600kg) by operator country, 2011–2020.

Source: BryceTech (2021b).

through reconfigurability on-orbit. Technology developments in areas such as antenna spot beams are significantly expanding satellite communications capacity on-orbit, while driving down the cost per data rate throughput. Among the numerous ongoing developments within the commercial ground equipment segment, two are significant. First, flat panel/phased-array antennas allow for better on the move connectivity. Second, integrated ground stations as part of a "space as a service" business model allow operators to command and control satellites and process and store data in cloud architectures without the need for dedicated ground infrastructure.

NewSpace companies are in the process of creating several new markets, including on-orbit servicing and space domain awareness (Klein 2019, 198–201). Established space companies and venture-backed start-ups alike are fielding capabilities for on-orbit servicing to extend the life, to repair, to augment, and to actively de-orbit spacecraft on-orbit. Several companies also seek to advance in-space transportation, through delivery to custom, specific orbits. Other NewSpace companies in the space domain awareness industry are developing ground- and space-based sensing capabilities to better track, catalog, and predict on orbit activity. If this transformation is realized, bringing additional capabilities, innovative technologies, and applications to market, NewSpace companies and space investors will affect the competitive advantage between countries, space security, and economic growth.

NEWSPACE AND NEW RISKS

Despite the significant increased capability anticipated from the contribution of NewSpace innovation to the space industry, analysts and other commentators highlight a number of perceived risks associated with these systems. The term *risk* here relates to the potential hazards, threats, challenges, and barriers that NewSpace actors could impose on space security. This section identifies five perceived risks that are frequently associated with NewSpace companies and capabilities.

Threat to Space Sustainability

An often-cited risk associated with NewSpace is the unprecedented number of satellites currently launching and proposed to be launched in the next several years, along with their corresponding impact on space sustainability (see Figure 40.4). Dozens of companies have proposed constellations of satellites in low Earth orbit (LEO) to provide a wide range of services. Some of the largest constellations such as SpaceX's Starlink, OneWeb, Amazon Kuiper, and Telesat LEO are deploying constellations to provide low-latency satellite broadband to a diverse set of customers. As of September 2021, Starlink has authority from the Federal Communications Commission to launch 4,408 satellites and is seeking to expand this satellite constellation to 30,000. Meanwhile, Amazon, OneWeb and Telesat have proposed 3,236, 648, and 298 satellites, respectively. Given that there were only 2,100 satellites active in space across all orbits in 2018 before these LEO constellations began deployment, regions in LEO are expected to become increasingly congested. For various reasons, including business viability and market conditions, not all proposed systems may fully deploy.

The proposed deployment of thousands, or even tens of thousands, of satellites creates a risk of increased congestion in critical regions of LEO, stress on governmental space domain awareness and space traffic management capabilities, and increased potential for orbital collisions and resulting debris generation. Some former officials suggest that with the deployment of these constellations "space will become too congested to be safe,"

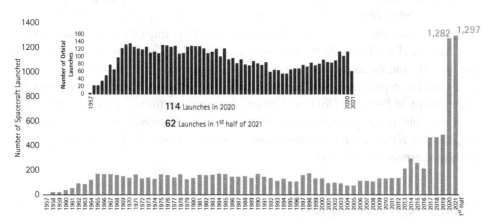

FIGURE 40.4 Number of spacecraft and launches, 1957–2021.

Source: BryceTech (2021b).

and the projected number of objects in LEO will strain "current capabilities to reliably model the risks" (Taverney 2020a). Others contend that the large numbers of satellites in LEO could add unnecessary burden for tracking and characterizing the orbital environment and increase the number of conjunction warnings issued by the Combined Space Operations Center, distracting the organization from its national security mission (Hallex and Cottom 2020, 24). Some security experts suggest that constellations would drive up costs borne by other satellite operators to carry out maneuvers or other operations to mitigate potential collisions (Weeden 2020).

In some cases, these fears are already becoming a reality. Some researchers highlight a significant increase in conjunctions among satellites in these constellations (Lewis 2021). High-profile collision risks with LEO broadband satellites have already been reported publicly, such as the risk of collision between a Starlink satellite and a European Space Agency (ESA) scientific satellite, Aeolus (Foust 2019). This event in particular highlighted difficulties in communication and collision avoidance in a region increasingly populated with commercial satellites.

Several studies conducted by space civil space agencies modeled the impacts of large constellations on the orbital environment. A LEO constellation study conducted by the National Aeronautics and Space Administration's (NASA) Orbital Debris Program Office models the number of objects larger than 10 cm over 200 years based on variations in constellation deployments and post mission disposal guideline adherence (Liou et al. 2018). Assuming three LEO constellations totaling 8,300 satellites (much fewer than are currently proposed to launch), NASA found that at 90 percent successful post mission disposal rate, the number of objects >10cm on orbit would reach over 100,000—about five times larger than the same disposal rate with scenario that excludes large constellations. Under this scenario, NASA projects 260 catastrophic collisions in 200 years, which is 8 times more collisions than the scenario excluding large constellations. The potential risk to the space environment is made even more clear given current compliance rates for post mission disposal are ~60 percent (ESA Space Debris Office 2021, 6).

The economic, military, and public-good value provided by satellites depends on the sustainability of the orbital environment in which they are located. Potential degradation of the orbital environment would have a direct impact on the US$271 billion in commercial satellite industry revenues, business plans, and investor confidence in the industry and the non-space industries and organization that rely on space services. It would also impact the ability for NASA, the United States Space Force (USSF), the Department of Defense (DoD) and other organizations to derive value from spacecraft on orbit. The unprecedented number of satellites launched and anticipated to be launched by NewSpace companies creates a significant perceived risk of the sustainability of the space environment.

Dual-Use Technologies

A general risk in the space domain is the dual-use nature of many space technologies—those that can be used for military or commercial purpose, or both at the same time.

Because of the dual-use nature of many of the products and services associated with satellite servicing and debris removal, some security professions highlight that it may be difficult, at times, to discriminate between purely military and commercial endeavors. NewSpace satellite servicing systems capable of maneuverability, rendezvous and proximity operations, and/or grappling may be ostensibly designed for peaceful purposes but also have the potential carry out military actions to inspect, disable, degrade, or destroy another satellite (Townsend 2020, 74). Some industry experts warn that the dual-use nature of these technologies is a risk to the national security community because anti-satellite "development, testing, and deployment could masquerade as non-threatening orbital applications" or advance space weapons capabilities (Vedda and Hays 2018, 44). Others highlight that the dual-use nature of these technologies could even lead to unintended escalation among adversaries because states would be unsure whether the systems were being used or leased by a hostile actor (Borowitz, Rubin, and Stewart 2020, 524). Given the lack of transparency between the United States and China or Russia in space, NewSpace actors providing satellite servicing or debris removal services may increase risk of misperceptions (Bateman 2021).

Increased Transparency in Space and on Earth

As noted above, commercial space domain awareness capabilities are advancing rapidly. The result is that space is becoming much more transparent, thereby improving the ability to understand a satellite system's disposition and potentially to understand a satellite's capabilities. This has led to a figurative "turning on the lights" in space. The democratization of the ability to identify, characterize, and understand the space environment through space situational awareness (SSA) and non-Earth imaging capabilities has curtailed the ability to maintain previous secrecy in areas once thought to be invisible to public view (Vedda and Hays 2018, 24).

Before NewSpace companies began fielding space domain awareness technologies, these capabilities were restricted only to governments, particularly states with significant space power (Morin and Wilson 2021, 4). The catalog of data on space objects that the USSF provides publicly excludes classified and sensitive US space objects to prevent identification and characterization of these national security systems (Borowitz, Rubin, and Stewart 2020, 522). The risk posed by NewSpace companies, industry professionals contend, is the erosion of secrecy regarding national security systems on orbit—potentially even the ability to determine a certain system's resolution, the signals it could collect, and methods of collection (522). Security professionals fear that the knowledge of national security satellites' activities and characteristics, if put into the wrong hands, could allow adversaries to mitigate the surveillance of their activities.

Much like the figurative "turning on the lights" in space described above, another cited NewSpace risk is the potential undermining of the state's monopoly on intelligence through the proliferation of commercial Earth observation satellite constellations.

With the increase in number of Earth observation satellites through commercial constellations like Planet, BlackSky, Hawkeye 360, Capella, and ICEYE, some analysts contend that the ability for all countries, including the United States, to remain undetected during military exercises or operations will be significantly reduced (Chin 2011). These constellations, analysts argue, democratize imagery and signals intelligence, challenging current government collection and analysis practices (Weinbaum, Berner, and McClinktock 2017, 1).

The US government historically has thought to control the distribution of commercial imagery through "shutter control," where the government could control imagery collection opportunities and/or collected imagery over a designated area (Hitchens 2021). Space security experts, however, contend that the United States is no longer able to exert this type of control (Hitchens 2021). Will Marshall, the CEO of Planet, asserts that commercial satellite imagery "might occasionally expose something inconvenient for them, but that's the new state of the world" (*Economist* 2021b). These views suggest that due to the increasing availability of commercial satellite imagery and analysis, governments, including the United States, China, and Russia, must contend with the potential risks associated with "mutually assured surveillance" (*Economist* 2021a).

Risks of Business Failure

Government organizations in the United States and abroad increasingly seek to leverage NewSpace capabilities to augment their own space systems and provide added value to their missions. As government actors begin to envision becoming customers of these products and services, and incorporate them in future planning and force development, there are risks that NewSpace companies will fail to deliver on some of these services or, generally, fail to reach business viability.

NewSpace companies have proposed revolutionary advances in launch, communications, Earth observation, satellite servicing, ground, and other space segments, from near real time all-day, all-night satellite imagery, to global low latency, high-speed broadband access, and responsive, low-cost launch, on timeframes much faster than typical government procurement cycles. The risk is that these capabilities may not be delivered at promised levels, on schedule, or at the proposed price.

A 2012 research study by Shikhar Ghosh finds that, "About three-quarters of venture-backed firms in the U.S. don't return investors' capital" (Gage 2012). Most venture capital backed space companies will inevitably fail. While this statistic should not be a surprise, it can be a risk to customers, particularly those in the national security community, if they begin incorporating these NewSpace capabilities into planning and force development and do not account for this uncertainty in future ability. The government can mitigate much of this risk by remaining flexible, being an informed customer, and understanding acceptable risk based upon specific mission area.

Failure to Take Advantage of Novel Capabilities

NewSpace companies are developing myriad capabilities that present opportunities for government customers, particularly the national security community. These customers have also expressed interest in leveraging these capabilities to augment their own systems and deliver significant value, including reducing costs and providing added resilience. Some government organizations—including the Defense Innovation Unit, Space Development Agency, and the USSF's Orbital Prime—are already working to promote and utilize NewSpace products and services. While governments are increasingly vocal about fielding NewSpace services and products, there is a risk that they will be unable to address existing barriers between government customer and NewSpace providers, resulting in significant missed opportunities.

Governments must determine which capabilities will remain wholly government, which capabilities can be augmented by commercial services and products, and which current government space mission areas can be transitioned to commercial services (Vedda and Hays 2018, 61; Loverro 2021). Absent these assessments, governments may continue to view NewSpace capabilities as "uncertain risks to our defense space enterprise," potentially leading to missed opportunities to leverage NewSpace developments for expanded or cost efficient space capability (Loverro 2021).

An additional risk is the potential disconnect between government customers' desire for control over requirements and parameters of a service or capability and the schedule and cost benefits of innovative procurement processes for NewSpace services. Commercial space providers frequently remark that the US military struggles to procure commercial services or products "as is" (Erwin 2021). These industry participants note that this inflexibility to adjust to services or products that are not directly catered to military customers could lead to a "strategic disadvantage," if military procurements cannot adapt (Erwin 2021).

A common criticism of increasing the government's utilization of NewSpace capabilities is that they will lack cyber and security protections compared to military space systems (Morin and Wilson 2021, 7). Taverney (2020a) illustrates this concern, writing that "comfort with existing processes and approaches drives traditionalists to make demands that commercial providers cannot rationally meet, including security classification of the development process, expensive and time consuming oversight, nuclear hardening requirements, and more." Due to the requirements of national security space missions, these spacecraft were often designed based on "worst-case analysis" so that potential failures or risks could be identified and mitigated (Taverney 2020b). The same prudence may not apply to select NewSpace companies. Concerns regarding the security and robustness of NewSpace systems are necessary to safeguard government customers' data and access to space, but potentially impede the governments' ability to leverage NewSpace capabilities and services.

Absent a coherent strategy of how government customers can adequately leverage commercial capabilities—while maintaining national systems where needed and relinquishing some control where acceptable—a risk exists that government customers may fail to reap the benefits coming from NewSpace innovations, leading to a strategic disadvantage.

Putting in Context: Balancing Risks with Benefits

The previous section identified some of the most frequently cited risks related to NewSpace ventures and security. While some of these risks are significant and should be considered by security practitioners, each identified risk also requires additional context to provide a balanced understanding of the risks relative to the net benefits incurred. While NewSpace initiatives may threaten space sustainability, they are also driving the establishment of norms of behavior and contributing to space sustainability. Dual-use technologies for applications such as on-orbit servicing generate concerns, but co-mingling of military and civilian technologies is not a phenomenon unique to the space domain. New sensors may complicate space operations by creating greater transparency, but increased transparency increases trust and deterrence efforts in the future space environment. There is a risk that these start-up businesses will fail to deliver on their promised products and services, but governments have proven abilities to mitigate market uncertainty while still seeking to utilize NewSpace capabilities.

Establishing Beneficial Norms of Behavior

A number of publications have discussed the potential risks that large constellations of LEO satellites could have on the space environment. This emphasis, however, ignores many of the NewSpace developments contributing to the creation of beneficial norms of behavior. NewSpace actors, and commercial space companies generally, have a significant role in the creation of norms of behavior. In a survey to national security space professionals conducted by Vedda and Hays (Vedda and Hays 2018), experts noted that "Behavioral norms will have a better chance of being accepted and sustained if they're bottom-up rather than top-down . . . Very likely the best chances are if this conversation [on international norms] begins not with arms control and security people, but rather with private operators who desire a stable environment" (39). Part of this bottom-up approach for what is considered norms will be how routine, day-to-day space operations are being conducted. The commercial space sector is intimately involved in this process.

The commercial sector's large number of satellites on-orbit—along with associated ground systems—shapes what is considered normal during day-to-day space operations. Carissa Christensen has called these day-to-day operations and associated commercial business practices *soft norms* (Klein 2019, 11). These soft norms are mostly not documented, officially agreed upon, or codified in writing. While industry business practices do not necessarily have quantitative metrics or hard thresholds for their use, they are significant nonetheless in shaping the perceptions of what is considered fair, equitable, and safe in space. Because commercial space constitutes a large percentage of on-orbit systems today, commercial space companies are critical in portraying standard day-to-day international and governmental behavior in space. As with other norms, the significance of soft norms is that any deviations from the standard business practices may highlight abnormal behavior or be used in cueing of possible nefarious activity or a potential hostile act.

Contributing to Space Sustainability

Many NewSpace companies place significant emphasis on space sustainability. Earth observation operator Planet has spoken about its commitment to sustainability in space and pledge to produce no long-lasting debris on orbit, while OneWeb has taken many measures to communicate its commitment to space sustainability hygiene, including the incorporation of technologies on its spacecraft that would facilitate active debris removal, if its spacecraft fail. NewSpace companies such as Astroscale, D-Orbit, and Clearspace are also currently leading efforts to develop active debris removal technologies to provide services to ensure the continued use of the space environment. Meanwhile companies such as LeoLabs are developing space situational awareness and space traffic management capabilities that could be used to provide enhanced conjunction assessments, event monitoring, and risk analysis. The actions of NewSpace companies could have a significant role in the maintenance and promotion of space sustainability. Several industry organizations, including the Space Data Association, the Satellite Industry Association, and the World Economic Forum are also emphasizing commitment to the space environment.

Analysts warn of the potential risk from commercial NewSpace constellations for the orbital environment; however, other experts contend that at present other actors, including governments, have contributed to the challenges of future space sustainability. A group of scholars identified the most dangerous objects in LEO, or those that pose the greatest debris-generating potential to operational satellites (McKnight et al. 2021). The fifty most dangerous objects are mainly of rocket stages and inoperable government spacecraft. The ESA reports on compliance with debris mitigation: its latest Space Environment Report finds that during the years 2010–2020 commercial operators in LEO were more compliant with debris mitigation guidelines than civil and government operators (ESA Space Debris Office 2021, 80). Commercial space actors appear to be leading in the development of space sustainability measures and solutions to debris growth on orbit. Also, other experts contend that governments, and the US government in particular, have been notably absent in progress toward greater space sustainability (Weeden 2020; NASA OIG 2021).

Growing Need for NewSpace Sensing Systems

Given the number of ground- and space-based non-Earth imaging, space domain awareness (SDA), and space traffic management (STM) capabilities, US and international national security space actors may not be able to operate under an assumption of privacy for much longer. However, NewSpace SDA and STM capabilities and services present governments with significant opportunities that must be considered, along with the risks due to increased transparency. By leveraging NewSpace sensors—geographically distributed on Earth and in space—governments can more accurately and completely capture the operational environment, thereby augmenting national capabilities. NewSpace SDA and STM systems also contribute to space security through advanced monitoring of the environment, debris tracking, and conjunction analyses, and these contributions aid in dispelling some of the concerns with commercial LEO constellations by providing these companies with robust situational awareness and analyses. Furthermore, governments may utilize NewSpace systems to "name and shame" irresponsible behavior in space, particularly nefarious activities conducted by adversaries (Vedda and Hays 2018, 8). NewSpace data and analysis also assists in breaking down classification impediments on sharing information with coalition partners (8). Distributed networks of sensors provide increased resiliency through redundancy and potentially interoperable systems, thereby adding additional layers of robustness to government owned and operated capabilities (Borowitz 2021, 116).

Moreover, governments have the ability to set guidelines and regulations to limit capture and distribution of data and information on sensitive assets, presenting an opportunity for balancing national security interests with commercial market growth (Vedda and Hays 2018, 116). Current US regulation permits imaging of consenting spacecraft with no limits on resolution, while imaging of non-consenting spacecraft is limited to a specific pixel size, and the US government has the ability to place dissemination restriction on some data (NOAA 2020). By seeking a balance between national security and nascent commercial market growth, government customers can realize the benefits of NewSpace SDA and STM data and services, while limiting security concerns regarding imaging the space environment.

Mitigating Market Uncertainty

Many NewSpace companies are venture capital backed organizations, seeking to realize potentially revolutionary new capabilities or markets. Though most venture capital backed space companies will inevitably fail. The government is a long-standing customer of commercial space capabilities and helped facilitate today's commercial space markets. The government has an opportunity to leverage emerging commercial space companies to help it to do more and spend less. However, the price of leveraging investor funded, NewSpace capabilities and services is uncertainty. Government customers must carefully consider how to best take advantage of this opportunity while ensuring long-term access to mission critical services.

Sometimes this uncertainty, including the uncertainty surrounding a company's business success, will create concerns regarding future availability. As US and international governments seek the best outcome for their mission objectives, customers will be well served by being flexible, informed, and partnering with industry. A clear example of this behavior was the award of the Agile Small Launch Operational Normalizer (ASLON)-45 mission to Vector, which was awarded shortly before the company suspended operations. The Air Force Space and Missile Systems Center was able to quickly re-award the contract through a Federal Acquisition Regulation simplified acquisition procedure, expediting the new agreement (Erwin 2019). The DoD's role in preserving the Iridium satellite constellation through indemnification and contracts for services when the company faced bankruptcy eventually enabled Iridium to restructure its debt and assist it in reaching its current status as a viable provider of commercial services to US government and commercial customers globally (Bloom 2016). Implementing acquisition processes and partnering mechanisms that recognize and specifically address this business uncertainty will help the government benefit while managing risk.

Benefits Outweighing Risks

The utilization of NewSpace capabilities and services presents governments with significant challenges. These systems will likely not be as protected as military systems; require governments to develop strategies balancing sovereign systems versus reliance on commercial solutions; compel governments to identify how to successfully integrate commercial data and services into architectures and concepts of operations; and place pressure on existing government acquisition and contracting mechanisms. However, the net benefit of integrating NewSpace capabilities and services into government frameworks and architectures far outweighs the potential risks and costs to governments.

Some of the notable contributions by commercial and NewSpace systems are the ability to quickly field novel technologies and capabilities and to help government customers do more while spending less. NewSpace systems can enable governments to circumnavigate traditional requirements, contracting, and development processes that significantly increases the time required to field government space capabilities. Current government approaches can result in timelines of over a decade to field complex space systems (Aerospace Corporation 2019, 2). By leveraging NewSpace systems, including off-the-shelf technologies and services, government customers can rapidly increase the agility of space procurements. Commercial capabilities also result in potential opportunities in cost savings compared to government owned and operated systems.

NewSpace systems may also enhance a state's deterrence posture through deterrence by denial. The growth in NewSpace capabilities means that denying space services or degrading another's access to or use of space will become even more challenging for space powers, particularly if those systems include proliferated architectures. Moreover, by utilizing NewSpace systems, governments can operate with spectrum diversity, challenging an adversary's ability to impede communications (Morin and Wilson 2021, 7). Agile manufacturing processes could also assist in reconstitution efforts (Hallex and Cottom 2020, 25). NewSpace capabilities can help convey the futility of conducting a hostile act in space, because it will be difficult to deny products or services through a hostile action. This fact may cause a potential adversary's leadership to avoid military confrontation in the first place. If conflict is not avoided, NewSpace systems can then provide support to space and terrestrial forces and enable a government's intra-war deterrence efforts.

NewSpace Technologies, International Relations, and Strategy

As NewSpace companies continue to drive trends and advances in technology and become further integrated into the traditional space ecosystem, a better understanding of these actors—along with their potential risks and benefits—is critical for a comprehensive appreciation of space security. For the international relations (IR) practitioner specifically, the rise of NewSpace companies as both contributors and key players in the space security environment deserves specific attention. This section details how IR practitioners can better understand the impact of NewSpace innovations on stability in the international environment by comprehending the role that technology and technological developments, such those being offered by NewSpace firms, has on the international system and strategy. This section first discusses common views and arguments regarding the role of technology—NewSpace technologies in particular—and its influence on IR and strategic stability, along with the likelihood for conflict. Then, these commonly held views are disputed, while an alternative argument on NewSpace technology's more limited impact on IR and strategy is offered.

Technology in IR and Strategy: Power Imbalances and Strategic Instability

In IR, power is often equated with material capabilities at disposal of the state. Kenneth Waltz (1979) discusses that "the political clout of nations correlates closely with their economic power and their military might" (153). NewSpace derived technological innovations contribute directly to a state's power, both through the economic power of space related commerce and non-space activities dependent on commercial space systems and directly to military power through their contribution to warfighting and deterrence (Drezner 2019, 288). As a contributor to national power, NewSpace technologies are significant to IR practitioners, as they contemplate what the potential technology driven power balances or imbalances between states mean for strategic stability between states.

A key concern is whether the dynamism of the innovative technologies under development by NewSpace companies generate greater risk for escalation and propensity for conflict (Borowitz et. al 2020). In IR literature, security dilemmas form when the accumulation of power creates insecurity among potential adversaries (Herz 1950, 157). As the NewSpace developments have largely taken place in the United States and its western allies, this increasing capability could impact the stability of the international system, as state-led space powers China and Russia lag behind. In his analysis of security dilemmas, Brad Townsend (2020, 64) notes that this type of dilemma for the space environment could result in arms races and potentially grave unintended outcomes.

Some IR scholars contend that innovation in technology, potentially including that currently driven by NewSpace firms, impacts bilateral or multilateral relationships among states, including through the reordering of hierarchies and distribution of power (Weiss 2005, 303). Daniel Drezner (2019) asserts that technologies can lead to radical shifts in the distribution of powers in states and that "any technological change is also an exercise in redistribution. It can create new winners and losers" (286–87). Following this line of reasoning, the international consequences of NewSpace innovative technological solutions would emerge as a key issue for future space strategists and IR practitioners, because shifts in relative power could have concrete effects on the balance of power (Goldman and Andres 1999, 79).

One way a NewSpace technology driven shift in power could manifest itself is through changes in the offense-defense balance in space, potentially impacting the likelihood for conflict. Robert Jervis (1978, 186–87) contends that the stability of the international system will be impacted by the distinguishability of "offensive" and "defensive" technologies and whether an offensive or defensive technology is advantaged in strategic relationship. Stephen Van Evera (1999, 13–14) notes that real or perceived shifts within the offense-defense balance increases the risk for conflict. Townsend explains that geography and technology are the typical determinants of offense or defense advantages, and because adversaries will share the geographical attributes of the space environment, technology will be the primary determinant in the dominance of offense or defense in space.

Both in terms of the impact on conflicts on Earth and conflicts extending into space, space warfare is perceived as largely offense dominant. One of the ways space power achieves strategic effect is through the concentration of satellite support services, in combination with terrestrial forces, to increase lethality and concentration of firepower of land, sea, and air power (Bowen 2015, 271; Sheldon 2005, 165; Smith 2016, 171). The result is an offensively focused strategic effect of space power on conflict on Earth.

In orbit, the common perception is that the offense dominates strategic considerations. Satellites follow predictable paths in orbit with limited ability to hide or defend themselves (Klein 2019, 28). The economics of launch and spacecraft size, weight, and power constraints create incentives to maximize mission payloads rather than defensive capabilities. Moreover, the anti-satellite weapon systems used to destroy or disrupt a satellite will likely be significantly less expensive than the satellite (Sheldon 2005, 199). Given the commonly accepted conclusion that space is an offense-dominated domain, the likelihood of heightened tensions and potential conflict appears increasingly likely.

A related concern for stability of the balance of power is the potential for NewSpace technologies, in an offense-dominated domain, to create incentives for states to take offensive actions through real or perceived first strike advantages. If a perceived advantage to strike first in a conflict is apparent, states are more likely to initiate conflict to utilize this advantage (Schneider 2019, 847). A key variable in the creation of first strike advantages is the vulnerability associated with the technologies that a state relies on.

In discussing information technologies and first strike advantages, Jacquelyn Schneider (2019) finds that certain technologies may generate significant benefits to the state that wields them, but these same technologies may also introduce reliance and vulnerabilities. In Schneider's example, the US military investments in information-enabled forces impart significant benefits on its military operations, but also introduce digital architectures subject to vulnerabilities (842). Dependency on information to support US military operations heightens the significance of the vulnerabilities of the systems and architectures that support it. In such situations, both sides of a conflict develop incentives to strike first. In theory, the less capable state is driven to strike first to exploit the more capable state's vulnerabilities and cripple it at the onset of conflict. The more capable state is also incentivized to strike first out of fear that the vulnerabilities in the technologies it depends on will be exploited and because the benefits it derives from the technologies would be nullified (848). This argument appears germane to the space domain as well. While many NewSpace capabilities are in the early stages of operationalization in military operations and planning, generally, the United States is dependent on space power for its conventional military capabilities (Townsend 2020, 65). Space systems are also vulnerable to adversary attack, for the reasons outlined above. Consequently, the dependency on and vulnerability of space systems and technologies introduces incentives for states to strike first at the onset of a conflict.

The final concern is the rapid diffusion of innovative space technologies. Earlier in this chapter, it was noted that the launch, communications, remote sensing, space domain awareness, and on-orbit servicing sectors are currently experiencing significant technological innovations. Moreover, this growth and innovation in NewSpace activity is concentrated largely in the United States, western Europe, and Japan. IR scholars write on the potential concerns of the proliferation of key technologies and the likelihood for war (Bas and Coe 2012). Muhammet Bas and Andrew Coe find that in some cases the diffusion of technologies may cause states to conduct preventive wars to halt the diffusion of a technology to a competitor (652). As innovative space technologies emerging from western NewSpace companies diffuse to rivals such as China and Russia, Bas and Coe would contend that this increases the potential for preventive war to halt technology proliferation and allow the United States and its western partners to maintain their technological advantages.

Setting the Record Straight: The Primacy of Politics and Limitations of Technology

The previous section outlined many of the prevalent views regarding technologies and their influence on IR, strategic stability, and the likelihood for conflict. Much of the IR scholarship presented posits that technologies—such as those being developed by NewSpace firms—can lead to inadvertent escalations of conflicts, specifically if those technologies shifted the offense-defense balance, created incentives to strike first in a conflict, or advanced likelihood of preventive wars. The findings paint a largely dismal picture that NewSpace technologies create significant risks for conflict materialization and escalation. While these arguments are notable, in many cases they are misguided and neglect an understanding of the primacy of politics in strategy and IR. Todd Sechser, Neil Narang, and Caitlin Talmadge (2019, 728) note that "Very few technologies fundamentally reshape the dynamics of international conflict. Historically, most technological innovations have amounted to incremental advancements, and some have disappeared into irrelevance despite widespread hype about their promise." NewSpace technology developments will likely have a limited effect on the future of IR and strategy due to the primacy of politics, the limitations of technology, and the diffusion of technology.

The concerns cited in the previous section emphasize the ability of specific technology to shape the international environment. This view neglects the essential role of political and strategic choices, the primary drivers of escalation and instability in the international system (Talmadge 2019, 865). In her exceptional assessment of the role of technology in escalation throughout the Cold War, Caitlin Talmadge finds escalation and the risk of escalation in the Cold War was largely independent of technology (866). Throughout the Cold War, she finds that in some cases technology enabled escalation, but that this escalation would have occurred, or indeed did occur, even in the absence of the technology in question (879). The emergence of particular technologies did not drive policymakers in the United States or the Soviet Union to engage in more escalatory strategies, instead states leveraged technologies when they decided politically or strategically to conduct actions that would be escalatory (866). Technology is merely a tool states leverage when they seek to escalate a conflict or relationship, actions they would likely take regardless of the availability of a specific technology (883).

The concern that space, as an offense-dominated domain based on satellite technologies, is at an increased risk for heightened tensions and potential escalation also fails to account for the primacy of politics. Because of the ubiquity of dual-use technologies, technology itself should not be considered a risk or threat. People and polities decide how technologies are employed. Colin Gray (2013, 179) explains that during the nineteenth and early twentieth centuries, technology largely favored defense over offense. Defense dominated during this period, yet wars—including the Crimean War, the American Civil War, and the First World War—were still waged (179). The presence of peace or war in the international system should not be determined by specific technologies. War and peace always have technological dimensions, yet Gray notes

"Polities do not fight because they are armed, even potentially decisively well-armed; rather they do fight for political reasons" (180).

A common shortcoming in the IR scholarship on the role of technology is an overstatement of the efficacy of new technologies in practice and a misunderstanding of the fundamental role of technology in strategy. The discussions cited above often cite technology as a near "silver bullet," destabilizing the international system. The strategic effect of technology will be highly dependent on the context and character of the potential conflict, and it may not live up to its promise (Sechser, Narang, and Talmadge 2019, 728). Adoption of superior technologies does not guarantee success in strategy. Because war and strategy have a distinct human element, the efficacy of specific technologies will often depend on the skill of those who wield them and the doctrine they follow (Gray 2013, 163). The silver bullet status that technology is granted in much of IR scholarship often fails to recognize that a technologically endowed state competes against an adversary that also has a vote. The efficacy of any technology is not a unilateral decision but will be decided through competition with an adversary that will seek to offset or fully mitigate the technology's potency (165).

The technology-focused IR concepts often fail to comprehend the role of technology in IR and strategy. Technology is one of several dimensions that must be considered in strategic planning and analysis (Gray 1999, 16–47). Gray communicates the role of technology concisely, "technology drives tactics, shapes operations, and enables strategy" (170). Some technologies are significant "game changers," altering how wars are waged. However, these developments and shifts take place at the tactical and operational level. At the level of strategy, policy ends driven by politics remain unchanged by technological developments (184).

The final factor limiting the actual effect of technologies on strategic stability and the likelihood for conflict is the typical rapid diffusion or proliferation of the technologies in question. Emily Goldman and Richard Andres (1999) note that following the logic of the neorealist school of thought "proven military methods, even if they are truly revolutionary, will have no lasting affect on the balance of international influence because diffusion occurs quickly among states that are within range of each other's war-making ability" (83). Also, this diffusion and proliferation of a technology does not mean that states find themselves in an escalatory or precarious arms race. The diffusion of certain technologies among states may simply be general military developments, not a specifically tailored amassing of capability (Huntington 1958, 42). For example, Barry Posen (1984) writes that following their debut in World War I, technologies supporting the development of tanks proliferated, absent the context of an arms race. If adversaries possess similar levels of scientific advancement, the technological advantage of one state is likely to be fleeting as the technology rapidly proliferates. Gray (2013) imparts the timeless wisdom that the unique advantages of specific technologies are unlikely to reach their promise because "a rising tide of technological sophistication raises all boats at home and abroad" (176).

Unlike some IR scholarship on the role of technology that concludes erroneously that technology development can lead to inadvertent escalation and increase the likelihood for conflict, the technologies being developed and fielded by NewSpace companies, in fact, will have a marginal impact on IR and strategy. Potential escalation in the strategic relationships between space powers will be driven by political considerations, not technological ones. The strategic effect of NewSpace technologies will be highly dependent on the context of a future conflict. It is possible that future conflicts will take place in locations or against adversaries that marginalize the benefits of space power or during miliary operations where space is inconsequential. Finally, the military advantages from wielding NewSpace derived technologies will be offset by the proliferation of these technologies among the global community.

CONCLUSION

NewSpace companies and the greater commercial space sector are currently playing a significant role in how polities protect security interests. This is because of primarily two reasons: the peaceful uses of space-relevant technologies enable commerce that is a vital national interest that needs to be protected; and the commercial space sector provides a means to help countries achieve their strategic goals. Governments are often long-standing customers of commercial space capabilities and help facilitate today's commercial space markets. While governments have an opportunity to leverage emerging commercial space companies to help it to do more and spend less, the potential downside of leveraging this investor funded, dynamic commercial innovation is greater uncertainty.

 While the rapid changes resulting in commercial space capabilities and services may be seen by some analysts as increasing national security risks and destabilizing to the global community's balance of power, such thinking is misguided. Ill-advised beliefs that NewSpace technologies will lead to inadvertent escalation and increase the likelihood for conflict neglect the fact that technology has a limited role in IR and strategy. When considering the security risks posed by innovative commercial space capabilities and services, policymakers and IR scholars must remember that technology in itself should not be considered a risk or threat. It is how people use such technology that determines if it is a risk to security or not. The fundamental role of people in determining risks to security is underscored by Carl von Clausewitz's observation that "war is a continuation of politics by other means" (Clausewitz 1989). People and polities most often decide how technologies are employed—whether for peace, conflict, or somewhere in between. Thus, peoples' intention matters in this regard. NewSpace, along with the novel technologies and space services that it brings, is no different in this regard.

DISCLAIMER

The views expressed in this article are solely those of the authors and do not necessarily reflect those of Falcon Research, Georgetown, and George Washington Universities, BryceTech, or the US government.

REFERENCES

Aerospace Corporation. 2019. "Outpacing the Threat with an Agile Defense Space Enterprise." The Aerospace Corporation. https://aerospace.org/sites/default/files/2020-11/Morin-Wilson_Leveraging_20201113.pdf.

Bas, Muhammet, and Andrew Coe. 2012. "Arms Diffusion and War." *Journal of Conflict Resolution* 56, no. 4: 651–74.

Bateman, Aaron. 2021. "Restraint, Not Superiority, in Space." *War on the Rocks*. March 4, 2021. https://warontherocks.com/2021/03/restraint-not-superiority-in-space/.

Bloom, John. 2016. *Eccentric Orbits: The Iridium Story*. New York: Atlantic Monthly Press.

Borowitz, Mariel John, Lawrence Rubin, and Briand Stewart. 2020. "National Security Implications of Emerging Satellite Technologies." *Foreign Policy Research Institute* Fall: 515–27.

Borowitz, Mariel. 2021. "An Interoperable Information Umbrella: Sharing Space Information Technology." *Strategic Studies Quarterly* (Spring): 116–32. https://www.airuniversity.af.edu/Portals/10/SSQ/documents/Volume-15_Issue-1/Borowitz.pdf.

Bowen, Bleddyn. 2015. "The Continuation of Terran Politics by Other Means." PhD. Diss., Department of International Politics, Aberystwyth University.

BryceTech. 2020. "Start-up Space: Update on Investment in Commercial Space Ventures." https://brycetech.com/reports/report-documents/Bryce_Start_Up_Space_2020.pdf.

BryceTech. 2021a. "Smallsats by the Numbers 2021." https://brycetech.com/reports/report-documents/Bryce_Smallsats_2021.pdf.

BryceTech. 2021b. "Start-up Space: Update on Investment in Commercial Space Ventures." https://brycetech.com/reports/report-documents/Bryce_Start_Up_Space_2021.pdf.

Chin, Carrey. 2011. "A Study on the Commercialization of Space-based Remote Sensing in the Twenty-First Century and Its Implications to United States National Security." Master's thesis, Naval Postgraduate School. https://apps.dtic.mil/sti/tr/pdf/ADA547960.pdf.

Clausewitz, Carl von. 1989. *On War*. Translated and edited by Michael Howard and Peter Paret. Princeton, NJ: Princeton University Press.

Consortium for Execution of Rendezvous and Servicing Operations (CONFERS). 2021. "CONFERS." https://www.satelliteconfers.org/.

Drezner, Daniel. 2019. "Technological Change and International Relations." *International Relations* 33, no. 2: 286–303.

Economist. 2021a. "The Promise of Open-Source Intelligence." *The Economist*. August 7, 2021. https://www.economist.com/leaders/2021/08/07/the-promise-of-open-source-intelligence.

Economist. 2021b. "Open-Source Intelligence Challenges State Monopolies on Information." *The Economist*. August 7, 2021. https://www.economist.com/briefing/2021/08/07/open-source-intelligence-challenges-state-monopolies-on-information?itm_source=parsely-api.

Erwin, Sandra. 2019. "Vector Relinquishes Air Force Launch Contract, Mission Re-awarded to Aevum." *Spacenews*. September 9, 2019. https://spacenews.com/vector-relinquishes-air-force-launch-contract-mission-re-awarded-to-aevum/.

Erwin, Sandra. 2021. "Military Building an Appetite for Commercial Space Services." *Spacenews*. June 25, 2021. https://spacenews.com/military-building-an-appetite-for-commercial-space-services/.

ESA Space Debris Office. 2021. "ESA's Annual Space Environment Report." European Space Agency. https://www.sdo.esoc.esa.int/environment_report/Space_Environment_Report_latest.pdf.

Foust, Jeff. 2019. "ESA Spacecraft Dodges Potential Collision with Starlink Satellite." *Spacenews.* September 2, 2019. https://spacenews.com/esa-spacecraft-dodges-potential-collision-with-starlink-satellite/.

Gage, Deborah. 2012. "The Venture Capital Secret: 3 Out of 4 Start-Ups Fail." *Wall Street Journal.* September 20, 2021. https://www.wsj.com/articles/SB10000872396390443720204578004980476429190.

Goldman, Emily, and Richard Andres. 1999. "Systemic Effects of Military Innovation and Diffusion." *Security Studies* 8, no. 4: 79–125.

Gray, Colin. 1999. *Modern Strategy.* Oxford: Oxford University Press.

Gray, Colin. 2013. *Perspectives on Strategy.* Oxford: Oxford University Press.

Hallex, Matthew, and Travis S. Cottom. 2020. "Proliferated Commercial Satellite Constellations: Implications for National Security." *Joint Force Quarterly* 97: 20–29. https://ndupress.ndu.edu/Portals/68/Documents/jfq/jfq-97/jfq-97_20-29_Hallex-Cottom.pdf?ver=2020-03-31-130614-940.

Herz, John. 1950. "Idealist Internationalism and the Security Dilemma." *World Politics* 2, no. 2: 157–80.

Hitchens, Theresa. 2021. "NRO Space 'Civil Reserve' Includes Shutter Control Option." *Breaking Defense.* July 30, 2021. https://breakingdefense.com/2021/07/exclusive-nro-space-civil-reserve-includes-shutter-control-option/.

Huntington, Samuel. 1958. "Arms Races: Prerequisites and Results." *Public Policy* 8: 41–86.

Jervis, Robert. 1978. "Cooperation Under the Security Dilemma." *World Politics* 30, no. 2: 167–214.

Johnson-Freese, Joan. 2017. *Space Warfare in the 21st Century: Arming the Heavens.* Abingdon, UK: Routledge.

Klein, John. 2019. *Understanding Space Strategy: The Art of War in Space.* Abingdon, UK: Routledge.

Lewis, Hugh. 2021. "Time for September's Update on Conjunctions Predicted by #SOCRATES (via http://celestrak.com) Involving #Starlink." Twitter. September 10, 2021. https://twitter.com/ProfHughLewis/status/1436334166447173640.

Liou, J. C, M. Matney, A. Varin, A. Manis, and D. Gates. 2018. "NASA ODPO's Large Constellation Study." *Orbital Debris Quarterly News,* 22, no. 3: 4–7.

Loverro, Doug. 2021. "If Commercial Space is Ready to Set Sail, Why Are We Still Missing the Boat?" *Breaking Defense.* August 25, 2021. https://breakingdefense.com/2021/08/if-commercial-space-is-ready-to-set-sail-why-are-we-still-missing-the-boat/.

McKnight, Darren, Rachel Witner, Francesca Letizia, Stijn Lemmens, Luciano Anselmo, Carmen Pardini, Alessandro Rossi, et al. 2021. "Identifying the 50 Statistically-Most-Concerning Derelict Objects in LEO." *Acta Astronautica* 181: 282–91. https://www.sciencedirect.com/science/article/abs/pii/S0094576521000217.

Morin, Jamie, and Robert Wilson. 2021. "Leveraging Commercial Space for National Security." The Aerospace Corporation. November 2021. https://aerospace.org/sites/default/files/2020-11/Morin-Wilson_Leveraging_20201113.pdf.

NASA Office of Inspector General. 2021. "NASA's Efforts to Mitigate the Risks Posed by Orbital Debris." Report No. IG-21-011. https://oig.nasa.gov/docs/IG-21-011.pdf.

NOAA (National Oceanic and Atmospheric Administration). 2020. "Licensing of Private Remote Sensing Space Systems." 15 CFR Part 960. Request for Comments. https://s3.amazonaws.com/public-inspection.federalregister.gov/2020-10703.pdf.

Posen, Barry. 1984. *The Sources of Military Doctrine: France, Britain, and Germany between the World Wars.* Ithaca, NY: Cornell University Press.

Satellite Industry Association. 2021. "State of the Satellite Industry Report." Satellite Industry Association. https://sia.org/news-resources/state-of-the-satellite-industry-report/.

Schneider, Jacquelyn. 2019. "The Capability/Vulnerability Paradox and Military Revolutions: Implications for Computing, Cyber, and the Onset of War." *Journal of Strategic Studies* 42, no. 6: 841–63.

Sechser, Todd, Neil Narang, and Caitlin Talmadge. 2019. "Emerging Technologies and Strategic Stability in Peacetime, Crisis, and War." *Journal of Strategic Studies* 42, no. 6: 727–35.

Sheldon, John. 2005. "Reasoning by Strategic Analogy: Classical Strategic Thought and the Foundations of a Theory of Space Power." PhD Diss., University of Reading.

Smith, M. V. 2016. "Spacepower and the Strategist." In *Strategy: Context and Adaptation from Archidamus to Airpower*, edited by Richard Bailey, James Forsyth, and Mark Yeisley, 157–85. Annapolis, MD: Naval Institute Press.

Talmadge, Caitlin. 2019. "Emerging Technology and Intra-War Escalation Risks: Evidence from the Cold War, Implications for Today." *Journal of Strategic Studies* 42, no. 6: 864–87.

Taverney, Thomas. 2020a. "Op-Ed | Proliferated LEO is Risky but Necessary." *Spacenews*. March 5, 2020. https://spacenews.com/op-ed-proliferated-leo-is-risky-but-necessary/.

Taverney, Thomas. 2020b. "Commercial Solutions Answer Space Force's Call." *Air Force Magazine*. December 1, 2020. https://www.airforcemag.com/article/commercial-solutions-answer-space-forces-call/.

Townsend, Brand. 2020. "Strategic Choice and the Orbital Security Dilemma." *Strategic Studies Quarterly* Spring: 64–90. https://www.airuniversity.af.edu/Portals/10/SSQ/documents/Volume-14_Issue-1/Townsend.pdf.

Van Evera, Stephen. 1999. *Causes of War*. Ithaca, NY: Cornell University Press.

Vedda, James, and Peter Hays. 2018. "Major Policy Issues in Evolving Global Space Operations." The Mitchell Institute of Aerospace Studies. https://aerospace.org/sites/default/files/2018-05/Space_Policy_FINAL_interactive_0.pdf.

Waltz, Kenneth. 1979. *Theory of International Politics*. Reading, UK: Addison-Wesley.

Weeden, Brian. 2020. "The United States is Losing Its Leadership Role in the Fight against Orbital Debris." *The Space Review*, February 24, 2020. https://www.thespacereview.com/article/3889/1.

Weinbaum, Cortney, Steven Berner, and Bruce McClintock. 2017. "SIGINT for Anyone." RAND Corporation. Perspective. https://www.rand.org/pubs/perspectives/PE273.html.

Weiss, Charles. 2005. "Science, Technology and International Relations." *Technology in Society* 27, no. 3: 295–313.

CHAPTER 41

PLANETARY DEFENSE

A Unique Opportunity to Practice Cosmopolitan
Security Principles in National Foreign Policies

NIKOLA SCHMIDT

INTRODUCTION

PLANETARY defense is a cooperative scientific, engineering, and policy initiative aimed at the observation of asteroid and comet populations in the solar system and the development of means capable of deflecting an asteroid or a comet on a collision course with Earth. While the threat is a natural phenomenon, the answer to it materializes certain dynamics in international relations (IR), including the problem of the development of dual-use technologies, the challenge to national sovereignties by an inherently transnational threat, or the liability dilemma posed by international space law in case of a deflection failure. On the other hand, planetary defense is a unique opportunity to develop a planetary-scale program in which each (willing) state would participate and which would secure the planet as whole and all the peoples living on it.

Scientists with various kinds of expertise have been working on planetary defense for decades (Morrison 2019b) and the whole effort has been significantly boosted in recent years with an enormous surge in solar system observations for asteroids (Vereš and Schmidt 2019) and, finally, with the demonstration missions DART by the US National Aeronautics and Space Agency (NASA), launched in 2021, and HERA by the European Space Agency (ESA), which is to be launched in October 2024.

However, to take the IR perspective in this chapter, we will discuss how the initiative is challenging the role of the state as a security guarantor on a delimited territory as it embraces the whole Earth. There could be various explanations for this, but we will argue that the decay of national sovereignty under the pressure of a deepening global consciousness will make the insensibility to the problem of planetary defense at the level of the national governments untenable. Scientists have been working hard to develop and continuously deepen the scientific knowledge about planetary defense so the emergence of the related policies on the national, and later on the global, level is inevitable. We consider planetary defense as a unique opportunity for humanity to shift its consciousness from a selfish, nationally divided global order to humanity thinking as a species. This can be done by the foreign policy of a cosmopolitan responsible state (Brown 2011), which is a concept realistically reflecting the current state-driven global governance, while injecting cosmopolitan ideas into the given policy. Cosmopolitan responsibility does not differentiate between people based on their nationality, ethnicity, or any other socially constructed category, following the core principles of cosmopolitan ethics (Pogge 1992). Cosmopolitan responsibility in foreign policy can be a constitutive practice toward cosmopolitan security as proposed by Anthony Burke (2013).

As we still live in an international global system, states have three options for how to proceed with the pressing scientific data that have been gathered so far:

(1) to participate in the global initiative in planetary defense by providing their scientific and engineering expertise and capacities and leave the planetary defense policy to the scientific community until a serious asteroid on a collision course is detected—this is the *international scenario* we can currently observe globally and is practiced at the Space Mission Planning Advisory Group (SMPAG), an expert group under the auspices of the United Nations Committee for the Peaceful Uses of Outer Space (COPUOS);

(2) to become significant players in planetary defense and announce their own self-supported program that would be capable of deflecting any incoming asteroid—this is the *national exceptionalism scenario* that could align with China's planetary defense policy, for example;

(3) to advocate a global policy program for planetary defense that would not only organize observations and build a standing multigenerational infrastructure of the deflection mission but also create a global ad-hoc decision-making body (or prepare a scenario for the decision-making process) for planetary defense—this is the *cosmopolitan scenario*, which the chapter will follow, assessing its practical and normative consequences under the light of the cosmopolitan theory in IR.

What is Planetary Defense?

This section lays out some basic considerations with respect to planetary defense.

Analyzing the Threat

The threat is posed by natural phenomena; it is becoming a *security* threat thanks to astronomical observations, subsequent impact modeling, the realization that there is an inevitable collision course, and the impact consequences. The substance of the threat is different to the *security* threat of possible catastrophic consequences imagined by the general public, politicians, radical religious groups, or economic advisers making evaluations of the costs of human lives. The former is about scientific efforts to explain the phenomena as objectively as possible, while the latter is about realizing what the natural phenomena can cause to humanity, cities, our way of life, and the biosphere. As such, near-Earth objects (asteroids and comets) become a security threat to each of these subjects. All of those groups, and plenty of others, will react to the announcement of a detected asteroid on a collision course differently, and the perception of the risk by each of them will be different. The risk of panic or an inappropriate reaction by governments without prepared scenarios could become another threat besides the asteroid strike itself.

When thinking about the risk, one of the greatest advantages of planetary defense is that the threat is predictable. However, as policy is about a desired outcome policymakers wish to achieve, it is inherently normative and cannot be reduced to the so-called single rational "solution" of an asteroid being deflected off its collision course. In this regard, limiting the policy to a mere evidence-based policy would be reductionist and probably even dangerous (Newman 2017; Standring 2017) because decisions and judgements have a whole complex of outcomes, even unintentional ones. Decisions should be focused on the practical context to reflect the normative dimension of the consequences rather than being based solely on scientific objectivity. Practical objectivity is an inclusive rather than an exclusive concept, it is aim-sensitive rather than aim-neutral and it is an achievement rather than a protocol of research (Montuschi 2017).

We need to take into consideration the following basic characteristics to understand the threat for the international security discussion: (1) the orbital mechanics—asteroids do not "fall from the sky" but cross the orbit of the Earth on an ecliptic plane; mostly, only a minority of asteroids deviate from the ecliptic (Crowe 2019). Some asteroids can be drawn by gravitational fluctuations of the big planets such as Jupiter and Saturn, which could change their orbit. Or more specifically, any approach of an asteroid toward a bigger object changes its orbit if they do not collide (Air University 2003). Therefore, while we can reach an almost perfect solar system awareness the predictability will never be 100 percent certain, and the orbits must be constantly clarified by follow up observations (Vereš and Schmidt 2019). (2) According to the International Asteroid Warning Network (IAWN) that collects all observational data, we already know the orbits of almost all (96–99 percent) asteroids bigger than 1 kilometer. Therefore, the probability of being hit by an extinction-size asteroid is negligible, which was actually the first project Spaceguard of NASA had answer when planetary defense had become an issue to study (Morrison 1992). However, asteroids capable of wiping out whole regions are about 140 meters wide and there could be around 25,000 of them. We estimate that we will be aware of 80 percent of them by 2032, and 60 percent remain to be discovered in 2022 according to IAWN. Asteroids bigger than 50 meters can still wipe out whole cities and there could be millions of them. In this regard, solar system observations will have to mature to a certain level and become permanent for follow-up observations. Therefore, we do not face an imminent extinction event, but an impact that would destroy a city could happen anytime. (3) Comets are significantly bigger than asteroids. They come to the center of the solar system on highly elliptical orbits and there could be trillions of them (Binzel, Reddy, and Dunn 2015). Comets lie in the Oort cloud beyond the solar system, and sometimes gravitational fluctuations of big planets can draw new ones close to Sun. While they are rare, their impact is barely predictable and deflectable, and as the Oort cloud is a sphere, they could come from anywhere, in contrast to the asteroids that are mostly on the ecliptic plane. Mapping all comets is a task for the next generations.

As any insurance of infrastructural systems is based on the cost-benefit principle, planetary defense can be perceived this way as well (Boslough 2019), while the probabilistic approach in this regard has also been developed (Mathias, Wheeler, and Dotson 2017). However, this probabilistic approach developed by astronomers has become a target of social scientists criticizing their occupation of the media space and their developing of misleading and inapplicable risk perceptions that draw on quantitative risk assessments (Mellor 2010). Mellor previously developed a solid critical insight into this expertise-driven discourse development by an isolated planetary defense scientific community (Mellor 2007). However, others argued that the fact that planetary defense requires various types of expertise (observation, study of the detected asteroids, development of mitigation methods) means that it has the potential to lead to the development of new modes of international cooperation (Bucknam and Gold 2008). We argue that planetary defense is not about the risk of impact but about the cosmopolitan responsibility that emerges with the produced knowledge and the capability to avoid the impact (Schmidt 2019). The probability is irrelevant from the perspective of cosmopolitan responsibility.

In summary, first, planetary defense is a low-probability/high-consequence event. Second, considering the sizes and orbital trajectories of asteroids, we are able to deflect most of the asteroids if they are detected sufficiently in advance (the required time greatly increases with the size, speed, and orbit of the asteroid), but we would struggle to defend Earth from comets, as a comet can barely be detected earlier than when it is on its final approach to the center of the solar system, on its collision course, weeks or months before impact. Third, planetary defense cannot be defended as a policy program until it has a normative framing over its practical objectivity, while it is still within the sphere of scientific objectivity. Fourth, regardless of the impact probability, we have the means to observe threatening asteroids and deflect them, which constitutes a cosmopolitan responsibility to act. From the perspective of cosmopolitan ethics, just the fact that we have the capacities to observe the solar system, map the asteroid population, and deflect a threatening asteroid on a collision course constitutes a cosmopolitan responsibility and, therefore, a moral obligation to act.

A Quick Summary of Deflection Methods

The social scientific problematization of asteroid observation is not as complex as the development of deflection methods. This is understandable, as deflection methods are an active technology with a maneuvering or even explosive capability. Five main deflection methods are discussed within the planetary defense community (Morrison 2019a).

First, a kinetic impactor is based on the momentum transfer caused by an impact of a heavy space craft. NASA's mission DART, launched in 2021, demonstrates this method (Cheng et al. 2018). Second, a gravity tractor is based on the principle that when a deployed (heavy) space craft is in the vicinity of an asteroid, its tiny gravity would pull the asteroid from its orbit so that it would miss the key hole (an abstract circle in space which confirms an upcoming collision if the asteroid goes through it) (Lu and Love 2005). Third, a nuclear explosive is certainly the most effective method. It does not depend on a shock wave as space lacks an atmosphere but rather on an evaporation of the surface of an asteroid caused by the enormous heat created by the nuclear explosion that pushes it in the opposite direction (Sarli et al. 2018). A nuclear explosive can be combined with a conventional explosive that would detonate a fraction of time before the nuclear explosion. The push momentum is then bigger, as the crater from the first explosion serves as a nozzle of the "rocket engine"; this method comes with the possibility to fully disintegrate the asteroid (Barbee et al. 2015). Fourth, laser or solar thermal methods use a similar approach, as they heat up the surface to emit particles of the target in a certain direction, similarly to the nuclear explosive devices, but due to the low energy methods in this case, they require a long period of time to be effective (Hughes et al. 2013) and the technology is not mature enough (Krůs and Schmidt 2022). Fifth, the final method is based on the idea that a space craft could land on an asteroid, hook itself to it, and move the asteroid with its ion engines.

Deflection methods vary in terms of their effectiveness, maturity, and security sensitivity. While kinetic impactors could possibly be used as weapons in hostile actions (as could any space craft with a capability to maneuver), high-power lasers could be used as distant weapons, and a major point is that nuclear explosive devices cannot even be tested due to the ban on nuclear explosions in space under the Test Ban Treaty of 1963. Therefore, in this regard, humanity depends mainly on kinetic impactors or gravity tractors along with ion beam-empowered space craft if it does not adopt a cooperative governance model in planetary defense.

Current National Planetary Defense Policies and Global Planetary Defense Efforts

Interestingly, states do not ignore planetary defense despite the general low public awareness of the global initiative. However, most states do not talk about "planetary defense" but rather about near-Earth objects, near-Earth asteroids, and space situational awareness (SSA). The reasons are clearly based on an assumption that the word "defense" is reserved for national security entities. Planetary defense is usually included in broader space safety programs. For example, the ESA understands space safety as a program aiming to mitigate and prevent the effects of hazards from space; it consists of four offices dealing with space weather, planetary defense, space debris, and clean space.

We have identified seven motivations for states deciding to pursue planetary defense policies in their national strategic documents (Lenkavska and Schmidt 2021). The motivations identified in the analyzed national policies should not be taken as a full analysis of all 200 states; even such an analysis would be biased by the varying sizes of states and their space programs. The prevalently observed motivation is still *national security* along with *scientific advancement* and *industrial growth*. *National welfare* significantly surpasses the motivation of *global welfare*, which emanates from the knowledge about the asteroid population and their possible mining opportunities. On the one hand, a desirable outcome from our study for the possible future cosmopolitan governance of planetary defense was the fact that states significantly prefer *global security* over *political leadership* as an outcome of their own national planetary defense programs or participation in the global broad planetary defense initiatives. On the other hand, pronouncements such as that by China stating that they will send 23 Long March 5 rockets to demonstrate a deflection of a large asteroid (Reuters 2021) do not contribute to global collaboration efforts but rather cause international security concerns. Pronouncements like that are certainly aimed to deepen feelings of national exceptionalism, because a year later, China published a paper on its planetary defense program consisting of a single kinetic impactor (Wang et al. 2021) and announced a serious mission based on it (Jones 2022).

The main international planetary defense project is the aforementioned double mission DART (NASA) and HERA (ESA). The United States has certainly the most developed planetary defense program, based in NASA's Planetary Defense Coordination Office (The White House 2018). ESA also has a strong focus and a dedicated planetary defense program within its space safety program (ESA 2021). The European Union (EU), at its newly established EUSPA headquarters in Prague, also focuses on planetary defense within its SSA program (Cemal 2021), which will be mainly implemented by ESA. In general, we can say that the aim is to have a significant portion of the solar system awareness program finished by 2030 and to have kinetic impactors prepared to deflect asteroids as small as 40 meters in terms of width and detect them weeks in advance. In recent years, planetary defense has been also making its way into the general disaster management sphere within civilian protection institutions (Ravan et al. 2022).

As this very brief introduction to the planetary defense programs shows, we can distinguish between the internationally driven initiative of mostly Western states and some newly emerging national initiatives such as the one in China. The political line in planetary defense is usually drawn between astronomical observations and participation in demonstration missions on one side and political motivations for planetary defense on the other. While the observations and even the participation in deflection demonstration missions are conducted by scientists, and funded from science grants or government programs that cooperate regardless of political ideologies (in the case of astronomers, this has been going on for centuries), the development of planetary defense as a global political program stalls because the political rationalization for its global scope is literally missing. The focus, even in US or EU strategies, in which one would expect an emphasis on global cooperation, is limited to instrumental cooperation in terms of observation and mitigation and ignores the socio-governance shift planetary defense policy could involve. If Anthony Burke sketches security cosmopolitanism as a theory, planetary defense is a perfect case in which to implement it as a practical policy—a reason and normative motivation for cosmopolitan responsible states.

ESA is a civilian institution and governs planetary defense under its space safety program, which also deals with space weather, space debris, and clean space. Space weather is understood comparably to Earth weather forecasts by the broader security community. Politicization and securitization could cause a shift of the understanding of planetary defense or space weather along with the whole space safety program; the security community's efforts to develop a global scale planetary defense policy is considered by the planetary defense scientific community as a possible menace to their hard scientific work. This position is quite ambiguous, however, because at the same time it is the planetary defense scientific community who call for a deepening of "asteroid threat awareness." This is also the reason why we do not find the asteroid threat as a part of national security strategies but as a part of science and technology strategies falling under general SSA programs.

The Drivers behind Planetary Defense Moving toward Cosmopolitan Governance

Planetary defense as a natural phenomenon has the potential to create unique dynamics in international politics. This is understandable, firstly, because asteroids and comets are a global threat per se but also because its natural characteristics make answers using technology inevitable, and this will affect international security given its security sensitivity. The following section lists some dynamics that the problem of planetary defense poses and that we understand as drivers toward its cosmopolitan governance. Some of the drivers are enabled by exogenous powers of nature that simply cannot be omitted, such as the risk corridor, and some have been created by people, such as the liability dilemma, which emerges from the fact of the current global governance by sovereign states. The following list demonstrates that a planetary defense governed through national policies would face a plethora of problems, while a global multilateral or, preferably, cosmopolitan governance can keep the Earth safe for the foreseeable future.

The Risk Corridor

A risk corridor crossing multiple states is the most obvious problem in planetary defense when addressed as a national security policy. When an asteroid is detected on a collision course, we do not know its exact spot of impact, but we know quite precisely the direction of its movement, as in the case of the well-known asteroid Apophis. It is 185 meters in diameter and will pass the Earth in 2029 at a distance of 38 kilometers, which will make it visible to the eye on the sky (Reddy et al. 2022). The risk corridor line surrounds the whole planet and crosses multiple states. The Earth's rotation makes the line wavy, and the uncertainty of the direction makes the risk corridor thick, while the site of impact can be somewhere along the whole line, but with a higher probability of being in its center.

Correction of the predicted impact site depends on measurements of numerous physical characteristics such as the thickness of the atmosphere according to the time of day that the object enters the atmosphere or the physical composition of the asteroid. Precise measurements of its trajectory and speed taken from the vicinity of the asteroid by a reconnaissance probe can help to significantly reduce the uncertainty and thus also the risk corridor. However, in the majority of cases, the risk corridor line will cross more than one country—asteroids do not discriminate. International cooperation in this regard is therefore more than just desirable; it is inevitable.

The National Security Policy Obstacle

The fact that planetary defense is making its way into national disaster strategies means that we can expect to have the asteroid threat dealt with alongside fires, floods, and other possible disasters in the coming decades. This is not necessarily bad if the "fire truck" consisting of asteroid deflection technology in standby mode is not considered a threat to the national security of other states. Some states even argued at ESA meetings that planetary defense should be reserved for national security agencies. This way of thinking would potentially create 200 planetary defense infrastructures with an inability to make decisions when needed. If security sensitive technologies were governed on national levels, they would create a classic neorealist security dilemma on the international level. Planetary defense simply cannot be governed by sovereign states alone. However, before 2013, the discussion about planetary defense governance at the United Nations considered the possibility of an ad-hoc decision-making body, the so-called MAOG—the Mission Authorization and Oversight Group. But this idea was ruled out in 2013, and power over decision making in planetary defense was kept in the hands of states. While this development could be considered as the most significant failure of attempts to build a planetary defense governance, the literature and the community continue their discussions on the topic of the "Decision to Act" and leave it open for ideas.

The Liability Treaty Dilemma

According to the Liability Treaty, states are liable for damage caused in space by space objects for which they are the launching state. Based on the legal principle of the causal nexus and the attributability of the chain of consequences to a launching state, the liability may apply also to some of the consequences of their actions regardless of the fact that the Liability Treaty is not explicit on the liability transfer through the causal chain. The SMPAG agreed on the principle of the causal chain in its legal report (SMPAG 2020).

Given the risk corridor dilemma the first confirmation that an asteroid is on a collision course with Earth will be of concern to more than one state. If one state acts and moves the asteroid inappropriately, it could hit another state, leading to an international conflict regardless of the deemed unintentionality. In this regard, a state or a group of states conducting a planetary defense mission that fails may be liable for the damages its actions caused. It would understandably be a subject of a discussion, but we can assume in an extensive legal interpretation that just a mere landing on an asteroid that would insignificantly nudge it can constitute potential liability for the foreseeable future of that asteroid on behalf of the state that landed the space craft. Consider the missions DART and HERA. They are not designed to hit a solitary asteroid but a small asteroid orbiting a bigger asteroid; so the small one is a moon to the bigger asteroid. Hitting the moon will not significantly move the whole two-object orbiting system because the smaller asteroid will be maintained around the larger asteroid. This mission design also helps to avoid possible discussions over liability in the future regardless the futility of the intended nudge as the discussions whether a failed hit of an asteroid in demonstration missions could constitute a liability is ongoing in the expert community.

Working on the current global planetary defense initiative does not constitute an obligation to act in case of a detected asteroid on a collision course. A multilateral regime, similar to the Washington Treaty establishing NATO, would but currently there is not even a glimpse of a political intention to open such a regime building discussion.

The Unilateral Mission Problem

The risk of a unilateral mission also comes from the preceding dilemma but frames slightly different situations. First, as planetary defense capabilities in deflection methods are developed on a national basis, it is reasonable to assume that some states will at least have the potential to act unilaterally against the interests or consent of other states within the risk corridor. Second, when unable to forge a broader international agreement, states resort to unilateral actions. Third, some states, such as China, could not even consider an international cooperation and would resort to a unilateral action because they are excluded from the international space community. Fourth, some states could be willing to demonstrate their national space capabilities to deepen their feeling of national exceptionalism, which is a problem that could emanate from just about every spacefaring authoritarian governed state (typically Russia but also Turkey, which mentions national leadership as a motivation in its strategy).

The Nuclear Explosive Device

The problem with nuclear explosive devices (NEDs) is another very delicate situation. Nuclear explosives in space are banned by the Partial Test Ban Treaty and recently any development of nuclear weapons has been banned by the Treaty on the Prohibition of Nuclear Weapons, which hampers any efforts to develop NEDs for planetary defense despite the fact that NEDs are the most effective means of asteroid (or comet) deflection. While not all treaties are in force or adopted by all nuclear states, the fact that international law could be considered as a normative plane (Bull 2002) that helps states to get oriented in the international order rather than being an enforceable system of binding rules makes any development of NEDs for planetary defense—and thus impacting everybody—impossible or at least politically unfeasible. The necessary power for deflecting an asteroid from its collision course increases as the time before the impact decreases. If an asteroid on a collision course is detected too late, the power of a nuclear explosive could be the only means of deflection. This is linked to the unilateral mission problem, because it is reasonable to assume that nuclear capable and spacefaring states working on planetary defense would develop means of last resort.

Another dimension of the nuclear question is the risk of destigmatizing the nuclear taboo (Smetana 2019) if nuclear weapons are rationalized as a planet saving technology. This problem can be linked to the rationalization of states obtaining nuclear weapons, especially rogue states such as North Korea. The fact that the scientific community behind planetary defense efforts visibly inclines toward "effective solutions" clearly shows the difference between scientific objectivization and practical objectivization. It is not a rare situation at the bi-annual planetary defense conferences that some scientists or engineers openly state that we should "solve politics" in order to be able to develop NEDs for planetary defense or "we are done." Securitizing an asteroid threat through a planetary defense initiative by destigmatizing the nuclear taboo could have horrible consequences for stability in world politics. Critics of these voices advocating NEDs for their effectivity take the current political system as granted, solid, and perpetual.

However, if humanity wants to be able to use last resort measures against a comet on a collision course, it should adopt the most effective means regardless of current taboos, such as the nuclear one, but that would require a significant change of the global governance system. Political systems change with philosophical thoughts, and our political system could change with thoughts that argue broadly for the reasons why we need to consider NEDs in planetary defense (Marks 2022) if they offer a new, more legitimate governance system that could feasibly be implemented. Taboos are part of the current political system, but they could fade out with its change (Price 1995). Therefore, both sources of ideas (philosophy and governance) should evolve mutually so as to unfold into particular new governance systems (Schmidt 2019; 2022a).

The nuclear question could be perceived as a problem that is not necessarily caused by the existence or effective rationalization of nuclear explosive technology as it is rather a problem of the dysfunctional international political system. A centralized global democracy would not have this problem, while it would understandably have different problems. But it is not necessary to discuss the achievability of a radically new political system here because having a perfectly internationally monitored global authority for planetary defense could be enough to keep the nuclear taboo untouched while enabling the discussion over using nuclear technology for planetary defense. We could imagine NEDs as a part of serious discussions on the standby technologies for planetary defense humanity should possess if we had a central authority for planetary defense over which all states, including nuclear states, would have a working oversight system with participation in its governance.

The idea for a centralized authority can be found in the legal report developed by the SMPAG (2020), in which the authors point to the possibility of an ad-hoc decision-making body should an asteroid be detected on a collision course. The idea of a centralized authority was promoted in reports by Action Team 14, where it was referred to as the aforementioned MAOG—the Mission Authorization and Oversight Group. Action Team 14 preceded (and recommended the establishment of) the SMPAG, but its vision of a centralized authority never materialized. States did not want a new authority above their national sovereignty and so only a coordination and advisory body (the SMPAG) was established.

The Large Technical System

A large technical system is a concept used in science and technology studies for technical systems of a large scale with significant social implications, regardless of whether they are networked (the internet, a road network, flight and airport infrastructure) or single machines (CERN, ITER, ISS, JWST). Planetary defense in the shape of multigenerational efforts will require a large infrastructure for observations and deflection.

Humanity is currently working with relatively small space craft to demonstrate impacts on asteroids but long-term safety from near Earth objects, including comets, will require a complex, large technical system. Observation systems could be perceived as surveillance, and deflection systems as possible weapons in the common dual-use technology dilemma. Deflecting comets might require dozens of standby rockets with NEDs. The problem of large technical system securitization in planetary defense is inevitable and will surface regardless of the low politicization of the issue when the planetary defense community simply proceeds further and begins discussions of what a complex planetary defense infrastructure should look like. Hundreds of planetary defense systems would certainly cause a new kind of security dilemma.

However, if they are not approached as threats to national security but as tools for forging global security, large technical systems requiring normative framing could have a positive and constitutive power in creating cosmopolitan governance (Schmidt and Ditrych 2022). In this regard, large technical systems can be drivers that would enable security cosmopolitanism in global governance.

The Multigenerational Inevitability

The planetary defense scientific community is rather small. Its bi-annual conference is visited by about 200 experts, and everybody in the field literally knows each other's work. Observations using various telescopes and engineers' concepts for future deflection missions significantly prevail over the social scientific interest in planetary defense, whose level can be computed in single experts studying the initiative. If we want to consider the current initiative as the beginning of the consciousness shift of the whole of humanity, we should think about how to make planetary defense a sustainable initiative, which is certainly a task for social scientists. First of all, humanity should stop discounting issues of a huge magnitude just because there is a low probability of solutions to them materializing within one generation (Gottlieb 2022).

Astronomers are currently studying asteroids, but they will be done one day, and following up on found asteroids will then be administrative rather than scientific work. Some parts of the observation activities such as following up on the orbital trajectories and their corrections currently need the development of a methodology, but one day, they will be conducted by automated systems reading data from telescopes. Deflection space craft will have to be built, but then they will have to be maintained, repaired, and rebuilt, which is also work for a not very specialized engineer rather than a high-end space engineer developing a unique machine. The scientific challenges planetary defense currently faces will lead to a shift to administrative work and disaster management consisting of prediction, deflection, or impact recovery. This shift of activities will require a global, sustainable, and multigenerational planetary defense governance system (Schmidt 2021).

FORGING A COSMOPOLITAN SECURITY FOR EARTH IN PLANETARY DEFENSE

Adopting a responsible foreign policy reflecting cosmopolitan values is a task for enlightened people who are willing to acquire cosmopolitan values and behave according to them in any democratic state.

Cosmopolitanism as a political theory is criticized for its allegedly too radical vision of global governance. Understandable criticism comes from classical realism, which argues that state alignment with international law (and thus also the cosmopolitan idea that people are equal) is (are) just a coincidence with states' interests (Goldsmith and Posner 2005), and therefore there are no normative powers. Another common criticism of cosmopolitanism argues that any version of cosmopolitan governance, even a cosmopolitan democracy, bears a risk of global dominion (Zolo 2000; 2013). Meanwhile some other authors think that cosmopolitan legitimacy in world politics is an unfeasible, misplaced, and dangerous idea (Hawthorn 2003). The EU did not emerge out of nowhere but was created by sovereign European states, which were willing to give up their sovereignty so that Europe would be governed according to shared values, with consent, more effectively and, finally, more legitimately. There is no reason why the same process cannot happen on the global level (Habermas 2008), especially if we accept that the arguments that the globalization process is inevitable and actually a continuous cosmopolitanization of the planet (Held 2010) that is slowly leading to an inevitable world state (Wendt 2003).

The most recent and elegant way to answer the overall criticism arguing that cosmo-politan ideas cannot be implemented in global governance due to their radicality is the concept of a *cosmopolitan responsible state*, which reflects the possibility of states directly changing the world from the perspective of cosmopolitan responsibility in the current inter-state system (Brown 2011; Beardsworth and Shapcott 2019).

The Crisis of Sovereignty

Sovereignty stands on authority, which is decreased by the incapability of the sover-eign to act, even in a situation where the sovereign is incapable of explaining certain unknown phenomena that could subsequently possibly challenge its sovereign power (Wendt and Duvall 2008). However, the traditional approach distinguishes authority from both violence and persuasion (Arendt 1993), and it is understood as a right to be obeyed (Anscombe 1990). Such an approach is not concerned with the grounds of the claim that to be obeyed requires a publicly accepted legitimacy of the sovereign as the nature of its authority. Sovereigns do not last long in authoritarian regimes; if they do, the source of their authority is derived from the divine power of the ruling family (e.g. North Korea). But democratic societies last thanks to the stability of the norma-tive framework the society stands on. Acceptance of the authority of the sovereign in democratic states could derive from plenty of sources; however, the critical ones are the ability and willingness to secure the principal moral values of the society, not only in constitutions but also in everyday practical politics, by continuously changing the politicians practicing democratic rule.

Cosmopolitanism as a political theory looks for the cosmopolitan moral values (Pogge 1992) such as individualism (the ultimate unit of concern is human beings), uni-versality (humans are equal regardless of any social category), and generality (this spe-cial status has global force for everyone). Efforts to define universal moral values look for the foundation of a legitimate and sustainable if not perpetual relation between the governed and the governor. Any sovereignty based on a one-directional power going from the sovereign to the public is, we argue, temporary. Looking for a multigenera-tional and sustainable planetary defense must be based firstly on the cosmopolitan moral values because they consider all as the main units of concern.

In this cosmopolitan sense, sovereignty is not about absolute power but about the acceptance by the governed people that the sovereign as a public entity is capable of securing these values. It is a normative approach for understanding sovereignty (Campos and Cadilha 2021). Moreover, there is pressure from globalization in the sense of the growing global interconnection between people. On every issue (migration, global threats, regional integrations, global markets, supply chains, etc.) globalization is a denominator that transcends single states' politics and is creating an environment in which a single state loses its capability to govern and therefore also its authority if it does not address global issues cooperatively (Campos 2021).

An asteroid strike that could happen anywhere on the planet opens up two options for states that are sovereign only on a delimited territory of the planet. On the one hand, states can completely ignore it, as accepting the possibility of an asteroid strike along with admitting to their inability to avoid it would constitute a loss of authority and subsequently a loss of sovereignty to govern. It is better and easier for a sovereign to denounce the problem as nonsense and science fiction to preserve its authority if it does not have the means to address it. Ignoring the possibility of an asteroid impact as a security issue while continuing the current contribution to the planetary defense initiative consisting of scientific research and procurement of some space craft–type instruments in space will sooner or later constitute a similar loss of authority under the pressure of newly produced knowledge. States will simply be pushed to act in the same way—under the pressure of the newly acquired knowledge—as they are with regard to climate change. On the other hand, states could begin conversations with other likeminded states to develop a global security regime on planetary defense that would fulfil the normative substance of sovereignty, which would strengthen their authority. This can happen if they accept the produced knowledge and exercise cosmopolitan responsibility in foreign policy.

The second option would fulfil the interpretation of sovereignty as a global responsibility, because sovereignty as autonomy is not about the authoritative absolute power of a state, in the sense of a radical autonomy that is not being influenced by others, but about its capability to change a course of events and act in a way that no other entity can (Geenens 2017). In this regard, the scientific community behind planetary defense proves that humanity has the capability to defend itself, actively develops the technical means for observation to objectivize the threat and justly securitize it (Floyd 2011), develops means to avoid the impact (Cheng et al. 2018), and, therefore, puts significant pressure on states, as sovereigns, to avoid the event of an asteroid impact. A foreign policy of a state that takes into consideration threats and challenges beyond its border, and is based on the generally available knowledge and acting in the name of global security because the state feels that it is part of the planet, has signs of cosmopolitan responsibility in planetary defense (Schmidt 2022b). Planetary defense sets forth a text-book example of the undergoing sovereignty transformation in the globalized world by the production of scientific knowledge.

Sovereignty in the traditional way of understanding it is in crisis. Democratic states in particular do not produce representatives exercising sovereignty as an absolute power of the respective state but rather look for modes of international cooperation and mutual recognition. The public in democratic states expect that states will develop conditions for continuous human flourishing, not that they would attack others to secure themselves.

Cosmopolitanism, Anthropocentrism, Positive Security, and Human Flourishing

Not only the climate crisis and its gravity but also the broad effects of globalization have influenced theoretical discussions about security in the discipline of IR. Security in the realist perception is a security of the territorial integrity of a state and the physical safety of its inhabitants, and the relation between states is anarchy (Morgenthau and Thompson 1985). Considering the drivers of planetary defense we sketched out above, an asteroid strike in a realist international order would be a total calamity. If we accept the above explanation of sovereignty, realism is losing ground under the pressure of global challenges.

Liberalism takes its core from cosmopolitan ideas, especially the emphasis on the individual, and develops a statist system of governance in which a state is the sovereign which is to secure individual desires (Owen 2010). The liberal approach solves the problem of legitimacy on the state level through democratic legitimacy, answering the problem of anarchy in IR by helping to develop the system of international institutions, which have a significant democratic deficit. However, liberalism is capable of delivering an international security regime (Ditrych and Schmidt 2022).

Most cosmopolitans are anti-statist because they identify the state as the center of international security tensions (Archibugi and Held 2011). For cosmopolitans such as Archibugi and Held, democracy is incomplete in the international world of nation-states because the relations between them are not governed by the democratic norms, rules, and principles delivering legitimacy to the governor. The arch-cosmopolitan David Held (2018) understands planetary defense as a possible driver of global democracy.

Ulrich Beck (1992) focuses on the world being at risk of a global catastrophe and argues that the planetary reality has shifted into a collective space. For that purpose he reconciles the statist and anti-statist debate by saying that "*cosmopolitanism without provincialism is empty, [and] provincialism without cosmopolitanism is blind*" (Beck 2006, 7). Ken Booth, alongside Beck, developed a theory of world security, in which he emphasizes the flourishing of humanity (Booth 1991; 2007). The core principle in Booth's approach is the normative shift from negative to positive security, or more specifically, from the *absence of threat* to the *conditions of human flourishing*.

Anthony Burke has developed the theory of security cosmopolitanism, in which he raises the argument for states and security actors of the necessity of responsibility in a deep and enduring positive security, multigenerational security, and security actions, reflecting on the future impacts of actions in his so-called *global categorical imperative*: "act as if both the principles and consequences of your action will become global, across space and through time, and act only in ways that will bring a more secure life for all human beings closer" (Burke 2013). Burke later moved forward and formulated his appeal to the need to shift the perspective of our responsibilities toward the *planetary reality* in which humans are flourishing and co-living with the biosphere (Burke et al. 2016) to avoid anthropocentrism in cosmopolitan thinking (Burke 2022). Interestingly such sparks beyond globalism and cosmopolitanism in so-called planetarism have evolved in isolation elsewhere (Pedersen 2021), demonstrating the moving shelves in the IR theory debate.

Cosmopolitanism might have limits on two levels: in its anthropocentrism and in the statism of the cosmopolitan responsible state concept. However, if we would like to develop a space security policy of planetary defense in the current international system, these two limits have to be accepted for the purpose of its current practicality. At the same time, states have to operate in space and in the context of international space law. Maybe it was a historical coincidence, or maybe it was intentional, but international space law certainly transformed some cosmopolitan ideas into legally binding rules (Svec 2022; Švec and Schmidt 2022).

Security as Responsibility: From Securing Space to Peaceful Use of Space

We argued that planetary defense is a unique opportunity for humanity to adopt a policy uniting states around one table on an issue with possibly massive consequences (Schmidt 2019), and later we argued that adopting a cosmopolitan responsible foreign policy with like-minded states would constitute a policy with broader cosmopolitan responsibilities (Schmidt 2022a). The planetary defense scientific community will put more pressure on states due to its continuously produced scientific knowledge, which is produced through observations or conducting missions that demonstrate existing means to avert an asteroid impact. The newly produced knowledge will have to later transform into an everyday practical politics dealing with our "everyday" struggles in the pragmatic sense (James 1910), which can be part of the ethical security policy of a state (Nyman 2016) that would later transform *a traditional nation-state* into *a responsible cosmopolitan state* (Brown 2011; Beardsworth and Shapcott 2019). Forging a predictable regime materializes the cosmopolitan responsibility. Not a mere statement that planetary defense requires international cooperation but forging the ideas into a solid international regime and a treaty is what constitutes the required peaceful use of space as it secures human flourishing. We need a policy enabling an open and inclusive collaborative technology development, the operation of technologies and a decision-making system enabling humanity to predictably act, which is based on the theoretical framework sketched above.

   The call for predictable state behavior clearly shows how important it is to normatively frame planetary defense efforts into any form of ethical state policy, but particularly into a cosmopolitan responsible policy that transcends a state's borders. Moreover, the normative framing can explain more practically "why we need planetary defenses" than mere scientific objectivity, which is actually why the pragmatic approach is not merely instrumental but inherently normative.

   The asteroid threat has been here for millions of years but thanks to the scientific community we have a unique historical opportunity to forge a cosmopolitan planetary defense policy that would contribute to cosmopolitan responsibility on the international level, to the emergence of a world society, to a cosmopolitan identity, and to securing the flourishing of the biosphere.

CONCLUSION

Planetary defense has been presented here not as a mere effort of the scientific community to detect and demonstrate the deflection of an asteroid on a collision course but as a unique historical opportunity to forge cosmopolitan governance on an issue that threatens us all equally. Planetary defense is currently developing mostly within the scientific community; it is already mentioned in national space strategies but mostly as a "scientific and technological international cooperation"; it still lacks a broader global policy approach. We have argued that planetary defense will inherently become a global policy under pressure from the growing knowledge developed by scientists and from being shown how these dynamics fulfil the core principles of peaceful use of space. In order to make the argument more persuasive, we have discussed practical problems with possibly negative international security consequences (the drivers) to demonstrate the necessity of planetary defense cosmopolitan governance. Planetary defense bears a powerful momentum for a possible global political change and awaits decision makers with a sense of cosmopolitan responsibility to act.

REFERENCES

Air University. 2003. "Orbital Mechanics." In *Space Primer*, 8-1–8-24. Maxwell AFB, AL: Air University Press.

Anscombe, G. E. M. 1990. "On the Source of the Authority of the State." In *Authority*, edited by Joseph Raz, 142–73. Oxford: Basil Blackwell.

Archibugi, Daniele, and David Held. 2011. "Cosmopolitan Democracy: Paths and Agents." *Ethics & International Affairs* 25, no. 4: 433–61. https://doi.org/10.1017/S0892679411000360.

Arendt, Hannah. 1993. "What Is Authority?" In *Between Past and Future: Six Exercises in Political Thought*, 91–141. New York: Penguin.

Barbee, Brent W., Bong Wie, Mark Steiner, and Kenneth Getzandanner. 2015. "Conceptual Design of a Flight Validation Mission for a Hypervelocity Asteroid Intercept Vehicle." *Acta Astronautica* 106: 139–59. https://doi.org/10.1016/j.actaastro.2014.10.043.

Beardsworth, Richard, and Richard Shapcott. 2019. *The State and Cosmopolitan Responsibilities*. Oxford: Oxford University Press.

Beck, Ulrich. 1992. "Risk Society: Towards a New Modernity." London: SAGE.

Beck, Ulrich. 2006. *The Cosmopolitan Vision*. Cambridge: Polity.

Binzel, Richard P., Vishnu Reddy, and Tasha Dunn. 2015. "The Near-Earth Object Population: Connections to Comets, Main-Belt Asteroids, and Meteorites." In *Asteroids IV*, edited by Patrick Michel, Francesca E. DeMeo, and William F. Bottke, 243–56. Huston: University of Arizona Press. https://doi.org/10.2458/azu_uapress_9780816532131-ch013.

Booth, Ken. 1991. "Security and Emancipation." *Review of International Studies* 17, no. 4: 313–26. https://doi.org/10.1017/S0260210500112033.

Booth, Ken. 2007. *Theory of World Security*. Melbourne: Cambridge University Press.

Boslough, Mark. 2019. "Uncertainty and Risk at the Catastrophe Threshold." In *Planetary Defense*, edited by Nikola Schmidt, 205–15. Space and Society. Cham: Springer International Publishing. https://doi.org/10.1007/978-3-030-01000-3_13.

Brown, Garrett Wallace. 2011. "Bringing the State Back into Cosmopolitanism: The Idea of Responsible Cosmopolitan States." *Political Studies Review* 9, no. 1: 53–66. https://doi.org/10.1111/j.1478-9302.2010.00226.x.

Bucknam, Mark, and Robert Gold. 2008. "Asteroid Threat? The Problem of Planetary Defence." *Survival* 50, no. 5: 141–56. https://doi.org/10.1080/00396330802456502.

Bull, Hedley. 2002. *The Anarchical Society: A Study of Order in World Politics*. 3rd ed. Basingstoke, UK: Palgrave.

Burke, Anthony. 2013. "Security Cosmopolitanism." *Critical Studies on Security* 1, no. 1: 13–28. https://doi.org/10.1080/21624887.2013.790194.

Burke, Anthony. 2022. "Interspecies Cosmopolitanism: Non-Human Power and the Grounds of World Order in the Anthropocene." *Review of International Studies* April: 1–22. https://doi.org/10.1017/S0260210522000171.

Burke, Anthony, Stefanie Fishel, Audra Mitchell, Simon Dalby, and Daniel J. Levine. 2016. "Planet Politics: A Manifesto from the End of IR." *Millennium: Journal of International Studies* 44, no. 3: 499–523. https://doi.org/10.1177/0305829816636674.

Campos, Andre Santos. 2021. "Sovereignty and Legitimate Authority." In *Sovereignty as Value*, edited by Andre Santos Campos and Susana Cadilha, 73–90. Lanham, MD: Rowman & Littlefield.

Campos, Andre Santos, and Susana Cadilha, eds. 2021. *Sovereignty as Value*. Values and Identities: Crossing Philosophical Borders. Lanham, MD: Rowman & Littlefield.

Cemal, KARAKAS. 2021. "EU Space Programme." EU Legislation in Progress Briefing. https://www.europarl.europa.eu/RegData/etudes/BRIE/2018/628300/EPRS_BRI(2018)628300_EN.pdf.

Cheng, Andrew F., Andrew S. Rivkin, Patrick Michel, Justin Atchison, Olivier Barnouin, Lance Benner, Nancy L. Chabot, et al. 2018. "AIDA DART Asteroid Deflection Test: Planetary Defense and Science Objectives." *Planetary and Space Science* 157: 104–15. https://doi.org/10.1016/j.pss.2018.02.015.

Crowe, William. 2019. "What Are NEOs and the Technical Means and Constraints of Solar System Mapping?" In *Planetary Defense*, edited by Nikola Schmidt, 33–48. Space and Society. Cham: Springer International Publishing. https://doi.org/10.1007/978-3-030-01000-3_3.

Ditrych, Ondřej, and Nikola Schmidt. 2022. "International Security Regimes, Space and Responsible Cosmopolitan States." In *Governance of Emerging Space Challenges*, edited by Nikola Schmidt, 29–47. Space and Society. Cham: Springer International Publishing. https://doi.org/10.1007/978-3-030-86555-9_3.

ESA. 2021. "ESA Agenda 2025." 2021. https://esamultimedia.esa.int/docs/ESA_Agenda_2025_final.pdf.

Floyd, Rita. 2011. "Can Securitization Theory Be Used in Normative Analysis? Towards a Just Securitization Theory." *Security Dialogue* 42, nos. 4–5: 427–39. https://doi.org/10.1177/0967010611418712.

Geenens, Raf. 2017. "Sovereignty as Autonomy." *Law and Philosophy* 36, no. 5: 495–524. https://doi.org/10.1007/s10982-017-9295-3.

Goldsmith, J. L., and E. A. Posner. 2005. *The Limits of International Law*. The Georgia Journal of International and Comparative Law. New York: Oxford University Press.

Gottlieb, Joseph. 2022. "Discounting, Buck-Passing, and Existential Risk Mitigation: The Case of Space Colonization." *Space Policy* March: 101486. https://doi.org/10.1016/j.space pol.2022.101486.

Habermas, Jürgen. 2008. "The Constitutionalization of International Law and the Legitimation Problems of a Constitution for World Society." *Constellations* 15, no. 4: 444–55. https://doi. org/10.1111/j.1467-8675.2008.00510.x.

Hawthorn, G. 2003. "Running the World through Windows." In *Debating Cosmopolitics*, edited by D. Archibugi, 16–26. Collection Verso. London; New York: Verso.

Held, David. 2010. *Cosmopolitanism: Ideals and Realities.* Cambridge, UK: Polity.

Held, David. 2018. Personal Email Conversation. July 2018.

Hughes, Gary B., Philip Lubin, Johanna Bible, Jesse Bublitz, Josh Arriola, Caio Motta, Jon Suen, et al. 2013. "DE-STAR: Phased-Array Laser Technology for Planetary Defense and Other Scientific Purposes." In *SPIE Optical Engineering+ Applications*, 88760J-88760J. International Society for Optics and Photonics. https://doi.org/10.1117/12.2026401.

James, William. 1910. *Pragmatism: A New Name for Some Old Ways of Thinking.* Cambridge: Cambridge University Press.

Jones, Andrew. 2022. "China to Target Near-Earth Object 2020 PN1 for Asteroid Deflection Mission." *SpaceNews.* July 12, 2022. https://spacenews.com/china-to-target-near-earth-obj ect-2020-pn1-for-asteroid-deflection-mission/.

Krůs, Miroslav, and Nikola Schmidt. 2022. "High-Energy Systems Today and Tomorrow." In *Governance of Emerging Space Challenges*, edited by Nikola Schmidt, 233–47. Space and Society. Cham: Springer International Publishing. https://doi.org/10.1007/978-3-030-86555-9_13.

Lenkavska, Adriana, and Nikola Schmidt. 2021. "Planetary Defense in National Space Documents." Study Produced as a Part of a Research Project: A Multidisciplinary Analysis of Planetary Defense from Asteroids as the Key National Policy Ensuring Further Flourishing and Prosperity Of Humankind both on Earth and in Space. https://planetary-defense.eu/ project-results/studies_and_reports/en-planetary-defense-in-national-space-documents/.

Lu, Edward T., and Stanley G. Love. 2005. "Gravitational Tractor for Towing Asteroids." *Nature* 438, no. 7065: 177.

Marks, Joel. 2022. "The Worst Case: Planetary Defense against a Doomsday Impactor." *Space Policy* June: 101493. https://doi.org/10.1016/j.spacepol.2022.101493.

Mathias, Donovan L., Lorien F. Wheeler, and Jessie L. Dotson. 2017. "A Probabilistic Asteroid Impact Risk Model: Assessment of Sub-300 m Impacts." *Icarus* 289: 106–19. https://doi.org/ 10.1016/j.icarus.2017.02.009.

Mellor, Felicity. 2007. "Colliding Worlds: Asteroid Research and the Legitimization of War in Space." *Social Studies of Science* 37, no. 4: 499–531. https://doi.org/10.1177/0306312706075336.

Mellor, Felicity. 2010. "Negotiating Uncertainty: Asteroids, Risk and the Media." *Public Understanding of Science* 19, no. 1: 16–33.

Montuschi, Eleonora. 2017. "Using Science, Making Policy: What Should We Worry About?" *European Journal for Philosophy of Science* 7, no. 1: 57–78. https://doi.org/10.1007/s13 194-016-0143-3.

Morgenthau, Hans, and Kenneth Thompson. 1985. *Politics Among Nations*, 6th ed. New York: McGraw-Hill.

Morrison, David. 1992. *The Spaceguard Survey Report of the NASA International Near-Earth-Object Detection Workshop.* NASA.

Morrison, David. 2019a. "Overview of Active Planetary Defense Methods." In *Planetary Defense— Global Collaboration for Saving Earth from Asteroids and Comets*, edited by Nikola Schmidt, 113–21. 1st ed. Cham: Springer International Publishing. https://doi.org/10.1007/978-3-030-01000-3_7.

Morrison, David. 2019b. "The Cosmic Impact Hazard." In *Planetary Defense*, edited by Nikola Schmidt, 15–32. Space and Society. Cham: Springer International Publishing. https://doi.org/10.1007/978-3-030-01000-3_2.

Newman, Joshua. 2017. "Deconstructing the Debate over Evidence-Based Policy." *Critical Policy Studies* 11, no. 2: 211–26. https://doi.org/10.1080/19460171.2016.1224724.

Nyman, Jonna. 2016. "Pragmatism, Practice and the Value of Security." In *Ethical Security Studies: A New Research Agenda*, edited by Jonna Nyman and Anthony Burke, 200–220. London; New York: Routledge.

Owen, John M., IV. 2010. "Liberalism and Security." In *Oxford Research Encyclopedia of International Studies*, edited by John M. Owen IV. Oxford University Press. https://doi.org/10.1093/acrefore/9780190846626.013.33.

Pedersen, Stefan. 2021. "Planetarism: A Paradigmatic Alternative to Internationalism." *Globalizations* 18, no. 2: 141–54. https://doi.org/10.1080/14747731.2020.1741901.

Pogge, Thomas. 1992. "Cosmopolitanism and Sovereignty." *Ethics* 103, no. 1: 48–75. https://doi.org/10.1086/293470.

Price, Richard. 1995. "A Genealogy of the Chemical Weapons Taboo." *International Organization* 49, no. 1: 73–103.

Ravan, Shirish, Tom De Groeve, Lara Mani, Einar Bjorgo, Richard Moissl, Jose Miguel Roncero, Katherine Rowan, David Schuld, Leviticus A. Lewis, and Romana Kofler. 2022. "When It Strikes, Are We Ready? Lessons Identified at the 7th Planetary Defense Conference in Preparing for a Near-Earth Object Impact Scenario." *International Journal of Disaster Risk Science* 13, no. 1: 151–59. https://doi.org/10.1007/s13753-021-00389-9.

Reddy, Vishnu, Michael S. Kelley, Jessie Dotson, Davide Farnocchia, Nicolas Erasmus, David Polishook, Joseph Masiero, et al. 2022. "Apophis Planetary Defense Campaign." *The Planetary Science Journal* 3, no. 5: 123. https://doi.org/10.3847/PSJ/ac66eb.

Reuters. 2021. "Chinese Researchers Propose Deflecting 'Armageddon' Asteroids with Rockets." *Reuters*. July 7, 2021, sec. Science. https://www.reuters.com/lifestyle/science/chinese-researchers-propose-deflecting-armageddon-asteroids-with-rockets-2021-07-07/.

Sarli, Bruno V., Jeremy M. Knittel, Jacob A. Englander, and Brent W. Barbee. 2018. "Mission Design and Optimal Asteroid Deflection for Planetary Defense." In *68th International Astronautical Congress*. International Astronautic Federation.

Schmidt, Nikola (ed.). 2019. *Planetary Defense—Global Collaboration for Saving Earth from Asteroids and Comets*. 1st ed. Space and Society. Cham: Springer International Publishing. https://doi.org/10.1007/978-3-030-01000-3.

Schmidt, Nikola. 2021. "Building Planetary Defense Governance: A Proposal for Multigenerational, Financially Sustainable and Scientifically Beneficial Planetary Defense Governance." Policy Paper. Prague: Institute of International Relations.

Schmidt, Nikola. (ed.). 2022a. *Governance of Emerging Space Challenges: The Benefits of a Responsible Cosmopolitan State Policy*. Space and Society. Cham: Springer International Publishing. https://doi.org/10.1007/978-3-030-86555-9.

Schmidt, Nikola. 2022b. "Responsible Cosmopolitan State in Space Politics." In *Governance of Emerging Space Challenges*, edited by Nikola Schmidt, 93–113. Space and Society. Cham: Springer International Publishing. https://doi.org/10.1007/978-3-030-86555-9_6.

Schmidt, Nikola, and Ondřej Ditrych. 2022. "Space Community as an Enabler of Cosmopolitan Ideas Through Large Technical Systems." *Space Policy* 60: 101485. https://doi.org/10.1016/j.spacepol.2022.101485.

Smetana, Michal. 2019. "Weapons of Mass Protection? Rogue Asteroids, Nuclear Explosions in Space, and the Norms of Global Nuclear Order." In *Planetary Defense*, edited by Nikola Schmidt, 231–44. Space and Society. Cham: Springer International Publishing. https://doi.org/10.1007/978-3-030-01000-3_15.

SMPAG. 2020. "Planetary Defence: Legal Overview and Assessment." Report by the Space Mission Planning Advisory Group (SMPAG) Ad-Hoc Working Group on Legal Issues to SMPAG.   https://www.cosmos.esa.int/documents/336356/336472/SMPAG-RP-004_1_0_SMPAG_legal_report_2020-04-08.pdf.

Standring, Adam. 2017. "Evidence-Based Policymaking and the Politics of Neoliberal Reason: A Response to Newman." *Critical Policy Studies* 11, no. 2: 227–34. https://doi.org/10.1080/19460171.2017.1304226.

Svec, Martin. 2022. "Outer Space, an Area Recognised as Res Communis Omnium: Limits of National Space Mining Law." *Space Policy* January: 101473. https://doi.org/10.1016/j.spacepol.2021.101473.

Švec, Martin, and Nikola Schmidt. 2022. "International Space Law as the Transiting Path to Cosmopolitan Order." In *Governance of Emerging Space Challenges*, edited by Nikola Schmidt, 65–91. Space and Society. Cham: Springer International Publishing. https://doi.org/10.1007/978-3-030-86555-9_5.

The White House. 2018. "National Near-Earth Object Preparedness Strategy and Action Plan." http://www.whitehouse.gov/ostp.

Vereš, Peter, and Nikola Schmidt. 2019. "Methods, Means and Governance of NEO Observation." In *Planetary Defense*, edited by Nikola Schmidt, 49–70. Space and Society. Cham: Springer International Publishing. https://doi.org/10.1007/978-3-030-01000-3_4.

Wang, Yirui, Mingtao Li, Zizheng Gong, Jianming Wang, Chuankui Wang, and Binghong Zhou. 2021. "Assembled Kinetic Impactor for Deflecting Asteroids by Combining the Spacecraft with the Launch Vehicle Upper Stage." *Icarus* 368: 114596. https://doi.org/10.1016/j.icarus.2021.114596.

Wendt, Alexander. 2003. "Why a World State Is Inevitable." *European Journal of International Relations* 9, no. 4: 491–542. https://doi.org/10.1177/135406610394001.

Wendt, Alexander, and Raymond Duvall. 2008. "Sovereignty and the UFO." *Political Theory* 36, no. 4: 607–33. https://doi.org/10.1177/0090591708317902.

Zolo, Danilo. 2000. "The Lords of Peace: From the Holy Alliance to the New International Criminal Tribunals." In *Global Democracy, Key Debate*, edited by B. Holden, 73–86. London; New York: Routledge.

Zolo, Danilo. 2013. *Cosmopolis: Prospects for World Government*. Cambridge, UK: Polity Press.

PART V

PROSPECTS

CHAPTER 42

....

THE FUTURE OF GLOBAL
SPACE GOVERNANCE

....

NATÁLIA ARCHINARD

INTRODUCTION

....

WITH the increased reliance on space technologies for many strategic aspects of society and sustainable economy, new states actors have emerged in space, rendering the need for enhanced global governance even stronger. States not only aim at accessing satellite services, many of them are developing their space capacities at a high pace while thoroughly looking after their national interests. The emergence of private actors conducting new kind of activities in space has extended traditional military and political alliances toward communities of commercial interests. Beyond the traditional bipolar rivalry inherited from the Cold War, new space powers have emerged, taking full leadership in the global governance of space activities.

The global governance of space activities, or global space governance, is understood in this chapter as the sets of international treaties, rules, standards, and guidelines that govern states' activities in outer space. As subjects of international space law, states are responsible for the space activities of all actors under their jurisdiction, hence they are traditionally considered as the rule-makers when it comes to global space governance. However, an evolution is being observed: as the private sector is taking an increased and new role in space in many countries, they are exercising a stronger influence on global space governance either through their direct action in setting standards or because their interests become interlinked with national interests and are represented by their governments in intergovernmental discussions. New kinds of space activities conducted by the private sector, such as large constellations, active debris removal, or on-orbit servicing, also bring new types of challenges in space governance that states will need to address, in particular with respect to sustainability, safety, and security.

The different equilibriums in the respective nations between public and private interests in space also make the international situation uneven, with differentiated

interests and priorities. The level of commercial or public-private space activities (including for military purposes) influences the strategies used by states to safeguard their
interests in global governance. Besides evolving commercial and national security
interests, geopolitical rivalries also have become more accute in recent times, with the
effect of increasing tensions in multilateral forums involved in the global governance
of space activities. These increasing tensions tend to reinforce positions that were already traditionally antagonistic in the areas of space security, safety, and sustainability.
This chapter will look at different approaches to space security and review several international initiatives in the last twenty years. While observing the priorities and the
positioning of states in the respective United Nations (UN) forums dealing with space
governance, special attention will be given to the interactions and interdependency between the security side and the safety and sustainability side. It will then look at possible avenues for making progress in enhancing space security, safety, and long-term
sustainability.

DIFFERENT APPROACHES TO SPACE
SECURITY AND SUSTAINABILITY

This section gives an outline of several international initiatives, which were brought
up at intergovernmental level in the last two decades. It will showcase the different
approaches taken by different groups of states, with one group conducted by Russia and
China and supported by the non-aligned movement setting priority on a legally binding
instrument to prohibit the placement of weapons in outer space and another group,
led by the United States and its allies, favoring another approach addressing space debris risks, threats to space systems and promoting responsible behaviors through non-
legally binding instruments, like possible codes of conduct, guidelines, or political
commitments.

Prevention of an Arms Race in Outer Space

Soon after the first human activities in space, the launch of Sputnik in 1957, the General
Assembly of the United Nations decided to discuss the technical and legal questions
associated with space activities. First constituted in 1958 as an ad hoc group of eighteen
states, the UN Committee on the Peaceful Uses of Outer Space (COPUOS) was established in 1959 as a permanent subsidiary body of the UN General Assembly (UNGA)
with a membership of twenty-eight. The states members of COPUOS developed the
five UN treaties dedicated to space activities: the so-called Outer Space Treaty (OST
1967), the Rescue Agreement (1968), the Liability Convention (1972), the Registration
Convention (1976) and the Moon Agreement (1984) (ST/SPACE/61/Rev.2). These

treaties constitute the basis of international space law (see Aoki, this volume). The Charter of the United Nations also applies to space activities in general (OST, Article III). Hence, the use of force against space systems is generally prohibited. In case of a conflict, international humanitarian law must be respected, preventing in particular the use of force against civilian targets. According to OST, Article IV, the establishment of military bases, installations, and fortifications, the testing of any type of weapons, and the conduct of military maneuvers shall be forbidden on celestial bodies. However, there is no prohibition of the placement of conventional weapons in Earth orbits according to the UN space treaties.

The regular testing of anti-satellite (ASAT) weapons by several space powers, including the United States and the USSR, was common in the 1970s and 1980s. After the Reagan administration had announced the Strategic Defense Initiative (the so-called "Star Wars" program), the discussions on the topic of the prevention of an arms race in outer space, since 1982 on the agenda of the Conference on Disarmament in Geneva, were revived. In 2002, Russia and China presented a working paper to the Conference on Disarmament containing possible elements for a future international legal agreement on the prevention of the deployment of weapons in outer space (CD/1679). This was followed by the submission of a draft Treaty on the Prevention of the Placement of Weapons in Outer Space and of the Threat or Use of Force Against Space Objects (PPWT) by Russia and China in 2008 (see West, this volume). The draft was commented by several member states (see for instance CD/1847) and presented again in a revised version in 2014 (CD/1985). However, several states felt that their concerns had not been addressed and the second draft still suffered from some major gaps and shortfalls (see for instance CD/1998). In particular, comments were raised on the difficulty of defining a weapon in outer space. That the testing and use of ground-based ASAT weapons were not addressed by the draft treaty was also criticized. The lack of a verification mechanism, even though the authors left the door open for discussing this at a later stage, was considered to be a major shortfall in a legally binding instrument. Western states remained critical and the functional difficulties prevailing at the Conference on Disarmament for more than twenty years did not allow for any progress to be made on this draft proposal. The draft PPWT was regularly brought to attention by its initiators, but no serious attempt on their part was conducted to address the major concerns expressed nor to organize negotiations in a different, better functioning setting. Instead of doing so, the initiators kept finger-pointing at their adversaries for not agreeing with the proposed draft treaty.

Bypassing the difficulties faced by the draft PPWT initiative within the Conference on Disarmament, the Russian Federation submitted a draft resolution entitled No First Placement of Weapons in Outer Space to the First Committee of the UNGA in 2014 (A/RES/69/32). This resolution entails a political commitment not to be the first state to place weapons in outer space. It was adopted by a majority of 126 states, mainly from the non-aligned movement, with many Western states either opposing or abstaining because of what they found to be a misleading approach. According to their views, such a commitment could be used to give a state a justification to place weapons in outer space after alleging another had done so and would not be instrumental in preventing an arms race in outer space as the development of weapons would not be stopped.

In 2017, Russia introduced a new resolution entitled "Further Practical Measures for the Prevention of an Arms Race in Outer Space " containing a proposal for the establishment of a Group of Governmental Experts mandated to exchange views on concrete measures and develop elements of a legally binding instrument aiming at preventing an arms race in outer space (A/RES/72/250). Despite many Western countries abstaining or voting against, the resolution was adopted with a majority of 121 positive votes. The group held extensive in-depth exchanges in 2018 and 2019 on this matter and produced a substantive report under the leadership of the Brazilian chair. However, the report could not be agreed upon by all members of the group, in particularly the United States, because of threat-like language they could not accept.

Transparency and Confidence-Building Measures

In its Resolutions A/RES/61/75 (2006) and A/RES/62/43 (2007), the UNGA invited Member States to submit proposals for international transparency and confidence-building measures for outer space. Two major initiatives of the 2010s were derived from this call. One did not conclude, while the other one set a reference, but both contributed to a more holistic approach to space security, safety, and sustainability by bringing space and disarmament experts to the same table, both at international and at national levels. This was progress.

The first initiative was led by the European Union (EU) in an ad hoc process outside of the UN. In response to the call by the UNGA, the EU started to work on a proposal for an International Code of Conduct for outer space activities, a voluntary instrument which would reflect a political commitment of the signatory states. It addressed all kinds of space activities, not distinguishing between their declared purposes, be they military or civilian. After presenting a contribution to the Report of the Secretary General on Transparency and Confidence-Building Measures in 2007 (A/62/114/Add.1), the EU Council adopted conclusions on a Draft Code of Conduct (ICOC) for Outer Space Activities (Council of the European Union, 2008), which served as a basis for consultations with third countries. In June 2012, the first official draft was presented to the Member States of the UN on the eve of COPUOS's 55th session in Vienna (European Union, 2012). At this stage already, many states criticized the process for not being transparent and inclusive, as they felt they had been left aside.

The EU then held multilateral consultations organized by the European External Action Service in different countries: in May 2013 in Kiev, Ukraine; in November 2013 in Bangkok, Thailand; and in May 2014 in Luxembourg, Luxembourg. The EU also funded the UN Institute for Disarmament Research (UNIDIR) to organize interactive workshops in different regions of the world to raise awareness and understanding of the project. Participating states were invited to provide written comments. While some of them were taken into account, many fundamental criticisms were not addressed, for instance, the explicit mention of Article 51 of the UN Charter, highlighting the right of self-defense, as a valuable exception to the application of the instrument. Some participating states felt that highlighting Article 51 was contrary to the spirit of the instrument and that recalling the applicability of the UN Charter as a whole was sufficient. The commitment not to create space debris unless it was deemed necessary was considered by these states an insufficient if not contradictory measure. In the end, many participating states did not feel ownership of the draft document and criticized the process for not being conducted under the UN umbrella. A final negotiation was organized by the EU in July 2015 at UN Headquarters in New York. However, this meeting was not able to gain enough support for the draft and the project somehow vanished. The EU had chosen the same approach as for the Den Haag Code of Conduct (HCOC) on ballistic missiles, which had been successful at the time, but reactions by many states around the world on the draft ICOC showed that inclusiveness in the development of the instrument had become essential for its success and that conducting such a process within the UN was necessary for its legitimacy and to ensure universal adhesion to the instrument. After some time for reflection, the EU resumed their efforts in 2019 by broadly advocating for the security, safety, and sustainability of outer space in multilateral forums, but no new process was launched.

The second initiative started in 2011 at the UNGA with the establishment of a Group of Governmental Experts to work on transparency and confidence-building measures for outer space. This group was able to develop a consensual report which was presented to, and welcomed by, the UNGA in 2013 (A/68/189). The report contains a set of criteria that any transparency and confidence-building measures should meet. These criteria are still considered as reference points when determining whether proposed measures could be considered as efficient for building confidence and transparency among states. The report also contains recommendations to states, international organizations, and UN entities, which address the peaceful and military uses of outer space alike. For instance, states are invited to make publicly available their space policy and their military space strategy. They are encouraged to exchange orbital information on their space objects and to pre-notify space launches, maneuvers, and break-ups. While recommendations related to the peaceful uses of outer space were implemented by COPUOS in the guidelines on the long-term sustainability of space activities, the recommendations addressing military activities were not concretely implemented by any intergovernmental body. In 2019 and 2022, the UN Disarmament Commission exchanged views on the implementation of the recommendations proposed by the group in relation with military uses of outer space.

These two initiatives, the draft International Code of Conduct and the Group of Governmental Experts on transparency and confidence-building measures, contributed in a significant manner to building bridges between the disarmament community (meeting in Geneva and New York) and the space community (meeting in Vienna). The Group of Governmental Experts in its composition itself gathered experts from the two communities and formulated overarching recommendations, while the International Code of Conduct project brought the two communities to the same table during multilateral consultations and at national level in the individual countries. This was a significant step forward toward enhanced coordination in global space governance.

Notably, the Group of Governmental Experts recommended that the First and Fourth Committees of the UNGA, dealing respectively with disarmament and international security and with international cooperation in the peaceful uses of outer space, hold joint meetings in order to address issues of common interest in space security and sustainability (A/68/189, para. 72). Such joint meetings were organized in 2015, 2017, 2019, and 2022. They were supported by the UN Office for Disarmament Affairs (ODA) and the UN Office for Outer Space Affairs (OOSA) in a collaboration that had also been encouraged by the Group of Governmental Experts.

Long-Term Sustainability of Outer Space Activities

The topic of the long-term sustainability of outer space activities was first promoted by Canada in 2004–2005 and by France under the French Chairmanship of COPUOS in 2006–2007. In 2008–2009, France proposed the establishment of a new agenda item on the long-term sustainability of outer space activities. After intensive discussions, COPUOS decided in 2010 to establish a working group under a new agenda item on the long-term sustainability of outer space activities. The first four-year workplan (2011–2014) had to be extended by two years, twice. After a total of eight years, the working group was able to achieve consensus on a preamble and twenty-one guidelines (see A/74/20, Annex II). The preamble establishes the voluntary and non-legally binding character of the guidelines as well as their objectives. It also provides a definition of the long-term sustainability of outer space activities, as the ability to conduct outer space activities indefinitely in the future and meeting the needs of currents generations in using outer space for peaceful purposes while preserving the ability to do so for future generations. The guidelines themselves are divided into four groups: (1) policy and regulatory frameworks for space activities; (2) safety of space operations; (3) international cooperation, capacity-building, and awareness; and (4) scientific and technical research development. They are directed at states, international organizations, and UN entities, but they contain recommendations that can be implemented by any space actors. Certain recommendations are meant to be implemented by states into legally binding requirements at national level. Others may be implemented without necessarily being integrated into national legal frameworks, as they may be part of space, research, education, or international cooperation policies or strategies.

While twenty-one guidelines were finalized and adopted consensually, seven projects of draft guidelines could not be agreed despite many rounds of negotiations between interested states (A/AC.105/C.1/L.367). Of these seven draft guidelines, one had been proposed by Brazil and six by Russia. The Brazilian proposal, which was supported by the Group of Latin America and Caribbean States (GRULAC), aimed at affirming the peaceful purpose of all space activities in a wording that was not considered customary by the United States and their closest allies. The draft guidelines proposed by Russia

contained elements that were deemed by other states as pertaining to international security and disarmament forums.

At the end of the extended mandate in June 2018, while COPUOS was celebrating the
fiftieth anniversary of the first UN Conference on the Peaceful Uses and Exploration
of Outer Space (UNISPACE), there was no consensus to adopt the guidelines, because
Russia wanted a guarantee that negotiations would continue on their draft proposals.
This position was shared by Brazil but opposed by Western states. That year, no consensus was reached but pressure remained, because results had long been expected
by the international community. Finally, an agreement was found in June 2019: while
adopting the twenty-one guidelines, COPUOS would establish a new working group
which would be guided by the following framework: identifying and studying new
challenges, sharing information on the implementation of the twenty-one guidelines,
and raising awareness and building capacities (A/74/20, para 165-167). This package decision was endorsed by the UNGA in the same year.

On the sensitive topic of long-term sustainability, consensus had never been—and
probably never would be—easy to reach. The election of the chair of a working group
was never so difficult at COPUOS. Four candidates were nominated (by India, Japan,
Switzerland, and the United Arab Emirates), but the membership of COPUOS could
not agree on a single composition, even envisaging a multiple chairpersonship. As chair
of the previous working group on this topic, South Africa facilitated the election process
during the fifty-seventh session of the Scientific and Technical Subcommittee and the
following intersessional period dominated by the Covid-19 pandemic. In the weeks before the fifty-eighth session of subcommittee, the candidates of Japan, Switzerland, and
the United Arab Emirates withdrew one after the other, leaving the subcommittee in a
position to elect the candidate of India during its fifty-eighth session.

In the course of these negotiations, one could see two different groups of states
holding together, with some nuanced positions however, and some states staying in between the two groups. On the one side, the group of so-called "like-minded" states (the
United States and its closest allies) were prioritizing the implementation of the twenty-
one adopted guidelines and did not want to see the draft guidelines proposed by Russia
come back in this new phase of work. Russia was supported by China and Iran. Some
in-between countries were favoring an equal treatment of the three pillars of the mandate given by COPUOS in June 2018. While the working group could adopt its terms of
reference, methods of work, and work-plan during the fifty-ninth session of the subcommittee in 2022, it became clear that these two groups (the like-minded states and
Russia and China with their allies) would continue to polarize antagonistic positions on
this, and other, topics within COPUOS.

The twenty-one COPUOS guidelines on the long-term sustainability of outer space
activities constitute a reference to guide legislators and space operators around the
world. They also encourage capacity-building and awareness-raising activities, which
are essential to enhance the implementation of the instrument. In this respect, initiatives
such as the Promoting Space Sustainability Project launched in 2021 by the UN Office
for Outer Space Affairs (OOSA) with the support of the United Kingdom (UK) are very

helpful (OOSA n.d). Another example are the workshops organized at European level by Finland and Switzerland in 2019 and 2022 to enhance the sharing of experience in the implementation of the twenty-one guidelines. Other such initiatives are popping up around the world.

Responsible Behavior in Outer Space

As a member of the EU until early 2020, the UK was a fervent advocate of the International Code of Conduct project. It also took part actively in the reflection process following the negotiation conference of July 2015 which marked the vanishing of the project. The UK started developing a behavioral approach toward ensuring security and stability in outer space. To explore further this approach with international partners, the UK government convened two conferences at Wilton Park in 2018 and 2019. They also organized regional conferences to create awareness around the world on this new approach to advance space security and stability while circumventing the difficulties met in disarmament forums. The report of the second Wilton Park conference on the topic "Operating in Space: Towards Developing Protocols on the Norms of Behaviour" was presented to COPUOS in June 2019 with the aim of informing discussions on the long-term sustainability of outer space activities (A/AC.105/2019/CRP.12).

In advance of the UNGA meetings in 2020, the UK circulated a draft resolution entitled "Reducing Threats through Norms, Rules and Principles of Responsible Behaviors" in outer space. By consulting largely and promoting an innovative, collaborative, and inclusive approach, the UK initiative succeeded in steering a large majority of states to adopt General Assembly Resolution A/RES/75/36. The success of the initiative is to be measured by the number of states as well as intergovernmental and non-governmental organizations who replied to the invitation of the secretary general (A/RES75/36, para. 6) and provided substantive views on threats to space systems and possible responsible behaviors in outer space (A/76/77). In the following year, the UK proposed the establishment of an open-ended working group with the mandate to (1) consider current and future threats by states to space systems and (2) make recommendations on possible norms, rules, and principles of responsible behaviors relating to threats by states to space systems. The corresponding resolution (A/RES/76/231) was adopted at the seventy-sixth session by a majority of 163 states despite of the opposition of Russia, China, Iran, and five other states. Russia, in particular, contested the legitimacy of the First Committee to deal with matters like the creation of space debris, which they felt lied in the mandate of COPUOS.

The open-ended working group was requested to meet twice in 2022 and twice in 2023 in Geneva, Switzerland and to present a consensual report to the UNGA in 2023. It held its first one-week meeting early May 2020 in Geneva under the chairpersonship of Chile after the first proposed dates had been postponed upon the request of Russia. It is difficult to predict how successful this initiative will eventually be, given the criticism by Russia and their allies. In particular, Russia may propose a follow-up to the Group of

Governmental Experts on the Prevention of an Arms Race in Outer Space that was not able to adopt its final report by consensus (see West, this volume). It seems that Russia does not go easily along with initiatives which may enter in concurrence with their own initiatives in the disarmament forums, such as the PPWT.

Through their numerous initiatives in recent years, the UK was able to endorse a leadership role in the global governance of outer space activities and to steer the agenda to create a new dynamic at the First Committee alongside the traditional PAROS approach. Together with their allies they aim to conceptualize a well-defined division of tasks between COPUOS and disarmament forums, making sure that the former would not address topics in the realm of the latter. It is to be noted that Russia has a reciprocal position, not agreeing on addressing outside of COPUOS topics they believe pertain to COPUOS. This ping-pong argument shows how difficult it is to reach common understanding and make progress in the global governance of space activities.

RECENT DEVELOPMENTS INFLUENCING MULTILATERAL PROCESSES IN SPACE GOVERNANCE

As outlined in the previous sections, states have different priorities as to how to enhance space security and sustainability. Correspondingly, they adopt different strategies for promoting and preserving their national interests in relation with outer space. These differences are grounded in history, reinforced by recent developments, and influenced by non-space sectors. This section goes through some of these developments.

The influence of global politics and strategic geopolitical interests on the governance of outer space activities is not to be underestimated. Outer space has long been the ultimate frontier for strategic and technological dominance. During the Cold War, the two major powers competed in a race to space, the USSR being the first to send an object, then a man, and finally a woman into Earth orbit, while the United States was the first to send men to the moon. This bi-power world has evolved toward a bipolar constellation in which international competition extends toward dominance in outer space. Space has become a central domain in which enhanced capacities allow for enhanced competitiveness in other domains such as the military, the economy, and technology. It has also become a domain of activities where commercial interests are growing strongly and being safeguarded by the corresponding states in space governance processes.

Space technologies have always supported military capacities. As satellites provide essential technologies in the areas of communication, positioning, navigation, and timing, space systems are at the core of military power. In certain countries, they contribute to national security and missile defense in essential ways. Hence, limiting the space capabilities of adversaries can be a determinant in the case of an armed conflict. This increased reliability on space systems is also a vulnerability, for some countries maybe more than for others. The United States for instance has long been working on the resilience of its space assets and the redundancy of its military systems to make them less vulnerable to targeted attacks. While developing their own (military) capacities, states may be looking at means to limit the development of their adversaries' capacities. The development of counter-space capacities is an established trend (see for instance UNIDIR 2020; or Secure World Foundation, 2022). The diplomatic positioning in multilateral forums is obviously influenced by such strategic military considerations. It is also guided by the objective of ensuring commercial dominance and strategic supremacy in outer space.

For instance, in their proposal for a draft treaty on the prevention of the placement of weapons in outer space and the use of force against space objects, Russia and China were not open to introducing a ban on the development and use of ground-based direct ascent ASAT weapons. Both countries developed and tested such kind of weapons against their own satellites. In January 2007, China destroyed Fengyun-1C leaving more than 2,000 trackable debris in a range of orbits at altitudes between 750 and 850 kilometers, a very busy orbital region. More recently, in November 2021, Russia destroyed Cosmos 1408 creating about 1,500 trackable debris in orbits at about 430 kilometers. Russia was the fourth country to demonstrate this capacity after the United States and India had done so in 2008 and 2019 respectively. But as the chosen targets were in much lower altitudes, the debris clouds generated have decayed rapidly in the latter two cases. The orbital area chosen by Russia for their recent ASAT test was heavily criticized, as the debris could have endangered the International Space Station whose crew was actually instructed to enter the emergency module. It also corresponded to the area of deployment of the Starlink constellation of the commercial company SpaceX (United States), while Russia itself had only a few satellites in this orbital area. With this test, Russia not only demonstrated military capacity, it also placed a hurdle in front of the commercial development of their competitors.

An important trend in recent years is the development of the so-called new space economy with lower costs both for satellites and launches, making orbital missions more affordable. Also supported by innovations in the downstream and uptake sectors, the space market was estimated at USD 371 billions in 2020 (PwC 2020). It is predicted to grow fast, carrying along a large span of investors and actors. A related trend is going to be a game changer in Earth orbit. Single commercial operators are deploying up to thousands of satellites many more than the numbers of objects placed in orbit in the previous era. Between 2016 and 2021, the number of operational satellites has doubled (ESA, 2022). This is due not only to the increased number of institutional operators, but to a few single commercial companies. A notable example is the Starlink constellation operated by the private actor SpaceX (United States) whose number of satellites has reached more than 2,000 in a few years from a total of about 8,000 satellites in orbit. For comparison, there were 5,000 satellites launched until 2010 from the beginning of the space era. Other companies such as Oneweb (UK) and Amazon Kuiper (United States) are operating or planning large constellations, with some countries presenting filing requests to the International Telecommunication Union in numbers never seen before (e.g., Rwanda submitted a request for 40,000 satellites).

While such projects may contribute to expanding access to digital technologies such as the internet, they raise several concerns with respect to the sustainable and equitable use of Earth orbits. In particular, concerns have been expressed about the potential saturation of specific orbital regions, which may limit the capacity of other actors to use the same regions, hence contradicting the principle of freedom of access enshrined in international space law. Furthermore, some level of international coordination seems to be required in order to prevent accidents and ensure safe mission disposal after orbital life. According to projections by ESA, the number of space objects is going to grow exponentially if no measures are taken. Another concern which was recently brought to light by the International Astronomical Union (IAU) is the impact of large constellation projects on the quality of ground-based astronomical (both optical and radio) observations (IAU, 2020). It is a concern not only for scientists and astronomical research infrastructures supported by governments but also for citizens, since the quality of dark skies is also impacted for the naked eye. After bringing this concern to the attention of COPUOS (A/AC.105/C.1/2021/CRP.17), the IAU recently established a new Centre for the Protection of the Dark and Quiet Sky from Satellite Constellation Interference in 2022 (CPS n.d.) with some partners like the Square Array Kilometer Organisation (SKAO). While states broadly share this concern, they aim at finding a balance between the interests of their private sector and that of their scientific communities.

Another trend is the development of new kind of activities in Earth orbit such as on-orbit servicing and active debris removal, by institutional and private actors alike, including through new types of partnerships between them. By extending operational life in orbit and removing pieces of debris that could break-up or create collisions with other space objects, such activities have the potential to contribute to the long-term sustainability of outer space activities and to preserve the orbital environment for future uses. However, they also raise questions of a legal and political nature. For instance, from the legal point of view, it is not clearly established who will be entitled to remove non-registered space objects once such technologies become largely available and less expensive. Such activities may also raise political conflicts since some states, like Russia, have warned that all their space objects and the pieces originating from fragmentation thereof must not be touched by other states. From the security point of view, on-orbit servicing, active debris removal, and any kind of rendezvous and proximity operations will need to be conducted with all safety precautions and in the most transparent way possible in order to avoid misunderstandings, misinterpretations, and possible counter-reactions. Under the Consortium Fostering the Satellite Servicing Industry (CONFERS) coalition, some private actors have established safety standards for such kinds of activities. At intergovernmental level too, coordination and possibly new norms, measures, or standards will be needed both from the security side and from the safety and sustainability side, meaning both in the disarmament forums and at COPUOS.

Another area in which states have demonstrated renewed ambitions is that of space exploration by human. In 2021, China and Russia announced their plan to establish an international research station on the moon's surface and called for international partnerships. The United States and their partners have negotiated an agreement for the establishment of the so-called Lunar Gateway, a space station orbiting the moon. Through the Artemis Accords, which have been signed to date by twenty states (as of June 2022), the United States and their partners are defining the basic principles of co-operation for states wishing to collaborate with them on the civil exploration and use of the moon, mars, comets, and asteroids and the exploitation of their resources. The utilization of space resources is deemed essential to sustain exploration missions on the moon's surface or further into the solar system (e.g., toward Mars). The United States was the first country to enact, in 2015, a national law allowing commercial entities to exploit, utilize, and sell mineral resources from celestial bodies including asteroids. Other countries have followed since then, e.g., Luxembourg in 2018 and the United Arab Emirates in 2020. These steps taken at national level and providing for unilateral interpretation of international law were put into question by other states from all around the world. Indeed, it is not universally agreed that the exploitation of space resources for commercial objectives is compatible with the "non-appropriation" principle enshrined in international space law (OST, Article II). In reaction, the legal subcommittee of COPUOS started discussing this topic as early as 2016 and unanimously decided in 2021 to establish a new working group on the utilization, exploration, and exploitation of space resources, to study elements of a corresponding international legal regime.

In recent years, outer space has been declared a domain of military operations by nations like the United States and France, and by the North Atlantic Treaty Organization (NATO). The establishment of military branches dedicated to space, so-called space forces, for instance by the United States (SPD-4, 2019) or France (ARMD1925270A, 2019) followed by the United States declaring not viewing outer space as a global commons (E.O. 13914, 2020), caused some criticism on the diplomatic level.

Commercial alliances, together with security and strategic stability coalitions, have had a tendency to reinforce the partisan positioning on space governance within the UN, especially within COPUOS and the UNGA. More often than not, observers can see Member States of NATO, the Five Eyes, or the Artemis Accords grouping, supporting each other and holding the same positions, with little national nuances. On the other side, one would witness Russia, China and other states such as Iran, Venezuela and Cuba supporting each other as a matter of principle against Western positions. This renewed kind of "group polarization" has been reinforced in the last few years at COPUOS, hence making any progress toward consensus very difficult.

In this context however, some states distinguish themselves by not supporting, per principle, the one or the other group. Their positions are usually more balanced and nuanced and seemingly more closely related to scientific findings. These states may have realized that their genuine interest lies in helping the major space powers—and their respective allies—find agreement toward making the use of space more equitable, more sustainable and safer, for all actors. Such states take an active role in multilateral space diplomacy and often remain the last guardians of common good and common interest in space. Benefiting from a well-established and influential diplomacy, they have been studied and characterized as Space Middle Powers by UNIDIR (UNIDIR 2015). According to this study, such states would include, for instance, Brazil, Mexico, South Africa, Switzerland, and Singapore.

Overall, the space sector has been evolving at a fast pace in the last years, bringing many recent developments to impact diplomatic efforts and multilateral initiatives in the global governance of outer space activities. With the increased strategic interest for outer space, both for military and commercial reasons, it is becoming ever more difficult to build consensus among an increasing number of states having space assets or a stake in space governance.

POSSIBLE WAYS FORWARD FOR THE GLOBAL GOVERNANCE OF OUTER SPACE ACTIVITIES

Given the strategic interests lying behind the increased use of outer space and the extreme geopolitical tensions, it seems that any progress will be hard to achieve in the coming years, as there is little readiness to compromise. Maintaining outer space as a global commons accessible and usable for the benefit of all humankind seems to be a utopia from the past. Even such a success as the adoption of the twenty-one guidelines on long-term sustainability of outer space activities seems to pertain to an era when international consensus in space governance was much easier to achieve. This is because geopolitical tensions have reached a peak not seen since the Cold War, especially with the attack on Ukraine by Russia in February 2022 (this chapter was written just before the start of the aggression). Confidence between the West and the East is the weakest it has been for a long time. The different priorities of states, as outlined earlier, are moving away from each other more acutely, making global consensus-building more difficult.

In this context, a "small step" approach seems the only way to make progress in global space governance. Inclusiveness throughout all processes appears to be essential in order to reach universal implementation of any new instrument or mechanism. Efforts should be pursued along different avenues of work, in a non-exclusive and simultaneous manner. For instance, preventing the placement of weapons in outer space need not be a prerequisite to developing a common understanding on which kinds of behavior should be declared irresponsible and should be avoided: both efforts are essential and can be conducted in parallel. Some proposed avenues and concrete steps are described below.

(1) *Improve the effective and systematic implementation of existing international instruments*: With a stronger adherence to the UN long-term sustainability guidelines and the space debris mitigation guidelines as recently updated by the Inter-Agency Space Debris Coordination Committee (IADC), increase in the space debris population could be controlled. Systematic notification prior to space launches (e.g., in accordance with the Den Haag Code of Conduct

for Ballistic Missiles) or prior to maneuvers in space would be an essential confidence-building measure, while the publication of military space strategies and expenditures would constitute a positive step toward more transparency (as for instance recommended in A/68/189, §§37–38).

(2) *Develop further common interpretation of international space law*: Unilateral interpretation of international space law should in principle be avoided. The legal subcommittee of the UN Committee on the Peaceful Uses of Outer Space is the global multilateral body mandated with the task of developing and interpreting international space law. Dedicated works could be conducted at the legal subcommittee to agree on common interpretation and develop further protocols based on the provisions of existing instruments (for instance, based on OST, Article IX, states could work toward establishing mechanisms for international consultations).

(3) *Involve all space actors, including the private sector and emerging space nations*: Standardization and rule-making need to be participative and inclusive. Commonly agreed rules, guidelines, and standards are the basis for equitable rules in outer space. Through uniformity, coherence, and efficiency, they should create the necessary incentive while limiting disadvantages for those being compliant. They should incentivize sustainable behaviors. Uniform and compatible standards could provide more accurate and transparent space situational awareness. Being an ever-growing actor in space, the private sector needs to be involved in providing inputs into multilateral processes, either directly or through the government of their jurisdiction. Mechanisms, such as those prevailing under the ITU in preparation of the World Radio Conferences, could be taken as models for setting up new rule-making processes including in the COPUOS framework. A mechanism for frequency and slot allocation in low Earth orbits (LEO) could be set up along the model of what is done at ITU for geostationary orbit. Instruments and mechanisms developed by consortia of private operators, such as the Space Data Association, the Global Satellite Operator Association (GSOA) and CONFERS could contribute to intergovernmental dialogue. Tools, such as the Space Sustainability Rating developed under the leadership of the World Economic Forum or the Orbital Capacity Index developed by ESA, should be used to set benchmarks and create incentives for all space actors.

(4) *Address urgent issues and emerging challenges by setting realistic common objectives*: The guidelines on the long-term sustainability of outer space activities call for further international collaboration in developing common standards and information exchange, for instance in the area of orbital data and contact information of operators—an area to start with. Further work also needs to be conducted in order to address risks such as the saturation of orbital regions and to coordinate safety aspects of rendezvous and proximity operations, including for purposes such as active debris removal and on-orbit servicing. Agreement should be reached urgently on banning intentional debris-creating actions, such as the test of direct-ascent ASAT weapons directed at space objects. Spontaneous unilateral

declarations in this area, as initiated in the spring 2022 by the United States and rapidly followed by other states, are constructive first steps.

(5) *Make efficient use of established avenues of work in multilateral settings*: Different processes have been established recently, such as the second working group on the long-term sustainability of outer space activities at COPUOS and the open-ended working group on reducing space threats through norms, rules, and principles of responsible behaviors under the First Committee of the UNGA. The joint meetings of the First and Fourth Committees on space security and sustainability also offer a setting whose potential could be used to achieve more concrete outcomes. By engaging genuinely in a constructive manner, states have a unique opportunity to make progress toward more security, safety, and sustainability in outer space. Failures, including because of procedural aspects, may suggest serious doubt on the real political will for finding tangible multilateral solutions. Civil society and private sectors are watching states' actions. It is states' responsibility to maintain space as a secure and sustainable environment where space activities can be conducted in a safe and affordable manner for the benefit of all nations.

Outer space is a highly attractive environment which brings unique opportunities for states in their quest for supremacy, military power, prosperity, and socio-economic development. Satellite systems and space technologies bring technological advancement to new frontiers, enabling many applications for society and economy. Therefore, competition is fierce, both between states and between private actors. Dominating outer space is the ultimate goal of the superpowers of this world, and they are competing for this. In this context, developing common understanding and agreements on traffic rules, or sustainable and responsible behaviors in space, is a very challenging task. States protect their immediate and future interests to the greatest extent possible, and their interests include the interests of the private sector under their jurisdiction. This is not only to promote prosperity and a stable economy, it is also because the private sector has become a major partner helping states to reach their goals in using and exploring outer space. And not the least, because the private sector is involved in the development of space missions to support military objectives and defense capabilities.

As space activities are flourishing and Earth orbits becoming congested, space actors may realize that their common as well as individual interest is to preserve the sustainability of the orbital environment and beyond. Common safety rules and international coordination of space traffic seem to be two prerequisites for ensuring the long-term use of outer space. The capacity to use outer space for peaceful purposes may suffer either from a lack of governance and proper measures or from the consequences of any conflict that would extend to outer space. As states remain very close to their national interests, civil society and end users could play a role in exercising pressure on governments and the diplomatic community, as is the case in the context of the climate crisis. Humanity should not replicate in the orbital environment, or beyond, what has been done to the environment on Earth, especially as there is no way to revert from orbital pollution. The clock is ticking; it is time for effective action, in the interest of all and everyone.

DISCLAIMER

The views and opinions expressed in this chapter are the author's own and do not necessarily reflect those of her employer or government.

REFERENCES

A/62/114/Add.1. 2007. "Transparency and Confidence-Building Measures in Outer Space Activities." Report of the Secretary General.

A/68/189. 2013. "Group of Governmental Experts on Transparency and Confidence-Building Measures in Outer Space Activities." Note by the Secretary General.

A/74/20. 2019. "Report of the Committee on the Peaceful Uses of Outer Space, 62nd Session."

A/76/77. 2021. "Reducing Space Threats through Norms, Rules and Principles of Responsible Behaviours." Report of the Secretary-General.

A/AC.105/2019/CRP.12. 2019. "Operating in Space: Towards Developing Protocols on the Norms of Behaviour." Conference Room Paper presented by the United Kingdom to COPUOS on its 62nd session.

A/AC.105/C.1/2021/CRP.17. 2021. "Recommendations to Keep Dark and Quiet Skies for Science and Society." Conference Room Paper submitted by Chile, Ethiopia, Jordan, Slovakia, Spain and the International Astronomical Union to COPUOS Scientific and Technical Subcommittee on its 58th Session.

A/AC.105/C.1/L.367. 2019. "Draft Guidelines for the Long-term Sustainability of Outer Space Activities." Working Paper by the Chair of the Working Group on the Long-Term Sustainability of Outer Space Activities.

A/RES/61/75. 2006. "Transparency and Confidence-Building Measures in Outer Space Activities." Resolution Adopted by the United Nations General Assembly.

A/RES/62/43. 2007. "Transparency and Confidence-Building Measures in Outer Space Activities." Resolution Adopted by the United Nations General Assembly.

A/RES/69/32. 2014. "No First Placement of Weapons in Outer Space." Resolution Adopted by the United Nations General Assembly.

A/RES/72/250. 2017. "Further Practical Measures for the Prevention of an Arms Race in Outer Space." Resolution Adopted by the United Nations General Assembly.

A/RES/75/36. 2020. "Reducing Space Threats through Norms, Rules and Principles of Responsible Behaviours." Resolution Adopted by the United Nations General Assembly.

A/RES/76/231. 2021. "Reducing Space Threats through Norms, Rules and Principles of Responsible Behaviours." Resolution Adopted by the United Nations General Assembly.

ARMD1925270A. 2019. Arrêté du 3 septembre 2019 portant création et organisation du commandement de l'espace (establishment of the French Space Command).

CD/1679. 2002. "Letter Dated 27 June 2002 from the Permanent Representative of the People's Republic of China and the Permanent Representative of the Russian Federation to the Conference on Disarmament Addressed to the Secretary-General of the Conference Transmitting the Chinese, English and Russian Texts of a Working Paper Entitled 'Possible Elements for a Future International Legal Agreement on the Prevention of the Deployment of Weapons in Outer Space, the Threat or Use of Force against Outer Space Objects.'"

CD/1847. 2008. "Letter Dated 19 August 2008 from the Permanent Representative of the United States of America Addressed to the Secretary-General of the Conference Transmitting

Comments on the Draft 'Treaty on Prevention of the Placement of Weapons in Outer Space and of the Threat or Use of Force against Outer Space Objects (PPWT)' as Contained in Document CD/1839 of 29 February 2008."

CD/1985. 2014. "Letter Dated 10 June 2014 from the Permanent Representative of the Russian Federation and the Permanent Representative of China to the Conference on Disarmament addressed to the Acting Secretary-General of the Conference Transmitting the Updated Russian and Chinese Texts of the Draft Treaty on Prevention of the Placement of Weapons in Outer Space and of the Threat or Use of Force against Outer Space Objects (PPWT) Introduced by the Russian Federation and China." Presented at the 1319th Plenary Meeting on June 10, 2014.

CD/1998. 2014. "Note verbale Dated 2 September 2014 from the Delegation of the United States of America to the Conference on Disarmament Addressed to the Acting Secretary-General of the Conference Transmitting the United States of America's Analysis of the 2014 Russian-Chinese Prevention of the Placement of Weapons in Outer Space and of the Threat or Use of Force against Outer Space Objects (PPWT) Introduced by the Russian Federation and China."

Council of the European Union. 2008. "Council Conclusions and Draft Code of Conduct for Outer Space Activities." 17175/08.

CPS. n.d. "IAU Center for the Protection of the Dark and Quiet Sky from Satellite Constellation Interferences." https://cps.iau.org/.

E.O. 13914. 2020. "Encouraging International Support for the Recovery and Use of Space Resources." Executive Order Signed by the President of the United States on April 6, 2020.

ESA. 2022. "ESA's Annual Space Environment Report 2022." Report by the European Space Agency.

European Union. 2012. "Revised Draft International Code of Conduct for Outer Space Activities." Working Document.

IAU. 2020. "Dark and Quiet Skies for Science and Society." Online Workshop, Report and Recommendations.

OOSA. n.d. "The Promoting Space Sustainability Project." https://www.unoosa.org/oosa/en/ourwork/topics/promoting-space-sustainability.html.

OST. 1967. "Treaty on Principles Governing the Activities of States in the Exploration and Use of Outer Space, Including the Moon and Other Celestial Bodies."

PwC. 2020. "Main Trends & Challenges in the Space Sector." 2nd ed. PricewaterhouseCoopers.

Secure World Foundation. 2022. "Global Counterspace Capabilities, an Open Source Assessment."

SPD-4. 2019. "Establishment of the United States Space Force." Space Policy Directive-4 of February 19, 2019, 84 FR 6049.

ST/SPACE/61/Rev.2. 2017. International Space Law: United Nations Instruments.

UNIDIR. 2015. "The Realities of Middle Power Space Reliance." 6/2015.

UNIDIR. 2020. "Alternative Approaches and Indicators for the Prevention of an Arms Race in Outer Space." 5/2020.

CHAPTER 43

....

THE FUTURE OF SPACE SECURITY

Assessing the Prospects for Peaceful Outcomes

....

JAMES CLAY MOLTZ

THE future of peaceful prospects in the space domain remains an open question more than sixty-five years since Sputnik's launch. While this decades-long initial period of space exploration and development passed without direct conflict between states, future trends are, arguably, more worrisome. The expansion of space actors, the rapid pace of technological developments, and the vast global increase in spending on military space activities are putting pressure on an international legal regime in space that dates largely to the Cold War.

This chapter seeks to understand—from the context of international relations theory—the set of factors that created Cold War space stability and the new dynamics that are fomenting concerns about emerging *in*stability. It begins by examining the international relations literature, identifying five main schools of thought and outlining their associated predictions regarding conflict in space. Then, it turns to the experience of space security to date, starting with a brief survey of the conditions that led to superpower space restraint during the Cold War, which was a highly unexpected outcome from the perspective of the late 1950s and early 1960s. The next section analyzes the set of political, technical, and geostrategic factors that are at the root of emerging current international concerns about twenty-first-century space insecurity. Finally, the chapter's conclusion considers possible indicators to watch over the next decade to assess whether space security is moving in the direction of more conflictual or cooperative outcomes. In terms of policy recommendation, the chapter suggests that a stepwise process of working from new norms to additional treaties—drawing on the peaceful interests of new space actors, especially in the commercial sector—may be a means of overcoming the existing stalemate at the international level.

International Relations: Recent Thinking about Space Security

As we seek to understand the sources of future space stability, it is instructive to review the main directions of recent scholarly thinking about space security. Five main schools of thought have emerged in the contemporary international relations literature about space over the past two decades or so. In general, the nature of the predictions has varied according to the author's assumptions about the broader causes of international conflict and the prospects for prevention. A brief survey of some of the leading perspectives helps clarify the range of ideas that have been offered on space security.

The first school of thought might be called "geopolitical pessimism." Rooted in classical theories of geopolitics, these theorists—represented by such authors as Everett Dolman and Daniel Deudney—see space as strategically favored over other domains and therefore uniquely attractive to states seeking to dominate Earth. For these reasons, they identify strong pressures for space's weaponization and see space warfare as virtually inevitable. Dolman's (2002) work is at the most extreme end of the conflict spectrum, representing the offensive realism tradition in political science in predicting that space will eventually fall to the control of a single major power, just as the oceans once did to the United Kingdom (UK) and now are under US naval hegemony. He believes that whichever country weaponizes space first will be able to use this new "high ground" to dominate both space and Earth. Deudney (2020) also uses geopolitics to predict the inevitability of space war, which he foresees risking the end of Earthly civilization as space colonies use superior weapons technology to attack Earth. From this school's perspective, preventing major war in space will be difficult, if not impossible, and crisis stability will also be low.

A second school of thought regarding space security draws on classical realism to predict a more nuanced outcome. Such varied authors as Michael O'Hanlon, Brad Townsend, Bleddyn Bowen, and John Klein sees space's weaponization as likely, but they do not necessarily predict large-scale conflict or the inevitability of a cataclysmic struggle for control of space, much less space being used to dominate Earth. Instead, O'Hanlon (2002) mixes an argument of technological determinism in the advancement of weaponry into space with traditional conservative (or defensive) realism in urging the United States to prepare for space war but not to start it. He is skeptical, however, about the prospects for international organizations or treaties to halt the weaponization of space. Klein (2006) has similar beliefs, but the focus of his argument draws on a maritime analogy of a medium with strategic lines of communication that need to be protected, rather than an environment that needs to be (or can be) dominated. In this regard, he makes an argument for a "maritime strategy" in space focusing on maintaining access to space data and communications through a "cruiser" approach and the ability to conduct selective attacks, rather than through full-scale weaponization, which he sees as inappropriate to the medium and possibly harmful. Bowen's (2020) work draws on geopolitics to predict space's weaponization, but—unlike Dolman and Deudney—he sees Earthly politics and militaries as remaining dominant, such that space war will not necessarily become cataclysmic. Townsend's (2020) work is based in realist principles of self-interest, the primacy of states, and the pursuit of power, but he sees space security moving from offense to defense dominance as satellite constellations become more dispersed and resilient.

The neoliberal institutionalist perspective on space security is perhaps best enunciated by the work of Nancy Gallagher and John Steinbruner and the writing of Detlev Wolter. These authors emphasize the need for new treaties to plug the loopholes in the space regime and bring enforceable, legal mechanisms to play to halt conflict in space. Gallagher and Steinbruner (2008) chart a path toward bans on interference with space assets and on "force application weapons" through formal treaties, supported by new forms of *international* verification. Similarly, Theresa Hitchens (2018) outlines a course via existing United Nations (UN) initiatives, such as the Group of Governmental Experts on Transparency and Confidence-Building Measures and the Committee on the Peaceful Uses of Outer Space, to build new rungs on the ladder of space security. Wolter (2006) emphasizes the need instead for a comprehensive treaty for collective space security, which would involve some of the same weapons bans but in a single document and implemented by a new world space organization.

Ideational and constructivist approaches look to the future in space and argue that a gradual norm-based approach may be the most realistic and, over the long run, most effective means of promoting security. Authors such as Michael Krepon (2010) put an emphasis on a code of conduct as a critical first step in creating a process-oriented regime involving consultations, steadily enhanced transparency, and eventual consensus building. Deganit Paikowsky's (2017) work on what she calls the "space club" points out that the motivations driving many states in space are focused on prestige and status, not offensive-oriented security goals. For this reason, conflict may not be a likely outcome. Finally, Max Mutschler's (2013) work focuses on prospects for improving space security via so-called "epistemic communities" of scientists and senior officials from spacefaring countries, who might raise awareness of the risks of space conflict and environmental degradation, thus leading to improved space security based on new arms control agreements.

Finally, a fifth school focuses on the increasing commercialization of space and the opportunities this might present for avoiding space conflict. Charles Pena (2002) uses a market-based approach for space to argue for a reorientation of national (and international) space policies away from military activities and instead toward space's commercial development by private companies. Wendy Whitman Cobb's (2021) work presents the case that states will be increasingly constrained from engaging in destructive military activities space because of the worsening cost-benefit calculations involved in harming the space-supported global economy by engaging in destructive military acts and spreading orbital debris (62). Instead, she sees a kind of "hidden hand" at work, with growing impact over time, in convincing state leaders to refrain from using weapons in space, although not necessarily from deploying them. To strengthen peaceful trends in space, she argues that "states should encourage further privatization of space activities and an expansion of space-related commerce" (129).

COLD WAR HISTORY AND SPACE STABILITY: A BRIEF OVERVIEW

Space security can be defined as "the ability to place and operate assets outside the Earth's atmosphere without external interference, damage, or destruction" (Moltz 2019, 11). The quality of space security in any period is affected by several factors (see Buono and Bateman, this volume). Primary among them are the international politics affecting space activity, the status of space weapons (their number, test experience, and deployment posture), and the safety of the physical environment of space (as influenced by human-generated impacts and natural forces, such as space weather) (Moltz 2019, 43–44). Each of these factors has changed at various points over time.

To set a baseline, it is instructive (albeit remarkably *hard* from our current historical vantage point) to think back to the pre-1957 period in space before the entry of human-made objects into orbit. "Space security" depended entirely on environmental factors because no human-made technologies or politics had yet penetrated the space domain. Once *Sputnik 1* entered orbit in October 1957 aboard a Soviet rocket, followed in January 1958 by the US *Explorer I*, international politics suddenly became a second critical factor affecting space security. Given the extreme hostility of the US-Soviet relationship, it is not surprising that space was quickly weaponized. In August 1958, less than a year after *Sputnik*'s launch, the United States began testing nuclear weapons in low Earth orbit (LEO) in anticipation of warfare in and through space. Similar Soviet and additional US tests followed suit, including several high-yield tests, most notably the 1.4 megaton US Starfish Prime test in July 1962. The electro-magnetic pulse effects of this explosion disabled seven first-generation US, Soviet, and UK satellites, while posing a serious threat to human spaceflight, which was just beginning (Moltz 2019, 132). The predictions of today's geopolitical pessimists seemed to prevail during this period.

The leaderships in Washington and Moscow faced a series of difficult trade-offs. Continued nuclear testing and weaponization (replete with orbital battle stations and Moon-based missile bases) would have precluded active human spaceflight programs and the fulfillment of Kennedy's geopolitical gambit to beat the Soviets to the lunar surface. The current course would also have made the budding revolution in commercial communications, witnessed in the first trans-Atlantic television broadcasts via *Telstar 1*, impossible. In fact, *Telstar*'s electronics ceased to function as a result of Starfish Prime. Finally, the just-realized revolution in secret space-based reconnaissance satellites (such as the Navy's GRAB and the Air Force/CIA Corona satellites) would have been jeopardized, denying the US government of priceless intelligence information on Soviet military bases, radar systems, and nuclear launch sites.

Given these costly trade-offs and fears of escalation generated by the dangerous nuclear crisis in Cuba that fall, the two leaderships stepped back from their prior course of space weaponization, deciding instead to build at least a basic framework for international space security. The arguments of today's neoliberal institutionalists began to emerge during this period. These initiatives included a ban on space nuclear testing in the 1963 Partial Test Ban Treaty (Bunn 1992, 18–48) and two resolutions adopted at the UN that fall supporting the application of international law to space, calling for countries not to claim territory in space or on the celestial bodies, and prohibiting the orbiting of weapons of mass destruction of any type (Stares 1985, 86–90).

Further protections emerged in the next decade, including a ban on lunar military bases in the 1967 Outer Space Treaty (Stares 1985, 101–104), a prohibition of the testing or stationing of ballistic missile defenses in space in the 1972 Anti-Ballistic Missile (ABM) Treaty, and a bilateral non-interference pledge regarding "national technical means" of verification (satellites) in both the ABM and Strategic Arms Limitation Talks treaties (Bunn 1992, 106–31). The 1972 UN Liability Convention also established a mechanism through which countries could sue for damages if another country's activities in space had harmed its nationals or their property in space or on the ground (Moltz 2019, 172). All of these mechanisms built a framework for predictability, general security, and mutual deterrence into the space environment, particularly as the dominant actors remained the only two nuclear-armed superpowers. Thus, in the language of today's constructivists, it is fair to say that a kind of limited "sanctuary" was created in space during the Cold War, although only after the two sides tried a weapons-based approach first.

As the Cold War wore on, however, the USSR conducted some two dozen tests of a conventionally armed, co-orbital anti-satellite (ASAT) weapon from 1968 to 1971 and from 1976 to 1982 (although many failed to destroy their apparent targets) (Johnson 1987, 140–56). But this weapon was not deployed in large numbers, was not space-based, and possessed only limited capabilities in terms of altitude and orbital inclination. Consistent with authors from the classical realist school, the arms dynamics seen during the Cold War show evidence of a security dilemma, although within certain limits. After the United States dismantled a small, ground-based, nuclear-armed interceptor program (Project 437) in the early 1970s (Chun 2000, 30–31), it eventually started a limited, kinetic ASAT program in the late 1970s in response to Soviet developments. However, it also pursued ASAT arms control measures as a second track of its policy during these years.

As the United States grew more fearful of large Soviet SS-18 multiple warhead missiles during the administration of Ronald Reagan, the announcement of the Strategic Defense Initiative (SDI) proposed the development and deployment of thousands of space-based missile defense interceptors, which would have violated the ABM Treaty and constituted a major weaponization of space, replete with likely large releases of orbital debris from testing. However, the system remained in the research and development stage, due to technical limitations, high costs, and strong opposition from the US Congress. Soviet systems to counter the proposed SDI program—the Skif-DM and

Kaskad space interceptors—never made it to the testing phase (Lantratov 2007). The one ASAT system tested by the United States during this period—the direct-ascent Miniature Homing Vehicle launched on a missile from an F-15 aircraft in 1985—created such a large field of orbital debris as a result of its one kinetic test that the United States eventually halted the test program altogether and instituted strict guidelines to mitigate future debris events (Moltz 2019, 202–203).

As both sides continued to deploy an increasing array of sensors, reconnaissance systems, missile early-warning satellites, and precision navigation and timing systems, it could be observed that space had become too valuable for warfare or, alternatively, too dangerous a domain to fight in given the risks to overall nuclear security. In the end, space weapons deployments remained minimal during the Cold War, and none of these systems were space based. No hostile shots were fired by either side from 1957 to 1991 and, despite some fears, generally robust space security was enjoyed by both sides.

Changes in Post–Cold War Space Security

With the break-up of the USSR in December 1991, conditions regarding space security changed dramatically, initially for the better. No hostile geopolitical rivalry now existed between Russia under President Boris Yeltsin and the United States. China's space capabilities were still quite modest, with almost no devoted military activity. For a decade and a half, the United States enjoyed a kind of space hegemony, which it chose not to exploit for military advantage in orbit. But the US use of GPS-guided munitions in the wars in Iraq, the Balkans, and Afghanistan during the 1990s showed how space was becoming valuable for tactical warfighting for the first time. China and Russia, among other countries, certainly took note of these developments and began to work toward their own capabilities. Similarly, as the risks of catastrophic nuclear war seemed to recede during the 1990s and early 2000s, the threshold for space war seemed to lower as well. Put simply, countries losing a conventional war fought by land, sea, and air forces supported from space now had an increased incentive to attack their adversary's space systems, including its early-warning, reconnaissance, communications, signals intelligence, and position, timing, and navigation satellites.

As the military's reliance on space increased, however, concomitant increases in international legal protections for space did not materialize. As the largest and most powerful space actor, the United States could have chosen to expand the framework for space security during its fifteen years of space hegemony. Instead, Washington actively opposed arms control agreements for space for fear of limiting its proposed missile defense programs, which were strongly supported by the conservative US senators who would have had to vote on any new space treaty. Negotiated forms of space security became even less likely after the Bush administration's 2001 decision to exit the ABM Treaty.

Loose talk by Air Force and Pentagon officials under the Bush administration about possible US development of "prompt global strike" capabilities employing proposed, futuristic, space-based interceptors and space-based missile defenses created new fears in Russian and Chinese military circles about US intentions. However, given the extreme costs of US anti-terrorist efforts, including the wars in Afghanistan and Iraq, after the September 11, 2001, attacks on the United States, the administration actually applied little funding to these programs. But skeptical military and political leaders in Russia and China acted on worst-case assumptions regarding US intentions and resumed or initiated counterspace programs (Mizin 2007, 93–94, 96).

China's 2007 ASAT test and a range of Chinese high-altitude experiments that followed (Weeden and Samson 2018, 1-2-1-24) raised great concerns in US military circles. Russia under Vladimir Putin also moved to reconstitute its military space capabilities, with a major upgrade of its Plesetsk launch facility, and warned of its readiness to meet any US actions to weaponize space with systems of its own (Moltz 2020, 21). The dramatic worsening of US-Russian political relations after Moscow's invasions of Ukraine in 2014 and 2022 and the application of increasingly strict Western sanctions on Russia only strengthened pressures for military space capabilities on both sides.

Other countries watching developments in the first decade and a half of the twenty-first century began to speak of their own possible needs for counterspace capabilities. Several countries in Asia reacted to China's 2007 ASAT test by radically altering the focus of previously peaceful space programs to include a military dimension. Japan passed new Diet legislation in 2008 allowing national security uses of space for the first time (Pekkanen and Kallender-Umezu 2010) and now has a multi-billion dollar military space program underway (Pekkanen 2022). Meanwhile, India initiated a military space organization in 2008 and promised to match China's space weapons program (Moltz 2012, 127–31). Making good on this threat, the Indian military tested a kinetic ASAT weapon in March 2019. Unfortunately, despite promises to the contrary, the test released considerably more orbital debris than had been predicted and in higher orbits. North Korea and South Korea also entered this growing Asian space race by testing their own rockets and launching their first satellites, fearing the geopolitical and military implications of being left behind (An 2020; Lee and Jeong, this volume). In the Middle East, Iran has conducted several satellite launches, prompting a number of its Persian Gulf rivals to purchase satellites and begin planning for enhanced, space-supported military operations. In Europe, France's foreign minister mentioned her country's interest in developing space-based laser weapons (Hitchens 2019). Separately, the North Atlantic Treaty Organization issued its first space policy in 2022, noting that "rapid advances in space technology have created . . . new risks, vulnerabilities, and potentially threats for the Alliance's and Allies' security and defence" (North Atlantic Treaty Organization 2022). These trends suggest a major shift in the focus of national space activities across the globe toward military purposes, which was the exclusive domain of the two superpowers during the Cold War.

Meanwhile, several factors have led to a dramatic increase in the number of commercial actors in space. First, the dramatic opening of the Russian space program in the 1990s to the international market led to an increased availability of a variety of space technologies as well as access to space on Russian boosters. Second, the information technology revolution that began to produce increasingly sophisticated and miniaturized technologies meant that small, start-up companies could now enter space at relatively low cost, making whole new sectors of activity—such as persistent Earth imaging through large constellations—possible for the first time. Similarly, new capabilities for space-delivered phone and internet communications from cheap satellites grouped into mega-constellations began to rapidly increase the number of satellites in orbit, creating crowding, not previously a concern in regard to space security. Companies like OneWeb, SpaceX (Starlink constellation), and the China Satellite Network Group (Guowang constellation) have all promised to deploy constellations of multiple thousands of satellites in the next decade. From a few dozen commercial actors in the 1990s, the commercial space sector has increased rapidly to hundreds of companies, with no signs of decreasing.

The resultant crowding of especially LEO means that controlling orbital debris, which circles the globe at speeds approximating 18,000 mph, is becoming an increasing imperative for safe use of this region of space. Besides putting pressure on the limited radio spectrum in which these satellites must broadcast, rules on traffic control remain vague and voluntary. The passage in December 2007 of Debris Mitigation Guidelines at the UN at least set up a list of objectives for debris control, including deorbiting of satellites after their service lives and calls for states to refrain from the intentional creation of long-lived debris. But the emergence, largely after 2007, of tiny cubesats (10 x 10 x 10 centimeters) without propulsion systems, meant that a significant portion of the expanded population of satellites lacked the capability of independent propulsion, making them subject only to weak forces of atmospheric drag and gravity in regard to deorbiting. While scientists fretted, entrepreneurs saw big profits from satellite broadband, which could be provided cheaply to users worldwide via large constellations of cubesats. The market beckoned, but at the risk of space security.

Changes in the launch marketplace have only accelerated these trends. Where launch services used to be few and very expensive, the emergence of SpaceX and a range of other private, low-cost launch companies since the early 2000s means that access to space is more readily available, thus lowering the bar to entry. The number of countries owning or operating spacecraft has increased dramatically since the end of the Cold War, from less than a dozen to nearly seventy, making countries more interested in space security but also making political agreements among "spacefaring" states more complicated.

This combination of changes in the space environment since the early 2000s—the multilateral proliferation of counterspace capabilities, the rapidly increasing number of commercial actors, and the explosive growth of cheap but often uncontrollable cubesats—means that a number of factors that previously promoted space security no longer exist. This situation raises two fundamental and yet very important questions: is space conflict preventable, and, if so, what new mechanisms for promoting space security might be achievable?

FACTORS TO WATCH IN FUTURE SPACE SECURITY

Given the generally negative predictions of recent IR theorists regarding prospects for future space security and the direction of proposals for those advocating new forms of space arms control, what are the possible "markers" students, analysts, and other observers should watch for to assess whether space security is improving or declining in the coming decade? Below, this chapter considers four factors as critical indicators of progress or setbacks toward improved space: space debris management; the status of ASAT weapons; progress toward norms or new treaties; and participation by scientific and commercial actors in space security solutions.

Orbital debris is arguably the single most dangerous threat to future space security, given existing (and seeming inexorable) trends toward greater numbers of operators and the expansion of mega-constellations of satellites (Moltz 2014). With the satellite population—especially in LEO—very likely to reach fifty thousand in the next five years and possibly one hundred thousand in the next decade, the ability of states and companies to use space safely is certainly at risk. As one recent study argues, besides the requirement to register with the International Telecommunications Union for a radio frequency, "No binding international rules exist on other aspects of mega-constellations" (Boley and Byers 2021).

New mechanisms for improved space security will require progress in three areas: limiting debris releases, characterizing (and avoiding) existing debris, and removing particularly dangerous debris. International progress on these three tasks to date can be graded: so-so (limiting debris), good (characterizing debris), and poor (removing debris). Since the passage of the 2007 UN Debris Mitigation Guidelines, countries have at least committed themselves on a voluntary basis toward the goal of not releasing long-lived debris, typically defined as debris that will remain in orbit for twenty-five years or more, and to de-orbiting their dead satellites. However, compliance with the guidelines has been spotty, with approximately 40 percent of space operators in LEO failing to follow de-orbiting guidelines for their satellites (European Space Agency 2021, 5). But even if the twenty-five-year goal is somehow met with improved compliance, there may simply be too many satellites in LEO in the future to carry out effective traffic control without enhanced measures. As Boley and Byers observe, "The widely accepted [twenty-five-year] guideline is poorly suited for mega-constellations made up of thousands of satellites with short operational lives" (Boley and Byers 2021). The risk, of course, is that increased debris could make LEO so cluttered that it sets off a Kessler Syndrome—a condition predicted in the 1970s by NASA scientist Donald Kessler where "cascading" collisions of debris hitting other debris become uncontrollable. Unfortunately, once this starts, there may be no return from this situation and near-Earth orbital space could be ruined.

Fortunately, compliance in geostationary orbit is considerably higher at 85 percent (European Space Agency 2021, 6), but there are fewer satellites in that region of space and they are not actually removed from orbit but simply boosted into higher orbits above the geostationary belt, where they will remain essentially forever. Getting an international agreement to require countries and their companies to remove satellites from critical orbits within five years overall or within one year of the end of the satellite's service life would go a long way toward improving future space security. A 2022 Federal Communications Commission rule that now requires deorbiting of US satellites from LEO within five years may stimulate such an effort.

In terms of characterizing existing debris, various nations and commercial companies are doing a good job of identifying what is in orbit, where it is, and what orbit it is traveling along. The US Space Surveillance Network and a number of other governmental systems around the world have been tracking space objects for years. Recently, a number of commercial companies—including the US LeoLabs and ExoAnalytical Solutions and the Canadian NorthStar Earth and Space—have developed networks of radars, telescopes, and space-based sensors, respectively, to build publicly available catalogues of satellites and debris. One advantage of these databases is that they could be used in international legal proceedings as evidence of irresponsible country or company debris releases or other intentional activities that harm space objects owned by others under the 1972 UN Liability Convention. The increased transparency of space activities promised by these commercial services could act as a deterrent in the future to harmful space activities in the areas of collision avoidance, interference, or debris creation.

Finally, in regard to removing orbital debris, especially large objects like rocket bodies that are the most likely to collide with other debris, very little has been accomplished to date, with the exception of a few experiments by scientists and commercial companies. Still, efforts by the UK University of Surrey's RemoveDEBRIS project and the Swiss firm ClearSpace are pointing the way to the possible future capture and de-orbiting of dead satellites and debris or the installation of drag sails or other mechanisms to assist in natural de-orbiting. Tracking progress in each of these areas of debris management will be critical to improving future space security.

A second factor in determining the status of space security—consistent with criteria outlined at the beginning of this chapter—will be the quantity of space weapons, the quality of their testing, and the nature of their deployment. A handful of the leading space powers seems intent on demonstrating offensive and defensive space capability for the possibility of future warfare. Whether or not these weapons are used in anger and how aggressively they are postured will certainly make a difference in regard to future space security. To date, space powers have limited themselves to ground-, sea-, and air-based weapons. That seems unlikely in the future. While the 2020 US National Space Policy calls for "responsible national security activities" in space, the definition does not preclude the development of "defensive" systems, including possibly those with dual-use offensive capabilities, as long as they are not tested in an irresponsible way or used against adversaries in peacetime. Chinese, Russian, Indian, and French plans and practices in regard to space weapons seem similar. While China and Russia are sponsors of a proposed treaty to ban deployment of space-based weapons, both continue to develop non-space-based systems, and could be developing space-based systems as well (Weeden and Samson 2018).

Active kinetic testing of any weapons in space will lead to a degradation of space security. Large-scale deployment of space-based weapons will certainly lead to heightened tensions and possibly increased likelihood of use, given the lack of warning time, particularly for on-orbit systems. It is also likely to further increase the field of orbital debris in LEO, thus raising the likelihood of collisions with spacecraft. Indeed, military deterrence in space in the presence of large-scale weaponization by multiple powers is likely to be much *less* stable than bilateral nuclear deterrence on Earth was during the Cold War (DeBlois 1998), not that those conditions felt especially "safe" at the time. By contrast, if governments were move in the future to adopt ASAT test limits or outright bans, or if they were to engage in mutual restraint in regard to weaponization, then space security as it has been enjoyed to date by the international community might continue. Unfortunately, current trends and the extensive secrecy guarding certain Chinese and Russian space systems make it hard to be optimistic about such limits. Watching for future weapons tests, releases of debris, and reactions by other states will provide clues as to whether a space arms race is emerging or whether countries are willing to limit themselves to "hedge" capabilities only. Fortunately, as noted above, prospects for national and commercial verification of many of these activities are growing, as is public knowledge of those who might be acting aggressively in space or harming the orbital environment. Also, the April 2022 announcement by the Biden administration of its adoption of a direct-ascent kinetic ASAT test moratorium is beginning to influence the international debate.

A third factor is new evidence of norm building, the signing of new treaties, or development of other enhanced governance mechanisms for space. Analysts generally agree that there are significant gaps in existing Cold War space treaties, which allowed activities (such as kinetic ASAT tests) that are obviously now very dangerous to safe use of space. While there have been a number of efforts led by states and non-governmental organizations to plug these loopholes, very little definitive progress has been made since the original space treaties were signed in the 1960s and 1970s. Of course, much has changed since then and there has been a vast proliferation of space actors and technologies. Evidence of progress in this category might include codes of conduct, pledges of non-interference with other countries' satellites, or formal treaties to outlaw specific classes of space weapons or harmful behaviors. Useful initial efforts are being made through the UN Committee on the Peaceful Uses of Outer Space's Scientific and Technical Subcommittee on Long-Term Sustainability, which issued a set of guidelines in 2019 (Martinez 2020). But more work is needed to translate these guidelines into national policies and to ensure worldwide compliance. Possible future steps might include bilateral, regional, or multilateral pledges to uphold and monitor compliance with these best practices or with additional measures that might be identified. Another route might be, as in the early 1960s, using UN resolutions to build a consensus for a future code of conduct or treaty, which would be binding. A US-backed resolution at the United Nations, first introduced in the fall of 2022, calling upon all countries to refrain from kinetic ASAT testing is a possible step in this direction. Despite widespread international support, China and Russia have so far rejected the initiative. Tracking the progress of this UN effort will be critical to understanding prospects for future space security.

A fourth factor to monitor in regard to future space security is the presence or absence of new scientific or commercial leadership in emerging policy debates. To date, governments and their militaries have dominated these discussions. Yet, in fields such as acid rain several decades ago and, more recently, climate change, scientists have helped shape international debates by providing critical, objective information that has led to collective action by governments. Information about orbital debris and possible risks of a Kessler Syndrome being triggered could raise the urgency among the general public and commercial companies for concerted action to combat this threat. One past example of such behavior occurred during the US debate over the ratification of the Chemical Weapons Convention (CWC) in 1997. Many US senators hinged their votes on the reaction of US chemical companies to the CWC, which would prohibit future production and sale of critical precursor chemicals used in the manufacture of dangerous chemical weapons. To the surprise of many observers, responsible chemical companies banded together in support of the CWC because they did not want to see their industry continue to face public criticism due to irresponsible behavior by a small number of producers. The CWC passed the US Senate and entered into force internationally as well. Commercial space companies could play a similar role in lobbying to prevent harmful activities in space and in providing enhanced space situational awareness through new commercial services (as mentioned above).

In terms of their motivations, commercial companies want to make money in space. Therefore, they have strong incentives to help create an orderly, predictable, and rule-based framework for space activity (Cobb 2021), not a military free-for-all, which is likely to increase space debris, heighten tensions, and, as a consequence, put their spacecraft (and their profits) at risk. On the other hand, a few companies may see strict limits on orbital debris releases as imposing costs on them, particularly as they test satellites for deployment in large constellations. Whether norms and rules for responsible debris behavior successfully pressure these outliers—and whether governments support those rules—will be critical factors to watch in terms of future space security.

In terms of prospects for peaceful outcomes in space, fortunately, there are at least a few promising developments to point to in recent years. In the fall of 2020, the UK introduced a resolution at the UN calling upon states to contribute to efforts to define "responsible" and "irresponsible" behavior in space (United Nations First Committee 2020). By the summer of 2021, a number of spacefaring countries—including China, Russia, and the United States—had submitted papers offering their perspectives on the subject. These submissions constituted one of the most meaningful "dialogues" about space security since the end of the Cold War. Drawing on this positive response, UN members met in a two-year Open Ended Working Group in 2022 and 2023, discussed further elaborations of these definitions, and proposed means of continuing this dialogue, despite a lack of consensus on specific steps forward.

In addition, in the fall of 2021, a Canadian non-governmental organization (the Outer Space Institute at the University of British Columbia) led the process of writing an open letter to the UN—signed by over one hundred space scientists and former government and UN officials—calling upon states to discuss negotiation of a kinetic weapons test ban for space and receiving considerable attention from diplomats. Subsequently, the release of 1,500 pieces of harmful debris as a result of the November 2021 Russia ASAT test stimulated a number of additional public proposals (including articles and letters signed by former senior officials and scientific experts) in support of an eventual international kinetic ASAT test ban (see, for example, Loverro et al. 2022). Perhaps these efforts will create the groundswell for increased public pressure for government action on space debris that has been missing in the past. These efforts might make it harder for those countries that are resisting commitments to put an end to kinetic weapons tests through a test ban or a new treaty.

Based on past experiences in space (such as during the 1960s), there may be a path forward of building from consensual knowledge about threats, to norm development, and finally to treaty formation and agreement. The role of the commercial sector may well be critical to the success of these developments, given its increasing activity in space, its growing share of the economic activity generated in space, and its possible influence on reluctant governments.

Conclusion: Charting Future Space Security

The maintenance of positive conditions of space security will be essential to the successful exploration and development of space, as well as its continued use for military support functions. If space instead becomes a battleground or if increased commercial activity leads to irresponsible behavior regarding the de-orbiting of satellites, the fragile environment of near-Earth space will become increasingly littered with orbital debris, possibly making critical orbits unusable. Then, space's future (and ours as a species) will face grim prospects.

Fortunately, there is growing understanding about the harmful implications of orbital debris releases and an increasing interest in at least some quarters in cleaning up near-Earth orbits. This shared interest among nations and companies may drive cooperation, even if this outcome currently appears unlikely. The same common fear of continued electro-magnetic pulse and radiation effects from nuclear tests in the period 1958–1962 led to successful collective action in banning space nuclear explosions once and for all. Therefore, positive precedents do exist, and scientists, space companies, and spacefaring countries have multiple venues today to share information and work out effective and verifiable mechanisms for limiting, avoiding, and reducing orbital debris.

In the end, much will depend, as it has in the past, on politics on Earth. If the leading spacefaring countries are cooperating to combat climate change and finding new ways of preventing conventional and nuclear conflicts, then prospects for space security will be enhanced. If instead mutual mistrust, cyber-attacks, trade wars, and conventional conflicts become the rule, then space activity is more likely to become an extension (rather than exception) to these dynamics. But the tools for cooperation exist and inter-national communications are at an all-time high. Let us hope that the political will to use these mechanisms for improving space security and sustaining it for future generations will emerge and eventually prevail.

References

An, Hyoung Joon. 2020. "South Korea's Space Program: Activities and Ambitions." *Asia Policy* 15, no. 2: 34–42.

Boley, Aaron C., and Michael Byers. 2021. "Satellite Mega-constellations Create Risks in Low Earth Orbit, the Atmosphere and on Earth." *Scientific Reports* 11:10642. https://doi.org/10.1038/s41598-021-89909-7.

Bowen, Bleddyn. 2020. *War in Space: Strategy, Spacepower, Geopolitics*. Edinburgh: Edinburgh University Press.

Bunn, George. 1992. *Arms Control by Committee: Managing Negotiations with the Russians*. Stanford, CA: Stanford University Press.

Cobb, Wendy N. Whitman. 2021. *Privatizing Peace: How Commerce Can Reduce Conflict in Space*. New York: Routledge.

Chun, Clayton K.S. 2000. *Shooting Down a "Star": Program 437, the US Nuclear ASAT System and Present-Day Copycat Killers*. Maxwell Air Force Base, AL: Air University Press.

DeBlois, Bruce M. 1998. "Space Sanctuary: A Viable National Strategy." *Airpower Journal* 12, no. 4: 41–57.

Deudney, Daniel. 2020. *Dark Skies: Space Expansionism, Planetary Geopolitics, and the Ends of Humanity*. New York: Oxford University Press.

Dolman, Everett C. 2002. *Astropolitik: Classical Geopolitics in the Space Age*. London: Frank Cass.

European Space Agency. 2021. *ESA's Annual Space Environment Report*. Darmstadt: European Space Agency, Space Debris Office.

Gallagher, Nancy, and John D. Steinbruner. 2008. *Reconsidering the Rules for Space Security*. Cambridge, MA: American Academy of Arts and Sciences.

Johnson, Nicholas L. 1987. *Soviet Military Strategy in Space*. New York: Jane's Publishing Company.

Hitchens, Theresa. 2018. "Forwarding Multilateral Space Governance: Next Steps for the International Community." College Park, MD: School of Public Policy, University of Maryland.

Hitchens, Theresa. 2019. "Space Lasers for Satellite Defense Top New French Space Strategy." *Breaking Defense*. July 26, 2019.

Klein, John J. 2006. *Space Warfare: Strategy, Principles and Policy*. London: Routledge.

Krepon, Michael, ed. 2010. *A Code of Conduct for Responsible Space-Faring Nations*. Washington, DC: Stimson Center.

Lantratov, Konstantin. 2007. "The 'Star Wars' That Never Happened: The True Story of the Soviet Union's Polyus (Skif-DM) Space-Based Battle Stations." *Quest* 14, no. 2: 5–18.

Loverro, Douglas, Brian Chow, Brandon Kelly, Brian Weeden, and Robert Cardillo. 2022. "The ASAT Prisoner's Dilemma: The Case for U.S. Leadership and a Unilateral Moratorium on Kinetic-Energy Antisatellite Testing." Center for Strategic and International Studies, Washington, D.C.

Martinez, Peter. 2020. "UN COPUOS Guidelines for Long-Term Sustainability of Outer Space Activities: Early implementation experiences and next steps in COPUOS." Paper for the 71st International Astronautical Congress. October 12–14, 2020.

Mizin, Victor. 2007. "Russian Perspectives on Space Security." In *Collective Security in Space: European Perspectives*, edited by John M. Logsdon, James Clay Moltz, and Emma Hinds, 75–108. Washington, DC: George Washington University, Space Policy Institute.

Moltz, James Clay. 2012. *Asia's Space Race: National Motivations, Regional Rivalries, and International Risks*. New York: Columbia University Press.

Moltz, James Clay. 2014. *Crowded Orbits: Conflict and Cooperation in Space*. New York: Columbia University Press.

Moltz, James Clay. 2019. *The Politics of Space Security: Strategic Restraint and the Pursuit of National Interests*. Stanford, CA: Stanford University Press.

Moltz, James Clay. 2020. "The Russian Space Program: In Search of a New Business Model." *Asia Policy* 15, no. 2: 19–26.

Mutschler, Max M. 2013. *Arms Control in Space: Exploring Conditions for Preventive Arms Control*. New York: Palgrave Macmillan.

North Atlantic Treaty Organization. 2022. "NATO's Overarching Space Policy."

O'Hanlon, Michael. 2002. *Neither Star Wars nor Sanctuary: Constraining the Military Uses of Space*. Washington, DC: Brookings Institution Press.

Outer Space Institute. 2021. Open Letter to H.E. Mr. Volkan Bozkir, President, United Nations General Assembly, Re: Kinetic ASAT Test Ban Treaty. September 2, 2021.

Paikowsky, Deganit. 2017. *The Power of the Space Club*. New York: Cambridge University Press.

Pekkanen, Saadia M. 2022. "Neoclassical Realism in Japan's Space Security." In *The Oxford Handbook of Japanese Politics*, edited by Robert J. Pekkanen and Saadia M. Pekkanen, 763–90. New York: Oxford University Press.

Pekkanen, Saadia M., and Paul Kallender-Umezu. 2010. *In Defense of Japan: From the Market to the Military in Space Policy*. Stanford, CA: Stanford University Press.

Pena, Charles V. 2002. "U.S. Commercial Space Programs: Future Priorities and Implications for National Security." In *Future Security in Space: Commercial, Military, and Arms Control Trade-Offs*, edited by James Clay Moltz, 8–10. Monterey, CA: Center for Nonproliferation Studies, Monterey Institute of International Studies, Occasional Paper No. 10.

Stares, Paul B. 1985. *The Militarization of Space: U.S. Policy, 1945–84*. Ithaca, NY: Cornell University Press.

Townsend, Brad. 2020. "Strategic Choice and the Orbital Security Dilemma." *Strategic Studies Quarterly* 14, no. 1: 64–90.

United Nations First Committee. 2020. "Reducing Space Threats through Norms, Rules and Principles of Responsible Behaviors." A/C.1/75/L.45/Rev. 1. October 20, 2020.

Weeden, Brian, and Victoria Samson, eds. 2018. *Global Counterspace Capabilities: An Open Source Assessment*. Washington, DC: Secure World Foundation.

Wolter, Detlev. 2006. *Common Security in Outer Space and International Law*. Geneva: United Nations Institute for Disarmament Research.

CHAPTER 44

THE FUTURE OF COOPERATION IN SPACE

Irreconcilable Differences?

ZHOU BO AND WANG GUOYU

INTRODUCTION

IN February 2021, Mars suddenly had three visitors from Earth: the United Arab Emirates' probe Amal, China's Tianwen-I, and NASA's (National Aeronautics and Space Agency) Perseverance. The question is: Why cannot nations pool their resources and work together on such gargantuan tasks that are extremely difficult and expensive?

Today, space is no longer the domain of a few spacefaring countries. All nations have grown increasingly reliant on space for, among other things, global communications, precision navigation, weather forecasting, and imagery provided by on-orbit systems that are vital for their national economies and security. Therefore, space is becoming more congested and even contested. But the biggest threat to outer space security is its weaponization and the arms race in outer space.

There are primarily two school of thoughts on space governance that are led by China and Russia on one side and the US-led western countries on the other side. China and Russia wish to make a binding treaty of non-weaponization in space while western countries claim that the weaponization of outer space is already unavoidable and propose to develop non-legally binding rules on responsible space behaviors.

The two views, like two sides of the same coin, are not necessarily incompatible. One way out of the impasse is to adopt a dual-track approach, that is, all parties agree to the goal of negotiating a binding treaty of no placement of weapons in outer space while encouraging discussions on responsible behaviors that serve the fundamental goal of preventing an arms race in outer space.

This is not impossible. So far, no countries have overtly declared possession of "weapons" in outer space. If all nations recognize that they are all vulnerable in outer space, then recognition and acceptance of "mutually assured vulnerability" (MAV) in outer space, a concept coined by Zhou Bo that first appeared in the *South China Morning Post* in March 2021, will make peaceful coexistence and necessary cooperation more likely. For that to happen, major powers should take the lead in cooperation wherever possible.

STUMBLING BLOCKS TO COOPERATION IN SPACE SECURITY

In outer space, all issues basically boil down to two categories: space security and space safety. Space security issues mainly refer to the risks of weaponization and an arms race in outer space. Space safety refers to the risks occurring in the process of peaceful uses of outer space, including orbit congestion, collision, and space debris (Note Verbale from the Permanent Mission of China 2021).

Regarding space security governance, the basic problem is that spacefaring nations disagree on what constitutes the biggest challenges to space security and the ways to best address them. No differences in thoughts are starker than those that are held by China and Russia on one side and the US-led western countries on the other side. Sadly, the differences appear irreconcilable since the positions are interpreted by some commentators as two totally different approaches.

China and Russia-Led Approach

China, along with Russia, wants a binding treaty of non-weaponization and stresses the avoidance of an arms race in space. In the "Document of the People's Republic of China Pursuant to UNGA Resolution 75/36 (2020)" (Ministry of Foreign Affairs 2021), China holds that the growing risks of weaponization and an arms race in outer space have become the greatest threat to outer space security. China believes that preventing an arms race in outer space is the precondition for safeguarding outer space security and ensuring peaceful uses of outer space, as well as being one of the most prominent and pressing issues for the international community. Since existing international legal instruments are insufficient to deal with new challenges, the conclusion of an arms control treaty on outer space becomes even more important and urgent and should be viewed as the priority and fundamental goal in related international agendas (Note verbale from the Permanent Mission of China 2021).

In 2008, China and Russia jointly submitted to the Conference on Disarmament (CD) the draft Treaty on the Prevention of the Placement of Weapons in Outer Space, the Threat or Use of Force against Outer Space Objects (PPWT) in its Plenary Session (CD/1839). The draft was renewed in 2014. According to China and Russia, "weapon in outer space" means any outer space object or its component produced or converted to eliminate, damage, or disrupt normal functioning of objects in outer space, on the Earth's surface, or in the air, as well as to eliminate populations or components of the biosphere important to human existence or to inflict damage to them by using any principles of physics. States Parties to this treaty shall not place any weapons in outer space nor resort to the threat or use of force against outer space objects of States Parties (PPWT 2014). Again, the two countries proposed to conclude a new international legal instrument through negotiation to prevent weaponization and an arms race in outer space.

The significance of the PPWT is that it is a huge step forward from the Treaty on the Principles Governing the Activities of States in the Exploration and Use of Outer Space, including the Moon and Other Celestial Bodies (1967) which is more commonly known as the Outer Space Treaty (OST). This treaty expressly prohibits placing any weapons of mass destruction in orbit, establishing military bases or installations, testing any type of weapons, or conducting military exercise on the moon and other celestial bodies, but does not include conventional weapons. The PPWT is also in line with the 1981 resolution of the United Nations General Assembly (UNGA) on "prevention of an arms race in outer space" that reaffirms the fundamental principles of the 1967 OST and advocates not placing any weapons in outer space. So far, the PPWT remains the only text to serve as the basis for negotiations of a new binding treaty.

US-Led Approach

However, the PPWT was rejected by some countries for a variety of reasons. For example, the US delegation opposes the PPWT because "there is no effective verification regime to monitor compliance, and terrestrially based anti-satellite systems posing the greatest and most imminent threat are not captured" (CD/1847). Instead, a totally different US-led western approach was proposed. It stressed making non-legally binding rules for responsible behaviors, transparency, and confidence building measures. It claims that it is difficult to define what is a weapon in space in that terrestrially based missile defense interceptors can be adopted to destroy satellites. Electronic jamming, directed energy weapons, and offensive cyber tools can also threaten satellites. Even if the definition of outer space weapons could be agreed, verifying these weapons is still challenging given the dual-use nature of satellites. In the future, defining an anti-satellite (ASAT) weapon will get even more problematic because a few spacefaring countries are developing the capability to service and refuel satellites on orbit. As a result, any system that maneuvers close enough to another satellite can pose an ASAT threat. Therefore, the weaponization of outer space is already unavoidable and discussions on the prevention of an arms race in outer space (PAROS) are no longer pertinent. It instead proposes to develop non-legally binding rules on responsible space behaviors that include best practices to avoid collisions and mitigate space debris (Lauder, Klotz, and Courtney 2020).

To support these claims, the Memorandum on the National Space Policy signed by President Trump in December 2020 calls upon the United States to "lead the enhancement of safety, stability, security, and long-term sustainability in space by promoting a framework for responsible behavior in outer space, including the pursuit and effective implementation of best practices, standards, and norms of behavior" (White House 2020). In March 2021, the Interim National Security Strategic Guidance, issued by President Biden, affirms that the United States will lead in promoting shared norms and forge new agreements on outer space (2020).

The United Kingdom (UK), in its respond under UNGA Resolution A/RES/75/36 on "Reducing Space Threats through Norms, Rules and Principles of Responsible Behavior," describes the call of China and Russia to not place weapons in space "an outdated concept," and calls instead for expert-level discussion on concrete technical points such as destruction of a satellite, direct ascent ASAT use, and rendezvous and proximity operations (United Kingdom 2021).

The Reality of Dual-Use Technology

Given the dual-use nature of satellites, many systems that have a civilian purpose can be used for military purposes, but most space systems are for civilian purposes. The numbers of military satellites in space are much smaller than those for civilian purposes,. For those satellites that are dual use in nature, we should take them as satellites for civilian use first until they are really found to be used militarily. Therefore, a prior verification of their nature is not necessary.

Although it is not realistic to get international consensus on the definition and scope of "space weapon" at this stage due to the dual-use nature of the technology, this is a question that could be considered within or beyond the PPWT. Take Active Debris Removal (ADR) technology for example. On one hand, on most occasions, the purpose of ADR differs from the purpose of use of a space weapon, which is to produce or convert to eliminate, damage, or disrupt the normal functioning of a space object (PPWT 2014). ADR is a complementary measure of space debris mitigation to "clean space," since mitigation alone cannot maintain a safe and stable debris environment in the long term. Therefore, if a state uses one space object to remove another non-functional space object under its jurisdiction and control, this could not be claimed as placing or using weapon in outer space.

Even if ADR is misused—a state removes functional space object of another state without its consent—the affected state may request the removal state to clarify the situation, assuming both of them are state parties of the PPWT (PPWT 2014). In this case, the removal state has the burden of proof to show that its ADR has not been used as space weapon.

On the other hand, the challenges brought by ADR should be settled by a pertinent international mechanism. For instance, under the Working Group of Long-term Sustainability for Outer Space Activities of the United Nations Committee on Peaceful

Uses of Outer Space (UNCOPUOS), the Russian delegation proposed a draft guideline entitled "Observe Criteria for Operations on Active Removal of Orbital Objects" (A/AC.105/C.1/2014/CRP.17). The discussions of other international platforms on ADR, such as the Inter-Agency of Space Debris Coordination Committee (IADC), will facilitate the consideration or implementation of the PPWT. Therefore, dual-use technology would not and should not be an obstacle to comprehensive recognition of the PPWT.

The definition of space weapon should not include weapons that are based on the ground, no matter if they are used through kinetic, electronic, directed energy, or cyber means. Although they could be used militarily against targets in space, they are not exclusively designed for space purposes. Almost all weapons can be used offensively and defensively. For example, an aircraft can attack a satellite with a missile at low Earth orbit, as was proven in a successful attack by a F-15A Eagle against an aging weather satellite in 1985, but we normally will not view an aircraft or a missile as a space weapon.

Non-Weaponization versus Responsible Behaviors

"Responsible behaviors" sounds slippery if compared with "no placement of weapons in outer space," which is clear-cut. It is reported that the United States, Russia, China, and India have all successfully demonstrated their ASAT capabilities (Secure World Foundation 2021, 7–16). While the United States condemned China's only ASAT weapon test in 2007 as irresponsible because it produced a large number of debris (Center for Strategic and Informational Studies 2020), China pointed out the United States was the first country to conduct an ASAT weapon test, and with the most tests conducted, it created the largest amount of space debris (Note Verbale from the Permanent Mission of China 2021).

To some extent, the PPWT is already inclusive of "responsible behaviors." It complements and expands the obligations established by the OST and embodies the principles of PAROS. On December 4, 2014, the UNGA passed two resolutions. For the first resolution, "Prevention of an Arms Race in Outer Space," 178 countries voted in favor to none against, with only 2 abstentions from Israel and United States (A/69/PV.62). For the second resolution, "No First Placement of Weapons in Outer Space," 126 countries voted in favor to 4 against (Georgia, Israel, Ukraine, United States), with 46 abstentions (A/69/PV.62). Although these two resolutions are not directly associated with the PPWT, one can see clearly that the PPWT is in line with the two resolutions in spirit. Even the UK, a country that first tabled "responsible behaviors," admits that many nations support a legally binding treaty and wish to prevent the "weaponization" of space (United Kingdom 2021).

The binary distinction between responsible and irresponsible behaviors in space amounts to seeing the trees without seeing the forest. If all countries agree to the prohibition of deployment and use of weapons in outer space, then the production, research and development, and testing of outer space weapons becomes impossible. This top-down approach is the most fundamental way of addressing the root cause of weaponization in outer space and therefore the most responsible behavior. As Chinese Ambassador Li Song pointed out in the CD on PAROS on June 14, 2019, "our aim is to prevent outer space from becoming a new battleground like the land, the seas and oceans and airspace, instead of merely formulating 'traffic rules' for outer space . . . no arms control and disarmament in any field can be achieved only through transparency and confidence building measures (TCBMs)" (The Permanent Mission of China 2019).

This does not mean China is against responsible outer space behaviors. On the contrary, it is in China's best national interests to welcome responsible behaviors. On December 3, 2021, China informed the UN secretary general of dangerous "close encounters" with Elon Musk's SpaceX Starlink satellites, which twice approached the Chinese Space Station (CSS) in orbit (Note Verbale from the Permanent Mission of China to the United Nations 2021). But without discussing the prevention of an arms race in outer space as required by the PAROS, the argument about responsible behaviors looks like a deliberate deviation from the agreed upon principles in the OST that "States Parties to the Treaty undertake not to place in orbit around the earth any objects carrying nuclear weapons or any other kinds of weapons of mass destruction, install such weapons on celestial bodies, or station such weapons in outer space in any other manner" (Art. IV). It also goes against PAROS, which "calls on all States, in particular those with major space capabilities, to contribute actively to the peaceful use of outer space, prevent an arms race there, and refrain from actions contrary to that objective" (A/RES/75/35).

The real purpose behind the push for "responsible behaviors" is that the United States wishes to maintain its large missile defense program and technical advantages in potential space weaponry so as to ensure its absolute supremacy in space as well as on Earth. Ever since 1985, when the CD established an ad hoc committee to identify and examine issues relevant to PAROS such as the legal protection of satellites, nuclear power systems in space, and various confidence-building measures, the United States has consistently opposed any talks on avoiding arms race in space in CD (Nuclear Threat Initiative 2020).

The great power competition since the Trump administration's taking of China and Russia as primary competitors makes compromises among major spacefaring nations more difficult. Donald Trump believes "we must have American dominance in space. And so we will" (Tobias 2018). The 2018 Nuclear Posture Review reserves the US right to use nuclear weapons in retaliation for "significant non-nuclear strategic attacks" against critical US infrastructure, including its space-based components (Department of Defense 2018). In 2019, the United States established an independent Space Force and Space Command. According to its first statement on doctrine, the primary purpose of military space forces is "to secure U.S. interests through deterrence and, when necessary, the application of force" (Lauder, Klotz, and Courtney 2020). In its 2019 Missile Defense Review, the United States stressed the importance of space in missile defense and its plans to build a network of space-based infrared sensors, develop new types of space sensors, and deploy space-based missile interceptors in space (Department of Defense 2019).

It seems impossible that the United States will accept any binding treaty that restricts, let alone, freezes its capabilities in an area where it wishes to maintain supremacy for good. It is no surprise that although prevention of an arms race in outer space is one of the main agenda items of the CD, differences resulted in recurring stalemate in negotiations of legally binding commitments on PAROS.

"Reducing Space Threats through Norms, Rules and Principles of Responsible Behaviors," an initiative initially put forward by the UK, was overwhelmingly adopted in UNGA Resolution 75/36 in December 2020 with 164 member states voting in favor. Admittedly, the initiative is useful in breaking through the decades-old diplomatic stagnation at the CD, but it should not be taken as a victory for the countries that advocate responsible behaviors or TCBMs.

In Brazil's submission on "existing and potential threats in outer space and behaviors that should be considered responsible, irresponsible and threatening in this environment" to the UN, it elaborates on how a country like Brazil, which has traditionally reasserted its commitment to the PAROS and to Non-First Placement of Weapons in Outer Space (NFP), has decided to support discussions on the gradual development of norms, rules, and principles based on political commitments, because "the discussion on modalities of negotiations of legally binding commitments on PAROS has been facing recurring stalemates" (Brazil's Submission 2021). In other words, Brazil changed its attitude because it believes some talk is better than no talk at all.

No Winners in Outer Space Arms Race

For countries to have cooperation rather than competition that threatens to slide into confrontation, the starting point is to realize every nation is vulnerable in space. In fact, if the environment becomes hostile among spacefarers, the more a country has satellites in outer space, the more vulnerable it will become. In this regard, the United States, being the largest spacefaring nation, is probably more vulnerable than any other country. No matter how the United States tries to stay ahead technologically in outer space, there is no guarantee that it will maintain its supremacy. Instead, it would find itself in a dilemma. In a preemptive strike against the ASAT weapons of an adversary on the ground, the US military can hardly eliminate all of them. In attacks launched against the satellites of an adversary with US ASAT weapons, enough debris could be produced to jeopardize the safety of its own satellites and the satellites of other nations. In defense against the ASAT attack of an adversary against US satellites, just changing position or increasing the maneuverability of these satellites in orbit are not necessarily effective in avoiding being attacked, since satellites moving on recognizable and commonly used orbits are more detectable than, say, submarines under the water. Even if the United States could place intercepting missiles in orbit, they are not guaranteed to be effective in preventing the ASAT attack of an adversary; and because these intercepting missiles are ostensible weapon systems placed in orbit, they could actually become the first targets of adversary ASAT weapons. As time goes on, at least theoretically, more countries could develop the capabilities to damage the satellites of other countries.

During the Cold War, mutually assured destruction (MAD), a gradually developed concept built upon a balance of terror, stabilized the relationship between two superpowers in constant rivalry. If all nations recognize that they are all vulnerable in outer space, then peaceful coexistence without an arms race in outer space is possible with recognition and acceptance of MAV in outer space.

A war in outer space is as consequential as a nuclear war, if it is not the prelude of a nuclear war. Attacking the satellites of an adversary is almost like launching a nuclear war, knowing this would be detectable and would almost certainly invite retaliation. The most common missions of military satellites are intelligence gathering, navigation, and military communications. It is meaningless to ascertain which type of military satellite is more valuable than the others, therefore, if a war in outer space starts, the probability is one nation might decide to launch a preemptive strike on as many satellites of the enemy as possible. This foretells that a war in outer space is intrinsically large in scale.

A war in space would almost certainly generate more than enough debris to cause third-party military or commercial systems to fail, thereby inflicting catastrophic damage on various platforms used on Earth, such as civilian and military communication, aviation, maritime navigation, cell phones, traffic-management systems, and railway operations. Simply put, an attack on one is an attack on all.

OPPORTUNITIES IN SPACE SECURITY COOPERATION

Needless to say, major powers should take the lead in cooperation wherever possible. The countries that have the strongest capabilities in outer space are the same countries that have the strongest military capabilities on Earth. One of the good lessons learnt from the Cold War is that even enemies can cooperate when their interests overlap, especially if they are technologically on an equal level. During the Cold War, in spite of seemingly irreconcilable hostilities, the two superpowers managed to cooperate successfully in outer space. In July 1975, the United States and the USSR jointly launched the Apollo-Soyuz Test Project, the first crewed international space mission. A United States Apollo module successfully docked with a Soviet Soyuz capsule. The three US astronauts and two Soviet cosmonauts performed both joint and separate scientific experiments, including an arranged eclipse of the sun by the Apollo module to allow instruments on the Soyuz to take photographs of the solar corona. Such collaboration helped in providing useful experience for the US–Russian joint space flights to follow, such as the Shuttle-Mir program and the International Space Station. The handshake in space, watched by millions of views on TV, best symbolized détente between the two superpowers. It was widely regarded as marking the end of the space race, which began in 1957 with the USSR's launch of Sputnik.

If enemies could cooperate then, why cannot competitors now? Unlike the zero-sum rivalry between the United States and the USSR, today the relationship between China and the United States is complex yet strong in an increasingly integrated global system. There is no guarantee that competitors are bound to become enemies.

Avoiding weaponization and an arms race in outer space is possible too, in that no countries have so far declared overtly that they possess "weapons" in outer space. The danger of weaponization in space makes any major space power hesitant in making such an announcement first, although they are invariably developing military capabilities that can be used in outer space. The dual-use nature of satellites also has a positive side in that the difficulties in identifying weapons in space make it harder to directly call any satellites "weapons," because their nature depends more on the intentions of the satellite users.

The definition of weaponization in space is not insurmountable as is alleged. The US submission to the UN secretary general pursuant to UNGA Resolution 75/36 includes a summary table of ASAT weapon types. They include kinetic, robotic arm, radiofrequency interference, directed–energy weapon (DEW), low power, DEW high power, nuclear weapons, orbital bombardment, C2 interference, on-orbit servicer, and active debris removal (United States of America 2021). The table shows that even from the US point of view, such weapon types can be defined. This could be used as a starting point for discussion on the definition of weaponization of outer space, leading to an eventual binding treaty.

A useful lesson from the UN Convention of the Law of the Sea is that countries were able to sign the convention with declarations on reservations for certain articles on which they disagreed. This approach could be applicable to a treaty of outer space. "Preventing weaponization and an arms race in outer space" and "responsible behaviors" are clearly different approaches in that one is top-down, while the other is bottom-up. But they do not necessarily conflict with each other. It is better see them as two sides of the same coin. China believes that TCBMs could play a certain positive role and serve as a useful supplement to legally binding arms control measures on outer space. Such TCBMS could include exchanges on space-related doctrines, strategies, and policies; notifications of scheduled maneuvers and predicted conjunctions; pre-launch notifications; sharing of space situational awareness data; notifications of active debris removal operations, etc. China also suggests that the UN should re-establish the Group of Governmental Experts (GGE) or establish an Open-Ended Working Group (OEWG) on PAROS, under which responsible behaviors in outer space could be included as one of the agenda items. However, the discussions on TCBMs should not replace the negotiation of an international legally binding instrument (Note Verbale from the Permanent Mission of China to the United Nations 2021).

One way out that addresses the concerns of all sides is to adopt a dual-track approach: that is, all parties agree to the goal of negotiating a binding treaty while encouraging discussions on responsible behaviors since they serve the fundamental goal of preventing an arms race in outer space. The core of the treaty should be no placement of weapons in the outer space and no use or threat of use of force anywhere against any celestial bodies.

Apparently, it is easier for China and Russia—two "strategic partners"—to cooperate and for the United States to cooperate with its allies. In March 2021, the China National Space Administration (CNSA) and Roscosmos, Russia's federal space agency, announced the construction of a moon outpost called the International Lunar Research Station (ILRS). According to CNSA, "the ILRS is a comprehensive scientific experiment base with the capability of long-term autonomous operation, built on the lunar surface and/or in lunar orbit that will carry out multi-disciplinary and multi-objective scientific research activities such as lunar exploration and utilization, lunar-based observation, basic scientific experiments and technical verification." What is equally important is that CNSA and Roscosmos will "facilitate extensive cooperation in the ILRS, open to all interested countries and international partners, strengthen scientific research exchanges, and promote humanity's exploration and use of outer space for peaceful purposes" (Wall 2021).

The United States working on NASA's Artemis program plans to send astronauts to the lunar surface in the mid-2020s and establish a long-term, sustainable human presence on and around the moon by the end of the decade. As of October 2021, thirteen countries have embraced the Artemis Accords, but Russia and China are not among the signatories.

Compared with the United States, China appears more open-minded about space cooperation with other nations. After the successful Chang'e-5 mission that collected moon samples in December 2020, China announced that it was ready to share her moon samples with international institutions and scientists (Crossley and Qiao 2020). It also declared in a memorandum with the UN that the Chinese Space Station, due to be completed in 2022, would be used for international scientific experiments and flights of international astronauts.

But China is not allowed to participate in any NASA program because of the Wolf Amendment. Passed by the US Congress in 2011, this prohibits NASA from using government funds to engage in direct, bilateral cooperation with the Chinese government and China-affiliated organizations without explicit authorization from the Federal Bureau of Investigation and Congress (Kohler 2015). Given that Washington has initiated the great power competition that takes China and Russia as primary competitors, it is understandably difficult to find room for cooperation between the United States, China and Russia now.

But the Wolf amendment does not completely prohibit China-US cooperation in selected civil space projects. In June 2017, there was a Chinese experiment on the International Space Station, having reached the orbiting lab aboard a SpaceX Dragon cargo spacecraft. NanoRacks, a Houston-based company that helps other companies and institutions make use of the space station, worked with the Beijing Institute of Technology to fly Chinese DNA research to the orbiting outpost (David 2017).

During China's 2019 moon exploration mission, NASA got congressional approval for a specific interaction with CNSA to monitor China's landing of a lunar probe on the dark side of the moon using NASA's Lunar Reconnaissance Orbiter (David 2020). Also, CNSA and NASA held working meetings and communications from January to March 2021 on exchanging ephemeris data to ensure the flight safety of Mars spacecraft (China National Space Administration 2021).

Whether China and the United States could cooperate more broadly in space depends partly on how quickly China could catch up technologically with the United States. Apollo–Soyuz Test Project was possible partly because the United States and the USSR were technologically on a par, therefore the United States did not really worry that the Soviets might "steal" its technical know-how. Backed by the political determination of the Chinese leadership, robust governmental investment, and accelerated technological improvement, the gap in space technology between China and the United States is more likely to narrow rather than widen. Both Chinese and US probes have explored the Mars. The Chinese government also announced crewed moon missions, although no timeline has been provided. In some areas, China has already overtaken the United States. The Chinese robotic spacecraft Chang'e 4 is the first ever to land in the far side of the moon. China's five-hundred-meter Aperture Spherical Telescope, larger than the now defunct US-run Arecibo spherical reflector dish in Puerto Rico, is the largest in the world. Almost ironically, on December 1, 2020, the same day that a Chinese lunar probe landed on the moon, the Arecibo dish collapsed.

A potential area of cooperation in transparency and confidence building between China and the United States is to agree on mutual notification of ballistic missile launches. China and Russia signed an agreement on mutual notification of missile launches in 2009. In fact, the China-Russia agreement is similar to a precedent concluded between the USSR and the United States in 1971 at the Strategic Arms Limitation Talks (SALT). That accord, known as the Accidents Measures Agreement, required pre-notification of the other side on launches of missiles that travel beyond the country's borders (Logan 2021). A similar agreement between China and the United States would be a major step in confidence building and risk reduction. In principle, it is also in line with the memorandum of understanding between China and the United States on notification of major military activities, in which both sides agree to establish a voluntary foundation for notifications of major military activities so as to "improve relations, deepen mutual understanding, reduce risk, and reduce the potential for misunderstanding and miscalculation" (U.S. Department of Defense 2014).

Because there is already agreement of mutual notification between Russia and the United States, and between China and Russia, on missile launch notification, an agreement on mutual notification between China and the United States, if made, could lead to an eventual trilateral notification agreement. By the same token, China, Russia, and the United States should bilaterally or multilaterally talk about no first placement of weapons in outer space. This might seem impossible in that the United States has rejected this idea time and again. But it is worth a second look. After the Indo-Pakistan nuclear test in 1998, China and the United States quickly came to a joint declaration of de-targeting their nuclear weapons against each other to show solidarity between two nuclear weapon states. This has led to five nuclear-weapon states jointly declaring that their nuclear weapons are not targeted at any country in May 2000 (Information Office of the State Council of China 2005).

Critics may argue that such de-targeting is symbolic only, in that it is not verifiable, but even symbolism is useful if it holds nuclear weapon states morally and ethnically responsible for their behaviors. If all nations believe they are invariably vulnerable in outer space and there are no winners in an arms race, then it is not impossible for major powers to pledge not to be the first one to place weapons in outer space.

During the 1985 Geneva Summit, President Ronald Reagan asked Soviet General Secretary Mikhail Gorbachev whether the USSR would help the United States if the United States were suddenly attacked by someone from outer space. Without hesitation, Gorbachev said no doubt about it. This is more than a lighthearted joke (Verma 2022). If climate change has started to make people to think about a possible new home in outer space, then no human folly is more monumental than attempting to place weapons in orbit to strike back on Earth, our only homeland, to eliminate adversaries. Yes, competition is part of human nature. But so is cooperation. Can the better angel in human nature prevail in outer space?

REFERENCES

Brazil's Submission. 2021. "Existing and Potential Threats in Outer Space and Behaviors That Should Be Considered Responsible, Irresponsible and Threatening in This Environment." https://front.un-arm.org/wp-content/uploads/2021/05/Brazils-submiss ion-A-RES-75-36.pdf.

Center for Strategic and Informational Studies. 2020. "Space Threat Assessment."

China National Space Administration. 2021. "CNSA and NASA Held Discussions on Exchanging the Ephemeris Data of Mars Spacecraft." March 31, 2021.

https://www.cnsa.gov.cn/english/n6465668/n6465670/c6811473/content.html#:~:text= China%20National%20Space%20Administration%20%28CNSA%29%20and%20Natio nal%20Aeronautics,to%20ensure%20the%20flight%20safety%20of%20Mars%20spacecraft.

Crossley, Gabriel, and Tina Qiao. 2020. "China Says to Share Part of Lunar Samples with Scientists from Other Countries." *Reuters*. December 17, 2020.

https://www.reuters.com/world/china/china-says-share-lunar-samples-with-other-countr ies-2020-12-17/.

David, Leonard. 2017. "Chinese Experiment Reaches Space Station in Historic First." *Space. com*. June 9, 2017.

https://www.space.com/37145-china-dna-experiment-international-space-station.html.

David, Leonard. 2019. "Farside Politics: The West Eyes Moon Cooperation with China." *Scientific American*. Feburary 7, 2020.

https://www.scientificamerican.com/article/farside-politics-the-west-eyes-moon-cooperat ion-with-china/.

Department of Defense. 2018. "Nuclear Posture Review Final Report."

Department of Defense. 2019. "Missile Defense Review."

Information Office of the State Council, China. 2005. "China's Endeavors for Arms Control, Disarmament and Non-Proliferation." White Paper.

Kohler, Hannah. 2015. "The Eagle and the Hare: U.S.-Chinese Relations, the Wolf Amendment, and the Future of International Cooperation in Space." *Georgetown Law Journal*, 103, no. 4: 1135–62.

Lauder, John, Frank G. Klotz, and William Courtney. 2020. "How to Avoid a Space Arms Race." Rand Blog. https://www.rand.org/blog/2020/10/how-to-avoid-a-space-arms-race.html.

Logan, David C. 2021. "Trilateral Arms Control: A Realistic Assessment of Chinese Participation." Stimson Center.

Ministry of Foreign Affairs. 2021. "Document of the People's Republic of China Pursuant to UNGA Resolution 75/36 (2020)." Office for Disarmament Affairs. https://front.un-arm.org/wp-content/uploads/2021/05/Chinas-Position-on-Outer-Space-SecurityEnglish.pdf.

The Permanent Mission of China. 2021. "Information Furnished in Conformity with the Treaty on Principles Governing the Activities of States in the Exploration and Use of Outer Space, Including the Moon and Other Celestial Bodies, Note Verbale dated 3 December 2021 from the Permanent Mission of China to the United Nations (Vienna) Addressed to the Secretary-General." United Nations Office for Outer Space Affairs. https://www.unoosa.org/res/oosa doc/data/documents/2021/aac_105/aac_1051262_0_html/AAC105_1262E.pdf.

Nuclear Threat Initiative. 2020. "Proposed Prevention of an Arms Race in Space (PAROS) Treaty, Permanent Mission of the People's Republic of China to the United Nations Office at Geneva and Other International Organizations in Switzerland. 2019. The CD Should Assume Its Historic Responsibility for PAROS: Remarks by H.E. Ambassador Li Song in the CD on PAROS." Washingtown, DC. https://www.nti.org/education-center/treaties-and-regimes/proposed-prevention-arms-race-space-paros-treaty/#2020.

PPWT. Treaty on the Prevention of the Placement of Weapons in Outer Space, the Threat or Use of Force against Outer Space Objects (Draft). 2014.

Secure World Foundation. 2021. "Global Counterspace Capabilities: An Open Source Assessment." Washingtown, DC. https://swfound.org/media/206118/swf_global_counter space_april2018.pdf.

The Permanent Mission of the People's Republic of China to the United Nations Office at Geneva and Other International Organisations in Switzerland. 2019. "The CD Should Assume Its Historic Responsibility for PAROS——Remarks by H.E. Ambassador Li Song in the CD on PAROS". http://geneva.china-mission.gov.cn/eng/dbdt/201906/t20190614_8192427.htm

Tobias, Manuela. 2018. "Trump Directed the Pentagon to Create a Space Force. What Would It Look Like." *POLITIFACT*. August 13, 2018. https://www.politifact.com/article/2018/aug/13/trump-directed-pentagon-create-space-force-what-mi/.

Treaty on Principles Governing the Activities of States in the Exploration and Use of Outer Space, including the Moon and Other Celestial Bodies. 1967.

United Kingdom. 2021. "United Kingdom National Submission on Space Threats to respond to the call from UN Secretary General under the UN GA Resolution A/RES/75/36 on Reducing Space Threats through norms, rules and principles of Responsible Behavior." Office for Disarmament Affairs. https://front.un-arm.org/wp-content/uploads/2021/05/national-sub mission-of-the-United-Kingdom-in-connection-with-resolution-75_36.pdf.

United States of America. 2021. "National Submission to the United Nations Secretary-General Pursuant to UN General Assembly Resolution 75/36 Reducing Space Threats through Norms, Rules and Principles of Responsible Behaviours." https://front.un-arm.org/wp-cont ent/uploads/2021/05/04292021-US-National-Submission-for-UNGA-Resolution-75.36.pdf.

U.S. Department of Defense. 2014. "Memorandum of Understanding Between the United States of America Department of Defense and the People's Republic of China Ministry of National Defense on Notification of Major Military Activities Confidence-Building Measures Mechanism." https://dod.defense.gov/Portals/1/Documents/pubs/141112_MemorandumOfUnderstandingOnNotification.pdf.

Verma, Vicky. 2022. "President Reagan Asked Russians to Unite with the US against Alien Attack In 1985." *How and Whys*. August 3, 2022. https://www.howandwhys.com/president-reagan-asked-russians-to-unite-with-the-us-against-alien-attack-in-1985/.

Wall, Mike. 2021. "Russia and China Just Agreed to Build a Research Station on the Moon Together." *Space.com*. March 17, 2021. https://www.space.com/russia-china-moon-research-station-agreement.

White House. 2020. "Memorandum on the National Space Policy." Washington, DC. https://trumpwhitehouse.archives.gov/presidential-actions/memorandum-national-space-policy/.

Zhou, Bo. 2021. "To Avoid the Folly of a US-China Space Race, the Two Competitors Should Learn Some Soviet-Era Cooperation." *South China Morning Post*. March 11, 2021. https://www.scmp.com/comment/opinion/article/3124789/avoid-folly-us-china-space-race-two-competitors-should-learn-some.

INDEX